weygandt
kimmel
kieso
team for success

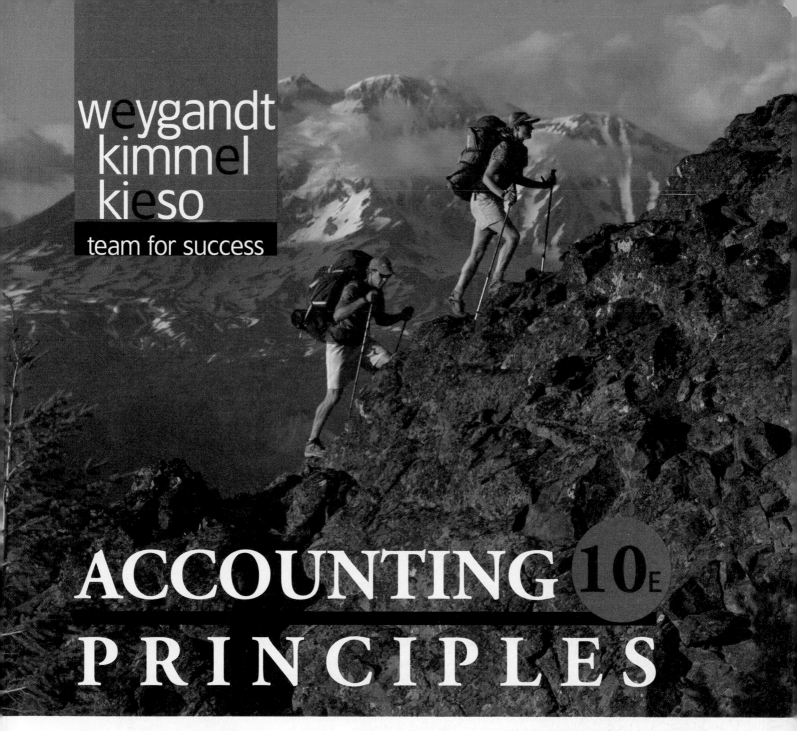

ACCOUNTING 10E
PRINCIPLES

Volume 1: Chapters 1–12

WILEY

John Wiley & Sons, Inc.

Jerry J. Weygandt PhD, CPA
University of Wisconsin—Madison
Madison, Wisconsin

Paul D. Kimmel PhD, CPA
University of Wisconsin—Milwaukee
Milwaukee, Wisconsin

Donald E. Kieso PhD, CPA
Northern Illinois University
DeKalb, Illinois

Dedicated to
the *Wiley sales representatives*
who sell our books and service
our adopters in a professional
and ethical manner and to
Enid, Merlynn, and Donna

Vice President & Executive Publisher	George Hoffman
Associate Publisher	Christopher DeJohn
Project Editor	Ed Brislin
Development Editor	Terry Ann Tatro
Project Editor	Yana Mermel
Production Manager	Dorothy Sinclair
Senior Production Editor	Valerie A. Vargas
Production Editor	Erin Bascom
Associate Director of Marketing	Amy Scholz
Senior Marketing Manager	Ramona Sherman
Executive Media Editor	Allison Morris
Media Editor	Greg Chaput
Creative Director	Harry Nolan
Senior Designer	Madelyn Lesure
Production Management Services	Ingrao Associates
Senior Photo Editor	Mary Ann Price
Editorial Assistant	Jacqueline Kepping
Marketing Assistant	Courtney Luzzi
Assistant Marketing Manager	Diane Mars
Cover Design	Maureen Eide
Cover Photo	©Bill Stevenson/Photolibrary

This book was set in Times Ten by Aptara®, Inc. and printed and bound by RR Donnelley. The cover was printed by RR Donnelley.

Founded in 1807, John Wiley & Sons, Inc. has been a valued source of knowledge and understanding for more than 200 years, helping people around the world meet their needs and fulfill their aspirations. Our company is built on a foundation of principles that include responsibility to the communities we serve and where we live and work. In 2008, we launched a Corporate Citizenship Initiative, a global effort to address the environmental, social, economic, and ethical challenges we face in our business. Among the issues we are addressing are carbon impact, paper specifications and procurement, ethical conduct within our business and among our vendors, and community and charitable support. For more information, please visit our website: www.wiley.com/go/citizenship.

Evaluation copies are provided to qualified academics and professionals for review purposes only, for use in their courses during the next academic year. These copies are licensed and may not be sold or transferred to a third party. Upon completion of the review period, please return the evaluation copy to Wiley. Return instructions and a free of charge return shipping label are available at www.wiley.com/go/returnlabel. Outside of the United States, please contact your local representative.

ISBN-13 978-1-118-00927-7

Printed in the United States of America

10 9 8 7 6 5 4 3 2

From the Authors

Dear Student,

Why This Course? *Remember your biology course in high school? Did you have one of those "invisible man" models (or maybe something more high-tech than that) that gave you the opportunity to look "inside" the human body? This accounting course offers something similar: To understand a business, you have to understand the financial insides of a business organization. An accounting course will help you understand the essential financial components of businesses. Whether you are looking at a large multinational company like Microsoft or Starbucks or a single-owner software consulting business or coffee shop, knowing the fundamentals of accounting will help you understand what is happening. As an employee, a manager, an investor, a business owner, or a director of your own personal finances—any of which roles you will have at some point in your life—you will be much the wiser for having taken this course.*

Why This Book? *Hundreds of thousands of students have used this textbook. Your instructor has chosen it for you because of its trusted reputation. The authors have worked hard to keep the book fresh, timely, and accurate.*

This textbook contains features to help you learn best, whatever your learning style. To understand what your learning style is, spend about ten minutes to take the learning style quiz at the book's companion website. Then, look at page vii for how you can apply an understanding of your learning style to this course. When you know more about your own learning style, browse through the Student Owner's Manual on pages viii–xi. It shows you the main features you will find in this textbook and explains their purpose.

How To Succeed? *We've asked many students and many instructors whether there is a secret for success in this course. The nearly unanimous answer turns out to be not much of a secret: "Do the homework." This is one course where doing is learning, and the more time you spend on the homework assignments—using the various tools that this textbook provides—the more likely you are to learn the essential concepts, techniques, and methods of accounting. Besides the textbook itself, the book's companion website offers various support resources.*

Good luck in this course. We hope you enjoy the experience and that you put to good use throughout a lifetime of success the knowledge you obtain in this course. We are sure you will not be disappointed.

Jerry J. Weygandt
Paul D. Kimmel
Donald E. Kieso

About the Authors

Jerry Weygandt

Jerry J. Weygandt, PhD, CPA, is Arthur Andersen Alumni Emeritus Professor of Accounting at the University of Wisconsin—Madison. He holds a Ph.D. in accounting from the University of Illinois. Articles by Professor Weygandt have appeared in the Accounting Review, Journal of Accounting Research, Accounting Horizons, Journal of Accountancy, and other academic and professional journals. These articles have examined such financial reporting issues as accounting for price-level adjustments, pensions, convertible securities, stock option contracts, and interim reports. Professor Weygandt is author of other accounting and financial reporting books and is a member of the American Accounting Association, the American Institute of Certified Public Accountants, and the Wisconsin Society of Certified Public Accountants. He has served on numerous committees of the American Accounting Association and as a member of the editorial board of the Accounting Review; he also has served as President and Secretary-Treasurer of the American Accounting Association. In addition, he has been actively involved with the American Institute of Certified Public Accountants and has been a member of the Accounting Standards Executive Committee (AcSEC) of that organization. He has served on the FASB task force that examined the reporting issues related to accounting for income taxes and served as a trustee of the Financial Accounting Foundation. Professor Weygandt has received the Chancellor's Award for Excellence in Teaching and the Beta Gamma Sigma Dean's Teaching Award. He is on the board of directors of M & I Bank of Southern Wisconsin. He is the recipient of the Wisconsin Institute of CPA's Outstanding Educator's Award and the Lifetime Achievement Award. In 2001 he received the American Accounting Association's Outstanding Educator Award.

Paul Kimmel

Paul D. Kimmel, PhD, CPA, received his bachelor's degree from the University of Minnesota and his doctorate in accounting from the University of Wisconsin. He is an Associate Professor at the University of Wisconsin—Milwaukee, and has public accounting experience with Deloitte & Touche (Minneapolis). He was the recipient of the UWM School of Business Advisory Council Teaching Award, the Reggie Taite Excellence in Teaching Award and a three-time winner of the Outstanding Teaching Assistant Award at the University of Wisconsin. He is also a recipient of the Elijah Watts Sells Award for Honorary Distinction for his results on the CPA exam. He is a member of the American Accounting Association and the Institute of Management Accountants and has published articles in Accounting Review, Accounting Horizons, Advances in Management Accounting, Managerial Finance, Issues in Accounting Education, Journal of Accounting Education, as well as other journals. His research interests include accounting for financial instruments and innovation in accounting education. He has published papers and given numerous talks on incorporating critical thinking into accounting education, and helped prepare a catalog of critical thinking resources for the Federated Schools of Accountancy.

Don Kieso

Donald E. Kieso, PhD, CPA, received his bachelor's degree from Aurora University and his doctorate in accounting from the University of Illinois. He has served as chairman of the Department of Accountancy and is currently the KPMG Emeritus Professor of Accountancy at Northern Illinois University. He has public accounting experience with Price Waterhouse & Co. (San Francisco and Chicago) and Arthur Andersen & Co. (Chicago) and research experience with the Research Division of the American Institute of Certified Public Accountants (New York). He has done post doctorate work as a Visiting Scholar at the University of California at Berkeley and is a recipient of NIU's Teaching Excellence Award and four Golden Apple Teaching Awards. Professor Kieso is the author of other accounting and business books and is a member of the American Accounting Association, the American Institute of Certified Public Accountants, and the Illinois CPA Society. He has served as a member of the Board of Directors of the Illinois CPA Society, then AACSB's Accounting Accreditation Committees, the State of Illinois Comptroller's Commission, as Secretary-Treasurer of the Federation of Schools of Accountancy, and as Secretary-Treasurer of the American Accounting Association. Professor Kieso is currently serving on the Board of Trustees and Executive Committee of Aurora University, as a member of the Board of Directors of Kishwaukee Community Hospital, and as Treasurer and Director of Valley West Community Hospital. From 1989 to 1993 he served as a charter member of the national Accounting Education Change Commission. He is the recipient of the Outstanding Accounting Educator Award from the Illinois CPA Society, the FSA's Joseph A. Silvoso Award of Merit, the NIU Foundation's Humanitarian Award for Service to Higher Education, a Distinguished Service Award from the Illinois CPA Society, and in 2003 an honorary doctorate from Aurora University.

What TYPE of learner are you?

	Intake: To take in the information	To make a study package	Text features that may help you the most	Output: To do well on exams
VISUAL	• Pay close attention to charts, drawings, and handouts your instructors use. • Underline. • Use different colors. • Use symbols, flow charts, graphs, different arrangements on the page, white spaces.	Convert your lecture notes into "page pictures." To do this: • Use the "Intake" strategies. • Reconstruct images in different ways. • Redraw pages from memory. • Replace words with symbols and initials. • Look at your pages.	The Navigator/Feature Story/Preview Infographics/Illustrations Accounting Equation Analyses Highlighted words Demonstration Problem/ Action Plan Questions/Exercises/Problems Financial Reporting Problem Comparative Analysis Problem On the Web Tutorials, video, iPod apps	• Recall your "page pictures." • Draw diagrams where appropriate. • Practice turning your visuals back into words.
AURAL	• Attend lectures and tutorials. • Discuss topics with students and instructors. • Explain new ideas to other people. • Use a tape recorder. • Leave spaces in your lecture notes for later recall. • Describe overheads, pictures, and visuals to somebody who was not in class.	You may take poor notes because you prefer to listen. Therefore: • Expand your notes by talking with others and with information from your textbook. • Tape-record summarized notes and listen. • Read summarized notes out loud. • Explain your notes to another "aural" person.	Preview Insight Boxes Review It/Do it!/Action Plan Summary of Study Objectives Glossary Demonstration Problem/Action Plan Self-Test Questions Questions/Exercises/Problems Financial Reporting Problem Comparative Analysis Problem On the Web Decision Making Across the Organization Tutorials, video	Communication Activity Ethics Case • Talk with the instructor. • Spend time in quiet places recalling the ideas. • Practice writing answers to old exam questions. • Say your answers out loud.
READING/ WRITING	• Use lists and headings. • Use dictionaries, glossaries, and definitions. • Read handouts, textbooks, and supplementary library readings. • Use lecture notes.	• Write out words again and again. • Reread notes silently. • Rewrite ideas and principles into other words. • Turn charts, diagrams, and other illustrations into statements.	The Navigator/Feature Story/Study Objectives/Preview Review It/Do it!/Action Plan Summary of Study Objectives Glossary/Self-Test Questions Questions/Exercises/Problems Writing Problems Financial Reporting Problem Comparative Analysis Problem "All About You" Activity On the Web Decision Making Across the Organization Communication Activity Flashcards	• Write exam answers. • Practice with multiple-choice questions. • Write paragraphs, beginnings and endings. • Write your lists in outline form. • Arrange your words into hierarchies and points.
KINESTHETIC	• Use all your senses. • Go to labs, take field trips. • Listen to real-life examples. • Pay attention to applications. • Use hands-on approaches. • Use trial-and-error methods.	You may take poor notes because topics do not seem concrete or relevant. Therefore: • Put examples in your summaries. • Use case studies and applications to help with principles and abstract concepts. • Talk about your notes with another "kinesthetic" person. • Use pictures and photographs that illustrate an idea.	The Navigator/Feature Story/Preview Infographics/Illustrations Review It/Do it!/Action Plan Summary of Study Objectives Demonstration Problem/ Action Plan Self-Test Questions Questions/Exercises/Problems Financial Reporting Problem Comparative Analysis Problem On the Web Decision Making Across the Organization Communication Activity "All About You" Activity	• Write practice answers. • Role-play the exam situation.

Student Owner's Manual

Using Your Textbook Effectively

The Navigator guides you through each chapter by pulling learning tools together into one learning system. Throughout the chapter, The Navigator prompts you to use listed learning aids and to set priorities as you study.

✔ The Navigator	
● Scan Study Objectives	○
● Read Feature Story	○
● Read Preview	○
● Read text and answer **Do it!** p. 102 ○ p. 110 ○ p. 116 ○ p. 121 ○	
● Work Comprehensive **Do it!** p. 122	○
● Review Summary of Study Objectives	○
● Answer Self-Test Questions	○
● Complete Assignments	○
● Go to *WileyPLUS* for practice and tutorials	○
● Read A Look at IFRS p. 148	○

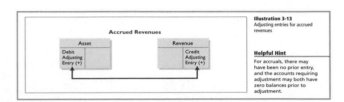

Helpful Hints in the margins further clarify concepts being discussed. They are like having an instructor with you as you read.

Ethics Notes and International Notes point out ethical and international points related to the nearby text discussion.

Insight examples give you more glimpses into how actual companies make decisions using accounting information. These high-interest boxes focus on various themes—ethics, international, and investor concerns.

A **critical thinking question** asks you to apply your accounting learning to the story in the example. *Guideline Answers* appear at the end of the chapter.

Accounting Across the Organization examples show the use of accounting by people in non-accounting functions—such as finance, marketing, or management. *Guideline Answers* appear at the end of the chapter.

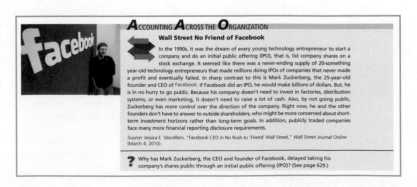

Anatomy of a Fraud boxes illustrate how a lack of specific internal controls resulted in real-world frauds.

ANATOMY OF A FRAUD

Bernie Ebbers was the founder and CEO of the phone company WorldCom. The company engaged in a series of increasingly large, debt-financed acquisitions of other companies. These acquisitions made the company grow quickly, which made the stock price increase dramatically. However, because the acquired companies all had different accounting systems, WorldCom's financial records were a mess. When WorldCom's performance started to flatten out, Bernie coerced WorldCom's accountants to engage in a number of fraudulent activities to make net income look better than it really was and thus prop up the stock price. One of these frauds involved treating $7 billion of line costs as capital expenditures. The line costs, which were rental fees paid to other phone companies to use their phone lines, had always been properly expensed in previous years. Capitalization delayed expense recognition to future periods and thus boosted current-period profits.

Total take: $7 billion

THE MISSING CONTROLS

Documentation procedures. The company's accounting system was a disorganized collection of nonintegrated systems, which resulted from a series of corporate acquisitions. Top management took advantage of this disorganization to conceal its fraudulent activities.

Independent internal verification. A fraud of this size should have been detected by a routine comparison of the actual physical assets with the list of physical assets shown in the accounting records.

Do it!

Adjusting Entries for Deferrals

The ledger of Hammond Company, on March 31, 2012, includes these selected accounts before adjusting entries are prepared.

	Debit	Credit
Prepaid Insurance	$ 3,600	
Supplies	2,800	
Equipment	25,000	
Accumulated Depreciation—Equipment		$5,000
Unearned Service Revenue		9,200

An analysis of the accounts shows the following.

1. Insurance expires at the rate of $100 per month.
2. Supplies on hand total $800.

Brief **Do it!** exercises ask you to put to work your newly acquired knowledge. They outline an **Action Plan** necessary to complete the exercise, and they show a **Solution**.

Comprehensive Do it! problem with **Action Plan** gives you an opportunity to see a detailed solution to a representative problem before you do your homework. Coincides with the Do it! problems within the chapter.

COMPREHENSIVE
Do it!

Terry Thomas opens the Green Thumb Lawn Care Company on April 1. At April 30, the trial balance shows the following balances for selected accounts.

Prepaid Insurance	$ 3,600
Equipment	28,000
Notes Payable	20,000
Unearned Service Revenue	4,200
Service Revenue	1,800

Do it! Review problems appear in the homework material and provide another way for you to determine whether you have mastered the content in the chapters.

Do it! Review

Do it! 3-1 Numerous timing concepts are discussed on pages 100–102. A list of concepts is provided below in the left column, with a description of the concept in the right column. There are more descriptions provided than concepts. Match the description of the concept to the concept.

Identify timing concepts.
(SO 1, 2)

1. ____ Cash-basis accounting.
2. ____ Fiscal year.
3. ____ Revenue recognition principle.
4. ____ Expense recognition principle.

(a) Monthly and quarterly time periods.
(b) Accountants divide the economic life of a business into artificial time periods.
(c) Efforts (expenses) should be matched with accomplishments (revenues).

What happens when no-par stock does not have a stated value? In that case, the corporation credits the entire proceeds to Common Stock. Thus, if Hydro-Slide does not assign a stated value to its no-par stock, it records the issuance of the 5,000 shares at $8 per share for cash as follows.

Cash	40,000	
Common Stock		40,000
(To record issue of 5,000 shares of no-par stock)		

A = L + SE
+40,000
+40,000 CS

Cash Flows
+40,000

Accounting equation analyses appear next to key journal entries. They will help you understand the impact of an accounting transaction on the components of the accounting equation, on the stockholders' equity accounts, and on the company's cash flows.

Financial statements appear regularly. Those from actual companies are identified by a company logo or a photo.

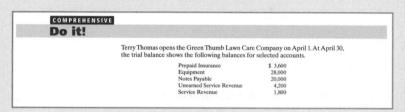

Illustration 14-11
Disclosure of restriction

Tektronix Inc.
Notes to the Financial Statements

Certain of the Company's debt agreements require compliance with debt covenants. Management believes that the Company is in compliance with such requirements. The Company had unrestricted retained earnings of $223.8 million after meeting those requirements.

Exercises: Set B are available online at *www.wiley.com/college/weygandt.*

Exercises: Set B
Visit the book's companion website, at **www.wiley.com/college/weygandt**, and choose the Student Companion site to access Exercise Set B.

In the textbook, two similar sets of **Problems—A** and **B**—are keyed to the same study objectives.

Selected problems, identified by this icon, can be solved using the **General Ledger Software (GLS)** package.

Journalize transactions and follow through accounting cycle to preparation of financial statements.

(SO 5, 6, 7)

GLS

P3-5A On September 1, 2012, the account balances of Moore Equipment Repair were as follows.

No.	Debits		No.	Credits	
101	Cash	$ 4,880	154	Accumulated Depreciation—Equipment	$ 1,500
112	Accounts Receivable	3,520	201	Accounts Payable	3,400
126	Supplies	2,000	209	Unearned Service Revenue	1,400
153	Equipment	15,000	212	Salaries and Wages Payable	500
			301	Owner's Capital	18,600
		$25,400			$25,400

Prepare correct income statement.

(SO 2, 5, 6, 7)

E3-10 The income statement of Brandon Co. for the month of July shows net income of $1,400 based on Service Revenue $5,500, Salaries and Wages Expense $2,300, Supplies Expense $1,200, and Utilities Expense $600. In reviewing the statement, you discover the following.

1. Insurance expired during July of $400 was omitted.
2. Supplies expense includes $250 of supplies that are still on hand at July 31.

An icon identifies **Exercises** and **Problems** that can be solved using Excel templates at the student website.

Those exercises and problems that focus on accounting situations faced by **service companies** are identified by the icon shown here.

Determine cost of jobs and ending balance in work in process and overhead accounts.

(SO 3, 4, 6)

SERVICE

E20-12 Alma Ortiz and Associates, a CPA firm, uses job order costing to capture the costs of its audit jobs. There were no audit jobs in process at the beginning of November. Listed below are data concerning the three audit jobs conducted during November.

	Perez	Rivera	Sota
Direct materials	$600	$400	$200
Auditor labor costs	$5,400	$6,600	$3,375
Auditor hours	72	88	45

Problems: Set C
Visit the book's companion website, at **www.wiley.com/college/weygandt**, and choose the Student Companion site to access Problem Set C.

An additional parallel set of **C Problems** appears at the book's companion website.

Comprehensive Problem: Chapters 3 to 7

CP7 Packard Company has the following opening account balances in its general and subsidiary ledgers on January 1 and uses the periodic inventory system. All accounts have normal debit and credit balances.

General Ledger

Account Number	Account Title	January 1 Opening Balance
101	Cash	$33,750

Comprehensive Problems combine material from the current chapter with previous chapters so that you understand how "it all fits together."

The **Continuing Cookie Chronicle** exercise follows the continuing saga of accounting for a small business begun by an entrepreneurial student.

Continuing Cookie Chronicle

(*Note:* This is a continuation of the Cookie Chronicle from Chapters 1 and 2. Use the information from the previous chapters and follow the instructions below using the general ledger accounts you have already prepared.)

Waterways Continuing Problem

(*Note:* The Waterways Problem begins in Chapter 19 and continues in the remaining chapters. You can also find this problem at the book's Student Companion site.)

The **Waterways Continuing Problem** uses the business activities of a fictional company, to help you apply managerial accounting topics to a realistic entrepreneurial situation.

The **Broadening Your Perspective** section helps to pull together concepts from the chapter and apply them to real-world business situations.

BROADENINGYOURPERSPECTIVE

The **Financial Reporting Problem** focuses on reading and understanding the financial statements of PepsiCo, which are available in Appendix A.

Financial Reporting and Analysis

Financial Reporting Problem: PepsiCo, Inc.

BYP3-1 The financial statements of PepsiCo, Inc. are presented in Appendix A at the end of this textbook.

Comparative Analysis Problem: PepsiCo, Inc. vs. The Coca-Cola Company

BYP3-2 PepsiCo's financial statements are presented in Appendix A. Financial statements for The Coca-Cola Company are presented in Appendix B.

A **Comparative Analysis Problem** compares and contrasts the financial reporting of PepsiCo and The Coca-Cola Company.

On the Web

BYP3-3 No financial decision maker should ever rely solely on the financial information reported in the annual report to make decisions. It is important to keep abreast of financial news. This activity demonstrates how to search for financial news on the Web.

Address: http://biz.yahoo.com/i, or go to **www.wiley.com/college/weygandt**

On the Web exercises guide you to websites where you can find and analyze information related to the chapter topic.

Decision Making Across the Organization cases help you build decision-making skills by analyzing accounting information in a less structured situation. These cases require you to work in teams.

Decision Making Across the Organization

BYP20-1 Burgio Parts Company uses a job order cost system. For a number of months, there has been an ongoing rift between the sales department and the production department concerning a special-order product, TC-1. TC-1 is a seasonal product that is manufactured in batches of 1,000 units. TC-1 is sold at cost plus a markup of 40% of cost.

Communication Activity

BYP3-5 In reviewing the accounts of Keri Ann Co. at the end of the year, you discover that adjusting entries have not been made.

Communication Activity problems help you to apply and practice business communication skills.

Ethics Cases ask you to reflect on typical ethical dilemmas, analyze the stakeholders and the issues involved, and decide on an appropriate course of action.

Ethics Case

BYP3-6 Bluestem Company is a pesticide manufacturer. Its sales declined greatly this year due to the passage of legislation outlawing the sale of several of Bluestem's chemical pesticides. In the coming year, Bluestem will have environmentally safe and competitive chemicals to replace these discontinued products. Sales in the next year are expected to greatly exceed any prior year's. The decline in sales and profits appears to be a one-year aberration. But even so, the company president fears a large dip in the current year's profits. He believes that such a dip could cause a significant drop in the market price of Bluestem's stock and make the company a takeover target.

"All About You" Activity

BYP3-7 Companies must report or disclose in their financial statements information about all liabilities, including potential liabilities related to environmental clean-up. There are many situations in which you will be asked to provide personal financial information about your assets, liabilities, revenue, and expenses. Sometimes you will face difficult decisions regarding what to disclose and how to disclose it.

All About You activities are designed to get you thinking and talking about how accounting impacts your personal life.

FASB Codification Activity offers you the opportunity to use this online system, which contains all the authoritative literature related to a particular topic.

FASB Codification Activity

BYP3-8 If your school has a subscription to the FASB Codification, go to *http://aaahq.org/asclogin.cfm* to log in and prepare responses to the following.

Instructions

Access the glossary ("Master Glossary") to answer the following.
(a) What is the definition of revenue?
(b) What is the definition of compensation?

Managerial Analysis

BYP19-2 B.J. King is a fairly large manufacturing company located in the southern United States. The company manufactures tennis rackets, tennis balls, tennis clothing, and tennis shoes, all bearing the company's distinctive logo, a large green question mark on a white-flocked tennis ball. The company's sales have been increasing over the past 10 years.

The tennis racket division has recently implemented several advanced manufacturing techniques. Robot arms hold the tennis rackets in place while glue dries, and machine vision systems check for defects. The engineering and design team uses computerized drafting and testing of new products. The following managers work in the tennis racket division.

Managerial Analysis assignments build analytical and decision-making skills in situations required by managers.

Real World Focus problems require you to apply techniques and concepts learned in the chapter to specific situations faced by actual companies.

Real-World Focus

BYP19-3 Anchor Glass Container Corporation, the third largest manufacturer of glass containers in the United States, supplies beverage and food producers and consumer products manufacturers nationwide. Parent company Consumers Packaging Inc. *(Toronto Stock Exchange: CGC)* is a leading international designer and manufacturer of glass containers.

The following management discussion appeared in a recent annual report of Anchor Glass.

IFRS   A Look at IFRS

It is often difficult for companies to determine in what time period they should report particular revenues and expenses. Both the IASB and FASB are working on a joint project to develop a common conceptual framework, as well as a revenue recognition project, that will enable companies to better use the same principles to record transactions consistently over time.

A Look at IFRS provides an overview of the International Financial Reporting Standards (IFRS) that relate to the chapter topics, highlights the differences between GAAP and IFRS, discusses IFRS/GAAP convergence efforts, and tests your understanding through *IFRS Self-Test Questions* and *IFRS Concepts and Application*.

Acknowledgments

Accounting Principles has benefited greatly from the input of focus group participants, manuscript reviewers, those who have sent comments by letter or e-mail, ancillary authors, and proofers. We greatly appreciate the constructive suggestions and innovative ideas of reviewers and the creativity and accuracy of the ancillary authors and checkers.

Prior Editions

Thanks to the following reviewers and focus group participants of prior editions of Accounting Principles:

John Ahmad, *Northern Virginia Community College—Annandale;* Sylvia Allen, *Los Angeles Valley College;* Matt Anderson, *Michigan State University;* Alan Applebaum, *Broward Community College;* Juanita Ardovany, *Los Angeles Valley College;* Yvonne Baker, *Cincinnati State Tech Community College;* Peter Battelle, *University of Vermont;* Colin Battle, *Broward Community College;* Jim Benedum; Beverly Beatty, *Anne Arundel Community College; Milwaukee Area Technical College;* Jaswinder Bhangal, *Chabot College;* Bernard Bieg, *Bucks County College;* Michael Blackett, *National American University;* Barry Bomboy, *J. Sargeant Reynolds Community College;* Kent D. Bowen, *Butler County Community College;* David Boyd, *Arkansas State University;* Greg Brookins, *Santa Monica College;* Kurt H. Buerger, *Angelo State University;* Leroy Bugger, *Edison Community College;* Leon Button, *Scottsdale Community College.*

Ann Cardozo, *Broward Community College;* Steve Carlson, *University of North Dakota;* Fatma Cebenoyan, *Hunter College;* Kimberly Charland, *Kansas State University;* Trudy Chiaravelli, *Lansing Community College;* Shifei Chung, *Rowan University;* Siu Chung, *Los Angeles Valley College;* Lisa Cole, *Johnson County Community College;* Kenneth Couvillion, *San Joaquin Delta College;* Alan B. Czyzewski, *Indiana State University;* Thomas Davies, *University of South Dakota;* Peggy DeJong, *Kirkwood Community College;* John Delaney, *Augustana College;* Tony Dellarte, *Luzerne Community College;* Kevin Dooley, *Kapi'olani Community College;* Pam Donahue, *Northern Essex Community College;* Edmond Douville, *Indiana University Northwest;* Pamela Druger, *Augustana College;* Russell Dunn, *Broward Community College;* John Eagan, *Erie Community College;* Richard Ellison, *Middlesex Community College;* Dora Estes, *Volunteer State Community College;* Mary Falkey, *Prince Georges Community College.*

Raymond Gardner, *Ocean County College;* Lori Grady, *Bucks County Community College;* Richard Ghio, *San Joaquin Delta College;* Joyce Griffin, *Kansas City Community College;* Amy Haas, *Kingsborough Community College, CUNY;* Lester Hall, *Danville Community College;* Becky Hancock, *El Paso Community College;* Jeannie Harrington, *Middle Tennessee State University;* Bonnie Harrison, *College of Southern Maryland;* William Harvey, *Henry Ford Community College;* Michelle Heard, *Metropolitan Community College;* Ruth Henderson, *Union Community College;* Ed Hess, *Butler County Community College;* Kathy Hill, *Leeward Community College;* Patty Holmes, *Des Moines Area Community College;* Zach Holmes, *Oakland Community College;* Paul Holt, *Texas A&M—Kingsville;* Audrey Hunter, *Broward Community College;* Verne Ingram, *Red Rocks Community College;* Joanne Johnson, *Caldwell Community College;* Naomi Karolinski, *Monroe Community College;* Anil Khatri, *Bowie State University;* Shirley Kleiner, *Johnson County Community College;* Jo Koehn, *Central Missouri State University;* Ken Koerber, *Bucks County Community College;* Adriana Kulakowski, *Mynderse Academy.*

Sandra Lang, *McKendree College;* Cathy Xanthaky Larsen, *Middlesex Community College;* David Laurel, *South Texas Community College;* Robert Laycock, *Montgomery College;* Natasha Librizzi, *Madison Area Technical College;* William P. Lovell, *Cayuga Community College;* Melanie Mackey, *Ocean County College;* Jerry Martens, *Community College of Aurora;* Maureen McBeth, *College of DuPage;* Francis McCloskey, *Community College of Philadelphia;* Chris McNamara, *Finger Lakes Community College;* Lori Major, *Luzerne County Community College;* Edwin Mah, *University of Maryland, University College;* Thomas Marsh, *Northern Virginia Community College—Annandale;* Jim Martin, *University of Montevallo;* Suneel Maheshwari, *Marshall University;* Shea Mears, *Des Moines Area Community College;* Pam Meyer, *University of Louisiana—Lafayette;* Cathy Montesarchio, *Broward Community College.*

Robin Nelson, *Community College of Southern Nevada;* Joseph M. Nicassio, *Westmoreland County Community College;* Michael O'Neill, *Seattle Central Community College;* Mike Palma, *Gwinnett Tech;* George Palz, *Erie Community College;* Michael Papke, *Kellogg Community College;* Ruth Parks, *Kellogg Community College;* Al Partington, *Los Angeles Pierce College;* Jennifer Patty, *Des Moines Area Community College;* Yvonne Phang, *Borough of Manhattan Community College;* Jan Pitera, *Broome Community College;* Mike Prockton, *Finger Lakes Community College;* Laura M. Prosser, *Black Hills State University;* Bill Rencher, *Seminole Community College;* Jenny Resnick, *Santa Monica College;* Renee Rigoni, *Monroe Community College;* Kathie Rogers, *SUNY Suffolk;* Al Ruggiero, *SUNY Suffolk;* Jill Russell, *Camden County College.*

Roger Sands, *Milwaukee Area Technical College;* Marcia Sandvold, *Des Moines Area Community College;* Richard Sarkisian, *Camden Community College;* Kent Schneider, *East Tennessee State University;* Karen Searle, Paul J. Shinal, *Cayuga Community College;* Beth Secrest, *Walsh University;* Kevin Sinclair, *Lehigh University;* Alice Sineath, *Forsyth Tech Community College;* Leon Singleton, *Santa Monica College;* Michael S. Skaff, *College of the Sequoias;* Jeff Slater, *North Shore Community College;* Lois Slutsky, *Broward Community College;* Dan Small, *J. Sargeant Reynolds Community College;* Lee Smart, *Southwest Tennessee Community College;* James Smith, *Ivy Tech State College;* Carol Springer, *Georgia State University;* Jeff Spoelman, *Grand Rapids Community College;* Norman Sunderman, *Angelo State University.*

Donald Terpstra, *Jefferson Community College;* Lynda Thompson, *Massasoit Community College;* Shafi Ullah, *Broward Community College;* Sue Van Boven, *Paradise Valley Community College;* Christian Widmer, *Tidewater Community College;* Wanda Wong, *Chabot College;* Pat Walczak, *Lansing Community College;* Kenton Walker, *University of Wyoming;* Patricia Wall, *Middle Tennessee State University;* Carol N. Welsh, *Rowan University;* Idalene Williams, *Metropolitan Community College;* Gloria Worthy, *Southwest Tennessee Community College.*

Thanks also to "perpetual reviewers" Robert Benjamin, *Taylor University;* Charles Malone, Tammy Wend, and Carol Wysocki, all of *Columbia Basin College;* and William Gregg of *Montgomery College.* We appreciate their continuing interest in the textbook and their regular contributions of ideas to improve it.

Tenth Edition

Thanks to the following reviewers, focus group participants, and others who provided suggestions for the Tenth Edition:

Sylvia Allen	Los Angeles Valley College
Juanita Ardavany	Los Angeles Valley College
Shele Bannon	Queensborough Community College
Amy Bentley	Tallahassee Community College
Timothy Bergsma	Davenport University
Teri Bernstein	Santa Monica College
Patrick Borja	Citrus College
Stanley Carroll	New York City College of Technology
Siu Chung	Los Angeles Valley College
Carol Collinsworth	University of Texas—Brownsville
Kelly Cranford	Hinds Community College—Raymond
Liz Diers	Black Hills State University
Samuel A. Duah	Bowie State University
Carle Essig	Montgomery County Community College
Annette Fisher	Glendale Community College
Kelly Ford	Queensborough Community College
Lori Grady	Bucks County Community College
Mary Halford	Prince Georges Community College
Thomas Kam	Hawaii Pacific University
Naomi Karolinski	Monroe Community College
Lynn Krausse	Bakersfield College
David Krug	Johnson County Community College
Cathy X. Larson	Middlesex Community College
David Laurel	South Texas College
Christina Manzo	Queensborough Community College
Beverly Mason	Front Range Community College
Robert Maxwell	College of the Canyons
Jill Mitchell	Northern Virginia Community College—Annandale
Ronald O'Brien	Fayetteville Technical Community College
Michael Motes	University of Maryland University College
Gregory L. Prescott	University of South Alabama
Jan Pitera	Broome Community College
Debra A. Sills Porter	Tidewater Community College
William Prosser	Cuyuga County Community College
Ada Rodriguez	Lehman College, The City University of New York
Eric Rothenburg	Kingsborough Community College, The City University of New York
Al Ruggiero	Suffolk County Community College
Marcia Sandvold	Des Moines Area Community College
Mary Jane Sauceda	University of Texas—Brownsville
Paul J. Shinal	Cayauga Community College
Bradley Smith	Des Moines Area Community College
Scott Stroher	Glendale Community College
Geoffrey Tickell	Indiana University of Pennsylvania
Pat Walczak	Lansing Community College
Wanda Wong	Chabot College
Jack Wiehler	San Joaquin Delta College

Ancillary Authors, Contributors, and Proofers

We sincerely thank the following individuals for their hard work in preparing the content that accompanies this textbook:

LuAnn Bean	Florida Institute of Technology
John C. Borke	University of Wisconsin—Platteville
Richard Campbell	Rio Grande College
Siu Chung	Los Angeles Valley College
Mel Coe	DeVry Institute of Technology, Atlanta
Chris Cole	Cole Creative Group
Joan Cook	Milwaukee Area Technical College
Larry Falcetto	Emporia State University
Mark Gleason	Metropolitan State University
Lori Grady	Bucks County Community College
Coby Harmon	University of California, Santa Barbara
Douglas W. Kieso	Aurora University
Yvonne Phang	Borough of Manhattan Community College
Rex A. Schildhouse	San Diego Community College—Miramar
Eileen Shifflett	James Madison University
Diane Tanner	University of North Florida
Sheila Viel	University of Wisconsin—Milwaukee
Dick Wasson	Southwestern College
Bernard Weinrich	Lindenwood University
Melanie Yon	

We also greatly appreciate the expert assistance provided by the following individuals in checking the accuracy of the content that accompanies this textbook:

LuAnn Bean	Florida Institute of Technology
Jack Borke	University of Wisconsin—Platteville
Sandee Cohen	Columbia College
Terry Elliott	Morehead State University
James Emig	Villanova University
Larry Falcetto	Emporia State University
Anthony Falgiani	Western Illinois University
Lori Grady	Bucks County Community College
Kirk Lynch	Sandhills Community College
Kevin McNelis	New Mexico State University
Jill Misuraca	Central Connecticut State University
Barbara Muller	Arizona State University
John Plouffe	California State University—Los Angeles
Ed Schell	University of Hawaii
Rex Schildhouse	San Diego Community College—Miramar
Alice Sineath	Forsyth Tech Community College
Teresa Speck	St. Mary's University
Lynn Stallworth	Appalachian State University
Sheila Viel	University of Wisconsin—Milwaukee
Dick Wasson	Southwestern College
Andrea Weickgenannt	Xavier University
Bernie Weinrich	Lindenwood University

Our thanks to the publishing "pros" who contribute to our efforts to publish high-quality products that benefit both teachers and students: Terry Ann Tatro, development editor; Ed Brislin, project editor; Yana Mermel, project editor; Allie K. Morris, executive media editor; Greg Chaput, media editor; Jacqueline Kepping, editorial assistant; Valerie A. Vargas, senior production editor; Maddy Lesure, textbook designer; Dorothy Sinclair, managing editor; Erin Bascom, production editor, Pam Kennedy, director of production and manufacturing; Ann Berlin, vice president of higher education production and manufacturing; Mary Ann Price, photo editor; Sandra Rigby, illustration editor; Suzanne Ingrao of Ingrao Associates, project manager; Jo-Anne Naples, permissions editor; Denise Showers of Aptara Inc., project manager at Aptara Inc.; Danielle Urban, project manager at Elm Street Publishing Services; and Cyndy Taylor. They provided innumerable services that helped this project take shape.

We also appreciate the exemplary support and professional commitment given us by Chris DeJohn, associate publisher, and the enthusiasm and ideas that Ramona Sherman, senior marketing manager, brings to the project.

Finally, our thanks to Amy Scholz, Susan Elbe, George Hoffman, Tim Stookesberry, Joe Heider, Bonnie Lieberman, and Will Pesce for their support and leadership in Wiley's College Division.

We thank PepsiCo, Inc. for permitting us the use of its 2009 annual reports for our specimen financial statements and accompanying notes. You can send your thoughts and ideas about the textbook to us via email at: *AccountingAuthors@yahoo.com*.

Jerry J. Weygandt
Madison, Wisconsin

Paul D. Kimmel
Milwaukee, Wisconsin

Donald E. Kieso
DeKalb, Illinois

Brief Contents

APPENDICES

Contents

chapter 18

Financial Statement Analysis 824

chapter 19

Managerial Accounting 876

chapter 20

Job Order Costing 922

chapter 21

Process Costing 964

CHAPTER 1

Accounting in Action

Study Objectives

After studying this chapter, you should be able to:

1. Explain what accounting is.
2. Identify the users and uses of accounting.
3. Understand why ethics is a fundamental business concept.
4. Explain generally accepted accounting principles.
5. Explain the monetary unit assumption and the economic entity assumption.
6. State the accounting equation, and define its components.
7. Analyze the effects of business transactions on the accounting equation.
8. Understand the four financial statements and how they are prepared.

Study Objectives give you a framework for learning the specific concepts covered in the chapter.

✔ The Navigator

✔ The Navigator

● Scan Study Objectives	○
● Read Feature Story	○
● Read Preview	○
● Read text and answer **Do it!** p. 11 ○ p. 14 ○ p. 21 ○ p. 25 ○	
● Work Comprehensive **Do it!** p. 26	○
● Review Summary of Study Objectives	○
● Answer Self-Test Questions	○
● Complete Assignments	○
● Go to *WileyPLUS* for practice and tutorials	○
● Read A Look at IFRS p. 46	○

The Navigator is a learning system designed to prompt you to use the learning aids in the chapter and set priorities as you study.

Feature Story

KNOWING THE NUMBERS

Many students who take this course do not plan to be accountants. If you are in that group, you might be thinking, "If I'm not going to be an accountant, why do I need to know accounting?" In response, consider the quote from Harold Geneen, the former chairman of IT&T: "To be good at your business, you have to know the numbers—cold." Success in any business comes back to the numbers. You will rely on them to make decisions, and managers will use them to evaluate your performance. That is true whether your job involves marketing, production, management, or information systems.

In business, accounting and financial statements are the means for communicating the numbers. If you don't know how to read financial statements, you can't really know your business.

Many companies spend significant resources teaching their employees basic accounting so

that they can read financial statements and understand how their actions affect the company's financial results. One such company is Springfield ReManufacturing Corporation (SRC). When Jack Stack and 11 other managers purchased SRC for 10 cents a share, it was a failing division of International Harvester. Jack's 119 employees, however, were counting on him for their livelihood. He decided that for the company to survive, every employee needed to think like a businessperson and to act like an owner. To accomplish this, all employees at SRC took basic accounting courses and participated in weekly reviews of the company's financial statements. SRC survived, and eventually thrived. To this day, every employee (now numbering more than 1,000) undergoes this same training.

Many other companies have adopted this approach, which is called "open-book management." Even in companies that do not practice open-book management, employers generally assume that managers in all areas of the company are "financially literate."

Taking this course will go a long way to making you financially literate. In this book, you will learn how to read and prepare financial statements, and how to use basic tools to evaluate financial results. Appendices A and B provide real financial statements of two well-known companies, PepsiCo, Inc. and The Coca-Cola Company. Throughout this textbook, we attempt to increase your familiarity with financial reporting by providing numerous references, questions, and exercises that encourage you to explore these financial statements.

The Feature Story helps you picture how the chapter topic relates to the real world of accounting and business. You will find references to the story throughout the chapter.

Inside**CHAPTER1**

"Inside Chapter x" lists boxes in the chapter that should be of special interest to you.

PreviewofCHAPTER1

The opening story about Springfield ReManufacturing Corporation highlights the importance of having good financial information to make effective business decisions. Whatever one's pursuits or occupation, the need for financial information is inescapable. You cannot earn a living, spend money, buy on credit, make an investment, or pay taxes without receiving, using, or dispensing financial information. Good decision making depends on good information.

The purpose of this chapter is to show you that accounting is the system used to provide useful financial information. The content and organization of Chapter 1 are as follows.

Accounting in Action

What Is Accounting?	The Building Blocks of Accounting	The Basic Accounting Equation	Using the Accounting Equation	Financial Statements
• Three activities • Who uses accounting data	• Ethics in financial reporting • Generally accepted accounting principles • Measurement principles • Assumptions	• Assets • Liabilities • Owner's equity	• Transaction analysis • Summary of transactions	• Income statement • Owner's equity statement • Balance sheet • Statement of cash flows

*The **Preview** describes and outlines the major topics and subtopics you will see in the chapter.*

The Navigator

What Is Accounting?

Study Objective [1]

Explain what accounting is.

Why is accounting so popular? What consistently ranks as one of the top career opportunities in business? What frequently rates among the most popular majors on campus? What was the undergraduate degree chosen by Nike founder Phil Knight, Home Depot co-founder Arthur Blank, former acting director of the Federal Bureau of Investigation (FBI) Thomas Pickard, and numerous members of Congress? Accounting.[1] Why did these people choose accounting? They wanted to understand what was happening financially to their organizations. Accounting is the financial information system that provides these insights. In short, to understand your organization, you have to know the numbers.

Accounting consists of three basic activities—it **identifies**, **records**, and **communicates** the economic events of an organization to interested users. Let's take a closer look at these three activities.

Three Activities

As a starting point to the accounting process, a company identifies the **economic events relevant to its business**. Examples of economic events are the sale of snack chips by PepsiCo, providing of telephone services by AT&T, and payment of wages by Ford Motor Company.

Once a company like PepsiCo identifies economic events, it **records** those events in order to provide a history of its financial activities. Recording consists of

---

[1]The appendix to this chapter describes job opportunities for accounting majors and explains why accounting is such a popular major.

keeping a **systematic**, **chronological diary of events**, measured in dollars and cents. In recording, PepsiCo also classifies and summarizes economic events.

Finally, PepsiCo **communicates** the collected information to interested users by means of **accounting reports**. The most common of these reports are called **financial statements**. To make the reported financial information meaningful, PepsiCo reports the recorded data in a standardized way. It accumulates information resulting from similar transactions. For example, PepsiCo accumulates all sales transactions over a certain period of time and reports the data as one amount in the company's financial statements. Such data are said to be reported **in the aggregate**. By presenting the recorded data in the aggregate, the accounting process simplifies a multitude of transactions and makes a series of activities understandable and meaningful.

A vital element in communicating economic events is the accountant's ability to **analyze and interpret** the reported information. Analysis involves use of ratios, percentages, graphs, and charts to highlight significant financial trends and relationships. Interpretation involves **explaining the uses**, **meaning**, **and limitations of reported data**. Appendix A of this textbook shows the financial statements of PepsiCo, Inc.; Appendix B illustrates the financial statements of The Coca-Cola Company. We refer to these statements at various places throughout the text. At this point, they probably strike you as complex and confusing. By the end of this course, you'll be surprised at your ability to understand, analyze, and interpret them.

Illustration 1-1 summarizes the activities of the accounting process.

Illustration 1-1
The activities of the accounting process

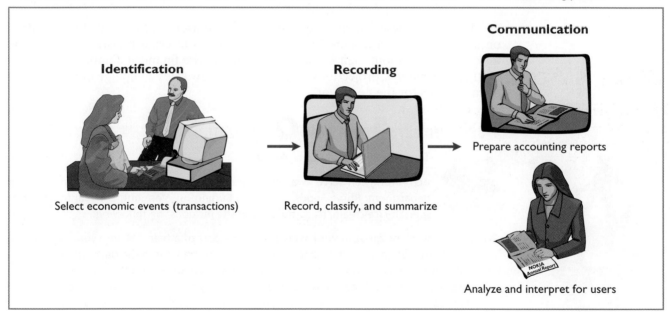

Identification

Select economic events (transactions)

Recording

Record, classify, and summarize

Communication

Prepare accounting reports

Analyze and interpret for users

You should understand that the accounting process **includes** the bookkeeping function. **Bookkeeping** usually involves **only** the recording of economic events. It is therefore just one part of the accounting process. In total, accounting involves **the entire process of identifying**, **recording**, **and communicating economic events**.[2]

Essential terms are printed in blue when they first appear, and are defined in the end-of-chapter glossary.

---

[2]The origins of accounting are generally attributed to the work of Luca Pacioli, an Italian Renaissance mathematician. Pacioli was a close friend and tutor to Leonardo da Vinci and a contemporary of Christopher Columbus. In his 1494 text *Summa de Arithmetica, Geometria, Proportione et Proportionalite*, Pacioli described a system to ensure that financial information was recorded efficiently and accurately.

Who Uses Accounting Data

Study Objective [2]
Identify the users and
uses of accounting.

The information that a user of financial information needs depends upon the kinds of decisions the user makes. There are two broad groups of users of financial information: internal users and external users.

INTERNAL USERS

Internal users of accounting information are managers who plan, organize, and run the business. These include marketing managers, production supervisors, finance directors, and company officers. In running a business, internal users must answer many important questions, as shown in Illustration 1-2.

Illustration 1-2
Questions that internal
users ask

Questions Asked by Internal Users

Finance	**Marketing**	**Human Resources**	**Management**
Is cash sufficient to pay dividends to Microsoft stockholders?	What price for an Apple iPod will maximize the company's net income?	Can we afford to give General Motors employees pay raises this year?	Which PepsiCo product line is the most profitable? Should any product lines be eliminated?

To answer these and other questions, internal users need detailed information on a timely basis. **Managerial accounting** provides internal reports to help users make decisions about their companies. Examples are financial comparisons of operating alternatives, projections of income from new sales campaigns, and forecasts of cash needs for the next year.

ACCOUNTING ACROSS THE ORGANIZATION

The Scoop on Accounting

Accounting can serve as a useful recruiting tool even for the human resources department. Rhino Foods, located in Burlington, Vermont, is a manufacturer of specialty ice cream. Its corporate website includes the following:

"Wouldn't it be great to work where you were part of a team? Where your input and hard work made a difference? Where you weren't kept in the dark about what management was thinking? . . . Well—it's not a dream! It's the way we do business . . . Rhino Foods believes in family, honesty and open communication—we really care about and appreciate our employees—and it shows. Operating results are posted and monthly group meetings inform all employees about what's happening in the Company. Employees also share in the Company's profits, in addition to having an excellent comprehensive benefits package."

Source: www.rhinofoods.com/workforus/workforus.html.

*Accounting Across the
Organization boxes
demonstrate applications of
accounting information in
various business functions.*

? What are the benefits to the company and to the employees of making the financial statements available to all employees? (See page 46.)

EXTERNAL USERS

External users are individuals and organizations outside a company who want financial information about the company. The two most common types of external users are investors and creditors. **Investors** (owners) use accounting information to make decisions to buy, hold, or sell ownership shares of a company. **Creditors** (such as suppliers and bankers) use accounting information to evaluate the risks of granting credit or lending money. Illustration 1-3 shows some questions that investors and creditors may ask.

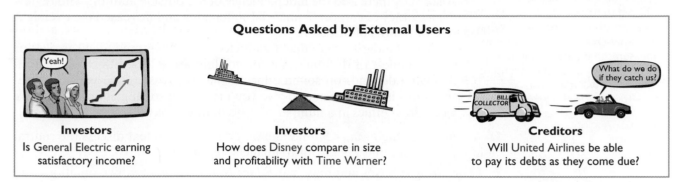

Questions Asked by External Users

Investors	**Investors**	**Creditors**
Is General Electric earning satisfactory income?	How does Disney compare in size and profitability with Time Warner?	Will United Airlines be able to pay its debts as they come due?

Illustration 1-3
Questions that external users ask

Financial accounting answers these questions. It provides economic and financial information for investors, creditors, and other external users. The information needs of external users vary considerably. **Taxing authorities**, such as the Internal Revenue Service, want to know whether the company complies with tax laws. **Regulatory agencies**, such as the Securities and Exchange Commission or the Federal Trade Commission, want to know whether the company is operating within prescribed rules. **Customers** are interested in whether a company like General Motors will continue to honor product warranties and support its product lines. **Labor unions** such as the Major League Baseball Players Association want to know whether the owners have the ability to pay increased wages and benefits.

The Building Blocks of Accounting

A doctor follows certain standards in treating a patient's illness. An architect follows certain standards in designing a building. An accountant follows certain standards in reporting financial information. For these standards to work, a fundamental business concept must be at work—ethical behavior.

Ethics in Financial Reporting

People won't gamble in a casino if they think it is "rigged." Similarly, people won't play the stock market if they think stock prices are rigged. In recent years the financial press has been full of articles about financial scandals at Enron, WorldCom, HealthSouth, AIG, and others. As the scandals came to light, mistrust of financial reporting in general grew. One article in the *Wall Street Journal* noted that "repeated disclosures about questionable accounting practices have bruised investors' faith in the reliability of earnings reports, which in turn has sent stock prices tumbling."[3] Imagine trying to carry on a business or invest money if you could not depend on the financial statements to be honestly prepared. Information would have no credibility. There is no doubt that a sound, well-functioning economy depends on accurate and dependable financial reporting.

United States regulators and lawmakers were very concerned that the economy would suffer if investors lost confidence in corporate accounting because of

Study Objective [3]
Understand why ethics is a fundamental business concept.

---

[3]"U.S. Share Prices Slump," *Wall Street Journal* (February 21, 2002).

unethical financial reporting. In response, Congress passed the **Sarbanes-Oxley Act of 2002** (SOX, or Sarbox). Its intent is to reduce unethical corporate behavior and decrease the likelihood of future corporate scandals. As a result of SOX, top management must now certify the accuracy of financial information. In addition, penalties for fraudulent financial activity are much more severe. Also, SOX increased the independence of the outside auditors who review the accuracy of corporate financial statements and increased the oversight role of boards of directors.

The standards of conduct by which one's actions are judged as right or wrong, honest or dishonest, fair or not fair, are **ethics**. Effective financial reporting depends on sound ethical behavior. To sensitize you to ethical situations in business and to give you practice at solving ethical dilemmas, we address ethics in a number of ways in this book:

1. A number of the *Feature Stories* and other parts of the text discuss the central importance of ethical behavior to financial reporting.

2. *Ethics Insight* boxes and marginal *Ethics Notes* highlight ethics situations and issues in actual business settings.

3. Many of the *All About You* topics (available on the book's companion website) focus on ethical issues you may face in your college and early-career years.

4. At the end of the chapter, an *Ethics Case* simulates a business situation and asks you to put yourself in the position of a decision maker in that case.

When analyzing these various ethics cases, as well as experiences in your own life, it is useful to apply the three steps outlined in Illustration 1-4.

Ethics Note

Circus-founder P.T. Barnum is alleged to have said, "Trust everyone, but cut the deck." What Sarbanes-Oxley does is to provide measures that (like cutting the deck of playing cards) help ensure that fraud will not occur.

Ethics Notes help sensitize you to some of the ethical issues in accounting.

Illustration 1-4
Steps in analyzing ethics cases and situations

1. **Recognize an ethical situation and the ethical issues involved.**	2. **Identify and analyze the principal elements in the situation.**	3. **Identify the alternatives, and weigh the impact of each alternative on various stakeholders.**
Use your personal ethics to identify ethical situations and issues. Some businesses and professional organizations provide written codes of ethics for guidance in some business situations.	Identify the *stakeholders*—persons or groups who may be harmed or benefited. Ask the question: What are the responsibilities and obligations of the parties involved?	Select the most ethical alternative, considering all the consequences. Sometimes there will be one right answer. Other situations involve more than one right solution; these situations require an evaluation of each and a selection of the best alternative.

Insights provide examples of business situations from various perspectives—ethics, investor, and international.

*E*THICS *I*NSIGHT

The Numbers Behind Not-for-Profit Organizations

Accounting plays an important role for a wide range of business organizations worldwide. Just as the integrity of the numbers matters for business, it matters at least as much for not-for-profit organizations. Proper control and reporting help ensure that money is used the way donors intended. Donors are less inclined to give to an organization if they think the organization is subject to waste or theft. The accounting challenges of some large international not-for-profits rival those of the world's largest businesses. For example, after the Haitian earthquake, the Haitian-born musician Wyclef Jean was criticized for the poor accounting controls in a relief fund that he founded. Since then, he has hired a new accountant and improved the transparency regarding funds raised and spent.

? What benefits does a sound accounting system provide to a not-for-profit organization? (See page 46.)

Generally Accepted Accounting Principles

The accounting profession has developed standards that are generally accepted and universally practiced. This common set of standards is called **generally accepted accounting principles (GAAP)**. These standards indicate how to report economic events.

The primary accounting standard-setting body in the United States is the **Financial Accounting Standards Board (FASB)**. The **Securities and Exchange Commission (SEC)** is the agency of the U.S. government that oversees U.S. financial markets and accounting standard-setting bodies. The SEC relies on the FASB to develop accounting standards, which public companies must follow. Many countries outside of the United States have adopted the accounting standards issued by the **International Accounting Standards Board (IASB)**. These standards are called International Financial Reporting Standards (IFRS).

As markets become more global, it is often desirable to compare the result of companies from different countries that report using different accounting standards. In order to increase comparability, in recent years the two standard-setting bodies have made efforts to reduce the differences between U.S. GAAP and IFRS. This process is referred to as **convergence**. As a result of these convergence efforts, it is likely that someday there will be a single set of high-quality accounting standards that are used by companies around the world. Because convergence is such an important issue, we highlight any major differences between GAAP and IFRS in *International Notes* (as shown in the margin here) and provide a more in-depth discussion in the *A Look at IRFS* section at the end of each chapter.

> **Study Objective [4]**
> Explain generally accepted accounting principles.

> **International Note**
>
> Over 100 countries use International Financial Reporting Standards (called IFRS). For example, all companies in the European Union follow international standards. The differences between U.S. and international standards are not generally significant.

International Notes highlight differences between U.S. and international accounting standards.

Measurement Principles

GAAP generally uses one of two measurement principles, the cost principle or the fair value principle. Selection of which principle to follow generally relates to trade-offs between relevance and faithful representation. **Relevance** means that financial information is capable of making a difference in a decision. **Faithful representation** means that the numbers and descriptions match what really existed or happened — it if factual.

> **Helpful Hint**
>
> *Relevance* and *faithful representation* are two primary qualities that make accounting information useful for decision making.
>
> *Helpful Hints further clarify concepts being discussed.*

COST PRINCIPLE

The **cost principle** (or historical cost principle) dictates that companies record assets at their cost. This is true not only at the time the asset is purchased, but also over the time the asset is held. For example if Best Buy purchases land for $300,000, the company initially reports it in its accounting records at $300,000. But what does Best Buy do if, by the end of the next year, the fair value of the land has increased to $400,000? Under the cost principle, it continues to report the land at $300,000.

FAIR VALUE PRINCIPLE

The **fair value principle** states that assets and liabilities should be reported at fair value (the price received to sell an asset or settle a liability). Fair value information may be more useful than historical cost for certain types of assets and liabilities. For example, certain investment securities are reported at fair value because market value information is usually readily available for these types of assets. In determining which measurement principle to use, companies weigh the factual nature of cost figures versus the relevance of fair value. In general, most companies choose to use cost. Only in situations where assets are actively traded, such as investment securities, do companies apply the fair value principle extensively.

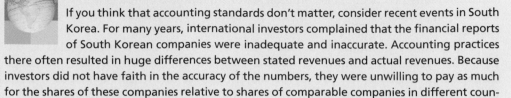

INTERNATIONAL INSIGHT

The Korean Discount

If you think that accounting standards don't matter, consider recent events in South Korea. For many years, international investors complained that the financial reports of South Korean companies were inadequate and inaccurate. Accounting practices there often resulted in huge differences between stated revenues and actual revenues. Because investors did not have faith in the accuracy of the numbers, they were unwilling to pay as much for the shares of these companies relative to shares of comparable companies in different countries. This difference in stock price was often referred to as the "Korean discount."

In response, Korean regulators decided that, beginning in 2011, companies will have to comply with international accounting standards. This change was motivated by a desire to "make the country's businesses more transparent" in order to build investor confidence and spur economic growth. Many other Asian countries, including China, India, Japan, and Hong Kong, have also decided either to adopt international standards or to create standards that are based on the international standards.

Source: Evan Ramstad, "End to 'Korea Discount'?" *Wall Street Journal* (March 16, 2007).

? What is meant by the phrase "make the country's businesses more transparent"? Why would increasing transparency spur economic growth? (See page 46.)

Assumptions

Study Objective [5]

Explain the monetary unit assumption and the economic entity assumption.

Assumptions provide a foundation for the accounting process. Two main assumptions are the **monetary unit assumption** and the **economic entity assumption**.

MONETARY UNIT ASSUMPTION

The monetary unit assumption requires that companies include in the accounting records only transaction data that can be expressed in money terms. This assumption enables accounting to quantify (measure) economic events. The monetary unit assumption is vital to applying the cost principle.

This assumption prevents the inclusion of some relevant information in the accounting records. For example, the health of a company's owner, the quality of service, and the morale of employees are not included. The reason: Companies cannot quantify this information in money terms. Though this information is important, companies record only events that can be measured in money.

ECONOMIC ENTITY ASSUMPTION

An economic entity can be any organization or unit in society. It may be a company (such as Crocs, Inc.), a governmental unit (the state of Ohio), a municipality (Seattle), a school district (St. Louis District 48), or a church (Southern Baptist). The economic entity assumption requires that the activities of the entity be kept separate and distinct from the activities of its owner and all other economic entities. To illustrate, Sally Rider, owner of Sally's Boutique, must keep her personal living costs separate from the expenses of the Boutique. Similarly, McDonald's, Coca-Cola, and Cadbury-Schweppes are segregated into separate economic entities for accounting purposes.

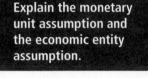

Ethics Note

The importance of the economic entity assumption is illustrated by scandals involving Adelphia. In this case, senior company employees entered into transactions that blurred the line between the employees' financial interests and those of the company. For example, Aldephia guaranteed over $2 billion of loans to the founding family.

Proprietorship. A business owned by one person is generally a proprietorship. The owner is often the manager/operator of the business. Small service-type businesses (plumbing companies, beauty salons, and auto repair shops), farms, and small retail stores (antique shops, clothing stores, and used-book stores) are often proprietorships. **Usually only a relatively small amount of money (capital) is necessary to start in business as a proprietorship. The owner (proprietor) receives any profits, suffers any losses, and is personally liable for all debts of the business.** There is no legal distinction between the business as an economic unit and the owner, but the accounting records of the business activities are kept separate from the personal records and activities of the owner.

Partnership. A business owned by two or more persons associated as partners is a partnership. In most respects a partnership is like a proprietorship except that more than one owner is involved. Typically a partnership agreement (written or oral) sets forth such terms as initial investment, duties of each partner, division of net income (or net loss), and settlement to be made upon death or withdrawal of a partner. Each partner generally has unlimited personal liability for the debts of the partnership. **Like a proprietorship, for accounting purposes the partnership transactions must be kept separate from the personal activities of the partners.** Partnerships are often used to organize retail and service-type businesses, including professional practices (lawyers, doctors, architects, and certified public accountants).

Corporation. A business organized as a separate legal entity under state corporation law and having ownership divided into transferable shares of stock is a corporation. The holders of the shares (stockholders) **enjoy limited liability**; that is, they are not personally liable for the debts of the corporate entity. Stockholders **may transfer all or part of their ownership shares to other investors at any time** (i.e., sell their shares). The ease with which ownership can change adds to the attractiveness of investing in a corporation. Because ownership can be transferred without dissolving the corporation, the corporation **enjoys an unlimited life**.

Although the combined number of proprietorships and partnerships in the United States is more than five times the number of corporations, the revenue produced by corporations is eight times greater. Most of the largest enterprises in the United States—for example, ExxonMobil, Ford, Wal-Mart, Citigroup, and Apple—are corporations.

The Do it! exercises ask you to put newly acquired knowledge to work. They outline the Action Plan necessary to complete the exercise, and they show a Solution.

Do it!

Indicate whether each of the five statements presented below is true or false.

Basic Concepts

1. The three steps in the accounting process are identification, recording, and communication.
2. The two most common types of external users are investors and company officers.
3. Congress passed the Sarbanes-Oxley Act of 2002 to reduce unethical behavior and decrease the likelihood of future corporate scandals.
4. The primary accounting standard-setting body in the United States is the Financial Accounting Standards Board (FASB).
5. The cost principle dictates that companies record assets at their cost. In later periods, however, the fair value of the asset must be used if fair value is higher than its cost.

action plan

✔ Review the basic concepts learned to date.

✔ Develop an understanding of the key terms used.

Solution

1. True   2. False. The two most common types of external users are investors and creditors.   3. True.   4. True.   5. False. The cost principle dictates that companies record assets at their cost. Under the cost principle, the company must also use cost in later periods as well.

Related exercise material: E1-1, E1-2, E1-3, E1-4, and **Do it!** 1-1.

✔
The Navigator

ACCOUNTING ACROSS THE ORGANIZATION

Spinning the Career Wheel

One question that students frequently ask is, "How will the study of accounting help me?" It should help you a great deal, because a working knowledge of accounting is desirable for virtually *every field* of endeavor. Some examples of how accounting is used in other careers include:

General management: Imagine running Ford Motors, Massachusetts General Hospital, Northern Virginia Community College, a Subway franchise, a Trek bike shop. All general managers need to understand accounting data in order to make wise business decisions.

Marketing: A marketing specialist at a company like Procter & Gamble develops strategies to help the sales force be successful. But making a sale is meaningless unless it is a profitable sale. Marketing people must be sensitive to costs and benefits, which accounting helps them quantify and understand.

Finance: Do you want to be a banker for Bank of America, an investment analyst for Goldman Sachs, a stock broker for Merrill Lynch? These fields rely heavily on accounting. In all of them you will regularly examine and analyze financial statements. In fact, it is difficult to get a good finance job without two or three courses in accounting.

Real estate: Are you interested in being a real estate broker for Prudential Real Estate? Because a third party—the bank—is almost always involved in financing a real estate transaction, brokers must understand the numbers involved: Can the buyer afford to make the payments to the bank? Does the cash flow from an industrial property justify the purchase price? What are the tax benefits of the purchase?

? How might accounting help you? (See page 46.)

The Basic Accounting Equation

Study Objective [6]
State the accounting equation, and define its components.

The two basic elements of a business are what it owns and what it owes. **Assets** are the resources a business owns. For example, Google has total assets of approximately $40.5 billion. Liabilities and owner's equity are the rights or claims against these resources. Thus, Google has $40.5 billion of claims against its $40.5 billion of assets. Claims of those to whom the company owes money (creditors) are called **liabilities**. Claims of owners are called **owner's equity**. Google has liabilities of $4.5 billion and owners' equity of $36 billion.

We can express the relationship of assets, liabilities, and owner's equity as an equation, as shown in Illustration 1-5.

Illustration 1-5
The basic accounting equation

Assets	=	Liabilities	+	Owner's Equity

This relationship is the **basic accounting equation**. Assets must equal the sum of liabilities and owner's equity. Liabilities appear before owner's equity in the basic accounting equation because they are paid first if a business is liquidated.

The accounting equation applies to all **economic entities** regardless of size, nature of business, or form of business organization. It applies to a small proprietorship such as a corner grocery store as well as to a giant corporation such as PepsiCo. The equation provides the **underlying framework** for recording and summarizing economic events.

Let's look in more detail at the categories in the basic accounting equation.

Assets

As noted above, assets are resources a business owns. The business uses its assets in carrying out such activities as production and sales. The common characteristic possessed by all assets is **the capacity to provide future services or benefits**. In a business, that service potential or future economic benefit eventually results in cash inflows (receipts). For example, Campus Pizza owns a delivery truck that provides economic benefits from delivering pizzas. Other assets of Campus Pizza are tables, chairs, jukebox, cash register, oven, tableware, and, of course, cash.

Liabilities

Liabilities are claims against assets—that is, existing debts and obligations. Businesses of all sizes usually borrow money and purchase merchandise on credit. These economic activities result in payables of various sorts:

- Campus Pizza, for instance, purchases cheese, sausage, flour, and beverages on credit from suppliers. These obligations are called **accounts payable**.
- Campus Pizza also has a **note payable** to First National Bank for the money borrowed to purchase the delivery truck.
- Campus Pizza may also have **salaries and wages payable** to employees and **sales and real estate taxes payable** to the local government.

All of these persons or entities to whom Campus Pizza owes money are its **creditors**.

Creditors may legally force the liquidation of a business that does not pay its debts. In that case, the law requires that creditor claims be paid **before** ownership claims.

Owner's Equity

The ownership claim on total assets is owner's equity. It is equal to total assets minus total liabilities. Here is why: The assets of a business are claimed by either creditors or owners. To find out what belongs to owners, we subtract the creditors' claims (the liabilities) from assets. The remainder is the owner's claim on the assets—the owner's equity. Since the claims of creditors must be paid **before** ownership claims, owner's equity is often referred to as **residual equity**.

INCREASES IN OWNER'S EQUITY

In a proprietorship, owner's investments and revenues increase owner's equity.

Investments by Owner. Investments by owner are the assets the owner puts into the business. These investments increase owner's equity. They are recorded in a category called **owner's capital**.

Revenues. Revenues are the **gross increase in owner's equity resulting from business activities entered into for the purpose of earning income**. Generally, revenues result from selling merchandise, performing services, renting property, and lending money. Common sources of revenue are sales, fees, services, commissions, interest, dividends, royalties, and rent.

Revenues usually result in an increase in an asset. They may arise from different sources and are called various names depending on the nature of the business. Campus Pizza, for instance, has two categories of sales revenues—pizza sales and beverage sales.

DECREASES IN OWNER'S EQUITY

In a proprietorship, owner's drawings and expenses decrease owner's equity.

Drawings. An owner may withdraw cash or other assets for personal use. We use a separate classification called drawings to determine the total withdrawals for each accounting period. **Drawings decrease owner's equity.** They are recorded in a category called owner's drawings.

Helpful Hint

In some places, we use the term "owner's equity" and in others we use "owners' equity." *Owner's* (singular, possessive) refers to one owner (the case with a sole proprietorship). *Owners'* (plural, possessive) refers to multiple owners (the case with partnerships or corporations).

Expenses. Expenses are the cost of assets consumed or services used in the process of earning revenue. They are **decreases in owner's equity that result from operating the business**. For example, Campus Pizza recognizes the following expenses: cost of ingredients (meat, flour, cheese, tomato paste, mushrooms, etc.); cost of beverages; salaries and wages expense; utilities expense (electric, gas, and water expense); delivery expense (gasoline, repairs, licenses, etc.); supplies expense (napkins, detergents, aprons, etc.); rent expense; interest expense; and property tax expense.

In summary, owner's equity is increased by an owner's investments and by revenues from business operations. Owner's equity is decreased by an owner's withdrawals of assets and by expenses. Illustration 1-6 expands the basic accounting equation by showing the accounts that comprise owner's equity. This format is referred to as the expanded accounting equation.

Illustration 1-6
Expanded accounting equation

Basic Equation:	Assets = Liabilities	+	Owner's Equity
Expanded Equation:	Assets = Liabilities	+	Owner's Capital − Owner's Drawings + Revenues − Expenses

Do it!

Owner's Equity Effects

action plan

✔ Understand the sources of revenue.

✔ Understand what causes expenses.

✔ Review the rules for changes in owner's equity: Investments and revenues increase owner's equity. Expenses and drawings decrease owner's equity.

✔ Recognize that drawings are withdrawals of cash or other assets from the business for personal use.

Classify the following items as investment by owner (I), owner's drawings (D), revenues (R), or expenses (E). Then indicate whether each item increases or decreases owner's equity.

(1) Rent Expense   (3) Drawings
(2) Service Revenue   (4) Salaries and Wages Expense

Solution

1. Rent Expense is an expense (E); it decreases owner's equity. 2. Service Revenue is revenue (R); it increases owner's equity. 3. Drawings is owner's drawings (D); it decreases owner's equity. 4. Salaries and Wages Expense is an expense (E); it decreases owner's equity.

Related exercise material: BE1-1, BE1-2, BE1-3, BE1-4, BE1-5, E1-5, E1-6, E1-7, and **Do it!** 1-2.

✔ The Navigator

Using the Accounting Equation

Study Objective [7]

Analyze the effects of business transactions on the accounting equation.

Transactions (**business transactions**) are a business's economic events recorded by accountants. Transactions may be external or internal. **External transactions** involve economic events between the company and some outside enterprise. For example, Campus Pizza's purchase of cooking equipment from a supplier, payment of monthly rent to the landlord, and sale of pizzas to customers are external transactions. **Internal transactions** are economic events that occur entirely within one company. The use of cooking and cleaning supplies are internal transactions for Campus Pizza.

Companies carry on many activities that do not represent business transactions. Examples are hiring employees, answering the telephone, talking with customers, and placing merchandise orders. Some of these activities may lead to business transactions: Employees will earn wages, and suppliers will deliver ordered merchandise. The company must analyze each event to find out if it affects the components of the accounting equation. If it does, the company will record the transaction. Illustration 1-7 demonstrates the transaction-identification process.

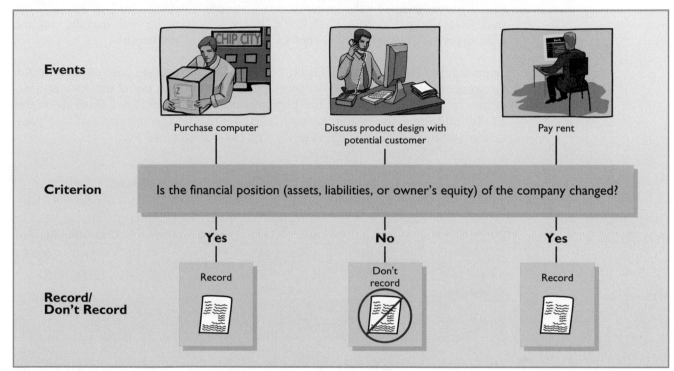

Illustration 1-7
Transaction-identification process

Each transaction must have a dual effect on the accounting equation. For example, if an asset is increased, there must be a corresponding: (1) decrease in another asset, or (2) increase in a specific liability, or (3) increase in owner's equity.

Two or more items could be affected. For example, as one asset is increased $10,000, another asset could decrease $6,000 and a liability could increase $4,000. Any change in a liability or ownership claim is subject to similar analysis.

Transaction Analysis

The following examples are business transactions for a computer programming business during its first month of operations.

Transaction (1). Investment by Owner. Ray Neal decides to open a computer programming service which he names Softbyte. On September 1, 2012, he invests $15,000 cash in the business. This transaction results in an equal increase in assets and owner's equity.

Helpful Hint

You will want to study these transactions until you are sure you understand them. They are not difficult, but understanding them is important to your success in this course. The ability to analyze transactions in terms of the basic accounting equation is essential in accounting.

Basic Analysis	The asset Cash increases $15,000, and owner's equity identified as Owner's Capital increases $15,000.

Equation Analysis		Assets	=	Liabilities	+	Owner's Equity

	Assets	**=**	**Liabilities**	**+**	**Owner's Equity**
	Cash	=			Owner's Capital
(1)	+$15,000	=			+$15,000 **Initial investment**

Observe that the equality of the accounting equation has been maintained. Note that the investments by the owner do not represent revenues, and they are excluded in determining net income. Therefore it is necessary to make clear that the increase is an investment (increasing Owner's Capital) rather than revenue.

Transaction (2). Purchase of Equipment for Cash. Softbyte purchases computer equipment for $7,000 cash. This transaction results in an equal increase and decrease in total assets, though the composition of assets changes. Cash decreases $7,000, and the asset Equipment increases $7,000. The specific effect of this transaction and the cumulative effect of the first two transactions are:

Basic Analysis	Cash decreases $7,000, and the asset Equipment increases $7,000.

Equation Analysis		**Assets**			**=**	**Liabilities**	**+**	**Owner's Equity**

	Cash	**+**	**Equipment**	**=**		**Owner's Capital**
	$15,000					$15,000
(2)	−7,000		+$7,000			
	$ 8,000	+	$7,000	=		$15,000
		$15,000				

Observe that total assets are still $15,000. Neal's equity also remains at $15,000, the amount of his original investment.

Transaction (3). Purchase of Supplies on Credit. Softbyte purchases for $1,600 from Acme Supply Company computer paper and other supplies expected to last several months. Acme agrees to allow Softbyte to pay this bill in October. This transaction is a purchase on account (a credit purchase). Assets increase because of the expected future benefits of using the paper and supplies, and liabilities increase by the amount due Acme Company.

Basic Analysis	The asset Supplies increases $1,600, and the liability Accounts Payable increases by $1,600.

			Assets			**=**	**Liabilities**	**+**	**Owner's Equity**

	Cash	**+**	**Supplies**	**+**	**Equipment**	**=**	**Accounts Payable**	**+**	**Owner's Capital**
	$8,000				$7,000				$15,000
(3)			+$1,600				+$1,600		
	$8,000	+	$1,600	+	$7,000	=	$1,600	+	$15,000
			$16,600					$16,600	

Total assets are now $16,600. This total is matched by a $1,600 creditor's claim and a $15,000 ownership claim.

Transaction (4). Services Provided for Cash.   Softbyte receives $1,200 cash from customers for programming services it has provided. This transaction represents Softbyte's principal revenue-producing activity. Recall that **revenue increases owner's equity**.

Basic Analysis	Cash increases $1,200, and revenues (specifically, Service Revenue) increase $1,200.

Equation Analysis		Assets			=	Liabilities	+	Owner's Equity		

		Assets			=	Liabilities	+	Owner's Equity			
	Cash	+	Supplies	+	Equipment	=	Accounts Payable	+	Owner's Capital	+	Revenues
	$8,000		$1,600		$7,000		$1,600		$15,000		
(4)	+$1,200										+$1,200 Service Revenue
	$9,200	+	$1,600	+	$7,000	=	$1,600	+	$15,000	+	$1,200
			$17,800						$17,800		

The two sides of the equation balance at $17,800. Service Revenue is included in determining Softbyte's net income.

Note that we do not have room to give details for each individual revenue and expense account in this illustration. Thus, revenues (and expenses when we get to them) are summarized under one column heading for Revenues and one for Expenses. However, it is important to keep track of the category (account) titles affected (e.g., Service Revenue) as they will be needed when we prepare financial statements later in the chapter.

Transaction (5). Purchase of Advertising on Credit. Softbyte receives a bill for $250 from the *Daily News* for advertising but postpones payment until a later date. This transaction results in an increase in liabilities and a decrease in owner's equity. The specific categories involved are Accounts Payable and expenses (specifically, Advertising Expense). The effect on the equation is:

Basic Analysis	Accounts Payable increases $250, and owner's equity decreases $250 due to Advertising Expense.

Equation Analysis

		Assets			=	Liabilities	+	Owner's Equity				
	Cash	+	Supplies	+	Equipment	=	Accounts Payable	+	Owner's Capital	+	Revenues	−	Expenses
	$9,200		$1,600		$7,000		$1,600		$15,000		$1,200		
(5)							+250						−$250 Advertising Expense
	$9,200	+	$1,600	+	$7,000	=	$1,850	+	$15,000	+	$1,200	−	$250
			$17,800						$17,800				

The two sides of the equation still balance at $17,800. Owner's equity decreases when Softbyte incurs the expense. Expenses are not always paid in cash at the time they are incurred. When Softbyte pays at a later date, the liability Accounts Payable will decrease, and the asset Cash will decrease [see Transaction (8)]. The cost of advertising is an expense (rather than an asset) because the company has *used* the benefits. Advertising Expense is included in determining net income.

Transaction (6). Services Provided for Cash and Credit. Softbyte provides $3,500 of programming services for customers. The company receives cash of $1,500 from customers, and it bills the balance of $2,000 on account. This transaction results in an equal increase in assets and owner's equity.

Basic Analysis	Three specific items are affected: Cash increases $1,500, Accounts Receivable increases $2,000, and Service Revenue increases $3,500.

Equation Analysis

	Assets				=	Liabilities	+	Owner's Equity			
	Cash	+ Accounts Receivable	+ Supplies	+ Equipment	=	Accounts Payable	+ Owner's Capital	+ Revenues	− Expenses		
	$9,200		$1,600	$7,000		$1,850	$15,000	$1,200	$250		
(6)	+1,500	+$2,000						+3,500			Service Revenue
	$10,700 +	$2,000 +	$1,600 +	$7,000	=	$1,850 +	$15,000 +	$4,700	− $250		
		$21,300					$21,300				

Softbyte earns revenues when it provides the service, and therefore it recognizes $3,500 in revenue. In exchange for this service, it received $1,500 in Cash and Accounts Receivable of $2,000. This Accounts Receivable represents customers' promise to pay $2,000 to Softbyte in the future. When it later receives collections on account, Softbyte will increase Cash and will decrease Accounts Receivable [see Transaction (9)].

Transaction (7). Payment of Expenses. Softbyte pays the following expenses in cash for September: store rent $600, salaries and wages of employees $900, and utilities $200. These payments result in an equal decrease in assets and expenses. Cash decreases $1,700, and the specific expense categories (Rent Expense, Salaries and Wages Expense, and Utilities Expense) decrease owner's equity by the same amount. The effect of these payments on the equation is:

	Assets				=	Liabilities	+	Owner's Equity			
	Cash	+ Accounts Receivable	+ Supplies	+ Equipment	=	Accounts Payable	+ Owner's Capital	+ Revenues	− Expenses		
	$10,700	$2,000	$1,600	$7,000		$1,850	$15,000	$4,700	$ 250		
(7)	−1,700								−600		Rent Expense
									−900		Sal. and Wages Exp.
									−200		Utilities Exp.
	$9,000 +	$2,000 +	$1,600 +	$7,000	=	$1,850 +	$15,000 +	$4,700	− $1,950		
		$19,600					$19,600				

The two sides of the equation now balance at $19,600. Three lines in the analysis indicate the different types of expenses that have been incurred.

Transaction (8). Payment of Accounts Payable. Softbyte pays its $250 *Daily News* bill in cash. The company previously [in Transaction (5)] recorded the bill as an increase in Accounts Payable and a decrease in owner's equity.

Basic Analysis	This cash payment "on account" decreases the asset Cash by $250 and also decreases the liability Accounts Payable by $250.

		Assets				=	Liabilities	+		Owner's Equity		
	Cash	+	Accounts Receivable	+	Supplies	+	Equipment	=	Accounts Payable	+	Owner's Capital	+	Revenues	−	Expenses
	$9,000		$2,000		$1,600		$7,000		$1,850		$15,000		$4,700		$1,950
(8)	−250								−250						
	$8,750	+	$2,000	+	$1,600	+	$7,000	=	$1,600	+	$15,000	+	$4,700	−	$1,950
			$19,350								$19,350				

Observe that the payment of a liability related to an expense that has previously been recorded does not affect owner's equity. The company recorded this expense in Transaction (5) and should not record it again.

Transaction (9). Receipt of Cash on Account. Softbyte receives $600 in cash from customers who had been billed for services [in Transaction (6)]. This does not change total assets, but it changes the composition of those assets.

Basic Analysis	Cash increases $600, and Accounts Receivable decreases $600.

		Assets				=	Liabilities	+		Owner's Equity		
	Cash	+	Accounts Receivable	+	Supplies	+	Equipment	=	Accounts Payable	+	Owner's Capital	+	Revenues	−	Expenses
	$8,750		$2,000		$1,600		$7,000		$1,600		$15,000		$4,700		$1,950
(9)	+600		−600												
	$9,350	+	$1,400	+	$1,600	+	$7,000	=	$1,600	+	$15,000	+	$4,700	−	$1,950
			$19,350								$19,350				

Note that the collection of an account receivable for services previously billed and recorded does not affect owner's equity. Softbyte already recorded this revenue in Transaction (6) and should not record it again.

Transaction (10). Withdrawal of Cash by Owner. Ray Neal withdraws $1,300 in cash from the business for his personal use. This transaction results in an equal decrease in assets and owner's equity. Both Cash and Owner's Drawings decrease $1,300, as shown on the next page.

Basic Analysis	Cash decreases $1,300, and Owner's Drawings decreases $1,300 due to owner's withdrawal.

			Assets			= **Liabilities** +			**Owner's Equity**			
	Cash	+	Accounts Receivable	+ Supplies	+ Equipment =	Accounts Payable	+	Owner's Capital	− Owner's Drawings	+ Revenues	− Expenses	
	$9,350		$1,400	$1,600	$7,000	$1,600		$15,000		$4,700	$1,950	
(10)	−1,300								−$1,300			**Drawings**
	$8,050 +		$1,400	+ $1,600 +	$7,000 =	$1,600	+	$15,000 −	$1,300 +	$4,700	− $1,950	
				$18,050					$18,050			

Observe that the effect of a cash withdrawal by the owner is the opposite of the effect of an investment by the owner. **Owner's drawings are not expenses.** Expenses are incurred for the purpose of earning revenue. Drawings do not generate revenue. They are a **disinvestment**. Like owner's investment, the company excludes owner's drawings in determining net income.

Summary of Transactions

Illustration 1-8 summarizes the September transactions of Softbyte to show their cumulative effect on the basic accounting equation. It also indicates the transaction number and the specific effects of each transaction.

			Assets			= **Liabilities** +			**Owner's Equity**			
	Cash	+	Accounts Receivable +	Supplies +	Equipment =	Accounts Payable	+	Owner's Capital	− Owner's Drawings	+ Rev.	− Exp.	
(1)	+$15,000						+	$15,000				Initial inv.
(2)	−7,000				+$7,000							
(3)				+$1,600		+$1,600						
(4)	+1,200									+$1,200		Ser. Rev.
(5)						+250					−$250	Adv. Exp.
(6)	+1,500		+$2,000							+3,500		Ser. Rev.
(7)	−600										−600	Rent Exp.
	−900										−900	Sal./Wages Exp.
	−200										−200	Utilities Exp.
(8)	−250					−250						
(9)	+600		−600									
(10)	−1,300								−$1,300			Drawings
	$ 8,050 +		$1,400 +	$1,600 +	$7,000 =	$1,600	+	$15,000 −	$1,300 +	$4,700 −	$1,950	
				$18,050					$18,050			

Illustration 1-8
Tabular summary of Softbyte transactions

Illustration 1-8 demonstrates some significant facts:

1. Each transaction is analyzed in terms of its effect on:
   (a) the three components of the basic accounting equation.
   (b) specific items within each component.
2. The two sides of the equation must always be equal.

There! You made it through your first transaction analysis. If you feel a bit shaky on any of the transactions, it might be a good idea at this point to get up, take a short break, and come back again for a 10- to 15-minute review of the transactions, to make sure you understand them before you go on to the next section.

Do it!

Transactions made by Virmari & Co., a public accounting firm, for the month of August are shown below. Prepare a tabular analysis which shows the effects of these transactions on the expanded accounting equation, similar to that shown in Illustration 1-8.

1. The owner invested $25,000 cash in the business.
2. The company purchased $7,000 of office equipment on credit.
3. The company received $8,000 cash in exchange for services performed.
4. The company paid $850 for this month's rent.
5. The owner withdrew $1,000 cash for personal use.

Tabular Analysis

action plan

✔ Analyze the effects of each transaction on the accounting equation.

✔ Use appropriate category names (not descriptions).

✔ Keep the accounting equation in balance.

Solution

	Assets		=	Liabilities	+			Owner's Equity			
	Cash	+ Equipment	=	Accounts Payable	+	Owner's Capital	−	Owner's Drawings	+ Revenues	−	Expenses
1.	+$25,000					+$25,000					
2.		+$7,000		+$7,000							
3.	+8,000								+$8,000		
4.	−850										−$850
5.	−1,000							−$1,000			
	$31,150	+ $7,000	=	$7,000	+	$25,000	−	$1,000	+ $8,000	−	$850
	$38,150							$38,150			

Related exercise material: BE1-6, BE1-7, BE1-8, BE1-9, E1-6, E1-7, E1-8, E1-10, E1-11, and **Do it!** 1-3.

✔ **The Navigator**

Financial Statements

Companies prepare four financial statements from the summarized accounting data:

1. An **income statement** presents the revenues and expenses and resulting net income or net loss for a specific period of time.
2. An **owner's equity statement** summarizes the changes in owner's equity for a specific period of time.
3. A **balance sheet** reports the assets, liabilities, and owner's equity at a specific date.
4. A **statement of cash flows** summarizes information about the cash inflows (receipts) and outflows (payments) for a specific period of time.

These statements provide relevant financial data for internal and external users. Illustration 1-9 (page 22) shows the financial statements of Softbyte.

Study Objective [8]
Understand the four financial statements and how they are prepared.

International Note

The primary types of financial statements required by GAAP and IFRS are the same. In practice, some format differences do exist in presentations commonly employed by GAAP companies compared to IFRS companies.

Illustration 1-9
Financial statements and their interrelationships

Helpful Hint

The heading of each statement identifies the company, the type of statement, and the specific date or time period covered by the statement.

Helpful Hint

Note that final sums are double-underlined, and negative amounts (in the statement of cash flows) are presented in parentheses.

Helpful Hint

The arrows in this illustration show the interrelationships of the four financial statements.

1. Net income is computed first and is needed to determine the ending balance in owner's equity.
2. The ending balance in owner's equity is needed in preparing the balance sheet.
3. The cash shown on the balance sheet is needed in preparing the statement of cash flows.

Softbyte
Income Statement
For the Month Ended September 30, 2012

Revenues		
Service revenue		$ 4,700
Expenses		
Salaries and wages expense	$900	
Rent expense	600	
Advertising expense	250	
Utilities expense	200	
Total expenses		1,950
Net income		$ 2,750

Softbyte
Owner's Equity Statement
For the Month Ended September 30, 2012

Owner's capital, September 1		$ –0–
Add: Investments	$15,000	
Net income	2,750	17,750
		17,750
Less: Drawings		1,300
Owner's capital, September 30		$16,450

Softbyte
Balance Sheet
September 30, 2012

Assets

Cash	$ 8,050
Accounts receivable	1,400
Supplies	1,600
Equipment	7,000
Total assets	$18,050

Liabilities and Owner's Equity

Liabilities	
Accounts payable	$ 1,600
Owner's equity	
Owner's capital	16,450
Total liabilities and owner's equity	$18,050

Softbyte
Statement of Cash Flows
For the Month Ended September 30, 2012

Cash flows from operating activities		
Cash receipts from revenues		$ 3,300
Cash payments for expenses		(1,950)
Net cash provided by operating activities		1,350
Cash flows from investing activities		
Purchase of equipment		(7,000)
Cash flows from financing activities		
Investments by owner	$15,000)	
Drawings by owner	(1,300)	13,700
Net increase in cash		8,050
Cash at the beginning of the period		0
Cash at the end of the period		$ 8,050

① ② ③

Note that the statements shown in Illustration 1-9 are interrelated:

Helpful Hint

The income statement, owner's equity statement, and statement of cash flows are all for a *period* of time, whereas the balance sheet is for a *point* in time.

1. Net income of $2,750 on the **income statement** is added to the beginning balance of owner's capital in the **owner's equity statement**.
2. Owner's capital of $16,450 at the end of the reporting period shown in the **owner's equity statement** is reported on the **balance sheet**.
3. Cash of $8,050 on the **balance sheet** is reported on the **statement of cash flows**.

Also, explanatory notes and supporting schedules are an integral part of every set of financial statements. We illustrate these notes and schedules in later chapters of this textbook.

Be sure to carefully examine the format and content of each statement in Illustration 1-9. We describe the essential features of each in the following sections.

Income Statement

The income statement reports the revenues and expenses for a specific period of time. (In Softbyte's case, this is "For the Month Ended September 30, 2012.") Softbyte's income statement is prepared from the data appearing in the owner's equity columns of Illustration 1-8 (page 20).

Alternative Terminology notes introduce other terms you might hear or read.

The income statement lists revenues first, followed by expenses. Finally the statement shows net income (or net loss). Net income results when revenues exceed expenses. A net loss occurs when expenses exceed revenues.

Alternative Terminology

The income statement is sometimes referred to as the *statement of operations, earnings statement,* or *profit and loss statement.*

Although practice varies, we have chosen in our illustrations and homework solutions to list expenses in order of magnitude. (We will consider alternative formats for the income statement in later chapters.)

Note that the income statement does **not** include investment and withdrawal transactions between the owner and the business in measuring net income. For example, as explained earlier, Ray Neal's withdrawal of cash from Softbyte was not regarded as a business expense.

Owner's Equity Statement

The owner's equity statement reports the changes in owner's equity for a specific period of time. The time period is the same as that covered by the income statement. Data for the preparation of the owner's equity statement come from the owner's equity columns of the tabular summary (Illustration 1-8) and from the income statement. The first line of the statement shows the beginning owner's equity amount (which was zero at the start of the business). Then come the owner's investments, net income (or loss), and the owner's drawings. This statement indicates *why* owner's equity has increased or decreased during the period.

What if Softbyte had reported a net loss in its first month? Let's assume that during the month of September 2012, Softbyte lost $10,000. Illustration 1-10 (page 24) shows the presentation of a net loss in the owner's equity statement.

Illustration 1-10
Presentation of net loss

Softbyte		
Owner's Equity Statement		
For the Month Ended September 30, 2012		
Owner's capital, September 1		$ –0–
Add: Investments		15,000
		15,000
Less: Drawings	$ 1,300	
Net loss	**10,000**	11,300
Owner's capital, September 30		$ 3,700

If the owner makes any additional investments, the company reports them in the owner's equity statement as investments.

Balance Sheet

Softbyte's balance sheet reports the assets, liabilities, and owner's equity at a specific date (in Softbyte's case, September 30, 2012). The company prepares the balance sheet from the column headings of the tabular summary (Illustration 1-8) and the month-end data shown in its last line.

Observe that the balance sheet lists assets at the top, followed by liabilities and owner's equity. Total assets must equal total liabilities and owner's equity. Softbyte reports only one liability—accounts payable—in its balance sheet. In most cases, there will be more than one liability. When two or more liabilities are involved, a customary way of listing is as follows.

Illustration 1-11
Presentation of liabilities

Liabilities	
Notes payable	$10,000
Accounts payable	63,000
Salaries and wages payable	18,000
Total liabilities	$91,000

The balance sheet is a snapshot of the company's financial condition at a specific moment in time (usually the month-end or year-end).

Statement of Cash Flows

Helpful Hint

Investing activities pertain to investments made by the company, not investments made by the owner.

The statement of cash flows provides information on the cash receipts and payments for a specific period of time. The statement of cash flows reports (1) the cash effects of a company's operations during a period, (2) its investing transactions, (3) its financing transactions, (4) the net increase or decrease in cash during the period, and (5) the cash amount at the end of the period.

Reporting the sources, uses, and change in cash is useful because investors, creditors, and others want to know what is happening to a company's most liquid resource. The statement of cash flows provides answers to the following simple but important questions.

1. Where did cash come from during the period?
2. What was cash used for during the period?
3. What was the change in the cash balance during the period?

As shown in Softbyte's statement of cash flows, cash increased $8,050 during the period. Net cash flow provided from operating activities increased cash $1,350. Cash flow from investing transactions decreased cash $7,000. And cash flow from financing transactions increased cash $13,700. At this time, you need not be concerned with how these amounts are determined. Chapter 17 will examine the statement of cash flows in detail.

Do it!

Presented below is selected information related to Flanagan Company at December 31, 2012. Flanagan reports financial information monthly.

Financial Statement Items

Equipment	$10,000	Utilities Expense	$ 4,000
Cash	8,000	Accounts Receivable	9,000
Service Revenue	36,000	Salaries and Wages Expense	7,000
Rent Expense	11,000	Notes Payable	16,500
Accounts Payable	2,000	Owner's Drawings	5,000

(a) Determine the total assets of Flanagan Company at December 31, 2012.

(b) Determine the net income that Flanagan Company reported for December 2012.

(c) Determine the owner's equity of Flanagan Company at December 31, 2012.

action plan

✔ Remember the basic accounting equation: assets must equal liabilities plus owner's equity.

✔ Review previous financial statements to determine how total assets, net income, and owner's equity are computed.

Solution

(a) The total assets are $27,000, comprised of Cash $8,000, Accounts Receivable $9,000, and Equipment $10,000.

(b) Net income is $14,000, computed as follows.

Revenues		
Service revenue		$36,000
Expenses		
Rent expense	$11,000	
Salaries and wages expense	7,000	
Utilities expense	4,000	
Total expenses		22,000
Net income		$14,000

(c) The ending owner's equity of Flanagan Company is $8,500. By rewriting the accounting equation, we can compute owner's equity as assets minus liabilities, as follows:

Total assets [as computed in (a)]		$27,000
Less: Liabilities		
Notes payable	$16,500	
Accounts payable	2,000	18,500
Owner's equity		$ 8,500

Note that it is not possible to determine the company's owner's equity in any other way, because the beginning total for owner's equity is not provided.

Related exercise material: BE1-10, BE1-11, E1-9, E1-12, E1-13, E1-14, E1-15, E1-16, and **Do it!** 1-4.

✔
The Navigator

Do it!

*The **Comprehensive Do it!** is a final review of the chapter. The **Action Plan** gives tips about how to approach the problem, and the **Solution** demonstrates both the form and content of complete answers.*

Joan Robinson opens her own law office on July 1, 2012. During the first month of operations, the following transactions occurred.

1. Joan invested $11,000 in cash in the law practice.
2. Paid $800 for July rent on office space.
3. Purchased office equipment on account $3,000.
4. Provided legal services to clients for cash $1,500.
5. Borrowed $700 cash from a bank on a note payable.
6. Performed legal services for client on account $2,000.
7. Paid monthly expenses: salaries and wages $500, utilities $300, and supplies $100.
8. Joan withdraws $1,000 cash for personal use.

Instructions

(a) Prepare a tabular summary of the transactions.
(b) Prepare the income statement, owner's equity statement, and balance sheet at July 31 for Joan Robinson, Attorney.

Solution to Comprehensive Do it!

(a)

Trans-action	Cash	+	Accounts Receivable	+	Equipment	=	Notes Payable	+	Accounts Payable	+	Owner's Capital	−	Owner's Drawings	+	Revenues	−	Expenses
(1)	+$11,000					=					+$11,000						
(2)	−800																−$800
(3)					+$3,000	=			+$3,000								
(4)	+1,500														+$1,500		
(5)	+700						+$700										
(6)			+$2,000												+2,000		
(7)	−500																−500
	−300																−300
	−100																−100
(8)	−1,000												−$1,000				
	$10,500	+	$2,000	+	$3,000	=	$700	+	$3,000	+	$11,000	−	$1,000	+	$3,500	−	$1,700

Assets = Liabilities + Owner's Equity

$15,500

$15,500

---

action plan

✔ Make sure that assets equal liabilities plus owner's equity after each transaction.

✔ Investments and revenues increase owner's equity. Withdrawals and expenses decrease owner's equity.

✔ Prepare the financial statements in the order listed.

✔ The income statement shows revenues and expenses for a period of time.

Joan Robinson, Attorney
Income Statement
Month Ended July 31, 2012

Revenues		
Service revenue		$3,500
Expenses		
Rent expense	$800	
Salaries and wages expense	500	
Utilities expense	300	
Supplies expense	100	
Total expenses		1,700
Net income		$1,800

Joan Robinson, Attorney
Owner's Equity Statement
Month Ended July 31, 2012

Owner's capital, July 1		$ 0
Add: Investments	$11,000	
Net income	1,800	12,800
		12,800
Less: Drawings		1,000
Owner's capital, July 31		$11,800

action plan (cont'd)

✔ The owner's equity statement shows the changes in owner's equity for the same period of time as the income statement.

✔ The balance sheet reports assets, liabilities, and owner's equity at a specific date.

Joan Robinson, Attorney
Balance Sheet
July 31, 2012

Assets

Cash	$10,500
Accounts receivable	2,000
Equipment	3,000
Total assets	$15,500

Liabilities and Owner's Equity

Liabilities		
Notes payable	$ 700	
Accounts payable	3,000	
Total liabilities		3,700
Owner's equity		
Owner's capital		11,800
Total liabilities and owner's equity		$15,500

The Navigator

*This would be a good time to return to the **Student Owner's Manual** at the beginning of the book (or look at it for the first time if you skipped it before) to read about the various types of assignment materials that appear at the end of each chapter. Knowing the purpose of the different assignments will help you appreciate what each contributes to your accounting skills and competencies.*

Summary of Study Objectives

[1] **Explain what accounting is.** Accounting is an information system that identifies, records, and communicates the economic events of an organization to interested users.

[2] **Identify the users and uses of accounting.** The major users and uses of accounting are as follows: (a) Management uses accounting information to plan, organize, and run the business. (b) Investors (owners) decide whether to buy, hold, or sell their financial interests on the basis of accounting data. (c) Creditors (suppliers and bankers) evaluate the risks of granting credit or lending money on the basis of accounting information. Other groups that use accounting information are taxing authorities, regulatory agencies, customers, and labor unions.

[3] **Understand why ethics is a fundamental business concept.** Ethics are the standards of conduct by which actions are judged as right or wrong. Effective financial reporting depends on sound ethical behavior.

[4] **Explain generally accepted accounting principles.** Generally accepted accounting principles are a common set of standards used by accountants.

[5] **Explain the monetary unit assumption and the economic entity assumption.** The monetary unit assumption requires that companies include in the accounting records only transaction data that can be expressed in terms of money. The economic entity assumption requires that the activities of each economic entity be kept separate from the activities of its owner(s) and other economic entities.

[6] State the accounting equation, and define its components. The basic accounting equation is:

$$\text{Assets} = \text{Liabilities} + \text{Owner's Equity}$$

Assets are resources a business owns. Liabilities are creditorship claims on total assets. Owner's equity is the ownership claim on total assets.

The expanded accounting equation is:

$$\text{Assets} = \text{Liabilities} + \text{Owner's Capital} - \text{Owner's}$$
$$\text{Drawings} + \text{Revenues} - \text{Expenses}$$

Owner's capital is assets the owner puts into the business. Owner's drawings are the assets the owner withdraws for personal use. Revenues are increases in assets resulting from income-earning activities. Expenses are the costs of assets consumed or services used in the process of earning revenue.

[7] Analyze the effects of business transactions on the accounting equation. Each business transaction must have a dual effect on the accounting equation. For example, if an individual asset increases, there must be a corresponding (1) decrease in another asset, or (2) increase in a specific liability, or (3) increase in owner's equity.

[8] Understand the four financial statements and how they are prepared. An income statement presents the revenues and expenses, and resulting net income or net loss, for a specific period of time. An owner's equity statement summarizes the changes in owner's equity for a specific period of time. A balance sheet reports the assets, liabilities, and owner's equity at a specific date. A statement of cash flows summarizes information about the cash inflows (receipts) and outflows (payments) for a specific period of time.

The Navigator

Glossary

Accounting The information system that identifies, records, and communicates the economic events of an organization to interested users. (p. 4).

Assets Resources a business owns. (p. 12).

Balance sheet A financial statement that reports the assets, liabilities, and owner's equity at a specific date. (p. 21).

Basic accounting equation Assets = Liabilities + Owner's Equity. (p. 12).

Bookkeeping A part of accounting that involves only the recording of economic events. (p. 5).

Convergence The process of reducing the differences between GAAP and IFRS. (p. 9).

Corporation A business organized as a separate legal entity under state corporation law, having ownership divided into transferable shares of stock. (p. 11).

Cost principle An accounting principle that states that companies should record assets at their cost. (p. 9).

Drawings Withdrawal of cash or other assets from an unincorporated business for the personal use of the owner(s). (p. 13).

Economic entity assumption An assumption that requires that the activities of the entity be kept separate and distinct from the activities of its owner and all other economic entities. (p. 10).

Ethics The standards of conduct by which one's actions are judged as right or wrong, honest or dishonest, fair or not fair. (p. 8).

Expanded accounting equation Assets = Liabilities + Owner's Capital − Owner's Drawings + Revenues − Expenses. (p. 14).

Expenses The cost of assets consumed or services used in the process of earning revenue. (p. 14).

Fair value principle An accounting principle stating that assets and liabilities should be reported at fair value (the price received to sell an asset or settle a liability). (p. 9).

Faithful representation Numbers and descriptions match what really existed or happened—it is factual. (p. 9).

Financial accounting The field of accounting that provides economic and financial information for investors, creditors, and other external users. (p. 7).

Financial Accounting Standards Board (FASB) A private organization that establishes generally accepted accounting principles (GAAP). (p. 9).

Generally accepted accounting principles (GAAP) Common standards that indicate how to report economic events. (p. 9).

Income statement financial statement that presents the revenues and expenses and resulting net income or net loss of a company for a specific period of time. (p. 21).

International Accounting Standards Board (IASB) An accounting standard-setting body that issues standards adopted by many countries outside of the United States. (p. 9).

Investments by owner The assets an owner puts into the business. (p. 13).

Liabilities Creditor claims on total assets. (p. 13).

Managerial accounting The field of accounting that provides internal reports to help users make decisions about their companies. (p. 6).

Monetary unit assumption An assumption stating that companies include in the accounting records only transaction data that can be expressed in terms of money. (p. 10).

Net income The amount by which revenues exceed expenses. (p. 23).

Net loss The amount by which expenses exceed revenues. (p. 23).

Owner's equity The ownership claim on total assets. (p. 13).

Owner's equity statement A financial statement that summarizes the changes in owner's equity for a specific period of time. (p. 21).

Partnership A business owned by two or more persons associated as partners. (p. 11).

Proprietorship A business owned by one person. (p. 10).

Relevance Financial information that is capable of making a difference in a decision. (p. 9).

Revenues   The gross increase in owner's equity resulting from business activities entered into for the purpose of earning income. (p. 13).

Sarbanes-Oxley Act of 2002 (SOX)   Law passed by Congress in 2002 intended to reduce unethical corporate behavior. (p. 8).

Securities and Exchange Commission (SEC)   A governmental agency that oversees U.S. financial markets and accounting standard-setting bodies. (p. 9).

Statement of cash flows   A financial statement that summarizes information about the cash inflows (receipts) and cash outflows (payments) for a specific period of time. (p. 21).

Transactions   The economic events of a business that are recorded by accountants. (p. 14).

APPENDIX1A

Accounting Career Opportunities

Study Objective [9]
Explain the career opportunities in accounting.

Why is accounting such a popular major and career choice? First, there are a lot of jobs. In many cities in recent years, the demand for accountants exceeded the supply. Not only are there a lot of jobs, but there are a wide array of opportunities. As one accounting organization observed, "accounting is one degree with 360 degrees of opportunity."

Accounting is also hot because it is obvious that accounting matters. Interest in accounting has increased, ironically, because of the attention caused by the accounting failures of companies such as Enron and WorldCom. These widely publicized scandals revealed the important role that accounting plays in society. Most people want to make a difference, and an accounting career provides many opportunities to contribute to society. Finally, the Sarbanes-Oxley Act of 2002 (SOX) (see page 8) significantly increased the accounting and internal control requirements for corporations. This dramatically increased demand for professionals with accounting training.

Accountants are in such demand that it is not uncommon for accounting students to have accepted a job offer a year before graduation. As the following discussion reveals, the job options of people with accounting degrees are virtually unlimited.

Public Accounting

Individuals in **public accounting** offer expert service to the general public, in much the same way that doctors serve patients and lawyers serve clients. A major portion of public accounting involves **auditing**. In auditing, a certified public accountant (CPA) examines company financial statements and provides an opinion as to how accurately the financial statements present the company's results and financial position. Analysts, investors, and creditors rely heavily on these "audit opinions," which CPAs have the exclusive authority to issue.

Taxation is another major area of public accounting. The work that tax specialists perform includes tax advice and planning, preparing tax returns, and representing clients before governmental agencies such as the Internal Revenue Service.

A third area in public accounting is **management consulting**. It ranges from installing basic accounting software or highly complex enterprise resource planning systems, to providing support services for major marketing projects or merger and acquisition activities.

Many CPAs are entrepreneurs. They form small- or medium-sized practices that frequently specialize in tax or consulting services.

Private Accounting

Instead of working in public accounting, you might choose to be an employee of a for-profit company such as Starbucks, Google, or PepsiCo. In **private** (or **managerial**) **accounting**, you would be involved in activities such as cost accounting (finding the cost of producing specific products), budgeting, accounting information system design and support, or tax planning and preparation. You might also be a member of your company's internal audit team. In response to SOX, the internal auditors' job of reviewing the company's operations to ensure compliance with company policies and to increase efficiency has taken on increased importance.

Alternatively, many accountants work for not-for-profit organizations such as the Red Cross or the Bill and Melinda Gates Foundation, or for museums, libraries, or performing arts organizations.

Opportunities in Government

Another option is to pursue one of the many accounting opportunities in governmental agencies. For example, the Internal Revenue Service (IRS), Federal Bureau of Investigation (FBI), and the Securities and Exchange Commission (SEC) all employ accountants. The FBI has a stated goal that at least 15 percent of its new agents should be CPAs. There is also a very high demand for accounting educators at public colleges and universities and in state and local governments.

Forensic Accounting

Forensic accounting uses accounting, auditing, and investigative skills to conduct investigations into theft and fraud. It is listed among the top 20 career paths of the future. The job of forensic accountants is to catch the perpetrators of the estimated $600 billion per year of theft and fraud occurring at U.S. companies. This includes tracing money-laundering and identity-theft activities as well as tax evasion. Insurance companies hire forensic accountants to detect insurance frauds such as arson, and law offices employ forensic accountants to identify marital assets in divorces. Forensic accountants often have FBI, IRS, or similar government experience.

"Show Me the Money"

How much can a new accountant make? Salary estimates are constantly changing, and salaries vary considerably across the country. At the time this text was written, the following general information was available from Robert Half International.

Illustration 1A-1
Salary estimates for jobs in public and corporate accounting

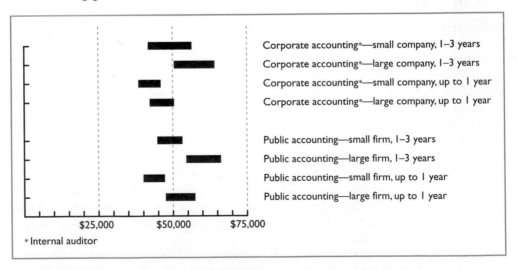

The average salary for a first-year partner in a CPA firm is close to $130,000, with experienced partners often making substantially more. On the corporate side, controllers (the head accountant) can earn $150,000, while chief financial officers can earn as much as $350,000.

For up-to-date salary estimates, as well as a wealth of additional information regarding accounting as a career, check out *www.startheregoplaces.com*.

Summary of Study Objective for Appendix 1A

[9] Explain the career opportunities in accounting. Accounting offers many different jobs in fields such as public and private accounting, government, and forensic accounting.

Accounting is a popular major because there are many different types of jobs, with unlimited potential for career advancement.

Glossary for Appendix 1A

Auditing   The examination of financial statements by a certified public accountant in order to express an opinion as to the fairness of presentation. (p. 29).

Forensic accounting   An area of accounting that uses accounting, auditing, and investigative skills to conduct investigations into theft and fraud. (p. 30).

Management consulting   An area of public accounting ranging from development of accounting and computer systems to support services for marketing projects and merger and acquisition activities. (p. 29).

Private (or managerial) accounting   An area of accounting within a company that involves such activities as cost accounting, budgeting, design and support of accounting information systems, and tax planning and preparation. (p. 29).

Public accounting   An area of accounting in which the accountant offers expert service to the general public. (p. 29).

Taxation   An area of public accounting involving tax advice, tax planning, preparing tax returns, and representing clients before governmental agencies. (p. 29).

 Self-Test, Brief Exercises, Exercises, Problem Set A, and many more components are available for practice in *WileyPLUS*

*****Note:** All asterisked Questions, Exercises, and Problems relate to material in the appendix to the chapter.

Self-Test Questions

Answers are on page 46.

(SO 1)   **1.** Which of the following is *not* a step in the accounting process?
   a. Identification.   **c.** Recording.
   b. Verification.   **d.** Communication.

(SO 2)   **2.** Which of the following statements about users of accounting information is *incorrect*?
   a. Management is an internal user.
   b. Taxing authorities are external users.
   c. Present creditors are external users.
   d. Regulatory authorities are internal users.

(SO 4)   **3.** The cost principle states that:
   a. assets should be initially recorded at cost and adjusted when the fair value changes.
   b. activities of an entity are to be kept separate and distinct from its owner.
   c. assets should be recorded at their cost.
   d. only transaction data capable of being expressed in terms of money be included in the accounting records.

(SO 5)   **4.** Which of the following statements about basic assumptions is *correct*?
   a. Basic assumptions are the same as accounting principles.
   b. The economic entity assumption states that there should be a particular unit of accountability.
   c. The monetary unit assumption enables accounting to measure employee morale.
   d. Partnerships are not economic entities.

(SO 5)   **5.** The three types of business entities are:
   a. proprietorships, small businesses, and partnerships.
   b. proprietorships, partnerships, and corporations.
   c. proprietorships, partnerships, and large businesses.
   d. financial, manufacturing, and service companies.

(SO 6)   **6.** Net income will result during a time period when:
   a. assets exceed liabilities.
   b. assets exceed revenues.
   c. expenses exceed revenues.
   d. revenues exceed expenses.

(SO 7)   **7.** Performing services on account will have the following effects on the components of the basic accounting equation:
   a. increase assets and decrease owner's equity.
   b. increase assets and increase owner's equity.
   c. increase assets and increase liabilities.
   d. increase liabilities and increase owner's equity.

(SO 7)   **8.** As of December 31, 2012, Stoneland Company has assets of $3,500 and owner's equity of $2,000. What are the liabilities for Stoneland Company as of December 31, 2012?
   a. $1,500.   **b.** $1,000.   **c.** $2,500.   **d.** $2,000.

(SO 7)   **9.** Which of the following events is *not* recorded in the accounting records?
   a. Equipment is purchased on account.
   b. An employee is terminated.
   c. A cash investment is made into the business.
   d. The owner withdraws cash for personal use.

(SO 7) **10.** During 2012, Gibson Company's assets decreased $50,000 and its liabilities decreased $90,000. Its owner's equity therefore:
   a. increased $40,000.
   b. decreased $140,000.
   c. decreased $40,000.
   d. increased $140,000.

(SO 7) **11.** Payment of an account payable affects the components of the accounting equation in the following way.
   a. Decreases owner's equity and decreases liabilities.
   b. Increases assets and decreases liabilities.
   c. Decreases assets and increases owner's equity.
   d. Decreases assets and decreases liabilities.

(SO 8) **12.** Which of the following statements is *false*?
   a. A statement of cash flows summarizes information about the cash inflows (receipts) and outflows (payments) for a specific period of time.
   b. A balance sheet reports the assets, liabilities, and owner's equity at a specific date.
   c. An income statement presents the revenues, expenses, changes in owner's equity, and resulting net income or net loss for a specific period of time.
   d. An owner's equity statement summarizes the changes in owner's equity for a specific period of time.

13. On the last day of the period, Jim Otto Company buys a (SO 8) $900 machine on credit. This transaction will affect the:
   a. income statement only.
   b. balance sheet only.
   c. income statement and owner's equity statement only.
   d. income statement, owner's equity statement, and balance sheet.

14. The financial statement that reports assets, liabilities, and (SO 8) owner's equity is the:
   a. income statement.
   b. owner's equity statement.
   c. balance sheet.
   d. statement of cash flows.

*15. Services provided by a public accountant include: (SO 9)
   a. auditing, taxation, and management consulting.
   b. auditing, budgeting, and management consulting.
   c. auditing, budgeting, and cost accounting.
   d. internal auditing, budgeting, and management consulting.

Go to the book's companion website, **www.wiley.com/college/weygandt**, for additional Self-Test Questions.

Questions

1. "Accounting is ingrained in our society and it is vital to our economic system." Do you agree? Explain.

2. Identify and describe the steps in the accounting process.

3. (a) Who are internal users of accounting data? (b) How does accounting provide relevant data to these users?

4. What uses of financial accounting information are made by (a) investors and (b) creditors?

5. "Bookkeeping and accounting are the same." Do you agree? Explain.

6. Eve Myles Travel Agency purchased land for $90,000 cash on December 10, 2012. At December 31, 2012, the land's value has increased to $93,000. What amount should be reported for land on Eve Myles's balance sheet at December 31, 2012? Explain.

7. What is the monetary unit assumption?

8. What is the economic entity assumption?

9. What are the three basic forms of business organizations for profit-oriented enterprises?

10. Maria Contreras is the owner of a successful printing shop. Recently, her business has been increasing, and Maria has been thinking about changing the organization of her business from a proprietorship to a corporation. Discuss some of the advantages Maria would enjoy if she were to incorporate her business.

11. What is the basic accounting equation?

12. (a) Define the terms assets, liabilities, and owner's equity.
   (b) What items affect owner's equity?

13. Which of the following items are liabilities of Karl Jewelry Stores?
   (a) Cash.
   (b) Accounts payable.
   (c) Owner's drawings.
   (d) Accounts receivable.
   (e) Supplies.
   (f) Equipment.

   (g) Salaries and wages payable.
   (h) Service revenue.
   (i) Rent expense.

14. Can a business enter into a transaction in which only the left side of the basic accounting equation is affected? If so, give an example.

15. Are the following events recorded in the accounting records? Explain your answer in each case.
   (a) The owner of the company dies.
   (b) Supplies are purchased on account.
   (c) An employee is fired.
   (d) The owner of the business withdraws cash from the business for personal use.

16. Indicate how the following business transactions affect the basic accounting equation.
   (a) Paid cash for janitorial services.
   (b) Purchased equipment for cash.
   (c) Invested cash in the business.
   (d) Paid accounts payable in full.

17. Listed below are some items found in the financial statements of Dave Ramsey Co. Indicate in which financial statement(s) the following items would appear.
   (a) Service revenue.
   (b) Equipment.
   (c) Advertising expense.
   (d) Accounts receivable.
   (e) Owner's capital.
   (f) Salaries and wages payable.

18. In February 2012, Betty King invested an additional $10,000 in her business, King's Pharmacy, which is organized as a proprietorship. King's accountant, Leroy James, recorded this receipt as an increase in cash and revenues. Is this treatment appropriate? Why or why not?

19. "A company's net income appears directly on the income statement and the owner's equity statement, and it is included indirectly in the company's balance sheet." Do you agree? Explain.

20. Torchwood Enterprises had a capital balance of $168,000 at the beginning of the period. At the end of the accounting period, the capital balance was $198,000.

(a) Assuming no additional investment or withdrawals during the period, what is the net income for the period?

(b) Assuming an additional investment of $13,000 but no withdrawals during the period, what is the net income for the period?

21. Summarized operations for J. R. Ewing Co. for the month of July are as follows.

Revenues earned: for cash $20,000; on account $70,000.
Expenses incurred: for cash $26,000; on account $40,000.
Indicate for J. R. Ewing Co. (a) the total revenues, (b) the total expenses, and (c) net income for the month of July.

22. The basic accounting equation is: Assets = Liabilities + Owner's Equity. Replacing the words in that equation with dollar amounts, what is Coca-Cola's accounting equation at December 31, 2009? (*Hint:* Owner's equity is equivalent to shareowners' equity.)

✔
The Navigator

Brief Exercises

BE1-1   Presented below is the basic accounting equation. Determine the missing amounts.

	Assets	=	Liabilities	+	Owner's Equity
(a)	$90,000		$50,000		?
(b)	?		$40,000		$70,000
(c)	$94,000		?		$53,000

Use basic accounting equation.
(SO 6)

BE1-2   Given the accounting equation, answer each of the following questions.

(a) The liabilities of Buerhle Company are $120,000 and the owner's equity is $232,000. What is the amount of Buerhle Company's total assets?

(b) The total assets of Buerhle Company are $190,000 and its owner's equity is $91,000. What is the amount of its total liabilities?

(c) The total assets of Buerhle Company are $800,000 and its liabilities are equal to one half of its total assets. What is the amount of Buerhle Company's owner's equity?

Use basic accounting equation.
(SO 6)

BE1-3   At the beginning of the year, Danks Company had total assets of $800,000 and total liabilities of $300,000. Answer the following questions.

(a) If total assets increased $150,000 during the year and total liabilities decreased $80,000, what is the amount of owner's equity at the end of the year?

(b) During the year, total liabilities increased $100,000 and owner's equity decreased $70,000. What is the amount of total assets at the end of the year?

(c) If total assets decreased $80,000 and owner's equity increased $120,000 during the year, what is the amount of total liabilities at the end of the year?

Use basic accounting equation.
(SO 6)

BE1-4   Use the expanded accounting equation to answer each of the following questions.

(a) The liabilities of Falk Company are $90,000. Owner's capital account is $150,000; drawings are $40,000; revenues, $450,000; and expenses, $320,000. What is the amount of Falk Company's total assets?

(b) The total assets of Pierogi Company are $57,000. Owner's capital account is $25,000; drawings are $7,000; revenues, $52,000; and expenses, $35,000. What is the amount of the company's total liabilities?

(c) The total assets of Yanko Co. are $600,000 and its liabilities are equal to two-thirds of its total assets. What is the amount of Yanko Co.'s owner's equity?

Solve expanded accounting equation.
(SO 6)

BE1-5   Indicate whether each of the following items is an asset (A), liability (L), or part of owner's equity (OE).

_____(a) Accounts receivable
_____(b) Salaries and wages payable
_____(c) Equipment

_____(d) Supplies
_____(e) Owner's capital
_____(f) Notes payable

Identify assets, liabilities, and owner's equity.
(SO 6)

BE1-6   Presented below are three business transactions. On a sheet of paper, list the letters (a), (b), and (c) with columns for assets, liabilities, and owner's equity. For each column, indicate whether the transactions increased (+), decreased (−), or had no effect (NE) on assets, liabilities, and owner's equity.

(a) Purchased supplies on account.
(b) Received cash for providing a service.
(c) Paid expenses in cash.

Determine effect of transactions on basic accounting equation.
(SO 7)

Determine effect of transactions on basic accounting equation.
(SO 7)

BE1-7 Follow the same format as BE1-6 on the previous page. Determine the effect on assets, liabilities, and owner's equity of the following three transactions.

(a) Invested cash in the business.
(b) Withdrawal of cash by owner.
(c) Received cash from a customer who had previously been billed for services provided.

Classify items affecting owner's equity.
(SO 7)

BE1-8 Classify each of the following items as owner's drawings (D), revenue (R), or expense (E).

_____ **(a)** Advertising expense   _____ **(e)** Owner's drawings
_____ **(b)** Service revenue   _____ **(f)** Rent revenue
_____ **(c)** Insurance expense   _____ **(g)** Utilities expense
_____ **(d)** Salaries and wages expense

Determine effect of transactions on basic owner's equity.
(SO 7)

BE1-9 Presented below are three transactions. Mark each transaction as affecting owner's investment (I), owner's drawings (D), revenue (R), expense (E), or not affecting owner's equity (NOE).

_____ **(a)** Received cash for services performed
_____ **(b)** Paid cash to purchase equipment
_____ **(c)** Paid employee salaries

Prepare a balance sheet.
(SO 8)

BE1-10 In alphabetical order below are balance sheet items for George Company at December 31, 2012. Kayla George is the owner of George Company. Prepare a balance sheet, following the format of Illustration 1-9.

Accounts payable	$90,000
Accounts receivable	$72,500
Cash	$49,000
Owner's capital	$31,500

Determine where items appear on financial statements.
(SO 8)

BE1-11 Indicate whether the following items would appear on the income statement (IS), balance sheet (BS), or owner's equity statement (OE).

_____ **(a)** Notes payable   _____ **(d)** Cash
_____ **(b)** Advertising expense   _____ **(e)** Service revenue
_____ **(c)** Owner's capital

Do it! Review

Review basic concepts.
(SO 1, 2, 4)

Do it! 1-1 Indicate whether each of the five statements presented below is true or false.

1. The three steps in the accounting process are identification, recording, and examination.
2. The two most common types of external users are investors and creditors.
3. Congress passed the Sarbanes-Oxley Act of 2002 to ensure that investors invest only in companies that will be profitable.
4. The primary accounting standard-setting body in the United States is the Securities and Exchange Commission (SEC).
5. The cost principle dictates that companies record assets at their cost and continue to report them at their cost over the time the asset is held.

Evaluate effects of transactions on owner's equity.
(SO 6)

Do it! 1-2 Classify the following items as investment by owner (I), owner's drawings (D), revenues (R), or expenses (E). Then indicate whether each item increases or decreases owner's equity.

(1) Drawings   (3) Advertising Expense
(2) Rent Revenue   (4) Owner puts personal assets into the business

Prepare tabular analysis.
(SO 7)

Do it! 1-3 Transactions made by Orlando Bloom and Co., a law firm, for the month of March are shown below. Prepare a tabular analysis which shows the effects of these transactions on the expanded accounting equation, similar to that shown in Illustration 1-8.

1. The company provided $20,000 of services for customers, on credit.
2. The company received $20,000 in cash from customers who had been billed for services [in transaction (1)].
3. The company received a bill for $2,300 of advertising, but will not pay it until a later date.
4. Orlando Bloom withdrew $3,600 cash from the business for personal use.

Do it! 1-4   Presented below is selected information related to Lance Company at December 31, 2012. Lance reports financial information monthly.

Calculate effects of transactions on financial statement items.
(SO 8)

Accounts Payable	$ 3,000	Salaries and Wages Expense	$16,500
Cash	4,500	Notes Payable	25,000
Advertising Expense	6,000	Rent Expense	10,500
Service Revenue	51,500	Accounts Receivable	13,500
Equipment	29,000	Owner's Drawings	7,500

(a) Determine the total assets of Lance Company at December 31, 2012.
(b) Determine the net income that Lance Company reported for December 2012.
(c) Determine the owner's equity of Lance Company at December 31, 2012.

Exercises

E1-1   Jenks Company performs the following accounting tasks during the year.

Classify the three activities of accounting.
(SO 1)

_____Analyzing and interpreting information.
_____Classifying economic events.
_____Explaining uses, meaning, and limitations of data.
_____Keeping a systematic chronological diary of events.
_____Measuring events in dollars and cents.
_____Preparing accounting reports.
_____Reporting information in a standard format.
_____Selecting economic activities relevant to the company.
_____Summarizing economic events.

Accounting is "an information system that **identifies**, **records**, and **communicates** the economic events of an organization to interested users."

Instructions
Categorize the accounting tasks performed by Jenks as relating to either the identification (I), recording (R), or communication (C) aspects of accounting.

E1-2   **(a)** The following are users of financial statements.

Identify users of accounting information.
(SO 2)

_____Customers   _____Securities and Exchange Commission
_____Internal Revenue Service   _____Store manager
_____Labor unions   _____Suppliers
_____Marketing manager   _____Vice president of finance
_____Production supervisor

Instructions
Identify the users as being either **external users** or **internal users**.

(b) The following questions could be asked by an internal user or an external user.

_____Can we afford to give our employees a pay raise?
_____Did the company earn a satisfactory income?
_____Do we need to borrow in the near future?
_____How does the company's profitability compare to other companies?
_____What does it cost us to manufacture each unit produced?
_____Which product should we emphasize?
_____Will the company be able to pay its short-term debts?

Instructions
Identify each of the questions as being more likely asked by an **internal user** or an **external user**.

E1-3   Lovie Smith, president of Smith Company, has instructed Michelle Martz, the head of the accounting department for Smith Company, to report the company's land in the company's accounting reports at its fair value of $170,000 instead of its cost of $100,000. Smith says, "Showing the land at $170,000 will make our company look like a better investment when we try to attract new investors next month."

Discuss ethics and the cost principle.
(SO 3)

Instructions

Explain the ethical situation involved for Michelle Martz, identifying the stakeholders and the alternatives.

Use accounting concepts.
(SO 4, 5)

E1-4   The following situations involve accounting principles and assumptions.

1. Rex Company owns buildings that are worth substantially more than they originally cost. In an effort to provide more relevant information, Rex reports the buildings at fair value in its accounting reports.
2. Levi Company includes in its accounting records only transaction data that can be expressed in terms of money.
3. Josh Borke, owner of Josh's Photography, records his personal living costs as expenses of the business.

Instructions

For each of the three situations, say if the accounting method used is correct or incorrect. If correct, identify which principle or assumption supports the method used. If incorrect, identify which principle or assumption has been violated.

Classify accounts as assets,
liabilities, and owner's equity.
(SO 6)

E1-5   Garcia Cleaners has the following balance sheet items.

Accounts payable	Accounts receivable
Cash	Notes payable
Equipment	Salaries and wages payable
Supplies	Owner's capital

Instructions

Classify each item as an asset, liability, or owner's equity.

Analyze the effect of
transactions.
(SO 6, 7)

E1-6   Selected transactions for Linebrink Lawn Care Company are listed below.

1. Made cash investment to start business.
2. Paid monthly rent.
3. Purchased equipment on account.
4. Billed customers for services performed.
5. Withdrew cash for owner's personal use.
6. Received cash from customers billed in (4).
7. Incurred advertising expense on account.
8. Purchased additional equipment for cash.
9. Received cash from customers when service was performed.

Instructions

List the numbers of the above transactions and describe the effect of each transaction on assets, liabilities, and owner's equity. For example, the first answer is: (1) Increase in assets and increase in owner's equity.

Analyze the effect of transac-
tions on assets, liabilities, and
owner's equity.
(SO 6, 7)

E1-7   Thornton Computer Timeshare Company entered into the following transactions during May 2012.

1. Purchased computer terminals for $20,000 from Digital Equipment on account.
2. Paid $4,000 cash for May rent on storage space.
3. Received $17,000 cash from customers for contracts billed in April.
4. Provided computer services to Fisher Construction Company for $3,000 cash.
5. Paid Northern States Power Co. $11,000 cash for energy usage in May.
6. Thornton invested an additional $29,000 in the business.
7. Paid Digital Equipment for the terminals purchased in (1) above.
8. Incurred advertising expense for May of $1,200 on account.

Instructions

Indicate with the appropriate letter whether each of the transactions above results in:

(a) An increase in assets and a decrease in assets.
(b) An increase in assets and an increase in owner's equity.
(c) An increase in assets and an increase in liabilities.
(d) A decrease in assets and a decrease in owner's equity.
(e) A decrease in assets and a decrease in liabilities.
(f) An increase in liabilities and a decrease in owner's equity.
(g) An increase in owner's equity and a decrease in liabilities.

E1-8   An analysis of the transactions made by Mark Kotsay & Co., a certified public accounting firm, for the month of August is shown below. The expenses were $650 for rent, $4,800 for salaries and wages, and $500 for utilities.

Analyze transactions and compute net income.
(SO 7)

	Cash	+	Accounts Receivable	+	Supplies	+	Equipment	=	Accounts Payable	+	Owner's Capital	−	Owner's Drawings	+	Revenues	−	Expenses
1.	+$15,000										+$15,000						
2.	−2,000						+$5,000		+$3,000								
3.	−750				+$750												
4.	+4,600		+$3,900												+$8,500		
5.	−1,500								−1,500								
6.	−2,000												−$2,000				
7.	−650																−$650
8.	+450		−450														
9.	−4,800																−4,800
10.									+500								−500

Instructions

(a) ◄█████ Describe each transaction that occurred for the month.
(b) Determine how much owner's equity increased for the month.
(c) Compute the amount of net income for the month.

E1-9   An analysis of transactions for Mark Kotsay & Co. was presented in E1–8.

Prepare financial statements.
(SO 8)

Instructions

Prepare an income statement and an owner's equity statement for August and a balance sheet at August 31, 2012.

E1-10   Andruw Company had the following assets and liabilities on the dates indicated.

Determine net income (or loss).
(SO 7)

December 31	Total Assets	Total Liabilities
2011	$400,000	$250,000
2012	$460,000	$300,000
2013	$590,000	$400,000

Andruw began business on January 1, 2011, with an investment of $100,000.

Instructions

From an analysis of the change in owner's equity during the year, compute the net income (or loss) for:

(a) 2011, assuming Andruw's drawings were $15,000 for the year.
(b) 2012, assuming Andruw made an additional investment of $45,000 and had no drawings in 2012.
(c) 2013, assuming Andruw made an additional investment of $15,000 and had drawings of $25,000 in 2013.

E1-11   Two items are omitted from each of the following summaries of balance sheet and income statement data for two proprietorships for the year 2012, Gavin's Goods and Floyd Enterprises.

Analyze financial statements items.
(SO 6, 7)

	Gavin's Goods	Floyd Enterprises
Beginning of year:		
Total assets	$110,000	$129,000
Total liabilities	85,000	(c)
Total owner's equity	(a)	80,000
End of year:		
Total assets	160,000	180,000
Total liabilities	120,000	50,000
Total owner's equity	40,000	130,000
Changes during year in owner's equity:		
Additional investment	(b)	25,000
Drawings	29,000	(d)
Total revenues	215,000	100,000
Total expenses	175,000	60,000

Instructions

Determine the missing amounts.

Prepare income statement and owner's equity statement.
(SO 8)

E1-12 The following information relates to Jake Peavy Co. for the year 2012.

Owner's capital, January 1, 2012	$48,000	Advertising expense	$ 1,800
Owner's drawings during 2012	6,000	Rent expense	10,400
Service revenue	63,600	Utilities expense	3,100
Salaries and wages expense	29,500		

Instructions

After analyzing the data, prepare an income statement and an owner's equity statement for the year ending December 31, 2012.

Correct an incorrectly prepared balance sheet.
(SO 8)

E1-13 Linda Puff is the bookkeeper for Sajuki Company. Linda has been trying to get the balance sheet of Sajuki Company to balance. Sajuki's balance sheet is shown below.

SAJUKI COMPANY
Balance Sheet
December 31, 2012

Assets		Liabilities	
Cash	$15,000	Accounts payable	$21,000
Supplies	8,000	Accounts receivable	(9,500)
Equipment	46,000	Owner's capital	67,500
Owner's drawings	10,000	Total liabilities and	
Total assets	$79,000	owner's equity	$79,000

Instructions

Prepare a correct balance sheet.

Compute net income and prepare a balance sheet.
(SO 8)

E1-14 Toni Pena is the sole owner of Deer Park, a public camping ground near the Lake Mead National Recreation Area. Toni has compiled the following financial information as of December 31, 2012.

Revenues during 2012—camping fees	$140,000	Fair value of equipment	$140,000
Revenues during 2012—general store	65,000	Notes payable	60,000
Accounts payable	11,000	Expenses during 2012	150,000
Cash on hand	23,000	Supplies on hand	17,500
Original cost of equipment	105,500		

Instructions

(a) Determine Toni Pena's net income from Deer Park for 2012.
(b) Prepare a balance sheet for Deer Park as of December 31, 2012.

Prepare an income statement.
(SO 8)

E1-15 Presented below is financial information related to the 2012 operations of J. J. Putz Cruise Company.

Maintenance and repairs expense	$ 95,000
Supplies expense	10,000
Salaries and wages expense	142,000
Advertising expense	24,500
Ticket revenue	410,000

Instructions

Prepare the 2012 income statement for J. J. Putz Cruise Company.

Prepare an owner's equity statement.
(SO 8)

E1-16 Presented below is information related to the sole proprietorship of Sergio Santos attorney.

Legal service revenue—2012	$335,000
Total expenses—2012	211,000
Assets, January 1, 2012	96,000
Liabilities, January 1, 2012	62,000
Assets, December 31, 2012	168,000
Liabilities, December 31, 2012	100,000
Drawings—2012	?

Instructions

Prepare the 2012 owner's equity statement for Sergio Santos' legal practice.

Exercises: Set B

Visit the book's companion website, at **www.wiley.com/college/weygandt**, and choose the Student Companion site to access Exercise Set B.

Problems: Set A

P1-1A   Threet's Repair Shop was started on May 1 by Erica Threet. A summary of May transactions is presented below.

1. Invested $10,000 cash to start the repair shop.
2. Purchased equipment for $5,000 cash.
3. Paid $400 cash for May office rent.
4. Paid $500 cash for supplies.
5. Incurred $250 of advertising costs in the *Beacon News* on account.
6. Received $6,100 in cash from customers for repair service.
7. Withdrew $1,000 cash for personal use.
8. Paid part-time employee salaries $2,000.
9. Paid utility bills $170.
10. Provided repair service on account to customers $750.
11. Collected cash of $120 for services billed in transaction (10).

Analyze transactions and compute net income.
(SO 6, 7)

Instructions
(a) Prepare a tabular analysis of the transactions, using the following column headings: Cash, Accounts Receivable, Supplies, Equipment, Accounts Payable, Owner's Capital, Owner's Drawings, Revenues, and Expenses.
(b) From an analysis of the owner's equity columns, compute the net income or net loss for May.

(a) Total assets $13,280

(b) Net income $4,030

P1-2A   Ramona Castro opened a veterinary business in Nashville, Tennessee, on August 1. On August 31, the balance sheet showed Cash $9,000, Accounts Receivable $1,700, Supplies $600, Equipment $6,000, Accounts Payable $3,600, and Owner's Capital $13,700. During September, the following transactions occurred.

1. Paid $2,900 cash on accounts payable.
2. Collected $1,300 of accounts receivable.
3. Purchased additional office equipment for $2,100, paying $800 in cash and the balance on account.
4. Earned revenue of $7,800, of which $2,500 is received in cash and the balance is due in October.
5. Withdrew $1,100 cash for personal use.
6. Paid salaries $1,700, rent for September $900, and advertising expense $450.
7. Incurred utilities expense for month on account $170.
8. Received $10,000 from Capital Bank (money borrowed on a note payable).

Analyze transactions and prepare income statement, owner's equity statement, and balance sheet.
(SO 6, 7, 8)

Instructions
(a) Prepare a tabular analysis of the September transactions beginning with August 31 balances. The column headings should be as follows: Cash + Accounts Receivable + Supplies + Equipment = Notes Payable + Accounts Payable + Owner's Capital − Owner's Drawings + Revenues − Expenses.
(b) Prepare an income statement for September, an owner's equity statement for September, and a balance sheet at September 30.

(a) Total assets $29,350

(b) Net income $4,580
   Ending capital $17,180

P1-3A   On May 1, A. J. Pierzynski started AJ Flying School, a company that provides flying lessons, by investing $40,000 cash in the business. Following are the assets and liabilities of the company on May 31, 2012, and the revenues and expenses for the month of May.

Prepare income statement, owner's equity statement, and balance sheet.
(SO 8)

Cash	$ 3,400	Notes Payable	$30,000
Accounts Receivable	4,900	Rent Expense	1,200
Equipment	64,000	Maintenance and Repairs Expense	400
Service Revenue	8,100	Gasoline Expense	2,500
Advertising Expense	600	Insurance Expense	400
		Accounts Payable	800

A. J. Pierzynski made no additional investment in May, but he withdrew $1,500 in cash for personal use.

Instructions

(a) Prepare an income statement and owner's equity statement for the month of May and a balance sheet at May 31.

(b) Prepare an income statement and owner's equity statement for May assuming the following data are not included above: (1) $900 of revenue was earned and billed but not collected at May 31, and (2) $1,500 of gasoline expense was incurred but not paid.

Analyze transactions and prepare financial statements.

(SO 6, 7, 8)

P1-4A Gordon Beckham started his own delivery service, Beckham Deliveries, on June 1, 2012. The following transactions occurred during the month of June.

June	1	Gordon invested $10,000 cash in the business.
	2	Purchased a used van for deliveries for $12,000. Gordon paid $2,000 cash and signed a note payable for the remaining balance.
	3	Paid $500 for office rent for the month.
	5	Performed $4,400 of services on account.
	9	Withdrew $200 cash for personal use.
	12	Purchased supplies for $150 on account.
	15	Received a cash payment of $1,250 for services provided on June 5.
	17	Purchased gasoline for $200 on account.
	20	Received a cash payment of $1,300 for services provided.
	23	Made a cash payment of $600 on the note payable.
	26	Paid $250 for utilities.
	29	Paid for the gasoline purchased on account on June 17.
	30	Paid $1,000 for employee salaries.

Instructions

(a) Show the effects of the previous transactions on the accounting equation using the following format.

			Assets			**Liabilities**		**Owner's Equity**			
Date	Cash	+ Accounts Receivable	+ Supplies	+ Equipment =	Notes Payable	+ Accounts Payable	+ Owner's Capital	− Owner's Drawings	+ Revenues	− Expenses	

(b) Prepare an income statement for the month of June.

(c) Prepare a balance sheet at June 30, 2012.

Determine financial statement amounts and prepare owner's equity statement.

(SO 7, 8)

P1-5A Financial statement information about four different companies is as follows.

	Alexei Company	Ramirez Company	Dayan Company	Viciedo Company
January 1, 2012				
Assets	$ 95,000	$110,000	(g)	$170,000
Liabilities	50,000	(d)	75,000	(j)
Owner's equity	(a)	60,000	45,000	90,000
December 31, 2012				
Assets	(b)	141,000	200,000	(k)
Liabilities	55,000	75,000	(h)	80,000
Owner's equity	63,000	(e)	130,000	162,000
Owner's equity changes in year				
Additional investment	(c)	15,000	10,000	15,000
Drawings	25,000	(f)	14,000	20,000
Total revenues	350,000	420,000	(i)	520,000
Total expenses	320,000	385,000	342,000	(l)

Instructions

(a) Determine the missing amounts. (*Hint:* For example, to solve for (a), Assets − Liabilities = Owner's equity = $45,000.)

(b) Prepare the owner's equity statement for Ramirez Company.

(c) ◄▬▬▬▬▬ Write a memorandum explaining the sequence for preparing financial statements and the interrelationship of the owner's equity statement to the income statement and balance sheet.

Problems: Set B

P1-1B   On April 1, Vince Morelli established Vince's Travel Agency. The following transactions were completed during the month.

Analyze transactions and compute net income.
(SO 6, 7)

1. Invested $15,000 cash to start the agency.
2. Paid $600 cash for April office rent.
3. Purchased office equipment for $3,000 cash.
4. Incurred $700 of advertising costs in the *Chicago Tribune,* on account.
5. Paid $800 cash for office supplies.
6. Earned $10,000 for services rendered: $3,000 cash is received from customers, and the balance of $7,000 is billed to customers on account.
7. Withdrew $500 cash for personal use.
8. Paid *Chicago Tribune* $500 of the amount due in transaction (4).
9. Paid employees' salaries $2,500.
10. Received $4,000 in cash from customers who have previously been billed in transaction (6).

Instructions

(a) Prepare a tabular analysis of the transactions using the following column headings: Cash, Accounts Receivable, Supplies, Equipment, Accounts Payable, Owner's Capital, Owner's Drawings, Revenues, and Expenses.

(b) From an analysis of the owner's equity columns, compute the net income or net loss for April.

(a) Total assets $20,900

(b) Net income $6,200

P1-2B   Juanita Pierre opened a law office, on July 1, 2012. On July 31, the balance sheet showed Cash $5,000, Accounts Receivable $1,500, Supplies $500, Equipment $6,000, Accounts Payable $4,200, and Owner's Capital $8,800. During August, the following transactions occurred.

Analyze transactions and prepare income statement, owner's equity statement, and balance sheet.
(SO 6, 7, 8)

1. Collected $1,200 of accounts receivable.
2. Paid $2,800 cash on accounts payable.
3. Earned revenue of $7,500 of which $3,000 is collected in cash and the balance is due in September.
4. Purchased additional office equipment for $2,000, paying $400 in cash and the balance on account.
5. Paid salaries $2,500, rent for August $900, and advertising expenses $400.
6. Withdrew $700 in cash for personal use.
7. Received $2,000 from Standard Federal Bank—money borrowed on a note payable.
8. Incurred utility expenses for month on account $270.

Instructions

(a) Prepare a tabular analysis of the August transactions beginning with July 31 balances. The column headings should be as follows: Cash + Accounts Receivable + Supplies + Equipment = Notes Payable + Accounts Payable + Owner's Capital − Owner's Drawings + Revenues − Expenses.

(b) Prepare an income statement for August, an owner's equity statement for August, and a balance sheet at August 31.

(a) Total assets $16,800

*(b) Net income $3,430
Ending capital $11,530*

P1-3B   On June 1, Alexia Rios started Crazy Creations Co., a company that provides craft opportunities, by investing $12,000 cash in the business. Following are the assets and liabilities of the company at June 30 and the revenues and expenses for the month of June.

Prepare income statement, owner's equity statement, and balance sheet.
(SO 8)

Cash	$10,150	Notes Payable	$9,000
Accounts Receivable	3,000	Accounts Payable	1,200
Service Revenue	6,700	Supplies Expense	1,600
Supplies	2,000	Gasoline Expense	200
Advertising Expense	500	Utilities Expense	150
Equipment	10,000		

Alexia made no additional investment in June but withdrew $1,300 in cash for personal use during the month.

Instructions

(a) Prepare an income statement and owner's equity statement for the month of June and a balance sheet at June 30, 2012.

(b) Prepare an income statement and owner's equity statement for June assuming the following data are not included above: (1) $900 of revenue was earned and billed but not collected at June 30, and (2) $150 of gasoline expense was incurred but not paid.

*(a) Net income $4,250
Owner's equity $14,950
Total assets $25,150*
*(b) Net income $5,000
Owner's equity $15,700*

Analyze transactions and prepare financial statements.
(SO 6, 7, 8)

P1-4B Carla Quentin started her own consulting firm, Quentin Consulting, on May 1, 2012. The following transactions occurred during the month of May.

May 1   Carla invested $7,000 cash in the business.
    2   Paid $900 for office rent for the month.
    3   Purchased $600 of supplies on account.
    5   Paid $125 to advertise in the *County News*.
    9   Received $4,000 cash for services provided.
    12   Withdrew $1,000 cash for personal use.
    15   Performed $5,400 of services on account.
    17   Paid $2,500 for employee salaries.
    20   Paid for the supplies purchased on account on May 3.
    23   Received a cash payment of $4,000 for services provided on account on May 15.
    26   Borrowed $5,000 from the bank on a note payable.
    29   Purchased office equipment for $4,200 on account.
    30   Paid $275 for utilities.

Instructions

(a) Total assets $20,800

(a) Show the effects of the previous transactions on the accounting equation using the following format.

	Assets			Liabilities		Owner's Equity				
Date	Cash +	Accounts Receivable +	Supplies +	Equipment =	Notes Payable +	Accounts Payable +	Owner's Capital −	Owner's Drawings +	Revenues −	Expenses

(b) Net income $5,600
(c) Cash $14,600

(b) Prepare an income statement for the month of May.
(c) Prepare a balance sheet at May 31, 2012.

Determine financial statement amounts and prepare owner's equity statement.
(SO 7, 8)

P1-5B Financial statement information about four different companies is as follows.

	Brent Company	Lillibridge Company	Omar Company	Vizquel Company
January 1, 2012				
Assets	$ 80,000	$ 90,000	(g)	$150,000
Liabilities	48,000	(d)	80,000	(j)
Owner's equity	(a)	40,000	49,000	90,000
December 31, 2012				
Assets	(b)	112,000	180,000	(k)
Liabilities	60,000	72,000	(h)	100,000
Owner's equity	50,000	(e)	82,000	151,000
Owner's equity changes in year				
Additional investment	(c)	8,000	10,000	15,000
Drawings	15,000	(f)	12,000	10,000
Total revenues	350,000	410,000	(i)	500,000
Total expenses	333,000	385,000	350,000	(l)

Instructions

(a) Determine the missing amounts. (*Hint:* For example, to solve for (a), Assets − Liabilities = Owner's equity = $32,000.)
(b) Prepare the owner's equity statement for Brent Company.
(c) ━━━ Write a memorandum explaining the sequence for preparing financial statements and the interrelationship of the owner's equity statement to the income statement and balance sheet.

Problems: Set C

Visit the book's companion website, at **www.wiley.com/college/weygandt**, and choose the Student Companion site to access Problem Set C.

Continuing Cookie Chronicle

CCC1 Natalie Koebel spent much of her childhood learning the art of cookie-making from her grandmother. They passed many happy hours mastering every type of cookie imaginable and later creating new recipes that were both healthy and delicious. Now at the start of her second year in college, Natalie is investigating various possibilities for starting her own business as part of the requirements of the entrepreneurship program in which she is enrolled.

*The **Continuing Cookie Chronicle** starts in this chapter and continues in every chapter. **You also can find this problem** at the book's Student Companion site.*

A long-time friend insists that Natalie has to somehow include cookies in her business plan. After a series of brainstorming sessions, Natalie settles on the idea of operating a cookie-making school. She will start on a part-time basis and offer her services in people's homes. Now that she has started thinking about it, the possibilities seem endless. During the fall, she will concentrate on holiday cookies. She will offer individual lessons and group sessions (which will probably be more entertainment than education for the participants). Natalie also decides to include children in her target market.

The first difficult decision is coming up with the perfect name for her business. In the end, she settles on "Cookie Creations" and then moves on to more important issues.

Instructions

(a) What form of business organization—proprietorship, partnership, or corporation—do you recommend that Natalie use for her business? Discuss the benefits and weaknesses of each form and give the reasons for your choice.

(b) Will Natalie need accounting information? If yes, what information will she need and why? How often will she need this information?

(c) Identify specific asset, liability, and owner's equity accounts that Cookie Creations will likely use to record its business transactions.

(d) Should Natalie open a separate bank account for the business? Why or why not?

BROADENINGYOURPERSPECTIVE

Financial Reporting and Analysis

Financial Reporting Problem: PepsiCo, Inc.

BYP1-1 The actual financial statements of PepsiCo, Inc., as presented in the company's 2009 annual report, are contained in Appendix A (at the back of the textbook).

 PEPSICO

Instructions

Refer to PepsiCo's financial statements and answer the following questions.

(a) What were PepsiCo's total assets at December 26, 2009? At December 27, 2008?

(b) How much cash (and cash equivalents) did PepsiCo have on December 26, 2009?

(c) What amount of accounts payable did PepsiCo report on December 26, 2009? On December 27, 2008?

(d) What were PepsiCo's net revenues in 2007? In 2008? In 2009?

(e) What is the amount of the change in PepsiCo's net income from 2008 to 2009?

Comparative Analysis Problem:
PepsiCo, Inc. vs. The Coca-Cola Company

BYP1-2 PepsiCo's financial statements are presented in Appendix A. Financial statements of The Coca-Cola Company are presented in Appendix B.

Instructions

(a) Based on the information contained in these financial statements, determine the following for each company.

(1) Total assets at December 26, 2009, for PepsiCo and for Coca-Cola at December 31, 2009.

(2) Accounts (notes) receivable, net at December 26, 2009, for PepsiCo and at December 31, 2009, for Coca-Cola.

(3) Net revenues for year ended in 2009.

(4) Net income for year ended in 2009.

(b) What conclusions concerning the two companies can be drawn from these data?

On the Web

BYP1-3 This exercise will familiarize you with skill requirements, job descriptions, and salaries for accounting careers.

Address: www.careers-in-accounting.com, or go to **www.wiley.com/college/weygandt**

Instructions

Go to the site shown above. Answer the following questions.

(a) What are the three broad areas of accounting (from "Skills and Talents")?

(b) List eight skills required in accounting.

(c) How do the three accounting areas differ in terms of these eight required skills?

(d) Explain one of the key job options in accounting.

(e) What is the overall salary range for a junior staff accountant?

Critical Thinking

Decision Making Across the Organization

BYP1-4 Mary and Jack Gray, local golf stars, opened the Chip-Shot Driving Range on March 1, 2012, by investing $25,000 of their cash savings in the business. A caddy shack was constructed for cash at a cost of $8,000, and $800 was spent on golf balls and golf clubs. The Grays leased five acres of land at a cost of $1,000 per month and paid the first month's rent. During the first month, advertising costs totaled $750, of which $150 was unpaid at March 31, and $400 was paid to members of the high-school golf team for retrieving golf balls. All revenues from customers were deposited in the company's bank account. On March 15, Mary and Jack withdrew a total of $1,000 in cash for personal living expenses. A $100 utility bill was received on March 31 but was not paid. On March 31, the balance in the company's bank account was $18,900.

Mary and Jack thought they had a pretty good first month of operations. But, their estimates of profitability ranged from a loss of $6,100 to net income of $2,450.

Instructions

With the class divided into groups, answer the following.

(a) How could the Grays have concluded that the business operated at a loss of $6,100? Was this a valid basis on which to determine net income?

(b) How could the Grays have concluded that the business operated at a net income of $2,450? (*Hint:* Prepare a balance sheet at March 31.) Was this a valid basis on which to determine net income?

(c) Without preparing an income statement, determine the actual net income for March.

(d) What was the revenue earned in March?

Communication Activity

BYP1-5 Lynn Benedict, the bookkeeper for New York Company, has been trying to get the balance sheet to balance. The company's balance sheet is shown below.

New York Company				
Balance Sheet				
For the Month Ended December 31, 2012				
Assets			**Liabilities**	
Equipment	$25,500		Owner's capital	$26,000
Cash	9,000		Accounts receivable	(6,000)
Supplies	2,000		Owner's drawings	(2,000)
Accounts payable	(8,000)		Notes payable	10,500
	$28,500			$28,500

Instructions

Explain to Lynn Benedict in a memo why the original balance sheet is incorrect, and what should be done to correct it.

Ethics Case

BYP1-6　After numerous campus interviews, Steve Baden, a senior at Great Northern College, received two office interview invitations from the Baltimore offices of two large firms. Both firms offered to cover his out-of-pocket expenses (travel, hotel, and meals). He scheduled the interviews for both firms on the same day, one in the morning and one in the afternoon. At the conclusion of each interview, he submitted to both firms his total out-of-pocket expenses for the trip to Baltimore: mileage $112 (280 miles at $0.40), hotel $130, meals $36, and parking and tolls $18, for a total of $296. He believes this approach is appropriate. If he had made two trips, his cost would have been two times $296. He is also certain that neither firm knew he had visited the other on that same trip. Within ten days, Steve received two checks in the mail, each in the amount of $296.

Instructions

(a) Who are the stakeholders (affected parties) in this situation?

(b) What are the ethical issues in this case?

(c) What would you do in this situation?

"All About You" Activity

BYP1-7　Some people are tempted to make their finances look worse to get financial aid. Companies sometimes also manage their financial numbers in order to accomplish certain goals. Earnings management is the planned timing of revenues, expenses, gains, and losses to smooth out bumps in net income. In managing earnings, companies' actions vary from being within the range of ethical activity, to being both unethical and illegal attempts to mislead investors and creditors.

Instructions

Provide responses for each of the following questions.

(a) Discuss whether you think each of the following actions (adapted from *www.finaid.org/fafsa/maximize.phtml*) to increase the chances of receiving financial aid is ethical.

　(i) Spend down the student's assets and income first, before spending parents' assets and income.

　(ii) Accelerate necessary expenses to reduce available cash. For example, if you need a new car, buy it before applying for financial aid.

　(iii) State that a truly financially dependent child is independent.

　(iv) Have a parent take an unpaid leave of absence for long enough to get below the "threshold" level of income.

(b) What are some reasons why a *company* might want to overstate its earnings?

(c) What are some reasons why a *company* might want to understate its earnings?

(d) Under what circumstances might an otherwise ethical person decide to illegally overstate or understate earnings?

FASB Codification Activity

BYP1-8　The FASB has developed the Financial Accounting Standards Board Accounting Standards Codification (or more simply "the Codification"). The FASB's primary goal in developing the Codification is to provide in one place all the authoritative literature related to a particular topic. To provide easy access to the Codification, the FASB also developed the Financial Accounting Standards Board Codification Research System (CRS). CRS is an online, real-time database that provides easy access to the Codification. The Codification and the related CRS provide a topically organized structure, subdivided into topic, subtopics, sections, and paragraphs, using a numerical index system.

　　You may find this system useful in your present and future studies, and so we have provided an opportunity to use this online system as part of the *Broadening Your Perspective* section.

Instructions

Academic access to the FASB Codification is available through university subscriptions, obtained from the American Accounting Association (at *http://aaahq.org/FASB/Access.cfm*), for an annual fee of $150. This subscription covers an unlimited number of students within a single institution. Once this access has been obtained by your school, you should log in (at *http://aaahq.org/ascLogin.cfm*) and familiarize yourself with the resources that are accessible at the FASB Codification site.

Answers to Insight and Accounting Across the Organization Questions

p. 6 The Scoop on Accounting   Q: What are the benefits to the company and to the employees of making the financial statements available to all employees? **A:** If employees can read and use financial reports, a company will benefit in the following ways. The *marketing department* will make better decisions about products to offer and prices to charge. The *finance department* will make better decisions about debt and equity financing and how much to distribute in dividends. The *production department* will make better decisions about when to buy new equipment and how much inventory to produce. The *human resources department* will be better able to determine whether employees can be given raises. Finally, *all employees* will be better informed about the basis on which they are evaluated, which will increase employee morale.

p. 8 The Numbers Behind Not-for-Profit Organizations   Q: What benefits does a sound accounting system provide to a not-for-profit organization? **A:** Accounting provides at least two benefits to not-for-profit organizations. First, it helps to ensure that money is used in the way that donors intended. Second, it assures donors that their money is not going to waste and thus increases the likelihood of future donations.

p. 10 The Korean Discount   Q: What is meant by the phrase "make the country's businesses more transparent"? Why would increasing transparency spur economic growth? **A:** Transparency refers to the extent to which outsiders have knowledge regarding a company's financial performance and financial position. If a company lacks transparency, its financial reports do not adequately inform investors of critical information that is needed to make investment decisions. If corporate transparency is increased, investors will be more willing to supply the financial capital that businesses need in order to grow, which would spur the country's economic growth.

p. 12 Spinning the Career Wheel   Q: How might accounting help you? **A:** You will need to understand financial reports in any enterprise with which you are associated. Whether you become a manager, a doctor, a lawyer, a social worker, a teacher, an engineer, an architect, or an entrepreneur, a working knowledge of accounting is relevant.

Answers to Self-Test Questions
1. b **2.** d **3.** c **4.** b **5.** b **6.** d **7.** b **8.** a ($3,500 − $2,000) **9.** b **10.** a ($90,000 − $50,000) **11.** d **12.** c **13.** b **14.** c *15. a

IFRS A Look at IFRS

Most agree that there is a need for one set of international accounting standards. Here is why:

Multinational corporations. Today's companies view the entire world as their market. For example, Coca-Cola, Intel, and McDonald's generate more than 50% of their sales outside the United States, and many foreign companies, such as Toyota, Nestlé, and Sony, find their largest market to be the United States.

Mergers and acquisitions. The mergers between Fiat/Chrysler and Vodafone/Mannesmann suggest that we will see even more such business combinations in the future.

Information technology. As communication barriers continue to topple through advances in technology, companies and individuals in different countries and markets are becoming more comfortable buying and selling goods and services from one another.

Financial markets. Financial markets are of international significance today. Whether it is currency, equity securities (stocks), bonds, or derivatives, there are active markets throughout the world trading these types of instruments.

Key Points

- International standards are referred to as *International Financial Reporting Standards (IFRS)*, developed by the International Accounting Standards Board (IASB).

- Recent events in the global capital markets have underscored the importance of financial disclosure and transparency not only in the United States but in markets around the world. As a result, many are examining which accounting and financial disclosure rules should be

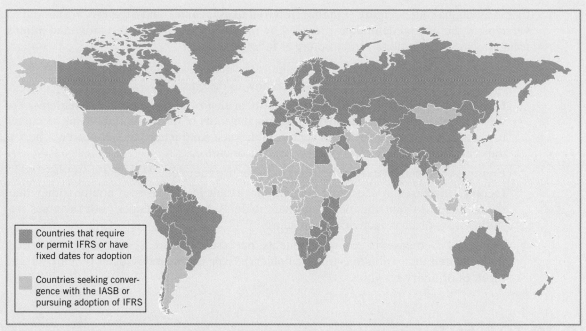

Source: http://www.pwc.com/us/en/issues/ifrs-reporting/country-adoption/index.jhtml.

followed. As indicated in the graphic above, much of the world has voted for the standards issued by the IASB. Over 115 countries require or permit use of IFRS.

- U.S standards, referred to as generally accepted accounting principles (GAAP), are developed by the Financial Accounting Standards Board (FASB). The fact that there are differences between what is in this textbook (which is based on U.S. standards) and IFRS should not be surprising because the FASB and IASB have responded to different user needs. In some countries, the primary users of financial statements are private investors; in others, the primary users are tax authorities or central government planners. It appears that the United States and the international standard-setting environment are primarily driven by meeting the needs of investors and creditors.

- The internal control standards applicable to Sarbanes-Oxley (SOX) apply only to large public companies listed on U.S. exchanges. There is a continuing debate as to whether non-U.S. companies should have to comply with this extra layer of regulation. Debate about international companies (non-U.S.) adopting SOX-type standards centers on whether the benefits exceed the costs. The concern is that the higher costs of SOX compliance are making the U.S. securities markets less competitive.

- The textbook mentions a number of ethics violations, such as Enron, WorldCom, and AIG. These problems have also occurred internationally, for example, at Satyam Computer Services (India), Parmalat (Italy), and Royal Ahold (the Netherlands).

- IFRS tends to be simpler in its accounting and disclosure requirements; some people say more "principles-based." GAAP is more detailed; some people say it is more "rules-based." This difference in approach has resulted in a debate about the merits of "principles-based" versus "rules-based" standards.

- U.S. regulators have recently eliminated the need for foreign companies that trade shares in U.S. markets to reconcile their accounting with GAAP.

- The three most common forms of business organization, proprietorships, partnerships, and corporations, are also found in countries that use IFRS. Because the choice of business organization is influenced by factors such as legal environment, tax rates and regulations, and degree of entrepreneurism, the relative use of each form will vary across countries.

- The conceptual framework that underlies IFRS is very similar to that used to develop GAAP. The basic definitions provided in this textbook for the key elements of financial statements, that is, assets, liabilities, equity, revenues (**referred to as income**), and expenses, are simplified versions of the official definitions provided by the FASB. The more substantive definitions, using the IASB definitional structure, are as follows.

Assets. A resource controlled by the entity as a result of past events and from which future economic benefits are expected to flow to the entity.

Liabilities. A present obligation of the entity arising from past events, the settlement of which is expected to result in an outflow from the entity of resources embodying economic benefits. Liabilities may be legally enforceable via a contract or law, but need not be, i.e., they can arise due to normal business practice or customs.

Equity. A residual interest in the assets of the entity after deducting all its liabilities.

Income. Increases in economic benefits that result in increases in equity (other than those related to contributions from shareholders). Income includes both revenues (resulting from ordinary activities) and gains.

Expenses. Decreases in economic benefits that result in decreases in equity (other than those related to distributions to shareholders). Expenses includes losses that are not the result of ordinary activities.

Looking to the Future

Both the IASB and the FASB are hard at work developing standards that will lead to the elimination of major differences in the way certain transactions are accounted for and reported. In fact, at one time the IASB stated that no new major standards would become effective until 2011. The major reason for this policy was to provide companies the time to translate and implement IFRS into practice, as much has happened in a very short period of time. Consider, for example, that as a result of a joint project on the conceptual framework, the definitions of the most fundamental elements (assets, liabilities, equity, revenues, and expenses) may actually change. However, whether the IASB adopts internal control provisions similar to those in SOX remains to be seen.

IFRS Self-Test Questions

1. Which of the following is *not* a reason why a single set of high-quality international accounting standards would be beneficial?
   (a) Mergers and acquisition activity.
   (b) Financial markets.
   (c) Multinational corporations.
   (d) GAAP is widely considered to be a superior reporting system.

2. The Sarbanes-Oxley Act determines:
   (a) international tax regulations.
   (b) internal control standards as enforced by the IASB.
   (c) internal control standards of U.S. publicly traded companies.
   (d) U.S. tax regulations.

3. IFRS is considered to be more:
   (a) principles-based and less rules-based than GAAP.
   (b) rules-based and less principles-based than GAAP.
   (c) detailed than GAAP.
   (d) None of the above.

4. Which of the following statements is *false*?
   (a) IFRS is based on a conceptual framework that is similar to that used to develop GAAP.
   (b) Assets are defined by the IASB as resources controlled by the entity as a result of past events and from which future economic benefits are expected to flow to the entity.

(c) Non-U.S. companies that trade shares in U.S. markets must reconcile their accounting with GAAP.

(d) Proprietorships, partnerships, and corporations are also found in countries that use IFRS.

5. Which of the following statements is *true*?

(a) Under IFRS, the term income refers to what would be called revenues and gains under GAAP.

(b) The term income is not used under IFRS.

(c) The term income refers only to gains on investments.

(d) Under IFRS, expenses include distributions to owners.

IFRS Concepts and Application

IFRS1-1   Who are the two key international players in the development of international accounting standards? Explain their role.

IFRS1-2   What might explain the fact that different accounting standard-setters have developed accounting standards that are sometimes quite different in nature?

IFRS1-3   What is the benefit of a single set of high-quality accounting standards?

IFRS1-4   Discuss the potential advantages and disadvantages that countries outside the United States should consider before adopting regulations, such as those in the Sarbanes-Oxley Act, that increase corporate internal control requirements.

International Financial Reporting Problem: Zetar plc

IFRS1-5   The financial statements of Zetar plc are presented in Appendix C. The company's complete annual report, including the notes to its financial statements, is available at *www.zetarplc.com*.

Instructions

Visit Zetar's corporate website and answer the following questions from Zetar's 2009 annual report.

(a) What accounting firm performed the audit of Zetar's financial statements?

(b) What is the address of the company's corporate headquarters?

(c) What is the company's reporting currency?

(d) What two segments does the company operate in, and what were the sales for each segment in the year ended April 30, 2009?

Answers to IFRS Self-Test Questions

1. d   2. c   3. a   4. c   5. a

✔
The Navigator

✔ **Remember to go back to the Navigator box on the chapter opening page and check off your completed work.**

CHAPTER2

The Recording Process

Study Objectives

After studying this chapter, you should be able to:

[1] Explain what an account is and how it helps in the recording process.

[2] Define debits and credits and explain their use in recording business transactions.

[3] Identify the basic steps in the recording process.

[4] Explain what a journal is and how it helps in the recording process.

[5] Explain what a ledger is and how it helps in the recording process.

[6] Explain what posting is and how it helps in the recording process.

[7] Prepare a trial balance and explain its purposes.

The Navigator

✔ The Navigator

● Scan Study Objectives	○
● Read Feature Story	○
● Read Preview	○
● Read text and answer **Do it!** p. 56 ○ p. 59 ○ p. 69 ○ p. 73 ○	
● Work Comprehensive **Do it!** p. 74	○
● Review Summary of Study Objectives	○
● Answer Self-Test Questions	○
● Complete Assignments	○
● Go to *WileyPLUS* for practice and tutorials	○
● Read A Look at IFRS p. 94	○

Feature Story

ACCIDENTS HAPPEN

How organized are you financially? Take a short quiz. Answer *yes* or *no* to each question:

• Does your wallet contain so many cash machine receipts that you've been declared a walking fire hazard?

• Is your wallet such a mess that it is often faster to fish for money in the crack of your car seat than to dig around in your wallet?

• Was Dwight Howard playing high school basketball the last time you balanced your checkbook?

• Have you ever been tempted to burn down your house so you don't have to try to find all of the receipts and records that you need to fill out your tax return?

If you think it is hard to keep track of the many transactions that make up *your* life, imagine what it is like for a major

corporation like Fidelity Investments. Fidelity is one of the largest mutual fund management firms in the world. If you had your life savings invested at Fidelity Investments, you might be just slightly displeased if, when you called to find out your balance, the representative said, "You know, I kind of remember someone with a name like yours sending us some money—now what did we do with that?"

To ensure the accuracy of your balance and the security of your funds, Fidelity Investments, like all other companies large and small, relies on a sophisticated accounting information system. That's not to say that Fidelity or any other company is error-free. In fact, if you've ever really messed up your checkbook register, you may take some comfort from one accountant's mistake at Fidelity Investments. The accountant failed to include a minus sign while doing a calculation, making what was actually a $1.3 billion loss look like a $1.3 billion—yes, *billion*—gain! Fortunately, like most accounting errors, it was detected before any real harm was done.

No one expects that kind of mistake at a company like Fidelity, which has sophisticated computer systems and top investment managers. In explaining the mistake to shareholders, a spokesperson wrote, "Some people have asked how, in this age of technology, such a mistake could be made. While many of our processes are computerized, accounting systems are complex and dictate that some steps must be handled manually by our managers and accountants, and people can make mistakes."

InsideCHAPTER2

Preview of CHAPTER 2

In Chapter 1, we analyzed business transactions in terms of the accounting equation, and we presented the cumulative effects of these transactions in tabular form. Imagine a company like Fidelity Investments (as in the Feature Story) using the same tabular format as Softbyte to keep track of its transactions. In a single day, Fidelity engages in thousands of business transactions. To record each transaction this way would be impractical, expensive, and unnecessary. Instead, companies use a set of procedures and records to keep track of transaction data more easily. This chapter introduces and illustrates these basic procedures and records.

The content and organization of Chapter 2 are as follows.

The Recording Process

The Account	Steps in the Recording Process	The Recording Process Illustrated	The Trial Balance
• Debits and credits • Summary of debit/credit rules	• Journal • Ledger	• Summary illustration of journalizing and posting	• Limitations of a trial balance • Locating errors • Use of dollar signs

The Navigator

The Account

Study Objective [1]

Explain what an account is and how it helps in the recording process.

An **account** is an individual accounting record of increases and decreases in a specific asset, liability, or owner's equity item. For example, Softbyte (the company discussed in Chapter 1) would have separate accounts for Cash, Accounts Receivable, Accounts Payable, Service Revenue, Salaries and Wages Expense, and so on. (Note that whenever we are referring to a specific account, we capitalize the name.)

In its simplest form, an account consists of three parts: (1) a title, (2) a left or debit side, and (3) a right or credit side. Because the format of an account resembles the letter T, we refer to it as a **T account**. Illustration 2-1 shows the basic form of an account.

Illustration 2-1
Basic form of account

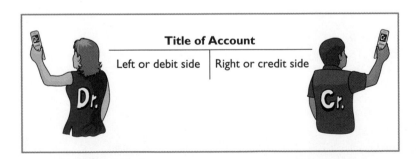

We use this form often throughout this book to explain basic accounting relationships.

Debits and Credits

Study Objective [2]

Define debits and credits and explain how they are used to record business transactions.

The term **debit** indicates the left side of an account, and **credit** indicates the right side. They are commonly abbreviated as **Dr.** for debit and **Cr.** for credit. They **do not** mean increase or decrease, as is commonly thought. We use the terms *debit* and *credit* repeatedly in the recording process to describe **where** entries are made in accounts. For example, the act of entering an amount on the left side of an account is called **debiting** the account. Making an entry on the right side is **crediting** the account.

When comparing the totals of the two sides, an account shows a **debit balance** if the total of the debit amounts exceeds the credits. An account shows a **credit balance** if the credit amounts exceed the debits. Note the position of the debit side and credit side in Illustration 2-1.

The procedure of recording debits and credits in an account is shown in Illustration 2-2 for the transactions affecting the Cash account of Softbyte. The data are taken from the Cash column of the tabular summary in Illustration 1-8 (page 20).

Illustration 2-2
Tabular summary and account form for Softbyte's Cash account

Tabular Summary		Account Form			
Cash		**Cash**			
$15,000		(Debits)	15,000	(Credits)	7,000
−7,000			1,200		1,700
1,200			1,500		250
1,500			600		1,300
−1,700		Balance	8,050		
−250		(Debit)			
600					
−1,300					
$ 8,050					

Every positive item in the tabular summary represents a receipt of cash; every negative amount represents a payment of cash. **Notice that in the account form we record the increases in cash as debits, and the decreases in cash as credits.** For example, the $15,000 receipt of cash (in red) is debited to Cash, and the −$7,000 payment of cash (in blue) is credited to Cash.

Having increases on one side and decreases on the other reduces recording errors and helps in determining the totals of each side of the account as well as the account balance. The balance is determined by netting the two sides (subtracting one amount from the other). The account balance, a debit of $8,050, indicates that Softbyte had $8,050 more increases than decreases in cash. That is, since it started with a balance of zero, it has $8,050 in its Cash account.

DEBIT AND CREDIT PROCEDURE

In Chapter 1, you learned the effect of a transaction on the basic accounting equation. Remember that each transaction must affect two or more accounts to keep the basic accounting equation in balance. In other words, for each transaction, debits must equal credits. The equality of debits and credits provides the basis for the **double-entry system** of recording transactions.

Under the double-entry system, the dual (two-sided) effect of each transaction is recorded in appropriate accounts. This system provides a logical method for recording transactions. The double-entry system also helps ensure the accuracy of the recorded amounts and helps to detect errors such as those at Fidelity Investments as discussed in the Feature Story. If every transaction is recorded with equal debits and credits, the sum of all the debits to the accounts must equal the sum of all the credits.

The double-entry system for determining the equality of the accounting equation is much more efficient than the plus/minus procedure used in Chapter 1. On the following pages, we will illustrate debit and credit procedures in the double-entry system.

International Note

Rules for accounting for specific events sometimes differ across countries. For example, European companies rely less on historical cost and more on fair value than U.S. companies. Despite the differences, the double-entry accounting system is the basis of accounting systems worldwide.

DR./CR. PROCEDURES FOR ASSETS AND LIABILITIES

In Illustration 2-2 for Softbyte, increases in Cash—an asset—were entered on the left side, and decreases in Cash were entered on the right side. We know that both sides of the basic equation (Assets = Liabilities + Owner's Equity) must be equal. It therefore follows that increases and decreases in liabilities will have to be recorded *opposite from* increases and decreases in assets. Thus, increases in liabilities must be entered on the right or credit side, and decreases in liabilities must be entered on the left or debit side. The effects that debits and credits have on assets and liabilities are summarized in Illustration 2-3.

Illustration 2-3
Debit and credit effects—assets and liabilities

Debits	Credits
Increase assets	Decrease assets
Decrease liabilities	Increase liabilities

Asset accounts normally show debit balances. That is, debits to a specific asset account should exceed credits to that account. Likewise, **liability accounts normally show credit balances**. That is, credits to a liability account should exceed debits to that account. The **normal balance** of an account is on the side where an increase in the account is recorded. Illustration 2-4 shows the normal balances for assets and liabilities.

Illustration 2-4
Normal balances—assets and liabilities

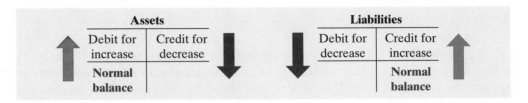

Knowing the normal balance in an account may help you trace errors. For example, a credit balance in an asset account such as Land or a debit balance in a liability account such as Salaries and Wages Payable usually indicates an error. Occasionally, though, an abnormal balance may be correct. The Cash account, for example, will have a credit balance when a company has overdrawn its bank balance (i.e., written a check that "bounced").

DR./CR. PROCEDURES FOR OWNER'S EQUITY

As Chapter 1 indicated, owner's investments and revenues increase owner's equity. Owner's drawings and expenses decrease owner's equity. Companies keep accounts for each of these types of transactions.

Owner's Capital. Investments by owners are credited to the Owner's Capital account. Credits increase this account, and debits decrease it. When an owner invests cash in the business, the company debits (increases) Cash and credits (increases) Owner's Capital. When the owner's investment in the business is reduced, Owner's Capital is debited (decreased).

Illustration 2-5 shows the rules of debit and credit for the Owner's Capital account.

Illustration 2-5
Debit and credit effects—Owner's Capital

Debits	Credits
Decrease Owner's Capital	Increase Owner's Capital

We can diagram the normal balance in Owner's Capital as follows.

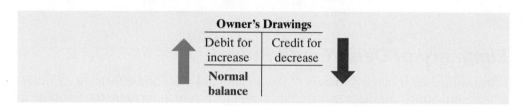

Illustration 2-6
Normal balance—Owner's Capital

Owner's Drawings. An owner may withdraw cash or other assets for personal use. Withdrawals could be debited directly to Owner's Capital to indicate a decrease in owner's equity. However, it is preferable to use a separate account, called Owner's Drawings. This separate account makes it easier to determine total withdrawals for each accounting period. Owner's Drawings is increased by debits and decreased by credits. Normally, the drawings account will have a debit balance.

Illustration 2-7 shows the rules of debit and credit for the drawings account.

Debits	Credits
Increase Owner's Drawings	Decrease Owner's Drawings

Illustration 2-7
Debit and credit effects—Owner's Drawings

We can diagram the normal balance as follows.

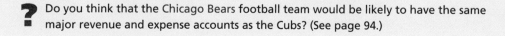

Illustration 2-8
Normal balance—Owner's Drawings

The Owner's Drawings account decreases owner's equity. It is not an income statement account like revenues and expenses.

 INVESTOR **I**NSIGHT

Keeping Score

The Chicago Cubs baseball team has these major revenue and expense accounts:

Revenues	Expenses
Admissions (ticket sales)	Players' salaries
Concessions	Administrative salaries
Television and radio	Travel
Advertising	Ballpark maintenance

? Do you think that the Chicago Bears football team would be likely to have the same major revenue and expense accounts as the Cubs? (See page 94.)

Revenues and Expenses. The purpose of earning revenues is to benefit the owner(s) of the business. When a company earns revenues, owner's equity increases. Therefore, **the effect of debits and credits on revenue accounts is the same as their effect on Owner's Capital.** That is, revenue accounts are increased by credits and decreased by debits.

Helpful Hint

Because revenues increase owner's equity, a revenue account has the same debit/credit rules as the Owner's Capital account. Expenses have the opposite effect.

Expenses have the opposite effect: Expenses decrease owner's equity. Since expenses decrease net income, and revenues increase it, it is logical that the increase and decrease sides of expense accounts should be the opposite of revenue accounts. Thus, expense accounts are increased by debits and decreased by credits. Illustration 2-9 shows the rules of debits and credits for revenues and expenses.

Illustration 2-9
Debit and credit effects—revenues and expenses

Debits	Credits
Decrease revenues	Increase revenues
Increase expenses	Decrease expenses

Credits to revenue accounts should exceed debits. Debits to expense accounts should exceed credits. Thus, revenue accounts normally show credit balances, and expense accounts normally show debit balances. We can diagram the normal balances as follows.

Illustration 2-10
Normal balances—revenues and expenses

	Revenues			Expenses	
	Debit for decrease	Credit for increase		Debit for increase	Credit for decrease
		Normal balance		**Normal balance**	

Summary of Debit/Credit Rules

Helpful Hint

You may want to bookmark Illustration 2-11. You probably will refer to it often.

Illustration 2-11 shows a summary of the debit/credit rules and effects on each type of account. Study this diagram carefully. It will help you understand the fundamentals of the double-entry system.

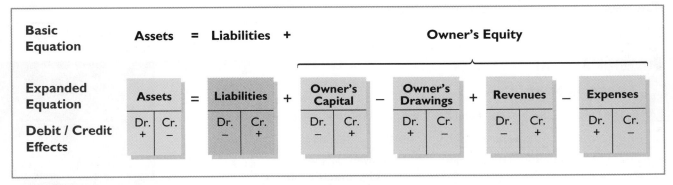

Illustration 2-11
Summary of debit/credit rules

Do it!

Normal Balances

Kate Browne has just rented space in a shopping mall. In this space, she will open a hair salon, to be called "Hair It Is." A friend has advised Kate to set up a double-entry set of accounting records in which to record all of her business transactions.

Identify the balance sheet accounts that Kate will likely need to record the transactions needed to open her business. Indicate whether the normal balance of each account is a debit or a credit.

Solution

Kate would likely need the following accounts in which to record the transactions necessary to ready her hair salon for opening day:

Cash (debit balance)

Equipment (debit balance)

Supplies (debit balance)

Accounts Payable (credit balance)

If she borrows money: Notes Payable (credit balance)

Owner's Capital (credit balance)

Related exercise material: BE2-1, BE2-2, BE2-5, E2-1, E2-2, E2-4, and **Do it!** 2-1.

action plan

✔ Determine the types of accounts needed: Kate will need asset accounts for each different type of asset she invests in the business, and liability accounts for any debts she incurs.

✔ Understand the types of owner's equity accounts: Only Owner's Capital will be needed when Kate begins the business. Other owner's equity accounts will be needed later.

Steps in the Recording Process

Although it is possible to enter transaction information directly into the accounts without using a journal, few businesses do so. Practically every business uses three basic steps in the recording process:

Study Objective [3]
Identify the basic steps in the recording process.

1. Analyze each transaction for its effects on the accounts.

2. Enter the transaction information in a *journal*.

3. Transfer the journal information to the appropriate accounts in the *ledger*.

The recording process begins with the transaction. **Business documents**, such as a sales slip, a check, a bill, or a cash register tape, provide evidence of the transaction. The company analyzes this evidence to determine the transaction's effects on specific accounts. The company then enters the transaction in the journal. Finally, it transfers the journal entry to the designated accounts in the ledger. Illustration 2-12 shows the recording process.

The steps in the recording process occur repeatedly. In Chapter 1, we illustrated the first step, the analysis of transactions, and will give further examples in this and later chapters. The other two steps in the recording process are explained in the next sections.

Ethics Note

Business documents provide evidence that transactions actually occurred. International Outsourcing Services, LLC, was accused of submitting fraudulent documents (store coupons) to companies such as Kraft Foods and PepsiCo for reimbursement of as much as $250 million. Ensuring that all recorded transactions are backed up by proper business documents reduces the likelihood of fraudulent activity.

Analyze each transaction

Enter transaction in a journal

Transfer journal information to ledger accounts

Illustration 2-12
The recording process

The Journal

Study Objective [4]

Explain what a journal is and how it helps in the recording process.

Companies initially record transactions in chronological order (the order in which they occur). Thus, the journal is referred to as the book of original entry. For each transaction the journal shows the debit and credit effects on specific accounts.

Companies may use various kinds of journals, but every company has the most basic form of journal, a general journal. Typically, a general journal has spaces for dates, account titles and explanations, references, and two amount columns. See the format of the journal in Illustration 2-13. *Whenever we use the term "journal" in this textbook without a modifying adjective, we mean the general journal.*

The journal makes several significant contributions to the recording process:

1. It discloses in one place the **complete effects of a transaction**.
2. It provides a **chronological record** of transactions.
3. It helps to **prevent or locate errors** because the debit and credit amounts for each entry can be easily compared.

JOURNALIZING

Entering transaction data in the journal is known as journalizing. Companies make separate journal entries for each transaction. A complete entry consists of (1) the date of the transaction, (2) the accounts and amounts to be debited and credited, and (3) a brief explanation of the transaction.

Illustration 2-13 shows the technique of journalizing, using the first two transactions of Softbyte. On September 1, Ray Neal invested $15,000 cash in the business, and Softbyte purchased computer equipment for $7,000 cash. The number J1 indicates that these two entries are recorded on the first page of the journal. Illustration 2-13 shows the standard form of journal entries for these two transactions. (The boxed numbers correspond to explanations in the list below the illustration.)

Illustration 2-13
Technique of journalizing

General Journal				J1
Date	**Account Titles and Explanation**	**Ref.**	**Debit**	**Credit**
2012		[5]		
Sept. 1 [2]	Cash		15,000	
[1] [3]	Owner's Capital			15,000
[4]	(Owner's investment of cash in business)			
1	Equipment		7,000	
	Cash			7,000
	(Purchase of equipment for cash)			

[1] The date of the transaction is entered in the Date column.

[2] The debit account title (that is, the account to be debited) is entered first at the extreme left margin of the column headed "Account Titles and Explanation," and the amount of the debit is recorded in the Debit column.

[3] The credit account title (that is, the account to be credited) is indented and entered on the next line in the column headed "Account Titles and Explanation," and the amount of the credit is recorded in the Credit column.

④ A brief explanation of the transaction appears on the line below the credit account title. A space is left between journal entries. The blank space separates individual journal entries and makes the entire journal easier to read.

⑤ The column titled Ref. (which stands for Reference) is left blank when the journal entry is made. This column is used later when the journal entries are transferred to the ledger accounts.

It is important to use correct and specific account titles in journalizing. Erroneous account titles lead to incorrect financial statements. However, some flexibility exists initially in selecting account titles. The main criterion is that each title must appropriately describe the content of the account. Once a company chooses the specific title to use, it should record under that account title all later transactions involving the account.[1]

SIMPLE AND COMPOUND ENTRIES

Some entries involve only two accounts, one debit and one credit. (See, for example, the entries in Illustration 2-13.) An entry like these is considered a **simple entry**. Some transactions, however, require more than two accounts in journalizing. An entry that requires three or more accounts is a **compound entry**. To illustrate, assume that on July 1, Butler Company purchases a delivery truck costing $14,000. It pays $8,000 cash now and agrees to pay the remaining $6,000 on account (to be paid later). The compound entry is as follows.

	General Journal			J1
Date	**Account Titles and Explanation**	**Ref.**	**Debit**	**Credit**
2012				
July 1	Equipment		14,000	
	Cash			8,000
	Accounts Payable			6,000
	(Purchased truck for cash with balance on account)			

Illustration 2-14
Compound journal entry

In a compound entry, the standard format requires that all debits be listed before the credits.

Do it!

Kate Browne engaged in the following activities in establishing her salon, Hair It Is:

1. Opened a bank account in the name of Hair It Is and deposited $20,000 of her own money in this account as her initial investment.

2. Purchased equipment on account (to be paid in 30 days) for a total cost of $4,800.

3. Interviewed three persons for the position of hair stylist.

In what form (type of record) should Kate record these three activities? Prepare the entries to record the transactions.

Recording Business Activities

---

[1]*In homework problems, you should use specific account titles when they are given.* When account titles are not given, you may select account titles that identify the nature and content of each account. The account titles used in journalizing should not contain explanations such as Cash Paid or Cash Received.

action plan

✔ Understand which activities need to be recorded and which do not. Any that affect assets, liabilities, or owner's capital should be recorded in a journal.

✔ Analyze the effects of transactions on asset, liability, and owner's equity accounts.

Solution

Each transaction that is recorded is entered in the general journal. The three activities would be recorded as follows.

1.	Cash	20,000	
	Owner's Capital		20,000
	(Owner's investment of cash in business)		
2.	Equipment	4,800	
	Accounts Payable		4,800
	(Purchase of equipment on account)		
3.	No entry because no transaction has occurred.		

Related exercise material: BE2-3, BE2-6, E2-3, E2-5, E2-6, E2-7, and **Do it!** 2-2.

The Navigator

The Ledger

Study Objective [5]

Explain what a ledger is and how it helps in the recording process.

The entire group of accounts maintained by a company is the **ledger**. The ledger keeps in one place all the information about changes in specific account balances.

Companies may use various kinds of ledgers, but every company has a general ledger. A **general ledger** contains all the asset, liability, and owner's equity accounts, as shown in Illustration 2-15 for J. Lind Company. *Whenever we use the term "ledger" in this textbook, we are referring to the general ledger, unless we specify otherwise.*

Illustration 2-15
The general ledger, which contains all of a company's accounts

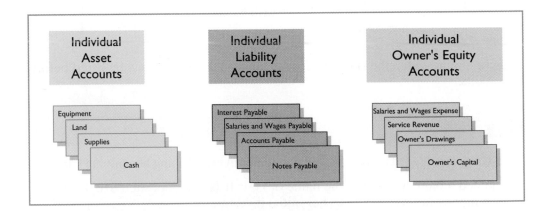

Companies arrange the ledger in the sequence in which they present the accounts in the financial statements, beginning with the balance sheet accounts. First in order are the asset accounts, followed by liability accounts, owner's capital, owner's drawings, revenues, and expenses. Each account is numbered for easier identification.

The ledger provides the balance in each of the accounts. For example, the Cash account shows the amount of cash available to meet current obligations. The Accounts Receivable account shows amounts due from customers. Accounts Payable shows amounts owed to creditors.

ACCOUNTING ACROSS THE ORGANIZATION

What Would Sam Do?

In his autobiography, Sam Walton described the double-entry accounting system he used when Wal-Mart was just getting started: "We kept a little pigeonhole on the wall for the cash receipts and paperwork of each [Wal-Mart] store. I had a blue binder ledger book for each store. When we added a store, we added a pigeonhole. We did this at least up to twenty stores. Then once a month, the bookkeeper and I would enter the merchandise, enter the sales, enter the cash, and balance it."

Source: Sam Walton, *Made in America* (New York: Doubleday, 1992), p. 53.

? Why did Sam Walton keep separate pigeonholes and blue binders? Why bother to keep separate records for each store? (See page 94.)

STANDARD FORM OF ACCOUNT

The simple T-account form used in accounting textbooks is often very useful for illustration purposes. However, in practice, the account forms used in ledgers are much more structured. Illustration 2-16 shows a typical form, using assumed data from a cash account.

Cash					No. 101
Date	**Explanation**	**Ref.**	**Debit**	**Credit**	**Balance**
2012					
June 1			25,000		25,000
2				8,000	17,000
3			4,200		21,200
9			7,500		28,700
17				11,700	17,000
20				250	16,750
30				7,300	9,450

Illustration 2-16
Three-column form of account

This format is called the **three-column form of account**. It has three money columns—debit, credit, and balance. The balance in the account is determined after each transaction. Companies use the explanation space and reference columns to provide special information about the transaction.

POSTING

Transferring journal entries to the ledger accounts is called posting. This phase of the recording process accumulates the effects of journalized transactions into the individual accounts. Posting involves the following steps.

Study Objective [6]

Explain what posting is and how it helps in the recording process.

1. In the **ledger**, in the appropriate columns of the account(s) debited, enter the date, journal page, and debit amount shown in the journal.
2. In the reference column of the **journal**, write the account number to which the debit amount was posted.
3. In the **ledger**, in the appropriate columns of the account(s) credited, enter the date, journal page, and credit amount shown in the journal.
4. In the reference column of the **journal**, write the account number to which the credit amount was posted.

Illustration 2-17 shows these four steps using Softbyte's first journal entry. The boxed numbers indicate the sequence of the steps.

Illustration 2-17
Posting a journal entry

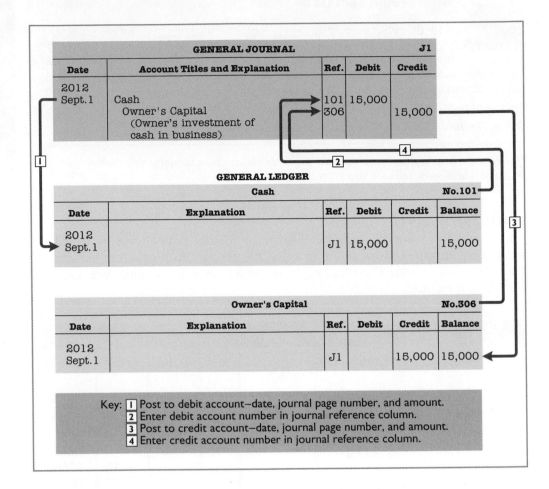

Posting should be performed in chronological order. That is, the company should post all the debits and credits of one journal entry before proceeding to the next journal entry. Postings should be made on a timely basis to ensure that the ledger is up to date.[2]

The reference column of a ledger account indicates the journal page from which the transaction was posted.[3] The explanation space of the ledger account is used infrequently because an explanation already appears in the journal.

CHART OF ACCOUNTS

The number and type of accounts differ for each company. The number of accounts depends on the amount of detail management desires. For example, the management of one company may want a single account for all types of utility expense. Another may keep separate expense accounts for each type of utility, such as gas, electricity, and water. Similarly, a small company like Softbyte will have fewer accounts than a corporate giant like Dell. Softbyte may be able to manage and report its activities in 20 to 30 accounts, while Dell may require thousands of accounts to keep track of its worldwide activities.

---

[2] *In homework problems, you can journalize all transactions before posting any of the journal entries.*
[3] After the last entry has been posted, the accountant should scan the reference column **in the journal**, to confirm that all postings have been made.

Most companies have a **chart of accounts**. This chart lists the accounts and the account numbers that identify their location in the ledger. The numbering system that identifies the accounts usually starts with the balance sheet accounts and follows with the income statement accounts.

In this and the next two chapters, we will be explaining the accounting for Pioneer Advertising Agency (a service company). Accounts 101–199 indicate asset accounts; 200–299 indicate liabilities; 301–350 indicate owner's equity accounts; 400–499, revenues; 601–799, expenses; 800–899, other revenues; and 900–999, other expenses. Illustration 2-18 shows Pioneer's chart of accounts. (C. R. Byrd is Pioneer's owner.) Accounts listed in red are used in this chapter; accounts shown in black are explained in later chapters.

Helpful Hint

On the book's endpapers, you also will find an expanded chart of accounts.

Illustration 2-18
Chart of accounts

Pioneer Advertising Agency
Chart of Accounts

Assets	Owner's Equity
101 Cash	301 Owner's Capital
112 Accounts Receivable	306 Owner's Drawings
126 Supplies	350 Income Summary
130 Prepaid Insurance	
157 Equipment	**Revenues**
158 Accumulated Depreciation—Equipment	400 Service Revenue
Liabilities	**Expenses**
200 Notes Payable	631 Supplies Expense
201 Accounts Payable	711 Depreciation Expense
209 Unearned Service Revenue	722 Insurance Expense
212 Salaries and Wages Payable	726 Salaries and Wages Expense
230 Interest Payable	729 Rent Expense
	905 Interest Expense

You will notice that there are gaps in the numbering system of the chart of accounts for Pioneer Advertising. Companies leave gaps to permit the insertion of new accounts as needed during the life of the business.

The Recording Process Illustrated

Illustrations 2-19 through 2-28 show the basic steps in the recording process, using the October transactions of Pioneer Advertising Agency. Pioneer's accounting period is a month. In these illustrations, a basic analysis, an equation analysis, and a debit-credit analysis precede the journal entry and posting of each transaction. For simplicity, we use the T-account form to show the posting instead of the standard account form.

Study these transaction analyses carefully. **The purpose of transaction analysis is first to identify the type of account involved, and then to determine whether to make a debit or a credit to the account.** You should always perform this type of analysis before preparing a journal entry. Doing so will help you understand the journal entries discussed in this chapter as well as more complex journal entries in later chapters.

Illustration 2-19
Investment of cash by owner

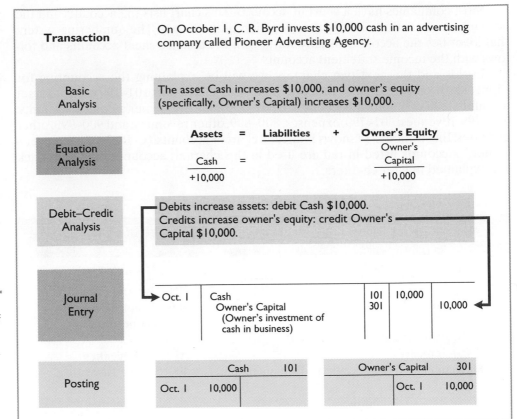

Helpful Hint

Follow these steps:
1. Determine what type of account is involved.
2. Determine what items increased or decreased and by how much.
3. Translate the increases and decreases into debits and credits.

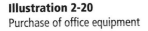

Illustration 2-20
Purchase of office equipment

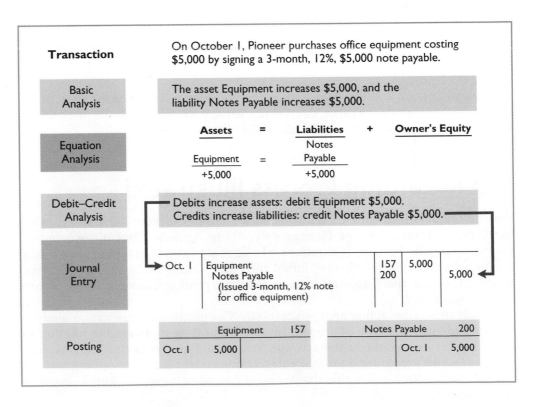

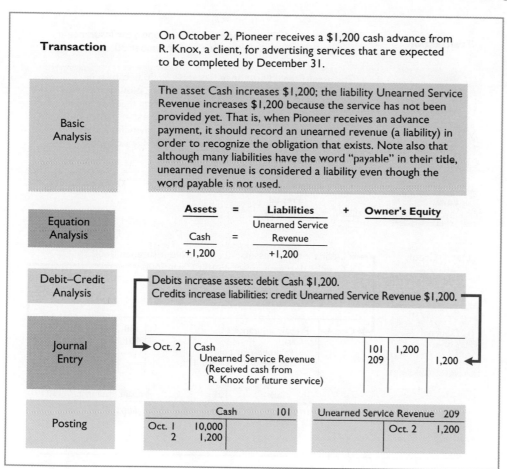

Illustration 2-21
Receipt of cash for future service

| Transaction | On October 2, Pioneer receives a $1,200 cash advance from R. Knox, a client, for advertising services that are expected to be completed by December 31. |

| Basic Analysis | The asset Cash increases $1,200; the liability Unearned Service Revenue increases $1,200 because the service has not been provided yet. That is, when Pioneer receives an advance payment, it should record an unearned revenue (a liability) in order to recognize the obligation that exists. Note also that although many liabilities have the word "payable" in their title, unearned revenue is considered a liability even though the word payable is not used. |

Equation Analysis

Assets	=	Liabilities	+	Owner's Equity
		Unearned Service		
Cash	=	Revenue		
+1,200		+1,200		

Debit–Credit Analysis

Debits increase assets: debit Cash $1,200.
Credits increase liabilities: credit Unearned Service Revenue $1,200.

Journal Entry

Oct. 2	Cash	101	1,200	
	Unearned Service Revenue	209		1,200
	(Received cash from			
	R. Knox for future service)			

Posting

Cash		101		Unearned Service Revenue	209
Oct. 1	10,000			Oct. 2	1,200
2	1,200				

Illustration 2-22
Payment of monthly rent

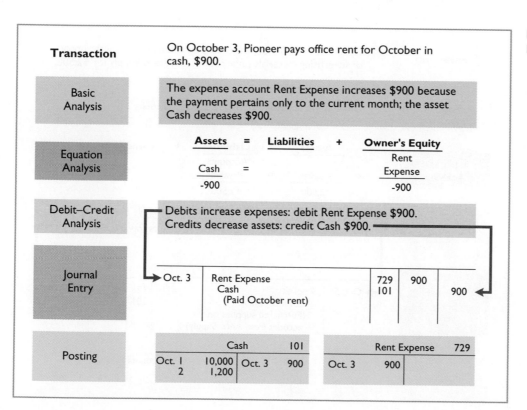

| Transaction | On October 3, Pioneer pays office rent for October in cash, $900. |

| Basic Analysis | The expense account Rent Expense increases $900 because the payment pertains only to the current month; the asset Cash decreases $900. |

Equation Analysis

Assets	=	Liabilities	+	Owner's Equity
				Rent
Cash	=			Expense
-900				-900

Debit–Credit Analysis

Debits increase expenses: debit Rent Expense $900.
Credits decrease assets: credit Cash $900.

Journal Entry

Oct. 3	Rent Expense	729	900	
	Cash	101		900
	(Paid October rent)			

Posting

Cash		101		Rent Expense		729
Oct. 1	10,000	Oct. 3	900	Oct. 3	900	
2	1,200					

Illustration 2-23
Payment for insurance

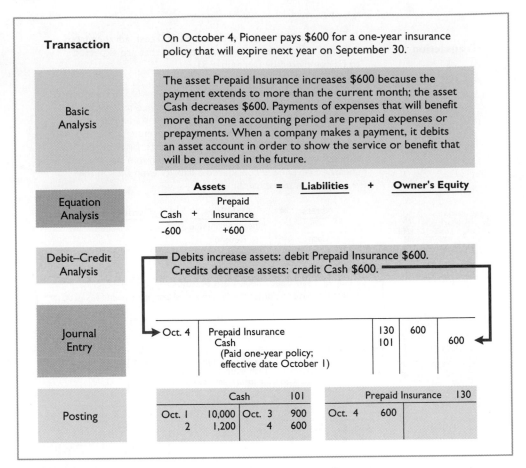

| Transaction | On October 4, Pioneer pays $600 for a one-year insurance policy that will expire next year on September 30. |

Basic Analysis

The asset Prepaid Insurance increases $600 because the payment extends to more than the current month; the asset Cash decreases $600. Payments of expenses that will benefit more than one accounting period are prepaid expenses or prepayments. When a company makes a payment, it debits an asset account in order to show the service or benefit that will be received in the future.

Equation Analysis

	Assets	=	Liabilities	+	Owner's Equity
Cash +	Prepaid Insurance				
-600	+600				

Debit–Credit Analysis

Debits increase assets: debit Prepaid Insurance $600.
Credits decrease assets: credit Cash $600.

Journal Entry

Oct. 4	Prepaid Insurance	130	600	
	Cash	101		600
	(Paid one-year policy; effective date October 1)			

Posting

	Cash	101			Prepaid Insurance	130
Oct. 1	10,000	Oct. 3	900	Oct. 4	600	
2	1,200	4	600			

Illustration 2-24
Purchase of supplies on credit

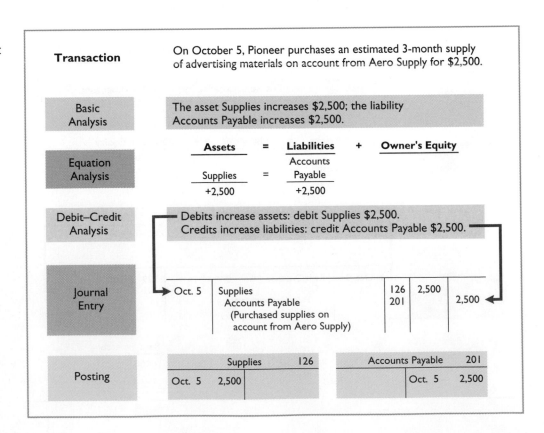

| Transaction | On October 5, Pioneer purchases an estimated 3-month supply of advertising materials on account from Aero Supply for $2,500. |

Basic Analysis

The asset Supplies increases $2,500; the liability Accounts Payable increases $2,500.

Equation Analysis

	Assets	=	Liabilities	+	Owner's Equity
			Accounts		
	Supplies	=	Payable		
	+2,500		+2,500		

Debit–Credit Analysis

Debits increase assets: debit Supplies $2,500.
Credits increase liabilities: credit Accounts Payable $2,500.

Journal Entry

Oct. 5	Supplies	126	2,500	
	Accounts Payable	201		2,500
	(Purchased supplies on account from Aero Supply)			

Posting

	Supplies	126		Accounts Payable	201
Oct. 5	2,500			Oct. 5	2,500

Illustration 2-25
Hiring of employees

Event	On October 9, Pioneer hires four employees to begin work on October 15. Each employee is to receive a weekly salary of $500 for a 5-day work week, payable every 2 weeks—first payment made on October 26.
Basic Analysis	A business transaction has not occurred. There is only an agreement between the employer and the employees to enter into a business transaction beginning on October 15. Thus, a debit–credit analysis is not needed because there is no accounting entry. (See transaction of October 26 for first entry.)

Illustration 2-26
Withdrawal of cash by owner

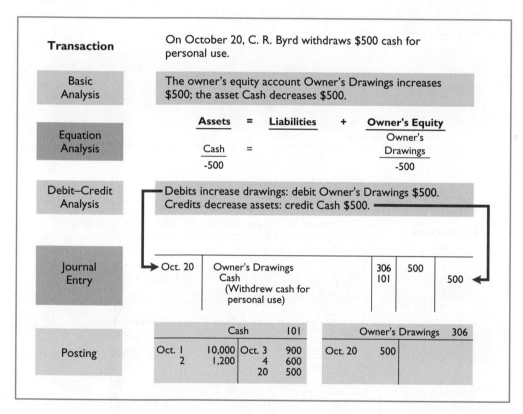

Transaction	On October 20, C. R. Byrd withdraws $500 cash for personal use.
Basic Analysis	The owner's equity account Owner's Drawings increases $500; the asset Cash decreases $500.

	Assets	=	Liabilities	+	Owner's Equity
Equation Analysis	Cash	=			Owner's Drawings
	-500				-500

Debit–Credit Analysis
Debits increase drawings: debit Owner's Drawings $500.
Credits decrease assets: credit Cash $500.

Journal Entry

Oct. 20	Owner's Drawings	306	500	
	Cash	101		500
	(Withdrew cash for personal use)			

Posting

	Cash		101		Owner's Drawings	306
Oct. 1	10,000	Oct. 3	900	Oct. 20	500	
2	1,200	4	600			
		20	500			

Illustration 2-27
Payment of salaries

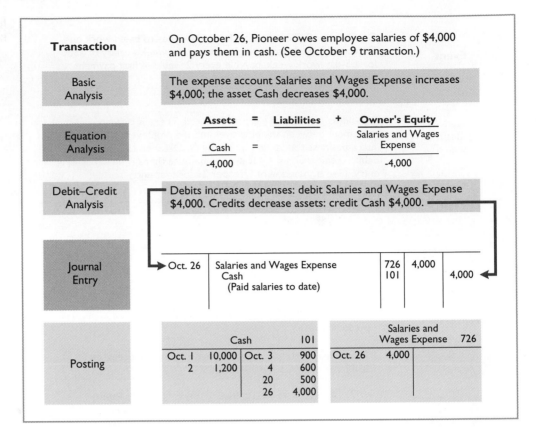

Transaction	On October 26, Pioneer owes employee salaries of $4,000 and pays them in cash. (See October 9 transaction.)
Basic Analysis	The expense account Salaries and Wages Expense increases $4,000; the asset Cash decreases $4,000.

Equation Analysis

Assets	=	Liabilities	+	Owner's Equity
Cash	=			Salaries and Wages Expense
-4,000				-4,000

Debit–Credit Analysis
Debits increase expenses: debit Salaries and Wages Expense $4,000. Credits decrease assets: credit Cash $4,000.

Journal Entry

Oct. 26	Salaries and Wages Expense	726	4,000	
	Cash	101		4,000
	(Paid salaries to date)			

Posting

Cash			101
Oct. 1	10,000	Oct. 3	900
2	1,200	4	600
		20	500
		26	4,000

Salaries and Wages Expense		726
Oct. 26	4,000	

Illustration 2-28
Receipt of cash for services provided

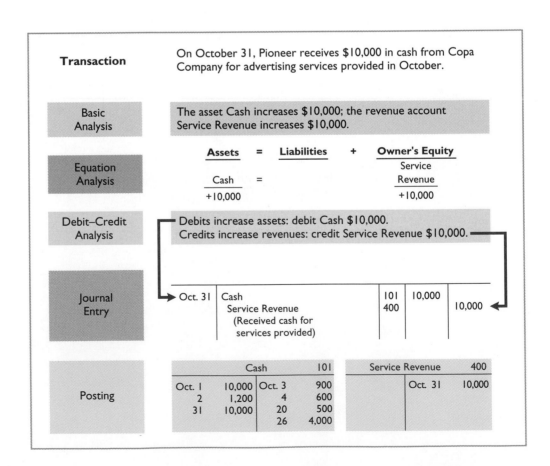

Transaction	On October 31, Pioneer receives $10,000 in cash from Copa Company for advertising services provided in October.
Basic Analysis	The asset Cash increases $10,000; the revenue account Service Revenue increases $10,000.

Equation Analysis

Assets	=	Liabilities	+	Owner's Equity
Cash	=			Service Revenue
+10,000				+10,000

Debit–Credit Analysis
Debits increase assets: debit Cash $10,000.
Credits increase revenues: credit Service Revenue $10,000.

Journal Entry

Oct. 31	Cash	101	10,000	
	Service Revenue	400		10,000
	(Received cash for services provided)			

Posting

Cash			101
Oct. 1	10,000	Oct. 3	900
2	1,200	4	600
31	10,000	20	500
		26	4,000

Service Revenue		400
	Oct. 31	10,000

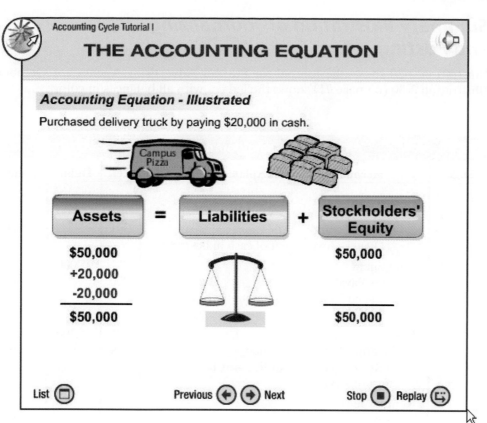

Accounting Cycle Tutorial I

THE ACCOUNTING EQUATION

Accounting Equation - Illustrated

Purchased delivery truck by paying $20,000 in cash.

Assets	=	Liabilities	+	Stockholders' Equity
$50,000				$50,000
+20,000				
-20,000				
$50,000				$50,000

List   Previous   Next   Stop   Replay

Accounting Cycle Tutorial

The diagrams in Illustrations 2-19 to 2-28 review the accounting cycle. If you would like additional practice, an Accounting Cycle Tutorial is available on *WileyPLUS*. The illustration to the left is an example of a screen from the tutorial.

Do it!

Posting

Kate Brown recorded the following transactions in a general journal during the month of March.

Mar.	4	Cash	2,280	
		Service Revenue		2,280
	15	Salaries and Wages Expense	400	
		Cash		400
	19	Utilities Expense	92	
		Cash		92

Post these entries to the Cash account of the general ledger to determine the ending balance in cash. The beginning balance of cash on March 1 was $600.

Solution

	Cash		
3/1	600	3/15	400
3/4	2,280	3/19	92
3/31 Bal.	2,388		

action plan

✔ Recall that posting involves transferring the journalized debits and credits to specific accounts in the ledger.

✔ Determine the ending balance by netting the total debits and credits.

Related exercise material: BE2-7, BE2-8, E2-8, E2-12 and **Do it!** 2-3.

The Navigator

Summary Illustration of Journalizing and Posting

Illustration 2-29 shows the journal for Pioneer Advertising Agency for October. Illustration 2-30 (on page 71) shows the ledger, with all balances in color.

Illustration 2-29
General journal entries

	General Journal			Page J1
Date	**Account Titles and Explanation**	**Ref.**	**Debit**	**Credit**
2012				
Oct. 1	Cash	101	10,000	
	Owner's Capital	301		10,000
	(Owner's investment of cash in business)			
1	Equipment	157	5,000	
	Notes Payable	200		5,000
	(Issued 3-month, 12% note for office equipment)			
2	Cash	101	1,200	
	Unearned Service Revenue	209		1,200
	(Received cash from R. Knox for future service)			
3	Rent Expense	729	900	
	Cash	101		900
	(Paid October rent)			
4	Prepaid Insurance	130	600	
	Cash	101		600
	(Paid one-year policy; effective date October 1)			
5	Supplies	126	2,500	
	Accounts Payable	201		2,500
	(Purchased supplies on account from Aero Supply)			
20	Owner's Drawings	306	500	
	Cash	101		500
	(Withdrew cash for personal use)			
26	Salaries and Wages Expense	726	4,000	
	Cash	101		4,000
	(Paid salaries to date)			
31	Cash	101	10,000	
	Service Revenue	400		10,000
	(Received cash for services provided)			

The Trial Balance

Study Objective [7]
Prepare a trial balance and explain its purposes.

A trial balance is a list of accounts and their balances at a given time. Customarily, companies prepare a trial balance at the end of an accounting period. They list accounts in the order in which they appear in the ledger. Debit balances appear in the left column and credit balances in the right column.

General Journal

Cash — No. 101

Date	Explanation	Ref.	Debit	Credit	Balance
2012					
Oct. 1		J1	10,000		10,000
2		J1	1,200		11,200
3		J1		900	10,300
4		J1		600	9,700
20		J1		500	9,200
26		J1		4,000	5,200
31		J1	10,000		15,200

Supplies — No. 126

Date	Explanation	Ref.	Debit	Credit	Balance
2012					
Oct. 5		J1	2,500		2,500

Prepaid Insurance — No. 130

Date	Explanation	Ref.	Debit	Credit	Balance
2012					
Oct. 4		J1	600		600

Equipment — No. 157

Date	Explanation	Ref.	Debit	Credit	Balance
2012					
Oct. 1		J1	5,000		5,000

Notes Payable — No. 200

Date	Explanation	Ref.	Debit	Credit	Balance
2012					
Oct. 1		J1		5,000	5,000

Accounts Payable — No. 201

Date	Explanation	Ref.	Debit	Credit	Balance
2012					
Oct. 5		J1		2,500	2,500

Unearned Service Revenue — No. 209

Date	Explanation	Ref.	Debit	Credit	Balance
2012					
Oct. 2		J1		1,200	1,200

Owner's Capital — No. 301

Date	Explanation	Ref.	Debit	Credit	Balance
2012					
Oct. 1		J1		10,000	10,000

Owner's Drawings — No. 306

Date	Explanation	Ref.	Debit	Credit	Balance
2012					
Oct. 20		J1	500		500

Service Revenue — No. 400

Date	Explanation	Ref.	Debit	Credit	Balance
2012					
Oct. 31		J1		10,000	10,000

Salaries and Wages Expense — No. 726

Date	Explanation	Ref.	Debit	Credit	Balance
2012					
Oct. 26		J1	4,000		4,000

Rent Expense — No. 729

Date	Explanation	Ref.	Debit	Credit	Balance
2012					
Oct. 3		J1	900		900

Illustration 2-30
General ledger

The trial balance proves the mathematical equality of debits and credits after posting. Under the double-entry system, this equality occurs when the sum of the debit account balances equals the sum of the credit account balances. A trial balance may also uncover errors in journalizing and posting. For example, a trial balance may well have detected the error at Fidelity Investments discussed in the Feature Story. In addition, a trial balance is useful in the preparation of financial statements, as we will explain in the next two chapters.

The steps for preparing a trial balance are:

1. List the account titles and their balances in the appropriate debit or credit column.

2. Total the debit and credit columns.

3. Prove the equality of the two columns.

Illustration 2-31 (on the next page) shows the trial balance prepared from Pioneer Advertising's ledger. Note that the total debits equal the total credits.

Illustration 2-31
A trial balance

Pioneer Advertising Agency		
Trial Balance		
October 31, 2012		
	Debit	**Credit**
Cash	$15,200	
Supplies	2,500	
Prepaid Insurance	600	
Equipment	5,000	
Notes Payable		$ 5,000
Accounts Payable		2,500
Unearned Service Revenue		1,200
Owner's Capital		10,000
Owner's Drawings	500	
Service Revenue		10,000
Salaries and Wages Expense	4,000	
Rent Expense	900	
	$28,700	**$28,700**

Helpful Hint

Note that the order of presentation in the trial balance is:
Assets
Liabilities
Owner's equity
Revenues
Expenses

A trial balance is a necessary checkpoint for uncovering certain types of errors. For example, if only the debit portion of a journal entry has been posted, the trial balance would bring this error to light.

Limitations of a Trial Balance

Ethics Note

An *error* is the result of an unintentional mistake; it is neither ethical nor unethical. An *irregularity* is an intentional misstatement, which *is* viewed as unethical.

A trial balance does not guarantee freedom from recording errors, however. Numerous errors may exist even though the trial balance columns agree. For example, the trial balance may balance even when:

1. a transaction is not journalized,
2. a correct journal entry is not posted,
3. a journal entry is posted twice,
4. incorrect accounts are used in journalizing or posting, or
5. offsetting errors are made in recording the amount of a transaction.

As long as equal debits and credits are posted, even to the wrong account or in the wrong amount, the total debits will equal the total credits. **The trial balance does not prove that the company has recorded all transactions or that the ledger is correct.**

Locating Errors

Errors in a trial balance generally result from mathematical mistakes, incorrect postings, or simply transcribing data incorrectly. What do you do if you are faced with a trial balance that does not balance? First determine the amount of the difference between the two columns of the trial balance. After this amount is known, the following steps are often helpful:

1. If the error is $1, $10, $100, or $1,000, re-add the trial balance columns and recompute the account balances.
2. If the error is divisible by 2, scan the trial balance to see whether a balance equal to half the error has been entered in the wrong column.

3. If the error is divisible by 9, retrace the account balances on the trial balance to see whether they are incorrectly copied from the ledger. For example, if a balance was $12 and it was listed as $21, a $9 error has been made. Reversing the order of numbers is called a **transposition error**.

4. If the error is not divisible by 2 or 9, scan the ledger to see whether an account balance in the amount of the error has been omitted from the trial balance, and scan the journal to see whether a posting of that amount has been omitted.

Use of Dollar Signs

Note that dollar signs do not appear in journals or ledgers. Dollar signs are typically used only in the trial balance and the financial statements. Generally, a dollar sign is shown only for the first item in the column and for the total of that column. A single line (a totaling rule) is placed under the column of figures to be added or subtracted. Total amounts are double-underlined to indicate they are final sums.

Insight boxes provide examples of business situations from various perspectives—ethics, investor, and international. Guideline answers are provided on the last page of the chapter.

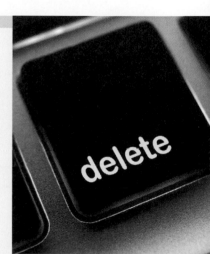

Do it!

The following accounts come from the ledger of SnowGo Company at December 31, 2012.

Trial Balance

157	Equipment	$88,000	301 Owner's Capital	$20,000
306	Owner's Drawings	8,000	212 Salaries and Wages	
201	Accounts Payable	22,000	Payable	2,000
726	Salaries and Wages		200 Notes Payable	19,000
	Expense	42,000	722 Insurance Expense	3,000
112	Accounts Receivable	4,000	130 Prepaid Insurance	6,000
400	Service Revenue	95,000	101 Cash	7,000

Prepare a trial balance in good form.

action plan

✔ Determine normal balances and list accounts in the order they appear in the ledger.

✔ Accounts with debit balances appear in the left column, and those with credit balances in the right column.

✔ Total the debit and credit columns to prove equality.

Solution

SNOWGO COMPANY
Trial Balance
December 31, 2012

	Debit	Credit
Cash	$ 7,000	
Accounts Receivable	4,000	
Prepaid Insurance	6,000	
Equipment	88,000	
Notes Payable		$ 19,000
Accounts Payable		22,000
Salaries and Wages Payable		2,000
Owner's Capital		20,000
Owner's Drawings	8,000	
Service Revenue		95,000
Insurance Expense	3,000	
Salaries and Wages Expense	42,000	
	$158,000	$158,000

Related exercise material: BE2-9, BE2-10, E2-9, E2-10, E2-11, E2-13, E2-14, and **Do it!** 2-4.

The Navigator

COMPREHENSIVE

Do it!

Transactions

Bob Sample opened the Campus Laundromat on September 1, 2012. During the first month of operations, the following transactions occurred.

Sept. 1 Bob invested $20,000 cash in the business.
2 The company paid $1,000 cash for store rent for September.
3 Purchased washers and dryers for $25,000, paying $10,000 in cash and signing a $15,000, 6-month, 12% note payable.
4 Paid $1,200 for a one-year accident insurance policy.
10 Received a bill from the *Daily News* for advertising the opening of the laundromat $200.
20 Bob withdrew $700 cash for personal use.
30 The company determined that cash receipts for laundry services for the month were $6,200.

The chart of accounts for the company is the same as that for Pioneer Advertising Agency plus No. 610 Advertising Expense.

Instructions

(a) Journalize the September transactions. (Use J1 for the journal page number.)
(b) Open ledger accounts and post the September transactions.
(c) Prepare a trial balance at September 30, 2012.

Solution to Comprehensive Do it!

(a)

	GENERAL JOURNAL			J1

Date	Account Titles and Explanation	Ref.	Debit	Credit
2012				
Sept. 1	Cash	101	20,000	
	Owner's Capital	301		20,000
	(Owner's investment of cash in business)			
2	Rent Expense	729	1,000	
	Cash	101		1,000
	(Paid September rent)			
3	Equipment	157	25,000	
	Cash	101		10,000
	Notes Payable	200		15,000
	(Purchased laundry equipment for cash and 6-month, 12% note payable)			
4	Prepaid Insurance	130	1,200	
	Cash	101		1,200
	(Paid one-year insurance policy)			
10	Advertising Expense	610	200	
	Accounts Payable	201		200
	(Received bill from Daily News for advertising)			
20	Owner's Drawings	306	700	
	Cash	101		700
	(Withdrew cash for personal use)			
30	Cash	101	6,200	
	Service Revenue	400		6,200
	(Received cash for services provided)			

action plan

✔ Make separate journal entries for each transaction.

✔ In journalizing, make sure debits equal credits.

✔ In journalizing, use specific account titles taken from the chart of accounts.

✔ Provide appropriate description of each journal entry.

✔ Arrange ledger in statement order, beginning with the balance sheet accounts.

✔ Post in chronological order.

✔ Use numbers in the reference column to indicate the amount has been posted.

✔ In the trial balance, list accounts in the order in which they appear in the ledger.

✔ List debit balances in the left column, and credit balances in the right column.

(b)   GENERAL LEDGER

Cash   No. 101

Date	Explanation	Ref.	Debit	Credit	Balance
2012					
Sept. 1		J1	20,000		20,000
2		J1		1,000	19,000
3		J1		10,000	9,000
4		J1		1,200	7,800
20		J1		700	7,100
30		J1	6,200		13,300

Prepaid Insurance   No. 130

Date	Explanation	Ref.	Debit	Credit	Balance
2012					
Sept. 4		J1	1,200		1,200

Equipment   No. 157

Date	Explanation	Ref.	Debit	Credit	Balance
2012					
Sept. 3		J1	25,000		25,000

Notes Payable   No. 200

Date	Explanation	Ref.	Debit	Credit	Balance
2012					
Sept. 3		J1		15,000	15,000

Accounts Payable   No. 201

Date	Explanation	Ref.	Debit	Credit	Balance
2012					
Sept. 10		J1		200	200

Owner's Capital   No. 301

Date	Explanation	Ref.	Debit	Credit	Balance
2012					
Sept. 1		J1		20,000	20,000

Owner's Drawings   No. 306

Date	Explanation	Ref.	Debit	Credit	Balance
2012					
Sept. 20		J1	700		700

(b)   **GENERAL LEDGER (Continued)**

Service Revenue					No. 400
Date	Explanation	Ref.	Debit	Credit	Balance
2012					
Sept. 30		J1		6,200	6,200

Advertising Expense					No. 610
Date	Explanation	Ref.	Debit	Credit	Balance
2012					
Sept. 10		J1	200		200

Rent Expense					No. 729
Date	Explanation	Ref.	Debit	Credit	Balance
2012					
Sept. 2		J1	1,000		1,000

(c)

CAMPUS LAUNDROMAT
Trial Balance
September 30, 2012

	Debit	Credit
Cash	$13,300	
Prepaid Insurance	1,200	
Equipment	25,000	
Notes Payable		$15,000
Accounts Payable		200
Owner's Capital		20,000
Owner's Drawings	700	
Service Revenue		6,200
Advertising Expense	200	
Rent Expense	1,000	
	$41,400	$41,400

✔ The Navigator

Summary of Study Objectives

[1] Explain what an account is and how it helps in the recording process. An account is a record of increases and decreases in specific asset, liability, and owner's equity items.

[2] Define debits and credits and explain their use in recording business transactions. The terms debit and credit are synonymous with left and right. Assets, drawings, and expenses are increased by debits and decreased by credits. Liabilities, owner's capital, and revenues are increased by credits and decreased by debits.

[3] Identify the basic steps in the recording process. The basic steps in the recording process are: (a) analyze each transaction for its effects on the accounts, (b) enter the transaction information in a journal, (c) transfer the journal information to the appropriate accounts in the ledger.

[4] Explain what a journal is and how it helps in the recording process. The initial accounting record of a transaction is entered in a journal before the data are entered in the accounts. A journal (a) discloses in one place the complete effects of a transaction, (b) provides a chronological record of transactions, and (c) prevents or locates errors

because the debit and credit amounts for each entry can be easily compared.

[5] Explain what a ledger is and how it helps in the recording process. The ledger is the entire group of accounts maintained by a company. The ledger keeps in one place all the information about changes in specific account balances.

[6] Explain what posting is and how it helps in the recording process. Posting is the transfer of journal entries to the ledger accounts. This phase of the recording process accumulates the effects of journalized transactions in the individual accounts.

[7] Prepare a trial balance and explain its purposes. A trial balance is a list of accounts and their balances at a given time. Its primary purpose is to prove the equality of debits and credits after posting. A trial balance also uncovers errors in journalizing and posting and is useful in preparing financial statements.

✔ The Navigator

Glossary

Account A record of increases and decreases in specific asset, liability, or owner's equity items. (p. 52).

Chart of accounts A list of accounts and the account numbers that identify their location in the ledger. (p. 63).

Compound entry A journal entry that involves three or more accounts. (p. 59).

Credit The right side of an account. (p. 52).

Debit The left side of an account. (p. 52).

Double-entry system A system that records in appropriate accounts the dual effect of each transaction. (p. 53).

General journal The most basic form of journal. (p. 58).

General ledger A ledger that contains all asset, liability, and owner's equity accounts. (p. 60).

Journal An accounting record in which transactions are initially recorded in chronological order. (p. 58).

Journalizing The entering of transaction data in the journal. (p. 58).

Ledger The entire group of accounts maintained by a company. (p. 60).

Normal balance An account balance on the side where an increase in the account is recorded. (p. 54).

Posting The procedure of transferring journal entries to the ledger accounts. (p. 61).

Simple entry A journal entry that involves only two accounts. (p. 59).

T account The basic form of an account. (p. 52).

Three-column form of account A form with columns for debit, credit, and balance amounts in an account. (p. 61).

Trial balance A list of accounts and their balances at a given time. (p. 70).

 Self-Test, Brief Exercises, Exercises, Problem Set A, and many more components are available for practice in *WileyPLUS*

Self-Test Questions

Answers are on page 94.

(SO 1) **1.** Which of the following statements about an account is *true*?
   a. In its simplest form, an account consists of two parts.
   b. An account is an individual accounting record of increases and decreases in specific asset, liability, and owner's equity items.
   c. There are separate accounts for specific assets and liabilities but only one account for owner's equity items.
   d. The left side of an account is the credit or decrease side.

(SO 2) **2.** Debits:
   a. increase both assets and liabilities.
   b. decrease both assets and liabilities.
   c. increase assets and decrease liabilities.
   d. decrease assets and increase liabilities.

(SO 2) **3.** A revenue account:
   a. is increased by debits.
   b. is decreased by credits.
   c. has a normal balance of a debit.
   d. is increased by credits.

(SO 2) **4.** Accounts that normally have debit balances are:
   a. assets, expenses, and revenues.
   b. assets, expenses, and owner's capital.
   c. assets, liabilities, and owner's drawings.
   d. assets, owner's drawings, and expenses.

(SO 2) **5.** The expanded accounting equation is:
   a. Assets + Liabilities = Owner's Capital + Owner's Drawings + Revenues + Expenses
   b. Assets = Liabilities + Owner's Capital + Owner's Drawings + Revenues − Expenses
   c. Assets = Liabilities − Owner's Capital − Owner's Drawings − Revenues − Expenses
   d. Assets = Liabilities + Owner's Capital − Owner's Drawings + Revenues − Expenses

6. Which of the following is *not* part of the recording process? (SO 3)
   a. Analyzing transactions.
   b. Preparing a trial balance.
   c. Entering transactions in a journal.
   d. Posting transactions.

7. Which of the following statements about a journal is *false*? (SO 4)
   a. It is not a book of original entry.
   b. It provides a chronological record of transactions.
   c. It helps to locate errors because the debit and credit amounts for each entry can be readily compared.
   d. It discloses in one place the complete effect of a transaction.

8. The purchase of supplies on account should result in: (SO 4)
   a. a debit to Supplies Expense and a credit to Cash.
   b. a debit to Supplies Expense and a credit to Accounts Payable.
   c. a debit to Supplies and a credit to Accounts Payable.
   d. a debit to Supplies and a credit to Accounts Receivable.

9. The order of the accounts in the ledger is: (SO 5)
   a. assets, revenues, expenses, liabilities, owner's capital, owner's drawings.
   b. assets, liabilities, owner's capital, owner's drawings, revenues, expenses.
   c. owner's capital, assets, revenues, expenses, liabilities, owner's drawings.
   d. revenues, assets, expenses, liabilities, owner's capital, owner's drawings.

(SO 5) **10.** A ledger:
  a. contains only asset and liability accounts.
  b. should show accounts in alphabetical order.
  c. is a collection of the entire group of accounts maintained by a company.
  d. is a book of original entry.

(SO 6) **11.** Posting:
  a. normally occurs before journalizing.
  b. transfers ledger transaction data to the journal.
  c. is an optional step in the recording process.
  d. transfers journal entries to ledger accounts.

(SO 6) **12.** Before posting a payment of $5,000, the Accounts Payable of Senator Company had a normal balance of $16,000. The balance after posting this transaction was:
  a. $21,000.   **c.** $11,000.
  b. $5,000.   **d.** Cannot be determined.

(SO 7) **13.** A trial balance:
  a. is a list of accounts with their balances at a given time.
  b. proves the mathematical accuracy of journalized transactions.
  c. will not balance if a correct journal entry is posted twice.
  d. proves that all transactions have been recorded.

14. A trial balance will not balance if: (SO 7)
  a. a correct journal entry is posted twice.
  b. the purchase of supplies on account is debited to Supplies and credited to Cash.
  c. a $100 cash drawing by the owner is debited to Owner's Drawings for $1,000 and credited to Cash for $100.
  d. a $450 payment on account is debited to Accounts Payable for $45 and credited to Cash for $45.

15. The trial balance of Clooney Company had accounts with   (SO 7) the following normal balances: Cash $5,000, Service Revenue $85,000, Salaries and Wages Payable $4,000, Salaries and Wages Expense $40,000, Rent Expense $10,000, Owner's Capital $42,000; Owner's Drawings $15,000; Equipment $61,000. In preparing a trial balance, the total in the debit column is:
  a. $131,000.   **c.** $91,000.
  b. $216,000.   **d.** $116,000.

Go to the book's companion website, **www.wiley.com/college/weygandt**, for additional Self-Test Questions.

Questions

1. Describe the parts of a T account.

2. "The terms *debit* and *credit* mean increase and decrease, respectively." Do you agree? Explain.

3. Jeff Hiller, a fellow student, contends that the double-entry system means each transaction must be recorded twice. Is Jeff correct? Explain.

4. Maria Alvarez, a beginning accounting student, believes debit balances are favorable and credit balances are unfavorable. Is Maria correct? Discuss.

5. State the rules of debit and credit as applied to (a) asset accounts, (b) liability accounts, and (c) the owner's equity accounts (revenue, expenses, owner's drawings, and owner's capital).

6. What is the normal balance for each of the following accounts? (a) Accounts Receivable. (b) Cash. (c) Owner's Drawings. (d) Accounts Payable. (e) Service Revenue. (f) Salaries and Wages Expense. (g) Owner's Capital.

7. Indicate whether each of the following accounts is an asset, a liability, or an owner's equity account and whether it has a normal debit or credit balance: (a) Accounts Receivable, (b) Accounts Payable, (c) Equipment, (d) Owner's Drawings, (e) Supplies.

8. For the following transactions, indicate the account debited and the account credited.
  (a) Supplies are purchased on account.
  (b) Cash is received on signing a note payable.
  (c) Employees are paid salaries in cash.

9. Indicate whether the following accounts generally will have (a) debit entries only, (b) credit entries only, or (c) both debit and credit entries.

  (1) Cash.   **(5)** Salaries and Wages
  (2) Accounts Receivable.   Expense.
  (3) Owner's Drawings.   **(6)** Service Revenue.
  (4) Accounts Payable.

10. What are the basic steps in the recording process?

11. What are the advantages of using a journal in the recording process?

12. (a) When entering a transaction in the journal, should the debit or credit be written first?
  (b) Which should be indented, the debit or credit?

13. Describe a compound entry, and provide an example.

14. (a) Should business transaction debits and credits be recorded directly in the ledger accounts?
  (b) What are the advantages of first recording transactions in the journal and then posting to the ledger?

15. The account number is entered as the last step in posting the amounts from the journal to the ledger. What is the advantage of this step?

16. Journalize the following business transactions.
  (a) Hector Molina invests $9,000 cash in the business.
  (b) Insurance of $800 is paid for the year.
  (c) Supplies of $2,000 are purchased on account.
  (d) Cash of $7,500 is received for services rendered.

17. (a) What is a ledger?
  (b) What is a chart of accounts and why is it important?

18. What is a trial balance and what are its purposes?

19. Jim Benes is confused about how accounting information flows through the accounting system. He believes the flow of information is as follows.
  (a) Debits and credits posted to the ledger.
  (b) Business transaction occurs.

(c) Information entered in the journal.
(d) Financial statements are prepared.
(e) Trial balance is prepared.

Is Jim correct? If not, indicate to Jim the proper flow of the information.

20. Two students are discussing the use of a trial balance. They wonder whether the following errors, each considered separately, would prevent the trial balance from balancing.

(a) The bookkeeper debited Cash for $600 and credited Salaries and Wages Expense for $600 for payment of wages.

(b) Cash collected on account was debited to Cash for $900 and Service Revenue was credited for $90.

What would you tell them?

21. **PEPSICO** What are the normal balances for PepsiCo's Cash, Accounts Payable, and Interest Expense accounts?

Brief Exercises

BE2-1 For each of the following accounts, indicate the effects of (a) a debit and (b) a credit on the accounts and (c) the normal balance of the account.

Indicate debit and credit effects and normal balance.
(SO 2)

1. Accounts Payable.
2. Advertising Expense.
3. Service Revenue.
4. Accounts Receivable.
5. Owner's Capital.
6. Owner's Drawings.

BE2-2 Transactions for the Daniel Hudson Company for the month of June are presented below. Identify the accounts to be debited and credited for each transaction.

Identify accounts to be debited and credited.
(SO 2)

June 1 Dan Hudson invests $5,000 cash in a small welding business of which he is the sole proprietor.
    2 Purchases equipment on account for $2,100.
    3 $800 cash is paid to landlord for June rent.
   12 Bills O. Guillen $300 for welding work done on account.

BE2-3 Using the data in BE2-2, journalize the transactions. (You may omit explanations.)

Journalize transactions.
(SO 4)

BE2-4 ⬤━━━ Kenny Williams a fellow student, is unclear about the basic steps in the recording process. Identify and briefly explain the steps in the order in which they occur.

Identify and explain steps in recording process.
(SO 3)

BE2-5 J. Reinsdorf has the following transactions during August of the current year. Indicate (a) the effect on the accounting equation and (b) the debit-credit analysis illustrated on pages 64–68 of the text.

Indicate basic and debit-credit analysis.
(SO 2)

Aug. 1 Opens an office as a financial advisor, investing $8,000 in cash.
    4 Pays insurance in advance for 6 months, $1,800 cash.
   16 Receives $3,400 from clients for services provided.
   27 Pays secretary $1,000 salary.

BE2-6 Using the data in BE2-5, journalize the transactions. (You may omit explanations.)

Journalize transactions.
(SO 4)

BE2-7 Selected transactions for the Anthony Adams Company are presented in journal form below. Post the transactions to T accounts. Make one T account for each item and determine each account's ending balance.

Post journal entries to T accounts.
(SO 6)

J1

Date	Account Titles and Explanation	Ref.	Debit	Credit
May 5	Accounts Receivable		4,100	
	Service Revenue			4,100
	(Billed for services provided)			
12	Cash		2,400	
	Accounts Receivable			2,400
	(Received cash in payment of account)			
15	Cash		3,000	
	Service Revenue			3,000
	(Received cash for services provided)			

Post journal entries to standard form of account.
(SO 6)

BE2-8 Selected journal entries for the Anthony Adams Company are presented in BE2-7. Post the transactions using the standard form of account.

Prepare a trial balance.
(SO 7)

BE2-9 From the ledger balances given below, prepare a trial balance for the Afalava Company at June 30, 2012. List the accounts in the order shown on page 63 of the text. All account balances are normal.

Accounts Payable $9,000, Cash $5,800, Owner's Capital $15,000, Owner's Drawings $1,200, Equipment $17,000, Service Revenue $10,000, Accounts Receivable $3,000, Salaries and Wages Expense $6,000, and Rent Expense $1,000.

Prepare a correct trial balance.
(SO 7)

BE2-10 An inexperienced bookkeeper prepared the following trial balance. Prepare a correct trial balance, assuming all account balances are normal.

WALTER COMPANY
Trial Balance
December 31, 2012

	Debit	Credit
Cash	$10,800	
Prepaid Insurance		$ 3,500
Accounts Payable		3,000
Unearned Service Revenue	2,200	
Owner's Capital		9,000
Owner's Drawings		4,500
Service Revenue		25,600
Salaries and Wages Expense	18,600	
Rent Expense		2,400
	$31,600	$48,000

Do it! Review

Identify normal balances.
(SO 1, 2)

Do it! 2-1 Joe Seacat has just rented space in a strip mall. In this space, he will open a photography studio, to be called "Picture This!" A friend has advised Joe to set up a double-entry set of accounting records in which to record all of his business transactions.

Identify the balance sheet accounts that Joe will likely need to record the transactions needed to open his business. Indicate whether the normal balance of each account is a debit or credit.

Record business activities.
(SO 4)

Do it! 2-2 Joe Seacat engaged in the following activities in establishing his photography studio, Picture This!:

1. Opened a bank account in the name of Picture This! and deposited $6,300 of his own money into this account as his initial investment.
2. Purchased photography supplies at a total cost of $1,100. The business paid $400 in cash and the balance is on account.
3. Obtained estimates on the cost of photography equipment from three different manufacturers.

In what form (type of record) should Joe record these three activities? Prepare the entries to record the transactions.

Post transactions.
(SO 6)

Do it! 2-3 Joe Seacat recorded the following transactions during the month of April.

April 3	Cash	3,400	
	Service Revenue		3,400
April 16	Rent Expense	700	
	Cash		700
April 20	Salaries and Wages Expense	300	
	Cash		300

Post these entries to the Cash T account of the general ledger to determine the ending balance in cash. The beginning balance in cash on April 1 was $1,600.

Do it! 2-4   The following accounts are taken from the ledger of Angulo Company at December 31, 2012.

200	Notes Payable	$20,000	101	Cash	$ 6,000
301	Owner's Capital	28,000	126	Supplies	6,000
157	Equipment	80,000	631	Supplies Expense	4,000
306	Owner's Drawings	8,000	212	Salaries and Wages Payable	3,000
726	Salaries and Wages Expense	38,000	201	Accounts Payable	11,000
400	Service Revenue	88,000	112	Accounts Receivable	8,000

Prepare a trial balance in good form.

Exercises

E2-1   Johan Aslata has prepared the following list of statements about accounts.

1. An account is an accounting record of either a specific asset or a specific liability.
2. An account shows only increases, not decreases, in the item it relates to.
3. Some items, such as Cash and Accounts Receivable, are combined into one account.
4. An account has a left, or credit side, and a right, or debit side.
5. A simple form of an account consisting of just the account title, the left side, and the right side, is called a T account.

Instructions
Identify each statement as true or false. If false, indicate how to correct the statement.

E2-2   Selected transactions for M. Anderson, an interior decorator, in her first month of business, are as follows.

Jan. 2   Invested $10,000 cash in business.
     3   Purchased used car for $4,000 cash for use in business.
     9   Purchased supplies on account for $500.
   11   Billed customers $2,100 for services performed.
   16   Paid $350 cash for advertising.
   20   Received $700 cash from customers billed on January 11.
   23   Paid creditor $300 cash on balance owed.
   28   Withdrew $1,000 cash for personal use by owner.

Instructions
For each transaction, indicate the following.
(a) The basic type of account debited and credited (asset, liability, owner's equity).
(b) The specific account debited and credited (cash, rent expense, service revenue, etc.).
(c) Whether the specific account is increased or decreased.
(d) The normal balance of the specific account.

Use the following format, in which the January 2 transaction is given as an example.

	Account Debited				Account Credited			
Date	**(a)** Basic Type	**(b)** Specific Account	**(c)** Effect	**(d)** Normal Balance	**(a)** Basic Type	**(b)** Specific Account	**(c)** Effect	**(d)** Normal Balance
Jan. 2	Asset	Cash	Increase	Debit	Owner's Equity	Owner's Capital	Increase	Credit

E2-3   Data for M. Anderson, interior decorator, are presented in E2-2.

Instructions
Journalize the transactions using journal page J1. (You may omit explanations.)

E2-4   Presented below is information related to Aromashodu Real Estate Agency.

Oct. 1   Devin Aromashodu begins business as a real estate agent with a cash investment of $15,000.
     2   Hires an administrative assistant.
     3   Purchases office furniture for $1,900, on account.

6   Sells a house and lot for H. Harrelson; bills H. Harrelson $3,600 for realty services provided.

27   Pays $1,100 on the balance related to the transaction of October 3.

30   Pays the administrative assistant $2,500 in salary for October.

Instructions

Prepare the debit-credit analysis for each transaction as illustrated on pages 64–68.

Journalize transactions.
(SO 4)

E2-5   Transaction data for Aromashodu Real Estate Agency are presented in E2-4.

Instructions

Journalize the transactions. (You may omit explanations.)

Analyze transactions and journalize.
(SO 2, 3, 4)

E2-6   Barnes Industries had the following transactions.

1. Borrowed $5,000 from the bank by signing a note.

2. Paid $3,100 cash for a computer.

3. Purchased $850 of supplies on account.

Instructions

(a) Indicate what accounts are increased and decreased by each transaction.

(b) Journalize each transaction. (Omit explanations.)

Analyze transactions and journalize.
(SO 2, 3, 4)

E2-7   Beekman Enterprises had the following selected transactions.

1. Jo Beekman invested $4,000 cash in the business.

2. Paid office rent of $950.

3. Performed consulting services and billed a client $5,200.

4. Jo Beekman withdrew $750 cash for personal use.

Instructions

(a) Indicate the effect each transaction has on the accounting equation (Assets = Liabilities + Owner's Equity), using plus and minus signs.

(b) Journalize each transaction. (Omit explanations.)

Analyze statements about the ledger.
(SO 5)

E2-8   Kahlil Bell has prepared the following list of statements about the general ledger.

1. The general ledger contains all the asset and liability accounts but no owner's equity accounts.

2. The general ledger is sometimes referred to as simply the ledger.

3. The accounts in the general ledger are arranged in alphabetical order.

4. Each account in the general ledger is numbered for easier identification.

5. The general ledger is a book of original entry.

Instructions

Identify each statement as true or false. If false, indicate how to correct the statement.

Post journal entries and prepare a trial balance.
(SO 6, 7)

E2-9   Selected transactions from the journal of Consuela Brown, investment broker, are presented below.

Date	Account Titles and Explanation	Ref.	Debit	Credit
Aug. 1	Cash		5,000	
	Owner's Capital			5,000
	(Owner's investment of cash in business)			
10	Cash		2,400	
	Service Revenue			2,400
	(Received cash for services provided)			
12	Equipment		5,000	
	Cash			3,000
	Notes Payable			2,000
	(Purchased equipment for cash and notes payable)			
25	Accounts Receivable		1,700	
	Service Revenue			1,700
	(Billed clients for services provided)			
31	Cash		900	
	Accounts Receivable			900
	(Receipt of cash on account)			

Instructions

(a) Post the transactions to T accounts.

(b) Prepare a trial balance at August 31, 2012.

E2-10 The T accounts below summarize the ledger of Bennet Landscaping Company at the end of the first month of operations.

Journalize transactions from account data and prepare a trial balance.

(SO 4, 7)

Cash			No. 101		Unearned Service Revenue		No. 209
4/1	12,000	4/15	1,300			4/30	1,000
4/12	900	4/25	1,500				
4/29	400						
4/30	1,000						

Accounts Receivable			No. 112		Owner's Capital		No. 301
4/7	3,200	4/29	400			4/1	12,000

Supplies		No. 126		Service Revenue		No. 400
4/4	1,800				4/7	3,200
					4/12	900

Accounts Payable			No. 201		Salaries and Wages Expense		No. 726
4/25	1,500	4/4	1,800		4/15	1,300	

Instructions

(a) Prepare the complete general journal (including explanations) from which the postings to Cash were made.

(b) Prepare a trial balance at April 30, 2012.

E2-11 Presented below is the ledger for Bowman Co.

Journalize transactions from account data and prepare a trial balance.

(SO 4, 7)

Cash			No. 101		Owner's Capital		No. 301
10/1	3,000	10/4	400			10/1	3,000
10/10	500	10/12	1,500			10/25	2,000
10/10	4,000	10/15	250				
10/20	500	10/30	300		Owner's Drawings		No. 306
10/25	2,000	10/31	500		10/30	300	

Accounts Receivable			No. 112		Service Revenue		No. 400
10/6	800	10/20	500			10/6	800
10/20	940					10/10	500
						10/20	940

Supplies		No. 126		Salaries and Wages Expense		No. 726
10/4	400			10/31	500	

Equipment		No. 157		Rent Expense		No. 729
10/3	2,000			10/15	250	

Notes Payable		No. 200
	10/10	4,000

Accounts Payable			No. 201
10/12	1,500	10/3	2,000

Instructions

(a) Reproduce the journal entries for the transactions that occurred on October 1, 10, and 20, and provide explanations for each.

(b) Determine the October 31 balance for each of the accounts above, and prepare a trial balance at October 31, 2012.

Prepare journal entries and post using standard account form.

(SO 4, 6)

E2-12 Selected transactions for Roberta Garza Company during its first month in business are presented below.

Sept. 1 Invested $10,000 cash in the business.
5 Purchased equipment for $12,000 paying $4,000 in cash and the balance on account.
25 Paid $3,000 cash on balance owed for equipment.
30 Withdrew $700 cash for personal use.

Garza's chart of accounts shows: No. 101 Cash, No. 157 Equipment, No. 201 Accounts Payable, No. 301 Owner's Capital, and No. 306 Owner's Drawings.

Instructions
(a) Journalize the transactions on page J1 of the journal. (Omit explanations.)
(b) Post the transactions using the standard account form.

Analyze errors and their effects on trial balance.

(SO 7)

E2-13 The bookkeeper for Lance Briggs Equipment Repair made a number of errors in journalizing and posting, as described below.

1. A credit posting of $525 to Accounts Receivable was omitted.
2. A debit posting of $750 for Prepaid Insurance was debited to Insurance Expense.
3. A collection from a customer of $100 in payment of its account owed was journalized and posted as a debit to Cash $100 and a credit to Service Revenue $100.
4. A credit posting of $415 to Property Taxes Payable was made twice.
5. A cash purchase of supplies for $250 was journalized and posted as a debit to Supplies $25 and a credit to Cash $25.
6. A debit of $475 to Advertising Expense was posted as $457.

Instructions
For each error:

(a) Indicate whether the trial balance will balance.
(b) If the trial balance will not balance, indicate the amount of the difference.
(c) Indicate the trial balance column that will have the larger total.

Consider each error separately. Use the following form, in which error (1) is given as an example.

Error	(a) In Balance	(b) Difference	(c) Larger Column
(1)	No	$525	debit

Prepare a trial balance.

(SO 2, 7)

E2-14 The accounts in the ledger of Bullucks Delivery Service contain the following balances on July 31, 2012.

Accounts Receivable	$ 7,642	Prepaid Insurance	$ 1,968
Accounts Payable	8,396	Maintenance and Repairs Expense	961
Cash	?	Service Revenue	10,610
Equipment	49,360	Owner's Drawings	700
Gasoline Expense	758	Owner's Capital	42,000
Insurance Expense	523	Salaries and Wages Expense	4,428
Notes Payable	17,000	Salaries and Wages Payable	815

Instructions
Prepare a trial balance with the accounts arranged as illustrated in the chapter and fill in the missing amount for Cash.

Exercises: Set B

Visit the book's companion website, at **www.wiley.com/college/weygandt**, and choose the Student Companion site to access Exercise Set B.

Problems: Set A

Journalize a series of transactions. **GLS**

(SO 2, 4)

P2-1A Frontier Park was started on April 1 by H. Hillenmeyer. The following selected events and transactions occurred during April.

Apr. 1   Hillenmeyer invested $35,000 cash in the business.
      4   Purchased land costing $27,000 for cash.
      8   Incurred advertising expense of $1,800 on account.
      11 Paid salaries to employees $1,500.
      12 Hired park manager at a salary of $4,000 per month, effective May 1.
      13 Paid $1,650 cash for a one-year insurance policy.
      17 Withdrew $1,000 cash for personal use.
      20 Received $6,800 in cash for admission fees.
      25 Sold 100 coupon books for $25 each. Each book contains 10 coupons that entitle the
          holder to one admission to the park.
      30 Received $8,900 in cash admission fees.
      30 Paid $900 on balance owed for advertising incurred on April 8.

Hillenmeyer uses the following accounts: Cash, Prepaid Insurance, Land, Accounts Payable, Unearned Service Revenue, Owner's Capital, Owner's Drawings, Service Revenue, Advertising Expense, and Salaries and Wages Expense.

Instructions
Journalize the April transactions.

P2-2A   Desiree Clark is a licensed CPA. During the first month of operations of her business, the following events and transactions occurred.

Journalize transactions, post, and prepare a trial balance.
(SO 2, 4, 6, 7)

GLS

May 1   Clark invested $20,000 cash in her business.
     2   Hired a secretary-receptionist at a salary of $2,000 per month.
     3   Purchased $2,500 of supplies on account from Read Supply Company.
     7   Paid office rent of $900 cash for the month.
     11 Completed a tax assignment and billed client $3,200 for services provided.
     12 Received $3,500 advance on a management consulting engagement.
     17 Received cash of $1,200 for services completed for C. Desmond Co.
     31 Paid secretary-receptionist $2,000 salary for the month.
     31 Paid 60% of balance due Read Supply Company.

Desiree uses the following chart of accounts: No. 101 Cash, No. 112 Accounts Receivable, No. 126 Supplies, No. 201 Accounts Payable, No. 209 Unearned Service Revenue, No. 301 Owner's Capital, No. 400 Service Revenue, No. 726 Salaries and Wages Expense, and No. 729 Rent Expense.

Instructions
(a) Journalize the transactions.
(b) Post to the ledger accounts.
(c) Prepare a trial balance on May 31, 2012.

Trial balance totals $28,900

P2-3A   Jay Cutler owns and manages a computer repair service, which had the following trial balance on December 31, 2011 (the end of its fiscal year).

Journalize transactions, post, and prepare a trial balance.
(SO 2, 4, 6, 7)

MEGA REPAIR SERVICE
Trial Balance
December 31, 2011

Cash	$ 8,000	
Accounts Receivable	15,000	
Supplies	13,000	
Prepaid Rent	3,000	
Equipment	20,000	
Accounts Payable		$19,000
Owner's Capital		40,000
	$59,000	$59,000

Summarized transactions for January 2012 were as follows.

1. Advertising costs, paid in cash, $1,000.
2. Additional supplies acquired on account $4,200.
3. Miscellaneous expenses, paid in cash, $2,000.
4. Cash collected from customers in payment of accounts receivable $14,000.
5. Cash paid to creditors for accounts payable due $15,000.

6. Supplies used during January $4,000.
7. Repair services performed during January: for cash $6,000; on account $9,000.
8. Wages for January, paid in cash, $3,500.
9. Jay's drawings during January were $3,000.

Instructions

(a) Open T accounts for each of the accounts listed in the trial balance, and enter the opening balances for 2012.
(b) Prepare journal entries to record each of the January transactions. (Omit explanations.)
(c) Post the journal entries to the accounts in the ledger. (Add accounts as needed.)

Trial balance totals $63,200

(d) Prepare a trial balance as of January 31, 2012.

Prepare a correct trial balance.
(SO 7)

P2-4A   The trial balance of the Kellen Davis Company shown below does not balance.

KELLEN DAVIS COMPANY
Trial Balance
May 31, 2012

	Debit	Credit
Cash	$ 5,850	
Accounts Receivable		$ 2,750
Prepaid Insurance	700	
Equipment	8,000	
Accounts Payable		4,500
Unearned Service Revenue	650	
Owner's Capital		11,700
Service Revenue	6,690	
Salaries and Wages Expense	4,200	
Advertising Expense		1,100
Insurance Expense	890	
	$26,980	$20,050

Your review of the ledger reveals that each account has a normal balance. You also discover the following errors.

1. The totals of the debit sides of Prepaid Insurance, Accounts Payable, and Insurance Expense were each understated $100.
2. Transposition errors were made in Accounts Receivable and Service Revenue. Based on postings made, the correct balances were $2,570 and $6,960, respectively.
3. A debit posting to Salaries and Wages Expense of $200 was omitted.
4. A $1,000 cash drawing by the owner was debited to Owner's Capital for $1,000 and credited to Cash for $1,000.
5. A $520 purchase of supplies on account was debited to Equipment for $520 and credited to Cash for $520.
6. A cash payment of $540 for advertising was debited to Advertising Expense for $54 and credited to Cash for $54.
7. A collection from a customer for $210 was debited to Cash for $210 and credited to Accounts Payable for $210.

Instructions

Trial balance totals $25,020

Prepare a correct trial balance. Note that the chart of accounts includes the following: Owner's Drawings and Supplies. (*Hint:* It helps to prepare the correct journal entry for the transaction described and compare it to the mistake made.)

Journalize transactions, post, and prepare a trial balance.
(SO 2, 4, 6, 7)

GLS

P2-5A   The Chicago Theater is owned by Rashied Davis. All facilities were completed on March 31. At this time, the ledger showed: No. 101 Cash $4,000, No. 140 Land $10,000, No. 145 Buildings (concession stand, projection room, ticket booth, and screen) $8,000, No. 157 Equipment $6,000, No. 201 Accounts Payable $2,000, No. 275 Mortgage Payable $8,000, and No. 301 Owner's Capital $18,000. During April, the following events and transactions occurred.

Apr. 2   Paid film rental of $1,100 on first movie.
      3   Ordered two additional films at $1,000 each.
      9   Received $2,800 cash from admissions.
     10   Made $2,000 payment on mortgage and $1,000 for accounts payable due.

11   Chicago Theater contracted with Virginia McCaskey to operate the concession stand. McCaskey is to pay 17% of gross concession receipts (payable monthly) for the rental of the concession stand.

12   Paid advertising expenses $500.

20   Received one of the films ordered on April 3 and was billed $1,000. The film will be shown in April.

25   Received $5,200 cash from admissions.

29   Paid salaries $2,000.

30   Received statement from Virginia McCaskey showing gross concession receipts of $1,000 and the balance due to The Chicago Theater of $170 ($1,000 × 17%) for April. McCaskey paid one-half of the balance due and will remit the remainder on May 5.

30   Prepaid $1,200 rental on special film to be run in May.

In addition to the accounts identified above, the chart of accounts shows: No. 112 Accounts Receivable, No. 136 Prepaid Rent, No. 400 Service Revenue, No. 429 Rent Revenue, No. 610 Advertising Expense, No. 726 Salaries and Wages Expense, and No. 729 Rent Expense.

Instructions

(a) Enter the beginning balances in the ledger as of April 1. Insert a check mark (✓) in the reference column of the ledger for the beginning balance.

Trial balance totals $34,170

(b) Journalize the April transactions. Chicago records admission revenue as service revenue, rental of the concession stand as rent revenue, and film rental expense as rent expense.

(c) Post the April journal entries to the ledger. Assume that all entries are posted from page 1 of the journal.

(d) Prepare a trial balance on April 30, 2012.

Problems: Set B

P2-1B   Forte Disc Golf Course was opened on March 1 by Matt Forte. The following selected events and transactions occurred during March.

Journalize a series of transactions.

(SO 2, 4)

Mar. 1   Invested $20,000 cash in the business.

3   Purchased Heeren's Golf Land for $15,000 cash. The price consists of land $12,000, shed $2,000, and equipment $1,000. (Make one compound entry.)

5   Paid advertising expenses of $700.

6   Paid cash $600 for a one-year insurance policy.

10   Purchased golf discs and other equipment for $1,050 from Innova Company payable in 30 days.

18   Received $1,100 in cash for golf fees earned (Forte records golf fees as service revenue).

19   Sold 150 coupon books for $10 each. Each book contains 4 coupons that enable the holder to play one round of disc golf.

25   Withdrew $800 cash for personal use.

30   Paid salaries of $250.

30   Paid Innova Company in full.

31   Received $2,100 cash for fees earned.

Matt Forte uses the following accounts: Cash, Prepaid Insurance, Land, Buildings, Equipment, Accounts Payable, Unearned Service Revenue, Owner's Capital, Owner's Drawings, Service Revenue, Advertising Expense, and Salaries and Wages Expense.

Instructions

Journalize the March transactions.

P2-2B   Victoria Hall is a licensed dentist. During the first month of the operation of her business, the following events and transactions occurred.

Journalize transactions, post, and prepare a trial balance.

(SO 2, 4, 6, 7)

April 1   Invested $20,000 cash in her business.

1   Hired a secretary-receptionist at a salary of $700 per week payable monthly.

2   Paid office rent for the month $1,100.

3   Purchased dental supplies on account from Smile Company $4,000.

10   Provided dental services and billed insurance companies $5,100.
11   Received $1,000 cash advance from Trudy Borke for an implant.
20   Received $2,100 cash for services completed and delivered to John Carl.
30   Paid secretary-receptionist for the month $2,800.
30   Paid $2,400 to Smile Company for accounts payable due.

Victoria uses the following chart of accounts: No. 101 Cash, No. 112 Accounts Receivable, No. 126 Supplies, No. 201 Accounts Payable, No. 209 Unearned Service Revenue, No. 301 Owner's Capital, No. 400 Service Revenue, No. 726 Salaries and Wages Expense, and No. 729 Rent Expense.

Instructions

Trial balance totals $29,800

(a) Journalize the transactions.
(b) Post to the ledger accounts.
(c) Prepare a trial balance on April 30, 2012.

Journalize transactions, post, and prepare a trial balance.

(SO 2, 4, 6, 7)

P2-3B   San Jose Services was formed on May 1, 2012. The following transactions took place during the first month.

Transactions on May 1:

1. Jarron Gilbert invested $40,000 cash in the company, as its sole owner.
2. Hired two employees to work in the warehouse. They will each be paid a salary of $3,050 per month.
3. Signed a 2-year rental agreement on a warehouse; paid $24,000 cash in advance for the first year.
4. Purchased furniture and equipment costing $30,000. A cash payment of $10,000 was made immediately; the remainder will be paid in 6 months.
5. Paid $1,800 cash for a one-year insurance policy on the furniture and equipment.

Transactions during the remainder of the month:

6. Purchased basic office supplies for $500 cash.
7. Purchased more office supplies for $1,500 on account.
8. Total revenues earned were $20,000—$8,000 cash and $12,000 on account.
9. Paid $400 to suppliers for accounts payable due.
10. Received $3,000 from customers in payment of accounts receivable.
11. Received utility bills in the amount of $350, to be paid next month.
12. Paid the monthly salaries of the two employees, totalling $6,100.

Instructions

Trial balance totals $81,450

(a) Prepare journal entries to record each of the events listed. (Omit explanations.)
(b) Post the journal entries to T accounts.
(c) Prepare a trial balance as of May 31, 2012.

Prepare a correct trial balance.

(SO 7)

P2-4B   The trial balance of Robbie Gould Co. shown below does not balance.

ROBBIE GOULD CO.
Trial Balance
June 30, 2012

	Debit	Credit
Cash		$ 3,340
Accounts Receivable	$ 2,812	
Supplies	1,200	
Equipment	2,600	
Accounts Payable		3,666
Unearned Service Revenue	1,100	
Owner's Capital		8,000
Owner's Drawings	800	
Service Revenue		2,480
Salaries and Wages Expense	3,200	
Supplies Expense	810	
	$12,522	$17,486

Each of the listed accounts has a normal balance per the general ledger. An examination of the ledger and journal reveals the following errors.

1. Cash received from a customer in payment of its account was debited for $580, and Accounts Receivable was credited for the same amount. The actual collection was for $850.
2. The purchase of a computer on account for $710 was recorded as a debit to Supplies for $710 and a credit to Accounts Payable for $710.
3. Services were performed on account for a client for $980. Accounts Receivable was debited for $980, and Service Revenue was credited for $98.
4. A debit posting to Salaries and Wages Expense of $700 was omitted.
5. A payment of a balance due for $306 was credited to Cash for $306 and credited to Accounts Payable for $360.
6. The withdrawal of $600 cash for Gould's personal use was debited to Salaries and Wages Expense for $600 and credited to Cash for $600.

Instructions

Prepare a correct trial balance. (*Hint:* It helps to prepare the correct journal entry for the transaction described and compare it to the mistake made.)

Trial balance totals $15,462

P2-5B The Cora Theater, owned by Cora Graham, will begin operations in March. The Cora will be unique in that it will show only triple features of sequential theme movies. As of March 1, the ledger of Cora showed: No. 101 Cash $3,000, No. 140 Land $24,000, No. 145 Buildings (concession stand, projection room, ticket booth, and screen) $10,000, No. 157 Equipment $10,000, No. 201 Accounts Payable $7,000, and No. 301 Owner's Capital $40,000. During the month of March the following events and transactions occurred.

Journalize transactions, post, and prepare a trial balance.
(SO 2, 4, 6, 7)

Mar. 2	Rented the three *Indiana Jones* movies to be shown for the first 3 weeks of March. The film rental was $3,500; $1,500 was paid in cash and $2,000 will be paid on March 10.
3	Ordered the *Lord of the Rings* movies to be shown the last 10 days of March. It will cost $200 per night.
9	Received $4,000 cash from admissions.
10	Paid balance due on *Indiana Jones* movies rental and $2,100 on March 1 accounts payable.
11	Cora Theater contracted with Caleb Hanie to operate the concession stand. Hanie is to pay 15% of gross concession receipts (payable monthly) for the rental of the concession stand.
12	Paid advertising expenses $800.
20	Received $5,000 cash from customers for admissions.
20	Received the *Lord of the Rings* movies and paid the rental fee of $2,000.
31	Paid salaries of $3,100.
31	Received statement from Caleb Hanie showing gross receipts from concessions of $6,000 and the balance due to Cora Theater of $900 ($6,000 × 15%) for March. Hanie paid one-half the balance due and will remit the remainder on April 5.
31	Received $9,000 cash from customers for admissions.

In addition to the accounts identified above, the chart of accounts includes: No. 112 Accounts Receivable, No. 400 Service Revenue, No. 429 Rent Revenue, No. 610 Advertising Expense, No. 726 Salaries and Wages Expense, and No. 729 Rent Expense.

Instructions

(a) Enter the beginning balances in the ledger. Insert a check mark (✓) in the reference column of the ledger for the beginning balance.
(b) Journalize the March transactions. Cora records admission revenue as service revenue, rental of the concession stand as rent revenue, and film rental expense as rent expense.
(c) Post the March journal entries to the ledger. Assume that all entries are posted from page 1 of the journal.
(d) Prepare a trial balance on March 31, 2012.

Trial balance totals $63,800

Problems: Set C

Visit the book's companion website, at **www.wiley.com/college/weygandt**, and choose the Student Companion site to access Problem Set C.

Continuing Cookie Chronicle

(*Note:* This is a continuation of the Cookie Chronicle from Chapter 1.)

CCC2 After researching the different forms of business organization. Natalie Koebel decides to operate "Cookie Creations" as a proprietorship. She then starts the process of getting the business running. In November 2011, the following activities take place.

Nov. 8 Natalie cashes her U.S. Savings Bonds and receives $520, which she deposits in her personal bank account.

8 She opens a bank account under the name "Cookie Creations" and transfers $500 from her personal account to the new account.

11 Natalie pays $65 for advertising.

13 She buys baking supplies, such as flour, sugar, butter, and chocolate chips, for $125 cash. (*Hint:* Use Supplies account.)

14 Natalie starts to gather some baking equipment to take with her when teaching the cookie classes. She has an excellent top-of-the-line food processor and mixer that originally cost her $750. Natalie decides to start using it only in her new business. She estimates that the equipment is currently worth $300. She invests the equipment in the business.

16 Natalie realizes that her initial cash investment is not enough. Her grandmother lends her $2,000 cash, for which Natalie signs a note payable in the name of the business. Natalie deposits the money in the business bank account. (*Hint:* The note does not have to be repaid for 24 months. As a result, the note payable should be reported in the accounts as the last liability and also on the balance sheet as the last liability.)

17 She buys more baking equipment for $900 cash.

20 She teaches her first class and collects $125 cash.

25 Natalie books a second class for December 4 for $150. She receives $30 cash in advance as a down payment.

30 Natalie pays $1,320 for a one-year insurance policy that will expire on December 1, 2011.

Instructions
(a) Prepare journal entries to record the November transactions.
(b) Post the journal entries to general ledger accounts.
(c) Prepare a trial balance at November 30.

BROADENINGYOURPERSPECTIVE

Financial Reporting and Analysis

Financial Reporting Problem: PepsiCo, Inc.

BYP2-1 The financial statements of PepsiCo, Inc. are presented in Appendix A. The notes accompanying the statements contain the following selected accounts, stated in millions of dollars.

Accounts Payable	Income Taxes Payable
Accounts Receivable	Interest Expense
Property, Plant, and Equipment	Inventory

Instructions
(a) Answer the following questions.
   (1) What is the increase and decrease side for each account?
   (2) What is the normal balance for each account?
(b) Identify the probable other account in the transaction and the effect on that account when:
   (1) Accounts Receivable is decreased.
   (2) Accounts Payable is decreased.
   (3) Inventory is increased.
(c) Identify the other account(s) that ordinarily would be involved when:
   (1) Interest Expense is increased.
   (2) Property, Plant, and Equipment is increased.

Comparative Analysis Problem: PepsiCo, Inc. vs. The Coca-Cola Company

BYP2-2 PepsiCo's financial statements are presented in Appendix A. Financial statements of The Coca-Cola Company are presented in Appendix B.

 **PEPSICO**

Instructions
(a) Based on the information contained in the financial statements, determine the normal balance of the listed accounts for each company.

PepsiCo	Coca-Cola
1. Inventory	**1.** Accounts Receivable
2. Property, Plant, and Equipment	**2.** Cash and Cash Equivalents
3. Accounts Payable	**3.** Cost of Goods Sold
4. Interest Expense	**4.** Sales (revenue)

(b) Identify the other account ordinarily involved when:
   (1) Accounts Receivable is increased.
   (2) Salaries and Wages Payable is decreased.
   (3) Property, Plant, and Equipment is increased.
   (4) Interest Expense is increased.

On the Web

BYP2-3 Much information about specific companies is available on the Internet. Such information includes basic descriptions of the company's location, activities, industry, financial health, and financial performance.

Address: biz.yahoo.com/i, or go to **www.wiley.com/college/weygandt**

Steps
1. Type in a company name, or use index to find company name.
2. Choose **Profile**. Perform instructions (a)–(c) below.
3. Click on the company's specific industry to identify competitors. Perform instructions (d)–(g) below.

Instructions
Answer the following questions.
(a) What is the company's industry?
(b) What was the company's total sales?
(c) What was the company's net income?
(d) What are the names of four of the company's competitors?
(e) Choose one of these competitors.
(f) What is this competitor's name? What were its sales? What was its net income?
(g) Which of these two companies is larger by size of sales? Which one reported higher net income?

Critical Thinking

Decision Making Across the Organization

BYP2-4 Lisa Ortega operates Ortega Riding Academy. The academy's primary sources of revenue are riding fees and lesson fees, which are paid on a cash basis. Lisa also boards horses for owners, who are billed monthly for boarding fees. In a few cases, boarders pay in advance of expected use. For its revenue transactions, the academy maintains the following accounts: No. 1 Cash, No. 5 Boarding Accounts Receivable, No. 27 Unearned Boarding Revenue, No. 51 Riding Revenue, No. 52 Lesson Revenue, and No. 53 Boarding Revenue.

The academy owns 10 horses, a stable, a riding corral, riding equipment, and office equipment. These assets are accounted for in accounts No. 11 Horses, No. 12 Building, No. 13 Riding Corral, No. 14 Riding Equipment, and No. 15 Office Equipment.

For its expenses, the academy maintains the following accounts: No. 6 Hay and Feed Supplies, No. 7 Prepaid Insurance, No. 21 Accounts Payable, No. 60 Salaries and Wages Expense, No. 61 Advertising Expense, No. 62 Utilities Expense, No. 63 Veterinary Expense, No. 64 Hay and Feed Expense, and No. 65 Insurance Expense.

Lisa makes periodic withdrawals of cash for personal living expenses. To record Lisa's equity in the business and her drawings, two accounts are maintained: No. 50 Owner's Capital, and No. 51 Owner's Drawings.

During the first month of operations an inexperienced bookkeeper was employed. Lisa Ortega asks you to review the following eight entries of the 50 entries made during the month. In each case, the explanation for the entry is correct.

Date	Account	Debit	Credit
May 1	Cash	18,000	
	Owner's Capital		18,000
	(Invested $18,000 cash in business)		
5	Cash	250	
	Riding Revenue		250
	(Received $250 cash for lessons provided)		
7	Cash	300	
	Boarding Revenue		300
	(Received $300 for boarding of horses beginning June 1)		
14	Riding Equipment	80	
	Cash		800
	(Purchased desk and other office equipment for $800 cash)		
15	Salaries and Wages Expense	400	
	Cash		400
	(Issued check to Lisa Ortega for personal use)		
20	Cash	148	
	Riding Revenue		184
	(Received $184 cash for riding fees)		
30	Veterinary Expense	75	
	Accounts Payable		75
	(Received bill of $75 from veterinarian for services rendered)		
31	Hay and Feed Expense	1,700	
	Cash		1,700
	(Purchased an estimated 2 months' supply of feed and hay for $1,700 on account)		

Instructions

With the class divided into groups, answer the following.

(a) Identify each journal entry that is correct. For each journal entry that is incorrect, prepare the entry that should have been made by the bookkeeper.

(b) Which of the incorrect entries would prevent the trial balance from balancing?

(c) What was the correct net income for May, assuming the bookkeeper reported net income of $4,500 after posting all 50 entries?

(d) What was the correct cash balance at May 31, assuming the bookkeeper reported a balance of $12,475 after posting all 50 entries (and the only errors occurred in the items listed above)?

Communication Activity

BYP2-5 Woderson's Maid Company offers home-cleaning service. Two recurring transactions for the company are billing customers for services rendered and paying employee salaries. For example, on March 15, bills totaling $6,000 were sent to customers and $2,000 was paid in salaries to employees.

Instructions

Write a memo to your instructor that explains and illustrates the steps in the recording process for each of the March 15 transactions. Use the format illustrated in the text under the heading, "The Recording Process Illustrated" (p. 64).

Ethics Case

BYP2-6 Mary Jansen is the assistant chief accountant at Casey Company, a manufacturer of computer chips and cellular phones. The company presently has total sales of $20 million. It is the end of the first quarter. Mary is hurriedly trying to prepare a general ledger trial balance so that quarterly financial statements can be prepared and released to management and the regulatory agencies. The total credits on the trial balance exceed the debits by $1,000. In order to meet the 4 p.m. deadline, Mary decides to force the debits and credits into balance by adding the amount of the difference to the Equipment account. She chose Equipment because it is one of the larger account balances; percentage-wise, it will be the least misstated. Mary "plugs" the difference! She believes that the difference will not affect anyone's decisions. She wishes that she had another few days to find the error but realizes that the financial statements are already late.

Instructions

(a) Who are the stakeholders in this situation?

(b) What are the ethical issues involved in this case?

(c) What are Mary's alternatives?

"All About You" Activity

BYP2-7 Every company needs to plan in order to move forward. Its top management must consider where it wants the company to be in three to five years. Like a company, you need to think about where you want to be three to five years from now, and you need to start taking steps now in order to get there. With some forethought, you can help yourself avoid a situation, like those described in the **All About You** feature (available online at the book's companion website) in which your résumé seems to need creative writing.

Instructions

Provide responses to each of the following items.

(a) Where would you like to be working in three to five years? Describe your plan for getting there by identifying between five and 10 specific steps that you need to take.

(b) In order to get the job you want, you will need a résumé. Your résumé is the equivalent of a company's annual report. It needs to provide relevant and reliable information about your past accomplishments so that employers can decide whether to "invest" in you. Do a search on the Internet to find a good résumé format. What are the basic elements of a résumé?

(c) A company's annual report provides information about a company's accomplishments. In order for investors to use the annual report, the information must be reliable; that is, users must have faith that the information is accurate and believable. How can you provide assurance that the information on your résumé is reliable?

(d) Prepare a résumé assuming that you have accomplished the five to 10 specific steps you identified in part (a). Also, provide evidence that would give assurance that the information is reliable.

Answers to Insight and Accounting Across the Organization Questions

p. 55 Keeping Score   Q: Do you think that the Chicago Bears football team would be likely to have the same major revenue and expense accounts as the Cubs? **A:** Because their businesses are similar—professional sports—many of the revenue and expense accounts for the baseball and football teams might be similar.

p. 61 What Would Sam Do?   Q: Why did Sam Walton keep separate pigeonholes and blue binders? **A:** Using separate pigeonholes and blue binders for each store enabled Walton to accumulate and track the performance of each individual store easily.   **Q:** Why bother to keep separate records for each store? **A:** Keeping separate records for each store provided Walton with more information about performance of individual stores and managers, and greater control. Walton would want and need the same advantages if he were starting his business today. The difference is that he might now use a computerized system for small businesses.

p. 73 Why Accuracy Matters   Q: In order for these companies to prepare and issue financial statements, their accounting equations (debit and credits) must have been in balance at year-end. How could these errors or misstatements have occurred? **A:** A company's accounting equation (its books) can be in balance yet its financial statements have errors or misstatements because of the following: entire transactions were not recorded; transactions were recorded at wrong amounts; transactions were recorded in the wrong accounts; transactions were recorded in the wrong accounting period. Audits of financial statements uncover some, but obviously not all, errors or misstatements.

Answers to Self-Test Questions
1. b **2.** c **3.** d **4.** d **5.** d **6.** b **7.** a **8.** c **9.** b **10.** c **11.** d **12.** c ($16,000 − $5,000) **13.** a **14.** c
15. a ($5,000 + $40,000 + $10,000 + $15,000 + $61,000)

IFRS A Look at IFRS

International companies use the same set of procedures and records to keep track of transaction data. Thus, the material in Chapter 2 dealing with the account, general rules of debit and credit, and steps in the recording process—the journal, ledger, and chart of accounts—is the same under both GAAP and IFRS.

Key Points

- Transaction analysis is the same under IFRS and GAAP but, as you will see in later chapters, different standards sometimes impact how transactions are recorded.

- Rules for accounting for specific events sometimes differ across countries. For example, European companies rely less on historical cost and more on fair value than U.S. companies. Despite the differences, the double-entry accounting system is the basis of accounting systems worldwide.

- Both the IASB and FASB go beyond the basic definitions provided in this textbook for the key elements of financial statements, that is, assets, liabilities, equity, revenues, and expenses. The more substantive definitions, using the IASB definitional structure, are provided in the Chapter 1 *A Look at IFRS* discussion.

- A trial balance under IFRS follows the same format as shown in the textbook.

- As shown in the textbook, dollars signs are typically used only in the trial balance and the financial statements. The same practice is followed under IFRS, using the currency of the country that the reporting company is headquartered.

- In February 2010, the SEC expressed a desire to continue working toward a single set of high-quality standards. In deciding whether the United States should adopt IFRS, some of the issues the SEC said should be considered are:

  ♦ Whether IFRS is sufficiently developed and consistent in application.

  ♦ Whether the IASB is sufficiently independent.

  ♦ Whether IFRS is established for the benefit of investors.

  ♦ The issues involved in educating investors about IFRS.

  ♦ The impact of a switch to IFRS on U.S. laws and regulations.

  ♦ The impact on companies including changes to their accounting systems, contractual arrangements, corporate governance, and litigation.

  ♦ The issues involved in educating accountants, so they can prepare statements under IFRS.

Looking to the Future

The basic recording process shown in this textbook is followed by companies across the globe. It is unlikely to change in the future. The definitional structure of assets, liabilities, equity, revenues, and expenses may change over time as the IASB and FASB evaluate their overall conceptual framework for establishing accounting standards.

IFRS Self-Test Questions

1. Which statement is *correct* regarding IFRS?
   (a) IFRS reverses the rules of debits and credits, that is, debits are on the right and credits are on the left.
   (b) IFRS uses the same process for recording transactions as GAAP.
   (c) The chart of accounts under IFRS is different because revenues follow assets.
   (d) None of the above statements are correct.

2. The expanded accounting equation under IFRS is as follows:
   (a) Assets = Liabilities + Owner's Capital + Owner's Drawings + Revenues − Expenses.
   (b) Assets + Liabilities = Owner's Capital + Owner's Drawings + Revenues − Expenses.
   (c) Assets = Liabilities + Owner's Capital − Owner's Drawings + Revenues − Expenses.
   (d) Assets = Liabilities + Owner's Capital + Owner's Drawings − Revenues − Expenses.

3. A trial balance:
   (a) is the same under IFRS and GAAP.
   (b) proves that transactions are recorded correctly.
   (c) proves that all transactions have been recorded.
   (d) will not balance if a correct journal entry is posted twice.

4. One difference between IFRS and GAAP is that:
   (a) GAAP uses accrual-accounting concepts and IFRS uses primarily the cash basis of accounting.
   (b) IFRS uses a different posting process than GAAP.
   (c) IFRS uses more fair value measurements than GAAP.
   (d) the limitations of a trial balance are different between IFRS and GAAP.

5. The general policy for using proper currency signs (dollar, yen, pound, etc.) is the same for both IFRS and this textbook. This policy is as follows:

(a) Currency signs only appear in ledgers and journal entries.

(b) Currency signs are only shown in the trial balance.

(c) Currency signs are shown for all compound journal entries.

(d) Currency signs are shown in trial balances and financial statements.

IFRS Concepts and Application

IFRS2-1   Describe some of the issues the SEC must consider in deciding whether the United States should adopt IFRS.

International Financial Reporting Problem: *Zetar plc*

IFRS2-2   The financial statements of Zetar plc are presented in Appendix C. The company's complete annual report, including the notes to its financial statements, is available at *www.zetarplc.com*.

Instructions

Describe in which statement each of the following items is reported, and the position in the statement (e.g., current asset).

(a) Other administrative expenses.

(b) Cash at bank.

(c) Borrowings and overdrafts.

(d) Finance costs.

Answers to IFRS Self-Test Questions

1. b   **2.** c   **3.** a   **4.** c   **5.** d

✔
The Navigator

✔   **Remember to go back to the Navigator box on the chapter opening page and check off your completed work.**

CHAPTER3

Adjusting the Accounts

Feature Story

WHAT WAS YOUR PROFIT?

The accuracy of the financial reporting system depends on answers to a few fundamental questions: At what point has revenue been earned? At what point is the earnings process complete? When have expenses really been incurred?

During the 1990s, the stock prices of dot-com companies boomed. Most dot-coms earned most of their revenue from selling advertising space on their websites. To boost reported revenue, some dot-coms began swapping website ad space. Company A would put an ad for its website on company B's website, and company B would put an ad for its website on company A's website. No money changed hands, but each company recorded revenue (for the value of the space that it gave the other company on its site). This practice did little to boost net income, and it resulted in no additional cash flow—but it did boost *reported revenue*.

Regulators eventually put an end to this misleading practice.

Another type of transgression results from companies recording revenues or expenses in the wrong year. In fact, shifting revenues and expenses is one of the most common abuses of financial accounting. Xerox admitted reporting billions of dollars of lease revenue in periods earlier than it should have been reported. And WorldCom stunned the financial markets with its admission that it had boosted net income by billions of dollars by delaying the recognition of expenses until later years.

Unfortunately, revelations such as these have become all too common in the corporate world. It is no wonder that a U.S. Trust survey of affluent Americans reported that 85% of respondents believed that there should be tighter regulation of financial disclosures; 66% said they did not trust the management of publicly traded companies.

Why did so many companies violate basic financial reporting rules and sound ethics? Many speculate that as stock prices climbed, executives were under increasing pressure to meet higher and higher earnings expectations. If actual results weren't as good as hoped for, some gave in to temptation and "adjusted" their numbers to meet market expectations.

Inside CHAPTER 3

PreviewofCHAPTER3

In Chapter 1, you learned a neat little formula: Net income = Revenues − Expenses. In Chapter 2, you learned some rules for recording revenue and expense transactions. Guess what? Things are not really that nice and neat. In fact, it is often difficult for companies to determine in what time period they should report some revenues and expenses. In other words, in measuring net income, timing is everything.

The content and organization of Chapter 3 are as follows.

Adjusting the Accounts

Timing Issues	The Basics of Adjusting Entries	The Adjusted Trial Balance and Financial Statements
• Fiscal and calendar years • Accrual- vs. cash-basis accounting • Recognizing revenues and expenses	• Types of adjusting entries • Adjusting entries for deferrals • Adjusting entries for accruals • Summary of basic relationships	• Preparing the adjusted trial balance • Preparing financial statements

✔ The Navigator

Timing Issues

Study Objective [1]
Explain the time period assumption.

We would need no adjustments if we could wait to prepare financial statements until a company ended its operations. At that point, we could easily determine its final balance sheet and the amount of lifetime income it earned.

However, most companies need immediate feedback about how well they are doing. For example, management usually wants monthly financial statements, and the Internal Revenue Service requires all businesses to file annual tax returns. Therefore, **accountants divide the economic life of a business into artificial time periods.** This convenient assumption is referred to as the time period assumption.

Many business transactions affect more than one of these arbitrary time periods. For example, the airplanes purchased by Southwest Airlines five years ago are still in use today. We must determine the relevance of each business transaction to specific accounting periods. (How much of the cost of an airplane contributed to operations this year?)

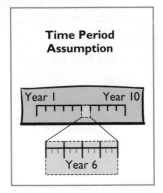

Time Period Assumption

Fiscal and Calendar Years

Alternative Terminology

The time period assumption is also called the *periodicity assumption*.

Both small and large companies prepare financial statements periodically in order to assess their financial condition and results of operations. **Accounting time periods are generally a month, a quarter, or a year.** Monthly and quarterly time periods are called **interim periods**. Most large companies must prepare both quarterly and annual financial statements.

An accounting time period that is one year in length is a **fiscal year**. A fiscal year usually begins with the first day of a month and ends twelve months later on the last day of a month. Most businesses use the **calendar year** (January 1 to December 31) as their accounting period. Some do not. Companies whose fiscal year differs from the calendar year include Delta Air Lines, June 30, and Walt Disney

Productions, September 30. Sometimes a company's year-end will vary from year to year. For example, PepsiCo's fiscal year ends on the Friday closest to December 31, which was December 30 in 2008 and December 29 in 2009.

Accrual- vs. Cash-Basis Accounting

What you will learn in this chapter is **accrual-basis accounting**. Under the accrual basis, companies record transactions that change a company's financial statements **in the periods in which the events occur.** For example, using the accrual basis to determine net income means companies recognize revenues when earned (rather than when they receive cash). It also means recognizing expenses when incurred (rather than when paid).

An alternative to the accrual basis is the cash basis. Under **cash-basis accounting**, companies record revenue when they receive cash. They record an expense when they pay out cash. The cash basis seems appealing due to its simplicity, but it often produces misleading financial statements. It fails to record revenue that a company has earned but for which it has not received the cash. Also, it does not match expenses with earned revenues. **Cash-basis accounting is not in accordance with generally accepted accounting principles (GAAP).**

Individuals and some small companies do use cash-basis accounting. The cash basis is justified for small businesses because they often have few receivables and payables. Medium and large companies use accrual-basis accounting.

Recognizing Revenues and Expenses

It can be difficult to determine the amount of revenues and expenses to report in a given accounting period. Two principles help in this task: the revenue recognition principle and the expense recognition principle.

REVENUE RECOGNITION PRINCIPLE

The **revenue recognition principle** requires that companies recognize revenue in the accounting period **in which it is earned.** In a service enterprise, revenue is considered to be earned at the time the service is performed. To illustrate, assume that Dave's Dry Cleaning cleans clothing on June 30 but customers do not claim and pay for their clothes until the first week of July. Under the revenue recognition principle, Dave's earns revenue in June when it performed the service, rather than in July when it received the cash. At June 30, Dave's would report a receivable on its balance sheet and revenue in its income statement for the service performed.

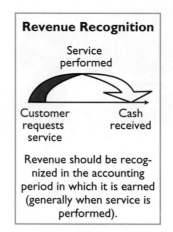

Revenue Recognition

Service performed

Customer requests service

Cash received

Revenue should be recognized in the accounting period in which it is earned (generally when service is performed).

EXPENSE RECOGNITION PRINCIPLE

Accountants follow a simple rule in recognizing expenses: "Let the expenses follow the revenues." Thus, expense recognition is tied to revenue recognition. In the dry cleaning example, this means that Dave's should report the salary expense incurred in performing the June 30 cleaning service in the same period in which it recognizes the service revenue. The critical issue in expense recognition is when the expense makes its contribution to revenue. This may or may not be the same period in which the expense is paid. If Dave's does not pay the salary incurred on June 30 until July, it would report salaries payable on its June 30 balance sheet.

This practice of expense recognition is referred to as the **expense recognition principle** (often referred to as the **matching principle**). It dictates that efforts (expenses) be matched with results (revenues). Illustration 3-1 (page 102) summarizes the revenue and expense recognition principles.

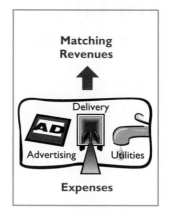

Matching Revenues

Delivery

AD Advertising

Utilities

Expenses

Illustration 3-1
GAAP relationships in revenue and expense recognition

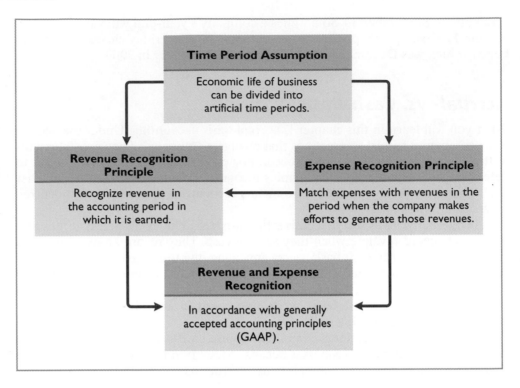

*E*THICS *I*NSIGHT

Cooking the Books?

Allegations of abuse of the revenue recognition principle have become all too common in recent years. For example, it was alleged that Krispy Kreme sometimes doubled the number of doughnuts shipped to wholesale customers at the end of a quarter to boost quarterly results. The customers shipped the unsold doughnuts back after the beginning of the next quarter for a refund. Conversely, Computer Associates International was accused of backdating sales—that is, saying that a sale that occurred at the beginning of one quarter occurred at the end of the previous quarter in order to achieve the previous quarter's sales targets.

? What motivates sales executives and finance and accounting executives to participate in activities that result in inaccurate reporting of revenues? (See page 148.)

Do it!

Timing Concepts

Numerous timing concepts are discussed on pages 100–102. A list of concepts is provided in the left column below, with a description of the concept in the right column below and on the next page. There are more descriptions provided than concepts. Match the description of the concept to the concept.

1. ____Accrual-basis accounting.

2. ____Calendar year.

3. ____Time period assumption.

4. ____Expense recognition principle.

(a) Monthly and quarterly time periods.

(b) Efforts (expenses) should be matched with results (revenues).

(c) Accountants divide the economic life of a business into artificial time periods.

(d) Companies record revenues when they receive cash and record expenses when they pay out cash.

(e) An accounting time period that starts on January 1 and ends on December 31.

(f) Companies record transactions in the period in which the events occur.

action plan

✔ Review the glossary terms identified on page 124.

✔ Study carefully the revenue recognition principle, the expense recognition principle, and the time period assumption.

Solution

1. f   2. e   3. c   4. b

Related exercise material: E3-1, E3-2, E3-3, and **Do it!** 3-1.

✔
The Navigator

The Basics of Adjusting Entries

In order for revenues to be recorded in the period in which they are earned, and for expenses to be recognized in the period in which they are incurred, companies make adjusting entries. Adjusting entries **ensure that the revenue recognition and expense recognition principles are followed.**

Adjusting entries are necessary because the **trial balance**—the first pulling together of the transaction data—may not contain up-to-date and complete data. This is true for several reasons:

1. Some events are not recorded daily because it is not efficient to do so. Examples are the use of supplies and the earning of wages by employees.

2. Some costs are not recorded during the accounting period because these costs expire with the passage of time rather than as a result of recurring daily transactions. Examples are charges related to the use of buildings and equipment, rent, and insurance.

3. Some items may be unrecorded. An example is a utility service bill that will not be received until the next accounting period.

Adjusting entries are required every time a company prepares financial statements. The company analyzes each account in the trial balance to determine whether it is complete and up to date for financial statement purposes. **Every adjusting entry will include one income statement account and one balance sheet account.**

Study Objective [3]
Explain the reasons for adjusting entries.

International Note

Internal controls are a system of checks and balances designed to detect and prevent fraud and errors. The Sarbanes-Oxley Act requires U.S. companies to enhance their systems of internal control. However, many foreign companies do not have to meet strict internal control requirements. Some U.S. companies believe that this gives foreign firms an unfair advantage because developing and maintaining internal controls can be very expensive.

Types of Adjusting Entries

Adjusting entries are classified as either deferrals or accruals. As Illustration 3-2 shows, each of these classes has two subcategories.

Study Objective [4]
Identify the major types of adjusting entries.

Deferrals:

1. Prepaid expenses: Expenses paid in cash and recorded as assets before they are used or consumed.

2. Unearned revenues: Cash received and recorded as liabilities before revenue is earned.

Accruals:

1. Accrued revenues: Revenues earned but not yet received in cash or recorded.

2. Accrued expenses: Expenses incurred but not yet paid in cash or recorded.

Illustration 3-2
Categories of adjusting entries

Subsequent sections give examples of each type of adjustment. Each example is based on the October 31 trial balance of Pioneer Advertising, from Chapter 2, reproduced in Illustration 3-3.

Illustration 3-3
Trial balance

Pioneer Advertising Agency		
Trial Balance		
October 31, 2012		
	Debit	**Credit**
Cash	$15,200	
Supplies	2,500	
Prepaid Insurance	600	
Equipment	5,000	
Notes Payable		$ 5,000
Accounts Payable		2,500
Unearned Service Revenue		1,200
Owner's Capital		10,000
Owner's Drawings	500	
Service Revenue		10,000
Salaries and Wages Expense	4,000	
Rent Expense	900	
	$28,700	**$28,700**

We assume that Pioneer Advertising uses an accounting period of one month. Thus, monthly adjusting entries are made. The entries are dated October 31.

Adjusting Entries For Deferrals

To defer means to postpone or delay. **Deferrals** are costs or revenues that are recognized at a date later than the point when cash was originally exchanged. Companies make adjusting entries for deferrals to record the portion of the deferred item that was incurred as an expense or earned as revenue during the current accounting period. The two types of deferrals are prepaid expenses and unearned revenues.

PREPAID EXPENSES

Companies record payments of expenses that will benefit more than one accounting period as assets called prepaid expenses or prepayments. When expenses are prepaid, an asset account is increased (debited) to show the service or benefit that the company will receive in the future. Examples of common prepayments are insurance, supplies, advertising, and rent. In addition, companies make prepayments when they purchase buildings and equipment.

Prepaid expenses are costs that expire either with the passage of time (e.g., rent and insurance) **or through use** (e.g., supplies). The expiration of these costs does not require daily entries, which would be impractical and unnecessary. Accordingly, companies postpone the recognition of such cost expirations until they prepare financial statements. At each statement date, they make adjusting entries to record the expenses applicable to the current accounting period and to show the remaining amounts in the asset accounts.

Prior to adjustment, assets are overstated and expenses are understated. Therefore, as shown in Illustration 3-4, **an adjusting entry for prepaid expenses results in an increase (a debit) to an expense account and a decrease (a credit) to an asset account.**

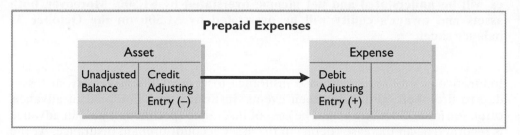

Illustration 3-4
Adjusting entries for prepaid expenses

Let's look in more detail at some specific types of prepaid expenses, beginning with supplies.

Supplies. The purchase of supplies, such as paper and envelopes, results in an increase (a debit) to an asset account. During the accounting period, the company uses supplies. Rather than record supplies expense as the supplies are used, companies recognize supplies expense at the **end** of the accounting period. At the end of the accounting period, the company counts the remaining supplies. The difference between the unadjusted balance in the Supplies (asset) account and the actual cost of supplies on hand represents the supplies used (an expense) for that period (page 106).

Recall from Chapter 2 that Pioneer Advertising purchased supplies costing $2,500 on October 5. Pioneer recorded the purchase by increasing (debiting) the asset Supplies. This account shows a balance of $2,500 in the October 31 trial balance. An inventory count at the close of business on October 31 reveals that $1,000 of supplies are still on hand. Thus, the cost of supplies used is $1,500 ($2,500 − $1,000). This use of supplies decreases an asset, Supplies. It also decreases owner's equity by increasing an expense account, Supplies Expense. This is shown in Illustration 3-5.

Supplies

Oct. 5

Supplies purchased; record asset

Oct. 31
Supplies used; record supplies expense

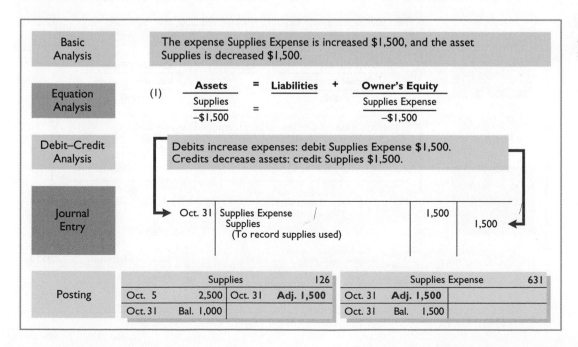

Illustration 3-5
Adjustment for supplies

Insurance

Oct. 4

Insurance purchased;
record asset

Insurance Policy			
Oct $50	Nov $50	Dec $50	Jan $50
Feb $50	March $50	April $50	May $50
June $50	July $50	Aug $50	Sept $50
I YEAR $600			

Oct. 31
Insurance expired;
record insurance expense

After adjustment, the asset account Supplies shows a balance of $1,000, which is equal to the cost of supplies on hand at the statement date. In addition, Supplies Expense shows a balance of $1,500, which equals the cost of supplies used in October. **If Pioneer does not make the adjusting entry, October expenses will be understated and net income overstated by $1,500. Moreover, both assets and owner's equity will be overstated by $1,500 on the October 31 balance sheet.**

Insurance. Companies purchase insurance to protect themselves from losses due to fire, theft, and unforeseen events. Insurance must be paid in advance, often for more than one year. The cost of insurance (premiums) paid in advance is recorded as an increase (debit) in the asset account prepaid insurance. At the financial statement date, companies increase (debit) Insurance expense and decrease (credit) Prepaid insurance for the cost of insurance that has expired during the period.

On October 4, Pioneer Advertising paid $600 for a one-year fire insurance policy. Coverage began on October 1. Pioneer recorded the payment by increasing (debiting) Prepaid Insurance. This account shows a balance of $600 in the October 31 trial balance. Insurance of $50 ($600 ÷ 12) expires each month. The expiration of prepaid insurance decreases an asset, Prepaid Insurance. It also decreases owner's equity by increasing an expense account, Insurance Expense.

As shown in Illustration 3-6, the asset Prepaid Insurance shows a balance of $550, which represents the unexpired cost for the remaining 11 months of coverage. At the same time, the balance in Insurance Expense equals the insurance cost that expired in October. If Pioneer does not make this adjustment, October expenses are understated by $50 and net income is overstated by $50. Moreover, as the accounting equation shows, both assets and owner's equity will be overstated by $50 on the October 31 balance sheet.

Illustration 3-6
Adjustment for insurance

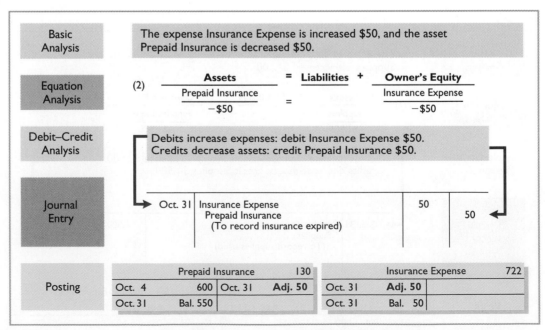

Basic Analysis	The expense Insurance Expense is increased $50, and the asset Prepaid Insurance is decreased $50.

Equation Analysis

(2)

Assets	=	Liabilities	+	Owner's Equity
Prepaid Insurance				Insurance Expense
−$50	=			−$50

Debit–Credit Analysis

Debits increase expenses: debit Insurance Expense $50.
Credits decrease assets: credit Prepaid Insurance $50.

Journal Entry

Oct. 31	Insurance Expense	50	
	Prepaid Insurance		50
	(To record insurance expired)		

Posting

Prepaid Insurance			130
Oct. 4	600	Oct. 31 Adj. 50	
Oct. 31 Bal. 550			

Insurance Expense			722
Oct. 31 Adj. 50			
Oct. 31 Bal. 50			

Depreciation. A company typically owns a variety of assets that have long lives, such as buildings, equipment, and motor vehicles. The period of service is referred to as the useful life of the asset. Because a building is expected to provide service for many years, it is recorded as an asset, rather than an expense, on the date it is acquired. As explained in Chapter 1, companies record such assets **at cost**, as required by the cost principle. To follow the expense recognition principle, companies allocate a portion of this cost as an expense during each period of the asset's useful life. Depreciation is the process of allocating the cost of an asset to expense over its useful life.

Depreciation

Oct. 2

Equipment purchased; record asset

Equipment			
Oct	Nov	Dec	Jan
$40	$40	$40	$40
Feb	March	April	May
$40	$40	$40	$40
June	July	Aug	Sept
$40	$40	$40	$40
Depreciation = $480/year			

Oct. 31
Depreciation recognized; record depreciation expense

Need for Adjustment. The acquisition of long-lived assets is essentially a long-term prepayment for the use of an asset. An adjusting entry for depreciation is needed to recognize the cost that has been used (an expense) during the period and to report the unused cost (an asset) at the end of the period. One very important point to understand: **Depreciation is an allocation concept, not a valuation concept.** That is, depreciation **allocates an asset's cost to the periods in which it is used. Depreciation does not attempt to report the actual change in the value of the asset.**

For Pioneer Advertising, assume that depreciation on the equipment is $480 a year, or $40 per month. As shown in Illustration 3-7 below, rather than decrease (credit) the asset account directly, Pioneer instead credits Accumulated Depreciation—Equipment. Accumulated Depreciation is called a contra asset account. Such an account is offset against an asset account on the balance sheet. Thus, the Accumulated Depreciation—Equipment account offsets the asset Equipment. This account keeps track of the total amount of depreciation expense taken over the life of the asset. To keep the accounting equation in balance, Pioneer decreases owner's equity by increasing an expense account, Depreciation Expense.

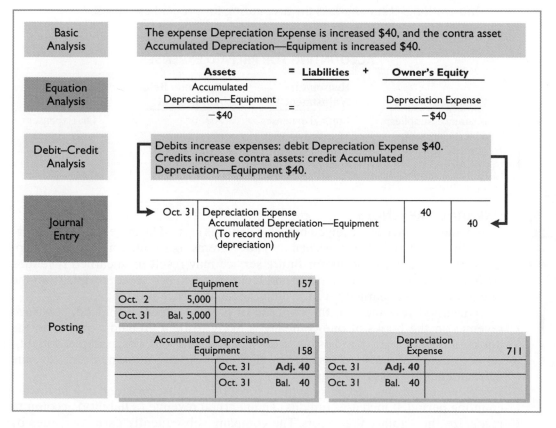

Illustration 3-7
Adjustment for depreciation

Basic Analysis The expense Depreciation Expense is increased $40, and the contra asset Accumulated Depreciation—Equipment is increased $40.

Equation Analysis

Assets	=	Liabilities	+	Owner's Equity
Accumulated Depreciation—Equipment	=			Depreciation Expense
−$40				−$40

Debit–Credit Analysis Debits increase expenses: debit Depreciation Expense $40. Credits increase contra assets: credit Accumulated Depreciation—Equipment $40.

Journal Entry

Oct. 31	Depreciation Expense	40	
	Accumulated Depreciation—Equipment		40
	(To record monthly depreciation)		

Posting

Equipment		157
Oct. 2	5,000	
Oct. 31	Bal. 5,000	

Accumulated Depreciation—Equipment		158
	Oct. 31	Adj. 40
	Oct. 31	Bal. 40

Depreciation Expense		711
Oct. 31	Adj. 40	
Oct. 31	Bal. 40	

Helpful Hint

All contra accounts have increases, decreases, and normal balances **opposite** to the account to which they relate.

The balance in the Accumulated Depreciation—Equipment account will increase $40 each month, and the balance in Equipment remains $5,000.

Statement Presentation. As indicated, Accumulated Depreciation—Equipment is a contra asset account. It is offset against Equipment on the balance sheet. The normal balance of a contra asset account is a credit. A theoretical alternative to using a contra asset account would be to decrease (credit) the asset account by the amount of depreciation each period. But using the contra account is preferable for a simple reason: It discloses *both* the original cost of the equipment *and* the total cost that has expired to date. Thus, in the balance sheet, Pioneer deducts Accumulated Depreciation—Equipment from the related asset account, as shown in Illustration 3-8.

Illustration 3-8
Balance sheet presentation of accumulated depreciation

Equipment	$5,000
Less: Accumulated depreciation—equipment	40
	$4,960

Alternative Terminology

Book value is also referred to as *carrying value*.

Book value is the difference between the cost of any depreciable asset and its related accumulated depreciation. In Illustration 3-8, the book value of the equipment at the balance sheet date is $4,960. The book value and the fair value of the asset are generally two different values. As noted earlier, **the purpose of depreciation is not valuation but a means of cost allocation.**

Depreciation expense identifies the portion of an asset's cost that expired during the period (in this case, in October). The accounting equation shows that without this adjusting entry, total assets, total owner's equity, and net income are overstated by $40 and depreciation expense is understated by $40.

Illustration 3-9 summarizes the accounting for prepaid expenses.

Illustration 3-9
Accounting for prepaid expenses

ACCOUNTING FOR PREPAID EXPENSES

Examples	Reason for Adjustment	Accounts Before Adjustment	Adjusting Entry
Insurance, supplies, advertising, rent, depreciation	Prepaid expenses recorded in asset accounts have been used.	Assets overstated. Expenses understated.	Dr. Expenses Cr. Assets

Unearned Revenues

Oct. 2

Thank you in advance for your work

I will finish by Dec. 31

~$1,200

Cash is received in advance; liability is recorded

Oct. 31

Some service has been provided; some revenue is recorded

UNEARNED REVENUES

Companies record cash received before revenue is earned by increasing (crediting) a liability account called **unearned revenues**. Items like rent, magazine subscriptions, and customer deposits for future service may result in unearned revenues. Airlines such as United, American, and Delta, for instance, treat receipts from the sale of tickets as unearned revenue until the flight service is provided.

Unearned revenues are the opposite of prepaid expenses. Indeed, unearned revenue on the books of one company is likely to be a prepaid expense on the books of the company that has made the advance payment. For example, if identical accounting periods are assumed, a landlord will have unearned rent revenue when a tenant has prepaid rent.

When a company receives payment for services to be provided in a future accounting period, it increases (credits) an unearned revenue (a liability) account to recognize the liability that exists. The company subsequently earns revenues by providing service. During the accounting period, it is not practical to make daily entries as the company earns the revenue. Instead, we delay recognition of earned revenue until the adjustment process. Then the company makes an adjusting entry to record the revenue earned during the period and to show the liability that remains at the end of the accounting period. Typically, prior to adjustment, liabilities are overstated and revenues are understated. Therefore, as shown in Illustration 3-10, **the adjusting entry for unearned revenues results in a decrease (a debit) to a liability account and an increase (a credit) to a revenue account.**

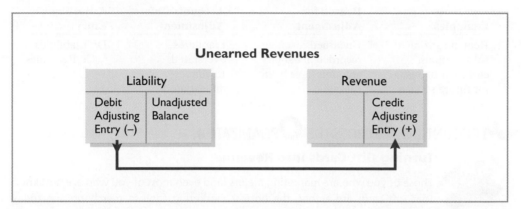

Illustration 3-10
Adjusting entries for unearned revenues

Pioneer Advertising received $1,200 on October 2 from R. Knox for advertising services expected to be completed by December 31. Pioneer credited the payment to Unearned Service Revenue, and this liability account shows a balance of $1,200 in the October 31 trial balance. From an evaluation of the service Pioneer performed for Knox during October, the company determines that it has earned $400 in October. The liability (Unearned Service Revenue) is therefore decreased, and owner's equity (Service Revenue) is increased.

As shown in Illustration 3-11, the liability Unearned Service Revenue now shows a balance of $800. That amount represents the remaining advertising services

Illustration 3-11
Service revenue accounts after adjustment

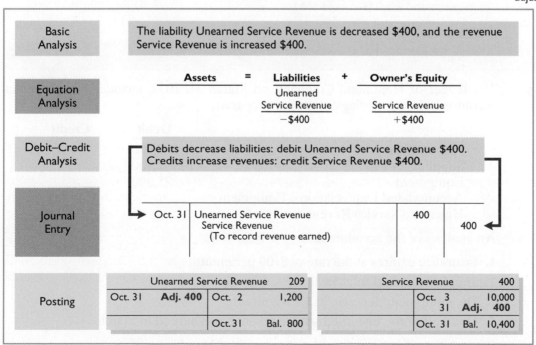

expected to be performed in the future. At the same time, Service Revenue shows total revenue earned in October of $10,400. **Without this adjustment, revenues and net income are understated by $400 in the income statement. Moreover, liabilities are overstated and owner's equity is understated by $400 on the October 31 balance sheet.**

Illustration 3-12 summarizes the accounting for unearned revenues.

Illustration 3-12
Accounting for unearned revenues

ACCOUNTING FOR UNEARNED REVENUES

Examples	Reason for Adjustment	Accounts Before Adjustment	Adjusting Entry
Rent, magazine subscriptions, customer deposits for future service	Unearned revenues recorded in liability accounts have been earned.	Liabilities overstated. Revenues understated.	Dr. Liabilities Cr. Revenues

ACCOUNTING ACROSS THE ORGANIZATION

Turning Gift Cards into Revenue

Those of you who are marketing majors (and even most of you who are not) know that gift cards are among the hottest marketing tools in merchandising today. Customers purchase gift cards and give them to someone for later use. In a recent year, gift-card sales topped $95 billion.

Although these programs are popular with marketing executives, they create accounting questions. Should revenue be recorded at the time the gift card is sold, or when it is exercised? How should expired gift cards be accounted for? In its 2009 balance sheet, Best Buy reported unearned revenue related to gift cards of $479 million.

Source: Robert Berner, "Gift Cards: No Gift to Investors," *BusinessWeek* (March 14, 2005), p. 86.

? Suppose that Robert Jones purchases a $100 gift card at Best Buy on December 24, 2011, and gives it to his wife, Mary Jones, on December 25, 2011. On January 3, 2012, Mary uses the card to purchase $100 worth of CDs. When do you think Best Buy should recognize revenue and why? (See page 148.)

Do it!

Adjusting Entries for Deferrals

The ledger of Hammond Company, on March 31, 2012, includes these selected accounts before adjusting entries are prepared.

	Debit	Credit
Prepaid Insurance	$ 3,600	
Supplies	2,800	
Equipment	25,000	
Accumulated Depreciation—Equipment		$5,000
Unearned Service Revenue		9,200

An analysis of the accounts shows the following.

1. Insurance expires at the rate of $100 per month.
2. Supplies on hand total $800.
3. The equipment depreciates $200 a month.
4. One-half of the unearned service revenue was earned in March.

Prepare the adjusting entries for the month of March.

Solution

1. Insurance Expense	100	
Prepaid Insurance		100
(To record insurance expired)		
2. Supplies Expense	2,000	
Supplies		2,000
(To record supplies used)		
3. Depreciation Expense	200	
Accumulated Depreciation—Equipment		200
(To record monthly depreciation)		
4. Unearned Service Revenue	4,600	
Service Revenue		4,600
(To record revenue earned)		

Related exercise material: BE3-3, BE3-4, BE3-6, and **Do it!** 3-2.

action plan

✔ Make adjusting entries at the end of the period for revenues earned and expenses incurred in the period.

✔ Don't forget to make adjusting entries for deferrals. Failure to adjust for deferrals leads to overstatement of the asset or liability and understatement of the related expense or revenue.

✔
The Navigator

Adjusting Entries for Accruals

The second category of adjusting entries is **accruals.** Prior to an accrual adjustment, the revenue account (and the related asset account) or the expense account (and the related liability account) are understated. Thus, the adjusting entry for accruals will **increase both a balance sheet and an income statement account.**

Study Objective [6]
Prepare adjusting entries for accruals.

ACCRUED REVENUES

Revenues earned but not yet recorded at the statement date are accrued revenues. Accrued revenues may accumulate (accrue) with the passing of time, as in the case of interest revenue. These are unrecorded because the earning of interest does not involve daily transactions. Companies do not record interest revenue on a daily basis because it is often impractical to do so. Accrued revenues also may result from services that have been performed but not yet billed nor collected, as in the case of commissions and fees. These may be unrecorded because only a portion of the total service has been provided and the clients won't be billed until the service has been completed.

An adjusting entry records the receivable that exists at the balance sheet date and the revenue earned during the period. Prior to adjustment, both assets and revenues are understated. As shown in Illustration 3-13, **an adjusting entry for accrued revenues results in an increase (a debit) to an asset account and an increase (a credit) to a revenue account.**

Accrued Revenues

Oct. 31

My fee is $200

Revenue and receivable are recorded for unbilled services

Nov. 10

Cash is received; receivable is reduced

Illustration 3-13
Adjusting entries for accrued revenues

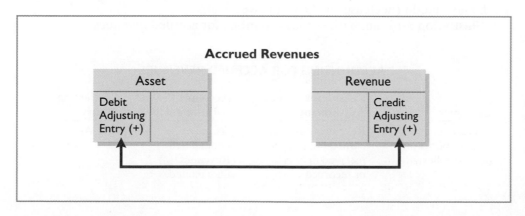

Accrued Revenues

Asset		Revenue	
Debit Adjusting Entry (+)			Credit Adjusting Entry (+)

Helpful Hint

For accruals, there may have been no prior entry, and the accounts requiring adjustment may both have zero balances prior to adjustment.

In October, Pioneer Advertising earned $200 for advertising services that were not billed to clients on or before October 31. Because these services are not billed, they are not recorded. The accrual of unrecorded service revenue increases an asset account, Accounts Receivable. It also increases owner's equity by increasing a revenue account, Service Revenue, as shown in Illustration 3-14.

Illustration 3-14
Adjustment for accrued revenue

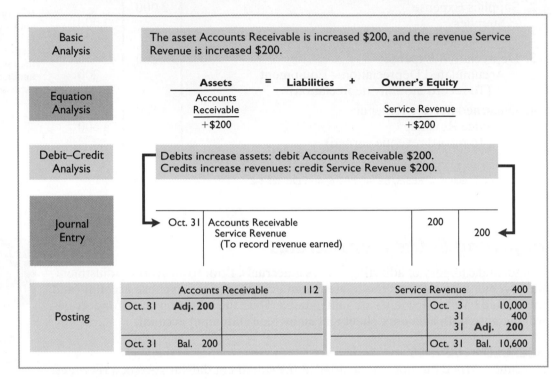

The asset Accounts Receivable shows that clients owe Pioneer $200 at the balance sheet date. The balance of $10,600 in Service Revenue represents the total revenue Pioneer earned during the month ($10,000 + $400 + $200). **Without the adjusting entry, assets and owner's equity on the balance sheet and revenues and net income on the income statement are understated.**

On November 10, Pioneer receives cash of $200 for the services performed in October and makes the following entry.

Equation analyses summarize the effects of transactions on the three elements of the accounting equation, as well as the effect on cash flows.

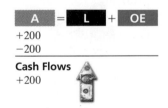

Nov. 10	Cash	200	
	Accounts Receivable		200
	(To record cash collected on account)		

The company records the collection of the receivables by a debit (increase) to Cash and a credit (decrease) to Accounts Receivable.

Illustration 3-15 summarizes the accounting for accrued revenues.

Illustration 3-15
Accounting for accrued revenues

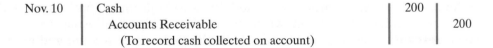

ACCOUNTING FOR ACCRUED REVENUES

Examples	Reason for Adjustment	Accounts Before Adjustment	Adjusting Entry
Interest, rent, services performed but not collected	Revenues have been earned but not yet received in cash or recorded.	Assets understated. Revenues understated.	Dr. Assets Cr. Revenues

ACCRUED EXPENSES

Expenses incurred but not yet paid or recorded at the statement date are called **accrued expenses**. Interest, taxes, and salaries are common examples of accrued expenses.

Companies make adjustments for accrued expenses to record the obligations that exist at the balance sheet date and to recognize the expenses that apply to the current accounting period. Prior to adjustment, both liabilities and expenses are understated. Therefore, as Illustration 3-16 shows, **an adjusting entry for accrued expenses results in an increase (a debit) to an expense account and an increase (a credit) to a liability account.**

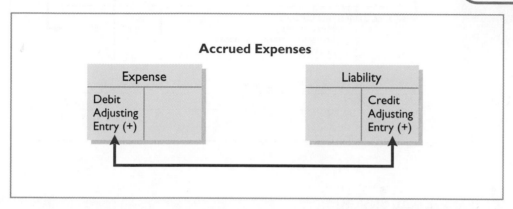

Illustration 3-16
Adjusting entries for accrued expenses

Let's look in more detail at some specific types of accrued expenses, beginning with accrued interest.

Accrued Interest. Pioneer Advertising signed a three-month note payable in the amount of $5,000 on October 1. The note requires Pioneer to pay interest at an annual rate of 12%.

The amount of the interest recorded is determined by three factors: (1) the face value of the note; (2) the interest rate, which is always expressed as an annual rate; and (3) the length of time the note is outstanding. For Pioneer, the total interest due on the $5,000 note at its maturity date three months in the future is $150 ($5,000 × 12% × $\frac{3}{12}$), or $50 for one month. Illustration 3-17 shows the formula for computing interest and its application to Pioneer for the month of October.

Face Value of Note	×	Annual Interest Rate	×	Time in Terms of One Year	=	Interest
$5,000	×	12%	×	$\frac{1}{12}$	=	**$50**

Illustration 3-17
Formula for computing interest

As Illustration 3-18 (page 114) shows, the accrual of interest at October 31 increases a liability account, Interest Payable. It also decreases owner's equity by increasing an expense account, Interest Expense.

Interest Expense shows the interest charges for the month of October. Interest Payable shows the amount of interest the company owes at the statement date. Pioneer will not pay the interest until the note comes due at the end of three months. Companies use the Interest Payable account, instead of crediting Notes Payable, to disclose the two different types of obligations—interest and principal—in the accounts and statements. **Without this adjusting entry, liabilities and interest expense are understated, and net income and owner's equity are overstated.**

Helpful Hint

In computing interest, we express the time period as a fraction of a year.

Illustration 3-18
Adjustment for
accrued interest

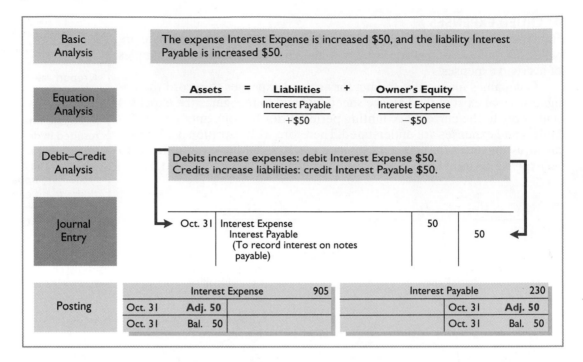

Cashing In on Accrual Accounting

The Chinese government, like most governments, uses cash accounting. It was therefore interesting when it was recently reported that for about $38 billion of expenditures in a recent budget projection, the Chinese government decided to use accrual accounting versus cash accounting. It decided to expense the amount in the year in which it was originally allocated rather than when the payments would be made. Why did it do this? It enabled the government to keep its projected budget deficit below a 3% threshold. While it was able to keep its projected shortfall below 3%, China did suffer some criticism for its inconsistent accounting. Critics charge that this inconsistent treatment reduces the transparency of China's accounting information. That is, it is not easy for outsiders to accurately evaluate what is really going on.

Source: Andrew Batson, "China Altered Budget Accounting to Reduce Deficit Figure," *Wall Street Journal Online* (March 15, 2010).

? Accrual accounting is often considered superior to cash accounting. Why, then, were some people critical of China's use of accrual accounting in this instance? (See page 148.)

Accrued Salaries and Wages. Companies pay for some types of expenses, such as employee salaries and wages, after the services have been performed. Pioneer paid salaries and wages on October 26 for its employees' first two weeks of work; the next payment of salaries will not occur until November 9. As Illustration 3-19 shows, three working days remain in October (October 29–31).

At October 31, the salaries and wages for these three days represent an accrued expense and a related liability to Pioneer. The employees receive total salaries and wages of $2,000 for a five-day work week, or $400 per day. Thus, accrued salaries and wages at October 31 are $1,200 ($400 × 3). This accrual increases a liability, Salaries and Wages Payable. It also decreases

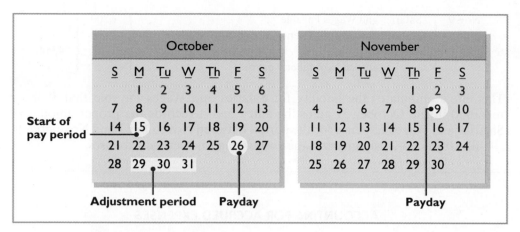

Illustration 3-19
Calendar showing Pioneer's
pay periods

owner's equity by increasing an expense account, Salaries and Wages Expense, as shown in Illustration 3-20.

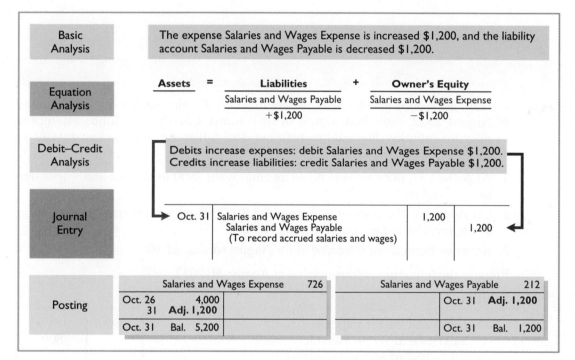

Illustration 3-20
Adjustment for accrued salaries
and wages

After this adjustment, the balance in Salaries and Wages Expense of $5,200 (13 days × $400) is the actual salary and wages expense for October. The balance in Salaries and Wages Payable of $1,200 is the amount of the liability for salaries and wages Pioneer owes as of October 31. **Without the $1,200 adjustment for salaries and wages, Pioneer's expenses are understated $1,200 and its liabilities are understated $1,200.**

Pioneer Advertising pays salaries and wages every two weeks. Consequently, the next payday is November 9, when the company will again pay total salaries and wages of $4,000. The payment consists of $1,200 of salaries and wages payable at October 31 plus $2,800 of salaries and wages expense for November (7 working days, as shown in the November calendar × $400). Therefore, Pioneer makes the following entry on November 9.

Nov. 9	Salaries and Wages Payable	1,200	
	Salaries and Wages Expense	2,800	
	Cash		4,000
	(To record November 9 payroll)		

This entry eliminates the liability for Salaries and Wages Payable that Pioneer recorded in the October 31 adjusting entry, and it records the proper amount of Salaries and Wages Expense for the period between November 1 and November 9. Illustration 3-21 summarizes the accounting for accrued expenses.

Illustration 3-21
Accounting for accrued expenses

ACCOUNTING FOR ACCRUED EXPENSES

Examples	Reason for Adjustment	Accounts Before Adjustment	Adjusting Entry
Interest, rent, salaries	Expenses have been incurred but not yet paid in cash or recorded.	Expenses understated. Liabilities understated.	Dr. Expenses Cr. Liabilities

Do it!

Adjusting Entries for Accruals

Calvin and Hobbs are the new owners of Micro Computer Services. At the end of August 2012, their first month of operations, Calvin and Hobbs attempted to prepare monthly financial statements. The following information relates to August.

1. At August 31, the company owed its employees $800 in salaries and wages that will be paid on September 1.

2. On August 1, the company borrowed $30,000 from a local bank on a 15-year mortgage. The annual interest rate is 10%.

3. Revenue earned but unrecorded for August totaled $1,100.

Prepare the adjusting entries needed at August 31, 2012.

action plan

✔ Make adjusting entries at the end of the period for revenues earned and expenses incurred in the period.

✔ Don't forget to make adjusting entries for accruals. Adjusting entries for accruals will increase both a balance sheet and an income statement account.

Solution

1. Salaries and Wages Expense	800	
Salaries and Wages Payable		800
(To record accrued salaries)		
2. Interest Expense	250	
Interest Payable		250
(To record accrued interest: $30,000 \times 10\% \times \frac{1}{12} = $250)		
3. Accounts Receivable	1,100	
Service Revenue		1,100
(To record revenue earned)		

Related exercise material: BE3-7, E3-5, E3-6, E3-7, E3-8, E3-9, E3-10, E3-11, E3-12, and **Do it!** 3-3.

✔
The Navigator

Summary of Basic Relationships

Illustration 3-22 summarizes the four basic types of adjusting entries. Take some time to study and analyze the adjusting entries. Be sure to note that **each adjusting entry affects one balance sheet account and one income statement account.**

Type of Adjustment	Accounts Before Adjustment	Adjusting Entry
Prepaid expenses	Assets overstated	Dr. Expenses
	Expenses understated	Cr. Assets
Unearned revenues	Liabilities overstated	Dr. Liabilities
	Revenues understated	Cr. Revenues
Accrued revenues	Assets understated	Dr. Assets
	Revenues understated	Cr. Revenues
Accrued expenses	Expenses understated	Dr. Expenses
	Liabilities understated	Cr. Liabilities

Illustration 3-22
Summary of adjusting entries

Illustrations 3-23 (below) and 3-24 (on page 118) show the journalizing and posting of adjusting entries for Pioneer Advertising Agency on October 31. The ledger identifies all adjustments by the reference J2 because they have been recorded on page 2 of the general journal. The company may insert a center caption "Adjusting Entries" between the last transaction entry and the first adjusting entry in the journal. When you review the general ledger in Illustration 3-24, note that the entries highlighted in color are the adjustments.

	General Journal			J2
Date	**Account Titles and Explanation**	**Ref.**	**Debit**	**Credit**
2012	*Adjusting Entries*			
Oct. 31	Supplies Expense	631	1,500	
	Supplies	126		1,500
	(To record supplies used)			
31	Insurance Expense	722	50	
	Prepaid Insurance	130		50
	(To record insurance expired)			
31	Depreciation Expense	711	40	
	Accumulated Depreciation—Equipment	158		40
	(To record monthly depreciation)			
31	Unearned Service Revenue	209	400	
	Service Revenue	400		400
	(To record revenue for services provided)			
31	Accounts Receivable	112	200	
	Service Revenue	400		200
	(To record revenue for services provided)			
31	Interest Expense	905	50	
	Interest Payable	230		50
	(To record interest on notes payable)			
31	Salaries and Wages Expense	726	1,200	
	Salaries and Wages Payable	212		1,200
	(To record accrued salaries and wages)			

Illustration 3-23
General journal showing adjusting entries

Helpful Hint

(1) Adjusting entries should not involve debits or credits to cash.
(2) Evaluate whether the adjustment makes sense. For example, an adjustment to recognize supplies used should increase supplies expense.
(3) Double-check all computations.
(4) Each adjusting entry affects one balance sheet account and one income statement account.

Illustration 3-24
General ledger after adjustment

General Journal

Cash — No. 101

Date	Explanation	Ref.	Debit	Credit	Balance
2012					
Oct. 1		J1	10,000		10,000
2		J1	1,200		11,200
3		J1		900	10,300
4		J1		600	9,700
20		J1		500	9,200
26		J1		4,000	5,200
31		J1	10,000		15,200

Accounts Receivable — No. 112

Date	Explanation	Ref.	Debit	Credit	Balance
2012					
Oct. 31	Adj. entry	J2	200		200

Supplies — No. 126

Date	Explanation	Ref.	Debit	Credit	Balance
2012					
Oct. 5		J1	2,500		2,500
31	Adj. entry	J2		1,500	1,000

Prepaid Insurance — No. 130

Date	Explanation	Ref.	Debit	Credit	Balance
2012					
Oct. 4		J1	600		600
31	Adj. entry	J2		50	550

Equipment — No. 157

Date	Explanation	Ref.	Debit	Credit	Balance
2012					
Oct. 1		J1	5,000		5,000

Accumulated Depreciation—Equipment — No. 158

Date	Explanation	Ref.	Debit	Credit	Balance
2012					
Oct. 31	Adj. entry	J2		40	40

Notes Payable — No. 200

Date	Explanation	Ref.	Debit	Credit	Balance
2012					
Oct. 1		J1		5,000	5,000

Accounts Payable — No. 201

Date	Explanation	Ref.	Debit	Credit	Balance
2012					
Oct. 5		J1		2,500	2,500

Unearned Service Revenue — No. 209

Date	Explanation	Ref.	Debit	Credit	Balance
2012					
Oct. 2		J1		1,200	1,200
31	Adj. entry	J2	400		800

Salaries and Wages Payable — No. 212

Date	Explanation	Ref.	Debit	Credit	Balance
2012					
Oct. 31	Adj. entry	J2		1,200	1,200

Interest Payable — No. 230

Date	Explanation	Ref.	Debit	Credit	Balance
2012					
Oct. 31	Adj. entry	J2		50	50

Owner's Capital — No. 301

Date	Explanation	Ref.	Debit	Credit	Balance
2012					
Oct. 1		J1		10,000	10,000

Owner's Drawings — No. 306

Date	Explanation	Ref.	Debit	Credit	Balance
2012					
Oct. 20		J1	500		500

Service Revenue — No. 400

Date	Explanation	Ref.	Debit	Credit	Balance
2012					
Oct. 31		J1		10,000	10,000
31	Adj. entry	J2		400	10,400
31	Adj. entry	J2		200	10,600

Supplies Expense — No. 631

Date	Explanation	Ref.	Debit	Credit	Balance
2012					
Oct. 31	Adj. entry	J2	1,500		1,500

Depreciation Expense — No. 711

Date	Explanation	Ref.	Debit	Credit	Balance
2012					
Oct. 31	Adj. entry	J2	40		40

Insurance Expense — No. 722

Date	Explanation	Ref.	Debit	Credit	Balance
2012					
Oct. 31	Adj. entry	J2	50		50

Salaries and Wages Expense — No. 726

Date	Explanation	Ref.	Debit	Credit	Balance
2012					
Oct. 26		J1	4,000		4,000
31	Adj. entry	J2	1,200		5,200

Rent Expense — No. 729

Date	Explanation	Ref.	Debit	Credit	Balance
2012					
Oct. 3		J1	900		900

Interest Expense — No. 905

Date	Explanation	Ref.	Debit	Credit	Balance
2012					
Oct. 31	Adj. entry	J2	50		50

118

The Adjusted Trial Balance and Financial Statements

After a company has journalized and posted all adjusting entries, it prepares another trial balance from the ledger accounts. This trial balance is called an **adjusted trial balance**. It shows the balances of all accounts, including those adjusted, at the end of the accounting period. The purpose of an adjusted trial balance is to **prove the equality** of the total debit balances and the total credit balances in the ledger after all adjustments. Because the accounts contain all data needed for financial statements, the adjusted trial balance is the **primary basis for the preparation of financial statements.**

Study Objective [7]

Describe the nature and purpose of an adjusted trial balance.

Preparing the Adjusted Trial Balance

Illustration 3-25 presents the adjusted trial balance for Pioneer Advertising Agency prepared from the ledger accounts in Illustration 3-24. The amounts affected by the adjusting entries are highlighted in color. Compare these amounts to those in the unadjusted trial balance in Illustration 3-3 on page 104. In this comparison, you will see that there are more accounts in the adjusted trial balance as a result of the adjusting entries made at the end of the month.

Illustration 3-25
Adjusted trial balance

Pioneer Advertising Agency Adjusted Trial Balance October 31, 2012		
	Dr.	**Cr.**
Cash	$15,200	
Accounts Receivable	200	
Supplies	1,000	
Prepaid Insurance	550	
Equipment	5,000	
Accumulated Depreciation—Equipment		$ 40
Notes Payable		5,000
Accounts Payable		2,500
Interest Payable		50
Unearned Service Revenue		800
Salaries and Wages Payable		1,200
Owner's Capital		10,000
Owner's Drawings	500	
Service Revenue		10,600
Salaries and Wages Expense	5,200	
Supplies Expense	1,500	
Rent Expense	900	
Insurance Expense	50	
Interest Expense	50	
Depreciation Expense	40	
	$30,190	$30,190

Preparing Financial Statements

Companies can prepare financial statements directly from the adjusted trial balance. Illustrations 3-26 and 3-27 present the interrelationships of data in the adjusted trial balance and the financial statements.

As Illustration 3-26 shows, companies prepare the income statement from the revenue and expense accounts. Next, they use the owner's capital and drawings accounts and the net income (or net loss) from the income statement to prepare the owner's equity statement. As Illustration 3-27 shows, companies then prepare the balance sheet from the asset and liability accounts and the ending owner's capital balance as reported in the owner's equity statement.

Illustration 3-26

Preparation of the income statement and owner's equity statement from the adjusted trial balance

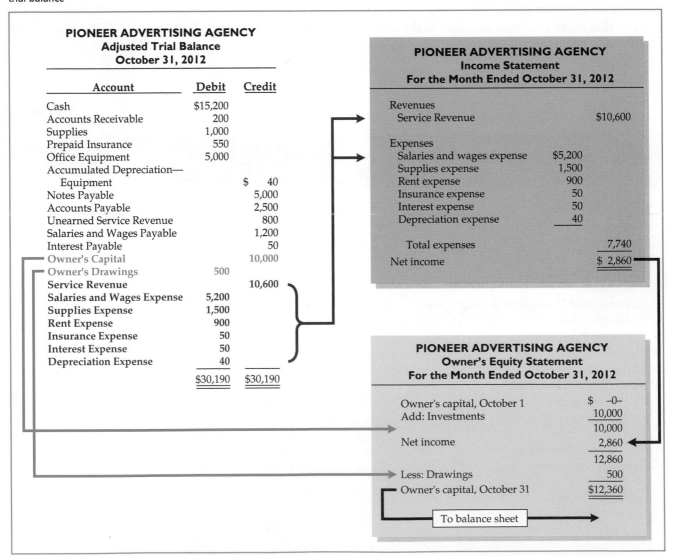

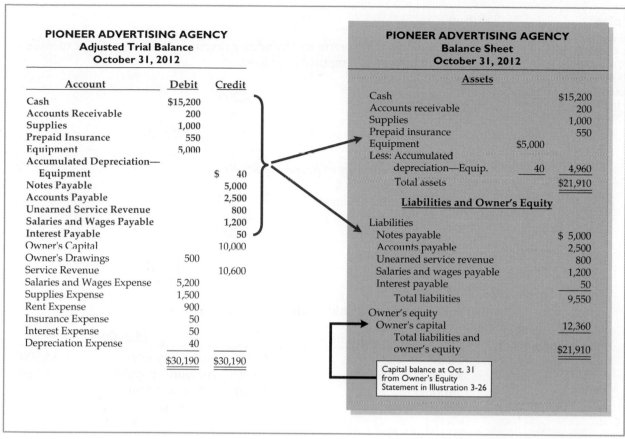

Illustration 3-27
Preparation of the balance sheet from the adjusted trial balance

Do it!

Skolnick Co. was organized on April 1, 2012. The company prepares quarterly financial statements. The adjusted trial balance amounts at June 30 are shown below.

Trial Balance

	Debits		Credits
Cash	$ 6,700	Accumulated Depreciation—Equipment	$ 850
Accounts Receivable	600	Notes Payable	5,000
Prepaid Rent	900	Accounts Payable	1,510
Supplies	1,000	Salaries and Wages Payable	400
Equipment	15,000	Interest Payable	50
Owner's Drawings	600	Unearned Rent Revenue	500
Salaries and Wages Expense	9,400	Owner's Capital	14,000
Rent Expense	1,500	Service Revenue	14,200
Depreciation Expense	850	Rent Revenue	800
Supplies Expense	200		
Utilities Expense	510		
Interest Expense	50		
Total debits	$37,310	Total credits	$37,310

(a) Determine the net income for the quarter April 1 to June 30.

(b) Determine the total assets and total liabilities at June 30, 2012, for Skolnick Co.

(c) Determine the amount that appears for Owner's Capital at June 30, 2012.

action plan

✔ In an adjusted trial balance, all asset, liability, revenue, and expense accounts are properly stated.

✔ To determine the ending balance in Owner's Capital, add net income and subtract dividends.

Solution

(a) The net income is determined by adding revenues and subtracting expenses. The net income is computed as follows.

Revenues		
Service revenue	$14,200	
Rent revenue	800	
Total revenues		$15,000
Expenses		
Salaries and wages expense	$ 9,400	
Rent expense	1,500	
Depreciation expense	850	
Utilities expense	510	
Supplies expense	200	
Interest expense	50	
Total expenses		12,510
Net income		$ 2,490

(b) Total assets and liabilities are computed as follows.

Assets			**Liabilities**	
Cash		$ 6,700	Notes payable	$5,000
Accounts receivable		600	Accounts payable	1,510
Supplies		1,000	Unearned rent	
Prepaid rent		900	revenue	500
			Salaries and wages	
Equipment	15,000		payable	400
Less: Accumulated			Interest payable	50
depreciation—				
equipment	850	14,150		
Total assets		$23,350	Total liabilities	$7,460

(c)
Owner's capital, April 1	$14,000
Add: Net income	2,490
Less: Drawings	600
Owner's capital, June 30	$15,890

Related exercise material: BE3-9, BE3-10, E3-11, E3-13, and **Do it!** 3-4.

✔
The Navigator

COMPREHENSIVE

Do it!

Terry Thomas opens the Green Thumb Lawn Care Company on April 1. At April 30, the trial balance shows the following balances for selected accounts.

Prepaid Insurance	$ 3,600
Equipment	28,000
Notes Payable	20,000
Unearned Service Revenue	4,200
Service Revenue	1,800

Analysis reveals the following additional data.

1. Prepaid insurance is the cost of a 2-year insurance policy, effective April 1.
2. Depreciation on the equipment is $500 per month.
3. The note payable is dated April 1. It is a 6-month, 12% note.
4. Seven customers paid for the company's 6 months' lawn service package of $600 beginning in April. The company performed services for these customers in April.
5. Lawn services provided other customers but not recorded at April 30 totaled $1,500.

Instructions

Prepare the adjusting entries for the month of April. Show computations.

action plan

✔ Note that adjustments are being made for one month.

✔ Make computations carefully.

✔ Select account titles carefully.

✔ Make sure debits are made first and credits are indented.

✔ Check that debits equal credits for each entry.

Solution to Comprehensive Do it!

GENERAL JOURNAL J1

Date	Account Titles and Explanation	Ref.	Debit	Credit
	Adjusting Entries			
Apr. 30	Insurance Expense		150	
	Prepaid Insurance			150
	(To record insurance expired: $3,600 \div 24 = \$150$ per month)			
30	Depreciation Expense		500	
	Accumulated Depreciation—Equipment			500
	(To record monthly depreciation)			
30	Interest Expense		200	
	Interest Payable			200
	(To record interest on notes payable: $\$20,000 \times 12\% \times 1/12 = \$200$)			
30	Unearned Service Revenue		700	
	Service Revenue			700
	(To record service revenue: $\$600 \div 6 = \$100$; $\$100$ per month $\times 7 = \$700$)			
30	Accounts Receivable		1,500	
	Service Revenue			1,500
	(To record revenue for services provided)			

Summary of Study Objectives

[1] **Explain the time period assumption.** The time period assumption assumes that the economic life of a business is divided into artificial time periods.

[2] **Explain the accrual basis of accounting.** Accrual-basis accounting means that companies record events that change a company's financial statements in the periods in which those events occur, rather than in the periods in which the company receives or pays cash.

[3] **Explain the reasons for adjusting entries.** Companies make adjusting entries at the end of an accounting period. Such

entries ensure that companies record revenues in the period in which they are earned and that they recognize expenses in the period in which they are incurred.

[4] **Identify the major types of adjusting entries.** The major types of adjusting entries are deferrals (prepaid expenses and unearned revenues), and accruals (accrued revenues and accrued expenses).

[5] **Prepare adjusting entries for deferrals.** Deferrals are either prepaid expenses or unearned revenues. Companies make adjusting entries for deferrals to record the portion of

the prepayment that represents the expense incurred or the revenue earned in the current accounting period.

[6] Prepare adjusting entries for accruals. Accruals are either accrued revenues or accrued expenses. Companies make adjusting entries for accruals to record revenues earned and expenses incurred in the current accounting period that have not been recognized through daily entries.

[7] Describe the nature and purpose of an adjusted trial balance. An adjusted trial balance shows the balances of all accounts, including those that have been adjusted, at the end of an accounting period. Its purpose is to prove the equality of the total debit balances and total credit balances in the ledger after all adjustments.

The Navigator

Glossary

Accrual-basis accounting Accounting basis in which companies record transactions that change a company's financial statements in the periods in which the events occur. (p. 101).

Accruals Adjusting entries for either accrued revenues or accrued expenses. (p. 103).

Accrued expenses Expenses incurred but not yet paid in cash or recorded. (p. 113).

Accrued revenues Revenues earned but not yet received in cash or recorded. (p. 111).

Adjusted trial balance A list of accounts and their balances after the company has made all adjustments. (p. 119).

Adjusting entries Entries made at the end of an accounting period to ensure that companies follow the revenue recognition and expense recognition principles. (p. 103).

Book value The difference between the cost of a depreciable asset and its related accumulated depreciation. (p. 108).

Calendar year An accounting period that extends from January 1 to December 31. (p. 100).

Cash-basis accounting Accounting basis in which companies record revenue when they receive cash and an expense when they pay cash. (p. 101).

Contra asset account An account offset against an asset account on the balance sheet. (p. 107).

Deferrals Adjusting entries for either prepaid expenses or unearned revenues. (p. 103).

Depreciation The allocation of the cost of an asset to expense over its useful life in a rational and systematic manner. (p. 107).

Expense recognition principle (matching principle) The principle that companies match efforts (expenses) with accomplishments (revenues). (p. 101).

Fiscal year An accounting period that is one year in length. (p. 100).

Interim periods Monthly or quarterly accounting time periods. (p. 100).

Prepaid expenses (prepayments) Expenses paid in cash that benefit more than one accounting period and that are recorded as assets. (p. 104).

Revenue recognition principle The principle that companies recognize revenue in the accounting period in which it is earned. (p. 101).

Time period assumption An assumption that accountants can divide the economic life of a business into artificial time periods. (p. 100).

Unearned revenues Cash received and recorded as liabilities before revenue is earned. (p. 108).

Useful life The length of service of a long-lived asset. (p. 107).

APPENDIX3A

Alternative Treatment of Prepaid Expenses and Unearned Revenues

Study Objective [8]
Prepare adjusting entries for the alternative treatment of deferrals.

In discussing adjusting entries for prepaid expenses and unearned revenues, we illustrated transactions for which companies made the initial entries to balance sheet accounts. In the case of prepaid expenses, the company debited the prepayment to an asset account. In the case of unearned revenue, the company credited a liability account to record the cash received.

Some companies use an alternative treatment: (1) When a company prepays an expense, it debits that amount to an expense account. (2) When it receives payment for future services, it credits the amount to a revenue account. In this appendix, we describe the circumstances that justify such entries and the different adjusting entries that may be required. This alternative treatment of prepaid expenses and unearned revenues has the same effect on the financial statements as the procedures described in the chapter.

Prepaid Expenses

Prepaid expenses become expired costs either through the passage of time (e.g., insurance) or through consumption (e.g., advertising supplies). If, at the time of purchase, the company expects to consume the supplies before the next financial statement date, **it may choose to debit (increase) an expense account rather than an asset account. This alternative treatment is simply more convenient.**

Assume that Pioneer Advertising expects that it will use before the end of the month all of the supplies purchased on October 5. A debit of $2,500 to Supplies Expense (rather than to the asset account Supplies) on October 5 will eliminate the need for an adjusting entry on October 31. At October 31, the Supplies Expense account will show a balance of $2,500, which is the cost of supplies used between October 5 and October 31.

But what if the company does not use all the supplies? For example, what if an inventory of $1,000 of advertising supplies remains on October 31? Obviously, the company would need to make an adjusting entry. Prior to adjustment, the expense account Supplies Expense is overstated $1,000, and the asset account Supplies is understated $1,000. Thus, Pioneer makes the following adjusting entry.

Oct. 31	Supplies	1,000	
	Supplies Expense		1,000
	(To record supplies inventory)		

A	=	L	+	OE
+1,000				
				+1,000 Exp

Cash Flows
no effect

After the company posts the adjusting entry, the accounts show:

Supplies			Supplies Expense			
10/31 **Adj.**	**1,000**		10/5	2,500	10/31 **Adj.**	**1,000**
			10/31 **Bal.**	**1,500**		

Illustration 3A-1
Prepaid expenses accounts after adjustment

After adjustment, the asset account Supplies shows a balance of $1,000, which is equal to the cost of supplies on hand at October 31. In addition, Supplies Expense shows a balance of $1,500. This is equal to the cost of supplies used between October 5 and October 31. Without the adjusting entry expenses are overstated and net income is understated by $1,000 in the October income statement. Also, both assets and owner's equity are understated by $1,000 on the October 31 balance sheet.

Illustration 3A-2 compares the entries and accounts for advertising supplies in the two adjustment approaches.

Prepayment Initially Debited to Asset Account (per chapter)			Prepayment Initially Debited to Expense Account (per appendix)		
Oct. 5 Supplies	2,500		Oct. 5 Supplies Expense	2,500	
Accounts Payable		2,500	Accounts Payable		2,500
Oct. 31 Supplies Expense	1,500		Oct. 31 Supplies	1,000	
Supplies		1,500	Supplies Expense		1,000

Illustration 3A-2
Adjustment approaches—a comparison

After Pioneer posts the entries, the accounts appear as follows.

Illustration 3A-3
Comparison of accounts

(per chapter) Supplies				(per appendix) Supplies		
10/5	2,500	10/31 **Adj.**	1,500	10/31 **Adj.**	1,000	
10/31 **Bal.**	1,000					

Supplies Expense				Supplies Expense		
10/31 **Adj.**	1,500			10/5	2,500	10/31 **Adj.**	1,000
				10/31 **Bal.**	1,500	

Note that the account balances under each alternative are the same at October 31: Supplies $1,000, and Supplies Expense $1,500.

Unearned Revenues

Unearned revenues become earned either through the passage of time (e.g., unearned rent revenue) or through providing the service (e.g., unearned service revenue). Similar to the case for prepaid expenses, companies may credit (increase) a revenue account when they receive cash for future services.

To illustrate, assume that Pioneer Advertising received $1,200 for future services on October 2. Pioneer expects to perform the services before October 31.[1] In such a case, the company credits Service Revenue. If it in fact earns the revenue before October 31, no adjustment is needed.

However, if at the statement date Pioneer has not performed $800 of the services, it would make an adjusting entry. Without the entry, the revenue account Service Revenue is overstated $800, and the liability account Unearned Service Revenue is understated $800. Thus, Pioneer makes the following adjusting entry.

Helpful Hint

The required adjusted balances here are Service Revenue $400 and Unearned Service Revenue $800.

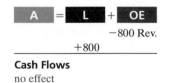

−800 Rev.

+800

Cash Flows
no effect

Oct. 31	Service Revenue	800	
	Unearned Service Revenue		800
	(To record unearned revenue)		

After Pioneer posts the adjusting entry, the accounts show:

Illustration 3A-4
Unearned service revenue accounts after adjstment

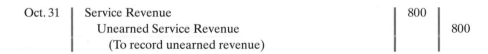

Unearned Service Revenue		Service Revenue			
	10/31 **Adj.**	800	10/31 **Adj.**	800	10/2	1,200
					10/31 **Bal.**	400

The liability account Unearned Service Revenue shows a balance of $800. This equals the services that will be provided in the future. In addition, the balance in Service Revenue equals the services provided in October. Without the adjusting entry, both revenues and net income are overstated by $800 in the October income statement. Also, liabilities are understated by $800, and owner's equity is overstated by $800 on the October 31 balance sheet.

Illustration 3A-5 compares the entries and accounts for service revenue earned and unearned in the two adjustment approaches.

---

[1]This example focuses only on the alternative treatment of unearned revenues. For simplicity, we have ignored the entries to Service Revenue pertaining to the immediate earning of revenue ($10,000) and the adjusting entry for accrued revenue ($200).

Unearned Service Revenue Initially Credited to Liability Account (per chapter)				Unearned Service Revenue Initially Credited to Revenue Account (per appendix)			
Oct. 2	Cash	1,200		Oct. 2	Cash	1,200	
	Unearned Service Revenue		1,200		Service Revenue		1,200
Oct. 31	Unearned Service Revenue	400		Oct. 31	Service Revenue	800	
	Service Revenue		400		Unearned Service Revenue		800

Illustration 3A-5
Adjustment approaches—a comparison

After Pioneer posts the entries, the accounts appear as follows.

Illustration 3A-6
Comparison of accounts

(per chapter)
Unearned Service Revenue

10/31 **Adj.**	400	10/2	1,200
		10/31 **Bal.**	800

(per appendix)
Unearned Service Revenue

		10/31 **Adj.**	800

Service Revenue

		10/31 **Adj.**	400

Service Revenue

10/31 **Adj.**	800	10/2	1,200
		10/31 **Bal.**	400

Note that the balances in the accounts are the same under the two alternatives: Unearned Service Revenue $800, and Service Revenue $400.

Summary of Additional Adjustment Relationships

Illustration 3A-7 provides a summary of basic relationships for deferrals.

Illustration 3A-7
Summary of basic relationships for deferrals

Type of Adjustment	Reason for Adjustment	Account Balances before Adjustment	Adjusting Entry
1. Prepaid expenses	(a) Prepaid expenses initially recorded in asset accounts have been used.	Assets overstated Expenses understated	Dr. Expenses Cr. Assets
	(b) **Prepaid expenses initially recorded in expense accounts have not been used.**	**Assets understated Expenses overstated**	**Dr. Assets Cr. Expenses**
2. Unearned revenues	(a) Unearned revenues initially recorded in liability accounts have been earned.	Liabilities overstated Revenues understated	Dr. Liabilities Cr. Revenues
	(b) **Unearned revenues initially recorded in revenue accounts have not been earned.**	**Liabilities understated Revenues overstated**	**Dr. Revenues Cr. Liabilities**

Alternative adjusting entries **do not apply** to accrued revenues and accrued expenses because **no entries occur before companies make these types of adjusting entries.**

Summary of Study Objective for Appendix 3A

[8] **Prepare adjusting entries for the alternative treatment of deferrals.** Companies may initially debit prepayments to an expense account. Likewise, they may credit unearned revenues to a revenue account. At the end of the period, these accounts may be overstated. The adjusting entries for prepaid expenses are a debit to an asset account and a credit to an expense account. Adjusting entries for unearned revenues are a debit to a revenue account and a credit to a liability account.

Note: All asterisked Questions, Exercises, and Problems relate to material in the appendix to the chapter.

Self-Test Questions

Answers are on page 148.

(SO 1) **1.** The time period assumption states that:
  a. revenue should be recognized in the accounting period in which it is earned.
  b. expenses should be matched with revenues.
  c. the economic life of a business can be divided into artificial time periods.
  d. the fiscal year should correspond with the calendar year.

(SO 1) **2.** The time period assumption states that:
  a. companies must wait until the calendar year is completed to prepare financial statements.
  b. companies use the fiscal year to report financial information.
  c. the economic life of a business can be divided into artificial time periods.
  d. companies record information in the time period in which the events occur.

(SO 2) **3.** Which of the following statements about the accrual basis of accounting is *false*?
  a. Events that change a company's financial statements are recorded in the periods in which the events occur.
  b. Revenue is recognized in the period in which it is earned.
  c. This basis is in accord with generally accepted accounting principles.
  d. Revenue is recorded only when cash is received, and expense is recorded only when cash is paid.

(SO 2) **4.** The principle or assumption dictating that efforts (expenses) be matched with accomplishments (revenues) is the:
  a. expense recognition principle.
  b. cost assumption.
  c. time period principle.
  d. revenue recognition principle.

(SO 3) **5.** Adjusting entries are made to ensure that:
  a. expenses are recognized in the period in which they are incurred.
  b. revenues are recorded in the period in which they are earned.
  c. balance sheet and income statement accounts have correct balances at the end of an accounting period.
  d. All of the above.

(SO 4) **6.** Each of the following is a major type (or category) of adjusting entries *except:*
  a. prepaid expenses.
  b. accrued revenues.
  c. accrued expenses.
  d. earned revenues.

(SO 5) **7.** The trial balance shows Supplies $1,350 and Supplies Expense $0. If $600 of supplies are on hand at the end of the period, the adjusting entry is:

  a. Supplies | 600 |
       Supplies Expense | | 600
  b. Supplies | 750 |
       Supplies Expense | | 750
  c. Supplies Expense | 750 |
       Supplies | | 750
  d. Supplies Expense | 600 |
       Supplies | | 600

8. Adjustments for prepaid expenses: (SO 5)
  a. decrease assets and increase revenues.
  b. decrease expenses and increase assets.
  c. decrease assets and increase expenses.
  d. decrease revenues and increase assets.

9. Accumulated Depreciation is: (SO 5)
  a. a contra asset account.
  b. an expense account.
  c. an owner's equity account.
  d. a liability account.

10. Queenan Company computes depreciation on delivery   (SO 5)
equipment at $1,000 for the month of June. The adjusting entry to record this depreciation is as follows.
  a. Depreciation Expense | 1,000 |
       Accumulated Depreciation—
         Queenan Company | | 1,000
  b. Depreciation Expense | 1,000 |
       Equipment | | 1,000
  c. Depreciation Expense | 1,000 |
       Accumulated Depreciation—
         Equipment | | 1,000
  d. Equipment Expense | 1,000 |
       Accumulated Depreciation—
         Equipment | | 1,000

11. Adjustments for unearned revenues: (SO 5)
  a. decrease liabilities and increase revenues.
  b. have an assets and revenues account relationship.
  c. increase assets and increase revenues.
  d. decrease revenues and decrease assets.

12. Adjustments for accrued revenues: (SO 6)
  a. have a liabilities and revenues account relationship.
  b. have an assets and revenues account relationship.
  c. decrease assets and revenues.
  d. decrease liabilities and increase revenues.

13. Kathy Siska earned a salary of $400 for the last week of   (SO 6)
September. She will be paid on October 1. The adjusting entry for Kathy's employer at September 30 is:
  a. No entry is required.
  b. Salaries and Wages Expense | 400 |
       Salaries and Wages Payable | | 400

c.	Salaries and Wages Expense	400	
	Cash		400
d.	Salaries and Wages Payable	400	
	Cash		400

(SO 7) **14.** Which of the following statements is *incorrect* concerning the adjusted trial balance?

    a. An adjusted trial balance proves the equality of the total debit balances and the total credit balances in the ledger after all adjustments are made.

    b. The adjusted trial balance provides the primary basis for the preparation of financial statements.

    c. The adjusted trial balance lists the account balances segregated by assets and liabilities.

    d. The adjusted trial balance is prepared after the adjusting entries have been journalized and posted.

*15. The trial balance shows Supplies $0 and Supplies Expense (SO 8) $1,500. If $800 of supplies are on hand at the end of the period, the adjusting entry is:

    a. Debit Supplies $800 and credit Supplies Expense $800.

    b. Debit Supplies Expense $800 and credit Supplies $800.

    c. Debit Supplies $700 and credit Supplies Expense $700.

    d. Debit Supplies Expense $700 and credit Supplies $700.

Go to the book's companion website, **www.wiley.com/college/weygandt**, for additional Self-Test Questions.

Questions

1. (a) How does the time period assumption affect an accountant's analysis of business transactions?

    (b) Explain the terms *fiscal year, calendar year,* and *interim periods.*

2. State two generally accepted accounting principles that relate to adjusting the accounts.

3. Chris Harris, a lawyer, accepts a legal engagement in March, performs the work in April, and is paid in May. If Harris's law firm prepares monthly financial statements, when should it recognize revenue from this engagement? Why?

4. Why do accrual-basis financial statements provide more useful information than cash-basis statements?

5. In completing the engagement in question 3, Harris pays no costs in March, $2,000 in April, and $2,500 in May (incurred in April). How much expense should the firm deduct from revenues in the month when it recognizes the revenue? Why?

6. "Adjusting entries are required by the cost principle of accounting." Do you agree? Explain.

7. Why may a trial balance not contain up-to-date and complete financial information?

8. Distinguish between the two categories of adjusting entries, and identify the types of adjustments applicable to each category.

9. What is the debit/credit effect of a prepaid expense adjusting entry?

10. "Depreciation is a valuation process that results in the reporting of the fair value of the asset." Do you agree? Explain.

11. Explain the differences between depreciation expense and accumulated depreciation.

12. T. Harris Company purchased equipment for $18,000. By the current balance sheet date, $6,000 had been depreciated. Indicate the balance sheet presentation of the data.

13. What is the debit/credit effect of an unearned revenue adjusting entry?

14. A company fails to recognize revenue earned but not yet received. Which of the following accounts are involved in the adjusting entry: (a) asset, (b) liability, (c) revenue, or (d) expense? For the accounts selected, indicate whether they would be debited or credited in the entry.

15. A company fails to recognize an expense incurred but not paid. Indicate which of the following accounts is debited and which is credited in the adjusting entry: (a) asset, (b) liability, (c) revenue, or (d) expense.

16. A company makes an accrued revenue adjusting entry for $900 and an accrued expense adjusting entry for $700. How much was net income understated prior to these entries? Explain.

17. On January 9, a company pays $5,000 for salaries, of which $2,000 was reported as Salaries and Wages Payable on December 31. Give the entry to record the payment.

18. For each of the following items before adjustment, indicate the type of adjusting entry (prepaid expense, unearned revenue, accrued revenue, or accrued expense) that is needed to correct the misstatement. If an item could result in more than one type of adjusting entry, indicate each of the types.

    (a) Assets are understated.

    (b) Liabilities are overstated.

    (c) Liabilities are understated.

    (d) Expenses are understated.

    (e) Assets are overstated.

    (f) Revenue is understated.

19. One-half of the adjusting entry is given below. Indicate the account title for the other half of the entry.

    (a) Salaries and Wages Expense is debited.

    (b) Depreciation Expense is debited.

    (c) Interest Payable is credited.

    (d) Supplies is credited.

    (e) Accounts Receivable is debited.

    (f) Unearned Service Revenue is debited.

20. "An adjusting entry may affect more than one balance sheet or income statement account." Do you agree? Why or why not?

21. Why is it possible to prepare financial statements directly from an adjusted trial balance?

*22. M. Harrison Company debits Supplies Expense for all purchases of supplies and credits Rent Revenue for all advanced rentals. For each type of adjustment, give the adjusting entry.

23. **PEPSICO** What was PepsiCo's depreciation and amortization expense for 2009 and 2008?

Brief Exercises

Indicate why adjusting entries are needed.

(SO 3)

BE3-1 The ledger of Levi Company includes the following accounts. Explain why each account may require adjustment.

(a) Prepaid Insurance
(b) Depreciation Expense
(c) Unearned Service Revenue
(d) Interest Payable

Identify the major types of adjusting entries.

(SO 4, 5, 6)

BE3-2 Horn Company accumulates the following adjustment data at December 31. Indicate (a) the type of adjustment (prepaid expense, accrued revenues and so on), and (b) the status of accounts before adjustment (overstated or understated).

1. Supplies of $100 are on hand.
2. Services provided but not recorded total $900.
3. Interest of $200 has accumulated on a note payable.
4. Rent collected in advance totaling $650 has been earned.

Prepare adjusting entry for supplies.

(SO 5)

BE3-3 Devin Advertising Company's trial balance at December 31 shows Supplies $6,700 and Supplies Expense $0. On December 31, there are $2,500 of supplies on hand. Prepare the adjusting entry at December 31, and using T accounts, enter the balances in the accounts, post the adjusting entry, and indicate the adjusted balance in each account.

Prepare adjusting entry for depreciation.

(SO 5)

BE3-4 At the end of its first year, the trial balance of Hester Company shows Equipment $30,000 and zero balances in Accumulated Depreciation—Equipment and Depreciation Expense. Depreciation for the year is estimated to be $4,000. Prepare the adjusting entry for depreciation at December 31, post the adjustments to T accounts, and indicate the balance sheet presentation of the equipment at December 31.

Prepare adjusting entry for prepaid expense.

(SO 5)

BE3-5 On July 1, 2012, Israel Co. pays $14,400 to Idonije Insurance Co. for a 3-year insurance contract. Both companies have fiscal years ending December 31. For Israel Co., journalize and post the entry on July 1 and the adjusting entry on December 31.

Prepare adjusting entry for unearned revenue.

(SO 5)

BE3-6 Using the data in BE3-5, journalize and post the entry on July 1 and the adjusting entry on December 31 for Idonije Insurance Co. Idonije uses the accounts Unearned Service Revenue and Service Revenue.

Prepare adjusting entries for accruals.

(SO 6)

BE3-7 The bookkeeper for Juaquin Company asks you to prepare the following accrued adjusting entries at December 31.

1. Interest on notes payable of $400 is accrued.
2. Services provided but not recorded total $1,900.
3. Salaries earned by employees of $900 have not been recorded.

Use the following account titles: Service Revenue, Accounts Receivable, Interest Expense, Interest Payable, Salaries and Wages Expense, and Salaries and Wages Payable.

Analyze accounts in an unadjusted trial balance.

(SO 4, 5, 6)

BE3-8 The trial balance of Iglesias Company includes the following balance sheet accounts, which may require adjustment. For each account that requires adjustment, indicate (a) the type of adjusting entry (prepaid expenses, unearned revenues, accrued revenues, and accrued expenses) and (b) the related account in the adjusting entry.

Accounts Receivable   Interest Payable
Prepaid Insurance   Unearned Service Revenue
Accumulated Depreciation—Equipment

Prepare an income statement from an adjusted trial balance.

(SO 7)

BE3-9 The adjusted trial balance of Iwuh Company at December 31, 2012, includes the following accounts: Owner's Capital $15,600; Owner's Drawings $7,000; Service Revenue $37,000; Salaries and Wages Expense $16,000; Insurance Expense $2,000; Rent Expense $4,000; Supplies Expense $1,500; and Depreciation Expense $1,300. Prepare an income statement for the year.

BE3-10 Partial adjusted trial balance data for Iwuh Company is presented in BE3-9. The balance in Owner's Capital is the balance as of January 1. Prepare an owner's equity statement for the year assuming net income is $12,200 for the year.

*BE3-11 Jennings Company records all prepayments in income statement accounts. At April 30, the trial balance shows Supplies Expense $2,800, Service Revenue $9,200, and zero balances in related balance sheet accounts. Prepare the adjusting entries at April 30 assuming (a) $700 of supplies on hand and (b) $3,000 of service revenue should be reported as unearned.

Prepare an owner's equity statement from an adjusted trial balance.
(SO 7)

Prepare adjusting entries under alternative treatment of deferrals.
(SO 8)

Do it! Review

Do it! 3-1 Numerous timing concepts are discussed on pages 100–102. A list of concepts is provided below in the left column, with a description of the concept in the right column. There are more descriptions provided than concepts. Match the description of the concept to the concept.

Identify timing concepts.
(SO 1, 2)

1. ____ Cash-basis accounting.
2. ____ Fiscal year.
3. ____ Revenue recognition principle.
4. ____ Expense recognition principle.

  (a) Monthly and quarterly time periods.
  (b) Accountants divide the economic life of a business into artificial time periods.
  (c) Efforts (expenses) should be matched with accomplishments (revenues).
  (d) Companies record revenues when they receive cash and record expenses when they pay out cash.
  (e) An accounting time period that is one year in length.
  (f) An accounting time period that starts on January 1 and ends on December 31.
  (g) Companies record transactions in the period in which the events occur.
  (h) Recognize revenue in the accounting period in which it is earned.

Do it! 3-2 The ledger of Lefevour, Inc. on March 31, 2012, includes the following selected accounts before adjusting entries.

Prepare adjusting entries for deferrals.
(SO 5)

	Debit	Credit
Prepaid Insurance	2,400	
Supplies	2,500	
Equipment	30,000	
Unearned Service Revenue		9,000

An analysis of the accounts shows the following.

1. Insurance expires at the rate of $300 per month.
2. Supplies on hand total $1,100.
3. The equipment depreciates $500 per month.
4. 2/5 of the unearned service revenue was earned in March.

Prepare the adjusting entries for the month of March.

Do it! 3-3 Johnny Knox is the new owner of Swift Computer Services. At the end of July 2012, his first month of ownership, Johnny is trying to prepare monthly financial statements. He has the following information for the month.

Prepare adjusting entries for accruals.
(SO 6)

1. At July 31, Knox owed employees $1,300 in salaries that the company will pay in August.
2. On July 1, Knox borrowed $20,000 from a local bank on a 10-year note. The annual interest rate is 12%.
3. Service revenue unrecorded in July totaled $2,400.

Prepare the adjusting entries needed at July 31, 2012.

Do it! 3-4 Kreutz Co. was organized on April 1, 2012. The company prepares quarterly financial statements. The adjusted trial balance amounts at June 30 are shown on the next page.

Calculate amounts from trial balance.
(SO 7)

Debits		**Credits**	
Cash	$ 5,360	Accumulated Depreciation—	$ 700
Accounts Receivable	480	Equipment	
Prepaid Rent	720	Notes Payable	4,000
Supplies	920	Accounts Payable	790
Equipment	12,000	Salaries and Wages Payable	300
Owner's Drawings	500	Interest Payable	40
Salaries and Wages Expense	7,400	Unearned Rent Revenue	400
Rent Expense	1,200	Owner's Capital	11,200
Depreciation Expense	700	Service Revenue	11,360
Supplies Expense	160	Rent Revenue	1,100
Utilities Expense	410	Total credits	$29,890
Interest Expense	40		
Total debits	$29,890		

(a) Determine the net income for the quarter April 1 to June 30.
(b) Determine the total assets and total liabilities at June 30, 2012 for Kreutz Company.
(c) Determine the amount that appears for Owner's Capital at June 30, 2012.

Exercises

Explain the time period assumption.

(SO 1)

E3-1 Lance Louis has prepared the following list of statements about the time period assumption.
1. Adjusting entries would not be necessary if a company's life were not divided into artificial time periods.
2. The IRS requires companies to file annual tax returns.
3. Accountants divide the economic life of a business into artificial time periods, but each transaction affects only one of these periods.
4. Accounting time periods are generally a month, a quarter, or a year.
5. A time period lasting one year is called an interim period.
6. All fiscal years are calendar years, but not all calendar years are fiscal years.

Instructions
Identify each statement as true or false. If false, indicate how to correct the statement.

Distinguish between cash and accrual basis of accounting.

(SO 2)

E3-2 On numerous occasions, proposals have surfaced to put the federal government on the accrual basis of accounting. This is no small issue. If this basis were used, it would mean that billions in unrecorded liabilities would have to be booked, and the federal deficit would increase substantially.

Instructions
(a) What is the difference between accrual-basis accounting and cash-basis accounting?
(b) Why would politicians prefer the cash basis over the accrual basis?
(c) Write a letter to your senator explaining why the federal government should adopt the accrual basis of accounting.

Compute cash and accrual accounting income.

(SO 2)

E3-3 Malast Industries collected $105,000 from customers in 2012. Of the amount collected, $25,000 was from revenue earned on account in 2011. In addition, Malast earned $40,000 of revenue in 2012, which will not be collected until 2013.

Malast Industries also paid $72,000 for expenses in 2012. Of the amount paid, $30,000 was for expenses incurred on account in 2011. In addition, Malast incurred $42,000 of expenses in 2012, which will not be paid until 2013.

Instructions
(a) Compute 2012 cash-basis net income.
(b) Compute 2012 accrual-basis net income.

Identify the type of adjusting entry needed.

(SO 4, 5, 6)

E3-4 Mannelly Corporation encounters the following situations:
1. Mannelly collects $1,300 from a customer in 2012 for services to be performed in 2013.
2. Mannelly incurs utility expense which is not yet paid in cash or recorded.

3. Mannelly's employees worked 3 days in 2012 but will not be paid until 2013.
4. Mannelly earned service revenue but has not yet received cash or recorded the transaction.
5. Mannelly paid $2,400 rent on December 1 for the 4 months starting December 1.
6. Mannelly received cash for future services and recorded a liability until the revenue was earned.
7. Mannelly performed consulting services for a client in December 2012. On December 31, it had not billed the client for services provided of $1,200.
8. Mannelly paid cash for an expense and recorded an asset until the item was used up.
9. Mannelly purchased $900 of supplies in 2012; at year-end, $400 of supplies remain unused.
10. Mannelly purchased equipment on January 1, 2012; the equipment will be used for 5 years.
11. Mannelly borrowed $10,000 on October 1, 2012, signing an 8% one-year note payable.

Instructions

Identify what type of adjusting entry (prepaid expense, unearned revenue, accrued expense, or accrued revenue) is needed in each situation, at December 31, 2012.

E3-5 Garrett Wolfe Company has the following balances in selected accounts on December 31, 2012.

Prepare adjusting entries from selected data.

(SO 5, 6)

Accounts Receivable	$ -0-
Accumulated Depreciation—Equipment	-0-
Equipment	7,000
Interest Payable	-0-
Notes Payable	10,000
Prepaid Insurance	2,100
Salaries and Wages Payable	-0-
Supplies	2,450
Unearned Service Revenue	30,000

All the accounts have normal balances. The information below has been gathered at December 31, 2012.

1. Garrett Wolfe Company borrowed $10,000 by signing a 12%, one-year note on September 1, 2012.
2. A count of supplies on December 31, 2012, indicates that supplies of $900 are on hand.
3. Depreciation on the equipment for 2012 is $1,000.
4. Garrett Wolfe Company paid $2,100 for 12 months of insurance coverage on June 1, 2012.
5. On December 1, 2012, Garrett Wolfe collected $30,000 for consulting services to be performed from December 1, 2012, through March 31, 2013.
6. Garrett Wolfe performed consulting services for a client in December 2012. The client will be billed $4,200.
7. Garrett Wolfe Company pays its employees total salaries of $9,000 every Monday for the preceding 5-day week (Monday through Friday). On Monday, December 29, employees were paid for the week ending December 26. All employees worked the last 3 days of 2012.

Instructions

Prepare adjusting entries for the seven items described above.

E3-6 J. Marten Company accumulates the following adjustment data at December 31.

Identify types of adjustments and account relationships.

(SO 4, 5, 6)

1. Services provided but not recorded total $1,000.
2. Supplies of $300 have been used.
3. Utility expenses of $225 are unpaid.
4. Unearned service revenue of $260 has been earned.
5. Salaries of $800 are unpaid.
6. Prepaid insurance totaling $350 has expired.

Instructions

For each of the above items indicate the following.

(a) The type of adjustment (prepaid expense, unearned revenue, accrued revenue, or accrued expense).
(b) The status of accounts before adjustment (overstatement or understatement).

E3-7 The ledger of Danieal Rental Agency on March 31 of the current year includes the selected accounts, shown on the next page, before adjusting entries have been prepared.

Prepare adjusting entries from selected account data.

(SO 5, 6)

	Debit	Credit
Prepaid Insurance	$ 3,600	
Supplies	2,800	
Equipment	25,000	
Accumulated Depreciation—Equipment		$ 8,400
Notes Payable		20,000
Unearned Rent Revenue		10,200
Rent Revenue		60,000
Interest Expense	–0–	
Salaries and Wages Expense	14,000	

An analysis of the accounts shows the following.

1. The equipment depreciates $400 per month.
2. One-third of the unearned rent revenue was earned during the quarter.
3. Interest of $500 is accrued on the notes payable.
4. Supplies on hand total $900.
5. Insurance expires at the rate of $200 per month.

Instructions

Prepare the adjusting entries at March 31, assuming that adjusting entries are made **quarterly**. Additional accounts are: Depreciation Expense, Insurance Expense, Interest Payable, and Supplies Expense.

Prepare adjusting entries.
(SO 5, 6)

E3-8   Danielle Manning, D.D.S., opened a dental practice on January 1, 2012. During the first month of operations, the following transactions occurred.

1. Performed services for patients who had dental plan insurance. At January 31, $875 of such services was earned but not yet recorded.
2. Utility expenses incurred but not paid prior to January 31 totaled $650.
3. Purchased dental equipment on January 1 for $80,000, paying $20,000 in cash and signing a $60,000, 3-year note payable. The equipment depreciates $400 per month. Interest is $500 per month.
4. Purchased a one-year malpractice insurance policy on January 1 for $24,000.
5. Purchased $1,600 of dental supplies. On January 31, determined that $400 of supplies were on hand.

Instructions

Prepare the adjusting entries on January 31. Account titles are: Accumulated Depreciation—Equipment, Depreciation Expense, Service Revenue, Accounts Receivable, Insurance Expense, Interest Expense, Interest Payable, Prepaid Insurance, Supplies, Supplies Expense, Utilities Expense, and Utilities Payable.

Prepare adjusting entries.
(SO 5, 6)

E3-9   The trial balance for Pioneer Advertising Agency is shown in Illustration 3-3, p. 104. In lieu of the adjusting entries shown in the text at October 31, assume the following adjustment data.

1. Supplies on hand at October 31 total $500.
2. Expired insurance for the month is $100.
3. Depreciation for the month is $50.
4. Unearned service revenue earned in October totals $600.
5. Services provided but not recorded at October 31 are $300.
6. Interest accrued at October 31 is $95.
7. Accrued salaries at October 31 are $1,625.

Instructions

Prepare the adjusting entries for the items above.

Prepare correct income statement.
(SO 2, 5, 6, 7)

E3-10   The income statement of Brandon Co. for the month of July shows net income of $1,400 based on Service Revenue $5,500, Salaries and Wages Expense $2,300, Supplies Expense $1,200, and Utilities Expense $600. In reviewing the statement, you discover the following.

1. Insurance expired during July of $400 was omitted.
2. Supplies expense includes $250 of supplies that are still on hand at July 31.

3. Depreciation on equipment of $150 was omitted.
4. Accrued but unpaid salaries and wages at July 31 of $300 were not included.
5. Services provided but unrecorded totaled $650.

Instructions
Prepare a correct income statement for July 2012.

E3-11 A partial adjusted trial balance of Manumaleuna Company at January 31, 2012, shows the following.

Analyze adjusted data.
(SO 4, 5, 6, 7)

MANUMALEUNA COMPANY
Adjusted Trial Balance
January 31, 2012

	Debit	Credit
Supplies	$ 850	
Prepaid Insurance	2,400	
Salaries and Wages Payable		$ 800
Unearned Service Revenue		750
Supplies Expense	950	
Insurance Expense	400	
Salaries and Wages Expense	2,900	
Service Revenue		2,000

Instructions
Answer the following questions, assuming the year begins January 1.

(a) If the amount in Supplies Expense is the January 31 adjusting entry, and $1,000 of supplies was purchased in January, what was the balance in Supplies on January 1?

(b) If the amount in Insurance Expense is the January 31 adjusting entry, and the original insurance premium was for one year, what was the total premium and when was the policy purchased?

(c) If $3,500 of salaries was paid in January, what was the balance in Salaries and Wages Payable at December 31, 2011?

E3-12 Selected accounts of Tabor Company are shown below.

Journalize basic transactions and adjusting entries.
(SO 5, 6, 7)

Supplies Expense

7/31	800	

Supplies

7/1 Bal.	1,100	7/31	800
7/10	650		

Salaries and Wages Payable

		7/31	1,200

Accounts Receivable

7/31	500		

Unearned Service Revenue

7/31	1,150	7/1 Bal.	1,500
		7/20	1,000

Salaries and Wages Expense

7/15	1,200		
7/31	1,200		

Service Revenue

		7/14	2,000
		7/31	1,150
		7/31	500

Instructions
After analyzing the accounts, journalize (a) the July transactions and (b) the adjusting entries that were made on July 31. (*Hint:* July transactions were for cash.)

E3-13 The trial balances before and after adjustment for Matthews Company at the end of its fiscal year are presented on the next page.

Prepare adjusting entries from analysis of trial balances.
(SO 5, 6, 7)

MATTHEWS COMPANY
Trial Balance
August 31, 2012

	Before Adjustment		After Adjustment	
	Dr.	**Cr.**	**Dr.**	**Cr.**
Cash	$10,400		$10,400	
Accounts Receivable	8,800		10,800	
Supplies	2,300		900	
Prepaid Insurance	4,000		2,500	
Equipment	14,000		14,000	
Accumulated Depreciation—Equipment		$ 3,600		$ 4,500
Accounts Payable		5,800		5,800
Salaries and Wages Payable		–0–		1,100
Unearned Rent Revenue		1,500		600
Owner's Capital		15,600		15,600
Service Revenue		34,000		36,000
Rent Revenue		11,000		11,900
Salaries and Wages Expense	17,000		18,100	
Supplies Expense	–0–		1,400	
Rent Expense	15,000		15,000	
Insurance Expense	–0–		1,500	
Depreciation Expense	–0–		900	
	$71,500	$71,500	$75,500	$75,500

Instructions
Prepare the adjusting entries that were made.

Prepare financial statements from adjusted trial balance.
(SO 7)

E3-14   The adjusted trial balance for Matthews Company is given in E3-13.

Instructions
Prepare the income and owner's equity statements for the year and the balance sheet at August 31.

Record transactions on accrual basis; convert revenue to cash receipts.
(SO 5, 6)

E3-15   The following data are taken from the comparative balance sheets of Mayberry Billiards Club, which prepares its financial statements using the accrual basis of accounting.

December 31	2012	2011
Accounts receivable from members	$14,000	$ 9,000
Unearned service revenue	17,000	25,000

Members are billed based upon their use of the club's facilities. Unearned service revenues arise from the sale of gift certificates, which members can apply to their future use of club facilities. The 2012 income statement for the club showed that service revenue of $161,000 was earned during the year.

Instructions
(*Hint:* You will probably find it helpful to use T accounts to analyze these data.)
(a) Prepare journal entries for each of the following events that took place during 2012.
  (1) Accounts receivable from 2011 were all collected.
  (2) Gift certificates outstanding at the end of 2011 were all redeemed.
  (3) An additional $38,000 worth of gift certificates were sold during 2012. A portion of these was used by the recipients during the year; the remainder was still outstanding at the end of 2012.
  (4) Services provided to members for 2012 were billed to members.
  (5) Accounts receivable for 2012 (i.e., those billed in item [4] above) were partially collected.
(b) Determine the amount of cash received by the club, with respect to member services, during 2012.

Journalize adjusting entries.
(SO 8)

*E3-16   Brad Maynard Company has the following balances in selected accounts on December 31, 2012.

Service Revenue	$40,000
Insurance Expense	2,700
Supplies Expense	2,450

All the accounts have normal balances. Brad Maynard Company debits prepayments to expense accounts when paid, and credits unearned revenues to revenue accounts when received. The following information below has been gathered at December 31, 2012.

1. Brad Maynard Company paid $2,700 for 12 months of insurance coverage on June 1, 2012.
2. On December 1, 2012, Brad Maynard Company collected $40,000 for consulting services to be performed from December 1, 2012, through March 31, 2013.
3. A count of supplies on December 31, 2012, indicates that supplies of $900 are on hand.

Instructions
Prepare the adjusting entries needed at December 31, 2012.

*E3-17   At Richmond Company, prepayments are debited to expense when paid, and unearned revenues are credited to revenue when received. During January of the current year, the following transactions occurred.

Journalize transactions and adjusting entries.
(SO 8)

Jan. 2   Paid $1,920 for fire insurance protection for the year.
   10   Paid $1,700 for supplies.
   15   Received $6,100 for services to be performed in the future.

On January 31, it is determined that $2,500 of the services are earned and that there are $650 of supplies on hand.

Instructions
(a) Journalize and post the January transactions. (Use T accounts.)
(b) Journalize and post the adjusting entries at January 31.
(c) Determine the ending balance in each of the accounts.

Exercises: Set B

Visit the book's companion website, at **www.wiley.com/college/weygandt**, and choose the Student Companion site to access Exercise Set B.

Problems: Set A

P3-1A   Tony Masasi started his own consulting firm, McGee Company, on June 1, 2012. The trial balance at June 30 is shown below.

Prepare adjusting entries, post to ledger accounts, and prepare adjusted trial balance.
(SO 5, 6, 7)

McGEE COMPANY
Trial Balance
June 30, 2012

Account Number		Debit	Credit
101	Cash	$ 7,150	
112	Accounts Receivable	6,000	
126	Supplies	2,000	
130	Prepaid Insurance	3,000	
157	Equipment	15,000	
201	Accounts Payable		$ 4,500
209	Unearned Service Revenue		4,000
301	Owner's Capital		21,750
400	Service Revenue		7,900
726	Salaries and Wages Expense	4,000	
729	Rent Expense	1,000	
		$38,150	$38,150

In addition to those accounts listed on the trial balance, the chart of accounts for McGee Company also contains the following accounts and account numbers: No. 158 Accumulated Depreciation—Equipment, No. 212 Salaries and Wages Payable, No. 631 Supplies Expense, No. 711 Depreciation Expense, No. 722 Insurance Expense, and No. 732 Utilities Expense.

Other data:

1. Supplies on hand at June 30 are $750.
2. A utility bill for $150 has not been recorded and will not be paid until next month.
3. The insurance policy is for a year.
4. $2,800 of unearned service revenue has been earned at the end of the month.
5. Salaries of $1,900 are accrued at June 30.
6. The equipment has a 5-year life with no salvage value. It is being depreciated at $250 per month for 60 months.
7. Invoices representing $1,200 of services performed during the month have not been recorded as of June 30.

Instructions

(a) Prepare the adjusting entries for the month of June. Use J3 as the page number for your journal.
(b) Post the adjusting entries to the ledger accounts. Enter the totals from the trial balance as beginning account balances and place a check mark in the posting reference column.

(c) Adj. trial balance $41,650   (c) Prepare an adjusted trial balance at June 30, 2012.

Prepare adjusting entries, post, and prepare adjusted trial balance, and financial statements.

(SO 5, 6, 7)

P3-2A   Melton River Resort opened for business on June 1 with eight air-conditioned units. Its trial balance before adjustment on August 31 is as follows.

MELTON RIVER RESORT
Trial Balance
August 31, 2012

Account Number		Debit	Credit
101	Cash	$ 19,600	
126	Supplies	3,300	
130	Prepaid Insurance	6,000	
140	Land	25,000	
143	Buildings	125,000	
149	Equipment	26,000	
201	Accounts Payable		$ 6,500
208	Unearned Rent Revenue		7,400
275	Mortgage Payable		80,000
301	Owner's Capital		100,000
306	Owner's Drawings	5,000	
429	Rent Revenue		80,000
622	Maintenance and Repairs Expense	3,600	
726	Salaries and Wages Expense	51,000	
732	Utilities Expense	9,400	
		$273,900	$273,900

In addition to those accounts listed on the trial balance, the chart of accounts for Melton River Resort also contains the following accounts and account numbers: No. 112 Accounts Receivable, No. 144 Accumulated Depreciation—Buildings, No. 150 Accumulated Depreciation—Equipment, No. 212 Salaries and Wages Payable, No. 230 Interest Payable, No. 620 Depreciation Expense, No. 631 Supplies Expense, No. 718 Interest Expense, and No. 722 Insurance Expense.

Other data:

1. Insurance expires at the rate of $300 per month.
2. A count on August 31 shows $800 of supplies on hand.

3. Annual depreciation is $6,000 on buildings and $2,400 on equipment.
4. Unearned rent revenue of $4,800 was earned prior to August 31.
5. Salaries of $400 were unpaid at August 31.
6. Rentals of $4,000 were due from tenants at August 31. (Use Accounts Receivable.)
7. The mortgage interest rate is 9% per year. (The mortgage was taken out on August 1.)

Instructions
(a) Journalize the adjusting entries on August 31 for the 3-month period June 1–August 31.
(b) Prepare a ledger using the three-column form of account. Enter the trial balance amounts and post the adjusting entries. (Use J1 as the posting reference.)
(c) Prepare an adjusted trial balance on August 31.
(d) Prepare an income statement and an owner's equity statement for the 3 months ending August 31 and a balance sheet as of August 31.

(c) Adj. trial balance
$281,000
(d) Net income $18,300
Ending capital balance
$113,300
Total assets $203,400

P3-3A Minor Advertising Agency was founded by Brandon Minor in January of 2011. Presented below are both the adjusted and unadjusted trial balances as of December 31, 2012.

Prepare adjusting entries and financial statements.
(SO 5, 6, 7)

MINOR ADVERTISING AGENCY
Trial Balance
December 31, 2012

	Unadjusted Dr.	Unadjusted Cr.	Adjusted Dr.	Adjusted Cr.
Cash	$ 11,000		$ 11,000	
Accounts Receivable	20,000		21,500	
Supplies	8,600		4,800	
Prepaid Insurance	3,350		2,500	
Equipment	60,000		60,000	
Accumulated Depreciation—Equipment		$ 28,000		$ 34,000
Accounts Payable		5,000		5,000
Interest Payable		–0–		150
Notes Payable		5,000		5,000
Unearned Service Revenue		7,200		5,900
Salaries and Wages Payable		–0–		2,100
Owner's Capital		25,500		25,500
Owner's Drawings	12,000		12,000	
Service Revenue		58,600		61,400
Salaries and Wages Expense	10,000		12,100	
Insurance Expense			850	
Interest Expense	350		500	
Depreciation Expense			6,000	
Supplies Expense			3,800	
Rent Expense	4,000		4,000	
	$129,300	$129,300	$139,050	$139,050

Instructions
(a) Journalize the annual adjusting entries that were made.
(b) Prepare an income statement and an owner's equity statement for the year ending December 31, 2012, and a balance sheet at December 31.
(c) Answer the following questions.
　(1) If the note has been outstanding 6 months, what is the annual interest rate on that note?
　(2) If the company paid $12,500 in salaries in 2012, what was the balance in Salaries and Wages Payable on December 31, 2011?

(b) Net income $34,150
Ending capital $47,650
Total assets $65,800
(c) (1) 6%
(2) $2,500

P3-4A A review of the ledger of D. J. Moore Company at December 31, 2012, produces the following data pertaining to the preparation of annual adjusting entries.

Preparing adjusting entries.
(SO 5, 6)

1. Salaries and Wages Payable $0. There are eight salaried employees. Salaries are paid every Friday for the current week. Five employees receive a salary of $900 each per week, and three

1. Salaries and wages
expense $2,640

employees earn $700 each per week. Assume December 31 is a Tuesday. Employees do not work weekends. All employees worked the last 2 days of December.

2. Rent revenue $84,000

2. Unearned Rent Revenue $354,000. The company began subleasing office space in its new building on November 1. At December 31, the company had the following rental contracts that are paid in full for the entire term of the lease.

Date	Term (in months)	Monthly Rent	Number of Leases
Nov. 1	6	$5,000	5
Dec. 1	6	$8,500	4

3. Advertising expense $5,200

3. Prepaid Advertising $15,600. This balance consists of payments on two advertising contracts. The contracts provide for monthly advertising in two trade magazines. The terms of the contracts are as follows.

Contract	Date	Amount	Number of Magazine Issues
A650	May 1	$6,000	12
B974	Oct. 1	9,600	24

The first advertisement runs in the month in which the contract is signed.

4. Interest expense $6,300

4. Notes Payable $120,000. This balance consists of a note for one year at an annual interest rate of 9%, dated June 1.

Instructions
Prepare the adjusting entries at December 31, 2012. (Show all computations.)

Journalize transactions and follow through accounting cycle to preparation of financial statements.

(SO 5, 6, 7)

GLS

P3-5A On September 1, 2012, the account balances of Moore Equipment Repair were as follows.

No.	Debits		No.	Credits	
101	Cash	$ 4,880	154	Accumulated Depreciation—Equipment	$ 1,500
112	Accounts Receivable	3,520	201	Accounts Payable	3,400
126	Supplies	2,000	209	Unearned Service Revenue	1,400
153	Equipment	15,000	212	Salaries and Wages Payable	500
			301	Owner's Capital	18,600
		$25,400			$25,400

During September, the following summary transactions were completed.

Sept. 8   Paid $1,400 for salaries due employees, of which $900 is for September.
10   Received $1,200 cash from customers on account.
12   Received $3,400 cash for services performed in September.
15   Purchased store equipment on account $3,000.
17   Purchased supplies on account $1,200.
20   Paid creditors $4,500 on account.
22   Paid September rent $500.
25   Paid salaries $1,250.
27   Performed services on account and billed customers for services provided $2,100.
29   Received $650 from customers for future service.

Adjustment data consist of:

1. Supplies on hand $1,300.
2. Accrued salaries payable $300.
3. Depreciation is $100 per month.
4. Unearned service revenue of $1,450 is earned.

Instructions
(a) Enter the September 1 balances in the ledger accounts.
(b) Journalize the September transactions.
(c) Post to the ledger accounts. Use J1 for the posting reference. Use the following additional accounts: No. 407 Service Revenue, No. 615 Depreciation Expense, No. 631 Supplies Expense, No. 726 Salaries and Wages Expense, and No. 729 Rent Expense.

(d) Prepare a trial balance at September 30.

(e) Journalize and post adjusting entries.

(f) Prepare an adjusted trial balance.

(g) Prepare an income statement and an owner's equity statement for September and a balance sheet at September 30.

*P3-6A Olsen Graphics Company was organized on January 1, 2012, by Gwen Olsen. At the end of the first 6 months of operations, the trial balance contained the accounts shown below.

Debits		Credits	
Cash	$ 8,600	Notes Payable	$ 20,000
Accounts Receivable	14,000	Accounts Payable	9,000
Equipment	45,000	Owner's Capital	22,000
Insurance Expense	2,700	Sales Revenue	52,100
Salaries and Wages Expense	30,000	Service Revenue	6,000
Supplies Expense	3,700		
Advertising Expense	1,900		
Rent Expense	1,500		
Utilities Expense	1,700		
	$109,100		$109,100

Analysis reveals the following additional data.

1. The $3,700 balance in Supplies Expense represents supplies purchased in January. At June 30, $1,500 of supplies was on hand.
2. The note payable was issued on February 1. It is a 9%, 6-month note.
3. The balance in Insurance Expense is the premium on a one-year policy, dated March 1, 2012.
4. Service revenues are credited to revenue when received. At June 30, service revenue of $1,300 is unearned.
5. Sales revenue earned but unrecorded at June 30 totals $2,000.
6. Depreciation is $2,250 per year.

Instructions

(a) Journalize the adjusting entries at June 30. (Assume adjustments are recorded every 6 months.)

(b) Prepare an adjusted trial balance.

(c) Prepare an income statement and owner's equity statement for the 6 months ended June 30 and a balance sheet at June 30.

(d) Trial balance $30,750
(f) Adj. trial balance $31,150
(g) Net income $2,000
    Ending capital $20,600
    Total assets $24,600

Prepare adjusting entries, adjusted trial balance, and financial statements using appendix.
(SO 5, 6, 7, 8)

(b) Adj. trial balance $112,975
(c) Net income $18,725
    Ending capital $40,725
    Total assets $71,775

Problems: Set B

P3-1B Fran Omiyale started her own consulting firm, Omiyale Consulting, on May 1, 2012. The trial balance at May 31 is as follows.

Prepare adjusting entries, post to ledger accounts, and prepare an adjusted trial balance.
(SO 5, 6, 7)

OMIYALE CONSULTING
Trial Balance
May 31, 2012

Account Number		Debit	Credit
101	Cash	$ 4,500	
112	Accounts Receivable	6,000	
126	Supplies	1,900	
130	Prepaid Insurance	3,600	
149	Equipment	11,400	
201	Accounts Payable		$ 4,500
209	Unearned Service Revenue		2,000
301	Owner's Capital		17,700
400	Service Revenue		7,500
726	Salaries and Wages Expense	3,400	
729	Rent Expense	900	
		$31,700	$31,700

In addition to those accounts listed on the trial balance, the chart of accounts for Omiyale Consulting also contains the following accounts and account numbers: No. 150 Accumulated Depreciation—Equipment, No. 212 Salaries and Wages Payable, No. 631 Supplies Expense, No. 717 Depreciation Expense, No. 722 Insurance Expense, and No. 736 Utilities Expense.

Other data:

1. $900 of supplies have been used during the month.
2. Utilities expense incurred but not paid on May 31, 2012, $250.
3. The insurance policy is for 2 years.
4. $400 of the balance in the unearned service revenue account remains unearned at the end of the month.
5. May 31 is a Wednesday, and employees are paid on Fridays. Omiyale Consulting has two employees, who are paid $900 each for a 5-day work week.
6. The office furniture has a 5-year life with no salvage value. It is being depreciated at $190 per month for 60 months.
7. Invoices representing $1,700 of services performed during the month have not been recorded as of May 31.

Instructions

(a) Prepare the adjusting entries for the month of May. Use J4 as the page number for your journal.
(b) Post the adjusting entries to the ledger accounts. Enter the totals from the trial balance as beginning account balances and place a check mark in the posting reference column.
(c) Prepare an adjusted trial balance at May 31, 2012.

(c) Adj. trial balance $34,920

Prepare adjusting entries, post, and prepare adjusted trial balance, and financial statements.

(SO 5, 6, 7)

P3-2B   The Bear Motel opened for business on May 1, 2012. Its trial balance before adjustment on May 31 is as follows.

BEAR MOTEL
Trial Balance
May 31, 2012

Account Number		Debit	Credit
101	Cash	$ 3,500	
126	Supplies	2,080	
130	Prepaid Insurance	2,400	
140	Land	12,000	
141	Buildings	60,000	
149	Equipment	15,000	
201	Accounts Payable		$ 4,800
208	Unearned Rent Revenue		3,300
275	Mortgage Payable		40,000
301	Owner's Capital		41,380
429	Rent Revenue		10,300
610	Advertising Expense	600	
726	Salaries and Wages Expense	3,300	
732	Utilities Expense	900	
		$99,780	$99,780

In addition to those accounts listed on the trial balance, the chart of accounts for Bear Motel also contains the following accounts and account numbers: No. 142 Accumulated Depreciation—Buildings, No. 150 Accumulated Depreciation—Equipment, No. 212 Salaries and Wages Payable, No. 230 Interest Payable, No. 619 Depreciation Expense, No. 631 Supplies Expense, No. 718 Interest Expense, and No. 722 Insurance Expense.

Other data:

1. Prepaid insurance is a 1-year policy starting May 1, 2012.
2. A count of supplies shows $750 of unused supplies on May 31.
3. Annual depreciation is $3,000 on the buildings and $1,500 on equipment.
4. The mortgage interest rate is 12%. (The mortgage was taken out on May 1.)
5. Two-thirds of the unearned rent revenue has been earned.
6. Salaries of $750 are accrued and unpaid at May 31.

Instructions
(a) Journalize the adjusting entries on May 31.
(b) Prepare a ledger using the three-column form of account. Enter the trial balance amounts and post the adjusting entries. (Use J1 as the posting reference.)
(c) Prepare an adjusted trial balance on May 31.
(d) Prepare an income statement and an owner's equity statement for the month of May and a balance sheet at May 31.

(c) Adj. trial balance
$101,305
(d) Net income $4,645
Ending capital balance
$46,025
Total assets $93,075

P3-3B Peterman Co. was organized on July 1, 2012. Quarterly financial statements are prepared. The unadjusted and adjusted trial balances as of September 30 are shown below.

Prepare adjusting entries and financial statements.
(SO 5, 6, 7)

PETERMAN CO.
Trial Balance
September 30, 2012

	Unadjusted Dr.	Unadjusted Cr.	Adjusted Dr.	Adjusted Cr.
Cash	$ 8,700		$ 8,700	
Accounts Receivable	10,400		11,500	
Supplies	1,500		650	
Prepaid Rent	2,200		1,200	
Equipment	18,000		18,000	
Accumulated Depreciation—Equipment		$ –0–		$ 700
Notes Payable		10,000		10,000
Accounts Payable		2,500		2,500
Salaries and Wages Payable		–0–		725
Interest Payable		–0–		100
Unearned Rent Revenue		1,900		1,050
Owner's Capital		22,000		22,000
Owner's Drawings	1,600		1,600	
Service Revenue		16,000		17,100
Rent Revenue		1,410		2,260
Salaries and Wages Expense	8,000		8,725	
Rent Expense	1,900		2,900	
Depreciation Expense			700	
Supplies Expense			850	
Utilities Expense	1,510		1,510	
Interest Expense			100	
	$53,810	$53,810	$56,435	$56,435

Instructions
(a) Journalize the adjusting entries that were made.
(b) Prepare an income statement and an owner's equity statement for the 3 months ending September 30 and a balance sheet at September 30.
(c) If the note bears interest at 12%, how many months has it been outstanding?

(b) Net income $4,575
Ending capital $24,975
Total assets $39,350

P3-4B A review of the ledger of Roach Company at December 31, 2012, produces the following data pertaining to the preparation of annual adjusting entries.

Prepare adjusting entries
(SO 5, 6)

1. Prepaid Insurance $10,440. The company has separate insurance policies on its buildings and its motor vehicles. Policy B4564 on the building was purchased on April 1, 2011, for $7,920. The policy has a term of 3 years. Policy A2958 on the vehicles was purchased on January 1, 2012, for $4,500. This policy has a term of 2 years.

1. Insurance expense $4,890

2. Unearned Rent Revenue $429,000. The company began subleasing office space in its new building on November 1. At December 31, the company had the following rental contracts that are paid in full for the entire term of the lease.

2. Rent revenue $84,000

Date	Term (in months)	Monthly Rent	Number of Leases
Nov. 1	9	$5,000	5
Dec. 1	6	$8,500	4

3. Interest expense $1,800

3. Notes Payable $120,000. This balance consists of a note for 9 months at an annual interest rate of 9%, dated November 1.

4. Salaries and wages
    expense $2,000

4. Salaries and Wages Payable $0. There are eight salaried employees. Salaries are paid every Friday for the current week. Five employees receive a salary of $700 each per week, and three employees earn $500 each per week. Assume December 31 is a Tuesday. Employees do not work weekends. All employees worked the last 2 days of December.

Instructions
Prepare the adjusting entries at December 31, 2012.

*Journalize transactions and
follow through accounting
cycle to preparation of financial
statements.*

(SO 5, 6, 7)

GLS

P3-5B On November 1, 2012, the account balances of Robinson Equipment Repair were as follows.

No.	Debits		No.	Credits	
101	Cash	$ 2,400	154	Accumulated Depreciation—Equipment	$ 2,000
112	Accounts Receivable	4,250	201	Accounts Payable	2,600
126	Supplies	1,800	209	Unearned Service Revenue	1,200
153	Equipment	12,000	212	Salaries and Wages Payable	700
			301	Owner's Capital	13,950
		$20,450			$20,450

During November, the following summary transactions were completed.

Nov. 8   Paid $1,700 for salaries due employees, of which $700 is for October salaries.
     10   Received $3,420 cash from customers on account.
     12   Received $3,100 cash for services performed in November.
     15   Purchased equipment on account $2,000.
     17   Purchased supplies on account $700.
     20   Paid creditors on account $2,700.
     22   Paid November rent $400.
     25   Paid salaries $1,700.
     27   Performed services on account and billed customers for services provided $1,900.
     29   Received $600 from customers for future service.

Adjustment data consist of:

1. Supplies on hand $1,400.
2. Accrued salaries payable $350.
3. Depreciation for the month is $200.
4. Unearned service revenue of $1,250 is earned.

Instructions
(a) Enter the November 1 balances in the ledger accounts.
(b) Journalize the November transactions.
(c) Post to the ledger accounts. Use J1 for the posting reference. Use the following additional accounts: No. 407 Service Revenue, No. 615 Depreciation Expense, No. 631 Supplies Expense, No. 726 Salaries and Wages Expense, and No. 729 Rent Expense.

(d) Trial balance $25,350

(d) Prepare a trial balance at November 30.
(e) Journalize and post adjusting entries.

(f) Adj. trial balance $25,900
(g) Net income $1,500;
    Ending capital $15,450
    Total assets $18,950

(f) Prepare an adjusted trial balance.
(g) Prepare an income statement and an owner's equity statement for November and a balance sheet at November 30.

Problems: Set C

Visit the book's companion website, at **www.wiley.com/college/weygandt**, and choose the Student Companion site to access Problem Set C.

Continuing Cookie Chronicle

(*Note:* This is a continuation of the Cookie Chronicle from Chapters 1 and 2. Use the information from the previous chapters and follow the instructions below using the general ledger accounts you have already prepared.)

CCC3   It is the end of November and Natalie has been in touch with her grandmother. Her grandmother asked Natalie how well things went in her first month of business. Natalie, too, would like to know if she has been profitable or not during November. Natalie realizes that in order to determine Cookie Creations' income, she must first make adjustments.

Natalie puts together the following additional information.

1. A count reveals that $35 of baking supplies were used during November.
2. Natalie estimates that all of her baking equipment will have a useful life of 5 years or 60 months. (Assume Natalie decides to record a full month's worth of depreciation, regardless of when the equipment was obtained by the business.)
3. Natalie's grandmother has decided to charge interest of 6% on the note payable extended on November 16. The loan plus interest is to be repaid in 24 months. (Assume that half a month of interest accrued during November.)
4. On November 30, a friend of Natalie's asks her to teach a class at the neighborhood school. Natalie agrees and teaches a group of 35 first-grade students how to make Santa Claus cookies. The next day, Natalie prepares an invoice for $300 and leaves it with the school principal. The principal says that he will pass the invoice along to the head office, and it will be paid sometime in December.
5. Natalie receives a utilities bill for $45. The bill is for utilities consumed by Natalie's business during November and is due December 15.

Instructions

Using the information that you have gathered through Chapter 2, and based on the new information above, do the following.

(a) Prepare and post the adjusting journal entries.
(b) Prepare an adjusting trial balance.
(c) Using the adjusted trial balance, calculate Cookie Creations' net income or net loss for the month of November. Do not prepare an income statement.

BROADENINGYOURPERSPECTIVE

Financial Reporting and Analysis

Financial Reporting Problem: PepsiCo, Inc.

BYP3-1   The financial statements of PepsiCo, Inc. are presented in Appendix A at the end of this textbook.

Instructions
(a) Using the consolidated financial statements and related information, identify items that may result in adjusting entries for prepayments.
(b) Using the consolidated financial statements and related information, identify items that may result in adjusting entries for accruals.
(c) Using the Selected Financial Data and 5-Year Summary, what has been the trend since 2005 for net income?

Comparative Analysis Problem: PepsiCo, Inc. vs. The Coca-Cola Company

BYP3-2   PepsiCo's financial statements are presented in Appendix A. Financial statements for The Coca-Cola Company are presented in Appendix B.

Instructions
Based on information contained in these financial statements, determine the following for each company.

(a) Net increase (decrease) in property, plant, and equipment (net) from 2008 to 2009.
(b) Increase (decrease) in selling, general, and administrative expenses from 2008 to 2009.

(c) Increase (decrease) in long-term debt (obligations) from 2008 to 2009.

(d) Increase (decrease) in net income from 2008 to 2009.

(e) Increase (decrease) in cash and cash equivalents from 2008 to 2009.

On the Web

BYP3-3   No financial decision maker should ever rely solely on the financial information reported in the annual report to make decisions. It is important to keep abreast of financial news. This activity demonstrates how to search for financial news on the Web.

Address: http://biz.yahoo.com/i, or go to **www.wiley.com/college/weygandt**

Steps:

1. Type in either Wal-Mart, Target Corp., or Kmart.
2. Choose **News**.
3. Select an article that sounds interesting to you and that would be relevant to an investor in these companies.

Instructions

(a) What was the source of the article (e.g., Reuters, Businesswire, Prnewswire)?

(b) Assume that you are a personal financial planner and that one of your clients owns stock in the company. Write a brief memo to your client summarizing the article and explaining the implications of the article for their investment.

Critical Thinking

Decision Making Across the Organization

BYP3-4   Happy Camper Park was organized on April 1, 2011, by Amaya Berge. Amaya is a good manager but a poor accountant. From the trial balance prepared by a part-time bookkeeper, Amaya prepared the following income statement for the quarter that ended March 31, 2012.

HAPPY CAMPER PARK
Income Statement
For the Quarter Ended March 31, 2012

Revenues		
Rent revenue		$90,000
Operating expenses		
Advertising	$ 5,200	
Salaries and wages	29,800	
Utilities	900	
Depreciation	800	
Maintenance and repairs	4,000	
Total operating expenses		40,700
Net income		$49,300

Amaya thought that something was wrong with the statement because net income had never exceeded $20,000 in any one quarter. Knowing that you are an experienced accountant, she asks you to review the income statement and other data.

You first look at the trial balance. In addition to the account balances reported above in the income statement, the ledger contains the following additional selected balances at March 31, 2012.

Supplies	$ 6,200
Prepaid Insurance	7,200
Notes Payable	12,000

You then make inquiries and discover the following.

1. Rent revenues include advanced rentals for summer occupancy $15,000.
2. There were $1,700 of supplies on hand at March 31.
3. Prepaid insurance resulted from the payment of a one-year policy on January 1, 2012.

4. The mail on April 1, 2012, brought the following bills: advertising for week of March 24, $110; repairs made March 10, $260; and utilities, $180.

5. There are four employees, who receive wages totaling $300 per day. At March 31, 2 days' salaries and wages have been incurred but not paid.

6. The note payable is a 3-month, 10% note dated January 1, 2012.

Instructions

With the class divided into groups, answer the following.

(a) Prepare a correct income statement for the quarter ended March 31, 2012.

(b) Explain to Amaya the generally accepted accounting principles that she did not recognize in preparing her income statement and their effect on her results.

Communication Activity

BYP3-5 In reviewing the accounts of Keri Ann Co. at the end of the year, you discover that adjusting entries have not been made.

Instructions

Write a memo to Keri Ann Nickels, the owner of Keri Ann Co., that explains the following: the nature and purpose of adjusting entries, why adjusting entries are needed, and the types of adjusting entries that may be made.

Ethics Case

BYP3-6 Bluestem Company is a pesticide manufacturer. Its sales declined greatly this year due to the passage of legislation outlawing the sale of several of Bluestem's chemical pesticides. In the coming year, Bluestem will have environmentally safe and competitive chemicals to replace these discontinued products. Sales in the next year are expected to greatly exceed any prior year's. The decline in sales and profits appears to be a one-year aberration. But even so, the company president fears a large dip in the current year's profits. He believes that such a dip could cause a significant drop in the market price of Bluestem's stock and make the company a takeover target.

To avoid this possibility, the company president calls in Cathi Bell, controller, to discuss this period's year-end adjusting entries. He urges her to accrue every possible revenue and to defer as many expenses as possible. He says to Cathi, "We need the revenues this year, and next year can easily absorb expenses deferred from this year. We can't let our stock price be hammered down!" Cathi didn't get around to recording the adjusting entries until January 17, but she dated the entries December 31 as if they were recorded then. Cathi also made every effort to comply with the president's request.

Instructions

(a) Who are the stakeholders in this situation?

(b) What are the ethical considerations of (1) the president's request and (2) Cathi's dating the adjusting entries December 31?

(c) Can Cathi accrue revenues and defer expenses and still be ethical?

"All About You" Activity

BYP3-7 Companies must report or disclose in their financial statements information about all liabilities, including potential liabilities related to environmental clean-up. There are many situations in which you will be asked to provide personal financial information about your assets, liabilities, revenue, and expenses. Sometimes you will face difficult decisions regarding what to disclose and how to disclose it.

Instructions

Suppose that you are putting together a loan application to purchase a home. Based on your income and assets, you qualify for the mortgage loan, but just barely. How would you address each of the following situations in reporting your financial position for the loan application? Provide responses for each of the following situations.

(a) You signed a guarantee for a bank loan that a friend took out for $20,000. If your friend doesn't pay, you will have to pay. Your friend has made all of the payments so far, and it appears he will be able to pay in the future.

(b) You were involved in an auto accident in which you were at fault. There is the possibility that you may have to pay as much as $50,000 as part of a settlement. The issue will not be resolved before the bank processes your mortgage request.

(c) The company at which you work isn't doing very well, and it has recently laid off employees. You are still employed, but it is quite possible that you will lose your job in the next few months.

FASB Codification Activity

BYP3-8   If your school has a subscription to the FASB Codification, go to *http://aaahq.org/asclogin.cfm* to log in and prepare responses to the following.

Instructions

Access the glossary ("Master Glossary") to answer the following.

(a) What is the definition of revenue?

(b) What is the definition of compensation?

Answers to Insight and Accounting Across the Organization Questions

p. 102 Cooking the Books?   **Q:** What motivates sales executives and finance and accounting executives to participate in activities that result in inaccurate reporting of revenues? **A:** Sales executives typically receive bonuses based on their ability to meet quarterly sales targets. In addition, they often face the possibility of losing their jobs if they miss those targets. Executives in accounting and finance are very aware of the earnings targets of Wall Street analysts and investors. If they fail to meet these targets, the company's stock price will fall. As a result of these pressures, executives sometimes knowingly engage in unethical efforts to misstate revenues. As a result of the Sarbanes-Oxley Act of 2002, the penalties for such behavior are now much more severe.

p. 110 Turning Gift Cards into Revenue   **Q:** Suppose that Robert Jones purchases a $100 gift card at Best Buy on December 24, 2011, and gives it to his wife, Mary Jones, on December 25, 2011. On January 3, 2012, Mary uses the card to purchase $100 worth of CDs. When do you think Best Buy should recognize revenue and why? **A:** According to the revenue recognition principle, companies should recognize revenue when earned. In this case, revenue is not earned until Best Buy provides the goods. Thus, when Best Buy receives cash in exchange for the gift card on December 24, 2011, it should recognize a liability, Unearned Revenue, for $100. On January 3, 2012, when Mary Jones exchanges the card for merchandise, Best Buy should recognize revenue and eliminate $100 from the balance in the Unearned Revenue account.

p. 114 Cashing In on Accrual Accounting   **Q:** Accrual accounting is often considered superior to cash accounting. Why, then, were some people critical of China's use of accrual accounting in this instance? **A:** In this case, some people were critical because, in general, China uses cash accounting. By switching to accrual accounting for this transaction, China was not being consistent in its accounting practices. Lack of consistency reduces the transparency and usefulness of accounting information.

Answers to Self-Test Questions

1. c   **2.** c   **3.** d   **4.** a   **5.** d   **6.** d   **7.** c ($1,350 − $600)   **8.** c   **9.** a   **10.** c   **11.** a   **12.** b   **13.** b
14. c   ***15.** a

IFRS A Look at IFRS

It is often difficult for companies to determine in what time period they should report particular revenues and expenses. Both the IASB and FASB are working on a joint project to develop a common conceptual framework, as well as a revenue recognition project, that will enable companies to better use the same principles to record transactions consistently over time.

Key Points

- In this chapter, you learned accrual-basis accounting applied under GAAP. Companies applying IFRS also use accrual-basis accounting to ensure that they record transactions that change a company's financial statements in the period in which events occur.

- Similar to GAAP, cash-basis accounting is not in accordance with IFRS.

- IFRS also divides the economic life of companies into artificial time periods. Under both GAAP and IFRS, this is referred to as the *time period assumption*.

- IFRS requires that companies present a complete set of financial statements, including comparative information annually.

- GAAP has more than 100 rules dealing with revenue recognition. Many of these rules are industry-specific. In contrast, revenue recognition under IFRS is determined primarily by a single standard. Despite this large disparity in the amount of detailed guidance devoted to revenue recognition, the **general** revenue recognition principles required by GAAP that are used in this textbook are similar to those under IFRS.

- As the Feature Story illustrates, revenue recognition fraud is a major issue in U.S. financial reporting. The same situation occurs in other countries, as evidenced by revenue recognition breakdowns at Dutch software company Baan NV, Japanese electronics giant NEC, and Dutch grocer Ahold NV.

- A specific standard exists for revenue recognition under IFRS *(IAS 18)*. In general, the standard is based on the **probability that the economic benefits associated with the transaction will flow to the company** selling the goods, providing the service, or receiving investment income. In addition, the revenues and costs **must be capable of being measured reliably**. GAAP uses concepts such as *realized, realizable* (that is, it is received, or expected to be received), and *earned* as a basis for revenue recognition.

- Under IFRS, revaluation of items such as land and buildings is permitted. IFRS allows depreciation based on revaluation of assets, which is not permitted under GAAP.

- The terminology used for revenues and gains, and expenses and losses, differs somewhat between IFRS and GAAP. For example, income is defined as:

  > Increases in economic benefits during the accounting period in the form of inflows or enhancements of assets or decreases of liabilities that result in increases in equity, other than those relating to contributions from shareholders.

  Income includes *both* revenues, which arise during the normal course of operating activities, and gains, which arise from activities outside of the normal sales of goods and services. The term income is not used this way under GAAP. Instead, under GAAP income refers to the net difference between revenues and expenses. Expenses are defined as:

  > Decreases in economic benefits during the accounting period in the form of outflows or depletions of assets or incurrences of liabilities that result in decreases in equity other than those relating to distributions to shareholders.

  Note that under IFRS, expenses include both those costs incurred in the normal course of operations, as well as losses that are not part of normal operations. This is in contrast to GAAP, which defines each separately.

Looking to the Future

The IASB and FASB are now involved in a joint project on revenue recognition. The purpose of this project is to develop comprehensive guidance on when to recognize revenue. Presently, the Boards are considering an approach that focuses on changes in assets and liabilities (rather than on earned and realized) as the basis for revenue recognition. It is hoped that this approach will lead to more consistent accounting in this area. For more on this topic, see *www.fasb.org/project/revenue_recognition.shtml*.

IFRS Self-Test Questions

1. GAAP:
   (a) provides very detailed, industry-specific guidance on revenue recognition, compared to the general guidance provided by IFRS.
   (b) provides only general guidance on revenue recognition, compared to the detailed guidance provided by IFRS.
   (c) allows revenue to be recognized when a customer makes an order.
   (d) requires that revenue not be recognized until cash is received.

2. Which of the following statements is *false*?
   (a) IFRS employs the time period assumption.
   (b) IFRS employs accrual accounting.
   (c) IFRS requires that revenues and costs must be capable of being measured reliably.
   (d) IFRS uses the cash basis of accounting.

3. As a result of the revenue recognition project being undertaken by the FASB and IASB:
   (a) revenue recognition will place more emphasis on when revenue is earned.
   (b) revenue recognition will place more emphasis on when revenue is realized.
   (c) revenue recognition will place more emphasis on when changes occur in assets and liabilities.
   (d) revenue will no longer be recorded unless cash has been received.

4. Which of the following is *false*?
   (a) Under IFRS, the term *income* describes both revenues and gains.
   (b) Under IFRS, the term *expenses* includes losses.
   (c) Under IFRS, firms do not engage in the closing process.
   (d) IFRS has fewer standards than GAAP that address revenue recognition.

5. Accrual-basis accounting:
   (a) is optional under IFRS.
   (b) results in companies recording transactions that change a company's financial statements in the period in which events occur.
   (c) will likely be eliminated as a result of the IASB/FASB joint project on revenue recognition.
   (d) is not consistent with the IASB conceptual framework.

IFRS Concepts and Application

IFRS3-1 Compare and contrast the rules regarding revenue recognition under IFRS versus GAAP.

IFRS3-2 Under IFRS, do the definitions of revenues and expenses include gains and losses? Explain.

International Financial Reporting Problem: Zetar plc

IFRS3-3 The financial statements of Zetar plc are presented in Appendix C. The company's complete annual report, including the notes to its financial statements, is available at *www.zetarplc.com*.

Instructions
Visit Zetar's corporate website and answer the following questions from Zetar's 2009 annual report.

(a) From the notes to the financial statements, how does the company determine the amount of revenue to record at the time of a sale?

(b) From the notes to the financial statements, how does the company determine whether a sale has occurred?

(c) Using the consolidated income statement and consolidated statement of financial position, identify items that may result in adjusting entries for deferrals.

(d) Using the consolidated income statement, identify two items that may result in adjusting entries for accruals.

Answers to IFRS Self-Test Questions
1. a   **2.** d   **3.** c   **4.** c   **5.** b

The Navigator

✔ **Remember to go back to the Navigator box on the chapter opening page and check off your completed work.**

CHAPTER4

Completing the Accounting Cycle

Study Objectives

After studying this chapter, you should be able to:

[1] Prepare a worksheet.

[2] Explain the process of closing the books.

[3] Describe the content and purpose of a post-closing trial balance.

[4] State the required steps in the accounting cycle.

[5] Explain the approaches to preparing correcting entries.

[6] Identify the sections of a classified balance sheet.

✔ The Navigator

✔ [The Navigator]

- Scan Study Objectives ○
- Read Feature Story ○
- Read Preview ○
- Read text and answer **Do it!** p. 160 ○ p. 164 ○ p. 174 ○ p. 176 ○
- Work Comprehensive **Do it!** p. 177 ○
- Review Summary of Study Objectives ○
- Answer Self-Test Questions ○
- Complete Assignments ○
- Go to *WileyPLUS* for practice and tutorials ○
- Read A Look at IFRS p. 204 ○

Feature Story

EVERYONE LIKES TO WIN

When Ted Castle was a hockey coach at the University of Vermont, his players were self-motivated by their desire to win. Hockey was a game you either won or lost. But at Rhino Foods, Inc., a bakery-foods company he founded in Burlington, Vermont, he discovered that manufacturing-line workers were not so self-motivated. Ted thought, what if he turned the food-making business into a game, with rules, strategies, and trophies?

Ted knew that in a game knowing the score is all-important. He felt that only if the employees know the score—know exactly how the business is doing daily, weekly, monthly—could he turn food-making into a game. But Rhino is a closely held, family-owned business, and its financial statements and profits were confidential. Ted wondered, should he open Rhino's books to the employees?

A consultant put Ted's concerns in perspective when he said, "Imagine you're playing touch football. You play for an hour or two, and the whole time I'm sitting there with a book, keeping score. All of a sudden I blow the whistle, and I say, 'OK, that's it. Everybody go home.' I close my book and walk away. How would you feel?" Ted opened his books and revealed the financial statements to his employees.

The next step was to teach employees the rules and strategies of how to "win" at making food. The first lesson: "Your opponent at Rhino is expenses. You must cut and control expenses." Ted and his staff distilled those lessons into daily scorecards—production reports and income statements—that keep Rhino's employees up-to-date on the game. At noon each day, Ted posts the previous day's results at the entrance to the production room. Everyone checks whether they made or lost money on what they produced the day before. And it's not just an academic exercise: There's a bonus check for each employee at the end of every four-week "game" that meets profitability guidelines.

Rhino has flourished since the first game. Employment has increased from 20 to 130 people, while both revenues and profits have grown dramatically.

Inside**CHAPTER**4

PreviewofCHAPTER4

At Rhino Foods, Inc., financial statements help employees understand what is happening in the business. In Chapter 3, we prepared financial statements directly from the adjusted trial balance. However, with so many details involved in the end-of-period accounting procedures, it is easy to make errors. One way to minimize errors in the records and to simplify the end-of-period procedures is to use a worksheet.

In this chapter, we will explain the role of the worksheet in accounting. We also will study the remaining steps in the accounting cycle, especially the closing process, again using Pioneer Advertising Agency as an example. Then we will consider correcting entries and classified balance sheets. The content and organization of Chapter 4 are as follows.

Completing the Accounting Cycle

Using a Worksheet	Closing the Books	Summary of Accounting Cycle	Classified Balance Sheet
• Steps in preparation • Preparing financial statements • Preparing adjusting entries	• Preparing closing entries • Posting closing entries • Preparing a post-closing trial balance	• Reversing entries—An optional step • Correcting entries—An avoidable step	• Current assets • Long-term investments • Property, plant, and equipment • Intangible assets • Current liabilities • Long-term liabilities • Owner's equity

✔ The Navigator

Using a Worksheet

Study Objective [1]
Prepare a worksheet.

A **worksheet** is a multiple-column form used in the adjustment process and in preparing financial statements. As its name suggests, the worksheet is a working tool. **It is not a permanent accounting record**; it is neither a journal nor a part of the general ledger. The worksheet is merely a device used in preparing adjusting entries and the financial statements. Companies generally computerize worksheets using an electronic spreadsheet program such as Excel.

Illustration 4-1 shows the basic form of a worksheet and the five steps for preparing it. Each step is performed in sequence. **The use of a worksheet is optional.** When a company chooses to use one, it prepares financial statements from the worksheet. It enters the adjustments in the worksheet columns and then journalizes and posts the adjustments after it has prepared the financial statements. Thus, worksheets make it possible to provide the financial statements to management and other interested parties at an earlier date.

Steps in Preparing a Worksheet

We will use the October 31 trial balance and adjustment data of Pioneer Advertising, from Chapter 3, to illustrate how to prepare a worksheet. We describe each step of the process and demonstrate these steps in Illustration 4-2 (page 156) and transparencies 4-3A, B, C, and D.

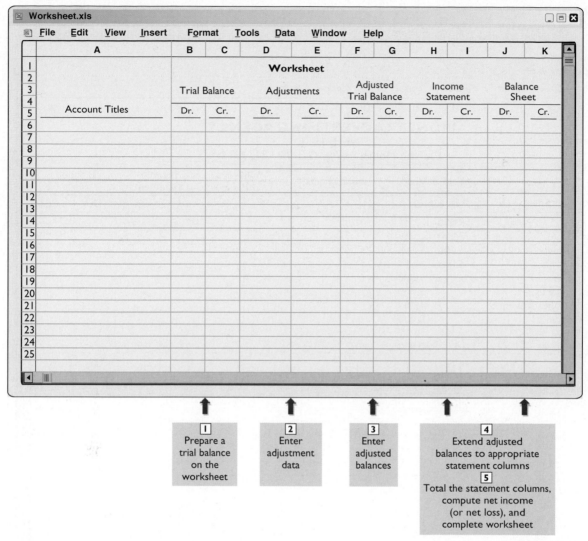

Illustration 4-1
Form and procedure for a worksheet

STEP 1. PREPARE A TRIAL BALANCE ON THE WORKSHEET

Enter all ledger accounts with balances in the account titles space. Enter debit and credit amounts from the ledger in the trial balance columns. Illustration 4-2 shows the worksheet trial balance for Pioneer Advertising Agency. This trial balance is the same one that appears in Illustration 2-31 (page 72) and Illustration 3-3 (page 104).

STEP 2. ENTER THE ADJUSTMENTS IN THE ADJUSTMENTS COLUMNS

Turn over the first transparency, Illustration 4-3A. When using a worksheet, enter all adjustments in the adjustments columns. In entering the adjustments, use applicable trial balance accounts. If additional accounts are needed, insert them on the lines immediately below the trial balance totals. A different letter identifies the debit and credit for each adjusting entry. The term used to describe this process is **keying. Companies do not journalize the adjustments until after they complete the worksheet and prepare the financial statements.**

(**Note:** Text continues on page 157, following acetate overlays.)

Illustration 4-2
Preparing a trial balance

Pioneer Advertising.xls

File　Edit　View　Insert　Format　Tools　Data　Window　Help

	A	B	C	D	E	F	G	H	I	J	K
1		**PIONEER ADVERTISING AGENCY**									
2		Worksheet									
3		For the Month Ended October 31, 2012									
4		Trial Balance		Adjustments		Adjusted Trial Balance		Income Statement		Balance Sheet	
5											
6	Account Titles										
7		Dr.	Cr.	Dr.	Cr.	Dr.	Cr.	Dr.	Cr.	Dr.	Cr.
8	Cash	15,200									
9	Supplies	2,500									
10	Prepaid Insurance	600									
11	Equipment	5,000									
12	Notes Payable		5,000								
13	Accounts Payable		2,500								
14	Unearned Service Revenue		1,200								
15	Owner's Capital		10,000								
16	Owner's Drawings	500									
17	Service Revenue		10,000								
18											
19	Salaries and Wages Expense	4,000									
20	Rent Expense	900									
21	Totals	28,700	28,700								
22											
23											
24											
25											
26											
27											
28											
29											
30											
31											
32											
33											
34											
35											
36											

Include all accounts with balances from ledger.

Trial balance amounts come directly from ledger accounts.

The adjustments for Pioneer Advertising Agency are the same as the adjustments illustrated on page 117. They are keyed in the adjustments columns of the worksheet as follows.

(a) Pioneer debits an additional account, Supplies Expense, $1,500 for the cost of supplies used, and credits Supplies $1,500.

(b) Pioneer debits an additional account, Insurance Expense, $50 for the insurance that has expired, and credits Prepaid Insurance $50.

(c) The company needs two additional depreciation accounts. It debits Depreciation Expense $40 for the month's depreciation, and credits Accumulated Depreciation—Equipment $40.

(d) Pioneer debits Unearned Service Revenue $400 for services provided, and credits Service Revenue $400.

(e) Pioneer debits an additional account, Accounts Receivable, $200 for services provided but not billed, and credits Service Revenue $200.

(f) The company needs two additional accounts relating to interest. It debits Interest Expense $50 for accrued interest, and credits Interest Payable $50.

(g) Pioneer debits Salaries and Wages Expense $1,200 for accrued salaries, and credits an additional account, Salaries and Wages Payable, $1,200.

After Pioneer has entered all the adjustments, the adjustments columns are totaled to prove their equality.

STEP 3. ENTER ADJUSTED BALANCES IN THE ADJUSTED TRIAL BALANCE COLUMNS

Turn over the second transparency, Illustration 4-3B. Pioneer determines the adjusted balance of an account by combining the amounts entered in the first four columns of the worksheet for each account. For example, the Prepaid Insurance account in the trial balance columns has a $600 debit balance and a $50 credit in the adjustments columns. The result is a $550 debit balance recorded in the adjusted trial balance columns. **For each account, the amount in the adjusted trial balance columns is the balance that will appear in the ledger after journalizing and posting the adjusting entries.** The balances in these columns are the same as those in the adjusted trial balance in Illustration 3-25 (page 119).

After Pioneer has entered all account balances in the adjusted trial balance columns, the columns are totaled to prove their equality. If the column totals do not agree, the financial statement columns will not balance and the financial statements will be incorrect.

STEP 4. EXTEND ADJUSTED TRIAL BALANCE AMOUNTS TO APPROPRIATE FINANCIAL STATEMENT COLUMNS

Turn over the third transparency, Illustration 4-3C. The fourth step is to extend adjusted trial balance amounts to the income statement and balance sheet columns of the worksheet. Pioneer enters balance sheet accounts in the appropriate balance sheet debit and credit columns. For instance, it enters Cash in the balance sheet debit column, and Notes Payable in the credit column. Pioneer extends Accumulated Depreciation—Equipment to the balance sheet credit column; the reason is that accumulated depreciation is a contra-asset account with a credit balance.

Because the worksheet does not have columns for the owner's equity statement, Pioneer extends the balance in owner's capital to the balance sheet credit column. In addition, it extends the balance in owner's drawings to the balance sheet debit column because it is an owner's equity account with a debit balance.

Helpful Hint

Every adjusted trial balance amount must be extended to one of the four statement columns.

The company enters the expense and revenue accounts such as Salaries and Wages Expense and Service Revenue in the appropriate income statement columns. Illustration 4-3C shows all of these extensions.

STEP 5. TOTAL THE STATEMENT COLUMNS, COMPUTE THE NET INCOME (OR NET LOSS), AND COMPLETE THE WORKSHEET

Turn over the fourth transparency, Illustration 4-3D. The company now must total each of the financial statement columns. The net income or loss for the period is the difference between the totals of the two income statement columns. If total credits exceed total debits, the result is net income. In such a case, as shown in Illustration 4-3D, the company inserts the words "Net Income" in the account titles space. It then enters the amount in the income statement debit column and the balance sheet credit column. **The debit amount balances the income statement columns; the credit amount balances the balance sheet columns.** In addition, the credit in the balance sheet column indicates the increase in owner's equity resulting from net income.

What if total debits in the income statement columns exceed total credits? In that case, the company has a net loss. It enters the amount of the net loss in the income statement credit column and the balance sheet debit column.

After entering the net income or net loss, the company determines new column totals. The totals shown in the debit and credit income statement columns will match. So will the totals shown in the debit and credit balance sheet columns. If either the income statement columns or the balance sheet columns are not equal after the net income or net loss has been entered, there is an error in the worksheet. Illustration 4-3D shows the completed worksheet for Pioneer Advertising Agency.

Preparing Financial Statements from a Worksheet

After a company has completed a worksheet, it has at hand all the data required for preparation of financial statements. The income statement is prepared from the income statement columns. The balance sheet and owner's equity statement are prepared from the balance sheet columns. Illustration 4-4 (page 159) shows the financial statements prepared from Pioneer's worksheet. At this point, the company has not journalized or posted adjusting entries. Therefore, ledger balances for some accounts are not the same as the financial statement amounts.

The amount shown for owner's capital on the worksheet is the account balance **before considering drawings and net income (or loss).** When the owner has made no additional investments of capital during the period, this worksheet amount for owner's capital is the balance at the beginning of the period.

Using a worksheet, companies can prepare financial statements before they journalize and post adjusting entries. **However, the completed worksheet is not a substitute for formal financial statements.** The format of the data in the financial statement columns of the worksheet is not the same as the format of the financial statements. **A worksheet is essentially a working tool of the accountant;** companies do not distribute it to management and other parties.

Preparing Adjusting Entries from a Worksheet

A worksheet is not a journal, and it cannot be used as a basis for posting to ledger accounts. To adjust the accounts, the company must journalize the adjustments and

Accounting Cycle Tutorial— Preparing Financial Statements and Closing the Books

Helpful Hint

Note that writing the explanation to the adjustment at the bottom of the worksheet is not required.

Illustration 4-4
Financial statements from a
worksheet

Pioneer Advertising Agency
Income Statement
For the Month Ended October 31, 2012

Revenues		
Service revenue		$10,600
Expenses		
Salaries and wages expense	$5,200	
Supplies expense	1,500	
Rent expense	900	
Insurance expense	50	
Interest expense	50	
Depreciation expense	40	
Total expenses		7,740
Net income		$ 2,860

Pioneer Advertising Agency
Owner's Equity Statement
For the Month Ended October 31, 2012

Owner's capital, October 1		$ –0–
Add: Investments	$10,000	
Net income	2,860	12,860
		12,860
Less: Drawings		500
Owner's capital, October 31		$12,360

Pioneer Advertising Agency
Balance Sheet
October 31, 2012

Assets

Cash		$15,200
Accounts receivable		200
Supplies		1,000
Prepaid insurance		550
Office equipment	$5,000	
Less: Accumulated depreciation—equipment	40	4,960
Total assets		$21,910

Liabilities and Owner's Equity

Liabilities		
Notes payable	$5,000	
Accounts payable	2,500	
Interest payable	50	
Unearned service revenue	800	
Salaries and wages payable	1,200	
Total liabilities		$ 9,550
Owner's equity		
Owner's capital		12,360
Total liabilities and owner's equity		$21,910

post them to the ledger. **The adjusting entries are prepared from the adjustments columns of the worksheet.** The reference letters in the adjustments columns and the explanations of the adjustments at the bottom of the worksheet help identify the adjusting entries. The journalizing and posting of adjusting entries **follows** the preparation of financial statements when a worksheet is used. The adjusting entries on October 31 for Pioneer Advertising Agency are the same as those shown in Illustration 3-23 (page 117).

Do it!

Worksheet

Susan Elbe is preparing a worksheet. Explain to Susan how she should extend the following adjusted trial balance accounts to the financial statement columns of the worksheet.

        Cash
        Accumulated Depreciation
        Accounts Payable
        Owner's Drawings
        Service Revenue
        Salaries and Wages Expense

action plan

✔ Balance sheet: Extend assets to debit column. Extend liabilities to credit column. Extend contra assets to credit column. Extend drawings account to debit column.

✔ Income statement: Extend expenses to debit column. Extend revenues to credit column.

Solution

Income statement debit column—Salaries and Wages Expense
Income statement credit column—Service Revenue
Balance sheet debit column—Cash; Owner's Drawings
Balance sheet credit column—Accumulated Depreciation; Accounts Payable

Related exercise material: BE4-1, BE4-2, BE4-3, E4-1, E4-2, E4-5, E4-6, and **Do it!** 4-1.

✔
The Navigator

Closing the Books

Study Objective [2]
Explain the process of closing the books.

At the end of the accounting period, the company makes the accounts ready for the next period. This is called **closing the books**. In closing the books, the company distinguishes between temporary and permanent accounts.

Temporary accounts relate only to a given accounting period. They include all income statement accounts and the owner's drawings account. **The company closes all temporary accounts at the end of the period.**

In contrast, permanent accounts relate to one or more future accounting periods. They consist of all balance sheet accounts, including the owner's capital account. **Permanent accounts are not closed from period to period.** Instead, the company carries forward the balances of permanent accounts into the next accounting period. Illustration 4-5 identifies the accounts in each category.

Alternative Terminology

Temporary accounts are sometimes called *nominal accounts*, and permanent accounts are sometimes called *real accounts*.

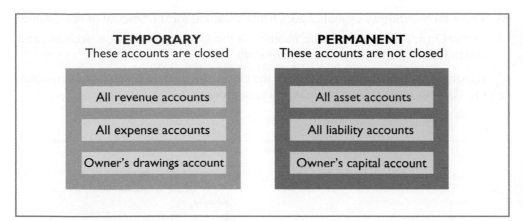

Illustration 4-5
Temporary versus permanent accounts

Helpful Hint

A contra-asset account, such as accumulated depreciation, is a permanent account also.

Preparing Closing Entries

At the end of the accounting period, the company transfers temporary account balances to the permanent owner's equity account, Owner's Capital, by means of closing entries.[1]

Closing entries formally recognize in the ledger the transfer of net income (or net loss) and owner's drawings to owner's capital. The owner's equity statement shows the results of these entries. **Closing entries also produce a zero balance in each temporary account.** The temporary accounts are then ready to accumulate data in the next accounting period separate from the data of prior periods. Permanent accounts are not closed.

Journalizing and posting closing entries is a required step in the accounting cycle. (See Illustration 4-12 on page 168.) The company performs this step after it has prepared financial statements. In contrast to the steps in the cycle that you have already studied, companies generally journalize and post closing entries **only at the end of the annual accounting period.** Thus, all temporary accounts will contain data for the entire year.

In preparing closing entries, companies could close each income statement account directly to owner's capital. However, to do so would result in excessive detail in the permanent Owner's Capital account. Instead, companies close the revenue and expense accounts to another temporary account, Income Summary, and they transfer the resulting net income or net loss from this account to owner's capital.

Companies **record closing entries in the general journal**. A center caption, Closing Entries, inserted in the journal between the last adjusting entry and the first closing entry, identifies these entries. Then the company posts the closing entries to the ledger accounts.

Companies generally prepare closing entries directly from the adjusted balances in the ledger. They could prepare separate closing entries for each nominal account, but the following four entries accomplish the desired result more efficiently:

1. Debit each revenue account for its balance, and credit Income Summary for total revenues.
2. Debit Income Summary for total expenses, and credit each expense account for its balance.

---

[1]We explain closing entries for a partnership and for a corporation in Chapters 12 and 13, respectively.

Helpful Hint

Owner's Drawings is closed directly to Owner's Capital and *not* to Income Summary; Owner's Drawings is not an expense.

3. Debit Income Summary and credit Owner's Capital for the amount of net income.

4. Debit Owner's Capital for the balance in the Owner's Drawings account, and credit Owner's Drawings for the same amount.

Illustration 4-6 presents a diagram of the closing process. In it, the boxed numbers refer to the four entries required in the closing process.

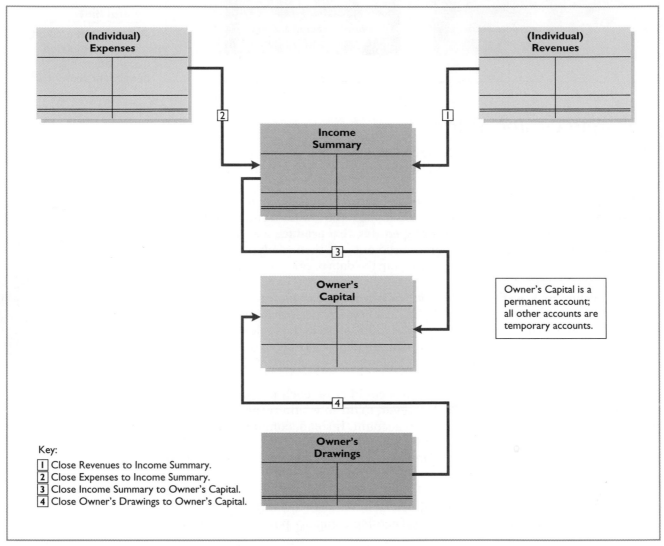

Illustration 4-6
Diagram of closing process—proprietorship

If there were a net loss (because expenses exceeded revenues), entry 3 in Illustration 4-6 would be reversed: there would be a credit to Income Summary and a debit to Owner's Capital.

CLOSING ENTRIES ILLUSTRATED

In practice, companies generally prepare closing entries only at the end of the annual accounting period. However, to illustrate the journalizing and posting of closing entries, we will assume that Pioneer Advertising Agency closes its books monthly. Illustration 4-7 shows the closing entries at October 31. (The numbers in parentheses before each entry correspond to the four entries diagrammed in Illustration 4-6.)

Illustration 4-7
Closing entries journalized

Date	Account Titles and Explanation	Ref.	Debit	Credit
	General Journal **J3**			
	<u>Closing Entries</u>			
2012	(1)			
Oct. 31	Service Revenue	400	10,600	
	Income Summary	350		10,600
	(To close revenue account)			
	(2)			
31	Income Summary	350	7,740	
	Supplies Expense	631		1,500
	Depreciation Expense	711		40
	Insurance Expense	722		50
	Salaries and Wages Expense	726		5,200
	Rent Expense	729		900
	Interest Expense	905		50
	(To close expense accounts)			
	(3)			
31	Income Summary	350	2,860	
	Owner's Capital	301		2,860
	(To close net income to capital)			
	(4)			
31	Owner's Capital	301	500	
	Owner's Drawings	306		500
	(To close drawings to capital)			

Note that the amounts for Income Summary in entries (1) and (2) are the totals of the income statement credit and debit columns, respectively, in the worksheet.

A couple of cautions in preparing closing entries: (1) Avoid unintentionally doubling the revenue and expense balances rather than zeroing them. (2) Do not close Owner's Drawings through the Income Summary account. **Owner's Drawings is not an expense, and it is not a factor in determining net income.**

Posting Closing Entries

Illustration 4-8 (page 164) shows the posting of the closing entries and the ruling of the accounts. Note that all temporary accounts have zero balances after posting the closing entries. In addition, notice that the balance in owner's capital (Owner's Capital) represents the total equity of the owner at the end of the accounting period. This balance is shown on the balance sheet and is the ending capital reported on the owner's equity statement, as shown in Illustration 4-4 on page 159. Pioneer uses the Income Summary account only in closing. It does not journalize and post entries to this account during the year.

As part of the closing process, Pioneer totals, balances, and double-rules its temporary accounts—revenues, expenses, and owner's drawings, as shown in T account form in Illustration 4-8. It does not close its permanent accounts—assets, liabilities, and owner's capital. Instead, Pioneer draws a single rule beneath the current-period entries for the permanent accounts. The account balance is then entered below the single rule and is carried forward to the next period. (For example, see Owner's Capital.)

Helpful Hint

The balance in Income Summary before it is closed must equal the net income or net loss for the period.

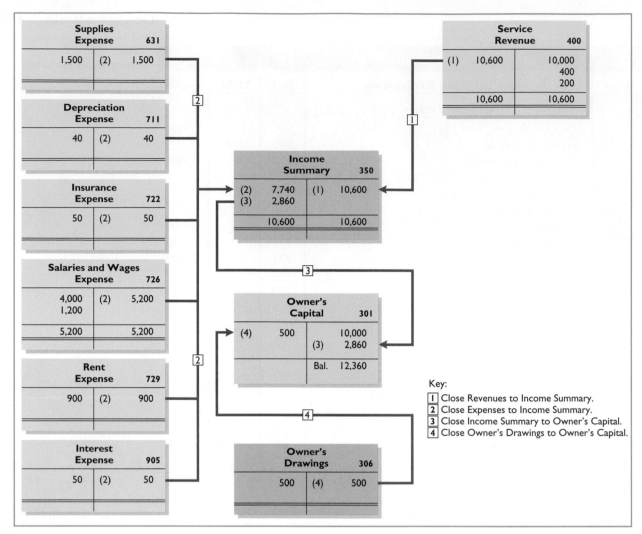

Illustration 4-8
Posting of closing entries

Do it!

Closing Entries

The worksheet for Hancock Company shows the following in the financial statement columns:

> Owner's drawings $15,000
>
> Owner's capital $42,000
>
> Net income $18,000

action plan

✔ Close Income Summary to Owner's Capital.

✔ Close Owner's Drawings to Owner's Capital.

Prepare the closing entries at December 31 that affect owner's capital.

Solution

Dec. 31	Income Summary	18,000	
	Owner's Capital		18,000
	(To close net income to capital)		
31	Owner's Capital	15,000	
	Owner's Drawings		15,000
	(To close drawings to capital)		

Related exercise material: BE4-4, BE4-5, BE4-6, BE4-7, BE4-8, E4-4, E4-7, E4-8, E4-10, E4-11, and **Do it!** 4-2.

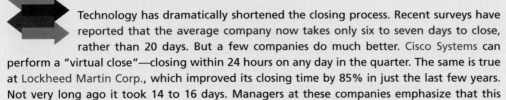

ACCOUNTING ACROSS THE ORGANIZATION

Cisco Performs the Virtual Close

Technology has dramatically shortened the closing process. Recent surveys have reported that the average company now takes only six to seven days to close, rather than 20 days. But a few companies do much better. Cisco Systems can perform a "virtual close"—closing within 24 hours on any day in the quarter. The same is true at Lockheed Martin Corp., which improved its closing time by 85% in just the last few years. Not very long ago it took 14 to 16 days. Managers at these companies emphasize that this increased speed has not reduced the accuracy and completeness of the data.

This is not just showing off. Knowing exactly where you are financially all of the time allows the company to respond faster than competitors. It also means that the hundreds of people who used to spend 10 to 20 days a quarter tracking transactions can now be more usefully employed on things such as mining data for business intelligence to find new business opportunities.

Source: "Reporting Practices: Few Do It All," *Financial Executive* (November 2003), p. 11.

? Who else benefits from a shorter closing process? (See page 204.)

Preparing a Post-Closing Trial Balance

After Pioneer has journalized and posted all closing entries, it prepares another trial balance, called a **post-closing trial balance**, from the ledger. The post-closing trial balance lists permanent accounts and their balances after journalizing and posting of closing entries. The purpose of the post-closing trial balance is **to prove the equality of the permanent account balances carried forward into the next accounting period**. Since all temporary accounts will have zero balances, **the post-closing trial balance will contain only permanent—balance sheet—accounts**.

Illustration 4-9 shows the post-closing trial balance for Pioneer Advertising Agency.

> **Study Objective [3]**
> Describe the content and purpose of a post-closing trial balance.

Illustration 4-9
Post-closing trial balance

Pioneer Advertising Agency Post-Closing Trial Balance October 31, 2012		
	Debit	**Credit**
Cash	$15,200	
Accounts Receivable	200	
Supplies	1,000	
Prepaid Insurance	550	
Office Equipment	5,000	
Accumulated Depreciation—Equipment		$ 40
Notes Payable		5,000
Accounts Payable		2,500
Unearned Service Revenue		800
Salaries and Wages Payable		1,200
Interest Payable		50
Owner's Capital		12,360
	$21,950	$21,950

Pioneer prepares the post-closing trial balance from the permanent accounts in the ledger. Illustration 4-10 shows the permanent accounts in Pioneer's general ledger.

Illustration 4-10
General ledger, permanent accounts

(Permanent Accounts Only)

General Ledger

Cash   No. 101

Date	Explanation	Ref.	Debit	Credit	Balance
2012					
Oct. 1		J1	10,000		10,000
2		J1	1,200		11,200
3		J1		900	10,300
4		J1		600	9,700
20		J1		500	9,200
26		J1		4,000	5,200
31		J1	10,000		**15,200**

Accounts Receivable   No. 112

Date	Explanation	Ref.	Debit	Credit	Balance
2012					
Oct. 31	Adj. entry	J2	**200**		**200**

Supplies   No. 126

Date	Explanation	Ref.	Debit	Credit	Balance
2012					
Oct. 5		J1	2,500		2,500
31	Adj. entry	J2		**1,500**	**1,000**

Prepaid Insurance   No. 130

Date	Explanation	Ref.	Debit	Credit	Balance
2012					
Oct. 4		J1	600		600
31	Adj. entry	J2		**50**	**550**

Equipment   No. 157

Date	Explanation	Ref.	Debit	Credit	Balance
2012					
Oct. 1		J1	5,000		**5,000**

Accumulated Depreciation—Equipment   No. 158

Date	Explanation	Ref.	Debit	Credit	Balance
2012					
Oct. 31	Adj. entry	J2		**40**	**40**

Notes Payable   No. 200

Date	Explanation	Ref.	Debit	Credit	Balance
2012					
Oct. 1		J1		5,000	**5,000**

Accounts Payable   No. 201

Date	Explanation	Ref.	Debit	Credit	Balance
2012					
Oct. 5		J1		2,500	**2,500**

Unearned Service Revenue   No. 209

Date	Explanation	Ref.	Debit	Credit	Balance
2012					
Oct. 2		J1		1,200	1,200
31	Adj. entry	J2	400		**800**

Salaries and Wages Payable   No. 212

Date	Explanation	Ref.	Debit	Credit	Balance
2012					
Oct. 31	Adj. entry	J2		**1,200**	**1,200**

Interest Payable   No. 230

Date	Explanation	Ref.	Debit	Credit	Balance
2012					
Oct. 31	Adj. entry	J2		**50**	**50**

Owner's Capital   No. 301

Date	Explanation	Ref.	Debit	Credit	Balance
2012					
Oct. 1		J1		10,000	10,000
31	Closing entry	J3		2,860	12,860
31	Closing entry	J3	500		12,360

Note: The permanent accounts for Pioneer Advertising Agency are shown here; Illustration 4-11 shows the temporary accounts. Both permanent and temporary accounts are part of the general ledger; they are segregated here to aid in learning.

A post-closing trial balance provides evidence that the company has properly journalized and posted the closing entries. It also shows that the accounting equation is in balance at the end of the accounting period. However, like the trial balance, it does not prove that Pioneer has recorded all transactions or that the ledger is correct.

For example, the post-closing trial balance still will balance even if a transaction is not journalized and posted or if a transaction is journalized and posted twice.

The remaining accounts in the general ledger are temporary accounts, shown in Illustration 4-11. After Pioneer correctly posts the closing entries, each temporary account has a zero balance. These accounts are double-ruled to finalize the closing process.

Illustration 4-11
General ledger, temporary accounts

(Temporary Accounts Only)

General Ledger

Owner's Drawings   No. 306

Date	Explanation	Ref.	Debit	Credit	Balance
2012					
Oct. 20		J1	500		500
31	Closing entry	J3		500	–0–

Income Summary   No. 350

Date	Explanation	Ref.	Debit	Credit	Balance
2012					
Oct. 31	Closing entry	J3		10,600	10,600
31	Closing entry	J3	7,740		2,860
31	Closing entry	J3	2,860		–0–

Service Revenue   No. 400

Date	Explanation	Ref.	Debit	Credit	Balance
2012					
Oct. 31		J1		10,000	10,000
31	Adj. entry	J2		400	10,400
31	Adj. entry	J2		200	10,600
31	Closing entry	J3	10,600		–0–

Supplies Expense   No. 631

Date	Explanation	Ref.	Debit	Credit	Balance
2012					
Oct. 31	Adj. entry	J2	1,500		1,500
31	Closing entry	J3		1,500	–0–

Depreciation Expense   No. 711

Date	Explanation	Ref.	Debit	Credit	Balance
2012					
Oct. 31	Adj. entry	J2	40		40
31	Closing entry	J3		40	–0–

Insurance Expense   No. 722

Date	Explanation	Ref.	Debit	Credit	Balance
2012					
Oct. 31	Adj. entry	J2	50		50
31	Closing entry	J3		50	–0–

Salaries and Wages Expense   No. 726

Date	Explanation	Ref.	Debit	Credit	Balance
2012					
Oct. 26		J1	4,000		4,000
31	Adj. entry	J2	1,200		5,200
31	Closing entry	J3		5,200	–0–

Rent Expense   No. 729

Date	Explanation	Ref.	Debit	Credit	Balance
2012					
Oct. 3		J1	900		900
31	Closing entry	J3		900	–0–

Interest Expense   No. 905

Date	Explanation	Ref.	Debit	Credit	Balance
2012					
Oct. 31	Adj. entry	J2	50		50
31	Closing entry	J3		50	–0–

Note: The temporary accounts for Pioneer Advertising Agency are shown here; Illustration 4-10 shows the permanent accounts. Both permanent and temporary accounts are part of the general ledger; they are segregated here to aid in learning.

Summary of the Accounting Cycle

Illustration 4-12 (page 168) summarizes the steps in the accounting cycle. You can see that the cycle begins with the analysis of business transactions and ends with the preparation of a post-closing trial balance.

Steps 1–3 may occur daily during the accounting period, as explained in Chapter 2. Companies perform Steps 4–7 on a periodic basis, such as monthly, quarterly, or annually. Steps 8 and 9—closing entries, and a post-closing trial balance—usually take place only at the end of a company's **annual** accounting period.

Study Objective [4]
State the required steps in the accounting cycle.

Illustration 4-12
Steps in the accounting cycle

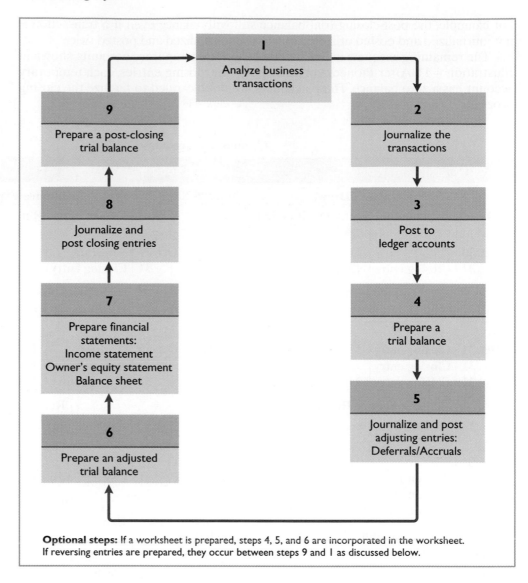

Optional steps: If a worksheet is prepared, steps 4, 5, and 6 are incorporated in the worksheet. If reversing entries are prepared, they occur between steps 9 and 1 as discussed below.

There are also two **optional steps** in the accounting cycle. As you have seen, companies may use a worksheet in preparing adjusting entries and financial statements. In addition, they may use reversing entries, as explained below.

Reversing Entries—An Optional Step

Some accountants prefer to reverse certain adjusting entries by making a **reversing entry** at the beginning of the next accounting period. A reversing entry is the exact opposite of the adjusting entry made in the previous period. **Use of reversing entries is an optional bookkeeping procedure; it is not a required step in the accounting cycle.** Accordingly, we have chosen to cover this topic in an appendix at the end of the chapter.

Study Objective [5]

Explain the approaches to preparing correcting entries.

Correcting Entries—An Avoidable Step

Unfortunately, errors may occur in the recording process. Companies should correct errors, **as soon as they discover them**, by journalizing and posting correcting entries. If the accounting records are free of errors, no correcting entries are needed.

You should recognize several differences between correcting entries and adjusting entries. First, adjusting entries are an integral part of the accounting cycle. Correcting entries, on the other hand, are unnecessary if the records are error-free. Second, companies journalize and post adjustments **only at the end of an accounting period**. In contrast, companies make correcting entries **whenever they discover an error**. Finally, adjusting entries always affect at least one balance sheet account and one income statement account. In contrast, correcting entries may involve any combination of accounts in need of correction. **Correcting entries must be posted before closing entries.**

To determine the correcting entry, it is useful to compare the incorrect entry with the correct entry. Doing so helps identify the accounts and amounts that should—and should not—be corrected. After comparison, the accountant makes an entry to correct the accounts. The following two cases for Mercato Co. illustrate this approach.

> **Ethics Note**
>
> When companies find errors in previously released income statements, they restate those numbers. Perhaps because of the increased scrutiny caused by Sarbanes-Oxley, in a recent year companies filed a record 1,195 restatements.

CASE 1

On May 10, Mercato Co. journalized and posted a $50 cash collection on account from a customer as a debit to Cash $50 and a credit to Service Revenue $50. The company discovered the error on May 20, when the customer paid the remaining balance in full.

Incorrect Entry (May 10)			Correct Entry (May 10)		
Cash	50		Cash	50	
Service Revenue		50	Accounts Receivable		50

Illustration 4-13
Comparison of entries

Comparison of the incorrect entry with the correct entry reveals that the debit to Cash $50 is correct. However, the $50 credit to Service Revenue should have been credited to Accounts Receivable. As a result, both Service Revenue and Accounts Receivable are overstated in the ledger. Mercato makes the following correcting entry.

	Correcting Entry		
May 20	Service Revenue	50	
	Accounts Receivable		50
	(To correct entry of May 10)		

Illustration 4-14
Correcting entry

A = L + OE
-50   -50 Rev

Cash Flows
no effect

CASE 2

On May 18, Mercato purchased on account equipment costing $450. The transaction was journalized and posted as a debit to Equipment $45 and a credit to Accounts Payable $45. The error was discovered on June 3, when Mercato received the monthly statement for May from the creditor.

Incorrect Entry (May 18)			Correct Entry (May 18)		
Equipment	45		Equipment	450	
Accounts Payable		45	Accounts Payable		450

Illustration 4-15
Comparison of entries

Comparison of the two entries shows that two accounts are incorrect. Equipment is understated $405, and Accounts Payable is understated $405. Mercato makes the following correcting entry.

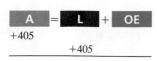

+405
　　　　+405

Cash Flows
no effect

Illustration 4-16
Correcting entry

		Correcting Entry		
June 3	Equipment		405	
	Accounts Payable			405
	(To correct entry of May 18)			

Instead of preparing a correcting entry, **it is possible to reverse the incorrect entry and then prepare the correct entry**. This approach will result in more entries and postings than a correcting entry, but it will accomplish the desired result.

ACCOUNTING ACROSS THE ORGANIZATION

Yale Express Loses Some Transportation Bills

Yale Express, a short-haul trucking firm, turned over much of its cargo to local truckers to complete deliveries. Yale collected the entire delivery charge; when billed by the local trucker, Yale sent payment for the final phase to the local trucker. Yale used a cutoff period of 20 days into the next accounting period in making its adjusting entries for accrued liabilities. That is, it waited 20 days to receive the local truckers' bills to determine the amount of the unpaid but incurred delivery charges as of the balance sheet date.

On the other hand, Republic Carloading, a nationwide, long-distance freight forwarder, frequently did not receive transportation bills from truckers to whom it passed on cargo until months after the year-end. In making its year-end adjusting entries, Republic waited for months in order to include all of these outstanding transportation bills.

When Yale Express merged with Republic Carloading, Yale's vice president employed the 20-day cutoff procedure for both firms. As a result, millions of dollars of Republic's accrued transportation bills went unrecorded. When the company detected the error and made correcting entries, these and other errors changed a reported profit of $1.14 million into a loss of $1.88 million!

? What might Yale Express's vice president have done to produce more accurate financial statements without waiting months for Republic's outstanding transportation bills? (See page 204.)

The Classified Balance Sheet

Study Objective [6]

Identify the sections of a classified balance sheet.

The balance sheet presents a snapshot of a company's financial position at a point in time. To improve users' understanding of a company's financial position, companies often use a classified balance sheet. A **classified balance sheet** groups together similar assets and similar liabilities, using a number of standard classifications and sections. This is useful because items within a group have similar economic characteristics. A classified balance sheet generally contains the standard classifications listed in Illustration 4-17.

Illustration 4-17
Standard balance sheet classifications

Assets	**Liabilities and Owner's Equity**
Current assets	Current liabilities
Long-term investments	Long-term liabilities
Property, plant, and equipment	Owner's (Stockholders') equity
Intangible assets	

These groupings help readers determine such things as (1) whether the company has enough assets to pay its debts as they come due, and (2) the claims of short- and long-term creditors on the company's total assets. Many of these groupings can be seen in the balance sheet of Franklin Company shown in Illustration 4-18 below. In the sections that follow, we explain each of these groupings.

Illustration 4-18
Classified balance sheet

Franklin Company
Balance Sheet
October 31, 2012

Assets

Current assets			
Cash		$ 6,600	
Short-term investments		2,000	
Accounts receivable		7,000	
Notes receivable		1,000	
Inventory		3,000	
Supplies		2,100	
Prepaid insurance		400	
Total current assets			$22,100
Long-term investments			
Investment in stock of Walters Corp.		5,200	
Investment in real estate		2,000	7,200
Property, plant, and equipment			
Land		10,000	
Equipment	$24,000		
Less: Accumulated depreciation— equipment	5,000	19,000	29,000
Intangible assets			
Patents			3,100
Total assets			$61,400

Liabilities and Owner's Equity

Current liabilities		
Notes payable	$11,000	
Accounts payable	2,100	
Salaries and wages payable	1,600	
Unearned service revenue	900	
Interest payable	450	
Total current liabilities		$16,050
Long-term liabilities		
Mortgage payable	10,000	
Notes payable	1,300	
Total long-term liabilities		11,300
Total liabilities		27,350
Owner's equity		
Owner's capital		34,050
Total liabilities and owner's equity		$61,400

Helpful Hint

Recall that the basic accounting equation is Assets = Liabilities + Owner's Equity.

Current Assets

Current assets are assets that a company expects to convert to cash or use up within one year or its operating cycle, whichever is longer. In Illustration 4-18, Franklin Company had current assets of $22,100. For most businesses the cutoff for classification as current assets is one year from the balance sheet date. For example, accounts receivable are current assets because the company will collect them and convert them to cash within one year. Supplies is a current asset because the company expects to use it up in operations within one year.

Some companies use a period longer than one year to classify assets and liabilities as current because they have an operating cycle longer than one year. The **operating cycle** of a company is the average time that it takes to purchase inventory, sell it on account, and then collect cash from customers. For most businesses this cycle takes less than a year, so they use a one-year cutoff. But, for some businesses, such as vineyards or airplane manufacturers, this period may be longer than a year. **Except where noted, we will assume that companies use one year to determine whether an asset or liability is current or long-term.**

Common types of current assets are (1) cash, (2) short-term investments (such as short-term U.S. government securities), (3) receivables (notes receivable, accounts receivable, and interest receivable), (4) inventories, and (5) prepaid expenses (insurance and supplies). **On the balance sheet, companies usually list these items in the order in which they expect to convert them into cash.**

Illustration 4-19 presents the current assets of Southwest Airlines Co.

Illustration 4-19
Current assets section

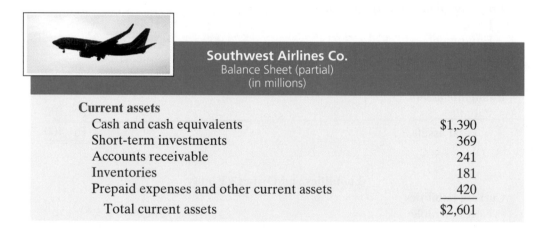

Southwest Airlines Co. Balance Sheet (partial) (in millions)	
Current assets	
Cash and cash equivalents	$1,390
Short-term investments	369
Accounts receivable	241
Inventories	181
Prepaid expenses and other current assets	420
Total current assets	$2,601

As explained later in the chapter, a company's current assets are important in assessing its short-term debt-paying ability.

Long-Term Investments

Alternative Terminology

Long-term investments are often referred to simply as *investments.*

Long-term investments are generally, (1) investments in stocks and bonds of other companies that are normally held for many years, and (2) long-term assets such as land or buildings that a company is not currently using in its operating activities. In Illustration 4-18, Franklin Company reported total long-term investments of $7,200 on its balance sheet.

Yahoo! Inc. reported long-term investments in its balance sheet as shown in Illustration 4-20.

Yahoo! Inc. Balance Sheet (partial) (in thousands)	
Long-term investments	
Long-term investments in marketable securities	$90,266

Illustration 4-20
Long-term investments
section

Property, Plant, and Equipment

Property, plant, and equipment are assets with relatively long useful lives that a company is currently using in operating the business. This category (sometimes called *fixed assets*) includes land, buildings, machinery and equipment, delivery equipment, and furniture. In Illustration 4-18, Franklin Company reported property, plant, and equipment of $29,000.

Depreciation is the practice of allocating the cost of assets to a number of years. Companies do this by systematically assigning a portion of an asset's cost as an expense each year (rather than expensing the full purchase price in the year of purchase). The assets that the company depreciates are reported on the balance sheet at cost less accumulated depreciation. The **accumulated depreciation** account shows the total amount of depreciation that the company has expensed thus far in the asset's life. In Illustration 4-18, Franklin Company reported accumulated depreciation of $5,000.

Illustration 4-21 presents the property, plant, and equipment of Cooper Tire & Rubber Company.

> **International Note**
>
> In 2007 China adopted International Financial Reporting Standards (IFRS). This was done in an effort to reduce fraud and increase investor confidence in financial reports. Under these standards, many items, such as property, plant, and equipment, may be reported at current fair values, rather than historical cost.

Cooper Tire & Rubber Company Balance Sheet (partial) (in thousands)		
Property, plant, and equipment		
Land and land improvements	$ 41,553	
Buildings	298,706	
Machinery and equipment	1,636,091	
Molds, cores, and rings	268,158	$2,244,508
Less: Accumulated depreciation		1,252,692
		$ 991,816

Illustration 4-21
Property, plant, and equipment section

Intangible Assets

Many companies have long-lived assets that do not have physical substance yet often are very valuable. We call these assets **intangible assets**. One common intangible asset is goodwill. Others include patents, copyrights, and trademarks or trade names that give the company **exclusive right** of use for a specified period of time. In Illustration 4-18, Franklin Company reported intangible assets of $3,100.

Helpful Hint

Sometimes intangible assets are reported under a broader heading called *"Other assets."*

Illustration 4-22 shows the intangible assets of media giant Time Warner, Inc.

Illustration 4-22
Intangible assets section

Time Warner, Inc.
Balance Sheet (partial)
(in millions)

Intangible assets	
Goodwill	$40,953
Film library	2,690
Customer lists	2,540
Cable television franchises	38,048
Sports franchises	262
Brands, trademarks, and other intangible assets	8,313
	$92,806

Do it!

Asset Section of Balance Sheet

Baxter Hoffman recently received the following information related to Hoffman Company's December 31, 2012, balance sheet.

Prepaid insurance	$ 2,300	Inventory	$3,400
Cash	800	Accumulated depreciation—	
Equipment	10,700	equipment	2,700
		Accounts receivable	1,100

Prepare the asset section of Hoffman Company's balance sheet.

action plan

✔ Present current assets first. Current assets are cash and other resources that the company expects to convert to cash or use up within one year.

✔ Present current assets in the order in which the company expects to convert them into cash.

✔ Subtract accumulated depreciation—equipment from equipment to determine net equipment.

Solution

Assets		
Current assets		
Cash	$ 800	
Accounts receivable	1,100	
Inventory	3,400	
Prepaid insurance	2,300	
Total current assets		$ 7,600
Equipment	10,700	
Less: Accumulated depreciation—equipment	2,700	8,000
Total assets		$15,600

Related exercise material: BE4-10 and **Do it!** 4-3.

The Navigator

Current Liabilities

Ethics Note

A company that has more current assets than current liabilities can increase the ratio of current assets to current liabilities by using cash to pay off some current liabilities. This gives the appearance of being more liquid. Do you think this move is ethical?

In the liabilities and owners' equity section of the balance sheet, the first grouping is current liabilities. **Current liabilities** are obligations that the company is to pay within the coming year or its operating cycle, whichever is longer. Common examples are accounts payable, wages payable, bank loans payable, interest payable, and taxes payable. Also included as current liabilities are current maturities of long-term obligations—payments to be made within the next year on long-term obligations. In Illustration 4-18, Franklin Company reported five different types of current liabilities, for a total of $16,050.

Within the current liabilities section, companies usually list notes payable first, followed by accounts payable. Other items then follow in the order of their magnitude. *In your homework, you should present notes payable first, followed by accounts payable, and then other liabilities in order of magnitude.*

Illustration 4-23 shows the current liabilities section adapted from the balance sheet of Marcus Corporation.

Illustration 4-23
Current liabilities section

Marcus Corporation Balance Sheet (partial) (in thousands)		
Current liabilities		
Notes payable	$	239
Accounts payable		24,242
Current maturities of long-term debt		57,250
Other current liabilities		27,477
Taxes payable		11,215
Accrued compensation payable		6,720
Total current liabilities		$127,143

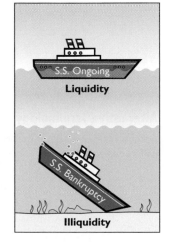

Users of financial statements look closely at the relationship between current assets and current liabilities. This relationship is important in evaluating a company's liquidity—its ability to pay obligations expected to be due within the next year. When current assets exceed current liabilities at the balance sheet date, the likelihood for paying the liabilities is favorable. When the reverse is true, short-term creditors may not be paid, and the company may ultimately be forced into bankruptcy.

ACCOUNTING ACROSS THE ORGANIZATION

Can a Company Be Too Liquid?

There actually is a point where a company can be too liquid—that is, it can have too much working capital (current assets less current liabilities). While it is important to be liquid enough to be able to pay short-term bills as they come due, a company does not want to tie up its cash in extra inventory or receivables that are not earning the company money.

By one estimate from the REL Consultancy Group, the thousand largest U.S. companies have on their books cumulative excess working capital of $764 billion. Based on this figure, companies could have reduced debt by 36% or increased net income by 9%. Given that managers throughout a company are interested in improving profitability, it is clear that they should have an eye toward managing working capital. They need to aim for a "Goldilocks solution"—not too much, not too little, but just right.

Source: K. Richardson, "Companies Fall Behind in Cash Management," *Wall Street Journal* (June 19, 2007).

? What can various company managers do to ensure that working capital is managed efficiently to maximize net income? (See page 204.)

Long-Term Liabilities

Long-term liabilities are obligations that a company expects to pay **after** one year. Liabilities in this category include bonds payable, mortgages payable, long-term notes payable, lease liabilities, and pension liabilities. Many companies report long-term debt maturing after one year as a single amount in the balance sheet and show the details of the debt in notes that accompany the financial statements. Others list the various types of long-term liabilities. In Illustration 4-18, Franklin Company reported long-term liabilities of $11,300. *In your homework, list long-term liabilities in the order of their magnitude.*

Illustration 4-24 shows the long-term liabilities that The Procter & Gamble Company reported in its balance sheet.

Illustration 4-24
Long-term liabilities section

The Procter & Gamble Company Balance Sheet (partial) (in millions)	
Long-term liabilities	
Long-term debt	$23,375
Deferred income taxes	12,015
Other noncurrent liabilities	5,147
Total long-term liabilities	$40,537

Owner's Equity

Alternative Terminology

Common stock is sometimes called *capital stock*.

The content of the owner's equity section varies with the form of business organization. In a proprietorship, there is one capital account. In a partnership, there is a capital account for each partner. Corporations divide owners' equity into two accounts— Common Stock (sometimes referred to as Capital Stock) and Retained Earnings. Corporations record stockholders' investments in the company by debiting an asset account and crediting the Common Stock account. They record in the Retained Earnings account income retained for use in the business. Corporations combine the Common Stock and Retained Earnings accounts and report them on the balance sheet as **stockholders' equity**. (We'll learn more about these corporation accounts in later chapters.) Nordstrom, Inc. recently reported its stockholders' equity section as follows.

Illustration 4-25
Stockholders' equity section

Nordstrom, Inc. Balance Sheet (partial) ($ in thousands)	
Stockholders' equity	
Common stock, 271,331 shares	$ 685,934
Retained earnings	1,406,747
Total stockholders' equity	$2,092,681

Do it!

Balance Sheet Classifications

The following accounts were taken from the financial statements of Callahan Company.

_____ Salaries and wages payable   _____ Investment in real estate
_____ Service revenue   _____ Equipment
_____ Interest payable   _____ Accumulated depreciation—
_____ Goodwill   equipment
_____ Short-term investments   _____ Depreciation expense
_____ Mortgage payable (due in 3 years)   _____ Owner's capital
                                          _____ Unearned service revenue

Match each of the following accounts to its proper balance sheet classification, shown below. If the item would not appear on a balance sheet, use "NA."

Current assets (CA)
Long-term investments (LTI)
Property, plant, and equipment (PPE)
Intangible assets (IA)

Current liabilities (CL)
Long-term liabilities (LTL)
Owner's equity (OE)

action plan

✔ Analyze whether each financial statement item is an asset, liability, or owner's equity.

✔ Determine if asset and liability items are short-term or long-term.

Solution

_CL_	Salaries and wages payable	_LTI_	Investment in real estate
_NA_	Service revenue	_PPE_	Equipment
_CL_	Interest payable	_PPE_	Accumulated depreciation—
_IA_	Goodwill		equipment
_CA_	Short-term investments	_NA_	Depreciation expense
LTL	Mortgage payable (due	_OE_	Owner's capital
	in 3 years)	_CL_	Unearned service revenue

Related exercise material: BE4-11, E4-14, E4-15, E4-16, E4-17, and **Do it!** 4-4.

✔
The Navigator

COMPREHENSIVE

Do it!

At the end of its first month of operations, Watson Answering Service has the following unadjusted trial balance.

WATSON ANSWERING SERVICE
August 31, 2012
Trial Balance

	Debit	Credit
Cash	$ 5,400	
Accounts Receivable	2,800	
Supplies	1,300	
Prepaid Insurance	2,400	
Equipment	60,000	
Notes Payable		$40,000
Accounts Payable		2,400
Owner's Capital		30,000
Owner's Drawings	1,000	
Service Revenue		4,900
Salaries and Wages Expense	3,200	
Utilities Expense	800	
Advertising Expense	400	
	$77,300	$77,300

action plan

✔ In completing the worksheet, be sure to (a) key the adjustments; (b) start at the top of the adjusted trial balance columns and extend adjusted balances to the correct statement columns; and (c) enter net income (or net loss) in the proper columns.

✔ In preparing a classified balance sheet, know the contents of each of the sections.

✔ In journalizing closing entries, remember that there are only four entries and that owner's drawings is closed to owner's capital.

Other data:

1. Insurance expires at the rate of $200 per month.
2. $1,000 of supplies are on hand at August 31.
3. Monthly depreciation on the equipment is $900.
4. Interest of $500 on the notes payable has accrued during August.

Instructions

(a) Prepare a worksheet.

(b) Prepare a classified balance sheet assuming $35,000 of the notes payable are long-term.

(c) Journalize the closing entries.

Solution to Comprehensive Do it!

(a)

WATSON ANSWERING SERVICE
Worksheet for the Month Ended August 31, 2012

Account Titles	Trial Balance Dr.	Trial Balance Cr.	Adjustments Dr.	Adjustments Cr.	Adjusted Trial Balance Dr.	Adjusted Trial Balance Cr.	Income Statement Dr.	Income Statement Cr.	Balance Sheet Dr.	Balance Sheet Cr.
Cash	5,400				5,400				5,400	
Accounts Receivable	2,800				2,800				2,800	
Supplies	1,300			(b) 300	1,000				1,000	
Prepaid Insurance	2,400			(a) 200	2,200				2,200	
Equipment	60,000				60,000				60,000	
Notes Payable		40,000				40,000				40,000
Accounts Payable		2,400				2,400				2,400
Owner's Capital		30,000				30,000				30,000
Owner's Drawings	1,000				1,000				1,000	
Service Revenue		4,900				4,900		4,900		
Salaries and										
Wages Expense	3,200				3,200		3,200			
Utilities Expense	800				800		800			
Advertising Expense	400				400		400			
Totals	77,300	77,300								
Insurance Expense			(a) 200		200		200			
Supplies Expense			(b) 300		300		300			
Depreciation Expense			(c) 900		900		900			
Accumulated Depreciation—										
Equipment				(c) 900		900				900
Interest Expense			(d) 500		500		500			
Interest Payable				(d) 500		500				500
Totals			1,900	1,900	78,700	78,700	6,300	4,900	72,400	73,800
Net Loss								1,400	1,400	
Totals							6,300	6,300	73,800	73,800

Explanation: (a) Insurance expired, (b) Supplies used, (c) Depreciation expensed, (d) Interest accrued.

(b)

WATSON ANSWERING SERVICE
Balance Sheet
August 31, 2012

Assets

Current assets		
Cash	$ 5,400	
Accounts receivable	2,800	
Supplies	1,000	
Prepaid insurance	2,200	
Total current assets		$11,400
Property, plant, and equipment		
Equipment	60,000	
Less: Accumulated depreciation—equipment	900	59,100
Total assets		$70,500

Liabilities and Owner's Equity

Current liabilities		
Notes payable	$ 5,000	
Accounts payable	2,400	
Interest payable	500	
Total current liabilities		$ 7,900
Long-term liabilities		
Notes payable		35,000
Total liabilities		42,900
Owner's equity		
Owner's capital		27,600*
Total liabilities and owner's equity		$70,500

*Owner's capital, $30,000 less drawings $1,000 and net loss $1,400.

(c)

Aug. 31	Service Revenue	4,900	
	Income Summary		4,900
	(To close revenue account)		
31	Income Summary	6,300	
	Salaries and Wages Expense		3,200
	Depreciation Expense		900
	Utilities Expense		800
	Interest Expense		500
	Advertising Expense		400
	Supplies Expense		300
	Insurance Expense		200
	(To close expense accounts)		
31	Owner's Capital	1,400	
	Income Summary		1,400
	(To close net loss to capital)		
31	Owner's Capital	1,000	
	Owner's Drawings		1,000
	(To close drawings to capital)		

The Navigator

Summary of Study Objectives

[1] Prepare a worksheet. The steps in preparing a worksheet are: (a) Prepare a trial balance on the worksheet. (b) Enter the adjustments in the adjustments columns. (c) Enter adjusted balances in the adjusted trial balance columns. (d) Extend adjusted trial balance amounts to appropriate financial statement columns. (e) Total the statement columns, compute net income (or net loss), and complete the worksheet.

[2] Explain the process of closing the books. Closing the books occurs at the end of an accounting period. The process is to journalize and post closing entries and then rule and balance all accounts. In closing the books, companies make separate entries to close revenues and expenses to Income Summary, Income Summary to Owner's Capital, and Owner's Drawings to Owner's Capital. Only temporary accounts are closed.

[3] Describe the content and purpose of a post-closing trial balance. A post-closing trial balance contains the balances in permanent accounts that are carried forward to the next accounting period. The purpose of this trial balance is to prove the equality of these balances.

[4] State the required steps in the accounting cycle. The required steps in the accounting cycle are: (1) analyze business transactions, (2) journalize the transactions, (3) post to ledger accounts, (4) prepare a trial balance, (5) journalize and post adjusting entries, (6) prepare an adjusted trial balance, (7) prepare financial statements, (8) journalize and post closing entries, and (9) prepare a post-closing trial balance.

[5] Explain the approaches to preparing correcting entries. One way to determine the correcting entry is to compare the incorrect entry with the correct entry. After comparison, the company makes a correcting entry to correct the accounts. An alternative to a correcting entry is to reverse the incorrect entry and then prepare the correct entry.

[6] Identify the sections of a classified balance sheet. A classified balance sheet categorizes assets as current assets; long-term investments; property, plant, and equipment; and intangibles. Liabilities are classified as either current or long-term. There is also an owner's (owners') equity section, which varies with the form of business organization.

The Navigator

Glossary

Classified balance sheet   A balance sheet that contains standard classifications or sections. (p. 170).

Closing entries   Entries made at the end of an accounting period to transfer the balances of temporary accounts to a permanent owner's equity account, Owner's Capital. (p. 161).

Correcting entries   Entries to correct errors made in recording transactions. (p. 168).

Current assets   Assets that a company expects to convert to cash or use up within one year. (p. 172).

Current liabilities   Obligations that a company expects to pay from existing current assets within the coming year. (p. 174).

Income Summary   A temporary account used in closing revenue and expense accounts. (p. 161).

Intangible assets   Noncurrent assets that do not have physical substance. (p. 173).

Liquidity   The ability of a company to pay obligations expected to be due within the next year. (p. 175).

Long-term investments   Generally, (1) investments in stocks and bonds of other companies that companies normally hold for many years, and (2) long-term assets, such as land and buildings, not currently being used in operations. (p. 172).

Long-term liabilities   Obligations that a company expects to pay after one year. (p. 175).

Operating cycle   The average time that it takes to go from cash to cash in producing revenues. (p. 172).

Permanent (real) accounts   Accounts that relate to one or more accounting periods. Consist of all balance sheet accounts. Balances are carried forward to next accounting period. (p. 160).

Post-closing trial balance   A list of permanent accounts and their balances after a company has journalized and posted closing entries. (p. 165).

Property, plant, and equipment   Assets with relatively long useful lives and currently being used in operations. (p. 173).

Reversing entry   An entry, made at the beginning of the next accounting period, that is the exact opposite of the adjusting entry made in the previous period. (p. 168).

Stockholders' equity   The ownership claim of shareholders on total assets. It is to a corporation what owner's equity is to a proprietorship. (p. 176).

Temporary (nominal) accounts   Accounts that relate only to a given accounting period. Consist of all income statement accounts and owner's drawings account. All temporary accounts are closed at end of the accounting period. (p. 160).

Worksheet   A multiple-column form that may be used in making adjusting entries and in preparing financial statements. (p. 154).

APPENDIX4A

Reversing Entries

After preparing the financial statements and closing the books, it is often helpful to reverse some of the adjusting entries before recording the regular transactions of the next period. Such entries are **reversing entries**. Companies make **a reversing entry at the beginning of the next accounting period**. Each reversing entry **is the exact opposite of the adjusting entry made in the previous period**. The recording of reversing entries is an **optional step** in the accounting cycle.

Study Objective [7]
Prepare reversing entries.

The purpose of reversing entries is to simplify the recording of a subsequent transaction related to an adjusting entry. For example, in Chapter 3 (page 116), the payment of salaries after an adjusting entry resulted in two debits: one to Salaries and Wages Payable and the other to Salaries and Wages Expense. With reversing entries, the company can debit the entire subsequent payment to Salaries and Wages Expense. **The use of reversing entries does not change the amounts reported in the financial statements.** What it does is simplify the recording of subsequent transactions.

Reversing Entries Example

Companies most often use reversing entries to reverse two types of adjusting entries: accrued revenues and accrued expenses. To illustrate the optional use of reversing entries for accrued expenses, we will use the salaries expense transactions for Pioneer Advertising Agency as illustrated in Chapters 2, 3, and 4. The transaction and adjustment data are as follows.

1. October 26 (initial salary entry): Pioneer pays $4,000 of salaries and wages earned between October 15 and October 26.

2. October 31 (adjusting entry): Salaries and wages earned between October 29 and October 31 are $1,200. The company will pay these in the November 9 payroll.

3. November 9 (subsequent salary entry): Salaries and wages paid are $4,000. Of this amount, $1,200 applied to accrued salaries and wages payable and $2,800 was earned between November 1 and November 9.

Illustration 4A-1 (page 182) shows the entries with and without reversing entries.

The first three entries are the same whether or not Pioneer uses reversing entries. The last two entries are different. The November 1 **reversing entry** eliminates the $1,200 balance in Salaries and Wages Payable created by the October 31 adjusting entry. The reversing entry also creates a $1,200 credit balance in the Salaries and Wages Expense account. As you know, it is unusual for an expense account to have a credit balance. The balance is correct in this instance, though, because it anticipates that the entire amount of the first salaries and wages payment in the new accounting period will be debited to Salaries and Wages Expense. This debit will eliminate the credit balance. The resulting debit balance in the expense account will equal the salaries and wages expense incurred in the new accounting period ($2,800 in this example).

If Pioneer makes reversing entries, it can debit all cash payments of expenses to the expense account. This means that on November 9 (and every payday) Pioneer can debit Salaries and Wages Expense for the amount paid, without regard to any accrued salaries and wages payable. Being able to make the **same entry each time**

Without Reversing Entries (per chapter)				**With Reversing Entries** (per appendix)			
Initial Salary Entry				**Initial Salary Entry**			
Oct. 26	Salaries and Wages Expense	4,000		Oct. 26	(Same entry)		
	Cash		4,000				
Adjusting Entry				**Adjusting Entry**			
Oct. 31	Salaries and Wages Expense	1,200		Oct. 31	(Same entry)		
	Salaries and Wages Payable		1,200				
Closing Entry				**Closing Entry**			
Oct. 31	Income Summary	5,200		Oct. 31	(Same entry)		
	Salaries and Wages Expense		5,200				
Reversing Entry				**Reversing Entry**			
Nov. 1	No reversing entry is made.			Nov. 1	**Salaries and Wages Payable**	**1,200**	
					Salaries and Wages Expense		**1,200**
Subsequent Salary Entry				**Subsequent Salary Entry**			
Nov. 9	Salaries and Wages Payable	1,200		Nov. 9	**Salaries and Wages Expense**	**4,000**	
	Salaries and Wages Expense	2,800			**Cash**		**4,000**
	Cash		4,000				

Illustration 4A-1
Comparative entries—not reversing vs. reversing

simplifies the recording process: The company can record subsequent transactions as if the related adjusting entry had never been made.

Illustration 4A-2 shows the posting of the entries with reversing entries.

Salaries and Wages Expense				**Salaries and Wages Payable**			
10/26 Paid	4,000	10/31 Closing	5,200	11/1 Reversing	1,200	10/31 Adjusting	1,200
31 Adjusting	1,200						
	5,200		5,200				
11/9 Paid	4,000	11/1 Reversing	1,200				

Illustration 4A-2
Postings with reversing entries

A company can also use reversing entries for accrued revenue adjusting entries. For Pioneer Advertising, the adjusting entry was: Accounts Receivable (Dr.) $200 and Service Revenue (Cr.) $200. Thus, the reversing entry on November 1 is:

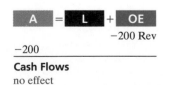

A	=	L	+	OE
				−200 Rev
−200				

Cash Flows
no effect

Nov. 1	Service Revenue	200	
	Accounts Receivable		200
	(To reverse October 31 adjusting entry)		

When Pioneer collects the accrued service revenue, it debits Cash and credits Service Revenue.

Summary of Study Objective for Appendix 4A

[7] **Prepare reversing entries.** Reversing entries are the opposite of the adjusting entries made in the preceding period. Some companies choose to make reversing entries at the beginning of a new accounting period to simplify the recording of later transactions related to the adjusting entries. In most cases, only accrued adjusting entries are reversed.

Self-Test, Brief Exercises, Exercises, Problem Set A, and many more components are available for practice in *WileyPLUS*

Note: All asterisked Questions, Exercises, and Problems relate to material in the appendix to the chapter.

Self-Test Questions

Answers are on page 204.

(SO 1) **1.** Which of the following statements is *incorrect* concerning the worksheet?
   a. The worksheet is essentially a working tool of the accountant.
   b. The worksheet is distributed to management and other interested parties.
   c. The worksheet cannot be used as a basis for posting to ledger accounts.
   d. Financial statements can be prepared directly from the worksheet before journalizing and posting the adjusting entries.

(SO 1) **2.** In a worksheet, net income is entered in the following columns:
   a. income statement (Dr) and balance sheet (Dr).
   b. income statement (Cr) and balance sheet (Dr).
   c. income statement (Dr) and balance sheet (Cr).
   d. income statement (Cr) and balance sheet (Cr).

(SO 1) **3.** In the unadjusted trial balance of its worksheet for the year ended December 31, 2012, Taitum Company reported Equipment of $120,000. The year-end adjusting entries require an adjustment of $15,000 for depreciation expense for the equipment. After adjustment, the following adjusted amount should be reported:
   a. A debit of $105,000 for Equipment in the balance sheet column.
   b. A credit of $15,000 for Depreciation Expense—Equipment in the income statement column.
   c. A debit of $120,000 for Equipment in the balance sheet column.
   d. A debit of $15,000 for Accumulated Depreciation—Equipment in the balance sheet column.

(SO 2) **4.** An account that will have a zero balance after closing entries have been journalized and posted is:
   a. Service Revenue.
   b. Supplies.
   c. Prepaid Insurance.
   d. Accumulated Depreciation—Equipment.

(SO 2) **5.** When a net loss has occurred, Income Summary is:
   a. debited and Owner's Capital is credited.
   b. credited and Owner's Capital is debited.
   c. debited and Owner's Drawings is credited.
   d. credited and Owner's Drawings is debited.

(SO 2) **6.** The closing process involves separate entries to close (1) expenses, (2) drawings, (3) revenues, and (4) income summary. The correct sequencing of the entries is:
   a. (4), (3), (2), (1)   **c.** (3), (1), (4), (2)
   b. (1), (2), (3), (4)   **d.** (3), (2), (1), (4)

(SO 3) **7.** Which types of accounts will appear in the post-closing trial balance?
   a. Permanent (real) accounts.
   b. Temporary (nominal) accounts.
   c. Accounts shown in the income statement columns of a worksheet.
   d. None of the above.

(SO 4) **8.** All of the following are required steps in the accounting cycle *except*:
   a. journalizing and posting closing entries.
   b. preparing financial statements.
   c. journalizing the transactions.
   d. preparing a worksheet.

(SO 4) **9.** The proper order of the following steps in the accounting cycle is:
   a. prepare unadjusted trial balance, journalize transactions, post to ledger accounts, journalize and post adjusting entries.
   b. journalize transactions, prepare unadjusted trial balance, post to ledger accounts, journalize and post adjusting entries.
   c. journalize transactions, post to ledger accounts, prepare unadjusted trial balance, journalize and post adjusting entries.
   d. prepare unadjusted trial balance, journalize and post adjusting entries, journalize transactions, post to ledger accounts.

(SO 5) **10.** When Alexander Company purchased supplies worth $500, it incorrectly recorded a credit to Supplies for $5,000 and a debit to Cash for $5,000. Before correcting this error:
   a. Cash is overstated and Supplies is overstated.
   b. Cash is understated and Supplies is understated.
   c. Cash is understated and Supplies is overstated.
   d. Cash is overstated and Supplies is understated.

(SO 5) **11.** Cash of $100 received at the time the service was provided was journalized and posted as a debit to Cash $100 and a credit to Accounts Receivable $100. Assuming the incorrect entry is not reversed, the correcting entry is:
   a. debit Service Revenue $100 and credit Accounts Receivable $100.
   b. debit Accounts Receivable $100 and credit Service Revenue $100.
   c. debit Cash $100 and credit Service Revenue $100.
   d. debit Accounts Receivable $100 and credit Cash $100.

(SO 6) **12.** The correct order of presentation in a classified balance sheet for the following current assets is:
   a. accounts receivable, cash, prepaid insurance, inventory.
   b. cash, inventory, accounts receivable, prepaid insurance.
   c. cash, accounts receivable, inventory, prepaid insurance.
   d. inventory, cash, accounts receivable, prepaid insurance.

(SO 6) **13.** A company has purchased a tract of land. It expects to build a production plant on the land in approximately 5 years. During the 5 years before construction, the land will be idle. The land should be reported as:
  a. property, plant, and equipment.
  b. land expense.
  c. a long-term investment.
  d. an intangible asset.

(SO 6) **14.** In a classified balance sheet, assets are usually classified using the following categories:
  a. current assets; long-term assets; property, plant, and equipment; and intangible assets.
  b. current assets; long-term investments; property, plant, and equipment; and tangible assets.
  c. current assets; long-term investments; tangible assets; and intangible assets.
  d. current assets; long-term investments; property, plant, and equipment; and intangible assets.

(SO 6) **15.** Current assets are listed:
  a. by expected conversion to cash.
  b. by importance.
  c. by longevity.
  d. alphabetically.

*16. On December 31, Frank Voris Company correctly made (SO 7) an adjusting entry to recognize $2,000 of accrued salaries payable. On January 8 of the next year, total salaries of $3,400 were paid. Assuming the correct reversing entry was made on January 1, the entry on January 8 will result in a credit to Cash $3,400 and the following debit(s):
  a. Salaries and Wages Payable $1,400, and Salaries and Wages Expense $2,000.
  b. Salaries and Wages Payable $2,000 and Salaries and Wages Expense $1,400.
  c. Salaries and Wages Expense $3,400.
  d. Salaries and Wages Payable $3,400.

Go to the book's companion website, **www.wiley.com/college/weygandt**, for additional Self-Test Questions.

 The Navigator

Questions

1. "A worksheet is a permanent accounting record and its use is required in the accounting cycle." Do you agree? Explain.

2. Explain the purpose of the worksheet.

3. What is the relationship, if any, between the amount shown in the adjusted trial balance column for an account and that account's ledger balance?

4. If a company's revenues are $125,000 and its expenses are $113,000, in which financial statement columns of the worksheet will the net income of $12,000 appear? When expenses exceed revenues, in which columns will the difference appear?

5. Why is it necessary to prepare formal financial statements if all of the data are in the statement columns of the worksheet?

6. Identify the account(s) debited and credited in each of the four closing entries, assuming the company has net income for the year.

7. Describe the nature of the Income Summary account and identify the types of summary data that may be posted to this account.

8. What are the content and purpose of a post-closing trial balance?

9. Which of the following accounts would not appear in the post-closing trial balance? Interest Payable; Equipment; Depreciation Expense; Owner's Drawings; Unearned Service Revenue; Accumulated Depreciation—Equipment; and Service Revenue.

10. Distinguish between a reversing entry and an adjusting entry. Are reversing entries required?

11. Indicate, in the sequence in which they are made, the three required steps in the accounting cycle that involve journalizing.

12. Identify, in the sequence in which they are prepared, the three trial balances that are often used to report financial information about a company.

13. How do correcting entries differ from adjusting entries?

14. What standard classifications are used in preparing a classified balance sheet?

15. What is meant by the term "operating cycle?"

16. Define current assets. What basis is used for arranging individual items within the current assets section?

17. Distinguish between long-term investments and property, plant, and equipment.

18. (a) What is the term used to describe the owner's equity section of a corporation? (b) Identify the two owners' equity accounts in a corporation and indicate the purpose of each.

19. **PEPSICO** Using PepsiCo's annual report, determine its current liabilities at December 26, 2009, and December 27, 2008. Were current liabilities higher or lower than current assets in these two years?

*20. Sanchez Company prepares reversing entries. If the adjusting entry for interest payable is reversed, what type of an account balance, if any, will there be in Interest Payable and Interest Expense after the reversing entry is posted?

*21. At December 31, accrued salaries payable totaled $3,500. On January 10, total salaries of $8,000 are paid. (a) Assume that reversing entries are made at January 1. Give the January 10 entry, and indicate the Salaries and Wages Expense account balance after the entry is posted. (b) Repeat part (a) assuming reversing entries are not made.

Brief Exercises

BE4-1 The steps in using a worksheet are presented in random order below. List the steps in the proper order by placing numbers 1–5 in the blank spaces.

(a) _____ Prepare a trial balance on the worksheet.
(b) _____ Enter adjusted balances.
(c) _____ Extend adjusted balances to appropriate statement columns.
(d) _____ Total the statement columns, compute net income (loss), and complete the worksheet.
(e) _____ Enter adjustment data.

List the steps in preparing a worksheet.
(SO 1)

BE4-2 The ledger of Saddler Company includes the following unadjusted balances: Prepaid Insurance $3,000, Service Revenue $58,000, and Salaries and Wages Expense $25,000. Adjusting entries are required for (a) expired insurance $1,800; (b) services provided $1,100, but unbilled and uncollected; and (c) accrued salaries payable $800. Enter the unadjusted balances and adjustments into a worksheet and complete the worksheet for all accounts. *Note:* You will need to add the following accounts: Accounts Receivable, Salaries and Wages Payable, and Insurance Expense.

Prepare partial worksheet.
(SO 1)

BE4-3 The following selected accounts appear in the adjusted trial balance columns of the worksheet for McQueen Company: Accumulated Depreciation; Depreciation Expense; Owner's Capital; Owner's Drawings; Service Revenue; Supplies; and Accounts Payable. Indicate the financial statement column (income statement Dr., balance sheet Cr., etc.) to which each balance should be extended.

Identify worksheet columns for selected accounts.
(SO 1)

BE4-4 The ledger of Quentin Company contains the following balances: Owner's Capital $30,000; Owner's Drawings $2,000; Service Revenue $50,000; Salaries and Wages Expense $27,000; and Supplies Expense $7,000. Prepare the closing entries at December 31.

Prepare closing entries from ledger balances.
(SO 2)

BE4-5 Using the data in BE4-4, enter the balances in T accounts, post the closing entries, and rule and balance the accounts.

Post closing entries; rule and balance T accounts.
(SO 2)

BE4-6 The income statement for Evergreen Golf Club for the month ending July 31 shows Service Revenue $16,400, Salaries and Wages Expense $8,200, Maintenance and Repairs Expense $2,500, and Net Income $5,700. Prepare the entries to close the revenue and expense accounts. Post the entries to the revenue and expense accounts, and complete the closing process for these accounts using the three-column form of account.

Journalize and post closing entries using the three-column form of account.
(SO 2)

BE4-7 Using the data in BE4-3, identify the accounts that would be included in a post-closing trial balance.

Identify post-closing trial balance accounts.
(SO 3)

BE4-8 The steps in the accounting cycle are listed in random order below. List the steps in proper sequence, assuming no worksheet is prepared, by placing numbers 1–9 in the blank spaces.

(a) _____ Prepare a trial balance.
(b) _____ Journalize the transactions.
(c) _____ Journalize and post closing entries.
(d) _____ Prepare financial statements.
(e) _____ Journalize and post adjusting entries.
(f) _____ Post to ledger accounts.
(g) _____ Prepare a post-closing trial balance.
(h) _____ Prepare an adjusted trial balance.
(i) _____ Analyze business transactions.

List the required steps in the accounting cycle in sequence.
(SO 4)

BE4-9 At Shaffer Company, the following errors were discovered after the transactions had been journalized and posted. Prepare the correcting entries.

1. A collection on account from a customer for $870 was recorded as a debit to Cash $870 and a credit to Service Revenue $870.
2. The purchase of store supplies on account for $1,570 was recorded as a debit to Supplies $1,750 and a credit to Accounts Payable $1,750.

Prepare correcting entries.
(SO 5)

BE4-10 The balance sheet debit column of the worksheet for Shaw Company includes the following accounts: Accounts Receivable $12,500; Prepaid Insurance $3,600; Cash $4,100; Supplies $5,200, and Short-term Investments $6,700. Prepare the current assets section of the balance sheet, listing the accounts in proper sequence.

Prepare the current assets section of a balance sheet.
(SO 6)

Classify accounts on balance sheet.
(SO 6)

BE4-11   The following are the major balance sheet classifications:

Current assets (CA)	Current liabilities (CL)
Long-term investments (LTI)	Long-term liabilities (LTL)
Property, plant, and equipment (PPE)	Owner's equity (OE)
Intangible assets (IA)	

Match each of the following accounts to its proper balance sheet classification.

_____ Accounts payable	_____ Income taxes payable
_____ Accounts receivable	_____ Debt investment (long-term)
_____ Accumulated depreciation—buildings	_____ Land
_____ Buildings	_____ Inventory
_____ Cash	_____ Patents
_____ Copyrights	_____ Supplies

Prepare reversing entries.
(SO 7)

***BE4-12**   At October 31, Steltz Company made an accrued expense adjusting entry of $2,100 for salaries. Prepare the reversing entry on November 1, and indicate the balances in Salaries and Wages Payable and Salaries and Wages Expense after posting the reversing entry.

Do it! Review

Prepare a worksheet.
(SO 1)

Do it! 4-1   Averell Spicer is preparing a worksheet. Explain to Averell how he should extend the following adjusted trial balance accounts to the financial statement columns of the worksheet.

Service Revenue	Accounts Receivable
Notes Payable	Accumulated Depreciation
Owner's Capital	Utilities Expense

Prepare closing entries.
(SO 5)

Do it! 4-2   The worksheet for Ta'ufo'ou Company shows the following in the financial statement columns.

Owner's drawings	$22,000
Owner's capital	70,000
Net income	41,000

Prepare the closing entries at December 31 that affect owner's capital.

Prepare assets section of the balance sheet.
(SO 6)

Do it! 4-3   Chester Taylor recently received the following information related to Taylor Company's December 31, 2012, balance sheet.

Inventory	$ 2,900	Short-term investments	$1,200
Cash	4,300	Accumulated depreciation	5,700
Equipment	21,700	Accounts receivable	4,300
Investments in stock (long-term)	6,500		

Prepare the assets section of Taylor Company's classified balance sheet.

Match accounts to balance sheet classifications.
(SO 6)

Do it! 4-4   The following accounts were taken from the financial statements of Tillman Company.

_____ Interest revenue	_____ Owner's capital
_____ Utilities payable	_____ Accumulated depreciation
_____ Accounts payable	_____ Equipment
_____ Supplies	_____ Salaries and wages expense
_____ Bonds payable	_____ Investment in real estate
_____ Trademarks	_____ Unearned rent revenue

Match each of the accounts to its proper balance sheet classification, as shown below. If the item would not appear on a balance sheet, use "NA."

Current assets (CA)	Current liabilities (CL)
Long-term investments (LTI)	Long-term liabilities (LTL)
Property, plant, and equipment (PPE)	Owner's equity (OE)
Intangible assets (IA)	

Exercises

E4-1 The trial balance columns of the worksheet for Tinoisamoa Company at June 30, 2012, are as follows.

Complete the worksheet.
(SO 1)

TINOISAMOA COMPANY
Worksheet
For the Month Ended June 30, 2012

Account Titles	Trial Balance	
	Dr.	Cr.
Cash	$2,320	
Accounts Receivable	2,440	
Supplies	1,880	
Accounts Payable		$1,120
Unearned Service Revenue		240
Owner's Capital		3,600
Service Revenue		2,400
Salaries and Wages Expense	560	
Miscellaneous Expense	160	
	$7,360	$7,360

Other data:

1. A physical count reveals $500 of supplies on hand.
2. $100 of the unearned revenue is still unearned at month-end.
3. Accrued salaries are $210.

Instructions
Enter the trial balance on a worksheet and complete the worksheet.

E4-2 The adjusted trial balance columns of the worksheet for Pisa Company are as follows.

Complete the worksheet.
(SO 1)

PISA COMPANY
Worksheet (partial)
For the Month Ended April 30, 2012

Account Titles	Adjusted Trial Balance		Income Statement		Balance Sheet	
	Dr.	Cr.	Dr.	Cr.	Dr.	Cr.
Cash	10,000					
Accounts Receivable	7,840					
Prepaid Rent	2,280					
Equipment	23,050					
Accumulated Depreciation—Equip.		4,921				
Notes Payable		5,700				
Accounts Payable		4,920				
Owner's Capital		27,960				
Owner's Drawings	3,650					
Service Revenue		15,590				
Salaries and Wages Expense	10,840					
Rent Expense	760					
Depreciation Expense	671					
Interest Expense	57					
Interest Payable		57				
Totals	59,148	59,148				

Instructions
Complete the worksheet.

Prepare financial statements from worksheet.
(SO 1, 6)

E4-3 Worksheet data for Pisa Company are presented in E4-2. The owner did not make any additional investments in the business in April.

Instructions
Prepare an income statement, an owner's equity statement, and a classified balance sheet.

Journalize and post closing entries and prepare a post-closing trial balance.
(SO 2, 3)

E4-4 Worksheet data for Pisa Company are presented in E4-2.

Instructions
(a) Journalize the closing entries at April 30.
(b) Post the closing entries to Income Summary and Owner's Capital. Use T accounts.
(c) Prepare a post-closing trial balance at April 30.

Prepare adjusting entries from a worksheet, and extend balances to worksheet columns.
(SO 1)

E4-5 The adjustments columns of the worksheet for Toeaina Company are shown below.

	Adjustments	
Account Titles	**Debit**	**Credit**
Accounts Receivable	1,100	
Prepaid Insurance		300
Accumulated Depreciation—Equipment		900
Salaries and Wages Payable		500
Service Revenue		1,100
Salaries and Wages Expense	500	
Insurance Expense	300	
Depreciation Expense	900	
	2,800	2,800

Instructions
(a) Prepare the adjusting entries.
(b) Assuming the adjusted trial balance amount for each account is normal, indicate the financial statement column to which each balance should be extended.

Derive adjusting entries from worksheet data.
(SO 1)

E4-6 Selected worksheet data for Woodny Company are presented below.

	Trial Balance		**Adjusted Trial Balance**	
Account Titles	**Dr.**	**Cr.**	**Dr.**	**Cr.**
Accounts Receivable	?		34,000	
Prepaid Insurance	26,000		20,000	
Supplies	7,000		?	
Accumulated Depreciation—Equipment		12,000		?
Salaries and Wages Payable		?		5,600
Service Revenue		88,000		97,000
Insurance Expense			?	
Depreciation Expense			10,000	
Supplies Expense			4,500	
Salaries and Wages Expense	?		49,000	

Instructions
(a) Fill in the missing amounts.
(b) Prepare the adjusting entries that were made.

Prepare closing entries, and prepare a post-closing trial balance.
(SO 2, 3)

E4-7 Willow Turenne Company had the following adjusted trial balance.

WILLOW TURENNE COMPANY
Adjusted Trial Balance
For the Month Ended June 30, 2012

Account Titles	Adjusted Trial Balance Debits	Credits
Cash	$ 3,712	
Accounts Receivable	3,904	
Supplies	480	
Accounts Payable		$ 1,556
Unearned Service Revenue		160
Owner's Capital		5,760
Owner's Drawings	628	
Service Revenue		4,300
Salaries and Wages Expense	1,344	
Miscellaneous Expense	256	
Supplies Expense	1,900	
Salaries and Wages Payable		448
	$12,224	$12,224

Instructions
(a) Prepare closing entries at June 30, 2012.
(b) Prepare a post-closing trial balance.

E4-8 Turner Company ended its fiscal year on July 31, 2012. The company's adjusted trial balance as of the end of its fiscal year is as shown below.

Journalize and post closing entries, and prepare a post-closing trial balance.
(SO 2, 3)

TURNER COMPANY
Adjusted Trial Balance
July 31, 2012

No.	Account Titles	Debits	Credits
101	Cash	$ 9,840	
112	Accounts Receivable	8,780	
157	Equipment	15,900	
167	Accumulated Depreciation—Equip.		$ 7,400
201	Accounts Payable		4,220
208	Unearned Rent Revenue		1,800
301	Owner's Capital		45,200
306	Owner's Drawings	16,000	
404	Service Revenue		64,000
429	Rent Revenue		6,500
711	Depreciation Expense	8,000	
720	Salaries and Wages Expense	55,700	
732	Utilities Expense	14,900	
		$129,120	$129,120

Instructions
(a) Prepare the closing entries using page J15.
(b) Post to Owner's Capital and No. 350 Income Summary accounts. (Use the three-column form.)
(c) Prepare a post-closing trial balance at July 31.

E4-9 The adjusted trial balance for Turner Company is presented in E4-8.

Prepare financial statements.
(SO 6)

Instructions
(a) Prepare an income statement and an owner's equity statement for the year. Turner did not make any capital investments during the year.
(b) Prepare a classified balance sheet at July 31.

Answer questions related to the accounting cycle.

(SO 4)

E4-10   Vince Vance has prepared the following list of statements about the accounting cycle.

1. "Journalize the transactions" is the first step in the accounting cycle.
2. Reversing entries are a required step in the accounting cycle.
3. Correcting entries do not have to be part of the accounting cycle.
4. If a worksheet is prepared, some steps of the accounting cycle are incorporated into the worksheet.
5. The accounting cycle begins with the analysis of business transactions and ends with the preparation of a post-closing trial balance.
6. All steps of the accounting cycle occur daily during the accounting period.
7. The step of "post to the ledger accounts" occurs before the step of "journalize the transactions."
8. Closing entries must be prepared before financial statements can be prepared.

Instructions

Identify each statement as true or false. If false, indicate how to correct the statement.

Prepare closing entries.

(SO 2)

E4-11   Selected accounts for Brianna's Salon are presented below. All June 30 postings are from closing entries.

Salaries and Wages Expense				Service Revenue					Owner's Capital			
6/10	3,200	6/30	8,800	6/30	18,100	6/15	9,700	6/30	2,500	6/1	12,000
6/28	5,600					6/24	8,400			6/30	5,000
										Bal.	14,500

Supplies Expense				Rent Expense				Owner's Drawings			
6/12	600	6/30	1,300	6/1	3,000	6/30	3,000	6/13	1,000	6/30	2,500
6/24	700							6/25	1,500		

Instructions

(a) Prepare the closing entries that were made.
(b) Post the closing entries to Income Summary.

Prepare correcting entries.

(SO 5)

E4-12   J'Morcus Webb Company discovered the following errors made in January 2012.

1. A payment of Salaries and Wages Expense of $700 was debited to Equipment and credited to Cash, both for $700.
2. A collection of $1,000 from a client on account was debited to Cash $100 and credited to Service Revenue $100.
3. The purchase of equipment on account for $760 was debited to Equipment $670 and credited to Accounts Payable $670.

Instructions

(a) Correct the errors by reversing the incorrect entry and preparing the correct entry.
(b) Correct the errors without reversing the incorrect entry.

Prepare correcting entries.

(SO 5)

E4-13   Williams Company has an inexperienced accountant. During the first 2 weeks on the job, the accountant made the following errors in journalizing transactions. All entries were posted as made.

1. A payment on account of $840 to a creditor was debited to Accounts Payable $480 and credited to Cash $480.
2. The purchase of supplies on account for $560 was debited to Equipment $56 and credited to Accounts Payable $56.
3. A $500 withdrawal of cash for C. Williams' personal use was debited to Salaries and Wages Expense $500 and credited to Cash $500.

Instructions

Prepare the correcting entries.

Prepare a classified balance sheet.

(SO 6)

E4-14   The adjusted trial balance for Wootton Bowling Alley at December 31, 2012, contains the following accounts.

Debits		Credits	
Buildings	$128,800	Owner's Capital	$115,000
Accounts Receivable	14,520	Accumulated Depreciation—Buildings	42,600
Prepaid Insurance	4,680	Accounts Payable	12,300
Cash	18,040	Notes Payable	97,780
Equipment	62,400	Accumulated Depreciation—Equipment	18,720
Land	67,000	Interest Payable	2,600
Insurance Expense	780	Service Revenue	17,180
Depreciation Expense	7,360		$306,180
Interest Expense	2,600		
	$306,180		

Instructions

(a) Prepare a classified balance sheet; assume that $22,000 of the note payable will be paid in 2013.

(b) ◄▬▬▬▬▶ Comment on the liquidity of the company.

E4-15 The following are the major balance sheet classifications.

Classify accounts on balance sheet.

(SO 6)

Current assets (CA)   Current liabilities (CL)
Long-term investments (LTI)   Long-term liabilities (LTL)
Property, plant, and equipment (PPE)   Owner's equity (OE)
Intangible assets (IA)

Instructions

Classify each of the following accounts taken from E. Williams Company's balance sheet.

_____ Accounts payable   _____ Accumulated depreciation
_____ Accounts receivable   _____ Buildings
_____ Cash   _____ Land
_____ Owner's capital   _____ Long-term debt
_____ Patents   _____ Supplies
_____ Salaries and wages payable   _____ Equipment
_____ Inventory   _____ Prepaid expenses
_____ Investments

E4-16 The following items were taken from the financial statements of M. Wright Company. (All dollars are in thousands.)

Prepare a classified balance sheet.

(SO 6)

Long-term debt	$ 1,000	Accumulated depreciation	5,655
Prepaid insurance	880	Accounts payable	1,444
Equipment	11,500	Notes payable (due after 2013)	400
Long-term investments	264	Owner's capital	12,955
Short-term investments	3,690	Accounts receivable	1,696
Notes payable (due in 2013)	500	Inventory	1,256
Cash	$ 2,668		

Instructions

Prepare a classified balance sheet in good form as of December 31, 2012.

E4-17 These financial statement items are for Major Company at year-end, July 31, 2012.

Prepare financial statements.

(SO 1, 6)

Salaries and wages payable	$ 2,080	Notes payable (long-term)	$ 1,800
Salaries and wages expense	51,700	Cash	14,200
Utilities expense	22,600	Accounts receivable	9,780
Equipment	30,400	Accumulated depreciation—equip.	6,000
Accounts payable	4,100	Owner's drawings	3,000
Service revenue	62,000	Depreciation expense	4,000
Rent revenue	8,500	Owner's Capital (beginning of the year)	51,200

Instructions

(a) Prepare an income statement and an owner's equity statement for the year. The owner did not make any new investments during the year.

(b) Prepare a classified balance sheet at July 31.

Use reversing entries.
(SO 7)

E4-18   Alexander Company pays salaries of $12,000 every Monday for the preceding 5-day week (Monday through Friday). Assume December 31 falls on a Tuesday, so Alexander's employees have worked 2 days without being paid.

Instructions
(a) Assume the company does not use reversing entries. Prepare the December 31 adjusting entry and the entry on Monday, January 6, when Alexander pays the payroll.
(b) Assume the company does use reversing entries. Prepare the December 31 adjusting entry, the January 1 reversing entry, and the entry on Monday, January 6, when Alexander pays the payroll.

Prepare closing and reversing entries.
(SO 2, 4, 7)

E4-19   On December 31, the adjusted trial balance of Johnson Employment Agency shows the following selected data.

Accounts Receivable	$24,500	Service Revenue	$92,500
Interest Expense	8,300	Interest Payable	2,000

Analysis shows that adjusting entries were made to (1) accrue $5,000 of service revenue and (2) accrue $2,000 interest expense.

Instructions
(a) Prepare the closing entries for the temporary accounts shown above at December 31.
(b) Prepare the reversing entries on January 1.
(c) Post the entries in (a) and (b). Rule and balance the accounts. (Use T accounts.)
(d) Prepare the entries to record (1) the collection of the accrued revenue on January 10 and (2) the payment of all interest due ($3,000) on January 15.
(e) Post the entries in (d) to the temporary accounts.

Exercises: Set B

Visit the book's companion website, at **www.wiley.com/college/weygandt**, and choose the Student Companion site to access Exercise Set B.

Problems: Set A

Prepare worksheet, financial statements, and adjusting and closing entries.
(SO 1, 2, 3, 6)

P4-1A   Omer Asik began operations as a private investigator on January 1, 2012. The trial balance columns of the worksheet for Omer Asik, P.I. at March 31 are as follows.

OMER ASIK, P.I.
Worksheet
For the Quarter Ended March 31, 2012

	Trial Balance	
Account Titles	**Dr.**	**Cr.**
Cash	11,400	
Accounts Receivable	5,620	
Supplies	1,050	
Prepaid Insurance	2,400	
Equipment	30,000	
Notes Payable		10,000
Accounts Payable		12,350
Owner's Capital		20,000
Owner's Drawings	600	
Service Revenue		13,620
Salaries and Wages Expense	2,200	
Travel Expense	1,300	
Rent Expense	1,200	
Miscellaneous Expense	200	
	55,970	55,970

Other data:

1. Supplies on hand total $480.
2. Depreciation is $800 per quarter.
3. Interest accrued on 6-month note payable, issued January 1, $300.
4. Insurance expires at the rate of $200 per month.
5. Services provided but unbilled at March 31 total $1,030.

Instructions

(a) Enter the trial balance on a worksheet and complete the worksheet.

(b) Prepare an income statement and owner's equity statement for the quarter and a classified balance sheet at March 31. O. Asik did not make any additional investments in the business during the quarter ended March 31, 2012.

(c) Journalize the adjusting entries from the adjustments columns of the worksheet.

(d) Journalize the closing entries from the financial statement columns of the worksheet.

(a) Adjusted trial balance $58,100

(b) Net income $7,480
    Total assets $49,530

P4-2A The adjusted trial balance columns of the worksheet for Boozer Company are as follows.

Complete worksheet; prepare financial statements, closing entries, and post-closing trial balance.

(SO 1, 2, 3, 6)

 GLS

BOOZER COMPANY
Worksheet
For the Year Ended December 31, 2012

Account No.	Account Titles	Adjusted Trial Balance Dr.	Adjusted Trial Balance Cr.
101	Cash	18,800	
112	Accounts Receivable	16,200	
126	Supplies	2,300	
130	Prepaid Insurance	4,400	
151	Equipment	46,000	
152	Accumulated Depreciation—Equipment		20,000
200	Notes Payable		20,000
201	Accounts Payable		8,000
212	Salaries and Wages Payable		2,600
230	Interest Payable		1,000
301	Owner's Capital		26,000
306	Owner's Drawings	12,000	
400	Service Revenue		87,800
610	Advertising Expense	10,000	
631	Supplies Expense	3,700	
711	Depreciation Expense	8,000	
722	Insurance Expense	4,000	
726	Salaries and Wages Expense	39,000	
905	Interest Expense	1,000	
	Totals	165,400	165,400

Instructions

(a) Complete the worksheet by extending the balances to the financial statement columns.

(b) Prepare an income statement, owner's equity statement, and a classified balance sheet. $5,000 of the notes payable become due in 2013. C. Boozer did not make any additional investments in the business during 2012.

(c) Prepare the closing entries. Use J14 for the journal page.

(d) Post the closing entries. Use the three-column form of account. Income Summary is account No. 350.

(e) Prepare a post-closing trial balance.

(a) Net income $22,100

(b) Current assets $41,700
    Current liabilities $16,600

(e) Post-closing trial balance $87,700

Prepare financial statements, closing entries, and post-closing trial balance.

(SO 1, 2, 3, 6)

P4-3A The completed financial statement columns of the worksheet for Carlos Company are shown on the next page.

CARLOS COMPANY
Worksheet
For the Year Ended December 31, 2012

Account No.	Account Titles	Income Statement Dr.	Income Statement Cr.	Balance Sheet Dr.	Balance Sheet Cr.
101	Cash			6,200	
112	Accounts Receivable			7,500	
130	Prepaid Insurance			1,800	
157	Equipment			33,000	
167	Accumulated Depreciation—Equip.				8,600
201	Accounts Payable				11,700
212	Salaries and Wages Payable				3,000
301	Owner's Capital				34,000
306	Owner's Drawings			7,200	
400	Service Revenue		46,000		
622	Maintenance and Repairs Expense	4,400			
711	Depreciation Expense	2,800			
722	Insurance Expense	1,200			
726	Salaries and Wages Expense	35,200			
732	Utilities Expense	4,000			
	Totals	47,600	46,000	55,700	57,300
	Net Loss		1,600	1,600	
		47,600	47,600	57,300	57,300

Instructions

(a) Net loss $1,600
  Ending capital $25,200
  Total assets $39,900

(d Post-closing trial balance $48,500

Complete worksheet; prepare classified balance sheet, entries, and post-closing trial balance.
(SO 1, 2, 3, 6)

(a) Prepare an income statement, owner's equity statement, and a classified balance sheet. B. Carlos made an additional investment in the business of $4,000 during 2012.
(b) Prepare the closing entries.
(c) Post the closing entries and rule and balance the accounts. Use T accounts. Income Summary is account No. 350.
(d) Prepare a post-closing trial balance.

P4-4A Noah Amusement Park has a fiscal year ending on September 30. Selected data from the September 30 worksheet are presented below.

NOAH AMUSEMENT PARK
Worksheet
For the Year Ended September 30, 2012

	Trial Balance Dr.	Trial Balance Cr.	Adjusted Trial Balance Dr.	Adjusted Trial Balance Cr.
Cash	41,400		41,400	
Supplies	18,600		2,200	
Prepaid Insurance	31,900		10,900	
Land	80,000		80,000	
Equipment	120,000		120,000	
Accumulated Depreciation—Equip.		36,200		42,200
Accounts Payable		14,600		14,600
Unearned Ticket Revenue		3,700		1,000
Mortgage Payable		50,000		50,000
Owner's Capital		109,700		109,700
Owner's Drawings	14,000		14,000	
Ticket Revenue		277,500		280,200
Salaries and Wages Expense	105,000		105,000	
Maintenance and Repairs Expense	30,500		30,500	
Advertising Expense	9,400		9,400	
Utilities Expense	16,900		16,900	

Property Tax Expense	18,000	21,000	
Interest Expense	6,000	10,000	
Totals	491,700	491,700	
Insurance Expense		21,000	
Supplies Expense		16,400	
Interest Payable			4,000
Depreciation Expense		6,000	
Property Taxes Payable			3,000
Totals		504,700	504,700

Instructions
(a) Prepare a complete worksheet.
(b) Prepare a classified balance sheet. (*Note*: $15,000 of the mortgage note payable is due for payment in the next fiscal year.)
(c) Journalize the adjusting entries using the worksheet as a basis.
(d) Journalize the closing entries using the worksheet as a basis.
(e) Prepare a post-closing trial balance.

(a) Net income $44,000
(b) Total current assets
    $54,500

(e) Post-closing trial balance
    $254,500

P4-5A   Devine Brown opened Devine's Carpet Cleaners on March 1. During March, the following transactions were completed.

Complete all steps in accounting cycle.
(SO 1, 2, 3, 4, 6)

Mar. 1 Invested $10,000 cash in the business.
     1 Purchased used truck for $6,000, paying $3,000 cash and the balance on account.
     3 Purchased cleaning supplies for $1,200 on account.
     5 Paid $1,200 cash on one-year insurance policy effective March 1.
    14 Billed customers $4,800 for cleaning services.
    18 Paid $1,500 cash on amount owed on truck and $500 on amount owed on cleaning supplies.
    20 Paid $1,800 cash for employee salaries.
    21 Collected $1,400 cash from customers billed on March 14.
    28 Billed customers $2,500 for cleaning services.
    31 Paid gasoline for month on truck $200.
    31 Withdrew $700 cash for personal use.

The chart of accounts for Devine's Carpet Cleaners contains the following accounts: No. 101 Cash, No. 112 Accounts Receivable, No. 128 Supplies, No. 130 Prepaid Insurance, No. 157 Equipment, No. 158 Accumulated Depreciation—Equipment, No. 201 Accounts Payable, No. 212 Salaries and Wages Payable, No. 301 Owner's Capital, No. 306 Owner's Drawings, No. 350 Income Summary, No. 400 Service Revenue, No. 633 Gasoline Expense, No. 634 Supplies Expense, No. 711 Depreciation Expense, No. 722 Insurance Expense, and No. 726 Salaries and Wages Expense.

Instructions
(a) Journalize and post the March transactions. Use page J1 for the journal and the three-column form of account.
(b) Prepare a trial balance at March 31 on a worksheet.
(c) Enter the following adjustments on the worksheet and complete the worksheet.
    (1) Earned but unbilled revenue at March 31 was $500.
    (2) Depreciation on equipment for the month was $300.
    (3) One-twelfth of the insurance expired.
    (4) An inventory count shows $250 of cleaning supplies on hand at March 31.
    (5) Accrued but unpaid employee salaries were $550.
(d) Prepare the income statement and owner's equity statement for March and a classified balance sheet at March 31.
(e) Journalize and post adjusting entries. Use page J2 for the journal.
(f) Journalize and post closing entries and complete the closing process. Use page J3 for the journal.
(g) Prepare a post-closing trial balance at March 31.

(b) Trial balance $19,500
(c) Adjusted trial balance
    $20,850

(d) Net income $3,900
    Total assets $15,950
(g) Post-closing trial balance
    $16,250

Analyze errors and prepare correcting entries and trial balance.
(SO 5)

P4-6A   Luol Deng CPA, was retained by Acie Cable to prepare financial statements for April 2012. Deng accumulated all the ledger balances per Acie's records and found the following.

ACIE CABLE
Trial Balance
April 30, 2012

	Debit	Credit
Cash	$ 4,100	
Accounts Receivable	3,200	
Supplies	800	
Equipment	10,600	
Accumulated Depreciation—Equip.		$ 1,350
Accounts Payable		2,100
Salaries and Wages Payable		700
Unearned Service Revenue		890
Owner's Capital		12,900
Service Revenue		5,450
Salaries and Wages Expense	3,300	
Advertising Expense	600	
Miscellaneous Expense	290	
Depreciation Expense	500	
	$23,390	$23,390

Luol Deng reviewed the records and found the following errors.

1. Cash received from a customer on account was recorded as $950 instead of $590.
2. A payment of $75 for advertising expense was entered as a debit to Miscellaneous Expense $75 and a credit to Cash $75.
3. The first salary payment this month was for $1,900, which included $700 of salaries payable on March 31. The payment was recorded as a debit to Salaries and Wages Expense $1,900 and a credit to Cash $1,900. (No reversing entries were made on April 1.)
4. The purchase on account of a printer costing $310 was recorded as a debit to Supplies and a credit to Accounts Payable for $310.
5. A cash payment of repair expense on equipment for $96 was recorded as a debit to Equipment $69 and a credit to Cash $69.

Instructions
(a) Prepare an analysis of each error showing (1) the incorrect entry, (2) the correct entry, and (3) the correcting entry. Items 4 and 5 occurred on April 30, 2012.

Trial balance $22,690
(b) Prepare a correct trial balance.

Problems: Set B

Prepare a worksheet, financial statements, and adjusting and closing entries.

(SO 1, 2, 3, 6)

P4-1B The trial balance columns of the worksheet for Gibson Roofing at March 31, 2012, are as follows.

GIBSON ROOFING
Worksheet
For the Month Ended March 31, 2012

	Trial Balance	
Account Titles	**Dr.**	**Cr.**
Cash	4,500	
Accounts Receivable	3,200	
Supplies	2,000	
Equipment	11,000	
Accumulated Depreciation—Equipment		1,250
Accounts Payable		2,500
Unearned Service Revenue		550
Owner's Capital		12,900
Owner's Drawings	1,100	
Service Revenue		6,300
Salaries and Wages Expense	1,300	
Miscellaneous Expense	400	
	23,500	23,500

Other data:

1. A physical count reveals only $550 of roofing supplies on hand.
2. Depreciation for March is $250.
3. Unearned revenue amounted to $210 at March 31.
4. Accrued salaries are $700.

Instructions

(a) Enter the trial balance on a worksheet and complete the worksheet.
(b) Prepare an income statement and owner's equity statement for the month of March and a classified balance sheet at March 31. T. Gibson did not make any additional investments in the business in March.
(c) Journalize the adjusting entries from the adjustments columns of the worksheet.
(d) Journalize the closing entries from the financial statement columns of the worksheet.

(a) Adjusted trial balance
    $24,450
(b) Net income $2,540
    Total assets $17,750

P4-2B The adjusted trial balance columns of the worksheet for Taj Company, owned by Gabby Taj, are as follows.

Complete worksheet; prepare financial statements, closing entries, and post-closing trial balance.

(SO 1, 2, 3, 6)

TAJ COMPANY
Worksheet
For the Year Ended December 31, 2012

Account No.	Account Titles	Adjusted Trial Balance Dr.	Adjusted Trial Balance Cr.
101	Cash	5,300	
112	Accounts Receivable	10,800	
126	Supplies	1,500	
130	Prepaid Insurance	2,000	
151	Equipment	27,000	
152	Accumulated Depreciation—Equipment		5,600
200	Notes Payable		15,000
201	Accounts Payable		6,100
212	Salaries and Wages Payable		2,400
230	Interest Payable		600
301	Owner's Capital		13,000
306	Owner's Drawings	7,000	
400	Service Revenue		61,000
610	Advertising Expense	8,400	
631	Supplies Expense	4,000	
711	Depreciation Expense	5,600	
722	Insurance Expense	3,500	
726	Salaries and Wages Expense	28,000	
905	Interest Expense	600	
	Totals	103,700	103,700

Instructions

(a) Complete the worksheet by extending the balances to the financial statement columns.
(b) Prepare an income statement, owner's equity statement, and a classified balance sheet. (*Note:* $5,000 of the notes payable become due in 2013.) Gabby Taj did not make any additional investments in the business during the year.
(c) Prepare the closing entries. Use J14 for the journal page.
(d) Post the closing entries. Use the three-column form of account. Income Summary is No. 350.
(e) Prepare a post-closing trial balance.

(a) Net income $10,900
(b) Current assets $19,600;
    Current liabilities $14,100

(e) Post-closing trial balance
    $46,600

Prepare financial statements, closing entries, and post-closing trial balance.

(SO 1, 2, 3, 6)

P4-3B The completed financial statement columns of the worksheet for Korver Company are shown on the next page.

KORVER COMPANY
Worksheet
For the Year Ended December 31, 2012

Account No.	Account Titles	Income Statement Dr.	Income Statement Cr.	Balance Sheet Dr.	Balance Sheet Cr.
101	Cash			8,900	
112	Accounts Receivable			10,800	
130	Prepaid Insurance			2,800	
157	Equipment			24,000	
167	Accumulated Depreciation—Equip.				4,500
201	Accounts Payable				9,000
212	Salaries and Wages Payable				2,400
301	Owner's Capital				19,500
306	Owner's Drawings			11,000	
400	Service Revenue		60,000		
622	Maintenance and Repairs Expense	1,600			
711	Depreciation Expense	3,100			
722	Insurance Expense	1,800			
726	Salaries and Wages Expense	30,000			
732	Utilities Expense	1,400			
	Totals	37,900	60,000	57,500	35,400
	Net Income	22,100			22,100
		60,000	60,000	57,500	57,500

Instructions

(a) Ending capital $30,600;
Total current assets
$22,500

(d) Post-closing trial balance
$46,500

Complete worksheet; prepare classified balance sheet, entries, and post-closing trial balance.
(SO 1, 2, 3, 6)

(a) Prepare an income statement, an owner's equity statement, and a classified balance sheet.
(b) Prepare the closing entries. Korver did not make any additional investments during the year.
(c) Post the closing entries and rule and balance the accounts. Use T accounts. Income Summary is account No. 350.
(d) Prepare a post-closing trial balance.

P4-4B Law Management Services began business on January 1, 2012, with a capital investment of $120,000. The company manages condominiums for owners (Service Revenue) and rents space in its own office building (Rent Revenue). The trial balance and adjusted trial balance columns of the worksheet at the end of the first year are as follows.

LAW MANAGEMENT SERVICES
Worksheet
For the Year Ended December 31, 2012

Account Titles	Trial Balance Dr.	Trial Balance Cr.	Adjusted Trial Balance Dr.	Adjusted Trial Balance Cr.
Cash	13,800		13,800	
Accounts Receivable	28,300		28,300	
Prepaid Insurance	3,600		2,400	
Land	67,000		67,000	
Buildings	127,000		127,000	
Equipment	59,000		59,000	
Accounts Payable		12,500		12,500
Unearned Rent Revenue		6,000		1,500
Mortgage Payable		120,000		120,000
Owner's Capital		144,000		144,000
Owner's Drawings	22,000		22,000	
Service Revenue		90,700		90,700
Rent Revenue		29,000		33,500
Salaries and Wages Expense	42,000		42,000	
Advertising Expense	20,500		20,500	
Utilities Expense	19,000		19,000	
Totals	402,200	402,200		

Insurance Expense	1,200	
Depreciation Expense	6,600	
Accumulated Depreciation—Buildings		3,000
Accumulated Depreciation—Equipment		3,600
Interest Expense	10,000	
Interest Payable		10,000
Totals	418,800	418,800

Instructions

(a) Prepare a complete worksheet.

(b) Prepare a classified balance sheet. (*Note*: $30,000 of the mortgage note payable is due for payment next year.)

(c) Journalize the adjusting entries.

(d) Journalize the closing entries.

(e) Prepare a post-closing trial balance.

(a) Net income $24,900

(b) Total current assets $44,500

(e) Post-closing trial balance $297,500

P4-5B   Jannero Pargo opened Pargo's Cleaning Service on July 1, 2012. During July the following transactions were completed.

Complete all steps in accounting cycle.

(SO 1, 2, 3, 4, 6)

GLS

July	1	Pargo invested $20,000 cash in the business.
	1	Purchased used truck for $9,000, paying $4,000 cash and the balance on account.
	3	Purchased cleaning supplies for $2,100 on account.
	5	Paid $1,800 cash on one-year insurance policy effective July 1.
	12	Billed customers $4,500 for cleaning services.
	18	Paid $1,500 cash on amount owed on truck and $1,400 on amount owed on cleaning supplies.
	20	Paid $2,500 cash for employee salaries.
	21	Collected $3,400 cash from customers billed on July 12.
	25	Billed customers $6,000 for cleaning services.
	31	Paid gasoline for month on truck $350.
	31	Withdraw $5,600 cash for personal use.

The chart of accounts for Pargo's Cleaning Service contains the following accounts: No. 101 Cash, No. 112 Accounts Receivable, No. 128 Supplies, No. 130 Prepaid Insurance, No. 157 Equipment, No. 158 Accumulated Depreciation—Equipment, No. 201 Accounts Payable, No. 212 Salaries and Wages Payable, No. 301 Owner's Capital, No. 306 Owner's Drawings, No. 350 Income Summary, No. 400 Service Revenue, No. 633 Gasoline Expense, No. 634 Supplies Expense, No. 711 Depreciation Expense, No. 722 Insurance Expense, and No. 726 Salaries and Wages Expense.

Instructions

(a) Journalize and post the July transactions. Use page J1 for the journal and the three-column form of account.

(b) Prepare a trial balance at July 31 on a worksheet.

(c) Enter the following adjustments on the worksheet and complete the worksheet.

    (1) Services provided but unbilled and uncollected at July 31 were $2,700.

    (2) Depreciation on equipment for the month was $500.

    (3) One-twelfth of the insurance expired.

    (4) An inventory count shows $600 of cleaning supplies on hand at July 31.

    (5) Accrued but unpaid employee salaries were $1,000.

(d) Prepare the income statement and owner's equity statement for July and a classified balance sheet at July 31.

(e) Journalize and post adjusting entries. Use page J2 for the journal.

(f) Journalize and post closing entries and complete the closing process. Use page J3 for the journal.

(g) Prepare a post-closing trial balance at July 31.

(b) Trial balance $34,700

(c) Adjusted trial balance $38,900

(d) Net income $7,200; Total assets $26,800

(g) Post-closing trial balance $27,300

Problems: Set C

Visit the book's companion website, at **www.wiley.com/college/weygandt**, and choose the Student Companion site to access Problem Set C.

Comprehensive Problem: Chapters 2 to 4

CP4   Julie Molony opened Julie's Maids Cleaning Service on July 1, 2012. During July, the company completed the following transactions.

July	1	Invested $14,000 cash in the business.
	1	Purchased a used truck for $10,000, paying $3,000 cash and the balance on account.
	3	Purchased cleaning supplies for $800 on account.
	5	Paid $1,800 on a one-year insurance policy, effective July 1.
	12	Billed customers $3,800 for cleaning services.
	18	Paid $1,000 of amount owed on truck, and $400 of amount owed on cleaning supplies.
	20	Paid $1,600 for employee salaries.
	21	Collected $1,400 from customers billed on July 12.
	25	Billed customers $1,500 for cleaning services.
	31	Paid gasoline for the month on the truck, $400.
	31	Withdrew $600 cash for personal use.

The chart of accounts for Julie's Maids Cleaning Service contains the following accounts: No. 101 Cash, No. 112 Accounts Receivable, No. 128 Supplies, No. 130 Prepaid Insurance, No. 157 Equipment, No. 158 Accumulated Depreciation—Equipment, No. 201 Accounts Payable, No. 212 Salaries and Wages Payable, No. 301 Owner's Capital, No. 306 Owner's Drawings, No. 350 Income Summary, No. 400 Service Revenue, No. 633 Gasoline Expense, No. 634 Supplies Expense, No. 711 Depreciation Expense, No. 722 Insurance Expense, and No. 726 Salaries and Wages Expense.

Instructions

(a) Journalize and post the July transactions. Use page J1 for the journal.

(b) Trial balance totals $25,700

(b) Prepare a trial balance at July 31 on a worksheet.

(c) Enter the following adjustments on the worksheet, and complete the worksheet.

  (1) Earned but unbilled fees at July 31 were $1,300.

  (2) Depreciation on equipment for the month was $200.

  (3) One-twelfth of the insurance expired.

  (4) An inventory count shows $100 of cleaning supplies on hand at July 31.

  (5) Accrued but unpaid employee salaries were $500.

(d) Net income $3,050
Total assets $23,350

(d) Prepare the income statement and owner's equity statement for July, and a classified balance sheet at July 31, 2012.

(e) Journalize and post the adjusting entries. Use page J2 for the journal.

(f) Journalize and post the closing entries, and complete the closing process. Use page J3 for the journal.

(g) Trial balance totals $23,550

(g) Prepare a post-closing trial balance at July 31.

Continuing Cookie Chronicle

(*Note:* This is a continuation of the Cookie Chronicle from Chapters 1 through 3.)

CCC4   Natalie had a very busy December. At the end of the month, after journalizing and posting the December transactions and adjusting entries, Natalie prepared the following adjusted trial balance.

COOKIE CREATIONS
Adjusted Trial Balance
December 31, 2011

	Debit	Credit
Cash	$1,180	
Accounts Receivable	875	
Supplies	350	
Prepaid Insurance	1,210	
Equipment	1,200	
Accumulated Depreciation—Equipment		$ 40
Accounts Payable		75
Salaries and Wages Payable		56

Interest Payable		15
Unearned Service Revenue		300
Notes Payable		2,000
Owner's Capital		800
Owner's Drawings	500	
Service Revenue		4,515
Salaries and Wages Expense	1,006	
Utilities Expense	125	
Advertising Expense	165	
Supplies Expense	1,025	
Depreciation Expense	40	
Insurance Expense	110	
Interest Expense	15	
	$7,801	$7,801

Instructions

Using the information in the adjusted trial balance, do the following.

(a) Prepare an income statement and an owner's equity statement for the 2 months ended December 31, 2011, and a classified balance sheet as at December 31, 2011. The note payable has a stated interest rate of 6%, and the principal and interest are due on November 16, 2013.

(b) Natalie has decided that her year-end will be December 31, 2011. Prepare and post closing entries as of December 31, 2011.

(c) Prepare a post-closing trial balance.

BROADENINGYOURPERSPECTIVE

Financial Reporting and Analysis

Financial Reporting Problem: PepsiCo, Inc.

BYP4-1 The financial statements of PepsiCo, Inc. are presented in Appendix A at the end of this textbook.

Instructions

Answer the questions on the following page using the Consolidated Balance Sheet and the Notes to Consolidated Financial Statements section.

(a) What were PepsiCo's total current assets at December 26, 2009, and December 27, 2008?
(b) Are assets that PepsiCo included under current assets listed in proper order? Explain.
(c) How are PepsiCo's assets classified?
(d) What are "cash equivalents"?
(e) What were PepsiCo's total current liabilities at December 26, 2009, and December 27, 2008?

Comparative Analysis Problem: PepsiCo, Inc. vs. The Coca-Cola Company

BYP4-2 PepsiCo's financial statements are presented in Appendix A. Financial statements for The Coca-Cola Company are presented in Appendix B.

Instructions

(a) Based on the information contained in these financial statements, determine each of the following for PepsiCo at December 26, 2009, and for Coca-Cola at December 31, 2009.
  (1) Total current assets.
  (2) Net amount of property, plant, and equipment (land, buildings, and equipment).
  (3) Total current liabilities.
  (4) Total equity.
(b) What conclusions concerning the companies' respective financial positions can be drawn?

On the Web

BYP4-3   Numerous companies have established home pages on the Internet, e.g., Capt'n Eli Root Beer Company *(www.captneli.com/rootbeer.php)* and Kodak *(www.kodak.com)*.

Instructions

Examine the home pages of any two companies and answer the following questions.

(a) What type of information is available?
(b) Is any accounting-related information presented?
(c) Would you describe the home page as informative, promotional, or both? Why?

Critical Thinking

Decision Making Across the Organization

BYP4-4   Whitegloves Janitorial Service was started 2 years ago by Nancy Kohl. Because business has been exceptionally good, Nancy decided on July 1, 2012, to expand operations by acquiring an additional truck and hiring two more assistants. To finance the expansion, Nancy obtained on July 1, 2012, a $25,000, 10% bank loan, payable $10,000 on July 1, 2013, and the balance on July 1, 2014. The terms of the loan require the borrower to have $10,000 more current assets than current liabilities at December 31, 2012. If these terms are not met, the bank loan will be refinanced at 15% interest. At December 31, 2012, the accountant for Whitegloves Janitorial Service Inc. prepared the balance sheet shown below.

Nancy presented the balance sheet to the bank's loan officer on January 2, 2013, confident that the company had met the terms of the loan. The loan officer was not impressed. She said, "We need financial statements audited by a CPA." A CPA was hired and immediately realized that the balance sheet had been prepared from a trial balance and not from an adjusted trial balance. The adjustment data at the balance sheet date consisted of the following.

(1) Earned but unbilled janitorial services were $3,700.
(2) Janitorial supplies on hand were $2,500.
(3) Prepaid insurance was a 3-year policy dated January 1, 2012.
(4) December expenses incurred but unpaid at December 31, $500.
(5) Interest on the bank loan was not recorded.
(6) The amounts for property, plant, and equipment presented in the balance sheet were reported net of accumulated depreciation (cost less accumulated depreciation). These amounts were $4,000 for cleaning equipment and $5,000 for delivery trucks as of January 1, 2012. Depreciation for 2012 was $2,000 for cleaning equipment and $5,000 for delivery trucks.

WHITEGLOVES JANITORIAL SERVICE
Balance Sheet
December 31, 2012

Assets			Liabilities and Owner's Equity	
Current assets			Current liabilities	
Cash	$ 6,500		Notes payable	$10,000
Accounts receivable	9,000		Accounts payable	2,500
Janitorial supplies	5,200		Total current liabilities	12,500
Prepaid insurance	4,800		Long-term liability	
Total current assets	25,500		Notes payable	15,000
Property, plant, and equipment			Total liabilities	27,500
Cleaning equipment (net)	22,000		Owner's equity	
Delivery trucks (net)	34,000		Owner's capital	54,000
Total property, plant, and equipment	56,000			
Total assets	$81,500		Total liabilities and owner's equity	$81,500

Instructions

With the class divided into groups, answer the following.

(a) Prepare a correct balance sheet.
(b) Were the terms of the bank loan met? Explain.

Communication Activity

BYP4-5   The accounting cycle is important in understanding the accounting process.

Instructions
Write a memo to your instructor that lists the steps of the accounting cycle in the order they should be completed. End with a paragraph that explains the optional steps in the cycle.

Ethics Case

BYP4-6   As the controller of Breathless Perfume Company, you discover a misstatement that overstated net income in the prior year's financial statements. The misleading financial statements appear in the company's annual report which was issued to banks and other creditors less than a month ago. After much thought about the consequences of telling the president, Jerry McNabb, about this misstatement, you gather your courage to inform him. Jerry says, "Hey! What they don't know won't hurt them. But, just so we set the record straight, we'll adjust this year's financial statements for last year's misstatement. We can absorb that misstatement better in this year than in last year anyway! Just don't make such a mistake again."

Instructions
(a) Who are the stakeholders in this situation?
(b) What are the ethical issues in this situation?
(c) What would you do as a controller in this situation?

"All About You" Activity

BYP4-7   Companies prepare balance sheets in order to know their financial position at a specific point in time. This enables them to make a comparison to their position at previous points in time, and gives them a basis for planning for the future. As discussed in the **All About You** feature (available on the book's companion website), in order to evaluate your financial position you need to prepare a personal balance sheet. Assume that you have compiled the following information regarding your finances. (*Hint:* Some of the items might not be used in your personal balance sheet.)

Amount owed on student loan balance (long-term)	$ 5,000
Balance in checking account	1,200
Certificate of deposit (6-month)	3,000
Annual earnings from part-time job	11,300
Automobile	7,000
Balance on automobile loan (current portion)	1,500
Balance on automobile loan (long-term portion)	4,000
Home computer	800
Amount owed to you by younger brother	300
Balance in money market account	1,800
Annual tuition	6,400
Video and stereo equipment	1,250
Balance owed on credit card (current portion)	150
Balance owed on credit card (long-term portion)	1,650

Instructions
Prepare a personal balance sheet using the format you have learned for a classified balance sheet for a company. For the capital account, use Owner's Capital.

FASB Codification Activity

BYP4-8   If your school has a subscription to the FASB Codification, go to *http://aaahq.org/ascLogin.cfm* to log in and prepare responses to the following.

Instructions
(a) Access the glossary ("Master Glossary") at the FASB Codification website to answer the following.
   (1) What is the definition of current assets?
   (2) What is the definition of current liabilities?
(b) A company wants to offset its accounts payable against its cash account and show a cash amount net of accounts payable on its balance sheet. Identify the criteria (found in the FASB Codification) under which a company has the right of set off. Does the company have the right to offset accounts payable against the cash account?

Answers to Insight and Accounting Across the Organization Questions

p. 165 Cisco Performs the Virtual Close   Q: Who else benefits from a shorter closing process? **A:** Investors benefit from a shorter closing process. The shorter the closing, the sooner the company can report its financial results. This means that the financial information is more timely and therefore more relevant to investors.

p. 170 Yale Express Loses Some Transportation Bills   Q: What might Yale Express's vice president have done to produce more accurate financial statements without waiting months for Republic's outstanding transportation bills? **A:** Yale's vice president could have engaged his accountants and auditors to prepare an adjusting entry based on an estimate of the outstanding transportation bills. (The estimate could have been made using past experience and the current volume of business.)

p. 175 Can a Company Be Too Liquid?   Q: What can various company managers do to ensure that working capital is managed efficiently to maximize net income? **A:** Marketing and sales managers must understand that by extending generous repayment terms, they are expanding the company's receivables balance and slowing the company's cash flow. Production managers must strive to minimize the amount of excess inventory on hand. Managers must coordinate efforts to speed up the collection of receivables, while also ensuring that the company pays its payables on time but never too early.

Answers to Self-Test Questions
1. b   **2.** c   **3.** c   **4.** a   **5.** b   **6.** c   **7.** a   **8.** d   **9.** c   **10.** d   **11.** b   **12.** c   **13.** c   **14.** d   **15.** a   *16. c

IFRS A Look at IFRS

The classified balance sheet, although generally required internationally, contains certain variations in format when reporting under IFRS.

Key Points

- The procedures of the closing process are applicable to all companies, whether they are using IFRS or GAAP.

- IFRS recommends but does not require the use of the title "statement of financial position" rather than balance sheet.

- The format of statement of financial position information is often presented differently under IFRS. Although no specific format is required, most companies that follow IFRS present statement of financial position information in this order:
  - ◆ Noncurrent assets
  - ◆ Current assets
  - ◆ Equity
  - ◆ Noncurrent liabilities
  - ◆ Current liabilities

- IFRS requires a classified statement of financial position except in very limited situations. IFRS follows the same guidelines as this textbook for distinguishing between current and noncurrent assets and liabilities.

- Under IFRS, current assets are usually listed in the reverse order of liquidity. For example, under GAAP cash is listed first, but under IFRS it is listed last.

- Some companies report the subtotal *net assets*, which equals total assets minus total liabilities. See, for example, the statement of financial position of Zetar plc in Appendix C.

- IFRS has many differences in terminology that you will notice in this textbook. For example, in the sample statement of financial position illustrated on the next page, notice in the investment category that stock is called shares.

Franklin Company
Statement of Financial Position
October 31, 2012

Assets

Intangible assets			
Patents			$ 3,100
Property, plant, and equipment			
Land		$10,000	
Equipment	$24,000		
Less: Accumulated depreciation	5,000	19,000	29,000
Long-term investments			
Investment in shares of Walters Corp.		5,200	
Investment in real estate		2,000	7,200
Current assets			
Prepaid insurance		400	
Supplies		2,100	
Inventories		3,000	
Notes receivable		1,000	
Accounts receivable		7,000	
Short-term investments		2,000	
Cash		6,600	22,100
Total assets			$61,400

Equity and Liabilities

Equity			
Owner's capital			$34,050
Non-current liabilities			
Mortgage payable		$10,000	
Notes payable		1,300	11,300
Current liabilities			
Notes payable		11,000	
Accounts payable		2,100	
Salaries payable		1,600	
Unearned service revenue		900	
Interest payable		450	16,050
Total equity and liabilities			$61,400

- Both IFRS and GAAP require disclosures about (1) accounting policies followed, (2) judgments that management has made in the process of applying the entity's accounting policies, and (3) the key assumptions and estimation uncertainty that could result in a material adjustment to the carrying amounts of assets and liabilities within the next financial year.

- Comparative prior-period information must be presented and financial statements must be prepared annually.

- Both GAAP and IFRS are increasing the use of fair value to report assets. However, at this point IFRS has adopted it more broadly. As examples, under IFRS companies can apply fair value to property, plant, and equipment; natural resources; and in some cases intangible assets.

Looking to the Future

The IASB and the FASB are working on a project to converge their standards related to financial statement presentation. A key feature of the proposed framework is that each of the statements will be organized in the same format, to separate an entity's financing activities from its operating and investing activities and, further, to separate financing activities into transactions with owners and creditors. Thus, the same classifications used in the statement of financial position would also be used in the income statement and the statement of cash flows. The project has three phases. You can follow the joint financial presentation project at the following link: *http://www.fasb.org/project/financial_statement_presentation.shtml.*

The IASB and the FASB face a difficult task in attempting to update, modify, and complete a converged conceptual framework. For example, how do companies choose between information that is highly relevant but difficult to verify versus information that is less relevant but easy to verify? How do companies define control when developing a definition of an asset? Is a liability the future sacrifice itself or the obligation to make the sacrifice? Should a single measurement method, such as historical cost or fair value, be used, or does it depend on whether it is an asset or liability that is being measured? It appears that the new document will be a significant improvement over its predecessors and will lead to principles-based standards, which will help financial statement users make better decisions.

IFRS Self-Test Questions

1. Which of the following statements is *false*?
   (a) Assets equals liabilities plus equity.
   (b) Under IFRS, companies sometimes net liabilities against assets to report "net assets."
   (c) The FASB and IASB are working on a joint conceptual framework project.
   (d) Under IFRS, the statement of financial position is usually referred to as the statement of assets and equity.

2. A company has purchased a tract of land and expects to build a production plant on the land in approximately 5 years. During the 5 years before construction, the land will be idle. Under IFRS, the land should be reported as:
   (a) land expense.
   (b) property, plant, and equipment.
   (c) an intangible asset.
   (d) a long-term investment.

3. Current assets under IFRS are listed generally:
   (a) by importance.
   (b) in the reverse order of their expected conversion to cash.
   (c) by longevity.
   (d) alphabetically.

4. Companies that use IFRS:
   (a) may report all their assets on the statement of financial position at fair value.
   (b) may offset assets against liabilities and show net assets and net liabilities on their statement of financial positions, rather than the underlying detailed line items.
   (c) may report noncurrent assets before current assets on the statement of financial position.
   (d) do not have any guidelines as to what should be reported on the statement of financial position.

5. Companies that follow IFRS to prepare a statement of financial position generally use the following order of classification:
   (a) current assets, current liabilities, noncurrent assets, noncurrent liabilities, equity.
   (b) noncurrent assets, noncurrent liabilities, current assets, current liabilities, equity.
   (c) noncurrent assets, current assets, equity, noncurrent liabilities, current liabilities.
   (d) equity, noncurrent assets, current assets, noncurrent liabilities, current liabilities.

IFRS Concepts and Application

IFRS4-1 In what ways does the format of a statement of financial of position under IFRS often differ from a balance sheet presented under GAAP?

IFRS4-2 What term is commonly used under IFRS in reference to the balance sheet?

IFRS4-3 The statement of financial position for Diaz Company includes the following accounts: Accounts Receivable £12,500; Prepaid Insurance £3,600; Cash £15,400; Supplies £5,200; and Short-Term Investments £6,700. Prepare the current assets section of the statement of financial position, listing the accounts in proper sequence.

IFRS4-4 Zurich Company recently received the following information related to the company's December 31, 2012, statement of financial position.

Inventories	CHF 2,900	Short-term investments	CHF 120
Cash	13,400	Accumulated depreciation—	
Equipment	21,700	equipment	5,700
Investments in shares		Accounts receivable	4,300
(long-term)	6,500		

Prepare the assets section of the company's classified statement of financial position.

IFRS4-5 The following information is available for Karr Bowling Alley at December 31, 2012.

Buildings	$128,800	Owner's Capital	$115,000
Accounts Receivable	14,520	Accumulated Depreciation—Buildings	42,600
Prepaid Insurance	4,680	Accounts Payable	12,300
Cash	18,040	Notes Payable	97,780
Equipment	62,400	Accumulated Depreciation—Equipment	18,720
Land	64,000	Interest Payable	2,600
Insurance Expense	780	Bowling Revenues	14,180
Depreciation Expense	7,360		
Interest Expense	2,600		

Prepare a classified statement of financial position; assume that $13,900 of the notes payable will be paid in 2013.

IFRS4-6 Brian Hopkins is interested in comparing the liquidity and solvency of a U.S. software company with a Chinese competitor. Is this possible if the two companies report using different currencies?

International Comparative Analysis Problem: PepsiCo vs. Zetar plc

IFRS4-7 The financial statements of Zetar plc are presented in Appendix C. The company's complete annual report, including the notes to its financial statements, is available at *www.zetarplc.com.*

Instructions
Identify five differences in the format of the statement of financial position used by Zetar plc compared to a company, such as PepsiCo, that follows GAAP. (PepsiCo's financial statements are available in Appendix A.)

Answers to IFRS Self-Test Questions
1. d   2. d   3. b   4. c   5. c

✔
The Navigator

✔ **Remember to go back to the Navigator box on the chapter opening page and check off your completed work.**

Study Objectives

After studying this chapter, you should be able to:

[1] Identify the differences between service and merchandising companies.

[2] Explain the recording of purchases under a perpetual inventory system.

[3] Explain the recording of sales revenues under a perpetual inventory system.

[4] Explain the steps in the accounting cycle for a merchandising company.

[5] Distinguish between a multiple-step and a single-step income statement.

[6] Explain the computation and importance of gross profit.

✔ **The Navigator**

✔ [The Navigator]

Feature Story

WHO DOESN'T SHOP AT WAL-MART?

In his book *The End of Work,* Jeremy Rifkin notes that until the 20th century the word *consumption* evoked negative images. To be labeled a "consumer" was an insult. (In fact, one of the deadliest diseases in history, tuberculosis, was often referred to as "consumption.") Twentieth-century merchants realized, however, that in order to prosper, they had to convince people of the need for things not previously needed. For example, General Motors made annual changes in its cars so that people would be discontented with the cars they already owned. Thus began consumerism.

Today, consumption describes the U.S. lifestyle in a nutshell. We consume twice as much today per person as we did at the end of World War II. The amount of U.S. retail space per person is vastly greater than that of any other country. It appears that we live to shop.

The first great retail giant was Sears Roebuck. It started as a catalog company enabling people in rural areas to buy things by mail. For decades, it was the uncontested merchandising leader.

Today, Wal-Mart Stores, Inc. is the undisputed champion provider of basic (and perhaps not-so-basic) human needs. Wal-Mart opened its first store in 1962, and it now has more than 8,000 stores, serving more than 100 million customers every week. A key cause of Wal-Mart's incredible growth is its amazing system of inventory control and distribution. Wal-Mart has a management information system that employs six satellite channels, from which company computers receive 8.4 million updates every minute on what items customers buy and the relationship among items sold to each person.

Measured by sales revenues, Wal-Mart is the largest company in the world. In six years, it went from selling almost no groceries to being America's largest grocery retailer.

It would appear that things have never looked better at Wal-Mart. On the other hand, a *Wall Street Journal* article entitled "How to Sell More to Those Who Think It's Cool to Be Frugal" suggests that consumerism as a way of life might be dying. Don't bet your high-definition 3D TV on it though.

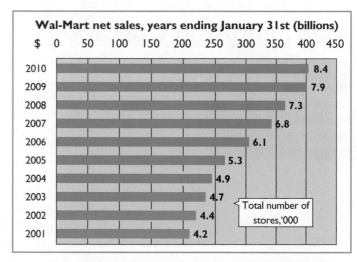

Wal-Mart net sales, years ending January 31st (billions)

Year	Net sales
2010	8.4
2009	7.9
2008	7.3
2007	6.8
2006	6.1
2005	5.3
2004	4.9
2003	4.7
2002	4.4
2001	4.2

Total number of stores,'000

Source: "How Big Can It Grow?" *The Economist* (April 17, 2004), pp. 67–69, and *www.walmart.com* (accessed November 23, 2010).

The Navigator

InsideCHAPTER5

PreviewofCHAPTER5

Merchandising is one of the largest and most influential industries in the United States. It is likely that a number of you will work for a merchandiser. Therefore, understanding the financial statements of merchandising companies is important. In this chapter, you will learn the basics about reporting merchandising transactions. In addition, you will learn how to prepare and analyze a commonly used form of the income statement—the multiple-step income statement. The content and organization of the chapter are as follows.

Accounting for Merchandising Operations

Merchandising Operations	Recording Purchases of Merchandise	Recording Sales of Merchandise	Completing the Accounting Cycle	Forms of Financial Statements
• Operating cycles • Flow of costs—perpetual and periodic inventory systems	• Freight costs • Purchase returns and allowances • Purchase discounts • Summary of purchasing transactions	• Sales returns and allowances • Sales discounts	• Adjusting entries • Closing entries • Summary of merchandising entries	• Multiple-step income statement • Single-step income statement • Classified balance sheet

✔ **The Navigator**

Merchandising Operations

Study Objective [1]

Identify the differences between service and merchandising companies.

Wal-Mart, Kmart, and Target are called merchandising companies because they buy and sell merchandise rather than perform services as their primary source of revenue. Merchandising companies that purchase and sell directly to consumers are called **retailers**. Merchandising companies that sell to retailers are known as **wholesalers**. For example, retailer Walgreens might buy goods from wholesaler McKesson; retailer Office Depot might buy office supplies from wholesaler United Stationers. The primary source of revenues for merchandising companies is the sale of merchandise, often referred to simply as **sales revenue** or **sales**. A merchandising company has two categories of expenses: cost of goods sold and operating expenses.

Cost of goods sold is the total cost of merchandise sold during the period. This expense is directly related to the revenue recognized from the sale of goods. Illustration 5-1 shows the income measurement process for a merchandising

Illustration 5-1
Income measurement process for a merchandising company

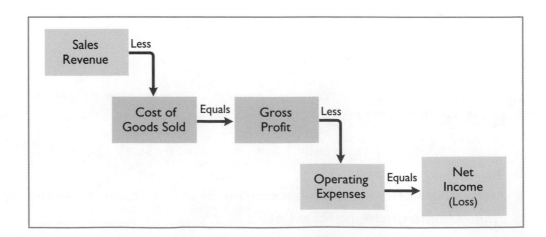

210

company. The items in the two blue boxes are unique to a merchandising company; they are not used by a service company.

Operating Cycles

The operating cycle of a merchandising company ordinarily is longer than that of a service company. The purchase of merchandise inventory and its eventual sale lengthen the cycle. Illustration 5-2 contrasts the operating cycles of service and merchandising companies. Note that the added asset account for a merchandising company is the Inventory account. Companies report inventory as a current asset on the balance sheet.

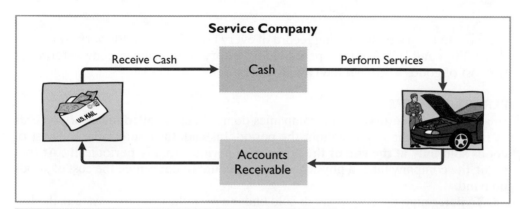

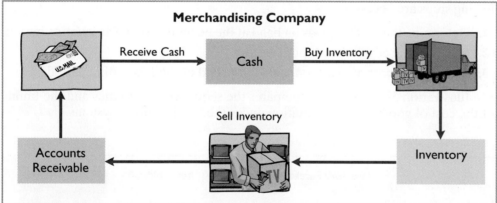

Illustration 5-2
Operating cycles for a service company and a merchandising company

Flow of Costs

The flow of costs for a merchandising company is as follows: Beginning inventory plus the cost of goods purchased is the cost of goods available for sale. As goods are sold, they are assigned to cost of goods sold. Those goods that are not sold by the end of the accounting period represent ending inventory. Illustration 5-3 (page 212) describes these relationships. Companies use one of two systems to account for inventory: a **perpetual inventory system** or a **periodic inventory system**.

PERPETUAL SYSTEM

In a **perpetual inventory system**, companies keep detailed records of the cost of each inventory purchase and sale. These records continuously—perpetually—show the inventory that should be on hand for every item. For example, a Ford dealership has separate inventory records for each automobile, truck, and van on its lot and showroom floor. Similarly, a Kroger grocery store uses bar codes and optical

Helpful Hint

For control purposes, companies take a physical inventory count under the perpetual system, even though it is not needed to determine cost of goods sold.

Illustration 5-3
Flow of costs

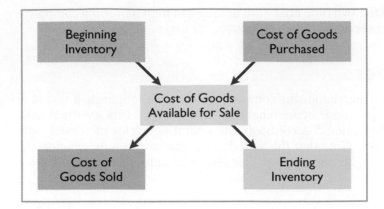

scanners to keep a daily running record of every box of cereal and every jar of jelly that it buys and sells. Under a perpetual inventory system, a company determines the cost of goods sold **each time a sale occurs**.

PERIODIC SYSTEM

In a periodic inventory system, companies do not keep detailed inventory records of the goods on hand throughout the period. Instead, they determine the cost of goods sold **only at the end of the accounting period**—that is, periodically. At that point, the company takes a physical inventory count to determine the cost of goods on hand.

To determine the cost of goods sold under a periodic inventory system, the following steps are necessary:

1. Determine the cost of goods on hand at the beginning of the accounting period.
2. Add to it the cost of goods purchased.
3. Subtract the cost of goods on hand at the end of the accounting period.

Illustration 5-4 graphically compares the sequence of activities and the timing of the cost of goods sold computation under the two inventory systems.

Illustration 5-4
Comparing perpetual and periodic inventory systems

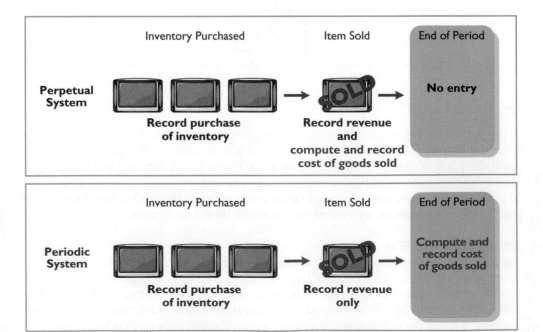

ADDITIONAL CONSIDERATIONS

Companies that sell merchandise with high unit values, such as automobiles, furniture, and major home appliances, have traditionally used perpetual systems. The growing use of computers and electronic scanners has enabled many more companies to install perpetual inventory systems. The perpetual inventory system is so named because the accounting records continuously—perpetually—show the quantity and cost of the inventory that should be on hand at any time.

A perpetual inventory system provides better control over inventories than a periodic system. Since the inventory records show the quantities that should be on hand, the company can count the goods at any time to see whether the amount of goods actually on hand agrees with the inventory records. If shortages are uncovered, the company can investigate immediately. Although a perpetual inventory system requires additional clerical work and additional cost to maintain the subsidiary records, a computerized system can minimize this cost. As noted in the Feature Story, much of Wal-Mart's success is attributed to its sophisticated inventory system.

Some businesses find it either unnecessary or uneconomical to invest in a computerized perpetual inventory system. Many small merchandising businesses, in particular, find that a perpetual inventory system costs more than it is worth. Managers of these businesses can control their merchandise and manage day-to-day operations using a periodic inventory system.

Because the perpetual inventory system is growing in popularity and use, we illustrate it in this chapter. Appendix 5A describes the journal entries for the periodic system.

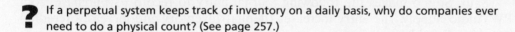

_I_NVESTOR _I_NSIGHT

Morrow Snowboards Improves Its Stock Appeal

Investors are often eager to invest in a company that has a hot new product. However, when snowboard maker Morrow Snowboards, Inc., issued shares of stock to the public for the first time, some investors expressed reluctance to invest in Morrow because of a number of accounting control problems. To reduce investor concerns, Morrow implemented a perpetual inventory system to improve its control over inventory. In addition, it stated that it would perform a physical inventory count every quarter until it felt that the perpetual inventory system was reliable.

? If a perpetual system keeps track of inventory on a daily basis, why do companies ever need to do a physical count? (See page 257.)

Recording Purchases of Merchandise

Companies purchase inventory using cash or credit (on account). They normally record purchases when they receive the goods from the seller. Business documents provide written evidence of the transaction. A canceled check or a cash register receipt, for example, indicates the items purchased and amounts paid for each cash purchase. Companies record cash purchases by an increase in Inventory and a decrease in Cash.

A **purchase invoice** should support each credit purchase. This invoice indicates the total purchase price and other relevant information. However, the purchaser does not prepare a separate purchase invoice. Instead, the purchaser uses as a

Study Objective [2]
Explain the recording of purchases under a perpetual inventory system.

purchase invoice a copy of the sales invoice sent by the seller. In Illustration 5-5, for example, Sauk Stereo (the buyer) uses as a purchase invoice the sales invoice prepared by PW Audio Supply, Inc. (the seller).

Illustration 5-5
Sales invoice used as purchase invoice by Sauk Stereo

Helpful Hint

To better understand the contents of this invoice, identify these items:
1. Seller
2. Invoice date
3. Purchaser
4. Salesperson
5. Credit terms
6. Freight terms
7. Goods sold: catalog number, description, quantity, price per unit
8. Total invoice amount

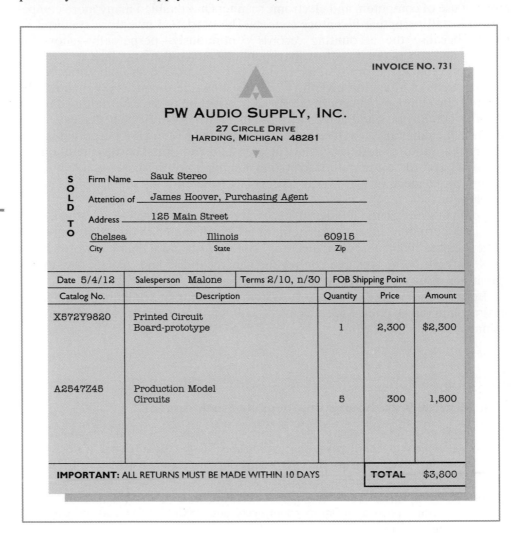

INVOICE NO. 731

PW AUDIO SUPPLY, INC.

27 CIRCLE DRIVE
HARDING, MICHIGAN 48281

SOLD TO

Firm Name ___ Sauk Stereo

Attention of ___ James Hoover, Purchasing Agent

Address ___ 125 Main Street

Chelsea   Illinois   60915
City   State   Zip

Date 5/4/12	Salesperson Malone	Terms 2/10, n/30	FOB Shipping Point		
Catalog No.	Description		Quantity	Price	Amount
X572Y9820	Printed Circuit Board-prototype		1	2,300	$2,300
A2547Z45	Production Model Circuits		5	300	1,500
IMPORTANT: ALL RETURNS MUST BE MADE WITHIN 10 DAYS				**TOTAL**	**$3,800**

Sauk Stereo makes the following journal entry to record its purchase from PW Audio Supply. The entry increases (debits) Inventory and increases (credits) Accounts Payable.

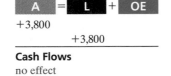

A	=	L	+	OE

+3,800
        +3,800

Cash Flows
no effect

May 4	Inventory	3,800	
	Accounts Payable		3,800
	(To record goods purchased on account from PW Audio Supply)		

Under the perpetual inventory system, companies record purchases of merchandise for sale in the Inventory account. Thus, Wal-Mart would increase (debit) Inventory for clothing, sporting goods, and anything else purchased for resale to customers.

Not all purchases are debited to Inventory, however. Companies record purchases of assets acquired for use and not for resale, such as supplies, equipment, and similar items, as increases to specific asset accounts rather than to Inventory. For example, to record the purchase of materials used to make shelf signs or for cash register receipt paper, Wal-Mart would increase Supplies.

Freight Costs

The sales agreement should indicate who—the seller or the buyer—is to pay for transporting the goods to the buyer's place of business. When a common carrier such as a railroad, trucking company, or airline transports the goods, the carrier prepares a freight bill in accord with the sales agreement.

Freight terms are expressed as either FOB shipping point or FOB destination. The letters FOB mean **free on board**. Thus, FOB shipping point means that the seller places the goods free on board the carrier, and the buyer pays the freight costs. Conversely, FOB destination means that the seller places the goods free on board to the buyer's place of business, and the seller pays the freight. For example, the sales invoice in Illustration 5-5 indicates FOB shipping point. Thus, the buyer (Sauk Stereo) pays the freight charges. Illustration 5-6 illustrates these shipping terms.

Illustration 5-6
Shipping terms

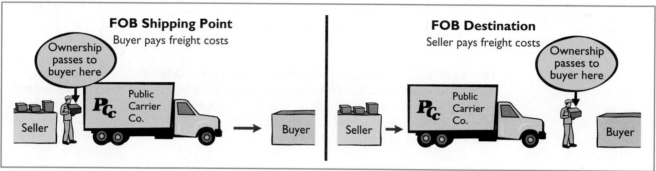

FREIGHT COSTS INCURRED BY THE BUYER

When the buyer incurs the transportation costs, these costs are considered part of the cost of purchasing inventory. Therefore, the buyer debits (increases) the account Inventory. For example, if upon delivery of the goods on May 6, Sauk Stereo (the buyer) pays Acme Freight Company $150 for freight charges, the entry on Sauk Stereo's books is:

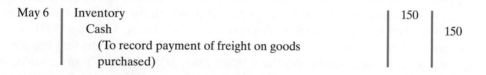

May 6	Inventory	150	
	Cash		150
	(To record payment of freight on goods purchased)		

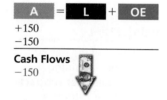

A = L + OE
+150
−150

Cash Flows
−150

Thus, any freight costs incurred by the buyer are part of the cost of merchandise purchased. The reason: Inventory cost should include any freight charges necessary to deliver the goods to the buyer.

FREIGHT COSTS INCURRED BY THE SELLER

In contrast, **freight costs incurred by the seller on outgoing merchandise are an operating expense to the seller.** These costs increase an expense account titled Freight-out or Delivery Expense. If the freight terms on the invoice had required PW Audio Supply (the seller) to pay the freight charges, the entry by PW Audio Supply would be:

May 4	Freight-out (or Delivery Expense)	150	
	Cash		150
	(To record payment of freight on goods sold)		

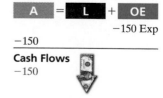

A = L + OE
−150 Exp
−150

Cash Flows
−150

When the seller pays the freight charges, it will usually establish a higher invoice price for the goods to cover the shipping expense.

Purchase Returns and Allowances

A purchaser may be dissatisfied with the merchandise received because the goods are damaged or defective, of inferior quality, or do not meet the purchaser's specifications. In such cases, the purchaser may return the goods to the seller for credit if the sale was made on credit, or for a cash refund if the purchase was for cash. This transaction is known as a **purchase return**. Alternatively, the purchaser may choose to keep the merchandise if the seller is willing to grant an allowance (deduction) from the purchase price. This transaction is known as a **purchase allowance**.

Assume that on May 8 Sauk Stereo returned goods costing $300 to PW Audio Supply. The following entry by Sauk Stereo for the returned merchandise decreases (debits) Accounts Payable and decreases (credits) Inventory.

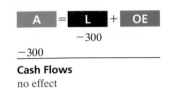

Cash Flows
no effect

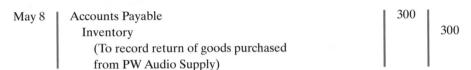

May 8	Accounts Payable	300	
	Inventory		300
	(To record return of goods purchased		
	from PW Audio Supply)		

Because Sauk Stereo increased Inventory when the goods were received, Inventory is decreased when Sauk Stereo returns the goods (or when it is granted an allowance).

Suppose instead that Sauk Stereo chose to keep the goods after being granted a $50 allowance (reduction in price). It would reduce (debit) Accounts Payable and reduce (credit) Inventory for $50.

Purchase Discounts

The credit terms of a purchase on account may permit the buyer to claim a cash discount for prompt payment. The buyer calls this cash discount a **purchase discount**. This incentive offers advantages to both parties: The purchaser saves money, and the seller shortens the operating cycle by more quickly converting the accounts receivable into cash.

Credit terms specify the amount of the cash discount and time period in which it is offered. They also indicate the time period in which the purchaser is expected to pay the full invoice price. In the sales invoice in Illustration 5-5 (page 214), credit terms are 2/10, n/30, which is read "two-ten, net thirty." This means that the buyer may take a 2% cash discount on the invoice price less ("net of") any returns or allowances, if payment is made within 10 days of the invoice date (the **discount period**). Otherwise, the invoice price, less any returns or allowances, is due 30 days from the invoice date.

Alternatively, the discount period may extend to a specified number of days following the month in which the sale occurs. For example, 1/10 EOM (end of month) means that a 1% discount is available if the invoice is paid within the first 10 days of the next month.

When the seller elects not to offer a cash discount for prompt payment, credit terms will specify only the maximum time period for paying the balance due. For example, the invoice may state the time period as n/30, n/60, or n/10 EOM. This means, respectively, that the buyer must pay the net amount in 30 days, 60 days, or within the first 10 days of the next month.

When the buyer pays an invoice within the discount period, the amount of the discount decreases Inventory. Why? Because companies record inventory at cost and, by paying within the discount period, the merchandiser has reduced that cost. To illustrate, assume Sauk Stereo pays the balance due of $3,500 (gross invoice price of $3,800 less purchase returns and allowances of $300) on May 14, the last

Helpful Hint

The term *net* in "net 30" means the remaining amount due after subtracting any sales returns and allowances and partial payments.

day of the discount period. The cash discount is $70 ($3,500 × 2%), and Sauk Stereo pays $3,430 ($3,500 − $70). The entry Sauk Stereo makes to record its May 14 payment decreases (debits) Accounts Payable by the amount of the gross invoice price, reduces (credits) Inventory by the $70 discount, and reduces (credits) Cash by the net amount owed.

May 14	Accounts Payable	3,500	
	Cash		3,430
	Inventory		70
	(To record payment within discount period)		

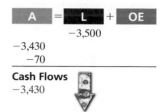

If Sauk Stereo failed to take the discount, and instead made full payment of $3,500 on June 3, it would debit Accounts Payable and credit Cash for $3,500 each.

June 3	Accounts Payable	3,500	
	Cash		3,500
	(To record payment with no discount taken)		

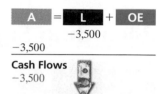

A merchandising company usually should take all available discounts. Passing up the discount may be viewed as **paying interest** for use of the money. For example, passing up the discount offered by PW Audio Supply would be comparable to Sauk Stereo paying an interest rate of 2% for the use of $3,500 for 20 days. This is the equivalent of an annual interest rate of approximately 36.5% (2% × 365/20). Obviously, it would be better for Sauk Stereo to borrow at prevailing bank interest rates of 6% to 10% than to lose the discount.

Summary of Purchasing Transactions

The following T account (with transaction descriptions in blue) provides a summary of the effect of the previous transactions on Inventory. Sauk Stereo originally purchased $3,800 worth of inventory for resale. It then returned $300 of goods. It paid $150 in freight charges, and finally, it received a $70 discount off the balance owed because it paid within the discount period. This results in a balance in Inventory of $3,580.

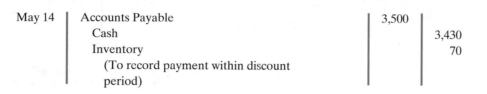

		Inventory			
Purchase	May 4	3,800	May 8	300	Purchase return
Freight-in	6	150	14	70	Purchase discount
		3,580			

Do it!

On September 5, De La Hoya Company buys merchandise on account from Junot Diaz Company. The selling price of the goods is $1,500, and the cost to Diaz Company was $800. On September 8, De La Hoya returns defective goods with a selling price of $200. Record the transactions on the books of De La Hoya Company.

Purchase Transactions

action plan

✔ Purchaser records goods at cost.

✔ When goods are returned, purchaser reduces Inventory.

Solution

Sept. 5	Inventory		1,500	
	Accounts Payable			1,500
	(To record goods purchased on account)			
8	Accounts Payable		200	
	Inventory			200
	(To record return of defective goods)			

Related exercise material: BE5-2, BE5-4, E5-2, E5-3, E5-4, and **Do it!** 5-1.

✔ The Navigator

Recording Sales of Merchandise

Study Objective [3]

Explain the recording of sales revenues under a perpetual inventory system.

Companies record sales revenues, like service revenues, when earned, in compliance with the revenue recognition principle. Typically, companies earn sales revenues when the goods transfer from the seller to the buyer. At this point, the sales transaction is complete and the sales price established.

Sales may be made on credit or for cash. A **business document** should support every sales transaction, to provide written evidence of the sale. **Cash register tapes** provide evidence of cash sales. A sales invoice, like the one shown in Illustration 5-5 (page 214), provides support for a credit sale. The original copy of the invoice goes to the customer, and the seller keeps a copy for use in recording the sale. The invoice shows the date of sale, customer name, total sales price, and other relevant information.

The seller makes two entries for each sale. **The first entry records the sale:** The seller increases (debits) Cash (or Accounts Receivable, if a credit sale), and also increases (credits) Sales Revenue. **The second entry records the cost of the merchandise sold:** The seller increases (debits) Cost of Goods Sold, and also decreases (credits) Inventory for the cost of those goods. As a result, the Inventory account will show at all times the amount of inventory that should be on hand.

To illustrate a credit sales transaction, PW Audio Supply records its May 4 sale of $3,800 to Sauk Stereo (see Illustration 5-5) as follows (assume the merchandise cost PW Audio Supply $2,400).

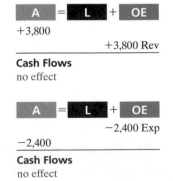

A	=	L	+	OE
+3,800				
				+3,800 Rev

Cash Flows
no effect

May 4	Accounts Receivable		3,800	
	Sales Revenue			3,800
	(To record credit sale to Sauk Stereo			
	per invoice #731)			

A	=	L	+	OE
				−2,400 Exp
−2,400				

Cash Flows
no effect

4	Cost of Goods Sold		2,400	
	Inventory			2,400
	(To record cost of merchandise sold on			
	invoice #731 to Sauk Stereo)			

For internal decision-making purposes, merchandising companies may use more than one sales account. For example, PW Audio Supply may decide to keep separate sales accounts for its sales of TV sets, DVD recorders, and microwave ovens. Wal-Mart might use separate accounts for sporting goods, children's clothing, and hardware—or it might have even more narrowly defined accounts. By using separate sales accounts for major product lines, rather than a single combined sales account, company management can more closely monitor sales trends and respond more strategically to changes in sales patterns. For example, if TV sales are increasing while microwave oven sales are decreasing, PW Audio Supply might reevaluate both its advertising and pricing policies on these items to ensure they are optimal.

On its income statement presented to outside investors, a merchandising company normally would provide only a single sales figure—the sum of all of its individual sales accounts. This is done for two reasons. First, providing detail on all of its individual sales accounts would add considerable length to its income statement. Second, companies do not want their competitors to know the details of their operating results. However, **Microsoft** recently expanded its disclosure of revenue from three to five types. The reason: The additional categories will better enable financial statement users to evaluate the growth of the company's consumer and Internet businesses.

Ethics Note

Many companies are trying to improve the quality of their financial reporting. For example, General Electric now provides more detail on its revenues and operating profits.

ANATOMY OF A FRAUD[1]

Holly Harmon was a cashier at a national superstore for only a short while when she began stealing merchandise using three methods. First, her husband or friends took UPC labels from cheaper items and put them on more expensive items. Holly then scanned the goods at the register. Second, Holly rang an item up but then voided the sale and left the merchandise in the shopping cart. A third approach was to put goods into large plastic containers. She rang up the plastic containers but not the goods within them. One day, Holly did not call in sick or show up for work. In such instances, the company reviews past surveillance tapes to look for suspicious activity by employees. This enabled the store to observe the thefts and to identify the participants.

Total take: $12,000

THE MISSING CONTROLS

Human resource controls. A background check would have revealed Holly's previous criminal record. She would not have been hired as a cashier.

Physical controls. Software can flag high numbers of voided transactions or a high number of sales of low-priced goods. Random comparisons of video records with cash register records can ensure that the goods reported as sold on the register are the same goods that are shown being purchased on the video recording. Finally, employees should be aware that they are being monitored.

Source: Adapted from Wells, *Fraud Casebook* (2007), pp. 251–259.

At the end of "Anatomy of a Fraud" stories, which describe some recent real-world frauds, we discuss the missing control activity that would likely have prevented or uncovered the fraud.

Sales Returns and Allowances

We now look at the "flipside" of purchase returns and allowances, which the seller records as **sales returns and allowances**. These are transactions where the seller either accepts goods back from the buyer (a return) or grants a reduction in the purchase price (an allowance) so the buyer will keep the goods. PW Audio Supply's entries to record credit for returned goods involve (1) an increase (debit) in Sales Returns and Allowances (a contra account to Sales Revenue) and a decrease (credit) in Accounts Receivable at the $300 selling price, and (2) an increase (debit) in

---

[1]The "Anatomy of a Fraud" stories in this textbook are adapted from *Fraud Casebook: Lessons from the Bad Side of Business,* edited by Joseph T. Wells (Hoboken, NJ: John Wiley & Sons, Inc., 2007). Used by permission. The names of some of the people and organizations in the stories are fictitious, but the facts in the stories are true.

Inventory (assume a $140 cost) and a decrease (credit) in Cost of Goods Sold, as shown below (assuming that the goods were not defective).

A = L + OE
−300 Rev
−300
Cash Flows
no effect

A = L + OE
+140
+140 Exp
Cash Flows
no effect

May 8	Sales Returns and Allowances	300	
	Accounts Receivable		300
	(To record credit granted to Sauk Stereo		
	for returned goods)		
8	Inventory	140	
	Cost of Goods Sold		140
	(To record cost of goods returned)		

If Sauk Stereo returns goods because they are damaged or defective, then PW Audio Supply's entry to Inventory and Cost of Goods Sold should be for the fair value of the returned goods, rather than their cost. For example, if the returned goods were defective and had a fair value of $50, PW Audio Supply would debit Inventory for $50, and would credit Cost of Goods Sold for $50.

What happens if the goods are not returned but the seller grants the buyer an allowance by reducing the purchase price? In this case, the seller debits Sales Returns and Allowances and credits Accounts Receivable for the amount of the allowance.

As mentioned above, Sales Returns and Allowances is a **contra-revenue account** to Sales Revenue. The normal balance of Sales Returns and Allowances is a debit. Companies use a contra account, instead of debiting Sales Revenue, to disclose in the accounts and in the income statement the amount of sales returns and allowances. Disclosure of this information is important to management: Excessive returns and allowances may suggest problems—inferior merchandise, inefficiencies in filling orders, errors in billing customers, or delivery or shipment mistakes. Moreover, a decrease (debit) recorded directly to Sales Revenue would obscure the relative importance of sales returns and allowances as a percentage of sales. It also could distort comparisons between total sales in different accounting periods.

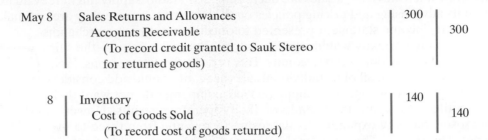

*A*CCOUNTING *A*CROSS THE *O*RGANIZATION

Should Costco Change Its Return Policy?

In most industries, sales returns are relatively minor. But returns of consumer electronics can really take a bite out of profits. Recently, the marketing executives at Costco Wholesale Corp. faced a difficult decision. Costco has always prided itself on its generous return policy. Most goods have had an unlimited grace period for returns. A new policy will require that certain electronics must be retuned within 90 days of their purchase. The reason? The cost of returned products such as high-definition TVs, computers, and iPods cut an estimated 8¢ per share off Costco's earnings per share, which was $2.30.

Source: Kris Hudson, "Costco Tightens Policy on Returning Electronics," *Wall Street Journal* (February 27, 2007), p. B4.

? If a company expects significant returns, what are the implications for revenue recognition? (See page 257.)

Sales Discounts

As mentioned in our discussion of purchase transactions, the seller may offer the customer a cash discount—called by the seller a **sales discount**—for the prompt payment of the balance due. Like a purchase discount, a sales discount is based on the invoice price less returns and allowances, if any. The seller increases (debits) the Sales Discounts account for discounts that are taken. For example, PW Audio

Supply makes the following entry to record the cash receipt on May 14 from Sauk Stereo within the discount period.

May 14	Cash	3,430	
	Sales Discounts	70	
	Accounts Receivable		3,500
	(To record collection within 2/10, n/30		
	discount period from Sauk Stereo)		

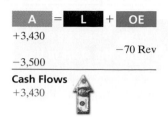

A = L + OE
+3,430
                   −70 Rev
−3,500
Cash Flows
+3,430

Like Sales Returns and Allowances, Sales Discounts is a **contra-revenue account** to Sales Revenue. Its normal balance is a debit. PW Audio Supply uses this account, instead of debiting Sales Revenue, to disclose the amount of cash discounts taken by customers. If Sauk Stereo does not take the discount, PW Audio Supply increases (debits) Cash for $3,500 and decreases (credits) Accounts Receivable for the same amount at the date of collection.

The following T accounts summarize the three sales-related transactions and show their combined effect on net sales.

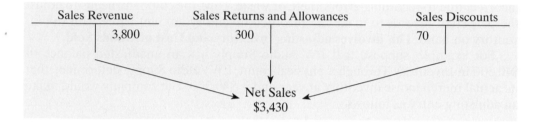

Sales Revenue	Sales Returns and Allowances	Sales Discounts
3,800	300	70

Net Sales
$3,430

Do it!

On September 5, De La Hoya Company buys merchandise on account from Junot Diaz Company. The selling price of the goods is $1,500, and the cost to Diaz Company was $800. On September 8, De La Hoya returns defective goods with a selling price of $200 and a fair value of $30. Record the transactions on the books of Junot Diaz Company.

Solution

Sept. 5	Accounts Receivable	1,500	
	Sales Revenue		1,500
	(To record credit sale)		
5	Cost of Goods Sold	800	
	Inventory		800
	(To record cost of goods sold on		
	account)		
8	Sales Returns and Allowances	200	
	Accounts Receivable		200
	(To record credit granted for receipt of		
	returned goods)		
8	Inventory	30	
	Cost of Goods Sold		30
	(To record fair value of goods		
	returned)		

Sales Transactions

action plan

✔ Seller records both the sale and the cost of goods sold at the time of the sale.

✔ When goods are returned, the seller records the return in a contra account, Sales Returns and Allowances, and reduces Accounts Receivable. Any goods returned increase Inventory and reduce Cost of Goods Sold.

✔ Defective or damaged inventory is recorded at fair value (scrap value).

Related exercise material: **BE5-2, BE5-3, E5-3, E5-4, E5-5,** and **Do it!** 5-2.

✔
The Navigator

Completing the Accounting Cycle

Up to this point, we have illustrated the basic entries for transactions relating to purchases and sales in a perpetual inventory system. Now we consider the remaining steps in the accounting cycle for a merchandising company. Each of the required steps described in Chapter 4 for service companies apply to merchandising companies. Appendix 5B to this chapter shows use of a worksheet by a merchandiser (an optional step).

Adjusting Entries

A merchandising company generally has the same types of adjusting entries as a service company. However, a merchandiser using a perpetual system will require one additional adjustment to make the records agree with the actual inventory on hand. Here's why: At the end of each period, for control purposes, a merchandising company that uses a perpetual system will take a physical count of its goods on hand. The company's unadjusted balance in Inventory usually does not agree with the actual amount of inventory on hand. The perpetual inventory records may be incorrect due to recording errors, theft, or waste. Thus, the company needs to adjust the perpetual records to make the recorded inventory amount agree with the inventory on hand. **This involves adjusting Inventory and Cost of Goods Sold.**

For example, suppose that PW Audio Supply has an unadjusted balance of $40,500 in Inventory. Through a physical count, PW Audio Supply determines that its actual merchandise inventory at year-end is $40,000. The company would make an adjusting entry as follows.

Cost of Goods Sold	500	
Inventory		500
(To adjust inventory to physical count)		

Closing Entries

A merchandising company, like a service company, closes to Income Summary all accounts that affect net income. In journalizing, the company credits all temporary accounts with debit balances, and debits all temporary accounts with credit balances, as shown below for PW Audio Supply. Note that PW Audio Supply closes Cost of Goods Sold to Income Summary.

Helpful Hint

The easiest way to prepare the first two closing entries is to identify the temporary accounts by their balances and then prepare one entry for the credits and one for the debits.

Dec. 31	Sales Revenue	480,000	
	Income Summary		480,000
	(To close income statement accounts with		
	credit balances)		
31	Income Summary	450,000	
	Sales Returns and Allowances		12,000
	Sales Discounts		8,000
	Cost of Goods Sold		316,000
	Salaries and Wages Expense		64,000
	Freight-out		7,000
	Advertising Expense		16,000
	Utilities Expense		17,000
	Depreciation Expense		8,000
	Insurance Expense		2,000
	(To close income statement accounts with		
	debit balances)		

31	Income Summary	30,000	
	Owner's Capital		30,000
	(To close net income to capital)		

31	Owner's Capital	15,000	
	Owner's Drawings		15,000
	(To close drawings to capital)		

After PW Audio Supply has posted the closing entries, all temporary accounts have zero balances. Also, Owner's Capital has a balance that is carried over to the next period.

Summary of Merchandising Entries

Illustration 5-7 summarizes the entries for the merchandising accounts using a perpetual inventory system.

Illustration 5-7
Daily recurring and adjusting and closing entries

	Transactions	Daily Recurring Entries	Dr.	Cr.
Sales Transactions	Selling merchandise to customers.	Cash or Accounts Receivable	XX	
		Sales Revenue		XX
		Cost of Goods Sold	XX	
		Inventory		XX
	Granting sales returns or allowances to customers.	Sales Returns and Allowances	XX	
		Cash or Accounts Receivable		XX
		Inventory	XX	
		Cost of Goods Sold		XX
	Paying freight costs on sales; FOB destination.	Freight-out	XX	
		Cash		XX
	Receiving payment from customers within discount period.	Cash	XX	
		Sales Discounts	XX	
		Accounts Receivable		XX
Purchase Transactions	Purchasing merchandise for resale.	Inventory	XX	
		Cash or Accounts Payable		XX
	Paying freight costs on merchandise purchased; FOB shipping point.	Inventory	XX	
		Cash		XX
	Receiving purchase returns or allowances from suppliers.	Cash or Accounts Payable	XX	
		Inventory		XX
	Paying suppliers within discount period.	Accounts Payable	XX	
		Inventory		XX
		Cash		XX

Events	Adjusting and Closing Entries	Dr.	Cr.
Adjust because book amount is higher than the inventory amount determined to be on hand.	Cost of Goods Sold	XX	
	Inventory		XX
Closing temporary accounts with credit balances.	Sales Revenue	XX	
	Income Summary		XX
Closing temporary accounts with debit balances.	Income Summary	XX	
	Sales Returns and Allowances		XX
	Sales Discounts		XX
	Cost of Goods Sold		XX
	Freight-out		XX
	Expenses		XX

Do it!

Closing Entries

action plan

✔ Close all temporary accounts with credit balances to Income Summary by debiting these accounts.

✔ Close all temporary accounts with debit balances, except drawings, to Income Summary by crediting these accounts.

The trial balance of Celine's Sports Wear Shop at December 31 shows Inventory $25,000, Sales Revenue $162,400, Sales Returns and Allowances $4,800, Sales Discounts $3,600, Cost of Goods Sold $110,000, Rent Revenue $6,000, Freight-out $1,800, Rent Expense $8,800, and Salaries and Wages Expense $22,000. Prepare the closing entries for the above accounts.

Solution

The two closing entries are:

Dec. 31	Sales Revenue	162,400	
	Rent Revenue	6,000	
	Income Summary		168,400
	(To close accounts with credit balances)		
31	Income Summary	151,000	
	Cost of Goods Sold		110,000
	Sales Returns and Allowances		4,800
	Sales Discounts		3,600
	Freight-out		1,800
	Rent Expense		8,800
	Salaries and Wages Expense		22,000
	(To close accounts with debit balances)		

Related exercise material: BE5-5, BE5-6, E5-6, E5-7, E5-8, and **Do it!** 5-3.

✔
The Navigator

Forms of Financial Statements

Study Objective [5]

Distinguish between a multiple-step and a single-step income statement.

Merchandising companies widely use the classified balance sheet introduced in Chapter 4 and one of two forms for the income statement. This section explains the use of these financial statements by merchandisers.

Multiple-Step Income Statement

The **multiple-step income statement** is so named because it shows several steps in determining net income. Two of these steps relate to the company's principal operating activities. A multiple-step statement also distinguishes between **operating** and **nonoperating activities**. Finally, the statement also highlights intermediate components of income and shows subgroupings of expenses.

INCOME STATEMENT PRESENTATION OF SALES

The multiple-step income statement begins by presenting **sales revenue**. It then deducts contra-revenue accounts—sales returns and allowances, and sales discounts— to arrive at **net sales**. Illustration 5-8 presents the sales revenues section for PW Audio Supply, using assumed data.

    This presentation discloses the key data about the company's principal revenue-producing activities.

Illustration 5-8
Computation of net sales

PW Audio Supply		
Income Statement (partial)		
Sales revenues		
Sales revenue		$480,000
Less: Sales returns and allowances	$12,000	
Sales discounts	8,000	20,000
Net sales		**$460,000**

GROSS PROFIT

From Illustration 5-1, you learned that companies deduct cost of goods sold from sales revenue in order to determine gross profit. For this computation, companies use **net sales** (which takes into consideration Sales Returns and Allowances and Sales Discounts) as the amount of sales revenue. On the basis of the sales data in Illustration 5-8 (net sales of $460,000) and cost of goods sold under the perpetual inventory system (assume $316,000), PW Audio Supply's gross profit is $144,000, computed as follows.

> **Study Objective [6]**
> Explain the computation and importance of gross profit.

Net sales	$460,000
Cost of goods sold	316,000
Gross profit	**$144,000**

Illustration 5-9
Computation of gross profit

We also can express a company's gross profit as a percentage, called the gross profit rate. To do so, we divide the amount of gross profit by net sales. For PW Audio Supply, the **gross profit rate** is 31.3%, computed as follows.

Gross Profit	÷	**Net Sales**	=	**Gross Profit Rate**
$144,000	÷	$460,000	=	31.3%

Illustration 5-10
Gross profit rate formula and computation

Analysts generally consider the gross profit **rate** to be more useful than the gross profit **amount**. The rate expresses a more meaningful (qualitative) relationship between net sales and gross profit. For example, a gross profit of $1,000,000 may sound impressive. But if it is the result of a gross profit rate of only 7%, it is not so impressive. The gross profit rate tells how many cents of each sales dollar go to gross profit.

Gross profit represents the **merchandising profit** of a company. It is not a measure of the overall profitability, because operating expenses are not yet deducted. But managers and other interested parties closely watch the amount and trend of gross profit. They compare current gross profit with amounts reported in past periods. They also compare the company's gross profit rate with rates of competitors and with industry averages. Such comparisons provide information about the effectiveness of a company's purchasing function and the soundness of its pricing policies.

OPERATING EXPENSES AND NET INCOME

Operating expenses are the next component in measuring net income for a merchandising company. They are the expenses incurred in the process of earning sales revenue. These expenses are similar in merchandising and service companies. At PW Audio Supply, operating expenses were $114,000. The company determines its net income by subtracting operating expenses from gross profit. Thus, net income is $30,000, as shown below.

Gross profit	$144,000
Operating expenses	**114,000**
Net income	$ 30,000

Illustration 5-11
Operating expenses in computing net income

The net income amount is the so-called "bottom line" of a company's income statement.

Ethics Note

Companies manage earnings in various ways. ConAgra Foods recorded a nonrecurring gain for $186 million from the sale of Pilgrim's Pride stock to help meet an earnings projection for the quarter.

NONOPERATING ACTIVITIES

Nonoperating activities consist of various revenues and expenses and gains and losses that are unrelated to the company's main line of operations. When nonoperating items are included, the label "**Income from operations**" (or "Operating income") precedes them. This label clearly identifies the results of the company's normal operations, an amount determined by subtracting cost of goods sold and operating expenses from net sales. The results of nonoperating activities are shown in the categories "**Other revenues and gains**" and "**Other expenses and losses**." Illustration 5-12 lists examples of each.

Illustration 5-12
Other items of nonoperating activities

Other Revenues and Gains
Interest revenue from notes receivable and marketable securities.
Dividend revenue from investments in common stock.
Rent revenue from subleasing a portion of the store.
Gain from the sale of property, plant, and equipment.

Other Expenses and Losses
Interest expense on notes and loans payable.
Casualty losses from recurring causes, such as vandalism and accidents.
Loss from the sale or abandonment of property, plant, and equipment.
Loss from strikes by employees and suppliers.

Merchandising companies report the nonoperating activities in the income statement immediately after the company's operating activities. Illustration 5-13 shows these sections for PW Audio Supply, Inc., using assumed data.

The distinction between operating and nonoperating activities is crucial to many external users of financial data. These users view operating income as sustainable and many nonoperating activities as nonrecurring. Therefore, when forecasting next year's income, analysts put the most weight on this year's operating income, and less weight on this year's nonoperating activities.

*E*THICS *I*NSIGHT

Disclosing More Details

After Enron, increased investor criticism and regulator scrutiny forced many companies to improve the clarity of their financial disclosures. For example, IBM announced that it would begin providing more detail regarding its "Other gains and losses." It had previously included these items in its selling, general, and administrative expenses, with little disclosure.

Disclosing other gains and losses in a separate line item on the income statement will not have any effect on bottom-line income. However, analysts complained that burying these details in the selling, general, and administrative expense line reduced their ability to fully understand how well IBM was performing. For example previously if IBM sold off one of its buildings at a gain, it would include this gain in the selling, general and administrative expense line item, thus reducing that expense. This made it appear that the company had done a better job of controlling operating expenses than it actually had.

Other companies that also recently announced changes to increase the informativeness of their income statements included PepsiCo and General Electric.

? Why have investors and analysts demanded more accuracy in isolating "Other gains and losses" from operating items? (See page 257.)

Illustration 5-13
Multiple-step income statement

PW Audio Supply, Inc.			
Income Statement			
For the Year Ended December 31, 2012			

Calculation of gross profit

Sales revenues		
Sales revenue		$480,000
Less: Sales returns and allowances	$12,000	
Sales discounts	8,000	20,000
Net sales		460,000
Cost of goods sold		316,000
Gross profit		144,000

Calculation of income from operations

Operating expenses		
Salaries and wages expense	64,000	
Utilities expense	17,000	
Advertising expense	16,000	
Depreciation expense	8,000	
Freight-out	7,000	
Insurance expense	2,000	
Total operating expenses		114,000
Income from operations		30,000
Other revenues and gains		
Interest revenue	3,000	
Gain on disposal of plant assets	600	3,600

Results of nonoperating activities

Other expenses and losses		
Interest expense	1,800	
Casualty loss from vandalism	200	2,000
Net income		$ 31,600

Single-Step Income Statement

Another income statement format is the **single-step income statement**. The statement is so named because only one step—subtracting total expenses from total revenues—is required in determining net income.

In a single-step statement, all data are classified into two categories: (1) **revenues**, which include both operating revenues and other revenues and gains; and (2) **expenses**, which include cost of goods sold, operating expenses, and other expenses and losses. Illustration 5-14 (page 228) shows a single-step statement for PW Audio Supply.

There are two primary reasons for using the single-step format: (1) A company does not realize any type of profit or income until total revenues exceed total expenses, so it makes sense to divide the statement into these two categories. (2) The format is simpler and easier to read. *For homework problems, however, you should use the single-step format only when specifically instructed to do so.*

Classified Balance Sheet

In the balance sheet, merchandising companies report inventory as a current asset immediately below accounts receivable. Recall from Chapter 4 that companies generally list current asset items in the order of their closeness to cash

Illustration 5-14
Single-step income statement

PW Audio Supply, Inc. Income Statement For the Year Ended December 31, 2012		
Revenues		
Net sales		$460,000
Interest revenue		3,000
Gain on disposal of plant assets		600
Total revenues		463,600
Expenses		
Cost of goods sold	$316,000	
Operating expenses	114,000	
Interest expense	1,800	
Casualty loss from vandalism	200	
Total expenses		432,000
Net income		$ 31,600

(liquidity). Inventory is less close to cash than accounts receivable because the goods must first be sold and then collection made from the customer. Illustration 5-15 presents the assets section of a classified balance sheet for PW Audio Supply.

Illustration 5-15
Assets section of a classified balance sheet

Helpful Hint
The $40,000 is the cost of the inventory on hand, not its expected selling price.

PW Audio Supply, Inc. Balance Sheet (Partial) December 31, 2012		
Assets		
Current assets		
Cash		$ 9,500
Accounts receivable		16,100
Inventory		40,000
Prepaid insurance		1,800
Total current assets		67,400
Property, plant, and equipment		
Equipment	$80,000	
Less: Accumulated depreciation—equipment	24,000	56,000
Total assets		$123,400

Do it!

Financial Statement Classifications

You are presented with the following list of accounts from the adjusted trial balance for merchandiser Gorman Company. Indicate in which financial statement and under what classification each of the following would be reported.

Accounts Payable
Accounts Receivable
Accumulated Depreciation—Buildings

Accumulated Depreciation—Equipment
Advertising Expense
Buildings

Cash
Depreciation Expense
Equipment
Freight-out
Gain on Disposal of Plant Assets
Insurance Expense
Interest Expense
Interest Payable
Inventory
Land

Notes Payable (due in 3 years)
Owner's Capital (beginning balance)
Owner's Drawings
Property Taxes Payable
Salaries and Wages Expense
Salaries and Wages Payable
Sales Returns and Allowances
Sales Revenue
Utilities Expense

Solution

Account	Financial Statement	Classification
Accounts Payable	Balance sheet	Current liabilities
Accounts Receivable	Balance sheet	Current assets
Accumulated Depreciation— Buildings	Balance sheet	Property, plant, and equipment
Accumulated Depreciation— Equipment	Balance sheet	Property, plant, and equipment
Advertising Expense	Income statement	Operating expenses
Buildings	Balance sheet	Property, plant, and equipment
Cash	Balance sheet	Current assets
Depreciation Expense	Income statement	Operating expenses
Equipment	Balance sheet	Property, plant, and equipment
Freight-out	Income statement	Operating expenses
Gain on Disposal of Plant Assets	Income statement	Other revenues and gains
Insurance Expense	Income statement	Operating expenses
Interest Expense	Income statement	Other expenses and losses
Interest Payable	Balance sheet	Current liabilities
Inventory	Balance sheet	Current assets
Land	Balance sheet	Property, plant, and equipment
Notes Payable	Balance sheet	Long-term liabilities
Owner's Capital	Owner's equity statement	Beginning balance
Owner's Drawings	Owner's equity statement	Deduction section
Property Taxes Payable	Balance sheet	Current liabilities
Salaries and Wages Expense	Income statement	Operating expenses
Salaries and Wages Payable	Balance sheet	Current liabilities
Sales Returns and Allowances	Income statement	Sales revenues
Sales Revenue	Income statement	Sales revenues
Utilities Expense	Income statement	Operating expenses

action plan

✔ Review the major sections of the income statement, sales revenues, cost of goods sold, operating expenses, other revenues and gains, and other expenses and losses.

✔ Add net income and investments to beginning capital and deduct drawings to arrive at ending capital in the owner's equity statement.

✔ Review the major sections of the balance sheet, income statement, and owner's equity statement.

Related exercise material: BE5-7, BE5-8, BE5-9, E5-9, E5-10, E5-12, E5-13, E5-14, and **Do it!** 5-4.

✔
The Navigator

The adjusted trial balance columns of Falcetto Company's worksheet for the year ended December 31, 2012, are as follows.

Debit		Credit	
Cash	14,500	Accumulated Depreciation—	18,000
Accounts Receivable	11,100	Equipment	
Inventory	29,000	Notes Payable	25,000
Prepaid Insurance	2,500	Accounts Payable	10,600
Equipment	95,000	Owner's Capital	81,000
Owner's Drawings	12,000	Sales Revenue	536,800
Sales Returns and Allowances	6,700	Interest Revenue	2,500
Sales Discounts	5,000		673,900
Cost of Goods Sold	363,400		
Freight-out	7,600		
Advertising Expense	12,000		
Salaries and Wages Expense	56,000		
Utilities Expense	18,000		
Rent Expense	24,000		
Depreciation Expense	9,000		
Insurance Expense	4,500		
Interest Expense	3,600		
	673,900		

Instructions

Prepare a multiple-step income statement for Falcetto Company.

action plan

✔ Remember that the key components of the income statement are net sales, cost of goods sold, gross profit, total operating expenses, and net income (loss). Report these components in the right-hand column of the income statement.

✔ Put nonoperating items after income from operations.

Solution to Comprehensive Do it!

FALCETTO COMPANY
Income Statement
For the Year Ended December 31, 2012

Sales revenues		
Sales revenue		$536,800
Less: Sales returns and allowances	$ 6,700	
Sales discounts	5,000	11,700
Net sales		525,100
Cost of goods sold		363,400
Gross profit		161,700
Operating expenses		
Salaries and wages expense	56,000	
Rent expense	24,000	
Utilities expense	18,000	
Advertising expense	12,000	
Depreciation expense	9,000	
Freight-out	7,600	
Insurance expense	4,500	
Total operating expenses		131,100
Income from operations		30,600
Other revenues and gains		
Interest revenue	2,500	
Other expenses and losses		
Interest expense	3,600	1,100
Net income		$ 29,500

The Navigator

Summary of Study Objectives

[1] Identify the differences between service and merchandising companies. Because of inventory, a merchandising company has sales revenue, cost of goods sold, and gross profit. To account for inventory, a merchandising company must choose between a perpetual and a periodic inventory system.

[2] Explain the recording of purchases under a perpetual inventory system. The company debits the Inventory account for all purchases of merchandise and freight-in, and credits it for purchase discounts and purchase returns and allowances.

[3] Explain the recording of sales revenues under a perpetual inventory system. When a merchandising company sells inventory, it debits Accounts Receivable (or Cash), and credits Sales Revenue for the **selling price** of the merchandise. At the same time, it debits Cost of Goods Sold, and credits Inventory for the **cost** of the inventory items sold.

[4] Explain the steps in the accounting cycle for a merchandising company. Each of the required steps in the accounting cycle for a service company applies to a merchandising company. A worksheet is again an optional step. Under a perpetual inventory system, the company must adjust the Inventory account to agree with the physical count.

[5] Distinguish between a multiple-step and a single-step income statement. A multiple-step income statement shows numerous steps in determining net income, including nonoperating activities sections. A single-step income statement classifies all data under two categories, revenues or expenses, and determines net income in one step.

[6] Explain the computation and importance of gross profit. Merchandising companies compute gross profit by subtracting cost of goods sold from net sales. Gross profit represents the merchandising profit of a company. Managers and other interested parties closely watch the amount and trend of gross profit and of the gross profit rate.

✔
The Navigator

Glossary

Contra-revenue account An account that is offset against a revenue account on the income statement. (p. 220).

Cost of goods sold The total cost of merchandise sold during the period. (p. 210).

FOB destination Freight terms indicating that the seller places the goods free on board to the buyer's place of business, and the seller pays the freight. (p. 215).

FOB shipping point Freight terms indicating that the seller places goods free on board the carrier, and the buyer pays the freight costs. (p. 215).

Gross profit The excess of net sales over the cost of goods sold. (p. 225).

Gross profit rate Gross profit expressed as a percentage, by dividing the amount of gross profit by net sales. (p. 225).

Income from operations Income from a company's principal operating activity; determined by subtracting cost of goods sold and operating expenses from net sales. (p. 226).

Multiple-step income statement An income statement that shows several steps in determining net income. (p. 224).

Net sales Sales less sales returns and allowances and less sales discounts. (p. 224).

Nonoperating activities Various revenues, expenses, gains, and losses that are unrelated to a company's main line of operations. (p. 226).

Operating expenses Expenses incurred in the process of earning sales revenues. (p. 225).

Other expenses and losses A nonoperating-activities section of the income statement that shows expenses and losses unrelated to the company's main line of operations. (p. 226).

Other revenues and gains A nonoperating-activities section of the income statement that shows revenues and gains unrelated to the company's main line of operations. (p. 226).

Periodic inventory system An inventory system under which the company does not keep detailed inventory records throughout the accounting period but determines the cost of goods sold only at the end of an accounting period. (p. 212).

Perpetual inventory system An inventory system under which the company keeps detailed records of the cost of each inventory purchase and sale, and the records continuously show the inventory that should be on hand. (p. 211).

Purchase allowance A deduction made to the selling price of merchandise, granted by the seller so that the buyer will keep the merchandise. (p. 216).

Purchase discount A cash discount claimed by a buyer for prompt payment of a balance due. (p. 216).

Purchase invoice A document that supports each credit purchase. (p. 213).

Purchase return A return of goods from the buyer to the seller for a cash or credit refund. (p. 216).

Sales discount A reduction given by a seller for prompt payment of a credit sale. (p. 220).

Sales invoice A document that supports each credit sale. (p. 218).

Sales returns and allowances Purchase returns and allowances from the seller's perspective. See *Purchase return* and *Purchase allowance*, above. (p. 219).

Sales revenue (Sales) The primary source of revenue in a merchandising company. (p. 210).

Single-step income statement An income statement that shows only one step in determining net income. (p. 227).

APPENDIX5A

Periodic Inventory System

Study Objective [7]
Explain the recording of purchases and sales of inventory under a periodic inventory system.

As described in this chapter, companies may use one of two basic systems of accounting for inventories: (1) the perpetual inventory system or (2) the periodic inventory system. In the chapter, we focused on the characteristics of the perpetual inventory system. In this appendix, we discuss and illustrate the **periodic inventory system**. One key difference between the two systems is the point at which the company computes cost of goods sold. For a visual reminder of this difference, refer back to Illustration 5-4 (on page 212).

Determining Cost of Goods Sold Under a Periodic System

Determining cost of goods sold is different when a periodic inventory system is used rather than a perpetual system. As you have seen, a company using a **perpetual system** makes an entry to record cost of goods sold and to reduce inventory *each time a sale is made*. A company using a **periodic system** does not determine cost of goods sold *until the end of the period*. At the end of the period the company performs a count to determine the ending balance of inventory. It then **calculates cost of goods sold by subtracting ending inventory from the goods available for sale**. Goods available for sale is the sum of beginning inventory plus purchases, as shown in Illustration 5A-1.

Illustration 5A-1
Basic formula for cost of goods sold using the periodic system

	Beginning Inventory
+	Cost of Goods Purchased
	Cost of Goods Available for Sale
−	Ending Inventory
	Cost of Goods Sold

Another difference between the two approaches is that the perpetual system directly adjusts the Inventory account for any transaction that affects inventory (such as freight costs, returns, and discounts). The periodic system does not do this. Instead, it creates different accounts for purchases, freight costs, returns, and discounts. These various accounts are shown in Illustration 5A-2, which presents the calculation of cost of goods sold for PW Audio Supply using the periodic approach.

Note that the basic elements from Illustration 5A-1 are highlighted in Illustration 5A-2. You will learn more in Chapter 6 about how to determine cost of goods sold using the periodic system.

The use of the periodic inventory system does not affect the form of presentation in the balance sheet. As under the perpetual system, a company reports inventory in the current assets section.

PW Audio Supply, Inc. Cost of Goods Sold For the Year Ended December 31, 2012			
Cost of goods sold			
Inventory, January 1			$ 36,000
Purchases		$325,000	
Less: Purchase returns and			
allowances	$10,400		
Purchase discounts	6,800	17,200	
Net purchases		307,800	
Add: Freight-in		12,200	
Cost of goods purchased			320,000
Cost of goods available for sale			356,000
Inventory, December 31			40,000
Cost of goods sold			$316,000

Illustration 5A-2
Cost of goods sold for a merchandiser using a periodic inventory system

Helpful Hint

The far right column identifies the primary items that make up cost of goods sold of $316,000. The middle column explains cost of goods purchased of $320,000. The left column reports contra purchase items of $17,200.

Recording Merchandise Transactions

In a **periodic inventory system**, companies record revenues from the sale of merchandise when sales are made, just as in a perpetual system. Unlike the perpetual system, however, companies **do not attempt on the date of sale to record the cost of the merchandise sold**. Instead, they take a physical inventory count at the **end of the period** to determine (1) the cost of the merchandise then on hand and (2) the cost of the goods sold during the period. And, **under a periodic system, companies record purchases of merchandise in the Purchases account rather than the Inventory account**. Also, in a periodic system, purchase returns and allowances, purchase discounts, and freight costs on purchases are recorded in separate accounts.

To illustrate the recording of merchandise transactions under a periodic inventory system, we will use purchase/sale transactions between PW Audio Supply, Inc. and Sauk Stereo, as illustrated for the perpetual inventory system in this chapter.

Recording Purchases of Merchandise

On the basis of the sales invoice (Illustration 5-5, shown on page 214) and receipt of the merchandise ordered from PW Audio Supply, Sauk Stereo records the $3,800 purchase as follows.

May 4	Purchases	3,800	
	Accounts Payable		3,800
	(To record goods purchased on account from PW Audio Supply)		

Purchases is a temporary account whose normal balance is a debit.

Helpful Hint

Be careful not to debit purchases of equipment or supplies to a Purchases account.

FREIGHT COSTS

When the purchaser directly incurs the freight costs, it debits the account Freight-in (or Transportation-in). For example, if Sauk Stereo pays Acme Freight Company $150 for freight charges on its purchase from PW Audio Supply on May 6, the entry on Sauk Stereo's books is:

May 6	Freight-in (Transportation-in)	150	
	Cash		150
	(To record payment of freight on goods purchased)		

Like Purchases, Freight-in is a temporary account whose normal balance is a debit. **Freight-in is part of cost of goods purchased.** The reason is that cost of goods purchased should include any freight charges necessary to bring the goods to the purchaser. Freight costs are not subject to a purchase discount. Purchase discounts apply only to the invoice cost of the merchandise.

PURCHASE RETURNS AND ALLOWANCES

Sauk Stereo returns $300 of goods to PW Audio Supply and prepares the following entry to recognize the return.

May 8	Accounts Payable	300	
	Purchase Returns and Allowances		300
	(To record return of goods purchased		
	from PW Audio Supply)		

Purchase Returns and Allowances is a temporary account whose normal balance is a credit.

PURCHASE DISCOUNTS

On May 14, Sauk Stereo pays the balance due on account to PW Audio Supply, taking the 2% cash discount allowed by PW Audio Supply for payment within 10 days. Sauk Stereo records the payment and discount as follows.

May 14	Accounts Payable ($3,800 − $300)	3,500	
	Purchase Discounts ($3,500 × .02)		70
	Cash		3,430
	(To record payment within the		
	discount period)		

Purchase Discounts is a temporary account whose normal balance is a credit.

Recording Sales of Merchandise

The seller, PW Audio Supply, records the sale of $3,800 of merchandise to Sauk Stereo on May 4 (sales invoice No. 731, Illustration 5-5, page 214) as follows.

May 4	Accounts Receivable	3,800	
	Sales Revenue		3,800
	(To record credit sales per invoice #731		
	to Sauk Stereo)		

SALES RETURNS AND ALLOWANCES

To record the returned goods received from Sauk Stereo on May 8, PW Audio Supply records the $300 sales return as follows.

May 8	Sales Returns and Allowances	300	
	Accounts Receivable		300
	(To record credit granted to Sauk		
	Stereo for returned goods)		

SALES DISCOUNTS

On May 14, PW Audio Supply receives payment of $3,430 on account from Sauk Stereo. PW Audio Supply honors the 2% cash discount and records the payment of Sauk Stereo's account receivable in full as follows.

May 14	Cash		3,430	
	Sales Discounts ($3,500 × .02)		70	
	Accounts Receivable ($3,800 − $300)			3,500
	(To record collection within 2/10, n/30 discount period from Sauk Stereo)			

COMPARISON OF ENTRIES—PERPETUAL VS. PERIODIC

Illustration 5A-3 summarizes the periodic inventory entries shown in this appendix and compares them to the perpetual-system entries from the chapter. Entries that differ in the two systems are shown in color.

Illustration 5A-3
Comparison of entries for perpetual and periodic inventory systems

Entries on Sauk Stereo's Books					
Transaction	**Perpetual Inventory System**			**Periodic Inventory System**	
May 4 Purchase of merchandise on credit.	Inventory	3,800		Purchases	3,800
	Accounts Payable		3,800	Accounts Payable		3,800
6 Freight costs on purchases.	Inventory	150		Freight-in	150
	Cash		150	Cash		150
8 Purchase returns and allowances.	Accounts Payable	300		Accounts Payable	300
	Inventory		300	Purchase Returns and Allowances		300
14 Payment on account with a discount.	Accounts Payable	3,500		Accounts Payable	3,500
	Cash		3,430	Cash		3,430
	Inventory		70	Purchase Discounts		70

Entries on PW Audio Supply's Books					
Transaction	**Perpetual Inventory System**			**Periodic Inventory System**	
May 4 Sale of merchandise on credit.	Accounts Receivable	3,800		Accounts Receivable	3,800
	Sales Revenue		3,800	Sales Revenue		3,800
	Cost of Goods Sold	2,400		No entry for cost of goods sold	
	Inventory		2,400		
8 Return of merchandise sold.	Sales Returns and Allowances	300		Sales Returns and Allowances	300
	Accounts Receivable		300	Accounts Receivable		300
	Inventory	140		No entry	
	Cost of Goods Sold		140		
14 Cash received on account with a discount.	Cash	3,430		Cash	3,430
	Sales Discounts	70		Sales Discounts	70
	Accounts Receivable		3,500	Accounts Receivable		3,500

Summary of Study Objective for Appendix 5A

[7] Explain the recording of purchases and sales of inventory under a periodic inventory system. In recording purchases under a periodic system, companies must make entries for (a) cash and credit purchases, (b) purchase returns and allowances, (c) purchase discounts, and (d) freight costs. In recording sales, companies must make entries for (a) cash and credit sales, (b) sales returns and allowances, and (c) sales discounts.

APPENDIX5B

Worksheet for a Merchandising Company

Using a Worksheet

Study Objective [8]

Prepare a worksheet for a merchandising company.

As indicated in Chapter 4, a worksheet enables companies to prepare financial statements before they journalize and post adjusting entries. The steps in preparing a worksheet for a merchandising company are the same as for a service company (see pages 154–158). Illustration 5B-1 shows the worksheet for PW Audio Supply (excluding nonoperating items). The unique accounts for a merchandiser using a perpetual inventory system are in boldface letters and in red.

PW Audio Supply.xls

File   Edit   View   Insert   Format   Tools   Data   Window   Help

PW AUDIO SUPPLY
Worksheet
For the Year Ended December 31, 2012

Accounts	Trial Balance Dr.	Trial Balance Cr.	Adjustments Dr.	Adjustments Cr.	Adjusted Trial Balance Dr.	Adjusted Trial Balance Cr.	Income Statement Dr.	Income Statement Cr.	Balance Sheet Dr.	Balance Sheet Cr.
Cash	9,500				9,500				9,500	
Accounts Receivable	16,100				16,100				16,100	
Inventory	**40,500**			(a) 500	**40,000**				**40,000**	
Prepaid Insurance	3,800			(b) 2,000	1,800				1,800	
Equipment	80,000				80,000				80,000	
Accumulated Depreciation—Equipment		16,000		(c) 8,000		24,000				24,000
Accounts Payable		20,400				20,400				20,400
Owner's Capital		83,000				83,000				83,000
Owner's Drawings	15,000				15,000				15,000	
Sales Revenue		**480,000**				**480,000**		**480,000**		
Sales Returns and Allowances	**12,000**				**12,000**		**12,000**			
Sales Discounts	**8,000**				**8,000**		**8,000**			
Cost of Goods Sold	**315,500**		(a) 500		**316,000**		**316,000**			
Freight-out	7,000				7,000		7,000			
Advertising Expense	16,000				16,000		16,000			
Salaries and Wages Expense	59,000		(d) 5,000		64,000		64,000			
Utilities Expense	17,000				17,000		17,000			
Totals	599,400	599,400								
Insurance Expense			(b) 2,000		2,000		2,000			
Depreciation Expense			(c) 8,000		8,000		8,000			
Salaries and Wages Payable				(d) 5,000		5,000				5,000
Totals			15,500	15,500	612,400	612,400	450,000	480,000	162,400	132,400
Net Income							30,000			30,000
Totals							480,000	480,000	162,400	162,400

Key: (a) Adjustment to inventory on hand. (b) Insurance expired. (c) Depreciation expense. (d) Salaries accrued.

Illustration 5B-1
Worksheet for merchandising company

TRIAL BALANCE COLUMNS

Data for the trial balance come from the ledger balances of PW Audio Supply at December 31. The amount shown for Inventory, $40,500, is the year-end inventory amount from the perpetual inventory system.

ADJUSTMENTS COLUMNS

A merchandising company generally has the same types of adjustments as a service company. As you see in the worksheet, adjustments (b), (c), and (d) are for insurance, depreciation, and salaries. Pioneer Advertising Agency, as illustrated in Chapters 3 and 4, also had these adjustments. Adjustment (a) was required to adjust the perpetual inventory carrying amount to the actual count.

After PW Audio Supply enters all adjustments data on the worksheet, it establishes the equality of the adjustments column totals. It then extends the balances in all accounts to the adjusted trial balance columns.

ADJUSTED TRIAL BALANCE

The adjusted trial balance shows the balance of all accounts after adjustment at the end of the accounting period.

INCOME STATEMENT COLUMNS

Next, the merchandising company transfers the accounts and balances that affect the income statement from the adjusted trial balance columns to the income statement columns. PW Audio Supply shows sales of $480,000 in the credit column. It shows the contra-revenue accounts Sales Returns and Allowances $12,000 and Sales Discounts $8,000 in the debit column. The difference of $460,000 is the net sales shown on the income statement (Illustration 5-13, page 227).

Finally, the company totals all the credits in the income statement column and compares those totals to the total of the debits in the income statement column. If the credits exceed the debits, the company has net income. PW Audio Supply has net income of $30,000. If the debits exceed the credits, the company would report a net loss.

BALANCE SHEET COLUMNS

The major difference between the balance sheets of a service company and a merchandiser is inventory. PW Audio Supply shows the ending inventory amount of $40,000 in the balance sheet debit column. The information to prepare the owner's equity statement is also found in these columns. That is, the Owner's Capital account is $83,000, Owner's Drawings are $15,000. Net income results when the total of the debit column exceeds the total of the credit column in the balance sheet columns. A net loss results when the total of the credits exceeds the total of the debit balances.

Summary of Study Objective for Appendix 5B

[8] Prepare a worksheet for a merchandising company. The steps in preparing a worksheet for a merchandising company are the same as for a service company. The unique accounts for a merchandiser are Inventory, Sales Revenue, Sales Returns and Allowances, Sales Discounts, and Cost of Goods Sold.

Self-Test, Brief Exercises, Exercises, Problem Set A, and many more components are available for practice in *WileyPLUS*

Note: All **asterisked** Questions, Exercises, and Problems relate to material in the appendices to the chapter.

Self-Test Questions

Answers are on page 257.

(SO 1) **1.** Gross profit will result if:
   a. operating expenses are less than net income.
   b. sales revenues are greater than operating expenses.
   c. sales revenues are greater than cost of goods sold.
   d. operating expenses are greater than cost of goods sold.

2. Under a perpetual inventory system, when goods are pur- (SO 2) chased for resale by a company:
   a. purchases on account are debited to Inventory.
   b. purchases on account are debited to Purchases.
   c. purchase returns are debited to Purchase Returns and Allowances.
   d. freight costs are debited to Freight-out.

(SO 3) **3.** The sales accounts that normally have a debit balance are:
   a. Sales Discounts.
   b. Sales Returns and Allowances.
   c. Both (a) and (b).
   d. Neither (a) nor (b).

(SO 3) **4.** A credit sale of $750 is made on June 13, terms 2/10, net/30. A return of $50 is granted on June 16. The amount received as payment in full on June 23 is:
   a. $700.   **c.** $685.
   b. $686.   **d.** $650.

(SO 2) **5.** Which of the following accounts will normally appear in the ledger of a merchandising company that uses a perpetual inventory system?
   a. Purchases.   **c.** Cost of Goods Sold.
   b. Freight-in.   **d.** Purchase Discounts.

(SO 3) **6.** To record the sale of goods for cash in a perpetual inventory system:
   a. only one journal entry is necessary to record cost of goods sold and reduction of inventory.
   b. only one journal entry is necessary to record the receipt of cash and the sales revenue.
   c. two journal entries are necessary: one to record the receipt of cash and sales revenue, and one to record the cost of goods sold and reduction of inventory.
   d. two journal entries are necessary: one to record the receipt of cash and reduction of inventory, and one to record the cost of goods sold and sales revenue.

(SO 4) **7.** The steps in the accounting cycle for a merchandising company are the same as those in a service company *except*:
   a. an additional adjusting journal entry for inventory may be needed in a merchandising company.
   b. closing journal entries are not required for a merchandising company.
   c. a post-closing trial balance is not required for a merchandising company.
   d. a multiple-step income statement is required for a merchandising company.

(SO 5) **8.** The multiple-step income statement for a merchandising company shows each of the following features *except*:
   a. gross profit.
   b. cost of goods sold.
   c. a sales revenue section.
   d. investing activities section.

9. If sales revenues are $400,000, cost of goods sold is $310,000, (SO 6) and operating expenses are $60,000, the gross profit is:
   a. $30,000.   **c.** $340,000.
   b. $90,000.   **d.** $400,000.

10. A single-step income statement: (SO 5)
   a. reports gross profit.
   b. does not report cost of goods sold.
   c. reports sales revenues and "Other revenues and gains" in the revenues section of the income statement.
   d. reports operating income separately.

11. Which of the following appears on both a single-step and (SO 5) a multiple-step income statement?
   a. inventory.
   b. gross profit.
   c. income from operations.
   d. cost of goods sold.

*12. In determining cost of goods sold: (SO 7)
   a. purchase discounts are deducted from net purchases.
   b. freight-out is added to net purchases.
   c. purchase returns and allowances are deducted from net purchases.
   d. freight-in is added to net purchases.

*13. If beginning inventory is $60,000, cost of goods purchased (SO 7) is $380,000, and ending inventory is $50,000, cost of goods sold is:
   a. $390,000.   **c.** $330,000.
   b. $370,000.   **d.** $420,000.

*14. When goods are purchased for resale by a company using (SO 7) a periodic inventory system:
   a. purchases on account are debited to Inventory.
   b. purchases on account are debited to Purchases.
   c. purchase returns are debited to Purchase Returns and Allowances.
   d. freight costs are debited to Purchases.

*15. In a worksheet, Inventory is shown in the following (SO 8) columns:
   a. Adjusted trial balance debit and balance sheet debit.
   b. Income statement debit and balance sheet debit.
   c. Income statement credit and balance sheet debit.
   d. Income statement credit and adjusted trial balance debit.

Go to the book's companion website, **www.wiley.com/college/weygandt**, for additional Self-Test Questions.

The Navigator

Questions

1. (a) "The steps in the accounting cycle for a merchandising company are different from the accounting cycle for a service company." Do you agree or disagree? (b) Is the measurement of net income for a merchandising company conceptually the same as for a service company? Explain.

2. Why is the normal operating cycle for a merchandising company likely to be longer than for a service company?

3. (a) How do the components of revenues and expenses differ between merchandising and service companies? (b)

Explain the income measurement process in a merchandising company.

4. How does income measurement differ between a merchandising and a service company?

5. When is cost of goods sold determined in a perpetual inventory system?

6. Distinguish between FOB shipping point and FOB destination. Identify the freight terms that will result in a debit to Inventory by the buyer and a debit to Freight-out by the seller.

7. Explain the meaning of the credit terms 2/10, n/30.

8. Goods costing $2,000 are purchased on account on July 15 with credit terms of 2/10, n/30. On July 18, a $200 credit memo is received from the supplier for damaged goods. Give the journal entry on July 24 to record payment of the balance due within the discount period using a perpetual inventory system.

9. Joan Roland believes revenues from credit sales may be earned before they are collected in cash. Do you agree? Explain.

10. (a) What is the primary source document for recording (1) cash sales, (2) credit sales. (b) Using XXs for amounts, give the journal entry for each of the transactions in part (a).

11. A credit sale is made on July 10 for $900, terms 2/10, n/30. On July 12, $100 of goods are returned for credit. Give the journal entry on July 19 to record the receipt of the balance due within the discount period.

12. Explain why the Inventory account will usually require adjustment at year-end.

13. Prepare the closing entries for the Sales Revenue account, assuming a balance of $200,000 and the Cost of Goods Sold account with a $145,000 balance.

14. What merchandising account(s) will appear in the post-closing trial balance?

15. Reese Co. has sales revenue of $105,000, cost of goods sold of $70,000, and operating expenses of $20,000. What is its gross profit and its gross profit rate?

16. Ann Fort Company reports net sales of $800,000, gross profit of $370,000, and net income of $240,000. What are its operating expenses?

17. Identify the distinguishing features of an income statement for a merchandising company.

18. Identify the sections of a multiple-step income statement that relate to (a) operating activities, and (b) nonoperating activities.

19. How does the single-step form of income statement differ from the multiple-step form?

20. ⬤ PEPSICO Determine PepsiCo's gross profit rate for 2009 and 2008. Indicate whether it increased or decreased from 2008 to 2009.

*21. Identify the accounts that are added to or deducted from Purchases to determine the cost of goods purchased. For each account, indicate whether it is added or deducted.

*22. Goods costing $3,000 are purchased on account on July 15 with credit terms of 2/10, n/30. On July 18, a $200 credit was received from the supplier for damaged goods. Give the journal entry on July 24 to record payment of the balance due within the discount period, assuming a periodic inventory system.

*23. Indicate the columns of the worksheet in which (a) inventory and (b) cost of goods sold will be shown.

Brief Exercises

BE5-1 Presented below are the components in Miller Company's income statement. Determine the missing amounts.

Compute missing amounts in determining net income.
(SO 1)

	Sales Revenue	Cost of Goods Sold	Gross Profit	Operating Expenses	Net Income
(a)	$75,000	?	$30,000	?	$10,800
(b)	$108,000	$70,000	?	?	$29,500
(c)	?	$83,900	$79,600	$39,500	?

BE5-2 Brad Company buys merchandise on account from Murray Company. The selling price of the goods is $780, and the cost of the goods is $470. Both companies use perpetual inventory systems. Journalize the transaction on the books of both companies.

Journalize perpetual inventory entries.
(SO 2, 3)

BE5-3 Prepare the journal entries to record the following transactions on Derrick Company's books using a perpetual inventory system.

Journalize sales transactions.
(SO 3)

(a) On March 2, Derrick Company sold $900,000 of merchandise to Rose Company, terms 2/10, n/30. The cost of the merchandise sold was $620,000.

(b) On March 6, Rose Company returned $90,000 of the merchandise purchased on March 2. The cost of the returned merchandise was $62,000.

(c) On March 12, Derrick Company received the balance due from Rose Company.

BE5-4 From the information in BE5-3, prepare the journal entries to record these transactions on Rose Company's books under a perpetual inventory system.

Journalize purchase transactions.
(SO 2)

BE5-5 At year-end, the perpetual inventory records of Brewer Company showed merchandise inventory of $98,000. The company determined, however, that its actual inventory on hand was $95,700. Record the necessary adjusting entry.

Prepare adjusting entry for merchandise inventory.
(SO 4)

BE5-6 Thibodeau Company has the following merchandise account balances: Sales Revenue $195,000, Sales Discounts $2,000, Cost of Goods Sold $117,000, and Inventory $40,000. Prepare the entries to record the closing of these items to Income Summary.

Prepare closing entries for merchandise accounts.
(SO 4)

Prepare sales revenues section of income statement.
(SO 5)

BE5-7   Myers Company provides the following information for the month ended October 31, 2012: sales on credit $280,000, cash sales $100,000, sales discounts $5,000, sales returns and allowances $11,000. Prepare the sales revenues section of the income statement based on this information.

Contrast presentation in multiple-step and single-step income statements.
(SO 5)

BE5-8 ⟨▬▬▬⟩   Explain where each of the following items would appear on (1) a multiple-step income statement, and on (2) a single-step income statement: (a) gain on sale of equipment, (b) interest expense, (c) casualty loss from vandalism, and (d) cost of goods sold.

Compute net sales, gross profit, income from operations, and gross profit rate.
(SO 5, 6)

BE5-9   Assume Adams Company has the following reported amounts: Sales revenue $510,000, Sales returns and allowances $15,000, Cost of goods sold $330,000, Operating expenses $110,000. Compute the following: (a) net sales, (b) gross profit, (c) income from operations, and (d) gross profit rate. (Round to one decimal place.)

Compute net purchases and cost of goods purchased.
(SO 7)

*BE5-10   Assume that Byars Company uses a periodic inventory system and has these account balances: Purchases $450,000; Purchase Returns and Allowances $13,000; Purchase Discounts $8,000; and Freight-in $16,000. Determine net purchases and cost of goods purchased.

Compute cost of goods sold and gross profit.
(SO 6, 7)

*BE5-11   Assume the same information as in BE5-10 and also that Byars Company has beginning inventory of $60,000, ending inventory of $90,000, and net sales of $730,000. Determine the amounts to be reported for cost of goods sold and gross profit.

Journalize purchase transactions.
(SO 7)

*BE5-12   Prepare the journal entries to record these transactions on Jerel Company's books using a periodic inventory system.

(a)   On March 2, Jerel Company purchased $900,000 of merchandise from McNeal Company, terms 2/10, n/30.
(b)   On March 6, Jerel Company returned $130,000 of the merchandise purchased on March 2.
(c)   On March 12, Jerel Company paid the balance due to McNeal Company.

Identify worksheet columns for selected accounts.
(SO 8)

*BE5-13   Presented below is the format of the worksheet presented in the chapter.

Trial Balance		Adjustments		Adjusted Trial Balance		Income Statement		Balance Sheet	
Dr.	Cr.	Dr.	Cr.	Dr.	Cr.	Dr.	Cr.	Dr.	Cr.

Indicate where the following items will appear on the worksheet: (a) Cash, (b) Inventory, (c) Sales revenue, and (d) Cost of goods sold.

Example:
Cash: Trial balance debit column; Adjusted trial balance debit column; and Balance sheet debit column.

Do it! Review

Record transactions of purchasing company.
(SO 2)

Do it! 5-1   On October 5, Bouldin Company buys merchandise on account from McClinton Company. The selling price of the goods is $5,000, and the cost to McClinton Company is $3,100. On October 8, Bouldin returns defective goods with a selling price of $650 and a fair value of $100. Record the transactions on the books of Bouldin Company.

Record transactions of selling company.
(SO 3)

Do it! 5-2   Assume information similar to that in **Do it!** 5-1. That is: On October 5, Bouldin Company buys merchandise on account from McClinton Company. The selling price of the goods is $5,000, and the cost to McClinton Company is $3,100. On October 8, Bouldin returns defective goods with a selling price of $650 and a fair value of $100. Record the transactions on the books of McClinton Company.

Prepare closing entries for a merchandising company.
(SO 4)

Do it! 5-3   The trial balance of Ogilvy's Boutique at December 31 shows Inventory $21,000, Sales Revenue $156,000, Sales Returns and Allowances $4,000, Sales Discounts $3,000, Cost of Goods Sold $92,400, Interest Revenue $5,000, Freight-out $1,500, Utilities Expense $7,400, and Salaries and Wages Expense $19,500. Prepare the closing entries for Ogilvy.

Classify financial statement accounts.
(SO 5)

Do it! 5-4   Richard Company is preparing its multiple-step income statement, owner's equity statement, and classified balance sheet. Using the column heads *Account, Financial Statement*, and

Classification, indicate in which financial statement and under what classification each of the following would be reported.

Account	Financial Statement	Classification
Accounts Payable		
Accounts Receivable		
Accumulated Depreciation— Buildings		
Cash		
Casualty Loss from Vandalism		
Cost of Goods Sold		
Depreciation Expense		
Equipment		
Freight-out		
Insurance Expense		
Interest Payable		
Inventory		
Land		
Notes Payable (due in 5 years)		
Owner's Capital (beginning balance)		
Owner's Drawings		
Property Taxes Payable		
Salaries and Wages Expense		
Salaries and Wages Payable		
Sales Returns and Allowances		
Sales Revenue		
Unearned Rent Revenue		
Utilities Expense		

Exercises

E5-1 Mr. Lucas has prepared the following list of statements about service companies and merchandisers.

Answer general questions about merchandisers.
(SO 1)

1. Measuring net income for a merchandiser is conceptually the same as for a service company.
2. For a merchandiser, sales less operating expenses is called gross profit.
3. For a merchandiser, the primary source of revenues is the sale of inventory.
4. Sales salaries and wages is an example of an operating expense.
5. The operating cycle of a merchandiser is the same as that of a service company.
6. In a perpetual inventory system, no detailed inventory records of goods on hand are maintained.
7. In a periodic inventory system, the cost of goods sold is determined only at the end of the accounting period.
8. A periodic inventory system provides better control over inventories than a perpetual system.

Instructions
Identify each statement as true or false. If false, indicate how to correct the statement.

E5-2 Information related to Almond Co. is presented below.

Journalize purchases transactions.
(SO 2)

1. On April 5, purchased merchandise from Morris Company for $23,000, terms 2/10, net/30, FOB shipping point.
2. On April 6, paid freight costs of $900 on merchandise purchased from Morris.
3. On April 7, purchased equipment on account for $26,000.
4. On April 8, returned damaged merchandise to Morris Company and was granted a $3,000 credit for returned merchandise.
5. On April 15, paid the amount due to Morris Company in full.

Instructions
(a) Prepare the journal entries to record these transactions on the books of Almond Co. under a perpetual inventory system.
(b) Assume that Almond Co. paid the balance due to Morris Company on May 4 instead of April 15. Prepare the journal entry to record this payment.

Journalize perpetual inventory entries.
(SO 2, 3)

E5-3   On September 1, Samardo Office Supply had an inventory of 30 calculators at a cost of $18 each. The company uses a perpetual inventory system. During September, the following transactions occurred.

Sept. 6   Purchased 80 calculators at $20 each from Samuels Co. for cash.
       9   Paid freight of $80 on calculators purchased from Samuels Co.
      10   Returned 3 calculators to Samuels Co. for $63 credit (including freight) because they did not meet specifications.
      12   Sold 26 calculators costing $21 (including freight) for $31 each to Trent Book Store, terms n/30.
      14   Granted credit of $31 to Trent Book Store for the return of one calculator that was not ordered.
      20   Sold 30 calculators costing $21 for $32 each to Plaisted's Card Shop, terms n/30.

Instructions
Journalize the September transactions.

Prepare purchase and sale entries.
(SO 2, 3)

E5-4   On June 10, Naveen Company purchased $8,000 of merchandise from Jarrah Company, FOB shipping point, terms 2/10, n/30. Naveen pays the freight costs of $400 on June 11. Damaged goods totaling $300 are returned to Jarrah for credit on June 12. The fair value of these goods is $70. On June 19, Naveen pays Jarrah Company in full, less the purchase discount. Both companies use a perpetual inventory system.

Instructions
(a) Prepare separate entries for each transaction on the books of Naveen Company.
(b) Prepare separate entries for each transaction for Jarrah Company. The merchandise purchased by Naveen on June 10 had cost Jarrah $4,800.

Journalize sales transactions.
(SO 3)

E5-5   Presented below are transactions related to Sayid Company.

1. On December 3, Sayid Company sold $570,000 of merchandise to Shephard Co., terms 2/10, n/30, FOB shipping point. The cost of the merchandise sold was $350,000.
2. On December 8, Shephard Co. was granted an allowance of $20,000 for merchandise purchased on December 3.
3. On December 13, Sayid Company received the balance due from Shephard Co.

Instructions
(a) Prepare the journal entries to record these transactions on the books of Sayid Company using a perpetual inventory system.
(b) Assume that Sayid Company received the balance due from Shephard Co. on January 2 of the following year instead of December 13. Prepare the journal entry to record the receipt of payment on January 2.

Prepare sales revenues section and closing entries.
(SO 4, 5)

E5-6   The adjusted trial balance of Garcia Company shows the following data pertaining to sales at the end of its fiscal year October 31, 2012: Sales Revenue $820,000, Freight-out $16,000, Sales Returns and Allowances $25,000, and Sales Discounts $13,000.

Instructions
(a) Prepare the sales revenues section of the income statement.
(b) Prepare separate closing entries for (1) sales, and (2) the contra accounts to sales.

Prepare adjusting and closing entries.
(SO 4)

E5-7   Hugo Reyes Company had the following account balances at year-end: Cost of Goods Sold $60,000; Inventory $15,000; Operating Expenses $29,000; Sales Revenue $115,000; Sales Discounts $1,200; and Sales Returns and Allowances $1,700. A physical count of inventory determines that merchandise inventory on hand is $13,900.

Instructions
(a) Prepare the adjusting entry necessary as a result of the physical count.
(b) Prepare closing entries.

Prepare adjusting and closing entries.
(SO 4)

E5-8   Presented below is information related to Hurley Co. for the month of January 2012.

Ending inventory per		Insurance expense	$ 12,000
perpetual records	$ 21,600	Rent expense	20,000
Ending inventory actually		Salaries and wages expense	55,000
on hand	21,000	Sales discounts	10,000
Cost of goods sold	218,000	Sales returns and allowances	13,000
Freight-out	7,000	Sales revenue	380,000

Instructions
(a) Prepare the necessary adjusting entry for inventory.
(b) Prepare the necessary closing entries.

E5-9 Presented below is information for Jorge Company for the month of March 2012.

Cost of goods sold	$212,000	Rent expense	$ 32,000
Freight-out	7,000	Sales discounts	8,000
Insurance expense	6,000	Sales returns and allowances	13,000
Salaries and wages expense	58,000	Sales revenue	380,000

Prepare multiple-step income statement.
(SO 5, 6)

Instructions
(a) Prepare a multiple-step income statement.
(b) Compute the gross profit rate.

E5-10 In its income statement for the year ended December 31, 2012, Fox Company reported the following condensed data.

Operating expenses	$ 725,000	Interest revenue	$ 28,000
Cost of goods sold	1,289,000	Loss on disposal of plant assets	17,000
Interest expense	70,000	Net sales	2,200,000

Prepare multiple-step and single-step income statements.
(SO 5)

Instructions
(a) Prepare a multiple-step income statement.
(b) Prepare a single-step income statement.

E5-11 An inexperienced accountant for Sawyer Company made the following errors in recording merchandising transactions.

1. A $195 refund to a customer for faulty merchandise was debited to Sales Revenue $195 and credited to Cash $195.
2. A $180 credit purchase of supplies was debited to Inventory $180 and credited to Cash $180.
3. A $215 sales discount was debited to Sales Revenue.
4. A cash payment of $20 for freight on merchandise purchases was debited to Freight-out $200 and credited to Cash $200.

Prepare correcting entries for sales and purchases.
(SO 2, 3)

Instructions
Prepare separate correcting entries for each error, assuming that the incorrect entry is not reversed. (Omit explanations.)

E5-12 In 2012, James Ford Company had net sales of $900,000 and cost of goods sold of $522,000. Operating expenses were $225,000, and interest expense was $11,000. Ford prepares a multiple-step income statement.

Compute various income measures.
(SO 5, 6)

Instructions
(a) Compute Ford's gross profit.
(b) Compute the gross profit rate. Why is this rate computed by financial statement users?
(c) What is Ford's income from operations and net income?
(d) If Ford prepared a single-step income statement, what amount would it report for net income?
(e) In what section of its classified balance sheet should Ford report merchandise inventory?

E5-13 Presented below is financial information for two different companies.

Compute missing amounts and compute gross profit rate.
(SO 5, 6)

	Dae Company	Kim Company
Sales revenue	$90,000	(d)
Sales returns	(a)	$ 5,000
Net sales	87,000	102,000
Cost of goods sold	56,000	(e)
Gross profit	(b)	41,500
Operating expenses	15,000	(f)
Net income	(c)	15,000

Instructions
(a) Determine the missing amounts.
(b) Determine the gross profit rates. (Round to one decimal place.)

Compute missing amounts.
(SO 5)

E5-14 Financial information is presented below for three different companies.

	Holloway Cosmetics	Jin Grocery	Kwon Wholesalers
Sales revenue	$90,000	$ (e)	$122,000
Sales returns and allowances	(a)	5,000	12,000
Net sales	86,000	95,000	(i)
Cost of goods sold	56,000	(f)	(j)
Gross profit	(b)	38,000	24,000
Operating expenses	15,000	(g)	18,000
Income from operations	(c)	(h)	(k)
Other expenses and losses	4,000	7,000	(l)
Net income	(d)	11,000	5,000

Instructions

Determine the missing amounts.

Prepare cost of goods sold section.
(SO 7)

*E5-15 The trial balance of S. Yunjin Company at the end of its fiscal year, August 31, 2012, includes these accounts: Inventory $17,200; Purchases $149,000; Sales Revenue $190,000; Freight-in $5,000; Sales Returns and Allowances $3,000; Freight-out $1,000; and Purchase Returns and Allowances $2,000. The ending merchandise inventory is $23,000.

Instructions

Prepare a cost of goods sold section for the year ending August 31 (periodic inventory).

Compute various income statement items.
(SO 7)

*E5-16 On January 1, 2012, Evangeline Lilly Corporation had merchandise inventory of $50,000. At December 31, 2012, Evangeline Lilly had the following account balances.

Freight-in	$ 4,000
Purchases	509,000
Purchase discounts	6,000
Purchase returns and allowances	2,000
Sales revenue	840,000
Sales discounts	5,000
Sales returns and allowances	10,000

At December 31, 2012, Evangeline Lilly determines that its ending inventory is $60,000.

Instructions

(a) Compute Evangeline Lilly's 2012 gross profit.
(b) Compute Evangeline Lilly's 2012 operating expenses if net income is $130,000 and there are no nonoperating activities.

Prepare cost of goods sold section.
(SO 7)

*E5-17 Below is a series of cost of goods sold sections for companies B, F, L, and R.

	B	F	L	R
Beginning inventory	$ 150	$ 70	$1,000	$ (j)
Purchases	1,620	1,060	(g)	43,590
Purchase returns and allowances	40	(d)	290	(k)
Net purchases	(a)	1,030	6,210	41,090
Freight-in	110	(e)	(h)	2,240
Cost of goods purchased	(b)	1,280	7,940	(l)
Cost of goods available for sale	1,840	1,350	(i)	49,530
Ending inventory	310	(f)	1,450	6,230
Cost of goods sold	(c)	1,230	7,490	43,300

Instructions

Fill in the lettered blanks to complete the cost of goods sold sections.

Journalize purchase transactions.
(SO 7)

*E5-18 This information relates to Locke Co.

1. On April 5, purchased merchandise from K. Austen Company for $25,000, terms 2/10, net/30, FOB shipping point.
2. On April 6, paid freight costs of $900 on merchandise purchased from K. Austen Company.
3. On April 7, purchased equipment on account for $30,000.
4. On April 8, returned some of April 5 merchandise, which cost $2,800, to K. Austen Company.
5. On April 15, paid the amount due to K. Austen Company in full.

Instructions

(a) Prepare the journal entries to record these transactions on the books of Locke Co. using a periodic inventory system.

(b) Assume that Locke Co. paid the balance due to K. Austen Company on May 4 instead of April 15. Prepare the journal entry to record this payment.

*E5-19 Presented below is information related to Emilie Co.

1. On April 5, purchased merchandise from De Ravin Company for $19,000, terms 2/10, net/30, FOB shipping point.
2. On April 6, paid freight costs of $800 on merchandise purchased from De Ravin.
3. On April 7, purchased equipment on account from Claire Littleton Mfg. Co. for $23,000.
4. On April 8, returned merchandise, which cost $4,000, to De Ravin Company.
5. On April 15, paid the amount due to De Ravin Company in full.

Journalize purchase transactions.

(SO 7)

Instructions

(a) Prepare the journal entries to record these transactions on the books of Emilie Co. using a periodic inventory system.

(b) Assume that Emilie Co. paid the balance due to De Ravin Company on May 4 instead of April 15. Prepare the journal entry to record this payment.

*E5-20 Presented below are selected accounts for Dawson Company as reported in the worksheet at the end of May 2012.

Complete worksheet.

(SO 8)

Accounts	Adjusted Trial Balance		Income Statement		Balance Sheet	
	Dr.	Cr.	Dr.	Cr.	Dr.	Cr.
Cash	11,000					
Inventory	76,000					
Sales Revenue		480,000				
Sales Returns and Allowances	10,000					
Sales Discounts	9,000					
Cost of Goods Sold	300,000					

Instructions

Complete the worksheet by extending amounts reported in the adjusted trial balance to the appropriate columns in the worksheet. Do not total individual columns.

*E5-21 The trial balance columns of the worksheet for Linus Company at June 30, 2012, are as follows.

Prepare a worksheet.

(SO 8)

LINUS COMPANY
Worksheet
For the Month Ended June 30, 2012

Account Titles	Trial Balance	
	Debit	Credit
Cash	$ 1,920	
Accounts Receivable	2,440	
Inventory	11,640	
Accounts Payable		$ 1,120
Owner's Capital		3,500
Sales Revenue		42,500
Cost of Goods Sold	20,560	
Operating Expenses	10,560	
	$47,120	$47,120

Other data:
Operating expenses incurred on account, but not yet recorded, total $1,500.

Instructions

Enter the trial balance on a worksheet and complete the worksheet.

Exercises: Set B

Visit the book's companion website, at **www.wiley.com/college/weygandt**, and choose the Student Companion site to access Exercise Set B.

Problems: Set A

Journalize purchase and sales transactions under a perpetual inventory system.

(SO 2, 3)

P5-1A   O'Quinn Co. distributes suitcases to retail stores and extends credit terms of 1/10, n/30 to all of its customers. At the end of June, O'Quinn's inventory consisted of suitcases costing $1,200. During the month of July, the following merchandising transactions occurred.

July   1   Purchased suitcases on account for $1,800 from Emerson Manufacturers, FOB destination, terms 2/10, n/30. The appropriate party also made a cash payment of $100 for freight on this date.

3   Sold suitcases on account to Straume Satchels for $2,000. The cost of suitcases sold is $1,200.

9   Paid Emerson Manufacturers in full.

12   Received payment in full from Straume Satchels.

17   Sold suitcases on account to The Going Concern for $1,800. The cost of the suitcases sold was $1,080.

18   Purchased suitcases on account for $1,900 from Hume Manufacturers, FOB shipping point, terms 1/10, n/30. The appropriate party also made a cash payment of $125 for freight on this date.

20   Received $300 credit (including freight) for suitcases returned to Hume Manufacturers.

21   Received payment in full from The Going Concern.

22   Sold suitcases on account to Desmond's for $2,250. The cost of suitcases sold was $1,350.

30   Paid Hume Manufacturers in full.

31   Granted Desmond's $200 credit for suitcases returned costing $120.

O'Quinn's chart of accounts includes the following: No. 101 Cash, No. 112 Accounts Receivable, No. 120 Inventory, No. 201 Accounts Payable, No. 401 Sales Revenue, No. 412 Sales Returns and Allowances, No. 414 Sales Discounts, and No. 505 Cost of Goods Sold.

Instructions

Journalize the transactions for the month of July for O'Quinn using a perpetual inventory system.

Journalize, post, and prepare a partial income statement.

(SO 2, 3, 5, 6)

P5-2A   Pace Distributing Company completed the following merchandising transactions in the month of April. At the beginning of April, the ledger of Pace showed Cash of $9,000 and Owner's Capital of $9,000.

Apr.   2   Purchased merchandise on account from Monaghan Supply Co. $6,900, terms 1/10, n/30.

4   Sold merchandise on account $6,500, FOB destination, terms 1/10, n/30. The cost of the merchandise sold was $3,900.

5   Paid $240 freight on April 4 sale.

6   Received credit from Monaghan Supply Co. for merchandise returned $500.

11   Paid Monaghan Supply Co. in full, less discount.

13   Received collections in full, less discounts, from customers billed on April 4.

14   Purchased merchandise for cash $3,800.

16   Received refund from supplier for returned goods on cash purchase of April 14, $500.

18   Purchased merchandise from Dominic Distributors $4,500, FOB shipping point, terms 2/10, n/30.

20   Paid freight on April 18 purchase $100.

23   Sold merchandise for cash $7,400. The merchandise sold had a cost of $4,120.

26   Purchased merchandise for cash $2,300.

27   Paid Dominic Distributors in full, less discount.

29   Made refunds to cash customers for defective merchandise $90. The returned merchandise had a fair value of $30.

30   Sold merchandise on account $3,700, terms n/30. The cost of the merchandise sold was $2,800.

Pace Distributing Company's chart of accounts includes the following: No. 101 Cash, No. 112 Accounts Receivable, No. 120 Inventory, No. 201 Accounts Payable, No. 301 Owner's Capital, No. 401 Sales Revenue, No. 412 Sales Returns and Allowances, No. 414 Sales Discounts, No. 505 Cost of Goods Sold, and No. 644 Freight-out.

Instructions
(a) Journalize the transactions using a perpetual inventory system.
(b) Enter the beginning cash and capital balances, and post the transactions. (Use J1 for the journal reference.)
(c) Prepare the income statement through gross profit for the month of April 2012.

(c) Gross profit $6,655

P5-3A Cusick Department Store is located near the Village Shopping Mall. At the end of the company's calendar year on December 31, 2012, the following accounts appeared in two of its trial balances.

Prepare financial statements and adjusting and closing entries.

(SO 4, 5)

	Unadjusted	Adjusted		Unadjusted	Adjusted
Accounts Payable	$ 79,300	$ 80,300	Inventory	$ 75,000	$ 75,000
Accounts Receivable	50,300	50,300	Mortgage Payable	80,000	80,000
Accumulated Depr.—Buildings	42,100	52,500	Owner's Capital	176,600	176,600
Accumulated Depr.—Equipment	29,600	42,900	Owner's Drawings	28,000	28,000
Buildings	290,000	290,000	Prepaid Insurance	9,600	2,400
Cash	23,800	23,800	Property Tax Expense		4,800
Cost of Goods Sold	412,700	412,700	Property Taxes Payable		4,800
Depreciation Expense		23,700	Salaries and Wages Expense	108,000	108,000
Equipment	110,000	110,000	Sales Revenue	728,000	728,000
Insurance Expense		7,200	Sales Commissions Expense	10,200	14,500
Interest Expense	3,000	12,000	Sales Commissions Payable		4,300
Interest Payable		9,000	Sales Returns and Allowances	8,000	8,000
Interest Revenue	4,000	4,000	Utilities Expense	11,000	12,000

Instructions
(a) Prepare a multiple-step income statement, an owner's equity statement, and a classified balance sheet. $25,000 of the mortgage payable is due for payment next year.
(b) Journalize the adjusting entries that were made.
(c) Journalize the closing entries that are necessary.

(a) Net income $129,100
Owner's capital $277,700
Total assets $456,100

P5-4A Juliet Burke, a former professional tennis star, operates Juliet's Tennis Shop at the Mitchell Lake Resort. At the beginning of the current season, the ledger of Juliet's Tennis Shop showed Cash $2,500, Inventory $1,700, and Owner's Capital $4,200. The following transactions were completed during April.

Journalize, post, and prepare a trial balance.

(SO 2, 3, 4)

Apr. 4   Purchased racquets and balls from Miles Co. $840, FOB shipping point, terms 2/10, n/30.
6   Paid freight on purchase from Miles Co. $40.
8   Sold merchandise to members $1,150, terms n/30. The merchandise sold had a cost of $790.
10   Received credit of $40 from Miles Co. for a racquet that was returned.
11   Purchased tennis shoes from Leung Sports for cash, $420.
13   Paid Miles Co. in full.
14   Purchased tennis shirts and shorts from Cyrena's Sportswear $900, FOB shipping point, terms 3/10, n/60.
15   Received cash refund of $50 from Leung Sports for damaged merchandise that was returned.
17   Paid freight on Cyrena's Sportswear purchase $30.
18   Sold merchandise to members $900, terms n/30. The cost of the merchandise sold was $540.
20   Received $600 in cash from members in settlement of their accounts.
21   Paid Cyrena's Sportswear in full.
27   Granted an allowance of $40 to members for tennis clothing that did not fit properly.
30   Received cash payments on account from members, $710.

The chart of accounts for the tennis shop includes the following: No. 101 Cash, No. 112 Accounts Receivable, No. 120 Inventory, No. 201 Accounts Payable, No. 301 Owner's Capital, No. 401 Sales Revenue, No. 412 Sales Returns and Allowances, and No. 505 Cost of Goods Sold.

Instructions

(a) Journalize the April transactions using a perpetual inventory system.
(b) Enter the beginning balances in the ledger accounts and post the April transactions. (Use J1 for the journal reference.)

(c) Total debits $6,250   (c) Prepare a trial balance on April 30, 2012.

Determine cost of goods sold and gross profit under periodic approach.
(SO 6, 7)

*P5-5A   At the end of Rutherford Department Store's fiscal year on December 31, 2012, these accounts appeared in its adjusted trial balance.

Freight-in	$ 5,600
Inventory	40,500
Purchases	447,000
Purchase Discounts	12,000
Purchase Returns and Allowances	6,400
Sales Revenue	725,000
Sales Returns and Allowances	11,000

Additional facts:

1. Merchandise inventory on December 31, 2012, is $65,000.
2. Rutherford Department Store uses a periodic system.

Instructions

Gross profit $304,300   Prepare an income statement through gross profit for the year ended December 31, 2012.

Calculate missing amounts and assess profitability.
(SO 6, 7)

*P5-6A   Ana Lucia operates a retail clothing operation. She purchases all merchandise inventory on credit and uses a periodic inventory system. The Accounts Payable account is used for recording inventory purchases only; all other current liabilities are accrued in separate accounts. You are provided with the following selected information for the fiscal years 2009–2012.

	2009	2010	2011	2012
Inventory (ending)	$13,000	$ 11,300	$ 14,700	$ 12,200
Accounts payable (ending)	20,000			
Sales revenue		239,000	237,000	235,000
Purchases of merchandise inventory on account		146,000	145,000	129,000
Cash payments to suppliers		135,000	161,000	127,000

Instructions

(a) 2011 $141,600   (a) Calculate cost of goods sold for each of the 2010, 2011, and 2012 fiscal years.
(b) Calculate the gross profit for each of the 2010, 2011, and 2012 fiscal years.

(c) 2011 Ending accts payable $15,000   (c) Calculate the ending balance of accounts payable for each of the 2010, 2011, and 2012 fiscal years.
(d) Sales declined in fiscal 2012. Does that mean that profitability, as measured by the gross profit rate, necessarily also declined? Explain, calculating the gross profit rate for each fiscal year to help support your answer. (Round to one decimal place.)

Journalize, post, and prepare trial balance and partial income statement using periodic approach.
(SO 7)

![GLS]

*P5-7A   At the beginning of the current season, the ledger of Alpert Tennis Shop showed Cash $2,500; Inventory $1,700; and Owner's Capital $4,200. The following transactions were completed during April.

Apr.	4	Purchased racquets and balls from Nestor Co. $740, terms 3/10, n/30.
	6	Paid freight on Nestor Co. purchase $60.
	8	Sold merchandise to members $900, terms n/30.
	10	Received credit of $40 from Nestor Co. for a racquet that was returned.
	11	Purchased tennis shoes from Carbonell Sports for cash $300.
	13	Paid Nestor Co. in full.
	14	Purchased tennis shirts and shorts from Faraday Sportswear $700, terms 2/10, n/60.
	15	Received cash refund of $50 from Carbonell Sports for damaged merchandise that was returned.
	17	Paid freight on Faraday Sportswear purchase $30.

18   Sold merchandise to members $1,000, terms n/30.
20   Received $500 in cash from members in settlement of their accounts.
21   Paid Faraday Sportswear in full.
27   Granted an allowance of $25 to members for tennis clothing that did not fit properly.
30   Received cash payments on account from members $550.

The chart of accounts for the tennis shop includes Cash, Accounts Receivable, Inventory, Accounts Payable, Owner's Capital, Sales Revenue, Sales Returns and Allowances, Purchases, Purchase Returns and Allowances, Purchase Discounts, and Freight-in.

Instructions
(a) Journalize the April transactions using a periodic inventory system.
(b) Using T accounts, enter the beginning balances in the ledger accounts and post the April transactions.
(c) Prepare a trial balance on April 30, 2012.
(d) Prepare an income statement through gross profit, assuming inventory on hand at April 30 is $2,296.

(c) Tot. trial balance $6,225
(d) Gross profit $766

*P5-8A   The trial balance of Mr. Eko Fashion Center contained the following accounts at November 30, the end of the company's fiscal year.

Complete accounting cycle beginning with a worksheet.
(SO 4, 5, 6, 8)

MR. EKO FASHION CENTER
Trial Balance
November 30, 2012

	Debit	Credit
Cash	$ 8,700	
Accounts Receivable	30,700	
Inventory	44,700	
Supplies	6,200	
Equipment	133,000	
Accumulated Depreciation—Equipment		$ 28,000
Notes Payable		51,000
Accounts Payable		48,500
Owner's Capital		90,000
Owner's Drawings	12,000	
Sales Revenue		755,200
Sales Returns and Allowances	8,800	
Cost of Goods Sold	497,400	
Salaries and Wages Expense	140,000	
Advertising Expense	24,400	
Utilities Expense	14,000	
Maintenance and Repairs Expense	12,100	
Freight-out	16,700	
Rent Expense	24,000	
Totals	$972,700	$972,700

Adjustment data:
1. Supplies on hand totaled $2,000.
2. Depreciation is $11,500 on the equipment.
3. Interest of $4,000 is accrued on notes payable at November 30.
4. Inventory actually on hand is $44,400.

Instructions
(a) Enter the trial balance on a worksheet, and complete the worksheet.
(b) Prepare a multiple-step income statement and an owner's equity statement for the year, and a classified balance sheet as of November 30, 2012. Notes payable of $20,000 are due in January 2013.
(c) Journalize the adjusting entries.
(d) Journalize the closing entries.
(e) Prepare a post-closing trial balance.

(a) Adj. trial balance
$988,200
Net loss $2,200
(b) Gross profit $248,700
Total assets $179,300

Problems: Set B

Journalize purchase and sales transactions under a perpetual inventory system.

(SO 2, 3)

P5-1B　Jeremy's Book Warehouse distributes hardcover books to retail stores and extends credit terms of 2/10, n/30 to all of its customers. At the end of May, Jeremy's inventory consisted of books purchased for $1,800. During June, the following merchandising transactions occurred.

June 1　Purchased books on account for $1,600 from Davies Publishers, FOB destination, terms 2/10, n/30. The appropriate party also made a cash payment of $50 for the freight on this date.

　3　Sold books on account to Reading Rainbow for $2,500. The cost of the books sold was $1,440.

　6　Received $100 credit for books returned to Davies Publishers.

　9　Paid Davies Publishers in full, less discount.

　15　Received payment in full from Reading Rainbow.

　17　Sold books on account to Lapidus Books for $1,800. The cost of the books sold was $1,080.

　20　Purchased books on account for $1,500 from Fahey Publishers, FOB destination, terms 2/15, n/30. The appropriate party also made a cash payment of $50 for the freight on this date.

　24　Received payment in full from Lapidus Books.

　26　Paid Fahey Publishers in full, less discount.

　28　Sold books on account to Carlyle Bookstore for $1,400. The cost of the books sold was $850.

　30　Granted Carlyle Bookstore $120 credit for books returned costing $72.

Jeremy's Book Warehouse's chart of accounts includes the following: No. 101 Cash, No. 112 Accounts Receivable, No. 120 Inventory, No. 201 Accounts Payable, No. 401 Sales Revenue, No. 412 Sales Returns and Allowances, No. 414 Sales Discounts, and No. 505 Cost of Goods Sold.

Instructions

Journalize the transactions for the month of June for Jeremy's Book Warehouse using a perpetual inventory system.

Journalize, post, and prepare a partial income statement.

(SO 2, 3, 5, 6)

P5-2B　Boone Hardware Store completed the following merchandising transactions in the month of May. At the beginning of May, the ledger of Boone showed Cash of $5,000 and Owner's Capital of $5,000.

May 1　Purchased merchandise on account from Adewale's Wholesale Supply $4,200, terms 2/10, n/30.

　2　Sold merchandise on account $2,100, terms 1/10, n/30. The cost of the merchandise sold was $1,300.

　5　Received credit from Adewale's Wholesale Supply for merchandise returned $300.

　9　Received collections in full, less discounts, from customers billed on sales of $2,100 on May 2.

　10　Paid Adewale's Wholesale Supply in full, less discount.

　11　Purchased supplies for cash $400.

　12　Purchased merchandise for cash $1,400.

　15　Received refund for poor quality merchandise from supplier on cash purchase $150.

　17　Purchased merchandise from Agbaje Distributors $1,300, FOB shipping point, terms 2/10, n/30.

　19　Paid freight on May 17 purchase $130.

　24　Sold merchandise for cash $3,200. The merchandise sold had a cost of $2,000.

　25　Purchased merchandise from Somerhalder, Inc. $620, FOB destination, terms 2/10, n/30.

　27　Paid Agbaje Distributors in full, less discount.

　29　Made refunds to cash customers for defective merchandise $70. The returned merchandise had a fair value of $30.

　31　Sold merchandise on account $1,000 terms n/30. The cost of the merchandise sold was $560.

Boone Hardware's chart of accounts includes the following: No. 101 Cash, No. 112 Accounts Receivable, No. 120 Inventory, No. 126 Supplies, No. 201 Accounts Payable, No. 301 Owner's Capital, No. 401 Sales Revenue, No. 412 Sales Returns and Allowances, No. 414 Sales Discounts, and No. 505 Cost of Goods Sold.

Instructions

(a) Journalize the transactions using a perpetual inventory system.
(b) Enter the beginning cash and capital balances and post the transactions. (Use J1 for the journal reference.)
(c) Prepare an income statement through gross profit for the month of May 2012.

(c) Gross profit $2,379

P5-3B The Akinnuoye Store is located in midtown Madison. During the past several years, net income has been declining because of suburban shopping centers. At the end of the company's fiscal year on November 30, 2012, the following accounts appeared in two of its trial balances.

Prepare financial statements and adjusting and closing entries.
(SO 4, 5)

	Unadjusted	Adjusted		Unadjusted	Adjusted
Accounts Payable	$ 25,200	$ 25,200	Notes Payable	$ 37,000	$ 37,000
Accounts Receivable	30,500	30,500	Owner's Capital	101,700	101,700
Accumulated Depr.—Equip.	34,000	45,000	Owner's Drawings	10,000	10,000
Cash	26,000	26,000	Prepaid Insurance	10,500	3,500
Cost of Goods Sold	507,000	507,000	Property Tax Expense		2,500
Freight-out	6,500	6,500	Property Taxes Payable		2,500
Equipment	146,000	146,000	Rent Expense	15,000	15,000
Depreciation Expense		11,000	Salaries and Wages Expense	96,000	96,000
Insurance Expense		7,000	Sales Revenue	700,000	700,000
Interest Expense	6,400	6,400	Sales Commissions Expense	6,500	11,000
Interest Revenue	8,000	8,000	Sales Commissions Payable		4,500
Inventory	29,000	29,000	Sales Returns and Allowances	8,000	8,000
			Utilities Expense	8,500	8,500

Instructions

(a) Prepare a multiple-step income statement, an owner's equity statement, and a classified balance sheet. Notes payable are due in 2015.
(b) Journalize the adjusting entries that were made.
(c) Journalize the closing entries that are necessary.

(a) Net income $29,100
Owner's capital $120,800
Total assets $190,000

P5-4B Ben Borke, a former disc golf star, operates Ben's Discorama. At the beginning of the current season on April 1, the ledger of Ben's Discorama showed Cash $1,800, Inventory $2,500, and Owner's Capital $4,300. The following transactions were completed during April.

Journalize, post, and prepare a trial balance.
(SO 2, 3, 4)

Apr. 5   Purchased golf discs, bags, and other inventory on account from Innova Co. $1,200, FOB shipping point, terms 2/10, n/60.
    7   Paid freight on the Innova purchase $50.
    9   Received credit from Innova Co. for merchandise returned $100.
   10   Sold merchandise on account for $900, terms n/30. The merchandise sold had a cost of $540.
   12   Purchased disc golf shirts and other accessories on account from Lightning Sportswear $670, terms 1/10, n/30.
   14   Paid Innova Co. in full, less discount.
   17   Received credit from Lightning Sportswear for merchandise returned $70.
   20   Made sales on account for $610, terms n/30. The cost of the merchandise sold was $370.
   21   Paid Lightning Sportswear in full, less discount.
   27   Granted an allowance to members for clothing that was flawed $20.
   30   Received payments on account from customers $900.

The chart of accounts for the store includes the following: No. 101 Cash, No. 112 Accounts Receivable, No. 120 Inventory, No. 201 Accounts Payable, No. 301 Owner's Capital, No. 401 Sales Revenue, No. 412 Sales Returns and Allowances, and No. 505 Cost of Goods Sold.

Instructions

(a) Journalize the April transactions using a perpetual inventory system.
(b) Enter the beginning balances in the ledger accounts and post the April transactions. (Use J1 for the journal reference.)
(c) Prepare a trial balance on April 30, 2012.

(c) Total debits $5,810

Determine cost of goods sold and gross profit under periodic approach.

(SO 6, 7)

*P5-5B At the end of Cortez Department Store's fiscal year on November 30, 2012, these accounts appeared in its adjusted trial balance.

Freight-in	$ 7,500
Inventory	40,000
Purchases	585,000
Purchase Discounts	6,300
Purchase Returns and Allowances	2,700
Sales Revenue	1,000,000
Sales Returns and Allowances	20,000

Additional facts:

1. Merchandise inventory on November 30, 2012, is $52,600.
2. Cortez Department Store uses a periodic system.

Instructions

Gross profit $409,100

Prepare an income statement through gross profit for the year ended November 30, 2012.

Calculate missing amounts and assess profitability.

(SO 6, 7)

*P5-6B Rodriguez Inc. operates a retail operation that purchases and sells home entertainment products. The company purchases all merchandise inventory on credit and uses a periodic inventory system. The Accounts Payable account is used for recording inventory purchases only; all other current liabilities are accrued in separate accounts. You are provided with the following selected information for the fiscal years 2009 through 2012, inclusive.

	2009	2010	2011	2012
Income Statement Data				
Sales revenue		$55,000	$ (e)	$47,000
Cost of goods sold		(a)	13,800	14,300
Gross profit		38,300	35,200	(i)
Operating expenses		34,900	(f)	28,600
Net income		$ (b)	$ 2,500	$ (j)
Balance Sheet Data				
Inventory	$7,200	$ (c)	$ 8,100	$ (k)
Accounts payable	3,200	3,600	2,500	(l)
Additional Information				
Purchases of merchandise inventory on account		$14,200	$ (g)	$13,200
Cash payments to suppliers		(d)	(h)	13,600

Instructions

(c) $4,700

(g) $17,200

(i) $32,700

(a) Calculate the missing amounts.

(b) Sales declined over the 3-year fiscal period, 2010–2012. Does that mean that profitability necessarily also declined? Explain, computing the gross profit rate and the profit margin ratio for each fiscal year to help support your answer. (Round to one decimal place.)

Journalize, post, and prepare trial balance and partial income statement using periodic approach.

(SO 7)

*P5-7B At the beginning of the current season on April 1, the ledger of Ilana Pro Shop showed Cash $3,000; Inventory $4,000; and Owner's Capital $7,000. These transactions occurred during April 2012.

Apr. 5 Purchased golf bags, clubs, and balls on account from Zuleikha Co. $1,200, FOB shipping point, terms 2/10, n/60.
    7 Paid freight on Zuleikha Co. purchases $50.
    9 Received credit from Zuleikha Co. for merchandise returned $100.
   10 Sold merchandise on account to members $600, terms n/30.
   12 Purchased golf shoes, sweaters, and other accessories on account from Libby Sportswear $450, terms 1/10, n/30.
   14 Paid Zuleikha Co. in full.
   17 Received credit from Libby Sportswear for merchandise returned $50.
   20 Made sales on account to members $600, terms n/30.

21   Paid Libby Sportswear in full.
27   Granted credit to members for clothing that had flaws $35.
30   Received payments on account from members $600.

The chart of accounts for the pro shop includes Cash, Accounts Receivable, Inventory, Accounts Payable, Owner's Capital, Sales Revenue, Sales Returns and Allowances, Purchases, Purchase Returns and Allowances, Purchase Discounts, and Freight-in.

Instructions

(a) Journalize the April transactions using a periodic inventory system.
(b) Using T accounts, enter the beginning balances in the ledger accounts and post the April transactions.
(c) Prepare a trial balance on April 30, 2012.
(d) Prepare an income statement through gross profit, assuming merchandise inventory on hand at April 30 is $4,824.

(c) Tot. trial
   balance $8,376
Gross profit $465

Problems: Set C

Visit the book's companion website, at **www.wiley.com/college/weygandt**, and choose the Student Companion site to access Problem Set C.

Comprehensive Problem

CP5   On December 1, 2012, Shiras Distributing Company had the following account balances.

	Debits		**Credits**
Cash	$ 7,200	Accumulated Depreciation—	
Accounts Receivable	4,600	Equipment	$ 2,200
Inventory	12,000	Accounts Payable	4,500
Supplies	1,200	Salaries and Wages Payable	1,000
Equipment	22,000	Owner's Capital	39,300
	$47,000		$47,000

During December, the company completed the following summary transactions.

Dec. 6   Paid $1,600 for salaries and wages due employees, of which $600 is for December and $1,000 is for November salaries and wages payable.
     8   Received $1,900 cash from customers in payment of account (no discount allowed).
    10   Sold merchandise for cash $6,300. The cost of the merchandise sold was $4,100.
    13   Purchased merchandise on account from Gong Co. $9,000, terms 2/10, n/30.
    15   Purchased supplies for cash $2,000.
    18   Sold merchandise on account $12,000, terms 3/10, n/30. The cost of the merchandise sold was $8,000.
    20   Paid salaries $1,800.
    23   Paid Gong Co. in full, less discount.
    27   Received collections in full, less discounts, from customers billed on December 18.

Adjustment data:

1. Accrued salaries payable $800.
2. Depreciation $200 per month.
3. Supplies on hand $1,500.

Instructions

(a) Journalize the December transactions using a perpetual inventory system.
(b) Enter the December 1 balances in the ledger T accounts and post the December transactions. Use Cost of Goods Sold, Depreciation Expense, Salaries and Wages Expense, Sales Revenue, Sales Discounts, and Supplies Expense.
(c) Journalize and post adjusting entries.
(d) Prepare an adjusted trial balance.
(e) Prepare an income statement and an owner's equity statement for December and a classified balance sheet at December 31.

(d) Totals $65,300
(e) Net income $740

Continuing Cookie Chronicle

(Note: This is a continuation of the Cookie Chronicle from Chapters 1 through 4.)

CCC5   Because Natalie has had such a successful first few months, she is considering other opportunities to develop her business. One opportunity is the sale of fine European mixers. The owner of Kzinski Supply Company has approached Natalie to become the exclusive U.S. distributor of these fine mixers in her state. The current cost of a mixer is approximately $525 (U.S.), and Natalie would sell each one for $1,050. Natalie comes to you for advice on how to account for these mixers.

Go to the book's companion website, **www.wiley.com/college/weygandt**, *to see the completion of this problem.*

BROADENINGYOURPERSPECTIVE

Financial Reporting and Analysis

Financial Reporting Problem: PepsiCo, Inc.

BYP5-1   The financial statements of PepsiCo, Inc. are presented in Appendix A at the end of this textbook.

Instructions

Answer the following questions using PepsiCo's Consolidated Statement of Income.

(a) What was the percentage change in (1) sales and in (2) net income from 2007 to 2008 and from 2008 to 2009?

(b) What was the company's gross profit rate in 2007, 2008, and 2009?

(c) What was the company's percentage of net income to net sales in 2007, 2008, and 2009? Comment on any trend in this percentage.

Comparative Analysis Problem: PepsiCo, Inc. vs. The Coca-Cola Company

BYP5-2   PepsiCo's financial statements are presented in Appendix A. Financial statements of The Coca-Cola Company are presented in Appendix B.

Instructions

(a) Based on the information contained in these financial statements, determine each of the following for each company.

(1) Gross profit for 2009.

(2) Gross profit rate for 2009.

(3) Operating income for 2009.

(4) Percent change in operating income from 2008 to 2009.

(b) What conclusions concerning the relative profitability of the two companies can you draw from these data?

On the Web

BYP5-3   No financial decision maker should ever rely solely on the financial information reported in the annual report to make decisions. It is important to keep abreast of financial news. This activity demonstrates how to search for financial news on the Web.

Address: biz.yahoo.com/i, or go to **www.wiley.com/college/weygandt**

Steps:

1. Type in either PepsiCo or Coca-Cola.

2. Choose **News**.

3. Select an article that sounds interesting to you.

Instructions

(a) What was the source of the article (e.g., Reuters, Businesswire, PR Newswire)?

(b) Assume that you are a personal financial planner and that one of your clients owns stock in the company. Write a brief memo to your client, summarizing the article and explaining the implications of the article for their investment.

Critical Thinking

Decision Making Across the Organization

BYP5-4   Three years ago, Carrie Dungy and her brother-in-law Luke Barber opened FedCo Department Store. For the first two years, business was good, but the following condensed income results for 2011 were disappointing.

FEDCO DEPARTMENT STORE
Income Statement
For the Year Ended December 31, 2011

Net sales		$700,000
Cost of goods sold		553,000
Gross profit		147,000
Operating expenses		
Selling expenses	$100,000	
Administrative expenses	20,000	120,000
Net income		$ 27,000

Carrie believes the problem lies in the relatively low gross profit rate (gross profit divided by net sales) of 21%. Luke believes the problem is that operating expenses are too high.

Carrie thinks the gross profit rate can be improved by making both of the following changes. She does not anticipate that these changes will have any effect on operating expenses.

1. Increase average selling prices by 17%. This increase is expected to lower sales volume so that total sales will increase only 6%.

2. Buy merchandise in larger quantities and take all purchase discounts. These changes are expected to increase the gross profit rate by 3 percentage points.

Luke thinks expenses can be cut by making both of the following changes. He feels that these changes will not have any effect on net sales.

1. Cut 2011 sales salaries of $60,000 in half and give sales personnel a commission of 2% of net sales.

2. Reduce store deliveries to one day per week rather than twice a week; this change will reduce 2011 delivery expenses of $30,000 by 40%.

Carrie and Luke come to you for help in deciding the best way to improve net income.

Instructions

With the class divided into groups, answer the following.

(a) Prepare a condensed income statement for 2012, assuming (1) Carrie's changes are implemented and (2) Luke's ideas are adopted.

(b) What is your recommendation to Carrie and Luke?

(c) Prepare a condensed income statement for 2012, assuming both sets of proposed changes are made.

Communication Activity

BYP5-5   The following situation is in chronological order.

1. Flutie decides to buy a surfboard.

2. He calls Surfing USA Co. to inquire about their surfboards.

3. Two days later, he requests Surfing USA Co. to make him a surfboard.

4. Three days later, Surfing USA Co. sends him a purchase order to fill out.

5. He sends back the purchase order.

6. Surfing USA Co. receives the completed purchase order.

7. Surfing USA Co. completes the surfboard.
8. Flutie picks up the surfboard.
9. Surfing USA Co. bills Flutie.
10. Surfing USA Co. receives payment from Flutie.

Instructions

In a memo to the president of Surfing USA Co., answer the following.

(a) When should Surfing USA Co. record the sale?

(b) Suppose that with his purchase order, Flutie is required to make a down payment. Would that change your answer?

Ethics Case

BYP5-6   Laura McAntee was just hired as the assistant treasurer of Dorchester Stores. The company is a specialty chain store with nine retail stores concentrated in one metropolitan area. Among other things, the payment of all invoices is centralized in one of the departments Laura will manage. Her primary responsibility is to maintain the company's high credit rating by paying all bills when due and to take advantage of all cash discounts.

Danny Feeney, the former assistant treasurer who has been promoted to treasurer, is training Laura in her new duties. He instructs Laura that she is to continue the practice of preparing all checks "net of discount" and dating the checks the last day of the discount period. "But," Danny continues, "we always hold the checks at least 4 days beyond the discount period before mailing them. That way, we get another 4 days of interest on our money. Most of our creditors need our business and don't complain. And, if they scream about our missing the discount period, we blame it on the mail room or the post office. We've only lost one discount out of every hundred we take that way. I think everybody does it. By the way, welcome to our team!"

Instructions

(a) What are the ethical considerations in this case?

(b) Who are the stakeholders that are harmed or benefitted in this situation?

(c) Should Laura continue the practice started by Danny? Does she have any choice?

"All About You" Activity

BYP5-7   There are many situations in business where it is difficult to determine the proper period in which to record revenue. Suppose that after graduation with a degree in finance, you take a job as a manager at a consumer electronics store called Atlantis Electronics. The company has expanded rapidly in order to compete with Best Buy. Atlantis has also begun selling gift cards for its electronic products. The cards are available in any dollar amount and allow the holder of the card to purchase an item for up to 2 years from the time the card is purchased. If the card is not used during that 2 years, it expires.

Instructions

Answer the following questions.

At what point should the revenue from the gift cards be recognized? Should the revenue be recognized at the time the card is sold, or should it be recorded when the card is redeemed? Explain the reasoning to support your answers.

FASB Codification Activity

BYP5-8   If your school has a subscription to the FASB Codification, go to *http://aaahq.org/ascLogin.cfm* to log in and prepare responses to the following

(a) Access the glossary ("Master Glossary") to answer the following.
   (1) What is the definition provided for inventory?
   (2) What is a customer?

(b) What guidance does the Codification provide concerning reporting inventories above cost?

Answers to Insight and Accounting Across the Organization Questions

p. 213 Morrow Snowboards Improves Its Stock Appeal   **Q:** If a perpetual system keeps track of inventory on a daily basis, why do companies ever need to do a physical count? **A:** A perpetual system keeps track of all sales and purchases on a continuous basis. This provides a constant record of the number of units in the inventory. However, if employees make errors in recording sales or purchases, or if there is theft, the inventory value will not be correct. As a consequence, all companies do a physical count of inventory at least once a year.

p. 220 Should Costco Change Its Return Policy?   **Q:** If a company expects significant returns, what are the implications for revenue recognition? **A:** If a company expects significant returns, it should make an adjusting entry at the end of the year reducing sales by the estimated amount of sales returns. This is necessary so as not to overstate the amount of revenue recognized in the period.

p. 226 Disclosing More Details   **Q:** Why have investors and analysts demanded more accuracy in isolating "Other gains and losses" from operating items? **A:** Greater accuracy in the classification of operating versus nonoperating ("Other gains and losses") items permits investors and analysts to judge the real operating margin, the results of continuing operations, and management's ability to control operating expenses.

Answers to Self-Test Questions

1. c   **2.** a   **3.** c   **4.** b (($750 − $50) × .98)   **5.** c   **6.** c   **7.** a   **8.** d   **9.** b ($400,000 − $310,000)   **10.** c   **11.** d   ***12.** d   ***13.** a ($60,000 + $380,000 − $50,000)   ***14.** b   ***15.** a

IFRS A Look at IFRS

The basic accounting entries for merchandising are the same under both GAAP and IFRS. The income statement is a required statement under both sets of standards. The basic format is similar although some differences do exist.

Key Points

- Under both GAAP and IFRS, a company can choose to use either a perpetual or a periodic system.

- Inventories are defined by IFRS as held-for-sale in the ordinary course of business, in the process of production for such sale, or in the form of materials or supplies to be consumed in the production process or in the providing of services.

- Under GAAP, companies generally classify income statement items by function. Classification by function leads to descriptions like administration, distribution, and manufacturing. Under IFRS, companies must classify expenses by either nature or function. Classification by nature leads to descriptions such as the following: salaries, depreciation expense, and utilities expense. If a company uses the functional-expense method on the income statement, disclosure by nature is required in the notes to the financial statements.

- Presentation of the income statement under GAAP follows either a single-step or multiple-step format. IFRS does not mention a single-step or multiple-step approach.

- Under IFRS, revaluation of land, buildings, and intangible assets is permitted. The initial gains and losses resulting from this revaluation are reported as adjustments to equity, often referred to as *other comprehensive income*. The effect of this difference is that the use of IFRS results in more transactions affecting equity (other comprehensive income) but not net income.

- *IAS 1*, "Presentation of Financial Statements," provides general guidelines for the reporting of income statement information. Subsequently, a number of international standards have been issued that provide additional guidance to issues related to income statement presentation.

- Similar to GAAP, comprehensive income under IFRS includes unrealized gains and losses (such as those on so-called "available-for-sale securities") that are not included in the calculation of net income.

- IFRS requires that two years of income statement information be presented, whereas GAAP requires three years.

Looking to the Future

The IASB and FASB are working on a project that would rework the structure of financial statements. Specifically, this project will address the issue of how to classify various items in the income statement. A main goal of this new approach is to provide information that better represents how businesses are run. In addition, this approach draws attention away from just one number—net income. It will adopt major groupings similar to those currently used by the statement of cash flows (operating, investing, and financing), so that numbers can be more readily traced across statements. For example, the amount of income that is generated by operations would be traceable to the assets and liabilities used to generate the income. Finally, this approach would also provide detail, beyond that currently seen in most statements (either GAAP or IFRS), by requiring that line items be presented both by function and by nature. The new financial statement format was heavily influenced by suggestions from financial statement analysts.

IFRS Self-Test Questions

1. Which of the following would *not* be included in the definition of inventory under IFRS?
   (a) Photocopy paper held for sale by an office-supply store.
   (b) Stereo equipment held for sale by an electronics store.
   (c) Used office equipment held for sale by the human relations department of a plastics company.
   (d) All of the above would meet the definition.

2. Which of the following would *not* be a line item of a company reporting costs by nature?
   (a) Depreciation expense.
   (b) Salaries expense.
   (c) Interest expense.
   (d) Manufacturing expense.

3. Which of the following would *not* be a line item of a company reporting costs by function?
   (a) Administration.
   (b) Manufacturing.
   (c) Utilities expense.
   (d) Distribution.

4. Which of the following statements is *false*?
   (a) IFRS specifically requires use of a multiple-step income statement.
   (b) Under IFRS, companies can use either a perpetual or periodic system.
   (c) The proposed new format for financial statements was heavily influenced by the suggestions of financial statement analysts.
   (d) The new income statement format will try to de-emphasize the focus on the "net income" line item.

5. Under the new format for financial statements being proposed under a joint IASB/FASB project:
   (a) all financial statements would adopt headings similar to the current format of the balance sheet.
   (b) financial statements would be presented consistent with the way management usually run companies.

(c) companies would be required to report income statement line items by function only.

(d) the amount of detail shown in the income statement would decrease compared to current presentations.

IFRS Concepts and Application

IFRS5-1 Explain the difference between the "nature-of-expense" and "function-of-expense" classifications.

IFRS5-2 For each of the following income statement line items, state whether the item is a "by nature" expense item or a "by function" expense item.

_____ Cost of goods sold
_____ Depreciation expense
_____ Salaries and wages expense
_____ Selling expenses
_____ Utilities expense
_____ Delivery expense
_____ General and administrative expenses

IFRS5-3 Gribble Company reported the following amounts in 2012: Net income, €150,000; Unrealized gain related to revaluation of buildings, €10,000; and Unrealized loss on available-for-sale securities, €(35,000). Determine Gribble's total comprehensive income for 2012.

International Financial Reporting Problem: Zetar plc

IFRS5-4 The financial statements of Zetar plc are presented in Appendix C. The company's complete annual report, including the notes to its financial statements, is available at *www.zetarplc.com*.

Instructions

(a) Is Zetar using a multiple-step or a single-step income statement format? Explain how you made your determination.

(b) Instead of "interest expense," what label does Zetar use for interest costs that it incurs?

(c) Using the notes to the company's financial statements, explain what each of the following are:

  (1) Adjusted results.

  (2) One-off items.

Answers to IFRS Self-Test Questions
1. c 2. d 3. c 4. a 5. b

✔
The Navigator

✔ **Remember to go back to the Navigator box on the chapter opening page and check off your completed work.**

CHAPTER6
Inventories

Study Objectives

After studying this chapter, you should be able to:

[1] Describe the steps in determining inventory quantities.

[2] Explain the accounting for inventories and apply the inventory cost flow methods.

[3] Explain the financial effects of the inventory cost flow assumptions.

[4] Explain the lower-of-cost-or-market basis of accounting for inventories.

[5] Indicate the effects of inventory errors on the financial statements.

[6] Compute and interpret the inventory turnover ratio.

✔ **The Navigator**

✔ [The Navigator]

● Scan Study Objectives	○
● Read Feature Story	○
● Read Preview	○
● Read text and answer **Do it!** p. 265 ○ p. 271 ○ p. 277 ○ p. 280 ○	
● Work Comprehensive **Do it!** **1** p. 280 ○ **2** p. 285 ○	
● Review Summary of Study Objectives	○
● Answer Self-Test Questions	○
● Complete Assignments	○
● Go to *WileyPLUS* for practice and tutorials	○
● Read A Look at IFRS p. 310	○

Feature Story

"WHERE IS THAT SPARE BULLDOZER BLADE?"

Let's talk inventory—big, bulldozer-size inventory. Caterpillar Inc. is the world's largest manufacturer of construction and mining equipment, diesel and natural gas engines, and industrial gas turbines. It sells its products in over 200 countries, making it one of the most successful U.S. exporters. More than 70% of its productive assets are located domestically, and nearly 50% of its sales are foreign.

During the 1980s, Caterpillar's profitability suffered, but today it is very successful. A big part of this turnaround can be attributed to effective management of its inventory. Imagine what it costs Caterpillar to have too many bulldozers sitting around in inventory—a situation the company definitely wants to avoid. Conversely, Caterpillar must make sure it has enough inventory to meet demand.

At one time during a 7-year period, Caterpillar's sales increased by 100%, while its inventory increased by only 50%. To achieve this dramatic reduction in the amount of resources tied up in inventory, while continuing to meet customers' needs, Caterpillar used a two-pronged approach. First, it completed a factory modernization program, which dramatically increased its production efficiency. The program reduced by 60% the amount of inventory the company processed at any one time. It also reduced by an incredible 75% the time it takes to manufacture a part.

Second, Caterpillar dramatically improved its parts distribution system. It ships more than 100,000 items daily from its 23 distribution centers strategically located around the world (10 *million* square feet of warehouse space—remember, we're talking bulldozers). The company can virtually guarantee that it can get any part to anywhere in the world within 24 hours.

After these changes, Caterpillar had record exports, profits, and revenues. It would seem that things couldn't be better. But industry analysts, as well as the company's managers, thought otherwise. In order to maintain Caterpillar's position as the industry leader, management began another major overhaul of inventory production and inventory management processes. The goal: to cut the number of repairs in half, increase productivity by 20%, and increase inventory turnover by 40%.

In short, Caterpillar's ability to manage its inventory has been a key reason for its past success, and inventory management will very likely play a huge part in its ability to succeed in the future.

The Navigator

Inside**CHAPTER6**

PreviewofCHAPTER6

In the previous chapter, we discussed the accounting for merchandise inventory using a perpetual inventory system. In this chapter, we explain the methods used to calculate the cost of inventory on hand at the balance sheet date and the cost of goods sold.

The content and organization of this chapter are as follows.

Inventories				
Classifying Inventory	**Determining Inventory Quantities**	**Inventory Costing**	**Inventory Errors**	**Statement Presentation and Analysis**
• Finished goods • Work in process • Raw materials	• Taking a physical inventory • Determining ownership of goods	• Specific identification • Cost flow assumptions • Financial statement and tax effects • Consistent use • Lower-of-cost-or-market	• Income statement effects • Balance sheet effects	• Presentation • Analysis

✔
The Navigator

Classifying Inventory

How a company classifies its inventory depends on whether the firm is a merchandiser or a manufacturer. In a *merchandising* company, such as those described in Chapter 5, inventory consists of many different items. For example, in a grocery store, canned goods, dairy products, meats, and produce are just a few of the inventory items on hand. These items have two common characteristics: (1) They are owned by the company, and (2) they are in a form ready for sale to customers in the ordinary course of business. Thus, merchandisers need only one inventory classification, **merchandise inventory**, to describe the many different items that make up the total inventory.

In a *manufacturing* company, some inventory may not yet be ready for sale. As a result, manufacturers usually classify inventory into three categories: finished goods, work in process, and raw materials. **Finished goods inventory** is manufactured items that are completed and ready for sale. **Work in process** is that portion of manufactured inventory that has been placed into the production process but is not yet complete. **Raw materials** are the basic goods that will be used in production but have not yet been placed into production.

For example, Caterpillar classifies earth-moving tractors completed and ready for sale as **finished goods**. It classifies the tractors on the assembly line in various stages of production as **work in process**. The steel, glass, tires, and other components that are on hand waiting to be used in the production of tractors are identified as **raw materials**.

By observing the levels and changes in the levels of these three inventory types, financial statement users can gain insight into management's production plans. For example, low levels of raw materials and high levels of finished goods suggest that management believes it has enough inventory on hand, and production will be slowing down—perhaps in anticipation of a recession. On the other hand, high levels of raw materials and low levels of finished goods probably indicate that management is planning to step up production.

Many companies have significantly lowered inventory levels and costs using **just-in-time (JIT) inventory** methods. Under a just-in-time method, companies

Helpful Hint

Regardless of the classification, companies report all inventories under Current Assets on the balance sheet.

manufacture or purchase goods just in time for use. Dell is famous for having developed a system for making computers in response to individual customer requests. Even though it makes each computer to meet each customer's particular specifications, Dell is able to assemble the computer and put it on a truck in less than 48 hours. The success of the JIT system depends on reliable suppliers. By integrating its information systems with those of its suppliers, Dell reduced its inventories to nearly zero. This is a huge advantage in an industry where products become obsolete nearly overnight.

The accounting concepts discussed in this chapter apply to the inventory classifications of both merchandising and manufacturing companies. Our focus here is on merchandise inventory.

ACCOUNTING ACROSS THE ORGANIZATION

A Big Hiccup

JIT can save a company a lot of money, but it isn't without risk. An unexpected disruption in the supply chain can cost a company a lot of money. Japanese automakers experienced just such a disruption when a 6.8-magnitude earthquake caused major damage to the company that produces 50% of their piston rings. The rings themselves cost only $1.50, but without them you cannot make a car. No other supplier could quickly begin producing sufficient quantities of the rings to match the desired specifications. As a result, the automakers were forced to shut down production for a few days—a loss of tens of thousands of cars.

Source: Amy Chozick, "A Key Strategy of Japan's Car Makers Backfires," *Wall Street Journal* (July 20, 2007).

? What steps might the companies take to avoid such a serious disruption in the future?
(See page 310.)

Determining Inventory Quantities

No matter whether they are using a periodic or perpetual inventory system, all companies need to determine inventory quantities at the end of the accounting period. If using a perpetual system, companies take a physical inventory for two reasons:

Study Objective [1]
Describe the steps in determining inventory quantities.

1. To check the accuracy of their perpetual inventory records.
2. To determine the amount of inventory lost due to wasted raw materials, shoplifting, or employee theft.

Companies using a periodic inventory system take a physical ⸺⸺ determine the inventory on hand at the balance sheet date, and to ⸺⸺ cost of goods sold for the period.

Determining inventory quantities involves two steps: (1) ta⸺ physical inventory of goods on hand and (2) determining the owners⸺ goods.

Taking a Physical Inventory

Companies take a physical inventory at the end of the accounting p⸺ Taking a physical inventory involves actually counting, weighi⸺ measuring each kind of inventory on hand. In many companies, t⸺ an inventory is a formidable task. Retailers such as Target, True ⸺

Hardware, or Home Depot have thousands of different inventory items. An inventory count is generally more accurate when goods are not being sold or received during the counting. Consequently, companies often "take inventory" when the business is closed or when business is slow. Many retailers close early on a chosen day in January—after the holiday sales and returns, when inventories are at their lowest level—to count inventory. Recall from Chapter 5 that Wal-Mart has a year-end of January 31.

*E*THICS *I*NSIGHT

Falsifying Inventory to Boost Income

Managers at women's apparel maker Leslie Fay were convicted of falsifying inventory records to boost net income—and consequently to boost management bonuses. In another case, executives at Craig Consumer Electronics were accused of defrauding lenders by manipulating inventory records. The indictment said the company classified "defective goods as new or refurbished" and claimed that it owned certain shipments "from overseas suppliers" when, in fact, Craig either did not own the shipments or the shipments did not exist.

? What effect does an overstatement of inventory have on a company's financial statements? (See page 310.)

Determining Ownership of Goods

One challenge in computing inventory quantities is determining what inventory a company owns. To determine ownership of goods, two questions must be answered: Do all of the goods included in the count belong to the company? Does the company own any goods that were not included in the count?

GOODS IN TRANSIT

A complication in determining ownership is **goods in transit** (on board a truck, train, ship, or plane) at the end of the period. The company may have purchased goods that have not yet been received, or it may have sold goods that have not yet been delivered. To arrive at an accurate count, the company must determine ownership of these goods.

Goods in transit should be included in the inventory of the company that has legal title to the goods. Legal title is determined by the terms of the sale, as shown in Illustration 6-1 and described below.

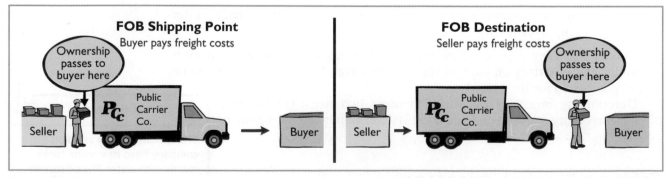

Illustration 6-1
Terms of sale

1. When the terms are FOB (free on board) shipping point, ownership of the goods passes to the buyer when the public carrier accepts the goods from the seller.
2. When the terms are FOB destination, ownership of the goods remains with the seller until the goods reach the buyer.

If goods in transit at the statement date are ignored, inventory quantities may be seriously miscounted. Assume, for example, that Hargrove Company has 20,000 units of inventory on hand on December 31. It also has the following goods in transit:

1. Sales of 1,500 units shipped December 31 FOB destination.
2. Purchases of 2,500 units shipped FOB shipping point by the seller on December 31.

Hargrove has legal title to both the 1,500 units sold and the 2,500 units purchased. If the company ignores the units in transit, it would understate inventory quantities by 4,000 units (1,500 + 2,500).

As we will see later in the chapter, inaccurate inventory counts affect not only the inventory amount shown on the balance sheet but also the cost of goods sold calculation on the income statement.

CONSIGNED GOODS

In some lines of business, it is common to hold the goods of other parties and try to sell the goods for them for a fee, but without taking ownership of the goods. These are called **consigned goods**.

For example, you might have a used car that you would like to sell. If you take the item to a dealer, the dealer might be willing to put the car on its lot and charge you a commission if it is sold. Under this agreement, the dealer **would not take ownership** of the car, which would still belong to you. Therefore, if an inventory count were taken, the car would not be included in the dealer's inventory.

Many car, boat, and antique dealers sell goods on consignment to keep their inventory costs down and to avoid the risk of purchasing an item that they won't be able to sell. Today even some manufacturers are making consignment agreements with their suppliers in order to keep their inventory levels low.

Do it!

Hasbeen Company completed its inventory count. It arrived at a total inventory value of $200,000. As a new member of Hasbeen's accounting department, you have been given the information listed below. Discuss how this information affects the reported cost of inventory.

1. Hasbeen included in the inventory goods held on consignment for Falls Co., costing $15,000.
2. The company did not include in the count purchased goods of $10,000 which were in transit (terms: FOB shipping point).
3. The company did not include in the count sold inventory with a cost of $12,000 which was in transit (terms: FOB shipping point).

Rules of Ownership

action plan

✔ Apply the rules of ownership to goods held on consignment.

✔ Apply the rules of ownership to goods in transit.

Solution

The goods of $15,000 held on consignment should be deducted from the inventory count. The goods of $10,000 purchased FOB shipping point should be added to the inventory count. Sold goods of $12,000 which were in transit FOB shipping point should not be included in the ending inventory. Thus, inventory should be carried at $195,000 ($200,000 − $15,000 + $10,000).

Related exercise material: BE6-1, E6-1, E6-2, and **Do it!** 6-1.

The Navigator

ANATOMY OF A FRAUD

Ted Nickerson, CEO of clock manufacturer Dally Industries, was feared by all of his employees. Ted had expensive tastes. To support his expensive tastes, Ted took out large loans, which he collateralized with his shares of Dally Industries stock. If the price of Dally's stock fell, he was required to provide the bank with more shares of stock. To achieve target net income figures and thus maintain the stock price, Ted coerced employees in the company to alter inventory figures. Inventory quantities were manipulated by changing the amounts on inventory control tags after the year-end physical inventory count. For example, if a tag said there were 20 units of a particular item, the tag was changed to 220. Similarly, the unit costs that were used to determine the value of ending inventory were increased from, for example, $125 per unit to $1,250. Both of these fraudulent changes had the effect of increasing the amount of reported ending inventory. This reduced cost of goods sold and increased net income.

Total take: $245,000

THE MISSING CONTROL

Independent internal verification. The company should have spot-checked its inventory records periodically, verifying that the number of units in the records agreed with the amount on hand and that the unit costs agreed with vendor price sheets.

Source: Adapted from Wells, *Fraud Casebook* (2007), pp. 502–509.

Inventory Costing

Inventory is accounted for at cost. Cost includes all expenditures necessary to acquire goods and place them in a condition ready for sale. For example, freight costs incurred to acquire inventory are added to the cost of inventory, but the cost of shipping goods to a customer are a selling expense.

After a company has determined the quantity of units of inventory, it applies unit costs to the quantities to compute the total cost of the inventory and the cost of goods sold. This process can be complicated if a company has purchased inventory items at different times and at different prices.

For example, assume that Crivitz TV Company purchases three identical 50-inch TVs on different dates at costs of $700, $750, and $800. During the year, Crivitz sold two sets at $1,200 each. These facts are summarized in Illustration 6-2.

Illustration 6-2
Data for inventory costing example

Purchases			
February 3	1 TV	at	$700
March 5	1 TV	at	$750
May 22	1 TV	at	$800
Sales			
June 1	2 TVs	for	$2,400 ($1,200 × 2)

Cost of goods sold will differ depending on which two TVs the company sold. For example, it might be $1,450 ($700 + $750), or $1,500 ($700 + $800), or $1,550 ($750 + $800). In this section, we discuss alternative costing methods available to Crivitz.

Specific Identification

If Crivitz can positively identify which particular units it sold and which are still in ending inventory, it can use the **specific identification method** of inventory costing. For example, if Crivitz sold the TVs it purchased on February 3 and May 22, then its cost of goods sold is $1,500 ($700 + $800), and its ending inventory is $750 (see Illustration 6-3). Using this method, companies can accurately determine ending inventory and cost of goods sold.

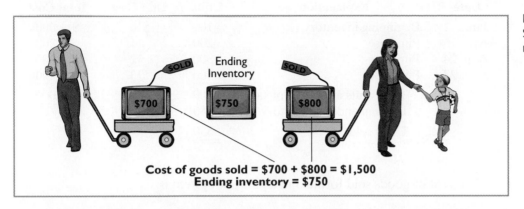

Illustration 6-3
Specific identification method

Specific identification requires that companies keep records of the original cost of each individual inventory item. Historically, specific identification was possible only when a company sold a limited variety of high-unit-cost items that could be identified clearly from the time of purchase through the time of sale. Examples of such products are cars, pianos, or expensive antiques.

Today, bar coding, electronic product codes, and radio frequency identification make it theoretically possible to do specific identification with nearly any type of product. The reality is, however, that this practice is still relatively rare. Instead, rather than keep track of the cost of each particular item sold, most companies make assumptions, called **cost flow assumptions**, about which units were sold.

Ethics Note

A major disadvantage of the specific identification method is that management may be able to manipulate net income. For example, it can boost net income by selling units purchased at a low cost, or reduce net income by selling units purchased at a high cost.

Cost Flow Assumptions

Because specific identification is often impractical, other cost flow methods are permitted. These differ from specific identification in that they **assume** flows of costs that may be unrelated to the physical flow of goods. There are three assumed cost flow methods:

1. First-in, first-out (FIFO)
2. Last-in, first-out (LIFO)
3. Average-cost

There is no accounting requirement that the cost flow assumption be consistent with the physical movement of the goods. Company management selects the appropriate cost flow method.

To demonstrate the three cost flow methods, we will use a *periodic* inventory system. We assume a periodic system for two main reasons. First, many small companies use periodic rather than perpetual systems. Second, **very few companies use** *perpetual* **LIFO, FIFO, or average-cost** to cost their inventory and related cost of goods sold. Instead, companies that use perpetual systems often use an assumed cost (called a standard cost) to record cost of goods sold at the time of sale. Then, at the end of the period when they count their inventory, they **recalculate cost of**

goods sold using *periodic* **FIFO, LIFO, or average-cost** and adjust cost of goods sold to this recalculated number.[1]

To illustrate the three inventory cost flow methods, we will use the data for Houston Electronics' Astro condensers, shown in Illustration 6-4.

Illustration 6-4
Data for Houston Electronics

Houston Electronics Astro Condensers				
Date	**Explanation**	**Units**	**Unit Cost**	**Total Cost**
Jan. 1	Beginning inventory	100	$10	$ 1,000
Apr. 15	Purchase	200	11	2,200
Aug. 24	Purchase	300	12	3,600
Nov. 27	Purchase	400	13	5,200
	Total units available for sale	1,000		$12,000
	Units in ending inventory	450		
	Units sold	550		

The cost of goods sold formula in a periodic system is:

(Beginning Inventory + Purchases) − Ending Inventory = Cost of Goods Sold

---

Houston Electronics had a total of 1,000 units available to sell during the period (beginning inventory plus purchases). The total cost of these 1,000 units is $12,000, referred to as *cost of goods available for sale*. A physical inventory taken at December 31 determined that there were 450 units in ending inventory. Therefore, Houston sold 550 units (1,000 − 450) during the period. To determine the cost of the 550 units that were sold (the cost of goods sold), we assign a cost to the ending inventory and subtract that value from the cost of goods available for sale. The value assigned to the ending inventory **will depend on which cost flow method we use**. No matter which cost flow assumption we use, though, the sum of cost of goods sold plus the cost of the ending inventory must equal the cost of goods available for sale—in this case, $12,000.

FIRST-IN, FIRST-OUT (FIFO)

The **first-in, first-out (FIFO) method** assumes that the **earliest goods** purchased are the first to be sold. FIFO often parallels the actual physical flow of merchandise; it generally is good business practice to sell the oldest units first. Under the FIFO method, therefore, the **costs** of the earliest goods purchased are the first to be recognized in determining cost of goods sold. (This does not necessarily mean that the oldest units *are* sold first, but that the costs of the oldest units are *recognized* first. In a bin of picture hangers at the hardware store, for example, no one really knows, nor would it matter, which hangers are sold first.) Illustration 6-5 shows the allocation of the cost of goods available for sale at Houston Electronics under FIFO.

---

[1]Also, some companies use a perpetual system to keep track of units, but they do not make an entry for perpetual cost of goods sold. In addition, firms that employ LIFO tend to use *dollar-value LIFO*, a method discussed in upper-level courses. FIFO periodic and FIFO perpetual give the same result; therefore firms should not incur the additional cost to use FIFO perpetual. Few firms use perpetual average-cost because of the added cost of record-keeping. Finally, for instructional purposes, we believe it is easier to demonstrate the cost flow assumptions under the periodic system, which makes it more pedagogically appropriate.

Illustration 6-5
Allocation of costs—FIFO method

Cost of Goods Available for Sale				
Date	**Explanation**	**Units**	**Unit Cost**	**Total Cost**
Jan. 1	Beginning inventory	100	$10	$ 1,000
Apr. 15	Purchase	200	11	2,200
Aug. 24	Purchase	300	12	3,600
Nov. 27	Purchase	400	13	5,200
	Total	1,000		**$12,000**

Step 1: Ending Inventory				Step 2: Cost of Goods Sold	
Date	**Units**	**Unit Cost**	**Total Cost**		
Nov. 27	400	$13	$5,200	Cost of goods available for sale	$12,000
Aug. 24	50	12	600	Less: Ending inventory	5,800
Total	450		**$5,800**	Cost of goods sold	**$ 6,200**

Helpful Hint

Note the sequencing of the allocation:
(1) Compute ending inventory, and
(2) determine cost of goods sold

Helpful Hint

Another way of thinking about the calculation of FIFO ending inventory is the *LISH assumption*—last in still here.

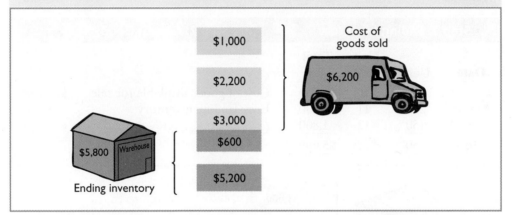

Under FIFO, since it is assumed that the first goods purchased were the first goods sold, ending inventory is based on the prices of the most recent units purchased. That is, **under FIFO, companies obtain the cost of the ending inventory by taking the unit cost of the most recent purchase and working backward until all units of inventory have been costed**. In this example, Houston Electronics prices the 450 units of ending inventory using the *most recent* prices. The last purchase was 400 units at $13 on November 27. The remaining 50 units are priced using the unit cost of the second most recent purchase, $12, on August 24. Next, Houston Electronics calculates cost of goods sold by subtracting the cost of the units **not sold** (ending inventory) from the cost of all goods available for sale.

Illustration 6-6 demonstrates that companies also can calculate cost of goods sold by pricing the 550 units sold using the prices of the first 550 units acquired. Note that of the 300 units purchased on August 24, only 250 units are assumed sold. This agrees with our calculation of the cost of ending inventory, where 50 of these units were assumed unsold and thus included in ending inventory.

Date	Units	Unit Cost	Total Cost
Jan. 1	100	$10	$1,000
Apr. 15	200	11	2,200
Aug. 24	250	12	3,000
Total	550		**$6,200**

Illustration 6-6
Proof of cost of goods sold

LAST-IN, FIRST-OUT (LIFO)

The **last-in, first-out (LIFO) method** assumes that the **latest goods** purchased are the first to be sold. LIFO seldom coincides with the actual physical flow of inventory. (Exceptions include goods stored in piles, such as coal or hay, where goods are removed from the top of the pile as they are sold.) Under the LIFO method, the **costs** of the latest goods purchased are the first to be recognized in determining cost of goods sold. Illustration 6-7 shows the allocation of the cost of goods available for sale at Houston Electronics under LIFO.

Illustration 6-7
Allocation of costs—LIFO method

Cost of Goods Available for Sale				
Date	**Explanation**	**Units**	**Unit Cost**	**Total Cost**
Jan. 1	Beginning inventory	100	$10	$ 1,000
Apr. 15	Purchase	200	11	2,200
Aug. 24	Purchase	300	12	3,600
Nov. 27	Purchase	400	13	5,200
	Total	1,000		$12,000

Step 1: Ending Inventory				Step 2: Cost of Goods Sold	
Date	**Units**	**Unit Cost**	**Total Cost**		
Jan. 1	100	$10	$1,000	Cost of goods available for sale	$12,000
Apr. 15	200	11	2,200	Less: Ending inventory	5,000
Aug. 24	150	12	1,800	Cost of goods sold	$ 7,000
Total	450		$5,000		

Helpful Hint

Another way of thinking about the calculation of LIFO **ending inventory** is the *FISH assumption*—first in still here.

Under LIFO, since it is assumed that the first goods sold were those that were most recently purchased, ending inventory is based on the prices of the oldest units purchased. That is, **under LIFO, companies obtain the cost of the ending inventory by taking the unit cost of the earliest goods available for sale and working forward until all units of inventory have been costed**. In this example, Houston Electronics prices the 450 units of ending inventory using the *earliest* prices. The first purchase was 100 units at $10 in the January 1 beginning inventory. Then 200 units were purchased at $11. The remaining 150 units needed are priced at $12 per unit (August 24 purchase). Next, Houston Electronics calculates cost of goods sold by subtracting the cost of the units **not sold** (ending inventory) from the cost of all goods available for sale.

Illustration 6-8 demonstrates that companies also can calculate cost of goods sold by pricing the 550 units sold using the prices of the last 550 units acquired. Note that of the 300 units purchased on August 24, only 150 units are assumed sold. This agrees with our calculation of the cost of ending inventory, where 150 of these units were assumed unsold and thus included in ending inventory.

Date	Units	Unit Cost	Total Cost
Nov. 27	400	$13	$5,200
Aug. 24	150	12	1,800
Total	550		$7,000

Illustration 6-8
Proof of cost of goods sold

Under a periodic inventory system, which we are using here, **all goods purchased during the period are assumed to be available for the first sale, regardless of the date of purchase**.

AVERAGE-COST

The **average-cost method** allocates the cost of goods available for sale on the basis of the **weighted-average unit cost** incurred. The average-cost method assumes that goods are similar in nature. Illustration 6-9 presents the formula and a sample computation of the weighted-average unit cost.

Cost of Goods Available for Sale	÷	**Total Units Available for Sale**	=	**Weighted-Average Unit Cost**
$12,000	÷	1,000	=	$12.00

Illustration 6-9
Formula for weighted-average unit cost

The company then applies the weighted-average unit cost to the units on hand to determine the cost of the ending inventory. Illustration 6-10 (page 272) shows the allocation of the cost of goods available for sale at Houston Electronics using average-cost.

We can verify the cost of goods sold under this method by multiplying the units sold times the weighted-average unit cost ($550 \times \$12 = \$6,600$). Note that this method does not use the average of the unit costs. That average is $11.50 ($10 + $11 + $12 + $13 = $46; $46 ÷ 4). The average-cost method instead uses the average **weighted by** the quantities purchased at each unit cost.

Do it!

The accounting records of Shumway Ag Implement show the following data.

Beginning inventory	4,000 units at $ 3
Purchases	6,000 units at $ 4
Sales	7,000 units at $12

Determine the cost of goods sold during the period under a periodic inventory system using (a) the FIFO method, (b) the LIFO method, and (c) the average-cost method.

Cost Flow Methods

Solution

Cost of goods available for sale = (4,000 × $3) + (6,000 × $4) = $36,000

Ending inventory = 10,000 − 7,000 = 3,000 units

(a) FIFO: $36,000 − (3,000 × $4) = $24,000

(b) LIFO: $36,000 − (3,000 × $3) = 27,000

(c) Average cost per unit: [(4,000 @ $3) + (6,000 @ $4)] ÷ 10,000 = $3.60
    Average-cost: $36,000 − (3,000 × $3.60) = $25,200

action plan

✔ Understand the periodic inventory system.

✔ Allocate costs between goods sold and goods on hand (ending inventory) for each cost flow method.

✔ Compute cost of goods sold for each method.

Related exercise material: BE6-3, BE6-4, BE6-5, E6-3, E6-4, E6-5, E6-6, E6-7, E6-8, and **Do it!** 6-2.

The Navigator

Illustration 6-10
Allocation of costs—
average-cost method

Cost of Goods Available for Sale				
Date	**Explanation**	**Units**	**Unit Cost**	**Total Cost**
Jan. 1	Beginning inventory	100	$10	$ 1,000
Apr. 15	Purchase	200	11	2,200
Aug. 24	Purchase	300	12	3,600
Nov. 27	Purchase	400	13	5,200
	Total	1,000		$12,000

Step 1: Ending Inventory			Step 2: Cost of Goods Sold	
$12,000 ÷ 1,000 = $12.00			Cost of goods available for sale	$12,000
			Less: Ending inventory	5,400
Units	**Unit Cost**	**Total Cost**	Cost of goods sold	$ 6,600
450	$12.00	**$5,400**		

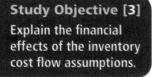
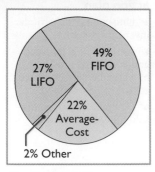

Financial Statement and Tax Effects of Cost Flow Methods

Study Objective [3]
Explain the financial
effects of the inventory
cost flow assumptions.

Each of the three assumed cost flow methods is acceptable for use. For example, Reebok International Ltd. and Wendy's International currently use the FIFO method of inventory costing. Campbell Soup Company, Krogers, and Walgreen Drugs use LIFO for part or all of their inventory. Bristol-Myers Squibb, Starbucks, and Motorola use the average-cost method. In fact, a company may also use more than one cost flow method at the same time. Stanley Black & Decker Manufacturing Company, for example, uses LIFO for domestic inventories and FIFO for foreign inventories. Illustration 6-11 (in the margin) shows the use of the three cost flow methods in the 500 largest U.S. companies.

The reasons companies adopt different inventory cost flow methods are varied, but they usually involve one of three factors: (1) income statement effects, (2) balance sheet effects, or (3) tax effects.

INCOME STATEMENT EFFECTS

To understand why companies might choose a particular cost flow method, let's examine the effects of the different cost flow assumptions on the financial statements of Houston Electronics. The condensed income statements in Illustration 6-12 assume that Houston sold its 550 units for $11,500, had operating expenses of $2,000, and is subject to an income tax rate of 30%.

Illustration 6-11
Use of cost flow methods in
major U.S. companies

49% FIFO
27% LIFO
22% Average-Cost
2% Other

Illustration 6-12
Comparative effects of cost
flow methods

Houston Electronics Condensed Income Statements			
	FIFO	**LIFO**	**Average-Cost**
Sales revenue	$11,500	$11,500	$11,500
Beginning inventory	1,000	1,000	1,000
Purchases	11,000	11,000	11,000
Cost of goods available for sale	12,000	12,000	12,000
Ending inventory	**5,800**	**5,000**	**5,400**
Cost of goods sold	6,200	7,000	6,600
Gross profit	5,300	4,500	4,900
Operating expenses	2,000	2,000	2,000
Income before income taxes[2]	3,300	2,500	2,900
Income tax expense (30%)	990	750	870
Net income	$ 2,310	$ 1,750	$ 2,303

Note the cost of goods available for sale ($12,000) is the same under each of the three inventory cost flow methods. However, the ending inventories and the costs of goods sold are different. This difference is due to the unit costs that the company allocated to cost of goods sold and to ending inventory. Each dollar of difference in ending inventory results in a corresponding dollar difference in income before income taxes. For Houston, an $800 difference exists between FIFO and LIFO cost of goods sold.

In periods of changing prices, the cost flow assumption can have a significant impact on income and on evaluations based on income. In most instances, prices are rising (inflation). In a period of inflation, FIFO produces a higher net income because the lower unit costs of the first units purchased are matched against revenues. In a period of rising prices (as is the case in the Houston example), FIFO reports the highest net income ($2,310) and LIFO the lowest ($1,750); average-cost falls in the middle ($2,030). If prices are falling, the results from the use of FIFO and LIFO are reversed: FIFO will report the lowest net income and LIFO the highest.

To management, higher net income is an advantage: It causes external users to view the company more favorably. In addition, management bonuses, if based on net income, will be higher. Therefore, when prices are rising (which is usually the case), companies tend to prefer FIFO because it results in higher net income.

Some argue that the use of LIFO in a period of inflation enables the company to avoid reporting **paper** (or **phantom**) **profit** as economic gain. To illustrate, assume that Kralik Company buys 200 units of a product at $20 per unit on January 10 and 200 more on December 31 at $24 each. During the year, Kralik sells 200 units at $30 each. Illustration 6-13 shows the results under FIFO and LIFO.

Illustration 6-13
Income statement effects
compared

	FIFO		**LIFO**	
Sales (200 × $30)	$6,000		$6,000	
Cost of goods sold	4,000	(200 × $20)	4,800	(200 × $24)
Gross profit	$2,000		$1,200	

---

[2]We are assuming that Houston Electronics is a corporation, and corporations are required to pay income taxes.

Under LIFO, Kralik Company has recovered the current replacement cost ($4,800) of the units sold. Thus, the gross profit in economic terms is real. However, under FIFO, the company has recovered only the January 10 cost ($4,000). To replace the units sold, it must reinvest $800 (200 × $4) of the gross profit. Thus, $800 of the gross profit is said to be phantom or illusory. As a result, reported net income is also overstated in real terms.

BALANCE SHEET EFFECTS

A major advantage of the FIFO method is that in a period of inflation, the costs allocated to ending inventory will approximate their current cost. For example, for Houston Electronics, 400 of the 450 units in the ending inventory are costed under FIFO at the higher November 27 unit cost of $13.

Conversely, a major shortcoming of the LIFO method is that in a period of inflation, the costs allocated to ending inventory may be significantly understated in terms of current cost. The understatement becomes greater over prolonged periods of inflation if the inventory includes goods purchased in one or more prior accounting periods. For example, Caterpillar has used LIFO for 50 years. Its balance sheet shows ending inventory of $6,360 million. But the inventory's actual current cost if FIFO had been used is $9,363 million.

TAX EFFECTS

We have seen that both inventory on the balance sheet and net income on the income statement are higher when companies use FIFO in a period of inflation. Yet, many companies have selected LIFO. Why? The reason is that LIFO results in the lowest income taxes (because of lower net income) during times of rising prices. For example, at Houston Electronics, income taxes are $750 under LIFO, compared to $990 under FIFO. The tax savings of $240 makes more cash available for use in the business.

Using Inventory Cost Flow Methods Consistently

Whatever cost flow method a company chooses, it should use that method consistently from one accounting period to another. This approach is often referred to as the **consistency principle**, which means that a company uses the same accounting principles and methods from year to year. Consistent application enhances the comparability of financial statements over successive time periods. In contrast, using the FIFO method one year and the LIFO method the next year would make it difficult to compare the net incomes of the two years.

Although consistent application is preferred, it does not mean that a company may *never* change its inventory costing method. When a company adopts a different method, it should disclose in the financial statements the change and its effects on net income. Illustration 6-14 shows a typical disclosure, using information from financial statements of Quaker Oats (now a unit of PepsiCo).

Helpful Hint

A tax rule, often referred to as the *LIFO conformity rule*, requires that if companies use LIFO for tax purposes they must also use it for financial reporting purposes. This means that if a company chooses the LIFO method to reduce its tax bills, it will also have to report lower net income in its financial statements.

Illustration 6-14
Disclosure of change in cost flow method

| Quaker Oats |
| Notes to the Financial Statements |

Note 1:   Effective July 1, the Company adopted the LIFO cost flow assumption for valuing the majority of U.S. Grocery Products inventories. The Company believes that the use of the LIFO method better matches current costs with current revenues. The effect of this change on the current year was to decrease net income by $16.0 million.

INTERNATIONAL INSIGHT

Is LIFO Fair?

ExxonMobil Corporation, like many U.S. companies, uses LIFO to value its inventory for financial reporting and tax purposes. In one recent year, this resulted in a cost of goods sold figure that was $5.6 billion higher than under FIFO. By increasing cost of goods sold, ExxonMobil reduces net income, which reduces taxes. Critics say that LIFO provides an unfair "tax dodge." As Congress looks for more sources of tax revenue, some lawmakers favor the elimination of LIFO. Supporters of LIFO argue that the method is conceptually sound because it matches current costs with current revenues. In addition, they point out that this matching provides protection against inflation.

International accounting standards do not allow the use of LIFO. Because of this, the net income of foreign oil companies such as BP and Royal Dutch Shell are not directly comparable to U.S. companies, which makes analysis difficult.

Source: David Reilly, "Big Oil's Accounting Methods Fuel Criticism," *Wall Street Journal* (August 8, 2006), p. C1.

? What are the arguments for and against the use of LIFO? (See page 310.)

Lower-of-Cost-or-Market

The value of inventory for companies selling high-technology or fashion goods can drop very quickly due to changes in technology or fashions. These circumstances sometimes call for inventory valuation methods other than those presented so far. For example, at one time purchasing managers at Ford decided to make a large purchase of palladium, a precious metal used in vehicle emission devices. They made this purchase because they feared a future shortage. The shortage did not materialize, and by the end of the year the price of palladium had plummeted. Ford's inventory was then worth $1 billion less than its original cost. Do you think Ford's inventory should have been stated at cost, in accordance with the cost principle, or at its lower replacement cost?

As you probably reasoned, this situation requires a departure from the cost basis of accounting. When the value of inventory is lower than its cost, companies can "write down" the inventory to its market value. This is done by valuing the inventory at the **lower-of-cost-or-market (LCM)** in the period in which the price decline occurs. LCM is an example of the accounting concept of **conservatism**, which means that the best choice among accounting alternatives is the method that is least likely to overstate assets and net income.

Companies apply LCM to the items in inventory after they have used one of the cost flow methods (specific identification, FIFO, LIFO, or average-cost) to determine cost. Under the LCM basis, market is defined as **current replacement cost**, not selling price. For a merchandising company, market is the cost of purchasing the same goods at the present time from the usual suppliers in the usual quantities. Current replacement cost is used because a decline in the replacement cost of an item usually leads to a decline in the selling price of the item.

To illustrate the application of LCM, assume that Ken Tuckie TV has the following lines of merchandise with costs and market values as indicated. LCM produces the results shown in Illustration 6-15 (page 276). Note that the amounts shown in the final column are the lower-of-cost-or-market amounts for each item.

> **Study Objective [4]**
> Explain the lower-of-cost-or-market basis of accounting for inventories.

> **International Note**
>
> Under U.S. GAAP, companies cannot reverse inventory write-downs if inventory increases in value in subsequent periods. IFRS permits companies to reverse write-downs in some circumstances.

Illustration 6-15
Computation of lower-of-cost-or-market

	Cost	Market	Lower-of-Cost-or-Market
Flatscreen TVs	$ 60,000	$ 55,000	$ 55,000
Satellite radios	45,000	52,000	45,000
DVD recorders	48,000	45,000	45,000
DVDs	15,000	14,000	14,000
Total inventory			**$159,000**

Inventory Errors

Study Objective [5]
Indicate the effects of inventory errors on the financial statements.

Unfortunately, errors occasionally occur in accounting for inventory. In some cases, errors are caused by failure to count or price the inventory correctly. In other cases, errors occur because companies do not properly recognize the transfer of legal title to goods that are in transit. When errors occur, they affect both the income statement and the balance sheet.

Income Statement Effects

Under a periodic inventory system, both the beginning and ending inventories appear in the income statement. The ending inventory of one period automatically becomes the beginning inventory of the next period. Thus, inventory errors affect the computation of cost of goods sold and net income in two periods.

The effects on cost of goods sold can be computed by entering incorrect data in the formula in Illustration 6-16 and then substituting the correct data.

Illustration 6-16
Formula for cost of goods sold

Beginning Inventory	+	Cost of Goods Purchased	−	Ending Inventory	=	Cost of Goods Sold

If the error understates *beginning* inventory, cost of goods sold will be understated. If the error understates *ending* inventory, cost of goods sold will be overstated. Illustration 6-17 shows the effects of inventory errors on the current year's income statement.

Illustration 6-17
Effects of inventory errors on current year's income statement

When Inventory Error:	Cost of Goods Sold Is:	Net Income Is:
Understates beginning inventory	Understated	Overstated
Overstates beginning inventory	Overstated	Understated
Understates ending inventory	Overstated	Understated
Overstates ending inventory	Understated	Overstated

Ethics Note

Inventory fraud increases during recessions. Such fraud includes pricing inventory at amounts in excess of its actual value, or claiming to have inventory when no inventory exists. Inventory fraud usually overstates ending inventory, thereby understating cost of goods sold and creating higher income.

So far, the effects of inventory errors are fairly straightforward. Now, though, comes the (at first) surprising part: An error in the ending inventory of the current period will have a **reverse effect on net income of the next accounting period**. Illustration 6-18 shows this effect. As you study the illustration, you will see that the reverse effect comes from the fact that understating ending inventory in 2011 results in understating beginning inventory in 2012 and overstating net income in 2012.

Over the two years, though, total net income is correct because the errors **offset each other**. Notice that total income using incorrect data is $35,000 ($22,000 + $13,000), which is the same as the total income of

	2011			2012	
Sample Company Condensed Income Statements					
	Incorrect	Correct		Incorrect	Correct
Sales revenue		$80,000		$80,000		$90,000		$90,000

Sample Company
Condensed Income Statements

	2011		2012	
	Incorrect	**Correct**	**Incorrect**	**Correct**
Sales revenue	$80,000	$80,000	$90,000	$90,000
Beginning inventory	$20,000	$20,000	**$12,000**	**$15,000**
Cost of goods purchased	40,000	40,000	68,000	68,000
Cost of goods available for sale	60,000	60,000	80,000	83,000
Ending inventory	**12,000**	**15,000**	23,000	23,000
Cost of goods sold	48,000	45,000	57,000	60,000
Gross profit	32,000	35,000	33,000	30,000
Operating expenses	10,000	10,000	20,000	20,000
Net income	$22,000	$25,000	$13,000	$10,000

$(3,000)
Net income
understated

$3,000
Net income
overstated

**The errors cancel. Thus the combined total
income for the 2-year period is correct.**

Illustration 6-18
Effects of inventory errors
on two years' income
statements

$35,000 ($25,000 + $10,000) using correct data. Also note in this example that an error in the beginning inventory does not result in a corresponding error in the ending inventory for that period. The correctness of the ending inventory depends entirely on the accuracy of taking and costing the inventory at the balance sheet date under the periodic inventory system.

Balance Sheet Effects

Companies can determine the effect of ending inventory errors on the balance sheet by using the basic accounting equation: Assets = Liabilities + Owner's Equity. Errors in the ending inventory have the effects shown in Illustration 6-19.

Illustration 6-19
Effects of ending inventory
errors on balance sheet

Ending Inventory Error	Assets	Liabilities	Owner's Equity
Overstated	Overstated	No effect	Overstated
Understated	Understated	No effect	Understated

The effect of an error in ending inventory on the subsequent period was shown in Illustration 6-18. Recall that if the error is not corrected, the combined total net income for the two periods would be correct. Thus, total owner's equity reported on the balance sheet at the end of 2012 will also be correct.

Do it!

(a) Tracy Company sells three different types of home heating stoves (wood, gas, and pellet). The cost and market value of its inventory of stoves are as follows.

**LCM Basis;
Inventory Errors**

	Cost	Market
Gas	$ 84,000	$ 79,000
Wood	250,000	280,000
Pellet	112,000	101,000

action plan

✔ Determine whether cost or market value is lower for each inventory type.

✔ Sum the lowest value of each inventory type to determine the total value of inventory.

Determine the value of the company's inventory under the lower-of-cost-or-market approach.

Solution

The lowest value for each inventory type is: gas $79,000, wood $250,000, and pellet $101,000. The total inventory value is the sum of these amounts, $430,000.

(b) Visual Company overstated its 2011 ending inventory by $22,000. Determine the impact this error has on ending inventory, cost of goods sold, and owner's equity in 2011 and 2012.

action plan

✔ An ending inventory error in one period will have an equal and opposite effect on cost of goods sold and net income in the next period.

✔ After two years, the errors have offset each other.

Solution

	2011	2012
Ending inventory	$22,000 overstated	No effect
Cost of goods sold	$22,000 understated	$22,000 overstated
Owner's equity	$22,000 overstated	No effect

Related exercise material: **BE6-7, BE6-8, E6-9, E6-10, E6-11, E6-12,** and **Do it!** 6-3.

Statement Presentation and Analysis

Presentation

As indicated in Chapter 5, inventory is classified in the balance sheet as a current asset immediately below receivables. In a multiple-step income statement, cost of goods sold is subtracted from sales. There also should be disclosure of (1) the major inventory classifications, (2) the basis of accounting (cost, or lower-of-cost-or-market), and (3) the cost method (FIFO, LIFO, or average).

Wal-Mart Stores, Inc., for example, in its January 31, 2010, balance sheet reported inventories of $33,160 million under current assets. The accompanying notes to the financial statements, as shown in Illustration 6-20, disclosed the following information.

Illustration 6-20
Inventory disclosures by Wal-Mart

Wal-Mart Stores, Inc.
Notes to the Financial Statements

Note 1. Summary of Significant Accounting Policies

Inventories

The Company values inventories at the lower of cost or market as determined primarily by the retail method of accounting, using the last-in, first-out ("LIFO") method for substantially all of the Wal-Mart Stores segments' merchandise inventories. SAM'S CLUB merchandise and merchandise in our distribution warehouses are valued based on the weighted average cost using the LIFO method. Inventories of international operations are primarily valued by the retail method of accounting, using the first-in, first-out ("FIFO") method. At January 31, 2010 and 2009, our inventories valued at LIFO approximate those inventories as if they were valued at FIFO.

As indicated in this note, Wal-Mart values its inventories at the lower-of-cost-or-market using LIFO and FIFO.

Analysis

The amount of inventory carried by a company has significant economic consequences. And inventory management is a double-edged sword that requires constant attention. On the one hand, management wants to have a great variety and quantity on hand so that customers have a wide selection and items are always in stock. But such a policy may incur high carrying costs (e.g., investment, storage, insurance, obsolescence, and damage). On the other hand, low inventory levels lead to stockouts and lost sales. Common ratios used to manage and evaluate inventory levels are inventory turnover and a related measure, days in inventory.

Inventory turnover measures the number of times on average the inventory is sold during the period. Its purpose is to measure the liquidity of the inventory. The inventory turnover is computed by dividing cost of goods sold by the average inventory during the period. Unless seasonal factors are significant, average inventory can be computed from the beginning and ending inventory balances. For example, Wal-Mart reported in its 2010 annual report a beginning inventory of $34,511 million, an ending inventory of $33,160 million, and cost of goods sold for the year ended January 31, 2010, of $304,657 million. The inventory turnover formula and computation for Wal-Mart are shown below.

> **Study Objective [6]**
> Compute and interpret the inventory turnover ratio.

Cost of Goods Sold	÷	Average Inventory	=	Inventory Turnover
$304,657	÷	$\dfrac{\$33,160 + \$34,511}{2}$	=	**9 times**

Illustration 6-21
Inventory turnover formula and computation for Wal-Mart

A variant of the inventory turnover ratio is **days in inventory**. This measures the average number of days inventory is held. It is calculated as 365 divided by the inventory turnover ratio. For example, Wal-Mart's inventory turnover of 9 times divided into 365 is approximately 40.6 days. This is the approximate time that it takes a company to sell the inventory once it arrives at the store.

There are typical levels of inventory in every industry. Companies that are able to keep their inventory at lower levels and higher turnovers and still satisfy customer needs are the most successful.

ACCOUNTING ACROSS THE ORGANIZATION

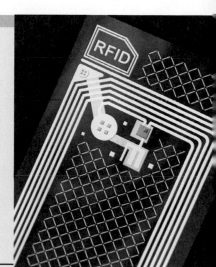

Improving Inventory Control with RFID

Wal-Mart improved its inventory control with the introduction of radio frequency identification (RFID). Much like bar codes, which tell a retailer the number of boxes of a specific product it has, RFID goes a step farther, helping to distinguish one box of a specific product from another. RFID uses technology similar to that used by keyless remotes that unlock car doors.

Companies currently use RFID to track shipments from supplier to distribution center to store. Other potential uses include monitoring product expiration dates and acting quickly on product recalls. Wal-Mart also anticipates faster returns and warranty processing using RFID. This technology will further assist Wal-Mart managers in their efforts to ensure that their store has just the right type of inventory, in just the right amount, in just the right place. Other companies are also interested in RFID. Best Buy has spent millions researching possible applications in its stores.

? Why is inventory control important to managers such as those at Wal-Mart and Best Buy? (See page 310.)

Do it!

Inventory Turnover

Early in 2012, Westmoreland Company switched to a just-in-time inventory system. Its sales, cost of goods sold, and inventory amounts for 2011 and 2012 are shown below.

	2011	2012
Sales revenue	$2,000,000	$1,800,000
Cost of goods sold	1,000,000	910,000
Beginning inventory	290,000	210,000
Ending inventory	210,000	50,000

Determine the inventory turnover and days in inventory for 2011 and 2012. Discuss the changes in the amount of inventory, the inventory turnover and days in inventory, and the amount of sales across the two years.

action plan

✔ To find the inventory turnover ratio, divide cost of goods sold by average inventory.

✔ To determine days in inventory, divide 365 days by the inventory turnover ratio.

✔ Just-in-time inventory reduces the amount of inventory on hand, which reduces carrying costs. Reducing inventory levels by too much has potential negative implications for sales.

Solution

	2011		2012	
Inventory turnover ratio	$\dfrac{\$1,000,000}{(\$290,000 + \$210,000)/2}$	= 4	$\dfrac{\$910,000}{(\$210,000 + \$50,000)/2}$	= 7
Days in inventory	365 ÷ 4 = 91.3 days		365 ÷ 7 = 52.1 days	

The company experienced a very significant decline in its ending inventory as a result of the just-in-time inventory. This decline improved its inventory turnover ratio and its days in inventory. However, its sales declined by 10%. It is possible that this decline was caused by the dramatic reduction in the amount of inventory that was on hand, which increased the likelihood of "stock-outs." To determine the optimal inventory level, management must weigh the benefits of reduced inventory against the potential lost sales caused by stock-outs.

Related exercise material: BE6-9, E6-13, E6-14, and **Do it!** 6-4.

The Navigator

Do it! 1

Gerald D. Englehart Company has the following inventory, purchases, and sales data for the month of March.

Inventory: March 1	200 units @ $4.00	$ 800
Purchases:		
March 10	500 units @ $4.50	2,250
March 20	400 units @ $4.75	1,900
March 30	300 units @ $5.00	1,500
Sales:		
March 15	500 units	
March 25	400 units	

The physical inventory count on March 31 shows 500 units on hand.

Instructions

Under a **periodic inventory system**, determine the cost of inventory on hand at March 31 and the cost of goods sold for March under (a) (FIFO), (b) (LIFO), and (c) average-cost.

action plan

✔ Compute the total goods available for sale, in both units and dollars.

✔ Compute the cost of ending inventory under the periodic FIFO method by allocating to the units on hand the **latest costs**.

✔ Compute the cost of ending inventory under the periodic LIFO method by allocating to the units on hand the **earliest costs**.

✔ Compute the cost of ending inventory under the periodic average-cost method by allocating to the units on hand a **weighted-average cost**.

Solution to Comprehensive Do it! 1

The cost of goods available for sale is $6,450, as follows.

Inventory:		200 units @ $4.00	$ 800
Purchases:			
	March 10	500 units @ $4.50	2,250
	March 20	400 units @ $4.75	1,900
	March 30	300 units @ $5.00	1,500
Total:		1,400	$6,450

Under a **periodic inventory system**, the cost of goods sold under each cost flow method is as follows.

FIFO Method

Ending inventory:

Date	Units	Unit Cost	Total Cost	
March 30	300	$5.00	$1,500	
March 20	200	4.75	950	$2,450

Cost of goods sold: $6,450 − $2,450 = $4,000

LIFO Method

Ending inventory:

Date	Units	Unit Cost	Total Cost	
March 1	200	$4.00	$ 800	
March 10	300	4.50	1,350	$2,150

Cost of goods sold: $6,450 − $2,150 = $4,300

Average-Cost Method

Average unit cost: $6,450 ÷ 1,400 = $4.607
Ending inventory: 500 × $4.607 = $2,303.50

Cost of goods sold: $6,450 − $2,303.50 = $4,146.50

✔ **The Navigator**

Summary of Study Objectives

[1] Describe the steps in determining inventory quantities. The steps are (1) take a physical inventory of goods on hand and (2) determine the ownership of goods in transit or on consignment.

[2] Explain the accounting for inventories and apply the inventory cost flow methods. The primary basis of accounting for inventories is cost. Cost of goods available for sale includes (a) cost of beginning inventory and (b) cost of goods purchased. The inventory cost flow methods are: specific identification and three assumed cost flow methods—FIFO, LIFO, and average-cost.

[3] Explain the financial effects of the inventory cost flow assumptions. Companies may allocate the cost of goods available for sale to cost of goods sold and ending inventory by specific identification or by a method based on an assumed cost flow. When prices are rising, the first-in, first-out (FIFO) method results in lower cost of goods sold and higher net income than the other methods. The reverse is true when prices are falling. In the balance sheet, FIFO results in an ending inventory that is closest to current value; inventory under LIFO is the farthest from current value. LIFO results in the lowest income taxes.

[4] Explain the lower-of-cost-or-market basis of accounting for inventories. Companies may use the lower-of-cost-or-market (LCM) basis when the current replacement cost (market) is less than cost. Under LCM,

companies recognize the loss in the period in which the price decline occurs.

[5] Indicate the effects of inventory errors on the financial statements. *In the income statement of the current year:* (a) An error in beginning inventory will have a reverse effect on net income. (b) An error in ending inventory will have a similar effect on net income. In the following period, its effect on net income for that period is reversed, and total net income for the two years will be correct.

In the balance sheet: Ending inventory errors will have the same effect on total assets and total owner's equity and no effect on liabilities.

[6] Compute and interpret the inventory turnover ratio. The inventory turnover ratio is cost of goods sold divided by average inventory. To convert it to average days in inventory, divide 365 days by the inventory turnover ratio.

Glossary

Average-cost method   Inventory costing method that uses the weighted-average unit cost to allocate to ending inventory and cost of goods sold the cost of goods available for sale. (p. 271).

Conservatism   Concept that dictates that when in doubt, choose the method that will be least likely to overstate assets and net income. (p. 275).

Consigned goods   Goods held for sale by one party although ownership of the goods is retained by another party. (p. 265).

Consistency principle   Dictates that a company use the same accounting principles and methods from year to year. (p. 274).

Current replacement cost   The current cost to replace an inventory item. (p. 275).

Days in inventory   Measure of the average number of days inventory is held; calculated as 365 divided by inventory turnover ratio. (p. 279).

Finished goods inventory   Manufactured items that are completed and ready for sale. (p. 262).

First-in, first-out (FIFO) method   Inventory costing method that assumes that the costs of the earliest goods purchased are the first to be recognized as cost of goods sold. (p. 268).

FOB (free on board) destination   Freight terms indicating that ownership of the goods remains with the seller until the goods reach the buyer. (p. 264).

FOB (free on board) shipping point   Freight terms indicating that ownership of the goods passes to the buyer

when the public carrier accepts the goods from the seller. (p. 264).

Inventory turnover   A ratio that measures the number of times on average the inventory sold during the period; computed by dividing cost of goods sold by the average inventory during the period. (p. 279).

Just-in-time (JIT) inventory method   Inventory system in which companies manufacture or purchase goods just in time for use. (p. 262).

Last-in, first-out (LIFO) method   Inventory costing method that assumes the costs of the latest units purchased are the first to be allocated to cost of goods sold. (p. 270).

Lower-of-cost-or-market (LCM) basis   A basis whereby inventory is stated at the lower of either its cost or its market value as determined by current replacement cost. (p. 275).

Raw materials   Basic goods that will be used in production but have not yet been placed into production. (p. 262).

Specific identification method   An actual physical flow costing method in which items still in inventory are specifically costed to arrive at the total cost of the ending inventory. (p. 267).

Weighted-average unit cost   Average cost that is weighted by the number of units purchased at each unit cost. (p. 271).

Work in process   That portion of manufactured inventory that has been placed into the production process but is not yet complete. (p. 262).

APPENDIX6A

Inventory Cost Flow Methods in Perpetual Inventory Systems

What inventory cost flow methods do companies employ if they use a perpetual inventory system? Simple—they can use any of the inventory cost flow methods described in the chapter. To illustrate the application of the three assumed cost flow methods (FIFO, LIFO, and average-cost), we will use the data shown in Illustration 6A-1 and in this chapter for Houston Electronic's Astro Condenser.

Study Objective [7]

Apply the inventory cost flow methods to perpetual inventory records.

Illustration 6A-1
Inventoriable units and costs

	Houston Electronics Astro Condensers				
Date	**Explanation**	**Units**	**Units Cost**	**Total Cost**	**Balance in Units**
1/1	Beginning inventory	100	$10	$ 1,000	100
4/15	Purchases	200	11	2,200	300
8/24	Purchases	300	12	3,600	600
9/10	Sale	550			50
11/27	Purchases	400	13	5,200	450
				$12,000	

First-In, First-Out (FIFO)

Under FIFO, the company charges to cost of goods sold the cost of the earliest goods on hand **prior to each sale**. Therefore, the cost of goods sold on September 10 consists of the units on hand January 1 and the units purchased April 15 and August 24. Illustration 6A-2 shows the inventory under a FIFO method perpetual system.

Illustration 6A-2
Perpetual system—FIFO

Date	Purchases		Cost of Goods Sold	Balance (in units and cost)	
January 1				(100 @ $10)	$1,000
April 15	(200 @ $11)	$2,200		(100 @ $10) (200 @ $11)	$3,200
August 24	(300 @ $12)	$3,600		(100 @ $10) (200 @ $11) (300 @ $12)	$6,800
September 10			(100 @ $10) (200 @ $11) (250 @ $12) $6,200	(50 @ $12)	$ 600
November 27	(400 @ $13)	$5,200		(50 @ $12) (400 @ $13)	$5,800

> **Cost of goods sold**

> **Ending inventory**

The ending inventory in this situation is $5,800, and the cost of goods sold is $6,200 [(100 @ $10) + (200 @ $11) + (250 @ $12)].

Compare Illustrations 6-5 (page 269) and 6A-2. You can see that the results under FIFO in a perpetual system are the **same as in a periodic system**. In both cases, the ending inventory is $5,800 and cost of goods sold is $6,200. Regardless of the system, the first costs in are the costs assigned to cost of goods sold.

Last-In, First-Out (LIFO)

Under the LIFO method using a perpetual system, the company charges to cost of goods sold the cost of the most recent purchase prior to sale. Therefore, the cost of the goods sold on September 10 consists of all the units from the August 24 and April 15 purchases plus 50 of the units in beginning inventory. Illustration 6A-3 shows the computation of the ending inventory under the LIFO method.

Illustration 6A-3
Perpetual system—LIFO

Date	Purchases		Cost of Goods Sold		Balance (in units and cost)	
January 1					(100 @ $10)	$1,000
April 15	(200 @ $11)	$2,200			(100 @ $10) (200 @ $11)	$3,200
August 24	(300 @ $12)	$3,600			(100 @ $10) (200 @ $11) (300 @ $12)	$6,800
September 10			(300 @ $12) (200 @ $11) (50 @ $10)		(50 @ $10)	$ 500
			$6,300			
November 27	(400 @ $13)	$5,200			(50 @ $10) (400 @ $13)	$5,700

Cost of goods sold

Ending inventory

The use of LIFO in a perpetual system will usually produce cost allocations that differ from those using LIFO in a periodic system. In a perpetual system, the company allocates the latest units purchased *prior to each sale* to cost of goods sold. In contrast, in a periodic system, the latest units purchased *during the period* are allocated to cost of goods sold. Thus, when a purchase is made after the last sale, the LIFO periodic system will apply this purchase to the previous sale. Compare Illustrations 6-7 (page 270) and 6A-3. Illustration 6-7 shows that the 400 units at $13 purchased on November 27 applied to the sale of 550 units on September 10. Under the LIFO perpetual system in Illustration 6A-3, the 400 units at $13 purchased on November 27 are all applied to the ending inventory.

The ending inventory in this LIFO perpetual illustration is $5,700, and cost of goods sold is $6,300, as compared to the LIFO periodic Illustration 6-7 (on page 270) where the ending inventory is $5,000 and cost of goods sold is $7,000.

Average-Cost

The average-cost method in a perpetual inventory system is called the **moving-average method**. Under this method, the company computes a new average **after each purchase**, by dividing the cost of goods available for sale by the units on hand. The average cost is then applied to: (1) the units sold, to determine the cost of goods sold, and (2) the remaining units on hand, to determine the ending inventory amount. Illustration 6A-4 shows the application of the moving-average cost method by Houston Electronics.

Illustration 6A-4
Perpetual system—average-cost method

Date	Purchases		Cost of Goods Sold	Balance (in units and cost)	
January 1				(100 @ $10)	$1,000
April 15	(200 @ $11)	$2,200		(300 @ $10.667)	$3,200
August 24	(300 @ $12)	$3,600		(600 @ $11.333)	$6,800
September 10			(550 @ $11.333)	(50 @ $11.333)	$ 567
			$6,233		
November 27	(400 @ $13)	$5,200		(450 @ $12.816)	$5,767

Cost of goods sold

Ending inventory

As indicated, Houston Electronics computes **a new average each time it makes a purchase**. On April 15, after it buys 200 units for $2,200, a total of 300 units costing $3,200 ($1,000 + $2,200) are on hand. The average unit cost is $10.667 ($3,200 ÷ 300). On August 24, after Houston Electronics buys 300 units for $3,600, a total of 600 units costing $6,800 ($1,000 + $2,200 + $3,600) are on hand, at an average cost per unit of $11.333 ($6,800 ÷ 600). Houston Electronics uses this unit cost of $11.333 in costing sales until it makes another purchase, when the company computes a new unit cost. Accordingly, the unit cost of the 550 units sold on September 10 is $11.333, and the total cost of goods sold is $6,233. On November 27, following the purchase of 400 units for $5,200, there are 450 units on hand costing $5,767 ($567 + $5,200) with a new average cost of $12.816 ($5,767 ÷ 450).

Compare this moving-average cost under the perpetual inventory system to Illustration 6-10 (on page 272) showing the average-cost method under a periodic inventory system.

COMPREHENSIVE
Do it! 2

Comprehensive Do it! 1 on page 280 showed cost of goods sold computations under a periodic inventory system. Now let's assume that Gerald D. Englehart Company uses a perpetual inventory system. The company has the same inventory, purchases, and sales data for the month of March as shown earlier:

Inventory:	March 1	200 units @ $4.00	$ 800
Purchases:	March 10	500 units @ $4.50	2,250
	March 20	400 units @ $4.75	1,900
	March 30	300 units @ $5.00	1,500
Sales:	March 15	500 units	
	March 25	400 units	

The physical inventory count on March 31 shows 500 units on hand.

Instructions

Under a **perpetual inventory system**, determine the cost of inventory on hand at March 31 and the cost of goods sold for March under (a) FIFO, (b) LIFO, and (c) average-cost.

action plan

✔ Compute the cost of goods sold under the perpetual FIFO method by allocating to the goods sold the **earliest** cost of goods purchased.

✔ Compute the cost of goods sold under the perpetual LIFO method by allocating to the goods sold the **latest** cost of goods purchased.

✔ Compute the cost of goods sold under the perpetual average-cost method by allocating to the goods sold a **moving-average** cost.

Solution to Comprehensive Do it! 2

The cost of goods available for sale is $6,450, as follows.

Inventory:		200 units @ $4.00	$ 800
Purchases:	March 10	500 units @ $4.50	2,250
	March 20	400 units @ $4.75	1,900
	March 30	300 units @ $5.00	1,500
Total:		1,400	$6,450

Under a **perpetual inventory system**, the cost of goods sold under each cost flow method is as follows.

FIFO Method

Date	Purchases		Cost of Goods Sold	Balance	
March 1				(200 @ $4.00)	$ 800
March 10	(500 @ $4.50)	$2,250		(200 @ $4.00) (500 @ $4.50) }	$3,050

Date	Purchases		Cost of Goods Sold		Balance	
March 15			(200 @ $4.00)			
			(300 @ $4.50)		(200 @ $4.50)	$ 900
			$2,150			
March 20	(400 @ $4.75)	$1,900			(200 @ $4.50) } (400 @ $4.75) }	$2,800
March 25			(200 @ $4.50)			
			(200 @ $4.75)		(200 @ $4.75)	$ 950
			$1,850			
March 30	(300 @ $5.00)	$1,500			(200 @ $4.75) } (300 @ $5.00) }	$2,450
	Ending inventory, $2,450		Cost of goods sold: $2,150 + $1,850 = $4,000			

LIFO Method

Date	Purchases		Cost of Goods Sold		Balance	
March 1					(200 @ $4.00)	$ 800
March 10	(500 @ $4.50)	$2,250			(200 @ $4.00) } (500 @ $4.50) }	$3,050
March 15			(500 @ $4.50)	$2,250	(200 @ $4.00)	$ 800
March 20	(400 @ $4.75)	$1,900			(200 @ $4.00) } (400 @ $4.75) }	$2,700
March 25			(400 @ $4.75)	$1,900	(200 @ $4.00)	$ 800
March 30	(300 @ $5.00)	$1,500			(200 @ $4.00) } (300 @ $5.00) }	$2,300
	Ending inventory, $2,300		Cost of goods sold: $2,250 + $1,900 = $4,150			

Moving-Average Cost Method

Date	Purchases		Cost of Goods Sold		Balance	
March 1					(200 @ $ 4.00)	$ 800
March 10	(500 @ $4.50)	$2,250			(700 @ $4.357)	$3,050
March 15			(500 @ $4.357)	$ 2,179	(200 @ $4.357)	$ 871
March 20	(400 @ $4.75)	$1,900			(600 @ $4.618)	$2,771
March 25			(400 @ $4.618)	$ 1,847	(200 @ $4.618)	$ 924
March 30	(300 @ $5.00)	$1,500			(500 @ $4.848)	$2,424
	Ending inventory, $2,424		Cost of goods sold: $2,179 + $1,847 = $4,026			

The Navigator

Summary of Study Objective for Appendix 6A

[7] Apply the inventory cost flow methods to perpetual inventory records. Under FIFO and a perpetual inventory system, companies charge to cost of goods sold the cost of the earliest goods on hand prior to each sale. Under LIFO and a perpetual system, companies charge to cost of goods sold the cost of the most recent purchase prior to sale. Under the moving-average (average cost) method and a perpetual system, companies compute a new average cost after each purchase.

APPENDIX6B

Estimating Inventories

Study Objective [8]

Describe the two methods of estimating inventories.

In the chapter, we assumed that a company would be able to physically count its inventory. What if it cannot? What if the inventory were destroyed by fire or flood, for example? In that case, the company would use an estimate.

Two circumstances explain why companies sometimes estimate inventories. First, a casualty such as fire, flood, or earthquake may make it impossible to take a physical inventory. Second, managers may want monthly or quarterly financial statements, but a physical inventory is taken only annually. The need for estimating inventories occurs primarily with a periodic inventory system because of the absence of perpetual inventory records.

There are two widely used methods of estimating inventories: (1) the gross profit method, and (2) the retail inventory method.

Gross Profit Method

The **gross profit method** estimates the cost of ending inventory by applying a gross profit rate to net sales. This method is relatively simple, but effective. Accountants, auditors, and managers frequently use the gross profit method to test the reasonableness of the ending inventory amount. It will detect large errors.

To use this method, a company needs to know its net sales, cost of goods available for sale, and gross profit rate. The company then can estimate its gross profit for the period. Illustration 6B-1 shows the formulas for using the gross profit method.

		Net Sales	−	Estimated Gross Profit	=	Estimated Cost of Goods Sold
Step 1:						

		Cost of Goods Available for Sale	−	Estimated Cost of Goods Sold	=	Estimated Cost of Ending Inventory
Step 2:						

Illustration 6B-1
Gross profit method formulas

To illustrate, assume that Kishwaukee Company wishes to prepare an income statement for the month of January. Its records show net sales of $200,000, beginning inventory $40,000, and cost of goods purchased $120,000. In the preceding year, the company realized a 30% gross profit rate. It expects to earn the same rate this year. Given these facts and assumptions, Kishwaukee can compute the estimated cost of the ending inventory at January 31 under the gross profit method as follows.

Illustration 6B-2
Example of gross profit method

Step 1:	
Net sales	$200,000
Less: Estimated gross profit (30% × $200,000)	60,000
Estimated cost of goods sold	**$140,000**
Step 2:	
Beginning inventory	$ 40,000
Cost of goods purchased	120,000
Cost of goods available for sale	160,000
Less: Estimated cost of goods sold	140,000
Estimated cost of ending inventory	**$ 20,000**

The gross profit method is based on the assumption that the gross profit rate will remain constant. But it may not remain constant, due to a change in merchandising policies or in market conditions. In such cases, the company should adjust the rate to reflect current operating conditions. In some cases, companies can obtain a more accurate estimate by applying this method on a department or product-line basis.

Note that companies should not use the gross profit method to prepare financial statements at the end of the year. These statements should be based on a physical inventory count.

Retail Inventory Method

A retail store such as Home Depot, Ace Hardware, or Wal-Mart has thousands of different types of merchandise at low unit costs. In such cases, it is difficult and time-consuming to apply unit costs to inventory quantities. An alternative is to use the **retail inventory method** to estimate the cost of inventory. Most retail companies can establish a relationship between cost and sales price. The company then applies the cost-to-retail percentage to the ending inventory at retail prices to determine inventory at cost.

Under the retail inventory method, a company's records must show both the cost and retail value of the goods available for sale. Illustration 6B-3 presents the formulas for using the retail inventory method.

Illustration 6B-3
Retail inventory method formulas

Step 1:	Goods Available for Sale at Retail	−	Net Sales	=	Ending Inventory at Retail
Step 2:	Goods Available for Sale at Cost	÷	Goods Available for Sale at Retail	=	Cost-to-Retail Ratio
Step 3:	Ending Inventory at Retail	×	Cost-to-Retail Ratio	=	Estimated Cost of Ending Inventory

We can demonstrate the logic of the retail method by using unit-cost data. Assume that Ortiz Inc. has marked 10 units purchased at $7 to sell for $10 per unit. Thus, the cost-to-retail ratio is 70% ($70 ÷ $100). If four units remain unsold, their retail value is $40 (4 × $10), and their cost is $28 ($40 × 70%). This amount agrees with the total cost of goods on hand on a per unit basis (4 × $7).

Illustration 6B-4 shows application of the retail method for Valley West Co. Note that it is not necessary to take a physical inventory to determine the estimated cost of goods on hand at any given time.

Illustration 6B-4
Application of retail inventory method

	At Cost	At Retail
Beginning inventory	$14,000	$ 21,500
Goods purchased	61,000	78,500
Goods available for sale	$75,000	100,000
Net sales		70,000
Step (1) Ending inventory at retail =		**$ 30,000**
Step (2) Cost-to-retail ratio $75,000 ÷ $100,000 = 75%		
Step (3) Estimated cost of ending inventory = $30,000 × 75% = $22,500		

The retail inventory method also facilitates taking a physical inventory at the end of the year. Valley West can value the goods on hand at the prices marked on the merchandise, and then apply the cost-to-retail ratio to the goods on hand at retail to determine the ending inventory at cost.

The major disadvantage of the retail method is that it is an averaging technique. Thus, it may produce an incorrect inventory valuation if the mix of the ending inventory is not representative of the mix in the goods available for sale. Assume, for example, that the cost-to-retail ratio of 75% for Valley West Co. consists of equal proportions of inventory items that have cost-to-retail ratios of 70%, 75%, and 80%. If the ending inventory contains only items with a 70% ratio, an incorrect inventory cost will result. Companies can minimize this problem by applying the retail method on a department or product-line basis.

Helpful Hint

In determining inventory at retail, companies use selling prices of the units.

Summary of Study Objective for Appendix 6B

[8] Describe the two methods of estimating inventories. The two methods of estimating inventories are the gross profit method and the retail inventory method. Under the gross profit method, companies apply a gross profit rate to net sales to determine estimated cost of goods sold. They then subtract estimated cost of goods sold from cost of goods available for sale to determine the estimated cost of the ending inventory.

Under the retail inventory method, companies compute a cost-to-retail ratio by dividing the cost of goods available for sale by the retail value of the goods available for sale. They then apply this ratio to the ending inventory at retail to determine the estimated cost of the ending inventory.

Glossary for Appendix 6B

Gross profit method A method for estimating the cost of the ending inventory by applying a gross profit rate to net sales and subtracting estimated cost of goods sold from cost of goods available for sale. (p. 287).

Retail inventory method A method for estimating the cost of the ending inventory by applying a cost-to-retail ratio to the ending inventory at retail. (p. 288).

Self-Test, Brief Exercises, Exercises, Problem Set A, and many more components are available for practice in *WileyPLUS*

*Note: All **asterisked** Questions, Exercises, and Problems relate to material in the appendix to the chapter.

Self-Test Questions

Answers are on page 310.

(SO 1) **1.** Which of the following should *not* be included in the physical inventory of a company?
  a. Goods held on consignment from another company.
  b. Goods shipped on consignment to another company.
  c. Goods in transit from another company shipped FOB shipping point.
  d. None of the above.

(SO 1) **2.** As a result of a thorough physical inventory, Railway Company determined that it had inventory worth $180,000 at December 31, 2012. This count did not take into consideration the following facts: Rogers Consignment store currently has goods worth $35,000 on its sales floor that belong to Railway but are being sold on consignment by Rogers. The selling price of these goods is $50,000. Railway purchased $13,000 of goods that were shipped on December 27, FOB destination, that will be received by Railway on January 3. Determine the correct amount of inventory that Railway should report.
  a. $230,000.   **c.** $228,000.
  b. $215,000.   **d.** $193,000.

3. Cost of goods available for sale consist of two elements: (SO 2) beginning inventory and
  a. ending inventory.
  b. cost of goods purchased.
  c. cost of goods sold.
  d. All of the above.

(SO 2) **4.** Tinker Bell Company has the following:

	Units	Unit Cost
Inventory, Jan. 1	8,000	$11
Purchase, June 19	13,000	12
Purchase, Nov. 8	5,000	13

If Tinker Bell has 9,000 units on hand at December 31, the cost of the ending inventory under FIFO is:
a. $99,000.   **c.** $113,000.
b. $108,000.   **d.** $117,000.

(SO 2) **5.** Using the data in Question 4 above, the cost of the ending inventory under LIFO is:
a. $113,000.   **c.** $99,000.
b. $108,000.   **d.** $100,000.

(SO 2) **6.** Davidson Electronics has the following:

	Units	Unit Cost
Inventory, Jan. 1	5,000	$ 8
Purchase, April 2	15,000	$10
Purchase, Aug. 28	20,000	$12

If Davidson has 7,000 units on hand at December 31, the cost of ending inventory under the average-cost method is:
a. $84,000.   **c.** $56,000.
b. $70,000.   **d.** $75,250.

(SO 3) **7.** In periods of rising prices, LIFO will produce:
a. higher net income than FIFO.
b. the same net income as FIFO.
c. lower net income than FIFO.
d. higher net income than average costing.

(SO 3) **8.** Factors that affect the selection of an inventory costing method do *not* include:
a. tax effects.
b. balance sheet effects.
c. income statement effects.
d. perpetual vs. periodic inventory system.

(SO 4) **9.** Rickety Company purchased 1,000 widgets and has 200 widgets in its ending inventory at a cost of $91 each and a current replacement cost of $80 each. The ending inventory under lower-of-cost-or-market is:
a. $91,000.   **c.** $18,200.
b. $80,000.   **d.** $16,000.

(SO 5) **10.** Atlantis Company's ending inventory is understated $4,000. The effects of this error on the current year's cost of goods sold and net income, respectively, are:
a. understated, overstated.
b. overstated, understated.

c. overstated, overstated.
d. understated, understated.

(SO 4) **11.** Harold Company overstated its inventory by $15,000 at December 31, 2011. It did not correct the error in 2011 or 2012. As a result, Harold's owner's equity was:
a. overstated at December 31, 2011, and understated at December 31, 2012.
b. overstated at December 31, 2011, and properly stated at December 31, 2012.
c. understated at December 31, 2011, and understated at December 31, 2012.
d. overstated at December 31, 2011, and overstated at December 31, 2012.

(SO 6) **12.** Which of these would cause the inventory turnover ratio to increase the most?
a. Increasing the amount of inventory on hand.
b. Keeping the amount of inventory on hand constant but increasing sales.
c. Keeping the amount of inventory on hand constant but decreasing sales.
d. Decreasing the amount of inventory on hand and increasing sales.

(SO 5) **13.** Carlos Company had beginning inventory of $80,000, ending inventory of $110,000, cost of goods sold of $285,000, and sales of $475,000. Carlos's days in inventory is:
a. 73 days.   **c.** 102.5 days.
b. 121.7 days.   **d.** 84.5 days.

(SO 8) *14. Songbird Company has sales of $150,000 and cost of goods available for sale of $135,000. If the gross profit rate is 30%, the estimated cost of the ending inventory under the gross profit method is:
a. $15,000.   **c.** $45,000.
b. $30,000.   **d.** $75,000.

(SO 7) *15. In a perpetual inventory system,
a. LIFO cost of goods sold will be the same as in a periodic inventory system.
b. average costs are based entirely on unit cost averages.
c. a new average is computed under the average-cost method after each sale.
d. FIFO cost of goods sold will be the same as in a periodic inventory system.

Go to the book's companion website,
www.wiley.com/college/weygandt,
for additional Self-Test Questions.

✔ **The Navigator**

Questions

1. "The key to successful business operations is effective inventory management." Do you agree? Explain.

2. An item must possess two characteristics to be classified as inventory by a merchandiser. What are these two characteristics?

3. Your friend Tom Witt has been hired to help take the physical inventory in Hawkeye Hardware Store. Explain to Tom Witt what this job will entail.

4. (a) Reeves Company ships merchandise to Cox Company on December 30. The merchandise reaches the buyer on January 6. Indicate the terms of sale that will result in the goods being included in (1) Reeves's December 31 inventory, and (2) Cox's December 31 inventory.

(b) Under what circumstances should Reeves Company include consigned goods in its inventory?

5. Jim's Hat Shop received a shipment of hats for which it paid the wholesaler $2,970. The price of the hats was $3,000 but Jim's was given a $30 cash discount and required to pay freight charges of $50. In addition, Jim's paid $130 to cover the travel expenses of an employee who negotiated the purchase of the hats. What amount will Jim's record for inventory? Why?

6. Explain the difference between the terms FOB shipping point and FOB destination.

7. David Shannon believes that the allocation of inventoriable costs should be based on the actual physical flow of the goods. Explain to David why this may be both impractical and inappropriate.

8. What is a major advantage and a major disadvantage of the specific identification method of inventory costing?

9. "The selection of an inventory cost flow method is a decision made by accountants." Do you agree? Explain. Once a method has been selected, what accounting requirement applies?

10. Which assumed inventory cost flow method:
    (a) usually parallels the actual physical flow of merchandise?
    (b) assumes that goods available for sale during an accounting period are identical?
    (c) assumes that the latest units purchased are the first to be sold?

11. In a period of rising prices, the inventory reported in Plato Company's balance sheet is close to the current cost of the inventory. Cecil Company's inventory is considerably below its current cost. Identify the inventory cost flow method being used by each company. Which company has probably been reporting the higher gross profit?

12. Casey Company has been using the FIFO cost flow method during a prolonged period of rising prices. During the same time period, Casey has been paying out all of its net income as dividends. What adverse effects may result from this policy?

13. Peter Lunde is studying for the next accounting mid-term examination. What should Peter know about (a) departing from the cost basis of accounting for inventories and (b) the meaning of "market" in the lower-of-cost-or-market method?

14. Garitson Music Center has 5 CD players on hand at the balance sheet date. Each cost $400. The current replace-

ment cost is $380 per unit. Under the lower-of-cost-or-market basis of accounting for inventories, what value should be reported for the CD players on the balance sheet? Why?

15. Ruthie Stores has 20 toasters on hand at the balance sheet date. Each cost $27. The current replacement cost is $30 per unit. Under the lower-of-cost-or-market basis of accounting for inventories, what value should Ruthie report for the toasters on the balance sheet? Why?

16. Mintz Company discovers in 2012 that its ending inventory at December 31, 2011, was $7,000 understated. What effect will this error have on (a) 2011 net income, (b) 2012 net income, and (c) the combined net income for the 2 years?

17. Willingham Company's balance sheet shows Inventory $162,800. What additional disclosures should be made?

18. Under what circumstances might inventory turnover be too high? That is, what possible negative consequences might occur?

19. **PEPSICO** What inventory cost flow does PepsiCo use for its inventories? (*Hint:* you will need to examine the notes for PepsiCo's financial statements.)

*20. "When perpetual inventory records are kept, the results under the FIFO and LIFO methods are the same as they would be in a periodic inventory system." Do you agree? Explain.

*21. How does the average-cost method of inventory costing differ between a perpetual inventory system and a periodic inventory system?

*22. When is it necessary to estimate inventories?

*23. Both the gross profit method and the retail inventory method are based on averages. For each method, indicate the average used, how it is determined, and how it is applied.

*24. Maureen Company has net sales of $400,000 and cost of goods available for sale of $300,000. If the gross profit rate is 35%, what is the estimated cost of the ending inventory? Show computations.

*25. Milo Shoe Shop had goods available for sale in 2012 with a retail price of $120,000. The cost of these goods was $84,000. If sales during the period were $80,000, what is the ending inventory at cost using the retail inventory method?

Brief Exercises

BE6-1 Bernard Company identifies the following items for possible inclusion in the taking of a physical inventory. Indicate whether each item should be included or excluded from the inventory taking.

Identify items to be included in taking a physical inventory.

(SO 1)

(a) Goods shipped on consignment by Bernard to another company.
(b) Goods in transit from a supplier shipped FOB destination.
(c) Goods sold but being held for customer pickup.
(d) Goods held on consignment from another company.

Identify the components of goods available for sale.
(SO 2)

BE6-2   The ledger of Charlotte Company includes the following items: (a) Freight-in, (b) Purchase Returns and Allowances, (c) Purchases, (d) Sales Discounts, (e) Purchase Discounts. Identify which items are included in goods available for sale.

Compute ending inventory using FIFO and LIFO.
(SO 2)

BE6-3   In its first month of operations, Danielle Company made three purchases of merchandise in the following sequence: (1) 300 units at $6, (2) 400 units at $7, and (3) 200 units at $8. Assuming there are 360 units on hand, compute the cost of the ending inventory under the (a) FIFO method and (b) LIFO method. Danielle uses a periodic inventory system.

Compute the ending inventory using average-cost.
(SO 2)

BE6-4   Data for Danielle Company are presented in BE6-3. Compute the cost of the ending inventory under the average-cost method, assuming there are 360 units on hand.

Explain the financial statement effect of inventory cost flow assumptions.
(SO 3)

BE6-5   The management of Rousseau Corp. is considering the effects of various inventory-costing methods on its financial statements and its income tax expense. Assuming that the price the company pays for inventory is increasing, which method will:

(a) provide the highest net income?
(b) provide the highest ending inventory?
(c) result in the lowest income tax expense?
(d) result in the most stable earnings over a number of years?

Explain the financial statement effect of inventory cost flow assumptions.
(SO 3)

BE6-6   In its first month of operation, Alex Company purchased 100 units of inventory for $6, then 200 units for $7, and finally 150 units for $8. At the end of the month, 180 units remained. Compute the amount of phantom profit that would result if the company used FIFO rather than LIFO. Explain why this amount is referred to as *phantom profit*. The company uses the periodic method.

Determine the LCM valuation using inventory categories.
(SO 4)

BE6-7   Tania Appliance Center accumulates the following cost and market data at December 31.

Inventory Categories	Cost Data	Market Data
Cameras	$12,000	$12,100
Camcorders	9,500	9,700
DVD players	14,000	12,800

Compute the lower-of-cost-or-market valuation for the company's total inventory.

Determine correct income statement amounts.
(SO 5)

BE6-8   Raymonde Company reports net income of $90,000 in 2012. However, ending inventory was understated $10,000. What is the correct net income for 2012? What effect, if any, will this error have on total assets as reported in the balance sheet at December 31, 2012?

Compute inventory turnover and days in inventory.
(SO 6)

BE6-9   At December 31, 2012, the following information was available for C. Widmore Company: ending inventory $40,000, beginning inventory $60,000, cost of goods sold $270,000, and sales revenue $380,000. Calculate inventory turnover and days in inventory for C. Widmore Company.

Apply cost flow methods to perpetual inventory records.
(SO 7)

*BE6-10   Pierre's Department Store uses a perpetual inventory system. Data for product E2-D2 include the following purchases.

Date	Number of Units	Unit Price
May 7	50	$10
July 28	30	13

On June 1, Pierre's sold 30 units, and on August 27, 40 more units. Prepare the perpetual inventory schedule for the above transactions using (a) FIFO, (b) LIFO, and (c) moving-average cost.

Apply the gross profit method.
(SO 8)

*BE6-11   At May 31, Chang Company has net sales of $330,000 and cost of goods available for sale of $230,000. Compute the estimated cost of the ending inventory, assuming the gross profit rate is 35%.

Apply the retail inventory method.
(SO 8)

*BE6-12   On June 30, Francois Fabrics has the following data pertaining to the retail inventory method: Goods available for sale: at cost $35,000, at retail $50,000; net sales $40,000, and ending inventory at retail $10,000. Compute the estimated cost of the ending inventory using the retail inventory method.

Do it! Review

Do it! 6-1   Chau Company just took its physical inventory. The count of inventory items on hand at the company's business locations resulted in a total inventory cost of $300,000. In reviewing the details of the count and related inventory transactions, you have discovered the following.

Apply rules of ownership to determine inventory cost.
(SO 1)

1. Chau has sent inventory costing $26,000 on consignment to Nikki Company. All of this inventory was at Nikki's showrooms on December 31.
2. The company did not include in the count inventory (cost, $20,000) that was sold on December 28, terms FOB shipping point. The goods were in transit on December 31.
3. The company did not include in the count inventory (cost, $17,000) that was purchased with terms of FOB shipping point. The goods were in transit on December 31.

Compute the correct December 31 inventory.

Do it! 6-2   The accounting records of Fernandez Electronics show the following data.

Compute cost of goods sold under different cost flow methods.
(SO 2)

Beginning inventory	3,000 units at $5
Purchases	8,000 units at $7
Sales	9,200 units at $10

Determine cost of goods sold during the period under a periodic inventory system using (a) the FIFO method, (b) the LIFO method, and (c) the average-cost method. (Round unit cost to nearest tenth of a cent.)

Do it! 6-3   (a) Kiele Company sells three different categories of tools (small, medium, and large). The cost and fair value of its inventory of tools are as follows.

Compute inventory value under LCM.
(SO 4)

	Cost	Fair Value
Small	$ 64,000	$ 73,000
Medium	290,000	260,000
Large	152,000	171,000

Determine the value of the company's inventory under the lower-of-cost-or-market approach.

(b) Sanchez Company understated its 2011 ending inventory by $31,000. Determine the impact this error has on ending inventory, cost of goods sold, and owner's equity in 2011 and 2012.

Do it! 6-4   Early in 2012, Paulo Company switched to a just-in-time inventory system. Its sales, cost of goods sold, and inventory amounts for 2011 and 2012 are shown below.

Compute inventory turnover ratio and assess inventory level.
(SO 6)

	2011	2012
Sales	$3,120,000	$3,713,000
Cost of goods sold	1,200,000	1,425,000
Beginning inventory	180,000	220,000
Ending inventory	220,000	80,000

Determine the inventory turnover and days in inventory for 2011 and 2012. Discuss the changes in the amount of inventory, the inventory turnover and days in inventory, and the amount of sales across the two years.

Exercises

E6-1   Balboa Bank and Trust is considering giving Rodrigo Company a loan. Before doing so, they decide that further discussions with Rodrigo's accountant may be desirable. One area of particular concern is the inventory account, which has a year-end balance of $297,000. Discussions with the accountant reveal the following.

Determine the correct inventory amount.
(SO 1)

1. Rodrigo sold goods costing $38,000 to Santoro Company, FOB shipping point, on December 28. The goods are not expected to arrive at Santoro until January 12. The goods were not included in the physical inventory because they were not in the warehouse.

2. The physical count of the inventory did not include goods costing $95,000 that were shipped to Rodrigo FOB destination on December 27 and were still in transit at year-end.
3. Rodrigo received goods costing $22,000 on January 2. The goods were shipped FOB shipping point on December 26 by Penelope Co. The goods were not included in the physical count.
4. Rodrigo sold goods costing $35,000 to Naomi Co., FOB destination, on December 30. The goods were received at Naomi on January 8. They were not included in Rodrigo's physical inventory.
5. Rodrigo received goods costing $44,000 on January 2 that were shipped FOB destination on December 29. The shipment was a rush order that was supposed to arrive December 31. This purchase was included in the ending inventory of $297,000.

Instructions

Determine the correct inventory amount on December 31.

Determine the correct inventory amount.

(SO 1)

E6-2 Marsha Thomason, an auditor with Dorrit CPAs, is performing a review of Mikhail Company's inventory account. Mikhail did not have a good year and top management is under pressure to boost reported income. According to its records, the inventory balance at year-end was $740,000. However, the following information was not considered when determining that amount.

1. Included in the company's count were goods with a cost of $250,000 that the company is holding on consignment. The goods belong to Bakunin Corporation.
2. The physical count did not include goods purchased by Mikhail with a cost of $40,000 that were shipped FOB destination on December 28 and did not arrive at Mikhail's warehouse until January 3.
3. Included in the inventory account was $17,000 of office supplies that were stored in the warehouse and were to be used by the company's supervisors and managers during the coming year.
4. The company received an order on December 29 that was boxed and was sitting on the loading dock awaiting pick-up on December 31. The shipper picked up the goods on January 1 and delivered them on January 6. The shipping terms were FOB shipping point. The goods had a selling price of $40,000 and a cost of $30,000. The goods were not included in the count because they were sitting on the dock.
5. On December 29, Mikhail shipped goods with a selling price of $80,000 and a cost of $60,000 to Omar Sales Corporation FOB shipping point. The goods arrived on January 3. Omar Sales had only ordered goods with a selling price of $10,000 and a cost of $8,000. However, a sales manager at Mikhail had authorized the shipment and said that if Omar wanted to ship the goods back next week, it could.
6. Included in the count was $40,000 of goods that were parts for a machine that the company no longer made. Given the high-tech nature of Mikhail's products, it was unlikely that these obsolete parts had any other use. However, management would prefer to keep them on the books at cost, "since that is what we paid for them, after all."

Instructions

Prepare a schedule to determine the correct inventory amount. Provide explanations for each item above, saying why you did or did not make an adjustment for each item.

Calculate cost of goods sold using specific identification and FIFO.

(SO 2, 3)

E6-3 On December 1, Nadia Electronics Ltd. has three DVD players left in stock. All are identical, all are priced to sell at $150. One of the three DVD players left in stock, with serial #1012, was purchased on June 1 at a cost of $100. Another, with serial #1045, was purchased on November 1 for $90. The last player, serial #1056, was purchased on November 30 for $80.

Instructions

(a) Calculate the cost of goods sold using the FIFO periodic inventory method assuming that two of the three players were sold by the end of December, Nadia Electronics' year-end.
(b) If Nadia Electronics used the specific identification method instead of the FIFO method, how might it alter its earnings by "selectively choosing" which particular players to sell to the two customers? What would Nadia's cost of goods sold be if the company wished to minimize earnings? Maximize earnings?
(c) Which of the two inventory methods do you recommend that Nadia use? Explain why.

Compute inventory and cost of goods sold using FIFO and LIFO.

(SO 2)

E6-4 Andrea's Boards sells a snowboard, Xpert, that is popular with snowboard enthusiasts. Information relating to Andrea's purchases of Xpert snowboards during September is shown on page 295.

During the same month, 121 Xpert snowboards were sold. Andrea's uses a periodic inventory system.

Date	Explanation	Units	Unit Cost	Total Cost
Sept. 1	Inventory	26	$ 97	$ 2,522
Sept. 12	Purchases	45	102	4,590
Sept. 19	Purchases	20	104	2,080
Sept. 26	Purchases	50	105	5,250
	Totals	141		$14,442

Instructions
(a) Compute the ending inventory at September 30 and cost of goods sold using the FIFO and LIFO methods. Prove the amount allocated to cost of goods sold under each method.
(b) For both FIFO and LIFO, calculate the sum of ending inventory and cost of goods sold. What do you notice about the answers you found for each method?

E6-5 Fionnula Co. uses a periodic inventory system. Its records show the following for the month of May, in which 65 units were sold.

Compute inventory and cost of goods sold using FIFO and LIFO.
(SO 2)

		Units	Unit Cost	Total Cost
May 1	Inventory	30	$ 8	$240
15	Purchases	25	11	275
24	Purchases	35	12	420
	Totals	90		$935

Instructions
Compute the ending inventory at May 31 and cost of goods sold using the FIFO and LIFO methods. Prove the amount allocated to cost of goods sold under each method.

E6-6 Flanagan Company reports the following for the month of June.

Compute inventory and cost of goods sold using FIFO and LIFO.
(SO 2, 3)

		Units	Unit Cost	Total Cost
June 1	Inventory	200	$5	$1,000
12	Purchase	300	6	1,800
23	Purchase	500	7	3,500
30	Inventory	120		

Instructions
(a) Compute the cost of the ending inventory and the cost of goods sold under (1) FIFO and (2) LIFO.
(b) Which costing method gives the higher ending inventory? Why?
(c) Which method results in the higher cost of goods sold? Why?

E6-7 Eloise Company had 100 units in beginning inventory at a total cost of $10,000. The company purchased 200 units at a total cost of $26,000. At the end of the year, Eloise had 80 units in ending inventory.

Compute inventory under FIFO, LIFO, and average-cost.
(SO 2, 3)

Instructions
(a) Compute the cost of the ending inventory and the cost of goods sold under (1) FIFO, (2) LIFO, and (3) average-cost.
(b) Which cost flow method would result in the highest net income?
(c) Which cost flow method would result in inventories approximating current cost in the balance sheet?
(d) Which cost flow method would result in Eloise paying the least taxes in the first year?

E6-8 Inventory data for Flanagan Company are presented in E6-6.

Compute inventory and cost of goods sold using average-cost.
(SO 2, 3)

Instructions
(a) Compute the cost of the ending inventory and the cost of goods sold using the average-cost method.
(b) Will the results in (a) be higher or lower than the results under (1) FIFO and (2) LIFO?
(c) Why is the average unit cost not $6?

Determine ending inventory under LCM.
(SO 4)

E6-9   Venden Camera Shop uses the lower-of-cost-or-market basis for its inventory. The following data are available at December 31.

Item	Units	Unit Cost	Market
Cameras:			
Minolta	5	$170	$156
Canon	6	150	152
Light meters:			
Vivitar	12	125	115
Kodak	14	120	135

Instructions
Determine the amount of the ending inventory by applying the lower-of-cost-or-market basis.

Compute lower-of-cost-or-market.
(SO 4)

E6-10   Radzinsky Company applied FIFO to its inventory and got the following results for its ending inventory.

Cameras	100 units at a cost per unit of $65
DVD players	150 units at a cost per unit of $75
iPods	125 units at a cost per unit of $80

The cost of purchasing units at year-end was cameras $71, DVD players $69, and iPods $78.

Instructions
Determine the amount of ending inventory at lower-of-cost-or-market.

Determine effects of inventory errors.
(SO 5)

E6-11   Jacob's Hardware reported cost of goods sold as follows.

	2011	2012
Beginning inventory	$ 20,000	$ 30,000
Cost of goods purchased	150,000	175,000
Cost of goods available for sale	170,000	205,000
Ending inventory	30,000	35,000
Cost of goods sold	$140,000	$170,000

Jacob's made two errors: (1) 2011 ending inventory was overstated $3,000, and (2) 2012 ending inventory was understated $6,000.

Instructions
Compute the correct cost of goods sold for each year.

Prepare correct income statements.
(SO 5)

E6-12   Pellegrino Watch Company reported the following income statement data for a 2-year period.

	2011	2012
Sales revenue	$210,000	$250,000
Cost of goods sold		
Beginning inventory	32,000	44,000
Cost of goods purchased	173,000	202,000
Cost of goods available for sale	205,000	246,000
Ending inventory	44,000	52,000
Cost of goods sold	161,000	194,000
Gross profit	$ 49,000	$ 56,000

Pellegrino uses a periodic inventory system. The inventories at January 1, 2011, and December 31, 2012, are correct. However, the ending inventory at December 31, 2011, was overstated $5,000.

Instructions
(a) Prepare correct income statement data for the 2 years.
(b) What is the cumulative effect of the inventory error on total gross profit for the 2 years?
(c) ⬛⬛⬛⬛ Explain in a letter to the president of Pellegrino Company what has happened—
i.e., the nature of the error and its effect on the financial statements.

E6-13 This information is available for Paik's Photo Corporation for 2010, 2011, and 2012.

Compute inventory turnover, days in inventory, and gross profit rate.
(SO 6)

	2010	2011	2012
Beginning inventory	$ 100,000	$ 300,000	$ 400,000
Ending inventory	300,000	400,000	480,000
Cost of goods sold	900,000	1,120,000	1,300,000
Sales revenue	1,200,000	1,600,000	1,900,000

Instructions

Calculate inventory turnover, days in inventory, and gross profit rate (from Chapter 5) for Paik's Photo Corporation for 2010, 2011, and 2012. Comment on any trends.

E6-14 The cost of goods sold computations for Target Company and Caesar Company are shown below.

Compute inventory turnover and days in inventory.
(SO 6)

	Target Company	Caesar Company
Beginning inventory	$ 45,000	$ 71,000
Cost of goods purchased	200,000	290,000
Cost of goods available for sale	245,000	361,000
Ending inventory	55,000	69,000
Cost of goods sold	$190,000	$292,000

Instructions

(a) Compute inventory turnover and days in inventory for each company.

(b) Which company moves its inventory more quickly?

*E6-15 Hiroyuki Appliance uses a perpetual inventory system. For its flat-screen television sets, the January 1 inventory was 3 sets at $600 each. On January 10, Hiroyuki purchased 6 units at $660 each. The company sold 2 units on January 8 and 4 units on January 15.

Apply cost flow methods to perpetual records.
(SO 7)

Instructions

Compute the ending inventory under (1) FIFO, (2) LIFO, and (3) moving-average cost.

*E6-16 Flanagan Company reports the following for the month of June.

Calculate inventory and cost of goods sold using three cost flow methods in a perpetual inventory system.
(SO 7)

Date	Explanation	Units	Unit Cost	Total Cost
June 1	Inventory	200	$5	$1,000
12	Purchase	300	6	1,800
23	Purchase	500	7	3,500
30	Inventory	120		

Instructions

(a) Calculate the cost of the ending inventory and the cost of goods sold for each cost flow assumption, using a perpetual inventory system. Assume a sale of 400 units occurred on June 15 for a selling price of $8 and a sale of 480 units on June 27 for $9.

(b) How do the results differ from E6-6 and E6-8?

(c) Why is the average unit cost not $6 [($5 + $6 + $7) ÷ 3 = $6]?

*E6-17 Information about Andrea's Boards is presented in E6-4. Additional data regarding Andrea's sales of Xpert snowboards are provided below. Assume that Andrea's uses a perpetual inventory system.

Apply cost flow methods to perpetual records.
(SO 7)

Date		Units	Unit Price	Total Cost
Sept. 5	Sale	12	$199	$ 2,388
Sept. 16	Sale	50	199	9,950
Sept. 29	Sale	59	209	12,331
	Totals	121		$24,669

Instructions

(a) Compute ending inventory at September 30 using FIFO, LIFO, and moving-average cost.

(b) Compare ending inventory using a perpetual inventory system to ending inventory using a periodic inventory system (from E6-4).

(c) Which inventory cost flow method (FIFO, LIFO) gives the same ending inventory value under both periodic and perpetual? Which method gives different ending inventory values?

Use the gross profit method to estimate inventory.

(SO 8)

*E6-18   Sanada Company reported the following information for November and December 2012.

	November	December
Cost of goods purchased	$500,000	$ 610,000
Inventory, beginning-of-month	100,000	120,000
Inventory, end-of-month	120,000	????
Sales revenue	800,000	1,000,000

Sanada's ending inventory at December 31 was destroyed in a fire.

Instructions

(a) Compute the gross profit rate for November.

(b) Using the gross profit rate for November, determine the estimated cost of inventory lost in the fire.

Determine merchandise lost using the gross profit method of estimating inventory.

(SO 8)

*E6-19   The inventory of Dogen Company was destroyed by fire on March 1. From an examination of the accounting records, the following data for the first 2 months of the year are obtained: Sales Revenue $51,000, Sales Returns and Allowances $1,000, Purchases $31,200, Freight-in $1,200, and Purchase Returns and Allowances $1,400.

Instructions

Determine the merchandise lost by fire, assuming:

(a) A beginning inventory of $20,000 and a gross profit rate of 40% on net sales.

(b) A beginning inventory of $30,000 and a gross profit rate of 30% on net sales.

Determine ending inventory at cost using retail method.

(SO 8)

*E6-20   Seamus Shoe Store uses the retail inventory method for its two departments, Women's Shoes and Men's Shoes. The following information for each department is obtained.

Item	Women's Shoes	Men's Shoes
Beginning inventory at cost	$ 32,000	$ 45,000
Cost of goods purchased at cost	148,000	136,300
Net sales	178,000	185,000
Beginning inventory at retail	46,000	60,000
Cost of goods purchased at retail	179,000	185,000

Instructions

Compute the estimated cost of the ending inventory for each department under the retail inventory method.

Exercises: Set B

Visit the book's companion website, at **www.wiley.com/college/weygandt**, and choose the Student Companion site to access Exercise Set B.

Problems: Set A

Determine items and amounts to be recorded in inventory.

(SO 1)

P6-1A   Toledo Limited is trying to determine the value of its ending inventory at February 28, 2012, the company's year-end. The accountant counted everything that was in the warehouse as of February 28, which resulted in an ending inventory valuation of $48,000. However, she didn't know how to treat the following transactions so she didn't record them.

(a) On February 26, Toledo shipped to a customer goods costing $800. The goods were shipped FOB shipping point, and the receiving report indicates that the customer received the goods on March 2.

(b) On February 26, Grisel Inc. shipped goods to Toledo FOB destination. The invoice price was $350. The receiving report indicates that the goods were received by Toledo on March 2.

(c) Toledo had $500 of inventory at a customer's warehouse "on approval." The customer was going to let Toledo know whether it wanted the merchandise by the end of the week, March 4.

(d) Toledo also had $400 of inventory on consignment at a Balboa craft shop.

(e) On February 26, Toledo ordered goods costing $750. The goods were shipped FOB shipping point on February 27. Toledo received the goods on March 1.

(f) On February 28, Toledo packaged goods and had them ready for shipping to a customer FOB destination. The invoice price was $350; the cost of the items was $250. The receiving report indicates that the goods were received by the customer on March 2.

(g) Toledo had damaged goods set aside in the warehouse because they are no longer saleable. These goods originally cost $400 and, originally, Toledo expected to sell these items for $600.

Instructions

For each of the above transactions, specify whether the item in question should be included in ending inventory, and if so, at what amount. For each item that is not included in ending inventory, indicate who owns it and what account, if any, it should have been recorded in.

P6-2A Kyoto Distribution markets CDs of the performing artist A. A. Bondy. At the beginning of March, Kyoto had in beginning inventory 1,500 Bondy CDs with a unit cost of $7. During March Kyoto made the following purchases of Bondy CDs.

Determine cost of goods sold and ending inventory using FIFO, LIFO, and average-cost with analysis.

(SO 2, 3)

| March 5 | 3,000 @ $8 | March 21 | 4,000 @ $10 |
| March 13 | 5,500 @ $9 | March 26 | 2,000 @ $11 |

During March 12,500 units were sold. Kyoto uses a periodic inventory system.

Instructions

(a) Determine the cost of goods available for sale.

(b) Determine (1) the ending inventory and (2) the cost of goods sold under each of the assumed cost flow methods (FIFO, LIFO, and average-cost). Prove the accuracy of the cost of goods sold under the FIFO and LIFO methods.

(c) Which cost flow method results in (1) the highest inventory amount for the balance sheet and (2) the highest cost of goods sold for the income statement?

(b)(2) Cost of goods sold:
FIFO $109,000
LIFO $119,500
Average $114,062

P6-3A Lu Company had a beginning inventory of 400 units of Product Ribo at a cost of $8 per unit. During the year, purchases were:

Determine cost of goods sold and ending inventory using FIFO, LIFO, and average-cost with analysis.

(SO 2, 3)

| Feb. 20 | 600 units at $9 | Aug. 12 | 300 units at $11 |
| May 5 | 500 units at $10 | Dec. 8 | 200 units at $12 |

Lu Company uses a periodic inventory system. Sales totaled 1,500 units.

Instructions

(a) Determine the cost of goods available for sale.

(b) Determine (1) the ending inventory, and (2) the cost of goods sold under each of the assumed cost flow methods (FIFO, LIFO, and average). Prove the accuracy of the cost of goods sold under the FIFO and LIFO methods.

(c) Which cost flow method results in (1) the lowest inventory amount for the balance sheet, and (2) the lowest cost of goods sold for the income statement?

(b) Cost of goods sold:
FIFO $13,600
LIFO $15,200
Average $14,475

P6-4A The management of Reiko Co. is reevaluating the appropriateness of using its present inventory cost flow method, which is average-cost. They request your help in determining the results of operations for 2012 if either the FIFO method or the LIFO method had been used. For 2012, the accounting records show the following data.

Compute ending inventory, prepare income statements, and answer questions using FIFO and LIFO.

(SO 2, 3)

Inventories		Purchases and Sales	
Beginning (15,000 units)	$32,000	Total net sales (215,000 units)	$865,000
Ending (30,000 units)		Total cost of goods purchased	
		(230,000 units)	595,000

Purchases were made quarterly as follows.

Quarter	Units	Unit Cost	Total Cost
1	60,000	$2.40	$144,000
2	50,000	2.50	125,000
3	50,000	2.60	130,000
4	70,000	2.80	196,000
	230,000		$595,000

Operating expenses were $147,000, and the company's income tax rate is 34%.

Instructions

(a) Prepare comparative condensed income statements for 2012 under FIFO and LIFO. (Show computations of ending inventory.)

(b) ⬤━━━━━▶ Answer the following questions for management.

(1) Which cost flow method (FIFO or LIFO) produces the more meaningful inventory amount for the balance sheet? Why?

(2) Which cost flow method (FIFO or LIFO) produces the more meaningful net income? Why?

(3) Which cost flow method (FIFO or LIFO) is more likely to approximate actual physical flow of the goods? Why?

(4) How much additional cash will be available for management under LIFO than under FIFO? Why?

(5) Will gross profit under the average-cost method be higher or lower than (i) FIFO and (ii) LIFO? (*Note:* It is not necessary to quantify your answer.)

Calculate ending inventory, cost of goods sold, gross profit, and gross profit rate under periodic method; compare results.

(SO 2, 3)

P6-5A You are provided with the following information for Aylesworth Inc. for the month ended October 31, 2012. Aylesworth uses a periodic method for inventory.

Date	Description	Units	Unit Cost or Selling Price
October 1	Beginning inventory	60	$25
October 9	Purchase	120	26
October 11	Sale	100	35
October 17	Purchase	70	27
October 22	Sale	60	40
October 25	Purchase	80	28
October 29	Sale	110	40

Instructions

(a) Calculate (i) ending inventory, (ii) cost of goods sold, (iii) gross profit, and (iv) gross profit rate under each of the following methods.

(1) LIFO.

(2) FIFO.

(3) Average-cost.

(b) Compare results for the three cost flow assumptions.

Compare specific identification, FIFO and LIFO under periodic method; use cost flow assumption to influence earnings.

(SO 2, 3)

P6-6A You have the following information for Goodspeed Diamonds. Goodspeed Diamonds uses the periodic method of accounting for its inventory transactions. Goodspeed only carries one brand and size of diamonds—all are identical. Each batch of diamonds purchased is carefully coded and marked with its purchase cost.

March 1 Beginning inventory 150 diamonds at a cost of $300 per diamond.
March 3 Purchased 200 diamonds at a cost of $350 each.
March 5 Sold 180 diamonds for $600 each.
March 10 Purchased 350 diamonds at a cost of $375 each.
March 25 Sold 400 diamonds for $650 each.

Instructions

(a) Assume that Goodspeed Diamonds uses the specific identification cost flow method.

(1) Demonstrate how Goodspeed Diamonds could maximize its gross profit for the month by specifically selecting which diamonds to sell on March 5 and March 25.

(2) Demonstrate how Goodspeed Diamonds could minimize its gross profit for the month by selecting which diamonds to sell on March 5 and March 25.

(b) Assume that Goodspeed Diamonds uses the FIFO cost flow assumption. Calculate cost of goods sold. How much gross profit would Goodspeed Diamonds report under this cost flow assumption?

(c) Assume that Goodspeed Diamonds uses the LIFO cost flow assumption. Calculate cost of goods sold. How much gross profit would the company report under this cost flow assumption?

Compute ending inventory, prepare income statements, and answer questions using FIFO and LIFO.

(SO 2, 3)

(d) Which cost flow method should Goodspeed Diamonds select? Explain.

P6-7A The management of Hillary Inc. asks your help in determining the comparative effects of the FIFO and LIFO inventory cost flow methods. For 2012, the accounting records provide the data shown on page 301.

Inventory, January 1 (10,000 units)	$ 35,000
Cost of 120,000 units purchased	504,500
Selling price of 100,000 units sold	665,000
Operating expenses	130,000

Units purchased consisted of 35,000 units at $4.00 on May 10; 60,000 units at $4.20 on August 15; and 25,000 units at $4.50 on November 20. Income taxes are 28%.

Instructions

(a) Prepare comparative condensed income statements for 2012 under FIFO and LIFO. (Show computations of ending inventory.)

(b) ◄━━━ Answer the following questions for management in the form of a business letter.

(1) Which inventory cost flow method produces the most meaningful inventory amount for the balance sheet? Why?

(2) Which inventory cost flow method produces the most meaningful net income? Why?

(3) Which inventory cost flow method is most likely to approximate the actual physical flow of the goods? Why?

(4) How much more cash will be available for management under LIFO than under FIFO? Why?

(5) How much of the gross profit under FIFO is illusionary in comparison with the gross profit under LIFO?

Gross profit:
FIFO $259,000
LIFO $240,500

*P6-8A Yemi Ltd. is a retailer operating in Edmonton, Alberta. Yemi uses the perpetual inventory method. All sales returns from customers result in the goods being returned to inventory; the inventory is not damaged. Assume that there are no credit transactions; all amounts are settled in cash. You are provided with the following information for Yemi Ltd. for the month of January 2012.

Calculate cost of goods sold and ending inventory for FIFO, moving-average cost, and LIFO under the perpetual system; compare gross profit under each assumption.
(SO 7)

Date	Description	Quantity	Unit Cost or Selling Price
December 31	Ending inventory	150	$17
January 2	Purchase	100	21
January 6	Sale	150	40
January 9	Sale return	10	40
January 9	Purchase	75	24
January 10	Purchase return	15	24
January 10	Sale	50	45
January 23	Purchase	100	28
January 30	Sale	110	50

Instructions

(a) For each of the following cost flow assumptions, calculate (i) cost of goods sold, (ii) ending inventory, and (iii) gross profit.

(1) LIFO.   (2) FIFO.   (3) Moving-average cost.

(b) Compare results for the three cost flow assumptions.

Gross profit:
LIFO $6,330
FIFO $7,500
Average $7,090

*P6-9A Farman Appliance Mart began operations on May 1. It uses a perpetual inventory system. During May, the company had the following purchases and sales for its Model 25 Sureshot camera.

Determine ending inventory under a perpetual inventory system.
(SO 7)

Date	Purchases Units	Purchases Unit Cost	Sales Units
May 1	7	$150	
4			4
8	8	$170	
12			5
15	6	$185	
20			3
25			4

Instructions

(a) Determine the ending inventory under a perpetual inventory system using (1) FIFO, (2) moving-average cost, and (3) LIFO.

(b) Which costing method produces (1) the highest ending inventory valuation and (2) the lowest ending inventory valuation?

(a) FIFO $925
Average $874
LIFO $790

Estimate inventory loss using gross profit method.
(SO 8)

*P6-10A   Jae Company lost 70% of its inventory in a fire on March 25, 2012. The accounting records showed the following gross profit data for February and March.

	February	March (to 3/25)
Net sales	$300,000	$250,000
Net purchases	197,800	191,000
Freight-in	2,900	4,000
Beginning inventory	4,500	13,200
Ending inventory	13,200	?

Jae Company is fully insured for fire losses but must prepare a report for the insurance company.

Instructions
(a) Compute the gross profit rate for the month of February.
(b) Using the gross profit rate for February, determine both the estimated total inventory and inventory lost in the fire in March.

Compute ending inventory using retail method.
(SO 8)

*P6-11A   Marin Department Store uses the retail inventory method to estimate its monthly ending inventories. The following information is available for two of its departments at August 31, 2012.

	Sporting Goods		Jewelry and Cosmetics	
	Cost	Retail	Cost	Retail
Net sales		$1,000,000		$1,160,000
Purchases	$675,000	1,066,000	$741,000	1,158,000
Purchase returns	(26,000)	(40,000)	(12,000)	(20,000)
Purchase discounts	(12,360)	—	(2,440)	—
Freight-in	9,000	—	14,000	—
Beginning inventory	47,360	74,000	39,440	62,000

At December 31, Marin Department Store takes a physical inventory at retail. The actual retail values of the inventories in each department are Sporting Goods $95,000, and Jewelry and Cosmetics $44,000.

Instructions
(a) Determine the estimated cost of the ending inventory for each department on **August 31**, 2012, using the retail inventory method.
(b) Compute the ending inventory at cost for each department at **December 31**, assuming the cost-to-retail ratios are 60% for Sporting Goods and 64% for Jewelry and Cosmetics.

Problems: Set B

Determine items and amounts to be recorded in inventory.
(SO 1)

P6-1B   Titus Manin Black Limited is trying to determine the value of its ending inventory as of February 28, 2012, the company's year-end. The following transactions occurred, and the accountant asked your help in determining whether they should be recorded or not.

(a) On February 26, Titus shipped goods costing $800 to a customer and charged the customer $1,000. The goods were shipped with terms FOB shipping point and the receiving report indicates that the customer received the goods on March 2.
(b) On February 26, Welliver Inc. shipped goods to Titus under terms FOB shipping point. The invoice price was $450 plus $30 for freight. The receiving report indicates that the goods were received by Titus on March 2.
(c) Titus had $650 of inventory isolated in the warehouse. The inventory is designated for a customer who has requested that the goods be shipped on March 10.
(d) Also included in Titus's warehouse is $700 of inventory that Ishii Producers shipped to Titus on consignment.
(e) On February 26, Titus issued a purchase order to acquire goods costing $900. The goods were shipped with terms FOB destination on February 27. Titus received the goods on March 2.

(f) On February 26, Titus shipped goods to a customer under terms FOB destination. The invoice price was $350; the cost of the items was $200. The receiving report indicates that the goods were received by the customer on March 2.

Instructions

For each of the above transactions, specify whether the item in question should be included in ending inventory, and if so, at what amount.

P6-2B Achilles Distribution markets CDs of the performing artist Vandyver. At the beginning of October, Achilles had in beginning inventory 2,000 of Vandyver's CDs with a unit cost of $7. During October Achilles made the following purchases of Vandyver's CDs.

Determine cost of goods sold and ending inventory using FIFO, LIFO, and average-cost with analysis.

(SO 2, 3)

Oct. 3	3,000 @ $8	Oct. 19	3,000 @ $10
Oct. 9	3,500 @ $9	Oct. 25	3,500 @ $11

During October, 11,400 units were sold. Achilles uses a periodic inventory system.

Instructions

(a) Determine the cost of goods available for sale.

(b) Determine (1) the ending inventory and (2) the cost of goods sold under each of the assumed cost flow methods (FIFO, LIFO, and average-cost). Prove the accuracy of the cost of goods sold under the FIFO and LIFO methods.

(c) Which cost flow method results in (1) the highest inventory amount for the balance sheet and (2) the highest cost of goods sold for the income statement?

(b)(2) Cost of goods sold:
FIFO $98,500
LIFO $111,200
Average $104,880

P6-3B Gacis Company had a beginning inventory on January 1 of 150 units of Product 4-18-15 at a cost of $20 per unit. During the year, the following purchases were made.

Determine cost of goods sold and ending inventory, using FIFO, LIFO, and average-cost with analysis.

(SO 2, 3)

Mar. 15	400 units at $23	Sept. 4	350 units at $26
July 20	250 units at $24	Dec. 2	100 units at $29

1,000 units were sold. Gacis Company uses a periodic inventory system.

Instructions

(a) Determine the cost of goods available for sale.

(b) Determine (1) the ending inventory, and (2) the cost of goods sold under each of the assumed cost flow methods (FIFO, LIFO, and average-cost). Prove the accuracy of the cost of goods sold under the FIFO and LIFO methods.

(c) Which cost flow method results in (1) the highest inventory amount for the balance sheet, and (2) the highest cost of goods sold for the income statement?

(b)(2) Cost of goods sold:
FIFO $23,400
LIFO $24,900
Average $24,160

P6-4B The management of Perrineau Inc. is reevaluating the appropriateness of using its present inventory cost flow method, which is average-cost. The company requests your help in determining the results of operations for 2012 if either the FIFO or the LIFO method had been used. For 2012, the accounting records show these data:

Compute ending inventory, prepare income statements, and answer questions using FIFO and LIFO.

(SO 2, 3)

Inventories		Purchases and Sales	
Beginning (8,000 units)	$16,000	Total net sales (180,000 units)	$747,000
Ending (18,000 units)		Total cost of goods purchased	
		(190,000 units)	468,000

Purchases were made quarterly as follows.

Quarter	Units	Unit Cost	Total Cost
1	50,000	$2.20	$110,000
2	40,000	2.40	96,000
3	40,000	2.50	100,000
4	60,000	2.70	162,000
	190,000		$468,000

Operating expenses were $130,000, and the company's income tax rate is 40%.

Instructions

(a) Prepare comparative condensed income statements for 2012 under FIFO and LIFO. (Show computations of ending inventory.)

(a) Gross profit:
FIFO $311,600
LIFO $301,000

(b) ◁▬▬▬▷ Answer the following questions for management.
   (1) Which cost flow method (FIFO or LIFO) produces the more meaningful inventory amount for the balance sheet? Why?
   (2) Which cost flow method (FIFO or LIFO) produces the more meaningful net income? Why?
   (3) Which cost flow method (FIFO or LIFO) is more likely to approximate the actual physical flow of goods? Why?
   (4) How much more cash will be available for management under LIFO than under FIFO? Why?
   (5) Will gross profit under the average-cost method be higher or lower than FIFO? Than LIFO? (*Note:* It is not necessary to quantify your answer.)

Calculate ending inventory, cost of goods sold, gross profit, and gross profit rate under periodic method; compare results.

(SO 2, 3)

P6-5B You are provided with the following information for Guillaume Inc. for the month ended June 30, 2012. Guillaume uses the periodic method for inventory.

Date	Description	Quantity	Unit Cost or Selling Price
June 1	Beginning inventory	40	$40
June 4	Purchase	135	44
June 10	Sale	110	70
June 11	Sale return	15	70
June 18	Purchase	55	46
June 18	Purchase return	10	46
June 25	Sale	65	75
June 28	Purchase	30	50

Instructions

(a)(iii) Gross profit:

LIFO	$4,215
FIFO	$4,645
Average	$4,414.60

(a) Calculate (i) ending inventory, (ii) cost of goods sold, (iii) gross profit, and (iv) gross profit rate under each of the following methods.
   (1) LIFO. **(2)** FIFO. **(3)** Average-cost.
(b) Compare results for the three cost flow assumptions.

Compare specific identification, FIFO, and LIFO under periodic method; use cost flow assumption to justify price increase.

(SO 2, 3)

P6-6B You are provided with the following information for Dabinpons Inc. Dabinpons Inc. uses the periodic method of accounting for its inventory transactions.

March 1 Beginning inventory 2,000 liters at a cost of 60¢ per liter.
March 3 Purchased 2,500 liters at a cost of 65¢ per liter.
March 5 Sold 2,200 liters for $1.05 per liter.
March 10 Purchased 4,000 liters at a cost of 72¢ per liter.
March 20 Purchased 2,500 liters at a cost of 80¢ per liter.
March 30 Sold 5,000 liters for $1.25 per liter.

Instructions

(a) Prepare partial income statements through gross profit, and calculate the value of ending inventory that would be reported on the balance sheet, under each of the following cost flow assumptions. Round ending inventory and cost of goods sold to the nearest dollar.

(a)(1) Gross profit:

Specific identification
$3,590

   (1) Specific identification method assuming:
      (i) The March 5 sale consisted of 1,100 liters from the March 1 beginning inventory and 1,100 liters from the March 3 purchase; and
      (ii) The March 30 sale consisted of the following number of units sold from beginning inventory and each purchase: 450 liters from March 1; 550 liters from March 3; 2,900 liters from March 10; 1,100 liters from March 20.

(2) FIFO $3,791
(3) LIFO $3,225

   (2) FIFO.
   (3) LIFO.

(b) How can companies use a cost flow method to justify price increases? Which cost flow method would best support an argument to increase prices?

Compute ending inventory, prepare income statements, and answer questions using FIFO and LIFO.

(SO 2, 3)

P6-7B The management of Tamara Co. asks your help in determining the comparative effects of the FIFO and LIFO inventory cost flow methods. For 2012, the accounting records provide the data shown on page 305.

Inventory, January 1 (10,000 units) $ 45,000
Cost of 100,000 units purchased   532,000
Selling price of 80,000 units sold   700,000
Operating expenses   140,000

Units purchased consisted of 35,000 units at $5.10 on May 10; 35,000 units at $5.30 on August 15; and 30,000 units at $5.60 on November 20. Income taxes are 30%.

Instructions

(a) Prepare comparative condensed income statements for 2012 under FIFO and LIFO. (Show computations of ending inventory.)

(b) ━━━ Answer the following questions for management.

    (1) Which inventory cost flow method produces the most meaningful inventory amount for the balance sheet? Why?

    (2) Which inventory cost flow method produces the most meaningful net income? Why?

    (3) Which inventory cost flow method is most likely to approximate actual physical flow of the goods? Why?

    (4) How much additional cash will be available for management under LIFO than under FIFO? Why?

    (5) How much of the gross profit under FIFO is illusory in comparison with the gross profit under LIFO?

(a) Net income
FIFO $105,700
LIFO $91,000

*P6-8B Ticotin Inc. is a retailer operating in British Columbia. Ticotin uses the perpetual inventory method. All sales returns from customers result in the goods being returned to inventory; the inventory is not damaged. Assume that there are no credit transactions; all amounts are settled in cash. You are provided with the following information for Ticotin Inc. for the month of January 2012.

Calculate cost of goods sold and ending inventory under LIFO, FIFO, and moving-average cost under the perpetual system; compare gross profit under each assumption.

(SO 7)

Date	Description	Quantity	Unit Cost or Selling Price
January 1	Beginning inventory	100	$15
January 5	Purchase	150	18
January 8	Sale	110	28
January 10	Sale return	10	28
January 15	Purchase	55	20
January 16	Purchase return	5	20
January 20	Sale	80	32
January 25	Purchase	30	22

Instructions

(a) For each of the following cost flow assumptions, calculate (i) cost of goods sold, (ii) ending inventory, and (iii) gross profit.

    (1) LIFO.   (2) FIFO.   (3) Moving-average cost.

(b) Compare results for the three cost flow assumptions.

Gross profit:
LIFO $2,020
FIFO $2,420
Average $2,272

*P6-9B Cortez Co. began operations on July 1. It uses a perpetual inventory system. During July, the company had the following purchases and sales.

Determine ending inventory under a perpetual inventory system.

(SO 7)

Date	Purchases Units	Purchases Unit Cost	Sales Units
July 1	5	$120	
July 6			4
July 11	7	$136	
July 14			3
July 21	8	$147	
July 27			6

Instructions

(a) Determine the ending inventory under a perpetual inventory system using (1) FIFO, (2) moving-average cost, and (3) LIFO.

(b) Which costing method produces the highest ending inventory valuation?

(a) Ending inventory
FIFO $1,029
Avg. $994
LIFO $958

Compute gross profit rate and inventory loss using gross profit method.

(SO 8)

*P6-10B   Bottitta Company lost all of its inventory in a fire on December 26, 2012. The accounting records showed the following gross profit data for November and December.

	November	December (to 12/26)
Net sales	$600,000	$700,000
Beginning inventory	32,000	36,000
Purchases	377,000	424,000
Purchase returns and allowances	13,300	14,900
Purchase discounts	8,500	9,500
Freight-in	8,800	9,900
Ending inventory	36,000	?

Bottitta is fully insured for fire losses but must prepare a report for the insurance company.

Instructions

(a) Compute the gross profit rate for November.

(b) Using the gross profit rate for November, determine the estimated cost of the inventory lost in the fire.

Compute ending inventory using retail method.

(SO 8)

*P6-11B   Farooqui Books uses the retail inventory method to estimate its monthly ending inventories. The following information is available for two of its departments at October 31, 2012.

	Hardcovers		Paperbacks	
	Cost	Retail	Cost	Retail
Beginning inventory	$ 420,000	$ 700,000	$ 280,000	$ 360,000
Purchases	2,135,000	3,200,000	1,155,000	1,540,000
Freight-in	24,000		12,000	
Purchase discounts	44,000		22,000	
Net sales		3,100,000		1,570,000

At December 31, Farooqui Books takes a physical inventory at retail. The actual retail values of the inventories in each department are Hardcovers $790,000 and Paperbacks $335,000.

Instructions

(a) Determine the estimated cost of the ending inventory for each department at **October 31**, 2012, using the retail inventory method.

(b) Compute the ending inventory at cost for each department at **December 31**, assuming the cost-to-retail ratios for the year are 65% for hardcovers and 75% for paperbacks.

Problems: Set C

Visit the book's companion website, at **www.wiley.com/college/weygandt**, and choose the Student Companion site to access Problem Set C.

Comprehensive Problem

CP6   On December 1, 2012, Ruggiero Company had the account balances shown below.

	Debits		Credits
Cash	$ 4,800	Accumulated Depreciation—Equipment	$ 1,500
Accounts Receivable	3,900	Accounts Payable	3,000
Inventory	1,800*	Owner's Capital	27,000
Equipment	21,000		$31,500
	$31,500		

*(3,000 × $0.60)

The following transactions occurred during December.

Dec. 3   Purchased 4,000 units of inventory on account at a cost of $0.72 per unit.
      5   Sold 4,400 units of inventory on account for $0.90 per unit. (It sold 3,000 of the $0.60 units and 1,400 of the $0.72.)
      7   Granted the December 5 customer $180 credit for 200 units of inventory returned costing $150. These units were returned to inventory.
     17   Purchased 2,200 units of inventory for cash at $0.80 each.
     22   Sold 2,000 units of inventory on account for $0.95 per unit. (It sold 2,000 of the $0.72 units.)

Adjustment data:

1. Accrued salaries payable $400.
2. Depreciation $200 per month.

Instructions

(a) Journalize the December transactions and adjusting entries, assuming Ruggiero uses the perpetual inventory method.
(b) Enter the December 1 balances in the ledger T accounts and post the December transactions. In addition to the accounts mentioned above, use the following additional accounts: Cost of Goods Sold, Depreciation Expense, Salaries and Wages Expense, Salaries and Wages Payable, Sales Revenue, and Sales Returns and Allowances.
(c) Prepare an adjusted trial balance as of December 31, 2012.
(d) Prepare an income statement for December 2012 and a classified balance sheet at December 31, 2012.
(e) Compute ending inventory and cost of goods sold under FIFO, assuming Ruggiero Company uses the periodic inventory system.
(f) Compute ending inventory and cost of goods sold under LIFO, assuming Ruggiero Company uses the periodic inventory system.

Continuing Cookie Chronicle

(*Note:* This is a continuation of the Cookie Chronicle from Chapters 1 through 5.)

CCC6   Natalie is busy establishing both divisions of her business (cookie classes and mixer sales) and completing her business degree. Her goals for the next 11 months are to sell one mixer per month and to give two to three classes per week.

The cost of the fine European mixers is expected to increase. Natalie has just negotiated new terms with Kzinski that include shipping costs in the negotiated purchase price (mixers will be shipped FOB destination). Natalie must choose a cost flow assumption for her mixer inventory.

Go to the book's companion website, **www.wiley.com/college/weygandt***, to see the completion of this problem.*

BROADENINGYOURPERSPECTIVE

Financial Reporting and Analysis

Financial Reporting Problem: PepsiCo, Inc.

BYP6-1   The notes that accompany a company's financial statements provide informative details that would clutter the amounts and descriptions presented in the statements. Refer to the financial statements of PepsiCo, Inc. and the Notes to Consolidated Financial Statements in Appendix A.

Instructions

Answer the following questions. Complete the requirements in millions of dollars, as shown in PepsiCo's annual report.

(a) What did PepsiCo report for the amount of inventories in its consolidated balance sheet at December 26, 2009? At December 27, 2008?

(b) Compute the dollar amount of change and the percentage change in inventories between 2008 and 2009. Compute inventory as a percentage of current assets at December 26, 2009.

(c) How does PepsiCo value its inventories? Which inventory cost flow method does PepsiCo use? (See Notes to the Financial Statements.)

(d) What is the cost of sales (cost of goods sold) reported by PepsiCo for 2009, 2008, and 2007? Compute the percentage of cost of sales to net sales in 2009.

Comparative Analysis Problem: PepsiCo, Inc. vs. The Coca-Cola Company

 PEPSICO

BYP6-2   PepsiCo's financial statements are presented in Appendix A. Financial statements of The Coca-Cola Company are presented in Appendix B.

Instructions

(a) Based on the information contained in these financial statements, compute the following 2009 ratios for each company.

(1) Inventory turnover ratio

(2) Days in inventory

(b) What conclusions concerning the management of the inventory can you draw from these data?

On the Web

BYP6-3   A company's annual report usually will identify the inventory method used. Knowing that, you can analyze the effects of the inventory method on the income statement and balance sheet.

Address: www.cisco.com, or go to **www.wiley.com/college/weygandt**

Instructions

Answer the following questions based on the current year's annual report on Cisco's website.

(a) At Cisco's fiscal year-end, what was the inventory on the balance sheet?

(b) How has this changed from the previous fiscal year-end?

(c) How much of the inventory was finished goods?

(d) What inventory method does Cisco use?

Critical Thinking

Decision Making Across the Organization

BYP6-4   On April 10, 2012, fire damaged the office and warehouse of Inwood Company. Most of the accounting records were destroyed, but the following account balances were determined as of March 31, 2012: Inventory (January 1), 2012, $80,000; Sales Revenue (January 1–March 31, 2012), $180,000; Purchases (January 1–March 31, 2012), $94,000.

The company's fiscal year ends on December 31. It uses a periodic inventory system.

From an analysis of the April bank statement, you discover cancelled checks of $4,200 for cash purchases during the period April 1–10. Deposits during the same period totaled $18,500. Of that amount, 60% were collections on accounts receivable, and the balance was cash sales.

Correspondence with the company's principal suppliers revealed $12,400 of purchases on account from April 1 to April 10. Of that amount, $1,600 was for merchandise in transit on April 10 that was shipped FOB destination.

Correspondence with the company's principal customers produced acknowledgments of credit sales totaling $37,000 from April 1 to April 10. It was estimated that $5,600 of credit sales will never be acknowledged or recovered from customers.

Inwood Company reached an agreement with the insurance company that its fire-loss claim should be based on the average of the gross profit rates for the preceding 2 years. The financial statements for 2010 and 2011 showed the following data.

	2011	2010
Net sales	$600,000	$480,000
Cost of goods purchased	404,000	356,000
Beginning inventory	60,000	40,000
Ending inventory	80,000	60,000

Inventory with a cost of $17,000 was salvaged from the fire.

Instructions
With the class divided into groups, answer the following.

(a) Determine the balances in (1) Sales Revenue and (2) Purchases at April 10.
*(b)** Determine the average gross profit rate for the years 2010 and 2011. (*Hint:* Find the gross profit rate for each year and divide the sum by 2.)
*(c)** Determine the inventory loss as a result of the fire, using the gross profit method.

Communication Activity

BYP6-5   You are the controller of Small Toys Inc. Janice LeMay, the president, recently mentioned to you that she found an error in the 2011 financial statements which she believes has corrected itself. She determined, in discussions with the Purchasing Department, that 2011 ending inventory was overstated by $1 million. Janice says that the 2012 ending inventory is correct. Thus, she assumes that 2012 income is correct. Janice says to you, "What happened has happened—there's no point in worrying about it anymore."

Instructions
You conclude that Janice is incorrect. Write a brief, tactful memo to Janice, clarifying the situation.

Ethics Case

BYP6-6   B. J. Ortiz Wholesale Corp. uses the LIFO method of inventory costing. In the current year, profit at B. J. Ortiz is running unusually high. The corporate tax rate is also high this year, but it is scheduled to decline significantly next year. In an effort to lower the current year's net income and to take advantage of the changing income tax rate, the president of B. J. Ortiz Wholesale instructs the plant accountant to recommend to the purchasing department a large purchase of inventory for delivery 3 days before the end of the year. The price of the inventory to be purchased has doubled during the year, and the purchase will represent a major portion of the ending inventory value.

Instructions
(a) What is the effect of this transaction on this year's and next year's income statement and income tax expense? Why?
(b) If B. J. Ortiz Wholesale had been using the FIFO method of inventory costing, would the president give the same directive?
(c) Should the plant accountant order the inventory purchase to lower income? What are the ethical implications of this order?

"All About You" Activity

BYP6-7   Some of the largest business frauds ever perpetrated have involved the misstatement of inventory. Two classics were at Leslie Fay Cos, and McKesson Corporation.

Instructions
There is considerable information regarding inventory frauds available on the Internet. Search for information about one of the two cases mentioned above, or inventory fraud at any other company, and prepare a short explanation of the nature of the inventory fraud.

FASB Codification Activity

BYP6-8 If your school has a subscription to the FASB Codification, go to *http://aaahq.org/ascLogin. cfm* to log in and prepare responses to the following.

(a) The primary basis for accounting for inventories is cost. How is cost defined in the Codification?

(b) What does the Codification state regarding the use of consistency in the selection or employment of a basis for inventory?

(c) What does the Codification indicate is a justification for the use of the lower-of-cost-or-market for inventory valuation?

Answers to Insight and Accounting Across the Organization Questions

p. 263 A Big Hiccup   Q: What steps might the companies take to avoid such a serious disruption in the future? **A:** The manufacturer of the piston rings should spread its manufacturing facilities across a few locations that are far enough apart that they would not all be at risk at once. In addition, the automakers might consider becoming less dependent on a single supplier.

p. 264 Falsifying Inventory to Boost Income   Q: What effect does an overstatement of inventory have on a company's financial statements? **A:** The balance sheet looks stronger because inventory and retained earnings are overstated. The income statement looks better because cost of goods sold is understated and income is overstated.

p. 275 Is LIFO Fair?   Q: What are the arguments for and against the use of LIFO? **A:** Proponents of LIFO argue that it is conceptually superior because it matches the most recent cost with the most recent selling price. Critics contend that it artificially understates the company's net income and consequently reduces tax payments. Also, because most foreign companies are not allowed to use LIFO, its use by U.S. companies reduces the ability of investors to compare U.S. companies with foreign companies.

p. 279 Improving Inventory Control with RFID   Q: Why is inventory control important to managers such as those at Wal-Mart and Best Buy? **A:** In the very competitive environment of discount retailing, where Wal-Mart and Best Buy are major players, small differences in price matter to the customer. Wal-Mart sells a high volume of inventory at a low gross profit rate. When operating in a high-volume, low-margin environment, small cost savings can mean the difference between being profitable or going out of business.

Answers to Self-Test Questions

1. a   **2.** b ($180,000 + $35,000)   **3.** b   **4.** c [(5,000 × $13) + (4,000 × $12)]   **5.** d [(8,000 × $11) + (1,000 × $12)]   **6.** d ((5,000 × $8) + (15,000 × $10) + (20,000 × $12)) ÷ 40,000 = $10.75; $10.75 × 7,000   **7.** c   **8.** d   **9.** d (200 × $80)   **10.** b   **11.** b   **12.** d   **13.** b $285,000 ÷ [($80,000 + $110,000) ÷ 2] = 3; 365 ÷ 3   ***14.** b [$150,000 − (30% × $150,000)] = $105,000; $135,000 − $105,000   ***15.** d

IFRS A Look at IFRS

The major IFRS requirements related to accounting and reporting for inventories are the same as GAAP. The major differences are that IFRS prohibits the use of the LIFO cost flow assumption and determines market in the lower-of-cost-or-market inventory valuation differently.

Key Points

- The requirements for accounting for and reporting inventories are more principles-based under IFRS. That is, GAAP provides more detailed guidelines in inventory accounting.

- The definitions for inventory are essentially similar under IFRS and GAAP. Both define inventory as assets held-for-sale in the ordinary course of business, in the process of production for sale (work in process), or to be consumed in the production of goods or services (e.g., raw materials).

- Who owns the goods—goods in transit or consigned goods—as well as the costs to include in inventory, are accounted for the same under IFRS and GAAP.
- Both GAAP and IFRS permit specific identification where appropriate. IFRS actually requires that the specific identification method be used where the inventory items are not interchangeable (i.e., can be specifically identified). If the inventory items are not specifically identifiable, a cost flow assumption is used. GAAP does not specify situations in which specific identification must be used.
- A major difference between IFRS and GAAP relates to the LIFO cost flow assumption. GAAP permits the use of LIFO for inventory valuation. IFRS prohibits its use. FIFO and average-cost are the only two acceptable cost flow assumptions permitted under IFRS.
- IFRS requires companies to use the same cost flow assumption for all goods of a similar nature. GAAP has no specific requirement in this area.
- In the lower-of-cost-or-market test for inventory valuation, IFRS defines market as net realizable value. Net realizable value is the estimated selling price in the ordinary course of business, less the estimated costs of completion and estimated selling expenses. In other words, net realizable value is the best estimate of the net amounts that inventories are expected to realize. GAAP, on the other hand, defines market as essentially replacement cost.
- Under GAAP, if inventory is written down under the lower-of-cost-or-market valuation, the new basis is now considered its cost. As a result, the inventory may not be written back up to its original cost in a subsequent period. Under IFRS, the write-down may be reversed in a subsequent period up to the amount of the previous write-down. Both the write-down and any subsequent reversal should be reported on the income statement as an expense. An item-by-item approach is generally followed under IFRS.
- An example of the use of lower-of-cost-or-net realizable value under IFRS follows.

Mendel Company has the following four items in its ending inventory as of December 31, 2012. The company uses the lower-of-cost-or-net realizable value approach for inventory valuation following IFRS.

Item No.	Cost	Net Realizable Value
1320	$3,600	$3,400
1333	4,000	4,100
1428	2,800	2,100
1510	5,000	4,700

The computation of the ending inventory value to be reported in the financial statements at December 31, 2012, is as follows.

Item No.	Cost	Net Realizable Value	LCNRV
1320	$ 3,600	$ 3,400	$ 3,400
1333	4,000	4,100	4,000
1428	2,800	2,100	2,100
1510	5,000	4,700	4,700
Total	$15,400	$14,300	$14,200

- Unlike property, plant, and equipment, IFRS does not permit the option of valuing inventories at fair value. As indicated above, IFRS requires inventory to be written down, but inventory cannot be written up above its original cost.
- Similar to GAAP, certain agricultural products and mineral products can be reported at net realizable value using IFRS.

Looking to the Future

One convergence issue that will be difficult to resolve relates to the use of the LIFO cost flow assumption. As indicated, IFRS specifically prohibits its use. Conversely, the LIFO cost flow assumption is widely used in the United States because of its favorable tax advantages. In addition, many argue that LIFO from a financial reporting point of view provides a better matching of current costs against revenue and, therefore, enables companies to compute a more realistic income.

With a new conceptual framework being developed, it is highly probable that the use of the concept of conservatism will be eliminated. Similarly, the concept of "prudence" in the IASB literature will also be eliminated. This may ultimately have implications for the application of the lower-of-cost-or-net realizable value.

IFRS Self-Test Questions

1. Which of the following should *not* be included in the inventory of a company using IFRS?
   (a) Goods held on consignment from another company.
   (b) Goods shipped on consignment to another company.
   (c) Goods in transit from another company shipped FOB shipping point.
   (d) None of the above.

2. Which method of inventory costing is prohibited under IFRS?
   (a) Specific identification.   (c) FIFO.
   (b) LIFO.   (d) Average-cost.

3. Yang Company purchased 2,000 widgets and has 400 widgets in its ending inventory at a cost of $90 each and a current replacement cost of $80 each. The net realizable value of each unit in the ending inventory is $70. The ending inventory under lower-of-cost-or-net realizable value is:
   (a) $36,000.   (c) $28,000.
   (b) $32,000.   (d) None of the above.

4. Specific identification:
   (a) must be used under IFRS if the inventory items are not interchangeable.
   (b) cannot be used under IFRS.
   (c) cannot be used under GAAP.
   (d) must be used under IFRS if it would result in the most conservative net income.

5. IFRS requires the following:
   (a) Ending inventory is written up and down to net realizable value each reporting period.
   (b) Ending inventory is written down to net realizable value but cannot be written up.
   (c) Ending inventory is written down to net realizable value and may be written up in future periods to its net realizable value but not above its original cost.
   (d) Ending inventory is written down to net realizable value and may be written up in future periods to its net realizable value.

IFRS Concepts and Application

IFRS6-1 Briefly describe some of the similarities and differences between GAAP and IFRS with respect to the accounting for inventories.

IFRS6-2 LaTour Inc. is based in France and prepares its financial statements in accordance with IFRS. In 2012, it reported cost of goods sold of €578 million and average inventory of €154 million. Briefly discuss how analysis of LaTour's inventory turnover ratio (and comparisons to a company using GAAP) might be affected by differences in inventory accounting between IFRS and GAAP.

IFRS6-3   Franklin Company has the following four items in its ending inventory as of December 31, 2012. The company uses the lower-of-cost-or-net realizable value approach for inventory valuation following IFRS.

Item No.	Cost	Net Realizable Value
AB	$1,700	$1,400
TRX	2,200	2,300
NWA	7,800	7,100
SGH	3,000	3,700

Compute the lower-of-cost-or-net realizable value.

International Financial Reporting Problem: *Zetar plc*

IFRS6-4   The financial statements of Zetar plc are presented in Appendix C. The company's complete annual report, including the notes to its financial statements, is available at *www.zetarplc.com.*

Instructions

Using the notes to the company's financial statements, answer the following questions.

(a) What cost flow assumption does the company use to value inventory?

(b) What was the amount of expense that the company reported for inventory write-downs during 2009?

(c) What amount of raw materials, work in process, and finished goods inventory did the company report at April 30, 2009?

Answers to IFRS Self-Test Questions
1. a   2. b   3. c   4. a   5. c

The Navigator

✔   **Remember to go back to the Navigator box on the chapter opening page and check off your completed work.**

CHAPTER7

Accounting Information Systems

Study Objectives

After studying this chapter, you should be able to:

[1] Identify the basic concepts of an accounting information system.

[2] Describe the nature and purpose of a subsidiary ledger.

[3] Explain how companies use special journals in journalizing.

[4] Indicate how companies post a multi-column journal.

The Navigator

✔ [The Navigator]

● Scan Study Objectives	○
● Read Feature Story	○
● Read Preview	○
● Read text and answer **Do it!** p. 321 ○ p. 335 ○	
● Work Comprehensive **Do it!** p. 335	○
● Review Summary of Study Objectives	○
● Answer Self-Test Questions	○
● Complete Assignments	○
● Go to *WileyPLUS* for practice and tutorials	○
● Read A Look at IFRS p. 357	○

Feature Story

QUICKBOOKS® HELPS THIS RETAILER SELL GUITARS

Starting a small business requires many decisions. For example, you have to decide where to locate, how much space you need, how much inventory to have, how many employees to hire, and where to advertise. Small business owners are typically so concerned about the product and sales side of their business that they often do not give enough thought to something that is critical to their success—how to keep track of financial results.

Small business owners today can choose either manual or computerized accounting systems. For example, Paul and Laura West are the owners of the first independent dealership of Carvin guitars and professional audio equipment. When they founded their company, in Sacramento, California, they decided to purchase a computerized accounting system that would integrate

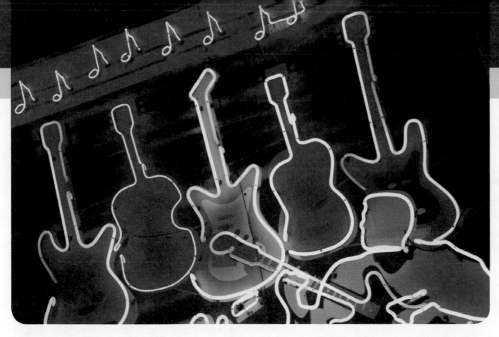

many aspects of their retail operations. They wanted their accounting software to manage their inventory of guitars and amplifiers, ring up sales, record and report financial data, and process credit card and debit card transactions. They evaluated a number of options and chose QuickBooks® by Intuit Inc.

QuickBooks®, like most other popular software packages, has programs designed for the needs of a specific business, which in this case is retailing. This QuickBooks® retailing package automatically collects sales information from its point-of-sale scanning devices. It also keeps track of inventory levels and automatically generates purchase orders for popular items when re-order points are reached. It even supports sales efforts by compiling a customer database from which the Wests send out targeted direct mailings to potential customers. The computerized system enables data files to be emailed to the company's accountant. This keeps costs down and makes it easier and more efficient to generate financial reports as needed. The Wests believe that the investment in the computerized system has saved them time and money, and allowed them to spend more time on other aspects of their business.

Source: Intuit Inc., "QuickBooks® and ProAdvisor® Help Make Guitar Store a Hit," *Journal of Accountancy* (May 2006), p. 101.

The Navigator

Inside CHAPTER7

As you see from the Feature Story, a reliable information system is a necessity for any company. Whether companies use pen, pencil, or computers in maintaining accounting records, certain principles and procedures apply. The purpose of this chapter is to explain and illustrate these features.

The content and organization of Chapter 7 are as follows.

Accounting Information Systems		
Basic Concepts of Accounting Information Systems	**Subsidiary Ledgers**	**Special Journals**
• Computerized accounting systems • Manual accounting systems	• Example • Advantages	• Sales journal • Cash receipts journal • Purchases journal • Cash payments journal • Effects of special journals on general journal

✔
The Navigator

Basic Concepts of Accounting Information Systems

Study Objective [1]
Identify the basic concepts of an accounting information system.

The **accounting information system** collects and processes transaction data and communicates financial information to decision makers. It includes each of the steps in the accounting cycle that you studied in earlier chapters. It also includes the documents that provide evidence of the transactions, and the records, trial balances, worksheets, and financial statements that result. An **accounting system** may be either manual or computerized. Most businesses these days use some sort of computerized accounting system, whether it is an off-the-shelf system for small businesses, like QuickBooks or Peachtree, or a more complex custom-made system.

Efficient and effective accounting information systems are based on certain basic principles. These principles, as described in Illustration 7-1, are (1) cost-effectiveness, (2) usefulness, and (3) flexibility. If the accounting system is cost-effective, provides useful output, and has the flexibility to meet future needs, it can contribute to both individual and organizational goals.

Computerized Accounting Systems

Many small businesses eventually replace their manual accounting system with a computerized general ledger accounting system. **General ledger accounting systems** are software programs that integrate the various accounting functions related to sales, purchases, receivables, payables, cash receipts and disbursements, and payroll. They also generate financial statements. Computerized systems have a number of advantages over manual systems. First, the company typically enters data only once in a computerized system. Second, because the computer does most steps automatically, many errors resulting from human intervention in a manual system,

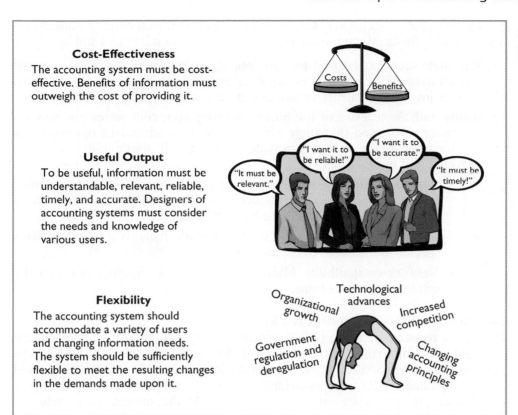

Cost-Effectiveness

The accounting system must be cost-effective. Benefits of information must outweigh the cost of providing it.

Useful Output

To be useful, information must be understandable, relevant, reliable, timely, and accurate. Designers of accounting systems must consider the needs and knowledge of various users.

Flexibility

The accounting system should accommodate a variety of users and changing information needs. The system should be sufficiently flexible to meet the resulting changes in the demands made upon it.

such as errors in posting or preparation of financial statements, are eliminated. Computerized systems also provide information up-to-the-minute. More timely information results in better business decisions. Many different general ledger software packages are available.

CHOOSING A SOFTWARE PACKAGE

To identify the right software for your business, you must understand your company's operations. For example, consider its needs with regard to inventory, billing, payroll, and cash management. In addition, the company might have specific needs that are not supported by all software systems. For example, you might want to track employees' hours on individual jobs or to extract information for determining sales commissions. Choosing the right system is critical because installation of even a basic system is time-consuming, and learning a new system will require many hours of employee time.

ENTRY-LEVEL SOFTWARE

Software publishers tend to classify businesses into groups based on revenue and the number of employees. Companies with revenues of less than $5 million and up to 20 employees generally use **entry-level programs**. The two leading entry-level programs are Intuit's QuickBooks and Sage Software's Peachtree. These programs control more than 90% of the market. Each of these entry-level programs comes in many different industry-specific versions. For example, some are designed for very specific industry applications such as restaurants, retailing, construction, manufacturing, or nonprofit. *(This textbook's general ledger system can be used in working many of the problems in this textbook.)*

Quality entry-level packages typically involve more than recording transactions and preparing financial statements. Here are some common features and benefits:

- **Easy data access and report preparation.** Users can easily access information related to specific customers or suppliers. For example, you can view all transactions, invoices, payments, as well as contact information for a specific client.
- **Audit trail.** As a result of the Sarbanes-Oxley Act, companies are now far more concerned that their accounting system minimizes opportunities for fraud. Many programs provide an "audit trail" that enables the tracking of all transactions.
  - **Internal controls.** Some systems have an internal accounting review that identifies suspicious transactions or likely mistakes such as wrong account numbers or duplicate transactions.
  - **Customization.** This feature enables the company to create data fields specific to the needs of its business.
  - **Network-compatibility.** Multiple users in the company can access the system at the same time.

Ethics Note

Entire books and movies have used computer-system tampering as a major theme. Most programmers would agree that tamper-proofing and debugging programs are the most difficult and time-consuming phases of their jobs.

ENTERPRISE RESOURCE PLANNING SYSTEMS

Enterprise resource planning (ERP) systems are typically used by manufacturing companies with more than 500 employees and $500 million in sales. The best-known of these systems are SAPAG's SAP (the most widely used), J.D. Edwards' ERP, and Oracle's Financials. ERP systems go far beyond the functions of an entry-level general ledger package. They integrate all aspects of the organization, including accounting, sales, human resource management, and manufacturing. Because of the complexity of an ERP system, implementation can take three years and cost five times as much as the purchase price of the system. Purchase and implementation of ERP systems can cost from $250,000 to as much as $50 million for the largest multinational corporations.

*E*THICS *I*NSIGHT

Curbing Fraudulent Activity with Software

The Sarbanes-Oxley Act (SOX) requires that companies demonstrate that they have adequate controls in place to detect significant fraudulent behavior by employees. Recently, about 15% of publicly traded companies reported at least one material weakness in their controls that needed to be remedied.

The SOX requirements have created a huge market for software that can monitor and trace every recorded transaction and adjusting entry. This enables companies to pinpoint who used the accounting system and when they used it. These systems also require "electronic signatures" by employees for all significant transactions. Such signatures verify that employees have followed all required procedures, and that all actions are properly authorized. SOX-related technology spending was estimated to be approximately $2 billion at one time. One firm that specializes in compliance software had 10 clients prior to SOX and 250 after SOX.

Source: W. M. Bulkeley and C. Forelle, "Anti-Crime Program: How Corporate Scandals Gave Tech Firms a New Business Line," *Wall Street Journal* (December 9, 2005), p. A1.

? Why might this software help reduce fraudulent activity by employees? (See page 357.)

Manual Accounting Systems

Manual accounting systems perform each of the steps in the accounting cycle by hand. For example, someone manually enters each accounting transaction in the journal and manually posts each to the ledger. Other manual computations must be made to obtain ledger account balances and to prepare a trial balance and financial statements. In the remainder of this chapter, we illustrate the use of a manual system.

You might be wondering, "Why cover manual accounting systems if the real world uses computerized systems?" First, small businesses still abound. Most of them begin operations with manual accounting systems and convert to computerized systems as the business grows. You may work in a small business, or start your own someday, so it is useful to know how a manual system works. Second, to understand what computerized accounting systems do, you also need to understand manual accounting systems.

The manual accounting system represented in the first six chapters of this textbook is satisfactory in a company with a low volume of transactions. However, in most companies, it is necessary to add additional ledgers and journals to the accounting system to record transaction data efficiently.

Subsidiary Ledgers

Imagine a business that has several thousand charge (credit) customers and shows the transactions with these customers in only one general ledger account—Accounts Receivable. It would be nearly impossible to determine the balance owed by an individual customer at any specific time. Similarly, the amount payable to one creditor would be difficult to locate quickly from a single Accounts Payable account in the general ledger.

Study Objective [2]
Describe the nature and purpose of a subsidiary ledger.

Instead, companies use subsidiary ledgers to keep track of individual balances. A **subsidiary ledger** is a group of accounts with a common characteristic (for example, all accounts receivable). It is an addition to, and an expansion of, the general ledger. The subsidiary ledger frees the general ledger from the details of individual balances.

Two common subsidiary ledgers are:

1. The **accounts receivable** (or **customers'**) **subsidiary ledger**, which collects transaction data of individual customers.

2. The **accounts payable** (or **creditors'**) **subsidiary ledger**, which collects transaction data of individual creditors.

In each of these subsidiary ledgers, companies usually arrange individual accounts in alphabetical order.

A general ledger account summarizes the detailed data from a subsidiary ledger. For example, the detailed data from the accounts receivable subsidiary ledger are summarized in Accounts Receivable in the general ledger. The general ledger account that summarizes subsidiary ledger data is called a **control account**. Illustration 7-2 (page 320) presents an overview of the relationship of subsidiary ledgers to the general ledger. There, the general ledger control accounts and subsidiary ledger accounts are in green. Note that cash and owner's capital in this illustration are not control accounts because there are no subsidiary ledger accounts related to these accounts.

At the end of an accounting period, each general ledger control account balance must equal the composite balance of the individual accounts in the related subsidiary ledger. For example, the balance in Accounts Payable in Illustration 7-2 must equal the total of the subsidiary balances of Creditors X + Y + Z.

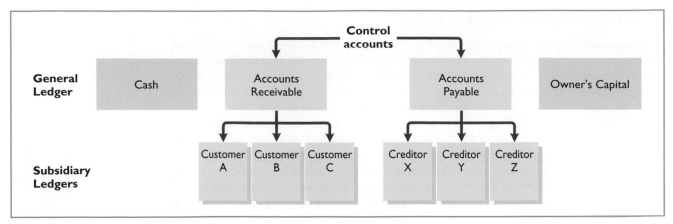

Illustration 7-2
Relationship of general ledger
and subsidiary ledgers

Subsidiary Ledger Example

Illustration 7-3
Relationship between general
and subsidiary ledgers

Illustration 7-3 provides an example of a control account and subsidiary ledger for Pujols Enterprises. (Due to space considerations, the explanation column in these accounts is not shown in this and subsequent illustrations.) Illustration 7-3 is based on the transactions listed in Illustration 7-4.

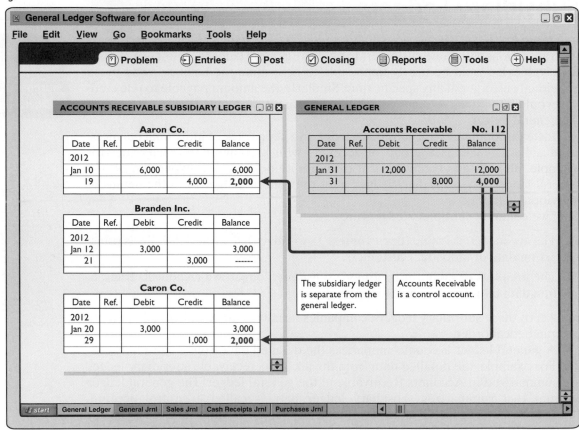

Illustration 7-4
Sales and collection
transactions

	Credit Sales			Collections on Account	
Jan. 10	Aaron Co.	$ 6,000	Jan. 19	Aaron Co.	$4,000
12	Branden Inc.	3,000	21	Branden Inc.	3,000
20	Caron Co.	3,000	29	Caron Co.	1,000
		$12,000			$8,000

Pujols can reconcile the total debits ($12,000) and credits ($8,000) in Accounts Receivable in the general ledger to the detailed debits and credits in the subsidiary accounts. Also, the balance of $4,000 in the control account agrees with the total of the balances in the individual accounts (Aaron Co. $2,000 + Branden Inc. $0 + Caron Co. $2,000) in the subsidiary ledger.

As Illustration 7-3 shows, companies make monthly postings to the control accounts in the general ledger. This practice allows them to prepare monthly financial statements. Companies post to the individual accounts in the subsidiary ledger daily. Daily posting ensures that account information is current. This enables the company to monitor credit limits, bill customers, and answer inquiries from customers about their account balances.

Advantages of Subsidiary Ledgers

Subsidiary ledgers have several advantages:

1. **They show in a single account transactions affecting one customer or one creditor**, thus providing up-to-date information on specific account balances.
2. **They free the general ledger of excessive details.** As a result, a trial balance of the general ledger does not contain vast numbers of individual account balances.
3. **They help locate errors in individual accounts** by reducing the number of accounts in one ledger and by using control accounts.
4. **They make possible a division of labor** in posting. One employee can post to the general ledger while someone else posts to the subsidiary ledgers.

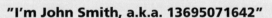

ACCOUNTING ACROSS THE ORGANIZATION

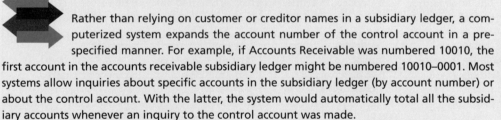

"I'm John Smith, a.k.a. 13695071642"

Rather than relying on customer or creditor names in a subsidiary ledger, a computerized system expands the account number of the control account in a pre-specified manner. For example, if Accounts Receivable was numbered 10010, the first account in the accounts receivable subsidiary ledger might be numbered 10010–0001. Most systems allow inquiries about specific accounts in the subsidiary ledger (by account number) or about the control account. With the latter, the system would automatically total all the subsidiary accounts whenever an inquiry to the control account was made.

? Why use numbers to identify names in a computerized system? (See page 357.)

Do it!

Subsidiary Ledgers

Presented below is information related to Sims Company for its first month of operations. Determine the balances that appear in the accounts payable subsidiary ledger. What Accounts Payable balance appears in the general ledger at the end of January?

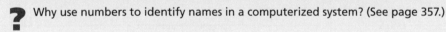

	Credit Purchases			Cash Paid	
Jan. 5	Devon Co.	$11,000	Jan. 9	Devon Co.	$7,000
11	Shelby Co.	7,000	14	Shelby Co.	2,000
22	Taylor Co.	14,000	27	Taylor Co.	9,000

action plan

✔ Subtract cash paid from credit purchases to determine the balances in the accounts payable subsidiary ledger.

✔ Sum the individual balances to determine the Accounts Payable balance.

Solution

Subsidiary ledger balances:

Devon Co. $4,000 ($11,000 − $7,000)

Shelby Co. $5,000 ($7,000 − $2,000)

Taylor Co. $5,000 ($14,000 − $9,000)

General ledger Accounts Payable balance: $14,000 ($4,000 + $5,000 + $5,000)

Related exercise material: BE7-4, BE7-5, E7-1, E7-2, E7-4, E7-5, and **Do it!** 7-1.

✔
The Navigator

Special Journals

Study Objective [3]

Explain how companies use special journals in journalizing.

So far you have learned to journalize transactions in a two-column general journal and post each entry to the general ledger. This procedure is satisfactory in only the very smallest companies. To expedite journalizing and posting, most companies use special journals **in addition to the general journal**.

Companies use special journals to record similar types of transactions. Examples are all sales of merchandise on account, or all cash receipts. The types of transactions that occur frequently in a company determine what special journals the company uses. Most merchandising enterprises record daily transactions using the journals shown in Illustration 7-5.

Illustration 7-5
Use of special journals and the general journal

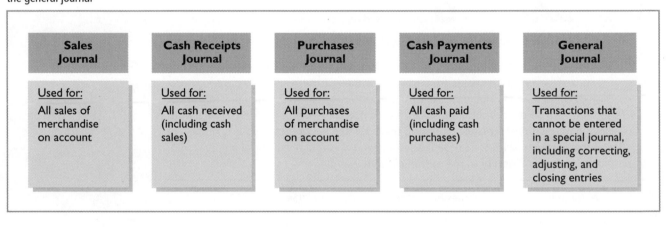

If a transaction cannot be recorded in a special journal, the company records it in the general journal. For example, if a company had special journals for only the four types of transactions listed above, it would record purchase returns and allowances in the general journal. Similarly, **correcting**, **adjusting**, **and closing entries are recorded in the general journal**. In some situations, companies might use special journals other than those listed above. For example, when sales returns and allowances are frequent, a company might use a special journal to record these transactions.

Special journals **permit greater division of labor** because several people can record entries in different journals at the same time. For example, one employee may journalize all cash receipts, and another may journalize all credit sales. Also, the use of special journals **reduces the time needed to complete the posting process**. With special journals, companies may post some accounts monthly, instead of daily, as we will illustrate later in the chapter. On the following pages, we discuss the four special journals shown in Illustration 7-5.

Sales Journal

In the sales journal, companies record **sales of merchandise on account**. Cash sales of merchandise go in the cash receipts journal. Credit sales of assets other than merchandise go in the general journal.

JOURNALIZING CREDIT SALES

To demonstrate use of a sales journal, we will use data for Karns Wholesale Supply, which uses a **perpetual inventory system**. Under this system, each entry in the sales journal results in one entry **at selling price** and another entry **at cost**. The entry at selling price is a debit to Accounts Receivable (a control account) and a credit of equal amount to Sales Revenue. The entry at cost is a debit to Cost of Goods Sold and a credit of equal amount to Inventory (a control account). Using a sales journal with two amount columns, the company can show on only one line a sales transaction at both selling price and cost. Illustration 7-6 shows this two-column sales journal of Karns Wholesale Supply, using assumed credit sales transactions (for sales invoices 101–107).

Helpful Hint

Postings are also made daily to individual ledger accounts in the inventory subsidiary ledger to maintain a perpetual inventory.

General Ledger Software for Accounting _ □ ☒

File   Edit   View   Go   Bookmarks   Tools   Help

⌇ Problem   ⌁ Entries   ▢ Post   ☑ Closing   ▦ Reports   ▤ Tools   ⊞ Help

SALES JOURNAL   SI ▢▢■

Date	Account Debited	Invoice No.	Ref.	Accts. Receivable Dr. Sales Revenue Cr.	Cost of Goods Sold Dr. Inventory Cr.
2012					
May 3	Abbot Sisters	101		10,600	6,360
7	Babson Co.	102		11,350	7,370
14	Carson Bros.	103		7,800	5,070
19	Deli Co.	104		9,300	6,510
21	Abbot Sisters	105		15,400	10,780
24	Deli Co.	106		21,210	15,900
27	Babson Co.	107		14,570	10,200
				90,230	62,190

▮ start   General Ledger   General Jrnl   Sales Jrnl   Cash Receipts Jrnl   Purchases Jrnl   ◄ ‖

Illustration 7-6
Journalizing the sales journal—perpetual inventory system

Note that, unlike the general journal, an explanation is not required for each entry in a special journal. Also, note that use of prenumbered invoices ensures that all invoices are journalized. Finally, note that the reference (Ref.) column is not used in journalizing. It is used in posting the sales journal, as explained in the next section.

POSTING THE SALES JOURNAL

Companies make daily postings from the sales journal **to the individual accounts receivable** in the subsidiary ledger. Posting **to the general ledger** is done **monthly**. Illustration 7-7 (page 324) shows both the daily and monthly postings.

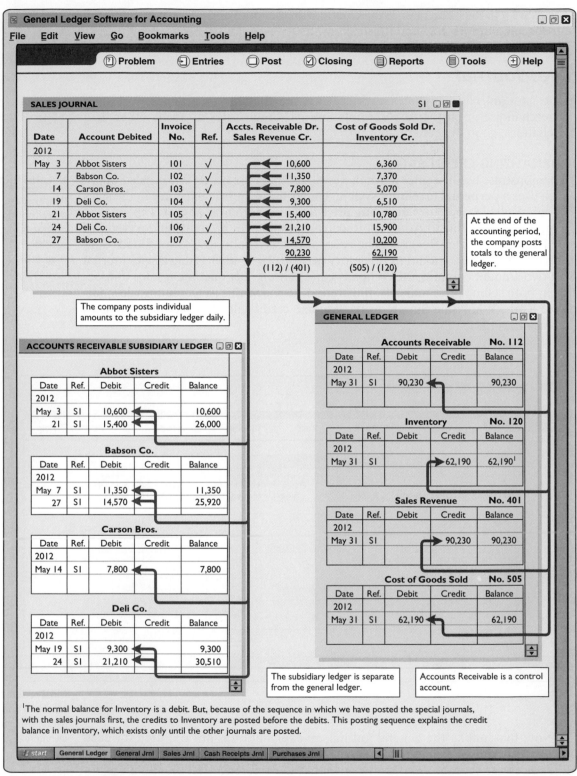

Illustration 7-7
Posting the sales journal

A check mark (✓) is inserted in the reference posting column to indicate that the daily posting to the customer's account has been made. If the subsidiary ledger accounts were numbered, the account number would be entered in place of the check mark. At the end of the month, Karns posts the column totals of the sales journal to the general ledger. Here, the column totals are as follows: From the selling-price column, a debit of $90,230 to Accounts Receivable (account No. 112), and a credit of \$90,230 to Sales Revenue (account No. 401). From the cost column, a debit of \$62,190 to Cost of Goods Sold (account No. 505), and a credit of \$62,190 to Inventory (account No. 120). Karns inserts the account numbers below the column totals to indicate that the postings have been made. In both the general ledger and subsidiary ledger accounts, the reference **S1** indicates that the posting came from page 1 of the sales journal.

PROVING THE LEDGERS

The next step is to "prove" the ledgers. To do so, Karns must determine two things: (1) The total of the general ledger debit balances must equal the total of the general ledger credit balances. (2) The sum of the subsidiary ledger balances must equal the balance in the control account. Illustration 7-8 shows the proof of the postings from the sales journal to the general and subsidiary ledgers.

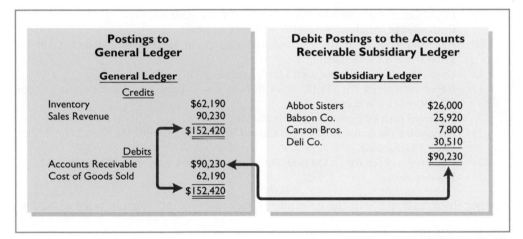

Illustration 7-8
Proving the equality of the postings from the sales journal

ADVANTAGES OF THE SALES JOURNAL

The use of a special journal to record sales on account has a number of advantages. First, the one-line entry for each sales transaction saves time. In the sales journal, it is not necessary to write out the four account titles for each transaction. Second, only totals, rather than individual entries, are posted to the general ledger. This saves posting time and reduces the possibilities of errors in posting. Finally, a division of labor results because one individual can take responsibility for the sales journal.

Cash Receipts Journal

In the **cash receipts journal**, companies record all receipts of cash. The most common types of cash receipts are cash sales of merchandise and collections of accounts receivable. Many other possibilities exist, such as receipt of money from bank loans and cash proceeds from disposal of equipment. A one- or two-column cash receipts journal would not have space enough for all possible cash receipt transactions. Therefore, companies use a multiple-column cash receipts journal.

Generally, a cash receipts journal includes the following columns: debit columns for Cash and Sales Discounts, and credit columns for Accounts Receivable, Sales Revenue, and "Other Accounts." Companies use the "Other Accounts" category when the cash receipt does not involve a cash sale or a collection of accounts receivable. Under a perpetual inventory system, each sales entry also is accompanied by an entry that debits Cost of Goods Sold and credits Inventory for the cost of the merchandise sold. Illustration 7-9 shows a six-column cash receipts journal.

Companies may use additional credit columns if these columns significantly reduce postings to a specific account. For example, a loan company, such as Household International, receives thousands of cash collections from customers. Using separate credit columns for Loans Receivable and Interest Revenue, rather than the Other Accounts credit column, would reduce postings.

JOURNALIZING CASH RECEIPTS TRANSACTIONS

To illustrate the journalizing of cash receipts transactions, we will continue with the May transactions of Karns Wholesale Supply. Collections from customers relate to the entries recorded in the sales journal in Illustration 7-6. The entries in the cash receipts journal are based on the following cash receipts.

May	1	D. A. Karns makes an investment of $5,000 in the business.
	7	Cash sales of merchandise total $1,900 (cost, $1,240).
	10	Received a check for $10,388 from Abbot Sisters in payment of invoice No. 101 for $10,600 less a 2% discount.
	12	Cash sales of merchandise total $2,600 (cost, $1,690).
	17	Received a check for $11,123 from Babson Co. in payment of invoice No. 102 for $11,350 less a 2% discount.
	22	Received cash by signing a note for $6,000.
	23	Received a check for $7,644 from Carson Bros. in full for invoice No. 103 for $7,800 less a 2% discount.
	28	Received a check for $9,114 from Deli Co. in full for invoice No. 104 for $9,300 less a 2% discount.

Further information about the columns in the cash receipts journal is listed below.

Debit Columns:

1. **Cash.** Karns enters in this column the amount of cash actually received in each transaction. The column total indicates the total cash receipts for the month.

2. **Sales Discounts.** Karns includes a Sales Discounts column in its cash receipts journal. By doing so, it does not need to enter sales discount items in the general journal. As a result, the cash receipts journal shows on one line the collection of an account receivable within the discount period.

Credit Columns:

3. **Accounts Receivable.** Karns uses the Accounts Receivable column to record cash collections on account. The amount entered here is the amount to be credited to the individual customer's account.

4. **Sales Revenue.** The Sales Revenue column records all cash sales of merchandise. Cash sales of other assets (plant assets, for example) are not reported in this column.

5. **Other Accounts.** Karns uses the Other Accounts column whenever the credit is other than to Accounts Receivable or Sales Revenue. For example, in the first entry, Karns enters $5,000 as a credit to Owner's Capital. This column is often referred to as the sundry accounts column.

Debit and Credit Column:

6. **Cost of Goods Sold and Inventory.** This column records debits to Cost of Goods Sold and credits to Inventory.

Helpful Hint

When is an account title entered in the "Account Credited" column of the cash receipts journal? Answer: A *subsidiary ledger* account is entered when the entry involves a collection of accounts receivable. A *general ledger* account is entered when the account is not shown in a special column (and an amount must be entered in the Other Accounts column). Otherwise, no account is shown in the "Account Credited" column.

Illustration 7-9
Journalizing and posting the cash receipts journal

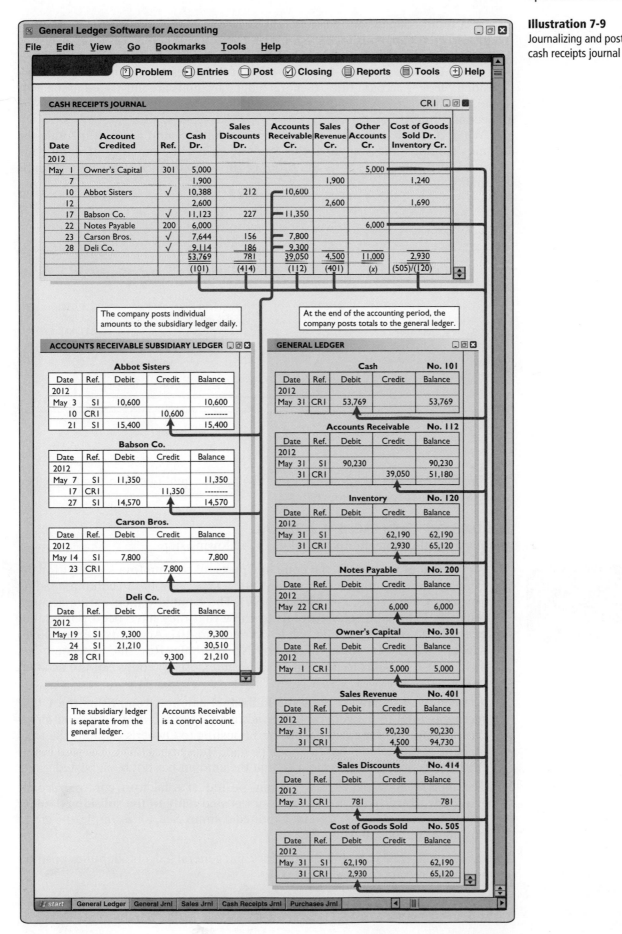

In a multi-column journal, generally only one line is needed for each entry. Debit and credit amounts for each line must be equal. When Karns journalizes the collection from Abbot Sisters on May 10, for example, three amounts are indicated. Note also that the Account Credited column identifies both general ledger and subsidiary ledger account titles. General ledger accounts are illustrated in the May 1 and May 22 entries. A subsidiary account is illustrated in the May 10 entry for the collection from Abbot Sisters.

When Karns has finished journalizing a multi-column journal, it totals the amount columns and compares the totals to prove the equality of debits and credits. Illustration 7-10 shows the proof of the equality of Karns's cash receipts journal.

Illustration 7-10
Proving the equality of the cash receipts journal

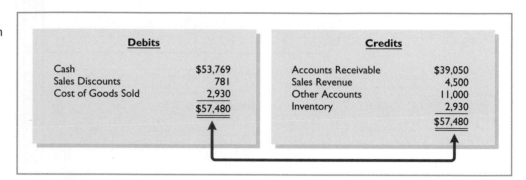

Debits		Credits	
Cash	$53,769	Accounts Receivable	$39,050
Sales Discounts	781	Sales Revenue	4,500
Cost of Goods Sold	2,930	Other Accounts	11,000
	$57,480	Inventory	2,930
			$57,480

Totaling the columns of a journal and proving the equality of the totals is called **footing** and **cross-footing** a journal.

POSTING THE CASH RECEIPTS JOURNAL

Posting a multi-column journal involves the following steps.

1. **At the end of the month**, the company posts all column totals, except for the Other Accounts total, to the account title(s) specified in the column heading (such as Cash or Accounts Receivable). The company then enters account numbers below the column totals to show that they have been posted. For example, Karns has posted Cash to account No. 101, Accounts Receivable to account No. 112, Inventory to account No. 120, Sales Revenue to account No. 401, Sales Discounts to account No. 414, and Cost of Goods Sold to account No. 505.

2. The company **separately posts the individual amounts comprising the Other Accounts total** to the general ledger accounts specified in the Account Credited column. See, for example, the credit posting to Owner's Capital. The total amount of this column has not been posted. The symbol (X) is inserted below the total to this column to indicate that the amount has not been posted.

3. The individual amounts in a column, posted in total to a control account (Accounts Receivable, in this case), are posted **daily to the subsidiary ledger** account specified in the Account Credited column. See, for example, the credit posting of $10,600 to Abbot Sisters.

The symbol **CR**, used in both the subsidiary and general ledgers, identifies postings from the cash receipts journal.

PROVING THE LEDGERS

After posting of the cash receipts journal is completed, Karns proves the ledgers. As shown in Illustration 7-11, the general ledger totals agree. Also, the sum of the subsidiary ledger balances equals the control account balance.

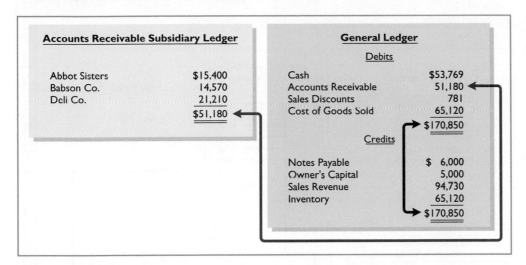

Illustration 7-11
Proving the ledgers after posting the sales and the cash receipts journals

Purchases Journal

In the **purchases journal**, companies record all purchases of merchandise on account. Each entry in this journal results in a debit to Inventory and a credit to Accounts Payable. Illustration 7-13 (on page 330) shows the purchases journal for Karns Wholesale Supply.

When using a one-column purchases journal (as in Illustration 7-13), a company cannot journalize other types of purchases on account or cash purchases in it. For example, in the purchases journal in Illustration 7-13, Karns would have to record credit purchases of equipment or supplies in the general journal. Likewise, all cash purchases would be entered in the cash payments journal. As illustrated later, companies that make numerous credit purchases for items other than merchandise often expand the purchases journal to a multi-column format. (See Illustration 7-15 on page 331.)

JOURNALIZING CREDIT PURCHASES OF MERCHANDISE

The journalizing procedure is similar to that for a sales journal. Companies make entries in the purchases journal from purchase invoices. In contrast to the sales journal, the purchases journal may not have an invoice number column, because invoices received from different suppliers will not be in numerical sequence. To ensure that they record all purchase invoices, some companies consecutively number each invoice upon receipt and then use an internal document number column in the purchases journal. The entries for Karns Wholesale Supply are based on the assumed credit purchases listed in Illustration 7-12.

Illustration 7-12
Credit purchases transactions

Date	Supplier	Amount
5/6	Jasper Manufacturing Inc.	$11,000
5/10	Eaton and Howe Inc.	7,200
5/14	Fabor and Son	6,900
5/19	Jasper Manufacturing Inc.	17,500
5/26	Fabor and Son	8,700
5/29	Eaton and Howe Inc.	12,600

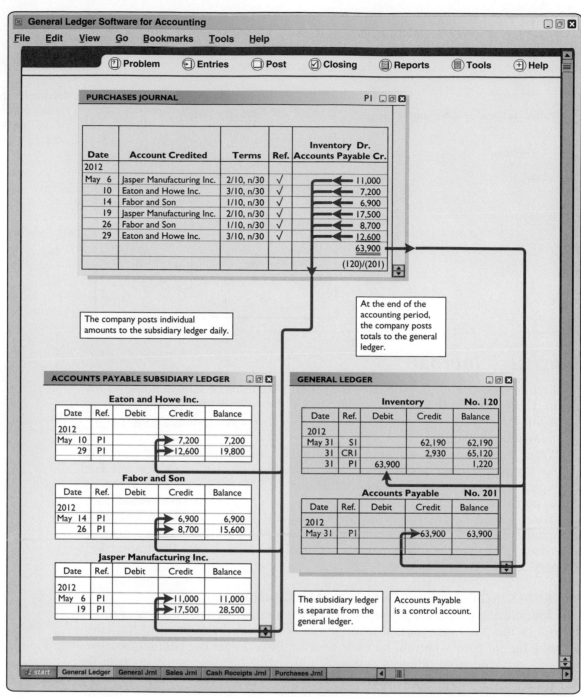

Illustration 7-13
Journalizing and posting the purchases journal

POSTING THE PURCHASES JOURNAL

The procedures for posting the purchases journal are similar to those for the sales journal. In this case, Karns makes **daily** postings to the **accounts payable ledger**; it makes **monthly** postings to Inventory and Accounts Payable in the general ledger. In both ledgers, Karns uses **P1** in the reference column to show that the postings are from page 1 of the purchases journal.

Proof of the equality of the postings from the purchases journal to both ledgers is shown in Illustration 7-14.

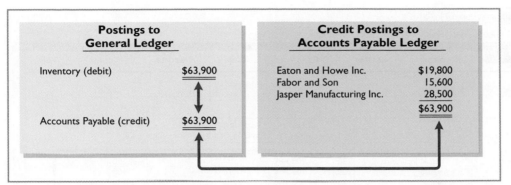

Illustration 7-14
Proving the equality of the
purchases journal

EXPANDING THE PURCHASES JOURNAL

As noted earlier, some companies expand the purchases journal to include all types of purchases on account. Instead of one column for inventory and accounts payable, they use a multiple-column format. This format usually includes a credit column for Accounts Payable and debit columns for purchases of Inventory, Supplies, and Other Accounts. Illustration 7-15 shows a multi-column purchases journal for Hanover Co. The posting procedures are similar to those shown earlier for posting the cash receipts journal.

Helpful Hint

A single-column purchases journal needs only to be footed to prove the equality of debits and credits.

Illustration 7-15
Multi-column purchases journal

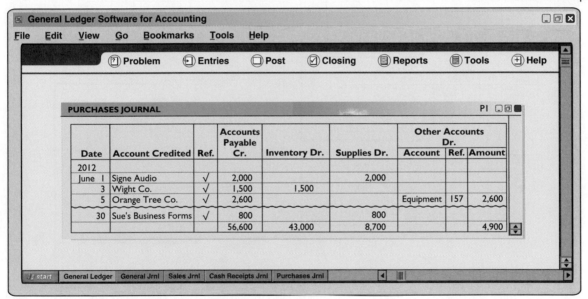

Cash Payments Journal

In a **cash payments (cash disbursements) journal**, companies record all disbursements of cash. Entries are made from prenumbered checks. Because companies make cash payments for various purposes, the cash payments journal has multiple columns. Illustration 7-16 (page 332) shows a four-column journal.

JOURNALIZING CASH PAYMENTS TRANSACTIONS

The procedures for journalizing transactions in this journal are similar to those for the cash receipts journal. Karns records each transaction on one line, and for each line there must be equal debit and credit amounts. The entries in the cash payments

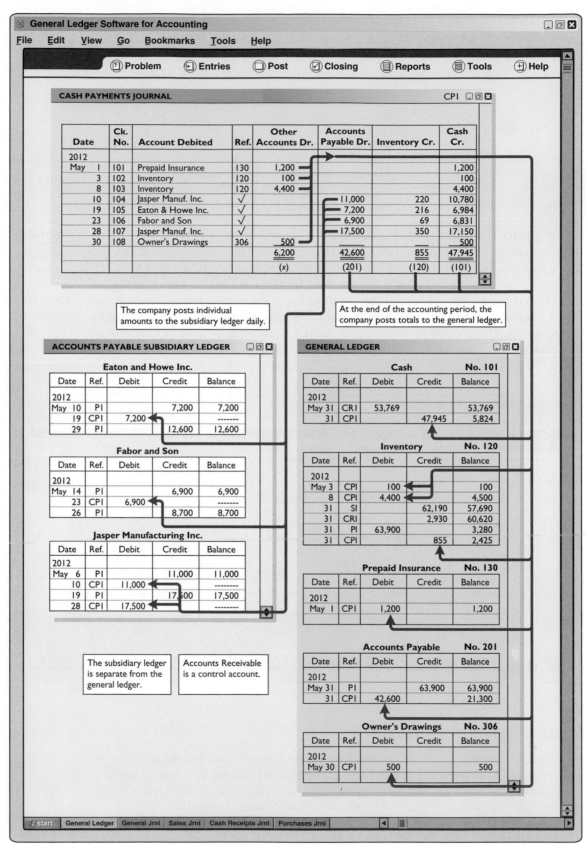

Illustration 7-16
Journalizing and posting the
cash payments journal

journal in Illustration 7-16 are based on the following transactions for Karns Whole-sale Supply.

May 1   Issued check No. 101 for $1,200 for the annual premium on a fire insurance policy.
      3   Issued check No. 102 for $100 in payment of freight when terms were FOB shipping point.
      8   Issued check No. 103 for $4,400 for the purchase of merchandise.
     10   Sent check No. 104 for $10,780 to Jasper Manufacturing Inc. in payment of May 6 invoice for $11,000 less a 2% discount.
     19   Mailed check No. 105 for $6,984 to Eaton and Howe Inc. in payment of May 10 invoice for $7,200 less a 3% discount.
     23   Sent check No. 106 for $6,831 to Fabor and Son in payment of May 14 invoice for $6,900 less a 1% discount.
     28   Sent check No. 107 for $17,150 to Jasper Manufacturing Inc. in payment of May 19 invoice for $17,500 less a 2% discount.
     30   Issued check No. 108 for $500 to D. A. Karns as a cash withdrawal for personal use.

Note that whenever Karns enters an amount in the Other Accounts column, it must identify a specific general ledger account in the Account Debited column. The entries for checks No. 101, 102, 103, and 108 illustrate this situation. Similarly, Karns must identify a subsidiary account in the Account Debited column whenever it enters an amount in the Accounts Payable column. See, for example, the entry for check No. 104.

After Karns journalizes the cash payments journal, it totals the columns. The totals are then balanced to prove the equality of debits and credits.

POSTING THE CASH PAYMENTS JOURNAL

The procedures for posting the cash payments journal are similar to those for the cash receipts journal. Karns posts the amounts recorded in the Accounts Payable column individually to the subsidiary ledger and in total to the control account. It posts Inventory and Cash only in total at the end of the month. Transactions in the Other Accounts column are posted individually to the appropriate account(s) affected. The company does not post totals for the Other Accounts column.

Illustration 7-16 shows the posting of the cash payments journal. Note that Karns uses the symbol **CP** as the posting reference. After postings are completed, the company proves the equality of the debit and credit balances in the general ledger. In addition, the control account balances should agree with the subsidiary ledger total balance. Illustration 7-17 shows the agreement of these balances.

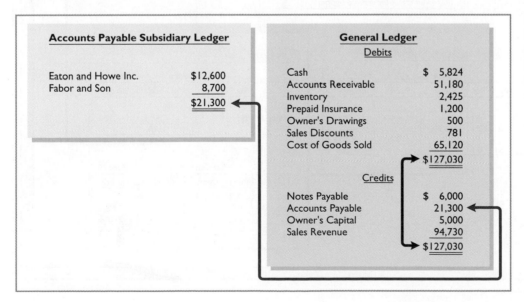

Illustration 7-17
Proving the ledgers after postings from the sales, cash receipts, purchases, and cash payments journals

Accounts Payable Subsidiary Ledger		General Ledger	
		Debits	
Eaton and Howe Inc.	$12,600	Cash	$ 5,824
Fabor and Son	8,700	Accounts Receivable	51,180
	$21,300	Inventory	2,425
		Prepaid Insurance	1,200
		Owner's Drawings	500
		Sales Discounts	781
		Cost of Goods Sold	65,120
			$127,030
		Credits	
		Notes Payable	$ 6,000
		Accounts Payable	21,300
		Owner's Capital	5,000
		Sales Revenue	94,730
			$127,030

Effects of Special Journals on the General Journal

Special journals for sales, purchases, and cash substantially reduce the number of entries that companies make in the general journal. **Only transactions that cannot be entered in a special journal are recorded in the general journal.** For example, a company may use the general journal to record such transactions as granting of credit to a customer for a sales return or allowance, granting of credit from a supplier for purchases returned, acceptance of a note receivable from a customer, and purchase of equipment by issuing a note payable. Also, **correcting, adjusting, and closing entries are made in the general journal**.

The general journal has columns for date, account title and explanation, reference, and debit and credit amounts. When control and subsidiary accounts are not involved, the procedures for journalizing and posting of transactions are the same as those described in earlier chapters. When control and subsidiary accounts *are* involved, companies make two changes from the earlier procedures:

1. In **journalizing**, they identify both the control and the subsidiary accounts.
2. In **posting**, there must be a **dual posting**: once to the control account and once to the subsidiary account.

To illustrate, assume that on May 31, Karns Wholesale Supply returns $500 of merchandise for credit to Fabor and Son. Illustration 7-18 shows the entry in the general journal and the posting of the entry. Note that if Karns receives cash instead of credit on this return, then it would record the transaction in the cash receipts journal.

Illustration 7-18
Journalizing and posting the general journal

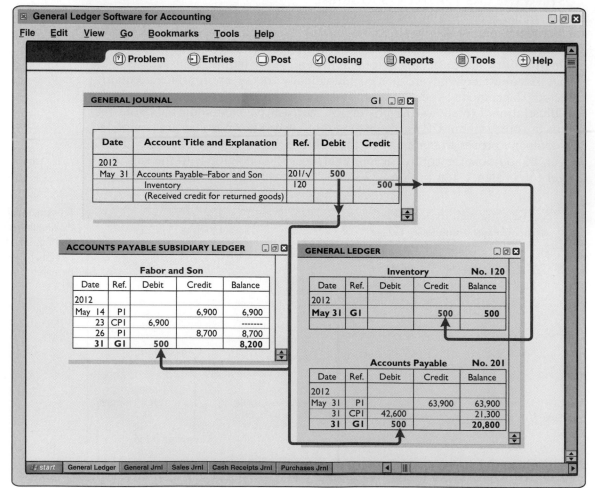

Note that the general journal indicates two accounts (Accounts Payable, and Fabor and Son) for the debit, and two postings ("201/✓") in the reference column. One debit is posted to the control account and another debit to the creditor's account in the subsidiary ledger.

Do it!

Swisher Company had the following transactions during March.

1. Collected cash on account from Oakland Company.
2. Purchased equipment by signing a note payable.
3. Sold merchandise on account.
4. Purchased merchandise on account.
5. Paid $2,400 for a 2-year insurance policy.

Identify the journal in which each of the transactions above is recorded.

Special Journals

action plan

✔ Determine if the transaction involves the receipt of cash (cash receipts journal) or the payment of cash (cash payments journal).

✔ Determine if the transaction is a sale of merchandise on account (sales journal) or a purchase of merchandise on account (purchases journal).

✔ All other transactions are recorded in the general journal.

Solution

1. Collected cash on account from Oakland Company.	Cash receipts journal
2. Purchased equipment by signing a note payable.	General journal
3. Sold merchandise on account.	Sales journal
4. Purchased merchandise on account.	Purchases journal
5. Paid $2,400 for a 2-year insurance policy.	Cash payments journal

Related exercise material: BE7-6, BE7-7, BE7-8, BE7-9, E7-6, E7-7, E7-8, E7-10, and **Do it!** 7-2.

The Navigator

COMPREHENSIVE

Do it!

Cassandra Wilson Company uses a six-column cash receipts journal with the following columns.

Cash (Dr.)   Other Accounts (Cr.)
Sales Discounts (Dr.)   Cost of Goods Sold (Dr.) and
Accounts Receivable (Cr.)   Inventory (Cr.)
Sales Revenue (Cr.)

Cash receipts transactions for the month of July 2012 are as follows.

July 3   Cash sales total $5,800 (cost, $3,480).
      5   Received a check for $6,370 from Jeltz Company in payment of an invoice dated June 26 for $6,500, terms 2/10, n/30.
      9   Cassandra Wilson, the proprietor, made an additional investment of $5,000 in cash in the business.
     10   Cash sales total $12,519 (cost, $7,511).
     12   Received a check for $7,275 from R. Eliot & Co. in payment of a $7,500 invoice dated July 3, terms 3/10, n/30.
     15   Received an advance of $700 cash for future services.
     20   Cash sales total $15,472 (cost, $9,283).
     22   Received a check for $5,880 from Beck Company in payment of $6,000 invoice dated July 13, terms 2/10, n/30.
     29   Cash sales total $17,660 (cost, $10,596).
     31   Received cash of $200 on interest earned for July.

action plan

✔ Record all cash receipts in the cash receipts journal.

✔ The "account credited" indicates items posted individually to the subsidiary ledger or to the general ledger.

✔ Record cash sales in the cash receipts journal—not in the sales journal.

✔ The total debits must equal the total credits.

Instructions

(a) Journalize the transactions in the cash receipts journal.

(b) Contrast the posting of the Accounts Receivable and Other Accounts columns.

Solution to Comprehensive Do it!

(a)

CASSANDRA WILSON COMPANY
Cash Receipts Journal   CR1

Date	Account Credited	Ref.	Cash Dr.	Sales Discounts Dr.	Accounts Receivable Cr.	Sales Revenue Cr.	Other Accounts Cr.	Cost of Goods Sold Dr. Inventory Cr.
2012								
7/3			5,800			5,800		3,480
5	Jeltz Company		6,370	130	6,500			
9	Owner's Capital		5,000				5,000	
10			12,519			12,519		7,511
12	R. Eliot & Co.		7,275	225	7,500			
15	Unearned Service Revenue		700				700	
20			15,472			15,472		9,283
22	Beck Company		5,880	120	6,000			
29			17,660			17,660		10,596
31	Interest Revenue		200				200	
			76,876	475	20,000	51,451	5,900	30,870

(b) The Accounts Receivable column total is posted as a credit to Accounts Receivable. The individual amounts are credited to the customers' accounts identified in the Account Credited column, which are maintained in the accounts receivable subsidiary ledger.

The amounts in the Other Accounts column are posted individually. They are credited to the account titles identified in the Account Credited column.

The Navigator

Summary of Study Objectives

[1] Identify the basic concepts of an accounting information system. The basic principles in developing an accounting information system are cost-effectiveness, useful output, and flexibility. Most companies use a computerized accounting system. Smaller companies use entry-level software such as QuickBooks or Peachtree. Larger companies use custom-made software packages, which often integrate all aspects of the organization.

[2] Describe the nature and purpose of a subsidiary ledger. A subsidiary ledger is a group of accounts with a common characteristic. It facilitates the recording process by freeing the general ledger from details of individual balances.

[3] Explain how companies use special journals in journalizing. Companies use special journals to group similar types of transactions. In a special journal, generally only one line is used to record a complete transaction.

[4] Indicate how companies post a multi-column journal. In posting a multi-column journal:

(a) Companies post all column totals except for the Other Accounts column once at the end of the month to the account title specified in the column heading.

(b) Companies do not post the total of the Other Accounts column. Instead, the individual amounts comprising the total are posted separately to the general ledger accounts specified in the Account Credited (Debited) column.

(c) The individual amounts in a column posted in total to a control account are posted daily to the subsidiary ledger accounts specified in the Account Credited (Debited) column.

The Navigator

Glossary

Accounting information system A system that collects and processes transaction data, and communicates financial information to decision makers. (p. 316).

Accounts payable (creditors') subsidiary ledger A subsidiary ledger that collects transaction data of individual creditors. (p. 319).

Accounts receivable (customers') subsidiary ledger A subsidiary ledger that collects transaction data of individual customers. (p. 319).

Cash payments (disbursements) journal A special journal that records all disbursements of cash. (p. 331).

Cash receipts journal A special journal that records all cash received. (p. 325).

Control account An account in the general ledger that summarizes subsidiary ledger data. (p. 319).

Manual accounting system A system in which someone performs each of the steps in the accounting cycle by hand. (p. 319).

Purchases journal A special journal that records all purchases of merchandise on account. (p. 329).

Sales journal A special journal that records all sales of merchandise on account. (p. 323).

Special journal A journal that records similar types of transactions, such as all credit sales. (p. 322).

Subsidiary ledger A group of accounts with a common characteristic. (p. 319).

 Self-Test, Brief Exercises, Exercises, Problem Set A, and many more components are available for practice in *WileyPLUS*

Self-Test Questions

Answers are on page 357.

(SO 1) **1.** The basic principles of an accounting information system include all of the following except:
  a. cost-effectiveness.   **c.** useful output.
  b. flexibility.   **d.** periodicity.

(SO 1) **2.** Which of the following is *not* an advantage of computerized accounting systems?
  a. Data is entered only once in computerized accounting systems.
  b. Computerized accounting systems provide up-to-date information.
  c. Computerized accounting systems eliminate entering of transaction information.
  d. Computerized accounting systems eliminate many errors resulting from human intervention.

(SO 2) **3.** Which of the following is *incorrect* concerning subsidiary ledgers?
  a. The purchases ledger is a common subsidiary ledger for creditor accounts.
  b. The accounts receivable ledger is a subsidiary ledger.
  c. A subsidiary ledger is a group of accounts with a common characteristic.
  d. An advantage of the subsidiary ledger is that it permits a division of labor in posting.

(SO 2) **4.** Two common subsidiary ledgers are:
  a. accounts receivable and cash receipts.
  b. accounts payable and cash payments.
  c. accounts receivable and accounts payable.
  d. sales and cost of goods sold.

(SO 2) **5.** At the beginning of the month, the accounts receivable subsidiary ledger showed balances for Apple Company $5,000 and Berry Company $7,000. During the month, credit sales were made to Apple $6,000, Berry $4,500, and Cantaloupe $8,500. Cash was collected on account from Berry $11,500 and Cantaloupe $3,000. At the end of the month, the control account Accounts Receivable in the general ledger should have a balance of:
  a. $11,000.   **c.** $16,500.
  b. $12,000.   **d.** $31,000.

6. A sales journal will be used for: (SO 3)

	Credit Sales	Cash Sales	Sales Discounts
a.	no	yes	yes
b.	yes	no	yes
c.	yes	no	no
d.	yes	yes	no

7. A purchase of equipment on account is recorded in the: (SO 3)
  a. cash receipts journal.   **c.** cash payments journal.
  b. purchases journal.   **d.** general journal.

8. A purchase of equipment using cash is recorded in the: (SO 3)
  a. cash receipts journal.   **c.** cash payments journal.
  b. purchases journal.   **d.** general journal.

9. Which of the following statements is *correct*?   (SO 3, 4)
  a. The sales discount column is included in the cash receipts journal.
  b. The purchases journal records all purchases of merchandise whether for cash or on account.
  c. The cash receipts journal records sales on account.
  d. Merchandise returned by the buyer is recorded by the seller in the purchases journal.

10. Dotel Company's cash receipts journal includes an   (SO 4) Accounts Receivable column and an Other Accounts column. At the end of the month, these columns are posted to the general ledger as:

	Accounts Receivable	Other Accounts
a.	a column total	a column total
b.	individual amounts	a column total
c.	individual amounts	individual amounts
d.	a column total	individual amounts

(SO 4) **11.** Which of the following is *incorrect* concerning the posting of the cash receipts journal?
  a. The total of the Other Accounts column is not posted.
  b. All column totals except the total for the Other Accounts column are posted once at the end of the month to the account title(s) specified in the column heading.
  c. The totals of all columns are posted daily to the accounts specified in the column heading.
  d. The individual amounts in a column posted in total to a control account are posted daily to the subsidiary ledger account specified in the Account Credited column.

(SO 4) **12.** Postings from the purchases journal to the subsidiary ledger are generally made:
  a. yearly.   **c.** weekly.
  b. monthly.   **d.** daily.

(SO 3) **13.** Which statement is *incorrect* regarding the general journal?
  a. Only transactions that cannot be entered in a special journal are recorded in the general journal.
  b. Dual postings are always required in the general journal.

  c. The general journal may be used to record acceptance of a note receivable in payment of an account receivable.
  d. Correcting, adjusting, and closing entries are made in the general journal.

14. When companies use special journals: (SO 3)
  a. they record all purchase transactions in the purchases journal.
  b. they record all cash received, except from cash sales, in the cash receipts journal.
  c. they record all cash disbursements in the cash payments journal.
  d. a general journal is not necessary.

15. If a customer returns goods for credit, the selling company   (SO 3)
normally makes an entry in the:
  a. cash payments journal.   **c.** general journal.
  b. sales journal.   **d.** cash receipts journal.

Go to the book's companion website, **www.wiley.com/college/weygandt**, for additional Self-Test Questions.

Questions

1. (a) What is an accounting information system? (b) "An accounting information system applies only to a manual system." Do you agree? Explain.

2. Certain principles should be followed in the development of an accounting information system. Identify and explain each of the principles.

3. What are common features of computerized accounting packages beyond recording transactions and preparing financial statements?

4. How does an enterprise resource planning (ERP) system differ from an entry-level computerized accounting system?

5. What are the advantages of using subsidiary ledgers?

6. (a) When do companies normally post to (1) the subsidiary accounts and (2) the general ledger control accounts? (b) Describe the relationship between a control account and a subsidiary ledger.

7. Identify and explain the four special journals discussed in the chapter. List an advantage of using each of these journals rather than using only a general journal.

8. Thogmartin Company uses special journals. It recorded in a sales journal a sale made on account to R. Peters for $435. A few days later, R. Peters returns $70 worth of merchandise for credit. Where should Thogmartin Company record the sales return? Why?

9. A $500 purchase of merchandise on account from Lore Company was properly recorded in the purchases journal. When posted, however, the amount recorded in the subsidiary ledger was $50. How might this error be discovered?

10. Why would special journals used in different businesses not be identical in format? What type of business would maintain a cash receipts journal but not include a column for accounts receivable?

11. The cash and the accounts receivable columns in the cash receipts journal were mistakenly overadded by $4,000 at the end of the month. (a) Will the customers' ledger agree with the Accounts Receivable control account? (b) Assuming no other errors, will the trial balance totals be equal?

12. One column total of a special journal is posted at month-end to only two general ledger accounts. One of these two accounts is Accounts Receivable. What is the name of this special journal? What is the other general ledger account to which that same month-end total is posted?

13. In what journal would the following transactions be recorded? (Assume that a two-column sales journal and a single-column purchases journal are used.)
  (a) Recording of depreciation expense for the year.
  (b) Credit given to a customer for merchandise purchased on credit and returned.
  (c) Sales of merchandise for cash.
  (d) Sales of merchandise on account.
  (e) Collection of cash on account from a customer.
  (f) Purchase of office supplies on account.

14. In what journal would the following transactions be recorded? (Assume that a two-column sales journal and a single-column purchases journal are used.)
  (a) Cash received from signing a note payable.
  (b) Investment of cash by the owner of the business.
  (c) Closing of the expense accounts at the end of the year.

(d) Purchase of merchandise on account.

(e) Credit received for merchandise purchased and returned to supplier.

(f) Payment of cash on account due a supplier.

15. What transactions might be included in a multiple-column purchases journal that would not be included in a single-column purchases journal?

16. Give an example of a transaction in the general journal that causes an entry to be posted twice (i.e., to two accounts), one in the general ledger, the other in the subsidiary ledger. Does this affect the debit/credit equality of the general ledger?

17. Give some examples of appropriate general journal transactions for an organization using special journals.

Brief Exercises

BE7-1 Indicate whether each of the following statements is true or false.

1. When designing an accounting system, we need to think about the needs and knowledge of both the top managers and various other users.

2. When the environment changes as a result of technological advances, increased competition, or government regulation, an accounting system does not have to be sufficiently flexible to meet the changes in order to save money.

3. In developing an accounting system, cost is relevant. The benefits obtained from the information disseminated must outweigh the cost of providing it.

Identify basic concepts of an accounting information system.
(SO 1)

BE7-2 Here is a list of words or phrases related to computerized accounting systems.

1. Entry-level software.

2. Enterprise resource planning systems.

3. Network-compatible.

4. Audit trail.

5. Internal control.

Identify basic concepts of an accounting information system.
(SO 1)

Instructions

Match each word or phrase with the best description of it.

_____**(a)** Allows multiple users to access the system at the same time.

_____**(b)** Enables the tracking of all transactions.

_____**(c)** Identifies suspicious transactions or likely mistakes such as wrong account numbers or duplicate transactions.

_____**(d)** Large-scale computer systems that integrate all aspects of the organization including accounting, sales, human resource management, and manufacturing.

_____**(e)** System for companies with revenues of less than $5 million and up to 20 employees.

BE7-3 Benji Borke has prepared the following list of statements about accounting information systems.

1. The accounting information system includes each of the steps of the accounting cycle, the documents that provide evidence of transactions that have occurred, and the accounting records.

2. The benefits obtained from information provided by the accounting information system need not outweigh the cost of providing that information.

3. Designers of accounting systems must consider the needs and knowledge of various users.

4. If an accounting information system is cost-effective and provides useful output, it does not need to be flexible.

Identify basic concepts of an accounting information system.
(SO 1)

Instructions

Identify each statement as true or false. If false, indicate how to correct the statement.

BE7-4 Presented below is information related to Montand Company for its first month of operations. Identify the balances that appear in the accounts receivable subsidiary ledger and the accounts receivable balance that appears in the general ledger at the end of January.

Identify subsidiary ledger balances.
(SO 2)

Credit Sales			Cash Collections		
Jan.	7 Ahuna Co.	$10,000	Jan.	17 Ahuna Co.	$7,000
	15 Aldo Co.	6,000		24 Aldo Co.	4,000
	23 Tito Co.	9,000		29 Tito Co.	9,000

Identify subsidiary ledger accounts.

(SO 2)

BE7-5   Identify in what ledger (general or subsidiary) each of the following accounts is shown.
1. Rent Expense
2. Accounts Receivable—Obileye
3. Notes Payable
4. Accounts Payable—Kolawole

Identify special journals.

(SO 3)

BE7-6   Identify the journal in which each of the following transactions is recorded.
1. Cash sales
2. Owner withdrawal of cash
3. Cash purchase of land
4. Credit sales
5. Purchase of merchandise on account
6. Receipt of cash for services performed

Identify entries to cash receipts journal.

(SO 3)

BE7-7   Indicate whether each of the following debits and credits is included in the cash receipts journal. (Use "Yes" or "No" to answer this question.)
1. Debit to Sales Revenue.
2. Credit to Inventory.
3. Credit to Accounts Receivable.
4. Debit to Accounts Payable.

Identify transactions for special journals.

(SO 3)

BE7-8   Olekan Co. uses special journals and a general journal. Identify the journal in which each of the following transactions is recorded.
(a) Purchased equipment on account.
(b) Purchased merchandise on account.
(c) Paid utility expense in cash.
(d) Sold merchandise on account.

Identify transactions for special journals.

(SO 3)

BE7-9   Identify the special journal(s) in which the following column headings appear.
1. Sales Discounts Dr.
2. Accounts Receivable Cr.
3. Cash Dr.
4. Sales Revenue Cr.
5. Inventory Dr.

Indicate postings for cash receipts journal.

(SO 4)

BE7-10   Bruni Computer Components Inc. uses a multi-column cash receipts journal. Indicate which column(s) is/are posted only in total, only daily, or both in total and daily.
1. Accounts Receivable
2. Sales Discounts
3. Cash
4. Other Accounts

Do it! Review

Determine subsidiary and general ledger balances.

(SO 2)

Do it! 7-1   Presented below is information related to Chung Company for its first month of operations. Determine the balances that appear in the accounts payable subsidiary ledger. What Accounts Payable balance appears in the general ledger at the end of January?

Credit Purchases			Cash Paid		
Jan. 6	Shada Company	$ 9,000	Jan. 11	Shada Company	$ 6,500
Jan. 10	Liam Company	12,000	Jan. 16	Liam Company	12,000
Jan. 23	Esmond Company	10,000	Jan. 29	Esmond Company	7,700

Identify special journals.

(SO 3)

Do it! 7-2   Tomiko Company had the following transactions during April.
1. Sold merchandise on account.
2. Purchased merchandise on account.
3. Collected cash from a sale to Kahale Company.
4. Recorded accrued interest on a note payable.
5. Paid $2,000 for supplies.

Identify the journal in which each of the transactions above is recorded.

Exercises

Determine control account balances, and explain posting of special journals.

(SO 2, 4)

E7-1   Ruz Company uses both special journals and a general journal as described in this chapter. On June 30, after all monthly postings had been completed, the Accounts Receivable control account in the general ledger had a debit balance of $320,000; the Accounts Payable control account had a credit balance of $77,000.

The July transactions recorded in the special journals are summarized below. No entries affecting accounts receivable and accounts payable were recorded in the general journal for July.

Sales journal	Total sales $161,400
Purchases journal	Total purchases $56,400
Cash receipts journal	Accounts receivable column total $131,000
Cash payments journal	Accounts payable column total $47,500

Instructions
(a) What is the balance of the Accounts Receivable control account after the monthly postings on July 31?
(b) What is the balance of the Accounts Payable control account after the monthly postings on July 31?
(c) To what account(s) is the column total of $161,400 in the sales journal posted?
(d) To what account(s) is the accounts receivable column total of $131,000 in the cash receipts journal posted?

E7-2 Presented below is the subsidiary accounts receivable account of Lana Parilla.

Explain postings to subsidiary ledger.

(SO 2)

Date	Ref.	Debit	Credit	Balance
2012				
Sept. 2	S31	61,000		61,000
9	G4		14,000	47,000
27	CR8		47,000	—

Instructions
Write a memo to Maya Henssens, chief financial officer, that explains each transaction.

E7-3 On September 1, the balance of the Accounts Receivable control account in the general ledger of Joss Whedon Company was $10,960. The customers' subsidiary ledger contained account balances as follows: Gareth $1,440, Gillum $2,640, Minear $2,060, Edlund $4,820. At the end of September, the various journals contained the following information.

Post various journals to control and subsidiary accounts.

(SO 2, 4)

Sales journal: Sales to Edlund $800; to Gareth $1,260; to Molina $1,330; to Minear $1,100.
Cash receipts journal: Cash received from Minear $1,310; from Edlund $2,300; from Molina $380; from Gillum $1,800; from Gareth $1,240.
General journal: An allowance is granted to Edlund $220.

Instructions
(a) Set up control and subsidiary accounts and enter the beginning balances. Do not construct the journals.
(b) Post the various journals. Post the items as individual items or as totals, whichever would be the appropriate procedure. (No sales discounts given.)
(c) Prepare a list of customers and prove the agreement of the controlling account with the subsidiary ledger at September 30, 2012.

E7-4 Malcolnn Reynolds Company has a balance in its Accounts Receivable control account of $11,000 on January 1, 2012. The subsidiary ledger contains three accounts: Nathan Company, balance $4,000; Fillion Company, balance $2,500; and Lassak Company. During January, the following receivable-related transactions occurred.

Determine control and subsidiary ledger balances for accounts receivable.

(SO 2)

	Credit Sales	Collections	Returns
Nathan Company	$9,000	$8,000	$ -0-
Fillion Company	7,000	2,500	3,000
Lassak Company	8,500	9,000	-0-

Instructions
(a) What is the January 1 balance in the Lassak Company subsidiary account?
(b) What is the January 31 balance in the control account?
(c) Compute the balances in the subsidiary accounts at the end of the month.
(d) Which January transaction would not be recorded in a special journal?

Determine control and subsidiary ledger balances for accounts payable.
(SO 2)

E7-5 Zoe Washburne Company has a balance in its Accounts Payable control account of $8,250 on January 1, 2012. The subsidiary ledger contains three accounts: Gina Company, balance $3,000; Torres Company, balance $1,875; and Wankum Company. During January, the following payable-related transactions occurred.

	Purchases	Payments	Returns
Gina Company	$6,750	$6,000	$ -0-
Torres Company	5,250	1,875	2,250
Wankum Company	6,375	6,750	-0-

Instructions

(a) What is the January 1 balance in the Wankum Company subsidiary account?

(b) What is the January 31 balance in the control account?

(c) Compute the balances in the subsidiary accounts at the end of the month.

(d) Which January transaction would not be recorded in a special journal?

Record transactions in sales and purchases journal.
(SO 2, 3)

E7-6 Hoban Company uses special journals and a general journal. The following transactions occurred during September 2012.

Sept. 2 Sold merchandise on account to H. Wash, invoice no. 101, $720, terms n/30. The cost of the merchandise sold was $420.

10 Purchased merchandise on account from A. Tudyk $600, terms 2/10, n/30.

12 Purchased office equipment on account from R. Press $6,500.

21 Sold merchandise on account to G. Edmonson, invoice no. 102 for $800, terms 2/10, n/30. The cost of the merchandise sold was $480.

25 Purchased merchandise on account from D. Boyd $860, terms n/30.

27 Sold merchandise to S. Miller for $700 cash. The cost of the merchandise sold was $400.

Instructions

(a) Prepare a sales journal (see Illustration 7-7) and a single-column purchases journal (see Illustration 7-13). (Use page 1 for each journal.)

(b) Record the transaction(s) for September that should be journalized in the sales journal and the purchases journal.

Record transactions in cash receipts and cash payments journal.
(SO 2, 3)

E7-7 Inara Serra Co. uses special journals and a general journal. The following transactions occurred during May 2012.

May 1 I. Serra invested $50,000 cash in the business.

2 Sold merchandise to Morena Co. for $6,300 cash. The cost of the merchandise sold was $4,200.

3 Purchased merchandise for $7,200 from J. DeLeon using check no. 101.

14 Paid salary to H. Potter $700 by issuing check no. 102.

16 Sold merchandise on account to K. Kimbell for $900, terms n/30. The cost of the merchandise sold was $630.

22 A check of $9,000 is received from M. Baccarin in full for invoice 101; no discount given.

Instructions

(a) Prepare a multiple-column cash receipts journal (see Illustration 7-9) and a multiple-column cash payments journal (see Illustration 7-16). (Use page 1 for each journal.)

(b) Record the transaction(s) for May that should be journalized in the cash receipts journal and cash payments journal.

Explain journalizing in cash journals.
(SO 3)

E7-8 Blue Glove Company uses the columnar cash journals illustrated in the textbook. In April, the following selected cash transactions occurred.

1. Made a refund to a customer as an allowance for damaged goods.

2. Received collection from customer within the 3% discount period.

3. Purchased merchandise for cash.

4. Paid a creditor within the 3% discount period.

5. Received collection from customer after the 3% discount period had expired.

6. Paid freight on merchandise purchased.

7. Paid cash for office equipment.

8. Received cash refund from supplier for merchandise returned.

9. Withdrew cash for personal use of owner.

10. Made cash sales.

Instructions

Indicate (a) the journal, and (b) the columns in the journal that should be used in recording each transaction.

E7-9   Jayne Cobb Company has the following selected transactions during March.

Mar. 2   Purchased equipment costing $9,400 from Adam Company on account.

5   Received credit of $410 from Baldwin Company for merchandise damaged in shipment to Jayne Cobb.

7   Issued credit of $400 to Cockrum Company for merchandise the customer returned. The returned merchandise had a cost of $260.

Jayne Cobb Company uses a one-column purchases journal, a sales journal, the columnar cash journals used in the text, and a general journal.

Journalize transactions in general journal and explain postings.

(SO 2, 4)

Instructions

(a) Journalize the transactions in the general journal.

(b) ▬▬▬ In a brief memo to the president of Jayne Cobb Company, explain the postings to the control and subsidiary accounts from each type of journal.

E7-10   Below are some typical transactions incurred by Ricketts Company.

1. Payment of creditors on account. *Cash Payment Journal*
2. Return of merchandise sold for credit. *General Journal*
3. Collection on account from customers. *Cash Recipes*
4. Sale of land for cash. *cash recipt*
5. Sale of merchandise on account.
6. Sale of merchandise for cash.
7. Received credit for merchandise purchased on credit.
8. Sales discount taken on goods sold.
9. Payment of employee wages.
10. Income summary closed to owner's capital.
11. Depreciation on building.
12. Purchase of office supplies for cash.
13. Purchase of merchandise on account.

Indicate journalizing in special journals.

(SO 3)

Instructions

For each transaction, indicate whether it would normally be recorded in a cash receipts journal, cash payments journal, sales journal, single-column purchases journal, or general journal.

E7-11   The general ledger of Fairman Company contained the following Accounts Payable control account (in T-account form). Also shown is the related subsidiary ledger.

Explain posting to control account and subsidiary ledger.

(SO 2, 4)

GENERAL LEDGER

Accounts Payable

Feb. 15	General journal	1,400	Feb. 1	Balance	26,025
28	?	?	5	General journal	265
			11	General journal	550
			28	Purchases	13,400
			Feb. 28	Balance	9,500

ACCOUNTS PAYABLE LEDGER

Adelai			**Niska**		
	Feb. 28	Bal. 4,600		Feb. 28	Bal. ?

Badger		
	Feb. 28	Bal. 2,300

Instructions

(a) Indicate the missing posting reference and amount in the control account, and the missing ending balance in the subsidiary ledger.

(b) Indicate the amounts in the control account that were dual-posted (i.e., posted to the control account and the subsidiary accounts).

Prepare purchases and general journals.

(SO 2, 3)

E7-12 Selected accounts from the ledgers of Kaylee Frye Company at July 31 showed the following.

GENERAL LEDGER

Equipment   No. 153

Date	Explanation	Ref.	Debit	Credit	Balance
July 1		G1	3,900		3,900

Accounts Payable   No. 201

Date	Explanation	Ref.	Debit	Credit	Balance
July 1		G1		3,900	3,900
15		G1		400	4,300
18		G1	100		4,200
25		G1	200		4,000
31		P1		8,300	12,300

Inventory   No. 120

Date	Explanation	Ref.	Debit	Credit	Balance
July 15		G1	400		400
18		G1		100	300
25		G1		200	100
31		P1	8,300		8,400

ACCOUNTS PAYABLE LEDGER

De Rovin Equipment Co.

Date	Explanation	Ref.	Debit	Credit	Balance
July 1		G1		3,900	3,900

Jewel Co.

Date	Explanation	Ref.	Debit	Credit	Balance
July 3		P1		2,400	2,400
20		P1		700	3,100

Hodge Corp

Date	Explanation	Ref.	Debit	Credit	Balance
July 17		P1		1,400	1,400
18		G1	100		1,300
29		P1		1,600	2,900

Staite Co.

Date	Explanation	Ref.	Debit	Credit	Balance
July 14		P1		1,100	1,100
25		G1	200		900

Sunny Co.

Date	Explanation	Ref.	Debit	Credit	Balance
July 12		P1		500	500
21		P1		600	1,100

Bernardo Inc.

Date	Explanation	Ref.	Debit	Credit	Balance
July 15		G1		400	400

Instructions

From the data prepare:

(a) The single-column purchases journal for July.

(b) The general journal entries for July.

Determine correct posting amount to control account.

(SO 4)

E7-13 Simon Products uses both special journals and a general journal as described in this chapter. Simon also posts customers' accounts in the accounts receivable subsidiary ledger. The postings for the most recent month are included in the subsidiary T accounts below.

Tam		
Bal.	340	250
	200	

Doctor		
Bal.	150	150
	240	

Sean		
Bal.	–0–	145
	145	

Maher		
Bal.	120	120
	190	
	150	

Instructions

Determine the correct amount of the end-of-month posting from the sales journal to the Accounts Receivable control account.

Compute balances in various accounts.

(SO 4)

E7-14 Selected account balances for R. Tam Company at January 1, 2012, are presented below.

Accounts Payable	$14,000
Accounts Receivable	22,000
Cash	17,000
Inventory	13,500

R. Tam's sales journal for January shows a total of $100,000 in the selling price column, and its one-column purchases journal for January shows a total of $72,000.

The column totals in R. Tam's cash receipts journal are: Cash Dr. $61,000; Sales Discounts Dr. $1,100; Accounts Receivable Cr. $45,000; Sales Revenue Cr. $6,000; and Other Accounts Cr. $11,100.

The column totals in R. Tam's cash payments journal for January are: Cash Cr. $55,000; Inventory Cr. $1,000; Accounts Payable Dr. $46,000; and Other Accounts Dr. $10,000. R. Tam's total cost of goods sold for January is $63,600.

Accounts Payable, Accounts Receivable, Cash, Inventory, and Sales Revenue are not involved in the "Other Accounts" column in either the cash receipts or cash payments journal, and are not involved in any general journal entries.

Instructions

Compute the January 31 balance for R. Tam in the following accounts.

(a) Accounts Payable.
(b) Accounts Receivable.
(c) Cash.
(d) Inventory.
(e) Sales Revenue.

Exercises: Set B

Visit the book's companion website, at **www.wiley.com/college/weygandt**, and choose the Student Companion site to access Exercise Set B.

Problems: Set A

P7-1A   River Company's chart of accounts includes the following selected accounts.

101 Cash	401 Sales Revenue
112 Accounts Receivable	414 Sales Discounts
120 Inventory	505 Cost of Goods Sold
301 Owner's Capital	

Journalize transactions in cash receipts journal; post to control account and subsidiary ledger.
(SO 2, 3, 4)

GLS

On April 1 the accounts receivable ledger of River Company showed the following balances: Summer $1,550, Glav $1,200, Sheppard Co. $2,900, and Book $1,800. The April transactions involving the receipt of cash were as follows.

Apr. 1   The owner, T. River, invested additional cash in the business $7,200.
   4   Received check for payment of account from Book less 2% cash discount.
   5   Received check for $920 in payment of invoice no. 307 from Sheppard Co.
   8   Made cash sales of merchandise totaling $7,245. The cost of the merchandise sold was $4,347.
   10   Received check for $600 in payment of invoice no. 309 from Summer.
   11   Received cash refund from a supplier for damaged merchandise $740.
   23   Received check for $1,500 in payment of invoice no. 310 from Sheppard Co.
   29   Received check for payment of account from Glav.

Instructions

(a) Journalize the transactions above in a six-column cash receipts journal with columns for Cash Dr., Sales Discounts Dr., Accounts Receivable Cr., Sales Revenue Cr., Other Accounts Cr., and Cost of Goods Sold Dr./Inventory Cr. Foot and crossfoot the journal.

(b) Insert the beginning balances in the Accounts Receivable control and subsidiary accounts, and post the April transactions to these accounts.

(c) Prove the agreement of the control account and subsidiary account balances.

(a) Balancing totals $21,205

(c) Accounts Receivable
 $1,430

P7-2A   Saffron Company's chart of accounts includes the following selected accounts.

101 Cash	201 Accounts Payable
120 Inventory	306 Owner's Drawings
130 Prepaid Insurance	505 Cost of Goods Sold
157 Equipment	

Journalize transactions in cash payments journal; post to control account and subsidiary ledgers.
(SO 2, 3, 4)

 GLS

On October 1, the accounts payable ledger of Saffron Company showed the following balances: Glass Company $2,700, Ron Co. $2,500, Hendricks Co. $1,800, and Christina Company $3,700. The October transactions involving the payment of cash were as follows.

Oct. 1   Purchased merchandise, check no. 63, $300.
     3   Purchased equipment, check no. 64, $800.
     5   Paid Glass Company balance due of $2,700, less 2% discount, check no. 65, $2,646.
     10   Purchased merchandise, check no. 66, $2,250.
     15   Paid Hendricks Co. balance due of $1,800, check no. 67.
     16   C. Saffron, the owner, pays his personal insurance premium of $400, check no. 68.
     19   Paid Ron Co. in full for invoice no. 610, $1,600 less 2% cash discount, check no. 69, $1,568.
     29   Paid Christina Company in full for invoice no. 264, $2,500, check no. 70.

Instructions

(a) Balancing totals $12,350

(a) Journalize the transactions above in a four-column cash payments journal with columns for Other Accounts Dr., Accounts Payable Dr., Inventory Cr., and Cash Cr. Foot and crossfoot the journal.

(b) Insert the beginning balances in the Accounts Payable control and subsidiary accounts, and post the October transactions to these accounts.

(c) Accounts Payable $2,100

(c) Prove the agreement of the control account and the subsidiary account balances.

Journalize transactions in multi-column purchases journal and sales journal; post to the general and subsidiary ledgers.

(SO 2, 3, 4)

P7-3A   The chart of accounts of IT Company includes the following selected accounts.

112	Accounts Receivable	401	Sales Revenue
120	Inventory	412	Sales Returns and Allowances
126	Supplies	505	Cost of Goods Sold
157	Equipment	610	Advertising Expense
201	Accounts Payable		

In July, the following selected transactions were completed. All purchases and sales were on account. The cost of all merchandise sold was 70% of the sales price.

July 1   Purchased merchandise from Roy Company $8,000.
     2   Received freight bill from Moss Shipping on Roy purchase $400.
     3   Made sales to Jen Company $1,300, and to O'Dowd Bros. $1,500.
     5   Purchased merchandise from Moon Company $3,200.
     8   Received credit on merchandise returned to Moon Company $300.
     13   Purchased store supplies from Cress Supply $720.
     15   Purchased merchandise from Roy Company $3,600 and from Anton Company $3,300.
     16   Made sales to Sager Company $3,450 and to O'Dowd Bros. $1,570.
     18   Received bill for advertising from Lynda Advertisements $600.
     21   Sales were made to Jen Company $310 and to Haddad Company $2,800.
     22   Granted allowance to Jen Company for merchandise damaged in shipment $40.
     24   Purchased merchandise from Moon Company $3,000.
     26   Purchased equipment from Cress Supply $900.
     28   Received freight bill from Moss Shipping on Moon purchase of July 24, $380.
     30   Sales were made to Sager Company $5,600.

Instructions

(a) Purchases journal— Accounts Payable $24,100 Sales column total $16,530

(a) Journalize the transactions above in a purchases journal, a sales journal, and a general journal. The purchases journal should have the following column headings: Date, Account Credited (Debited), Ref., Accounts Payable Cr., Inventory Dr., and Other Accounts Dr.

(c) Accounts Receivable $16,490 Accounts Payable $23,800

(b) Post to both the general and subsidiary ledger accounts. (Assume that all accounts have zero beginning balances.)

(c) Prove the agreement of the control and subsidiary accounts.

Journalize transactions in special journals.

(SO 2, 3, 4)

P7-4A   Selected accounts from the chart of accounts of Ayoade Company are shown below.

101	Cash	126	Supplies
112	Accounts Receivable	157	Equipment
120	Inventory	201	Accounts Payable

401 Sales Revenue
412 Sales Returns and Allowances
414 Sales Discounts

505 Cost of Goods Sold
726 Salaries and Wages Expense

The cost of all merchandise sold was 60% of the sales price. During January, Ayoade completed the following transactions.

Jan. 3   Purchased merchandise on account from Parkinson Co. $10,000.
4   Purchased supplies for cash $80.
4   Sold merchandise on account to Douglas $5,250, invoice no. 371, terms 1/10, n/30.
5   Returned $300 worth of damaged goods purchased on account from Parkinson Co. on January 3.
6   Made cash sales for the week totaling $3,150.
8   Purchased merchandise on account from Denholm Co. $4,500.
9   Sold merchandise on account to Connor Corp. $6,400, invoice no. 372, terms 1/10, n/30.
11   Purchased merchandise on account from Betz Co. $3,700.
13   Paid in full Parkinson Co. on account less a 2% discount.
13   Made cash sales for the week totaling $6,260.
15   Received payment from Connor Corp. for invoice no. 372.
15   Paid semi-monthly salaries of $14,300 to employees.
17   Received payment from Douglas for invoice no. 371.
17   Sold merchandise on account to Bullock Co. $1,200, invoice no. 373, terms 1/10, n/30.
19   Purchased equipment on account from Murphy Corp. $5,500.
20   Cash sales for the week totaled $3,200.
20   Paid in full Denholm Co. on account less a 2% discount.
23   Purchased merchandise on account from Parkinson Co. $7,800.
24   Purchased merchandise on account from Forgetta Corp. $5,100.
27   Made cash sales for the week totaling $4,230.
30   Received payment from Bullock Co. for invoice no. 373.
31   Paid semi-monthly salaries of $13,200 to employees.
31   Sold merchandise on account to Douglas $9,330, invoice no. 374, terms 1/10, n/30.

Ayoade Company uses the following journals.

1. Sales journal.
2. Single-column purchases journal.
3. Cash receipts journal with columns for Cash Dr., Sales Discounts Dr., Accounts Receivable Cr., Sales Revenue Cr., Other Accounts Cr., and Cost of Goods Sold Dr./Inventory Cr.
4. Cash payments journal with columns for Other Accounts Dr., Accounts Payable Dr., Inventory Cr., and Cash Cr.
5. General journal.

Instructions
Using the selected accounts provided:

(a) Record the January transactions in the appropriate journal noted.
(b) Foot and crossfoot all special journals.
(c) Show how postings would be made by placing ledger account numbers and checkmarks as needed in the journals. (Actual posting to ledger accounts is not required.)

(a) Sales journal $22,180
   Purchases journal $31,100
   Cash receipts journal
     balancing total $29,690
   Cash payments journal
     balancing total $41,780

P7-5A Presented below and on page 348 are the purchases and cash payments journals for Richmond Co. for its first month of operations.

Journalize in sales and cash receipts journals; post; prepare a trial balance; prove control to subsidiary; prepare adjusting entries; prepare an adjusted trial balance.

(SO 2, 3, 4)

	PURCHASES JOURNAL		P1
Date	**Account Credited**	**Ref.**	**Inventory Dr.** **Accounts Payable Cr.**
July 4	N. Fielding		6,800
5	F. Noel		8,100
11	J. Shaggy		5,920
13	C. Tabor		15,300
20	M. Sneezy		7,900
			44,020

CASH PAYMENTS JOURNAL CP1

Date	Account Debited	Ref	Other Accounts Dr.	Accounts Payable Dr.	Inventory Cr.	Cash Cr.
July 4	Supplies		600			600
10	F. Noel			8,100	81	8,019
11	Prepaid Rent		6,000			6,000
15	N. Fielding			6,800		6,800
19	Owner's Drawings		2,500			2,500
21	C. Tabor			15,300	153	15,147
			9,100	30,200	234	39,066

In addition, the following transactions have not been journalized for July. The cost of all merchandise sold was 65% of the sales price.

July 1 The founder, N. Richmond, invests $80,000 in cash.
  6 Sell merchandise on account to Abi Co. $6,200 terms 1/10, n/30.
  7 Make cash sales totaling $6,000.
  8 Sell merchandise on account to S. Beauty $3,600, terms 1/10, n/30.
  10 Sell merchandise on account to W. Pitts $4,900, terms 1/10, n/30.
  13 Receive payment in full from S. Beauty.
  16 Receive payment in full from W. Pitts.
  20 Receive payment in full from Abi Co.
  21 Sell merchandise on account to H. Prince $5,000, terms 1/10, n/30.
  29 Returned damaged goods to N. Fielding and received cash refund of $420.

Instructions

(a) Open the following accounts in the general ledger.

101 Cash
112 Accounts Receivable
120 Inventory
127 Supplies
131 Prepaid Rent
201 Accounts Payable
301 Owner's Capital
306 Owner's Drawings
401 Sales Revenue
414 Sales Discounts
505 Cost of Goods Sold
631 Supplies Expense
729 Rent Expense

(b) Sales journal total
$19,700
Cash receipts journal
balancing totals $101,120

(e) Totals $119,520
(f) Accounts Receivable
$5,000
Accounts Payable $13,820
(h) Totals $119,520

Journalize in special journals; post; prepare a trial balance.

(SO 2, 3, 4)   GLS

(b) Journalize the transactions that have not been journalized in the sales journal, the cash receipts journal (see Illustration 7-9), and the general journal.
(c) Post to the accounts receivable and accounts payable subsidiary ledgers. Follow the sequence of transactions as shown in the problem.
(d) Post the individual entries and totals to the general ledger.
(e) Prepare a trial balance at July 31, 2012.
(f) Determine whether the subsidiary ledgers agree with the control accounts in the general ledger.
(g) The following adjustments at the end of July are necessary.
  (1) A count of supplies indicates that $140 is still on hand.
  (2) Recognize rent expense for July, $500.
  Prepare the necessary entries in the general journal. Post the entries to the general ledger.
(h) Prepare an adjusted trial balance at July 31, 2012.

P7-6A The post-closing trial balance for Bugeja Co. is shown on page 349.

BUGEJA CO.
Post-Closing Trial Balance
December 31, 2012

	Debit	Credit
Cash	$ 41,500	
Accounts Receivable	15,000	
Notes Receivable	45,000	
Inventory	23,000	
Equipment	6,450	
Accumulated Depreciation—Equipment		$ 1,500
Accounts Payable		43,000
Owner's Capital		86,450
	$130,950	$130,950

The subsidiary ledgers contain the following information: (1) accounts receivable— B. Cordelia $2,500, I. Togo $7,500, T. Dudley $5,000; (2) accounts payable—T. Igawa $10,000, D. Miranda $18,000, and K. Inwood $15,000. The cost of all merchandise sold was 60% of the sales price.

The transactions for January 2013 are as follows.

Jan. 3   Sell merchandise to M. Rensing $5,000, terms 2/10, n/30.
   5   Purchase merchandise from E. Vietti $2,000, terms 2/10, n/30.
   7   Receive a check from T. Dudley $3,500.
   11   Pay freight on merchandise purchased $300.
   12   Pay rent of $1,000 for January.
   13   Receive payment in full from M. Rensing.
   14   Post all entries to the subsidiary ledgers. Issued credit of $300 to B. Cordelia for returned merchandise.
   15   Send K. Inwood a check for $14,850 in full payment of account, discount $150.
   17   Purchase merchandise from G. Marley $1,600, terms 2/10, n/30.
   18   Pay sales salaries of $2,800 and office salaries $2,000.
   20   Give D. Miranda a 60-day note for $18,000 in full payment of account payable.
   23   Total cash sales amount to $9,100.
   24   Post all entries to the subsidiary ledgers. Sell merchandise on account to I. Togo $7,400, terms 1/10, n/30.
   27   Send E. Vietti a check for $950.
   29   Receive payment on a note of $40,000 from B. Lemke.
   30   Post all entries to the subsidiary ledgers. Return merchandise of $300 to G. Marley for credit.

Instructions

(a) Open general and subsidiary ledger accounts for the following.

101	Cash	301	Owner's Capital
112	Accounts Receivable	401	Sales Revenue
115	Notes Receivable	412	Sales Returns and Allowances
120	Inventory	414	Sales Discounts
157	Equipment	505	Cost of Goods Sold
158	Accumulated Depreciation—Equipment	726	Salaries and Wages Expense
200	Notes Payable	729	Rent Expense
201	Accounts Payable		

(b) Record the January transactions in a sales journal, a single-column purchases journal, a cash receipts journal (see Illustration 7-9), a cash payments journal (see Illustration 7-16), and a general journal.

(c) Post the appropriate amounts to the general ledger.

(d) Prepare a trial balance at January 31, 2013.

(e) Determine whether the subsidiary ledgers agree with controlling accounts in the general ledger.

(b) Sales journal $12,400
  Purchases journal $3,600
  Cash receipts journal (balancing) $57,600
  Cash payments journal (balancing) $22,050
(d) Totals $139,800
(e) Accounts Receivable $18,600
  Accounts Payable $12,350

Problems: Set B

Journalize transactions in cash receipts journal; post to control account and subsidiary ledger.

(SO 2, 3, 4)

P7-1B Feig Company's chart of accounts includes the following selected accounts.

101	Cash	401	Sales Revenue
112	Accounts Receivable	414	Sales Discounts
120	Inventory	505	Cost of Goods Sold
301	Owner's Capital		

On June 1, the accounts receivable ledger of Feig Company showed the following balances: Kwapis & Son $3,500, Einhorn Co. $2,800, Randall Bros. $2,400, and Daniels Co. $2,000. The June transactions involving the receipt of cash were as follows.

June 1   The owner, Paul Feig, invested additional cash in the business $12,000.
     3   Received check in full from Daniels Co. less 2% cash discount.
     6   Received check in full from Einhorn Co. less 2% cash discount.
     7   Made cash sales of merchandise totaling $8,700. The cost of the merchandise sold was $5,000.
     9   Received check in full from Kwapis & Son less 2% cash discount.
    11   Received cash refund from a supplier for damaged merchandise $450.
    15   Made cash sales of merchandise totaling $6,500. The cost of the merchandise sold was $4,000.
    20   Received check in full from Randall Bros. $2,400.

Instructions

(a) Balancing totals $38,350

(a) Journalize the transactions above in a six-column cash receipts journal with columns for Cash Dr., Sales Discounts Dr., Accounts Receivable Cr., Sales Revenue Cr., Other Accounts Cr., and Cost of Goods Sold Dr./Inventory Cr. Foot and crossfoot the journal.

(b) Insert the beginning balances in the Accounts Receivable control and subsidiary accounts, and post the June transactions to these accounts.

(c) Accounts Receivable $0

(c) Prove the agreement of the control account and subsidiary account balances.

Journalize transactions in cash payments journal and sales journal; post to the general and subsidiary ledgers.

(SO 2, 3, 4)

P7-2B Dunder Mifflin Company's chart of accounts includes the following selected accounts.

101	Cash	157	Equipment
120	Inventory	201	Accounts Payable
130	Prepaid Insurance	306	Owner's Drawings

On November 1, the accounts payable ledger of Dunder Mifflin Company showed the following balances: S. Carell $4,000, D. Schrute $2,100, R. Wilson $800, and W. Rainn $1,300. The November transactions involving the payment of cash were as follows.

Nov. 1   Purchased merchandise, check no. 11, $950.
     3   Purchased store equipment, check no. 12, $1,400.
     5   Paid W. Rainn balance due of $1,300, less 1% discount, check no. 13, $1,287.
    11   Purchased merchandise, check no. 14, $1,700.
    15   Paid R. Wilson balance due of $800, less 3% discount, check no. 15, $776.
    16   M. Scott, the owner, withdrew $400 cash for own use, check no. 16.
    19   Paid D. Schrute in full for invoice no. 1245, $2,100 less 2% discount, check no. 17, $2,058.
    25   Paid premium due on one-year insurance policy, check no. 18, $2,400.
    30   Paid S. Carell in full for invoice no. 832, $2,900, check no. 19.

Instructions

(a) Balancing totals $13,950

(a) Journalize the transactions above in a four-column cash payments journal with columns for Other Accounts Dr., Accounts Payable Dr., Inventory Cr., and Cash Cr. Foot and crossfoot the journal.

(b) Insert the beginning balances in the Accounts Payable control and subsidiary accounts, and post the November transactions to these accounts.

(c) Accounts Payable $1,100

(c) Prove the agreement of the control account and the subsidiary account balances.

Journalize transactions in multi-column purchases journal; post to the general and subsidiary ledgers.

(SO 2, 3, 4)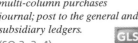

P7-3B The chart of accounts of Sabre Company includes the following selected accounts.

112	Accounts Receivable	401	Sales Revenue
120	Inventory	412	Sales Returns and Allowances
126	Supplies	505	Cost of Goods Sold
157	Equipment	610	Advertising Expense
201	Accounts Payable		

In May, the following selected transactions were completed. All purchases and sales were on account except as indicated. The cost of all merchandise sold was 60% of the sales price.

May 2 Purchased merchandise from Halpert Company $5,000.
3 Received freight bill from Fast Freight on Halpert purchase $250.
5 Sales were made to Krasinski Company $1,300, Coen Bros. $1,800, and Lucy Company $1,000.
8 Purchased merchandise from Beesly Company $5,400 and Fischer Company $3,000.
10 Received credit on merchandise returned to Fischer Company $350.
15 Purchased supplies from Jenna's Supplies $600.
16 Purchased merchandise from Halpert Company $3,100, and Beesly Company $4,800.
17 Returned supplies to Jenna's Supplies, receiving credit $70. (*Hint:* Credit Supplies.)
18 Received freight bills on May 16 purchases from Fast Freight $325.
20 Returned merchandise to Halpert Company receiving credit $200.
23 Made sales to Coen Bros. $1,600 and to Lucy Company $2,500.
25 Received bill for advertising from Ole Advertising $620.
26 Granted allowance to Lucy Company for merchandise damaged in shipment $140.
28 Purchased equipment from Jenna's Supplies $400.

Instructions

(a) Journalize the transactions above in a purchases journal, a sales journal, and a general journal. The purchases journal should have the following column headings: Date, Account Credited (Debited), Ref., Accounts Payable Cr., Inventory Dr., and Other Accounts Dr.

(b) Post to both the general and subsidiary ledger accounts. (Assume that all accounts have zero beginning balances.)

(c) Prove the agreement of the control and subsidiary accounts.

(a) Purchases journal—
Accounts Payable, Cr.
$23,495
Sales column total $8,200
(c) Accounts Receivable
$8,060
Accounts Payable $22,875

P7-4B Selected accounts from the chart of accounts of Malone Company are shown below.

101 Cash	201 Accounts Payable
112 Accounts Receivable	401 Sales Revenue
120 Inventory	414 Sales Discounts
126 Supplies	505 Cost of Goods Sold
140 Land	610 Advertising Expense
145 Buildings	

Journalize transactions in special journals.

(SO 2, 3, 4)

The cost of all merchandise sold was 65% of the sales price. During October, Malone Company completed the following transactions.

Oct. 2 Purchased merchandise on account from Ryan Company $12,000.
4 Sold merchandise on account to Howard Co. $5,600. Invoice no. 204, terms 2/10, n/30.
5 Purchased supplies for cash $60.
7 Made cash sales for the week totaling $6,700.
9 Paid in full the amount owed Ryan Company less a 2% discount.
10 Purchased merchandise on account from Arduino Corp. $2,600.
12 Received payment from Howard Co. for invoice no. 204.
13 Returned $150 worth of damaged goods purchased on account from Arduino Corp. on October 10.
14 Made cash sales for the week totaling $6,000.
16 Sold a parcel of land for $20,000 cash, the land's original cost.
17 Sold merchandise on account to BJ's Warehouse $3,900, invoice no. 205, terms 2/10, n/30.
18 Purchased merchandise for cash $1,600.
21 Made cash sales for the week totaling $6,000.
23 Paid in full the amount owed Arduino Corp. for the goods kept (no discount).
25 Purchased supplies on account from Paul Martin Co. $190.
25 Sold merchandise on account to David Corp. $3,800, invoice no. 206, terms 2/10, n/30.
25 Received payment from BJ's Warehouse for invoice no. 205.
26 Purchased for cash a small parcel of land and a building on the land to use as a storage facility. The total cost of $26,000 was allocated $16,000 to the land and $10,000 to the building.
27 Purchased merchandise on account from Novak Co. $6,200.
28 Made cash sales for the week totaling $5,500.
30 Purchased merchandise on account from Ryan Company $10,000.
30 Paid advertising bill for the month from the *Gazette*, $290.
30 Sold merchandise on account to BJ's Warehouse $3,400, invoice no. 207, terms 2/10, n/30.

Malone Company uses the following journals.

1. Sales journal.
2. Single-column purchases journal.
3. Cash receipts journal with columns for Cash Dr., Sales Discounts Dr., Accounts Receivable Cr., Sales Revenue Cr., Other Accounts Cr., and Cost of Goods Sold Dr./Inventory Cr.
4. Cash payments journal with columns for Other Accounts Dr., Accounts Payable Dr., Inventory Cr., and Cash Cr.
5. General journal.

(b) Sales journal $16,700
    Purchases journal
    $30,800
    Cash receipts journal—
    Cash, Dr. $53,510
    Cash payments journal,
    Cash, Cr. $42,160

*Journalize in purchases and
cash payments journals; post;
prepare a trial balance; prove
control to subsidiary; prepare
adjusting entries; prepare an
adjusted trial balance.*

(SO 2, 3, 4)

Instructions
Using the selected accounts provided:

(a) Record the October transactions in the appropriate journals.
(b) Foot and crossfoot all special journals.
(c) Show how postings would be made by placing ledger account numbers and check marks as needed in the journals. (Actual posting to ledger accounts is not required.)

P7-5B   Presented below are the sales and cash receipts journals for Hudson Co. for its first month of operations.

SALES JOURNAL   S1

Date	Account Debited	Ref.	Accounts Receivable Dr. Sales Revenue Cr.	Cost of Goods Sold Dr. Inventory Cr.
Feb. 3	C. Leslie		4,000	2,400
9	S. David		5,000	3,000
12	T. Baker		6,500	3,900
26	W. Oz		5,500	3,300
			21,000	12,600

CASH RECEIPTS JOURNAL   CR1

Date	Owner's Account Credited	Ref.	Cash Dr.	Sales Discounts Dr.	Accounts Receivable Cr.	Sales Revenue Cr.	Other Accounts Cr.	Cost of Goods Sold Dr. Inventory Cr.
Feb. 1	Owner's Capital		23,000				23,000	
2			4,500			4,500		2,700
13	C. Leslie		3,960	40	4,000			
18	Inventory		120				120	
26	S. David		5,000		5,000			
			36,580	40	9,000	4,500	23,120	2,700

In addition, the following transactions have not been journalized for February 2012.

Feb. 2   Purchased merchandise on account from B. Baumgartner for $3,600, terms 2/10, n/30.
   7   Purchased merchandise on account from A. Martin for $23,000, terms 1/10, n/30.
   9   Paid cash of $980 for purchase of supplies.
   12   Paid $3,528 to B. Baumgartner in payment for $3,600 invoice, less 2% discount.
   15   Purchased equipment for $5,500 cash.
   16   Purchased merchandise on account from D. Gale $1,900, terms 2/10, n/30.
   17   Paid $22,770 to A. Martin in payment of $23,000 invoice, less 1% discount.
   20   S. Hudson withdrew cash of $800 from the business for personal use.
   21   Purchased merchandise on account from Kansas Company for $6,000, terms 1/10, n/30.
   28   Paid $1,900 to D. Gale in payment of $1,900 invoice.

Instructions

(a) Open the following accounts in the general ledger.

101	Cash	301	Owner's Capital
112	Accounts Receivable	306	Owner's Drawings
120	Inventory	401	Sales Revenue
126	Supplies	414	Sales Discounts
157	Equipment	505	Cost of Goods Sold
158	Accumulated Depreciation—Equipment	631	Supplies Expense
201	Accounts Payable	711	Depreciation Expense

(b) Journalize the transactions that have not been journalized in a one-column purchases journal and the cash payments journal (see Illustration 7-16).

(c) Post to the accounts receivable and accounts payable subsidiary ledgers. Follow the sequence of transactions as shown in the problem.

(d) Post the individual entries and totals to the general ledger.

(e) Prepare a trial balance at February 28, 2012.

(f) Determine that the subsidiary ledgers agree with the control accounts in the general ledger.

(g) The following adjustments at the end of February are necessary.

  (1) A count of supplies indicates that $200 is still on hand.

  (2) Depreciation on equipment for February is $150.

  Prepare the adjusting entries and then post the adjusting entries to the general ledger.

(h) Prepare an adjusted trial balance at February 28, 2012.

(b) Purchases journal total $34,500
Cash payments journal—Cash, Cr. $35,478

(e) Totals $54,500
(f) Accounts Receivable $12,000
Accounts Payable $6,000

(h) Totals $54,650

Problems: Set C

Visit the book's companion website, at **www.wiley.com/college/weygandt**, and choose the Student Companion site to access Problem Set C.

Comprehensive Problem: Chapters 3 to 7

CP7 Packard Company has the following opening account balances in its general and subsidiary ledgers on January 1 and uses the periodic inventory system. All accounts have normal debit and credit balances.

General Ledger

Account Number	Account Title	January 1 Opening Balance
101	Cash	$33,750
112	Accounts Receivable	13,000
115	Notes Receivable	39,000
120	Inventory	20,000
125	Supplies	1,000
130	Prepaid Insurance	2,000
157	Equipment	6,450
158	Accumulated Depreciation—Equip.	1,500
201	Accounts Payable	35,000
301	Owner's Capital	78,700

Accounts Receivable Subsidiary Ledger

Customer	January 1 Opening Balance
R. Draves	$1,500
B. Hachinski	7,500
S. Ingles	4,000

Accounts Payable Subsidiary Ledger

Creditor	January 1 Opening Balance
S. Kosko	$ 9,000
R. Mikush	15,000
D. Moreno	11,000

Jan. 3 Sell merchandise on account to B. Remy $3,100, invoice no. 510, and J. Fine $1,800, invoice no. 511.

    5 Purchase merchandise on account from S. Yost $3,000 and D. Laux $2,700.

7   Receive checks for $4,000 from S. Ingles and $2,000 from B. Hachinski.
8   Pay freight on merchandise purchased $180.
9   Send checks to S. Kosko for $9,000 and D. Moreno for $11,000.
9   Issue credit of $300 to J. Fine for merchandise returned.
10   Summary cash sales total $15,500.
11   Sell merchandise on account to R. Draves for $1,900, invoice no. 512, and to S. Ingles $900, invoice no. 513.
     Post all entries to the subsidiary ledgers.
12   Pay rent of $1,000 for January.
13   Receive payment in full from B. Remy and J. Fine.
15   Withdraw $800 cash by I. Packard for personal use.
16   Purchase merchandise on account from D. Moreno for $15,000, from S. Kosko for $13,900, and from S. Yost for $1,500.
17   Pay $400 cash for supplies.
18   Return $200 of merchandise to S. Kosko and receive credit.
20   Summary cash sales total $17,500.
21   Issue $15,000 note to R. Mikush in payment of balance due.
21   Receive payment in full from S. Ingles.
     Post all entries to the subsidiary ledgers.
22   Sell merchandise on account to B. Remy for $3,700, invoice no. 514, and to R. Draves for $800, invoice no. 515.
23   Send checks to D. Moreno and S. Kosko in full payment.
25   Sell merchandise on account to B. Hachinski for $3,500, invoice no. 516, and to J. Fine for $6,100, invoice no. 517.
27   Purchase merchandise on account from D. Moreno for $12,500, from D. Laux for $1,200, and from S. Yost for $2,800.
28   Pay $200 cash for office supplies.
31   Summary cash sales total $22,920.
31   Pay sales salaries of $4,300 and office salaries of $3,600.

Instructions

(a) Record the January transactions in the appropriate journal—sales, purchases, cash receipts, cash payments, and general.

(b) Post the journals to the general and subsidiary ledgers. Add and number new accounts in an orderly fashion as needed.

(c) Trial balance totals $196,820; Adj. T/B totals $196,975

(c) Prepare a trial balance at January 31, 2012, using a worksheet. Complete the worksheet using the following additional information.
   (1) Supplies at January 31 total $700.
   (2) Insurance coverage expires on October 31, 2012.
   (3) Annual depreciation on the equipment is $1,500.
   (4) Interest of $30 has accrued on the note payable.
   (5) Inventory at January 31 is $15,000.

(d) Net income $9,685 Total assets $126,315

(d) Prepare a multiple-step income statement and an owner's equity statement for January and a classified balance sheet at the end of January.

(e) Prepare and post the adjusting and closing entries.

(f) Post-closing T/B totals $127,940

(f) Prepare a post-closing trial balance, and determine whether the subsidiary ledgers agree with the control accounts in the general ledger.

BROADENINGYOURPERSPECTIVE

Financial Reporting and Analysis

Financial Reporting Problem—Mini Practice Set

BYP7-1 **(You may use the working papers that accompany this textbook to work this mini practice set.)** Bluma Co. uses a perpetual inventory system and both an accounts receivable and an accounts payable subsidiary ledger. Balances related to both the general ledger and the subsidiary ledger for Bluma are indicated in the working papers. Presented on the next page are a series of transactions for Bluma Co. for the month of January. Credit sales terms are 2/10, n/30. The cost of all merchandise sold was 60% of the sales price.

Jan. 3 Sell merchandise on account to B. Richey $3,100, invoice no. 510, and to J. Forbes $1,800, invoice no. 511.

5 Purchase merchandise from S. Vogel $5,000 and D. Lynch $2,200, terms n/30.

7 Receive checks from S. LaDew $4,000 and B. Garcia $2,000 after discount period has lapsed.

8 Pay freight on merchandise purchased $235.

9 Send checks to S. Hoyt for $9,000 less 2% cash discount, and to D. Omara for $11,000 less 1% cash discount.

9 Issue credit of $300 to J. Forbes for merchandise returned.

10 Summary daily cash sales total $15,500.

11 Sell merchandise on account to R. Dvorak $1,600, invoice no. 512, and to S. LaDew $900, invoice no. 513.

12 Pay rent of $1,000 for January.

13 Receive payment in full from B. Richey and J. Forbes less cash discounts.

15 Withdraw $800 cash by M. Bluma for personal use.

15 Post all entries to the subsidiary ledgers.

16 Purchase merchandise from D. Omara $18,000, terms 1/10, n/30; S. Hoyt $14,200, terms 2/10, n/30; and S. Vogel $1,500, terms n/30.

17 Pay $400 cash for office supplies.

18 Return $200 of merchandise to S. Hoyt and receive credit.

20 Summary daily cash sales total $20,100.

21 Issue $15,000 note, maturing in 90 days, to R. Moses in payment of balance due.

21 Receive payment in full from S. LaDew less cash discount.

22 Sell merchandise on account to B. Richey $2,700, invoice no. 514, and to R. Dvorak $1,300, invoice no. 515.

22 Post all entries to the subsidiary ledgers.

23 Send checks to D. Omara and S. Hoyt in full payment less cash discounts.

25 Sell merchandise on account to B. Garcia $3,500, invoice no. 516, and to J. Forbes $6,100, invoice no. 517.

27 Purchase merchandise from D. Omara $14,500, terms 1/10, n/30; D. Lynch $1,200, terms n/30; and S. Vogel $5,400, terms n/30.

27 Post all entries to the subsidiary ledgers.

28 Pay $200 cash for office supplies.

31 Summary daily cash sales total $21,300.

31 Pay sales salaries $4,300 and office salaries $3,800.

Instructions

(a) Record the January transactions in a sales journal, a single-column purchases journal, a cash receipts journal as shown on page 327, a cash payments journal as shown on page 332, and a two-column general journal.

(b) Post the journals to the general ledger.

(c) Prepare a trial balance at January 31, 2012, in the trial balance columns of the worksheet. Complete the worksheet using the following additional information.

    (1) Office supplies at January 31 total $900.

    (2) Insurance coverage expires on October 31, 2012.

    (3) Annual depreciation on the equipment is $1,500.

    (4) Interest of $50 has accrued on the note payable.

(d) Prepare a multiple-step income statement and an owner's equity statement for January and a classified balance sheet at the end of January.

(e) Prepare and post adjusting and closing entries.

(f) Prepare a post-closing trial balance, and determine whether the subsidiary ledgers agree with the control accounts in the general ledger.

On the Web

BYP7-2 Intuit provides some of the leading accounting software packages. Information related to its products are found at its website.

Address: http://quickbooks.intuit.com or go to **www.wiley.com/college/weygandt**

Instructions

Look under product and services for the product QuickBooks Premier for Accountants. Be ready to discuss its new features with the class.

Critical Thinking

Decision Making Across the Organization

BYP7-3 Hughey & Payne is a wholesaler of small appliances and parts. Hughey & Payne is operated by two owners, Rich Hughey and Kristen Payne. In addition, the company has one employee, a repair specialist, who is on a fixed salary. Revenues are earned through the sale of appliances to retailers (approximately 75% of total revenues), appliance parts to do-it-yourselfers (10%), and the repair of appliances brought to the store (15%). Appliance sales are made on both a credit and cash basis. Customers are billed on prenumbered sales invoices. Credit terms are always net/30 days. All parts sales and repair work are cash only.

Merchandise is purchased on account from the manufacturers of both the appliances and the parts. Practically all suppliers offer cash discounts for prompt payments, and it is company policy to take all discounts. Most cash payments are made by check. Checks are most frequently issued to suppliers, to trucking companies for freight on merchandise purchases, and to newspapers, radio, and TV stations for advertising. All advertising bills are paid as received. Rich and Kristen each make a monthly drawing in cash for personal living expenses. The salaried repairman is paid twice monthly. Hughey & Payne currently has a manual accounting system.

Instructions
With the class divided into groups, answer the following.
(a) Identify the special journals that Hughey & Payne should have in its manual system. List the column headings appropriate for each of the special journals.
(b) What control and subsidiary accounts should be included in Hughey & Payne's manual system? Why?

Communication Activity

BYP7-4 Barb Doane, a classmate, has a part-time bookkeeping job. She is concerned about the inefficiencies in journalizing and posting transactions. Jim Houser is the owner of the company where Barb works. In response to numerous complaints from Barb and others, Jim hired two additional bookkeepers a month ago. However, the inefficiencies have continued at an even higher rate. The accounting information system for the company has only a general journal and a general ledger. Jim refuses to install a computerized accounting system.

Instructions
Now that Barb is an expert in manual accounting information systems, she decides to send a letter to Jim Houser explaining (1) why the additional personnel did not help and (2) what changes should be made to improve the efficiency of the accounting department. Write the letter that you think Barb should send.

Ethics Case

BYP7-5 Roniger Products Company operates three divisions, each with its own manufacturing plant and marketing/sales force. The corporate headquarters and central accounting office are in Roniger, and the plants are in Freeport, Rockport, and Bayport, all within 50 miles of Roniger. Corporate management treats each division as an independent profit center and encourages competition among them. They each have similar but different product lines. As a competitive incentive, bonuses are awarded each year to the employees of the fastest-growing and most-profitable division.

Jose Molina is the manager of Roniger's centralized computerized accounting operation that enters the sales transactions and maintains the accounts receivable for all three divisions. Jose came up in the accounting ranks from the Bayport division where his wife, several relatives, and many friends still work. As sales documents are entered into the computer, the originating division is identified by code. Most sales documents (95%) are coded, but some (5%) are not coded or are coded incorrectly. As the manager, Jose has instructed the data-entry personnel to assign the Bayport code to all uncoded and incorrectly coded sales documents. This is done he says, "in order to expedite processing and to keep the computer files current since they are updated daily." All receivables and cash collections for all three divisions are handled by Roniger as one subsidiary accounts receivable ledger.

Instructions
(a) Who are the stakeholders in this situation?
(b) What are the ethical issues in this case?
(c) How might the system be improved to prevent this situation?

"All About You" Activity

BYP7-6 In this chapter, you learned about a basic manual accounting information system. Computerized accounting systems range from the very basic and inexpensive to the very elaborate and expensive. However, even the most sophisticated systems are based on the fundamental structures and relationships that you learned in this chapter.

Instructions

Go to the book companion site for this text, **www.wiley.com/college/weygandt**, and review the demonstration that is provided for the general ledger software package that is used with this text. Prepare a brief explanation of how the general ledger system works—that is, how it is used, and what information it provides.

Answers to Insight and Accounting Across the Organization Questions

p. 318 Curbing Fraudulent Activity with Software **Q:** Why might this software help reduce fraudulent activity by employees? **A:** By pinpointing who used the accounting system and when they used it, the software can hold employees more accountable for their actions. Companies hope that this will reduce efforts by employees to enter false accounting entries, change the dates of transactions, or create unauthorized expenditures. If employees do engage in these activities, there will be significant evidence of their activities.

p. 321 "I'm John Smith, a.k.a. 13695071642" **Q:** Why use numbers to identify names in a computerized system? **A:** Computerized systems process numbers faster than letters. Also, letters sometimes cause problems because you may have two people with the same name. Computerized systems avoid this problem by giving different customers, including those with the same names, different account numbers.

Answers to Self-Test Questions

1. d **2.** c **3.** a **4.** c **5.** c ($5,000 + $7,000 + $6,000 + $4,500 + $8,500 − $11,500 − $3,000) **6.** c **7.** d
8. c **9.** a **10.** d **11.** c **12.** d **13.** b **14.** c **15.** c

IFRS A Look at IFRS

As discussed in Chapter 1, IFRS is growing in acceptance around the world. For example, recent statistics indicate 40% of the Global Fortune 500 companies use IFRS. And the chair of the IASB predicts that IFRS adoption will grow from its current level of 115 countries to nearly 150 countries in the near future.

When countries accept IFRS for use as accepted accounting policies, companies need guidance to ensure that their first IFRS financial statements contain high-quality information. Specifically, *IFRS 1* requires that information in a company's first IFRS statements (1) be transparent, (2) provide a suitable starting point, and (3) have a cost that does not exceed the benefits.

Key Points

- The basic concepts related to an accounting information system are the same under GAAP and IFRS.

- The use of subsidiary ledgers and control accounts, as well as the system used for recording transactions, are the same under GAAP and IFRS.

- Many companies will be going through a substantial conversion process to switch from their current reporting standards to IFRS.

- The overriding principle in converting to IFRS is full retrospective application of IFRS. Retrospective application—recasting prior financial statements on the basis of IFRS—provides financial statement users with comparable information.

- As indicated, the objective of the conversion process is to present a set of IFRS statements as if the company always reported under IFRS. To achieve this objective, a company follows these steps.

  1. Identify the timing of its first IFRS statements.

  2. Prepare an opening balance sheet at the date of transition to IFRS.

3. Select accounting principles that comply with IFRS, and apply these principles retrospectively.

4. Make extensive disclosures to explain the transition to IFRS.

- Once a company decides to convert to IFRS, it must decide on the transition date and the reporting date. The transition date is the beginning of the earliest period for which full comparative IFRS information is presented. The reporting date is the closing balance sheet date for the first IFRS financial statements.

- To illustrate, assume that FirstChoice Company plans to provide its first IFRS statements for the year ended December 31, 2014. FirstChoice decides to present comparative information for one year only. Therefore, its date of transition to IFRS is January 1, 2013, and its reporting date is December 31, 2014.

- The timeline for first-time adoption is presented in the following graphic.

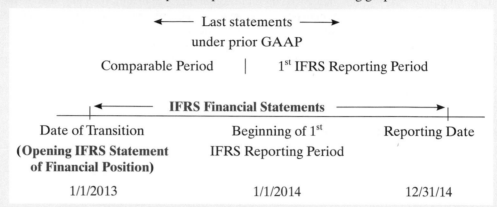

The graphic shows the following.

1. The opening IFRS statement of financial position for FirstChoice on January 1, 2013, serves as the starting point (date of transition) for the company's accounting under IFRS.

2. The first full IFRS statements are shown for FirstChoice for December 31, 2014. In other words, a minimum of two years of IFRS statements must be presented before a conversion to IFRS occurs. As a result, FirstChoice must prepare at least one year of comparative financial statements for 2013 using IFRS.

3. FirstChoice presents financial statements in accordance with U.S. GAAP annually to December 31, 2013.

Following this conversion process, FirstChoice provides users of the financial statements with comparable IFRS statements for 2013 and 2014.

- Upon first-time adoption of IFRS, a company must present at least one year of comparative information under IFRS.

Looking to the Future

The basic recording process shown in this textbook is followed by companies around the globe. It is unlikely to change in the future. The definitional structure of assets, liabilities, equity, revenues, and expenses may change over time as the IASB and FASB evaluate their overall conceptual framework for establishing accounting standards. In addition, high-quality international accounting requires both high-quality accounting standards and high-quality auditing. Similar to the convergence of U.S. GAAP and IFRS, there is a movement to improve international auditing standards. The International Auditing and Assurance Standards Board (IAASB) functions as an independent standard-setting body. It works to establish high-quality auditing and assurance and quality-control standards throughout the world. Whether the IAASB adopts internal control provisions similar to those in SOX remains to be seen. You can follow developments in the international audit arena at *http://www.ifac.org/laasb/*.

Self-Test Questions

1. Information in a company's first IFRS statements must:
   (a) have a cost that does not exceed the benefits.
   (b) be transparent.
   (c) provide a suitable starting point.
   (d) All the above.

2. Indicate which of these statements is *false*.
   (a) The use of subsidiary ledgers is the same under IFRS and GAAP.
   (b) GAAP and IFRS use the same accounting principles.
   (c) The use of special journals is the same under IFRS and GAAP.
   (d) At conversion, companies should retrospectively adjust the financial statements presented following IFRS.

3. The transition date is the date:
   (a) when a company no longer reports under its national standards.
   (b) when the company issues its most recent financial statement under IFRS.
   (c) three years prior to the reporting date.
   (d) None of the above.

4. When converting to IFRS, a company must:
   (a) recast previously issued financial statements in accordance with IFRS.
   (b) use U.S. GAAP in the reporting period but subsequently use IFRS.
   (c) prepare at least three years of comparative statements.
   (d) use U.S. GAAP in the transition year, but IFRS in the reporting year.

5. The purpose of presenting comparative information in the transition to IFRS is:
   (a) to ensure that the information is reliable.
   (b) in accordance with the Sarbanes-Oxley Act.
   (c) to provide users of the financial statements with information on U.S. GAAP in one period and IFRS in the other period.
   (d) to provide users of the financial statements with information on IFRS for at least two periods.

IFRS Concepts and Applications

IFRS7-1   How is the date of transition and the date of reporting determined in first-time adoption of IFRS?

IFRS7-2   What are the characteristics of high-quality information in a company's first IFRS financial statements?

IFRS7-3   What are the steps to be completed in preparing the opening IFRS statement of financial position?

IFRS7-4   Becker Ltd. is planning to adopt IFRS and prepare its first IFRS financial statements at December 31, 2013. What is the date of Becker's opening balance sheet assuming one year of comparative information? What periods will be covered in Becker's first IFRS financial statements?

IFRS7-5   Stengel plc is preparing its opening IFRS balance sheet on January 1, 2012. Under its previous GAAP, Stengel used the LIFO inventory method. Under LIFO, its inventory is reported at £250,000; under FIFO, which Stengel will use upon adoption of IFRS, the inventory is valued at £265,000. Explain what Stengel must do.

Answers to IFRS Self-Test Questions
1. d   2. b   3. d   4. a   5. d

The Navigator

✔ **Remember to go back to the Navigator box on the chapter opening page and check off your completed work.**

CHAPTER8

Fraud, Internal Control, and Cash

Study Objectives

After studying this chapter, you should be able to:

[1] Define fraud and internal control.

[2] Identify the principles of internal control activities.

[3] Explain the applications of internal control principles to cash receipts.

[4] Explain the applications of internal control principles to cash disbursements.

[5] Describe the operation of a petty cash fund.

[6] Indicate the control features of a bank account.

[7] Prepare a bank reconciliation.

[8] Explain the reporting of cash.

The Navigator

✔ [The Navigator]

Feature Story

MINDING THE MONEY IN MOOSE JAW

If you're ever looking for a cappuccino in Moose Jaw, Saskatchewan, stop by Stephanie's Gourmet Coffee and More, located on Main Street. Staff there serve, on average, 650 cups of coffee a day, including both regular and specialty coffees, not to mention soups, Italian sandwiches, and a wide assortment of gourmet cheesecakes.

"We've got high school students who come here, and students from the community college," says owner/manager Stephanie Mintenko, who has run the place since opening it in 1995. "We have customers who are retired, and others who are working people and have only 30 minutes for lunch. We have to be pretty quick."

That means that the cashiers have to be efficient. Like most businesses where purchases are low-cost and high-volume, cash control has to be simple.

"We have an electronic cash register, but it's not the fancy new kind where you just punch in the item," explains Ms. Mintenko. "You have to punch in the prices." The machine does keep track of sales in several categories, however. Cashiers punch a button to indicate whether each item is a beverage, a meal, or a charge for the cafe's Internet connections. An internal tape in the machine keeps a record of all transactions; the customer receives a receipt only upon request.

There is only one cash register. "Up to three of us might operate it on any given shift, including myself," says Ms. Mintenko.

She and her staff do two "cashouts" each day—one with the shift change at 5:00 p.m. and one when the shop closes at 10:00 p.m. At each cashout, they count the cash in the register drawer. That amount, minus the cash change carried forward (the float), should match the shift total on the register tape. If there's a discrepancy, they do another count. Then, if necessary, "we go through the whole tape to find the mistake," she explains. "It usually turns out to be someone who punched in $18 instead of $1.80, or something like that."

Ms. Mintenko sends all the cash tapes and float totals to a bookkeeper, who double-checks everything and provides regular reports. "We try to keep the accounting simple, so we can concentrate on making great coffee and food."

Inside**CHAPTER8**

As the story about recording cash sales at Stephanie's Gourmet Coffee and More indicates, control of cash is important to ensure that fraud does not occur. Companies also need controls to safeguard other types of assets. For example, Stephanie's undoubtedly has controls to prevent the theft of food and supplies, and controls to prevent the theft of tableware and dishes from its kitchen.

In this chapter, we explain the essential features of an internal control system and how it prevents fraud. We also describe how those controls apply to a specific asset—cash. The applications include some controls with which you may be already familiar, such as the use of a bank.

The content and organization of Chapter 8 are as follows.

Fraud, Internal Control, and Cash			
Fraud and Internal Control	**Cash Controls**	**Control Features: Use of a Bank**	**Reporting Cash**
• Fraud • The Sarbanes-Oxley Act • Internal control • Principles of internal control activities • Limitations	• Cash receipts controls • Cash disbursements controls	• Making deposits • Writing checks • Bank statements • Reconciling the bank account • Electronic funds transfer (EFT) system	• Cash equivalents • Restricted cash

The Navigator

Fraud and Internal Control

Study Objective [1]
Define fraud and internal control.

The Feature Story describes many of the internal control procedures used by Stephanie's Gourmet Coffee and More. These procedures are necessary to discourage employees from fraudulent activities.

Fraud

A **fraud** is a dishonest act by an employee that results in personal benefit to the employee at a cost to the employer. Examples of fraud reported in the financial press include:

- A bookkeeper in a small company diverted $750,000 of bill payments to a personal bank account over a three-year period.
- A shipping clerk with 28 years of service shipped $125,000 of merchandise to himself.
- A computer operator embezzled $21 million from Wells Fargo Bank over a two-year period.
- A church treasurer "borrowed" $150,000 of church funds to finance a friend's business dealings.

Why does fraud occur? The three main factors that contribute to fraudulent activity are depicted by the **fraud triangle** in Illustration 8-1.

The most important element of the fraud triangle is **opportunity**. For an employee to commit fraud, the workplace environment must provide opportunities that an employee can take advantage of. Opportunities occur when the workplace lacks sufficient controls to deter and detect fraud. For example, inadequate monitoring of employee actions can create opportunities for theft and can embolden employees because they believe they will not be caught.

A second factor that contributes to fraud is **financial pressure**. Employees sometimes commit fraud because of personal financial problems caused by too much debt. Or they might commit fraud because they want to lead a lifestyle that they cannot afford on their current salary.

The third factor that contributes to fraud is **rationalization**. In order to justify their fraud, employees rationalize their dishonest actions. For example, employees sometimes justify fraud because they believe they are underpaid while the employer is making lots of money. Employees feel justified in stealing because they believe they deserve to be paid more.

Illustration 8-1
Fraud triangle

The Sarbanes-Oxley Act

What can be done to prevent or to detect fraud? After numerous corporate scandals came to light in the early 2000s, Congress addressed this issue by passing the Sarbanes-Oxley Act of 2002 (SOX). Under SOX, all publicly traded U.S. corporations are required to maintain an adequate system of internal control. Corporate executives and boards of directors must ensure that these controls are reliable and effective. In addition, independent outside auditors must attest to the adequacy of the internal control system. Companies that fail to comply are subject to fines, and company officers can be imprisoned. SOX also created the Public Company Accounting Oversight Board (PCAOB), to establish auditing standards and regulate auditor activity.

One poll found that 60% of investors believe that SOX helps safeguard their stock investments. Many say they would be unlikely to invest in a company that fails to follow SOX requirements. Although some corporate executives have criticized the time and expense involved in following the SOX requirements, SOX appears to be working well. For example, the chief accounting officer of Eli Lily noted that SOX triggered a comprehensive review of how the company documents controls. This review uncovered redundancies and pointed out controls that needed to be added. In short, it added up to time and money well spent. And the finance chief at General Electric noted, "We have seen value in SOX. It helps build investors' trust and gives them more confidence."[1]

Internal Control

Internal control consists of all the related methods and measures adopted within an organization to safeguard its assets, enhance the reliability of its accounting records, increase efficiency of operations, and ensure compliance with laws and regulations. Internal control systems have five primary components as listed below.[2]

- **A control environment.** It is the responsibility of top management to make it clear that the organization values integrity and that unethical activity will not be tolerated. This component is often referred to as the "tone at the top."

---

[1]"Corporate Regulation Must Be Working—There's a Backlash," *Wall Street Journal,* June 16, 2004, p. C1; and Judith Burns, "Is Sarbanes-Oxley Working?" *Wall Street Journal,* June 21, 2004, pp. R8–R9.

[2]The Committee of Sponsoring Organizations of the Treadway Commission, "Internal Control—Integrated Framework," *www.coso.org/publications/executive_summary_integrated_framework.htm* (accessed March 2008).

- **Risk assessment.** Companies must identify and analyze the various factors that create risk for the business and must determine how to manage these risks.
- **Control activities.** To reduce the occurrence of fraud, management must design policies and procedures to address the specific risks faced by the company.
- **Information and communication.** The internal control system must capture and communicate all pertinent information both down and up the organization, as well as communicate information to appropriate external parties.
- **Monitoring.** Internal control systems must be monitored periodically for their adequacy. Significant deficiencies need to be reported to top management and/or the board of directors.

Principles of Internal Control Activities

Study Objective [2]

Identify the principles of internal control activities.

Each of the five components of an internal control system is important. Here, we will focus on one component, the control activities. The reason? These activities are the backbone of the company's efforts to address the risks it faces, such as fraud. The specific control activities used by a company will vary, depending on management's assessment of the risks faced. This assessment is heavily influenced by the size and nature of the company.

The six principles of control activities are as follows.

- Establishment of responsibility
- Segregation of duties
- Documentation procedures
- Physical controls
- Independent internal verification
- Human resource controls

We explain these principles in the following sections. You should recognize that they apply to most companies and are relevant to both manual and computerized accounting systems.

It's your shift now. I'm turning in my cash drawer and heading home.

Transfer of cash drawers

ESTABLISHMENT OF RESPONSIBILITY

An essential principle of internal control is to assign responsibility to specific employees. **Control is most effective when only one person is responsible for a given task.**

To illustrate, assume that the cash on hand at the end of the day in a Safeway supermarket is $10 short of the cash rung up on the cash register. If only one person has operated the register, the shift manager can quickly determine responsibility for the shortage. If two or more individuals have worked the register, it may be impossible to determine who is responsible for the error. In the Feature Story, the principle of establishing responsibility does not appear to be strictly applied by Stephanie's, since three people operate the cash register on any given shift.

Establishing responsibility often requires limiting access only to authorized personnel, and then identifying those personnel. For example, the automated systems used by many companies have mechanisms such as identifying passcodes that keep track of who made a journal entry, who rang up a sale, or who entered an inventory storeroom at a particular time. Use of identifying passcodes enables the company to establish responsibility by identifying the particular employee who carried out the activity.

Maureen Frugali was a training supervisor for claims processing at Colossal Healthcare. As a standard part of the claims processing training program, Maureen created fictitious claims for use by trainees. These fictitious claims were then sent to the accounts payable department. After the training claims had been processed, she was to notify Accounts Payable of all fictitious claims, so that they would not be paid. However, she did not inform Accounts Payable about every fictitious claim. She created some fictitious claims for entities that she controlled (that is, she would receive the payment), and she let Accounts Payable pay her.

Total take: $11 million

THE MISSING CONTROL

Establishment of responsibility. The healthcare company did not adequately restrict the responsibility for authoring and approving claims transactions. The training supervisor should not have been authorized to create claims in the company's "live" system.

Source: Adapted from Wells, *Fraud Casebook* (2007), pp. 61–70.

SEGREGATION OF DUTIES

Segregation of duties is indispensable in an internal control system. There are two common applications of this principle:

1. Different individuals should be responsible for related activities.
2. The responsibility for record-keeping for an asset should be separate from the physical custody of that asset.

The rationale for segregation of duties is this: **The work of one employee should, without a duplication of effort, provide a reliable basis for evaluating the work of another employee.** For example, the personnel that design and program computerized systems should not be assigned duties related to day-to-day use of the system. Otherwise, they could design the system to benefit them personally and conceal the fraud through day-to-day use.

Segregation of Related Activities.   **Making one individual responsible for related activities increases the potential for errors and irregularities.** For example, companies should assign related *purchasing activities* to different individuals. Related purchasing activities include ordering merchandise, order approval, receiving goods, authorizing payment, and paying for goods or services. Various frauds are possible when one person handles related purchasing activities. For example:

- If a purchasing agent is allowed to order goods without obtaining supervisory approval, the likelihood of the purchasing agent receiving kickbacks from suppliers increases.
- If an employee who orders goods also handles receipt of the goods and invoice, as well as payment authorization, he or she might authorize payment for a fictitious invoice.

These abuses are less likely to occur when companies divide the purchasing tasks. Similarly, companies should assign related *sales activities* to different individuals. Related selling activities include making a sale, shipping (or delivering) the goods to the customer, billing the customer, and receiving payment. Various frauds are possible when one person handles related sales transactions. For example:

- If a salesperson can make a sale without obtaining supervisory approval, he or she might make sales at unauthorized prices to increase sales commissions.
- A shipping clerk who also has access to accounting records could ship goods to himself.
- A billing clerk who handles billing and receipt could understate the amount billed for sales made to friends and relatives.

These abuses are less likely to occur when companies divide the sales tasks: The salespeople make the sale; the shipping department ships the goods on the basis of the sales order; and the billing department prepares the sales invoice after comparing the sales order with the report of goods shipped.

ANATOMY OF A FRAUD

Lawrence Fairbanks, the assistant vice-chancellor of communications at Aesop University, was allowed to make purchases of under $2,500 for his department without external approval. Unfortunately, he also sometimes bought items for himself, such as expensive antiques and other collectibles. How did he do it? He replaced the vendor invoices he received with fake vendor invoices that he created. The fake invoices had descriptions that were more consistent with the communications department's purchases. He submitted these fake invoices to the accounting department as the basis for their journal entries and to the accounts payable department as the basis for payment.

Total take: $475,000

THE MISSING CONTROL

Segregation of duties. The university had not properly segregated related purchasing activities. Lawrence was ordering items, receiving the items, and receiving the invoice. By receiving the invoice, he had control over the documents that were used to account for the purchase and thus was able to substitute a fake invoice.

Source: Adapted from Wells, *Fraud Casebook* (2007), pp. 3–15.

Accounting Employee A
Maintains cash balances per books

Segregation of Duties
(Accountability for assets)

Assistant Cashier B
Maintains custody of cash on hand

Segregation of Record-Keeping from Physical Custody. The accountant should have neither physical custody of the asset nor access to it. Likewise, the custodian of the asset should not maintain or have access to the accounting records. **The custodian of the asset is not likely to convert the asset to personal use when one employee maintains the record of the asset, and a different employee has physical custody of the asset.** The separation of accounting responsibility from the custody of assets is especially important for cash and inventories because these assets are very vulnerable to fraud.

ANATOMY OF A FRAUD

Angela Bauer was an accounts payable clerk for Aggasiz Construction Company. She prepared and issued checks to vendors and reconciled bank statements. She perpetrated a fraud in this way: She wrote checks for costs that the company had not actually incurred (e.g., fake taxes). A supervisor then approved and signed the checks. Before issuing the check, though, she would "white-out" the payee line on the check and change it to personal accounts that she controlled. She was able to conceal the theft because she also reconciled the bank account. That is, nobody else ever saw that the checks had been altered.

Total take: $570,000

THE MISSING CONTROL

Segregation of duties. Aggasiz Construction Company did not properly segregate record-keeping from physical custody. Angela had physical custody of the checks, which essentially was control of the cash. She also had record-keeping responsibility because she prepared the bank reconciliation.

Source: Adapted from Wells, *Fraud Casebook* (2007), pp. 100–107.

DOCUMENTATION PROCEDURES

Documents provide evidence that transactions and events have occurred. At Stephanie's Gourmet Coffee and More, the cash register tape is the restaurant's documentation for the sale and the amount of cash received. Similarly, a shipping document indicates that the goods have been shipped, and a sales invoice indicates that the company has billed the customer for the goods. By requiring signatures (or initials) on the documents, the company can identify the individual(s) responsible for the transaction or event. Companies should document transactions when the transaction occurs.

Companies should establish procedures for documents. First, whenever possible, companies should use **prenumbered documents, and all documents should be accounted for**. Prenumbering helps to prevent a transaction from being recorded more than once, or conversely, from not being recorded at all. Second, the control system should require that employees **promptly forward source documents for accounting entries to the accounting department. This control measure helps to ensure timely recording of the transaction** and contributes directly to the accuracy and reliability of the accounting records.

Prenumbered invoices

ANATOMY OF A FRAUD

To support their reimbursement requests for travel costs incurred, employees at Mod Fashions Corporation's design center were required to submit receipts. The receipts could include the detailed bill provided for a meal, or the credit card receipt provided when the credit card payment is made, or a copy of the employee's monthly credit card bill that listed the item. A number of the designers who frequently traveled together came up with a fraud scheme: They submitted claims for the same expenses. For example, if they had a meal together that cost $200, one person submitted the detailed meal bill, another submitted the credit card receipt, and a third submitted a monthly credit card bill showing the meal as a line item. Thus, all three received a $200 reimbursement.

Total take: $75,000

THE MISSING CONTROL

Documentation procedures. Mod Fashions should require the original, detailed receipt. It should not accept photocopies, and it should not accept credit card statements. In addition, documentation procedures could be further improved by requiring the use of a corporate credit card (rather than a personal credit card) for all business expenses.

Source: Adapted from Wells, *Fraud Casebook* (2007), pp. 79–90.

PHYSICAL CONTROLS

Use of physical controls is essential. *Physical controls* relate to the safeguarding of assets and enhance the accuracy and reliability of the accounting records. Illustration 8-2 shows examples of these controls.

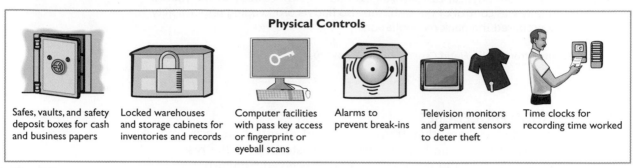

Physical Controls

| Safes, vaults, and safety deposit boxes for cash and business papers | Locked warehouses and storage cabinets for inventories and records | Computer facilities with pass key access or fingerprint or eyeball scans | Alarms to prevent break-ins | Television monitors and garment sensors to deter theft | Time clocks for recording time worked |

Illustration 8-2
Physical controls

ANATOMY OF A FRAUD

At Centerstone Health, a large insurance company, the mailroom each day received insurance applications from prospective customers. Mailroom employees scanned the applications into electronic documents before the applications were processed. Once the applications are scanned they can be accessed online by authorized employees.

Insurance agents at Centerstone Health earn commissions based upon successful applications. The sales agent's name is listed on the application. However, roughly 15% of the applications are from customers who did not work with a sales agent. Two friends—Alex, an employee in record keeping, and Parviz, a sales agent—thought up a way to perpetrate a fraud. Alex identified scanned applications that did not list a sales agent. After business hours, he entered the mailroom and found the hardcopy applications that did not show a sales agent. He wrote in Parviz's name as the sales agent and then rescanned the application for processing. Parviz received the commission, which the friends then split.

Total take: $240,000

THE MISSING CONTROL

Physical controls. Centerstone Health lacked two basic physical controls that could have prevented this fraud. First, the mailroom should have been locked during nonbusiness hours, and access during business hours should have been tightly controlled. Second, the scanned applications supposedly could be accessed only by authorized employees using their passwords. However, the password for each employee was the same as the employee's user ID. Since employee user-ID numbers were available to all other employees, all employees knew all other employees' passwords. Unauthorized employees could access the scanned applications. Thus, Alex could enter the system using another employee's password and access the scanned applications.

Source: Adapted from Wells, *Fraud Casebook* (2007), pp. 316–326.

INDEPENDENT INTERNAL VERIFICATION

Most internal control systems provide for **independent internal verification**. This principle involves the review of data prepared by employees. To obtain maximum benefit from independent internal verification:

1. Companies should verify records periodically or on a surprise basis.
2. An employee who is independent of the personnel responsible for the information should make the verification.
3. Discrepancies and exceptions should be reported to a management level that can take appropriate corrective action.

Independent internal verification is especially useful in comparing recorded accountability with existing assets. The reconciliation of the cash register tape with the cash in the register at Stephanie's Gourmet Coffee and More is an example of this internal control principle. Another common example is the reconciliation of a company's cash balance per books with the cash balance per bank and the verification of the perpetual inventory records through a count of physical inventory. Illustration 8-3 shows the relationship between this principle and the segregation of duties principle.

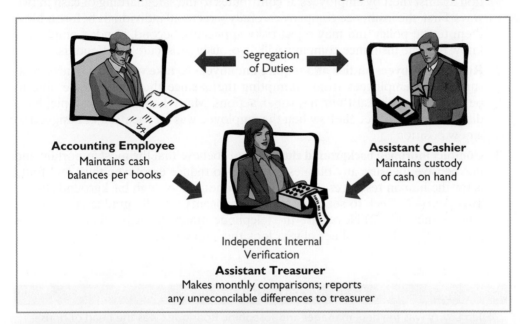

Accounting Employee
Maintains cash balances per books

Segregation of Duties

Assistant Cashier
Maintains custody of cash on hand

Independent Internal Verification
Assistant Treasurer
Makes monthly comparisons; reports any unreconcilable differences to treasurer

Illustration 8-3
Comparison of segregation of duties principle with independent internal verification principle

ANATOMY OF A FRAUD

Bobbi Jean Donnelly, the office manager for Mod Fashions Corporations design center, was responsible for preparing the design center budget and reviewing expense reports submitted by design center employees. Her desire to upgrade her wardrobe got the better of her, and she enacted a fraud that involved filing expense-reimbursement requests for her own personal clothing purchases. She was able to conceal the fraud because she was responsible for reviewing all expense reports, including her own. In addition, she sometimes was given ultimate responsibility for signing off on the expense reports when her boss was "too busy." Also, because she controlled the budget, when she submitted her expenses, she coded them to budget items that she knew were running under budget, so that they would not catch anyone's attention.

Total take: $275,000

THE MISSING CONTROL

Independent internal verification. Bobbi Jean's boss should have verified her expense reports. When asked what he thought her expenses for a year were, the boss said about $10,000. At $115,000 per year, her actual expenses were more than ten times what would have been expected. However, because he was "too busy" to verify her expense reports or to review the budget, he never noticed.

Source: Adapted from Wells, *Fraud Casebook* (2007), pp. 79–90.

Large companies often assign independent internal verification to internal auditors. **Internal auditors** are company employees who continuously evaluate the effectiveness of the company's internal control systems. They review the activities of departments and individuals to determine whether prescribed internal controls are being followed. They also recommend improvements when needed. In fact, most fraud is discovered by the company through internal mechanisms such as existing internal controls and internal audits. For example, the alleged fraud at WorldCom, involving billions of dollars, was uncovered by an internal auditor.

HUMAN RESOURCE CONTROLS

Human resource control activities include the following.

1. **Bond employees who handle cash. Bonding** involves obtaining insurance protection against theft by employees. It contributes to the safeguarding of cash in two ways: First, the insurance company carefully screens all individuals before adding them to the policy and may reject risky applicants. Second, bonded employees know that the insurance company will vigorously prosecute all offenders.

2. **Rotate employees' duties and require employees to take vacations.** These measures deter employees from attempting thefts since they will not be able to permanently conceal their improper actions. Many banks, for example, have discovered employee thefts when the employee was on vacation or assigned to a new position.

3. **Conduct thorough background checks.** Many believe that the most important and inexpensive measure any business can take to reduce employee theft and fraud is for the human resources department to conduct thorough background checks. Two tips: (1) Check to see whether job applicants actually graduated from the schools they list. (2) Never use the telephone numbers for previous employers given on the reference sheet; always look them up yourself.

ANATOMY OF A FRAUD

Ellen Lowry was the desk manager and Josephine Rodriquez was the head of housekeeping at the Excelsior Inn, a luxury hotel. The two best friends were so dedicated to their jobs that they never took vacations, and they frequently filled in for other employees. In fact, Ms. Rodriquez, whose job as head of housekeeping did not include cleaning rooms, often cleaned rooms herself, "just to help the staff keep up." These two "dedicated" employees, working as a team, found a way to earn a little more cash. Ellen, the desk manager, provided significant discounts to guests who paid with cash. She kept the cash and did not register the guest in the hotel's computerized system. Instead, she took the room out of circulation "due to routine maintenance." Because the room did not show up as being used, it did not receive a normal housekeeping assignment. Instead, Josephine, the head of housekeeping, cleaned the rooms during the guests' stay.

Total take: $95,000

THE MISSING CONTROL

Human resource controls. Ellen, the desk manager, had been fired by a previous employer after being accused of fraud. If the Excelsior Inn had conducted a thorough background check, it would not have hired her. The hotel fraud was detected when Ellen missed work for a few days due to illness. A system of mandatory vacations and rotating days off would have increased the chances of detecting the fraud before it became so large.

Source: Adapted from Wells, *Fraud Casebook* (2007), pp. 145–155.

SOX Boosts the Role of Human Resources

Under SOX, a company needs to keep track of employees' degrees and certifications to ensure that employees continue to meet the specified requirements of a job. Also, to ensure proper employee supervision and proper separation of duties, companies must develop and monitor an organizational chart. When one corporation went through this exercise, it found that out of 17,000 employees, there were 400 people who did not report to anyone, and they had 35 people who reported to each other. In addition, if an employee complains of an unfair firing and mentions financial issues at the company, HR must refer the case to the company audit committee and possibly to its legal counsel.

 Why would unsupervised employees or employees who report to each other represent potential internal control threats? (See page 410.)

Limitations of Internal Control

Companies generally design their systems of internal control to provide **reasonable assurance** of proper safeguarding of assets and reliability of the accounting records. The concept of reasonable assurance rests on the premise that the costs of establishing control procedures should not exceed their expected benefit.

To illustrate, consider shoplifting losses in retail stores. Stores could eliminate such losses by having a security guard stop and search customers as they leave the store. But store managers have concluded that the negative effects of such a procedure cannot be justified. Instead, stores have attempted to control shoplifting losses by less costly procedures: They post signs saying, "We reserve the right to inspect all packages" and "All shoplifters will be prosecuted." They use hidden TV cameras and store detectives to monitor customer activity, and they install sensor equipment at exits.

The **human element** is an important factor in every system of internal control. A good system can become ineffective as a result of employee fatigue, carelessness, or indifference. For example, a receiving clerk may not bother to count goods received and may just "fudge" the counts. Occasionally, two or more individuals may work together to get around prescribed controls. Such **collusion** can significantly reduce the effectiveness of a system, eliminating the protection offered by segregation of duties. No system of internal control is perfect.

The size of the business also may impose limitations on internal control. A small company, for example, may find it difficult to segregate duties or to provide for independent internal verification.

Helpful Hint

Controls may vary with the risk level of the activity. For example, management may consider cash to be high risk and maintaining inventories in the stockroom as low risk. Thus, management would have stricter controls for cash.

Big Theft at Small Companies

A study by the Association of Certified Fraud Examiners indicates that businesses with fewer than 100 employees are most at risk for employee theft. In fact, 38% of frauds occurred at companies with fewer than 100 employees. The median loss at small companies was $200,000, which was higher than the median fraud at companies with more than 10,000 employees ($147,000). A $200,000 loss can threaten the very existence of a small company.

Source: 2008 Report to the Nation on Occupational Fraud and Abuse, Association of Certified Fraud Examiners, www.acfe.com/documents/2008-rttn.pdf, p. 26.

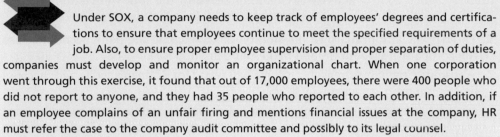

? Why are small companies more susceptible to employee theft? (See page 410.)

Do it!

Control Activities

Identify which control activity is violated in each of the following situations, and explain how the situation creates an opportunity for a fraud.

1. The person with primary responsibility for reconciling the bank account is also the company's accountant and makes all bank deposits.
2. Wellstone Company's treasurer received an award for distinguished service because he had not taken a vacation in 30 years.
3. In order to save money spent on order slips, and to reduce time spent keeping track of order slips, a local bar/restaurant does not buy prenumbered order slips.

action plan

✔ Familiarize yourself with each of the control activities summarized on page xxx.

✔ Understand the nature of the frauds that each control activity is intended to address.

Solution

1. Violates the control activity of segregation of duties. Record-keeping should be separate from physical custody. As a consequence, the employee could embezzle cash and make journal entries to hide the theft.
2. Violates the control activity of human resource controls. Key employees must take vacations. Otherwise, the treasurer, who manages the company's cash, might embezzle cash and use his position to conceal the theft.
3. Violates the control activity of documentation procedures. If pre-numbered documents are not used, then it is virtually impossible to account for the documents. As a consequence, an employee could write up a dinner sale, receive the cash from the customer, and then throw away the order slip and keep the cash.

Related exercise material: BE8-1, BE8-2, BE8-3, E8-1, and **Do it!** 8-1.

✔
The Navigator

Cash Controls

Cash is the one asset that is readily convertible into any other type of asset. It also is easily concealed and transported, and is highly desired. Because of these characteristics, **cash is the asset most susceptible to fraudulent activities**. In addition, because of the large volume of cash transactions, numerous errors may occur in executing and recording them. To safeguard cash and to ensure the accuracy of the accounting records for cash, effective internal control over cash is critical.

Cash Receipts Controls

Study Objective [3]

Explain the applications of internal control principles to cash receipts.

Illustration 8-4 shows how the internal control principles explained earlier apply to cash receipts transactions. As you might expect, companies vary considerably in how they apply these principles. To illustrate internal control over cash receipts, we will examine control activities for a retail store with both over-the-counter and mail receipts.

OVER-THE-COUNTER RECEIPTS

In retail businesses, control of over-the-counter receipts centers on cash registers that are visible to customers. A cash sale is rung up on a cash register, with the amount clearly visible to the customer. This activity prevents the cashier from ringing up a lower amount and pocketing the difference. The customer receives an itemized cash register receipt slip and is expected to count the change received. The

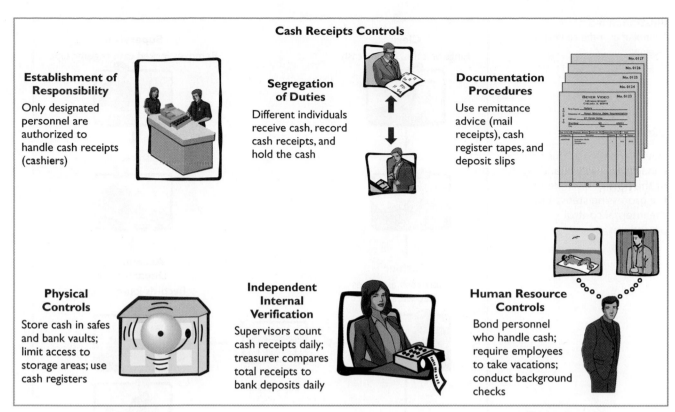

Cash Receipts Controls

Establishment of Responsibility

Only designated personnel are authorized to handle cash receipts (cashiers)

Segregation of Duties

Different individuals receive cash, record cash receipts, and hold the cash

Documentation Procedures

Use remittance advice (mail receipts), cash register tapes, and deposit slips

Physical Controls

Store cash in safes and bank vaults; limit access to storage areas; use cash registers

Independent Internal Verification

Supervisors count cash receipts daily; treasurer compares total receipts to bank deposits daily

Human Resource Controls

Bond personnel who handle cash; require employees to take vacations; conduct background checks

Illustration 8-4
Application of internal control principles to cash receipts

cash register's tape is locked in the register until a supervisor removes it. This tape accumulates the daily transactions and totals.

At the end of the clerk's shift, the clerk counts the cash and sends the cash and the count to the cashier. The cashier counts the cash, prepares a deposit slip, and deposits the cash at the bank. The cashier also sends a duplicate of the deposit slip to the accounting department to indicate cash received. The supervisor removes the cash register tape and sends it to the accounting department as the basis for a journal entry to record the cash received. Illustration 8-5 (page 374) summarizes this process.

This system for handling cash receipts uses an important internal control principle—segregation of record-keeping from physical custody. The supervisor has access to the cash register tape, but **not** to the cash. The clerk and the cashier have access to the cash, but **not** to the register tape. In addition, the cash register tape provides documentation and enables independent internal verification. Use of these three principles of internal control (segregation of record-keeping from physical custody, documentation, and independent internal verification) provides an effective system of internal control. Any attempt at fraudulent activity should be detected unless there is collusion among the employees.

In some instances, the amount deposited at the bank will not agree with the cash recorded in the accounting records based on the cash register tape. These differences often result because the clerk hands incorrect change back to the retail customer. In this case, the difference between the actual cash and the amount reported on the cash register tape is reported in a Cash Over and Short account. For example, suppose that the cash register tape indicated sales of $6,956.20 but the amount of cash was only $6,946.10. A cash shortfall of $10.10 exists. To account for this cash shortfall and related cash, the company makes the following entry.

Illustration 8-5
Control of over-the-counter
receipts

Helpful Hint

Flowcharts such as this one
enhance the understanding
of the flow of documents,
the processing steps, and
the internal control
procedures.

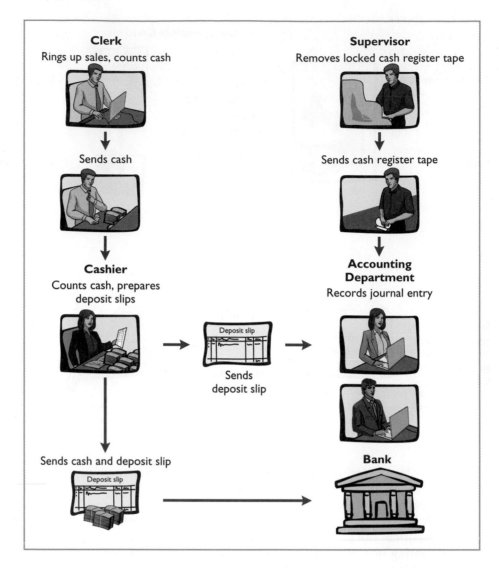

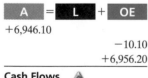
+6,946.10
$\quad$ −10.10
$\quad$ +6,956.20

Cash Flows
+6,946.10

Cash	6,946.10	
Cash Over and Short	10.10	
$\quad$ Sales Revenue		6,956.20
$\quad\quad$ (To record cash shortfall)		

Cash Over and Short is an income statement item. It is reported as miscellaneous expense when there is a cash shortfall, and as miscellaneous revenue when there is an overage. Clearly, the amount should be small. Any material amounts in this account should be investigated.

MAIL RECEIPTS

All mail receipts should be opened in the presence of at least two mail clerks. These receipts are generally in the form of checks. A mail clerk should endorse each check "For Deposit Only." This restrictive endorsement reduces the likelihood that someone could divert the check to personal use. Banks will not give an individual cash when presented with a check that has this type of endorsement.

The mail-receipt clerks prepare, in triplicate, a list of the checks received each day. This list shows the name of the check issuer, the purpose of the payment, and the amount of the check. Each mail clerk signs the list to establish responsibility for the data. The original copy of the list, along with the checks, is then sent to the cashier's department. A copy of the list is sent to the accounting department for recording in the accounting records. The clerks also keep a copy.

This process provides excellent internal control for the company. By employing two clerks, the chance of fraud is reduced; each clerk knows he or she is being observed by the other clerk(s). To engage in fraud, they would have to collude. The customers who submit payments also provide control, because they will contact the company with a complaint if they are not properly credited for payment. Because the cashier has access to cash but not the records, and the accounting department has access to records but not cash, neither can engage in undetected fraud.

Do it!

L. R. Cortez is concerned about the control over cash receipts in his fast-food restaurant, Big Cheese. The restaurant has two cash registers. At no time do more than two employees take customer orders and ring up sales. Work shifts for employees range from 4 to 8 hours. Cortez asks your help in installing a good system of internal control over cash receipts.

Solution

Cortez should assign a cash register to each employee at the start of each work shift, with register totals set at zero. Each employee should be instructed to use only the assigned register and to ring up all sales. Each customer should be given a receipt. At the end of the shift, the employee should do a cash count. A separate employee should compare the cash count with the register tape, to be sure they agree. In addition, Cortez should install an automated system that would enable the company to compare orders rung up on the register to orders processed by the kitchen.

Related exercise material: BE8-5, E8-2, and **Do it!** 8-2.

Control over Cash Receipts

action plan

✔ Differentiate among the internal control principles of (1) establishing responsibility, (2) using physical controls, and (3) independent internal verification.

✔ Design an effective system of internal control over cash receipts.

The Navigator

Cash Disbursements Controls

Companies disburse cash for a variety of reasons, such as to pay expenses and liabilities or to purchase assets. **Generally, internal control over cash disbursements is more effective when companies pay by check, rather than by cash.** One exception is **for incidental amounts that are paid out of petty cash.**[3]

Companies generally issue checks only after following specified control procedures. Illustration 8-6 (page 376) shows how principles of internal control apply to cash disbursements.

Study Objective [4]
Explain the applications of internal control principles to cash disbursements.

VOUCHER SYSTEM CONTROLS

Most medium and large companies use vouchers as part of their internal control over cash disbursements. A **voucher system** is a network of approvals by authorized individuals, acting independently, to ensure that all disbursements by check are proper.

---

[3]We explain the operation of a petty cash fund on pages 377–380.

Cash Disbursements Controls

Establishment of Responsibility

Only designated personnel are authorized to sign checks (treasurer) and approve vendors

Physical Controls

Store blank checks in safes, with limited access; print check amounts by machine in indelible ink

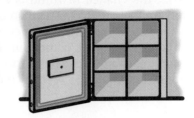

Segregation of Duties

Different individuals approve and make payments; check signers do not record disbursements

Independent Internal Verification

Compare checks to invoices; reconcile bank statement monthly

Documentation Procedures

Use prenumbered checks and account for them in sequence; each check must have an approved invoice; require employees to use corporate credit cards for reimbursable expenses; stamp invoices "paid"

Human Resource Controls

Bond personnel who handle cash; require employees to take vacations; conduct background checks

Illustration 8-6
Application of internal control principles to cash disbursements

The system begins with the authorization to incur a cost or expense. It ends with the issuance of a check for the liability incurred. A **voucher** is an authorization form prepared for each expenditure. Companies require vouchers for all types of cash disbursements except those from petty cash.

The starting point in preparing a voucher is to fill in the appropriate information about the liability on the face of the voucher. The vendor's invoice provides most of the needed information. Then, an employee in accounts payable records the voucher (in a journal called a **voucher register**) and files it according to the date on which it is to be paid. The company issues and sends a check on that date, and stamps the voucher "paid." The paid voucher is sent to the accounting department for recording (in a journal called the **check register**). A voucher system involves two journal entries, one to record the liability when the voucher is issued and a second to pay the liability that relates to the voucher.

The use of a voucher system improves internal control over cash disbursements. First, the authorization process inherent in a voucher system establishes responsibility. Each individual has responsibility to review the underlying documentation to ensure that it is correct. In addition, the voucher system keeps track of the documents that back up each transaction. By keeping these documents in one place, a supervisor can independently verify the authenticity of each transaction. Consider, for example, the case of Aesop University presented on page 366. Aesop did not use a voucher system for transactions under $2,500. As a consequence, there was no independent verification of the documents, which enabled the employee to submit fake invoices to hide his unauthorized purchases.

PETTY CASH FUND CONTROLS

As you learned earlier in the chapter, better internal control over cash disbursements is possible when companies make payments by check. However, using checks to pay small amounts is both impractical and a nuisance. For instance, a company would not want to write checks to pay for postage due, working lunches, or taxi fares. A common way of handling such payments, while maintaining satisfactory control, is to use a **petty cash fund** to pay relatively small amounts. The operation of a petty cash fund, often called an **imprest system**, involves (1) establishing the fund, (2) making payments from the fund, and (3) replenishing the fund.[4]

Establishing the Petty Cash Fund. Two essential steps in establishing a petty cash fund are: (1) appointing a petty cash custodian who will be responsible for the fund, and (2) determining the size of the fund. Ordinarily, a company expects the amount in the fund to cover anticipated disbursements for a three- to four-week period.

To establish the fund, a company issues a check payable to the petty cash custodian for the stipulated amount. For example, if Laird Company decides to establish a $100 fund on March 1, the general journal entry is:

Mar. 1	Petty Cash	100	
	Cash		100
	(To establish a petty cash fund)		

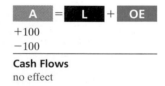

A	=	L	+	OE
+100				
−100				

Cash Flows
no effect

The fund custodian cashes the check and places the proceeds in a locked petty cash box or drawer. Most petty cash funds are established on a fixed-amount basis. The company will make no additional entries to the Petty Cash account unless management changes the stipulated amount of the fund. For example, if Laird Company decides on July 1 to increase the size of the fund to $250, it would debit Petty Cash $150 and credit Cash $150.

Ethics Note

Petty cash funds are authorized and legitimate. In contrast, "slush" funds are unauthorized and hidden (under the table).

Making Payments from the Petty Cash Fund. The petty cash fund custodian has the authority to make payments from the fund that conform to prescribed management policies. Usually, management limits the size of expenditures that come from petty cash. Likewise, it may not permit use of the fund for certain types of transactions (such as making short-term loans to employees).

Each payment from the fund must be documented on a prenumbered petty cash receipt (or petty cash voucher), as shown in Illustration 8-7 (page 378). The signatures of both the fund custodian and the person receiving payment are required on the receipt. If other supporting documents such as a freight bill or invoice are available, they should be attached to the petty cash receipt.

Helpful Hint

The petty cash receipt satisfies two internal control procedures: (1) establishing responsibility (signature of custodian), and (2) documentation procedures.

---

[4]The term "imprest" means an advance of money for a designated purpose.

Illustration 8-7
Petty cash receipt

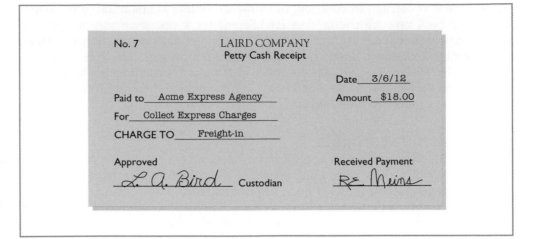

No. 7   LAIRD COMPANY
                                   Petty Cash Receipt

                                                    Date___3/6/12___

Paid to___Acme Express Agency___   Amount___$18.00___

For___Collect Express Charges___

CHARGE TO_____Freight-in_____

Approved   Received Payment

_L. A. Bird___ Custodian   _R. E. Meins___

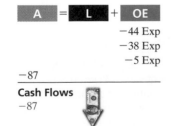

Ethics Note

Internal control over a petty cash fund is strengthened by: (1) having a supervisor make surprise counts of the fund to confirm whether the paid petty cash receipts and fund cash equal the imprest amount, and (2) canceling or mutilating the paid petty cash receipts so they cannot be resubmitted for reimbursement.

The fund custodian keeps the receipts in the petty cash box until the fund is replenished. The sum of the petty cash receipts and the money in the fund should equal the established total at all times. Management can (and should) make surprise counts at any time to determine whether the fund is being maintained correctly.

The company does not make an accounting entry to record a payment when it is made from petty cash. It is considered both inexpedient and unnecessary to do so. Instead, the company recognizes the accounting effects of each payment when it replenishes the fund.

Replenishing the Petty Cash Fund. When the money in the petty cash fund reaches a minimum level, the company replenishes the fund. The petty cash custodian initiates a request for reimbursement. The individual prepares a schedule (or summary) of the payments that have been made and sends the schedule, supported by petty cash receipts and other documentation, to the treasurer's office. The treasurer's office examines the receipts and supporting documents to verify that proper payments from the fund were made. The treasurer then approves the request and issues a check to restore the fund to its established amount. At the same time, all supporting documentation is stamped "paid" so that it cannot be submitted again for payment.

To illustrate, assume that on March 15 Laird's petty cash custodian requests a check for $87. The fund contains $13 cash and petty cash receipts for postage $44, freight-out $38, and miscellaneous expenses $5. The general journal entry to record the check is:

A = L + OE
−44 Exp
−38 Exp
−5 Exp
−87

Cash Flows
−87

Mar. 15	Postage Expense	44	
	Freight-out	38	
	Miscellaneous Expense	5	
	Cash		87
	(To replenish petty cash fund)		

Note that the reimbursement entry does not affect the Petty Cash account. Replenishment changes the composition of the fund by replacing the petty cash receipts with cash. It does not change the balance in the fund.

Occasionally, in replenishing a petty cash fund, the company may need to recognize a cash shortage or overage. This results when the total of the cash plus receipts in the petty cash box does not equal the established amount of the petty cash fund. To illustrate, assume that Laird's petty cash custodian has only $12 in cash in the fund plus the receipts as listed. The request for reimbursement would therefore be for $88, and Laird would make the following entry.

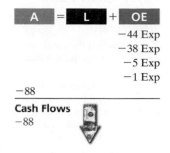

Mar. 15	Postage Expense	44	
	Freight-out	38	
	Miscellaneous Expense	5	
	Cash Over and Short	1	
	Cash		88
	(To replenish petty cash fund)		

−44 Exp
−38 Exp
−5 Exp
−1 Exp
−88

Cash Flows
−88

Conversely, if the custodian has $14 in cash, the reimbursement request would be for $86, and the company would credit Cash Over and Short for $1 (overage). A company reports a debit balance in Cash Over and Short in the income statement as miscellaneous expense. It reports a credit balance in the account as miscellaneous revenue. The company closes Cash Over and Short to Income Summary at the end of the year.

Companies should replenish a petty cash fund at the end of the accounting period, regardless of the cash in the fund. Replenishment at this time is necessary in order to recognize the effects of the petty cash payments on the financial statements.

Helpful Hint

Cash over and short situations result from mathematical errors or from failure to keep accurate records.

*E*THICS *I*NSIGHT

How Employees Steal

A recent study by the Association of Certified Fraud Examiners found that two-thirds of all employee thefts involved a fraudulent disbursement by an employee. The most common form (28.3% of cases) was fraudulent billing schemes. In these, the employee causes the company to issue a payment to the employee by submitting a bill for nonexistent goods or services, purchases of personal goods by the employee, or inflated invoices. The following graph shows various types of fraudulent disbursements and the median loss from each.

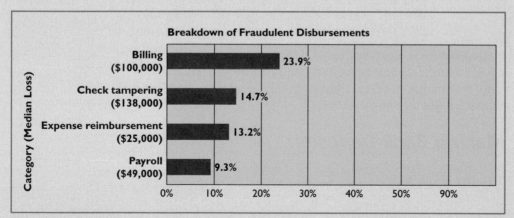

Source: 2008 Report to the Nation on Occupational Fraud and Abuse, Association of Certified Fraud Examiners, *www.acfe.com/documents/2008_rttn.pdf,* p.13.

? How can companies reduce the likelihood of fraudulent disbursements? (See page 410.)

Do it!

Petty Cash Fund

action plan

✔ To establish the fund, set up a separate general ledger account.

✔ Determine how much cash is needed to replenish the fund: subtract the cash remaining from the petty cash fund balance.

✔ Total the petty cash receipts. Determine any cash over or short—the difference between the cash needed to replenish the fund and the total of the petty cash receipts.

✔ Record the expenses incurred according to the petty cash receipts when replenishing the fund.

Bateer Company established a $50 petty cash fund on July 1. On July 30, the fund had $12 cash remaining and petty cash receipts for postage $14, office supplies $10, and delivery expense $15. Prepare journal entries to establish the fund on July 1 and to replenish the fund on July 30.

Solution

July 1	Petty Cash		50	
	Cash			50
	(To establish petty cash fund)			
30	Postage Expense		14	
	Supplies		10	
	Delivery Expense		15	
	Cash Over and Short			1
	Cash ($50 – $12)			38
	(To replenish petty cash)			

Related exercise material: BE8-9, E8-7, E8-8, and **Do it!** 8-3.

The Navigator

Control Features: Use of a Bank

Study Objective [6]

Indicate the control features of a bank account.

The use of a bank contributes significantly to good internal control over cash. A company can safeguard its cash by using a bank as a depository and as a clearing house for checks received and written. Use of a bank minimizes the amount of currency that a company must keep on hand. Also, use of a bank facilitates the control of cash because it creates a double record of all bank transactions—one by the company and the other by the bank. The asset account Cash maintained by the company should have the same balance as the bank's liability account for that company. A **bank reconciliation** compares the bank's balance with the company's balance and explains any differences to make them agree.

Many companies have more than one bank account. For efficiency of operations and better control, national retailers like Wal-Mart and Target may have regional bank accounts. Large companies, with tens of thousands of employees, may have a payroll bank account, as well as one or more general bank accounts. Also, a company may maintain several bank accounts in order to have more than one source for short-term loans when needed.

Making Bank Deposits

An authorized employee, such as the head cashier, should make a company's bank deposits. Each deposit must be documented by a deposit slip (ticket), as shown in Illustration 8-8.

Deposit slips are prepared in duplicate. The bank retains the original; the depositor keeps the duplicate, machine-stamped by the bank to establish its authenticity.

Writing Checks

Most of us write checks, without thinking very much about them. A **check** is a written order signed by the depositor directing the bank to pay a specified sum of money to

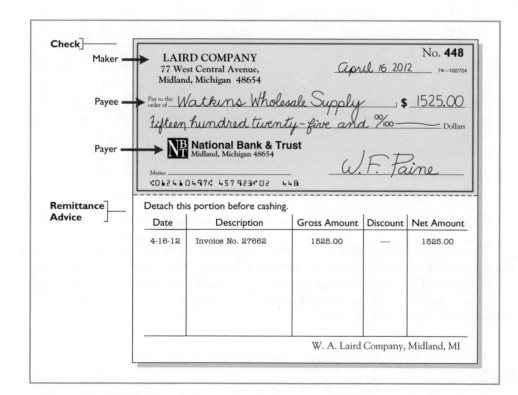

Illustration 8-8
Deposit slip

a designated recipient. There are three parties to a check: (1) the **maker** (or drawer) who issues the check, (2) the **bank** (or payer) on which the check is drawn, and (3) the **payee** to whom the check is payable. A check is a **negotiable instrument** that one party can transfer to another party by endorsement. Each check should be accompanied by an explanation of its purpose. In many companies, a remittance advice attached to the check, as shown in Illustration 8-9 explains the check's purpose.

Illustration 8-9
Check with remittance advice

It is important to know the balance in the checking account at all times. To keep the balance current, the depositor should enter each deposit and check on running-balance memo forms provided by the bank or on the check stubs in the checkbook.

Bank Statements

If you have a personal checking account, you are probably familiar with bank statements. A **bank statement** shows the depositor's bank transactions and balances.[5] Each month, a depositor receives a statement from the bank. Illustration 8-10 presents a typical bank statement. It shows: (1) checks paid and other debits that reduce the balance in the depositor's account, (2) deposits and other credits that increase the balance in the account, and (3) the account balance after each day's transactions.

Illustration 8-10
Bank statement

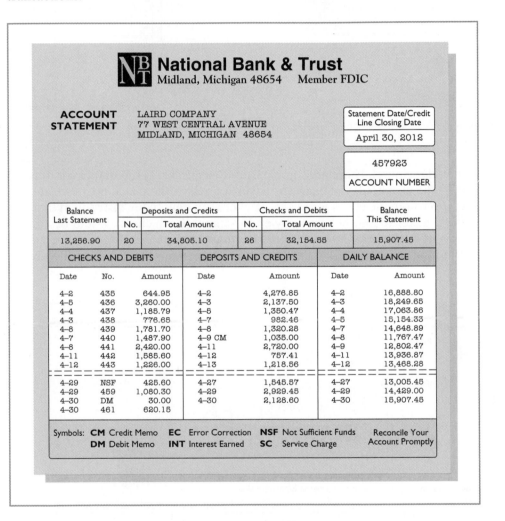

The bank statement lists in numerical sequence all "paid" checks, along with the date the check was paid and its amount. Upon paying a check, the bank stamps the check "paid"; a paid check is sometimes referred to as a **canceled** check. On the statement the bank also includes memoranda explaining other debits and credits it made to the depositor's account.

---

[5] Our presentation assumes that the depositor makes all adjustments at the end of the month. In practice, a company may also make journal entries during the month as it receives information from the bank regarding its account.

DEBIT MEMORANDUM

Some banks charge a monthly fee for their services. Often they charge this fee only when the average monthly balance in a checking account falls below a specified amount. They identify the fee, called a **bank service charge**, on the bank statement by a symbol such as **SC**. The bank also sends with the statement a debit memorandum explaining the charge noted on the statement. Other debit memoranda may also be issued for other bank services such as the cost of printing checks, issuing traveler's checks, and wiring funds to other locations. The symbol **DM** is often used for such charges.

Banks also use a debit memorandum when a deposited check from a customer "bounces" because of insufficient funds. For example, assume that Scott Company, a customer of Laird Company, sends a check for $800 to Laird Company for services provided. Unfortunately, Scott does not have sufficient funds at its bank to pay for these services. In such a case, Scott's bank marks the check **NSF** (not sufficient funds) and returns it to Laird's (the depositor's) bank. Laird's bank then debits Laird's account, as shown by the symbol NSF on the bank statement in Illustration 8-10. The bank sends the NSF check and debit memorandum to Laird as notification of the charge. Laird then records an Account Receivable from Scott Company (the writer of the bad check) and reduces cash for the NSF check.

CREDIT MEMORANDUM

Sometimes a depositor asks the bank to collect its notes receivable. In such a case, the bank will credit the depositor's account for the cash proceeds of the note. This is illustrated by the symbol **CM** on the Laird Company bank statement. The bank issues and sends with the statement a credit memorandum to explain the entry. Many banks also offer interest on checking accounts. The interest earned may be indicated on the bank statement by the symbol **CM** or **INT**.

Reconciling the Bank Account

The bank and the depositor maintain independent records of the depositor's checking account. People tend to assume that the respective balances will always agree. In fact, the two balances are seldom the same at any given time, and both balances differ from the "correct" or "true" balance. Therefore, it is necessary to make the balance per books and the balance per bank agree with the correct or true amount—a process called **reconciling the bank account**. The need for agreement has two causes:

Study Objective [7]
Prepare a bank reconciliation.

1. **Time lags** that prevent one of the parties from recording the transaction in the same period as the other party.
2. **Errors** by either party in recording transactions.

Time lags occur frequently. For example, several days may elapse between the time a company mails a check to a payee and the date the bank pays the check. Similarly, when the depositor uses the bank's night depository to make its deposits, there will be a difference of at least one day between the time the depositor records the deposit and the time the bank does so. A time lag also occurs whenever the bank mails a debit or credit memorandum to the depositor.

The incidence of errors depends on the effectiveness of the internal controls of the depositor and the bank. Bank errors are infrequent. However, either party could accidentally record a $450 check as $45 or $540. In addition, the bank might mistakenly charge a check to a wrong account by keying in an incorrect account name or number.

RECONCILIATION PROCEDURE

The bank reconciliation should be prepared by an employee who has no other responsibilities pertaining to cash. If a company fails to follow this internal control principle of independent internal verification, cash embezzlements may go unnoticed. For example, a cashier who prepares the reconciliation can embezzle cash and conceal the embezzlement by misstating the reconciliation. Thus, the bank accounts would reconcile, and the embezzlement would not be detected.

In reconciling the bank account, it is customary to reconcile the balance per books and balance per bank to their adjusted (correct or true) cash balances. The starting point in preparing the reconciliation is to enter the balance per bank statement and balance per books on the reconciliation schedule. The company then makes various adjustments, as shown in Illustration 8-11.

The following steps should reveal all the reconciling items that cause the difference between the two balances.

Helpful Hint

Deposits in transit and outstanding checks are reconciling items because of time lags.

Step 1. Deposits in transit. Compare the individual deposits listed on the bank statement with deposits in transit from the preceding bank reconciliation and with the deposits per company records or duplicate deposit slips. Deposits recorded by the depositor that have not been recorded by the bank are the **deposits in transit**. Add these deposits to the balance per bank.

Step 2. Outstanding checks. Compare the paid checks shown on the bank statement with (a) checks outstanding from the previous bank reconciliation,

Illustration 8-11
Bank reconciliation adjustments

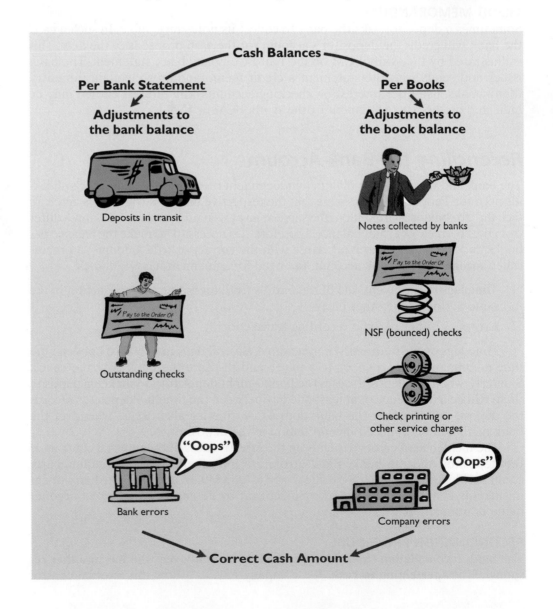

and (b) checks issued by the company as recorded in the cash payments journal (or in the check register in your personal checkbook). Issued checks recorded by the company but that have not yet been paid by the bank are **outstanding checks**. Deduct outstanding checks from the balance per the bank.

Step 3. Errors. Note any errors discovered in the foregoing steps and list them in the appropriate section of the reconciliation schedule. For example, if the company mistakenly recorded as $169 a paid check correctly written for $196, it would deduct the error of $27 from the balance per books. All errors made by the depositor are reconciling items in determining the adjusted cash balance per books. In contrast, all errors made by the bank are reconciling items in determining the adjusted cash balance per the bank.

Step 4. Bank memoranda. Trace bank memoranda to the depositor's records. List in the appropriate section of the reconciliation schedule any unrecorded memoranda. For example, the company would deduct from the balance per books a $5 debit memorandum for bank service charges. Similarly, it would add to the balance per books $32 of interest earned.

BANK RECONCILIATION ILLUSTRATED

The bank statement for Laird Company, in Illustration 8-10, shows a balance per bank of $15,907.45 on April 30, 2012. On this date the balance of cash per books is $11,589.45. Using the four reconciliation steps, Laird determines the following reconciling items.

Step 1.	**Deposits in transit:** April 30 deposit (received by bank on May 1).	$2,201.40
Step 2.	**Outstanding checks:** No. 453, $3,000.00; no. 457, $1,401.30; no. 460, $1,502.70.	5,904.00
Step 3.	**Errors:** Laird wrote check no. 443 for $1,226.00 and the bank correctly paid that amount. However, Laird recorded the check as $1,262.00.	36.00
Step 4.	**Bank memoranda:**	
	a. Debit—NSF check from J. R. Baron for $425.60	425.60
	b. Debit—Charge for printing company checks $30.00	30.00
	c. Credit—Collection of note receivable for $1,000 plus interest earned $50, less bank collection fee $15.00	1,035.00

Illustration 8-12 (page 386) shows Laird's bank reconciliation.

Helpful Hint

Note in the bank statement on page 382 that checks no. 459 and 461 have been paid but check no. 460 is not listed. Thus, this check is outstanding. If a complete bank statement were provided, checks no. 453 and 457 would also not be listed. The amounts for these three checks are obtained from the company's cash payments records.

ENTRIES FROM BANK RECONCILIATION

The company records each reconciling item used to determine the **adjusted cash balance per books. If the company does not journalize and post these items, the Cash account will not show the correct balance.** Laird Company would make the following entries on April 30.

Collection of Note Receivable. This entry involves four accounts. Assuming that the interest of $50 has not been accrued and the collection fee is charged to Miscellaneous Expense, the entry is:

Helpful Hint

The entries that follow are adjusting entries. In prior chapters, Cash was an account that did not require adjustment. That was a simplifying assumption for learning purposes, because we had not yet explained a bank reconciliation.

Apr. 30	Cash	1,035.00	
	Miscellaneous Expense	15.00	
	Notes Receivable		1,000.00
	Interest Revenue		50.00
	(To record collection of note receivable by bank)		

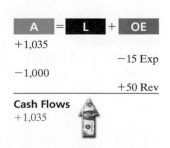

A = L + OE
+1,035
−15 Exp
−1,000
+50 Rev

Cash Flows
+1,035

Illustration 8-12
Bank reconciliation

Laird Company		
Bank Reconciliation		
April 30, 2012		
Cash balance per bank statement		$ 15,907.45
Add: Deposits in transit		2,201.40
		18,108.85
Less: Outstanding checks		
No. 453	$3,000.00	
No. 457	1,401.30	
No. 460	1,502.70	5,904.00
Adjusted cash balance per bank		**$12,204.85**
Cash balance per books		$11,589.45
Add: Collection of note receivable $1,000, plus		
interest earned $50, less collection fee $15	$1,035.00	
Error in recording check no. 443	36.00	1,071.00
		12,660.45
Less: NSF check	425.60	
Bank service charge	30.00	455.60
Adjusted cash balance per books		**$12,204.85**

Alternative Terminology

The terms *adjusted cash balance*, *true cash balance*, and *correct cash balance* are used interchangeably.

Book Error. The cash disbursements journal shows that check no. 443 was a payment on account to Andrea Company, a supplier. The correcting entry is:

A = L + OE
+36
      +36
Cash Flows
+36

Apr. 30	Cash	36.00	
	Accounts Payable—Andrea Company		36.00
	(To correct error in recording check no. 443)		

NSF Check. As indicated earlier, an NSF check becomes an account receivable to the depositor. The entry is:

A = L + OE
+425.60
−425.60
Cash Flows
−425.60

Apr. 30	Accounts Receivable—J. R. Baron	425.60	
	Cash		425.60
	(To record NSF check)		

Bank Service Charges. Depositors debit check printing charges (DM) and other bank service charges (SC) to Miscellaneous Expense because they are usually nominal in amount. The entry is:

A = L + OE
                  −30 Exp
−30
Cash Flows
−30

Apr. 30	Miscellaneous Expense	30.00	
	Cash		30.00
	(To record charge for printing company checks)		

Instead of making four separate entries, Laird could combine them into one compound entry.

After Laird has posted the entries, the Cash account will show the following.

Illustration 8-13
Adjusted balance in cash account

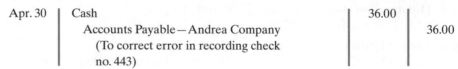

Cash			
Apr. 30 Bal.	11,589.45	Apr. 30	425.60
30	1,035.00	30	30.00
30	36.00		
Apr. 30 Bal.	**12,204.85**		

The adjusted cash balance in the ledger should agree with the adjusted cash balance per books in the bank reconciliation in Illustration 8-12 (page 386).

What entries does the bank make? If the company discovers any bank errors in preparing the reconciliation, it should notify the bank. The bank then can make the necessary corrections in its records. The bank does not make any entries for deposits in transit or outstanding checks. Only when these items reach the bank will the bank record these items.

Electronic Funds Transfer (EFT) System

It is not surprising that companies and banks have developed approaches to transfer funds among parties without the use of paper (deposit tickets, checks, etc.). Such procedures, called **electronic funds transfers (EFT)**, are disbursement systems that use wire, telephone, or computers to transfer cash balances from one location to another. Use of EFT is quite common. For example, many employees receive no formal payroll checks from their employers. Instead, employers send electronic payroll data to the appropriate banks. Also, individuals now frequently make regular payments such as those for house, car, and utilities by EFT.

EFT transfers normally result in better internal control since no cash or checks are handled by company employees. This does not mean that opportunities for fraud are eliminated. In fact, the same basic principles related to internal control apply to EFT transfers. For example, without proper segregation of duties and authorizations, an employee might be able to redirect electronic payments into a personal bank account and conceal the theft with fraudulent accounting entries.

*I*NVESTOR *I*NSIGHT

Madoff's Ponzi Scheme

No recent fraud has generated more interest and rage than the one perpetrated by Bernard Madoff. Madoff was an elite New York investment fund manager who was highly regarded by securities regulators. Investors flocked to him because he delivered very steady returns of between 10% and 15%, no matter whether the market was going up or going down. However, for many years, Madoff did not actually invest the cash that people gave to him. Instead, he was running a Ponzi scheme: He paid returns to existing investors using cash received from new investors. As long as the size of his investment fund continued to grow from new investments at a rate that exceeded the amounts that he needed to pay out in returns, Madoff was able to operate his fraud smoothly. To conceal his misdeeds, he fabricated false investment statements that were provided to investors. In addition, Madoff hired an auditor that never verified the accuracy of the investment records but automatically issued unqualified opinions each year. Although a competing fund manager warned the SEC a number of times over a nearly 10-year period that he thought Madoff was engaged in fraud, the SEC never aggressively investigated the allegations. Investors, many of which were charitable organizations, lost more than $18 billion. Madoff was sentenced to a jail term of 150 years.

? How was Madoff able to conceal such a giant fraud? (See page 410.)

Do it!

Sally Kist owns Linen Kist Fabrics. Sally asks you to explain how she should treat the following reconciling items when reconciling the company's bank account: (1) a debit memorandum for an NSF check, (2) a credit memorandum for a note collected by the bank, (3) outstanding checks, and (4) a deposit in transit.

Bank Reconciliation

action plan

✔ Understand the purpose of a bank reconciliation.

✔ Identify time lags and explain how they cause reconciling items.

Solution

Sally should treat the reconciling items as follows.

(1) NSF check: Deduct from balance per books.

(2) Collection of note: Add to balance per books.

(3) Outstanding checks: Deduct from balance per bank.

(4) Deposit in transit: Add to balance per bank.

Related exercise material: BE8-11, BE8-12, BE8-13, BE8-14, E8-9, E8-10, E8-11, E8-12, E8-13, and **Do it!** 8-4.

Reporting Cash

Study Objective [8]
Explain the reporting of cash.

Cash consists of coins, currency (paper money), check, money orders, and money on hand or on deposit in a bank or similar depository. Companies report cash in two different statements: the balance sheet and the statement of cash flows. The balance sheet reports the amount of cash available at a given point in time. The statement of cash flows shows the sources and uses of cash during a period of time. The cash flow statement was introduced in Chapter 1 and will be discussed in much detail in Chapter 17. In this section, we discuss some important points regarding the presentation of cash in the balance sheet.

When presented in a balance sheet, cash on hand, cash in banks, and petty cash are often combined and reported simply as **Cash**. Because it is the most liquid asset owned by the company, cash is listed first in the current assets section of the balance sheet.

Cash Equivalents

Many companies use the designation "Cash and cash equivalents" in reporting cash. (See Illustration 8-14 for an example.) **Cash equivalents** are short-term, highly liquid investments that are both:

1. Readily convertible to known amounts of cash, and
2. So near their maturity that their market value is relatively insensitive to changes in interest rates.

Illustration 8-14
Balance sheet presentation of cash

Delta Air Lines, Inc. Balance Sheet (partial) December 31, 2009 (in millions)	
Assets	
Current assets	
Cash and cash equivalents	**$4,607**
Short-term investments	71
Restricted cash	**423**
Accounts receivable and other net	1,360
Parts inventories	327
Prepaid expenses and other	953
Total current assets	$7,741

Examples of cash equivalents are Treasury bills, commercial paper (short-term corporate notes), and money market funds. All typically are purchased with cash that is in excess of immediate needs.

Occasionally, a company will have a net negative balance in its bank account. In this case, the company should report the negative balance among current liabilities. For example, farm equipment manufacturer Ag-Chem recently reported "Checks outstanding in excess of cash balances" of $2,145,000 among its current liabilities.

Restricted Cash

A company may have **restricted cash**, cash that is not available for general use but rather is restricted for a special purpose. For example, landfill companies are often required to maintain a fund of restricted cash to ensure they will have adequate resources to cover closing and clean-up costs at the end of a landfill site's useful life. McKessor Corp. recently reported restricted cash of $962 million to be paid out as the result of investor lawsuits.

Cash restricted in use should be reported separately on the balance sheet as restricted cash. If the company expects to use the restricted cash within the next year, it reports the amount as a current asset. When this is not the case, it reports the restricted funds as a noncurrent asset.

Illustration 8-14 shows restricted cash reported in the financial statements of Delta Air Lines. The company is required to maintain restricted cash as collateral to support insurance obligations related to workers' compensation claims. Delta does not have access to these funds for general use, and so it must report them separately, rather than as part of cash and cash equivalents.

Ethics Note

Recently, some companies were forced to restate their financial statements because they had too broadly interpreted which types of investments could be treated as cash equivalents. By reporting these items as cash equivalents, the companies made themselves look more liquid.

COMPREHENSIVE

Do it!

Poorten Company's bank statement for May 2012 shows the following data.

Balance 5/1	$12,650	Balance 5/31	$14,280
Debit memorandum:		Credit memorandum:	
NSF check	$175	Collection of note receivable	$505

The cash balance per books at May 31 is $13,319. Your review of the data reveals the following.

1. The NSF check was from Copple Co., a customer.
2. The note collected by the bank was a $500, 3-month, 12% note. The bank charged a $10 collection fee. No interest has been accrued.
3. Outstanding checks at May 31 total $2,410.
4. Deposits in transit at May 31 total $1,752.
5. A Poorten Company check for $352, dated May 10, cleared the bank on May 25. The company recorded this check, which was a payment on account, for $325.

Instructions

(a) Prepare a bank reconciliation at May 31.

(b) Journalize the entries required by the reconciliation.

action plan

✔ Follow the four steps in the reconciliation procedure (pp. 384–385).

✔ Work carefully to minimize mathematical errors in the reconciliation.

✔ Prepare entries from reconciling items per books.

✔ Make sure the cash ledger balance after posting the reconciling entries agrees with the adjusted cash balance per books.

Solution to Comprehensive Do it!

(a)

POORTEN COMPANY
Bank Reconciliation
May 31, 2012

Cash balance per bank statement		$14,280
Add: Deposits in transit		1,752
		16,032
Less: Outstanding checks		2,410
Adjusted cash balance per bank		$13,622
Cash balance per books		$13,319
Add: Collection of note receivable $500, plus $15		
interest, less collection fee $10		505
		13,824
Less: NSF check	$175	
Error in recording check	27	202
Adjusted cash balance per books		$13,622

(b)

May 31	Cash		505	
	Miscellaneous Expense		10	
		Notes Receivable		500
		Interest Revenue		15
		(To record collection of note by bank)		
31	Accounts Receivable—Copple Co.		175	
		Cash		175
		(To record NSF check from Copple Co.)		
31	Accounts Payable		27	
		Cash		27
		(To correct error in recording check)		

✔ **The Navigator**

Summary of Study Objectives

[1] Define fraud and internal control. A fraud is a dishonest act by an employee that results in personal benefit to the employee at a cost to the employer. The fraud triangle refers to the three factors that contribute to fraudulent activity by employees: opportunity, financial pressure, and rationalization. Internal control consists of all the related methods and measures adopted within an organization to safeguard its assets, enhance the reliability of its accounting records, increase efficiency of operations, and ensure compliance with laws and regulations.

[2] Identify the principles of internal control activities. The principles of internal control are: establishment of responsibility; segregation of duties; documentation procedures; physical controls; independent internal verification; and human resource controls such as bonding and requiring employees to take vacations.

[3] Explain the applications of internal control principles to cash receipts. Internal controls over cash receipts include: (a) designating specific personnel to handle cash; (b) assigning different individuals to receive cash, record cash, and

maintain custody of cash; (c) using remittance advices for mail receipts, cash register tapes for over-the-counter receipts, and deposit slips for bank deposits; (d) using company safes and bank vaults to store cash with access limited to authorized personnel, and using cash registers in executing over-the-counter receipts; (e) making independent daily counts of register receipts and daily comparison of total receipts with total deposits; and (f) bonding personnel that handle cash and requiring them to take vacations.

[4] Explain the applications of internal control principles to cash disbursements. Internal controls over cash disbursements include: (a) having specific individuals such as the treasurer authorized to sign checks and approve invoices; (b) assigning different individuals to approve items for payment, pay the items, and record the payment; (c) using prenumbered checks and accounting for all checks, with each check supported by an approved invoice; (d) storing blank checks in a safe or vault with access restricted to authorized personnel, and using a checkwriting machine to imprint amounts on checks; (e) comparing each check with the approved invoice before issuing the check, and making monthly reconciliations of bank and book balances; and (f) bonding personnel who handle cash, requiring employees to take vacations, and conducting background checks.

[5] Describe the operation of a petty cash fund. Companies operate a petty cash fund to pay relatively small amounts of cash. They must establish the fund, make payments from the fund, and replenish the fund when the cash in the fund reaches a minimum level.

[6] Indicate the control features of a bank account. A bank account contributes to good internal control by providing physical controls for the storage of cash. It minimizes the amount of currency that a company must keep on hand, and it creates a double record of a depositor's bank transactions.

[7] Prepare a bank reconciliation. It is customary to reconcile the balance per books and balance per bank to their adjusted balances. The steps in the reconciling process are to determine deposits in transit, outstanding checks, errors by the depositor or the bank, and unrecorded bank memoranda.

[8] Explain the reporting of cash. Companies list cash first in the current assets section of the balance sheet. In some cases, they report cash together with cash equivalents. Cash restricted for a special purpose is reported separately as a current asset or as a noncurrent asset, depending on when the cash is expected to be used.

Glossary

Bank reconciliation The process of comparing the bank's balance of an account with the company's balance and explaining any differences to make them agree. (p. 380).

Bank service charge A fee charged by a bank for the use of its services. (p. 383).

Bank statement A monthly statement from the bank that shows the depositor's bank transactions and balances. (p. 382).

Bonding Obtaining insurance protection against misappropriation of assets by employees. (p. 370).

Cash Resources that consist of coins, currency, checks, money orders, and money on hand or on deposit in a bank or similar depository. (p. 388).

Cash equivalents Short-term, highly liquid investments that can be converted to a specific amount of cash. (p. 388).

Check A written order signed by a bank depositor, directing the bank to pay a specified sum of money to a designated recipient. (p. 380).

Deposits in transit Deposits recorded by the depositor but not yet been recorded by the bank. (p. 384).

Electronic funds transfer (EFT) A disbursement system that uses wire, telephone, or computers to transfer funds from one location to another. (p. 387).

Fraud A dishonest act by an employee that results in personal benefit to the employee at a cost to the employer. (p. 362).

Fraud triangle The three factors that contribute to fraudulent activity by employees: opportunity, financial pressure, and rationalization. (p. 362).

Internal auditors Company employees who continuously evaluate the effectiveness of the company's internal control system. (p. 370).

Internal control All of the related methods and activities adopted within an organization to safeguard its assets and enhance the accuracy and reliability of its accounting records. (p. 363).

NSF check A check that is not paid by a bank because of insufficient funds in a customer's bank account. (p. 383).

Outstanding checks Checks issued and recorded by a company but not yet paid by the bank. (p. 385).

Petty cash fund A cash fund used to pay relatively small amounts. (p. 377).

Restricted cash Cash that must be used for a special purpose. (p. 389).

Sarbanes-Oxley Act of 2002 (SOX) Regulations passed by Congress to try to reduce unethical corporate behavior. (p. 363).

Voucher An authorization form prepared for each payment in a voucher system. (p. 376).

Voucher system A network of approvals by authorized individuals acting independently to ensure that all disbursements by check are proper. (p. 375).

Self-Test, Brief Exercises, Exercises, Problem Set A, and many more components are available for practice in *WileyPLUS*

Self-Test Questions

Answers are on page 410.

(SO 1) **1.** Which of the following is *not* an element of the fraud triangle?
  a. Rationalization.   **c.** Segregation of duties.
  b. Financial pressure.   **d.** Opportunity.

2. An organization uses internal control to enhance the (SO 1) accuracy and reliability of its accounting records and to:
  a. safeguard its assets.
  b. prevent fraud.

   c. produce correct financial statements.
   d. deter employee dishonesty.

(SO 1)   **3.** Which of the following was *not* a result of the Sarbanes-Oxley Act?
   a. Companies must file financial statements with the Internal Revenue Service.
   b. All publicly traded companies must maintain adequate internal controls.
   c. The Public Company Accounting Oversight Board was created to establish auditing standards and regulate auditor activity.
   d. Corporate executives and board of directors must ensure that controls are reliable and effective, and they can be fined or imprisoned for failure to do so.

(SO 2)   **4.** The principles of internal control do *not* include:
   a. establishment of responsibility.
   b. documentation procedures.
   c. management responsibility.
   d. independent internal verification.

(SO 2)   **5.** Physical controls do *not* include:
   a. safes and vaults to store cash.
   b. independent bank reconciliations.
   c. locked warehouses for inventories.
   d. bank safety deposit boxes for important papers.

(SO 3)   **6.** Permitting only designated personnel to handle cash receipts is an application of the principle of:
   a. segregation of duties.
   b. establishment of responsibility.
   c. independent check.
   d. human resource controls.

(SO 3)   **7.** Which of the following control activities is *not* relevant to when a company uses a computerized (rather than manual) accounting system?
   a. Establishment of responsibility.
   b. Segregation of duties.
   c. Independent internal verification.
   d. All of these control activities are relevant to a computerized system.

(SO 4)   **8.** The use of prenumbered checks in disbursing cash is an application of the principle of:
   a. establishment of responsibility.
   b. segregation of duties.

   c. physical controls.
   d. documentation procedures.

(SO 5)   **9.** A company writes a check to replenish a $100 petty cash fund when the fund contains receipts of $94 and $4 in cash. In recording the check, the company should:
   a. debit Cash Over and Short for $2.
   b. debit Petty Cash for $94.
   c. credit Cash for $94.
   d. credit Petty Cash for $2.

(SO 6)   **10.** The control features of a bank account do *not* include:
   a. having bank auditors verify the correctness of the bank balance per books.
   b. minimizing the amount of cash that must be kept on hand.
   c. providing a double record of all bank transactions.
   d. safeguarding cash by using a bank as a depository.

(SO 7)   **11.** In a bank reconciliation, deposits in transit are:
   a. deducted from the book balance.
   b. added to the book balance.
   c. added to the bank balance.
   d. deducted from the bank balance.

(SO 7)   **12.** The reconciling item in a bank reconciliation that will result in an adjusting entry by the depositor is:
   a. outstanding checks.   **c.** a bank error.
   b. deposit in transit.   **d.** bank service charges.

(SO 8)   **13.** Which of the following items in a cash drawer at November 30 is *not* cash?
   a. Money orders.
   b. Coins and currency.
   c. A customer check dated December 1.
   d. A customer check dated November 28.

(SO 8)   **14.** Which of the following statements correctly describes the reporting of cash?
   a. Cash cannot be combined with cash equivalents.
   b. Restricted cash funds may be combined with Cash.
   c. Cash is listed first in the current assets section.
   d. Restricted cash funds cannot be reported as a current asset.

Go to the book's companion website, **www.wiley.com/college/weygandt**, for additional Self-Test Questions.

The Navigator

Questions

1. A local bank reported that it lost $150,000 as the result of an employee fraud. Randal Smith is not clear on what is meant by an "employee fraud." Explain the meaning of fraud to Randal and give an example of frauds that might occur at a bank.

2. Fraud experts often say that there are three primary factors that contribute to employee fraud. Identify the three factors and explain what is meant by each.

3. Identify and describe the five components of a good internal control system.

4. "Internal control is concerned only with enhancing the accuracy of the accounting records." Do you agree? Explain.

5. What principles of internal control apply to most organizations?

6. At the corner grocery store, all sales clerks make change out of one cash register drawer. Is this a violation of internal control? Why?

7. Meg Lucas is reviewing the principle of segregation of duties. What are the two common applications of this principle?

8. How do documentation procedures contribute to good internal control?

9. What internal control objectives are met by physical controls?

10. (a) Explain the control principle of independent internal verification. (b) What practices are important in applying this principle?

11. The management of Sewell Company asks you, as the company accountant, to explain (a) the concept of reasonable assurance in internal control and (b) the importance of the human factor in internal control.

12. McCartney Fertilizer Co. owns the following assets at the balance sheet date.

Cash in bank savings account	$ 8,000
Cash on hand	850
Cash refund due from the IRS	1,000
Checking account balance	12,000
Postdated checks	500

What amount should McCartney report as cash in the balance sheet?

13. What principle(s) of internal control is (are) involved in making daily cash counts of over-the-counter receipts?

14. Jacobs Department Stores has just installed new electronic cash registers in its stores. How do cash registers improve internal control over cash receipts?

15. At Hummel Wholesale Company, two mail clerks open all mail receipts. How does this strengthen internal control?

16. "To have maximum effective internal control over cash disbursements, all payments should be made by check." Is this true? Explain.

17. Joe Griswold Company's internal controls over cash disbursements provide for the treasurer to sign checks imprinted by a check-writing machine in indelible ink after comparing the check with the approved invoice. Identify the internal control principles that are present in these controls.

18. How do the principles of (a) physical controls and (b) documentation controls apply to cash disbursements?

19. (a) What is a voucher system? (b) What principles of internal control apply to a voucher system?

20. What is the essential feature of an electronic funds transfer (EFT) procedure?

21. (a) Identify the three activities that pertain to a petty cash fund, and indicate an internal control principle that is applicable to each activity. (b) When are journal entries required in the operation of a petty cash fund?

22. "The use of a bank contributes significantly to good internal control over cash." Is this true? Why or why not?

23. Lori Figgs is confused about the lack of agreement between the cash balance per books and the balance per the bank. Explain the causes for the lack of agreement to Lori, and give an example of each cause.

24. What are the four steps involved in finding differences between the balance per books and balance per bank?

25. Kristen Hope asks your help concerning an NSF check. Explain to Kristen (a) what an NSF check is, (b) how it is treated in a bank reconciliation, and (c) whether it will require an adjusting entry.

26. (a) "Cash equivalents are the same as cash." Do you agree? Explain. (b) How should restricted cash funds be reported on the balance sheet?

27. **PEPSICO** At what amount does PepsiCo report cash and cash equivalents in its 2009 consolidated balance sheet?

Brief Exercises

BE8-1 Match each situation with the fraud triangle factor—opportunity, financial pressure, or rationalization—that best describes it.

1. An employee's monthly credit card payments are nearly 75% of his or her monthly earnings.
2. An employee earns minimum wage at a firm that has reported record earnings for each of the last five years.
3. An employee has an expensive gambling habit.
4. An employee has check-writing and signing responsibilities for a small company, as well as reconciling the bank account.

Identify fraud triangle concepts.
(SO 1)

BE8-2 Angela Kinsey has prepared the following list of statements about internal control.

1. One of the objectives of internal control is to safeguard assets from employee theft, robbery, and unauthorized use.
2. One of the objectives of internal control is to enhance the accuracy and reliability of the accounting records.
3. No laws require U.S. corporations to maintain an adequate system of internal control.

Identify each statement as true or false. If false, indicate how to correct the statement.

Indicate internal control concepts.
(SO 1)

BE8-3 Phyllis Lapin is the new owner of Ready Parking. She has heard about internal control but is not clear about its importance for her business. Explain to Phyllis the four purposes of internal control and give her one application of each purpose for Ready Parking.

Explain the importance of internal control.
(SO 1)

Identify internal control principles.
(SO 2)

BE8-4 The internal control procedures in Meredith Palmer Company provide that:

1. Employees who have physical custody of assets do not have access to the accounting records.
2. Each month the assets on hand are compared to the accounting records by an internal auditor.
3. A prenumbered shipping document is prepared for each shipment of goods to customers.

Identify the principles of internal control that are being followed.

Identify the internal control principles applicable to cash receipts.
(SO 3)

BE8-5 Kate Flannery Company has the following internal control procedures over cash receipts. Identify the internal control principle that is applicable to each procedure.

1. All over-the-counter receipts are registered on cash registers.
2. All cashiers are bonded.
3. Daily cash counts are made by cashier department supervisors.
4. The duties of receiving cash, recording cash, and custody of cash are assigned to different individuals.
5. Only cashiers may operate cash registers.

Make journal entries for cash overage and shortfall.
(SO 3)

BE8-6 The cash register tape for Kelly Kapoor Industries reported sales of $6,891.50. Record the journal entry that would be necessary for each of the following situations. (a) Cash to be accounted for exceeds cash on hand by $50.75. (b) Cash on hand exceeds cash to be accounted for by $28.32.

Make journal entry using cash count sheet.
(SO 3)

BE8-7 While examining cash receipts information, the accounting department determined the following information: opening cash balance $150, cash on hand $1,125.74, and cash sales per register tape $990.83. Prepare the required journal entry based upon the cash count sheet.

Identify the internal control principles applicable to cash disbursements.
(SO 4)

BE8-8 Mindy Kaliny Company has the following internal control procedures over cash disbursements. Identify the internal control principle that is applicable to each procedure.

1. Company checks are prenumbered.
2. The bank statement is reconciled monthly by an internal auditor.
3. Blank checks are stored in a safe in the treasurer's office.
4. Only the treasurer or assistant treasurer may sign checks.
5. Check signers are not allowed to record cash disbursement transactions.

Prepare entry to replenish a petty cash fund.
(SO 5)

BE8-9 On March 20, Toby's petty cash fund of $100 is replenished when the fund contains $7 in cash and receipts for postage $52, freight-out $26, and travel expense $10. Prepare the journal entry to record the replenishment of the petty cash fund.

Identify the control features of a bank account.
(SO 6)

BE8-10 Creed Bratton is uncertain about the control features of a bank account. Explain the control benefits of (a) a check and (b) a bank statement.

Indicate location of reconciling items in a bank reconciliation.
(SO 7)

BE8-11 The following reconciling items are applicable to the bank reconciliation for Flenderson Company: (1) outstanding checks, (2) bank debit memorandum for service charge, (3) bank credit memorandum for collecting a note for the depositor, (4) deposits in transit. Indicate how each item should be shown on a bank reconciliation.

Identify reconciling items that require adjusting entries.
(SO 7)

BE8-12 Using the data in BE8-11, indicate (a) the items that will result in an adjustment to the depositor's records and (b) why the other items do not require adjustment.

Prepare partial bank reconciliation.
(SO 7)

BE8-13 At July 31, Martinez Company has the following bank information: cash balance per bank $7,420, outstanding checks $762, deposits in transit $1,120, and a bank service charge $20. Determine the adjusted cash balance per bank at July 31.

Prepare partial bank reconciliation.
(SO 7)

BE8-14 At August 31, Oscar Company has a cash balance per books of $8,500 and the following additional data from the bank statement: charge for printing Oscar Company checks $35, interest earned on checking account balance $40, and outstanding checks $800. Determine the adjusted cash balance per books at August 31.

Explain the statement presentation of cash balances.
(SO 8)

BE8-15 Nunez Company has the following cash balances: Cash in Bank $15,742, Payroll Bank Account $6,000, and Plant Expansion Fund Cash $25,000. Explain how each balance should be reported on the balance sheet.

Do it! Review

Do it! 8-1   Identify which control activity is violated in each of the following situations, and explain how the situation creates an opportunity for fraud or inappropriate accounting practices.

1. Once a month, the sales department sends sales invoices to the accounting department to be recorded.
2. Leah Hutcherson orders merchandise for Rice Lake Company; he also receives merchandise and authorizes payment for merchandise.
3. Several clerks at Pig Foods use the same cash register drawer.

Identify violations of control activities.
(SO 2)

Do it! 8-2   Andy Bernard is concerned with control over mail receipts at Andy's Sporting Goods. All mail receipts are opened by Ed Helms. Ed sends the checks to the accounting department, where they are stamped "For Deposit Only." The accounting department records and deposits the mail receipts weekly. Andy asks for your help in installing a good system of internal control over mail receipts.

Design system of internal control over cash receipts.
(SO 3)

Do it! 8-3   Craig Robinson Company established a $100 petty cash fund on August 1. On August 30, the fund had $9 cash remaining and petty cash receipts for postage $31, office supplies $42, and miscellaneous expense $16. Prepare journal entries to establish the fund on August 1 and replenish the fund on August 30.

Make journal entries for petty cash fund.
(SO 5)

Do it! 8-4   Daryl Philbin owns Philbin Blankets. Philbin asks you to explain how he should treat the following reconciling items when reconciling the company's bank account.

1. Outstanding checks
2. A deposit in transit
3. The bank charged to our account a check written by another company
4. A debit memorandum for a bank service charge

Explain treatment of items in bank reconciliation.
(SO 7)

Exercises

E8-1   Jan Levinson is the owner of Levinson's Pizza. Levinson's is operated strictly on a carryout basis. Customers pick up their orders at a counter where a clerk exchanges the pizza for cash. While at the counter, the customer can see other employees making the pizzas and the large ovens in which the pizzas are baked.

Identify the principles of internal control.
(SO 2)

Instructions
Identify the six principles of internal control and give an example of each principle that you might observe when picking up your pizza. (*Note:* It may not be possible to observe all the principles.)

E8-2   The following control procedures are used at Melora Company for over-the-counter cash receipts.

1. To minimize the risk of robbery, cash in excess of $100 is stored in an unlocked attaché case in the stock room until it is deposited in the bank.
2. All over-the-counter receipts are registered by three clerks who use a cash register with a single cash drawer.
3. The company accountant makes the bank deposit and then records the day's receipts.
4. At the end of each day, the total receipts are counted by the cashier on duty and reconciled to the cash register total.
5. Cashiers are experienced; they are not bonded.

Identify internal control weaknesses over cash receipts and suggest improvements.
(SO 2, 3)

Instructions
(a) For each procedure, explain the weakness in internal control, and identify the control principle that is violated.
(b) For each weakness, suggest a change in procedure that will result in good internal control.

Identify internal control weaknesses over cash disbursements and suggest improvements.
(SO 2, 4)

E8-3 The following control procedures are used in Kelly Erin's Boutique Shoppe for cash disbursements.

1. The company accountant prepares the bank reconciliation and reports any discrepancies to the owner.
2. The store manager personally approves all payments before signing and issuing checks.
3. Each week, Kelly leaves 100 company checks in an unmarked envelope on a shelf behind the cash register.
4. After payment, bills are filed in a paid invoice folder.
5. The company checks are unnumbered.

Instructions

(a) For each procedure, explain the weakness in internal control, and identify the internal control principle that is violated.

(b) For each weakness, suggest a change in the procedure that will result in good internal control.

Identify internal control weaknesses for cash disbursements and suggest improvements.
(SO 4)

E8-4 At Hannon Company, checks are not prenumbered because both the purchasing agent and the treasurer are authorized to issue checks. Each signer has access to unissued checks kept in an unlocked file cabinet. The purchasing agent pays all bills pertaining to goods purchased for resale. Prior to payment, the purchasing agent determines that the goods have been received and verifies the mathematical accuracy of the vendor's invoice. After payment, the invoice is filed by the vendor, and the purchasing agent records the payment in the cash disbursements journal. The treasurer pays all other bills following approval by authorized employees. After payment, the treasurer stamps all bills PAID, files them by payment date, and records the checks in the cash disbursements journal. Hannon Company maintains one checking account that is reconciled by the treasurer.

Instructions

(a) List the weaknesses in internal control over cash disbursements.

(b) ◖━━━▶ Write a memo to the company treasurer indicating your recommendations for improvement.

Indicate whether procedure is good or weak internal control.
(SO 2, 3, 4)

E8-5 Listed below are five procedures followed by Ellie Kempet Company.

1. Several individuals operate the cash register using the same register drawer.
2. A monthly bank reconciliation is prepared by someone who has no other cash responsibilities.
3. Roy Anderson writes checks and also records cash payment journal entries.
4. One individual orders inventory, while a different individual authorizes payments.
5. Unnumbered sales invoices from credit sales are forwarded to the accounting department every four weeks for recording.

Instructions

Indicate whether each procedure is an example of good internal control or of weak internal control. If it is an example of good internal control, indicate which internal control principle is being followed. If it is an example of weak internal control, indicate which internal control principle is violated. Use the table below.

Procedure	IC Good or Weak?	Related Internal Control Principle
1.		
2.		
3.		
4.		
5.		

Indicate whether procedure is good or weak internal control.
(SO 2, 3, 4)

E8-6 Listed below are five procedures followed by Wallace Company.

1. Employees are required to take vacations.
2. Any member of the sales department can approve credit sales.
3. Andy Buckley ships goods to customers, bills customers, and receives payment from customers.
4. Total cash receipts are compared to bank deposits daily by someone who has no other cash responsibilities.
5. Time clocks are used for recording time worked by employees.

Instructions

Indicate whether each procedure is an example of good internal control or of weak internal control. If it is an example of good internal control, indicate which internal control principle is being followed. If it is an example of weak internal control, indicate which internal control principle is violated. Use the table below.

Procedure	IC Good or Weak?	Related Internal Control Principle
1.		
2.		
3.		
4.		
5.		

E8-7 Karen Filippelli Company established a petty cash fund on May 1, cashing a check for $100. The company reimbursed the fund on June 1 and July 1 with the following results.

> June 1: Cash in fund $2.75. Receipts: delivery expense $31.25; postage expense $39.00; and miscellaneous expense $25.00.
> July 1: Cash in fund $3.25. Receipts: delivery expense $21.00; entertainment expense $51.00; and miscellaneous expense $24.75.

On July 10, Karen Filippelli increased the fund from $100 to $150.

Prepare journal entries for a petty cash fund.
(SO 5)

Instructions

Prepare journal entries for Karen Filippelli Company for May 1, June 1, July 1, and July 10.

E8-8 Rashida Company uses an imprest petty cash system. The fund was established on March 1 with a balance of $100. During March, the following petty cash receipts were found in the petty cash box.

Prepare journal entries for a petty cash fund.
(SO 5)

Date	Receipt No.	For	Amount
3/5	1	Stamp Inventory	$39
7	2	Freight-out	21
9	3	Miscellaneous Expense	6
11	4	Travel Expense	24
14	5	Miscellaneous Expense	5

The fund was replenished on March 15 when the fund contained $3 in cash. On March 20, the amount in the fund was increased to $150.

Instructions

Journalize the entries in March that pertain to the operation of the petty cash fund.

E8-9 Bob Vance is unable to reconcile the bank balance at January 31. Bob's reconciliation is as follows.

Prepare bank reconciliation and adjusting entries.
(SO 7)

Cash balance per bank	$3,560.20
Add: NSF check	690.00
Less: Bank service charge	25.00
Adjusted balance per bank	$4,225.20
Cash balance per books	$3,875.20
Less: Deposits in transit	530.00
Add: Outstanding checks	930.00
Adjusted balance per books	$4,275.20

Instructions

(a) Prepare a correct bank reconciliation.
(b) Journalize the entries required by the reconciliation.

E8-10 On April 30, the bank reconciliation of Gabe Lewis Company shows three outstanding checks: no. 254, $650; no. 255, $820; and no. 257, $410. The May bank statement and the May cash payments journal show the following.

Determine outstanding checks.
(SO 7)

Bank Statement			Cash Payments Journal		
Checks Paid			Checks Issued		
Date	Check No.	Amount	Date	Check No.	Amount
5/4	254	650	5/2	258	159
5/2	257	410	5/5	259	275
5/17	258	159	5/10	260	890
5/12	259	275	5/15	261	500
5/20	261	500	5/22	262	750
5/29	263	480	5/24	263	480
5/30	262	750	5/29	264	560

Instructions

Using step 2 in the reconciliation procedure, list the outstanding checks at May 31.

Prepare bank reconciliation and adjusting entries.

(SO 7)

E8-11   The following information pertains to Miner Video Company.

1. Cash balance per bank, July 31, $7,263.
2. July bank service charge not recorded by the depositor $28.
3. Cash balance per books, July 31, $7,284.
4. Deposits in transit, July 31, $1,500.
5. Bank collected $900 note for Miner in July, plus interest $36, less fee $20. The collection has not been recorded by Miner, and no interest has been accrued.
6. Outstanding checks, July 31, $591.

Instructions

(a) Prepare a bank reconciliation at July 31.
(b) Journalize the adjusting entries at July 31 on the books of Miner Video Company.

Prepare bank reconciliation and adjusting entries.

(SO 7)

E8-12   The information below relates to the Cash account in the ledger of Porter Company.

Balance September 1—$17,150; Cash deposited—$64,000.
Balance September 30—$17,404; Checks written—$63,746.

The September bank statement shows a balance of $16,422 on September 30 and the following memoranda.

Credits		Debits	
Collection of $1,500 note plus interest $30	$1,530	NSF check: Charles Esten	$425
Interest earned on checking account	$45	Safety deposit box rent	$65

At September 30, deposits in transit were $4,450, and outstanding checks totaled $2,383.

Instructions

(a) Prepare the bank reconciliation at September 30.
(b) Prepare the adjusting entries at September 30, assuming (1) the NSF check was from a customer on account, and (2) no interest had been accrued on the note.

Compute deposits in transit and outstanding checks for two bank reconciliations.

(SO 7)

E8-13   The cash records of Holly Company show the following four situations.

1. The June 30 bank reconciliation indicated that deposits in transit total $720. During July, the general ledger account Cash shows deposits of $15,750, but the bank statement indicates that only $15,600 in deposits were received during the month.
2. The June 30 bank reconciliation also reported outstanding checks of $680. During the month of July, Holly Company books show that $17,200 of checks were issued. The bank statement showed that $16,400 of checks cleared the bank in July.
3. In September, deposits per the bank statement totaled $26,700, deposits per books were $25,400, and deposits in transit at September 30 were $2,100.
4. In September, cash disbursements per books were $23,700, checks clearing the bank were $25,000, and outstanding checks at September 30 were $2,100.

There were no bank debit or credit memoranda. No errors were made by either the bank or Holly Company.

Instructions

Answer the following questions.

(a) In situation (1), what were the deposits in transit at July 31?
(b) In situation (2), what were the outstanding checks at July 31?
(c) In situation (3), what were the deposits in transit at August 31?
(d) In situation (4), what were the outstanding checks at August 31?

E8-14   Flax Company has recorded the following items in its financial records.

Cash in bank	$ 47,000
Cash in plant expansion fund	100,000
Cash on hand	12,000
Highly liquid investments	34,000
Petty cash	500
Receivables from customers	89,000
Stock investments	61,000

Show presentation of cash in financial statements.
(SO 8)

The cash in bank is subject to a compensating balance of $5,000. The highly liquid investments had maturities of 3 months or less when they were purchased. The stock investments will be sold in the next 6 to 12 months. The plant expansion project will begin in 3 years.

Instructions

(a) What amount should Flax report as "Cash and cash equivalents" on its balance sheet?
(b) Where should the items not included in part (a) be reported on the balance sheet?
(c) What disclosures should Flax make in its financial statements concerning "cash and cash equivalents"?

Exercises: Set B

Visit the book's companion website, at **www.wiley.com/college/weygandt**, and choose the Student Companion site to access Exercise Set B.

Problems: Set A

P8-1A   Mose Office Supply Company recently changed its system of internal control over cash disbursements. The system includes the following features.

Identify internal control principles over cash disbursements.
(SO 2, 4)

Instead of being unnumbered and manually prepared, all checks must now be prenumbered and written by using the new checkwriting machine purchased by the company. Before a check can be issued, each invoice must have the approval of Linda Purl, the purchasing agent, and Idris Elba, the receiving department supervisor. Checks must be signed by either Vivianne Collins, the treasurer, or Nick D'Agosto, the assistant treasurer. Before signing a check, the signer is expected to compare the amount of the check with the amount on the invoice.

After signing a check, the signer stamps the invoice PAID and inserts within the stamp, the date, check number, and amount of the check. The "paid" invoice is then sent to the accounting department for recording.

Blank checks are stored in a safe in the treasurer's office. The combination to the safe is known only by the treasurer and assistant treasurer. Each month, the bank statement is reconciled with the bank balance per books by the assistant chief accountant. All employees who handle or account for cash are bonded.

Instructions

Identify the internal control principles and their application to cash disbursements of Mose Office Supply Company.

P8-2A   Ursula Company maintains a petty cash fund for small expenditures. The following transactions occurred over a 2-month period.

Journalize and post petty cash fund transactions.
(SO 5)

July	1	Established petty cash fund by writing a check on Scranton Bank for $200.
	15	Replenished the petty cash fund by writing a check for $196.00. On this date the fund consisted of $4.00 in cash and the following petty cash receipts: freight-out $94.00, postage expense $42.40, entertainment expense $46.60, and miscellaneous expense $11.20.

31 Replenished the petty cash fund by writing a check for $192.00. At this date, the fund consisted of $8.00 in cash and the following petty cash receipts: freight-out $82.10, charitable contributions expense $45.00, postage expense $25.50, and miscellaneous expense $39.40.

Aug. 15 Replenished the petty cash fund by writing a check for $187.00. On this date, the fund consisted of $13.00 in cash and the following petty cash receipts: freight-out $75.60, entertainment expense $43.00, postage expense $33.00, and miscellaneous expense $37.00.

16 Increased the amount of the petty cash fund to $300 by writing a check for $100.

31 Replenished petty cash fund by writing a check for $284.00. On this date, the fund consisted of $16 in cash and the following petty cash receipts: postage expense $140.00, travel expense $95.60, and freight-out $47.10.

Instructions

(a) July 15, Cash short $1.80

(b) Aug. 31 balance $300

(a) Journalize the petty cash transactions.

(b) Post to the Petty Cash account.

(c) What internal control features exist in a petty cash fund?

Prepare a bank reconciliation and adjusting entries.

(SO 7)

P8-3A On May 31, 2012, Sabre Company had a cash balance per books of $6,781.50. The bank statement from New York State Bank on that date showed a balance of $6,404.60. A comparison of the statement with the cash account revealed the following facts.

1. The statement included a debit memo of $40 for the printing of additional company checks.

2. Cash sales of $836.15 on May 12 were deposited in the bank. The cash receipts journal entry and the deposit slip were incorrectly made for $886.15. The bank credited Sabre Company for the correct amount.

3. Outstanding checks at May 31 totaled $576.25. Deposits in transit were $1,916.15.

4. On May 18, the company issued check No. 1181 for $685 to Carol Stills on account. The check, which cleared the bank in May, was incorrectly journalized and posted by Sabre Company for $658.

5. A $2,500 note receivable was collected by the bank for Sabre Company on May 31 plus $80 interest. The bank charged a collection fee of $20. No interest has been accrued on the note.

6. Included with the cancelled checks was a check issued by Rapier Company to Tom Lujak for $800 that was incorrectly charged to Sabre Company by the bank.

7. On May 31, the bank statement showed an NSF charge of $680 for a check issued by Jo Bennett, a customer, to Sabre Company on account.

Instructions

(a) Adjusted cash balance per bank $8,544.50

(a) Prepare the bank reconciliation at May 31, 2012.

(b) Prepare the necessary adjusting entries for Sabre Company at May 31, 2012.

Prepare a bank reconciliation and adjusting entries from detailed data.

(SO 7)

P8-4A The bank portion of the bank reconciliation for Helene Company at November 30, 2012, was as follows.

HELENE COMPANY
Bank Reconciliation
November 30, 2012

Cash balance per bank		$14,367.90
Add: Deposits in transit		2,530.20
		16,898.10

Less: Outstanding checks		
Check Number	Check Amount	
3451	$2,260.40	
3470	720.10	
3471	844.50	
3472	1,426.80	
3474	1,050.00	6,301.80
Adjusted cash balance per bank		$10,596.30

The adjusted cash balance per bank agreed with the cash balance per books at November 30.

The December bank statement showed the following checks and deposits.

Bank Statement				
Checks			**Deposits**	
Date	Number	Amount	Date	Amount
12-1	3451	$ 2,260.40	12-1	$ 2,530.20
12-2	3471	844.50	12-4	1,211.60
12-7	3472	1,426.80	12-8	2,365.10
12-4	3475	1,640.70	12-16	2,672.70
12-8	3476	1,300.00	12-21	2,945.00
12-10	3477	2,130.00	12-26	2,567.30
12-15	3479	3,080.00	12-29	2,836.00
12-27	3480	600.00	12-30	1,025.00
12-30	3482	475.50	Total	$18,152.90
12-29	3483	1,140.00		
12-31	3485	540.80		
	Total	$15,438.70		

The cash records per books for December showed the following.

Cash Payments Journal						Cash Receipts Journal	
Date	Number	Amount	Date	Number	Amount	Date	Amount
12-1	3475	$1,640.70	12-20	3482	$ 475.50	12-3	$ 1,211.60
12-2	3476	1,300.00	12-22	3483	1,140.00	12-7	2,365.10
12-2	3477	2,130.00	12-23	3484	798.00	12-15	2,672.70
12-4	3478	621.30	12-24	3485	450.80	12-20	2,954.00
12-8	3479	3,080.00	12-30	3486	1,889.50	12-25	2,567.30
12-10	3480	600.00	Total		$14,933.20	12-28	2,836.00
12-17	3481	807.40				12-30	1,025.00
						12-31	1,690.40
						Total	$17,322.10

The bank statement contained two memoranda:

1. A credit of $4,145 for the collection of a $4,000 note for Helene Company plus interest of $160 and less a collection fee of $15. Helene Company has not accrued any interest on the note.
2. A debit of $572.80 for an NSF check written by L. Purl, a customer. At December 31, the check had not been redeposited in the bank.

At December 31, the cash balance per books was $12,485.20, and the cash balance per the bank statement was $20,154.30. The bank did not make any errors, but two errors were made by Helene Company.

Instructions
(a) Using the four steps in the reconciliation procedure, prepare a bank reconciliation at December 31.
(b) Prepare the adjusting entries based on the reconciliation. (*Hint:* The correction of any errors pertaining to recording checks should be made to Accounts Payable. The correction of any errors relating to recording cash receipts should be made to Accounts Receivable.)

(a) Adjusted balance per books $15,958.40

Prepare a bank reconciliation and adjusting entries.

(SO 7)

P8-5A Hidetoshi Company maintains a checking account at the Imura Bank. At July 31, selected data from the ledger balance and the bank statement are shown below.

	Cash in Bank	
	Per Books	**Per Bank**
Balance, July 1	$17,600	$16,800
July receipts	81,400	
July credits		82,470
July disbursements	77,150	
July debits		74,756
Balance, July 31	$21,850	$24,514

Analysis of the bank data reveals that the credits consist of $79,000 of July deposits and a credit memorandum of $3,470 for the collection of a $3,400 note plus interest revenue of $70. The July debits per bank consist of checks cleared $74,700 and a debit memorandum of $56 for printing additional company checks.

You also discover the following errors involving July checks: (1) A check for $230 to a creditor on account that cleared the bank in July was journalized and posted as $320. (2) A salary check to an employee for $255 was recorded by the bank for $155.

The June 30 bank reconciliation contained only two reconciling items: deposits in transit $7,000 and outstanding checks of $6,200.

Instructions

(a) Adjusted balance per books $25,354

(a) Prepare a bank reconciliation at July 31, 2012.

(b) Journalize the adjusting entries to be made by Hidetoshi Company. Assume that interest on the note has not been accrued.

Identify internal control weaknesses in cash receipts and cash disbursements.

(SO 2, 3, 4)

P8-6A Hasagama Middle School wants to raise money for a new sound system for its auditorium. The primary fund-raising event is a dance at which the famous disc jockey D.J. Rivet will play classic and not-so-classic dance tunes. Will Schuester, the music and theater instructor, has been given the responsibility for coordinating the fund-raising efforts. This is Will's first experience with fund-raising. He decides to put the eighth-grade choir in charge of the event; he will be a relatively passive observer.

Will had 500 unnumbered tickets printed for the dance. He left the tickets in a box on his desk and told the choir students to take as many tickets as they thought they could sell for $5 each. In order to ensure that no extra tickets would be floating around, he told them to dispose of any unsold tickets. When the students received payment for the tickets, they were to bring the cash back to Will and he would put it in a locked box in his desk drawer.

Some of the students were responsible for decorating the gymnasium for the dance. Will gave each of them a key to the money box and told them that if they took money out to purchase materials, they should put a note in the box saying how much they took and what it was used for. After 2 weeks the money box appeared to be getting full, so Will asked Luke Gilmor to count the money, prepare a deposit slip, and deposit the money in a bank account Will had opened.

The day of the dance, Will wrote a check from the account to pay the DJ. D.J. Rivet, however, said that he accepted only cash and did not give receipts. So Will took $200 out of the cash box and gave it to D.J. At the dance Will had Mel Harris working at the entrance to the gymnasium, collecting tickets from students, and selling tickets to those who had not prepurchased them. Will estimated that 400 students attended the dance.

The following day Will closed out the bank account, which had $250 in it, and gave that amount plus the $180 in the cash box to Principal Foran. Principal Foran seemed surprised that, after generating roughly $2,000 in sales, the dance netted only $430 in cash. Will did not know how to respond.

Instructions

Identify as many internal control weaknesses as you can in this scenario, and suggest how each could be addressed.

Problems: Set B

P8-1B Magical Elves Theater is located in the Brooklyn Mall. A cashier's booth is located near the entrance to the theater. Three cashiers are employed. One works from 1–5 P.M., another from 5–9 P.M. The shifts are rotated among the three cashiers. The cashiers receive cash from customers and operate a machine that ejects serially numbered tickets. The rolls of tickets are inserted and locked into the machine by the theater manager at the beginning of each cashier's shift.

Identify internal control weaknesses over cash receipts.
(SO 2, 3)

After purchasing a ticket, the customer takes the ticket to an usher stationed at the entrance of the theater lobby some 60 feet from the cashier's booth. The usher tears the ticket in half, admits the customer, and returns the ticket stub to the customer. The other half of the ticket is dropped into a locked box by the usher.

At the end of each cashier's shift, the theater manager removes the ticket rolls from the machine and makes a cash count. The cash count sheet is initialed by the cashier. At the end of the day, the manager deposits the receipts in total in a bank night deposit vault located in the mall. The manager also sends copies of the deposit slip and the initialed cash count sheets to the theater company treasurer for verification and to the company's accounting department. Receipts from the first shift are stored in a safe located in the manager's office.

Instructions
(a) Identify the internal control principles and their application to the cash receipts transactions of the Magical Elves Theater.
(b) If the usher and cashier decide to collaborate to misappropriate cash, what actions might they take?

P8-2B Chow Company maintains a petty cash fund for small expenditures. The following transactions occurred over a 2-month period.

Journalize and post petty cash find transactions.
(SO 5)

July   1   Established petty cash fund by writing a check on China Bank for $100.
    15   Replenished the petty cash fund by writing a check for $96.90. On this date, the fund consisted of $3.10 in cash and the following petty cash receipts: freight-out $51.00, postage expense $20.50, entertainment expense $23.10, and miscellaneous expense $4.10.
    31   Replenished the petty cash fund by writing a check for $95.90. At this date, the fund consisted of $4.10 in cash and the following petty cash receipts: freight-out $43.50, charitable contributions expense $20.00, postage expense $20.10, and miscellaneous expense $12.30.
Aug. 15   Replenished the petty cash fund by writing a check for $98.00. On this date, the fund consisted of $2.00 in cash and the following petty cash receipts: freight-out $40.20, entertainment expense $21.00, postage expense $14.00, and miscellaneous expense $19.80.
    16   Increased the amount of the petty cash fund to $150 by writing a check for $50.
    31   Replenished the petty cash fund by writing a check for $137.00. On this date, the fund consisted of $13 in cash and the following petty cash receipts: freight-out $74.00, entertainment expense $43.20, and postage expense $17.70.

Instructions
(a) Journalize the petty cash transactions.
(b) Post to the Petty Cash account.
(c) What internal control features exist in a petty cash fund?

(a) July 15 Cash over $1.80
(b) Aug. 31 balance $150

P8-3B Rohatyn Genetics Company of Lancaster, Wisconsin, spreads herbicides and applies liquid fertilizer for local farmers. On May 31, 2012, the company's Cash account per its general ledger showed the following balance.

Prepare a bank reconciliation and adjusting entries.
(SO 7)

	CASH				NO. 101
Date	**Explanation**	**Ref.**	**Debit**	**Credit**	**Balance**
May 31	Balance				13,287

The bank statement from Lancaster State Bank on that date showed the following balance.

LANCASTER STATE BANK

Checks and Debits	Deposits and Credits	Daily Balance
XXX	XXX	5/31 13,332

A comparison of the details on the bank statement with the details in the cash account revealed the following facts.

1. The statement included a debit memo of $35 for the printing of additional company checks.
2. Cash sales of $1,720 on May 12 were deposited in the bank. The cash receipts journal entry and the deposit slip were incorrectly made for $1,820. The bank credited Rohatyn Genetics Company for the correct amount.
3. Outstanding checks at May 31 totaled $1,225, and deposits in transit were $2,100.
4. On May 18, the company issued check no. 1181 for $911 to J. Greenberg on account. The check, which cleared the bank in May, was incorrectly journalized and posted by Rohatyn Genetics Company for $119.
5. A $4,000 note receivable was collected by the bank for Rohatyn Genetics Company on May 31 plus $80 interest. The bank charged a collection fee of $25. No interest has been accrued on the note.
6. Included with the cancelled checks was a check issued by Powers Company to Jerry Saltz for $900 that was incorrectly charged to Rohatyn Genetics Company by the bank.
7. On May 31, the bank statement showed an NSF charge of $1,308 for a check issued by Simon de Pury, a customer, to Rohatyn Genetics Company on account.

Instructions

(a) Adj. cash bal. $15,107

(a) Prepare the bank reconciliation at May 31, 2012.
(b) Prepare the necessary adjusting entries for Rohatyn Genetics Company at May 31, 2012.

Prepare a bank reconciliation and adjusting entries from detailed data.

(SO 7)

P8-4B   The bank portion of the bank reconciliation for Williams Company at October 31, 2012, was as follows.

WILLIAMS COMPANY
Bank Reconciliation
October 31, 2012

Cash balance per bank		$6,000
Add: Deposits in transit		842
		6,842
Less: Outstanding checks		

Check Number	Check Amount	
2451	$700	
2470	396	
2471	464	
2472	270	
2474	578	2,408

Adjusted cash balance per bank		$4,434

The adjusted cash balance per bank agreed with the cash balance per books at October 31.
The November bank statement showed the following checks and deposits:

Bank Statement

Checks			Deposits	
Date	Number	Amount	Date	Amount
11-1	2470	$ 396	11-1	$ 842
11-2	2471	464	11-4	666
11-5	2474	578	11-8	545
11-4	2475	903	11-13	1,416
11-8	2476	1,556	11-18	810
11-10	2477	330	11-21	1,624
11-15	2479	980	11-25	1,412
11-18	2480	714	11-28	908
11-27	2481	382	11-30	652
11-30	2483	317	Total	$8,875
11-29	2486	495		
	Total	$7,115		

The cash records per books for November showed the following.

Cash Payments Journal

Date	Number	Amount	Date	Number	Amount
11-1	2475	$ 903	11-20	2483	$ 317
11-2	2476	1,556	11-22	2484	460
11-2	2477	330	11-23	2485	525
11-4	2478	300	11-24	2486	495
11-8	2479	890	11-29	2487	210
11-10	2480	714	11-30	2488	635
11-15	2481	382	Total		$8,067
11-18	2482	350			

Cash Receipts Journal

Date	Amount
11-3	$ 666
11-7	545
11-12	1,416
11-17	810
11-20	1,642
11-24	1,412
11-27	908
11-29	652
11-30	1,541
Total	$9,592

The bank statement contained two bank memoranda:

1. A credit of $1,375 for the collection of a $1,300 note for Williams Company plus interest of $91 and less a collection fee of $16. Williams Company has not accrued any interest on the note.
2. A debit for the printing of additional company checks $34.

At November 30, the cash balance per books was $5,958, and the cash balance per the bank statement was $9,100. The bank did not make any errors, but two errors were made by Williams Company.

Instructions

(a) Using the four steps in the reconciliation procedure described on pages 384–385, prepare a bank reconciliation at November 30.

(b) Prepare the adjusting entries based on the reconciliation. (*Hint:* The correction of any errors pertaining to recording checks should be made to Accounts Payable. The correction of any errors relating to recording cash receipts should be made to Accounts Receivable).

(a) Adjusted cash balance per bank $7,191

P8-5B Trong Company's bank statement from Nguyen National Bank at August 31, 2012, shows the information below.

Prepare a bank reconciliation and adjusting entries.

(SO 7)

Balance, August 1	$11,284	Bank credit memoranda:	
August deposits	47,521	Collection of note	
Checks cleared in August	46,475	receivable plus $105	
Balance, August 31	16,856	interest	$4,505
		Interest earned	41
		Bank debit memorandum:	
		Safety deposit box rent	20

A summary of the Cash account in the ledger for August shows: Balance, August 1, $10,959; receipts $50,050; disbursements $47,794; and balance, August 31, $13,215. Analysis reveals that the only reconciling items on the July 31 bank reconciliation were a deposit in transit for $2,600 and outstanding checks of $2,925. The deposit in transit was the first deposit recorded by the bank in August. In addition, you determine that there were two errors involving company checks drawn in August: (1) A check for $340 to a creditor on account that cleared the bank in August was journalized and posted for $430. (2) A salary check to an employee for $275 was recorded by the bank for $277.

Instructions

(a) Adjusted balance per
books $17,831

(a) Prepare a bank reconciliation at August 31.
(b) Journalize the adjusting entries to be made by Trong Company at August 31. Assume that interest on the note has not been accrued by the company.

*Prepare a comprehensive bank
reconciliation with theft and
internal control deficiencies.*
(SO 2, 3, 4, 7)

P8-6B   Braun Company is a very profitable small business. It has not, however, given much consideration to internal control. For example, in an attempt to keep clerical and office expenses to a minimum, the company has combined the jobs of cashier and bookkeeper. As a result, Judith Tan handles all cash receipts, keeps the accounting records, and prepares the monthly bank reconciliations.

The balance per the bank statement on October 31, 2012, was $15,453. Outstanding checks were: no. 62 for $107.74, no. 183 for $127.50, no. 284 for $215.26, no. 862 for $162.10, no. 863 for $192.78, and no. 864 for $140.49. Included with the statement was a credit memorandum of $340 indicating the collection of a note receivable for Braun Company by the bank on October 25. This memorandum has not been recorded by Braun Company.

The company's ledger showed one cash account with a balance of $18,608.81. The balance included undeposited cash on hand. Because of the lack of internal controls, Tan took for personal use all of the undeposited receipts in excess of $3,226.18. She then prepared the following bank reconciliation in an effort to conceal her theft of cash.

BANK RECONCILIATION

Cash balance per books, October 31		$18,608.81
Add: Outstanding checks		
No. 862	$162.10	
No. 863	192.78	
No. 864	140.49	410.37
		19,019.18
Less: Undeposited receipts		3,226.18
Unadjusted balance per bank, October 31		15,793.00
Less: Bank credit memorandum		340.00
Cash balance per bank statement, October 31		$15,453.00

Instructions

(a) Adjusted balance per
books $17,733.31

(a) Prepare a correct bank reconciliation. (*Hint:* Deduct the amount of the theft from the adjusted balance per books.)
(b) Indicate the three ways that Tan attempted to conceal the theft and the dollar amount pertaining to each method.
(c) What principles of internal control were violated in this case?

Problems: Set C

Visit the book's companion website, at **www.wiley.com/college/weygandt**, and choose the Student Companion site to access Problem Set C.

Comprehensive Problem

CP8 On December 1, 2012, Bluemound Company had the following account balances.

	Debits		**Credits**
Cash	$18,200	Accumulated Depreciation—	
Notes Receivable	2,200	Equipment	$ 3,000
Accounts Receivable	7,500	Accounts Payable	6,100
Inventory	16,000	Owner's Capital	64,400
Prepaid Insurance	1,600		$73,500
Equipment	28,000		
	$73,500		

During December, the company completed the following transactions.

Dec. 7 Received $3,600 cash from customers in payment of account (no discount allowed).
   12 Purchased merchandise on account from Klump Co. $12,000, terms 1/10, n/30.
   17 Sold merchandise on account $15,000, terms 2/10, n/30. The cost of the merchandise sold was $10,000.
   19 Paid salaries $2,500.
   22 Paid Klump Co. in full, less discount.
   26 Received collections in full, less discounts, from customers billed on December 17.

Adjustment data:
1. Depreciation $200 per month.
2. Insurance expired $400.

Instructions
(a) Journalize the December transactions. (Assume a perpetual inventory system.)
(b) Enter the December 1 balances in the ledger T accounts and post the December transactions. Use Cost of Goods Sold, Depreciation Expense, Insurance Expense, Salaries and Wages Expense, Sales Revenue, and Sales Discounts.
(c) The statement from Jackson County Bank on December 31 showed a balance of $21,994. A comparison of the bank statement with the Cash account revealed the following facts.
   1. The bank collected a note receivable of $2,200 for Bluemound Company on December 15.
   2. The December 31 receipts of $2,736 were not included in the bank deposits for December. The company deposited these receipts in a night deposit vault on December 31.
   3. Checks outstanding on December 31 totaled $1,210.
   4. On December 31, the bank statement showed a NSF charge of $800 for a check received by the company from L. Shur, a customer, on account.

Prepare a bank reconciliation as of December 31 based on the available information. (*Hint:* The cash balance per books is $22,120. This can be proven by finding the balance in the Cash account from parts (a) and (b).)
(d) Journalize the adjusting entries resulting from the bank reconciliation and adjustment data.
(e) Post the adjusting entries to the ledger T accounts.
(f) Prepare an adjusted trial balance.
(g) Prepare an income statement for December and a classified balance sheet at December 31.

Continuing Cookie Chronicle

(*Note:* This is a continuation of the Cookie Chronicle from Chapters 1 through 7.)

CCC8   Part 1   Natalie is struggling to keep up with the recording of her accounting transactions. She is spending a lot of time marketing and selling mixers and giving her cookie classes. Her friend John is an accounting student who runs his own accounting service. He has asked Natalie if she would like to have him do her accounting. John and Natalie meet and discuss her business.
Part 2   Natalie decides that she cannot afford to hire John to do her accounting. One way that she can ensure that her cash account does not have any errors and is accurate and up-to-date is to prepare a bank reconciliation at the end of each month. Natalie would like you to help her.

Go to the book's companion website, **www.wiley.com/college/weygandt**, *to see the completion of this problem.*

BROADENINGYOURPERSPECTIVE

Financial Reporting and Analysis

Financial Reporting Problem: PepsiCo, Inc.

BYP8-1   The financial statements of PepsiCo, Inc. are presented in Appendix A at the end of this textbook.

Instructions
(a) What comments, if any, are made about cash in the report of the independent registered public accounting firm?
(b) What data about cash and cash equivalents are shown in the consolidated balance sheet?
(c) In its notes to Consolidated Financial Statements, how does PepsiCo define cash equivalents?
(d) In management's letter that assumes "Responsibility for Financial Reporting," what does PepsiCo's management say about internal control? (See page A31 in Appendix A of the back of the book.)

Comparative Analysis Problem:
PepsiCo, Inc. vs. The Coca-Cola Company

BYP8-2   PepsiCo's financial statements are presented in Appendix A. Financial statements of The Coca-Cola Company are presented in Appendix B.

Instructions
(a) Based on the information contained in these financial statements, determine each of the following for each company:
    (1) Cash and cash equivalents balance at December 26, 2009, for PepsiCo and at December 31, 2009, for Coca-Cola.
    (2) Increase (decrease) in cash and cash equivalents from 2008 to 2009.
    (3) Cash provided by operating activities during the year ended December 2009 (from statement of cash flows).
(b) What conclusions concerning the management of cash can be drawn from these data?

On the Web

BYP8-3   All organizations should have systems of internal control. Universities are no exception. This site discusses the basics of internal control in a university setting.

Address: www.bc.edu/offices/audit/controls, or go to **www.wiley.com/college/weygandt**

Steps: Go to the site shown above.

Instructions
The front page of this site provides links to pages that answer six critical questions. Use these links to answer the following questions.
(a) In a university setting, who has responsibility for evaluating the adequacy of the system of internal control?
(b) What do reconciliations ensure in the university setting? Who should review the reconciliation?
(c) What are some examples of physical controls?
(d) What are two ways to accomplish inventory counts?

Critical Thinking

Decision Making Across the Organization

BYP8-4   The board of trustees of a local church is concerned about the internal accounting controls for the offering collections made at weekly services. The trustees ask you to serve on a three-person audit team with the internal auditor of a local college and a CPA who has just joined the church.

At a meeting of the audit team and the board of trustees, you learn the following.

1. The church's board of trustees has delegated responsibility for the financial management and audit of the financial records to the finance committee. This group prepares the annual budget and approves major disbursements. It is not involved in collections or record-keeping. No audit has been made in recent years because the same trusted employee has kept church records and served as financial secretary for 15 years. The church does not carry any fidelity insurance.

2. The collection at the weekly service is taken by a team of ushers who volunteer to serve one month. The ushers take the collection plates to a basement office at the rear of the church. They hand their plates to the head usher and return to the church service. After all plates have been turned in, the head usher counts the cash received. The head usher then places the cash in the church safe along with a notation of the amount counted. The head usher volunteers to serve for 3 months.

3. The next morning, the financial secretary opens the safe and recounts the collection. The secretary withholds $150–$200 in cash, depending on the cash expenditures expected for the week, and deposits the remainder of the collections in the bank. To facilitate the deposit, church members who contribute by check are asked to make their checks payable to "Cash."

4. Each month, the financial secretary reconciles the bank statement and submits a copy of the reconciliation to the board of trustees. The reconciliations have rarely contained any bank errors and have never shown any errors per books.

Instructions

With the class divided into groups, answer the following.

(a) Indicate the weaknesses in internal accounting control over the handling of collections.

(b) List the improvements in internal control procedures that you plan to make at the next meeting of the audit team for (1) the ushers, (2) the head usher, (3) the financial secretary, and (4) the finance committee.

(c) What church policies should be changed to improve internal control?

Communication Activity

BYP8-5 As a new auditor for the CPA firm of Croix, Marais, and Kale, you have been assigned to review the internal controls over mail cash receipts of Manhattan Company. Your review reveals the following: Checks are promptly endorsed "For Deposit Only," but no list of the checks is prepared by the person opening the mail. The mail is opened either by the cashier or by the employee who maintains the accounts receivable records. Mail receipts are deposited in the bank weekly by the cashier.

Instructions

Write a letter to Jerry Mays, owner of Manhattan Company, explaining the weaknesses in internal control and your recommendations for improving the system.

Ethics Case

BYP8-6 You are the assistant controller in charge of general ledger accounting at Riverside Bottling Company. Your company has a large loan from an insurance company. The loan agreement requires that the company's cash account balance be maintained at $200,000 or more, as reported monthly.

At June 30, the cash balance is $80,000, which you report to Gena Schmitt, the financial vice president. Gena excitedly instructs you to keep the cash receipts book open for one additional day for purposes of the June 30 report to the insurance company. Gena says, "If we don't get that cash balance over $200,000, we'll default on our loan agreement. They could close us down, put us all out of our jobs!" Gena continues, "I talked to Oconto Distributors (one of Riverside's largest customers) this morning. They said they sent us a check for $150,000 yesterday. We should receive it tomorrow. If we include just that one check in our cash balance, we'll be in the clear. It's in the mail!"

Instructions

(a) Who will suffer negative effects if you do not comply with Gena Schmitt's instructions? Who will suffer if you do comply?

(b) What are the ethical considerations in this case?

(c) What alternatives do you have?

"All About You" Activity

BYP8-7   The **All About You** feature (available on the book's companion website) indicates potential security risks that may arise from your personal computer. It is important to keep in mind, however, that there are also many other ways that your identity can be stolen other than from your computer. The federal government provides many resources to help protect you from identity thieves.

Instructions
Go to **http://onguardonline.gov/idtheft.html**, and click on **ID Theft Faceoff**. Complete the quiz provided there.

FASB Codification Activity

BYP8-8   If your school has a subscription to the FASB Codification, go to *http://aaahq.org/ascLogin.cfm* to log in and prepare responses to the following.

(a) How is cash defined in the Codification?
(b) How are cash equivalents defined in the Codification?
(c) What are the disclosure requirements related to cash and cash equivalents?

Answers to Insight and Accounting Across the Organization Questions

p. 371 SOX Boosts the Role of Human Resources   Q: Why would unsupervised employees or employees who report to each other represent potential internal control threats? **A:** An unsupervised employee may have a fraudulent job (or may even be a fictitious person), e.g., a person drawing a paycheck without working. Or, if two employees supervise each other, there is no real separation of duties, and they can conspire to defraud the company.

p. 371 Big Theft at Small Companies   Q: Why are small companies more susceptible to employee theft? **A:** The high degree of trust often found in small companies makes them more vulnerable. Also, small companies tend to have less sophisticated systems of internal control, and they usually lack internal auditors. In addition, it is very hard to achieve some internal control features, such as segregation of duties, when you have very few employees.

p. 379 How Employees Steal   Q: How can companies reduce the likelihood of fraudulent disbursements? **A:** To reduce the occurrence of fraudulent disbursements, a company should follow the procedures discussed in this chapter. These include having only designated personnel sign checks; having different personnel approve payments and make payments; ensuring that check signers do not record disbursements; using prenumbered checks and matching each check to an approved invoice; storing blank checks securely; reconciling the bank statement; and stamping invoices PAID.

p. 387 Madoff's Ponzi Scheme   Q: How was Madoff able to conceal such a giant fraud? **A:** Madoff fabricated false investment statements that were provided to investors. In addition, his auditor never verified these investment statements even though the auditor gave him an unqualified opinion each year.

Answers to Self-Test Questions

1. c   **2.** a   **3.** a   **4.** c   **5.** b   **6.** b   **7.** d   **8.** d   **9.** a ($100 – ($94 + $4))   **10.** a   **11.** c   **12.** d   **13.** c   **14.** c

IFRS A Look at IFRS

Fraud can occur anywhere. And because the three main factors that contribute to fraud are universal in nature, the principles of internal control activities are used globally by companies. While Sarbanes-Oxley (SOX) does not apply to international companies, most large international companies have internal controls similar to those indicated in the chapter. IFRS and GAAP are very similar in accounting for cash. *IAS No. 1 (revised),* "Presentation of Financial Statements," is the only standard that discusses issues specifically related to cash.

Key Points

- The fraud triangle discussed in this chapter is applicable to all international companies. Some of the major frauds on an international basis are Parmalat (Italy), Royal Ahold (the Netherlands), and Satyam Computer Services (India).

- Rising economic crime poses a growing threat to companies, with nearly half of all organizations worldwide being victims of fraud in a recent two-year period (*PricewaterhouseCoopers' Global Economic Crime Survey,* 2005). Specifically, 44% of Romanian companies surveyed experienced fraud in the past two years.

- Globally, the number of companies reporting fraud increased from 37% to 45% since 2003, a 22% increase. The cost to companies was an average US$1.7 million in losses from "tangible frauds," that is, those that result in an immediate and direct financial loss. These include asset misappropriation, false pretenses, and counterfeiting (*PricewaterhouseCoopers' Global Economic Crime Survey,* 2005).

- Accounting scandals both in the United States and internationally have re-ignited the debate over the relative merits of GAAP, which takes a "rules-based" approach to accounting, versus IFRS, which takes a "principles-based" approach. The FASB announced that it intends to introduce more principles-based standards.

- On a lighter note, at one time Ig Nobel Prize in Economics went to the CEOs of those companies involved in the corporate accounting scandals of that year for "adapting the mathematical concept of imaginary numbers for use in the business world." The Ig Nobel Prizes (read Ignoble, as not noble) are a parody of the Nobel Prizes and are given each year in early October for 10 achievements that "first make people laugh, and then make them think." Organized by the scientific humor magazine *Annals of Improbable Research* (*AIR*), they are presented by a group that includes genuine Nobel laureates at a ceremony at Harvard University's Sanders Theater. (See *en.wikipedia.org/wiki/Ig_Nobel_Prize.*)

- Internal controls are a system of checks and balances designed to prevent and detect fraud and errors. While most companies have these systems in place, many have never completely documented them, nor had an independent auditor attest to their effectiveness. Both of these actions are required under SOX.

- Companies find that internal control review is a costly process but badly needed. One study estimates the cost of SOX compliance for U.S. companies at over $35 billion, with audit fees doubling in the first year of compliance. At the same time, examination of internal controls indicates lingering problems in the way companies operate. One study of first compliance with the internal-control testing provisions documented material weaknesses for about 13% of companies reporting in a two-year period (*PricewaterhouseCoopers' Global Economic Crime Survey,* 2005).

- The SOX internal control standards apply only to companies listed on U.S. exchanges. There is continuing debate over whether foreign issuers should have to comply with this extra layer of regulation.

- The accounting and internal control procedures related to cash are essentially the same under both IFRS and this textbook. In addition, the definition used for cash equivalents is the same.

- Most companies report cash and cash equivalents together under IFRS, as shown in this textbook. In addition, IFRS follows the same accounting policies related to the reporting of restricted cash.

- IFRS defines cash and cash equivalents as follows.
    - **Cash** is comprised of cash on hand and demand deposits.
    - **Cash equivalents** are short-term, highly liquid investments that are readily convertible to known amounts of cash and which are subject to an insignificant risk of changes in value.

Looking to the Future

Ethics has become a very important aspect of reporting. Different cultures have different perspectives on bribery and other questionable activities, and consequently penalties for engaging in such activities vary considerably across countries.

High-quality international accounting requires both high-quality accounting standards and high-quality auditing. Similar to the convergence of GAAP and IFRS, there is movement to improve international auditing standards. The International Auditing and Assurance Standards Board (IAASB) functions as an independent standard-setting body. It works to establish high-quality auditing and assurance and quality-control standards throughout the world. Whether the IAASB adopts internal control provisions similar to those in SOX remains to be seen. You can follow developments in the international audit arena at *http://www.ifac.org/iaasb/*.

Under proposed new standards for financial statements, companies would not be allowed to combine cash equivalents with cash.

IFRS Self-Test Questions

1. Non-U.S companies that follow IFRS:
   (a) do not normally use the principles of internal control activities used in this textbook.
   (b) often offset cash with accounts payable on the balance sheet.
   (c) are not required to follow SOX.
   (d) None of the above.

2. Which of the following is the correct accounting under IFRS for cash?
   (a) Cash cannot be combined with cash equivalents.
   (b) Restricted cash funds may be reported as a current or non-current asset depending on the circumstances.
   (c) Restricted cash funds cannot be reported as a current asset.
   (d) Cash on hand is not reported on the balance sheet as Cash.

3. The Sarbanes-Oxley Act of 2002 applies to:
   (a) all U.S. companies listed on U.S. exchanges.
   (b) all companies that list stock on any stock exchange in any country.
   (c) all European companies listed on European exchanges.
   (d) Both (a) and (c).

4. High-quality international accounting requires both high-quality accounting standards and:
   (a) a reconsideration of SOX to make it less onerous.
   (b) high-quality auditing standards.
   (c) government intervention to ensure that the public interest is protected.
   (d) the development of new principles of internal control activities.

5. Cash equivalents under IFRS:
   (a) are significantly different than the cash equivalents discussed in the textbook.
   (b) are generally disclosed separately from cash.
   (c) may be required to be reported separately from cash in the future.
   (d) None of the above.

IFRS Concepts and Application

IFRS8-1 Some people argue that the internal control requirements of the Sarbanes-Oxley Act (SOX) put U.S. companies at a competitive disadvantage to companies outside the United States. Discuss the competitive implications (both pros and cons) of SOX.

IFRS8-2   State whether each of the following is true or false. For those that are false, explain why.

(a) A proposed new financial accounting standard would not allow cash equivalents to be reported in combination with cash.

(b) Perspectives on bribery and penalties for engaging in bribery are the same across all countries.

(c) Cash equivalents are comprised of cash on hand and demand deposits.

(d) SOX was created by the International Accounting Standards Board.

International Financial Reporting Problem: *Zetar plc*

IFRS8-3   The financial statements of Zetar plc are presented in Appendix C. The company's complete annual report, including the notes to its financial statements, is available at *www.zetarplc.com.*

Instructions

Using the notes to the company's financial statements, answer the following questions.

(a) Which committee of the board of directors is responsible for considering management's reports on internal control?

(b) What are the company's key control procedures?

(c) Does the company have an internal audit department?

(d) In what section or sections does Zetar report its bank overdrafts?

Answers to IFRS Self-Test Questions

1. c   **2.** b   **3.** a   **4.** b   **5.** c

✔
The Navigator

✔   **Remember to go back to the Navigator box on the chapter opening page and check off your completed work.**

CHAPTER 9

Accounting for Receivables

Study Objectives

After studying this chapter, you should be able to:

[1] Identify the different types of receivables.

[2] Explain how companies recognize accounts receivable.

[3] Distinguish between the methods and bases companies use to value accounts receivable.

[4] Describe the entries to record the disposition of accounts receivable.

[5] Compute the maturity date of and interest on notes receivable.

[6] Explain how companies recognize notes receivable.

[7] Describe how companies value notes receivable.

[8] Describe the entries to record the disposition of notes receivable.

[9] Explain the statement presentation and analysis of receivables.

✔ **The Navigator**

✔ [The Navigator]

- Scan Study Objectives ○
- Read Feature Story ○
- Read Preview ○
- Read text and answer **Do it!** p. 425 ○ p. 427 ○ p. 433 ○ p. 434 ○
- Work Comprehensive **Do it!** p. 435 ○
- Review Summary of Study Objectives ○
- Answer Self-Test Questions ○
- Complete Assignments ○
- Go to *WileyPLUS* for practice and tutorials ○
- Read A Look at IFRS p. 453 ○

Feature Story

A DOSE OF CAREFUL MANAGEMENT KEEPS RECEIVABLES HEALTHY

"Sometimes you have to know when to be very tough, and sometimes you can give them a bit of a break," says Vivi Su. She's not talking about her children, but about the customers of a subsidiary of pharmaceutical company Whitehall-Robins, where she works as supervisor of credit and collections.

For example, while the company's regular terms are 1/15, n/30 (1% discount if paid within 15 days), a customer might ask for and receive a few days of grace and still get the discount. Or a customer might place orders above its credit limit, in which case, depending on its payment history and the circumstances, Ms. Su might authorize shipment of the goods anyway.

"It's not about drawing a line in the sand, and that's all," she explains. "You want a good relationship with your customers—but you also need to bring in the money."

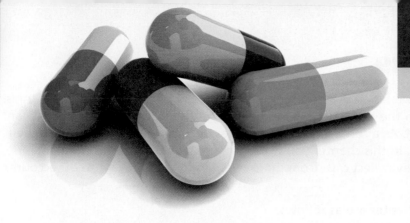

"The money," in Whitehall-Robins's case, amounts to some $170 million in sales a year. Nearly all of it comes in through the credit accounts Ms. Su manages. The process starts with the decision to grant a customer an account in the first place, Ms. Su explains. The sales rep gives the customer a credit application. "My department reviews this application very carefully; a customer needs to supply three good references, and we also run a check with a credit firm like Equifax. If we accept them, then based on their size and history, we assign a credit limit."

Once accounts are established, the company supervises them very carefully. "I get an aging report every single day," says Ms. Su.

"The rule of thumb is that we should always have at least 85% of receivables current—meaning they were billed less than 30 days ago," she continues. "But we try to do even better than that—I like to see 90%." Similarly, her guideline is never to have more than 5% of receivables at over 90 days. But long before that figure is reached, "we jump on it," she says firmly.

At 15 days overdue, Whitehall-Robins phones the client. Often there's a reasonable explanation for the delay—an invoice may have gone astray, or the payables clerk is away. "But if a customer keeps on delaying, and tells us several times that it'll only be a few more days, we know there's a problem," says Ms. Su. After 45 days, "I send a letter. Then a second notice is sent in writing. After the third and final notice, the client has 10 days to pay, and then I hand it over to a collection agency, and it's out of my hands."

Ms. Su's boss, Terry Norton, records an estimate for bad debts every year, based on a percentage of receivables. The percentage depends on the current aging history. He also calculates and monitors the company's receivables turnover ratio, which the company reports in its financial statements. "I think of it in terms of collection period of DSO—days of sales outstanding," he explains.

Ms. Su knows that she and Mr. Norton are crucial to the profitability of Whitehall-Robins. "Receivables are generally the second-largest asset of any company (after its capital assets)," she points out. "So it's no wonder we keep a very close eye on them."

Inside CHAPTER 9

PreviewofCHAPTER9

As indicated in the Feature Story, receivables are a significant asset for many pharmaceutical companies. Because a significant portion of sales in the United States are done on credit, receivables are significant to companies in other industries as well. As a consequence, companies must pay close attention to their receivables and manage them carefully. In this chapter you will learn what journal entries companies make when they sell products, when they collect cash from those sales, and when they write off accounts they cannot collect.

The content and organization of the chapter are as follows.

Accounting for Receivables			
Types of Receivables	**Accounts Receivable**	**Notes Receivable**	**Statement Presentation and Analysis**
• Accounts receivable • Notes receivable • Other receivables	• Recognizing accounts receivable • Valuing accounts receivable • Disposing of accounts receivable	• Determining maturity date • Computing interest • Recognizing notes receivable • Valuing notes receivable • Disposing of notes receivable	• Presentation • Analysis

The Navigator

Types of Receivables

Study Objective [1]
Identify the different types of receivables.

The term **receivables** refers to amounts due from individuals and companies. Receivables are claims that are expected to be collected in cash. The management of receivables is a very important activity for any company that sells goods or services on credit.

Receivables are important because they represent one of a company's most liquid assets. For many companies, receivables are also one of the largest assets. For example, receivables represented 30.8% of the current assets of pharmaceutical giant Rite Aid in 2009. Illustration 9-1 lists receivables as a percentage of total assets for five other well-known companies in a recent year.

Illustration 9-1
Receivables as a percentage of assets

Company	Receivables as a Percentage of Total Assets
General Electric	52%
Ford Motor Company	42%
Minnesota Mining and Manufacturing Company (3M)	14%
DuPont Co.	17%
Intel Corporation	5%

The relative significance of a company's receivables as a percentage of its assets depends on various factors: its industry, the time of year, whether it extends long-term financing, and its credit policies. To reflect important differences among receivables, they are frequently classified as (1) accounts receivable, (2) notes receivable, and (3) other receivables.

Accounts receivable are amounts customers owe on account. They result from the sale of goods and services. Companies generally expect to collect accounts receivable within 30 to 60 days. They are usually the most significant type of claim held by a company.

Notes receivable represent claims for which formal instruments of credit are issued as evidence of the debt. The credit instrument normally requires the debtor to pay interest and extends for time periods of 60–90 days or longer. Notes and accounts receivable that result from sales transactions are often called **trade receivables**.

Other receivables include nontrade receivables such as interest receivable, loans to company officers, advances to employees, and income taxes refundable. These do not generally result from the operations of the business. Therefore, they are generally classified and reported as separate items in the balance sheet.

> **Ethics Note**
>
> Companies report receivables from employees separately in the financial statements. The reason: Sometimes those assets are not the result of an "arm's-length" transaction.

Accounts Receivable

Three accounting issues associated with accounts receivable are:

1. Recognizing accounts receivable.
2. Valuing accounts receivable.
3. Disposing of accounts receivable.

Recognizing Accounts Receivable

Recognizing accounts receivable is relatively straightforward. A service organization records a receivable when it provides service on account. A merchandiser records accounts receivable at the point of sale of merchandise on account. When a merchandiser sells goods, it increases (debits) Accounts Receivable and increases (credits) Sales Revenue.

> **Study Objective [2]**
> Explain how companies recognize accounts receivable.

The seller may offer terms that encourage early payment by providing a discount. Sales returns also reduce receivables. The buyer might find some of the goods unacceptable and choose to return the unwanted goods.

To review, assume that Jordache Co. on July 1, 2012, sells merchandise on account to Polo Company for $1,000, terms 2/10, n/30. On July 5, Polo returns merchandise worth $100 to Jordache Co. On July 11, Jordache receives payment from Polo Company for the balance due. The journal entries to record these transactions on the books of Jordache Co. are as follows. **(Cost of goods sold entries are omitted.)**

> **Ethics Note**
>
> In exchange for lower interest rates, some companies have eliminated the 25-day grace period before finance charges kick in. Be sure you read the fine print in any credit agreement you sign.

July 1	Accounts Receivable—Polo Company	1,000	
	Sales Revenue		1,000
	(To record sales on account)		
July 5	Sales Returns and Allowances	100	
	Accounts Receivable—Polo Company		
	(To record merchandise returned)		100
July 11	Cash ($900 − $18)	882	
	Sales Discounts ($900 × .02)	18	
	Accounts Receivable—Polo Company		900
	(To record collection of accounts receivable)		

> **Helpful Hint**
>
> These entries are the same as those described in Chapter 5. For simplicity, we have omitted inventory and cost of goods sold from this set of journal entries and from end-of-chapter material.

Some retailers issue their own credit cards. When you use a retailer's credit card (JCPenney, for example), the retailer charges interest on the balance due if not paid within a specified period (usually 25–30 days).

To illustrate, assume that you use your JCPenney Company credit card to purchase clothing with a sales price of $300. JCPenney will increase (debit) Accounts Receivable for $300 and increase (credit) Sales Revenue for $300 (cost of goods sold entry omitted) as follows.

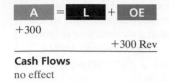

+300

+300 Rev

Cash Flows
no effect

Accounts Receivable	300	
Sales Revenue		300
(To record sale of merchandise)		

Assuming that you owe $300 at the end of the month, and JCPenney charges 1.5% per month on the balance due, the adjusting entry that JCPenney makes to record interest revenue of $4.50 ($300 × 1.5%) is as follows.

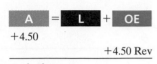

+4.50

+4.50 Rev

Cash Flows
no effect

Accounts Receivable	4.50	
Interest Revenue		4.50
(To record interest on amount due)		

Interest revenue is often substantial for many retailers.

ANATOMY OF A FRAUD

Tasanee was the accounts receivable clerk for a large non-profit foundation that provided performance and exhibition space for the performing and visual arts. Her responsibilities included activities normally assigned to an accounts receivable clerk, such as recording revenues from various sources that included donations, facility rental fees, ticket revenue, and bar receipts. However, she was also responsible for handling all cash and checks from the time they were received until the time she deposited them, as well as preparing the bank reconciliation. Tasanee took advantage of her situation by falsifying bank deposits and bank reconciliations so that she could steal cash from the bar receipts. Since nobody else logged the donations or matched the donation receipts to pledges prior to Tasanee receiving them, she was able to offset the cash that was stolen against donations that she received but didn't record. Her crime was made easier by the fact that her boss, the company's controller, only did a very superficial review of the bank reconciliation and thus didn't notice that some numbers had been cut out from other documents and taped onto the bank reconciliation.

Total take: $1.5 million

THE MISSING CONTROL

Segregation of duties. The foundation should not have allowed an accounts receivable clerk, whose job was to record receivables, to also handle cash, record cash, make deposits, and especially prepare the bank reconciliation.

Independent internal verification. The controller was supposed to perform a thorough review of the bank reconciliation. Because he did not, he was terminated from his position.

Source: Adapted from Wells, *Fraud Casebook* (2007), pp. 183–194.

Study Objective [3]

Distinguish between the methods and bases companies use to value accounts receivable.

Valuing Accounts Receivable

Once companies record receivables in the accounts, the next question is: How should they report receivables in the financial statements? Companies report accounts receivable on the balance sheet as an asset. But determining the **amount** to report is sometimes difficult because some receivables will become uncollectible.

Each customer must satisfy the credit requirements of the seller before the credit sale is approved. Inevitably, though, some accounts receivable become uncollectible. For example, a customer may not be able to pay because of a decline in its sales revenue due to a downturn in the economy. Similarly, individuals may be laid off from their jobs or faced with unexpected hospital bills. Companies record credit losses as debits to **Bad Debts Expense** (or Uncollectible Accounts Expense). Such losses are a normal and necessary risk of doing business on a credit basis.

Alternative Terminology

You will sometimes see *Bad Debts Expense* called *Uncollectible Accounts Expense*.

Recently, when U.S. home prices fell, home foreclosures rose, and the economy in general slowed, lenders experienced huge increases in their bad debts expense. For example, during a recent quarter Wachovia, the fourth largest U.S. bank, increased bad debts expense from $108 million to $408 million. Similarly, American Express increased its bad debts expense by 70%.

Two methods are used in accounting for uncollectible accounts: (1) the direct write-off method and (2) the allowance method. The following sections explain these methods.

DIRECT WRITE-OFF METHOD FOR UNCOLLECTIBLE ACCOUNTS

Under the **direct write-off method**, when a company determines a particular account to be uncollectible, it charges the loss to Bad Debts Expense. Assume, for example, that Warden Co. writes off as uncollectible M. E. Doran's $200 balance on December 12. Warden's entry is:

Dec. 12	Bad Debts Expense	200	
	Accounts Receivable—M. E. Doran		200
	(To record write-off of M. E. Doran account)		

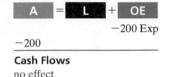

−200 Exp

−200

Cash Flows
no effect

Under this method, Bad Debts Expense will show only **actual losses** from uncollectibles. The company will report accounts receivable at its gross amount.

Although this method is simple, its use can reduce the usefulness of both the income statement and balance sheet. Consider the following example. Assume that in 2012, Quick Buck Computer Company decided it could increase its revenues by offering computers to college students without requiring any money down and with no credit-approval process. On campuses across the country, it distributed one million computers with a selling price of $800 each. This increased Quick Buck's revenues and receivables by $800 million. The promotion was a huge success! The 2012 balance sheet and income statement looked great. Unfortunately, during 2013, nearly 40% of the customers defaulted on their loans. This made the 2013 income statement and balance sheet look terrible. Illustration 9-2 shows the effect of these events on the financial statements if the direct write-off method is used.

Illustration 9-2
Effects of direct write-off method

Year 2012

Net income

Huge sales promotion.
Sales increase dramatically.
Accounts receivable increases dramatically.

Year 2013

Net income

Customers default on loans.
Bad debts expense increases dramatically.
Accounts receivable plummets.

Under the direct write-off method, companies often record bad debts expense in a period different from the period in which they record the revenue. The method does not attempt to match bad debts expense to sales revenues in the income statement. Nor does the direct write-off method show accounts receivable in the balance sheet at the amount the company actually expects to receive. **Consequently, unless bad debts losses are insignificant, the direct write-off method is not acceptable for financial reporting purposes.**

ALLOWANCE METHOD FOR UNCOLLECTIBLE ACCOUNTS

The allowance method of accounting for bad debts involves estimating uncollectible accounts at the end of each period. This provides better matching on the income statement. It also ensures that companies state receivables on the balance sheet at their cash (net) realizable value. Cash (net) realizable value is the net amount the company expects to receive in cash. It excludes amounts that the company estimates it will not collect. Thus, this method reduces receivables in the balance sheet by the amount of estimated uncollectible receivables.

GAAP requires the allowance method for financial reporting purposes when bad debts are material in amount. This method has three essential features:

1. Companies **estimate** uncollectible accounts receivable. They match this estimated expense **against revenues** in the same accounting period in which they record the revenues.

2. Companies debit estimated uncollectibles to Bad Debts Expense and credit them to Allowance for Doubtful Accounts through an adjusting entry at the end of each period. Allowance for Doubtful Accounts is a contra account to Accounts Receivable.

3. When companies write off a specific account, they debit actual uncollectibles to Allowance for Doubtful Accounts and credit that amount to Accounts Receivable.

Recording Estimated Uncollectibles.   To illustrate the allowance method, assume that Hampson Furniture has credit sales of $1,200,000 in 2012. Of this amount, $200,000 remains uncollected at December 31. The credit manager estimates that $12,000 of these sales will be uncollectible. The adjusting entry to record the estimated uncollectibles increases (debits) Bad Debts Expense and increases (credits) Allowance for Doubtful Accounts, as follows.

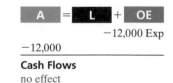

−12,000 Exp

−12,000

Cash Flows
no effect

Dec. 31	Bad Debts Expense	12,000	
	Allowance for Doubtful Accounts		12,000
	(To record estimate of uncollectible		
	accounts)		

Hampson reports Bad Debts Expense in the income statement as an operating expense (usually as a selling expense). Thus, the estimated uncollectibles are matched with sales in 2012. Hampson records the expense in the same year it made the sales.

Allowance for Doubtful Accounts shows the estimated amount of claims on customers that the company expects will become uncollectible in the future. Companies use a contra account instead of a direct credit to Accounts Receivable because they do not know *which* customers will not pay. The credit balance in the allowance account will absorb the specific write-offs when they occur. As Illustration 9-3 shows, the company deducts the allowance account from accounts receivable in the current assets section of the balance sheet.

The amount of $188,000 in Illustration 9-3 represents the expected **cash realizable value** of the accounts receivable at the statement date. **Companies do not close Allowance for Doubtful Accounts at the end of the fiscal year.**

Illustration 9-3
Presentation of allowance
for doubtful accounts

Hampson Furniture Balance Sheet (partial)		
Current assets		
Cash		$ 14,800
Accounts receivable	**$200,000**	
Less: Allowance for doubtful accounts	**12,000**	188,000
Inventory		310,000
Supplies		25,000
Total current assets		$537,800

Recording the Write-Off of an Uncollectible Account. As described in the Feature Story, companies use various methods of collecting past-due accounts, such as letters, calls, and legal action. When they have exhausted all means of collecting a past-due account and collection appears impossible, the company should write off the account. In the credit card industry, for example, it is standard practice to write off accounts that are 210 days past due. To prevent premature or unauthorized write-offs, authorized management personnel should formally approve each write-off. To maintain good internal control, companies should not authorize someone to write off accounts who also has daily responsibilities related to cash or receivables.

To illustrate a receivables write-off, assume that the financial vice president of Hampson Furniture authorizes a write-off of the $500 balance owed by R. A. Ware on March 1, 2013. The entry to record the write-off is:

Mar. 1	Allowance for Doubtful Accounts	500	
	Accounts Receivable—R. A. Ware		500
	(Write-off of R. A. Ware account)		

A = L + OE
+500
−500

Cash Flows
no effect

Bad Debts Expense does not increase when the write-off occurs. **Under the allowance method, companies debit every bad debt write-off to the allowance account rather than to Bad Debts Expense.** A debit to Bad Debts Expense would be incorrect because the company has already recognized the expense when it made the adjusting entry for estimated bad debts. Instead, the entry to record the write-off of an uncollectible account reduces both Accounts Receivable and Allowance for Doubtful Accounts. After posting, the general ledger accounts will appear as in Illustration 9-4.

Illustration 9-4
General ledger balances
after write-off

Accounts Receivable				Allowance for Doubtful Accounts			
Jan. 1 Bal.	200,000	Mar. 1	500	Mar. 1	500	Jan. 1 Bal.	12,000
Mar. 1 Bal.	199,500					Mar. 1 Bal.	11,500

A write-off affects **only balance sheet accounts**—not income statement accounts. The write-off of the account reduces both Accounts Receivable and Allowance for Doubtful Accounts. Cash realizable value in the balance sheet, therefore, remains the same, as Illustration 9-5 shows.

Illustration 9-5
Cash realizable value
comparison

	Before Write-Off	After Write-Off
Accounts receivable	$200,000	$199,500
Allowance for doubtful accounts	12,000	11,500
Cash realizable value	**$188,000**	**$188,000**

Recovery of an Uncollectible Account. Occasionally, a company collects from a customer after it has written off the account as uncollectible. The company makes two entries to record the recovery of a bad debt: (1) It reverses the entry made in writing off the account. This reinstates the customer's account. (2) It journalizes the collection in the usual manner.

To illustrate, assume that on July 1, R. A. Ware pays the $500 amount that Hampson had written off on March 1. Hampson makes these entries:

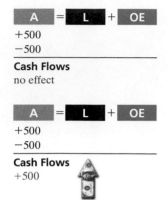

Cash Flows
no effect

Cash Flows
+500

			(1)			
July 1		Accounts Receivable—R. A. Ware			500	
		Allowance for Doubtful Accounts				500
		(To reverse write-off of R. A. Ware account)				

			(2)			
July 1		Cash			500	
		Accounts Receivable—R. A. Ware				500
		(To record collection from R. A. Ware)				

Note that the recovery of a bad debt, like the write-off of a bad debt, affects **only balance sheet accounts**. The net effect of the two entries above is a debit to Cash and a credit to Allowance for Doubtful Accounts for $500. Accounts Receivable and the Allowance for Doubtful Accounts both increase in entry (1) for two reasons: First, the company made an error in judgment when it wrote off the account receivable. Second, after R. A. Ware did pay, Accounts Receivable in the general ledger and Ware's account in the subsidiary ledger should show the collection for possible future credit purposes.

Estimating the Allowance. For Hampson Furniture in Illustration 9-3, the amount of the expected uncollectibles was given. However, in "real life," companies must estimate that amount when they use the allowance method. Two bases are used to determine this amount: **(1) percentage of sales**, and **(2) percentage of receivables**. Both bases are generally accepted. The choice is a management decision. It depends on the relative emphasis that management wishes to give to expenses and revenues on the one hand or to cash realizable value of the accounts receivable on the other. The choice is whether to emphasize income statement or balance sheet relationships. Illustration 9-6 compares the two bases.

Illustration 9-6
Comparison of bases for estimating uncollectibles

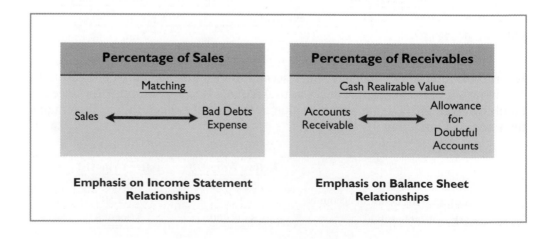

The percentage-of-sales basis results in a better matching of expenses with revenues—an income statement viewpoint. The percentage-of-receivables basis produces the better estimate of cash realizable value—a balance sheet viewpoint. Under both bases, the company must determine its past experience with bad debt losses.

Percentage-of-Sales. In the **percentage-of-sales basis**, management estimates what percentage of credit sales will be uncollectible. This percentage is based on past experience and anticipated credit policy.

The company applies this percentage to either total credit sales or net credit sales of the current year. To illustrate, assume that Gonzalez Company elects to use the percentage-of-sales basis. It concludes that 1% of net credit sales will become uncollectible. If net credit sales for 2012 are $800,000, the estimated bad debts expense is $8,000 (1% × $800,000). The adjusting entry is:

Dec. 31	Bad Debts Expense	8,000	
	Allowance for Doubtful Accounts		8,000
	(To record estimated bad debts for year)		

A	=	L	+	OE
				−8,000 Exp
−8,000				

Cash Flows
no effect

After the adjusting entry is posted, assuming the allowance account already has a credit balance of $1,723, the accounts of Gonzalez Company will show the following:

Bad Debts Expense		**Allowance for Doubtful Accounts**	
Dec. 31 Adj. **8,000**		Jan. 1 Bal. 1,723	
		Dec. 31 Adj. **8,000**	
		Dec. 31 Bal. 9,723	

Illustration 9-7
Bad debts accounts after posting

This basis of estimating uncollectibles emphasizes the matching of expenses with revenues. As a result, Bad Debts Expense will show a direct percentage relationship to the sales base on which it is computed. **When the company makes the adjusting entry, it disregards the existing balance in Allowance for Doubtful Accounts.** The adjusted balance in this account should be a reasonable approximation of the realizable value of the receivables. If actual write-offs differ significantly from the amount estimated, the company should modify the percentage for future years.

Percentage-of-Receivables. Under the **percentage-of-receivables basis**, management estimates what percentage of receivables will result in losses from uncollectible accounts. The company prepares an **aging schedule**, in which it classifies customer balances by the length of time they have been unpaid. Because of its emphasis on time, the analysis is often called **aging the accounts receivable**. In the Feature Story, Whitehall-Robins prepared an aging report daily.

After the company arranges the accounts by age, it determines the expected bad debt losses. It applies percentages based on past experience to the totals in each category. The longer a receivable is past due, the less likely it is to be collected. Thus, the estimated percentage of uncollectible debts increases as the number of days past due increases. Illustration 9-8 (page 424) shows an aging schedule for Dart Company. Note that the estimated percentage uncollectible increases from 2 to 40% as the number of days past due increases.

Illustration 9-8
Aging schedule

Worksheet.xls

File   Edit   View   Insert   Format   Tools   Data   Window   Help

	A	B	C	D	E	F	G
1					**Number of Days Past Due**		
2			**Not**				
3	**Customer**	**Total**	**Yet Due**	**1–30**	**31–60**	**61–90**	**Over 90**
4	T. E. Adert	$ 600		$ 300		$ 200	$ 100
5	R. C. Bortz	300	$ 300				
6	B. A. Carl	450		200	$ 250		
7	O. L. Diker	700	500			200	
8	T. O. Ebbet	600			300		300
9	Others	36,950	26,200	5,200	2,450	1,600	1,500
10		$39,600	$27,000	$5,700	$3,000	$2,000	$1,900
11	Estimated Percentage Uncollectible			2%	4%	10%	20%	40%
12	Total Estimated Bad Debts	$ 2,228	$ 540	$ 228	$ 300	$ 400	$ 760
13							

Helpful Hint

The older categories have higher percentages because the longer an account is past due, the less likely it is to be collected.

Total estimated bad debts for Dart Company ($2,228) represent the amount of existing customer claims the company expects will become uncollectible in the future. This amount represents the **required balance** in Allowance for Doubtful Accounts at the balance sheet date. **The amount of the bad debt adjusting entry is the difference between the required balance and the existing balance in the allowance account.** If the trial balance shows Allowance for Doubtful Accounts with a credit balance of $528, the company will make an adjusting entry for $1,700 ($2,228 − $528), as shown here.

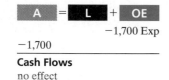

A = L + OE
−1,700 Exp
−1,700

Cash Flows
no effect

Dec. 31	Bad Debts Expense	1,700	
	Allowance for Doubtful Accounts		1,700
	(To adjust allowance account to total estimated uncollectibles)		

After Dart posts its adjusting entry, its accounts will appear as follows.

Illustration 9-9
Bad debts accounts after posting

Bad Debts Expense		**Allowance for Doubtful Accounts**	
Dec. 31 Adj. **1,700**			Bal. 528
			Dec. 31 Adj. **1,700**
			Bal. 2,228

Occasionally, the allowance account will have a **debit balance** prior to adjustment. This occurs when write-offs during the year have exceeded previous provisions for bad debts. In such a case, the company **adds the debit balance to the required balance** when it makes the adjusting entry. Thus, if there had been a $500 debit balance in the allowance account before adjustment, the adjusting entry would have been for $2,728 ($2,228 + $500) to arrive at a credit balance of $2,228. The percentage-of-receivables basis will normally result in the better approximation of cash realizable value.

Do it!

Brule Co. has been in business five years. The ledger at the end of the current year shows:

Accounts Receivable	$30,000 Dr.
Sales Revenue	$180,000 Cr.
Allowance for Doubtful Accounts	$2,000 Dr.

Bad debts are estimated to be 10% of receivables. Prepare the entry to adjust Allowance for Doubtful Accounts.

Solution

The following entry should be made to bring the balance in Allowance for Doubtful Accounts up to a balance of $3,000 (0.1 × $30,000):

Bad Debts Expense [(0.1 × $30,000) + $2,000]	5,000	
Allowance for Doubtful Accounts		5,000
(To record estimate of uncollectible accounts)		

Related exercise material: BE9-3, BE9-4, BE9-5, BE9-6, BE9-7, E9-3, E9-4, E9-5, E9-6, and **Do it!** 9-1.

Uncollectible Accounts Receivable

action plan

✔ Report receivables at their cash (net) realizable value.

✔ Estimate the amount the company does not expect to collect.

✔ Consider the existing balance in the allowance account when using the percentage-of-receivables basis.

The Navigator

Disposing of Accounts Receivable

In the normal course of events, companies collect accounts receivable in cash and remove the receivables from the books. However, as credit sales and receivables have grown in significance, the "normal course of events" has changed. Companies now frequently sell their receivables to another company for cash, thereby shortening the cash-to-cash operating cycle.

Companies sell receivables for two major reasons. First, **they may be the only reasonable source of cash**. When money is tight, companies may not be able to borrow money in the usual credit markets. Or, if money is available, the cost of borrowing may be prohibitive.

A second reason for selling receivables is that **billing and collection are often time-consuming and costly**. It is often easier for a retailer to sell the receivables to another party with expertise in billing and collection matters. Credit card companies such as MasterCard, Visa, and Discover specialize in billing and collecting accounts receivable.

Study Objective [4]
Describe the entries to record the disposition of accounts receivable.

SALE OF RECEIVABLES

A common sale of receivables is a sale to a factor. A **factor** is a finance company or bank that buys receivables from businesses and then collects the payments directly from the customers. Factoring is a multibillion dollar business.

Factoring arrangements vary widely. Typically the factor charges a commission to the company that is selling the receivables. This fee ranges from 1–3% of the amount of receivables purchased. To illustrate, assume that Hendredon Furniture factors $600,000 of receivables to Federal Factors. Federal Factors assesses a service charge of 2% of the amount of receivables sold. The journal entry to record the sale by Hendredon Furniture is as follows.

Cash	588,000	
Service Charge Expense (2% × $600,000)	12,000	
Accounts Receivable		600,000
(To record the sale of accounts receivable)		

A	=	L	+	OE
+588,000				
				−12,000 Exp
−600,000				

Cash Flows
+588,000

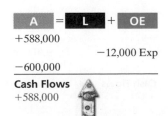

If the company often sells its receivables, it records the service charge expense (such as that incurred by Hendredon) as selling expense. If the company infrequently sells receivables, it may report this amount in the "Other expenses and losses" section of the income statement.

CREDIT CARD SALES

Over one billion credit cards are in use in the United States—more than three credit cards for every man, woman, and child in this country. Visa, MasterCard, and American Express are the national credit cards that most individuals use. Three parties are involved when national credit cards are used in retail sales: (1) the credit card issuer, who is independent of the retailer, (2) the retailer, and (3) the customer. A retailer's acceptance of a national credit card is another form of selling (factoring) the receivable.

Illustration 9-10 shows the major advantages of national credit cards to the retailer. In exchange for these advantages, the retailer pays the credit card issuer a fee of 2–6% of the invoice price for its services.

Illustration 9-10
Advantages of credit cards to the retailer

Accounting for Credit Card Sales.   The retailer generally considers sales from the use of national credit card sales as *cash sales*. The retailer must pay to the bank that issues the card a fee for processing the transactions. The retailer records the credit card slips in a similar manner as checks deposited from a cash sale.

To illustrate, Anita Ferreri purchases $1,000 of compact discs for her restaurant from Karen Kerr Music Co., using her Visa First Bank Card. First Bank charges a service fee of 3%. The entry to record this transaction by Karen Kerr Music is as follows.

A	=	L	+	OE
+970				
				−30 Exp
				+1,000 Rev

Cash Flows
+970

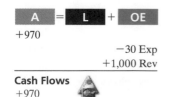

Cash	970	
Service Charge Expense	30	
Sales Revenue		1,000
(To record Visa credit card sales)		

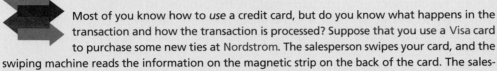

ACCOUNTING ACROSS THE ORGANIZATION

How Does a Credit Card Work?

Most of you know how to *use* a credit card, but do you know what happens in the transaction and how the transaction is processed? Suppose that you use a Visa card to purchase some new ties at Nordstrom. The salesperson swipes your card, and the swiping machine reads the information on the magnetic strip on the back of the card. The salesperson then types in the amount of the purchase. The machine contacts the Visa computer, which routes the call back to the bank that issued your Visa card. The issuing bank verifies that the account exists, that the card is not stolen, and that you have not exceeded your credit limit. At this point, the slip is printed, which you sign.

Visa acts as the clearing agent for the transaction. It transfers funds from the issuing bank to Nordstrom's bank account. Generally this transfer of funds, from sale to the receipt of funds in the merchant's account, takes two to three days.

In the meantime, Visa puts a pending charge on your account for the amount of the tie purchase; that amount counts immediately against your available credit limit. At the end of the billing period, Visa sends you an invoice (your credit card bill) which shows the various charges you made, and the amounts that Visa expended on your behalf, for the month. You then must "pay the piper" for your stylish new ties.

? Assume that Nordstrom prepares a bank reconciliation at the end of each month. If some credit card sales have not been processed by the bank, how should Nordstrom treat these transactions on its bank reconciliation? (See page 453.)

Do it!

Mehl Wholesalers Co. has been expanding faster than it can raise capital. According to its local banker, the company has reached its debt ceiling. Mehl's suppliers (creditors) are demanding payment within 30 days of the invoice date for goods acquired, but Mehl's customers are slow in paying (60–90 days). As a result, Mehl has a cash flow problem.

Mehl needs $120,000 in cash to safely cover next Friday's payroll. Its balance of outstanding accounts receivables totals $750,000. What might Mehl do to alleviate this cash crunch? Record the entry that Mehl would make when it raises the needed cash.

Disposition of Accounts Receivable

action plan

✔ To speed up the collection of cash, sell receivables to a factor.

✔ Calculate service charge expense as a percentage of the factored receivables.

Solution

Assuming that Mehl Wholesalers factors $125,000 of its accounts receivable at a 1% service charge, it would make the following entry.

Cash	123,750	
Service Charge Expense	1,250	
Accounts Receivable		125,000
(To record sale of receivables to factor)		

Related exercise material: BE9-8, E9-7, E9-8, E9-9, and **Do it!** 9-2.

✔ The Navigator

Notes Receivable

Companies may also grant credit in exchange for a formal credit instrument known as a **promissory note**. A **promissory note** is a written promise to pay a specified amount of money on demand or at a definite time. Promissory notes may be used

(1) when individuals and companies lend or borrow money, (2) when the amount of the transaction and the credit period exceed normal limits, or (3) in settlement of accounts receivable.

In a promissory note, the party making the promise to pay is called the **maker**. The party to whom payment is to be made is called the **payee**. The note may specifically identify the payee by name or may designate the payee simply as the bearer of the note.

In the note shown in Illustration 9-11, Calhoun Company is the maker, Wilma Company is the payee. To Wilma Company, the promissory note is a note receivable; to Calhoun Company, it is a note payable.

Illustration 9-11
Promissory note

Helpful Hint

Who are the two key parties to a note, and what entry does each party make when the note is issued?

Answer:
1. The maker, Calhoun Company, credits Notes Payable.
2. The payee, Wilma Company, debits Notes Receivable.

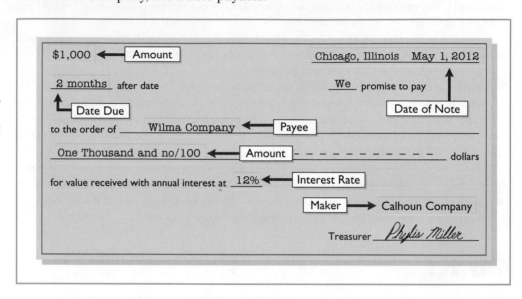

Notes receivable give the holder a stronger legal claim to assets than do accounts receivable. Like accounts receivable, notes receivable can be readily sold to another party. Promissory notes are negotiable instruments (as are checks), which means that they can be transferred to another party by endorsement.

Companies frequently accept notes receivable from customers who need to extend the payment of an outstanding account receivable. They often require such notes from high-risk customers. In some industries (such as the pleasure and sport boat industry), all credit sales are supported by notes. The majority of notes, however, originate from loans.

The basic issues in accounting for notes receivable are the same as those for accounts receivable:

1. **Recognizing** notes receivable.
2. **Valuing** notes receivable.
3. **Disposing of** notes receivable.

On the following pages, we will look at these issues. Before we do, we need to consider two issues that did not apply to accounts receivable: maturity date and computing interest.

Determining the Maturity Date

Study Objective [5]

Compute the maturity date of and interest on notes receivable.

When the life of a note is expressed in terms of months, you find the date when it matures by counting the months from the date of issue. For example, the maturity date of a three-month note dated May 1 is August 1. A note drawn on the last day of a month matures on the last day of a subsequent month. That is, a July 31 note due in two months matures on September 30.

When the due date is stated in terms of days, you need to count the exact number of days to determine the maturity date. In counting, **omit the date the note is issued but include the due date**. For example, the maturity date of a 60-day note dated July 17 is September 15, computed as follows.

Term of note		60 days
July (31−17)	14	
August	31	45
Maturity date: September		**15**

Illustration 9-12
Computation of maturity date

Illustration 9-13 shows three ways of stating the maturity date of a promissory note.

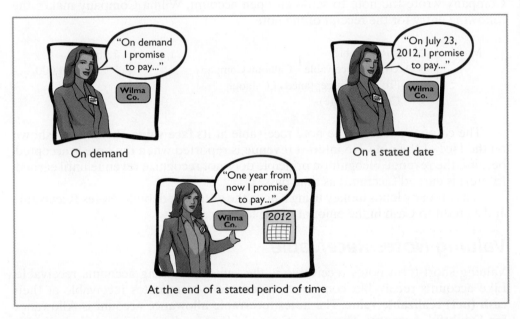

On demand

On a stated date

At the end of a stated period of time

Illustration 9-13
Maturity date of different notes

Computing Interest

Illustration 9-14 gives the basic formula for computing interest on an interest-bearing note.

Face Value of Note	×	Annual Interest Rate	×	Time in Terms of One Year	=	Interest

Illustration 9-14
Formula for computing interest

The interest rate specified in a note is an **annual** rate of interest. The time factor in the computation in Illustration 9-14 expresses the fraction of a year that the note is outstanding. When the maturity date is stated in days, the time factor is often the number of days divided by 360. When counting days, omit the date that the note is issued but include the due date. When the due date is stated in months, the time factor is the number of months divided by 12. Illustration 9-15 (page 430) shows computation of interest for various time periods.

Helpful Hint

The interest rate specified is the *annual* rate.

Illustration 9-15
Computation of interest

Terms of Note	Interest Computation
	Face × Rate × Time = Interest
$ 730, 18%, 120 days	$ 730 × 18% × 120/360 = $ 43.80
$1,000, 15%, 6 months	$1,000 × 15% × 6/12 = $ 75.00
$2,000, 12%, 1 year	$2,000 × 12% × 1/1 = $240.00

There are different ways to calculate interest. For example, the computation in Illustration 9-15 assumed 360 days for the length of the year. Most financial instruments use 365 days to compute interest. *For homework problems, assume 360 days to simplify computations.*

Recognizing Notes Receivable

Study Objective [6]

Explain how companies recognize notes receivable.

A = L + OE
+1,000
−1,000

Cash Flows
no effect

To illustrate the basic entry for notes receivable, we will use Calhoun Company's $1,000, two-month, 12% promissory note dated May 1. Assuming that Calhoun Company wrote the note to settle an open account, Wilma Company makes the following entry for the receipt of the note.

May 1	Notes Receivable	1,000	
	Accounts Receivable—Calhoun Company		1,000
	(To record acceptance of Calhoun		
	Company note)		

The company records the note receivable at its **face value**, the amount shown on the face of the note. No interest revenue is reported when the note is accepted, because the revenue recognition principle does not recognize revenue until earned. Interest is earned (accrued) as time passes.

If a company lends money using a note, the entry is a debit to Notes Receivable and a credit to Cash in the amount of the loan.

Valuing Notes Receivable

Study Objective [7]

Describe how companies value notes receivable.

Valuing short-term notes receivable is the same as valuing accounts receivable. Like accounts receivable, companies report short-term notes receivable at their **cash (net) realizable value**. The notes receivable allowance account is Allowance for Doubtful Accounts. The estimations involved in determining cash realizable value and in recording bad debts expense and the related allowance are done similarly to accounts receivable.

INTERNATIONAL INSIGHT

Can Fair Value Be Unfair?

The FASB and the International Accounting Standards Board (IASB) are considering proposals for how to account for financial instruments. The FASB has proposed that loans and receivables be accounted for at their fair value (the amount they could currently be sold for), as are most investments. The FASB believes that this would provide a more accurate view of a company's financial position. It might be especially useful as an early warning when a bank is in trouble because of poor-quality loans. But, banks argue that fair values are difficult to estimate accurately. They are also concerned that volatile fair values could cause large swings in a bank's reported net income.

Source: David Reilly, "Banks Face a Mark-to-Market Challenge," *Wall Street Journal Online* (March 15, 2010).

? What are the arguments in favor of and against fair value accounting for loans and receivables? (See page 453.)

Disposing of Notes Receivable

Notes may be held to their maturity date, at which time the face value plus accrued interest is due. In some situations, the maker of the note defaults, and the payee must make an appropriate adjustment. In other situations, similar to accounts receivable, the holder of the note speeds up the conversion to cash by selling the receivables as described later in this chapter.

HONOR OF NOTES RECEIVABLE

A note is **honored** when its maker pays in full at its maturity date. For each interest-bearing note, the **amount due at maturity** is the face value of the note plus interest for the length of time specified on the note.

To illustrate, assume that Wolder Co. lends Higley Co. $10,000 on June 1, accepting a five-month, 9% interest note. In this situation, interest is $375 ($10,000 × 9% × $\frac{5}{12}$). The amount due, the maturity value, is $10,375 ($10,000 + $375). To obtain payment, Wolder (the payee) must present the note either to Higley Co. (the maker) or to the maker's agent, such as a bank. If Wolder presents the note to Higley Co. on November 1, the maturity date, Wolder's entry to record the collection is:

Nov. 1	Cash	10,375	
	Notes Receivable		10,000
	Interest Revenue ($10,000 × 9% × $\frac{5}{12}$)		375
	(To record collection of Higley note and interest)		

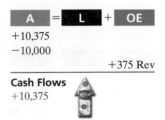

A = L + OE

+10,375
−10,000
+375 Rev

Cash Flows
+10,375

ACCRUAL OF INTEREST RECEIVABLE

Suppose instead that Wolder Co. prepares financial statements as of September 30. The timeline in Illustration 9-16 presents this situation.

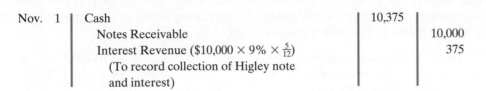

Illustration 9-16
Timeline of interest earned

To reflect interest earned but not yet received, Wolder must accrue interest on September 30. In this case, the adjusting entry by Wolder is for four months of interest, or $300, as shown below.

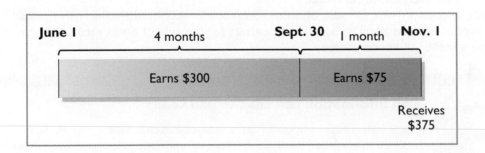

Sept. 30	Interest Receivable ($10,000 × 9% × $\frac{4}{12}$)	300	
	Interest Revenue		300
	(To accrue 4 months' interest on Higley note)		

A = L + OE

+300
+300 Rev

Cash Flows
no effect

At the note's maturity on November 1, Wolder receives $10,375. This amount represents repayment of the $10,000 note as well as five months of interest, or $375, as shown on the next page. The $375 is comprised of the $300 Interest Receivable accrued on September 30 plus $75 earned during October. Wolder's entry to record the honoring of the Higley note on November 1 is:

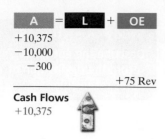

A	=	L	+	OE
+10,375				
−10,000				
−300				
				+75 Rev

Cash Flows
+10,375

Nov. 1	Cash [$10,000 + ($10,000 × 9% × $\frac{5}{12}$)]	10,375	
	Notes Receivable		10,000
	Interest Receivable		300
	Interest Revenue ($10,000 × 9% × $\frac{1}{12}$)		75
	(To record collection of Higley note and interest)		

In this case, Wolder credits Interest Receivable because the receivable was established in the adjusting entry on September 30.

DISHONOR OF NOTES RECEIVABLE

A **dishonored note** is a note that is not paid in full at maturity. A dishonored note receivable is no longer negotiable. However, the payee still has a claim against the maker of the note for both the note and the interest. Therefore the note holder usually transfers the Notes Receivable account to an Account Receivable.

To illustrate, assume that Higley Co. on November 1 indicates that it cannot pay at the present time. The entry to record the dishonor of the note depends on whether Wolder Co. expects eventual collection. If it does expect eventual collection, Wolder Co. debits the amount due (face value and interest) on the note to Accounts Receivable. It would make the following entry at the time the note is dishonored (assuming no previous accrual of interest).

A	=	L	+	OE
+10,375				
−10,000				
				+375 Rev

Cash Flows
no effect

Nov. 1	Accounts Receivable—Higley	10,375	
	Notes Receivable		10,000
	Interest Revenue		375
	(To record the dishonor of Higley note)		

If instead, on November 1, there is no hope of collection, the note holder would write off the face value of the note by debiting Allowance for Doubtful Accounts. No interest revenue would be recorded because collection will not occur.

SALE OF NOTES RECEIVABLE

The accounting for the sale of notes receivable is recorded similarly to the sale of accounts receivable. The accounting entries for the sale of notes receivable are left for a more advanced course.

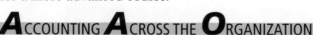

*A*CCOUNTING *A*CROSS THE *O*RGANIZATION

Bad Information Can Lead to Bad Loans

Many factors have contributed to the recent credit crisis. One significant factor that resulted in many bad loans was a failure by lenders to investigate loan customers sufficiently. For example, Countrywide Financial Corporation wrote many loans under its "Fast and Easy" loan program. That program allowed borrowers to provide little or no documentation for their income or their assets. Other lenders had similar programs, which earned the nickname "liars' loans." One study found that in these situations 60% of applicants overstated their incomes by more than 50% in order to qualify for a loan. Critics of the banking industry say that because loan officers were compensated for loan volume, and because banks were selling the loans to investors rather than holding them, the lenders had little incentive to investigate the borrowers' creditworthiness.

Source: Glenn R. Simpson and James R. Hagerty, "Countrywide Loss Focuses Attention on Underwriting," *Wall Street Journal* (April 30, 2008), p. B1; and Michael Corkery, "Fraud Seen as Driver in Wave of Foreclosures," *Wall Street Journal* (December 21, 2007), p. A1.

? What steps should the banks have taken to ensure the accuracy of financial information provided on loan applications? (See page 453.)

Do it!

Gambit Stores accepts from Leonard Co. a $3,400, 90-day, 6% note dated May 10 in settlement of Leonard's overdue account. (a) What is the maturity date of the note? (b) What entry does Gambit make at the maturity date, assuming Leonard pays the note and interest in full at that time?

Notes Receivable

action plan

✔ Count the exact number of days to determine the maturity date. Omit the date the note is issued, but include the due date.

Solution

(a) The maturity date is August 8, computed as follows.

Term of note:		90 days
May (31–10)	21	
June	30	
July	31	82
Maturity date: August		8

✔ Determine whether interest was accrued.

✔ Compute the accrued interest.

✔ Prepare the entry for payment of the note and interest.

(b) The interest payable at the maturity date is $51, computed as follows.

Face × Rate × Time = Interest
$3,400 × 6% × 90/360 = $51

✔ The entry to record interest at maturity in this solution assumes no interest has been previously accrued on this note.

The entry recorded by Gambit Stores at the maturity date is:

Cash	3,451	
Notes Receivable		3,400
Interest Revenue		51
(To record collection of Leonard note)		

Related exercise material: BE9-9, BE9-10, BE9-11, E9-10, E9-11, E9-12, E9-13, and **Do it!** 9-3.

The Navigator

Statement Presentation and Analysis

Presentation

Companies should identify in the balance sheet or in the notes to the financial statements each of the major types of receivables. Short-term receivables appear in the current assets section of the balance sheet. Short-term investments appear before short-term receivables because these investments are more liquid (nearer to cash). Companies report both the gross amount of receivables and the allowance for doubtful accounts.

In a multiple-step income statement, companies report bad debts expense and service charge expense as selling expenses in the operating expenses section. Interest revenue appears under "Other revenues and gains" in the nonoperating activities section of the income statement.

Study Objective [9]
Explain the statement presentation and analysis of receivables.

Analysis

Investors and corporate managers compute financial ratios to evaluate the liquidity of a company's accounts receivable. They use the **accounts receivable turnover ratio** to assess the liquidity of the receivables. This ratio measures the number of times, on average, the company collects accounts receivable during the period. It is computed by dividing net credit sales (net sales less cash sales) by the average net accounts receivable during the year. Unless seasonal factors are significant, average net accounts receivable outstanding can be computed from the beginning and ending balances of net accounts receivable.

For example, in 2009 Cisco Systems had net sales of $29,131 million for the year. It had a beginning accounts receivable (net) balance of $3,821 million and an ending accounts receivable (net) balance of $3,177 million. Assuming that Cisco's sales were all on credit, its accounts receivable turnover ratio is computed as follows.

Illustration 9-17
Accounts receivable turnover ratio and computation

Net Credit Sales	÷	Average Net Accounts Receivable	=	Accounts Receivable Turnover
$29,131	÷	$\dfrac{\$3{,}821 + \$3{,}177}{2}$	=	**8.3 times**

The result indicates an accounts receivable turnover ratio of 8.3 times per year. The higher the turnover ratio the more liquid the company's receivables.

A variant of the accounts receivable turnover ratio that makes the liquidity even more evident is its conversion into an **average collection period** in terms of days. This is done by dividing the turnover ratio into 365 days. For example, Cisco's turnover of 8.3 times is divided into 365 days, as shown in Illustration 9-18, to obtain approximately 44 days. This means that it takes Cisco 44 days to collect its accounts receivable.

Illustration 9-18
Average collection period for receivables formula and computation

Days in Year	÷	Accounts Receivable Turnover	=	Average Collection Period in Days
365 days	÷	8.3 times	=	**44 days**

Companies frequently use the average collection period to assess the effectiveness of a company's credit and collection policies. The general rule is that the collection period should not greatly exceed the credit term period (that is, the time allowed for payment).

Do it!

Analysis of Receivables

action plan

✔ Review the formula to compute the accounts receivable turnover.

✔ Make sure that both the beginning and ending accounts receivable balances are considered in the computation.

✔ Review the formula to compute the average collection period in days.

In 2012, Phil Mickelson Company has net credit sales of $923,795 for the year. It had a beginning accounts receivable (net) balance of $38,275 and an ending accounts receivable (net) balance of $35,988. Compute Phil Mickelson Company's (a) accounts receivable turnover and (b) average collection period in days.

Solution

(a)	Net credit sales	÷	Average net accounts receivable	=	Accounts receivable turnover	
	$923,795	÷	$\dfrac{38{,}275 + 35{,}988}{2}$	=	24.9 times	
(b)	Days in year	÷	Accounts receivable turnover	=	Average collection period in days	
	365	÷	24.9 times	=	14.7 days	

Related exercise material: BE9-12, E9-14, and **Do it!** 9-4.

✔
The Navigator

COMPREHENSIVE

Do it!

The following selected transactions relate to Dylan Company.

Mar. 1 Sold $20,000 of merchandise to Potter Company, terms 2/10, n/30.

11 Received payment in full from Potter Company for balance due.

12 Accepted Juno Company's $20,000, 6-month, 12% note for balance due.

13 Made Dylan Company credit card sales for $13,200.

15 Made Visa credit card sales totaling $6,700. A 3% service fee is charged by Visa.

Apr. 11 Sold accounts receivable of $8,000 to Harcot Factor. Harcot Factor assesses a service charge of 2% of the amount of receivables sold.

13 Received collections of $8,200 on Dylan Company credit card sales and added finance charges of 1.5% to the remaining balances.

May 10 Wrote off as uncollectible $16,000 of accounts receivable. Dylan uses the percentage-of-sales basis to estimate bad debts.

June 30 Credit sales recorded during the first 6 months total $2,000,000. The bad debt percentage is 1% of credit sales. At June 30, the balance in the allowance account is $3,500.

July 16 One of the accounts receivable written off in May was from J. Simon, who pays the amount due, $4,000, in full.

Instructions

Prepare the journal entries for the transactions.

action plan

✔ Generally, record accounts receivable at invoice price.

✔ Recognize that sales returns and allowances and cash discounts reduce the amount received on accounts receivable.

✔ Record service charge expense on the seller's books when accounts receivable are sold.

✔ Prepare an adjusting entry for bad debts expense.

✔ Ignore any balance in the allowance account under the percentage-of-sales basis. Recognize the balance in the allowance account under the percentage-of-receivables basis.

✔ Record write-offs of accounts receivable only in balance sheet accounts.

Solution to Comprehensive Do it!

Mar. 1	Accounts Receivable–Potter	20,000	
	Sales Revenue		20,000
	(To record sales on account)		
11	Cash	19,600	
	Sales Discounts (2% × $20,000)	400	
	Accounts Receivable—Potter		20,000
	(To record collection of accounts receivable)		
12	Notes Receivable	20,000	
	Accounts Receivable—Juno		20,000
	(To record acceptance of Juno Company note)		
13	Accounts Receivable	13,200	
	Sales Revenue		13,200
	(To record company credit card sales)		
15	Cash	6,499	
	Service Charge Expense (3% × $6,700)	201	
	Sales		6,700
	(To record credit card sales)		
Apr. 11	Cash	7,840	
	Service Charge Expense (2% × $8,000)	160	
	Accounts Receivable		8,000
	(To record sale of receivables to factor)		
13	Cash	8,200	
	Accounts Receivable		8,200
	(To record collection of accounts receivable)		
	Accounts Receivable [($13,200 − $8,200) × 1.5%]	75	
	Interest Revenue		75
	(To record interest on amount due)		
May 10	Allowance for Doubtful Accounts	16,000	
	Accounts Receivable		16,000
	(To record write-off of accounts receivable)		

June 30	Bad Debts Expense ($2,000,000 × 1%)	20,000	
	Allowance for Doubtful Accounts		20,000
	(To record estimate of uncollectible accounts)		
July 16	Accounts Receivable—J. Simon	4,000	
	Allowance for Doubtful Accounts		4,000
	(To reverse write-off of accounts receivable)		
	Cash	4,000	
	Accounts Receivable—J. Simon		4,000
	(To record collection of accounts receivable)		

✔ The Navigator

Summary of Study Objectives

[1] Identify the different types of receivables. Receivables are frequently classified as (1) accounts, (2) notes, and (3) other. Accounts receivable are amounts customers owe on account. Notes receivable are claims for which lenders issue formal instruments of credit as proof of the debt. Other receivables include nontrade receivables such as interest receivable, loans to company officers, advances to employees, and income taxes refundable.

[2] Explain how companies recognize accounts receivable. Companies record accounts receivable at invoice price. They are reduced by sales returns and allowances. Cash discounts reduce the amount received on accounts receivable. When interest is charged on a past due receivable, the company adds this interest to the accounts receivable balance and recognizes it as interest revenue.

[3] Distinguish between the methods and bases companies use to value accounts receivable. There are two methods of accounting for uncollectible accounts: the allowance method and the direct write-off method. Companies may use either the percentage-of-sales or the percentage-of-receivables basis to estimate uncollectible accounts using the allowance method. The percentage-of-sales basis emphasizes the expense recognition (matching) principle. The percentage-of-receivables basis emphasizes the cash realizable value of the accounts receivable. An aging schedule is often used with this basis.

[4] Describe the entries to record the disposition of accounts receivable. When a company collects an account receivable, it credits Accounts Receivable. When a company sells (factors) an account receivable, a service charge expense reduces the amount received.

[5] Compute the maturity date of and interest on notes receivable. For a note stated in months, the maturity date is found by counting the months from the date of issue. For a note stated in days, the number of days is counted, omitting the issue date and counting the due date. The formula for computing interest is: Face value × Interest rate × Time.

[6] Explain how companies recognize notes receivable. Companies record notes receivable at face value. In some cases, it is necessary to accrue interest prior to maturity. In this case, companies debit Interest Receivable and credit Interest Revenue.

[7] Describe how companies value notes receivable. As with accounts receivable, companies report notes receivable at their cash (net) realizable value. The notes receivable allowance account is Allowance for Doubtful Accounts. The computation and estimations involved in valuing notes receivable at cash realizable value, and in recording the proper amount of bad debts expense and related allowance are similar to those for accounts receivable.

[8] Describe the entries to record the disposition of notes receivable. Notes can be held to maturity. At that time the face value plus accrued interest is due, and the note is removed from the accounts. In many cases, the holder of the note speeds up the conversion by selling the receivable to another party (a factor). In some situations, the maker of the note dishonors the note (defaults), in which case the company transfers the note and accrued interest to an account receivable or writes off the note.

[9] Explain the statement presentation and analysis of receivables. Companies should identify in the balance sheet or in the notes to the financial statements each major type of receivable. Short-term receivables are considered current assets. Companies report the gross amount of receivables and the allowance for doubtful accounts. They report bad debts and service charge expenses in the multiple-step income statement as operating (selling) expenses; interest revenue appears under other revenues and gains in the nonoperating activities section of the statement. Managers and investors evaluate accounts receivable for liquidity by computing a turnover ratio and an average collection period.

✔ The Navigator

Glossary

Accounts receivable Amounts owed by customers on account. (p. 416).

Accounts receivable turnover ratio A measure of the liquidity of accounts receivable; computed by dividing net credit sales by average net accounts receivable. (p. 433).

Aging the accounts receivable The analysis of customer balances by the length of time they have been unpaid. (p. 423).

Allowance method A method of accounting for bad debts that involves estimating uncollectible accounts at the end of each period. (p. 420).

Average collection period The average amount of time that a receivable is outstanding; calculated by dividing 365 days by the accounts receivables turnover ratio. (p. 434).

Bad Debts Expense An expense account to record uncollectible receivables. (p. 419).

Cash (net) realizable value The net amount a company expects to receive in cash. (p. 420).

Direct write-off method A method of accounting for bad debts that involves expensing accounts at the time they are determined to be uncollectible. (p. 419).

Dishonored note A note that is not paid in full at maturity. (p. 432).

Factor A finance company or bank that buys receivables from businesses and then collects the payments directly from the customers. (p. 425).

Maker The party in a promissory note who is making the promise to pay. (p. 428).

Notes receivable Claims for which formal instruments of credit are issued as proof of the debt. (p. 417).

Other receivables Various forms of nontrade receivables, such as interest receivable and income taxes refundable. (p. 417).

Payee The party to whom payment of a promissory note is to be made. (p. 428).

Percentage-of-receivables basis Management estimates what percentage of receivables will result in losses from uncollectible accounts. (p. 423).

Percentage-of-sales basis Management estimates what percentage of credit sales will be uncollectible. (p. 423).

Promissory note A written promise to pay a specified amount of money on demand or at a definite time. (p. 427).

Receivables Amounts due from individuals and other companies. (p. 416).

Trade receivables Notes and accounts receivable that result from sales transactions. (p. 417).

 Self-Test, Brief Exercises, Exercises, Problem Set A, and many more components are available for practice in *WileyPLUS*

Self-Test Questions

Answers are on page 453.

(SO 1) **1.** Receivables are frequently classified as:
  a. accounts receivable, company receivables, and other receivables.
  b. accounts receivable, notes receivable, and employee receivables.
  c. accounts receivable and general receivables.
  d. accounts receivable, notes receivable, and other receivables.

(SO 2) **2.** Buehler Company on June 15 sells merchandise on account to Chaz Co. for $1,000, terms 2/10, n/30. On June 20, Chaz Co. returns merchandise worth $300 to Buehler Company. On June 24, payment is received from Chaz Co. for the balance due. What is the amount of cash received?
  a. $700.   **c.** $686.
  b. $680.   **d.** None of the above.

(SO 3) **3.** Which of the following approaches for bad debts is best described as a balance sheet method?
  a. Percentage-of-receivables basis.
  b. Direct write-off method.
  c. Percentage-of-sales basis.
  d. Both a and b.

(SO 3) **4.** Hughes Company has a credit balance of $5,000 in its Allowance for Doubtful Accounts before any adjustments are made at the end of the year. Based on review and aging of its accounts receivable at the end of the year, Hughes estimates that $60,000 of its receivables are uncollectible. The amount of bad debts expense which should be reported for the year is:
  a. $5,000.   **c.** $60,000.
  b. $55,000.   **d.** $65,000.

5. Use the same information as in question 4, except that (SO 3) Hughes has a debit balance of $5,000 in its Allowance for Doubtful Accounts before any adjustments are made at the end of the year. In this situation, the amount of bad debts expense that should be reported for the year is:
  a. $5,000.   **c.** $60,000.
  b. $55,000.   **d.** $65,000.

6. Net sales for the month are $800,000, and bad debts are (SO 3) expected to be 1.5% of net sales. The company uses the percentage-of-sales basis. If Allowance for Doubtful Accounts has a credit balance of $15,000 before adjustment, what is the balance after adjustment?
  a. $15,000.   **c.** $23,000.
  b. $27,000.   **d.** $31,000.

7. In 2012, Roso Carlson Company had net credit sales of (SO 3) $750,000. On January 1, 2012, Allowance for Doubtful Accounts had a credit balance of $18,000. During 2012, $30,000 of uncollectible accounts receivable were written off. Past experience indicates that 3% of net credit sales become uncollectible. What should be the adjusted balance of Allowance for Doubtful Accounts at December 31, 2012?

a. $10,050.   c. $22,500.
b.. $10,500.   d. $40,500.

(SO 3) **8.** An analysis and aging of the accounts receivable of Prince Company at December 31 reveals the following data.

Accounts receivable	$800,000
Allowance for doubtful accounts per books before adjustment	50,000
Amounts expected to become uncollectible	65,000

The cash realizable value of the accounts receivable at December 31, after adjustment, is:

a. $685,000.   c. $800,000.
b. $750,000.   d. $735,000.

(SO 6) **9.** One of the following statements about promissory notes is incorrect. The *incorrect* statement is:

a. The party making the promise to pay is called the maker.
b. The party to whom payment is to be made is called the payee.
c. A promissory note is not a negotiable instrument.
d. A promissory note is often required from high-risk customers.

(SO 4) **10.** Which of the following statements about Visa credit card sales is *incorrect*?

a. The credit card issuer makes the credit investigation of the customer.
b. The retailer is not involved in the collection process.
c. Two parties are involved.
d. The retailer receives cash more quickly than it would from individual customers on account.

(SO 4) **11.** Blinka Retailers accepted $50,000 of Citibank Visa credit card charges for merchandise sold on July 1. Citibank charges 4% for its credit card use. The entry to record this transaction by Blinka Retailers will include a credit to Sales Revenue of $50,000 and a debit(s) to:

a. Cash	$48,000
and Service Charge Expense	$2,000
b. Accounts Receivable	$48,000
and Service Charge Expense	$2,000

c. Cash	$50,000
d. Accounts Receivable	$50,000

(SO 6) **12.** Foti Co. accepts a $1,000, 3-month, 6% promissory note in settlement of an account with Bartelt Co. The entry to record this transaction is as follows.

a. Notes Receivable	1,015	
Accounts Receivable		1,015
b. Notes Receivable	1,000	
Accounts Receivable		1,000
c. Notes Receivable	1,000	
Sales Revenue		1,000
d. Notes Receivable	1,030	
Accounts Receivable		1,030

(SO 8) **13.** Ginter Co. holds Kolar Inc.'s $10,000, 120-day, 9% note. The entry made by Ginter Co. when the note is collected, assuming no interest has been previously accrued, is:

a. Cash	10,300	
Notes Receivable		10,300
b. Cash	10,000	
Notes Receivable		10,000
c. Accounts Receivable	10,300	
Notes Receivable		10,000
Interest Revenue		300
d. Cash	10,300	
Notes Receivable		10,000
Interest Revenue		300

(SO 9) **14.** Accounts and notes receivable are reported in the current assets section of the balance sheet at:

a. cash (net) realizable value
b. net book value.
c. lower-of-cost-or-market value.
d. invoice cost.

(SO 9) **15.** Oliveras Company had net credit sales during the year of $800,000 and cost of goods sold of $500,000. The balance in accounts receivable at the beginning of the year was $100,000, and the end of the year it was $150,000. What were the accounts receivable turnover ratio and the average collection period in days?

a. 4.0 and 91.3 days.   c. 6.4 and 57 days.
b. 5.3 and 68.9 days.   d. 8.0 and 45.6 days.

Go to the book's companion website, **www.wiley.com/college/weygandt**, for additional Self-Test Questions.

Questions

1. What is the difference between an account receivable and a note receivable?

2. What are some common types of receivables other than accounts receivable and notes receivable?

3. Texaco Oil Company issues its own credit cards. Assume that Texaco charges you $40 interest on an unpaid balance. Prepare the journal entry that Texaco makes to record this revenue.

4. What are the essential features of the allowance method of accounting for bad debts?

5. Jerry Gatewood cannot understand why cash realizable value does not decrease when an uncollectible account is

written off under the allowance method. Clarify this point for Jerry Gatewood.

6. Distinguish between the two bases that may be used in estimating uncollectible accounts.

7. Eaton Company has a credit balance of $3,500 in Allowance for Doubtful Accounts. The estimated bad debts expense under the percentage-of-sales basis is $4,100. The total estimated uncollectibles under the percentage-of-receivables basis is $5,800. Prepare the adjusting entry under each basis.

8. How are bad debts accounted for under the direct write-off method? What are the disadvantages of this method?

9. DeVito Company accepts both its own credit cards and national credit cards. What are the advantages of accepting both types of cards?

10. An article recently appeared in the *Wall Street Journal* indicating that companies are selling their receivables at a record rate. Why are companies selling their receivables?

11. Pinkston Textiles decides to sell $600,000 of its accounts receivable to First Factors Inc. First Factors assesses a service charge of 3% of the amount of receivables sold. Prepare the journal entry that Pinkston Textiles makes to record this sale.

12. Your roommate is uncertain about the advantages of a promissory note. Compare the advantages of a note receivable with those of an account receivable.

13. How may the maturity date of a promissory note be stated?

14. Indicate the maturity date of each of the following promissory notes:

Date of Note	Terms
(a) March 13	one year after date of note
(b) May 4	3 months after date
(c) June 20	30 days after date
(d) July 1	60 days after date

15. Compute the missing amounts for each of the following notes.

	Principal	Annual Interest Rate	Time	Total Interest
(a)	?	9%	120 days	$ 600
(b)	$30,000	10%	3 years	?
(c)	$60,000	?	5 months	$2,000
(d)	$45,000	8%	?	$1,200

16. In determining interest revenue, some financial institutions use 365 days per year and others use 360 days. Why might a financial institution use 360 days?

17. Cain Company dishonors a note at maturity. What are the options available to the lender?

18. General Motors Corporation has accounts receivable and notes receivable. How should the receivables be reported on the balance sheet?

19. The accounts receivable turnover ratio is 8.14, and average net receivables during the period are $400,000. What is the amount of net credit sales for the period?

20. **PEPSICO** What percentage does PepsiCo's allowance for doubtful accounts represent as a percent of its gross receivables?

Brief Exercises

BE9-1 Presented below are three receivables transactions. Indicate whether these receivables are reported as accounts receivable, notes receivable, or other receivables on a balance sheet.

(a) Sold merchandise on account for $64,000 to a customer.
(b) Received a promissory note of $57,000 for services performed.
(c) Advanced $10,000 to an employee.

Identify different types of receivables.
(SO 1)

BE9-2 Record the following transactions on the books of Nao Co.

(a) On July 1, Nao Co. sold merchandise on account to Bustamante Inc. for $15,200, terms 2/10, n/30.
(b) On July 8, Bustamante Inc. returned merchandise worth $3,800 to Nao Co.
(c) On July 11, Bustamante Inc. paid for the merchandise.

Record basic accounts receivable transactions.
(SO 2)

BE9-3 During its first year of operations, Parot Company had credit sales of $3,000,000; $600,000 remained uncollected at year-end. The credit manager estimates that $35,000 of these receivables will become uncollectible.

(a) Prepare the journal entry to record the estimated uncollectibles.
(b) Prepare the current assets section of the balance sheet for Parot Company. Assume that in addition to the receivables it has cash of $90,000, inventory of $130,000, and prepaid insurance of $7,500.

Prepare entry for allowance method and partial balance sheet.
(SO 3, 9)

BE9-4 At the end of 2012, Henderson Co. has accounts receivable of $700,000 and an allowance for doubtful accounts of $54,000. On January 24, 2013, the company learns that its receivable from Jaime Lynn is not collectible, and management authorizes a write-off of $5,400.

(a) Prepare the journal entry to record the write-off.
(b) What is the cash realizable value of the accounts receivable (1) before the write-off and (2) after the write-off?

Prepare entry for write-off; determine cash realizable value.
(SO 3)

BE9-5 Assume the same information as BE9-4. On March 4, 2013, Henderson Co. receives payment of $5,400 in full from Jaime Lynn. Prepare the journal entries to record this transaction.

Prepare entries for collection of bad debts write-off.
(SO 3)

BE9-6 Erik Co. elects to use the percentage-of-sales basis in 2012 to record bad debts expense. It estimates that 2% of net credit sales will become uncollectible. Sales revenues are $800,000 for 2012, sales returns and allowances are $45,000, and the allowance for doubtful accounts has a credit balance of $9,000. Prepare the adjusting entry to record bad debts expense in 2012.

Prepare entry using percentage-of-sales method.
(SO 3)

Prepare entry using percentage-of-receivables method.

(SO 3)

BE9-7 Johnson Co. uses the percentage-of-receivables basis to record bad debts expense. It estimates that 1% of accounts receivable will become uncollectible. Accounts receivable are $450,000 at the end of the year, and the allowance for doubtful accounts has a credit balance of $1,500.

(a) Prepare the adjusting journal entry to record bad debts expense for the year.

(b) If the allowance for doubtful accounts had a debit balance of $800 instead of a credit balance of $1,500, determine the amount to be reported for bad debts expense.

Prepare entries to dispose of accounts receivable.

(SO 4)

BE9-8 Presented below are two independent transactions.

(a) Ryan's Restaurant accepted a Visa card in payment of a $150 lunch bill. The bank charges a 4% fee. What entry should Ryan's make?

(b) Shultz Company sold its accounts receivable of $60,000. What entry should Shultz make, given a service charge of 3% on the amount of receivables sold?

Compute interest and determine maturity dates on notes.

(SO 5)

BE9-9 Compute interest and find the maturity date for the following notes.

	Date of Note	Principal	Interest Rate (%)	Terms
(a)	June 10	$80,000	6%	60 days
(b)	July 14	$50,000	7%	90 days
(c)	April 27	$12,000	8%	75 days

Determine maturity dates and compute interest and rates on notes.

(SO 5)

BE9-10 Presented below are data on three promissory notes. Determine the missing amounts.

Date of Note	Terms	Maturity Date	Principal	Annual Interest Rate	Total Interest
(a) April 1	60 days	?	$600,000	9%	?
(b) July 2	30 days	?	90,000	?	$600
(c) March 7	6 months	?	120,000	10%	?

Prepare entry for notes receivable exchanged for account receivable.

(SO 6)

BE9-11 On January 10, 2012, Honig Co. sold merchandise on account to Peregrine Co. for $13,600, n/30. On February 9, Peregrine Co. gave Honig Co. a 10% promissory note in settlement of this account. Prepare the journal entry to record the sale and the settlement of the account receivable.

Compute ratios to analyze receivables.

(SO 9)

BE9-12 The financial statements of Minnesota Mining and Manufacturing Company (3M) report net sales of $20.0 billion. Accounts receivable (net) are $2.7 billion at the beginning of the year and $2.8 billion at the end of the year. Compute 3M's receivables turnover ratio. Compute 3M's average collection period for accounts receivable in days.

Do it! Review

Prepare entry for uncollectible accounts.

(SO 3)

Do it! 9-1 Valasquez Company has been in business several years. At the end of the current year, the ledger shows:

Accounts Receivable	$ 310,000 Dr.
Sales Revenue	2,200,000 Cr.
Allowance for Doubtful Accounts	6,100 Cr.

Bad debts are estimated to be 7% of receivables. Prepare the entry to adjust Allowance for Doubtful Accounts.

Prepare entry for factored accounts.

(SO 4)

Do it! 9-2 Mark Distributors is a growing company whose ability to raise capital has not been growing as quickly as its expanding assets and sales. Mark's local banker has indicated that the company cannot increase its borrowing for the foreseeable future. Mark's suppliers are demanding payment for goods acquired within 30 days of the invoice date, but Mark's customers are slow in paying for their purchases (60–90 days). As a result, Mark has a cash flow problem.

Mark needs $160,000 to cover next Friday's payroll. Its balance of outstanding accounts receivable totals $1,000,000. What might Mark do to alleviate this cash crunch? Record the entry that Mark would make when it raises the needed cash. (Assume a 2% service charge.)

Prepare entries for notes receivable.

(SO 5, 8)

Do it! 9-3 Nadeau Wholesalers accepts from Nicole Stores a $6,200, 4-month, 12% note dated May 31 in settlement of Nicole's overdue account. (a) What is the maturity date of the note?

(b) What is the entry made by Nadeau at the maturity date, assuming Nicole pays the note and interest in full at that time?

Do it! 9-4 In 2012, Abdi Farah Company has net credit sales of $1,600,000 for the year. It had a beginning accounts receivable (net) balance of $101,000 and an ending accounts receivable (net) balance of $107,000. Compute Abdi Farah Company's (a) accounts receivable turnover and (b) average collection period in days.

Compute ratios for receivables.
(SO 9)

Exercises

E9-1 Presented below are selected transactions of Santos Company. Santos sells in large quantities to other companies and also sells its product in a small retail outlet.

Journalize entries related to accounts receivable.
(SO 2)

March   1   Sold merchandise on account to Jaclyn Company for $3,000, terms 2/10, n/30.
        3   Jaclyn Company returned merchandise worth $500 to Santos.
        9   Santos collected the amount due from Jaclyn Company from the March 1 sale.
      15   Santos sold merchandise for $400 in its retail outlet. The customer used his Santos credit card.
      31   Santos added 1.5% monthly interest to the customer's credit card balance.

Instructions
Prepare journal entries for the transactions above.

E9-2 Presented below are two independent situations.

Journalize entries for recognizing accounts receivable.
(SO 2)

(a) On January 6, Mendenhall Co. sells merchandise on account to Miles Inc. for $9,000, terms 2/10, n/30. On January 16, Miles Inc. pays the amount due. Prepare the entries on Mendenhall's books to record the sale and related collection.

(b) On January 10, Markus Klinko uses his Indrani Co. credit card to purchase merchandise from Indrani Co. for $9,000. On February 10, Klinko is billed for the amount due of $9,000. On February 12, Klinko pays $5,000 on the balance due. On March 10, Klinko is billed for the amount due, including interest at 2% per month on the unpaid balance as of February 12. Prepare the entries on Indrani Co.'s books related to the transactions that occurred on January 10, February 12, and March 10.

E9-3 The ledger of G.K. Reid Company at the end of the current year shows Accounts Receivable $120,000, Sales Revenue $840,000, and Sales Returns and Allowances $30,000.

Journalize entries to record allowance for doubtful accounts using two different bases.
(SO 3)

Instructions
(a) If G.K. Reid uses the direct write-off method to account for uncollectible accounts, journalize the adjusting entry at December 31, assuming G.K. Reid determines that L. Gaga's $1,400 balance is uncollectible.

(b) If Allowance for Doubtful Accounts has a credit balance of $2,100 in the trial balance, journalize the adjusting entry at December 31, assuming bad debts are expected to be (1) 1% of net sales, and (2) 10% of accounts receivable.

(c) If Allowance for Doubtful Accounts has a debit balance of $200 in the trial balance, journalize the adjusting entry at December 31, assuming bad debts are expected to be (1) 0.75% of net sales and (2) 6% of accounts receivable.

E9-4 Lohan Company has accounts receivable of $93,100 at March 31. An analysis of the accounts shows the following information.

Determine bad debts expense; prepare the adjusting entry for bad debts expense.
(SO 3)

Month of Sale	Balance, March 31
March	$60,000
February	17,600
January	8,500
Prior to January	7,000
	$93,100

Credit terms are 2/10, n/30. At March 31, Allowance for Doubtful Accounts has a credit balance of $1,200 prior to adjustment. The company uses the percentage-of-receivables basis for estimating uncollectible accounts. The company's estimate of bad debts is shown on the next page.

Age of Accounts	Estimated Percentage Uncollectible
1–30 days	2.0%
31–60 days	5.0%
61–90 days	30.0%
Over 90 days	50.0%

Instructions

(a) Determine the total estimated uncollectibles.

(b) Prepare the adjusting entry at March 31 to record bad debts expense.

Journalize write-off and recovery.

(SO 3)

E9-5 At December 31, 2011, Kardashian Company had a balance of $15,000 in Allowance for Doubtful Accounts. During 2012, Kardashian wrote off accounts totaling $13,000. One of those accounts ($1,800) was later collected. At December 31, 2012, an aging schedule indicated that the balance in Allowance for Doubtful Accounts should be $19,000.

Instructions

Prepare journal entries to record the 2012 transactions of Kardashian Company.

Journalize percentage of sales basis, write-off, recovery.

(SO 3)

E9-6 On December 31, 2012, Dita Co. estimated that 2% of its net sales of $400,000 will become uncollectible. The company recorded this amount as an addition to Allowance for Doubtful Accounts. On May 11, 2013, Dita Co. determined that the Alex Lundquist account was uncollectible and wrote off $1,100. On June 12, 2013, Lundquist paid the amount previously written off.

Instructions

Prepare the journal entries on December 31, 2012, May 11, 2013, and June 12, 2013.

Journalize entries for the sale of accounts receivable.

(SO 4)

E9-7 Presented below are two independent situations.

(a) On March 3, Van Teese Appliances sells $680,000 of its receivables to Naomi Factors Inc. Naomi Factors assesses a finance charge of 3% of the amount of receivables sold. Prepare the entry on Van Teese Appliances' books to record the sale of the receivables.

(b) On May 10, Campbell Company sold merchandise for $3,500 and accepted the customer's America Bank MasterCard. America Bank charges a 4% service charge for credit card sales. Prepare the entry on Campbell Company's books to record the sale of merchandise.

Journalize entries for credit card sales.

(SO 4)

E9-8 Presented below are two independent situations.

(a) On April 2, Brooklyn Decker uses her J. C. Penney Company credit card to purchase merchandise from a J. C. Penney store for $1,500. On May 1, Decker is billed for the $1,500 amount due. Decker pays $700 on the balance due on May 3. On June 1, Decker receives a bill for the amount due, including interest at 1.0% per month on the unpaid balance as of May 3. Prepare the entries on J. C. Penney Co.'s books related to the transactions that occurred on April 2, May 3, and June 1.

(b) On July 4, Vanderloo's Restaurant accepts a Visa card for a $200 dinner bill. Visa charges a 3% service fee. Prepare the entry on Vanderloo's books related to this transaction.

Journalize credit card sales, and indicate the statement presentation of financing charges and service charge expense.

(SO 4)

E9-9 Bowie Stores accepts both its own and national credit cards. During the year, the following selected summary transactions occurred.

Jan. 15	Made Bowie credit card sales totaling $18,000. (There were no balances prior to January 15.)
20	Made Visa credit card sales (service charge fee 2%) totaling $4,300.
Feb. 10	Collected $10,000 on Bowie credit card sales.
15	Added finance charges of 1% to Bowie credit card balance.

Instructions

(a) Journalize the transactions for Bowie Stores.

(b) Indicate the statement presentation of the financing charges and the credit card service charge expense for Bowie Stores.

Journalize entries for notes receivable transactions.

(SO 5, 6)

E9-10 Stroup Supply Co. has the following transactions related to notes receivable during the last 2 months of 2012.

Nov. 1	Loaned $15,000 cash to Jorge Perez on a 1-year, 10% note.
Dec. 11	Sold goods to Armle Hammer, Inc., receiving a $6,750, 90-day, 8% note.
16	Received a $4,000, 6-month, 9% note in exchange for Max Weinberg's outstanding accounts receivable.
31	Accrued interest revenue on all notes receivable.

Instructions

(a) Journalize the transactions for Stroup Supply Co.
(b) Record the collection of the Perez note at its maturity in 2013.

E9-11 Record the following transactions for Conando Co. in the general journal.

Journalize entries for notes receivable.
(SO 5, 6)

2012

May 1 Received a $7,500, 1-year, 10% note in exchange for Andy Richter's outstanding accounts receivable.
Dec.31 Accrued interest on the Richter note.
Dec.31 Closed the interest revenue account.

2013

May 1 Received principal plus interest on the Richter note. (No interest has been accrued in 2013.)

E9-12 La Bamba Company had the following select transactions.

Prepare entries for note receivable transactions.
(SO 5, 6, 8)

Apr. 1, 2012 Accepted Shatner Company's 1-year, 12% note in settlement of a $20,000 account receivable.
July 1, 2012 Loaned $25,000 cash to Richie Rosenberg on a 9-month, 10% note.
Dec. 31, 2012 Accrued interest on all notes receivable.
Apr. 1, 2013 Received principal plus interest on the Shatner note.
Apr. 1, 2013 Richie Rosenberg dishonored its note; La Bamba expects it will eventually collect.

Instructions

Prepare journal entries to record the transactions. La Bamba prepares adjusting entries once a year on December 31.

E9-13 On May 2, George Company lends $7,600 to Takei, Inc., issuing a 6-month, 9% note. At the maturity date, November 2, Takei indicates that it cannot pay.

Journalize entries for dishonor of notes receivable.
(SO 5, 8)

Instructions

(a) Prepare the entry to record the issuance of the note.
(b) Prepare the entry to record the dishonor of the note, assuming that George Company expects collection will occur.
(c) Prepare the entry to record the dishonor of the note, assuming that George Company does not expect collection in the future.

E9-14 Nachito Company had accounts receivable of $100,000 on January 1, 2012. The only transactions that affected accounts receivable during 2012 were net credit sales of $1,000,000, cash collections of $900,000, and accounts written off of $30,000.

Compute receivables turnover and average collection period.
(SO 9)

Instructions

(a) Compute the ending balance of accounts receivable.
(b) Compute the accounts receivable turnover ratio for 2012.
(c) Compute the average collection period in days.

Exercises: Set B

Visit the book's companion website, at **www.wiley.com/college/weygandt**, and choose the Student Companion site to access Exercise Set B.

Problems: Set A

P9-1A At December 31, 2011, Mernt Co. reported the following information on its balance sheet.

Prepare journal entries related to bad debts expense.
(SO 2, 3, 9)

| Accounts receivable | $960,000 |
| Less: Allowance for doubtful accounts | 80,000 |

During 2012, the company had the following transactions related to receivables.

1.	Sales on account	$3,200,000
2.	Sales returns and allowances	50,000
3.	Collections of accounts receivable	2,810,000
4.	Write-offs of accounts receivable deemed uncollectible	90,000
5.	Recovery of bad debts previously written off as uncollectible	24,000

Instructions

(a) Prepare the journal entries to record each of these five transactions. Assume that no cash discounts were taken on the collections of accounts receivable.

(b) Accounts receivable $1,210,000 ADA $14,000

(b) Enter the January 1, 2012, balances in Accounts Receivable and Allowance for Doubtful Accounts, post the entries to the two accounts (use T accounts), and determine the balances.

(c) Bad debts expense $101,000

(c) Prepare the journal entry to record bad debts expense for 2012, assuming that an aging of accounts receivable indicates that expected bad debts are $115,000.

(d) Compute the accounts receivable turnover ratio for 2012.

Compute bad debts amounts.
(SO 3)

P9-2A Information related to Jordan Schlansky Company for 2012 is summarized below.

Total credit sales	$2,200,000
Accounts receivable at December 31	825,000
Bad debts written off	33,000

Instructions

(a) What amount of bad debts expense will Jordan Schlansky Company report if it uses the direct write-off method of accounting for bad debts?

(b) Assume that Jordan Schlansky Company estimates its bad debts expense to be 2% of credit sales. What amount of bad debts expense will Jordan Schlansky record if it has an Allowance for Doubtful Accounts credit balance of $4,000?

(c) Assume that Jordan Schlansky Company estimates its bad debts expense based on 6% of accounts receivable. What amount of bad debts expense will Jordan Schlansky record if it has an Allowance for Doubtful Accounts credit balance of $3,000?

(d) Assume the same facts as in (c), except that there is a $3,000 debit balance in Allowance for Doubtful Accounts. What amount of bad debts expense will Jordan Schlansky record?

(e) What is the weakness of the direct write-off method of reporting bad debts expense?

Journalize entries to record transactions related to bad debts.
(SO 2, 3)

P9-3A Presented below is an aging schedule for McCann Company.

⊠ Worksheet.xls							▢▣☒
⊠ **File** **Edit** **View** **Insert** **Format** **Tools** **Data** **Window** **Help**							
	A	**B**	**C**	**D**	**E**	**F**	**G**
1				**Number of Days Past Due**			
2			**Not**				
3	**Customer**	**Total**	**Yet Due**	**1–30**	**31–60**	**61–90**	**Over 90**
4	Amos	$ 22,000		$10,000	$12,000		
5	Brian	40,000	$ 40,000				
6	Chevy	57,000	16,000	6,000		$35,000	
7	Drake	34,000					$34,000
8	Others	132,000	96,000	16,000	14,000		6,000
9		$285,000	$152,000	$32,000	$26,000	$35,000	$40,000
10	Estimated Percentage Uncollectible		3%	6%	13%	25%	60%
11	Total Estimated Bad Debts	$ 42,610	$ 4,560	$ 1,920	$ 3,380	$ 8,750	$24,000
12							

At December 31, 2012, the unadjusted balance in Allowance for Doubtful Accounts is a credit of $12,000.

Instructions

(a) Bad debts expense $30,610

(a) Journalize and post the adjusting entry for bad debts at December 31, 2012.

(b) Journalize and post to the allowance account the following events and transactions in the year 2013.

(1) On March 31, a $1,000 customer balance originating in 2012 is judged uncollectible.

(2) On May 31, a check for $1,000 is received from the customer whose account was written off as uncollectible on March 31.

(c) Journalize the adjusting entry for bad debts on December 31, 2013, assuming that the unadjusted balance in Allowance for Doubtful Accounts is a debit of $800 and the aging schedule indicates that total estimated bad debts will be $28,600.

(c) Bad debts expense $29,400

P9-4A   Pender Inc. uses the allowance method to estimate uncollectible accounts receivable. The company produced the following aging of the accounts receivable at year-end.

Journalize transactions related to bad debts.

(SO 2, 3)

Worksheet.xls							
File Edit View Insert Format Tools Data Window Help							
	A	B	C	D	E	F	G
1			Number of Days Outstanding				
2							
3		Total	0–30	31–60	61–90	91–120	Over 120
4	Accounts receivable	200,000	77,000	46,000	39,000	23,000	$15,000
5	% uncollectible		1%	4%	5%	8%	10%
6	Estimated bad debts						
7							

Instructions

(a) Calculate the total estimated bad debts based on the above information.

(b) Prepare the year-end adjusting journal entry to record the bad debts using the aged uncollectible accounts receivable determined in (a). Assume the current balance in Allowance for Doubtful Accounts is a $8,000 debit.

(c) Of the above accounts, $5,000 is determined to be specifically uncollectible. Prepare the journal entry to write off the uncollectible account.

(d) The company collects $5,000 subsequently on a specific account that had previously been determined to be uncollectible in (c). Prepare the journal entry(ies) necessary to restore the account and record the cash collection.

(e) Comment on how your answers to (a)–(d) would change if Pender Inc. used 3% of *total* accounts receivable, rather than aging the accounts receivable. What are the advantages to the company of aging the accounts receivable rather than applying a percentage to total accounts receivable?

(a) Tot. est. bad debts $11,510

P9-5A   At December 31, 2012, the trial balance of Stack Company contained the following amounts before adjustment.

Journalize entries to record transactions related to bad debts.

(SO 3)

	Debits	Credits
Accounts Receivable	$385,000	
Allowance for Doubtful Accounts		$ 2,000
Sales Revenue		950,000

Instructions

(a) Based on the information given, which method of accounting for bad debts is Stack Company using—the direct write-off method or the allowance method? How can you tell?

(b) Prepare the adjusting entry at December 31, 2012, for bad debts expense under each of the following independent assumptions.

(b) (2) $9,500

(1) An aging schedule indicates that $11,750 of accounts receivable will be uncollectible.

(2) The company estimates that 1% of sales will be uncollectible.

(c) Repeat part (b) assuming that instead of a credit balance there is an $2,000 debit balance in Allowance for Doubtful Accounts.

(d) During the next month, January 2013, a $3,000 account receivable is written off as uncollectible. Prepare the journal entry to record the write-off.

(e) Repeat part (d) assuming that Stack uses the direct write-off method instead of the allowance method in accounting for uncollectible accounts receivable.

(f) ◄━━━━━━━ What type of account is Allowance for Doubtful Accounts? How does it affect how accounts receivable is reported on the balance sheet at the end of the accounting period?

Prepare entries for various notes receivable transactions.

(SO 2, 4, 5, 8, 9)

P9-6A   Manatee Company closes its books monthly. On September 30, selected ledger account balances are:

Notes Receivable	$33,000
Interest Receivable	170

Notes Receivable include the following.

Date	Maker	Face	Term	Interest
Aug. 16	M. Bear Inc.	$ 8,000	60 days	8%
Aug. 25	Pope Co.	9,000	60 days	10%
Sept. 30	Quackers Corp.	16,000	6 months	9%

Interest is computed using a 360-day year. During October, the following transactions were completed.

Oct.   7   Made sales of $6,900 on Manatee credit cards.
    12   Made sales of $900 on MasterCard credit cards. The credit card service charge is 3%.
    15   Added $460 to Manatee customer balance for finance charges on unpaid balances.
    15   Received payment in full from M. Bear Inc. on the amount due.
    24   Received notice that the Pope note has been dishonored. (Assume that Pope is expected to pay in the future.)

Instructions
(a) Journalize the October transactions and the October 31 adjusting entry for accrued interest receivable.

(b) Accounts receivable $16,510

(b) Enter the balances at October 1 in the receivable accounts. Post the entries to all of the receivable accounts.

(c) Total receivables $32,630

(c) Show the balance sheet presentation of the receivable accounts at October 31.

Prepare entries for various receivable transactions.

(SO 2, 4, 5, 6, 7, 8)

P9-7A   On January 1, 2012, Pierre Company had Accounts Receivable $139,000, Notes Receivable $25,000, and Allowance for Doubtful Accounts $13,200. The note receivable is from Stacy Richter Company. It is a 4-month, 12% note dated December 31, 2011. Pierre Company prepares financial statements annually. During the year, the following selected transactions occurred.

Jan.   5   Sold $20,000 of merchandise to Bernard Company, terms n/15.
    20   Accepted Bernard Company's $20,000, 3-month, 9% note for balance due.
Feb. 18   Sold $8,000 of merchandise to LaBamba Company and accepted LaBamba's $8,000, 6-month, 9% note for the amount due.
Apr. 20   Collected Bernard Company note in full.
    30   Received payment in full from Stacy Richter Company on the amount due.
May 25   Accepted Cloppy Inc.'s $4,000, 3-month, 7% note in settlement of a past-due balance on account.
Aug. 18   Received payment in full from LaBamba Company on note due.
    25   The Cloppy Inc. note was dishonored. Cloppy Inc. is not bankrupt; future payment is anticipated.
Sept. 1   Sold $12,000 of merchandise to Bessie Lou Company and accepted a $12,000, 6-month, 10% note for the amount due.

Instructions
Journalize the transactions.

Problems: Set B

Prepare journal entries related to bad debts expense.

(SO 2, 3, 9)

P9-1B   At December 31, 2011, Artie Kendall Imports reported the following information on its balance sheet.

Accounts receivable	$250,000
Less: Allowance for doubtful accounts	15,000

During 2012, the company had the following transactions related to receivables.

1. Sales on account	$2,400,000
2. Sales returns and allowances	45,000

3. Collections of accounts receivable   2,250,000
4. Write-offs of accounts receivable deemed uncollectible   12,000
5. Recovery of bad debts previously written off as uncollectible   3,000

Instructions
(a) Prepare the journal entries to record each of these five transactions. Assume that no cash discounts were taken on the collections of accounts receivable.
(b) Enter the January 1, 2012, balances in Accounts Receivable and Allowance for Doubtful Accounts. Post the entries to the two accounts (use T accounts), and determine the balances.
(c) Prepare the journal entry to record bad debts expense for 2012, assuming that an aging of accounts receivable indicates that estimated bad debts are $22,000.
(d) Compute the accounts receivable turnover ratio for the year 2012.

(b) Accounts receivable
$343,000
ADA $6,000
(c) Bad debts expense
$16,000

P9-2B Information related to Gustavo Company for 2012 is summarized below.

Compute bad debts amounts.
(SO 3)

Total credit sales	$1,100,000
Accounts receivable at December 31	369,000
Bad debts written off	22,150

Instructions
(a) What amount of bad debts expense will Gustavo Company report if it uses the direct write-off method of accounting for bad debts?
(b) Assume that Gustavo Company decides to estimate its bad debts expense to be 2% of credit sales. What amount of bad debts expense will Gustavo record if Allowance for Doubtful Accounts has a credit balance of $3,000?
(c) Assume that Gustavo Company decides to estimate its bad debts expense based on 6% of accounts receivable. What amount of bad debts expense will Gustavo Company record if Allowance for Doubtful Accounts has a credit balance of $4,000?
(d) Assume the same facts as in (c), except that there is a $2,000 debit balance in Allowance for Doubtful Accounts. What amount of bad debts expense will Gustavo record?
(e) What is the weakness of the direct write-off method of reporting bad debts expense?

P9-3B Presented below is an aging schedule for Stol Company.

Journalize entries to record transactions related to bad debts.
(SO 2, 3)

Worksheet.xls

File   Edit   View   Insert   Format   Tools   Data   Window   Help

	A	B	C	D	E	F	G
1				**Number of Days Past Due**			
2			**Not**				
3	**Customer**	**Total**	**Yet Due**	**1–30**	**31–60**	**61–90**	**Over 90**
4	Ang	$ 30,000		$ 13,500	$16,500		
5	Bistro	45,000	$ 45,000				
6	Conesie	75,000	22,500	7,500		$45,000	
7	Dagova	57,000					$57,000
8	Others	189,000	138,000	22,500	19,500		9,000
9		$396,000	$205,500	$43,500	$36,000	$45,000	$66,000
10	Estimated Percentage Uncollectible		2%	6%	10%	25%	50%
11	Total Estimated Bad Debts	$ 54,570	$ 4,110	$ 2,610	$ 3,600	$ 11,250	$33,000
12							

At December 31, 2012, the unadjusted balance in Allowance for Doubtful Accounts is a credit of $16,000.

Instructions
(a) Journalize and post the adjusting entry for bad debts at December 31, 2012.
(b) Journalize and post to the allowance account the following events and transactions in the year 2013.
  (1) March 1, a $1,900 customer balance originating in 2012 is judged uncollectible.
  (2) May 1, a check for $1,900 is received from the customer whose account was written off as uncollectible on March 1.

(a) Bad debts expense
$38,570

(c) Bad debts expense
$44,300

(c) Journalize the adjusting entry for bad debts on December 31, 2013. Assume that the unadjusted balance in Allowance for Doubtful Accounts is a debit of $2,000, and the aging schedule indicates that total estimated bad debts will be $42,300.

Journalize transactions related to bad debts.
(SO 2, 3)

P9-4B The following represents selected information taken from a company's aging schedule to estimate uncollectible accounts receivable at year-end.

Worksheet.xls

File Edit View Insert Format Tools Data Window Help

	A	B	C	D	E	F	G
1			Number of Days Outstanding				
2							
3		Total	0–30	31–60	61–90	91–120	Over 120
4	Accounts receivable	$375,000	$220,000	$90,000	$40,000	$10,000	$15,000
5	% uncollectible		1%	4%	5%	8%	10%
6	Estimated bad debts						
7							

Instructions

(a) Tot. est.
bad debts $10,100

(a) Calculate the total estimated bad debts based on the above information.
(b) Prepare the year-end adjusting journal entry to record the bad debts using the allowance method and the aged uncollectible accounts receivable determined in (a). Assume the current balance in Allowance for Doubtful Accounts is a $3,000 credit.
(c) Of the above accounts, $1,600 is determined to be specifically uncollectible. Prepare the journal entry to write off the uncollectible accounts.
(d) The company subsequently collects $700 on a specific account that had previously been determined to be uncollectible in (c). Prepare the journal entry(ies) necessary to restore the account and record the cash collection.
(e) Explain how establishing an allowance account satisfies the expense recognition principle.

Journalize entries to record transactions related to bad debts.
(SO 3)

P9-5B At December 31, 2012, the trial balance of Flexenfusser Company contained the following amounts before adjustment.

	Debits	**Credits**
Accounts Receivable	$250,000	
Allowance for Doubtful Accounts		$ 1,100
Sales Revenue		600,000

Instructions

(a) (2) $12,000

(a) Prepare the adjusting entry at December 31, 2012, to record bad debts expense under each of the following independent assumptions.
  (1) An aging schedule indicates that $12,500 of accounts receivable will be uncollectible.
  (2) The company estimates that 2% of sales will be uncollectible.
(b) Repeat part (a) assuming that instead of a credit balance, there is a $1,100 debit balance in Allowance for Doubtful Accounts.
(c) During the next month, January 2013, a $3,200 account receivable is written off as uncollectible. Prepare the journal entry to record the write-off.
(d) Repeat part (c) assuming that Flexenfusser Company uses the direct write-off method instead of the allowance method in accounting for uncollectible accounts receivable.
(e) ◀▬▬▬ What are the advantages of using the allowance method in accounting for uncollectible accounts as compared to the direct write-off method?

Prepare entries for various notes receivable transactions.
(SO 2, 4, 5, 8, 9)

GLS

P9-6B Mr. T Co. closes its books monthly. On June 30, selected ledger account balances are:

Notes Receivable	$57,000
Interest Receivable	420

Notes Receivable include the following.

Date	Maker	Face	Term	Interest
May 16	Abe Inc.	$12,000	60 days	10%
May 26	Vigoda Co.	30,000	60 days	9%
June 30	Lipton Corp.	15,000	6 months	12%

During July, the following transactions were completed.

July 5 Made sales of $7,200 on Mr. T Co. credit cards.
     14 Made sales of $1,000 on Visa credit cards. The credit card service charge is 3%.
     14 Added $510 to Mr. T Co. credit card customer balances for finance charges on unpaid balances.
     15 Received payment in full from Abe Inc. on the amount due.
     25 Received notice that the Vigoda Co. note has been dishonored. (Assume that Vigoda Co. is expected to pay in the future.)

Instructions

(a) Journalize the July transactions and the July 31 adjusting entry for accrued interest receivable. (Interest is computed using 360 days.)

(b) Enter the balances at July 1 in the receivable accounts. Post the entries to all of the receivable accounts.

(c) Show the balance sheet presentation of the receivable accounts at July 31.

(b) Accounts receivable $38,160

(c) Total receivables $53,310

P9-7B On January 1, 2012, DeCarlo Company had Accounts Receivable $98,000 and Allowance for Doubtful Accounts $8,100. DeCarlo Company prepares financial statements annually. During the year, the following selected transactions occurred.

Prepare entries for various receivable transactions.

(SO 2, 4, 5, 6, 7, 8)

Jan. 5 Sold $10,800 of merchandise to Kelly Company, terms n/30.
Feb. 2 Accepted a $10,800, 4-month, 10% promissory note from Kelly Company for the balance due.
     12 Sold $13,500 of merchandise to Raymond Company and accepted Raymond's $13,500, 2-month, 10% note for the balance due.
     26 Sold $7,000 of merchandise to Ringspin Co., terms n/10.
Apr. 5 Accepted a $7,000, 3-month, 8% note from Ringspin Co. for the balance due.
     12 Collected Raymond Company note in full.
June 2 Collected Kelly Company note in full.
July 5 Ringspin Co. dishonors its note of April 5. It is expected that Ringspin will eventually pay the amount owed.
     15 Sold $12,000 of merchandise to Butter Co. and accepted Butter's $12,000, 3-month, 12% note for the amount due.
Oct. 15 Butter Co.'s note was dishonored. Butter Co. is bankrupt, and there is no hope of future settlement.

Instructions

Journalize the transactions.

Problems: Set C

Visit the book's companion website, at **www.wiley.com/college/weygandt**, and choose the Student Companion site to access Problem Set C.

Comprehensive Problem

CP9 Porter Company's balance sheet at December 31, 2011, is presented below.

PORTER COMPANY
Balance Sheet
December 31, 2011

Cash	$13,100	Accounts payable	$ 8,750
Accounts receivable	19,780	Owner's capital	32,730
Allowance for doubtful accounts	(800)		$41,480
Inventory	9,400		
	$41,480		

During January 2012, the following transactions occurred. Porter uses the perpetual inventory method.

Jan. 1 Porter accepted a 4-month, 8% note from Anderko Company in payment of Anderko's $1,200 account.

3 Porter wrote off as uncollectible the accounts of Elrich Corporation ($450) and Rios Company ($280).

8 Porter purchased $17,200 of inventory on account.

11 Porter sold for $25,000 on account inventory that cost $17,500.

15 Porter sold inventory that cost $700 to Fred Berman for $1,000. Berman charged this amount on his Visa First Bank card. The service fee charged Porter by First Bank is 3%.

17 Porter collected $22,900 from customers on account.

21 Porter paid $16,300 on accounts payable.

24 Porter received payment in full ($280) from Rios Company on the account written off on January 3.

27 Porter purchased advertising supplies for $1,400 cash.

31 Porter paid other operating expenses, $3,218.

Adjustment data:

1. Interest is recorded for the month on the note from January 1.
2. Bad debts are expected to be 6% of the January 31, 2012, accounts receivable.
3. A count of advertising supplies on January 31, 2012, reveals that $560 remains unused.

Instructions

(You may want to set up T accounts to determine ending balances.)

(a) Prepare journal entries for the transactions listed above and adjusting entries. (Include entries for cost of goods sold using the perpetual system.)

(b) Prepare an adjusted trial balance at January 31, 2012.

(c) Prepare an income statement and an owner's equity statement for the month ending January 31, 2012, and a classified balance sheet as of January 31, 2012.

Continuing Cookie Chronicle

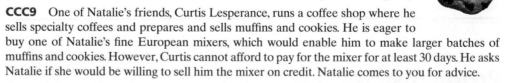

(*Note:* This is a continuation of the Cookie Chronicle from Chapters 1 through 8.)

CCC9 One of Natalie's friends, Curtis Lesperance, runs a coffee shop where he sells specialty coffees and prepares and sells muffins and cookies. He is eager to buy one of Natalie's fine European mixers, which would enable him to make larger batches of muffins and cookies. However, Curtis cannot afford to pay for the mixer for at least 30 days. He asks Natalie if she would be willing to sell him the mixer on credit. Natalie comes to you for advice.

Go to the book's companion website, **www.wiley.com/college/weygandt**, *to see the completion of this problem.*

BROADENINGYOURPERSPECTIVE

Financial Reporting and Analysis

Financial Reporting Problem: SEK Company

BYP9-1 SEK Company sells office equipment and supplies to many organizations in the city and surrounding area on contract terms of 2/10, n/30. In the past, over 75% of the credit customers have taken advantage of the discount by paying within 10 days of the invoice date.

The number of customers taking the full 30 days to pay has increased within the last year. Current indications are that less than 60% of the customers are now taking the discount. Bad debts as a percentage of gross credit sales have risen from the 2.5% provided in past years to about 4.5% in the current year.

The company's Finance Committee has requested more information on the collections of accounts receivable. The controller responded to this request with the report reproduced below.

SEK COMPANY
Accounts Receivable Collections
May 31, 2012

The fact that some credit accounts will prove uncollectible is normal. Annual bad debts write-offs have been 2.5% of gross credit sales over the past 5 years. During the last fiscal year, this percentage increased to slightly less than 4.5%. The current Accounts Receivable balance is $1,400,000. The condition of this balance in terms of age and probability of collection is as follows.

Proportion of Total	Age Categories	Probability of Collection
62%	not yet due	98%
20%	less than 30 days past due	96%
9%	30 to 60 days past due	94%
5%	61 to 120 days past due	91%
$2^{1}/_{2}$%	121 to 180 days past due	75%
$1^{1}/_{2}$%	over 180 days past due	30%

Allowance for Doubtful Accounts had a credit balance of $29,500 on June 1, 2011. SEK has provided for a monthly bad debts expense accrual during the current fiscal year based on the assumption that 4.5% of gross credit sales will be uncollectible. Total gross credit sales for the 2011–2012 fiscal year amounted to $2,900,000. Write-offs of bad accounts during the year totaled $102,000.

Instructions

(a) Prepare an accounts receivable aging schedule for SEK Company using the age categories identified in the controller's report to the Finance Committee showing the following.
  (1) The amount of accounts receivable outstanding for each age category and in total.
  (2) The estimated amount that is uncollectible for each category and in total.
(b) Compute the amount of the year-end adjustment necessary to bring Allowance for Doubtful Accounts to the balance indicated by the age analysis. Then prepare the necessary journal entry to adjust the accounting records.
(c) In a recessionary environment with tight credit and high interest rates:
  (1) Identify steps SEK Company might consider to improve the accounts receivable situation.
  (2) Then evaluate each step identified in terms of the risks and costs involved.

Comparative Analysis Problem:
PepsiCo, Inc. vs. The Coca-Cola Company

BYP9-2 PepsiCo, Inc.'s financial statements are presented in Appendix A. Financial statements of The Coca-Cola Company are presented in Appendix B.

Instructions

(a) Based on the information in these financial statements, compute the following 2009 ratios for each company. (Assume all sales are credit sales and that PepsiCo's receivables on its balance sheet are all trade receivables.)
  (1) Accounts receivable turnover ratio.
  (2) Average collection period for receivables.
(b) What conclusions about managing accounts receivable can you draw from these data?

On the Web

BYP9-3 **Purpose:** To learn more about factoring services.

Address: www.invoicebankers.com, or go to **www.wiley.com/college/weygandt**

Steps: Go to the website and answer the following questions.

(a) What are some of the benefits of factoring?
(b) What is the range of the percentages of the typical discount rate?
(c) If a company factors its receivables, what percentage of the value of the receivables can it expect to receive from the factor in the form of cash, and how quickly will it receive the cash?

Critical Thinking

Decision Making Across the Organization

BYP9-4   Molly and Joe Mayne own Campus Fashions. From its inception Campus Fashions has sold merchandise on either a cash or credit basis, but no credit cards have been accepted. During the past several months, the Maynes have begun to question their sales policies. First, they have lost some sales because of refusing to accept credit cards. Second, representatives of two metropolitan banks have been persuasive in almost convincing them to accept their national credit cards. One bank, City National Bank, has stated that its credit card fee is 4%.

The Maynes decide that they should determine the cost of carrying their own credit sales. From the accounting records of the past 3 years, they accumulate the following data.

	2012	2011	2010
Net credit sales	$500,000	$600,000	$400,000
Collection agency fees for slow-paying customers	2,450	2,500	2,400
Salary of part-time accounts receivable clerk	4,100	4,100	4,100

Credit and collection expenses as a percentage of net credit sales are: uncollectible accounts 1.6%, billing and mailing costs 0.5%, and credit investigation fee on new customers 0.15%.

Molly and Joe also determine that the average accounts receivable balance outstanding during the year is 5% of net credit sales. The Maynes estimate that they could earn an average of 8% annually on cash invested in other business opportunities.

Instructions
With the class divided into groups, answer the following.

(a) Prepare a table showing, for each year, total credit and collection expenses in dollars and as a percentage of net credit sales.
(b) Determine the net credit and collection expense in dollars and as a percentage of sales after considering the revenue not earned from other investment opportunities.
(c) Discuss both the financial and nonfinancial factors that are relevant to the decision.

Communication Activity

BYP9-5   Rene Mai, a friend of yours, overheard a discussion at work about changes her employer wants to make in accounting for uncollectible accounts. Rene knows little about accounting, and she asks you to help make sense of what she heard. Specifically, she asks you to explain the differences between the percentage-of-sales, percentage-of-receivables, and the direct write-off methods for uncollectible accounts.

Instructions
In a letter of one page (or less), explain to Rene the three methods of accounting for uncollectibles. Be sure to discuss differences among these methods.

Ethics Case

BYP9-6   The controller of Ruiz Co. believes that the yearly allowance for doubtful accounts for Ruiz Co. should be 2% of net credit sales. The president of Ruiz Co., nervous that the stockholders might expect the company to sustain its 10% growth rate, suggests that the controller increase the allowance for doubtful accounts to 4%. The president thinks that the lower net income, which reflects a 6% growth rate, will be a more sustainable rate for Ruiz Co.

Instructions
(a) Who are the stakeholders in this case?
(b) Does the president's request pose an ethical dilemma for the controller?
(c) Should the controller be concerned with Ruiz Co.'s growth rate? Explain your answer.

"All About You" Activity

BYP9-7 As the **All About You** feature (available on the book's companion website) indicates, credit card usage in the United States is substantial. Many startup companies use credit cards as a way to help meet short-term financial needs. The most common forms of debt for startups are use of credit cards and loans from relatives.

Suppose that you start up Brothers Sandwich Shop. You invested your savings of $20,000 and borrowed $70,000 from your relatives. Although sales in the first few months are good, you see that you may not have sufficient cash to pay expenses and maintain your inventory at acceptable levels, at least in the short term. You decide you may need to use one or more credit cards to fund the possible cash shortfall.

Instructions

(a) Go to the Internet and find two sources that provide insight into how to compare credit card terms.

(b) Develop a list, in descending order of importance, as to what features are most important to you in selecting a credit card for your business.

(c) Examine the features of your present credit card. (If you do not have a credit card, select a likely one online for this exercise.) Given your analysis above, what are the three major disadvantages of your present credit card?

FASB Codification Activity

BYP9-8 If your school has a subscription to the FASB Codification, go to *http://aaahq.org/ascLogin.cfm* to log in and prepare responses to the following.

(a) How are receivables defined in the Codification?

(b) What are the conditions under which losses from uncollectible receivables (Bad Debts Expense) should be reported?

Answers to Insight and Accounting Across the Organization Questions

p. 427 How Does a Credit Card Work? Q: Assume that Nordstrom prepares a bank reconciliation at the end of each month. If some credit card sales have not been processed by the bank, how should Nordstrom treat these transactions on its bank reconciliation? **A:** Nordstrom would treat the credit card receipts as deposits in transit. It has already recorded the receipts as cash. Its bank will increase Nordstrom's cash account when it receives the receipts.

p. 430 Can Fair Value Be Unfair? Q: What are the arguments in favor of and against fair value accounting for loans and receivables? **A:** Arguments in favor of fair value accounting for loans and receivables are that fair value would provide a more accurate view of a company's financial position. This might provide a useful early warning of when a bank or other financial institution was in trouble because its loans were of poor quality. But, banks argue that estimating fair values is very difficult to do accurately. They are also concerned that volatile fair values could cause large swings in a bank's reported net income.

p. 432 Bad Information Can Lead to Bad Loans Q: What steps should the banks have taken to ensure the accuracy of financial information provided on loan applications? **A:** At a minimum, the bank should have requested copies of recent income tax forms and contacted the supposed employer to verify income. To verify ownership and value of assets, it should have examined bank statements, investment statements, and title documents and should have employed appraisers.

Answers to Self-Test Questions

1. d **2.** c ($1,000 − $300) × (100% − 2%) **3.** a **4.** b ($60,000 − $5,000) **5.** d ($60,000 + $5,000) **6.** b ($800,000 × 1.5%) + $15,000 **7.** b ($750,000 × 3%) + ($18,000 − $30,000) **8.** d ($800,000 − $65,000) **9.** c **10.** c **11.** a **12.** b **13.** d $10,000 + ($10,000 × 120/360 × 9%) **14.** a **15.** c $800,000 ÷ [($100,000 + $15,000) ÷ 2]

IFRS A Look at IFRS

The basic accounting and reporting issues related to recognition and measurement of receivables, such as the use of allowance accounts, how to record discounts, use of the allowance method to account for bad debts, and factoring, are essentially the same between IFRS and GAAP.

Key Points

- IFRS requires that loans and receivables be accounted for at amortized cost, adjusted for allowances for doubtful accounts. IFRS sometimes refers to these allowances as *provisions*. The entry to record the allowance would be:

Bad Debts Expense	xxxxxx	
Allowance for Doubtful Accounts		xxxxxx

- Although IFRS implies that receivables with different characteristics should be reported separately, there is no standard that mandates this segregation.

- The FASB and IASB have worked to implement fair value measurement (the amount they currently could be sold for) for financial instruments. Both Boards have faced bitter opposition from various factions. As a consequence, the Boards have adopted a piecemeal approach; the first step is disclosure of fair value information in the notes. The second step is the fair value option, which permits, but does not require, companies to record some types of financial instruments at fair values in the financial statements.

- IFRS requires a two-tiered approach to test whether the value of loans and receivables are impaired. First, a company should look at specific loans and receivables to determine whether they are impaired. Then, the loans and receivables as a group should be evaluated for impairment. GAAP does not prescribe a similar two-tiered approach.

- IFRS and GAAP differ in the criteria used to determine how to record a factoring transaction. IFRS is a combination of an approach focused on risks and rewards and loss of control. GAAP uses loss of control as the primary criterion. In addition, IFRS permits partial derecognition of receivables; GAAP does not.

Looking to the Future

It appears likely that the question of recording fair values for financial instruments will continue to be an important issue to resolve as the Boards work toward convergence. Both the IASB and the FASB have indicated that they believe that financial statements would be more transparent and understandable if companies recorded and reported all financial instruments at fair value. That said, in *IFRS 9*, which was issued in 2009, the IASB created a split model, where some financial instruments are recorded at fair value, but other financial assets, such as loans and receivables, can be accounted for at amortized cost if certain criteria are met. Critics say that this can result in two companies with identical securities accounting for those securities in different ways. A proposal by the FASB would require that nearly all financial instruments, including loans and receivables, be accounted for at fair value. It has been suggested that *IFRS 9* will likely be changed or replaced as the FASB and IASB continue to deliberate the best treatment for financial instruments. In fact, one past member of the IASB said that companies should ignore *IFRS 9* and continue to report under the old standard, because in his opinion, it was extremely likely that it would be changed before the mandatory adoption date of the standard arrived in 2013.

IFRS Self-Test Questions

1. Under IFRS, loans and receivables are to be reported on the balance sheet at:
   (a) amortized cost.
   (b) amortized cost adjusted for estimated loss provisions.
   (c) historical cost.
   (d) replacement cost.

2. Which of the following statements is *false*?
   (a) Loans and receivables include equity securities purchased by the company.
   (b) Loans and receivables include credit card receivables.

(c) Loans and receivables include amounts owed by employees as a result of company loans to employees.

(d) Loans and receivables include amounts resulting from transactions with customers.

3. In recording a factoring transaction:
   (a) IFRS focuses on loss of control.
   (b) GAAP focuses on loss of control and risks and rewards.
   (c) IFRS and GAAP allow partial derecognition.
   (d) IFRS allows partial derecognition

4. Under IFRS:
   (a) the entry to record estimated uncollected accounts is the same as GAAP.
   (b) loans and receivables should only be tested for impairment as a group.
   (c) it is always acceptable to use the direct write-off method.
   (d) all financial instruments are recorded at fair value.

5. Which of the following statements is *true*?
   (a) The fair value option requires that some types of financial instruments be recorded at fair value.
   (b) The fair value option allows, but does not require, that some types of financial instruments be recorded at amortized cost.
   (c) The fair value option allows, but does not require, that some types of financial instruments be recorded at fair value.
   (d) The FASB and IASB would like to reduce the reliance on fair value accounting for financial instruments in the future.

IFRS Concepts and Application

IFRS9-1 What are some steps taken by both the FASB and IASB to move to fair value measurement for financial instruments? In what ways have some of the approaches differed?

International Financial Reporting Problem: Zetar plc

IFRS9-2 The financial statements of Zetar plc are presented in Appendix C. The company's complete annual report, including the notes to its financial statements, is available at *www.zetarplc.com*.

Instructions
Use the company's annual report to answer the following questions.

(a) According to the Operational Review of Financial Performance, what was one reason why the balance in receivables increased relative to the previous year?

(b) According to the notes to the financial statements, how are loans and receivables defined?

(c) In the notes to the financial statements, the company reports a "one off item" related to receivables. Explain what this item was.

(d) Using information in the notes to the financial statements, determine what percentage the provision for impairment of receivables was as a percentage of total trade receivables for 2009 and 2008. How did the ratio change from 2008 to 2009, and what does this suggest about the company's receivables?

Answers to IFRS Self-Test Questions
1. b   **2.** a   **3.** d   **4.** a   **5.** c

✔ Remember to go back to the Navigator box on the chapter opening page and check off your completed work.

CHAPTER10

Plant Assets, Natural Resources, and Intangible Assets

Study Objectives

After studying this chapter, you should be able to:

[1] Describe how the cost principle applies to plant assets.

[2] Explain the concept of depreciation.

[3] Compute periodic depreciation using different methods.

[4] Describe the procedure for revising periodic depreciation.

[5] Distinguish between revenue and capital expenditures, and explain the entries for each.

[6] Explain how to account for the disposal of a plant asset.

[7] Compute periodic depletion of natural resources.

[8] Explain the basic issues related to accounting for intangible assets.

[9] Indicate how plant assets, natural resources, and intangible assets are reported.

✔ The Navigator

Feature Story

HOW MUCH FOR A RIDE TO THE BEACH?

It's spring break. Your plane has landed, you've finally found your bags, and you're dying to hit the beach—but first you need a "vehicular unit" to get you there. As you turn away from baggage claim you see a long row of rental agency booths. Many are names you are familiar with—Hertz, Avis, and Budget. But a booth at the far end catches your eye—Rent-A-Wreck. Now there's a company making a clear statement!

Any company that relies on equipment to generate revenues must make decisions about what kind of equipment to buy, how long to keep it, and how vigorously to maintain it. Rent-A-Wreck has decided to rent used rather than new cars and trucks. It rents these vehicles across the United States, Europe, and Asia. While the big-name agencies push vehicles with that "new car smell," Rent-A-Wreck competes on price. The message is simple: Rent a used car and

save some cash. It's not a message that appeals to everyone. If you're a marketing executive wanting to impress a big client, you probably don't want to pull up in a Rent-A-Wreck car. But if you want to get from point A to point B for the minimum cash per mile, then they are playing your tune. The company's message seems to be getting across to the right clientele. Revenues have increased significantly.

When you rent a car from Rent-A-Wreck, you are renting from an independent business person who has paid a "franchise fee" for the right to use the Rent-A-Wreck name. In order to gain a franchise, he or she must meet financial and other criteria, and must agree to run the rental agency according to rules prescribed by Rent-A-Wreck. Some of these rules require that each franchise maintain its cars in a reasonable fashion. This ensures that, though you won't be cruising down Daytona Beach's Atlantic Avenue in a Mercedes convertible, you can be reasonably assured that you won't be calling a towtruck.

Inside CHAPTER 10

PreviewofCHAPTER10

The accounting for long-term assets has important implications for a company's reported results. In this chapter, we explain the application of the cost principle of accounting to property, plant, and equipment, such as Rent-A-Wreck vehicles, as well as to natural resources and intangible assets such as the "Rent-A-Wreck" trademark. We also describe the methods that companies may use to allocate an asset's cost over its useful life. In addition, we discuss the accounting for expenditures incurred during the useful life of assets, such as the cost of replacing tires and brake pads on rental cars.

The content and organization of Chapter 10 are as follows.

Plant Assets, Natural Resources, and Intangible Assets

Plant Assets	Natural Resources	Intangible Assets	Statement Presentation and Analysis
• Determining the cost of plant assets • Depreciation • Expenditures during useful life • Plant asset disposals	• Depletion	• Accounting for intangibles • Research and development costs	• Presentation • Analysis

✔ The Navigator

SECTION1 PLANT ASSETS

Plant assets are resources that have three characteristics: they have a physical substance (a definite size and shape), are used in the operations of a business, and are not intended for sale to customers. They are also called **property, plant, and equipment; plant and equipment;** and **fixed assets**. These assets are expected to provide services to the company for a number of years. Except for land, plant assets decline in service potential over their useful lives.

Because plant assets play a key role in ongoing operations, companies keep plant assets in good operating condition. They also replace worn-out or outdated plant assets, and expand productive resources as needed. Many companies have substantial investments in plant assets. Illustration 10-1 shows the

Illustration 10-1
Percentages of plant assets in relation to total assets

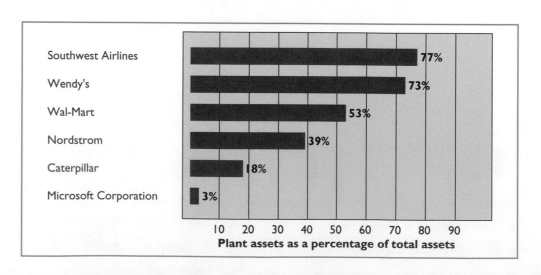

Plant assets as a percentage of total assets

percentages of plant assets in relation to total assets of companies in a number of industries.

Determining the Cost of Plant Assets

The cost principle requires that companies record plant assets at cost. Thus Rent-A-Wreck records its vehicles at cost. **Cost consists of all expenditures necessary to acquire the asset and make it ready for its intended use.** For example, the cost of factory machinery includes the purchase price, freight costs paid by the purchaser, and installation costs. Once cost is established, the company uses that amount as the basis of accounting for the plant asset over its useful life.

In the following sections, we explain the application of the cost principle to each of the major classes of plant assets.

Study Objective [1]
Describe how the cost principle applies to plant assets.

Land

Companies often use **land** as a building site for a manufacturing plant or office site. The cost of land includes (1) the cash purchase price, (2) closing costs such as title and attorney's fees, (3) real estate brokers' commissions, and (4) accrued property taxes and other liens assumed by the purchaser. For example, if the cash price is $50,000 and the purchaser agrees to pay accrued taxes of $5,000, the cost of the land is $55,000.

Companies record as debits (increases) to the Land account all necessary costs incurred to make land **ready for its intended use.** When a company acquires vacant land, these costs include expenditures for clearing, draining, filling, and grading. Sometimes the land has a building on it that must be removed before construction of a new building. In this case, the company debits to the Land account all demolition and removal costs, less any proceeds from salvaged materials.

Helpful Hint
Management's intended use is important in applying the cost principle.

To illustrate, assume that Hayes Manufacturing Company acquires real estate at a cash cost of $100,000. The property contains an old warehouse that is razed at a net cost of $6,000 ($7,500 in costs less $1,500 proceeds from salvaged materials). Additional expenditures are the attorney's fee, $1,000, and the real estate broker's commission, $8,000. The cost of the land is $115,000, computed as shown in Illustration 10-2.

Illustration 10-2
Computation of cost of land

Land	
Cash price of property	$100,000
Net removal cost of warehouse	6,000
Attorney's fee	1,000
Real estate broker's commission	8,000
Cost of land	**$115,000**

When Hayes records the acquisition, it debits Land for $115,000 and credits Cash for $115,000.

Land Improvements

Land improvements are structural additions made to land. Examples are driveways, parking lots, fences, landscaping, and underground sprinklers. The cost of land improvements includes all expenditures necessary to make the improvements ready for their intended use. For example, the cost of a new parking lot for Home Depot includes the amount paid for paving, fencing, and lighting. Thus, Home Depot debits to Land Improvements the total of all of these costs.

Land improvements have limited useful lives, and their maintenance and replacement are the responsibility of the company. Because of their limited useful life, companies expense (depreciate) the cost of land improvements over their useful lives.

Buildings

Buildings are facilities used in operations, such as stores, offices, factories, warehouses, and airplane hangars. Companies debit to the Buildings account all necessary expenditures related to the purchase or construction of a building. When a building is **purchased**, such costs include the purchase price, closing costs (attorney's fees, title insurance, etc.) and real estate broker's commission. Costs to make the building ready for its intended use include expenditures for remodeling and replacing or repairing the roof, floors, electrical wiring, and plumbing. When a new building is **constructed**, cost consists of the contract price plus payments for architects' fees, building permits, and excavation costs.

In addition, companies charge certain interest costs to the Buildings account: Interest costs incurred to finance the project are included in the cost of the building when a significant period of time is required to get the building ready for use. In these circumstances, interest costs are considered as necessary as materials and labor. However, the inclusion of interest costs in the cost of a constructed building is **limited to the construction period**. When construction has been completed, the company records subsequent interest payments on funds borrowed to finance the construction as debits (increases) to Interest Expense.

Equipment

Equipment includes assets used in operations, such as store check-out counters, office furniture, factory machinery, delivery trucks, and airplanes. The cost of equipment, such as Rent-A-Wreck vehicles, consists of the **cash purchase price, sales taxes, freight charges, and insurance during transit paid by the purchaser**. It also includes expenditures required in assembling, installing, and testing the unit. However, Rent-A-Wreck does not include motor vehicle licenses and accident insurance on company vehicles in the cost of equipment. These costs **represent annual recurring expenditures and do not benefit future periods**. Thus, they are treated as expenses as they are incurred.

To illustrate, assume Merten Company purchases factory machinery at a cash price of $50,000. Related expenditures are for sales taxes $3,000, insurance during shipping $500, and installation and testing $1,000. The cost of the factory machinery is $54,500, computed in Illustration 10-3.

Illustration 10-3
Computation of cost of factory machinery

Factory Machinery	
Cash price	$50,000
Sales taxes	3,000
Insurance during shipping	500
Installation and testing	1,000
Cost of factory machinery	**$54,500**

Merten makes the following summary entry to record the purchase and related expenditures.

Equipment	54,500	
Cash		54,500
(To record purchase of factory machine)		

A = L + OE
+54,500
−54,500
Cash Flows
−54,500

For another example, assume that Lenard Company purchases a delivery truck at a cash price of $22,000. Related expenditures consist of sales taxes $1,320, painting and lettering $500, motor vehicle license $80, and a three-year accident insurance policy $1,600. The cost of the delivery truck is $23,820, computed as follows.

Delivery Truck	
Cash price	$22,000
Sales taxes	1,320
Painting and lettering	500
Cost of delivery truck	**$23,820**

Illustration 10-4
Computation of cost of delivery truck

Lenard treats the cost of the motor vehicle license as an expense, and the cost of the insurance policy as a prepaid asset. Thus, Lenard makes the following entry to record the purchase of the truck and related expenditures:

Equipment	23,820	
License Expense	80	
Prepaid Insurance	1,600	
Cash		25,500
(To record purchase of delivery truck and related expenditures)		

A = L + OE
+23,820
        −80 Exp
+1,600
−25,500
Cash Flows
−25,500

ACCOUNTING ACROSS THE ORGANIZATION

Many U.S. Firms Use Leases

Leasing is big business for U.S. companies. For example, business investment in equipment in a recent year totaled $709 billion. Leasing accounted for about 31% of all business investment ($218 billion).

Who does the most leasing? Interestingly major banks, such as Continental Bank, J.P. Morgan Leasing, and US Bancorp Equipment Finance, are the major lessors. Also, many companies have established separate leasing companies, such as Boeing Capital Corporation, Dell Financial Services, and John Deere Capital Corporation. And, as an excellent example of the magnitude of leasing, leased planes account for nearly 40% of the U.S. fleet of commercial airlines. In addition, leasing is becoming increasingly common in the hotel industry. Marriott, Hilton, and InterContinental are increasingly choosing to lease hotels that are owned by someone else.

? Why might airline managers choose to lease rather than purchase their planes?
(See page 503.)

Do it!

Cost of Plant Assets

action plan

✔ Identify expenditures made in order to get delivery equipment ready for its intended use.

✔ Treat operating costs as expenses.

Assume that Drummond Heating and Cooling Co. purchases a delivery truck for $15,000 cash, plus sales taxes of $900 and delivery costs of $500. The buyer also pays $200 for painting and lettering, $600 for an annual insurance policy, and $80 for a motor vehicle license. Explain how each of these costs would be accounted for.

Solution

The first four payments ($15,000, $900, $500, and $200) are expenditures necessary to make the truck ready for its intended use. Thus, the cost of the truck is $16,600. The payments for insurance and the license are operating costs and therefore are expensed.

Related exercise material: BE10-1, BE10-2, E10-1, E10-2, E10-3, and **Do it!** 10-1.

The Navigator

Depreciation

As explained in Chapter 3, depreciation **is the process of allocating to expense the cost of a plant asset over its useful (service) life in a rational and systematic manner**. Cost allocation enables companies to properly match expenses with revenues in accordance with the expense recognition principle (see Illustration 10-5).

Illustration 10-5
Depreciation as a cost allocation concept

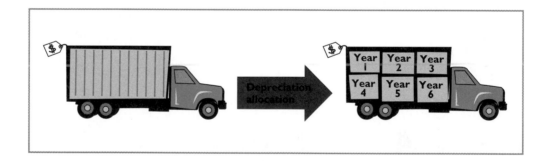

It is important to understand that **depreciation is a process of cost allocation. It is not a process of asset valuation**. No attempt is made to measure the change in an asset's fair value during ownership. So, the **book value** (cost less accumulated depreciation) of a plant asset may be quite different from its fair value. In fact, if an asset is fully depreciated, it can have a zero book value but still have a significant fair value.

Depreciation applies to three classes of plant assets: land improvements, buildings, and equipment. Each asset in these classes is considered to be a **depreciable asset**. Why? Because the usefulness to the company and revenue-producing ability of each asset will decline over the asset's useful life. Depreciation **does not apply to land** because its usefulness and revenue-producing ability generally remain intact over time. In fact, in many cases, the usefulness of land is greater over time because of the scarcity of good land sites. Thus, **land is not a depreciable asset**.

Ethics Note

When a business is acquired, proper allocation of the purchase price to various asset classes is important, since different depreciation treatment can materially affect income. For example, buildings are depreciated, but land is not.

During a depreciable asset's useful life, its revenue-producing ability declines because of **wear and tear**. A delivery truck that has been driven 100,000 miles will be less useful to a company than one driven only 800 miles.

Revenue-producing ability may also decline because of obsolescence. **Obsolescence** is the process of becoming out of date before the asset physically wears out. For example, major airlines moved from Chicago's Midway Airport to Chicago-O'Hare International Airport because Midway's runways were too short for jumbo jets. Similarly, many companies replace their computers long before they originally planned to do so because improvements in new computing technology make the old computers obsolete.

Recognizing depreciation on an asset does not result in an accumulation of cash for replacement of the asset. The balance in Accumulated Depreciation represents the total amount of the asset's cost that the company has charged to expense. It is not a cash fund.

Note that the concept of depreciation is consistent with the going-concern assumption. The **going-concern assumption** states that the company will continue in operation for the foreseeable future. If a company does not use a going-concern assumption, then plant assets should be stated at their fair value. In that case, depreciation of these assets is not needed.

Factors in Computing Depreciation

Three factors affect the computation of depreciation, as shown in Illustration 10-6.

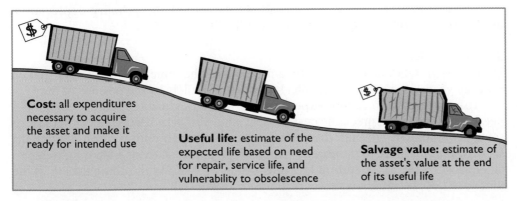

Cost: all expenditures necessary to acquire the asset and make it ready for intended use

Useful life: estimate of the expected life based on need for repair, service life, and vulnerability to obsolescence

Salvage value: estimate of the asset's value at the end of its useful life

Illustration 10-6
Three factors in computing depreciation

Helpful Hint

Depreciation expense is reported on the income statement. Accumulated depreciation is reported on the balance sheet as a deduction from plant assets.

1. **Cost.** Earlier, we explained the issues affecting the cost of a depreciable asset. Recall that companies record plant assets at cost, in accordance with the cost principle.

2. **Useful life.** Useful life is an estimate of the expected *productive life*, also called *service life*, of the asset for its owner. Useful life may be expressed in terms of time, units of activity (such as machine hours), or units of output. Useful life is an estimate. In making the estimate, management considers such factors as the intended use of the asset, its expected repair and maintenance, and its vulnerability to obsolescence. Past experience with similar assets is often helpful in deciding on expected useful life. We might reasonably expect Rent-A-Wreck and Avis to use different estimated useful lives for their vehicles.

3. **Salvage value.** Salvage value is an estimate of the asset's value at the end of its useful life. This value may be based on the asset's worth as scrap or on its expected trade-in value. Like useful life, salvage value is an estimate. In making the estimate, management considers how it plans to dispose of the asset and its experience with similar assets.

Alternative Terminology

Another term sometimes used for salvage value is *residual value*.

Depreciation Methods

Depreciation is generally computed using one of the following methods:

1. Straight-line
2. Units-of-activity
3. Declining-balance

Each method is acceptable under generally accepted accounting principles. Management selects the method(s) it believes to be appropriate. The objective is to select the method that best measures an asset's contribution to revenue over its useful life. Once a company chooses a method, it should apply it consistently over the useful life of the asset. Consistency enhances the comparability of financial statements. Depreciation affects the balance sheet through accumulated depreciation and the income statement through depreciation expense.

We will compare the three depreciation methods using the following data for a small delivery truck purchased by Barb's Florists on January 1, 2012.

Illustration 10-7
Delivery truck data

Cost	$13,000
Expected salvage value	$ 1,000
Estimated useful life in years	5
Estimated useful life in miles	100,000

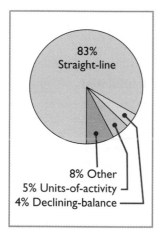

Illustration 10-8
Use of depreciation methods in 600 large U.S. companies

83% Straight-line

8% Other
5% Units-of-activity
4% Declining-balance

Illustration 10-8 (in the margin) shows the use of the primary depreciation methods in 600 of the largest companies in the United States.

STRAIGHT-LINE

Under the **straight-line method**, companies expense the same amount of depreciation for each year of the asset's useful life. It is measured solely by the passage of time.

To compute depreciation expense under the straight-line method, companies need to determine depreciable cost. **Depreciable cost** is the cost of the asset less its salvage value. It represents the total amount subject to depreciation. Under the straight-line method, to determine annual depreciation expense, we divide depreciable cost by the asset's useful life. Illustration 10-9 shows the computation of the first year's depreciation expense for Barb's Florists.

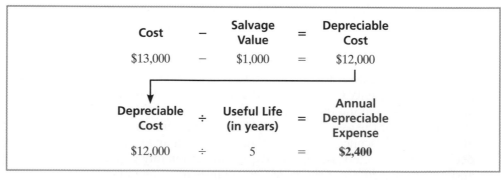

Illustration 10-9
Formula for straight-line method

Alternatively, we also can compute an annual **rate** of depreciation. In this case, the rate is 20% (100% ÷ 5 years). When a company uses an annual straight-line rate, it applies the percentage rate to the depreciable cost of the asset. Illustration 10-10 shows a **depreciation schedule** using an annual rate.

	Computation				End of Year	
Barb's Florists						
Year	Depreciable Cost	× Depreciation Rate =	Annual Depreciation Expense	Accumulated Depreciation	Book Value
2012	$12,000	20%	**$2,400**	$ 2,400	$10,600*
2013	12,000	20	**2,400**	4,800	8,200
2014	12,000	20	**2,400**	7,200	5,800
2015	12,000	20	**2,400**	9,600	3,400
2016	12,000	20	**2,400**	12,000	**1,000**

*Book Value = Cost − Accumulated depreciation = ($13,000 − $2,400).

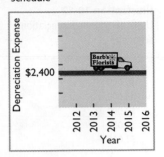

Illustration 10-10
Straight-line depreciation schedule

Note that the depreciation expense of $2,400 is the same each year. The book value (computed as cost minus accumulated depreciation) at the end of the useful life is equal to the expected $1,000 salvage value.

What happens to these computations for an asset purchased **during** the year, rather than on January 1? In that case, it is necessary to **prorate the annual depreciation** on a time basis. If Barb's Florists had purchased the delivery truck on April 1, 2012, the company would own the truck for nine months of the first year (April–December). Thus, depreciation for 2012 would be $1,800 ($12,000 × 20% × 9/12 of a year).

The straight-line method predominates in practice. Such large companies as Campbell Soup, Marriott, and General Mills use the straight-line method. It is simple to apply, and it matches expenses with revenues when the use of the asset is reasonably uniform throughout the service life.

UNITS-OF-ACTIVITY

Under the units-of-activity method, useful life is expressed in terms of the total units of production or use expected from the asset, rather than as a time period. The units-of-activity method is ideally suited to factory machinery. Manufacturing companies can measure production in units of output or in machine hours. This method can also be used for such assets as delivery equipment (miles driven) and airplanes (hours in use). The units-of-activity method is generally not suitable for buildings or furniture, because depreciation for these assets is more a function of time than of use.

To use this method, companies estimate the total units of activity for the entire useful life, and then divide these units into depreciable cost. The resulting number represents the depreciation cost per unit. The depreciation cost per unit is then applied to the units of activity during the year to determine the annual depreciation expense.

To illustrate, assume that Barb's Florists drives its delivery truck 15,000 miles in the first year. Illustration 10-11 shows the units-of-activity formula and the computation of the first year's depreciation expense.

Alternative Terminology

Another term often used is the *units-of-production method*.

Helpful Hint

Under any method, depreciation stops when the asset's book value equals expected salvage value.

Depreciable Cost	÷	Total Units of Activity	=	Depreciable Cost per Unit
$12,000	÷	100,000 miles	=	$0.12

Depreciable Cost per Unit	×	Units of Activity during the Year	=	Annual Depreciable Expense
$0.12	×	15,000 miles	=	**$1,800**

Illustration 10-11
Formula for units-of-activity method

The units-of-activity depreciation schedule, using assumed mileage, is as follows.

Illustration 10-12
Units-of-activity depreciation schedule

	Computation			Annual	End of Year	
Year	Units of Activity	× Depreciation Cost/Unit	=	Depreciation Expense	Accumulated Depreciation	Book Value
2012	15,000	$0.12		**$1,800**	$ 1,800	$11,200*
2013	30,000	0.12		**3,600**	5,400	7,600
2014	20,000	0.12		**2,400**	7,800	5,200
2015	25,000	0.12		**3,000**	10,800	2,200
2016	10,000	0.12		**1,200**	12,000	**1,000**

($13,000 − $1,800).

Table header: **Barb's Florists**

This method is easy to apply for assets purchased mid-year. In such a case, the company computes the depreciation using the productivity of the asset for the partial year.

The units-of-activity method is not nearly as popular as the straight-line method (see Illustration 10-8, page 464), primarily because it is often difficult for companies to reasonably estimate total activity. However, some very large companies, such as Chevron and Boise Cascade (a forestry company), do use this method. When the productivity of an asset varies significantly from one period to another, the units-of-activity method results in the best matching of expenses with revenues.

DECLINING-BALANCE

The **declining-balance method** produces a decreasing annual depreciation expense over the asset's useful life. The method is so named because the periodic depreciation is based on a **declining book value** (cost less accumulated depreciation) of the asset. With this method, companies compute annual depreciation expense by multiplying the book value at the beginning of the year by the declining-balance depreciation rate. **The depreciation rate remains constant from year to year, but the book value to which the rate is applied declines each year.**

At the beginning of the first year, book value is the cost of the asset. This is so because the balance in accumulated depreciation at the beginning of the asset's useful life is zero. In subsequent years, book value is the difference between cost and accumulated depreciation to date. Unlike the other depreciation methods, the declining-balance method does not use depreciable cost. That is, **it ignores salvage value in determining the amount to which the declining-balance rate is applied**. Salvage value, however, does limit the total depreciation that can be taken. Depreciation stops when the asset's book value equals expected salvage value.

A common declining-balance rate is double the straight-line rate. The method is often called the **double-declining-balance method**. If Barb's Florists uses the double-declining-balance method, it uses a depreciation rate of 40% (2 × the straight-line rate of 20%). Illustration 10-13 shows the declining-balance formula and the computation of the first year's depreciation on the delivery truck.

Illustration 10-13
Formula for declining-balance method

Book Value at Beginning of Year	×	Declining-Balance Rate	=	Annual Depreciation Expense
$13,000	×	40%	=	$5,200

The depreciation schedule under this method is as follows.

Barb's Florists					
	Computation		Annual	End of Year	
Year	Book Value Beginning of Year	× Depreciation Rate	= Depreciation Expense	Accumulated Depreciation	Book Value
2012	$13,000	40%	**$5,200**	$ 5,200	$7,800
2013	7,800	40	**3,120**	8,320	4,680
2014	4,680	40	**1,872**	10,192	2,808
2015	2,808	40	**1,123**	11,315	1,685
2016	1,685	40	**685***	12,000	**1,000**

*Computation of $674 ($1,685 × 40%) is adjusted to $685 in order for book value to equal salvage value.

Illustration 10-14
Double-declining-balance depreciation schedule

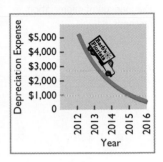

The delivery equipment is 69% depreciated ($8,320 ÷ $12,000) at the end of the second year. Under the straight-line method, the truck would be depreciated 40% ($4,800 ÷ $12,000) at that time. Because the declining-balance method produces higher depreciation expense in the early years than in the later years, it is considered an **accelerated-depreciation method**. The declining-balance method is compatible with the expense recognition principle. It matches the higher depreciation expense in early years with the higher benefits received in these years. It also recognizes lower depreciation expense in later years, when the asset's contribution to revenue is less. Some assets lose usefulness rapidly because of obsolescence. In these cases, the declining-balance method provides the most appropriate depreciation amount.

When a company purchases an asset during the year, it must prorate the first year's declining-balance depreciation on a time basis. For example, if Barb's Florists had purchased the truck on April 1, 2012, depreciation for 2012 would become $3,900 ($13,000 × 40% × 9/12). The book value at the beginning of 2013 is then $9,100 ($13,000 − $3,900), and the 2013 depreciation is $3,640 ($9,100 × 40%). Subsequent computations would follow from those amounts.

Helpful Hint

The method recommended for an asset that is expected to be significantly more productive in the first half of its useful life is the declining-balance method.

Do it!

On January 1, 2012, Iron Mountain Ski Corporation purchased a new snow-grooming machine for $50,000. The machine is estimated to have a 10-year life with a $2,000 salvage value. What journal entry would Iron Mountain Ski Corporation make at December 31, 2012, if it uses the straight-line method of depreciation?

Straight-Line Depreciation

action plan

✔ Calculate depreciable cost (Cost − Salvage value).

✔ Divide the depreciable cost by the asset's estimated useful life.

Solution

$$\text{Depreciation expense} = \frac{\text{Cost} - \text{Salvage value}}{\text{Useful life}} = \frac{\$50,000 - \$2,000}{10} = \$4,800$$

The entry to record the first year's depreciation would be:

Dec. 31	Depreciation Expense	4,800	
	Accumulated Depreciation—Equipment		4,800
	(To record annual depreciation on snow-grooming machine)		

Related exercise material: BE10-3, BE10-4, BE10-5, BE10-6, BE10-7, E10-5, E10-6, E10-7, E10-8, and **Do it!** 10-2.

The Navigator

COMPARISON OF METHODS

Illustration 10-15 compares annual and total depreciation expense under each of the three methods for Barb's Florists.

Illustration 10-15
Comparison of depreciation methods

Year	Straight-Line	Units-of-Activity	Declining-Balance
2012	$ 2,400	$ 1,800	$ 5,200
2013	2,400	3,600	3,120
2014	2,400	2,400	1,872
2015	2,400	3,000	1,123
2016	2,400	1,200	685
	$12,000	$12,000	$12,000

Annual depreciation varies considerably among the methods, but **total depreciation is the same for the five-year period** under all three methods. Each method is acceptable in accounting because each recognizes in a rational and systematic manner the decline in service potential of the asset. Illustration 10-16 graphs the depreciation expense pattern under each method.

Illustration 10-16
Patterns of depreciation

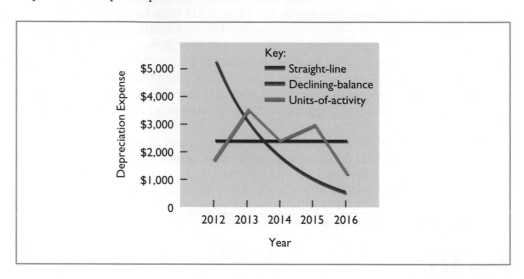

Depreciation and Income Taxes

The Internal Revenue Service (IRS) allows corporate taxpayers to deduct depreciation expense when they compute taxable income. However, the IRS does not require the taxpayer to use the same depreciation method on the tax return that is used in preparing financial statements.

Many corporations use straight-line in their financial statements to maximize net income. At the same time, they use a special accelerated-depreciation method on their tax returns to minimize their income taxes. Taxpayers must use on their tax returns either the straight-line method or a special accelerated-depreciation method called the **Modified Accelerated Cost Recovery System** (MACRS).

Revising Periodic Depreciation

Study Objective [4]

Describe the procedure for revising periodic depreciation.

Depreciation is one example of the use of estimation in the accounting process. Management should periodically review annual depreciation expense. If wear and tear or obsolescence indicate that annual depreciation estimates are inadequate or excessive, the company should change the amount of depreciation expense.

When a change in an estimate is required, the company makes the change in **current and future years. It does not change depreciation in prior periods.** The rationale is that continual restatement of prior periods would adversely affect confidence in financial statements.

To determine the new annual depreciation expense, the company first computes the asset's depreciable cost at the time of the revision. It then allocates the revised depreciable cost to the remaining useful life.

To illustrate, assume that Barb's Florists decides on January 1, 2015, to extend the useful life of the truck one year (a total life of six years) and increase its salvage value to $2,200. The company has used the straight-line method to depreciate the asset to date. Depreciation per year was $2,400 (($13,000 − $1,000) ÷ 5). Accumulated depreciation after three years (2012–2014) is $7,200 ($2,400 × 3), and book value is $5,800 ($13,000 − $7,200). The new annual depreciation is $1,200, computed as follows.

Helpful Hint

Use a step-by-step approach: (1) determine new depreciable cost; (2) divide by remaining useful life.

Book value, 1/1/15	$ 5,800
Less: Salvage value	2,200
Depreciable cost	$ 3,600
Remaining useful life	3 years (2015–2017)
Revised annual depreciation ($3,600 ÷ 3)	**$ 1,200**

Illustration 10-17
Revised depreciation computation

Barb's Florists makes no entry for the change in estimate. On December 31, 2015, during the preparation of adjusting entries, it records depreciation expense of $1,200. Companies must describe in the financial statements significant changes in estimates.

Do it!

Chambers Corporation purchased a piece of equipment for $36,000. It estimated a 6-year life and $6,000 salvage value. Thus, straight-line depreciation was $5,000 per year (($36,000 − $6,000) ÷ 6). At the end of year three (before the depreciation adjustment), it estimated the new total life to be 10 years and the new salvage value to be $2,000. Compute the revised depreciation.

Revised Depreciation

Solution

action plan
✔ Calculate remaining depreciable cost.
✔ Divide remaining depreciable cost by new remaining life.

Original depreciation expense = [($36,000 − $6,000) ÷ 6] = $5,000
Accumulated depreciation after 2 years = 2 × $5,000 = $10,000
Book value = $36,000 − $10,000 = $26,000

Book value after 2 years of depreciation	$26,000
Less: New salvage value	2,000
Depreciable cost	24,000
Remaining useful life	8 years
Revised annual depreciation ($24,000 ÷ 8)	$ 3,000

Related exercise material: BE10-7, E10-8, and **Do it!** 10-3.

Expenditures During Useful Life

During the useful life of a plant asset, a company may incur costs for ordinary repairs, additions, or improvements. Ordinary repairs are expenditures to **maintain** the operating efficiency and productive life of the unit. They usually are fairly small amounts that occur frequently. Examples are motor tune-ups and oil changes, the painting of buildings, and the replacing of worn-out gears on machinery. Companies record such repairs as debits to Maintenance and Repairs Expense as they are incurred. Because they are immediately charged as an expense against revenues, these costs are often referred to as revenue expenditures.

In contrast, additions and improvements are costs incurred to **increase** the operating efficiency, productive capacity, or useful life of a plant asset. They are usually material in amount and occur infrequently. Additions and improvements increase the company's investment in productive facilities. Companies generally debit these amounts to the plant asset affected. They are often referred to as capital expenditures.

Companies must use good judgment in deciding between a revenue expenditure and capital expenditure. For example, assume that Rodriguez Co. purchases a number of wastepaper baskets. Although the proper accounting would appear to be to capitalize and then depreciate these wastepaper baskets over their useful life, it would be more usual for Rodriguez to expense them immediately. This practice is justified on the basis of **materiality**. Materiality refers to the impact of an item's size on a company's financial operations. The materiality principle states that if an item would not make a difference in decision making, the company does not have to follow GAAP in reporting that item.

ANATOMY OF A FRAUD

Bernie Ebbers was the founder and CEO of the phone company WorldCom. The company engaged in a series of increasingly large, debt-financed acquisitions of other companies. These acquisitions made the company grow quickly, which made the stock price increase dramatically. However, because the acquired companies all had different accounting systems, WorldCom's financial records were a mess. When WorldCom's performance started to flatten out, Bernie coerced WorldCom's accountants to engage in a number of fraudulent activities to make net income look better than it really was and thus prop up the stock price. One of these frauds involved treating $7 billion of line costs as capital expenditures. The line costs, which were rental fees paid to other phone companies to use their phone lines, had always been properly expensed in previous years. Capitalization delayed expense recognition to future periods and thus boosted current-period profits.

Total take: $7 billion

THE MISSING CONTROLS

Documentation procedures. The company's accounting system was a disorganized collection of non-integrated systems, which resulted from a series of corporate acquisitions. Top management took advantage of this disorganization to conceal its fraudulent activities.

Independent internal verification. A fraud of this size should have been detected by a routine comparison of the actual physical assets with the list of physical assets shown in the accounting records.

Plant Asset Disposals

Companies dispose of plant assets that are no longer useful to them. Illustration 10-18 below shows the three ways in which companies make plant asset disposals.

Whatever the disposal method, the company must determine the book value of the plant asset at the disposal date to determine the gain or loss. Recall that the book value is the difference between the cost of the plant asset and the accumulated depreciation to date. If the disposal occurs at any time during the year, the company must record depreciation for the fraction of the year to the date of disposal. The company then eliminates the book value by reducing (debiting) Accumulated Depreciation for the total depreciation associated with that asset to the date of disposal and reducing (crediting) the asset account for the cost of the asset.

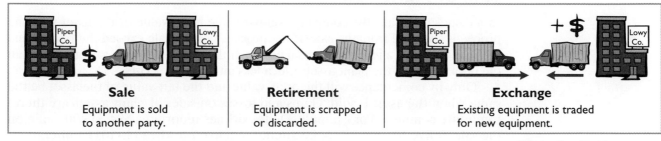

Study Objective [6]
Explain how to account for the disposal of a plant asset.

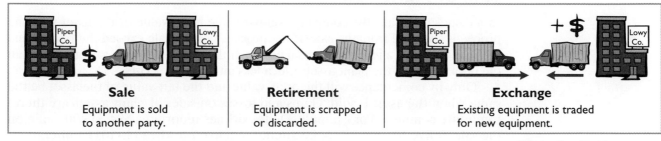

Sale
Equipment is sold to another party.

Retirement
Equipment is scrapped or discarded.

Exchange
Existing equipment is traded for new equipment.

Illustration 10-18
Methods of plant asset disposal

In this chapter, we examine the accounting for the retirement and sale of plant assets. In the appendix to the chapter, we discuss and illustrate the accounting for exchanges of plant assets.

Retirement of Plant Assets

To illustrate the retirement of plant assets, assume that Hobart Enterprises retires its computer printers, which cost $32,000. The accumulated depreciation on these printers is $32,000. The equipment, therefore, is fully depreciated (zero book value). The entry to record this retirement is as follows.

Accumulated Depreciation—Equipment	32,000	
Equipment		32,000
(To record retirement of fully depreciated equipment)		

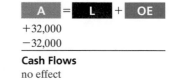

A = L + OE
+32,000
−32,000
—————————
Cash Flows
no effect

What happens if a fully depreciated plant asset is still useful to the company? In this case, the asset and its accumulated depreciation continue to be reported on the balance sheet, without further depreciation adjustment, until the company retires the asset. Reporting the asset and related accumulated depreciation on the balance sheet informs the financial statement reader that the asset is still in use. Once fully depreciated, no additional depreciation should be taken, even if an asset is still being used. In no situation can the accumulated depreciation on a plant asset exceed its cost.

If a company retires a plant asset before it is fully depreciated, and no cash is received for scrap or salvage value, a loss on disposal occurs. For example, assume

Helpful Hint

When a company disposes of a plant asset, the company must remove from the accounts all amounts related to the asset. This includes the original cost in the asset account and the total depreciation to date in the accumulated depreciation account.

that Sunset Company discards delivery equipment that cost $18,000 and has accumulated depreciation of $14,000. The entry is as follows.

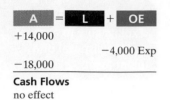

+14,000

     −4,000 Exp

−18,000

Cash Flows

no effect

Accumulated Depreciation—Equipment	14,000	
Loss on Disposal of Plant Assets	4,000	
Equipment		18,000
(To record retirement of delivery equipment at a loss)		

Companies report a loss on disposal of plant assets in the "Other expenses and losses" section of the income statement.

Sale of Plant Assets

In a disposal by sale, the company compares the book value of the asset with the proceeds received from the sale. If the proceeds of the sale **exceed** the book value of the plant asset, **a gain on disposal occurs**. If the proceeds of the sale **are less than** the book value of the plant asset sold, **a loss on disposal occurs**.

Only by coincidence will the book value and the fair value of the asset be the same when the asset is sold. Gains and losses on sales of plant assets are therefore quite common. For example, Delta Airlines reported a $94,343,000 gain on the sale of five Boeing B727-200 aircraft and five Lockheed L-1011-1 aircraft.

GAIN ON SALE

To illustrate a gain on sale of plant assets, assume that on July 1, 2012, Wright Company sells office furniture for $16,000 cash. The office furniture originally cost $60,000. As of January 1, 2012, it had accumulated depreciation of $41,000. Depreciation for the first six months of 2012 is $8,000. Wright records depreciation expense and updates accumulated depreciation to July 1 with the following entry.

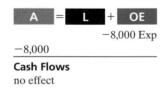

     −8,000 Exp

−8,000

Cash Flows

no effect

July 1	Depreciation Expense	8,000	
	Accumulated Depreciation—Equipment		8,000
	(To record depreciation expense for the first		
	6 months of 2012)		

After the accumulated depreciation balance is updated, the company computes the gain or loss. The gain or loss is the difference between the proceeds from the sale and the book value at the date of disposal. Illustration 10-19 shows this computation for Wright Company, which has a gain on disposal of $5,000.

Illustration 10-19

Computation of gain on disposal

Cost of office furniture	$60,000
Less: Accumulated depreciation ($41,000 + $8,000)	49,000
Book value at date of disposal	11,000
Proceeds from sale	16,000
Gain on disposal of plant asset	**$ 5,000**

Wright records the sale and the gain on disposal of the plant asset as follows.

July 1	Cash	16,000	
	Accumulated Depreciation—Equipment	49,000	
	Equipment		60,000
	Gain on Disposal of Plant Assets		5,000
	(To record sale of office furniture		
	at a gain)		

A = L + OE
+16,000
+49,000
−60,000
              +5,000 Rev

Cash Flows
+16,000

Companies report a gain on disposal of plant assets in the "Other revenues and gains" section of the income statement.

LOSS ON SALE

Assume that instead of selling the office furniture for $16,000, Wright sells it for $9,000. In this case, Wright computes a loss of $2,000 as follows.

Cost of office furniture	$60,000
Less: Accumulated depreciation	49,000
Book value at date of disposal	11,000
Proceeds from sale	9,000
Loss on disposal of plant asset	**$ 2,000**

Illustration 10-20
Computation of loss on disposal

Wright records the sale and the loss on disposal of the plant asset as follows.

July 1	Cash	9,000	
	Accumulated Depreciation—Equipment	49,000	
	Loss on Disposal of Plant Assets	2,000	
	Equipment		60,000
	(To record sale of office furniture at a loss)		

A = L + OE
+ 9,000
+49,000
            −2,000 Exp
+60,000

Cash Flows
+9,000

Companies report a loss on disposal of plant assets in the "Other expenses and losses" section of the income statement.

Do it!

Overland Trucking has an old truck that cost $30,000, and it has accumulated depreciation of $16,000 on this truck. Overland has decided to sell the truck. (a) What entry would Overland Trucking make to record the sale of the truck for $17,000 cash? (b) What entry would Overland trucking make to record the sale of the truck for $10,000 cash?

Solution

(a) Sale of truck for cash at a gain:

Cash	17,000	
Accumulated Depreciation—Equipment	16,000	
Equipment		30,000
Gain on Disposal of Plant Assets [$17,000 − ($30,000 − $16,000)]		3,000
(To record sale of truck at a gain)		

Plant Asset Disposal

action plan

✔ At the time of disposal, determine the book value of the asset.

✔ Compare the asset's book value with the proceeds received to determine whether a gain or loss has occurred.

(b) Sale of truck for cash at a loss:

Cash	10,000	
Loss on Disposal of Plant Assets [$10,000 − ($30,000 − $16,000)]	4,000	
Accumulated Depreciation—Equipment	16,000	
Equipment		30,000
(To record sale of truck at a loss)		

Related exercise material: BE10-9, BE10-10, E10-9, E10-10, and **Do it!** 10-3.

✔
The Navigator

SECTION2 NATURAL RESOURCES

Helpful Hint

On a balance sheet, natural resources may be described more specifically as *timberlands*, *mineral deposits*, *oil reserves*, and so on.

Natural resources consist of standing timber and underground deposits of oil, gas, and minerals. These long-lived productive assets have two distinguishing characteristics: (1) They are physically extracted in operations (such as mining, cutting, or pumping). (2) They are replaceable only by an act of nature.

The acquisition cost of a natural resource is the price needed to acquire the resource **and** prepare it for its intended use. For an already-discovered resource, such as an existing coal mine, cost is the price paid for the property.

The allocation of the cost of natural resources to expense in a rational and systematic manner over the resource's useful life is called **depletion**. (That is, *depletion* is to natural resources as *depreciation* is to plant assets.) **Companies generally use the units-of-activity method** (learned earlier in the chapter) **to compute depletion**. The reason is that **depletion generally is a function of the units extracted during the year**.

Study Objective [7]
Compute periodic depletion of natural resources.

Under the units-of-activity method, companies divide the total cost of the natural resource minus salvage value by the number of units estimated to be in the resource. The result is a **depletion cost per unit of product**. They then multiply the depletion cost per unit by the number of units extracted and sold. The result is the **annual depletion expense**. Illustration 10-21 shows the formula to compute depletion expense.

Illustration 10-21
Formula to compute depletion expense

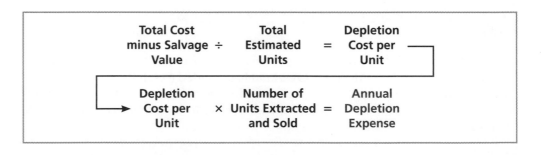

Ethics Note

Investors were stunned at news that Royal Dutch/Shell Group had significantly overstated its reported oil reserves—and perhaps had done so intentionally.

To illustrate, assume that Lane Coal Company invests $5 million in a mine estimated to have 10 million tons of coal and no salvage value. In the first year, Lane extracts and sells 800,000 tons of coal. Using the formulas above, Lane computes the depletion expense as follows:

$5,000,000 ÷ 10,000,000 = $0.50 depletion cost per ton

$0.50 × 800,000 = $400,000 annual depletion expense

Lane records depletion expense for the first year of operation as follows.

Dec. 31	Depletion Expense	400,000	
	Accumulated Depletion		400,000
	(To record depletion expense on coal deposits)		

A = L + OE
−400,000 Exp
−400,000
Cash Flows
no effect

The company reports the account Depletion Expense as a part of the cost of producing the product. Accumulated Depletion is a contra-asset account, similar to accumulated depreciation. It is deducted from the cost of the natural resource in the balance sheet, as Illustration 10-22 shows.

Lane Coal Company
Balance Sheet (partial)

Coal mine	$5,000,000	
Less: Accumulated depletion	**400,000**	$4,600,000

Illustration 10-22
Statement presentation of accumulated depletion

Many companies do not use an Accumulated Depletion account. In such cases, the company credits the amount of depletion directly to the natural resources account.

Sometimes, a company will extract natural resources in one accounting period but not sell them until a later period. In this case, the company does not expense the depletion until it sells the resource. It reports the amount not sold as inventory in the current assets section.

SECTION3 INTANGIBLE ASSETS

Intangible assets are rights, privileges, and competitive advantages that result from the ownership of long-lived assets that do not possess physical substance. Evidence of intangibles may exist in the form of contracts or licenses. Intangibles may arise from the following sources:

1. Government grants, such as patents, copyrights, licenses, trademarks, and trade names.
2. Acquisition of another business, in which the purchase price includes a payment for *goodwill*.
3. Private monopolistic arrangements arising from contractual agreements, such as franchises and leases.

Some widely known intangibles are Microsoft's patents, McDonald's franchises, Apple's trade name iPod, J.K. Rowlings' copyrights on the Harry Potter books, and the trademark Rent-A-Wreck in the Feature Story.

Accounting for Intangible Assets

Companies record intangible assets at cost. Intangibles are categorized as having either a limited life or an indefinite life. If an intangible has a **limited life**, the company allocates its cost over the asset's useful life using a process similar to depreciation. The process of allocating the cost of intangibles is referred to as amortization. The cost of intangible assets with **indefinite lives should not be amortized**.

Study Objective [8]
Explain the basic issues related to accounting for intangible assets.

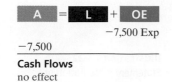

−7,500

Cash Flows
no effect

To record amortization of an intangible asset, a company increases (debits) Amortization Expense, and decreases (credits) the specific intangible asset. (Unlike depreciation, no contra account, such as Accumulated Amortization, is usually used.)

Intangible assets are typically amortized on a straight-line basis. For example, the legal life of a patent is 20 years. Companies **amortize the cost of a patent over its 20-year life or its useful life, whichever is shorter.** To illustrate the computation of patent amortization, assume that National Labs purchases a patent at a cost of $60,000. If National estimates the useful life of the patent to be eight years, the annual amortization expense is $7,500 ($60,000 ÷ 8). National records the annual amortization as follows.

Dec. 31	Amortization Expense	7,500	
	Patents		7,500
	(To record patent amortization)		

Companies classify Amortization Expense as an operating expense in the income statement.

There is a difference between intangible assets and plant assets in determining cost. For plant assets, cost includes both the purchase price of the asset and the costs incurred in designing and constructing the asset. In contrast, cost for an intangible asset includes **only the purchase price.** Companies expense any costs incurred in developing an intangible asset.

Patents

A **patent** is an exclusive right issued by the U.S. Patent Office that enables the recipient to manufacture, sell, or otherwise control an invention for a period of 20 years from the date of the grant. A patent is nonrenewable. But companies can extend the legal life of a patent by obtaining new patents for improvements or other changes in the basic design. **The initial cost of a patent is the cash or cash equivalent price paid to acquire the patent.**

The saying, "A patent is only as good as the money you're prepared to spend defending it" is very true. Most patents are subject to litigation by competitors. Any legal costs an owner incurs in successfully defending a patent in an infringement suit are considered necessary to establish the patent's validity. **The owner adds those costs to the Patents account and amortizes them over the remaining life of the patent.**

The patent holder amortizes the cost of a patent over its 20-year legal life or its useful life, whichever is shorter. Companies consider obsolescence and inadequacy in determining useful life. These factors may cause a patent to become economically ineffective before the end of its legal life.

Copyrights

The federal government grants **copyrights** which give the owner the exclusive right to reproduce and sell an artistic or published work. Copyrights extend for the life of the creator plus 70 years. The cost of a copyright is the **cost of acquiring and defending it.** The cost may be only the small fee paid to the U.S. Copyright Office. Or it may amount to much more if an infringement suit is involved.

The useful life of a copyright generally is significantly shorter than its legal life. Therefore, copyrights usually are amortized over a relatively short period of time.

Trademarks and Trade Names

A **trademark** or **trade name** is a word, phrase, jingle, or symbol that identifies a particular enterprise or product. Trade names like Wheaties, Monopoly, Big Mac,

Kleenex, Coca-Cola, and Jeep create immediate product identification. They also generally enhance the sale of the product. The creator or original user may obtain exclusive legal right to the trademark or trade name by registering it with the U.S. Patent Office. Such registration provides 20 years of protection. The registration may be renewed indefinitely as long as the trademark or trade name is in use.

If a company purchases the trademark or trade name, its cost is the purchase price. If a company develops and maintains the trademark or trade name, any costs related to these activities are expensed as incurred. Because trademarks and trade names have indefinite lives, they are not amortized.

Franchises and Licenses

When you fill up your tank at the corner Shell station, eat lunch at Subway, or rent a car from Rent-A-Wreck, you are dealing with franchises. A **franchise** is a contractual arrangement between a franchisor and a franchisee. The franchisor grants the franchisee the right to sell certain products, provide specific services, or use certain trademarks or trade names, usually within a designated geographical area.

Another type of franchise is that entered into between a governmental body (commonly municipalities) and a company. This franchise permits the company to use public property in performing its services. Examples are the use of city streets for a bus line or taxi service, use of public land for telephone and electric lines, and the use of airwaves for radio or TV broadcasting. Such operating rights are referred to as **licenses**. Franchises and licenses may by granted for a definite period of time, an indefinite period, or perpetually.

When a company can identify costs with the purchase of a franchise or license, it should recognize an intangible asset. Companies should amortize the cost of a limited-life franchise (or license) over its useful life. If the life is indefinite, the cost is not amortized. Annual payments made under a franchise agreement are recorded as **operating expenses** in the period in which they are incurred.

Goodwill

Usually, the largest intangible asset that appears on a company's balance sheet is goodwill. **Goodwill** represents the value of all favorable attributes that relate to a company that are not attributable to any other specific asset. These include exceptional management, desirable location, good customer relations, skilled employees, high-quality products, and harmonious relations with labor unions. Goodwill is unique: Unlike assets such as investments and plant assets, which can be sold *individually* in the marketplace, goodwill can be identified only with the business as a whole.

If goodwill can be identified only with the business as a whole, how can its amount be determined? One could try to put a dollar value on the factors listed above (exceptional management, desirable location, and so on). But the results would be very subjective, and such subjective valuations would not contribute to the reliability of financial statements. **Therefore, companies record goodwill only when an entire business is purchased. In that case, goodwill is the excess of cost over the fair value of the net assets (assets less liabilities) acquired.**

In recording the purchase of a business, the company debits (increases) the identifiable acquired assets, and credits liabilities at their fair values, credits cash for the purchase price, and records the difference as goodwill. **Goodwill is not amortized** because it is considered to have an indefinite life. Companies report goodwill in the balance sheet under intangible assets.

*I*NTERNATIONAL *I*NSIGHT

Should Companies Write Up Goodwill?

Softbank Corp. is Japan's biggest Internet company. At one time, it boosted the profit margin of its mobile-phone unit from 3.2% to 11.2% through what appeared to some as accounting tricks. What did it do? It wrote down the value of its mobile-phone-unit assets by half. This would normally result in a huge loss. But rather than take a loss, the company wrote up goodwill by the same amount. How did this move increase earnings? The assets were being depreciated over 10 years, but the company amortizes goodwill over 20 years. (Amortization of goodwill was allowed under the accounting standards it followed at that time.) While the new treatment did not break any rules, the company was criticized by investors for not providing sufficient justification or a detailed explanation for the sudden shift in policy.

Source: Andrew Morse and Yukari Iwatani Kane, "Softbank's Accounting Shift Raises Eyebrows," *Wall Street Journal* (August 28, 2007), p. C1.

? Do you think that this treatment would be allowed under U.S. GAAP? (See page 503.)

Research and Development Costs

Helpful Hint

Research and development (R&D) costs are not intangible assets. But because they may lead to patents and copyrights, we discuss them in this section.

Research and development costs are expenditures that may lead to patents, copyrights, new processes, and new products. Many companies spend considerable sums of money on research and development (R&D). For example, in a recent year IBM spent over $5.1 billion on R&D.

Research and development costs present accounting problems. For one thing, it is sometimes difficult to assign the costs to specific projects. Also, there are uncertainties in identifying the extent and timing of future benefits. As a result, companies usually record R&D costs **as an expense when incurred**, whether the research and development is successful or not.

To illustrate, assume that Laser Scanner Company spent $3 million on R&D that resulted in two highly successful patents. It spent $20,000 on legal fees for the patents. The company would add the lawyers' fees to the patent account. The R&D costs, however, cannot be included in the cost of the patent. Instead, the company would record the R&D costs as an expense when incurred.

Many disagree with this accounting approach. They argue that expensing R&D costs leads to understated assets and net income. Others, however, argue that capitalizing these costs will lead to highly speculative assets on the balance sheet. Who is right is difficult to determine.

Do it!

Classification Concepts

Match the statement with the term most directly associated with it.

Copyrights	Depletion
Intangible assets	Franchises
Research and development costs	

1. _____ The allocation of the cost of a natural resource to expense in a rational and systematic manner.

2. _____ Rights, privileges, and competitive advantages that result from the ownership of long-lived assets that do not possess physical substance.

3. _____An exclusive right granted by the federal government to reproduce and sell an artistic or published work.

4. _____A right to sell certain products or services or to use certain trademarks or trade names within a designated geographic area.

5. _____Costs incurred by a company that often lead to patents or new products. These costs must be expensed as incurred.

Solution

1. Depletion
2. Intangible assets
3. Copyrights
4. Franchises
5. Research and development costs

Related exercise material: **BE10-11, BE10-12, E10-11, E10-12, E10-13,** and **Do it!** 10-4.

Statement Presentation and Analysis

Presentation

Usually, companies combine plant assets and natural resources under "Property, plant, and equipment" in the balance sheet. They show intangibles separately. Companies disclose either in the balance sheet or the notes the balances of the major classes of assets, such as land, buildings, and equipment, and accumulated depreciation by major classes or in total. In addition, they should describe the depreciation and amortization methods that were used, as well as disclose the amount of depreciation and amortization expense for the period.

Illustration 10-23 shows a typical financial statement presentation of property, plant, and equipment and intangibles for The Procter & Gamble Company

Study Objective [9]
Indicate how plant assets, natural resources, and intangible assets are reported.

Illustration 10-23
P&G's presentation of property, plant, and equipment, and intangible assets

P&G

The Procter & Gamble Company Balance Sheet (partial) (in millions)		
	June 30	
	2009	**2008**
Property, plant, and equipment		
Buildings	$ 6,724	$ 7,052
Machinery and equipment	29,042	30,145
Land	885	889
	36,651	38,086
Accumulated depreciation	(17,189)	(17,446)
Net property, plant, and equipment	19,462	20,640
Goodwill and other intangible assets		
Goodwill	56,512	59,767
Trademarks and other intangible assets, net	32,606	34,233
Net goodwill and other intangible assets	$89,118	$94,000

(P&G) in its 2009 balance sheet. The notes to P&G's financial statements present greater details about the accounting for its long-term tangible and intangible assets.

Illustration 10-24 shows another comprehensive presentation of property, plant, and equipment, from the balance sheet of Owens-Illinois. The notes to the financial statements of Owens-Illinois identify the major classes of property, plant, and equipment. They also indicate that depreciation and amortization are by the straight-line method, and depletion is by the units-of-activity method.

Illustration 10-24
Owens-Illinois' presentation of property, plant, and equipment, and intangible assets

Owens-Illinois, Inc.
Balance Sheet (partial)
(in millions)

Property, plant, and equipment			
Timberlands, at cost, less accumulated depletion		$ 95.4	
Buildings and equipment, at cost	$2,207.1		
Less: Accumulated depreciation	1,229.0	978.1	
Total property, plant, and equipment			$1,073.5
Intangibles			
Patents			410.0
Total			$1,483.5

Analysis

Using ratios, we can analyze how efficiently a company uses its assets to generate sales. The **asset turnover ratio** analyzes the productivity of a company's assets. It tells us how many dollars of sales a company generates for each dollar invested in assets. This ratio is computed by dividing net sales by average total assets for the period. The formula in Illustration 10-25 shows the computation of the asset turnover ratio for The Procter & Gamble Company. P&G's net sales for 2009 were $79,029 million. Its total ending assets were $134,833 million, and beginning assets were $143,992 million.

Illustration 10-25
Asset turnover formula and computation

$$\text{Net Sales} \div \text{Average Total Assets} = \text{Asset Turnover Ratio}$$

$$\$79,029 \div \frac{\$134,833 + \$143,992}{2} = \textbf{.57 times}$$

Thus, each dollar invested in assets produced $0.57 in sales for P&G. If a company is using its assets efficiently, each dollar of assets will create a high amount of sales. This ratio varies greatly among different industries—from those that are asset intensive (utilities) to those that are not (services).

COMPREHENSIVE

Do it!   1

DuPage Company purchases a factory machine at a cost of $18,000 on January 1, 2012. DuPage expects the machine to have a salvage value of $2,000 at the end of its 4-year useful life.

During its useful life, the machine is expected to be used 160,000 hours. Actual annual hourly use was: 2012, 40,000; 2013, 60,000; 2014, 35,000; and 2015, 25,000.

Instructions

Prepare depreciation schedules for the following methods: (a) straight-line, (b) units-of-activity, and (c) declining-balance using double the straight-line rate.

action plan

✔ Under the straight-line method, apply the depreciation rate to depreciable cost.

✔ Under the units-of-activity method, compute the depreciation cost per unit by dividing depreciable cost by total units of activity.

✔ Under the declining-balance method, apply the depreciation rate to **book value** at the beginning of the year.

Solution to Comprehensive Do it! 1

(a)

Straight-Line Method

| | Computation | | | Annual | End of Year | |
Year	Depreciable Cost*	×	Depreciation Rate	= Depreciation Expense	Accumulated Depreciation	Book Value
2012	$16,000		25%	$4,000	$ 4,000	$14,000**
2013	16,000		25%	4,000	8,000	10,000
2014	16,000		25%	4,000	12,000	6,000
2015	16,000		25%	4,000	16,000	2,000

*$18,000 − $2,000.
**$18,000 − $4,000.

(b)

Units-of-Activity Method

| | Computation | | | Annual | End of Year | |
Year	Units of Activity	×	Depreciation Cost/Unit	= Depreciation Expense	Accumulated Depreciation	Book Value
2012	40,000		$0.10*	$4,000	$ 4,000	$14,000
2013	60,000		0.10	6,000	10,000	8,000
2014	35,000		0.10	3,500	13,500	4,500
2015	25,000		0.10	2,500	16,000	2,000

*($18,000 − $2,000) ÷ 160,000.

(c)

Declining-Balance Method

| | Computation | | | Annual | End of Year | |
Year	Book Value Beginning of Year	×	Depreciation Rate*	= Depreciation Expense	Accumulated Depreciation	Book Value
2012	$18,000		50%	$9,000	$ 9,000	$9,000
2013	9,000		50%	4,500	13,500	4,500
2014	4,500		50%	2,250	15,750	2,250
2015	2,250		50%	250**	16,000	2,000

*¼ × 2.
**Adjusted to $250 because ending book value should not be less than expected salvage value.

The Navigator

COMPREHENSIVE

Do it!   2

On January 1, 2012, Skyline Limousine Co. purchased a limo at an acquisition cost of $28,000. The vehicle has been depreciated by the straight-line method using a 4-year service life and a $4,000 salvage value. The company's fiscal year ends on December 31.

Instructions

Prepare the journal entry or entries to record the disposal of the limousine assuming that it was:

(a) Retired and scrapped with no salvage value on January 1, 2016.

(b) Sold for $5,000 on July 1, 2015.

action plan

✔ At the time of disposal, determine the book value of the asset.

✔ Recognize any gain or loss from disposal of the asset.

✔ Remove the book value of the asset from the records by debiting Accumulated Depreciation for the total depreciation to date of disposal and crediting the asset account for the cost of the asset.

Solution to Comprehensive Do it! 2

(a)	1/1/16	Accumulated Depreciation—Equipment	24,000	
		Loss on Disposal of Plant Assets	4,000	
		Equipment		28,000
		(To record retirement of limousine)		
(b)	7/1/15	Depreciation Expense	3,000	
		Accumulated Depreciation—Equipment		3,000
		(To record depreciation to date of disposal)		
		Cash	5,000	
		Accumulated Depreciation—Equipment	21,000	
		Loss on Disposal of Plant Assets	2,000	
		Equipment		28,000
		(To record sale of limousine)		

✔

The Navigator

Summary of Study Objectives

[1] Describe how the cost principle applies to plant assets. The cost of plant assets includes all expenditures necessary to acquire the asset and make it ready for its intended use. Cost is measured by the cash or cash equivalent price paid.

[2] Explain the concept of depreciation. Depreciation is the allocation of the cost of a plant asset to expense over its useful (service) life in a rational and systematic manner. Depreciation is not a process of valuation, nor is it a process that results in an accumulation of cash.

[3] Compute periodic depreciation using different methods. Three depreciation methods are:

Method	Effect on Annual Depreciation	Formula
Straight-line	Constant amount	Depreciable cost ÷ Useful life (in years)
Units-of-activity	Varying amount	Depreciation cost per unit × Units of activity during the year
Declining-balance	Decreasing amount	Book value at beginning of year × Declining-balance rate

[4] Describe the procedure for revising periodic depreciation. Companies make revisions of periodic depreciation in present and future periods, not retroactively. They determine the new annual depreciation by dividing the depreciable cost at the time of the revision by the remaining useful life.

[5] Distinguish between revenue and capital expenditures, and explain the entries for each. Companies incur revenue expenditures to maintain the operating efficiency and productive life of an asset. They debit these expenditures to Maintenance and Repairs Expense as incurred. Capital expenditures increase the operating efficiency, productive capacity, or expected useful life of the asset. Companies generally debit these expenditures to the plant asset affected.

[6] Explain how to account for the disposal of a plant asset. The accounting for disposal of a plant asset through retirement or sale is as follows.

(a) Eliminate the book value of the plant asset at the date of disposal.

(b) Record cash proceeds, if any.

(c) Account for the difference between the book value and the cash proceeds as a gain or loss on disposal.

[7] Compute periodic depletion of natural resources. Companies compute depletion cost per unit by dividing the total cost of the natural resource minus salvage value by the number of units estimated to be in the resource. They then multiply the depletion cost per unit by the number of units extracted and sold.

[8] Explain the basic issues related to accounting for intangible assets. The process of allocating the cost of an intangible asset is referred to as amortization. The cost of intangible assets with indefinite lives are not amortized. Companies normally use the straight-line method for amortizing intangible assets.

[9] Indicate how plant assets, natural resources, and intangible assets are reported. Companies usually combine plant assets and natural resources under property, plant, and equipment; they show intangibles separately under intangible assets. Either within the balance sheet or in the notes, companies should disclose the balances of the major classes of assets, such as land, buildings, and equipment, and accumulated depreciation by major classes or in total. They also should describe the depreciation and amortization methods used, and should disclose the amount of depreciation and amortization expense for the period. The asset turnover ratio measures the productivity of a company's assets in generating sales.

Glossary

Accelerated-depreciation method   Depreciation method that produces higher depreciation expense in the early years than in the later years. (p. 467).

Additions and improvements   Costs incurred to increase the operating efficiency, productive capacity, or useful life of a plant asset. (p. 470).

Amortization   The allocation of the cost of an intangible asset to expense over its useful life in a systematic and rational manner. (p. 475).

Asset turnover ratio   A measure of how efficiently a company uses its assets to generate sales; calculated as net sales divided by average total assets. (p. 480).

Capital expenditures   Expenditures that increase the company's investment in productive facilities. (p. 470).

Copyrights   Exclusive grant from the federal government that allows the owner to reproduce and sell an artistic or published work. (p. 476).

Declining-balance method   Depreciation method that applies a constant rate to the declining book value of the asset and produces a decreasing annual depreciation expense over the useful life of the asset. (p. 466).

Depletion   The allocation of the cost of a natural resource to expense in a rational and systematic manner over the resource's useful life. (p. 474).

Depreciation   The process of allocating to expense the cost of a plant asset over its useful (service) life in a rational and systematic manner. (p. 462).

Depreciable cost   The cost of a plant asset less its salvage value. (p. 464).

Franchise (license)   A contractual arrangement under which the franchisor grants the franchisee the right to sell certain products, provide specific services, or use certain trademarks or trade names, usually within a designated geographical area. (p. 477).

Going-concern assumption   States that the company will continue in operation for the foreseeable future. (p. 463).

Goodwill   The value of all favorable attributes that relate to a company that is not attributable to any other specific asset. (p. 477).

Intangible assets   Rights, privileges, and competitive advantages that result from the ownership of long-lived assets that do not possess physical substance. (p. 475).

Licenses   Operating rights to use public property, granted to a business by a governmental agency. (p. 477).

Materiality principle   If an item would not make a difference in decision making, a company does not have to follow GAAP in reporting it. (p. 470).

Natural resources   Assets that consist of standing timber and underground deposits of oil, gas, or minerals. (p. 474).

Ordinary repairs   Expenditures to maintain the operating efficiency and productive life of the unit. (p. 470).

Patent   An exclusive right issued by the U.S. Patent Office that enables the recipient to manufacture, sell, or otherwise control an invention for a period of 20 years from the date of the grant. (p. 476).

Plant assets   Tangible resources that are used in the operations of the business and are not intended for sale to customers. (p. 458).

Research and development (R&D) costs   Expenditures that may lead to patents, copyrights, new processes, or new products. (p. 478).

Revenue expenditures   Expenditures that are immediately charged against revenues as an expense. (p. 470).

Salvage value   An estimate of an asset's value at the end of its useful life. (p. 463).

Straight-line method   Depreciation method in which periodic depreciation is the same for each year of the asset's useful life. (p. 464).

Trademark (trade name)   A word, phrase, jingle, or symbol that identifies a particular enterprise or product. (p. 476).

Units-of-activity method   Depreciation method in which useful life is expressed in terms of the total units of production or use expected from an asset. (p. 465).

Useful life   An estimate of the expected productive life, also called service life, of an asset. (p. 463).

APPENDIX10A

Exchange of Plant Assets

Study Objective [10]

Explain how to account for the exchange of plant assets.

Ordinarily, companies record a gain or loss on the exchange of plant assets. The rationale for recognizing a gain or loss is that most exchanges have **commercial substance**. An exchange has commercial substance if the future cash flows change as a result of the exchange.

To illustrate, Ramos Co. exchanges some of its equipment for land held by Brodhead Inc. It is likely that the timing and amount of the cash flows arising from the land will differ significantly from the cash flows arising from the equipment. As a result, both Ramos and Brodhead are in different economic positions. Therefore **the exchange has commercial substance**, and the companies recognize a gain or loss in the exchange. Because most exchanges have commercial substance (even when similar assets are exchanged), we illustrate only this type of situation, for both a loss and a gain.

Loss Treatment

To illustrate an exchange that results in a loss, assume that Roland Company exchanged a set of used trucks plus cash for a new semi-truck. The used trucks have a combined book value of $42,000 (cost $64,000 less $22,000 accumulated depreciation). Roland's purchasing agent, experienced in the second-hand market, indicates that the used trucks have a fair value of $26,000. In addition to the trucks, Roland must pay $17,000 for the semi-truck. Roland computes the cost of the semi-truck as follows.

Illustration 10A-1
Cost of semi-truck

Fair value of used trucks	$26,000
Cash paid	17,000
Cost of semi-truck	$43,000

Roland incurs a loss on disposal of plant assets of $16,000 on this exchange. The reason is that the book value of the used trucks is greater than the fair value of these trucks. The computation is as follows.

Illustration 10A-2
Computation of loss on disposal

Book value of used trucks ($64,000 − $22,000)	$42,000
Fair value of used trucks	26,000
Loss on disposal of plant assets	**$16,000**

In recording an exchange at a loss, three steps are required: (1) Eliminate the book value of the asset given up, (2) record the cost of the asset acquired, and (3) recognize the loss on disposal of plant assets. Roland Company thus records the exchange on the loss as follows.

A	=	L	+	OE
+43,000				
+22,000				
				−16,000 Exp
−64,000				
−17,000				

Cash Flows
−17,000

Equipment (new)	43,000	
Accumulated Depreciation—Equipment	22,000	
Loss on Disposal of Plant Assets	16,000	
Equipment (old)		64,000
Cash		17,000
(To record exchange of used trucks for semi-truck)		

Gain Treatment

To illustrate a gain situation, assume that Mark Express Delivery decides to exchange its old delivery equipment plus cash of $3,000 for new delivery equipment. The book value of the old delivery equipment is $12,000 (cost $40,000 less accumulated depreciation $28,000). The fair value of the old delivery equipment is $19,000.

The cost of the new asset is the fair value of the old asset exchanged plus any cash paid (or other consideration given up). The cost of the new delivery equipment is $22,000, computed as follows.

Fair value of old delivery equipment	$19,000
Cash paid	3,000
Cost of new delivery equipment	**$22,000**

Illustration 10A-3
Cost of new delivery equipment

A gain results when the fair value of the old delivery equipment is greater than its book value. For Mark Express, there is a gain of $7,000 on disposal of plant assets, computed as follows.

Fair value of old delivery equipment	$19,000
Book value of old delivery equipment ($40,000 − $28,000)	12,000
Gain on disposal of plant assets	**$ 7,000**

Illustration 10A-4
Computation of gain on disposal

Mark Express Delivery records the exchange as follows.

Equipment (new)	22,000	
Accumulated Depreciation—Equipment (old)	28,000	
Equipment (old)		40,000
Gain on Disposal of Plant Assets		7,000
Cash		3,000
(To record exchange of old delivery equipment for new delivery equipment)		

A = L + OE
+22,000
+28,000
−40,000
           +7,000 Rev
−3,000

Cash Flows
−3,000

In recording an exchange at a gain, the following three steps are involved: (1) Eliminate the book value of the asset given up, (2) record the cost of the asset acquired, and (3) recognize the gain on disposal of plant assets. Accounting for exchanges of plant assets becomes more complex if the transaction does not have commercial substance. This issue is discussed in more advanced accounting classes.

Summary of Study Objective for Appendix 10A

[10] Explain how to account for the exchange of plant assets. Ordinarily, companies record a gain or loss on the exchange of plant assets. The rationale for recognizing a gain or loss is that most exchanges have commercial substance. An exchange has commercial substance if the future cash flows change as a result of the exchange.

Note: All **asterisked** Questions, Exercises, and Problems relate to material in the appendix to the chapter.

Self-Test Questions

Answers are on page 503.

(SO 1) **1.** Erin Danielle Company purchased equipment and incurred the following costs.

Cash price	$24,000
Sales taxes	1,200
Insurance during transit	200
Installation and testing	400
Total costs	$25,800

What amount should be recorded as the cost of the equipment?
   a. $24,000.   **c.** $25,400.
   b. $25,200.   **d.** $25,800.

(SO 2) **2.** Depreciation is a process of:
   a. valuation.
   b. cost allocation.
   c. cash accumulation.
   d. appraisal.

(SO 3) **3.** Micah Bartlett Company purchased equipment on January 1, 2011, at a total invoice cost of $400,000. The equipment has an estimated salvage value of $10,000 and an estimated useful life of 5 years. The amount of accumulated depreciation at December 31, 2012, if the straight-line method of depreciation is used, is:
   a. $80,000.   **c.** $78,000.
   b. $160,000.   **d.** $156,000.

(SO 3) **4.** Ann Torbert purchased a truck for $11,000 on January 1, 2011. The truck will have an estimated salvage value of $1,000 at the end of 5 years. Using the units-of-activity method, the balance in accumulated depreciation at December 31, 2012, can be computed by the following formula:
   a. ($11,000 ÷ Total estimated activity) × Units of activity for 2012.
   b. ($10,000 ÷ Total estimated activity) × Units of activity for 2012.
   c. ($11,000 ÷ Total estimated activity) × Units of activity for 2011 and 2012.
   d. ($10,000 ÷ Total estimated activity) × Units of activity for 2011 and 2012.

(SO 3) **5.** Jefferson Company purchased a piece of equipment on January 1, 2012. The equipment cost $60,000 and has an estimated life of 8 years and a salvage value of $8,000. What was the depreciation expense for the asset for 2013 under the double-declining-balance method?
   a. $6,500.   **c.** $15,000.
   b. $11,250.   **d.** $6,562.

6. When there is a change in estimated depreciation: (SO 4)
   a. previous depreciation should be corrected.
   b. current and future years' depreciation should be revised.
   c. only future years' depreciation should be revised.
   d. None of the above.

7. Able Towing Company purchased a tow truck for $60,000   (SO 4)
on January 1, 2010. It was originally depreciated on a straight-line basis over 10 years with an assumed salvage value of $12,000. On December 31, 2012, before adjusting entries had been made, the company decided to change the remaining estimated life to 4 years (including 2012) and the salvage value to $2,000. What was the depreciation expense for 2012?
   a. $6,000.   **c.** $15,000.
   b. $4,800.   **d.** $12,100.

8. Additions to plant assets are: (SO 5)
   a. revenue expenditures.
   b. debited to the Maintenance and Repairs Expense account.
   c. debited to the Purchases account.
   d. capital expenditures.

9. Bennie Razor Company has decided to sell one of its old   (SO 6)
manufacturing machines on June 30, 2012. The machine was purchased for $80,000 on January 1, 2008, and was depreciated on a straight-line basis for 10 years assuming no salvage value. If the machine was sold for $26,000, what was the amount of the gain or loss recorded at the time of the sale?
   a. $18,000.   **c.** $22,000.
   b. $54,000.   **d.** $46,000.

10. Maggie Sharrer Company expects to extract 20 million   (SO 7)
tons of coal from a mine that cost $12 million. If no salvage value is expected and 2 million tons are mined and sold in the first year, the entry to record depletion will include a:
   a. debit to Accumulated Depletion of $2,000,000.
   b. credit to Depletion Expense of $1,200,000.
   c. debit to Depletion Expense of $1,200,000.
   d. credit to Accumulated Depletion of $2,000,000.

11. Which of the following statements is *false*?   (SO 8)
   a. If an intangible asset has a finite life, it should be amortized.
   b. The amortization period of an intangible asset can exceed 20 years.
   c. Goodwill is recorded only when a business is purchased.
   d. Research and development costs are expensed when incurred, except when the research and development expenditures result in a successful patent.

(SO 8) **12.** Martha Beyerlein Company incurred $150,000 of research and development costs in its laboratory to develop a patent granted on January 2, 2012. On July 31, 2012, Beyerlein paid $35,000 for legal fees in a successful defense of the patent. The total amount debited to Patents through July 31, 2012, should be:
    a. $150,000.
    b. $35,000.
    c. $185,000.
    d. $170,000.

(SO 9) **13.** Indicate which of the following statements is *true*.
    a. Since intangible assets lack physical substance, they need be disclosed only in the notes to the financial statements.
    b. Goodwill should be reported as a contra-account in the owner's equity section.
    c. Totals of major classes of assets can be shown in the balance sheet, with asset details disclosed in the notes to the financial statements.
    d. Intangible assets are typically combined with plant assets and natural resources and shown in the property, plant, and equipment section.

(SO 9) **14.** Lake Coffee Company reported net sales of $180,000, net income of $54,000, beginning total assets of $200,000, and ending total assets of $300,000. What was the company's asset turnover ratio?
    a. 0.90
    b. 0.20
    c. 0.72
    d. 1.39

*15. Schopenhauer Company exchanged an old machine, with (SO 10)
a book value of $39,000 and a fair value of $35,000, and paid $10,000 cash for a similar new machine. The transaction has commercial substance. At what amount should the machine acquired in the exchange be recorded on Schopenhauer's books?
    a. $45,000.
    b. $46,000.
    c. $49,000.
    d. $50,000.

*16. In exchanges of assets in which the exchange has commer- (SO 10)
cial substance:
    a. neither gains nor losses are recognized immediately.
    b. gains, but not losses, are recognized immediately.
    c. losses, but not gains, are recognized immediately.
    d. both gains and losses are recognized immediately.

Go to the book's companion website, **www.wiley.com/college/weygandt**, for additional Self-Test Questions.

Questions

1. Tim Hoover is uncertain about the applicability of the cost principle to plant assets. Explain the principle to Tim.

2. What are some examples of land improvements?

3. Dain Company acquires the land and building owned by Corrs Company. What types of costs may be incurred to make the asset ready for its intended use if Dain Company wants to use (a) only the land, and (b) both the land and the building?

4. In a recent newspaper release, the president of Keene Company asserted that something has to be done about depreciation. The president said, "Depreciation does not come close to accumulating the cash needed to replace the asset at the end of its useful life." What is your response to the president?

5. Robert is studying for the next accounting examination. He asks your help on two questions: (a) What is salvage value? (b) Is salvage value used in determining periodic depreciation under each depreciation method? Answer Robert's questions.

6. Contrast the straight-line method and the units-of-activity method as to (a) useful life, and (b) the pattern of periodic depreciation over useful life.

7. Contrast the effects of the three depreciation methods on annual depreciation expense.

8. In the fourth year of an asset's 5-year useful life, the company decides that the asset will have a 6-year service life. How should the revision of depreciation be recorded? Why?

9. Distinguish between revenue expenditures and capital expenditures during useful life.

10. How is a gain or loss on the sale of a plant asset computed?

11. Mendez Corporation owns a machine that is fully depreciated but is still being used. How should Mendez account for this asset and report it in the financial statements?

12. What are natural resources, and what are their distinguishing characteristics?

13. Explain what depletion is and how it is computed.

14. What are the similarities and differences between the terms depreciation, depletion, and amortization?

15. Pendergrass Company hires an accounting intern who says that intangible assets should always be amortized over their legal lives. Is the intern correct? Explain.

16. Goodwill has been defined as the value of all favorable attributes that relate to a business. What types of attributes could result in goodwill?

17. Kenny Sain, a business major, is working on a case problem for one of his classes. In the case problem, the company needs to raise cash to market a new product it developed. Joe Morris, an engineering major, takes one look at the company's balance sheet and says, "This company has an awful lot of goodwill. Why don't you recommend that they sell some of it to raise cash?" How should Kenny respond to Joe?

18. Under what conditions is goodwill recorded?

19. Often research and development costs provide companies with benefits that last a number of years. (For example, these costs can lead to the development of a patent that will increase the company's income for many years.) However, generally accepted accounting principles require that such costs be recorded as an expense when incurred. Why?

20. McDonald's Corporation reports total average assets of $28.9 billion and net sales of $20.5 billion. What is the company's asset turnover ratio?

21. Resco Corporation and Yapan Corporation operate in the same industry. Resco uses the straight-line method to account for depreciation; Yapan uses an accelerated method. Explain what complications might arise in trying to compare the results of these two companies.

22. Lopez Corporation uses straight-line depreciation for financial reporting purposes but an accelerated method for tax purposes. Is it acceptable to use different methods for the two purposes? What is Lopez's motivation for doing this?

23. You are comparing two companies in the same industry. You have determined that May Corp. depreciates its plant assets over a 40-year life, whereas Won Corp. depreciates its plant assets over a 20-year life. Discuss the implications this has for comparing the results of the two companies.

24. Wade Company is doing significant work to revitalize its warehouses. It is not sure whether it should capitalize these costs or expense them. What are the implications for current-year net income and future net income of expensing versus capitalizing these costs?

25. **PEPSICO** What classifications and amounts are shown in PepsiCo's Note 4 to explain its total property, plant, and equipment (net) of $12,671 million?

26. When assets are exchanged in a transaction involving commercial substance, how is the gain or loss on disposal of plant assets computed?

*27. Tatum Refrigeration Company trades in an old machine on a new model when the fair value of the old machine is greater than its book value. The transaction has commercial substance. Should Tatum recognize a gain on disposal of plant assets? If the fair value of the old machine is less than its book value, should Tatum recognize a loss on disposal of plant assets?

Brief Exercises

Determine the cost of land.
(SO 1)

BE10-1 The following expenditures were incurred by Krunk Company in purchasing land: cash price $70,000, accrued taxes $3,000, attorneys' fees $2,500, real estate broker's commission $2,000, and clearing and grading $3,500. What is the cost of the land?

Determine the cost of a truck.
(SO 1)

BE10-2 Mick Ferguson Company incurs the following expenditures in purchasing a truck: cash price $30,000, accident insurance $2,000, sales taxes $1,500, motor vehicle license $100, and painting and lettering $400. What is the cost of the truck?

Compute straight-line depreciation.
(SO 3)

BE10-3 Tomorry Company acquires a delivery truck at a cost of $42,000. The truck is expected to have a salvage value of $6,000 at the end of its 4-year useful life. Compute annual depreciation for the first and second years using the straight-line method.

Compute depreciation and evaluate treatment.
(SO 3)

BE10-4 String Dance Company purchased land and a building on January 1, 2012. Management's best estimate of the value of the land was $100,000 and of the building $200,000. But management told the accounting department to record the land at $220,000 and the building at $80,000. The building is being depreciated on a straight-line basis over 20 years with no salvage value. Why do you suppose management requested this accounting treatment? Is it ethical?

Compute declining-balance depreciation.
(SO 3)

BE10-5 Depreciation information for Tomorry Company is given in BE10-3. Assuming the declining-balance depreciation rate is double the straight-line rate, compute annual depreciation for the first and second years under the declining-balance method.

Compute depreciation using the units-of-activity method.
(SO 3)

BE10-6 Koman Taxi Service uses the units-of-activity method in computing depreciation on its taxicabs. Each cab is expected to be driven 150,000 miles. Taxi no. 10 cost $33,500 and is expected to have a salvage value of $500. Taxi no. 10 is driven 30,000 miles in year 1 and 20,000 miles in year 2. Compute the depreciation for each year.

Compute revised depreciation.
(SO 4)

BE10-7 On January 1, 2012, the Dancing Gorillas Company ledger shows Equipment $29,000 and Accumulated Depreciation—Equipment $9,000. The depreciation resulted from using the straight-line method with a useful life of 10 years and salvage value of $2,000. On this date, the company concludes that the equipment has a remaining useful life of only 4 years with the same salvage value. Compute the revised annual depreciation.

Prepare entries for delivery truck costs.
(SO 5)

BE10-8 Euro Guy Company had the following two transactions related to its delivery truck.
1. Paid $45 for an oil change.
2. Paid $400 to install special gear unit, which increases the operating efficiency of the truck.

Prepare Euro Guy's journal entries to record these two transactions.

Prepare entries for disposal by retirement.
(SO 6)

BE10-9 Prepare journal entries to record the following.
(a) Twitter Tracker Company retires its delivery equipment, which cost $41,000. Accumulated depreciation is also $41,000 on this delivery equipment. No salvage value is received.
(b) Assume the same information as (a), except that accumulated depreciation is $39,000, instead of $41,000, on the delivery equipment.

BE10-10 Wing Pang Company sells equipment on September 30, 2012, for $20,000 cash. The equipment originally cost $72,000 and as of January 1, 2012, had accumulated depreciation of $42,000. Depreciation for the first 9 months of 2012 is $5,250. Prepare the journal entries to (a) update depreciation to September 30, 2012, and (b) record the sale of the equipment.

Prepare entries for disposal by sale.
(SO 6)

BE10-11 Deon Cole Mining Co. purchased for $7 million a mine that is estimated to have 35 million tons of ore and no salvage value. In the first year, 6 million tons of ore are extracted and sold.

(a) Prepare the journal entry to record depletion expense for the first year.
(b) Show how this mine is reported on the balance sheet at the end of the first year.

Prepare depletion expense entry and balance sheet presentation for natural resources.
(SO 7)

BE10-12 Pevensie Company purchases a patent for $120,000 on January 2, 2012. Its estimated useful life is 10 years.

(a) Prepare the journal entry to record amortization expense for the first year.
(b) Show how this patent is reported on the balance sheet at the end of the first year.

Prepare amortization expense entry and balance sheet presentation for intangibles.
(SO 8)

BE10-13 Information related to plant assets, natural resources, and intangibles at the end of 2012 for Lucy Company is as follows: buildings $1,100,000; accumulated depreciation—buildings $650,000; goodwill $410,000; coal mine $500,000; accumulated depletion—coal mine $108,000. Prepare a partial balance sheet of Lucy Company for these items.

Classify long-lived assets on balance sheet.
(SO 9)

BE10-14 In its 2009 annual report, Target reported beginning total assets of $44.1 billion; ending total assets of $44.5 billion; and net sales of $63.4 billion. Compute Target's asset turnover ratio.

Analyze long-lived assets.
(SO 9)

*BE10-15 Edmund Company exchanges old delivery equipment for new delivery equipment. The book value of the old delivery equipment is $31,000 (cost $61,000 less accumulated depreciation $30,000). Its fair value is $19,000, and cash of $5,000 is paid. Prepare the entry to record the exchange, assuming the transaction has commercial substance.

Prepare entry for disposal by exchange.
(SO 10)

*BE10-16 Assume the same information as BE10-15, except that the fair value of the old delivery equipment is $38,000. Prepare the entry to record the exchange.

Prepare entry for disposal by exchange.
(SO 10)

Do it! Review

Do it! 10-1 Henley Company purchased a delivery truck. The total cash payment was $27,900, including the following items.

Explain accounting for cost of plant assets.
(SO 1)

Negotiated purchase price	$24,000
Installation of special shelving	1,100
Painting and lettering	900
Motor vehicle license	100
Annual insurance policy	500
Sales tax	1,300
Total paid	$27,900

Explain how each of these costs would be accounted for.

Do it! 10-2 On January 1, 2012, Skandar Country Club purchased a new riding mower for $15,000. The mower is expected to have an 8-year life with a $1,000 salvage value. What journal entry would Skandar make at December 31, 2012, if it uses straight-line depreciation?

Calculate depreciation expense and make journal entry.
(SO 2)

Do it! 10-3 Whistler Corporation purchased a piece of equipment for $50,000. It estimated an 8-year life and $2,000 salvage value. At the end of year four (before the depreciation adjustment), it estimated the new total life to be 10 years and the new salvage value to be $4,000. Compute the revised depreciation.

Calculated revised depreciation
(SO 4)

Do it! 10-4 Keynes Manufacturing has old equipment that cost $50,000. The equipment has accumulated depreciation of $28,000 and a fair value of $26,000. Keynes has decided to sell the equipment.

(a) What entry would Keynes make to record the sale of the equipment for $26,000 cash?
(b) What entry would Keynes make to record the sale of the equipment for $15,000 cash?

Make journal entries to record plant asset disposal.
(SO 6)

Match intangibles classifications concepts.

(SO 7, 8)

Do it! 10-5   Match the statement with the term most directly associated with it.

Goodwill   Amortization
Intangible assets   Franchises
Research and development costs

1. _____ Rights, privileges, and competitive advantages that result from the ownership of long-lived assets that do not possess physical substance.
2. _____ The allocation of the cost of an intangible asset to expense in a rational and systematic manner.
3. _____ A right to sell certain products or services, or use certain trademarks or trade names within a designated geographic area.
4. _____ Costs incurred by a company that often lead to patents or new products. These costs must be expensed as incurred.
5. _____ The excess of the cost of a company over the fair value of the net assets acquired.

Exercises

Determine cost of plant acquisitions.

(SO 1)

E10-1   The following expenditures relating to plant assets were made by Georgie Company during the first 2 months of 2012.

1. Paid $5,000 of accrued taxes at time plant site was acquired.
2. Paid $200 insurance to cover possible accident loss on new factory machinery while the machinery was in transit.
3. Paid $850 sales taxes on new delivery truck.
4. Paid $17,500 for parking lots and driveways on new plant site.
5. Paid $250 to have company name and advertising slogan painted on new delivery truck.
6. Paid $8,000 for installation of new factory machinery.
7. Paid $900 for one-year accident insurance policy on new delivery truck.
8. Paid $75 motor vehicle license fee on the new truck.

Instructions
(a) ◖▬▬▬▬▷ Explain the application of the cost principle in determining the acquisition cost of plant assets.
(b) List the numbers of the foregoing transactions, and opposite each indicate the account title to which each expenditure should be debited.

Determine property, plant, and equipment costs.

(SO 1)

E10-2   Moseley Company incurred the following costs.

1. Sales tax on factory machinery purchased	$ 5,000
2. Painting of and lettering on truck immediately upon purchase	700
3. Installation and testing of factory machinery	2,000
4. Real estate broker's commission on land purchased	3,500
5. Insurance premium paid for first year's insurance on new truck	880
6. Cost of landscaping on property purchased	7,200
7. Cost of paving parking lot for new building constructed	17,900
8. Cost of clearing, draining, and filling land	13,300
9. Architect's fees on self-constructed building	10,000

Instructions
Indicate to which account Moseley would debit each of the costs.

Determine acquisition costs of land.

(SO 1)

E10-3   On March 1, 2012, Popplewell Company acquired real estate on which it planned to construct a small office building. The company paid $80,000 in cash. An old warehouse on the property was razed at a cost of $8,600; the salvaged materials were sold for $1,700. Additional expenditures before construction began included $1,100 attorney's fee for work concerning the land purchase, $5,000 real estate broker's fee, $7,800 architect's fee, and $14,000 to put in driveways and a parking lot.

Instructions
(a) Determine the amount to be reported as the cost of the land.
(b) For each cost not used in part (a), indicate the account to be debited.

E10-4 Jim McAvoy has prepared the following list of statements about depreciation.

1. Depreciation is a process of asset valuation, not cost allocation.
2. Depreciation provides for the proper matching of expenses with revenues.
3. The book value of a plant asset should approximate its fair value.
4. Depreciation applies to three classes of plant assets: land, buildings, and equipment.
5. Depreciation does not apply to a building because its usefulness and revenue-producing ability generally remain intact over time.
6. The revenue-producing ability of a depreciable asset will decline due to wear and tear and to obsolescence.
7. Recognizing depreciation on an asset results in an accumulation of cash for replacement of the asset.
8. The balance in accumulated depreciation represents the total cost that has been charged to expense.
9. Depreciation expense and accumulated depreciation are reported on the income statement.
10. Four factors affect the computation of depreciation: cost, useful life, salvage value, and residual value.

Understand depreciation concepts.
(SO 2)

Instructions

Identify each statement as true or false. If false, indicate how to correct the statement.

E10-5 Tilda Bus Lines uses the units-of-activity method in depreciating its buses. One bus was purchased on January 1, 2012, at a cost of $168,000. Over its 4-year useful life, the bus is expected to be driven 100,000 miles. Salvage value is expected to be $8,000.

Compute depreciation under units-of-activity method.
(SO 3)

Instructions

(a) Compute the depreciation cost per unit.
(b) Prepare a depreciation schedule assuming actual mileage was: 2012, 26,000; 2013, 32,000; 2014, 25,000; and 2015, 17,000.

E10-6 Swinton Company purchased a new machine on October 1, 2012, at a cost of $120,000. The company estimated that the machine will have a salvage value of $12,000. The machine is expected to be used for 10,000 working hours during its 5-year life.

Determine depreciation for partial periods.
(SO 3)

Instructions

Compute the depreciation expense under the following methods for the year indicated.

(a) Straight-line for 2012.
(b) Units-of-activity for 2012, assuming machine usage was 1,700 hours.
(c) Declining-balance using double the straight-line rate for 2012 and 2013.

E10-7 Tumnus Company purchased a delivery truck for $30,000 on January 1, 2012. The truck has an expected salvage value of $2,000, and is expected to be driven 100,000 miles over its estimated useful life of 8 years. Actual miles driven were 15,000 in 2012 and 12,000 in 2013.

Compute depreciation using different methods.
(SO 3)

Instructions

(a) Compute depreciation expense for 2012 and 2013 using (1) the straight-line method, (2) the units-of-activity method, and (3) the double-declining-balance method.
(b) Assume that Tumnus uses the straight-line method.
    (1) Prepare the journal entry to record 2012 depreciation.
    (2) Show how the truck would be reported in the December 31, 2012, balance sheet.

E10-8 Kiran Shah, the new controller of Ginarrbrik Company, has reviewed the expected useful lives and salvage values of selected depreciable assets at the beginning of 2012. His findings are as follows.

Compute revised annual depreciation.
(SO 4)

Type of Asset	Date Acquired	Cost	Accumulated Depreciation 1/1/12	Useful Life in Years		Salvage Value	
				Old	Proposed	Old	Proposed
Building	1/1/06	$800,000	$114,000	40	50	$40,000	$37,000
Warehouse	1/1/07	100,000	19,000	25	20	5,000	3,600

All assets are depreciated by the straight-line method. Ginarrbrik Company uses a calendar year in preparing annual financial statements. After discussion, management has agreed to accept Kiran's proposed changes.

Instructions

(a) Compute the revised annual depreciation on each asset in 2012. (Show computations.)

(b) Prepare the entry (or entries) to record depreciation on the building in 2012.

Journalize entries for disposal of plant assets.
(SO 6)

E10-9 Presented below are selected transactions at Kirke Company for 2012.

Jan. 1   Retired a piece of machinery that was purchased on January 1, 2002. The machine cost $62,000 on that date. It had a useful life of 10 years with no salvage value.

June 30   Sold a computer that was purchased on January 1, 2009. The computer cost $40,000. It had a useful life of 5 years with no salvage value. The computer was sold for $14,000.

Dec. 31   Discarded a delivery truck that was purchased on January 1, 2008. The truck cost $39,000. It was depreciated based on a 6-year useful life with a $3,000 salvage value.

Instructions

Journalize all entries required on the above dates, including entries to update depreciation, where applicable, on assets disposed of. Kirke Company uses straight-line depreciation. (Assume depreciation is up to date as of December 31, 2011.)

Journalize entries for disposal of equipment.
(SO 6)

E10-10 Cosmo Company owns equipment that cost $50,000 when purchased on January 1, 2009. It has been depreciated using the straight-line method based on estimated salvage value of $5,000 and an estimated useful life of 5 years.

Instructions

Prepare Cosmo Company's journal entries to record the sale of the equipment in these four independent situations.

(a) Sold for $28,000 on January 1, 2012.

(b) Sold for $28,000 on May 1, 2012.

(c) Sold for $11,000 on January 1, 2012.

(d) Sold for $11,000 on October 1, 2012.

Journalize entries for natural resources depletion.
(SO 7)

E10-11 On July 1, 2012, Macready Inc. invested $720,000 in a mine estimated to have 800,000 tons of ore of uniform grade. During the last 6 months of 2012, 100,000 tons of ore were mined and sold.

Instructions

(a) Prepare the journal entry to record depletion expense.

(b) Assume that the 100,000 tons of ore were mined, but only 80,000 units were sold. How are the costs applicable to the 20,000 unsold units reported?

Prepare adjusting entries for amortization.
(SO 8)

E10-12 The following are selected 2012 transactions of Oveius Corporation.

Jan. 1   Purchased a small company and recorded goodwill of $150,000. Its useful life is indefinite.

May 1   Purchased for $90,000 a patent with an estimated useful life of 5 years and a legal life of 20 years.

Instructions

Prepare necessary adjusting entries at December 31 to record amortization required by the events above.

Prepare entries to set up appropriate accounts for different intangibles; amortize intangible assets.
(SO 8)

E10-13 Kake Company, organized in 2012, has the following transactions related to intangible assets.

1/2/12	Purchased patent (7-year life)	$560,000
4/1/12	Goodwill purchased (indefinite life)	360,000
7/1/12	10-year franchise; expiration date 7/1/2022	440,000
9/1/12	Research and development costs	185,000

Instructions

Prepare the necessary entries to record these intangibles. All costs incurred were for cash. Make the adjusting entries as of December 31, 2012, recording any necessary amortization and reflecting all balances accurately as of that date.

Calculate asset turnover ratio.
(SO 9)

E10-14 During 2012 Otmin Corporation reported net sales of $4,900,000 and net income of $1,500,000. Its balance sheet reported average total assets of $1,400,000.

Instructions

Calculate the asset turnover ratio.

*E10-15 Presented below are two independent transactions. Both transactions have commercial substance.

Journalize entries for exchanges.
(SO 10)

1. Rangi Co. exchanged old trucks (cost $64,000 less $22,000 accumulated depreciation) plus cash of $17,000 for new trucks. The old trucks had a fair value of $36,000.
2. Dryad Inc. trades its used machine (cost $12,000 less $4,000 accumulated depreciation) for a new machine. In addition to exchanging the old machine (which had a fair value of $9,000), Dryad also paid cash of $3,000.

Instructions
(a) Prepare the entry to record the exchange of assets by Rangi Co.
(b) Prepare the entry to record the exchange of assets by Dryad Inc.

*E10-16 Jaxin's Delivery Company and Felicity's Express Delivery exchanged delivery trucks on January 1, 2012. Jaxin's truck cost $22,000. It has accumulated depreciation of $15,000 and a fair value of $4,000. Felicity's truck cost $10,000. It has accumulated depreciation of $8,000 and a fair value of $4,000. The transaction has commercial substance.

Journalize entries for the exchange of plant assets.
(SO 10)

Instructions
(a) Journalize the exchange for Jaxin's Delivery Company.
(b) Journalize the exchange for Felicity's Express Delivery.

Exercises: Set B

Visit the book's companion website, at **www.wiley.com/college/weygandt**, and choose the Student Companion site to access Exercise Set B.

Problems: Set A

P10-1A Rumblebuffin Company was organized on January 1. During the first year of operations, the following plant asset expenditures and receipts were recorded in random order.

Determine acquisition costs of land and building.
(SO 1)

Debits

1. Cost of filling and grading the land	$ 4,000
2. Full payment to building contractor	700,000
3. Real estate taxes on land paid for the current year	5,000
4. Cost of real estate purchased as a plant site (land $100,000 and building $45,000)	145,000
5. Excavation costs for new building	35,000
6. Architect's fees on building plans	10,000
7. Accrued real estate taxes paid at time of purchase of real estate	2,000
8. Cost of parking lots and driveways	14,000
9. Cost of demolishing building to make land suitable for construction of new building	15,000
	$930,000

Credit

10. Proceeds from salvage of demolished building	$ 3,500

Instructions
Analyze the foregoing transactions using the following column headings. Insert the number of each transaction in the Item space, and insert the amounts in the appropriate columns. For amounts entered in the Other Accounts column, also indicate the account titles.

Item	Land	Buildings	Other Accounts

Totals
Land $162,500
Buildings $745,000

P10-2A In recent years, Sonya Transportation purchased three used buses. Because of frequent turnover in the accounting department, a different accountant selected the depreciation method for each bus, and various methods were selected. Information concerning the buses is summarized on page 494.

Compute depreciation under different methods.
(SO 3)

Bus	Acquired	Cost	Salvage Value	Useful Life in Years	Depreciation Method
1	1/1/10	$ 96,000	$ 6,000	5	Straight-line
2	1/1/10	120,000	10,000	4	Declining-balance
3	1/1/11	80,000	8,000	5	Units-of-activity

For the declining-balance method, the company uses the double-declining rate. For the units-of-activity method, total miles are expected to be 120,000. Actual miles of use in the first 3 years were: 2011, 24,000; 2012, 34,000; and 2013, 30,000.

Instructions

(a) Bus 2, 2011, $90,000

(a) Compute the amount of accumulated depreciation on each bus at December 31, 2012.

(b) If bus no. 2 was purchased on April 1 instead of January 1, what is the depreciation expense for this bus in (1) 2010 and (2) 2011?

Compute depreciation under different methods.

(SO 3)

P10-3A On January 1, 2012, Tiggy Company purchased the following two machines for use in its production process.

Machine A: The cash price of this machine was $38,000. Related expenditures included: sales tax $1,700, shipping costs $150, insurance during shipping $80, installation and testing costs $70, and $100 of oil and lubricants to be used with the machinery during its first year of operations. Tiggy estimates that the useful life of the machine is 5 years with a $5,000 salvage value remaining at the end of that time period. Assume that the straight-line method of depreciation is used.

Machine B: The recorded cost of this machine was $160,000. Tiggy estimates that the useful life of the machine is 4 years with a $10,000 salvage value remaining at the end of that time period.

Instructions

(a) Prepare the following for Machine A.

(1) The journal entry to record its purchase on January 1, 2012.

(2) The journal entry to record annual depreciation at December 31, 2012.

(b) Calculate the amount of depreciation expense that Tiggy should record for machine B each year of its useful life under the following assumptions.

(1) Tiggy uses the straight-line method of depreciation.

(b) (2) 2012 DDB depreciation $80,000

(2) Tiggy uses the declining-balance method. The rate used is twice the straight-line rate.

(3) Tiggy uses the units-of-activity method and estimates that the useful life of the machine is 125,000 units. Actual usage is as follows: 2012, 45,000 units; 2013, 35,000 units; 2014, 25,000 units; 2015, 20,000 units.

(c) Which method used to calculate depreciation on machine B reports the highest amount of depreciation expense in year 1 (2012)? The highest amount in year 4 (2015)? The highest total amount over the 4-year period?

Calculate revisions to depreciation expense.

(SO 3, 4)

P10-4A At the beginning of 2010, Sarofim Company acquired equipment costing $90,000. It was estimated that this equipment would have a useful life of 6 years and a residual value of $9,000 at that time. The straight-line method of depreciation was considered the most appropriate to use with this type of equipment. Depreciation is to be recorded at the end of each year.

During 2012 (the third year of the equipment's life), the company's engineers reconsidered their expectations, and estimated that the equipment's useful life would probably be 7 years (in total) instead of 6 years. The estimated residual value was not changed at that time. However, during 2015 the estimated residual value was reduced to $5,000.

Instructions

Indicate how much depreciation expense should be recorded each year for this equipment, by completing the following table.

Year	Depreciation Expense	Accumulated Depreciation
2010		
2011		
2012		
2013		
2014		
2015		
2016		

2016 depreciation expense, $12,800

P10-5A At December 31, 2012, Alina Company reported the following as plant assets.

Journalize a series of equipment transactions related to purchase, sale, retirement, and depreciation.

(SO 3, 6, 9)

Land		$ 4,000,000
Buildings	$28,500,000	
Less: Accumulated depreciation—buildings	12,100,000	16,400,000
Equipment	48,000,000	
Less: Accumulated depreciation—equipment	5,000,000	43,000,000
Total plant assets		$63,400,000

During 2013, the following selected cash transactions occurred.

April	1	Purchased land for $2,130,000.
May	1	Sold equipment that cost $780,000 when purchased on January 1, 2009. The equipment was sold for $450,000.
June	1	Sold land purchased on June 1, 2003 for $1,500,000. The land cost $400,000.
July	1	Purchased equipment for $2,000,000.
Dec. 31		Retired equipment that cost $500,000 when purchased on December 31, 2003. No salvage value was received.

Instructions

(a) Journalize the above transactions. The company uses straight-line depreciation for buildings and equipment. The buildings are estimated to have a 50-year life and no salvage value. The equipment is estimated to have a 10-year useful life and no salvage value. Update depreciation on assets disposed of at the time of sale or retirement.

(b) Record adjusting entries for depreciation for 2013.

(c) Prepare the plant assets section of Alina's balance sheet at December 31, 2013.

(b) Depreciation Expense—
Buildings $570,000;
Equipment $4,772,000
(c) Total plant assets
$61,270,000

P10-6A Faun Co. has equipment that cost $75,000 and that has been depreciated $50,000. Record the disposal under the following assumptions.

Record disposals.

(SO 6)

(a) It was scrapped as having no value.

(b) It was sold for $21,000.

(c) It was sold for $31,000.

P10-7A The intangible assets section of Centaur Company at December 31, 2012, is presented below.

Prepare entries to record transactions related to acquisition and amortization of intangibles; prepare the intangible assets section.

(SO 8, 9)

Patents ($70,000 cost less $7,000 amortization)	$63,000
Franchises ($48,000 cost less $19,200 amortization)	28,800
Total	$91,800

The patent was acquired in January 2012 and has a useful life of 10 years. The franchise was acquired in January 2009 and also has a useful life of 10 years. The following cash transactions may have affected intangible assets during 2013.

Jan. 2	Paid $45,000 legal costs to successfully defend the patent against infringement by another company.
Jan.–June	Developed a new product, incurring $140,000 in research and development costs. A patent was granted for the product on July 1. Its useful life is equal to its legal life.
Sept. 1	Paid $50,000 to an extremely large defensive lineman to appear in commercials advertising the company's products. The commercials will air in September and October.
Oct. 1	Acquired a franchise for $100,000. The franchise has a useful life of 50 years.

Instructions

(a) Prepare journal entries to record the transactions above.

(b) Prepare journal entries to record the 2013 amortization expense.

(c) Prepare the intangible assets section of the balance sheet at December 31, 2013.

(b) Amortization Expense
(patents) $12,000
Amortization Expense
(franchises) $5,300
(c) Total intangible assets
$219,500

P10-8A Due to rapid turnover in the accounting department, a number of transactions involving intangible assets were improperly recorded by the Satyr Company in 2012.

Prepare entries to correct errors made in recording and amortizing intangible assets.

(SO 8)

1. Satyr developed a new manufacturing process, incurring research and development costs of $136,000. The company also purchased a patent for $60,000. In early January, Satyr capitalized $196,000 as the cost of the patents. Patent amortization expense of $9,800 was recorded based on a 20-year useful life.

2. On July 1, 2012, Satyr purchased a small company and as a result acquired goodwill of $92,000. Satyr recorded a half-year's amortization in 2012, based on a 50-year life ($920 amortization). The goodwill has an indefinite life.

Instructions

1. R&D Exp. $136,000

Prepare all journal entries necessary to correct any errors made during 2012. Assume the books have not yet been closed for 2012.

Calculate and comment on asset turnover ratio.
(SO 9)

P10-9A Ratial Company and Navi Corporation, two corporations of roughly the same size, are both involved in the manufacture of in-line skates. Each company depreciates its plant assets using the straight-line approach. An investigation of their financial statements reveals the following information.

	Ratial Co.	**Navi Corp.**
Net income	$ 800,000	$1,000,000
Sales revenue	1,200,000	1,080,000
Average total assets	2,500,000	2,000,000
Average plant assets	1,800,000	1,000,000

Instructions

(a) For each company, calculate the asset turnover ratio.
(b) ◄━━━► Based on your calculations in part (a), comment on the relative effectiveness of the two companies in using their assets to generate sales and produce net income.

Problems: Set B

Determine acquisition costs of land and building.
(SO 1)

P10-1B Bhaja Company was organized on January 1. During the first year of operations, the following plant asset expenditures and receipts were recorded in random order.

Debits

1. Accrued real estate taxes paid at time of purchase of real estate	$ 5,000
2. Real estate taxes on land paid for the current year	7,500
3. Full payment to building contractor	500,000
4. Excavation costs for new building	19,000
5. Cost of real estate purchased as a plant site (land $75,000 and building $25,000)	100,000
6. Cost of parking lots and driveways	18,000
7. Architect's fees on building plans	9,000
8. Installation cost of fences around property	6,000
9. Cost of demolishing building to make land suitable for construction of new building	17,000
	$681,500

Credit

10. Proceeds from salvage of demolished building	$ 3,500

Instructions

Analyze the foregoing tranactions using the following column headings. Insert the number of each transaction in the Item space, and insert the amounts in the appropriate columns. For amounts entered in the Other Accounts column, also indicate the account title.

Totals

Land $118,500
Buildings $528,000

Item	**Land**	**Buildings**	**Other Accounts**

Compute depreciation under different methods.
(SO 3)

P10-2B In recent years, Kannada Company purchased three machines. Because of heavy turnover in the accounting department, a different accountant was in charge of selecting the depreciation method for each machine, and each selected a different method. Information concerning the machines is summarized below.

Machine	**Acquired**	**Cost**	**Salvage Value**	**Useful Life in Years**	**Depreciation Method**
1	1/1/09	$105,000	$ 5,000	10	Straight-line
2	1/1/10	150,000	10,000	8	Declining-balance
3	11/1/12	100,000	15,000	6	Units-of-activity

For the declining-balance method, the company uses the double-declining rate. For the units-of-activity method, total machine hours are expected to be 25,000. Actual hours of use in the first 3 years were: 2012, 2,000; 2013, 4,500; and 2014, 5,500.

Instructions
(a) Compute the amount of accumulated depreciation on each machine at December 31, 2012.

(a) Machine 2, 2011, $28,125

(b) If machine 2 had been purchased on May 1 instead of January 1, what would be the depreciation expense for this machine in (1) 2010 and (2) 2011?

P10-3B On January 1, 2012, Zakiuddin Company purchased the following two machines for use in its production process.

Compute depreciation under different methods.
(SO 3)

Machine A: The cash price of this machine was $55,000. Related expenditures included: sales tax $2,750, shipping costs $100, insurance during shipping $75, installation and testing costs $75, and $90 of oil and lubricants to be used with the machinery during its first year of operation. Zakiuddin estimates that the useful life of the machine is 4 years with a $5,000 salvage value remaining at the end of that time period.

Machine B: The recorded cost of this machine was $100,000. Zakiuddin estimates that the useful life of the machine is 4 years with a $10,000 salvage value remaining at the end of that time period.

Instructions
(a) Prepare the following for Machine A.
   (1) The journal entry to record its purchase on January 1, 2012.
   (2) The journal entry to record annual depreciation at December 31, 2012, assuming the straight-line method of depreciation is used.

(a) (2) $13,250

(b) Calculate the amount of depreciation expense that Zakiuddin should record for machine B each year of its useful life under the following assumption.
   (1) Zakiuddin uses the straight-line method of depreciation.
   (2) Zakiuddin uses the declining-balance method. The rate used is twice the straight-line rate.
   (3) Zakiuddin uses the units-of-activity method and estimates the useful life of the machine is 25,000 units. Actual usage is as follows: 2012, 5,500 units; 2013, 7,000 units; 2014, 8,000 units; 2015, 4,500 units.
(c) Which method used to calculate depreciation on machine B reports the lowest amount of depreciation expense in year 1 (2012)? The lowest amount in year 4 (2015)? The lowest total amount over the 4-year period?

P10-4B At the beginning of 2010, Farooque Company acquired equipment costing $200,000. It was estimated that this equipment would have a useful life of 6 years and a residual value of $20,000 at that time. The straight-line method of depreciation was considered the most appropriate to use with this type of equipment. Depreciation is to be recorded at the end of each year.

Calculate revisions to depreciation expense.
(SO 3, 4)

During 2012 (the third year of the equipment's life), the company's engineers reconsidered their expectations, and estimated that the equipment's useful life would probably be 7 years (in total) instead of 6 years. The estimated residual value was not changed at that time. However, during 2015 the estimated residual value was reduced to $5,000.

Instructions
Indicate how much depreciation expense should be recorded for this equipment each year by completing the following table.

Year	Depreciation Expense	Accumulated Depreciation
2010		
2011		
2012		
2013		
2014		
2015		
2016		

2016 depreciation expense, $31,500

P10-5B At December 31, 2012, Ramaswami Company reported the following as plant assets.

Land		$ 2,000,000
Buildings	$20,000,000	
Less: Accumulated depreciation—buildings	8,000,000	12,000,000
Equipment	30,000,000	
Less: Accumulated depreciation—equipment	4,000,000	26,000,000
Total plant assets		$40,000,000

During 2013, the following selected cash transactions occurred.

April	1	Purchased land for $1,200,000.
May	1	Sold equipment that cost $420,000 when purchased on January 1, 2009. The equipment was sold for $240,000.
June	1	Sold land purchased on June 1, 2003, for $1,000,000. The land cost $340,000.
July	1	Purchased equipment for $1,100,000.
Dec.	31	Retired equipment that cost $300,000 when purchased on December 31, 2003. No salvage value was received.

Instructions

(a) Journalize the above transactions. Ramaswami uses straight-line depreciation for buildings and equipment. The buildings are estimated to have a 50-year useful life and no salvage value. The equipment is estimated to have a 10-year useful life and no salvage value. Update depreciation on assets disposed of at the time of sale or retirement.

(b) Record adjusting entries for depreciation for 2013.

(c) Prepare the plant assets section of Ramaswami's balance sheet at December 31, 2013.

P10-6B Nikhom's has equipment that cost $40,000 and that has been depreciated $26,000. Record the disposal under the following assumptions.

(a) It was scrapped as having no value.

(b) It was sold for $29,000.

(c) It was sold for $10,000.

P10-7B The intangible assets section of Praphaphorn Company at December 31, 2012, is presented below.

Patents ($100,000 cost less $10,000 amortization)	$ 90,000
Copyrights ($60,000 cost less $24,000 amortization)	36,000
Total	$126,000

The patent was acquired in January 2012 and has a useful life of 10 years. The copyright was acquired in January 2009 and also has a useful life of 10 years. The following cash transactions may have affected intangible assets during 2013.

Jan. 2	Paid $45,000 legal costs to successfully defend the patent against infringement by another company.
Jan.–June	Developed a new product, incurring $230,000 in research and development costs. A patent was granted for the product on July 1. Its useful life is equal to its legal life.
Sept. 1	Paid $125,000 to an Xgames star to appear in commercials advertising the company's products. The commercials will air in September and October.
Oct. 1	Acquired a copyright for $200,000. The copyright has a useful life of 50 years.

Instructions

(a) Prepare journal entries to record the transactions above.

(b) Prepare journal entries to record the 2013 amortization expense for intangible assets.

(c) Prepare the intangible assets section of the balance sheet at December 31, 2013.

(d) Prepare the note to the financials on Praphaphorn's intangibles as of December 31, 2013.

P10-8B Due to rapid turnover in the accounting department, a number of transactions involving intangible assets were improperly recorded by Chansantor Company in 2012.

1. Chansantor developed a new manufacturing process, incurring research and development costs of $110,000. The company also purchased a patent for $50,000. In early January, Chansantor capitalized $160,000 as the cost of the patents. Patent amortization expense of $8,000 was recorded based on a 20-year useful life.

2. On July 1, 2012, Chansantor purchased a small company and as a result acquired goodwill of $200,000. Chansantor recorded a half-year's amortization in 2012, based on a 50-year life ($2,000 amortization). The goodwill has an indefinite life.

Instructions

Prepare all journal entries necessary to correct any errors made during 2012. Assume the books have not yet been closed for 2012.

R&D Exp. $110,000

P10-9B Liam Corporation and Aslan Corporation, two corporations of roughly the same size, are both involved in the manufacture of canoes and sea kayaks. Each company depreciates its plant assets using the straight-line approach. An investigation of their financial statements reveals the following information.

Calculate and comment on asset turnover ratio.
(SO 9)

	Liam Corp.	**Aslan Corp.**
Net income	$ 300,000	$ 325,000
Sales revenue	1,100,000	990,000
Average total assets	1,000,000	1,050,000
Average plant assets	750,000	770,000

Instructions

(a) For each company, calculate the asset turnover ratio.
(b) ⬤━━━━▶ Based on your calculations in part (a), comment on the relative effectiveness of the two companies in using their assets to generate sales and produce net income.

Problems: Set C

Visit the book's companion website, at **www.wiley.com/college/weygandt**, and choose the Student Companion site to access Problem Set C.

Comprehensive Problem: Chapters 3 to 10

CP10   Winterschid Company's trial balance at December 31, 2012, is presented below. All 2012 transactions have been recorded except for the items described on page 500.

	Debit	**Credit**
Cash	$ 28,000	
Accounts Receivable	36,800	
Notes Receivable	10,000	
Interest Receivable	–0–	
Inventory	36,200	
Prepaid Insurance	3,600	
Land	20,000	
Buildings	150,000	
Equipment	60,000	
Patents	9,000	
Allowance for Doubtful Accounts		$ 500
Accumulated Depreciation—Buildings		50,000
Accumulated Depreciation—Equipment		24,000
Accounts Payable		27,300
Salaries and Wages Payable		–0–
Unearned Rent Revenue		6,000
Notes Payable (due in 2013)		11,000
Interest Payable		–0–
Notes Payable (due after 2013)		35,000
Owner's Capital		113,600
Owner's Drawings	12,000	

	Debit	Credit
Sales Revenue		900,000
Interest Revenue		–0–
Rent Revenue		–0–
Gain on Disposal of Plant Assets		–0–
Bad Debts Expense	–0–	
Cost of Goods Sold	630,000	
Depreciation Expense	–0–	
Insurance Expense	–0–	
Interest Expense	–0–	
Other Operating Expenses	61,800	
Amortization Expense	–0–	
Salaries and Wages Expense	110,000	
Total	$1,167,400	$1,167,400

Unrecorded transactions:

1. On May 1, 2012, Winterschid purchased equipment for $13,200 plus sales taxes of $600 (all paid in cash).
2. On July 1, 2012, Winterschid sold for $3,500 equipment which originally cost $5,000. Accumulated depreciation on this equipment at January 1, 2012, was $1,800; 2012 depreciation prior to the sale of the equipment was $450.
3. On December 31, 2012, Winterschid sold for $9,000 on account inventory that cost $6,300.
4. Winterschid estimates that uncollectible accounts receivable at year-end is $4,000.
5. The note receivable is a one-year, 8% note dated April 1, 2012. No interest has been recorded.
6. The balance in prepaid insurance represents payment of a $3,600 6-month premium on September 1, 2012.
7. The building is being depreciated using the straight-line method over 30 years. The salvage value is $30,000.
8. The equipment owned prior to this year is being depreciated using the straight-line method over 5 years. The salvage value is 10% of cost.
9. The equipment purchased on May 1, 2012, is being depreciated using the straight-line method over 5 years, with a salvage value of $1,800.
10. The patent was acquired on January 1, 2012, and has a useful life of 10 years from that date.
11. Unpaid salaries and wages at December 31, 2012, total $2,200.
12. The unearned rent revenue of $6,000 was received on December 1, 2012, for 3 months rent.
13. Both the short-term and long-term notes payable are dated January 1, 2012, and carry a 9% interest rate. All interest is payable in the next 12 months.

Instructions

(a) Prepare journal entries for the transactions listed above.

(b) Totals $1,201,290

(b) Prepare an updated December 31, 2012, trial balance.

(c) Prepare a 2012 income statement and an owner's equity statement.

(d) Total assets $260,400

(d) Prepare a December 31, 2012, classified balance sheet.

Continuing Cookie Chronicle

(*Note:* This is a continuation of the Cookie Chronicle from Chapters 1 through 9.)

CCC10   Natalie is also thinking of buying a van that will be used only for business. Natalie is concerned about the impact of the van's cost on her income statement and balance sheet. She has come to you for advice on calculating the van's depreciation.

Go to the book's companion website, **www.wiley.com/college/weygandt,** *to see the completion of this problem.*

BROADENINGYOURPERSPECTIVE

Financial Reporting and Analysis

Financial Reporting Problem: PepsiCo, Inc.

BYP10-1 The financial statements and the Notes to Consolidated Financial Statements of PepsiCo, Inc. are presented in Appendix A. **PEPSICO**

Instructions

Refer to PepsiCo's financial statements and answer the following questions.

(a) What was the total cost and book value of property, plant, and equipment at December 26, 2009?
(b) What method or methods of depreciation are used by the company for financial reporting purposes?
(c) What was the amount of depreciation and amortization expense for each of the three years 2007–2009?
(d) Using the statement of cash flows, what is the amount of capital spending in 2009 and 2008?
(e) Where does the company disclose its intangible assets, and what types of intangibles did it have at December 26, 2009?

Comparative Analysis Problem: PepsiCo, Inc. vs. The Coca-Cola Company

BYP10-2 PepsiCo's financial statements are presented in Appendix A. Financial statements of The Coca-Cola Company are presented in Appendix B. **PEPSICO**

Instructions

(a) Compute the asset turnover ratio for each company for 2009.
(b) What conclusions concerning the efficiency of assets can be drawn from these data?

On the Web

BYP10-3 A company's annual report identifies the amount of its plant assets and the depreciation method used.

Address: www.reportgallery.com, or go to **www.wiley.com/college/weygandt**

Steps

1. From Report Gallery Homepage, choose **Search by Alphabet**, and pick a letter.
2. Select a particular company.
3. Choose the most recent **Annual Report**.
4. Follow instructions below.

Instructions

(a) What is the name of the company?
(b) At fiscal year-end, what is the net amount of its plant assets?
(c) What is the accumulated depreciation?
(d) Which method of depreciation does the company use?

Critical Thinking

Decision Making Across the Organization

BYP10-4 Reimer Company and Lingo Company are two proprietorships that are similar in many respects. One difference is that Reimer Company uses the straight-line method and Lingo Company uses the declining-balance method at double the straight-line rate. On January 2, 2010, both companies acquired the depreciable assets shown on page 502.

Asset	Cost	Salvage Value	Useful Life
Buildings	$320,000	$20,000	40 years
Equipment	110,000	10,000	10 years

Including the appropriate depreciation charges, annual net income for the companies in the years 2010, 2011, and 2012 and total income for the 3 years were as follows.

	2010	2011	2012	Total
Reimer Company	$84,000	$88,400	$90,000	$262,400
Lingo Company	68,000	76,000	85,000	229,000

At December 31, 2012, the balance sheets of the two companies are similar except that Lingo Company has more cash than Reimer Company.

Sally Vogts is interested in buying one of the companies. She comes to you for advice.

Instructions

With the class divided into groups, answer the following.

(a) Determine the annual and total depreciation recorded by each company during the 3 years.

(b) Assuming that Lingo Company also uses the straight-line method of depreciation instead of the declining-balance method as in (a), prepare comparative income data for the 3 years.

(c) Which company should Sally Vogts buy? Why?

Communication Activity

BYP10-5 The following was published with the financial statements to American Exploration Company.

American Exploration Company
Notes to the Financial Statements

Property, Plant, and Equipment—The Company accounts for its oil and gas exploration and production activities using the successful efforts method of accounting. Under this method, acquisition costs for proved and unproved properties are capitalized when incurred.... The costs of drilling exploratory wells are capitalized pending determination of whether each well has discovered proved reserves. If proved reserves are not discovered, such drilling costs are charged to expense.... Depletion of the cost of producing oil and gas properties is computed on the units-of-activity method.

Instructions

Write a brief memo to your instructor discussing American Exploration Company's note regarding property, plant, and equipment. Your memo should address what is meant by the "successful efforts method" and "units-of-activity method."

Ethics Case

BYP10-6 Buster Container Company is suffering declining sales of its principal product, nonbiodegradeable plastic cartons. The president, Dennis Harwood, instructs his controller, Shelly McGlone, to lengthen asset lives to reduce depreciation expense. A processing line of automated plastic extruding equipment, purchased for $3.1 million in January 2012, was originally estimated to have a useful life of 8 years and a salvage value of $300,000. Depreciation has been recorded for 2 years on that basis. Dennis wants the estimated life changed to 12 years total, and the straight-line method continued. Shelly is hesitant to make the change, believing it is unethical to increase net income in this manner. Dennis says, "Hey, the life is only an estimate, and I've heard that our competition uses a 12-year life on their production equipment."

Instructions

(a) Who are the stakeholders in this situation?

(b) Is the change in asset life unethical, or is it simply a good business practice by an astute president?

(c) What is the effect of Dennis Harwood's proposed change on income before taxes in the year of change?

"All About You" Activity

BYP10-7 Both the **All About You** feature (available at the book's companion website) and the Feature Story at the beginning of the chapter discussed the company Rent-A-Wreck. Note that the trade name Rent-A-Wreck is a very important asset to the company, as it creates immediate product identification. As indicated in the chapter, companies invest substantial sums to ensure that their product is well-known to the consumer. Test your knowledge of who owns some famous brands and their impact on the financial statements.

Instructions

(a) Provide an answer to the five multiple-choice questions below.

    (1) Which company owns both Taco Bell and Pizza Hut?
        (a) McDonald's.   **(c)** Yum Brands.
        (b) CKE.   **(d)** Wendy's.

    (2) Dairy Queen belongs to:
        (a) Breyer.   **(c)** GE.
        (b) Berkshire Hathaway.   **(d)** The Coca-Cola Company.

    (3) Phillip Morris, the cigarette maker, is owned by:
        (a) Altria.   **(c)** Boeing.
        (b) GE.   **(d)** ExxonMobil.

    (4) AOL, a major Internet provider, belongs to:
        (a) Microsoft.   **(c)** NBC.
        (b) Cisco.   **(d)** Time Warner.

    (5) ESPN, the sports broadcasting network, is owned by:
        (a) Procter & Gamble.   **(c)** Walt Disney.
        (b) Altria.   **(d)** The Coca-Cola Company.

(b) How do you think the value of these brands is reported on the appropriate company's balance sheet?

FASB Codification Activity

BYP10-8 If your school has a subscription to the FASB Codification, go to *http://aaahq.org/ascLogin.cfm* to log in and prepare responses to the following.

(a) What does it mean to capitalize an item?

(b) What is the definition provided for an intangible asset?

(c) Your great-uncle, who is a CPA, is impressed that you are taking an accounting class. Based on his experience, he believes that depreciation is something that companies do based on past practice, not on the basis of authoritative guidance. Provide the authoritative literature to support the practice of fixed-asset depreciation.

Answers to Insight and Accounting Across the Organization Questions

p. 461 Many U.S. Firms Use Leases **Q:** Why might airline managers choose to lease rather than purchase their planes? **A:** The reasons for leasing include favorable tax treatment, better financing options, increased flexibility, reduced risk of obsolescence, and low airline income.

p. 478 Should Companies Write Up Goodwill? **Q:** Do you think that this treatment would be allowed under U.S. GAAP? **A:** The write-down of assets would have been allowed if it could be shown that the assets had declined in value (an impairment). However, the creation of goodwill to offset the write-down would not have been allowed. Goodwill can be recorded only when it results from the acquisition of a business. It cannot be recorded as the result of being created internally.

Answers to Self-Test Questions

1. d ($24,000 + $1,200 + $200 + $400)   **2.** b   **3.** d [($400,000 − $10,000) ÷ 5] × 2   **4.** d   **5.** b $60,000 × 25% = $15,000; ($60,000 − $15,000) × 25% = $11,250   **6.** b   **7.** d [($60,000 − $12,000) ÷ 10] × 2 = $9,600; ($60,000 − $9,600 − $2,000) ÷ 4   **8.** d   **9.** a [($80,000 ÷ 10) × 4.5] = $36,000; ($80,000 − $36,000) − $26,000   **10.** c ($12 million ÷ 20 million) × 2 million   **11.** d   **12.** b   **13.** c   **14.** c $180,000 ÷ [($200,000 + $300,000) ÷ 2]   ***15.** a ($35,000 + $10,000)   ***16.** d

IFRS A Look at IFRS

IFRS follows most of the same principles as GAAP in the accounting for property, plant, and equipment. There are, however, some significant differences in the implementation: IFRS allows the use of revaluation of property, plant, and equipment, and it also requires the use of component depreciation. In addition, there are some significant differences in the accounting for both intangible assets and impairments.

Key Points

- The definition for plant assets for both IFRS and GAAP is essentially the same.

- Both international standards and GAAP follow the cost principle when accounting for property, plant, and equipment at date of acquisition. Cost consists of all expenditures necessary to acquire the asset and make it ready for its intended use.

- Under both IFRS and GAAP, interest costs incurred during construction are capitalized. Recently, IFRS converged to GAAP requirements in this area.

- IFRS, like GAAP, capitalizes all direct costs in self-constructed assets such as raw materials and labor. IFRS does not address the capitalization of fixed overhead, although in practice these costs are generally capitalized.

- IFRS also views depreciation as an allocation of cost over an asset's useful life. IFRS permits the same depreciation methods (e.g., straight-line, accelerated, and units-of-activity) as GAAP. However, a major difference is that IFRS requires component depreciation. *Component depreciation* specifies that any significant parts of a depreciable asset that have different estimated useful lives should be separately depreciated. Component depreciation is allowed under GAAP but is seldom used.

  To illustrate, assume that Lexure Construction builds an office building for $4,000,000, not including the cost of the land. If the $4,000,000 is allocated over the 40-year useful life of the building, Lexure reports $100,000 of depreciation per year, assuming straight-line depreciation and no disposal value. However, assume that $320,000 of the cost of the building relates to personal property and $600,000 relates to land improvements. The personal property has a depreciable life of 5 years, and the land improvements have a depreciable life of 10 years. In accordance with IFRS, Lexure must use component depreciation. It must reclassify $320,000 of the cost of the building to personal property and $600,000 to the cost of land improvements. Assuming that Lexure uses straight-line depreciation, component depreciation for the first year of the office building is computed as follows.

Building cost adjusted ($4,000,000 − $320,000 − $600,000)	$3,080,000
Building cost depreciation per year ($3,080,000/40)	$ 77,000
Personal property depreciation ($320,000/5)	64,000
Land improvements depreciation ($600,000/10)	60,000
Total component depreciation in first year	$ 201,000

- IFRS uses the term *residual value*, rather than salvage value, to refer to an owner's estimate of an asset's value at the end of its useful life for that owner.

- IFRS allows companies to revalue plant assets to fair value at the reporting date. Companies that choose to use the revaluation framework must follow revaluation procedures. If revaluation is used, it must be applied to all assets in a class of assets. Assets that are experiencing rapid price changes must be revalued on an annual basis, otherwise less frequent revaluation is acceptable.

  To illustrate asset revaluation accounting, assume that Pernice Company applies revaluation to plant assets with a carrying value of $1,000,000, a useful life of 5 years, and no residual value. Pernice makes the following journal entries in year 1, assuming straight-line depreciation.

Depreciation Expense	200,000	
Accumulated Depreciation—Plant Assets		200,000
(To record depreciation expense in year 1)		

After this entry, Pernice's plant assets have a carrying amount of $800,000 ($1,000,000 − $200,000). At the end of year 1, independent appraisers determine that the asset has a fair value of $850,000. To report the plant assets at fair value, or $850,000, Pernice eliminates the Accumulated Depreciation—Plant Assets account, reduces Plant Assets to its fair value of $850,000, and records Revaluation Surplus of $50,000. The entry to record the revaluation is as follows.

Accumulated Depreciation—Plant Assets	200,000	
Plant Assets		150,000
Revaluation Surplus		50,000
(To record adjusting the plant assets to fair value)		

Thus, Pernice follows a two-step process. First, Pernice records depreciation based on the cost basis of $1,000,000. As a result, it reports depreciation expense of $200,000 on the income statement. Second, it records the revaluation. It does this by eliminating any accumulated depreciation, adjusting the recorded value of the plant assets to fair value, and debiting or crediting the Revaluation Surplus account. In this example, the revaluation surplus is $50,000, which is the difference between the fair value of $850,000 and the book value of $800,000. Revaluation surplus is an example of an item reported as other comprehensive income, as discussed in the *A Look at IFRS* section of Chapter 5. Pernice now reports the following information in its statement of financial position at the end of year 1.

Plant assets ($1,000,000 − $150,000)	$850,000
Accumulated depreciation—plant assets	0
	$850,000
Revaluation surplus (equity)	$ 50,000

As indicated, $850,000 is the new basis of the asset. Pernice reports depreciation expense of $200,000 in the income statement and $50,000 in other comprehensive income. Assuming no change in the total useful life, depreciation in year 2 will be $212,500 ($850,000 ÷ 4).

- Under both GAAP and IFRS, changes in the depreciation method used and changes in useful life are handled in current and future periods. Prior periods are not affected. GAAP recently conformed to international standards in the accounting for changes in depreciation methods.

- The accounting for subsequent expenditures, such as ordinary repairs and additions, are essentially the same under IFRS and GAAP.

- The accounting for plant asset disposals is essentially the same under IFRS and GAAP.

- Initial costs to acquire natural resources are essentially the same under IFRS and GAAP.

- The definition of intangible assets is essentially the same under IFRS and GAAP.

- As in GAAP, under IFRS the costs associated with research and development are segregated into the two components. Costs in the research phase are always expensed under both IFRS and GAAP. Under IFRS, however, costs in the development phase are capitalized as Development Costs once technological feasibility is achieved.

  To illustrate, assume that Laser Scanner Company spent $1 million on research and $2 million on development of new products. Of the $2 million in development costs, $500,000 was incurred prior to technological feasibility and $1,500,000 was incurred after technological feasibility had been demonstrated. The company would record these costs as follows.

Research Expense	1,000,000	
Development Expense	500,000	
Development Costs	1,500,000	
Cash		3,000,000
(To record research and development costs)		

- IFRS permits revaluation of intangible assets (except for goodwill). GAAP prohibits revaluation of intangible assets.

- IFRS requires an impairment test at each reporting date for plant assets and intangibles and records an impairment if the asset's carrying amount exceeds its recoverable amount. The recoverable amount is the higher of the asset's fair value less costs to sell or its value-in-use. Value-in-use is the future cash flows to be derived from the particular asset, discounted to present value. Under GAAP, impairment loss is measured as the excess of the carrying amount over the asset's fair value.

- IFRS allows reversal of impairment losses when there has been a change in economic conditions or in the expected use of the asset. Under GAAP, impairment losses cannot be reversed for assets to be held and used; the impairment loss results in a new cost basis for the asset. IFRS and GAAP are similar in the accounting for impairments of assets held for disposal.

- The accounting for exchanges of nonmonetary assets has recently converged between IFRS and GAAP. GAAP now requires that gains on exchanges of nonmonetary assets be recognized if the exchange has commercial substance. This is the same framework used in IFRS.

Looking to the Future

With respect to revaluations, as part of the conceptual framework project, the Boards will examine the measurement bases used in accounting. It is too early to say whether a converged conceptual framework will recommend fair value measurement (and revaluation accounting) for plant assets and intangibles. However, this is likely to be one of the more contentious issues, given the long-standing use of historical cost as a measurement basis in GAAP.

The IASB and FASB have identified a project that would consider expanded recognition of internally generated intangible assets. IFRS permits more recognition of intangibles compared to GAAP. Thus, it will be challenging to develop converged standards for intangible assets, given the long-standing prohibition on capitalizing internally generated intangible assets and research and development costs in GAAP.

IFRS Self-Test Questions

1. Which of the following statements is *correct*?
   (a) Both IFRS and GAAP permit revaluation of property, plant, and equipment and intangible assets (except for goodwill).
   (b) IFRS permits revaluation of property, plant, and equipment and intangible assets (except for goodwill).
   (c) Both IFRS and GAAP permit revaluation of property, plant, and equipment but not intangible assets.
   (d) GAAP permits revaluation of property, plant, and equipment but not intangible assets.

2. International Company has land that cost $450,000 but now has a fair value of $600,000. International Company decides to use the revaluation method specified in IFRS to account for the land. Which of the following statements is *correct*?
   (a) International Company must continue to report the land at $450,000.
   (b) International Company would report a net income increase of $150,000 due to an increase in the value of the land.
   (c) International Company would debit Revaluation Surplus for $150,000.
   (d) International Company would credit Revaluation Surplus by $150,000.

3. Francisco Corporation is constructing a new building at a total initial cost of $10,000,000. The building is expected to have a useful live of 50 years with no residual value. The building's finished surfaces (e.g., roof cover and floor cover) are 5% of this cost and have a useful life of 20 years. Building services systems (e.g., electric, heating, and plumbing) are 20% of the cost and have a useful life of 25 years. The depreciation in the first year using component depreciation, assuming straight-line depreciation with no residual value, is:
   (a) $200,000.   (c) $255,000.
   (b) $215,000.   (d) None of the above.

4. Research and development costs are:
(a) expensed under GAAP.
(c) expensed under both GAAP and IFRS.
(b) expensed under IFRS.
(d) None of the above.

5. Under IFRS, value-in-use is defined as:
(a) net realizable value.
(c) future cash flows discounted to present value.
(b) fair value.
(d) total future undiscounted cash flows.

IFRS Concepts and Application

IFRS10-1 What is component depreciation, and when must it be used?

IFRS10-2 What is revaluation of plant assets? When should revaluation be applied?

IFRS10-3 Some product development expenditures are recorded as development expenses and others as development costs. Explain the difference between these accounts and how a company decides which classification is appropriate.

IFRS10-4 Mandall Company constructed a warehouse for $280,000. Mandall estimates that the warehouse has a useful life of 20 years and no residual value. Construction records indicate that $40,000 of the cost of the warehouse relates to its heating, ventilation, and air conditioning (HVAC) system, which has an estimated useful life of only 10 years. Compute the first year of depreciation expense using straight-line component depreciation.

IFRS10-5 At the end of its first year of operations, Brianna Company chose to use the revaluation framework allowed under IFRS. Brianna's ledger shows Plant Assets $480,000 and Accumulated Depreciation—Plant Assets $60,000. Prepare journal entries to record the following.
(a) Independent appraisers determine that the plant assets have a fair value of $460,000.
(b) Independent appraisers determine that the plant assets have a fair value of $400,000.

IFRS10-6 Newell Industries spent $300,000 on research and $600,000 on development of a new product. Of the $600,000 in development costs, $400,000 was incurred prior to technological feasibility and $200,000 after technological feasibility had been demonstrated. Prepare the journal entry to record research and development costs.

International Financial Statement Analysis: Zetar plc

IFRS10-7 The financial statements of Zetar plc are presented in Appendix C.

Instructions
Use the company's annual report, available at *www.zetarplc.com*, to answer the following questions.

(a) According to the notes to the financial statements, what method or methods does the company use to depreciate "plant and equipment?" What rate does it use to depreciate plant and equipment?

(b) According to the notes to the financial statements, how often is goodwill tested for impairment?

(c) Using the notes to the financial statements, as well as information from the statement of cash flows, prepare the journal entry to record the disposal of property, plant, and equipment during 2009. (Round your amounts to the nearest thousand.)

Answers to IFRS Self-Test Questions
1. b **2.** d **3.** c ($10,000,000 $\times$ .05/20) + ($10,000,000 $\times$ .20/25) + ($10,000,000 $\times$ .75/50) **4.** a **5.** c

The Navigator

✔ **Remember to go back to the Navigator box on the chapter opening page and check off your completed work.**

CHAPTER11

Current Liabilities and Payroll Accounting

Study Objectives

After studying this chapter, you should be able to:

[1] Explain a current liability, and identify the major types of current liabilities.

[2] Describe the accounting for notes payable.

[3] Explain the accounting for other current liabilities.

[4] Explain the financial statement presentation and analysis of current liabilities.

[5] Describe the accounting and disclosure requirements for contingent liabilities.

[6] Compute and record the payroll for a pay period.

[7] Describe and record employer payroll taxes.

[8] Discuss the objectives of internal control for payroll.

✔ **The Navigator**

✔ [The Navigator]

● Scan Study Objectives	○
● Read Feature Story	○
● Read Preview	○
● Read text and answer **Do it!** p. 513 ○ p. 518 ○ p. 525 ○ p. 527 ○	
● Work Comprehensive **Do it!** p. 530	○
● Review Summary of Study Objectives	○
● Answer Self-Test Questions	○
● Complete Assignments	○
● Go to *WileyPLUS* for practice and tutorials	○
● Read A Look at IFRS p. 549	○

Feature Story

FINANCING HIS DREAMS

What would you do if you had a great idea for a new product, but couldn't come up with the cash to get the business off the ground? Small businesses often cannot attract investors. Nor can they obtain traditional debt financing through bank loans or bond issuances. Instead, they often resort to unusual, and costly, forms of nontraditional financing.

Such was the case for Wilbert Murdock. Murdock grew up in a New York housing project, and always had great ambitions. This ambitious spirit led him into some business ventures that failed: a medical diagnostic tool, a device to eliminate carpal-tunnel syndrome, custom-designed sneakers, and a device to keep people from falling asleep while driving.

Another idea was computerized golf clubs that analyze a golfer's swing and provide immediate feedback. Murdock saw great

potential in the idea: Many golfers are willing to shell out considerable sums of money for devices that might improve their game. But Murdock had no cash to develop his product, and banks and other lenders had shied away. Rather than give up, Murdock resorted to credit cards—in a big way. He quickly owed $25,000 to credit card companies.

While funding a business with credit cards might sound unusual, it isn't. A recent study found that one-third of businesses with fewer than 20 employees financed at least part of their operations with credit cards. As Murdock explained, credit cards are an appealing way to finance a start-up because "credit-card companies don't care how the money is spent." However, they do care how they are paid. And so Murdock faced high interest charges and a barrage of credit card collection letters.

Murdock's debt forced him to sacrifice nearly everything in order to keep his business afloat. His car stopped running, he barely had enough money to buy food, and he lived and worked out of a dimly lit apartment in his mother's basement. Through it all he tried to maintain a positive spirit, joking that, if he becomes successful, he might some day get to appear in an American Express commercial.

Source: Rodney Ho, "Banking on Plastic: To Finance a Dream, Many Entrepreneurs Binge on Credit Cards," *Wall Street Journal* (March 9, 1998), p. A1.

Inside**CHAPTER**11

PreviewofCHAPTER11

Inventor-entrepreneur Wilbert Murdock, as you can tell from the Feature Story, had to use multiple credit cards to finance his business ventures. Murdock's credit card debts would be classified as *current liabilities* because they are due every month. Yet by making minimal payments and paying high interest each month, Murdock used this credit source long-term. Some credit card balances remain outstanding for years as they accumulate interest.

Earlier, we defined liabilities as creditors' claims on total assets and as existing debts and obligations. These claims, debts, and obligations must be settled or paid at some time **in the future** by the transfer of assets or services. The future date on which they are due or payable (maturity date) is a significant feature of liabilities. This "future date" feature gives rise to two basic classifications of liabilities: (1) current liabilities and (2) long-term liabilities. We will explain current liabilities, along with payroll accounting, in this chapter. We will explain long-term liabilities in Chapter 15.

The content and organization of Chapter 11 are as follows.

Current Liabilities and Payroll Accounting		
Accounting for Current Liabilities	**Contingent Liabilities**	**Payroll Accounting**
• Notes payable • Sales taxes payable • Unearned revenues • Current maturities of long-term debt • Statement presentation and analysis	• Recording • Disclosure	• Determining payroll • Recording payroll • Employer payroll taxes • Filing and remitting payroll taxes • Internal control for payroll

The Navigator

Accounting for Current Liabilities

Study Objective [1]

Explain a current liability, and identify the major types of current liabilities.

As explained in Chapter 4, a **current liability** is a debt with two key features: (1) The company reasonably expects to pay the debt from existing current assets or through the creation of other current liabilities. (2) The company will pay the debt within one year or the operating cycle, whichever is longer. Debts that do not meet **both criteria** are classified as long-term liabilities.

Companies must carefully monitor the relationship of current liabilities to current assets. This relationship is critical in evaluating a company's short-term debt-paying ability. A company that has more current liabilities than current assets may not be able to meet its current obligations when they become due.

Current liabilities include notes payable, accounts payable, and unearned revenues. They also include accrued liabilities such as taxes, salaries and wages, and interest payable. In the sections that follow, we discuss a few of the common types of current liabilities.

Notes Payable

Study Objective [2]

Describe the accounting for notes payable.

Companies record obligations in the form of written notes as **notes payable**. Notes payable are often used instead of accounts payable because they give the lender formal proof of the obligation in case legal remedies are needed to collect the debt. Companies frequently issue notes payable to meet short-term financing needs. Notes payable usually require the borrower to pay interest.

Notes are issued for varying periods of time. **Those due for payment within one year of the balance sheet date are usually classified as current liabilities.**

To illustrate the accounting for notes payable, assume that First National Bank agrees to lend $100,000 on September 1, 2012, if Cole Williams Co. signs a $100,000, 12%, four-month note maturing on January 1. When a company issues an interest-bearing note, the amount of assets it receives upon issuance of the note generally equals the note's face value. Cole Williams Co. therefore will receive $100,000 cash and will make the following journal entry.

Sept. 1	Cash	100,000	
	Notes Payable		100,000
	(To record issuance of 12%, 4 month note		
	to First National Bank)		

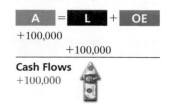

A = L + OE
+100,000
        +100,000

Cash Flows
+100,000

Interest accrues over the life of the note, and the company must periodically record that accrual. If Cole Williams Co. prepares financial statements annually, it makes an adjusting entry at December 31 to recognize interest expense and interest payable of $4,000 ($100,000 × 12% × 4/12). Illustration 11-1 shows the formula for computing interest, and its application to Cole Williams Co.'s note.

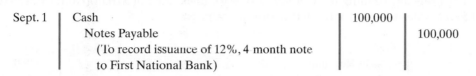

Face Value of Note	×	Annual Interest Rate	×	Time in Terms of One Year	=	Interest
$100,000	×	12%	×	4/12	=	**$4,000**

Illustration 11-1
Formula for computing interest

Cole Williams makes an adjusting entry as follows:

Dec. 31	Interest Expense	4,000	
	Interest Payable		4,000
	(To accrue interest for 4 months on		
	First National Bank note)		

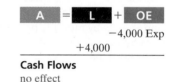

A = L + OE
        −4,000 Exp
    +4,000

Cash Flows
no effect

In the December 31 financial statements, the current liabilities section of the balance sheet will show notes payable $100,000 and interest payable $4,000. In addition, the company will report interest expense of $4,000 under "Other expenses and losses" in the income statement. If Cole Williams Co. prepared financial statements monthly, the adjusting entry at the end of each month would have been $1,000 ($100,000 × 12% × 1/12).

At maturity (January 1, 2013), Cole Williams Co. must pay the face value of the note ($100,000) plus $4,000 interest ($100,000 × 12% × 4/12). It records payment of the note and accrued interest as follows.

Jan. 1	Notes Payable	100,000	
	Interest Payable	4,000	
	Cash		104,000
	(To record payment of First National Bank		
	interest-bearing note and accrued interest		
	at maturity)		

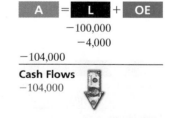

A = L + OE
        −100,000
        −4,000
−104,000

Cash Flows
−104,000

Sales Taxes Payable

As a consumer, you know that many of the products you purchase at retail stores are subject to sales taxes. Many states also are now collecting sales taxes on purchases made on the Internet as well. Sales taxes are expressed as a percentage of the sales price. The selling company collects the tax from the customer when the

Study Objective [3]
Explain the accounting for other current liabilities.

sale occurs. Periodically (usually monthly), the retailer remits the collections to the state's department of revenue.

Under most state sales tax laws, the selling company must ring up separately on the cash register the amount of the sale and the amount of the sales tax collected. (Gasoline sales are a major exception.) The company then uses the cash register readings to credit Sales Revenue and Sales Taxes Payable. For example, if the March 25 cash register reading for Cooley Grocery shows sales of $10,000 and sales taxes of $600 (sales tax rate of 6%), the journal entry is:

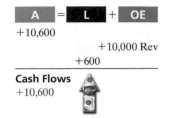

Mar. 25	Cash	10,600	
	Sales Revenue		10,000
	Sales Taxes Payable		600
	(To record daily sales and sales taxes)		

When the company remits the taxes to the taxing agency, it debits Sales Taxes Payable and credits Cash. The company does not report sales taxes as an expense. It simply forwards to the government the amount paid by the customers. Thus, Cooley Grocery serves only as a **collection agent** for the taxing authority.

Sometimes, companies do not ring up sales taxes separately on the cash register. To determine the amount of sales in such cases, divide total receipts by 100% plus the sales tax percentage. To illustrate, assume that in the above example Cooley Grocery rings up total receipts of $10,600. The receipts from the sales are equal to the sales price (100%) plus the tax percentage (6% of sales), or 1.06 times the sales total. We can compute the sales amount as follows.

$$\$10,600 \div 1.06 = \$10,000$$

Thus, Cooley Grocery could find the sales tax amount it must remit to the state ($600) by subtracting sales from total receipts ($10,600 − $10,000).

Helpful Hint

Alternatively, Cooley could find the tax by multiplying sales by the sales tax rate ($10,000 × .06).

Unearned Revenues

A magazine publisher, such as Sports Illustrated, receives customers' checks when they order magazines. An airline company, such as American Airlines, often receives cash when it sells tickets for future flights. Season tickets for concerts, sporting events, and theater programs are also paid for in advance. How do companies account for unearned revenues that are received before goods are delivered or services are provided?

1. When a company receives the advance payment, it debits Cash, and credits a current liability account identifying the source of the unearned revenue.

2. When the company earns the revenue, it debits an unearned revenue account, and credits an earned revenue account.

To illustrate, assume that Superior University sells 10,000 season football tickets at $50 each for its five-game home schedule. The university makes the following entry for the sale of season tickets.

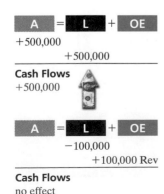

Aug. 6	Cash	500,000	
	Unearned Ticket Revenue		500,000
	(To record sale of 10,000 season tickets)		

As each game is completed, Superior records the earning of revenue with the following entry.

Sept. 7	Unearned Ticket Revenue	100,000	
	Ticket Revenue		100,000
	(To record football ticket revenue earned)		

The account Unearned Ticket Revenue represents unearned revenue, and Superior reports it as a current liability. As the school earns the revenue, it reclassifies the amount from unearned revenue to earned revenue. Unearned revenue is material for some companies. In the airline industry, for example, tickets sold for future flights represent almost 50% of total current liabilities. At United Air Lines, unearned ticket revenue was its largest current liability, recently amounting to over $1 billion.

Illustration 11-2 shows specific unearned and earned revenue accounts used in selected types of businesses.

Illustration 11-2
Unearned and earned
revenue accounts

Type of Business	Account Title	
	Unearned Revenue	**Earned Revenue**
Airline	Unearned Ticket Revenue	Ticket Revenue
Magazine publisher	Unearned Subscription Revenue	Subscription Revenue
Hotel	Unearned Rent Revenue	Rent Revenue

Current Maturities of Long-Term Debt

Companies often have a portion of long-term debt that comes due in the current year. That amount is considered a current liability. As an example, assume that Wendy Construction issues a five-year interest-bearing $25,000 note on January 1, 2011. This note specifies that each January 1, starting January 1, 2012, Wendy should pay $5,000 of the note. When the company prepares financial statements on December 31, 2011, it should report $5,000 as a current liability and $20,000 as a long-term liability. (The $5,000 amount is the portion of the note that is due to be paid within the next 12 months.) Companies often identify current maturities of long-term debt on the balance sheet as **long-term debt due within one year**.

It is not necessary to prepare an adjusting entry to recognize the current maturity of long-term debt. At the balance sheet date, all obligations due within one year are classified as current, and all other obligations as long-term.

Do it!

You and several classmates are studying for the next accounting examination. They ask you to answer the following questions.

Current Liabilities

1. If cash is borrowed on a $50,000, 6-month, 12% note on September 1, how much interest expense would be incurred by December 31?

2. How is the sales tax amount determined when the cash register total includes sales taxes?

3. If $15,000 is collected in advance on November 1 for 3-months' rent, what amount of rent revenue is earned by December 31?

action plan

✔ Use the interest formula: Face value of note × Annual interest rate × Time in terms of one year.

Solution

1. $50,000 × 12% × 4/12 = $2,000

2. First, divide the total cash register receipts by 100% plus the sales tax percentage to find the sales amount. Second, subtract the sales amount from the total cash register receipts to determine the sales taxes.

3. $15,000 × 2/3 = $10,000

✔ Divide total receipts by 100% plus the tax rate to determine sales; then subtract sales from the total receipts.

✔ Determine what fraction of the total unearned rent was earned this year.

Related exercise material: BE11-2, BE11-3, BE11-4, E11-1, E11-2, E11-3, E11-4, and **Do it!** 11-1.

The Navigator

Statement Presentation and Analysis

PRESENTATION

As indicated in Chapter 4, current liabilities are the first category under liabilities on the balance sheet. Each of the principal types of current liabilities is listed separately. In addition, companies disclose the terms of notes payable and other key information about the individual items in the notes to the financial statements.

Companies seldom list current liabilities in the order of liquidity. The reason is that varying maturity dates may exist for specific obligations such as notes payable. A more common method of presenting current liabilities is to list them by **order of magnitude**, with the largest ones first. Or, as a matter of custom, many companies show notes payable first, and then accounts payable, regardless of amount. Then the remaining current liabilities are listed by magnitude. (*Use this approach in your homework.*) The following adapted excerpt from the balance sheet of Caterpillar Inc. illustrates its order of presentation.

Illustration 11-3
Balance sheet presentation of current liabilities

Caterpillar Inc.
Balance Sheet
December 31, 2009
(in millions)

Assets

Current assets	$26,789
Property, plant and equipment (net)	12,386
Other long-term assets	20,863
Total assets	$60,038

Liabilities and Stockholders' Equity

Current liabilities	
Short-term borrowings (notes payable)	$ 4,083
Accounts payable	2,993
Accrued expenses	3,351
Accrued wages, salaries, and employee benefits	797
Customer advances	1,217
Dividends payable	262
Other current liabilities	888
Long-term debt due within one year	5,701
Total current liabilities	19,292
Noncurrent liabilities	31,446
Total liabilities	50,738
Stockholders' equity	9,300
Total liabilities and stockholders' equity	$60,038

Helpful Hint

For other examples of current liabilities sections, refer to the PepsiCo and Coca-Cola balance sheets in Appendixes A and B.

ANALYSIS

Use of current and noncurrent classifications makes it possible to analyze a company's liquidity. **Liquidity** refers to the ability to pay maturing obligations and meet unexpected needs for cash. The relationship of current assets to current liabilities is critical in analyzing liquidity. We can express this relationship as a dollar amount (working capital) and as a ratio (the current ratio).

The excess of current assets over current liabilities is **working capital**. Illustration 11-4 shows the formula for the computation of Caterpillar's working capital (dollar amounts in millions).

Illustration 11-4
Working capital formula and computation

Current Assets	−	Current Liabilities	=	Working Capital
$26,789	−	$19,292	=	**$7,497**

As an absolute dollar amount, working capital offers limited informational value. For example, $1 million of working capital may be far more than needed for a small company but be inadequate for a large corporation. Also, $1 million of working capital may be adequate for a company at one time but inadequate at another time.

The **current ratio** permits us to compare the liquidity of different-sized companies and of a single company at different times. The current ratio is calculated as current assets divided by current liabilities. The formula for this ratio is illustrated below, along with its computation using Caterpillar's current asset and current liability data (dollar amounts in millions).

Illustration 11-5
Current ratio formula and computation

Current Assets	÷	Current Liabilities	=	Current Ratio
$26,789	÷	$19,292	=	**1.39:1**

Historically, companies and analysts considered a current ratio of 2:1 to be the standard for a good credit rating. In recent years, however, many healthy companies have maintained ratios well below 2:1 by improving management of their current assets and liabilities. Caterpillar's ratio of 1.39:1 is adequate but certainly below the standard of 2:1.

Contingent Liabilities

With notes payable, interest payable, accounts payable, and sales taxes payable, we know that an obligation to make a payment exists. But suppose that your company is involved in a dispute with the Internal Revenue Service (IRS) over the amount of its income tax liability. Should you report the disputed amount as a liability on the balance sheet? Or suppose your company is involved in a lawsuit which, if you lose, might result in bankruptcy. How should you report this major contingency? The answers to these questions are difficult, because these liabilities are dependent—contingent—upon some future event. In other words, a **contingent liability** is a potential liability that may become an actual liability in the future.

How should companies report contingent liabilities? They use the following guidelines:

1. If the contingency is **probable** (if it is *likely* to occur) **and** the amount can be **reasonably estimated**, the liability should be recorded in the accounts.
2. If the contingency is only **reasonably possible** (if it *could* happen), then it needs to be disclosed only in the notes that accompany the financial statements.
3. If the contingency is **remote** (if it is *unlikely* to occur), it need not be recorded or disclosed.

Recording a Contingent Liability

Product warranties are an example of a contingent liability that companies should record in the accounts. Warranty contracts result in future costs that companies may incur in replacing defective units or repairing malfunctioning units. Generally, a manufacturer, such as Stanley Black & Decker, knows that it will incur some warranty costs. From prior experience with the product, the company usually can reasonably estimate the anticipated cost of servicing (honoring) the warranty.

The accounting for warranty costs is based on the expense recognition principle. **The estimated cost of honoring product warranty contracts should be recognized as an expense in the period in which the sale occurs.** To illustrate, assume that in 2012 Denson Manufacturing Company sells 10,000 washers and dryers at an average price of $600 each. The selling price includes a one-year warranty on parts. Denson expects that 500 units (5%) will be defective and that warranty repair costs will average $80 per unit. In 2012, the company honors warranty contracts on 300 units, at a total cost of $24,000.

At December 31, it is necessary to accrue the estimated warranty costs on the 2012 sales. Denson computes the estimated warranty liability as follows.

Illustration 11-6
Computation of estimated product warranty liability

Number of units sold	10,000
Estimated rate of defective units	× 5%
Total estimated defective units	500
Average warranty repair cost	× $80
Estimated product warranty liability	**$40,000**

The company makes the following adjusting entry.

A	=	L	+	OE
				−40,000 Exp
		+40,000		

Cash Flows
no effect

Dec. 31	Warranty Expense	40,000	
	Warranty Liability		40,000
	(To accrue estimated warranty costs)		

Denson records those repair costs incurred in 2012 to honor warranty contracts on 2012 sales as shown below.

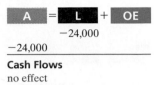

Jan. 1–	Warranty Liability	24,000	
Dec. 31	Repair Parts		24,000
	(To record honoring of 300 warranty		
	contracts on 2012 sales)		

A = L + OE
      −24,000
−24,000

Cash Flows
no effect

The company reports warranty expense of $40,000 under selling expenses in the income statement. It classifies warranty liability of $16,000 ($40,000 − $24,000) as a current liability on the balance sheet.

In the following year, Denson should debit to Warranty Liability all expenses incurred in honoring warranty contracts on 2012 sales. To illustrate, assume that the company replaces 20 defective units in January 2013, at an average cost of $80 in parts and labor. The summary entry for the month of January 2013 is:

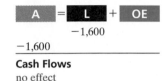

Jan. 31	Warranty Liability	1,600	
	Repair Parts		1,600
	(To record honoring of 20 warranty		
	contracts on 2012 sales)		

A = L + OE
      −1,600
−1,600

Cash Flows
no effect

Disclosure of Contingent Liabilities

When it is probable that a company will incur a contingent liability but it cannot reasonably estimate the amount, or when the contingent liability is only reasonably possible, only disclosure of the contingency is required. Examples of contingencies that may require disclosure are pending or threatened lawsuits and assessment of additional income taxes pending an IRS audit of the tax return.

The disclosure should identify the nature of the item and, if known, the amount of the contingency and the expected outcome of the future event. Disclosure is usually accomplished through a note to the financial statements, as illustrated by the following.

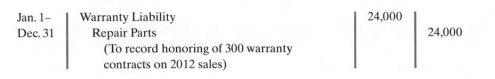

Yahoo! Inc.
Notes to the Financial Statements

Illustration 11-7
Disclosure of contingent liability

Contingencies. From time to time, third parties assert patent infringement claims against the company. Currently the company is engaged in several lawsuits regarding patent issues and has been notified of a number of other potential patent disputes. In addition, from time to time the company is subject to other legal proceedings and claims in the ordinary course of business, including claims for infringement of trademarks, copyrights and other intellectual property rights.... The Company does not believe, based on current knowledge, that any of the foregoing legal proceedings or claims are likely to have a material adverse effect on the financial position, results of operations or cash flows.

The required disclosure for contingencies is a good example of the use of the full-disclosure principle. The **full-disclosure principle** requires that companies disclose all circumstances and events that would make a difference to financial statement users. Some important financial information, such as contingencies, is not easily reported in the financial statements. Reporting information on contingencies in the notes to the financial statements will help investors be aware of events that can affect the financial health of a company.

Do it!

Current Liabilities

Lepid Company has the following account balances at December 31, 2012.

Notes payable ($80,000 due after 12/31/13)	$200,000
Unearned service revenue	75,000
Other long-term debt ($30,000 due in 2013)	150,000
Salaries and wages payable	22,000
Other accrued expenses	15,000
Accounts payable	100,000

In addition, Lepid is involved in a lawsuit. Legal counsel feels it is probable Lepid will pay damages of $38,000 in 2013.

(a) Prepare the current liability section of Lepid's December 31, 2012, balance sheet.

(b) Lepid's current assets are $504,000. Compute Lepid's working capital and current ratio.

action plan

✔ Determine which liabilities will be paid within one year or the operating cycle and include those as current liabilities.

✔ If the contingent liability is probable and reasonably estimable, include it as a current liability.

✔ Use the formula for working capital: Current assets − Current liabilities.

✔ Use the formula for the current ratio: Current assets ÷ Current liabilities.

Solution

(a) Current liabilities

Notes payable	$120,000
Accounts payable	100,000
Unearned service revenue	75,000
Lawsuit liability	38,000
Salaries and wages payable	22,000
Other accrued expenses	15,000
Long-term debt due within one year	30,000
Total current liabilities	$400,000

(b) Working capital = Current assets − Current liabilities = $504,000 − $400,000 = $104,000
Current ratio: Current assets ÷ Current liabilities = $504,000 ÷ $400,000 = 1.26:1

Related exercise material: BE11-5, E11-7, E11-8, E11-9, and **Do it!** 11-2.

✔ **The Navigator**

Payroll Accounting

Payroll and related fringe benefits often make up a large percentage of current liabilities. Employee compensation is often the most significant expense that a company incurs. For example, Costco recently reported total employees of 103,000 and labor and fringe benefits costs which approximated 70% of the company's total cost of operations.

Payroll accounting involves more than paying employees' wages. Companies are required by law to maintain payroll records for each employee, to file and pay payroll taxes, and to comply with state and federal tax laws related to employee compensation.

The term "payroll" **pertains to both salaries and wages of employees**. Managerial, administrative, and sales personnel are generally paid salaries. Salaries are often expressed in terms of a specified amount per month or per year rather than an hourly rate. Store clerks, factory employees, and manual laborers are normally paid wages.

Wages are based on a rate per hour or on a piecework basis (such as per unit of product). Frequently, people use the terms "salaries" and "wages" interchangeably.

The term "payroll" **does not apply to payments made for services of professionals** such as certified public accountants, attorneys, and architects. Such professionals are independent contractors rather than salaried employees. Payments to them are called **fees**. This distinction is important because government regulations relating to the payment and reporting of payroll taxes apply only to employees.

Determining the Payroll

Determining the payroll involves computing three amounts: (1) gross earnings, (2) payroll deductions, and (3) net pay.

Study Objective [6]
Compute and record the payroll for a pay period.

GROSS EARNINGS

Gross earnings is the total compensation earned by an employee. It consists of wages or salaries, plus any bonuses and commissions.

Companies determine total **wages** for an employee by multiplying the hours worked by the hourly rate of pay. In addition to the hourly pay rate, most companies are required by law to pay hourly workers a minimum of 1½ times the regular hourly rate for overtime work in excess of eight hours per day or 40 hours per week. In addition, many employers pay overtime rates for work done at night, on weekends, and on holidays.

For example, assume that Michael Jordan, an employee of Academy Company, worked 44 hours for the weekly pay period ending January 14. His regular wage is $12 per hour. For any hours in excess of 40, the company pays at one-and-a-half times the regular rate. Academy computes Jordan's gross earnings (total wages) as follows.

Type of Pay	Hours	×	Rate	=	Gross Earnings
Regular	40	×	$12	=	$480
Overtime	4	×	18	=	72
Total wages					**$552**

Illustration 11-8
Computation of total wages

This computation assumes that Jordan receives 1½ times his regular hourly rate ($12 × 1.5) for his overtime hours. Union contracts often require that overtime rates be as much as twice the regular rates.

An employee's **salary** is generally based on a monthly or yearly rate. The company then prorates these rates to its payroll periods (e.g., biweekly or monthly). Most executive and administrative positions are salaried. Federal law does not require overtime pay for employees in such positions.

Many companies have **bonus** agreements for employees. One survey found that over 94% of the largest U.S. manufacturing companies offer annual bonuses to key executives. Bonus arrangements may be based on such factors as increased sales or net income. Companies may pay bonuses in cash and/or by granting employees the opportunity to acquire shares of company stock at favorable prices (called stock option plans).

Ethics Note

Bonuses often reward outstanding individual performance, but successful corporations also need considerable teamwork. A challenge is to motivate individuals while preventing an unethical employee from taking another's idea for his or her own advantage.

PAYROLL DEDUCTIONS

As anyone who has received a paycheck knows, gross earnings are usually very different from the amount actually received. The difference is due to **payroll deductions**.

Payroll deductions may be mandatory or voluntary. **Mandatory deductions are required by law and consist of FICA taxes and income taxes.** Voluntary deductions are at the option of the employee. Illustration 11-9 (page 520) summarizes common

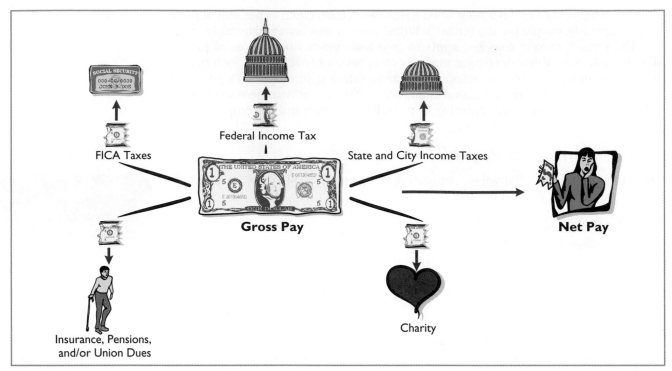

Illustration 11-9
Payroll deductions

types of payroll deductions. Such deductions do not result in payroll tax expense to the employer. The employer is merely a collection agent, and subsequently transfers the deducted amounts to the government and designated recipients.

FICA Taxes. In 1937, Congress enacted the Federal Insurance Contribution Act (FICA). **FICA taxes are designed to provide workers with supplemental retirement, employment disability, and medical benefits.** In 1965, Congress extended benefits to include Medicare for individuals over 65 years of age. The benefits are financed by a tax levied on employees' earnings. FICA taxes are commonly referred to as **Social Security taxes**.

Congress sets the tax rate and the tax base for FICA taxes. When FICA taxes were first imposed, the rate was 1% on the first $3,000 of gross earnings, or a maximum of $30 per year. The rate and base have changed dramatically since that time! In 2010, the rate was 7.65% (6.2% Social Security plus 1.45% Medicare) on the first $106,800 of gross earnings for each employee.[1] For purpose of illustration in this chapter, we will assume a rate of 8% on the first $100,000 of gross earnings, or a maximum of $8,000. Using the 8% rate, the FICA withholding for Jordan for the weekly pay period ending January 14 is $44.16 ($552 × 8%).

Income Taxes. Under the U.S. pay-as-you-go system of federal income taxes, employers are required to withhold income taxes from employees each pay period. Three variables determine the amount to be withheld: (1) the employee's gross earnings; (2) the number of allowances claimed by the employee; and (3) the length of the pay period. The number of allowances claimed typically includes the employee, his or her spouse, and other dependents.

---

[1]The Medicare provision also includes a tax of 1.45% on gross earnings in excess of $106,800. In the interest of simplification, we ignore this 1.45% charge in our end-of-chapter assignment material. We assume zero FICA withholdings on gross earnings above $100,000.

Withholding tables furnished by the Internal Revenue Service indicate the amount of income tax to be withheld. Withholding amounts are based on gross wages and the number of allowances claimed. Separate tables are provided for weekly, biweekly, semimonthly, and monthly pay periods. Illustration 11-10 shows the withholding tax table for Michael Jordan (assuming he earns $552 per week and claims two allowances). For a weekly salary of $552 with two allowances, the income tax to be withheld is $49.

Illustration 11-10
Withholding tax table

MARRIED Persons — **WEEKLY** Payroll Period
(For Wages Paid in 2010)

If the wages are —		And the number of withholding allowances claimed is —										
At least	But less than	0	1	2	3	4	5	6	7	8	9	10
		The amount of income tax to be withheld is —										
490	500	56	48	40	32	24	17	9	1	0	0	0
500	510	57	49	42	34	26	18	10	3	0	0	0
510	520	59	51	43	35	27	20	12	4	0	0	0
520	530	60	52	45	37	29	21	13	6	0	0	0
530	540	62	54	46	38	30	23	15	7	0	0	0
540	550	63	55	48	40	32	24	16	9	1	0	0
550	560	65	57	49	41	33	26	18	10	2	0	0
560	570	66	58	51	43	35	27	19	12	4	0	0
570	580	68	60	52	44	36	29	21	13	5	0	0
580	590	69	61	54	46	38	30	22	15	7	0	0
590	600	71	63	55	47	39	32	24	16	8	1	0
600	610	72	64	57	49	41	33	25	18	10	2	0
610	620	74	66	58	50	42	35	27	19	11	4	0
620	630	75	67	60	52	44	36	28	21	13	5	0
630	640	77	69	61	53	45	38	30	22	14	7	0
640	650	78	70	63	55	47	39	31	24	16	8	0
650	660	80	72	64	56	48	41	33	25	17	10	2
660	670	81	73	66	58	50	42	34	27	19	11	3
670	680	83	75	67	59	51	44	36	28	20	13	5
680	690	84	76	69	61	53	45	37	30	22	14	6

In addition, most states (and some cities) require **employers** to withhold income taxes from employees' earnings. As a rule, the amounts withheld are a percentage (specified in the state revenue code) of the amount withheld for the federal income tax. Or they may be a specified percentage of the employee's earnings. For the sake of simplicity, we have assumed that Jordan's wages are subject to state income taxes of 2%, or $11.04 (2% × $552) per week.

There is no limit on the amount of gross earnings subject to income tax withholdings. In fact, under our progressive system of taxation, the higher the earnings, the higher the percentage of income withheld for taxes.

Other Deductions.   Employees may voluntarily authorize withholdings for charitable organizations, retirement, and other purposes. All voluntary deductions from gross earnings should be authorized in writing by the employee. The authorization(s) may be made individually or as part of a group plan. Deductions for charitable organizations, such as the United Fund, or for financial arrangements, such as U.S. savings bonds and repayment of loans from company credit unions, are made individually. Deductions for union dues, health and life insurance, and pension plans are often made on a group basis. We will assume that Jordan has weekly voluntary deductions of $10 for the United Fund and $5 for union dues.

NET PAY

Academy determines **net pay** by subtracting payroll deductions from gross earnings. Illustration 11-11 shows the computation of Jordan's net pay for the pay period.

Illustration 11-11
Computation of net pay

Gross earnings		$552.00
Payroll deductions:		
FICA taxes	$44.16	
Federal income taxes	49.00	
State income taxes	11.04	
United Fund	10.00	
Union dues	5.00	119.20
Net pay		**$432.80**

Assuming that Michael Jordan's wages for each week during the year are $552, total wages for the year are $28,704 (52 × $552). Thus, all of Jordan's wages are subject to FICA tax during the year. In comparison, let's assume that Jordan's department head earns $2,000 per week, or $104,000 for the year. Since we assume that only the first $100,000 is subject to FICA taxes, the maximum FICA withholdings on the department head's earnings would be $8,000 ($100,000 × 8%).

Recording the Payroll

Recording the payroll involves maintaining payroll department records, recognizing payroll expenses and liabilities, and recording payment of the payroll.

MAINTAINING PAYROLL DEPARTMENT RECORDS

To comply with state and federal laws, an employer must keep a cumulative record of each employee's gross earnings, deductions, and net pay during the year. The record that provides this information is the **employee earnings record**. Illustration 11-12 (page 523) shows Michael Jordan's employee earnings record.

Companies keep a separate earnings record for each employee, and update these records after each pay period. The employer uses the cumulative payroll data on the earnings record to: (1) determine when an employee has earned the maximum earnings subject to FICA taxes, (2) file state and federal payroll tax returns (as explained later), and (3) provide each employee with a statement of gross earnings and tax withholdings for the year. Illustration 11-16 on page 529 shows this statement.

In addition to employee earnings records, many companies find it useful to prepare a **payroll register**. This record accumulates the gross earnings, deductions, and net pay by employee for each pay period. Illustration 11-13 (page 523) presents Academy Company's payroll register. It provides the documentation for preparing a paycheck for each employee. For example, it shows the data for Michael Jordan in the wages section. In this example, Academy Company's total weekly payroll is $17,210, as shown in the gross earnings column (column E, row 24).

Note that this record is a listing of each employee's payroll data for the pay period. In some companies, a payroll register is a journal or book of original entry. Postings are made from it directly to ledger accounts. In other companies, the payroll register is a memorandum record that provides the data for a general journal entry and subsequent posting to the ledger accounts. At Academy Company, the latter procedure is followed.

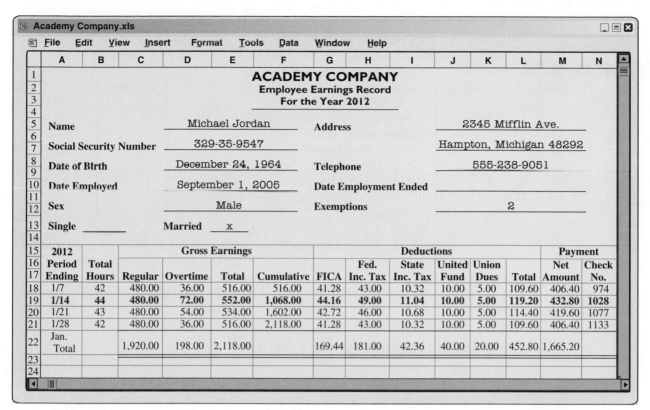

Illustration 11-12
Employee earnings record

ACADEMY COMPANY.xls

File Edit View Insert Format Tools Data Window Help

ACADEMY COMPANY
Employee Earnings Record
For the Year 2012

Name: Michael Jordan   Address: 2345 Mifflin Ave.

Social Security Number: 329-35-9547   Hampton, Michigan 48292

Date of Birth: December 24, 1964   Telephone: 555-238-9051

Date Employed: September 1, 2005   Date Employment Ended:

Sex: Male   Exemptions: 2

Single _____   Married x

2012 Period Ending	Total Hours	Gross Earnings Regular	Overtime	Total	Cumulative	FICA	Fed. Inc. Tax	State Inc. Tax	United Fund	Union Dues	Total	Net Amount	Check No.
1/7	42	480.00	36.00	516.00	516.00	41.28	43.00	10.32	10.00	5.00	109.60	406.40	974
1/14	44	480.00	72.00	552.00	1,068.00	44.16	49.00	11.04	10.00	5.00	119.20	432.80	1028
1/21	43	480.00	54.00	534.00	1,602.00	42.72	46.00	10.68	10.00	5.00	114.40	419.60	1077
1/28	42	480.00	36.00	516.00	2,118.00	41.28	43.00	10.32	10.00	5.00	109.60	406.40	1133
Jan. Total		1,920.00	198.00	2,118.00		169.44	181.00	42.36	40.00	20.00	452.80	1,665.20	

Illustration 11-13
Payroll register

ACADEMY COMPANY.xls

File Edit View Insert Format Tools Data Window Help

ACADEMY COMPANY
Payroll Register
For the Week Ending January 14, 2012

Employee	Total Hours	Earnings Regular	Over-time	Gross	FICA	Deductions Federal Income Tax	State Income Tax	United Fund	Union Dues	Total	Paid Net Pay	Check No.	Account Debited Salaries and Wages Expense
Arnold, Patricia	40	580.00		580.00	46.40	61.00	11.60	15.00		134.00	446.00	998	580.00
Canton, Matthew	40	590.00		590.00	47.20	63.00	11.80	20.00		142.00	448.00	999	590.00
Mueller, William	40	530.00		530.00	42.40	54.00	10.60	11.00		118.00	412.00	1000	530.00
Bennett, Robin	42	480.00	36.00	516.00	41.28	43.00	10.32	18.00	5.00	117.60	398.40	1025	516.00
Jordan, Michael	44	480.00	72.00	552.00	44.16	49.00	11.04	10.00	5.00	119.20	432.80	1028	552.00
Milroy, Lee	43	480.00	54.00	534.00	42.72	46.00	10.68	10.00	5.00	114.40	419.60	1029	534.00
Total		16,200.00	1,010.00	17,210.00	1,376.80	3,490.00	344.20	421.50	115.00	5,747.50	11,462.50		17,210.00

RECOGNIZING PAYROLL EXPENSES AND LIABILITIES

From the payroll register in Illustration 11-13, Academy Company makes a journal entry to record the payroll. For the week ending January 14, the entry is:

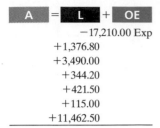

A = L + OE

−17,210.00 Exp
+1,376.80
+3,490.00
+344.20
+421.50
+115.00
+11,462.50

Cash Flows
no effect

Jan. 14	Salaries and Wages Expense	17,210.00	
	FICA Taxes Payable		1,376.80
	Federal Income Taxes Payable		3,490.00
	State Income Taxes Payable		344.20
	United Fund Payable		421.50
	Union Dues Payable		115.00
	Salaries and Wages Payable		11,462.50
	(To record payroll for the week ending January 14)		

The company credits specific liability accounts for the mandatory and voluntary deductions made during the pay period. In the example, Academy debits Salaries and Wages Expense for the gross earnings of its employees. The amount credited to Salaries and Wages Payable is the sum of the individual checks the employees will receive.

RECORDING PAYMENT OF THE PAYROLL

A company makes payments by check (or electronic funds transfer) either from its regular bank account or a payroll bank account. Each paycheck is usually accompanied by a detachable **statement of earnings** document. This shows the employee's gross earnings, payroll deductions, and net pay, both for the period and for the year-to-date. Academy Company uses its regular bank account for payroll checks. Illustration 11-14 shows the paycheck and statement of earnings for Michael Jordan.

Illustration 11-14
Paycheck and statement of earnings

Helpful Hint

Do any of the income tax liabilities result in payroll tax expense for the employer?

Answer: No. The employer is acting only as a collection agent for the government.

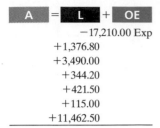

		NO. 1028
	ACADEMY COMPANY	
AC	19 Center St.	
	Hampton, MI 48291	January 14, 2012 62—1113 / 610

Pay to the order of _Michael Jordan_ $ 432.80

Four Hundred Thirty-two and 80/100 _____ Dollars

City Bank & Trust
P.O. Box 3000
Hampton, MI 48291

For _Payroll_   _Randall E. Barnes_

⑆00324477⑆ ⑈1028

- -
DETACH AND RETAIN THIS PORTION FOR YOUR RECORDS

NAME				SOC. SEC. NO.	EMPL. NUMBER	NO. EXEMP	PAY PERIOD ENDING
Michael Jordan				329-35-9547		2	1/14/12

REG. HRS.	O.T. HRS.	OTH. HRS. (1)	OTH. HRS. (2)	REG. EARNINGS	O.T. EARNINGS	OTH. EARNINGS (1)	OTH. EARNINGS (2)	GROSS
40	4			480.00	72.00			$552.00

FED. W/H TAX	FICA	STATE TAX	LOCAL TAX	OTHER DEDUCTIONS				NET PAY
49.00	44.16	11.04		(1) 10.00	(2) 5.00	(3)	(4)	432.80

			YEAR TO DATE				
FED. W/H TAX	FICA	STATE TAX	LOCAL TAX	OTHER DEDUCTIONS				NET PAY
92.00	85.44	21.36		(1) 20.00	(2) 10.00	(3)	(4)	$839.20

Following payment of the payroll, the company enters the check numbers in the payroll register. Academy Company records payment of the payroll as follows.

Jan. 14	Salaries and Wages Payable	11,462.50	
	Cash		11,462.50
	(To record payment of payroll)		

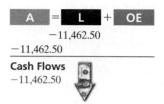

A = L + OE
−11,462.50
−11,462.50
Cash Flows
−11,462.50

Many medium- and large-size companies use a payroll processing center that provides payroll record-keeping services. Companies send the center payroll information about employee pay rates and hours worked. The center maintains the payroll records and prepares the payroll checks. In most cases, it costs less to process the payroll through the center than if the company did so internally.

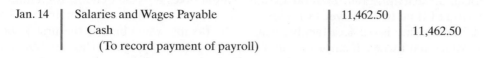

Do it!

In January, gross earnings in Ramirez Company were $40,000. All earnings are subject to 8% FICA taxes. Federal income tax withheld was $9,000, and state income tax withheld was $1,000. (a) Calculate net pay for January, and (b) record the payroll.

Payroll

action plan

✔ Determine net pay by subtracting payroll deductions from gross earnings.

✔ Record gross earnings as Salaries and Wages Expense, record payroll deductions as liabilities, and record net pay as Salaries and Wages Payable.

Solution

(a) Net pay: $40,000 − (8% × $40,000) − $9,000 − $1,000 = $26,800

(b)	Salaries and Wages Expense	40,000	
	FICA Taxes Payable		3,200
	Federal Income Taxes Payable		9,000
	State Income Taxes Payable		1,000
	Salaries and Wages Payable		26,800
	(To record payroll)		

Related exercise material: BE11-7, BE11-8, E11-10, E11-11, E11-12, E11-13, and **Do it!** 11-3.

The Navigator

Employer Payroll Taxes

Payroll tax expense for businesses results from three taxes that governmental agencies levy **on employers**. These taxes are: (1) FICA, (2) federal unemployment tax, and (3) state unemployment tax. These taxes plus such items as paid vacations and pensions (discussed in the appendix to this chapter) are collectively referred to as **fringe benefits**. As indicated earlier, the cost of fringe benefits in many companies is substantial. The pie chart in the margin shows the pieces of the benefits "pie."

Study Objective [7]
Describe and record employer payroll taxes.

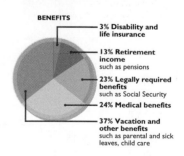

BENEFITS
3% Disability and life insurance
13% Retirement income such as pensions
23% Legally required benefits such as Social Security
24% Medical benefits
37% Vacation and other benefits such as parental and sick leaves, child care

FICA TAXES

Each employee must pay FICA taxes. In addition, employers must match each employee's FICA contribution. This means the employer must remit to the federal government 12.4% of each employee's first $106,800 of taxable earnings, plus 2.9% of each employee's earnings, regardless of amount. The matching contribution results in **payroll tax expense** to the employer. The employer's tax is subject to the same rate and maximum earnings as the employee's. The company uses the same account, FICA Taxes Payable, to record both the employee's and the employer's FICA contributions. For the January 14 payroll, Academy Company's FICA tax contribution is $1,376.80 ($17,210.00 × 8%).

FEDERAL UNEMPLOYMENT TAXES

The Federal Unemployment Tax Act (FUTA) is another feature of the federal Social Security program. **Federal unemployment taxes** provide benefits for a limited period of time to employees who lose their jobs through no fault of their own. The FUTA tax rate is 6.2% of taxable wages. The taxable wage base is the first $7,000 of wages paid to each employee in a calendar year. Employers who pay the state unemployment tax on a timely basis will receive an offset credit of up to 5.4%. Therefore, the net federal tax rate is generally 0.8% (6.2%–5.4%). This rate would equate to a maximum of $56 of federal tax per employee per year (0.8% × $7,000). State tax rates are based on state law.

The **employer** bears the entire federal unemployment tax. There is no deduction or withholding from employees. Companies use the account Federal Unemployment Taxes Payable to recognize this liability. The federal unemployment tax for Academy Company for the January 14 payroll is $137.68 ($17,210.00 × 0.8%).

STATE UNEMPLOYMENT TAXES

All states have unemployment compensation programs under state unemployment tax acts (SUTA). Like federal unemployment taxes, **state unemployment taxes** provide benefits to employees who lose their jobs. These taxes are levied on employers.[2] The basic rate is usually 5.4% on the first $7,000 of wages paid to an employee during the year. The state adjusts the basic rate according to the employer's experience rating: Companies with a history of stable employment may pay less than 5.4%. Companies with a history of unstable employment may pay more than the basic rate. Regardless of the rate paid, the company's credit on the federal unemployment tax is still 5.4%.

Companies use the account State Unemployment Taxes Payable for this liability. The state unemployment tax for Academy Company for the January 14 payroll is $929.34 ($17,210.00 × 5.4%). Illustration 11-15 summarizes the types of employer payroll taxes.

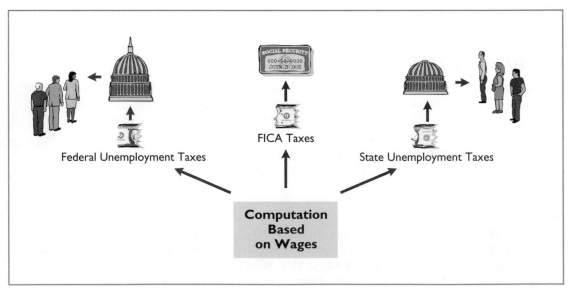

Illustration 11-15
Employer payroll taxes

---

[2]In a few states, the employee is also required to make a contribution. *In this textbook, including the homework, we will assume that the tax is only on the employer.*

RECORDING EMPLOYER PAYROLL TAXES

Companies usually record employer payroll taxes at the same time they record the payroll. The entire amount of gross pay ($17,210.00) shown in the payroll register in Illustration 11-13 is subject to each of the three taxes mentioned above. Accordingly, Academy records the payroll tax expense associated with the January 14 payroll with the following entry.

Jan. 14	Payroll Tax Expense	2,443.82	
	FICA Taxes Payable		1,376.80
	Federal Unemployment Taxes Payable		137.68
	State Unemployment Taxes Payable		929.34
	(To record employer's payroll taxes on January 14 payroll)		

A	=	L	+	OE

−2,443.82 Exp
+1,376.80
+137.68
+929.34

Cash Flows
no effect

Note that Academy uses separate liability accounts instead of a single credit to Payroll Taxes Payable. Why? Because these liabilities are payable to different taxing authorities at different dates. Companies classify the liability accounts in the balance sheet as current liabilities since they will be paid within the next year. They classify Payroll Tax Expense on the income statement as an operating expense.

ACCOUNTING ACROSS THE ORGANIZATION

It Costs $74,000 to Put $44,000 in Sally's Pocket

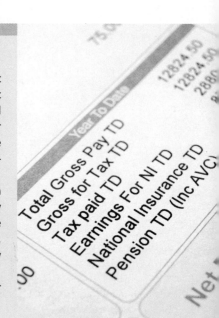

Sally works for Bogan Communications, a small company in New Jersey that provides audio systems. She makes $59,000 a year but only nets $44,000. What happened to the other $15,000? Well, $2,376 goes for Sally's share of the medical and dental insurance that Bogan provides, $126 for state unemployment insurance, $149 for disability insurance, and $856 for Medicare. New Jersey takes $1,893 in income taxes, and the federal government gets $3,661 for Social Security and another $6,250 for income tax withholding. All of this adds up to some 22% of Sally's gross pay going to Washington or Trenton.

Employing Sally costs Bogan plenty too. Bogan has to write checks for $74,000 so Sally can receive her $59,000 in base pay. Health insurance is the biggest cost: While Sally pays nearly $2,400 for coverage, Bogan pays the rest—$9,561. Then, the federal and state governments take $56 for federal unemployment coverage, $149 for disability insurance, $300 for workers' comp, and $505 for state unemployment insurance. Finally, the government requires Bogan to pay $856 for Sally's Medicare and $3,661 for her Social Security.

When you add it all up, it costs $74,000 to put $44,000 in Sally's pocket and to give her $12,000 in benefits.

Source: Michael P. Fleischer, "Why I'm Not Hiring," *Wall Street Journal* (August 9, 2010), p. A17.

? How are the Social Security and Medicare taxes computed for Sally's salary? (See page 549.)

Do it!

In January, the payroll supervisor determines that gross earnings for Halo Company are $70,000. All earnings are subject to 8% FICA taxes, 5.4% state unemployment taxes, and 0.8% federal unemployment taxes. Halo asks you to record the employer's payroll taxes.

Employer's Payroll Taxes

action plan

✔ Compute the employer's payroll taxes on the period's gross earnings.

✔ Identify the expense account(s) to be debited.

✔ Identify the liability account(s) to be credited.

Solution

The entry to record the employer's payroll taxes is:

Payroll Tax Expense	9,940	
FICA Taxes Payable ($70,000 × 8%)		5,600
Federal Unemployment Taxes Payable ($70,000 × 0.8%)		560
State Unemployment Taxes Payable ($70,000 × 5.4%)		3,780
(To record employer's payroll taxes		
on January payroll)		

Related exercise material: BE11-9, E11-12, E11-14, and **Do it!** 11-4.

Filing and Remitting Payroll Taxes

Preparation of payroll tax returns is the responsibility of the payroll department. The treasurer's department makes the tax payment. Much of the information for the returns is obtained from employee earnings records.

For purposes of reporting and remitting to the IRS, the company combines the FICA taxes and federal income taxes that it withheld. **Companies must report the taxes quarterly**, no later than one month following the close of each quarter. The remitting requirements depend on the amount of taxes withheld and the length of the pay period. Companies remit funds through deposits in either a Federal Reserve bank or an authorized commercial bank.

Companies generally file and remit federal unemployment taxes **annually** on or before January 31 of the subsequent year. Earlier payments are required when the tax exceeds a specified amount. Companies usually must file and pay state unemployment taxes by the **end of the month following each quarter**. When payroll taxes are paid, companies debit payroll liability accounts, and credit Cash.

ANATOMY OF A FRAUD

Art was a custodial supervisor for a large school district. The district was supposed to employ between 35 and 40 regular custodians, as well as 3 or 4 substitute custodians to fill in when regular custodians were missing. Instead, in addition to the regular custodians, Art "hired" 77 substitutes. In fact, almost none of these people worked for the district. Instead, Art submitted time cards for these people, collected their checks at the district office, and personally distributed the checks to the "employees." If a substitute's check was for $1,200, that person would cash the check, keep $200, and pay Art $1,000.

Total take: $150,000

THE MISSING CONTROLS

Human Resource Controls. Thorough background checks should be performed. No employees should begin work until they have been approved by the Board of Education and entered into the payroll system. No employees should be entered into the payroll system until they have been approved by a supervisor. All paychecks should be distributed directly to employees at the official school locations by designated employees.

Independent internal verification. Budgets should be reviewed monthly to identify situations where actual costs significantly exceed budgeted amounts.

Source: Adapted from Wells, *Fraud Casebook* (2007), pp. 164–171.

Employers also must provide each employee with a **Wage and Tax Statement (Form W-2)** by January 31 following the end of a calendar year. This statement shows gross earnings, FICA taxes withheld, and income taxes withheld for the year. The required W-2 form for Michael Jordan, using assumed annual data, is shown in Illustration 11-16. The employer must send a copy of each employee's Wage and Tax Statement (Form W-2) to the Social Security Administration. This agency subsequently furnishes the Internal Revenue Service with the income data required.

22222	Void ☐	**a** Employee's social security number 329-36-9547	For Official Use Only ▶ OMB No. 1545-0008	
b Employer identification number (EIN) 36-2167852			**1** Wages, tips, other compensation 26,300.00	**2** Federal income tax withheld 2,248.00
c Employer's name, address, and ZIP code Academy Company 19 Center St. Hampton, MI 48291			**3** Social security wages 26,300.00	**4** Social security tax withheld 2,104.00
			5 Medicare wages and tips 26,300.00	**6** Medicare tax withheld
			7 Social security tips	**8** Allocated tips
d Control number			**9** Advance EIC payment	**10** Dependent care benefits
e Employee's first name and initial Michael	Last name Jordan	Suff.	**11** Nonqualified plans	**12a** See instructions for box 12
			13 Statutory employee ☐ Retirement plan ☐ Third-party sick pay ☐	**12b**
2345 Mifflin Ave. Hampton, MI 48292			**14** Other	**12c**
				12d
f Employee's address and ZIP code				
15 State MI Employer's state ID number 423-1466-3	**16** State wages, tips, etc. 26,300.00	**17** State income tax 526.00	**18** Local wages, tips, etc.	**19** Local income tax **20** Locality name

Form **W-2** Wage and Tax Statement   **2010**   Department of the Treasury—Internal Revenue Service

Copy A For Social Security Administration — Send this entire page with Form W-3 to the Social Security Administration; photocopies are **not** acceptable.

For Privacy Act and Paperwork Reduction Act Notice, see back of Copy D.

Cat. No. 10134D

Illustration 11-16
W-2 form

Internal Control for Payroll

Chapter 8 introduced internal control. As applied to payrolls, the objectives of internal control are (1) to safeguard company assets against unauthorized payments of payrolls, and (2) to ensure the accuracy and reliability of the accounting records pertaining to payrolls.

Irregularities often result if internal control is lax. Frauds involving payroll include overstating hours, using unauthorized pay rates, adding fictitious employees to the payroll, continuing terminated employees on the payroll, and distributing duplicate payroll checks. Moreover, inaccurate records will result in incorrect paychecks, financial statements, and payroll tax returns.

Payroll activities involve four functions: hiring employees, timekeeping, preparing the payroll, and paying the payroll. For effective internal control, companies should assign these four functions to different departments or individuals. Illustration 11-17 (page 530) highlights these functions and illustrates their internal control features.

Study Objective [8]
Discuss the objectives of internal control for payroll.

Payroll Function

Payroll Function

Hiring Employees

Human Resources

Internal control feature:
Human Resources department documents and authorizes employment.

Fraud prevented:
Fictitious employees are not added to payroll.

Preparing the Payroll

Internal control feature:
Two (or more) employees verify payroll amounts; supervisor approves.

Fraud prevented:
Payroll calculations are accurate and relevant.

Timekeeping

Internal control feature:
Supervisors monitor hours worked through time cards and time reports.

Fraud prevented:
Employee works appropriate hours.

Paying the Payroll

Internal control feature:
Treasurer signs and distributes prenumbered checks.

Fraud prevented:
Checks are not lost from theft; endorsed check provides proof of payment.

Illustration 11-17
Internal control for payroll

COMPREHENSIVE
Do it!

Indiana Jones Company had the following selected transactions.

Feb. 1 Signs a $50,000, 6-month, 9%-interest-bearing note payable to CitiBank and receives $50,000 in cash.

10 Cash register sales total $43,200, which includes an 8% sales tax.

28 The payroll for the month consists of salaries and wages of $50,000. All wages are subject to 8% FICA taxes. A total of $8,900 federal income taxes are withheld. The salaries are paid on March 1.

28 The company develops the following adjustment data.
1. Interest expense of $375 has been incurred on the note.
2. Employer payroll taxes include 8% FICA taxes, a 5.4% state unemployment tax, and a 0.8% federal unemployment tax.
3. Some sales were made under warranty. Of the units sold under warranty, 350 are expected to become defective. Repair costs are estimated to be $40 per unit.

Instructions

(a) Journalize the February transactions.

(b) Journalize the adjusting entries at February 28.

action plan

✔ To determine sales, divide the cash register total by 100% plus the sales tax percentage.

✔ Base payroll taxes on gross earnings.

✔ Expense warranty costs in the period in which the sale occurs.

Solution to Comprehensive Do it!

(a) Feb. 1	Cash		50,000	
	Notes Payable			50,000
	(Issued 6-month, 9%-interest-bearing note to CitiBank)			
	10	Cash		43,200	
	Sales Revenue ($43,200 ÷ 1.08)			40,000
	Sales Taxes Payable ($40,000 × 8%)			3,200
	(To record sales and sales taxes payable)			

28	Salaries and Wages Expense		50,000	
	FICA Taxes Payable (8% × $50,000)			4,000
	Federal Income Taxes Payable			8,900
	Salaries and Wages Payable			37,100
	(To record February salaries)			
(b) Feb. 28	Interest Expense		375	
	Interest Payable			375
	(To record accrued interest for February)			
28	Payroll Tax Expense		7,100	
	FICA Taxes Payable			4,000
	Federal Unemployment Taxes Payable			400
	(0.8% × $50,000)			
	State Unemployment Taxes Payable			2,700
	(5.4% × $50,000)			
	(To record employer's payroll taxes on			
	February payroll)			
28	Warranty Expense (350 × $40)		14,000	
	Warranty Liability			14,000
	(To record estimated product warranty			
	liability)			

Summary of Study Objectives

[1] Explain a current liability, and identify the major types of current liabilities. A current liability is a debt that a company can reasonably expect to pay (1) from existing current assets or through the creation of other current liabilities, and (2) within one year or the operating cycle, whichever is longer. The major types of current liabilities are notes payable, accounts payable, sales taxes payable, unearned revenues, and accrued liabilities such as taxes, salaries and wages, and interest payable.

[2] Describe the accounting for notes payable. When a promissory note is interest-bearing, the amount of assets received upon the issuance of the note is generally equal to the face value of the note. Interest expense accrues over the life of the note. At maturity, the amount paid equals the face value of the note plus accrued interest.

[3] Explain the accounting for other current liabilities. Companies record sales taxes payable at the time the related sales occur. The company serves as a collection agent for the taxing authority. Sales taxes are not an expense to the company. Companies initially record unearned revenues in an Unearned Revenue account. As the company earns the revenue, a transfer from unearned revenue to earned revenue occurs. Companies report the current maturities of long-term debt as a current liability in the balance sheet.

[4] Explain the financial statement presentation and analysis of current liabilities. Companies should report the nature and amount of each current liability in the balance sheet or in schedules in the notes accompanying the statements. The liquidity of a company may be analyzed by computing working capital and the current ratio.

[5] Describe the accounting and disclosure requirements for contingent liabilities. If the contingency is *probable* (likely to occur) and the amount is reasonably estimable, the company should record the liability in the accounts. If the contingency is only *reasonably possible* (it could happen), then it should be disclosed only in the notes to the financial statements. If the possibility that the contingency will happen is *remote* (unlikely to occur), it need not be recorded or disclosed.

[6] Compute and record the payroll for a pay period. The computation of the payroll involves gross earnings, payroll deductions, and net pay. In recording the payroll, companies debit salaries (or wages) expense for gross earnings, credit individual tax and other liability accounts for payroll deductions, and credit salaries (wages) payable for net pay. When the payroll is paid, companies debit Salaries and Wages Payable, and credit Cash.

[7] Describe and record employer payroll taxes. Employer payroll taxes consist of FICA, federal unemployment taxes, and state unemployment taxes. The taxes are usually accrued at the time the company records the payroll, by debiting Payroll Tax Expense and crediting separate liability accounts for each type of tax.

[8] Discuss the objectives of internal control for payroll. The objectives of internal control for payroll are (1) to safeguard company assets against unauthorized payments of payrolls, and (2) to ensure the accuracy of the accounting records pertaining to payrolls.

Glossary

Bonus Compensation to management and other personnel, based on factors such as increased sales or the amount of net income. (p. 519).

Contingent liability A potential liability that may become an actual liability in the future. (p. 515).

Current ratio A measure of a company's liquidity; computed as current assets divided by current liabilities. (p. 515).

Employee earnings record A cumulative record of each employee's gross earnings, deductions, and net pay during the year. (p. 522).

Federal unemployment taxes Taxes imposed on the employer by the federal government that provide benefits for a limited time period to employees who lose their jobs through no fault of their own. (p. 526).

Fees Payments made for the services of professionals. (p. 519).

FICA taxes Taxes designed to provide workers with supplemental retirement, employment disability, and medical benefits. (p. 520).

Full-disclosure principle Requires that companies disclose all circumstances and events that would make a difference to financial statement users. (p. 517).

Gross earnings Total compensation earned by an employee. (p. 519).

Net pay Gross earnings less payroll deductions. (p. 522).

Notes payable Obligations in the form of written notes. (p. 510).

Payroll deductions Deductions from gross earnings to determine the amount of a paycheck. (p. 519).

Payroll register A payroll record that accumulates the gross earnings, deductions, and net pay by employee for each pay period. (p. 522).

Salaries Employee pay based on a specified amount rather than an hourly rate. (p. 518).

Statement of earnings A document attached to a paycheck that indicates the employee's gross earnings, payroll deductions, and net pay. (p. 524).

State unemployment taxes Taxes imposed on the employer by states that provide benefits to employees who lose their jobs. (p. 526).

Wage and Tax Statement (Form W-2) A form showing gross earnings, FICA taxes withheld, and income taxes withheld, prepared annually by an employer for each employee. (p. 528).

Wages Amounts paid to employees based on a rate per hour or on a piecework basis. (p. 518).

Working capital A measure of a company's liquidity; computed as current assets minus current liabilities. (p. 515).

APPENDIX11A

Additional Fringe Benefits

Study Objective [9]
Identify additional fringe benefits associated with employee compensation.

In addition to the three payroll-tax fringe benefits, employers incur other substantial fringe benefit costs. Two of the most important are paid absences and post-retirement benefits.

Paid Absences

Employees often are given rights to receive compensation for absences when they meet certain conditions of employment. The compensation may be for paid vacations, sick pay benefits, and paid holidays. When the payment for such absences is **probable** and the amount can be **reasonably estimated**, the company should accrue a liability for paid future absences. When the amount cannot be reasonably estimated, the company should instead disclose the potential liability. Ordinarily, vacation pay is the only paid absence that is accrued. The other types of paid absences are only disclosed.

To illustrate, assume that Academy Company employees are entitled to one day's vacation for each month worked. If 30 employees earn an average of $110 per day in a given month, the accrual for vacation benefits in one month is $3,300. Academy records the liability at the end of the month by the following adjusting entry.

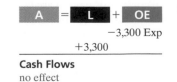

A = L + OE
−3,300 Exp
+3,300

Cash Flows
no effect

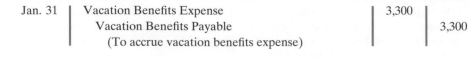

Jan. 31	Vacation Benefits Expense	3,300	
	Vacation Benefits Payable		3,300
	(To accrue vacation benefits expense)		

This accrual is required by the expense recognition principle. Academy would report Vacation Benefits Expense as an operating expense in the income statement, and Vacation Benefits Payable as a current liability in the balance sheet.

Later, when Academy pays vacation benefits, it debits Vacation Benefits Payable and credits Cash. For example, if employees take 10 days of vacation in July, the entry is:

July 31	Vacation Benefits Payable	1,100	
	Cash		1,100
	(To record payment of vacation benefits)		

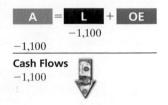

The magnitude of unpaid absences has gained employers' attention. Consider the case of an assistant superintendent of schools who worked for 20 years and rarely took a vacation or sick day. A month or so before she retired, the school district discovered that she was due nearly $30,000 in accrued benefits. Yet the school district had never accrued the liability.

Post-Retirement Benefits

Post-retirement benefits are benefits that employers provide to retired employees for (1) pensions and (2) health care and life insurance. Companies account for both types of post-retirement benefits on the accrual basis. The cost of post-retirement benefits is getting steep. For example, states and localities must deal with a $1 trillion deficit in public employees' retirement benefit funds. The shortfall amounts to more than $8,800 for every household in the nation.

The average American has debt of approximately $10,000 (not counting the mortgage on their home) and has little in the way of savings. What will happen at retirement for these people? The picture is not pretty—people are living longer, the future of Social Security is unclear, and companies are cutting back on post-retirement benefits. This situation may lead to one of the great social and moral dilemmas this country faces in the next 40 years. The more you know about post-retirement benefits, the better you will understand the issues involved in this dilemma.

PENSIONS

A **pension plan** is an agreement whereby employers provide benefits (payments) to employees after they retire. The most popular type of pension plan used is the 401(k) plan. A 401(k) plan works as follows: As an employee, you can contribute up to a certain percentage of your pay into a 401(k) plan, and your employer will match a percentage of your contribution. These contributions are then generally invested in stocks and bonds through mutual funds. These funds will grow without being taxed and can be withdrawn beginning at age 59-1/2. If you must access the funds earlier, you may be able to do so, but a penalty usually occurs along with a payment of tax on the proceeds. Any time you have the opportunity to be involved in a 401(k) plan, you should avail yourself of this benefit!

The accounting for a 401(k) plan by the company is straightforward. When the company makes a contribution on behalf of the employee, it debits Pension Expense and credits Cash for the amount contributed. For example, Mark Hatfield, an employee of Veri Company, contributes $11,000 to his 401(k) plan. Veri Company matches this contribution, and records the expense with the following entry.

Pension Expense	11,000	
Cash		11,000
(To record contribution to 401(k) plan)		

If the pension expense is not funded during the year, the company credits Pension Liability.

A 401(k) plan is often referred to as a **defined-contribution plan**. In a defined-contribution plan, the plan defines the contribution that an employer will make but not the benefit that the employee will receive at retirement.

The other type of pension plan is a **defined-benefit plan**. In a defined-benefit plan, the employer agrees to pay a defined amount to retirees, based on employees meeting certain eligibility standards. The amount of the benefit is usually based on years of service and average salary over a period of years. Employers are at risk with defined-benefit plans because they must contribute enough to meet the cost of benefits that the plan defines. Many large companies have defined-benefit plans. The accounting for these plans is complex. Many companies are starting to utilize 401(k) plans more extensively instead.

POST-RETIREMENT HEALTH-CARE AND LIFE INSURANCE BENEFITS

Providing medical and related health-care benefits for retirees was at one time an inexpensive and highly effective way of generating employee goodwill. This practice has now turned into one of corporate America's most worrisome financial problems. Runaway medical costs, early retirement, and increased longevity are sending the liability for retiree health plans through the roof.

Companies estimate and expense post-retirement costs during the working years of the employee because the company benefits from the employee's services during this period. However, the company rarely sets up funds to meet the cost of the future benefits. It follows a pay-as-you-go basis for these costs. The major reason is that the company does not receive a tax deduction until it actually pays the medical bill.

Summary of Study Objective for Appendix 11A

[9] Identify additional fringe benefits associated with employee compensation. Additional fringe benefits associated with wages are paid absences (paid vacations, sick pay benefits, and paid holidays), and post-retirement benefits (pensions, health care, and life insurance).

Glossary for Appendix 11A

Pension plan   An agreement whereby an employer provides benefits to employees after they retire. (p. 533).

Post-retirement benefits   Payments by employers to retired employees for health care, life insurance, and pensions. (p. 533).

Self-Test, Brief Exercises, Exercises Problem Set A, and many more components are available for practice in *WileyPLUS*

***Note:** All **asterisked** Questions, Exercises, and Problems relate to material in the appendix to the chapter.

Self-Test Questions

Answers are on page 549.

(SO 1)   **1.** The time period for classifying a liability as current is one year or the operating cycle, whichever is:
   a. longer.   **c.** probable.
   b. shorter.   **d.** possible.

2. To be classified as a current liability, a debt must be ex-   (SO 1)
pected to be paid:
   a. out of existing current assets.
   b. by creating other current liabilities.
   c. within 2 years.
   d. Both (a) and (b).

(SO 2) 3. Maggie Sharrer Company borrows $88,500 on September 1, 2012, from Sandwich State Bank by signing an $88,500, 12%, one-year note. What is the accrued interest at December 31, 2012?
- **a.** $2,655.
- **b.** $3,540.
- **c.** $4,425.
- **d.** $10,620.

(SO 2) 4. RS Company borrowed $70,000 on December 1 on a 6-month, 6% note. At December 31:
- **a.** neither the note payable nor the interest payable is a current liability.
- **b.** the note payable is a current liability, but the interest payable is not.
- **c.** the interest payable is a current liability but the note payable is not.
- **d.** both the note payable and the interest payable are current liabilities.

(SO 3) 5. Becky Sherrick Company has total proceeds from sales of $4,515. If the proceeds include sales taxes of 5%, the amount to be credited to Sales Revenue is:
- **a.** $4,000.
- **b.** $4,300.
- **c.** $4,289.25.
- **d.** No correct answer given.

(SO 3) 6. Sensible Insurance Company collected a premium of $18,000 for a 1-year insurance policy on April 1. What amount should Sensible report as a current liability for Unearned Insurance Premiums at December 31?
- **a.** $0.
- **b.** $4,500.
- **c.** $13,500.
- **d.** $18,000.

(SO 4) 7. Working capital is calculated as:
- **a.** current assets minus current liabilities.
- **b.** total assets minus total liabilities.
- **c.** long-term liabilities minus current liabilities.
- **d.** Both (b) and (c).

(SO 4) 8. The current ratio is computed as:
- **a.** total assets divided by total liabilities.
- **b.** total assets divided by current liabilities.
- **c.** current assets divided by total liabilities.
- **d.** current assets divided by current liabilities.

(SO 5) 9. A contingent liability should be recorded in the accounts when:
- **a.** it is probable the contingency will happen, but the amount cannot be reasonably estimated.
- **b.** it is reasonably possible the contingency will happen, and the amount can be reasonably estimated.
- **c.** it is probable the contingency will happen, and the amount can be reasonably estimated.

- **d.** it is reasonably possible the contingency will happen, but the amount cannot be reasonably estimated.

(SO 5) 10. At December 31, Hanes Company prepares an adjusting entry for a product warranty contract. Which of the following accounts is/are included in the entry?
- **a.** Miscellaneous Expense.
- **b.** Warranty Liability.
- **c.** Repair Parts.
- **d.** Both (a) and (b).

(SO 6) 11. Andy Manion earns $14 per hour for a 40-hour week and $21 per hour for any overtime work. If Manion works 45 hours in a week, gross earnings are:
- **a.** $560.
- **b.** $630.
- **c.** $650.
- **d.** $665.

(SO 6) 12. When recording payroll:
- **a.** gross earnings are recorded as salaries and wages payable.
- **b.** net pay is recorded as salaries and wages expense.
- **c.** payroll deductions are recorded as liabilities.
- **d.** More than one of the above.

(SO 7) 13. Employer payroll taxes do *not* include:
- **a.** federal unemployment taxes.
- **b.** state unemployment taxes.
- **c.** federal income taxes.
- **d.** FICA taxes.

(SO 7) 14. FICA Taxes Payable was credited for $7,500 in the entry when Antonio Company recorded payroll. When Antonio Company records employer's payroll taxes, FICA Taxes Payable should be credited for:
- **a.** $0.
- **b.** $7,500.
- **c.** $15,000.
- **d.** Some other amount.

(SO 8) 15. The department that should pay the payroll is the:
- **a.** timekeeping department.
- **b.** human resources department.
- **c.** payroll department.
- **d.** treasurer's department.

(SO 9) *16. Which of the following is *not* an additional fringe benefit?
- **a.** Post-retirement pensions.
- **b.** Paid absences.
- **c.** Paid vacations.
- **d.** Salaries.

Go to the book's companion website, **www.wiley.com/college/weygandt**, for additional Self-Test Questions.

Questions

1. Jill Loomis believes a current liability is a debt that can be expected to be paid in one year. Is Jill correct? Explain.

2. Frederickson Company obtains $40,000 in cash by signing a 9%, 6-month, $40,000 note payable to First Bank on July 1. Frederickson's fiscal year ends on September 30. What information should be reported for the note payable in the annual financial statements?

3. (a) Your roommate says, "Sales taxes are reported as an expense in the income statement." Do you agree? Explain.

(b) Planet Hollywood has cash proceeds from sales of $7,400. This amount includes $400 of sales taxes. Give the entry to record the proceeds.

4. Baylor University sold 10,000 season football tickets at $80 each for its five-game home schedule. What entries should be made (a) when the tickets were sold, and (b) after each game?

5. What is liquidity? What are two measures of liquidity?

6. What is a contingent liability? Give an example of a contingent liability that is usually recorded in the accounts.

7. Under what circumstances is a contingent liability disclosed only in the notes to the financial statements? Under what circumstances is a contingent liability not recorded in the accounts nor disclosed in the notes to the financial statements?

8. What is the difference between gross pay and net pay? Which amount should a company record as wages and salaries expense?

9. Which payroll tax is levied on both employers and employees?

10. Are the federal and state income taxes withheld from employee paychecks a payroll tax expense for the employer? Explain your answer.

11. What do the following acronyms stand for: FICA, FUTA, and SUTA?

12. What information is shown in a W-2 statement?

13. Distinguish between the two types of payroll deductions and give examples of each.

14. What are the primary uses of the employee earnings record?

15. (a) Identify the three types of employer payroll taxes.
    (b) How are tax liability accounts and payroll tax expense accounts classified in the financial statements?

16. You are a newly hired accountant with Batista Company. On your first day, the controller asks you to identify the main internal control objectives related to payroll accounting. How would you respond?

17. What are the four functions associated with payroll activities?

*18. Identify two additional types of fringe benefits associated with employees' compensation.

*19. Often during job interviews, the candidate asks the potential employer about the firm's paid absences policy. What are paid absences? How are they accounted for?

*20. What are two types of post-retirement benefits?

*21. Explain how a 401(k) plan works.

*22. What is the difference between a defined-contribution pension plan and a defined-benefit pension plan?

Brief Exercises

Identify whether obligations are current liabilities.
(SO 1)

BE11-1 Sanford Company has the following obligations at December 31: (a) a note payable for $100,000 due in 2 years, (b) a 10-year mortgage payable of $300,000 payable in ten $30,000 annual payments, (c) interest payable of $15,000 on the mortgage, and (d) accounts payable of $60,000. For each obligation, indicate whether it should be classified as a current liability. (Assume an operating cycle of less than one year.)

Prepare entries for an interest-bearing note payable.
(SO 2)

BE11-2 Douglas Company borrows $80,000 on July 1 from the bank by signing a $80,000, 10%, one-year note payable.

(a) Prepare the journal entry to record the proceeds of the note.
(b) Prepare the journal entry to record accrued interest at December 31, assuming adjusting entries are made only at the end of the year.

Compute and record sales taxes payable.
(SO 3)

BE11-3 Savango Auto Supply does not segregate sales and sales taxes at the time of sale. The register total for March 16 is $15,540. All sales are subject to a 5% sales tax. Compute sales taxes payable, and make the entry to record sales taxes payable and sales.

Prepare entries for unearned revenues.
(SO 3)

BE11-4 Frost University sells 4,000 season basketball tickets at $180 each for its 12-game home schedule. Give the entry to record (a) the sale of the season tickets and (b) the revenue earned by playing the first home game.

Analyze liquidity.
(SO 4)

BE11-5 Yahoo! Inc.'s 2009 financial statements contain the following selected data (in thousands).

Current assets	$ 4,594,772	Current liabilities	$1,717,728
Total assets	14,936,030	Total liabilities	2,417,394

Compute (a) working capital and (b) current ratio.

Prepare adjusting entry for warranty costs.
(SO 5)

BE11-6 On December 1, Beaver Company introduces a new product that includes a one-year warranty on parts. In December, 1,000 units are sold. Management believes that 5% of the units will be defective and that the average warranty costs will be $80 per unit. Prepare the adjusting entry at December 31 to accrue the estimated warranty cost.

Compute gross earnings and net pay.
(SO 6)

BE11-7 Dawn French's regular hourly wage rate is $16, and she receives an hourly rate of $24 for work in excess of 40 hours. During a January pay period, Dawn works 47 hours. Dawn's federal income tax withholding is $95, and she has no voluntary deductions. Compute Dawn French's gross earnings and net pay for the pay period.

Record a payroll and the payment of wages.
(SO 6)

BE11-8 Data for Dawn French are presented in BE11-7. Prepare the journal entries to record (a) Dawn's pay for the period and (b) the payment of Dawn's wages. Use January 15 for the end of the pay period and the payment date.

BE11-9   In January, gross earnings in Gyro Company totaled $70,000. All earnings are subject to 8% FICA taxes, 5.4% state unemployment taxes, and 0.8% federal unemployment taxes. Prepare the entry to record January payroll tax expense.

Record employer payroll taxes.
(SO 7)

BE11-10   Vardan Company has the following payroll procedures.

(a) Supervisor approves overtime work.
(b) The human resources department prepares hiring authorization forms for new hires.
(c) A second payroll department employee verifies payroll calculations.
(d) The treasurer's department pays employees.

Identify the payroll function to which each procedure pertains.

Identify payroll functions.
(SO 8)

*BE11-11   At Wolf Company, employees are entitled to one day's vacation for each month worked. In January, 80 employees worked the full month. Record the vacation pay liability for January assuming the average daily pay for each employee is $120.

Record estimated vacation benefits.
(SO 9)

Do it! Review

Do it! 11-1   You and several classmates are studying for the next accounting examination. They ask you to answer the following questions:

Answer questions about current liabilities.
(SO 2, 3)

1. If cash is borrowed on a $70,000, 9-month, 12% note on August 1, how much interest expense would be incurred by December 31?
2. The cash register total including sales taxes is $42,000, and the sales tax rate is 5%. What is the sales taxes payable?
3. If $42,000 is collected in advance on November 1 for 6-month magazine subscriptions, what amount of subscription revenue is earned by December 31?

Do it! 11-2   Goblin Company, has the following account balances at December 31, 2012.

Prepare current liabilities section and compute liquidity measures.
(SO 4, 5)

Notes payable ($60,000 due after 12/31/13)	$100,000
Unearned service revenue	70,000
Other long-term debt ($90,000 due in 2013)	250,000
Salaries and wages payable	32,000
Accounts payable	63,000

In addition, Goblin is involved in a lawsuit. Legal counsel feels it is probable Goblin will pay damages of $85,000 in 2013.

(a) Prepare the current liability section of Goblin's 12/31/12 balance sheet.
(b) Goblin's current assets are $570,000. Compute Goblin's working capital and current ratio.

Do it! 11-3   In January, gross earnings in Centaur Company were $60,000. All earnings are subject to 8% FICA taxes. Federal income tax withheld was $14,000, and state income tax withheld was $1,600. (a) Calculate net pay for January, and (b) record the payroll.

Calculate net pay and record payroll.
(SO 6)

Do it! 11-4   In January, the payroll supervisor determines that gross earnings for Maugrim Company are $110,000. All earnings are subject to 8% FICA taxes, 5.4% state unemployment taxes, and 0.8% federal unemployment taxes. Bond asks you to record the employer's payroll taxes.

Record employer's payroll taxes.
(SO 7)

Exercises

E11-1   C.S. Lewis Company had the following transactions involving notes payable.

Prepare entries for interest-bearing notes.
(SO 2)

July 1, 2012	Borrows $50,000 from Fourth National Bank by signing a 9-month, 12% note.
Nov. 1, 2012	Borrows $60,000 from Livingston State Bank by signing a 3-month, 10% note.
Dec. 31, 2012	Prepares adjusting entries.
Feb. 1, 2013	Pays principal and interest to Livingston State Bank.
Apr. 1, 2013	Pays principal and interest to Fourth National Bank.

Instructions
Prepare journal entries for each of the transactions.

E11-2   On June 1, Caspian Company borrows $90,000 from First Bank on a 6-month, $90,000, 12% note.

Prepare entries for interest-bearing notes.
(SO 2)

Instructions

(a) Prepare the entry on June 1.

(b) Prepare the adjusting entry on June 30.

(c) Prepare the entry at maturity (December 1), assuming monthly adjusting entries have been made through November 30.

(d) What was the total financing cost (interest expense)?

Journalize sales and related taxes.

(SO 3)

E11-3 In providing accounting services to small businesses, you encounter the following situations pertaining to cash sales.

1. Miraz Company rings up sales and sales taxes separately on its cash register. On April 10, the register totals are sales $30,000 and sales taxes $1,500.

2. Trumpkin Company does not segregate sales and sales taxes. Its register total for April 15 is $23,540, which includes a 7% sales tax.

Instructions

Prepare the entry to record the sales transactions and related taxes for each client.

Journalize unearned subscription revenue.

(SO 3)

E11-4 Sergio Company publishes a monthly sports magazine, *Fishing Preview*. Subscriptions to the magazine cost $20 per year. During November 2012, Sergio sells 12,000 subscriptions beginning with the December issue. Sergio prepares financial statements quarterly and recognizes subscription revenue earned at the end of the quarter. The company uses the accounts Unearned Subscription Revenue and Subscription Revenue.

Instructions

(a) Prepare the entry in November for the receipt of the subscriptions.

(b) Prepare the adjusting entry at December 31, 2012, to record sales revenue earned in December 2012.

(c) Prepare the adjusting entry at March 31, 2013, to record sales revenue earned in the first quarter of 2013.

Record estimated liability and expense for warranties.

(SO 5)

E11-5 Castellitto Company sells automatic can openers under a 75-day warranty for defective merchandise. Based on past experience, Castellitto estimates that 3% of the units sold will become defective during the warranty period. Management estimates that the average cost of replacing or repairing a defective unit is $20. The units sold and units defective that occurred during the last 2 months of 2012 are as follows.

Month	Units Sold	Units Defective Prior to December 31
November	30,000	600
December	32,000	400

Instructions

(a) Determine the estimated warranty liability at December 31 for the units sold in November and December.

(b) Prepare the journal entries to record the estimated liability for warranties and the costs incurred in honoring 1,000 warranty claims. (Assume actual costs of $20,000.)

(c) Give the entry to record the honoring of 500 warranty contracts in January at an average cost of $20.

Record and disclose contingent liabilities.

(SO 5)

E11-6 Nikabrik Co. is involved in a lawsuit as a result of an accident that took place September 5, 2012. The lawsuit was filed on November 1, 2012, and claims damages of $1,000,000.

Instructions

(a) At December 31, 2012, Nikabrik's attorneys feel it is remote that Nikabrik will lose the lawsuit. How should the company account for the effects of the lawsuit?

(b) Assume instead that at December 31, 2012, Nikabrik's attorneys feel it is probable that Nikabrik will lose the lawsuit and be required to pay $1,000,000. How should the company account for this lawsuit?

(c) Assume instead that at December 31, 2012, Nikabrik's attorneys feel it is reasonably possible that Nikabrik could lose the lawsuit and be required to pay $1,000,000. How should the company account for this lawsuit?

Prepare the current liability section of the balance sheet.

(SO 1, 2, 3, 4, 5)

E11-7 Warwick Online Company has the following liability accounts after posting adjusting entries: Accounts Payable $63,000, Unearned Ticket Revenue $24,000, Estimated Warranty Liability $18,000, Interest Payable $8,000, Mortgage Payable $120,000, Notes Payable $80,000, and Sales Taxes Payable $10,000. Assume the company's operating cycle is less than 1 year, ticket revenue will be earned within 1 year, warranty costs are expected to be incurred within 1 year, and the notes mature in 3 years.

Instructions

(a) Prepare the current liabilities section of the balance sheet, assuming $30,000 of the mortgage is payable next year.

(b) Comment on Warwick Online Company's liquidity, assuming total current assets are $300,000.

E11-8 Kroger Co.'s 2009 financial statements contained the following data (in millions).

Calculate liquidity ratios.
(SO 4)

Current assets	$ 7,450	Accounts receivable	$909
Total assets	23,093	Interest expense	502
Current liabilities	7,714	Income tax expense	532
Total liabilities	18,187	Net income	70
Cash	424		

Instructions

Compute these values:

(a) Working capital.   (b) Current ratio.

E11-9 The following financial data were reported by 3M Company for 2008 and 2009 (dollars in millions).

Calculate current ratio and working capital before and after paying accounts payable.
(SO 4)

3M Company
Balance Sheets (partial)

	2009	2008
Current assets		
Cash and cash equivalents	$ 3,040	$1,849
Accounts receivable, net	3,250	3,195
Inventories	2,639	3,013
Other current assets	1,866	1,541
Total current assets	$10,795	$9,598
Current liabilities	$ 4,897	$5,839

Instructions

(a) Calculate the current ratio and working capital for 3M for 2008 and 2009.

(b) Suppose that at the end of 2009, 3M management used $200 million cash to pay off $200 million of accounts payable. How would its current ratio and working capital have changed?

E11-10 Pedja Belic's regular hourly wage rate is $15, and she receives a wage of 1½ times the regular hourly rate for work in excess of 40 hours. During a March weekly pay period, Pedja worked 42 hours. Her gross earnings prior to the current week were $6,000. Pedja is married and claims three withholding allowances. Her only voluntary deduction is for group hospitalization insurance at $25 per week.

Compute net pay and record pay for one employee.
(SO 6)

Instructions

(a) Compute the following amounts for Pedja's wages for the current week.
   (1) Gross earnings.
   (2) FICA taxes. (Assume an 8% rate on maximum of $90,000.)
   (3) Federal income taxes withheld. (Use the withholding table in the text, page 521.)
   (4) State income taxes withheld. (Assume a 2.0% rate.)
   (5) Net pay.
(b) Record Pedja's pay.

E11-11 Employee earnings records for Cornelius Company reveal the following gross earnings for four employees through the pay period of December 15.

Compute maximum FICA deductions.
(SO 6)

J. Glozelle	$93,500	L. Schooler	$96,100
R. Jen	$97,600	T. Crier	$104,000

For the pay period ending December 31, each employee's gross earnings is $4,000. The FICA tax rate is 8% on gross earnings of $100,000.

Instructions
Compute the FICA withholdings that should be made for each employee for the December 31 pay period. (Show computations.)

Prepare payroll register and record payroll and payroll tax expense.
(SO 6, 7)

E11-12   Alvarez Company has the following data for the weekly payroll ending January 31.

| Employee | Hours | | | | | | Hourly Rate | Federal Income Tax Withholding | Health Insurance |
	M	T	W	T	F	S			
L. Donnon	8	8	9	8	10	3	$12	$34	$10
L. Gregoire	8	8	8	8	8	2	13	37	25
D. Alcazar	9	10	8	8	9	0	15	58	25

Employees are paid 1½ times the regular hourly rate for all hours worked in excess of 40 hours per week. FICA taxes are 8% on the first $100,000 of gross earnings. Alvarez Company is subject to 5.4% state unemployment taxes and 0.8% federal unemployment taxes on the first $7,000 of gross earnings.

Instructions
(a) Prepare the payroll register for the weekly payroll.
(b) Prepare the journal entries to record the payroll and Alvarez's payroll tax expense.

Compute missing payroll amounts and record payroll.
(SO 6)

E11-13   Selected data from a February payroll register for Favino Company are presented below. Some amounts are intentionally omitted.

Gross earnings:		State income taxes	$ (3)
Regular	$8,900	Union dues	100
Overtime	(1)	Total deductions	(4)
Total	(2)	Net pay	$7,660
Deductions:		Account debited:	
FICA taxes	$ 800	Salaries and wages expense	(5)
Federal income taxes	1,140		

FICA taxes are 8%. State income taxes are 3% of gross earnings.

Instructions
(a) Fill in the missing amounts.
(b) Journalize the February payroll and the payment of the payroll.

Determine employer's payroll taxes; record payroll tax expense.
(SO 7)

E11-14   According to a payroll register summary of Pierfrancesco Company, the amount of employees' gross pay in December was $850,000, of which $90,000 was not subject to FICA tax and $750,000 was not subject to state and federal unemployment taxes.

Instructions
(a) Determine the employer's payroll tax expense for the month, using the following rates: FICA 8%, state unemployment 5.4%, federal unemployment 0.8%.
(b) Prepare the journal entry to record December payroll tax expense.

Prepare adjusting entries for fringe benefits.
(SO 9)

*E11-15   Borrachero Company has two fringe benefit plans for its employees:
1. It grants employees 2 days' vacation for each month worked. Ten employees worked the entire month of March at an average daily wage of $120 per employee.
2. In its pension plan, the company recognizes 10% of gross earnings as a pension expense. Gross earnings in March were $40,000. No contribution has been made to the pension fund.

Instructions
Prepare the adjusting entries at March 31.

Prepare journal entries for fringe benefits.
(SO 9)

*E11-16   Glenstorm Corporation has 20 employees who each earn $120 a day. The following information is available.
1. At December 31, Glenstorm recorded vacation benefits. Each employee earned 5 vacation days during the year.

2. At December 31, Glenstorm recorded pension expense of $100,000, and made a contribution of $70,000 to the pension plan.

3. In January, 18 employees used one vacation day each.

Instructions
Prepare Glenstorm's journal entries to record these transactions.

Exercises: Set B

Visit the book's companion website, at **www.wiley.com/college/weygandt**, and choose the Student Companion site to access Exercise Set B.

Problems: Set A

P11-1A On January 1, 2012, the ledger of Montoya Company contains the following liability accounts.

Accounts Payable	$52,000
Sales Taxes Payable	7,700
Unearned Service Revenue	16,000

During January, the following selected transactions occurred.

Jan. 5 Sold merchandise for cash totaling $22,680, which includes 8% sales taxes.
   12 Provided services for customers who had made advance payments of $10,000. (Credit Service Revenue.)
   14 Paid state revenue department for sales taxes collected in December 2011 ($7,700).
   20 Sold 800 units of a new product on credit at $50 per unit, plus 8% sales tax. This new product is subject to a 1-year warranty.
   21 Borrowed $18,000 from DeKalb Bank on a 3-month, 8%, $18,000 note.
   25 Sold merchandise for cash totaling $12,420, which includes 8% sales taxes.

Instructions
(a) Journalize the January transactions.
(b) Journalize the adjusting entries at January 31 for (1) the outstanding notes payable, and (2) estimated warranty liability, assuming warranty costs are expected to equal 7% of sales of the new product. (*Hint:* Use one-third of a month for the DeKalb Bank note.)
(c) Prepare the current liabilities section of the balance sheet at January 31, 2012. Assume no change in accounts payable.

P11-2A The following are selected transactions of Andreu Company. Andreu prepares financial statements quarterly.

Jan. 2 Purchased merchandise on account from Diego Company, $30,000, terms 2/10, n/30. (Andreu uses the perpetual inventory system.)
Feb. 1 Issued a 9%, 2-month, $30,000 note to Diego in payment of account.
Mar. 31 Accrued interest for 2 months on Diego note.
Apr. 1 Paid face value and interest on Diego note.
July 1 Purchased equipment from Garcia Equipment paying $11,000 in cash and signing a 10%, 3-month, $40,000 note.
Sept. 30 Accrued interest for 3 months on Garcia note.
Oct. 1 Paid face value and interest on Garcia note.
Dec. 1 Borrowed $15,000 from the Isova Bank by issuing a 3-month, 8% note with a face value of $15,000.
Dec. 31 Recognized interest expense for 1 month on Isova Bank note.

Instructions
(a) Prepare journal entries for the listed transactions and events.
(b) Post to the accounts Notes Payable, Interest Payable, and Interest Expense.
(c) Show the balance sheet presentation of notes and interest payable at December 31.
(d) What is total interest expense for the year?

Prepare current liability entries, adjusting entries, and current liabilities section.
(SO 1, 2, 3, 4, 5)

(c) Current liability total $84,640

Journalize and post note transactions; show balance sheet presentation.
(SO 2)

(d) $1,550

Prepare payroll register and payroll entries.

(SO 6, 7)

P11-3A   Hira Hardware has four employees who are paid on an hourly basis plus time-and-a half for all hours worked in excess of 40 a week. Payroll data for the week ended March 15, 2012, are presentd below.

Employee	Hours Worked	Hourly Rate	Federal Income Tax Withholdings	United Fund
Joe Hana	40	$15.00	$?	$5.00
Mary Alina	42	15.00	?	5.00
Andy Silva	44	13.00	60	8.00
Kim Gomez	46	13.00	61	5.00

Hana and Alina are married. They claim 0 and 4 withholding allowances, respectively. The following tax rates are applicable: FICA 8%, state income taxes 3%, state unemployment taxes 5.4%, and federal unemployment 0.8%.

Instructions

(a) Net pay $1,944.20

(a) Prepare a payroll register for the weekly payroll. (Use the wage-bracket withholding table in the text for federal income tax withholdings.)

(b) Payroll tax expense
   $352.16

(b) Journalize the payroll on March 15, 2012, and the accrual of employer payroll taxes.

(c) Journalize the payment of the payroll on March 16, 2012.

(d) Cash paid $636.80

(d) Journalize the deposit in a Federal Reserve bank on March 31, 2012, of the FICA and federal income taxes payable to the government.

Journalize payroll transactions and adjusting entries.

(SO 6, 7, 9)

P11-4A   The following payroll liability accounts are included in the ledger of Wimble Company on January 1, 2012.

FICA Taxes Payable	$ 760.00
Federal Income Taxes Payable	1,204.60
State Income Taxes Payable	108.95
Federal Unemployment Taxes Payable	288.95
State Unemployment Taxes Payable	1,954.40
Union Dues Payable	870.00
U.S. Savings Bonds Payable	360.00

In January, the following transactions occurred.

Jan. 10   Sent check for $870.00 to union treasurer for union dues.

12   Remitted check for $1,964.60 to the Federal Reserve bank for FICA taxes and federal income taxes withheld.

15   Purchased U.S. Savings Bonds for employees by writing check for $360.00.

17   Paid state income taxes withheld from employees.

20   Paid federal and state unemployment taxes.

31   Completed monthly payroll register, which shows office salaries $26,600, store wages $28,400, FICA taxes withheld $4,400, federal income taxes payable $2,158, state income taxes payable $454, union dues payable $400, United Fund contributions payable $1,888, and net pay $45,700.

31   Prepared payroll checks for the net pay and distributed checks to employees.

At January 31, the company also makes the following accrued adjustments pertaining to employee compensation.

1. Employer payroll taxes: FICA taxes 8%, federal unemployment taxes 0.8%, and state unemployment taxes 5.4%.

*2. Vacation pay: 6% of gross earnings.

(b) Payroll tax expense
   $7,810; Vacation benefits
   expense $3,300

Instructions

(a) Journalize the January transactions.

Prepare entries for payroll and payroll taxes; prepare W-2 data.

(SO 6, 7)

(b) Journalize the adjustments pertaining to employee compensation at January 31.

P11-5A   For the year ended December 31, 2012, Telmarine Electrical Repair Company reports the following summary payroll data.

Gross earnings:

Administrative salaries	$200,000
Electricians' wages	370,000
Total	$570,000

Deductions:

FICA taxes	$ 38,800
Federal income taxes withheld	174,400
State income taxes withheld (3%)	17,100
United Fund contributions payable	27,500
Health insurance premiums	17,200
Total	$275,000

Telmarine Company's payroll taxes are: FICA 8%, state unemployment 2.5% (due to a stable employment record), and 0.8% federal unemployment. Gross earnings subject to FICA taxes total $485,000, and gross earnings subject to unemployment taxes total $135,000.

Instructions
(a) Prepare a summary journal entry at December 31 for the full year's payroll.
(b) Journalize the adjusting entry at December 31 to record the employer's payroll taxes.
(c) The W-2 Wage and Tax Statement requires the following dollar data.

(a) Salaries and wages payable $295,000

(b) Payroll tax expense $43,255

Wages, Tips, Other Compensation	Federal Income Tax Withheld	State Income Tax Withheld	FICA Wages	FICA Tax Withheld

Complete the required data for the following employees.

Employee	Gross Earnings	Federal Income Tax Withheld
Lucie Solarava	$59,000	$28,500
Kristina Madericova	26,000	10,200

Problems: Set B

P11-1B On January 1, 2012, the ledger of Tyrus Company contains the following liability accounts.

Prepare current liability entries, adjusting entries, and current liabilities section.

(SO 1, 2, 3, 4, 5)

Accounts Payable	$30,000
Sales Taxes Payable	5,000
Unearned Service Revenue	12,000

During January, the following selected transactions occurred.

Jan. 1   Borrowed $20,000 in cash from Platteville Bank on a 4-month, 6%, $20,000 note.
     5   Sold merchandise for cash totaling $9,752, which includes 6% sales taxes.
    12   Provided services for customers who had made advance payments of $8,000. (Credit Service Revenue.)
    14   Paid state treasurer's department for sales taxes collected in December 2011, $5,000.
    20   Sold 900 units of a new product on credit at $44 per unit, plus 6% sales tax. This new product is subject to a 1-year warranty.
    25   Sold merchandise for cash totaling $16,536, which includes 6% sales taxes.

Instructions
(a) Journalize the January transactions.
(b) Journalize the adjusting entries at January 31 for (1) the outstanding notes payable, and (2) estimated warranty liability, assuming warranty costs are expected to equal 5% of sales of the new product.
(c) Prepare the current liabilities section of the balance sheet at January 31, 2012. Assume no change in accounts payable.

(c) Current liability total $59,944

P11-2B The following are selected transactions of Karolina Company. Karolina prepares financial statements *quarterly*.

Journalize and post note transactions and show balance sheet presentation.

(SO 2)

Jan. 2   Purchased merchandise on account from Pavel Company, $20,000, terms 2/10, n/30. (Karolina uses the perpetual inventory system.)

Feb. 1	Issued a 12%, 2-month, $20,000 note to Pavel in payment of account.
Mar. 31	Accrued interest for 2 months on Pavel note.
Apr. 1	Paid face value and interest on Pavel note.
July 1	Purchased equipment from Filipensky Equipment paying $12,000 in cash and signing a 10%, 3-month, $25,000 note.
Sept. 30	Accrued interest for 3 months on Filipensky note.
Oct. 1	Paid face value and interest on Filipensky note.
Dec. 1	Borrowed $15,000 from the Federated Bank by issuing a 3-month, 12% note with a face value of $15,000.
Dec. 31	Recognized interest expense for 1 month on Federated Bank note.

Instructions

(a) Prepare journal entries for the above transactions and events.

(b) Post to the accounts, Notes Payable, Interest Payable, and Interest Expense.

(c) Show the balance sheet presentation of notes and interest payable at December 31.

(d) $1,175

(d) What is total interest expense for the year?

Prepare payroll register and payroll entries.

(SO 6, 7)

P11-3B   Yemi's Drug Store has four employees who are paid on an hourly basis plus time-and-a-half for all hours worked in excess of 40 a week. Payroll data for the week ended February 15, 2012, are shown below.

Employee	Hours Worked	Hourly Rate	Federal Income Tax Withholdings	United Fund Contributions
M. Dvorska	39	$12.00	$34	$ –0–
D. Mottl	42	11.00	20	10.00
L. Abbasova	44	10.00	51	5.00
A. Lee	46	10.00	36	5.00

The following tax rates are applicable: FICA 8%, state income taxes 3%, state unemployment taxes 5.4%, and federal unemployment 0.8%. The first three employees are sales clerks (store wages expense). The fourth employee performs administrative duties (office wages expense).

Instructions

(a) Net pay $1,521.99

(a) Prepare a payroll register for the weekly payroll.

(b) Payroll tax expense $268.52

(b) Journalize the payroll on February 15, 2012, and the accrual of employer payroll taxes.

(c) Journalize the payment of the payroll on February 16, 2012.

(d) Cash paid $443.56

(d) Journalize the remittance to the Federal Reserve bank on February 28, 2012, of the FICA and federal income taxes payable to the government.

Journalize payroll transactions and adjusting entries.

(SO 6, 7, 9)

P11-4B   The following payroll liability accounts are included in the ledger of Patteri Company on January 1, 2012.

FICA Taxes Payable	$ 540
Federal Income Taxes Payable	1,100
State Income Taxes Payable	210
Federal Unemployment Taxes Payable	54
State Unemployment Taxes Payable	365
Union Dues Payable	200
U.S. Savings Bonds Payable	300

In January, the following transactions occurred.

Jan. 10	Sent check for $200 to union treasurer for union dues.
12	Remitted check for $1,640 to the Federal Reserve bank for FICA taxes and federal income taxes withheld.
15	Purchased U.S. Savings Bonds for employees by writing check for $300.
17	Paid state income taxes withheld from employees.
20	Paid federal and state unemployment taxes.
31	Completed monthly payroll register, which shows office salaries $17,400, store wages $22,500, FICA taxes withheld $3,192, federal income taxes payable $2,540, state income taxes payable $500, union dues payable $300, United Fund contributions payable $1,300, and net pay $32,068.
31	Prepared payroll checks for the net pay and distributed checks to employees.

At January 31, the company also makes the following accruals pertaining to employee compensation.

1. Employer payroll taxes: FICA taxes 8%, state unemployment taxes 5.4%, and federal unemployment taxes 0.8%.
*2. Vacation pay: 5% of gross earnings.

Instructions
(a) Journalize the January transactions.
(b) Journalize the adjustments pertaining to employee compensation at January 31.

(b) Payroll tax expense $5,665.80; Vacation benefits expense $1,995

P11-5B For the year ended December 31, 2012, Radar Company reports the following summary payroll data.

Prepare entries for payroll and payroll taxes; prepare W-2 data.
(SO 6, 7)

Gross earnings:		Deductions:	
Administrative salaries	$150,000	FICA taxes	$ 29,600
Electricians' wages	240,000	Federal income taxes withheld	78,000
Total	$390,000	State income taxes withheld (3%)	11,700
		United Fund contributions payable	17,000
		Health insurance premiums	12,000
		Total	$148,300

Radar Company's payroll taxes are: FICA 8%, state unemployment 2.5% (due to a stable employment record), and 0.8% federal unemployment. Gross earnings subject to FICA taxes total $370,000, and gross earnings subject to unemployment taxes total $90,000.

Instructions
(a) Prepare a summary journal entry at December 31 for the full year's payroll.
(b) Journalize the adjusting entry at December 31 to record the employer's payroll taxes.
(c) The W-2 Wage and Tax Statement requires the dollar data shown below.

(a) Salaries and wages payable $241,700
(b) Payroll tax expense $32,570

Wages, Tips, Other Compensation	Federal Income Tax Withheld	State Income Tax Withheld	FICA Wages	FICA Tax Withheld

Complete the required data for the following employees.

Employee	Gross Earnings	Federal Income Tax Withheld
A. Valdez	$50,000	$18,300
E. Izzard	24,000	4,800

Problems: Set C

Visit the book's companion website, at **www.wiley.com/college/weygandt**, and choose the Student Companion site to access Problem Set C.

Comprehensive Problem

CP11 Wright Company's balance sheet at December 31, 2011, is presented below.

WRIGHT COMPANY
Balance Sheet
December 31, 2011

Cash	$ 30,000	Accounts Payable	$ 13,750
Inventory	30,750	Interest Payable	250
Prepaid Insurance	6,000	Notes Payable	50,000
Equipment	38,000	Owner's Capital	40,750
	$104,750		$104,750

During January 2012, the following transactions occurred. (Wright Company uses the perpetual inventory system.)

1. Wright paid $250 interest on the note payable on January 1, 2012. The note is due December 31, 2013.

2. Wright purchased $241,100 of inventory on account.
3. Wright sold for $480,000 cash, inventory which cost $265,000. Wright also collected $28,800 in sales taxes.
4. Wright paid $230,000 in accounts payable.
5. Wright paid $17,000 in sales taxes to the state.
6. Paid other operating expenses of $20,000.
7. On January 31, 2012, the payroll for the month consists of salaries and wages of $60,000. All salaries and wages are subject to 8% FICA taxes. A total of $8,900 federal income taxes are withheld. The salaries and wages are paid on February 1.

Adjustment data:

8. Interest expense of $250 has been incurred on the notes payable.
9. The insurance for the year 2012 was prepaid on December 31, 2011.
10. The equipment was acquired on December 31, 2011, and will be depreciated on a straight-line basis over 5 years with a $2,000 salvage value.
11. Employer's payroll taxes include 8% FICA taxes, a 5.4% state unemployment tax, and an 0.8% federal unemployment tax.

Instructions

(You may need to set up T accounts to determine ending balances.)

(a) Prepare journal entries for the transactions listed above and the adjusting entries.
(b) Prepare an adjusted trial balance at January 31, 2012.
(c) Prepare an income statement, an owner's equity statement for the month ending January 31, 2012, and a classified balance sheet as of January 31, 2012.

Continuing Cookie Chronicle

(*Note:* This is a continuation of the Cookie Chronicle from Chapters 1 through 10.)

CCC11 Recall that Cookie Creations sells fine European mixers that it purchases from Kzinski Supply Co. Kzinski warrants the mixers to be free of defects in material and workmanship for a period of one year from the date of original purchase. If the mixer has such a defect, Kzinski will repair or replace the mixer free of charge for parts and labor.

Go to the book's companion website, **www.wiley.com/college/weygandt**, *to see the completion of this problem.*

BROADENINGYOURPERSPECTIVE

Financial Reporting and Analysis

Financial Reporting Problem: PepsiCo, Inc.

BYP11-1 The financial statements of PepsiCo, Inc. and the notes to consolidated financial statements appear in Appendix A.

Instructions

Refer to PepsiCo's financial statements and answer the following questions about current and contingent liabilities and payroll costs.

(a) What were PepsiCo's total current liabilities at December 26, 2009? What was the increase/decrease in PepsiCo's total current liabilities from the prior year?
(b) In PepsiCo's Note 2 ("Our Significant Accounting Policies"), the company explains the nature of its contingencies. Under what conditions does PepsiCo recognize (record and report) liabilities for contingencies?
(c) What were the components of total current liabilities on December 26, 2009?

Comparative Analysis Problem:
PepsiCo, Inc. vs. The Coca-Cola Company

BYP11-2 PepsiCo, Inc.'s financial statements are presented in Appendix A. Financial statements of The Coca-Cola Company are presented in Appendix B.

Instructions

(a) At December 26, 2009, what was PepsiCo's largest current liability account? What were its total current liabilities? At December 31, 2009, what was Coca-Cola's largest current liability account? What were its total current liabilities?

(b) Based on information contained in those financial statements, compute the following 2009 values for each company.
  (1) Working capital.
  (2) Current ratio.

(c) What conclusions concerning the relative liquidity of these companies can be drawn from these data?

On the Web

BYP11-3 The Internal Revenue Service provides considerable information over the Internet. The following site answers payroll tax questions faced by employers.

Address: www.irs.ustreas.gov/formspubs/index.html, or go to **www.wiley.com/college/weygandt**

Steps

1. Go to the site shown above.
2. Choose **View Online, Tax Publications**.
3. Choose **Publication 15, Circular E, Employer's Tax Guide**.

Instructions

Answer each of the following questions.

(a) How does the government define "employees"?

(b) What are the special rules for Social Security and Medicare regarding children who are employed by their parents?

(c) How can an employee obtain a Social Security card if he or she doesn't have one?

(d) Must employees report to their employer tips received from customers? If so, how?

(e) Where should the employer deposit Social Security taxes withheld or contributed?

Critical Thinking

Decision Making Across the Organization

BYP11-4 Kensingtown Processing Company provides word-processing services for business clients and students in a university community. The work for business clients is fairly steady throughout the year. The work for students peaks significantly in December and May as a result of term papers, research project reports, and dissertations.

Two years ago, the company attempted to meet the peak demand by hiring part-time help. This led to numerous errors and much customer dissatisfaction. A year ago, the company hired four experienced employees on a permanent basis in place of part-time help. This proved to be much better in terms of productivity and customer satisfaction. But, it has caused an increase in annual payroll costs and a significant decline in annual net income.

Recently, Valarie Flynn, a sales representative of Metcalfe Services Inc., has made a proposal to the company. Under her plan, Metcalfe will provide up to four experienced workers at a daily rate of $75 per person for an 8-hour workday. Metcalfe workers are not available on an hourly basis. Kensingtown would have to pay only the daily rate for the workers used.

The owner of Kensingtown Processing, Donna Bell, asks you, as the company's accountant, to prepare a report on the expenses that are pertinent to the decision. If the Metcalfe plan is adopted, Donna will terminate the employment of two permanent employees and will keep two permanent employees. At the moment, each employee earns an annual income of $21,000. Kensingtown pays 8% FICA taxes, 0.8% federal unemployment taxes, and 5.4% state unemployment taxes. The unemployment taxes apply to only the first $7,000 of gross earnings. In addition, Kensingtown pays $40 per month for each employee for medical and dental insurance. Donna indicates that if the Metcalfe Services plan is accepted, her needs for temporary workers will be as follows.

Months	Number of Employees	Working Days per Month
January–March	2	20
April–May	3	25
June–October	2	18
November–December	3	23

Instructions

With the class divided into groups, answer the following.

(a) Prepare a report showing the comparative payroll expense of continuing to employ permanent workers compared to adopting the Metcalfe Services Inc. plan.

(b) What other factors should Donna consider before finalizing her decision?

Communication Activity

BYP11-5   Jack Quaney, president of the Ramsberg Company, has recently hired a number of additional employees. He recognizes that additional payroll taxes will be due as a result of this hiring, and that the company will serve as the collection agent for other taxes.

Instructions

In a memorandum to Jack Quaney, explain each of the taxes, and identify the taxes that result in payroll tax expense to Ramsberg Company.

Ethics Case

BYP11-6   Daniel Longan owns and manages Daniel's Restaurant, a 24-hour restaurant near the city's medical complex. Daniel employs 9 full-time employees and 16 part-time employees. He pays all of the full-time employees by check, the amounts of which are determined by Daniel's public accountant, Gina Watt. Daniel pays all of his part-time employees in currency. He computes their wages and withdraws the cash directly from his cash register.

Gina has repeatedly urged Daniel to pay all employees by check. But as Daniel has told his competitor and friend, Steve Hill, who owns the Greasy Diner, "My part-time employees prefer the currency over a check. Also, I don't withhold or pay any taxes or worker's compensation insurance on those cash wages because they go totally unrecorded and unnoticed."

Instructions

(a) Who are the stakeholders in this situation?

(b) What are the legal and ethical considerations regarding Daniel's handling of his payroll?

(c) Gina Watt is aware of Daniel's payment of the part-time payroll in currency. What are her ethical responsibilities in this case?

(d) What internal control principle is violated in this payroll process?

"All About You" Activity

BYP11-7   As indicated in the **All About You** feature (available on the book's companion website), medical costs are substantial and rising. But will they be the most substantial expense over your lifetime? Not likely. Will it be housing or food? Again, not likely. The answer is taxes. On average, Americans work 99 days to afford their taxes. Companies, too, have large tax burdens. They look very hard at tax issues in deciding where to build their plants and where to locate their administrative headquarters.

Instructions

(a) Determine what your state income taxes are if your taxable income is $60,000 and you file as a single taxpayer in the state in which you live.

(b) Assume that you own a home worth $200,000 in your community and the tax rate is 2.1%. Compute the property taxes you would pay.

(c) Assume that the total gasoline bill for your automobile is $1,200 a year (300 gallons at $4 per gallon). What are the amounts of state and federal taxes that you pay on the $1,200?

(d) Assume that your purchases for the year total $9,000. Of this amount, $5,000 was for food and prescription drugs. What is the amount of sales tax you would pay on these purchases? (Many states do not levy a sales tax on food or prescription drugs. Does yours?)

(e) Determine what your Social Security taxes are if your income is $60,000.

(f) Determine what your federal income taxes are if your taxable income is $60,000 and you file as a single taxpayer.

(g) Determine your total taxes paid based on the above calculations, and determine the percentage of income that you would pay in taxes based on the following formula: Total taxes paid ÷ Total income.

FASB Codification Activity

BYP11-8 If your school has a subscription to the FASB Codification, go to *http://aaahq.org/ascLogin. cfm* to log in and prepare responses to the following.

(a) What is the definition of current liabilities?

(b) What is the definition of a *contingent liability*?

(c) What guidance does the Codification provide for the disclosure of contingent liabilities?

Answers to Accounting Across the Organization Questions

p. 516 Contingencies: How Big Are They? **Q:** Why do you think most companies disclose, but do not record, contingent liabilities? **A:** A contingent liability may be probable, but often its amount is difficult to determine. If it cannot be determined, the company is not required to accrue it as a liability.

p. 527 It Costs $74,000 to Put $44,000 in Sally's Pocket **Q:** How are the Social Security and Medicare taxes computed for Sally's salary? **A:** As indicated in the story, Sally's gross earnings were $59,000. The Social Security tax is 6.2% for both employee and employer up to gross earnings of $106,800 (2010 guidelines). As shown, both Sally and Bogan pay $3,661, which is 6.2% × $59,000. In addition, the Medicare tax is 1.45% on all gross earnings for both employee and employer. As shown, both Sally and Bogan pay $856, which is 1.45% × $59,000.

Answers to Self-Test Questions

1. a **2.** d **3.** b ($88,500 × 12% × 4/12) **4.** d **5.** b ($4,515 ÷ 1.05) **6.** b ($18,000 × 3/12) **7.** a **8.** d **9.** c
10. b **11.** d ($14 × 40) + ($21 × 5) **12.** c **13.** c **14.** b **15.** d *****16.** d

IFRS A Look at IFRS

IFRS and GAAP have similar definitions of liabilities. IFRS related to reporting and recognition of liabilities are found in *IAS 1 (revised)* ("Presentation of Financial Statements") and *IAS 37* ("Provisions, Contingent Liabilities, and Contingent Assets"). The general recording procedures for payroll are similar, although differences occur depending on the types of benefits that are provided in different countries. For example, companies in other countries often have different forms of pensions, unemployment benefits, welfare payments, and so on. The accounting for various forms of compensation plans under IFRS is found in *IAS 19* ("Employee Benefits") and *IFRS 2* ("Share-based Payments"). *IAS 19* addresses the accounting for a wide range of compensation elements, including wages, bonuses, post-employment benefits, and compensated absences. Both of these standards were recently amended, resulting in significant convergence between IFRS and GAAP.

Key Points

• The basic definition of a liability under GAAP and IFRS is very similar. In a more technical way, liabilities are defined by the IASB as a present obligation of the entity arising from past events, the settlement of which is expected to result in an outflow from the entity of resources embodying economic benefits. Liabilities may be legally enforceable via a contract or law but need not be; that is, they can arise due to normal business practice or customs.

- IFRS requires that companies classify liabilities as current or noncurrent on the face of the statement of financial position (balance sheet), except in industries where a *presentation* based on liquidity would be considered to provide more useful information (such as financial institutions).When current liabilities (also called short-term liabilities) are presented, they are generally presented in order of liquidity.

- Under IFRS, liabilities are classified as current if they are expected to be paid within 12 months.

- Similar to GAAP, items are normally reported in order of liquidity. Companies sometimes show liabilities before assets. Also, they will sometimes show long-term liabilities before current liabilities.

- Under IFRS, companies sometimes will net current liabilities against current assets to show working capital on the face of the statement of financial position. (This is evident in the Zetar financial statements in Appendix C.)

- Under GAAP, some contingent liabilities are recorded in the financial statements, others are disclosed, and in some cases no disclosure is required. Unlike GAAP, IFRS reserves the use of the term *contingent liability* to refer only to possible obligations that are *not* recognized in the financial statements but may be disclosed if certain criteria are met. Contingent liabilities are defined in *IAS 37* as being:

  ◆ A possible obligation that arises from past events and whose existence will be confirmed only by the occurrence or nonoccurrence of one or more uncertain future events not wholly within the control of the entity; or

  ◆ A present obligation that arises from past events but is not recognized because:

    • It is not probable that an outflow of resources embodying economic benefits will be required to settle the obligation; or

    • The amount of the obligation cannot be measured with sufficient reliability.

- For those items that GAAP would treat as recordable contingent liabilities, IFRS instead uses the term *provisions*. **Provisions** are defined as liabilities of uncertain timing or amount. Examples of provisions would be provisions for warranties, employee vacation pay, or anticipated losses. Under IFRS, the measurement of a provision related to an uncertain obligation is based on the best estimate of the expenditure required to settle the obligation.

- IFRS and GAAP separate plans into defined benefit and defined contribution. The accounting for defined contribution plans is similar. For defined benefit plans, there are still some significant technical differences in the reporting between GAAP and IFRS. However, the IASB and FASB are working on a joint project on pensions that will most likely eliminate the differences between the two, while dramatically changing the approach used by both.

Looking to the Future

The FASB and IASB are currently involved in two projects, each of which has implications for the accounting for liabilities. One project is investigating approaches to differentiate between debt and equity instruments. The other project, the elements phase of the conceptual framework project, will evaluate the definitions of the fundamental building blocks of accounting. The results of these projects could change the classification of many debt and equity securities.

IFRS Self-Test Questions

1. Which of the following is *false*?
   (a) Under IFRS, current liabilities must always be presented before noncurrent liabilities.
   (b) Under IFRS, an item is a current liability if it will be paid within the next 12 months.
   (c) Under IFRS, current liabilities are shown in order of liquidity.
   (d) Under IFRS, a liability is only recognized if it is a present obligation.

2. Under IFRS, a contingent liability is:
   (a) disclosed in the notes if certain criteria are met.
   (b) reported on the face of the financial statements if certain criteria are met.
   (c) the same as a provision.
   (d) not covered by IFRS.

3. Under IFRS, obligations related to warranties are considered:
   (a) contingent liabilities.
   (b) provisions.
   (c) possible obligations.
   (d) None of these.

4. Which of the following statements is *true*?
   (a) Under IFRS, the accounting for issues related to payroll are not covered in any IFRS.
   (b) The accounting for payrolls is similar under IFRS and U.S. GAAP.
   (c) Salary and wages payable is considered a contingent liability under IFRS.
   (d) IFRS does not normally report liabilities in order of liquidity.

5. The joint projects of the FASB and IASB could potentially:
   (a) change the definition of liabilities.
   (b) change the definition of equity.
   (c) change the definition of assets.
   (d) All of the above.

IFRS Concepts and Application

IFRS11-1 Define a provision and give an example.

IFRS11-2 Define a contingent liability and give an example.

IFRS11-3 Briefly describe some of the similarities and differences between GAAP and IFRS with respect to the accounting for liabilities.

International Financial Statement Analysis: Zetar plc

IFRS11-4 The financial statements of Zetar plc are presented in Appendix C.

Instructions
Use the company's complete annual report, available at *www.zetarplc.com*, to answer the following questions.

(a) According to the notes to the financial statements, what types of transactions do trade payables relate to? What was the average amount of time it took the company to pay its payables?

(b) Note 2(B) discusses provisions that the company records for certain types of activities. What do the provisions relate to, what are the estimates based on, and what could cause those estimates to change in subsequent periods?

(c) What was the average interest rate paid on bank loans and overdrafts?

Answers to IFRS Self-Test Questions
1. a   2. a   3. b   4. b   5. d

The Navigator

✔ **Remember to go back to the Navigator box on the chapter opening page and check off your completed work.**

CHAPTER12

Accounting for Partnerships

Study Objectives

After studying this chapter, you should be able to:

[1] Identify the characteristics of the partnership form of business organization.

[2] Explain the accounting entries for the formation of a partnership.

[3] Identify the bases for dividing net income or net loss.

[4] Describe the form and content of partnership financial statements.

[5] Explain the effects of the entries to record the liquidation of a partnership.

✔ **The Navigator**

✔ [The Navigator]

- ● Scan Study Objectives ○
- ● Read Feature Story ○
- ● Read Preview ○
- ● Read text and answer **Do it!** p. 558 ○ p. 564 ○ p. 567 ○ p. 570 ○
- ● Work Comprehensive **Do it!** p. 571 ○
- ● Review Summary of Study Objectives ○
- ● Answer Self-Test Questions ○
- ● Complete Assignments ○
- ● Go to *WileyPLUS* for practice and tutorials ○

Feature Story

FROM TRIALS TO THE TOP TEN

In 1990, Cliff Chenfield and Craig Balsam gave up the razors, ties, and six-figure salaries they had become accustomed to as New York lawyers. Instead, they set up a partnership, Razor & Tie Music, in Cliff's living room. Ten years later, it became the only record company in the country that had achieved success in selling music both on television and in stores. Razor & Tie's entertaining and effective TV commercials have yielded unprecedented sales for multi-artist music compilations. At the same time, its hot retail label has been behind some of the most recent original, progressive releases from artists such as Kelly Sweet, All That Remains, EndeverafteR, Angelique Kidjo, Ryan Shaw, Dave Barnes, Twisted Sister, Dar Williams, Danko Jones, and Yerba Buena.

Razor & Tie may be best known for its wildly popular *Kidz Bop* CD series, the top-selling children's audio product in the United States. Advertised on Nickelodeon, the

Cartoon Network, and elsewhere, *Kidz Bop* titles have sold millions of copies. Many of its releases in the series have "gone Gold."

Razor & Tie got its start with its first TV release, *Those Fabulous '70s* (100,000 copies sold), followed by *Disco Fever* (over 300,000 sold).

After restoring the respectability of the oft-maligned music of the 1970s, the partners forged into the musical '80s with the same zeal that elicited success with their first releases. In 1993, Razor & Tie released *Totally '80s*, a collection of Top-10 singles from the 1980s that has sold over 450,000 units. Featuring the tag line, "The greatest hits from the decade when communism died and music videos were born," *Totally '80s* was the best-selling direct-response album in the country in 1993.

In 1995, Razor & Tie broke into the contemporary music world with *Living in the '90s*, the most successful record in the history of the company. Featuring a number of songs that were still hits on the radio at the time the package initially aired, *Living in the '90s* was a blockbuster. It received Gold certification in less than nine months and rewrote the rules on direct-response albums. For the first time, contemporary music was available through an album offered only through direct-response spots. Razor & Tie pursued that same strategy with its 2002 introduction of the *Kidz Bop* titles.

In fact, Razor & Tie is now a vertically integrated business that includes a music company with major label distribution, a music publishing business, a media buying company, a home video company, a direct marketing operation, and a growing database of entertainment consumers.

Razor & Tie has carved out a sizable piece of the market through the complementary talents of the two partners. Their imagination and savvy, along with exciting new releases planned for the coming years, ensure Razor & Tie's continued growth.

✔ The Navigator

InsideCHAPTER12

PreviewofCHAPTER12

It is not surprising that when Cliff Chenfield and Craig Balsam began Razor & Tie, they decided to use the partnership form of organization. Both saw the need for hands-on control of their product and its promotion. In this chapter, we will discuss reasons why businesses select the partnership form of organization. We also will explain the major issues in accounting for partnerships.

The content and organization of Chapter 12 are as follows.

Accounting for Partnerships

Partnership Form of Organization	Basic Partnership Accounting	Liquidation of a Partnership
• Characteristics • Organizations with partnership characteristics • Advantages/disadvantages • Partnership agreement	• Forming a partnership • Dividing net income/loss • Financial statements	• No capital deficiency • Capital deficiency

The Navigator

Partnership Form of Organization

A **partnership** is an association of two or more persons to carry on as co-owners of a business for profit. Partnerships are sometimes used in small retail, service, or manufacturing companies. Also accountants, lawyers, and doctors find it desirable to form partnerships with other professionals in the field.

Study Objective [1]

Identify the characteristics of the partnership form of business organization.

Characteristics of Partnerships

Partnerships are fairly easy to form. People form partnerships simply by a verbal agreement, or more formally, by written agreement. We explain the principal characteristics of partnerships in the following sections.

ASSOCIATION OF INDIVIDUALS

A partnership is a legal entity. A partnership can own property (land, buildings, equipment), and can sue or be sued. **A partnership also is an accounting entity.** Thus, the personal assets, liabilities, and transactions of the partners are excluded from the accounting records of the partnership, just as they are in a proprietorship.

The net income of a partnership is not taxed as a separate entity. But, a partnership must file an information tax return showing partnership net income and each partner's share of that net income. Each partner's share is taxable at **personal tax rates**, regardless of the amount of net income each withdraws from the business during the year.

Association of Individuals

MUTUAL AGENCY

Mutual agency means that each partner acts on behalf of the partnership when engaging in partnership business. The act of any partner is binding on all other partners. This is true even when partners act beyond the scope of their authority, so long as the act appears to be appropriate for the partnership. For example, a partner of a

Mutual Agency

grocery store who purchases a delivery truck creates a binding contract in the name of the partnership, even if the partnership agreement denies this authority. On the other hand, if a partner in a law firm purchased a snowmobile for the partnership, such an act would not be binding on the partnership. The purchase is clearly outside the scope of partnership business.

LIMITED LIFE

Corporations have unlimited life. Partnerships do not. A partnership may be ended voluntarily at any time through the acceptance of a new partner or the withdrawal of a partner. It may be ended involuntarily by the death or incapacity of a partner. **Partnership dissolution** occurs whenever a partner withdraws or a new partner is admitted. Dissolution does not necessarily mean that the business ends. If the continuing partners agree, operations can continue without interruption by forming a new partnership.

Limited Life

UNLIMITED LIABILITY

Each partner is **personally and individually liable** for all partnership liabilities. Creditors' claims attach first to partnership assets. If these are insufficient, the claims then attach to the personal resources of any partner, irrespective of that partner's equity in the partnership. Because each partner is responsible for all the debts of the partnership, each partner is said to have **unlimited liability**.

Unlimited Liability

CO-OWNERSHIP OF PROPERTY

Partners jointly own partnership assets. If the partnership is dissolved, each partner has a claim on total assets equal to the balance in his or her respective capital account. This claim does not attach to **specific assets** that an individual partner contributed to the firm. Similarly, if a partner invests a building in the partnership valued at $100,000 and the building is later sold at a gain of $20,000, the partners all share in the gain.

Partnership net income (or net loss) is also co-owned. **If the partnership contract does not specify to the contrary, all net income or net loss is shared equally by the partners.** As you will see later, though, partners may agree to unequal sharing of net income or net loss.

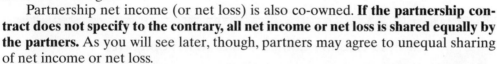
Co-ownership of Property

Organizations with Partnership Characteristics

If you are starting a business with a friend and each of you has little capital and your business is not risky, you probably want to use a partnership. As indicated above, the partnership is easy to establish and its cost is minimal. These types of partnerships are often called **regular partnerships**. However if your business is risky—say, roof repair or providing some type of professional service—you will want to limit your liability and not use a regular partnership. As a result, special forms of business organizations with partnership characteristics are now often used to provide protection from unlimited liability for people who wish to work together in some activity.

The special partnership forms are: limited partnerships, limited liability partnerships, and limited liability companies. These special forms use the same accounting procedures as those described for a regular partnership. In addition, for taxation purposes, all the profits and losses pass through these organizations (similar to the regular partnership) to the owners, who report their share of partnership net income or losses on their personal tax returns.

LIMITED PARTNERSHIPS

In a **limited partnership**, one or more partners have **unlimited liability** and one or more partners have **limited liability** for the debts of the firm. Those with unlimited

International Note

Much of the funding for successful new U.S. businesses comes from "venture capital" firms, which are organized as limited partnerships. To develop its own venture capital industry, China believes that it needs the limited liability form. Therefore, China has taken steps to model its partnership laws to allow for limited partnerships like those in the United States.

Helpful Hint

In an LLP, *all* partners have limited liability. There are no general partners.

liability are **general partners**. Those with limited liability are **limited partners**. Limited partners are responsible for the debts of the partnership up to the limit of their investment in the firm.

The words "Limited Partnership," or "Ltd.," or "LP" identify this type of organization. For the privilege of limited liability, the limited partner usually accepts less compensation than a general partner and exercises less influence in the affairs of the firm. If the limited partners get involved in management, they risk their liability protection.

LIMITED LIABILITY PARTNERSHIP

Most states allow professionals such as lawyers, doctors, and accountants to form a **limited liability partnership** or "LLP." The LLP is designed to protect innocent partners from malpractice or negligence claims resulting from the acts of another partner. LLPs generally carry large insurance policies as protection against malpractice suits. These professional partnerships vary in size from a medical partnership of three to five doctors, to 150 to 200 partners in a large law firm, to more than 2,000 partners in an international accounting firm.

LIMITED LIABILITY COMPANIES

A hybrid form of business organization with certain features like a corporation and others like a limited partnership is the **limited liability company**, or "LLC." An LLC usually has a limited life. The owners, called **members**, have limited liability like owners of a corporation. Whereas limited partners do not actively participate in the management of a limited partnership (LP), the members of a limited liability company (LLC) can assume an active management role. For income tax purposes, the IRS usually classifies an LLC as a partnership.

ACCOUNTING ACROSS THE ORGANIZATION

Limited Liability Companies Gain in Popularity

The proprietorship form of business organization is still the most popular, followed by the corporate form. But whenever a group of individuals wants to form a partnership, the limited liability company is usually the popular choice.

One other form of business organization is a *subchapter S corporation*. A subchapter S corporation has many of the characteristics of a partnership—especially, taxation as a partnership—but it is losing its popularity. The reason: It involves more paperwork and expense than a limited liability company, which in most cases offers similar advantages.

? Why do you think that the use of the limited liability company is gaining in popularity?
(See page 591.)

Illustration 12-1 summarizes different forms of organizations that have partnership characteristics.

Advantages and Disadvantages of Partnerships

Why do people choose partnerships? One major advantage of a partnership is to combine the skills and resources of two or more individuals. In addition, partnerships are easily formed and are relatively free from government regulations and restrictions. A partnership does not have to contend with the "red tape" that a

	Major Advantages	Major Disadvantages
Regular Partnership General Partners	Simple and inexpensive to create and operate.	Owners (partners) personally liable for business debts.
Limited Partnership General Partners　Limited Partners	Limited partners have limited personal liability for business debts as long as they do not participate in management. General partners can raise cash without involving outside investors in management of business.	General partners personally liable for business debts. More expensive to create than regular partnership. Suitable mainly for companies that invest in real estate.
Limited Liability Partnership	Mostly of interest to partners in old-line professions such as law, medicine, and accounting. Owners (partners) are not personally liable for the malpractice of other partners.	Unlike a limited liability company, owners (partners) remain personally liable for many types of obligations owed to business creditors, lenders, and landlords. Often limited to a short list of professions.
Limited Liability Company	Owners have limited personal liability for business debts even if they participate in management.	More expensive to create than regular partnership.

Source: www.nolo.com (accessed June 2010).

Illustration 12-1
Different forms of organizations with partnership characteristics

corporation must face. Also, partners generally can make decisions quickly on substantive business matters without having to consult a board of directors.

On the other hand, partnerships also have some major disadvantages. **Unlimited liability** is particularly troublesome. Many individuals fear they may lose not only their initial investment but also their personal assets, if those assets are needed to pay partnership creditors.

Illustration 12-2 summarizes the advantages and disadvantages of the regular partnership form of business organization. As indicated in the previous section,

Advantages	Disadvantages
Combining skills and resources of two or more individuals	Mutual agency
Ease of formation	Limited life
Freedom from governmental regulations and restrictions	Unlimited liability
Ease of decision making	

Illustration 12-2
Advantages and disadvantages of a partnership

different types of partnership forms have evolved to reduce some of the disadvantages.

Do it!

Partnership Organization

Indicate whether each of the following statements is true or false.

_____ **1.** Partnerships have unlimited life. Corporations do not.

_____ **2.** Partners jointly own partnership assets. A partner's claim on partnership assets does not attach to specific assets.

_____ **3.** In a limited partnership, the general partners have unlimited liability.

_____ **4.** The members of a limited liability company have limited liability, like shareholders of a corporation, and they are taxed like corporate shareholders.

_____ **5.** Because of mutual agency, the act of any partner is binding on all other partners.

action plan

✔ When forming a business, carefully consider what type of organization would best suit the needs of the business.

✔ Keep in mind the new, "hybrid" organizational forms that have many of the best characteristics of partnerships and corporations.

Solution

1. False. Corporations have unlimited life. Partnerships do not.
2. True.
3. True.
4. False. The members of a limited liability company are taxed like partners in a partnership.
5. True.

Related exercise material: E12-1 and **Do it!** 12-1.

✔
The Navigator

Ethics Note

A well-developed partnership agreement reduces ethical conflict among partners. It specifies in clear and concise language the process by which the partners will resolve ethical and legal problems. This issue is especially significant when the partnership experiences financial distress.

The Partnership Agreement

Ideally, the agreement of two or more individuals to form a partnership should be expressed in a written contract, called the **partnership agreement** or **articles of co-partnership**. The partnership agreement contains such basic information as the name and principal location of the firm, the purpose of the business, and date of inception. In addition, it should specify relationships among the partners, such as:

1. Names and capital contributions of partners.
2. Rights and duties of partners.
3. Basis for sharing net income or net loss.
4. Provision for withdrawals of assets.
5. Procedures for submitting disputes to arbitration.
6. Procedures for the withdrawal or addition of a partner.
7. Rights and duties of surviving partners in the event of a partner's death.

We cannot overemphasize the importance of a written contract. The agreement should attempt to anticipate all possible situations, contingencies, and disagreements. The help of a lawyer is highly desirable in preparing the agreement.

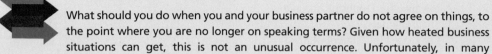

ACCOUNTING ACROSS THE ORGANIZATION

How to Part Ways Nicely

What should you do when you and your business partner do not agree on things, to the point where you are no longer on speaking terms? Given how heated business situations can get, this is not an unusual occurrence. Unfortunately, in many instances the partners do everything they can to undermine the other partner, eventually destroying the business. In some instances people even steal from the partnership because they either feel that they "deserve it" or they assume that the other partners are stealing from them.

It would be much better to follow the example of Jennifer Appel and her partner. They found that after opening a successful bakery and writing a cookbook, they couldn't agree on how the business should be run. The other partner bought out Ms. Appel's share of the business, and Ms. Appel went on to start her own style of bakery, which she ultimately franchised.

Source: Paulette Thomas, "As Partnership Sours, Parting Is Sweet," *Wall Street Journal*, (July 6, 2004), p. A20.

 How can partnership conflicts be minimized and more easily resolved? (See page 591.)

Basic Partnership Accounting

We now turn to the basic accounting for partnerships. The major accounting issues relate to forming the partnership, dividing income or loss, and preparing financial statements.

Study Objective [2]
Explain the accounting entries for the formation of a partnership.

Forming a Partnership

Each partner's initial investment in a partnership is entered in the partnership records. The partnership should record these investments at the **fair value of the assets at the date of their transfer to the partnership**. All partners must agree to the values assigned.

To illustrate, assume that A. Rolfe and T. Shea combine their proprietorships to start a partnership named U.S. Software. The firm will specialize in developing financial modeling software packages. Rolfe and Shea have the following assets prior to the formation of the partnership.

	Book Value		Fair Value	
	A. Rolfe	T. Shea	A. Rolfe	T. Shea
Cash	$ 8,000	$ 9,000	$ 8,000	$ 9,000
Equipment	5,000		4,000	
Accumulated depreciation	(2,000)			
Accounts receivable		4,000		4,000
Allowance for doubtful accounts		(700)		(1,000)
	$11,000	$12,300	$12,000	$12,000

Illustration 12-3
Book and fair values of assets invested

*Items under **owners' equity** (OE) in the accounting equation analyses (in margins) are not labeled in this partnership chapter. Nearly all affect partners' **capital** accounts.*

The partnership records the investments as follows.

Investment of A. Rolfe

Cash	8,000	
Equipment	4,000	
A. Rolfe, Capital		12,000
(To record investment of Rolfe)		

A = L + OE
+8,000
+4,000
+12,000
Cash Flows
+8,000

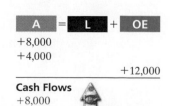

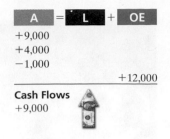

A	=	L	+	OE
+9,000				
+4,000				
−1,000				
				+12,000

Cash Flows
+9,000

Investment of T. Shea

Cash	9,000	
Accounts Receivable	4,000	
Allowance for Doubtful Accounts		1,000
T. Shea, Capital		12,000
(To record investment of Shea)		

> **International Note**
>
> Partnership accounting under GAAP and IFRS are essentially the same.

Note that the partnership records neither the original cost of the office equipment ($5,000) nor its book value ($5,000 − $2,000). It records the equipment at its fair value, $4,000. The partnership does not carry forward any accumulated depreciation from the books of previous entities (in this case, the two proprietorships).

In contrast, the gross claims on customers ($4,000) are carried forward to the partnership. The partnership adjusts the allowance for doubtful accounts to $1,000, to arrive at a cash (net) realizable value of $3,000. A partnership may start with an allowance for doubtful accounts because it will continue to collect existing accounts receivable, some of which are expected to be uncollectible. In addition, this procedure maintains the control and subsidiary relationship between Accounts Receivable and the accounts receivable subsidiary ledger.

After formation of the partnership, the accounting for transactions is similar to any other type of business organization. For example, the partners record all transactions with outside parties, such as the purchase or sale of merchandise inventory and the payment or receipt of cash, the same as would a sole proprietor.

The steps in the accounting cycle described in Chapter 4 for a proprietorship also apply to a partnership. For example, the partnership prepares a trial balance and journalizes and posts adjusting entries. A worksheet may be used. There are minor differences in journalizing and posting closing entries and in preparing financial statements, as we explain in the following sections. The differences occur because there is more than one owner.

Dividing Net Income or Net Loss

Partners equally share partnership net income or net loss unless the partnership contract indicates otherwise. The same basis of division usually applies to both net income and net loss. It is customary to refer to this basis as the **income ratio**, the **income and loss ratio**, or the **profit and loss (P&L) ratio**. Because of its wide acceptance, we will use the term income ratio to identify the basis for dividing net income and net loss. The partnership recognizes a partner's share of net income or net loss in the accounts through closing entries.

CLOSING ENTRIES

As in the case of a proprietorship, a partnership must make four entries in preparing closing entries. The entries are:

1. Debit each revenue account for its balance, and credit Income Summary for total revenues.
2. Debit Income Summary for total expenses, and credit each expense account for its balance.
3. Debit Income Summary for its balance, and credit each partner's capital account for his or her share of net income. Or, credit Income Summary, and debit each partner's capital account for his or her share of net loss.
4. Debit each partner's capital account for the balance in that partner's drawing account, and credit each partner's drawing account for the same amount.

The first two entries are the same as in a proprietorship. The last two entries are different because (1) there are two or more owners' capital and drawing accounts, and (2) it is necessary to divide net income (or net loss) among the partners.

To illustrate the last two closing entries, assume that AB Company has net income of $32,000 for 2012. The partners, L. Arbor and D. Barnett, share net income and net loss equally. Drawings for the year were Arbor $8,000 and Barnett $6,000. The last two closing entries are:

Dec. 31	Income Summary	32,000	
	L. Arbor, Capital ($32,000 × 50%)		16,000
	D. Barnett, Capital ($32,000 × 50%)		16,000
	(To transfer net income to partners' capital accounts)		
Dec. 31	L. Arbor, Capital	8,000	
	D. Barnett, Capital	6,000	
	L. Arbor, Drawings		8,000
	D. Barnett, Drawings		6,000
	(To close drawing accounts to capital accounts)		

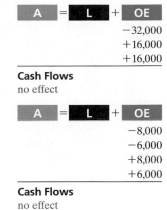

A = L + OE
−32,000
+16,000
+16,000

Cash Flows
no effect

A = L + OE
−8,000
−6,000
+8,000
+6,000

Cash Flows
no effect

Assume that the beginning capital balance is $47,000 for Arbor and $36,000 for Barnett. After posting the closing entries, the capital and drawing accounts will appear as shown in Illustration 12-4.

Illustration 12-4
Partners' capital and drawing accounts after closing

L. Arbor, Capital					**D. Barnett, Capital**			
12/31 **Clos.**	**8,000**	1/1 Bal.	47,000	12/31 **Clos.**	**6,000**	1/1 Bal.	36,000
		12/31 **Clos.**	**16,000**			12/31 **Clos.**	**16,000**
		12/31 Bal.	55,000			12/31 Bal.	46,000
L. Arbor, Drawings				**D. Barnett, Drawings**			
12/31 Bal.	8,000	12/31 **Clos.**	**8,000**	12/31 Bal.	6,000	12/31 **Clos.**	**6,000**

As in a proprietorship, the partners' capital accounts are permanent accounts; their drawing accounts are temporary accounts. Normally, the capital accounts will have credit balances, and the drawing accounts will have debit balances. Drawing accounts are debited when partners withdraw cash or other assets from the partnership for personal use.

INCOME RATIOS

As noted earlier, the partnership agreement should specify the basis for sharing net income or net loss. The following are typical income ratios.

Study Objective [3]
Identify the bases for dividing net income or net loss.

1. A fixed ratio, expressed as a proportion (6:4), a percentage (70% and 30%), or a fraction (2/3 and 1/3).
2. A ratio based either on capital balances at the beginning of the year or on average capital balances during the year.
3. Salaries to partners and the remainder on a fixed ratio.
4. Interest on partners' capital balances and the remainder on a fixed ratio.
5. Salaries to partners, interest on partners' capital, and the remainder on a fixed ratio.

The objective is to settle on a basis that will equitably reflect the partners' capital investment and service to the partnership.

A **fixed ratio** is easy to apply, and it may be an equitable basis in some circumstances. Assume, for example, that Hughes and Lane are partners. Each contributes the same amount of capital, but Hughes expects to work full-time in the partnership and Lane expects to work only half-time. Accordingly, the partners agree to a fixed ratio of 2/3 to Hughes and 1/3 to Lane.

A **ratio based on capital balances** may be appropriate when the funds invested in the partnership are considered the critical factor. Capital ratios may also be equitable when the partners hire a manager to run the business and do not plan to take an active role in daily operations.

The three remaining ratios (items 3, 4, and 5) give specific recognition to differences among partners. These ratios provide salary allowances for time worked and interest allowances for capital invested. Then, the partnership allocates any remaining net income or net loss on a fixed ratio.

Salaries to partners and interest on partners' capital are not expenses of the partnership. Therefore, these items do not enter into the matching of expenses with revenues and the determination of net income or net loss. For a partnership, as for other entities, salaries and wages expense pertains to the cost of services performed by employees. Likewise, interest expense relates to the cost of borrowing from creditors. But partners, as owners, are not considered either **employees** or **creditors**. When the partnership agreement permits the partners to make monthly withdrawals of cash based on their "salary," the partnership debits these withdrawals to the partner's drawing account.

SALARIES, INTEREST, AND REMAINDER ON A FIXED RATIO

Under income ratio (5) in the list above, the partnership must apply salaries and interest **before** it allocates the remainder on the specified fixed ratio. **This is true even if the provisions exceed net income. It is also true even if the partnership has suffered a net loss for the year.** The partnership's income statement should show, below net income, detailed information concerning the division of net income or net loss.

To illustrate, assume that King and Lee are co-partners in the Kingslee Company. The partnership agreement provides for: (1) salary allowances of $8,400 to King and $6,000 to Lee, (2) interest allowances of 10% on capital balances at the beginning of the year, and (3) the remainder equally. Capital balances on January 1 were King $28,000, and Lee $24,000. In 2012, partnership net income is $22,000. The division of net income is as follows.

Illustration 12-5
Division of net income schedule

Kingslee Company Division of Net Income For the Year Ended December 31, 2012			
Net income			$ 22,000
Division of Net Income			
	Sara King	**Ray Lee**	**Total**
Salary allowance	$ 8,400	$6,000	$14,400
Interest allowance on partners' capital			
Sara King ($28,000 × 10%)	2,800		
Ray Lee ($24,000 × 10%)		2,400	
Total interest allowance			5,200
Total salaries and interest	11,200	8,400	19,600
Remaining income, $2,400			
($22,000 − $19,600)			
Sara King ($2,400 × 50%)	1,200		
Ray Lee ($2,400 × 50%)		1,200	
Total remainder			2,400
Total division of net income	**$12,400**	**$9,600**	**$22,000**

Kingslee records the division of net income as follows.

Dec. 31	Income Summary	22,000	
	Sara King, Capital		12,400
	Ray Lee, Capital		9,600
	(To close net income to partners' capital)		

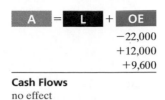

A	=	L	+	OE

−22,000
+12,000
+9,600

Cash Flows
no effect

Now let's look at a situation in which the salary and interest allowances *exceed* net income. Assume that Kingslee Company's net income is only $18,000. In this case, the salary and interest allowances will create a deficiency of $1,600 ($19,600 − $18,000). The computations of the allowances are the same as those in the preceding example. Beginning with total salaries and interest, we complete the division of net income as shown in Illustration 12-6.

	Sara King	Ray Lee	Total
Total salaries and interest	$11,200	$8,400	$19,600
Remaining deficiency ($1,600)			
($18,000 − $19,600)			
Sara King ($1,600 × 50%)	(800)		
Ray Lee ($1,600 × 50%)		(800)	
Total remainder			(1,600)
Total division	**$10,400**	**$7,600**	**$18,000**

Illustration 12-6
Division of net income—income deficiency

Partnership Financial Statements

The financial statements of a partnership are similar to those of a proprietorship. The differences are due to the number of owners involved. The income statement for a partnership is identical to the income statement for a proprietorship except for the division of net income, as shown earlier.

The owners' equity statement for a partnership is called the **partners' capital statement**. It explains the changes in each partner's capital account and in total partnership capital during the year. Illustration 12-7 shows the partners' capital statement for Kingslee Company. It is based on the division of $22,000 of net income in Illustration 12-5. The statement includes assumed data for the additional investment and drawings. The partnership prepares the partners' capital statement from the income statement and the partners' capital and drawing accounts.

Study Objective [4]
Describe the form and content of partnership financial statements.

Kingslee Company Partners' Capital Statement For the Year Ended December 31, 2012			
	Sara King	Ray Lee	Total
Capital, January 1	$28,000	$24,000	$52,000
Add: Additional investment	2,000		2,000
Net income	12,400	9,600	22,000
	42,400	33,600	76,000
Less: Drawings	7,000	5,000	12,000
Capital, December 31	**$35,400**	**$28,600**	**$64,000**

Illustration 12-7
Partners' capital statement

Helpful Hint

As in a proprietorship, partners' capital may change due to (1) additional investment, (2) drawings, and (3) net income or net loss.

The balance sheet for a partnership is the same as for a proprietorship except for the owner's equity section. For a partnership, the balance sheet shows the capital balances of each partner. The owners' equity section for Kingslee Company would show the following.

Illustration 12-8
Owners' equity section of a partnership balance sheet

Kingslee Company Balance Sheet (partial) December 31, 2012		
Total liabilities (assumed amount)		$115,000
Owners' equity		
Sara King, capital	$35,400	
Ray Lee, capital	28,600	
Total owners' equity		64,000
Total liabilities and owners' equity		$179,000

Do it!

Division of Net Income

action plan

✔ Compute net income exclusive of any salaries to partners and interest on partners' capital.

✔ Deduct salaries to partners from net income.

✔ Apply the partners' income ratios to the remaining net income.

✔ Prepare the closing entry distributing net income or net loss among the partners' capital accounts.

LeeMay Company reports net income of $57,000. The partnership agreement provides for salaries of $15,000 to L. Lee and $12,000 to R. May. They will share the remainder on a 60:40 basis (60% to Lee). L. Lee asks your help to divide the net income between the partners and to prepare the closing entry.

Solution

The division of net income is as follows.

	L. Lee	R. May	Total
Salary allowance	$15,000	$12,000	$27,000
Remaining income $30,000 ($57,000 − $27,000)			
L. Lee (60% × $30,000)	18,000		
R. May (40% × $30,000)		12,000	
Total remaining income			30,000
Total division of net income	$33,000	$24,000	$57,000

The closing entry for net income therefore is:

Income Summary	57,000	
L. Lee, Capital		33,000
R. May, Capital		24,000
(To close net income to partners' capital accounts)		

Related exercise material: BE12-3, BE12-4, BE12-5, E12-4, E12-5, and **Do it!** 12-2.

The Navigator

Liquidation of a Partnership

Study Objective [5]
Explain the effects of the entries to record the liquidation of a partnership.

Liquidation of a business involves selling the assets of the firm, paying liabilities, and distributing any remaining assets. Liquidation may result from the sale of the business by mutual agreement of the partners, from the death of a partner, or from bankruptcy. Partnership liquidation ends both the legal and economic life of the entity.

From an accounting standpoint, the partnership should complete the accounting cycle for the final operating period prior to liquidation. This includes preparing adjusting entries and financial statements. It also involves preparing closing entries and a post-closing trial balance. Thus, only balance sheet accounts should be open as the liquidation process begins.

In liquidation, the sale of noncash assets for cash is called **realization**. Any difference between book value and the cash proceeds is called the **gain or loss on realization**. To liquidate a partnership, it is necessary to:

1. Sell noncash assets for cash and recognize a gain or loss on realization.
2. Allocate gain/loss on realization to the partners based on their income ratios.
3. Pay partnership liabilities in cash.
4. Distribute remaining cash to partners on the basis of their **capital balances**.

Each of the steps must be performed in sequence. The partnership must pay creditors **before** partners receive any cash distributions. Also, an accounting entry must record each step.

When a partnership is liquidated, all partners may have credit balances in their capital accounts. This situation is called **no capital deficiency**. Or, one or more partners may have a debit balance in the capital account. This situation is termed a **capital deficiency**. To illustrate each of these conditions, assume that Ace Company is liquidated when its ledger shows the following assets, liabilities, and owners' equity accounts.

> **Ethics Note**
>
> The process of selling noncash assets and then distributing the cash reduces the likelihood of partner disputes. If, instead, the partnership distributes noncash assets to partners to liquidate the firm, the partners would need to agree on the value of the noncash assets, which can be very difficult to determine.

Assets		Liabilities and Owners' Equity	
Cash	$ 5,000	Notes payable	$15,000
Accounts receivable	15,000	Accounts payable	16,000
Inventory	18,000	R. Arnet, capital	15,000
Equipment	35,000	P. Carey, capital	17,800
Accum. depr.—equipment	(8,000)	W. Eaton, capital	1,200
	$65,000		$65,000

Illustration 12-9
Account balances prior to liquidation

No Capital Deficiency

The partners of Ace Company agree to liquidate the partnership on the following terms: (1) The partnership will sell its noncash assets to Jackson Enterprises for $75,000 cash. (2) The partnership will pay its partnership liabilities. The income ratios of the partners are 3:2:1, respectively. The steps in the liquidation process are as follows.

1. Ace sells the noncash assets (accounts receivable, inventory, and equipment) for $75,000. The book value of these assets is $60,000 ($15,000 + $18,000 + $35,000 − $8,000). Thus, Ace realizes a gain of $15,000 on the sale. The entry is:

(1)		
Cash	75,000	
Accumulated Depreciation–Equipment	8,000	
Accounts Receivable		15,000
Inventory		18,000
Equipment		35,000
Gain on Realization		15,000
(To record realization of noncash assets)		

A = L + OE
+75,000
+8,000
−15,000
−18,000
−35,000
+15,000

Cash Flows
+75,000

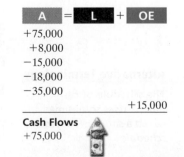

2. Ace allocates the $15,000 gain on realization to the partners based on their income ratios, which are 3:2:1. The entry is:

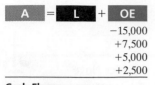

Cash Flows
no effect

(2)

Gain on Realization	15,000	
R. Arnet, Capital ($15,000 × 3/6)		7,500
P. Carey, Capital ($15,000 × 2/6)		5,000
W. Eaton, Capital ($15,000 × 1/6)		2,500
(To allocate gain to partners' capital accounts)		

3. Partnership liabilities consist of Notes Payable $15,000 and Accounts Payable $16,000. Ace pays creditors in full by a cash payment of $31,000. The entry is:

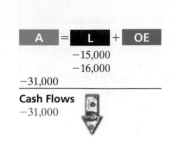

Cash Flows
−31,000

(3)

Notes Payable	15,000	
Accounts Payable	16,000	
Cash		31,000
(To record payment of partnership liabilities)		

4. Ace distributes the remaining cash to the partners on the basis of **their capital balances**. After posting the entries in the first three steps, all partnership accounts, including Gain on Realization, will have zero balances except for four accounts: Cash $49,000; R. Arnet, Capital $22,500; P. Carey, Capital $22,800; and W. Eaton, Capital $3,700, as shown below.

Cash				R. Arnet, Capital			P. Carey, Capital			W. Eaton, Capital	
Bal.	5,000	(3)	31,000	Bal.	15,000		Bal.	17,800		Bal.	1,200
(1)	75,000			(2)	7,500		(2)	5,000		(2)	2,500
Bal.	**49,000**			**Bal.**	**22,500**		**Bal.**	**22,800**		**Bal.**	**3,700**

Illustration 12-10
Ledger balances before distribution of cash

Ace records the distribution of cash as follows.

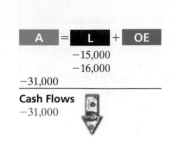

Cash Flows
−49,000

(4)

R. Arnet, Capital	22,500	
P. Carey, Capital	22,800	
W. Eaton, Capital	3,700	
Cash		49,000
(To record distribution of cash to partners)		

After posting this entry, all partnership accounts will have zero balances.

A word of caution: **Partnerships should not distribute remaining cash to partners on the basis of their income-sharing ratios.** On this basis, Arnet would receive three-sixths, or $24,500, which would produce an erroneous debit balance of $2,000. The income ratio is the proper basis for allocating net income or loss. **It is not a proper basis for making the final distribution of cash to the partners.**

Alternative Terminology

The schedule of cash payments is sometimes called a *safe cash payments schedule.*

SCHEDULE OF CASH PAYMENTS

The schedule of cash payments shows the distribution of cash to the partners in a partnership liquidation. A cash payments schedule is sometimes prepared to determine the distribution of cash to the partners in the liquidation of a partnership.

The schedule of cash payments is organized around the basic accounting equation. Illustration 12-11 shows the schedule for Ace Company. The numbers in parentheses refer to the four required steps in the liquidation of a partnership. They also identify the accounting entries that Ace must make. The cash payments schedule is especially useful when the liquidation process extends over a period of time.

ACE Company.xls

File Edit View Insert Format Tools Data Window Help

ACE COMPANY
Schedule of Cash Payments

Item		Cash	+	Noncash Assets	=	Liabilities	+	R. Arnet, Capital	+	P. Carey, Capital	+	W. Eaton, Capital
Balances before liquidation		5,000	+	60,000	=	31,000	+	15,000	+	17,800	+	1,200
Sale of noncash assets and allocation of gain	(1)&(2)	75,000	+	(60,000)	=			7,500	+	5,000	+	2,500
New balances		80,000	+	–0–	=	31,000	+	22,500	+	22,800	+	3,700
Pay liabilities	(3)	(31,000)			=	(31,000)						
New balances		49,000	+	–0–	=	–0–	+	22,500	+	22,800	+	3,700
Cash distribution to partners	(4)	(49,000)			=			(22,500)	+	(22,800)	+	(3,700)
Final balances		–0–		–0–		–0–		–0–		–0–		–0–

Illustration 12-11
Schedule of cash payments, no capital deficiency

Do it!

The partners of Grafton Company have decided to liquidate their business. Noncash assets were sold for $115,000. The income ratios of the partners Kale D., Croix D., and Marais K. are 2:3:3, respectively. Complete the following schedule of cash payments for Grafton Company.

GRAFTON Company.xls

File Edit View Insert Format Tools Data Window Help

Item	Cash	+	Noncash Assets	=	Liabilities	+	Kale D., Capital	+	Croix D., Capital	+	Marais K., Capital
Balances before liquidation	10,000		85,000		40,000		15,000		35,000		5,000
Sale of noncash assets and allocation of gain											
New balances											
Pay liabilities											
New balances											
Cash distribution to partners											
Final balances											

Partnership Liquidation

action plan

✔ First, sell the noncash assets and determine the gain.

✔ Allocate the gain to the partners based on their income ratios.

✔ Use cash to pay off liabilities.

✔ Distribute remaining cash on the basis of their capital balances.

Solution

Item	Cash	+	Noncash Assets	=	Liabilities	+	Kale D., Capital	+	Croix D., Capital	+	Marais K., Capital
1											
2 Balances before liquidation	10,000		85,000		40,000		15,000		35,000		5,000
3 Sale of noncash assets and allocation of gain	115,000		(85,000)				7,500ᵃ		11,250ᵇ		11,250ᵇ
4 New balances	125,000		–0–		40,000		22,500		46,250		16,250
5 Pay liabilities	(40,000)				(40,000)						
6 New balances	85,000		–0–		–0–		22,500		46,250		16,250
7 Cash distribution to partners	85,000						(22,500)		(46,250)		(16,250)
8 Final balances	–0–		–0–		–0–		–0–		–0–		–0–

ᵃ$30,000 \times 2/8$
ᵇ$30,000 \times 3/8$

Related exercise material: BE12-6, E12-8, E12-9, E12-10, and **Do it!** 12-3.

✔ The Navigator

Capital Deficiency

A capital deficiency may result from recurring net losses, excessive drawings, or losses from realization suffered during liquidation. To illustrate, assume that Ace Company is on the brink of bankruptcy. The partners decide to liquidate by having a "going-out-of-business" sale. They sell merchandise at substantial discounts, and sell the equipment at auction. Cash proceeds from these sales and collections from customers total only $42,000. Thus, the loss from liquidation is $18,000 ($60,000 − $42,000). The steps in the liquidation process are as follows.

1. The entry for the realization of noncash assets is:

(1)

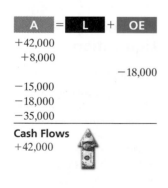

Cash	42,000	
Accumulated Depreciation—Equipment	8,000	
Loss on Realization	18,000	
Accounts Receivable		15,000
Inventory		18,000
Equipment		35,000
(To record realization of noncash assets)		

A = L + OE
+42,000
+8,000
−18,000
−15,000
−18,000
−35,000
Cash Flows
+42,000

2. Ace allocates the loss on realization to the partners on the basis of their income ratios. The entry is:

(2)

R. Arnet, Capital ($18,000 × 3/6)	9,000	
P. Carey, Capital ($18,000 × 2/6)	6,000	
W. Eaton, Capital ($18,000 × 1/6)	3,000	
Loss on Realization		18,000
(To allocate loss on realization to partners)		

A = L + OE
−9,000
−6,000
−3,000
+18,000
Cash Flows
no effect

3. Ace pays the partnership liabilities. This entry is the same as the previous one.

(3)

Notes Payable	15,000	
Accounts Payable	16,000	
Cash		31,000
(To record payment of partnership liabilities)		

A	=	L	+	OE

−15,000
−16,000
_____
−31,000

Cash Flows
−31,000

4. After posting the three entries, two accounts will have debit balances—Cash $16,000, and W. Eaton, Capital $1,800. Two accounts will have credit balances— R. Arnet, Capital $6,000, and P. Carey, Capital $11,800. All four accounts are shown below.

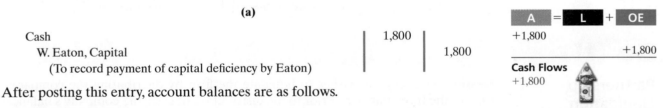

Cash			R. Arnet, Capital			P. Carey, Capital			W. Eaton, Capital		
Bal. 5,000	(3) 31,000	(2) 9,000	Bal. 15,000	(2) 6,000	Bal. 17,800	(2) 3,000	Bal. 1,200
(1) 42,000			Bal. 6,000		Bal. 11,800	Bal. 1,800	
Bal. 16,000							

Illustration 12-12
Ledger balances before distribution of cash

Eaton has a capital deficiency of $1,800, and so owes the partnership $1,800. Arnet and Carey have a legally enforceable claim for that amount against Eaton's personal assets. Note that the distribution of cash is still made on the basis of capital balances. But the amount will vary depending on how Eaton settles the deficiency. Two alternatives are presented in the following sections.

PAYMENT OF DEFICIENCY

If the partner with the capital deficiency pays the amount owed the partnership, the deficiency is eliminated. To illustrate, assume that Eaton pays $1,800 to the partnership. The entry is:

(a)

Cash	1,800	
W. Eaton, Capital		1,800
(To record payment of capital deficiency by Eaton)		

A	=	L	+	OE

+1,800
+1,800

Cash Flows
+1,800

After posting this entry, account balances are as follows.

Cash			R. Arnet, Capital			P. Carey, Capital			W. Eaton, Capital		
Bal. 5,000	(3) 31,000	(2) 9,000	Bal. 15,000	(2) 6,000	Bal. 17,800	(2) 3,000	Bal. 1,200
(1) 42,000			Bal. 6,000		Bal. 11,800		(a) 1,800
(a) 1,800							Bal. —0—
Bal. 17,800							

Illustration 12-13
Ledger balances after paying capital deficiency

The cash balance of $17,800 is now equal to the credit balances in the capital accounts (Arnet $6,000 + Carey $11,800). Ace now distributes cash on the basis of these balances. The entry is:

R. Arnet, Capital	6,000	
P. Carey, Capital	11,800	
Cash		17,800
(To record distribution of cash to the partners)		

A	=	L	+	OE

−6,000
−11,800
_____
−17,800

Cash Flows
−17,800

After posting this entry, all accounts will have zero balances.

NONPAYMENT OF DEFICIENCY

If a partner with a capital deficiency is unable to pay the amount owed to the partnership, the partners with credit balances must absorb the loss. The partnership allocates the loss on the basis of the income ratios that exist between the partners with credit balances.

The income ratios of Arnet and Carey are 3:2, or 3/5 and 2/5, respectively. Thus, Ace would make the following entry to remove Eaton's capital deficiency.

(a)

R. Arnet, Capital ($1,800 × 3/5)	1,080	
P. Carey, Capital ($1,800 × 2/5)	720	
W. Eaton, Capital		1,800
(To record write-off of capital deficiency)		

Cash Flows
no effect

After posting this entry, the cash and capital accounts will have the following balances.

Cash				R. Arnet, Capital				P. Carey, Capital				W. Eaton, Capital			
Bal.	5,000	(3)	31,000	(2)	9,000	Bal.	15,000	(2)	6,000	Bal.	17,800	(2)	3,000	Bal.	1,200
(1)	42,000			(a)	1,080			(a)	720					(a)	1,800
Bal.	16,000					Bal.	4,920			Bal.	11,080			Bal.	—0—

Illustration 12-14
Ledger balances after nonpayment of capital deficiency

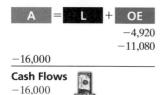

Cash Flows
−16,000

The cash balance ($16,000) now equals the sum of the credit balances in the capital accounts (Arnet $4,920 + Carey $11,080). Ace records the distribution of cash as:

R. Arnet, Capital	4,920	
P. Carey, Capital	11,080	
Cash		16,000
(To record distribution of cash to the partners)		

After posting this entry, all accounts will have zero balances.

Do it!

Partnership Liquidation

Kessington Company wishes to liquidate the firm by distributing the company's cash to the three partners. Prior to the distribution of cash, the company's balances are: Cash $45,000; Rollings, Capital (Cr.) $28,000; Havens, Capital (Dr.) $12,000; and Ostergard, Capital (Cr.) $29,000. The income ratios of the three partners are 4:4:2, respectively. Prepare the entry to record the absorption of Havens' capital deficiency by the other partners and the distribution of cash to the partners with credit balances.

action plan

✔ Allocate any unpaid capital deficiency to the partners with credit balances, based on their income ratios.

✔ After distribution of the deficiency, distribute cash to the remaining partners, based on their capital balances.

Solution

Rollings, Capital ($12,000 × 4/6)	8,000	
Ostergard, Capital ($12,000 × 2/6)	4,000	
Havens, Capital		12,000
(To record write-off of capital deficiency)		
Rollings, Capital ($28,000 − $8,000)	20,000	
Ostergard, Capital ($29,000 − $4,000)	25,000	
Cash		45,000
(To record distribution of cash to partners)		

Related exercise material: **E12-10** and **Do it!** 12-4.

The Navigator

COMPREHENSIVE
Do it!

On January 1, 2012, the capital balances in Hollingsworth Company are Lois Holly $26,000, and Jim Worth $24,000. In 2012 the partnership reports net income of $30,000. The income ratio provides for salary allowances of $12,000 for Holly and $10,000 to Worth and the remainder equally. Neither partner had any drawings in 2012.

Instructions

(a) Prepare a schedule showing the distribution of net income in 2012.

(b) Journalize the division of 2012 net income to the partners.

action plan

✔ Compute the net income of the partnership.

✔ Allocate the partners' salaries.

✔ Divide the remaining net income among the partners, applying the income/loss ratio.

✔ Journalize the division of net income in a closing entry.

Solution to Comprehensive Do it!

(a)   Net income   30,000

Division of Net Income

	Lois Holly	Jim Worth	Total
Salary allowance	$12,000	$10,000	$22,000
Remaining income $8,000 ($30,000 − $22,000)			
Lois Holly ($8,000 × 50%)	4,000		
Jim Worth ($8,000 × 50%)		4,000	
Total remainder			8,000
Total division of net income	$16,000	$14,000	$30,000

(b) 12/31/12

Income Summary	30,000	
Lois Holly, Capital		16,000
Jim Worth, Capital		14,000
(To close net income to partners' capital)		

The Navigator

Summary of Study Objectives

[1] **Identify the characteristics of the partnership form of business organization.** The principal characteristics of a partnership are: (a) association of individuals, (b) mutual agency, (c) limited life, (d) unlimited liability, and (e) co-ownership of property.

[2] **Explain the accounting entries for the formation of a partnership.** When formed, a partnership records each partner's initial investment at the fair value of the assets at the date of their transfer to the partnership.

[3] **Identify the bases for dividing net income or net loss.** Partnerships divide net income or net loss on the basis of the income ratio, which may be (a) a fixed ratio, (b) a ratio based on beginning or average capital balances, (c) salaries to partners and the remainder on a fixed ratio, (d) interest on partners' capital and the remainder on a fixed ratio, and (e) salaries to partners, interest on partners' capital, and the remainder on a fixed ratio.

[4] **Describe the form and content of partnership financial statements.** The financial statements of a partnership are similar to those of a proprietorship. The principal differences are: (a) The partnership shows the division of net income on the income statement. (b) The owners' equity statement is called a partners' capital statement. (c) The partnership reports each partner's capital on the balance sheet.

[5] **Explain the effects of the entries to record the liquidation of a partnership.** When a partnership is liquidated, it is necessary to record the (a) sale of noncash assets, (b) allocation of the gain or loss on realization, (c) payment of partnership liabilities, and (d) distribution of cash to the partners on the basis of their capital balances.

The Navigator

Glossary

Capital deficiency A debit balance in a partner's capital account after allocation of gain or loss. (p. 565).

General partners Partners who have unlimited liability for the debts of the firm. (p. 556).

Income ratio The basis for dividing net income and net loss in a partnership. (p. 560).

Limited liability company A form of business organization, usually classified as a partnership for tax purposes and usually with limited life, in which partners, who are called *members*, have limited liability. (p. 556).

Limited liability partnership A partnership of professionals in which partners are given limited liability and the public is protected from malpractice by insurance carried by the partnership. (p. 556).

Limited partners Partners whose liability for the debts of the firm is limited to their investment in the firm. (p. 556).

Limited partnership A partnership in which one or more general partners have unlimited liability and one or more partners have limited liability for the obligations of the firm. (p. 555).

No capital deficiency All partners have credit balances after allocation of gain or loss. (p. 565).

Partners' capital statement The owners' equity statement for a partnership which shows the changes in each partner's capital account and in total partnership capital during the year. (p. 563).

Partnership An association of two or more persons to carry on as co-owners of a business for profit. (p. 554).

Partnership agreement A written contract expressing the voluntary agreement of two or more individuals in a partnership. (p. 558).

Partnership dissolution A change in partners due to withdrawal or admission, which does not necessarily terminate the business. (p. 555).

Partnership liquidation An event that ends both the legal and economic life of a partnership. (p. 564).

Schedule of cash payments A schedule showing the distribution of cash to the partners in a partnership liquidation. (p. 566).

APPENDIX12A

Admission and Withdrawal of Partners

The chapter explained how the basic accounting for a partnership works. We now look at how to account for a common occurrence in partnerships—the addition or withdrawal of a partner.

Admission of a Partner

Study Objective [6]

Explain the effects of the entries when a new partner is admitted.

The admission of a new partner results in the **legal dissolution** of the existing partnership and the beginning of a new one. From an economic standpoint, however, the admission of a new partner (or partners) may be of minor significance in the continuity of the business. For example, in large public accounting or law firms, partners are admitted annually without any change in operating policies. **To recognize the economic effects, it is necessary only to open a capital account for each new partner.** In the entries illustrated in this appendix, we assume that the accounting records of the predecessor firm will continue to be used by the new partnership.

Helpful Hint

In a purchase of an interest, the partnership is not a participant in the transaction. In this transaction, the new partner contributes *no* cash to the partnership.

A new partner may be admitted either by (1) purchasing the interest of one or more existing partners or (2) investing assets in the partnership. The former affects only the capital accounts of the partners who are parties to the transaction. The latter increases both net assets and total capital of the partnership.

PURCHASE OF A PARTNER'S INTEREST

The **admission** of a partner **by purchase of an interest** is a personal transaction between one or more existing partners and the new partner. Each party acts as an individual separate from the partnership entity. The individuals involved negotiate the price paid. It may be equal to or different from the capital equity acquired. The purchase price passes directly from the new partner to the partners who are giving up part or all of their ownership claims.

Any money or other consideration exchanged is the personal property of the participants and **not** the property of the partnership. Upon purchase of an interest, the new partner acquires each selling partner's capital interest and income ratio.

Accounting for the purchase of an interest is straightforward. The partnership records record only the changes in partners' capital. **Partners' capital accounts are debited for any ownership claims sold.** At the same time, the new partner's capital account is credited for the capital equity purchased. Total assets, total liabilities, and total capital remain unchanged, as do all individual asset and liability accounts.

To illustrate, assume that L. Carson agrees to pay $10,000 each to C. Ames and D. Barker for 33⅓% (one-third) of their interest in the Ames–Barker partnership. At the time of the admission of Carson, each partner has a $30,000 capital balance. Both partners, therefore, give up $10,000 of their capital equity. The entry to record the admission of Carson is:

C. Ames, Capital	10,000	
D. Barker, Capital	10,000	
L. Carson, Capital		20,000
(To record admission of Carson by purchase)		

Illustration 12A-1
Ledger balances after purchase of a partner's interest

The effect of this transaction on net assets and partners' capital is shown below.

Net Assets	C. Ames, Capital		D. Barker, Capital		L. Carson, Capital
60,000	**10,000**	30,000	**10,000**	30,000	**20,000**
		Bal. 20,000		Bal. 20,000	

Note that net assets remain unchanged at $60,000, and each partner has a $20,000 capital balance. Ames and Barker continue as partners in the firm, but the capital interest of each has changed. The cash paid by Carson goes directly to the individual partners and not to the partnership.

Regardless of the amount paid by Carson for the one-third interest, the entry is exactly the same. If Carson pays $12,000 each to Ames and Barker for one-third of the partnership, the partnership still makes the entry shown above.

INVESTMENT OF ASSETS IN A PARTNERSHIP

The admission of a partner by an investment of assets is a transaction between the new partner and the partnership. Often referred to simply as admission by investment, the transaction **increases both the net assets and total capital of the partnership**.

Assume, for example, that instead of purchasing an interest, Carson invests $30,000 in cash in the Ames–Barker partnership for a 33⅓% capital interest. In such a case, the entry is:

Cash	30,000	
L. Carson, Capital		30,000
(To record admission of Carson by investment)		

Illustration 12A-2
Ledger balances after investment of assets

The effects of this transaction on the partnership accounts would be:

Net Assets	C. Ames, Capital	D. Barker, Capital	L. Carson, Capital
60,000	30,000	30,000	**30,000**
30,000			
Bal. 90,000			

Note that both net assets and total capital have increased by $30,000.

Remember that Carson's one-third capital interest might not result in a one-third income ratio. The new partnership agreement should specify Carson's income ratio, and it may or may not be equal to the one-third capital interest.

The comparison of the net assets and capital balances in Illustration 12A-3 shows the different effects of the purchase of an interest and admission by investment.

Illustration 12A-3
Comparison of purchase of an interest and admission by investment

Purchase of an Interest		Admission by Investment	
Net assets	$60,000	Net assets	$90,000
Capital		Capital	
C. Ames	$20,000	C. Ames	$30,000
D. Barker	20,000	D. Barker	30,000
L. Carson	20,000	L. Carson	30,000
Total capital	**$60,000**	**Total capital**	**$90,000**

When a new partner purchases an interest, the total net assets and total capital of the partnership *do not change*. When a partner is admitted by investment, both the total net assets and the total capital *change*.

In the case of admission by investment, further complications occur when the new partner's investment differs from the capital equity acquired. When those amounts are not the same, the difference is considered a **bonus** either to (1) the existing (old) partners or (2) the new partner.

Bonus to Old Partners. For both personal and business reasons, the existing partners may be unwilling to admit a new partner without receiving a bonus. In an established firm, existing partners may insist on a bonus as compensation for the work they have put into the company over the years. Two accounting factors underlie the business reason: First, total partners' capital equals the **book value** of the recorded net assets of the partnership. When the new partner is admitted, the fair values of assets such as land and buildings may be higher than their book values. The bonus will help make up the difference between fair value and book value. Second, when the partnership has been profitable, goodwill may exist. But, the partnership balance sheet does not report goodwill. The new partner is usually willing to pay the bonus to become a partner.

A bonus to old partners results when the new partner's investment in the firm is greater than the capital credit on the date of admittance. The bonus results in **an increase in the capital balances of the old partners. The partnership allocates the bonus to them on the basis of their income ratios before the admission of the new partner.** To illustrate, assume that the Bart–Cohen partnership, owned by Sam Bart and Tom Cohen, has total capital of $120,000. Lea Eden acquires a 25% ownership (capital) interest in the partnership by making a cash investment of $80,000. The procedure for determining Eden's capital credit and the bonus to the old partners is as follows.

1. **Determine the total capital of the new partnership:** Add the new partner's investment to the total capital of the old partnership. In this case, the total capital of the new firm is $200,000, computed as follows.

Total capital of existing partnership	$120,000
Investment by new partner, Eden	80,000
Total capital of new partnership	$200,000

2. **Determine the new partner's capital credit:** Multiply the total capital of the new partnership by the new partner's ownership interest. Eden's capital credit is $50,000 ($200,000 × 25%).

3. **Determine the amount of bonus:** Subtract the new partner's capital credit from the new partner's investment. The bonus in this case is $30,000 ($80,000 − $50,000).

4. **Allocate the bonus to the old partners on the basis of their income ratios:** Assuming the ratios are Bart 60%, and Cohen 40%, the allocation is: Bart $18,000 ($30,000 × 60%) and Cohen $12,000 ($30,000 × 40%).

The entry to record the admission of Eden is:

Cash	80,000	
Sam Bart, Capital		18,000
Tom Cohen, Capital		12,000
Lea Eden, Capital		50,000
(To record admission of Eden and bonus to old partners)		

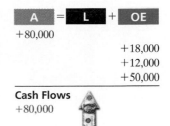

A = L + OE
+80,000
            +18,000
            +12,000
            +50,000

Cash Flows
+80,000

Bonus to New Partner. A bonus to a new partner results when the new partner's investment in the firm is less than his or her capital credit. This may occur when the new partner possesses special attributes that the partnership wants. For example, the new partner may be able to supply cash that the firm needs for expansion or to meet maturing debts. Or the new partner may be a recognized expert in a relevant field. Thus, an engineering firm may be willing to give a renowned engineer a bonus to join the firm. The partners of a restaurant may offer a bonus to a sports celebrity in order to add the athlete's name to the partnership. A bonus to a new partner may also result when recorded book values on the partnership books are higher than their fair values.

A bonus to a new partner results in a **decrease in the capital balances of the old partners. The amount of the decrease for each partner is based on the income ratios before the admission of the new partner.** To illustrate, assume that Lea Eden invests $20,000 in cash for a 25% ownership interest in the Bart–Cohen partnership. The computations for Eden's capital credit and the bonus are as follows, using the four procedures described in the preceding section.

1. Total capital of Bart–Cohen partnership		$120,000
Investment by new partner, Eden		20,000
Total capital of new partnership		$140,000
2. **Eden's capital credit** (25% × $140,000)		**$ 35,000**
3. **Bonus to Eden** ($35,000 − $20,000)		**$ 15,000**
4. Allocation of bonus to old partners:		
Bart ($15,000 × 60%)	$9,000	
Cohen ($15,000 × 40%)	6,000	$ 15,000

Illustration 12A-4
Computation of capital credit and bonus to new partner

The partnership records the admission of Eden as follows.

Cash	20,000	
Sam Bart, Capital	9,000	
Tom Cohen, Capital	6,000	
Lea Eden, Capital		35,000
(To record Eden's admission and bonus)		

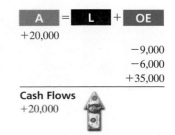

A = L + OE
+20,000
            −9,000
            −6,000
            +35,000

Cash Flows
+20,000

Withdrawal of a Partner

Study Objective [7]
Describe the effects of the entries when a partner withdraws from the firm.

Now let's look at the opposite situation—the withdrawal of a partner. A partner may withdraw from a partnership **voluntarily**, by selling his or her equity in the firm. Or, he or she may withdraw **involuntarily**, by reaching mandatory retirement age or by dying. The withdrawal of a partner, like the admission of a partner, legally dissolves the partnership. The legal effects may be recognized by dissolving the firm. However, it is customary to record only the economic effects of the partner's withdrawal, while the firm continues to operate and reorganizes itself legally.

As indicated earlier, the partnership agreement should specify the terms of withdrawal. The withdrawal of a partner may be accomplished by (1) payment from partners' personal assets or (2) payment from partnership assets. The former affects only the partners' capital accounts. The latter decreases total net assets and total capital of the partnership.

PAYMENT FROM PARTNERS' PERSONAL ASSETS

Withdrawal by payment from partners' personal assets is a personal transaction between the partners. **It is the direct opposite of admitting a new partner who purchases a partner's interest.** The remaining partners pay the retiring partner directly from their personal assets. **Partnership assets are not involved in any way, and total capital does not change.** The effect on the partnership is limited to changes in the partners' capital balances.

To illustrate, assume that partners Morz, Nead, and Odom have capital balances of $25,000, $15,000, and $10,000, respectively. Morz and Nead agree to buy out Odom's interest. Each of them agrees to pay Odom $8,000 in exchange for one-half of Odom's total interest of $10,000. The entry to record the withdrawal is:

A	=	L	+	OE
−10,000				
+5,000				
+5,000				

Cash Flows
no effect

J. Odom, Capital	10,000	
A. Morz, Capital		5,000
M. Nead, Capital		5,000
(To record purchase of Odom's interest)		

The effect of this entry on the partnership accounts is shown below.

Net Assets		A. Morz, Capital		M. Nead, Capital		J. Odom, Capital	
50,000			25,000		15,000	**10,000**	10,000
			5,000		**5,000**		
						Bal.	–0–
		Bal. 30,000		Bal. 20,000			

Illustration 12A-5
Ledger balances after payment from partners' personal assets

Note that net assets and total capital remain the same at $50,000.

What about the $16,000 paid to Odom? You've probably noted that it is not recorded. The entry debited Odom's capital only for $10,000, not for the $16,000 that she received. Similarly, both Morz and Nead credit their capital accounts for only $5,000, not for the $8,000 they each paid.

After Odom's withdrawal, Morz and Nead will share net income or net loss equally unless they indicate another income ratio in the partnership agreement.

PAYMENT FROM PARTNERSHIP ASSETS

Withdrawal by payment from partnership assets is a transaction that involves the partnership. **Both partnership net assets and total capital decrease as a result.** Using partnership assets to pay for a withdrawing partner's interest is the **reverse** of admitting a partner through the investment of assets in the partnership.

Many partnership agreements provide that the amount paid should be based on the fair value of the assets at the time of the partner's withdrawal. When this basis is required, some maintain that any differences between recorded asset balances and their fair values should be (1) recorded by an adjusting entry, and (2) allocated to all partners on the basis of their income ratios. This position has serious flaws. Recording the revaluations violates the cost principle, which requires that assets be stated at original cost. It also violates the going-concern assumption, which assumes the entity will continue indefinitely. The terms of the partnership contract should not dictate the accounting for this event.

In accounting for a withdrawal by payment from partnership assets, the partnership should not record asset revaluations. Instead, it should consider any difference between the amount paid and the withdrawing partner's capital balance as **a bonus** to the retiring partner or to the remaining partners.

Bonus to Retiring Partner.   A partnership may pay a bonus to a retiring partner when:

1. The fair value of partnership assets is more than their book value,
2. There is unrecorded goodwill resulting from the partnership's superior earnings record, or
3. The remaining partners are eager to remove the partner from the firm.

The partnership deducts the bonus from the remaining partners' capital balances on the basis of their income ratios at the time of the withdrawal.

To illustrate, assume that the following capital balances exist in the RST partnership: Roman $50,000, Sand $30,000, and Terk $20,000. The partners share income in the ratio of 3 : 2 : 1, respectively. Terk retires from the partnership and receives a cash payment of $25,000 from the firm. The procedure for determining the bonus to the retiring partner and the allocation of the bonus to the remaining partners is as follows.

1. **Determine the amount of the bonus:** Subtract the retiring partner's capital balance from the cash paid by the partnership. The bonus in this case is $5,000 ($25,000 − $20,000).

2. **Allocate the bonus to the remaining partners on the basis of their income ratios:** The ratios of Roman and Sand are 3 : 2. Thus, the allocation of the $5,000 bonus is: Roman $3,000 ($5,000 × 3/5) and Sand $2,000 ($5,000 × 2/5).

The partnership records the withdrawal of Terk as follows.

B. Terk, Capital	20,000	
F. Roman, Capital	3,000	
D. Sand, Capital	2,000	
Cash		25,000
(To record withdrawal of and bonus to Terk)		

The remaining partners, Roman and Sand, will recover the bonus given to Terk as the partnership sells or uses the undervalued assets.

Helpful Hint

Compare this entry to the one on page 578.

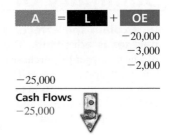

A	=	L	+	OE
				−20,000
				−3,000
				−2,000
−25,000				

Cash Flows
−25,000

Bonus to Remaining Partners.   The retiring partner may give a bonus to the remaining partners when:

1. Recorded assets are overvalued,
2. The partnership has a poor earnings record, or
3. The partner is eager to leave the partnership.

In such cases, the cash paid to the retiring partner will be less than the retiring partner's capital balance. **The partnership allocates (credits) the bonus to the capital accounts of the remaining partners on the basis of their income ratios.**

To illustrate, assume instead that the partnership pays Terk only $16,000 for her $20,000 equity when she withdraws from the partnership. In that case:

1. The bonus to remaining partners is $4,000 ($20,000 − $16,000).
2. The allocation of the $4,000 bonus is: Roman $2,400 ($4,000 × 3/5) and Sand $1,600 ($4,000 × 2/5).

Under these circumstances, the entry to record the withdrawal is:

Helpful Hint

Compare this entry to the one on page 577.

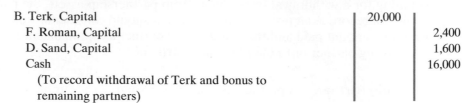

B. Terk, Capital	20,000	
F. Roman, Capital		2,400
D. Sand, Capital		1,600
Cash		16,000
(To record withdrawal of Terk and bonus to remaining partners)		

Note that if Sand had withdrawn from the partnership, Roman and Terk would divide any bonus on the basis of their income ratio, which is 3 : 1 or 75% and 25%.

DEATH OF A PARTNER

The death of a partner dissolves the partnership. But partnership agreements usually contain a provision for the surviving partners to continue operations. When a partner dies, it usually is necessary to determine the partner's equity at the date of death. This is done by (1) determining the net income or loss for the year to date, (2) closing the books, and (3) preparing financial statements. The partnership agreement may also require an independent audit and a revaluation of assets.

The surviving partners may agree to purchase the deceased partner's equity from their personal assets. Or they may use partnership assets to settle with the deceased partner's estate. In both instances, the entries to record the withdrawal of the partner are similar to those presented earlier.

To facilitate payment from partnership assets, some partnerships obtain life insurance policies on each partner, with the partnership named as the beneficiary. The partnership then uses the proceeds from the insurance policy on the deceased partner to settle with the estate.

Summary of Study Objectives for Appendix 12A

[6] Explain the effects of the entries when a new partner is admitted. The entry to record the admittance of a new partner by purchase of a partner's interest affects only partners' capital accounts. The entries to record the admittance by investment of assets in the partnership (a) increase both net assets and total capital and (b) may result in recognition of a bonus to either the old partners or the new partner.

[7] Describe the effects of the entries when a partner withdraws from the firm. The entry to record a withdrawal from the firm when the partners pay from their personal assets affects only partners' capital accounts. The entry to record a withdrawal when payment is made from partnership assets (a) decreases net assets and total capital and (b) may result in recognizing a bonus either to the retiring partner or the remaining partners.

Glossary for Appendix 12A

Admission by investment Admission of a partner by investing assets in the partnership, causing both partnership net assets and total capital to increase. (p. 573).

Admission by purchase of an interest Admission of a partner in a personal transaction between one or more existing partners and the new partner; does not change total partnership assets or total capital. (p. 572).

Withdrawal by payment from partners' personal assets Withdrawal of a partner in a personal transaction between partners; does not change total partnership assets or total capital. (p. 576).

Withdrawal by payment from partnership assets Withdrawal of a partner in a transaction involving the partnership, causing both partnership net assets and total capital to decrease. (p. 576).

*Note: All **asterisked** Questions, Exercises, and Problems relate to material in the appendix to the chapter.

Self-Test Questions

Answers are on page 591.

(SO 1) **1.** Which of the following is *not* a characteristic of a partnership?
    a. Taxable entity.
    b. Co-ownership of property.
    c. Mutual agency.
    d. Limited life.

(SO 1) **2.** A partnership agreement should include each of the following except:
    a. names and capital contributions of partners.
    b. rights and duties of partners as well as basis for sharing net income or loss.
    c. basis for splitting partnership income taxes.
    d. provision for withdrawal of assets.

(SO 1) **3.** The advantages of a partnership do *not* include:
    a. ease of formation.
    b. unlimited liability.
    c. freedom from government regulation.
    d. ease of decision making.

(SO 2) **4.** Upon formation of a partnership, each partner's initial investment of assets should be recorded at their:
    a. book values.
    b. cost.
    c. fair values.
    d. appraised values.

(SO 2) **5.** Ben and Sam Jenkins formed a partnership. Ben contributed $8,000 cash and a used truck that originally cost $35,000 and had accumulated depreciation of $15,000. The truck's fair value was $16,000. Sam, a builder, contributed a new storage garage. His cost of construction was $40,000. The garage has a fair value of $55,000. What is the combined total capital that would be recorded on the partnership books for the two partners?
    a. $79,000.
    b. $60,000.
    c. $75,000.
    d. $90,000.

(SO 3) **6.** The NBC Company reports net income of $60,000. If partners N, B, and C have an income ratio of 50%, 30%, and 20%, respectively, C's share of the net income is:
    a. $30,000.
    b. $12,000.
    c. $18,000.
    d. No correct answer is given.

(SO 3) **7.** Using the data in (6) above, what is B's share of net income if the percentages are applicable after each partner receives a $10,000 salary allowance?
    a. $12,000.
    b. $20,000.
    c. $19,000.
    d. $21,000.

(SO 3) **8.** To close a partner's drawing account, an entry must be made that:
    a. debits that partner's drawing account and credits Income Summary.
    b. debits that partner's drawing account and credits that partner's capital account.
    c. credits that partner's drawing account and debits that partner's capital account.
    d. credits that partner's drawing account and debits the firm's dividend account.

9. Which of the following statements about partnership (SO 4) financial statements is *true*?
    a. Details of the distribution of net income are shown in the owners' equity statement.
    b. The distribution of net income is shown on the balance sheet.
    c. Only the total of all partner capital balances is shown in the balance sheet.
    d. The owners' equity statement is called the partners' capital statement.

10. In the liquidation of a partnership, it is necessary to (1) (SO 5) distribute cash to the partners, (2) sell noncash assets, (3) allocate any gain or loss on realization to the partners, and (4) pay liabilities. These steps should be performed in the following order:
    a. (2), (3), (4), (1).
    c. (3), (2), (1), (4).
    b. (2), (3), (1), (4).
    d. (3), (2), (4), (1).

Use the following account balance information for Creekville Partnership to answer questions 11 and 12. Income ratios are 2 : 4 : 4 for Harriet, Mike, and Elly, respectively.

Assets		Liabilities and Owners' Equity	
Cash	$ 9,000	Accounts payable	$ 21,000
Accounts		Harriet, capital	23,000
receivable	22,000	Mike, capital	8,000
Inventory	73,000	Elly, capital	52,000
	$104,000		$104,000

11. Assume that, as part of liquidation proceedings, (SO 5) Creekville sells its noncash assets for $85,000. The amount of cash that would ultimately be distributed to Elly would be:
    a. $52,000.
    b. $48,000.
    c. $34,000.
    d. $86,000.

12. Assume that, as part of liquidation proceedings, Creekville (SO 5) sells its noncash assets for $60,000. As a result, one of the partners has a capital deficiency which that partner decides not to repay. The amount of cash that would ultimately be distributed to Elly would be:
    a. $52,000.
    b. $38,000.
    c. $24,000.
    d. $34,000.

*13.** Louisa Santiago purchases 50% of Leo Lemon's capital (SO 6) interest in the K & L partnership for $22,000. If the capital

balance of Kate Kildare and Leo Lemon are $40,000 and $30,000, respectively, Santiago's capital balance following the purchase is:
a. $22,000.   c. $20,000.
b. $35,000.   d. $15,000.

(SO 6) *14. Capital balances in the MEM partnership are Mary, Capital $60,000; Ellen, Capital $50,000; and Mills, Capital $40,000, and income ratios are 5 : 3 : 2, respectively. The MEMO partnership is formed by admitting Oleg to the firm with a cash investment of $60,000 for a 25% capital interest. The bonus to be credited to Mills, Capital in admitting Oleg is:
a. $10,000.   c. $3,750.
b. $7,500.   d. $1,500.

*15. Capital balances in the MURF partnership are Molly, (SO 7) Capital $50,000; Ursula, Capital $40,000; Ray, Capital $30,000; and Fred, Capital $20,000, and income ratios are 4 : 3 : 2 : 1, respectively. Fred withdraws from the firm following payment of $29,000 in cash from the partnership. Ursula's capital balance after recording the withdrawal of Fred is:
a. $36,000.   c. $38,000.
b. $37,000.   d. $40,000.

Go to the book's companion website, **www.wiley.com/college/weygandt**, for additional Self-Test Questions.

The Navigator

Questions

1. The characteristics of a partnership include the following: (a) association of individuals, (b) limited life, and (c) co-ownership of property. Explain each of these terms.

2. Jerry Kerwin is confused about the partnership characteristics of (a) mutual agency and (b) unlimited liability. Explain these two characteristics for Jerry.

3. Brent Houghton and Dick Kreibach are considering a business venture. They ask you to explain the advantages and disadvantages of the partnership form of organization.

4. Why might a company choose to use a limited partnership?

5. Sampson and Stevens form a partnership. Sampson contributes land with a book value of $50,000 and a fair value of $65,000. Sampson also contributes equipment with a book value of $52,000 and a fair value of $57,000. The partnership assumes a $20,000 mortgage on the land. What should be the balance in Sampson's capital account upon formation of the partnership?

6. W. Mantle, N. Cash, and W. DiMaggio have a partnership called Outlaws. A dispute has arisen among the partners. Mantle has invested twice as much in assets as the other two partners, and he believes net income and net losses should be shared in accordance with the capital ratios. The partnership agreement does not specify the division of profits and losses. How will net income and net loss be divided?

7. Blue and Grey are discussing how income and losses should be divided in a partnership they plan to form. What factors should be considered in determining the division of net income or net loss?

8. M. Carson and R. Leno have partnership capital balances of $40,000 and $80,000, respectively. The partnership agreement indicates that net income or net loss should be shared equally. If net income for the partnership is $36,000, how should the net income be divided?

9. S. McMurray and F. Kohl share net income and net loss equally. (a) Which account(s) is (are) debited and credited to record the division of net income between the partners? (b) If S. McMurray withdraws $30,000 in cash for personal use in lieu of salary, which account is debited and which is credited?

10. Partners T. Evans and R. Meloy are provided salary allowances of $30,000 and $25,000, respectively. They divide the remainder of the partnership income in a ratio of 3 : 2. If partnership net income is $45,000, how much is allocated to Evans and Meloy?

11. Are the financial statements of a partnership similar to those of a proprietorship? Discuss.

12. How does the liquidation of a partnership differ from the dissolution of a partnership?

13. Bobby Donal and Bill Spader are discussing the liquidation of a partnership. Bobby maintains that all cash should be distributed to partners on the basis of their income ratios. Is he correct? Explain.

14. In continuing their discussion from Question 13, Bill says that even in the case of a capital deficiency, all cash should still be distributed on the basis of capital balances. Is Bill correct? Explain.

15. Lowery, Keegan, and Feeney have income ratios of 5 : 3 : 2 and capital balances of $34,000, $31,000, and $28,000, respectively. Noncash assets are sold at a gain. After creditors are paid, $109,000 of cash is available for distribution to the partners. How much cash should be paid to Keegan?

16. Before the final distribution of cash, account balances are: Cash $23,000; S. Penn, Capital $19,000 (Cr.); L. Pattison, Capital $12,000 (Cr.); and M. Jeter, Capital $8,000 (Dr.). Jeter is unable to pay any of the capital deficiency. If the income-sharing ratios are 5 : 3 : 2, respectively, how much cash should be paid to L. Pattison?

*17. Linda Ratzlaff decides to purchase from an existing partner for $50,000 a one-third interest in a partnership. What effect does this transaction have on partnership net assets?

*18. Steve Renn decides to invest $25,000 in a partnership for a one-sixth capital interest. How much do the partnership's net assets increase? Does Renn also acquire a one-sixth income ratio through this investment?

*19. Kate Robidou purchases for $72,000 Grant's interest in the Sharon-Grant partnership. Assuming that Grant has a $66,000 capital balance in the partnership, what journal entry is made by the partnership to record this transaction?

*20. Tracy Harper has a $39,000 capital balance in a partnership. She sells her interest to Kim Remington for $45,000 cash. What entry is made by the partnership for this transaction?

*21. Debbie Perry retires from the partnership of Garland, Newlin, and Perry. She receives $85,000 of partnership assets in settlement of her capital balance of $77,000. Assuming that the income-sharing ratios are 5 : 3 : 2,

respectively, how much of Perry's bonus is debited to Newlin's capital account?

*22. Your roommate argues that partnership assets should be revalued in situations like those in question 21. Why is this generally not done?

*23. How is a deceased partner's equity determined?

24. ⬢ **PEPSICO** Why is PepsiCo not a partnership?

Brief Exercises

BE12-1   Eustace Scrubb and Will Poulter decide to organize the ALL-Star partnership. Scrubb invests $15,000 cash, and Poulter contributes $10,000 cash and equipment having a book value of $3,500. Prepare the entry to record Poulter's investment in the partnership, assuming the equipment has a fair value of $5,000.

Journalize entries in forming a partnership.
(SO 2)

BE12-2   Rhince and Rynelf decide to merge their proprietorships into a partnership called Dawn Treader Company. The balance sheet of Rynelf Co. shows:

Prepare portion of opening balance sheet for partnership.
(SO 2)

Accounts receivable	$16,000	
Less: Allowance for doubtful accounts	1,200	$14,800
Equipment	20,000	
Less: Accumulated depreciation—equip.	7,000	13,000

The partners agree that the net realizable value of the receivables is $13,500 and that the fair value of the equipment is $11,000. Indicate how the accounts should appear in the opening balance sheet of the partnership.

BE12-3   Pug Bern Co. reports net income of $70,000. The income ratios are Pug 60% and Bern 40%. Indicate the division of net income to each partner, and prepare the entry to distribute the net income.

Journalize the division of net income using fixed income ratios.
(SO 3)

BE12-4   SDT Co. reports net income of $55,000. Partner salary allowances are Sweet $15,000, Drinian $5,000, and Tavros $5,000. Indicate the division of net income to each partner, assuming the income ratio is 50 : 30 : 20, respectively.

Compute division of net income with a salary allowance and fixed ratios.
(SO 3)

BE12-5   Lill & Dil Co. reports net income of $28,000. Interest allowances are Lill $7,000 and Dil $5,000; salary allowances are Lill $15,000 and Dil $10,000; the remainder is shared equally. Show the distribution of income on the income statement.

Show division of net income when allowances exceed net income.
(SO 3)

BE12-6   After liquidating noncash assets and paying creditors, account balances in the Kidz Co. are Cash $19,000, A Capital (Cr.) $8,000, B Capital (Cr.) $7,000, and C Capital (Cr.) $4,000. The partners share income equally. Journalize the final distribution of cash to the partners.

Journalize final cash distribution in liquidation.
(SO 5)

*****BE12-7**   Beta Co. capital balances are: Acc $30,000, Bly $25,000, and Gumpus $20,000. The partners share income equally. Rhoop is admitted to the firm by purchasing one-half of Gumpus's interest for $13,000. Journalize the admission of Rhoop to the partnership.

Journalize admission by purchase of an interest.
(SO 6)

*****BE12-8**   In Coriakin Co., capital balances are Gael $40,000 and Nausus $50,000. The partners share income equally. Slaver is admitted to the firm with a 45% interest by an investment of cash of $52,000. Journalize the admission of Slaver.

Journalize admission by investment.
(SO 6)

*****BE12-9**   Capital balances in Midway Co. are Mirko $40,000, Neil $30,000, and Grillini $18,000. Mirko and Neil each agree to pay Grillini $12,000 from their personal assets. Mirko and Neil each receive 50% of Grillini's equity. The partners share income equally. Journalize the withdrawal of Grillini.

Journalize withdrawal paid by personal assets.
(SO 7)

*****BE12-10**   Data pertaining to Midway Co. are presented in BE12-9. Instead of payment from personal assets, assume that Grillini receives $24,000 from partnership assets in withdrawing from the firm. Journalize the withdrawal of Grillini.

Journalize withdrawal paid by partnership assets.
(SO 7)

Do it! Review

Analyze statements about part-nership organization.

(SO 1)

Do it! 12-1   Indicate whether each of the following statements is true or false.

_____ **1.** Each partner is personally and individually liable for all partnership liabilities.

_____ **2.** If a partnership dissolves, each partner has a claim to the specific assets he/she contrib-uted to the firm.

_____ **3.** In a limited partnership, all partners have limited liability.

_____ **4.** A major advantage of regular partnership is that it is simple and inexpensive to create and operate.

_____ **5.** Members of a limited liability company can take an active management role.

Divide net income and prepare closing entry.

(SO 3)

Do it! 12-2   Villa America Company reported net income of $85,000. The partnership agree-ment provides for salaries of $25,000 to Kibra and $18,000 to Devrish. They divide the remainder 40% to Kibra and 60% to Devrish. Kibra asks your help to divide the net income between the partners and to prepare the closing entry.

Complete schedule of partner-ship liquidation payments.

(SO 5)

Do it! 12-3   The partners of CS Company have decided to liquidate their business. Noncash assets were sold for $125,000. The income ratios of the partners Arabella, Dufflepud, and Davies are 3 : 2 : 3, respectively. Complete the following schedule of cash payments for CS Company

CS Company.xls

File   Edit   View   Insert   Format   Tools   Data   Window   Help

	A	B	C	D	E	F	G	H	I	J	K	L
1	Item	Cash	+	Noncash Assets	=	Liabilities	+	Arabella, Capital	+	Dufflepud, Capital	+	Davies, Capital
2	Balances before liquidation	15,000		90,000		40,000		20,000		32,000		13,000
3	Sale of noncash assets and allocation of gain											
4	New balances											
5	Pay liabilities											
6	New balances											
7	Cash distribution to partners											
8	Final balances											

Prepare entries to record absorption of capital deficiency and distribution of cash.

(SO 5)

Do it! 12-4   Granger Company wishes to liquidate the firm by distributing the company's cash to the three partners. Prior to the distribution of cash, the company's balances are: Cash $66,000; Moffit, Capital (Cr.) $47,000; Nation, Capital (Dr.) $21,000; and Davis, Capital (Cr.) $40,000. The income ratios of the three partners are 3 : 3 : 4, respectively. Prepare the entry to record the absorption of Nation's capital deficiency by the other partners and the distribution of cash to the partners with credit balances.

Exercises

Identify characteristics of partnership.

(SO 1)

E12-1   David Tennant has prepared the following list of statements about partnerships.

1. A partnership is an association of three or more persons to carry on as co-owners of a business for profit.

2. The legal requirements for forming a partnership can be quite burdensome.

3. A partnership is not an entity for financial reporting purposes.

4. The net income of a partnership is taxed as a separate entity.

5. The act of any partner is binding on all other partners, even when partners perform business acts beyond the scope of their authority.

6. Each partner is personally and individually liable for all partnership liabilities.

7. When a partnership is dissolved, the assets legally revert to the original contributor.

X 8. In a limited partnership, one or more partners have unlimited liability and one or more partners have limited liability for the debts of the firm.

F 9. Mutual agency is a major advantage of the partnership form of business.

Instructions
Identify each statement as true or false. If false, indicate how to correct the statement.

E12-2 K. Billie, S. Piper, and E. Rose are forming a partnership. Billie is transferring $50,000 of personal cash to the partnership. Piper owns land worth $15,000 and a small building worth $80,000, which she transfers to the partnership. Rose transfers to the partnership cash of $9,000, accounts receivable of $32,000 and equipment worth $19,000. The partnership expects to collect $29,000 of the accounts receivable.

Journalize entry for formation of a partnership.
(SO 2)

Instructions
(a) Prepare the journal entries to record each of the partners' investments.
(b) What amount would be reported as total owners' equity immediately after the investments?

E12-3 Rose Tyler has owned and operated a proprietorship for several years. On January 1, she decides to terminate this business and become a partner in the firm of Tyler and Sigma. Tyler's investment in the partnership consists of $12,000 in cash, and the following assets of the proprietorship: accounts receivable $14,000 less allowance for doubtful accounts of $2,000, and equipment $20,000 less accumulated depreciation of $4,000. It is agreed that the allowance for doubtful accounts should be $3,000 for the partnership. The fair value of the equipment is $13,500.

Journalize entry for formation of a partnership.
(SO 2)

Instructions
Journalize Tyler's admission to the firm of Tyler and Sigma.

E12-4 Martha and Jones have capital balances on January 1 of $50,000 and $40,000, respectively. The partnership income-sharing agreement provides for (1) annual salaries of $20,000 for Martha and $12,000 for Jones, (2) interest at 10% on beginning capital balances, and (3) remaining income or loss to be shared 60% by Martha and 40% by Jones.

Prepare schedule showing distribution of net income and closing entry.
(SO 3)

Instructions
(a) Prepare a schedule showing the distribution of net income, assuming net income is (1) $50,000 and (2) $36,000.
(b) Journalize the allocation of net income in each of the situations above.

E12-5 Aikman (beginning capital, $60,000) and Rory (beginning capital $90,000) are partners. During 2012, the partnership earned net income of $70,000, and Aikman made drawings of $18,000 while Rory made drawings of $24,000.

Prepare journal entries to record allocation of net income.
(SO 3)

Instructions
(a) Assume the partnership income-sharing agreement calls for income to be divided 45% to Aikman and 55% to Rory. Prepare the journal entry to record the allocation of net income.
(b) Assume the partnership income-sharing agreement calls for income to be divided with a salary of $30,000 to Aikman and $25,000 to Rory, with the remainder divided 45% to Aikman and 55% to Rory. Prepare the journal entry to record the allocation of net income.
(c) Assume the partnership income-sharing agreement calls for income to be divided with a salary of $40,000 to Aikman and $35,000 to Rory, interest of 10% on beginning capital, and the remainder divided 50%–50%. Prepare the journal entry to record the allocation of net income.
(d) Compute the partners' ending capital balances under the assumption in part (c).

E12-6 For Starrite Co., beginning capital balances on January 1, 2012, are Donna Noble $20,000 and Amy Bond $18,000. During the year, drawings were Noble $8,000 and Bond $5,000. Net income was $30,000, and the partners share income equally.

Prepare partners' capital statement and partial balance sheet.
(SO 4)

Instructions
(a) Prepare the partners' capital statement for the year.
(b) Prepare the owners' equity section of the balance sheet at December 31, 2012.

E12-7 David, Matt, and Chris are forming The Doctor Partnership. David is transferring $30,000 of personal cash and equipment worth $25,000 to the partnership. Matt owns land worth $18,000 and a small building worth $75,000, which he transfers to the partnership. There is a long-term mortgage of $20,000 on the land and building, which the partnership assumes. Chris transfers cash of $7,000, accounts receivable of $36,000, supplies worth $3,000, and equipment

Prepare a classified balance sheet of a partnership.
(SO 4)

worth $22,000 to the partnership. The partnership expects to collect $32,000 of the accounts receivable.

Instructions

Prepare a classified balance sheet for the partnership after the partners' investments on December 31, 2012.

Prepare cash payments schedule.
(SO 5)

E12-8 The Freema Company at December 31 has cash $20,000, noncash assets $100,000, liabilities $55,000, and the following capital balances: Dalek $45,000 and Briggs $20,000. The firm is liquidated, and $110,000 in cash is received for the noncash assets. Dalek and Briggs income ratios are 60% and 40%, respectively.

Instructions

Prepare a schedule of cash payments.

Journalize transactions in a liquidation.
(SO 5)

E12-9 Data for The Freema Company are presented in E12-8.

Instructions

Prepare the entries to record:

(a) The sale of noncash assets.
(b) The allocation of the gain or loss on realization to the partners.
(c) Payment of creditors.
(d) Distribution of cash to the partners.

Journalize transactions with a capital deficiency.
(SO 5)

E12-10 Prior to the distribution of cash to the partners, the accounts in the TSM Company are: Cash $28,000; Tyler, Capital (Cr.) $17,000; Smith, Capital (Cr.) $15,000; and Mott, Capital (Dr.) $4,000. The income ratios are 5 : 3 : 2, respectively.

Instructions

(a) Prepare the entry to record (1) Mott's payment of $4,000 in cash to the partnership and (2) the distribution of cash to the partners with credit balances.
(b) Prepare the entry to record (1) the absorption of Mott's capital deficiency by the other partners and (2) the distribution of cash to the partners with credit balances.

Journalize admission of a new partner by purchase of an interest.
(SO 6)

*E12-11 K. Gillan, C. Coduri, and C. Tate share income on a 5 : 3 : 2 basis. They have capital balances of $30,000, $26,000, and $18,000, respectively, when Cap Harkness is admitted to the partnership.

Instructions

Prepare the journal entry to record the admission of Cap Harkness under each of the following assumptions.

(a) Purchase of 50% of Gillan's equity for $19,000.
(b) Purchase of 50% of Coduri's equity for $12,000.
(c) Purchase of 33⅓% of Tate's equity for $9,000.

Journalize admission of a new partner by investment.
(SO 6)

*E12-12 S. Noble and T. Wells share income on a 6 : 4 basis. They have capital balances of $100,000 and $70,000, respectively, when W. Trinity is admitted to the partnership.

Instructions

Prepare the journal entry to record the admission of W. Trinity under each of the following assumptions.

(a) Investment of $90,000 cash for a 30% ownership interest with bonuses to the existing partners.
(b) Investment of $50,000 cash for a 30% ownership interest with a bonus to the new partner.

Journalize withdrawal of a partner with payment from partners' personal assets.
(SO 7)

*E12-13 N. Clark, C. Camille, and C. Eccleston have capital balances of $50,000, $40,000, and $32,000, respectively. Their income ratios are 5 : 3 : 2. Eccleston withdraws from the partnership under each of the following independent conditions.

1. Clark and Camille agree to purchase Eccleston's equity by paying $17,000 each from their personal assets. Each purchaser receives 50% of Eccleston's equity.
2. Camille agrees to purchase all of Eccleston's equity by paying $22,000 cash from her personal assets.
3. Clark agrees to purchase all of Eccleston's equity by paying $26,000 cash from his personal assets.

Instructions

Journalize the withdrawal of Eccleston under each of the assumptions above.

*E12-14 B. Edwards, J. King, and N. Pegg have capital balances of $95,000, $75,000, and $60,000, respectively. They share income or loss on a 5 : 3 : 2 basis. Pegg withdraws from the partnership under each of the following conditions.

Journalize withdrawal of a partner with payment from partnership assets.
(SO 7)

1. Pegg is paid $68,000 in cash from partnership assets, and a bonus is granted to the retiring partner.

2. Pegg is paid $56,000 in cash from partnership assets, and bonuses are granted to the remaining partners.

Instructions
Journalize the withdrawal of Pegg under each of the assumptions above.

*E12-15 Carl, Barrowman, and Cribbins are partners who share profits and losses 50%, 30%, and 20%, respectively. Their capital balances are $100,000, $60,000, and $40,000, respectively.

Journalize entry for admission and withdrawal of partners.
(SO 6, 7)

Instructions
(a) Assume Darvill joins the partnership by investing $80,000 for a 25% interest with bonuses to the existing partners. Prepare the journal entry to record his investment.
(b) Assume instead that Carl leaves the partnership. Carl is paid $120,000 with a bonus to the retiring partner. Prepare the journal entry to record Carl's withdrawal.

Exercises: Set B

Visit the book's companion website, at **www.wiley.com/college/weygandt**, and choose the Student Companion site to access Exercise Set B.

Problems: Set A

P12-1A The post-closing trial balances of two proprietorships on January 1, 2012, are presented below.

Prepare entries for formation of a partnership and a balance sheet.
(SO 2, 4)

	Williams Company		Jones Company	
	Dr.	**Cr.**	**Dr.**	**Cr.**
Cash	$ 14,000		$12,000	
Accounts receivable	17,500		26,000	
Allowance for doubtful accounts		$ 3,000		$ 4,400
Inventory	26,500		18,400	
Equipment	45,000		29,000	
Accumulated depreciation—equipment		24,000		11,000
Notes payable		18,000		15,000
Accounts payable		22,000		31,000
Williams, capital		36,000		
Jones, capital				24,000
	$103,000	$103,000	$85,400	$85,400

Williams and Jones decide to form a partnership, Wijo Company, with the following agreed upon valuations for noncash assets.

	Williams Company	Jones Company
Accounts receivable	$17,500	$26,000
Allowance for doubtful accounts	4,500	4,000
Inventory	28,000	20,000
Equipment	23,000	16,000

All cash will be transferred to the partnership, and the partnership will assume all the liabilities of the two proprietorships. Further, it is agreed that Williams will invest an additional $5,000 in cash, and Jones will invest an additional $19,000 in cash.

Instructions
(a) Prepare separate journal entries to record the transfer of each proprietorship's assets and liabilities to the partnership.
(b) Journalize the additional cash investment by each partner.
(c) Prepare a classified balance sheet for the partnership on January 1, 2012.

(a) Williams, Capital $38,000
Jones, Capital $24,000

(c) Total assets $172,000

Journalize divisions of net income and prepare a partners' capital statement.

(SO 3, 4)

P12-2A   At the end of its first year of operations on December 31, 2012, LAD Company's accounts show the following.

Partner	Drawings	Capital
Rory Lachelle	$23,000	$48,000
Andy Andoh	14,000	30,000
Francine Dalek	10,000	25,000

The capital balance represents each partner's initial capital investment. Therefore, net income or net loss for 2012 has not been closed to the partners' capital accounts.

Instructions

(a) Journalize the entry to record the division of net income for the year 2012 under each of the following independent assumptions.

(a) (1) Lachelle $18,000
    (2) Lachelle $19,000
    (3) Lachelle $15,700

  (1) Net income is $30,000. Income is shared 6 : 3 : 1.
  (2) Net income is $37,000. Lachelle and Andoh are given salary allowances of $15,000 and $10,000, respectively. The remainder is shared equally.
  (3) Net income is $19,000. Each partner is allowed interest of 10% on beginning capital balances. Lachelle is given a $12,000 salary allowance. The remainder is shared equally.

(b) Prepare a schedule showing the division of net income under assumption (3) above.

(c) Lachelle $40,700

(c) Prepare a partners' capital statement for the year under assumption (3) above.

Prepare entries with a capital deficiency in liquidation of a partnership.

(SO 5)

P12-3A   The partners in River Song Company decide to liquidate the firm when the balance sheet shows the following.

RIVER SONG COMPANY
Balance Sheet
May 31, 2012

Assets		Liabilities and Owners' Equity	
Cash	$ 27,500	Notes payable	$ 13,500
Accounts receivable	25,000	Accounts payable	27,000
Allowance for doubtful accounts	(1,000)	Salaries and wages payable	4,000
Inventory	34,500	A. Mangold, capital	33,000
Equipment	21,000	S. Otis, capital	21,000
Accumulated depreciation—equipment	(5,500)	P. Tyler, capital	3,000
Total	$101,500	Total	$101,500

The partners share income and loss 5 : 3 : 2. During the process of liquidation, the following transactions were completed in the following sequence.

1. A total of $55,000 was received from converting noncash assets into cash.
2. Gain or loss on realization was allocated to partners.
3. Liabilities were paid in full.
4. P. Tyler paid his capital deficiency.
5. Cash was paid to the partners with credit balances.

Instructions

(a) Loss on realization
    $19,000
    Cash paid: to Mangold
    $23,500; to Otis
    $15,300

(a) Prepare the entries to record the transactions.
(b) Post to the cash and capital accounts.
(c) Assume that Tyler is unable to pay the capital deficiency.
  (1) Prepare the entry to allocate Tyler's debit balance to Mangold and Otis.
  (2) Prepare the entry to record the final distribution of cash.

Journalize admission of a partner under different assumptions.

(SO 6)

*P12-4A   At April 30, partners' capital balances in SCJ Company are: G. Cooper $52,000, C. Jones $54,000, and J. Simmonds $18,000. The income sharing ratios are 5 : 4 : 1, respectively. On May 1, the SCJR Company is formed by admitting J. Redfern to the firm as a partner.

Instructions

(a) Journalize the admission of Redfern under each of the following independent assumptions.

(a) (1) Redfern $9,000
    (2) Redfern $18,000
    (3) Redfern $57,000
    (4) Redfern $51,000

  (1) Redfern purchases 50% of Simmonds's ownership interest by paying Simmonds $16,000 in cash.
  (2) Redfern purchases 33⅓% of Jones's ownership interest by paying Jones $15,000 in cash.

(3) Redfern invests $66,000 for a 30% ownership interest, and bonuses are given to the old partners.

(4) Redfern invests $46,000 for a 30% ownership interest, which includes a bonus to the new partner.

(b) Jones's capital balance is $32,000 after admitting Redfern to the partnership by investment. If Jones's ownership interest is 20% of total partnership capital, what were (1) Redfern's cash investment and (2) the bonus to the new partner?

*P12-5A On December 31, the capital balances and income ratios in SAR Company are as follows.

Journalize withdrawal of a partner under different assumptions.
(SO 7)

Partner	Capital Balance	Income Ratio
Spargo	$60,000	50%
Ames	40,000	30%
Ruscoe	26,000	20%

Instructions

(a) Journalize the withdrawal of Ruscoe under each of the following assumptions.

(1) Each of the continuing partners agrees to pay $18,000 in cash from personal funds to purchase Ruscoe's ownership equity. Each receives 50% of Ruscoe's equity.

(2) Ames agrees to purchase Ruscoe's ownership interest for $25,000 cash.

(3) Ruscoe is paid $34,000 from partnership assets, which includes a bonus to the retiring partner.

(4) Ruscoe is paid $22,000 from partnership assets, and bonuses to the remaining partners are recognized.

(b) If Ames's capital balance after Ruscoe's withdrawal is $42,400, what were (1) the total bonus to the remaining partners and (2) the cash paid by the partnership to Ruscoe?

(a) (1) Ames, Capital
       $13,000
    (2) Ames, Capital
       $26,000
    (3) Bonus $8,000
    (4) Bonus $4,000

Problems: Set B

P12-1B The post-closing trial balances of two proprietorships on January 1, 2012, are presented below.

Prepare entries for formation of a partnership and a balance sheet.
(SO 2, 4)

	Skorr Company		Crane Company	
	Dr.	Cr.	Dr.	Cr.
Cash	$ 10,000		$ 8,000	
Accounts receivable	18,000		30,000	
Allowance for doubtful accounts		$ 2,000		$ 3,000
Inventory	35,000		20,000	
Equipment	60,000		35,000	
Accumulated depreciation—equipment		28,000		15,000
Notes payable		20,000		
Accounts payable		30,000		40,000
Skorr, capital		43,000		
Crane, capital				35,000
	$123,000	$123,000	$93,000	$93,000

Skorr and Crane decide to form a partnership, Commander Company, with the following agreed upon valuations for noncash assets.

	Skorr Company	Crane Company
Accounts receivable	$18,000	$30,000
Allowance for doubtful accounts	2,500	4,000
Inventory	38,000	25,000
Equipment	40,000	22,000

All cash will be transferred to the partnership, and the partnership will assume all the liabilities of the two proprietorships. Further, it is agreed that Skorr will invest an additional $3,500 in cash, and Crane will invest an additional $16,000 in cash.

Instructions

(a) Skorr, Capital $53,500
    Crane, Capital $41,000

(c) Total assets $204,000

(a) Prepare separate journal entries to record the transfer of each proprietorship's assets and liabilities to the partnership.

(b) Journalize the additional cash investment by each partner.

(c) Prepare a classified balance sheet for the partnership on January 1, 2012.

Journalize divisions of net income and prepare a partners' capital statement.

(SO 3, 4)

P12-2B At the end of its first year of operations on December 31, 2012, SHB Company's accounts show the following.

Partner	Drawings	Capital
Staal	$15,000	$40,000
Harris	10,000	25,000
Blaine	5,000	15,000

The capital balance represents each partner's initial capital investment. Therefore, net income or net loss for 2012 has not been closed to the partners' capital accounts.

Instructions

(a) (1) Staal $25,000
    (2) Staal $20,000
    (3) Staal $27,000

(a) Journalize the entry to record the division of net income for 2012 under each of the independent assumptions shown on the next page.

(1) Net income is $50,000. Income is shared 5 : 3 : 2.

(2) Net income is $40,000. Staal and Harris are given salary allowances of $15,000 and $10,000, respectively. The remainder is shared equally.

(3) Net income is $37,000. Each partner is allowed interest of 10% on beginning capital balances. Staal is given a $20,000 salary allowance. The remainder is shared equally.

(b) Prepare a schedule showing the division of net income under assumption (3) above.

(c) Staal $52,000

(c) Prepare a partners' capital statement for the year under assumption (3) above.

Prepare entries and schedule of cash payments in liquidation of a partnership

(SO 5)

  GLS

P12-3B The partners in Tallis Company decide to liquidate the firm when the balance sheet shows the following.

TALLIS COMPANY
Balance Sheet
April 30, 2012

Assets		Liabilities and Owners' Equity	
Cash	$30,000	Notes payable	$20,000
Accounts receivable	25,000	Accounts payable	30,000
Allowance for doubtful accounts	(2,000)	Salaries and wages payable	2,500
Inventory	35,000	Laszlo, capital	28,000
Equipment	20,000	Alaya, capital	13,650
Accumulated depreciation—equipment	(8,000)	Octavian, capital	5,850
Total	$100,000	Total	$100,000

The partners share income and loss 5 : 3 : 2. During the process of liquidation, the transactions below were completed in the following sequence.

1. A total of $57,000 was received from converting noncash assets into cash.
2. Gain or loss on relization was allocated to partners.
3. Liabilities were paid in full.
4. Cash was paid to the partners with credit balances.

Instructions

(a) Loss on realization
    $13,000
    Cash paid: to Laszlo
    $21,500; to Octavian
    $3,250

(a) Prepare a schedule of cash payments.

(b) Prepare the entries to record the transactions.

(c) Post to the cash and capital accounts.

Journalize admission of a partner under different assumptions.

(SO 6)

*P12-4B At April 30, partners' capital balances in ZCF Company are: Zachary $30,000. Cross $16,000, and Flane $15,000. The income-sharing ratios are 5 : 3 : 2, respectively. On May 1, the ZCFC Company is formed by admitting Chantho to the firm as a partner.

Instructions

(a) (1) Chantho, Capital
    $7,500
    (2) Chantho $8,000
    (3) Chantho $36,000

(a) Journalize the admission of Chantho under each of the following independent assumptions.

(1) Chantho purchases 50% of Flane's ownership interest by paying Flane $6,000 in cash.

(2) Chantho purchases 50% of Cross's ownership interest by paying Cross $10,000 in cash.

(3) Chantho invests $29,000 cash in the partnership for a 40% ownership interest that includes a bonus to the new partner.

(4) Chantho invests $24,000 in the partnership for a 20% ownership interest, and bonuses are given to the old partners.

(4) Chantho $17,000

(b) Cross's capital balance is $24,000 after admitting Chantho to the partnership by investment. If Cross's ownership interest is 24% of total partnership capital, what were (1) Chantho's cash investment and (2) the total bonus to the old partners?

*P12-5B   On December 31, the capital balances and income ratios in Noma Company are as follows.

Journalize withdrawal of a partner under different assumptions.

(SO 7)

Partner	Capital Balance	Income Ratio
Morgan	$100,000	60%
White	51,000	30
Ogden	25,000	10

Instructions

(a) Journalize the withdrawal of Ogden under each of the following independent assumptions.

(1) Each of the remaining partners agrees to pay $15,000 in cash from personal funds to purchase Ogden's ownership equity. Each receives 50% of Ogden's equity.

(2) White agrees to purchase Ogden's ownership interest for $22,000 in cash.

(3) From partnership assets, Ogden is paid $34,000, which includes a bonus to the retiring partner.

(4) Ogden is paid $19,000 from partnership assets. Bonuses to the remaining partners are recognized.

(a) (1) White, Capital $12,500
(2) White, Capital $25,000
(3) Bonus $9,000
(4) Bonus $6,000

(b) If White's capital balance after Ogden's withdrawal is $55,000, what were (1) the total bonus to the remaining partners and (2) the cash paid by the partnership to Ogden?

Problems: Set C

Visit the book's companion website, at **www.wiley.com/college/weygandt**, and choose the Student Companion site to access Problem Set C.

Continuing Cookie Chronicle

(*Note:* This is a continuation of the Cookie Chronicle from Chapters 1 through 11.)

CCC12   Natalie's high school friend, Katy Peterson, has been operating a bakery for approximately 18 months. Because Natalie has been so successful operating Cookie Creations, Katy would like to have Natalie become her partner. Katy believes that together they will create a thriving cookie-making business. Natalie is quite happy with her current business set-up. Up until now, she had not considered joining forces with anyone. However, Natalie thinks that it may be a good idea to establish a partnership with Katy, and decides to look into it.

Go to the book's companion website, **www.wiley.com/college/weygandt,** *to see the completion of this problem.*

BROADENINGYOURPERSPECTIVE

Financial Reporting and Analysis

On the Web

BYP12-1   This exercise is an introduction to the Big Four accounting firms, all of which are partnerships.

Addresses

Deloitte & Touche	**www.deloitte.com/**
Ernst & Young	**www.ey.com/**
KPMG	**www.us.kpmg.com/**
PricewaterhouseCoopers	**www.pw.com/**
or go to **www.wiley.com/college/weygandt**	

Steps

1. Select a firm that is of interest to you.
2. Go to the firm's homepage.

Instructions

(a) Name two services provided by the firm.
(b) What is the firm's total annual revenue?
(c) How many clients does it service?
(d) How many people are employed by the firm?
(e) How many partners are there in the firm?

Critical Thinking

Decision Making Across the Organization

BYP12-2 Richard Powers and Jane Keckley, two professionals in the finance area, have worked for Eberhart Leasing for a number of years. Eberhart Leasing is a company that leases high-tech medical equipment to hospitals. Richard and Jane have decided that, with their financial expertise, they might start their own company to provide consulting services to individuals interested in leasing equipment. One form of organization they are considering is a partnership.

If they start a partnership, each individual plans to contribute $50,000 in cash. In addition, Richard has a used IBM computer that originally cost $3,700, which he intends to invest in the partnership. The computer has a present fair value of $1,500.

Although both Richard and Jane are financial wizards, they do not know a great deal about how a partnership operates. As a result, they have come to you for advice.

Instructions

With the class divided into groups, answer the following.

(a) What are the major disadvantages of starting a partnership?
(b) What type of document is needed for a partnership, and what should this document contain?
(c) Both Richard and Jane plan to work full-time in the new partnership. They believe that net income or net loss should be shared equally. However, they are wondering how they can provide compensation to Richard Powers for his additional investment of the computer. What would you tell them?
(d) Richard is not sure how the computer equipment should be reported on his tax return. What would you tell him?
(e) As indicated above, Richard and Jane have worked together for a number of years. Richard's skills complement Jane's and vice versa. If one of them dies, it will be very difficult for the other to maintain the business, not to mention the difficulty of paying the deceased partner's estate for his or her partnership interest. What would you advise them to do?

Communication Activity

BYP12-3 You are an expert in the field of forming partnerships. Daniel Ortman and Sue Stafford want to establish a partnership to start "Pasta Shop," and they are going to meet with you to discuss their plans. Prior to the meeting, you will send them a memo discussing the issues they need to consider before their visit.

Instructions

Write a memo in good form to be sent to Ortman and Stafford.

Ethics Case

BYP12-4 Elizabeth and Laurie operate a beauty salon as partners who share profits and losses equally. The success of their business has exceeded their expectations; the salon is operating quite profitably. Laurie is anxious to maximize profits and schedules appointments from 8 a.m. to 6 p.m. daily, even sacrificing some lunch hours to accommodate regular customers. Elizabeth schedules her appointments from 9 a.m. to 5 p.m. and takes long lunch hours. Elizabeth regularly makes significantly larger withdrawals of

cash than Laurie does, but, she says, "Laurie, you needn't worry, I never make a withdrawal without you knowing about it, so it is properly recorded in my drawing account and charged against my capital at the end of the year." Elizabeth's withdrawals to date are double Laurie's.

Instructions
(a) Who are the stakeholders in this situation?
(b) Identify the problems with Elizabeth's actions and discuss the ethical considerations of her actions.
(c) How might the partnership agreement be revised to accommodate the differences in Elizabeth's and Laurie's work and withdrawal habits?

"All About You" Activity

BYP12-5   As the text in this chapter indicates, the partnership form of organization has advantages and disadvantages. The chapter noted that different types of partnerships have been developed to minimize some of these disadvantages. Alternatively, an individual or company can choose the proprietorship or corporate form of organization.

Instructions
Go to two local businesses that are different, such as a restaurant, a retailer, a construction company, or a professional office (dentist, doctor, etc.), and find the answers to the following questions.
(a) What form of organization do you use in your business?
(b) What do you believe are the two major advantages of this form of organization for your business?
(c) What do you believe are the two major disadvantages of this form of organization for your business?
(d) Do you believe that eventually you may choose another form of organization?
(e) Did you have someone help you form this organization (attorney, accountant, relative, etc.)?

Answers to Insight and Accounting Across the Organization Questions
p. 556 Limited Liability Companies Gain in Popularity   Q: Why do you think that the use of the limited liability company is gaining in popularity? **A:** The LLC is gaining in popularity because owners in such companies have limited liability for business debts even if they participate in management. As a result, the LLC form has a distinct advantage over regular partnerships. In addition, the other limited-type partnerships discussed in Illustration 12-1 are restrictive as to their use. As a result, it is not surprising that limited liability companies are now often used as the form of organization when individuals want to set up a partnership.
p. 559 How to Part Ways Nicely   Q: How can partnership conflicts be minimized and more easily resolved? **A:** First, it is important to develop a business plan that all parties agree to. Second, it is vital to have a well-thought-out partnership agreement. Third, it can be useful to set up a board of mutually agreed upon and respected advisors to consult when making critical decisions.

Answers to Self-Test Questions
1. a   **2.** c   **3.** b   **4.** c   **5.** a ($8,000 + $16,000 + $55,000)   **6.** b ($60,000 × 20%)   **7.** c [$60,000 − ($10,000 × 3)] × 30% = $9,000   **8.** c   **9.** d   **10.** a   **11.** b ($22,000 + $73,000) − $85,000 = $10,000 loss; Ely $52,000 − (40% × 10,000)   **12.** d ($22,000 + $73,000) − $60,000 = $35,000 loss; loss allocation Harriett $23,000 − (20% × 35,000); Mike $8,000 − (40% × 35,000); Elly $52,000 − (40% × 35,000); Mike deficiency is $6,000; allocated to Elly $38,000 − ($6,000 × 4/6)   ***13.** d ($30,000 × 50%)   ***14.** d ($60,000 + $50,000 + $40,000 + $60,000) = $210,000; $210,000 × 25% = $52,500; ($60,000 − $52,500) × 20%   ***15.** b ($29,000 − $20,000) = $9,000 loss; $40,000 − ($9,000 × 3/9)

✔
The Navigator

✔   **Remember to go back to the Navigator box on the chapter opening page and check off your completed work.**

APPENDIXA

Specimen Financial Statements:

PepsiCo, Inc.

The Annual Report

Once each year a corporation communicates to its stockholders and other interested parties by issuing a complete set of audited financial statements. The **annual report**, as this communication is called, summarizes the financial results of the company's operations for the year and its plans for the future. Many annual reports are attractive, multicolored, glossy public relations pieces, containing pictures of corporate officers and directors as well as photos and descriptions of new products and new buildings. Yet the basic function of every annual report is to report financial information, almost all of which is a product of the corporation's accounting system.

The content and organization of corporate annual reports have become fairly standardized. Excluding the public relations part of the report (pictures, products, etc.), the following are the traditional financial portions of the annual report:

- Financial Highlights
- Letter to the Stockholders
- Management's Discussion and Analysis
- Financial Statements
- Notes to the Financial Statements

- Management's Responsibility for Financial Reporting
- Management's Report on Internal Control over Financial Reporting
- Report of Independent Registered Public Accounting Firm
- Selected Financial Data

In this appendix we illustrate current financial reporting with a comprehensive set of corporate financial statements that are prepared in accordance with generally accepted accounting principles and audited by an international independent certified public accounting firm. We are grateful for permission to use the actual financial statements and other accompanying financial information from the annual report of a large, publicly held company, PepsiCo, Inc.

Financial Highlights

Companies usually present the financial highlights section inside the front cover of the annual report or on its first two pages. This section generally reports the total or per share amounts for five to fifteen financial items for the current year and one or more previous years. Financial items from the income statement and the balance sheet that typically are presented are sales, income from continuing operations, net income, net income per share, net cash provided by operating activities, dividends per common share, and the amount of capital expenditures. The financial highlights section from PepsiCo's Annual Report is shown on page A2.

The financial information herein is reprinted with permission from the PepsiCo, Inc. 2009 Annual Report. The complete financial statements are available through a link at the book's companion website.

Financial Highlights

PepsiCo, Inc. and subsidiaries
(in millions except per share data, all per share amounts assume dilution)

Summary of Operations	2009	2008	Chg(a)	Chg Constant Currency(a)(e)
Total net revenue	$43,232	$43,251	–%	5%
Core division operating profit (b)	$ 8,647	$ 8,499	2%	6%
Core total operating profit (c)	$ 7,856	$ 7,848	–%	
Core net income attributable to PepsiCo (c)	$ 5,846	$ 5,887	(1)%	
Core earnings per share (c)	$ 3.71	$ 3.68	1%	6%
Other Data				
Management operating cash flow, excluding certain items (d)	$ 5,583	$ 4,831	16%	
Net cash provided by operating activities	$ 6,796	$ 6,999	(3)%	
Capital spending	$ 2,128	$ 2,446	(13)%	
Common share repurchases	$ –	$ 4,720	n/m	
Dividends paid	$ 2,732	$ 2,541	8%	
Long-term debt	$ 7,400	$ 7,858	(6)%	

(a) Percentage changes are based on unrounded amounts.

(b) Excludes corporate unallocated expenses, restructuring and impairment charges and PBG and PAS merger costs. See page 91 for a reconciliation to the most directly comparable financial measure in accordance with GAAP.

(c) Excludes restructuring and impairment charges, PBG and PAS merger costs and the net mark-to-market impact of our commodity hedges. See pages 91 and 92 for a reconciliation to the most directly comparable financial measure in accordance with GAAP.

(d) Includes the impact of net capital spending, and excludes the impact of a discretionary pension contribution, cash payments for PBG and PAS merger costs and restructuring-related cash payments. See also "Our Liquidity and Capital Resources" in Management's Discussion and Analysis. See page 92 for a reconciliation to the most directly comparable financial measure in accordance with GAAP.

(e) Assumes constant currency exchange rates used for translation based on the rates in effect in 2008. See pages 91 and 92 for a reconciliation to the most directly comparable financial measure in accordance with GAAP.

Core Earnings Per Share*

$3.37 $3.68 $3.71

07   08   09

*See page 92 for a reconciliation to the most directly comparable financial measure in accordance with GAAP.

Management Operating Cash Flow, Excluding Certain Items**

(in millions)

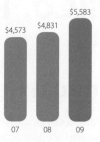

$4,573 $4,831 $5,583

07   08   09

**See page 92 for a reconciliation to the most directly comparable financial measure in accordance with GAAP.

Cumulative Total Shareholder Return

Return on PepsiCo stock investment (including dividends), the S&P 500 and the S&P Average of Industry Groups.***

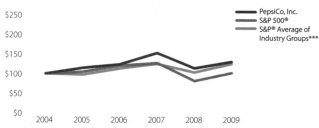

PepsiCo, Inc.
S&P 500®
S&P® Average of Industry Groups***

***The S&P Average of Industry Groups is derived by weighting the returns of two applicable S&P Industry Groups (Non-Alcoholic Beverages and Food) by PepsiCo's sales in its beverage and foods businesses. The returns for PepsiCo, the S&P 500 and the S&P Average indices are calculated through December 31, 2009.

	Dec-04	Dec-05	Dec-06	Dec-07	Dec-08	Dec-09
PepsiCo, Inc.	$100	$115	$124	$154	$114	$131
S&P 500®	$100	$105	$121	$128	$ 81	$102
S&P® Avg. of Industry Groups***	$100	$ 97	$113	$125	$103	$125

PepsiCo Estimated Worldwide Retail Sales: $108 Billion

Includes estimated retail sales of all PepsiCo products, including those sold by our partners and franchised bottlers.

Net Revenues

16%   13%   23%   48%

● PepsiCo Americas Foods – 48%
● PepsiCo Americas Beverages – 23%
  PepsiCo International – 29%
    ● Europe – 16%
    ● AMEA – 13%

Mix of Net Revenue

37%   63%

● Food – 63%
● Beverage – 37%

52%   48%

● U.S. – 52%
● Outside the U.S. – 48%

Pro Forma Revenue Percentage by Segment

10%   36%   16%   38%

● PepsiCo Americas Foods – 36%
● PepsiCo Americas Beverages – 38%
  PepsiCo International – 26%
    ● Europe – 16%
    ● AMEA – 10%

The above pro forma 2009 revenue chart has been prepared to illustrate the effect of the PBG and PAS mergers as if the mergers had been completed as of the beginning of PepsiCo's 2009 fiscal year. The pro forma revenue presented above is not indicative of the future operating results or financial position of PBG, PAS and PepsiCo and is based upon preliminary estimates. The final amounts recorded may differ from the information presented and are subject to change.

Letter to the Shareholders

Nearly every annual report contains a letter to the shareholders from the chairman of the board or the president, or both. This letter typically discusses the company's accomplishments during the past year and highlights significant events such as mergers and acquisitions, new products, operating achievements, business philosophy, changes in officers or directors, financing commitments, expansion plans, and future prospects. The letter to the stockholders is signed by Indra Nooyi, Chairman of the Board and Chief Executive Officer, of PepsiCo.

Only a short summary of the letter is provided below. The full letter can be accessed at the book's companion website at **www.wiley.com/college/weygandt**.

Indra K. Nooyi, *Chairman and Chief Executive Officer*

Dear Fellow Shareholders,

Our commitment to the principles and values of *Performance with Purpose* has helped us earn trust and respect from our consumers and partners, and the communities in which we operate across the world. By staying true to this foundation and continuing to execute on our strategies, we are sure that PepsiCo will continue to provide long-term sustainable growth for all stakeholders.

The *Performance with Purpose* initiatives that we have chosen to showcase in this year's annual report demonstrate that what's right for society is also what's right for business. It is a belief to which we are deeply committed. It has stood the test in difficult years, and we believe it will stand the test of time to come.

INDRA K. NOOYI
Chairman and Chief Executive Officer

Management's Discussion and Analysis

The **management's discussion and analysis (MD&A)** section covers three financial aspects of a company: its results of operations, its ability to pay near-term obligations, and its ability to fund operations and expansion. Management must highlight favorable or unfavorable trends and identity significant events and uncertainties that affect these three factors. This discussion obviously involves a number of subjective estimates and opinions. In its MD&A section, PepsiCo breaks its discussion into three major headings: Our Business, Our Critical Accounting Policies, and Our Financial Results. You can access the full MD&A section at **www.wiley.com/college/weygandt**.

Financial Statements and Accompanying Notes

The standard set of financial statements consists of: (1) a comparative income statement for three years, (2) a comparative statement of cash flows for three years, (3) a comparative balance sheet for two years, (4) a statement of equity for three years, and (5) a set of accompanying notes that are considered an integral part of the financial statements. The auditor's report, unless stated otherwise, covers the financial statements and the accompanying notes. PepsiCo's financial statements and accompanying notes plus supplementary data and analyses follow.

Consolidated Statement of Income

PepsiCo, Inc. and Subsidiaries
(in millions except per share amounts)

Fiscal years ended December 26, 2009, December 27, 2008 and December 29, 2007	2009	2008	2007
Net Revenue	**$43,232**	$43,251	$39,474
Cost of sales	**20,099**	20,351	18,038
Selling, general and administrative expenses	**15,026**	15,877	14,196
Amortization of intangible assets	**63**	64	58
Operating Profit	**8,044**	6,959	7,182
Bottling equity income	**365**	374	560
Interest expense	**(397)**	(329)	(224)
Interest income	**67**	41	125
Income before Income Taxes	**8,079**	7,045	7,643
Provision for Income Taxes	**2,100**	1,879	1,973
Net Income	**5,979**	5,166	5,670
Less: Net income attributable to noncontrolling interests	**33**	24	12
Net Income Attributable to PepsiCo	**$ 5,946**	$ 5,142	$ 5,658
Net Income Attributable to PepsiCo per Common Share			
Basic	**$ 3.81**	$ 3.26	$ 3.48
Diluted	**$ 3.77**	$ 3.21	$ 3.41

See accompanying notes to consolidated financial statements.

Consolidated Statement of Cash Flows

PepsiCo, Inc. and Subsidiaries
(in millions)

Fiscal years ended December 26, 2009, December 27, 2008 and December 29, 2007	2009	2008	2007
Operating Activities			
Net income	$ 5,979	$ 5,166	$ 5,670
Depreciation and amortization	1,635	1,543	1,426
Stock-based compensation expense	227	238	260
Restructuring and impairment charges	36	543	102
Cash payments for restructuring charges	(196)	(180)	(22)
PBG/PAS merger costs	50	–	–
Cash payments for PBG/PAS merger costs	(49)	–	–
Excess tax benefits from share-based payment arrangements	(42)	(107)	(208)
Pension and retiree medical plan contributions	(1,299)	(219)	(310)
Pension and retiree medical plan expenses	423	459	535
Bottling equity income, net of dividends	(235)	(202)	(441)
Deferred income taxes and other tax charges and credits	284	573	118
Change in accounts and notes receivable	188	(549)	(405)
Change in inventories	17	(345)	(204)
Change in prepaid expenses and other current assets	(127)	(68)	(16)
Change in accounts payable and other current liabilities	(133)	718	522
Change in income taxes payable	319	(180)	128
Other, net	(281)	(391)	(221)
Net Cash Provided by Operating Activities	6,796	6,999	6,934
Investing Activities			
Capital spending	(2,128)	(2,446)	(2,430)
Sales of property, plant and equipment	58	98	47
Proceeds from finance assets	–	–	27
Acquisitions and investments in noncontrolled affiliates	(500)	(1,925)	(1,320)
Divestitures	99	6	–
Cash restricted for pending acquisitions	15	(40)	–
Cash proceeds from sale of PBG and PAS stock	–	358	315
Short-term investments, by original maturity			
More than three months—purchases	(29)	(156)	(83)
More than three months—maturities	71	62	113
Three months or less, net	13	1,376	(413)
Net Cash Used for Investing Activities	(2,401)	(2,667)	(3,744)
Financing Activities			
Proceeds from issuances of long-term debt	1,057	3,719	2,168
Payments of long-term debt	(226)	(649)	(579)
Short-term borrowings, by original maturity			
More than three months—proceeds	26	89	83
More than three months—payments	(81)	(269)	(133)
Three months or less, net	(963)	625	(345)
Cash dividends paid	(2,732)	(2,541)	(2,204)
Share repurchases—common	–	(4,720)	(4,300)
Share repurchases—preferred	(7)	(6)	(12)
Proceeds from exercises of stock options	413	620	1,108
Excess tax benefits from share-based payment arrangements	42	107	208
Other financing	(26)	–	–
Net Cash Used for Financing Activities	(2,497)	(3,025)	(4,006)
Effect of exchange rate changes on cash and cash equivalents	(19)	(153)	75
Net Increase/(Decrease) in Cash and Cash Equivalents	1,879	1,154	(741)
Cash and Cash Equivalents, Beginning of Year	2,064	910	1,651
Cash and Cash Equivalents, End of Year	$ 3,943	$ 2,064	$ 910

See accompanying notes to consolidated financial statements.

Consolidated Balance Sheet

PepsiCo, Inc. and Subsidiaries
(in millions except per share amounts)

December 26, 2009 and December 27, 2008	2009	2008
ASSETS		
Current Assets		
Cash and cash equivalents	$ 3,943	$ 2,064
Short-term investments	192	213
Accounts and notes receivable, net	4,624	4,683
Inventories	2,618	2,522
Prepaid expenses and other current assets	1,194	1,324
Total Current Assets	12,571	10,806
Property, Plant and Equipment, net	12,671	11,663
Amortizable Intangible Assets, net	841	732
Goodwill	6,534	5,124
Other nonamortizable intangible assets	1,782	1,128
Nonamortizable Intangible Assets	8,316	6,252
Investments in Noncontrolled Affiliates	4,484	3,883
Other Assets	965	2,658
Total Assets	$ 39,848	$ 35,994
LIABILITIES AND EQUITY		
Current Liabilities		
Short-term obligations	$ 464	$ 369
Accounts payable and other current liabilities	8,127	8,273
Income taxes payable	165	145
Total Current Liabilities	8,756	8,787
Long-Term Debt Obligations	7,400	7,858
Other Liabilities	5,591	6,541
Deferred Income Taxes	659	226
Total Liabilities	22,406	23,412
Commitments and Contingencies		
Preferred Stock, no par value	41	41
Repurchased Preferred Stock	(145)	(138)
PepsiCo Common Shareholders' Equity		
Common stock, par value 1 2/3¢ per share (authorized 3,600 shares, issued 1,782 shares)	30	30
Capital in excess of par value	250	351
Retained earnings	33,805	30,638
Accumulated other comprehensive loss	(3,794)	(4,694)
Repurchased common stock, at cost (217 and 229 shares, respectively)	(13,383)	(14,122)
Total PepsiCo Common Shareholders' Equity	16,908	12,203
Noncontrolling interests	638	476
Total Equity	17,442	12,582
Total Liabilities and Equity	$ 39,848	$ 35,994

See accompanying notes to consolidated financial statements.

Consolidated Statement of Equity

PepsiCo, Inc. and Subsidiaries
(in millions)

Fiscal years ended December 26, 2009, December 27, 2008 and December 29, 2007	2009 Shares	2009 Amount	2008 Shares	2008 Amount	2007 Shares	2007 Amount
Preferred Stock	0.8	$ 41	0.8	$ 41	0.8	$ 41
Repurchased Preferred Stock						
Balance, beginning of year	(0.5)	(138)	(0.5)	(132)	(0.5)	(120)
Redemptions	(0.1)	(7)	(–)	(6)	(–)	(12)
Balance, end of period	(0.6)	(145)	(0.5)	(138)	(0.5)	(132)
Common Stock	1,782	30	1,782	30	1,782	30
Capital in Excess of Par Value						
Balance, beginning of year		351		450		584
Stock-based compensation expense		227		238		260
Stock option exercises/RSUs converted[a]		(292)		(280)		(347)
Withholding tax on RSUs converted		(36)		(57)		(47)
Balance, end of year		250		351		450
Retained Earnings						
Balance, beginning of year		30,638		28,184		24,837
Adoption of guidance on accounting for uncertainty in income taxes		–		–		7
Measurement date change		–		(89)		–
Adjusted balance, beginning of year		30,638		28,095		24,844
Net income attributable to PepsiCo		5,946		5,142		5,658
Cash dividends declared—common		(2,768)		(2,589)		(2,306)
Cash dividends declared—preferred		(2)		(2)		(2)
Cash dividends declared—RSUs		(9)		(8)		(10)
Balance, end of year		33,805		30,638		28,184
Accumulated Other Comprehensive Loss						
Balance, beginning of year		(4,694)		(952)		(2,246)
Measurement date change		–		51		–
Adjusted balance, beginning of year		(4,694)		(901)		(2,246)
Currency translation adjustment		800		(2,484)		719
Cash flow hedges, net of tax:						
Net derivative (losses)/gains		(55)		16		(60)
Reclassification of losses to net income		28		5		21
Pension and retiree medical, net of tax:						
Net pension and retiree medical gains/(losses)		86		(1,376)		464
Reclassification of net losses to net income		21		73		135
Unrealized gains/(losses) on securities, net of tax		20		(21)		9
Other		–		(6)		6
Balance, end of year		(3,794)		(4,694)		(952)
Repurchased Common Stock						
Balance, beginning of year	(229)	(14,122)	(177)	(10,387)	(144)	(7,758)
Share repurchases	–	–	(68)	(4,720)	(64)	(4,300)
Stock option exercises	11	649	15	883	28	1,582
Other, primarily RSUs converted	1	90	1	102	3	89
Balance, end of year	(217)	(13,383)	(229)	(14,122)	(177)	(10,387)
Total Common Shareholders' Equity		16,908		12,203		17,325
Noncontrolling Interests						
Balance, beginning of year		476		62		45
Net income attributable to noncontrolling interests		33		24		12
Purchase of subsidiary shares from noncontrolling interests, net		150		450		9
Currency translation adjustment		(12)		(48)		2
Other		(9)		(12)		(6)
Balance, end of year		638		476		62
Total Equity		$ 17,442		$ 12,582		$ 17,296
Comprehensive Income						
Net income		$ 5,979		$ 5,166		$ 5,670
Other Comprehensive Income/(Loss)						
Currency translation adjustment		788		(2,532)		721
Cash flow hedges, net of tax		(27)		21		(39)
Pension and retiree medical, net of tax						
Net prior service (cost)/credit		(3)		55		(105)
Net gains/(losses)		110		(1,358)		704
Unrealized gains/(losses) on securities, net of tax		20		(21)		9
Other		–		(6)		6
		888		(3,841)		1,296
Comprehensive Income		6,867		1,325		6,966
Comprehensive (income)/loss attributable to noncontrolling interests		(21)		24		(14)
Comprehensive Income Attributable to PepsiCo		$ 6,846		$ 1,349		$ 6,952

(a) Includes total tax benefits of $31 million in 2009, $95 million in 2008 and $216 million in 2007.

See accompanying notes to consolidated financial statements.

Notes to Consolidated Financial Statements

Note 1 Basis of Presentation and Our Divisions

BASIS OF PRESENTATION

Our financial statements include the consolidated accounts of PepsiCo, Inc. and the affiliates that we control. In addition, we include our share of the results of certain other affiliates based on our economic ownership interest. We do not control these other affiliates, as our ownership in these other affiliates is generally less than 50%. Equity income or loss from our anchor bottlers is recorded as bottling equity income in our income statement. Bottling equity income also includes any changes in our ownership interests of our anchor bottlers. Bottling equity income includes $147 million of pre-tax gains on our sales of PBG and PAS stock in 2008 and $174 million of pre-tax gains on our sales of PBG stock in 2007. There were no sales of PBG or PAS stock in 2009. See Notes 8 and 15 for additional information on our significant noncontrolled bottling affiliates. Income or loss from other noncontrolled affiliates is recorded as a component of selling, general and administrative expenses. Intercompany balances and transactions are eliminated. Our fiscal year ends on the last Saturday of each December, resulting in an additional week of results every five or six years.

Raw materials, direct labor and plant overhead, as well as purchasing and receiving costs, costs directly related to production planning, inspection costs and raw material handling facilities, are included in cost of sales. The costs of moving, storing and delivering finished product are included in selling, general and administrative expenses.

The preparation of our consolidated financial statements in conformity with generally accepted accounting principles requires us to make estimates and assumptions that affect reported amounts of assets, liabilities, revenues, expenses and disclosure of contingent assets and liabilities. Estimates are used in determining, among other items, sales incentives accruals, tax reserves, stock-based compensation, pension and retiree medical accruals, useful lives for intangible assets, and future cash flows associated with impairment testing for perpetual brands, goodwill and other long-lived assets. We evaluate our estimates on an on-going basis using our historical experience, as well as other factors we believe appropriate under the circumstances, such as current economic conditions, and adjust or revise our estimates as circumstances change. As future events and their effect cannot be determined with precision, actual results could differ significantly from these estimates.

While the majority of our results are reported on a weekly calendar basis, most of our international operations report on a monthly calendar basis. The following chart details our quarterly reporting schedule:

Quarter	U.S. and Canada	International
First Quarter	12 weeks	January, February
Second Quarter	12 weeks	March, April and May
Third Quarter	12 weeks	June, July and August
Fourth Quarter	16 weeks	September, October, November and December

See "Our Divisions" below and for additional unaudited information on items affecting the comparability of our consolidated results, see "Items Affecting Comparability" in Management's Discussion and Analysis of Financial Condition and Results of Operations.

Tabular dollars are in millions, except per share amounts. All per share amounts reflect common per share amounts, assume dilution unless noted, and are based on unrounded amounts. Certain reclassifications were made to prior years' amounts to conform to the 2009 presentation.

OUR DIVISIONS

We manufacture or use contract manufacturers, market and sell a variety of salty, convenient, sweet and grain-based snacks, carbonated and non-carbonated beverages, and foods in over 200 countries with our largest operations in North America (United States and Canada), Mexico and the United Kingdom. Division results are based on how our Chief Executive Officer assesses the performance of and allocates resources to our divisions. For additional unaudited information on our divisions, see "Our Operations" in Management's Discussion and Analysis of Financial Condition and Results of Operations. The accounting policies for the divisions are the same as those described in Note 2, except for the following allocation methodologies:

- stock-based compensation expense,
- pension and retiree medical expense, and
- derivatives.

Stock-Based Compensation Expense

Our divisions are held accountable for stock-based compensation expense and, therefore, this expense is allocated to our divisions as an incremental employee compensation cost. The allocation of stock-based compensation expense in 2009 was approximately 27% to FLNA, 3% to QFNA, 6% to LAF, 21% to PAB, 13% to Europe, 13% to AMEA and 17% to corporate unallocated expenses. We had similar allocations of stock-based compensation expense to our divisions in 2008 and 2007. The expense allocated to our divisions excludes any impact of changes in our assumptions during the year which reflect market conditions over which division management has no control. Therefore, any variances between allocated expense and our actual expense are recognized in corporate unallocated expenses.

Pension and Retiree Medical Expense

Pension and retiree medical service costs measured at a fixed discount rate, as well as amortization of gains and losses due to demographics, including salary experience, are reflected in division results for North American employees. Division results also include interest costs, measured at a fixed discount rate, for retiree medical plans. Interest costs for the pension plans, pension asset returns and the impact of pension funding, and gains and losses other than those due to demographics, are all reflected in corporate unallocated expenses. In addition, corporate unallocated expenses include the difference between the service costs measured at a fixed discount rate (included in division results as noted above) and the total service costs determined using the Plans' discount rates as disclosed in Note 7.

Derivatives

We centrally manage commodity derivatives on behalf of our divisions. These commodity derivatives include energy, fruit and other raw materials. Certain of these commodity derivatives do not qualify for hedge accounting treatment and are marked to market with the resulting gains and losses reflected in corporate unallocated expenses. These gains and losses are subsequently reflected in division results when the divisions take delivery of the underlying commodity. Therefore, the divisions realize the economic effects of the derivative without experiencing any resulting mark-to-market volatility, which remains in corporate unallocated expenses. These derivatives hedge underlying commodity price risk and were not entered into for speculative purposes.

In 2007, we expanded our commodity hedging program to include derivative contracts used to mitigate our exposure to price changes associated with our purchases of fruit. In addition, in 2008, we entered into additional contracts to further reduce our exposure to price fluctuations in our raw material and energy costs. The majority of these contracts do not qualify for hedge accounting treatment and are marked to market with the resulting gains and losses recognized in corporate unallocated expenses within selling, general and administrative expenses. These gains and losses are subsequently reflected in division results.

PepsiCo		
PepsiCo Americas Foods (PAF)	**PepsiCo Americas Beverages (PAB)**	**PepsiCo International (PI)**
Frito-Lay North America (FLNA)		**Europe**
Quaker Foods North America (QFNA)		**Asia, Middle East & Africa (AMEA)**
Latin America Foods (LAF)		

	2009	2008	2007	2009	2008	2007
		Net Revenue			Operating Profit[a]	
FLNA	**$13,224**	$12,507	$11,586	**$3,258**	$2,959	$2,845
QFNA	**1,884**	1,902	1,860	**628**	582	568
LAF	**5,703**	5,895	4,872	**904**	897	714
PAB	**10,116**	10,937	11,090	**2,172**	2,026	2,487
Europe	**6,727**	6,891	5,896	**932**	910	855
AMEA	**5,578**	5,119	4,170	**716**	592	466
Total division	43,232	43,251	39,474	8,610	7,966	7,935
Corporate—net impact of mark-to-market on commodity hedges	–	–	–	274	(346)	19
Corporate—PBG/PAS merger costs	–	–	–	(49)	–	–
Corporate—restructuring	–	–	–	–	(10)	–
Corporate—other	–	–	–	(791)	(651)	(772)
	$43,232	$43,251	$39,474	**$8,044**	$6,959	$7,182

(a) *For information on the impact of restructuring and impairment charges on our divisions, see Note 3.*

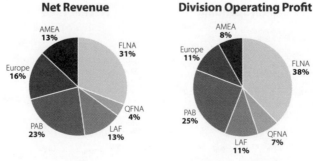

Net Revenue

AMEA 13%
FLNA 31%
Europe 16%
QFNA 4%
PAB 23%
LAF 13%

Division Operating Profit

AMEA 8%
Europe 11%
FLNA 38%
PAB 25%
QFNA 7%
LAF 11%

Notes to Consolidated Financial Statements

CORPORATE

Corporate includes costs of our corporate headquarters, centrally managed initiatives, such as our ongoing business transformation initiative and research and development projects, unallocated insurance and benefit programs, foreign exchange transaction gains and losses, certain commodity derivative gains and losses and certain other items.

OTHER DIVISION INFORMATION

	2009	2008	2007	2009	2008	2007
	Total Assets			Capital Spending		
FLNA	$ 6,337	$ 6,284	$ 6,270	$ 490	$ 553	$ 624
QFNA	997	1,035	1,002	33	43	41
LAF	3,575	3,023	3,084	310	351	326
PAB	7,670	7,673	7,780	182	344	450
Europe	9,321	8,840	7,330	357	401	369
AMEA	4,937	3,756	3,683	585	479	393
Total division	32,837	30,611	29,149	1,957	2,171	2,203
Corporate(a)	3,933	2,729	2,124	171	275	227
Investments in bottling affiliates	3,078	2,654	3,355	–	–	–
	$39,848	$35,994	$34,628	$2,128	$2,446	$2,430

(a) Corporate assets consist principally of cash and cash equivalents, short-term investments, derivative instruments and property, plant and equipment.

	2009	2008	2007	2009	2008	2007
	Amortization of Intangible Assets			Depreciation and Other Amortization		
FLNA	$ 7	$ 9	$ 9	$ 440	$ 441	$ 437
QFNA	–	–	–	36	34	34
LAF	5	6	4	189	194	166
PAB	18	16	16	345	334	321
Europe	22	23	20	227	210	190
AMEA	11	10	9	248	213	189
Total division	63	64	58	1,485	1,426	1,337
Corporate	–	–	–	87	53	31
	$63	$64	$58	$1,572	$1,479	$1,368

	2009	2008	2007	2009	2008	2007
	Net Revenue(a)			Long-Lived Assets(b)		
U.S.	$22,446	$22,525	$21,978	$12,496	$12,095	$12,498
Mexico	3,210	3,714	3,498	1,044	904	1,067
Canada	1,996	2,107	1,961	688	556	699
United Kingdom	1,826	2,099	1,987	1,358	1,509	2,090
All other countries	13,754	12,806	10,050	10,726	7,466	6,441
	$43,232	$43,251	$39,474	$26,312	$22,530	$22,795

(a) Represents net revenue from businesses operating in these countries.
(b) Long-lived assets represent property, plant and equipment, nonamortizable intangible assets, amortizable intangible assets, and investments in noncontrolled affiliates. These assets are reported in the country where they are primarily used.

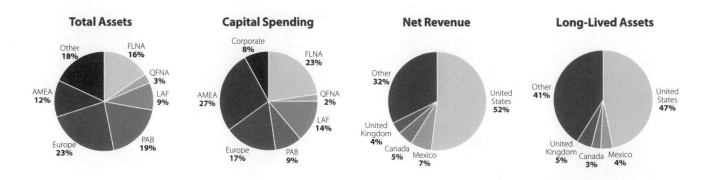

Note 2 Our Significant Accounting Policies

REVENUE RECOGNITION

We recognize revenue upon shipment or delivery to our customers based on written sales terms that do not allow for a right of return. However, our policy for DSD and certain chilled products is to remove and replace damaged and out-of-date products from store shelves to ensure that our consumers receive the product quality and freshness that they expect. Similarly, our policy for certain warehouse-distributed products is to replace damaged and out-of-date products. Based on our experience with this practice, we have reserved for anticipated damaged and out-of-date products. For additional unaudited information on our revenue recognition and related policies, including our policy on bad debts, see "Our Critical Accounting Policies" in Management's Discussion and Analysis of Financial Condition and Results of Operations. We are exposed to concentration of credit risk by our customers, Wal-Mart and PBG. In 2009, Wal-Mart (including Sam's) represented approximately 13% of our total net revenue, including concentrate sales to our bottlers which are used in finished goods sold by them to Wal-Mart; and PBG represented approximately 6%. We have not experienced credit issues with these customers.

SALES INCENTIVES AND OTHER MARKETPLACE SPENDING

We offer sales incentives and discounts through various programs to our customers and consumers. Sales incentives and discounts are accounted for as a reduction of revenue and totaled $12.9 billion in 2009, $12.5 billion in 2008 and $11.3 billion in 2007. While most of these incentive arrangements have terms of no more than one year, certain arrangements, such as fountain pouring rights, may extend beyond one year. Costs incurred to obtain these arrangements are recognized over the shorter of the economic or contractual life, as a reduction of revenue, and the remaining balances of $296 million as of December 26, 2009 and $333 million as of December 27, 2008 are included in current assets and other assets on our balance sheet. For additional unaudited information on our sales incentives, see "Our Critical Accounting Policies" in Management's Discussion and Analysis of Financial Condition and Results of Operations.

Other marketplace spending, which includes the costs of advertising and other marketing activities, totaled $2.8 billion in 2009 and $2.9 billion in both 2008 and 2007 and is reported as selling, general and administrative expenses. Included in these amounts were advertising expenses of $1.7 billion in both 2009

and 2008 and $1.8 billion in 2007. Deferred advertising costs are not expensed until the year first used and consist of:

* media and personal service prepayments,
* promotional materials in inventory, and
* production costs of future media advertising.

Deferred advertising costs of $143 million and $172 million at year-end 2009 and 2008, respectively, are classified as prepaid expenses on our balance sheet.

DISTRIBUTION COSTS

Distribution costs, including the costs of shipping and handling activities, are reported as selling, general and administrative expenses. Shipping and handling expenses were $5.6 billion in both 2009 and 2008 and $5.2 billion in 2007.

CASH EQUIVALENTS

Cash equivalents are investments with original maturities of three months or less which we do not intend to rollover beyond three months.

SOFTWARE COSTS

We capitalize certain computer software and software development costs incurred in connection with developing or obtaining computer software for internal use when both the preliminary project stage is completed and it is probable that the software will be used as intended. Capitalized software costs include only (i) external direct costs of materials and services utilized in developing or obtaining computer software, (ii) compensation and related benefits for employees who are directly associated with the software project and (iii) interest costs incurred while developing internal-use computer software. Capitalized software costs are included in property, plant and equipment on our balance sheet and amortized on a straight-line basis when placed into service over the estimated useful lives of the software, which approximate five to ten years. Software amortization totaled $119 million in 2009, $58 million in 2008 and $30 million in 2007. Net capitalized software and development costs were $1.1 billion as of December 26, 2009 and $940 million as of December 27, 2008.

COMMITMENTS AND CONTINGENCIES

We are subject to various claims and contingencies related to lawsuits, certain taxes and environmental matters, as well as commitments under contractual and other commercial obligations. We recognize liabilities for contingencies and commitments when a loss is probable and estimable. For additional information on our commitments, see Note 9.

Notes to Consolidated Financial Statements

RESEARCH AND DEVELOPMENT

We engage in a variety of research and development activities. These activities principally involve the development of new products, improvement in the quality of existing products, improvement and modernization of production processes, and the development and implementation of new technologies to enhance the quality and value of both current and proposed product lines. Consumer research is excluded from research and development costs and included in other marketing costs. Research and development costs were $414 million in 2009, $388 million in 2008 and $364 million in 2007 and are reported within selling, general and administrative expenses.

OTHER SIGNIFICANT ACCOUNTING POLICIES

Our other significant accounting policies are disclosed as follows:

- *Property, Plant and Equipment and Intangible Assets*—Note 4, and for additional unaudited information on brands and goodwill, see "Our Critical Accounting Policies" in Management's Discussion and Analysis of Financial Condition and Results of Operations.
- *Income Taxes*—Note 5, and for additional unaudited information, see "Our Critical Accounting Policies" in Management's Discussion and Analysis of Financial Condition and Results of Operations.
- *Stock-Based Compensation*—Note 6.
- *Pension, Retiree Medical and Savings Plans*—Note 7, and for additional unaudited information, see "Our Critical Accounting Policies" in Management's Discussion and Analysis of Financial Condition and Results of Operations.
- *Financial Instruments*—Note 10, and for additional unaudited information, see "Our Business Risks" in Management's Discussion and Analysis of Financial Condition and Results of Operations.

RECENT ACCOUNTING PRONOUNCEMENTS

In December 2007, the FASB amended its guidance on accounting for business combinations to improve, simplify and converge internationally the accounting for business combinations. The new accounting guidance continues the movement toward the greater use of fair value in financial reporting and increased transparency through expanded disclosures. We adopted the provisions of the new guidance as of the beginning of our 2009 fiscal year. The new accounting guidance changes how business acquisitions are accounted for and will impact financial statements both on the acquisition date and in subsequent periods. Additionally, under the new guidance, transaction costs are expensed rather than capitalized. Future adjustments made to valuation allowances on deferred taxes and acquired tax contingencies associated with acquisitions that closed prior to the beginning of our 2009 fiscal year apply the new provisions and will be evaluated based on the outcome of these matters.

In December 2007, the FASB issued new accounting and disclosure guidance on noncontrolling interests in consolidated financial statements. This guidance amends the accounting literature to establish new standards that will govern the accounting for and reporting of (1) noncontrolling interests in partially owned consolidated subsidiaries and (2) the loss of control of subsidiaries. We adopted the accounting provisions of the new guidance on a prospective basis as of the beginning of our 2009 fiscal year, and the adoption did not have a material impact on our financial statements. In addition, we adopted the presentation and disclosure requirements of the new guidance on a retrospective basis in the first quarter of 2009.

In June 2009, the FASB amended its accounting guidance on the consolidation of VIEs. Among other things, the new guidance requires a qualitative rather than a quantitative assessment to determine the primary beneficiary of a VIE based on whether the entity (1) has the power to direct matters that most significantly impact the activities of the VIE and (2) has the obligation to absorb losses or the right to receive benefits of the VIE that could potentially be significant to the VIE. In addition, the amended guidance requires an ongoing reconsideration of the primary beneficiary. The provisions of this new guidance are effective as of the beginning of our 2010 fiscal year, and we do not expect the adoption to have a material impact on our financial statements.

Note 3 Restructuring and Impairment Charges

2009 AND 2008 RESTRUCTURING AND IMPAIRMENT CHARGES

In 2009, we incurred a charge of $36 million ($29 million after-tax or $0.02 per share) in conjunction with our Productivity for Growth program that began in 2008. The program includes actions in all divisions of the business, including the closure of six plants that we believe will increase cost competitiveness across the supply chain, upgrade and streamline our product portfolio, and simplify the organization for more effective and timely decision-making. These charges were recorded in selling, general and administrative expenses. These initiatives were completed in the second quarter of 2009, and substantially all cash payments related to these charges are expected to be paid by 2010.

In 2008, we incurred a charge of $543 million ($408 million after-tax or $0.25 per share) in conjunction with our Productivity for Growth program. Approximately $455 million of the charge was recorded in selling, general and administrative expenses, with the remainder recorded in cost of sales.

A summary of the restructuring and impairment charge in 2009 is as follows:

	Severance and Other Employee Costs (a)	Other Costs	Total
FLNA	$ –	$ 2	$ 2
QFNA	–	1	1
LAF	3	–	3
PAB	6	10	16
Europe	1	–	1
AMEA	7	6	13
	$17	$19	$36

(a) *Primarily reflects termination costs for approximately 410 employees.*

A summary of the restructuring and impairment charge in 2008 is as follows:

	Severance and Other Employee Costs	Asset Impairments	Other Costs	Total
FLNA	$ 48	$ 38	$ 22	$108
QFNA	14	3	14	31
LAF	30	8	2	40
PAB	68	92	129	289
Europe	39	6	5	50
AMEA	11	2	2	15
Corporate	2	–	8	10
	$212	$149	$182	$543

Severance and other employee costs primarily reflect termination costs for approximately 3,500 employees. Asset impairments relate to the closure of six plants and changes to our beverage product portfolio. Other costs include contract exit costs and third-party incremental costs associated with upgrading our product portfolio and our supply chain.

A summary of our Productivity for Growth program activity is as follows:

	Severance and Other Employee Costs	Asset Impairments	Other Costs	Total
2008 restructuring and impairment charge	$ 212	$ 149	$ 182	$ 543
Cash payments	(50)	–	(109)	(159)
Non-cash charge	(27)	(149)	(9)	(185)
Currency translation	(1)	–	–	(1)
Liability as of December 27, 2008	134	–	64	198
2009 restructuring and impairment charge	17	12	7	36
Cash payments	(128)	–	(68)	(196)
Currency translation and other	(14)	(12)	25	(1)
Liability as of December 26, 2009	$ 9	$ –	$ 28	$ 37

2007 RESTRUCTURING AND IMPAIRMENT CHARGE

In 2007, we incurred a charge of $102 million ($70 million after-tax or $0.04 per share) in conjunction with restructuring actions primarily to close certain plants and rationalize other production lines across FLNA, LAF, PAB, Europe and AMEA. The charge was recorded in selling, general and administrative expenses. All cash payments related to this charge were paid by the end of 2008.

A summary of the restructuring and impairment charge is as follows:

	Severance and Other Employee Costs	Asset Impairments	Other Costs	Total
FLNA	$ –	$19	$ 9	$ 28
LAF	14	25	–	39
PAB	12	–	–	12
Europe	2	4	3	9
AMEA	5	9	–	14
	$33	$57	$12	$102

Severance and other employee costs primarily reflect termination costs for approximately 1,100 employees.

Note 4   Property, Plant and Equipment and Intangible Assets

	Average Useful Life	2009	2008	2007
Property, plant and equipment, net				
Land and improvements	10–34yrs.	$ 1,208	$ 868	
Buildings and improvements	20–44	5,080	4,738	
Machinery and equipment, including fleet and software	5–14	17,183	15,173	
Construction in progress		1,441	1,773	
		24,912	22,552	
Accumulated depreciation		(12,241)	(10,889)	
		$ 12,671	$ 11,663	
Depreciation expense		$ 1,500	$ 1,422	$1,304
Amortizable intangible assets, net				
Brands	5–40	$ 1,465	$ 1,411	
Other identifiable intangibles	10–24	505	360	
		1,970	1,771	
Accumulated amortization		(1,129)	(1,039)	
		$ 841	$ 732	
Amortization expense		$ 63	$ 64	$ 58

Property, plant and equipment is recorded at historical cost. Depreciation and amortization are recognized on a straight-line basis over an asset's estimated useful life. Land is not depreciated and construction in progress is not depreciated until ready for service. Amortization of intangible assets for each of the next five years, based on existing intangible assets as of December 26, 2009 and using average 2009 foreign exchange rates, is expected to be $65 million in both 2010 and 2011, $61 million in 2012, $58 million in 2013 and $52 million in 2014.

Notes to Consolidated Financial Statements

Depreciable and amortizable assets are only evaluated for impairment upon a significant change in the operating or macroeconomic environment. In these circumstances, if an evaluation of the undiscounted cash flows indicates impairment, the asset is written down to its estimated fair value, which is based on discounted future cash flows. Useful lives are periodically evaluated to determine whether events or circumstances have occurred which indicate the need for revision. For additional unaudited information on our amortizable brand policies, see "Our Critical Accounting Policies" in Management's Discussion and Analysis of Financial Condition and Results of Operations.

NONAMORTIZABLE INTANGIBLE ASSETS

Perpetual brands and goodwill are assessed for impairment at least annually. If the carrying amount of a perpetual brand exceeds its fair value, as determined by its discounted cash flows, an impairment loss is recognized in an amount equal to that excess. No impairment charges resulted from these impairment evaluations. The change in the book value of nonamortizable intangible assets is as follows:

	Balance, Beginning 2008	Acquisitions	Translation and Other	Balance, End of 2008	Acquisitions	Translation and Other	Balance, End of 2009
FLNA							
Goodwill	$ 311	$ –	$ (34)	$ 277	$ 6	$ 23	$ 306
Brands	–	–	–	–	26	4	30
	311	–	(34)	277	32	27	336
QFNA							
Goodwill	175	–	–	175	–	–	175
LAF							
Goodwill	147	338	(61)	424	17	38	479
Brands	22	118	(13)	127	1	8	136
	169	456	(74)	551	18	46	615
PAB							
Goodwill	2,369	–	(14)	2,355	62	14	2,431
Brands	59	–	–	59	48	5	112
	2,428	–	(14)	2,414	110	19	2,543
Europe							
Goodwill	1,642	45	(218)	1,469	1,291	(136)	2,624
Brands	1,041	14	(211)	844	572	(38)	1,378
	2,683	59	(429)	2,313	1,863	(174)	4,002
AMEA							
Goodwill	525	1	(102)	424	4	91	519
Brands	126	–	(28)	98	–	28	126
	651	1	(130)	522	4	119	645
Total goodwill	5,169	384	(429)	5,124	1,380	30	6,534
Total brands	1,248	132	(252)	1,128	647	7	1,782
	$6,417	$516	$(681)	$6,252	$2,027	$ 37	$8,316

Note 5 Income Taxes

	2009	2008	2007
Income before income taxes			
U.S.	$4,209	$3,274	$4,085
Foreign	3,870	3,771	3,558
	$8,079	$7,045	$7,643
Provision for income taxes			
Current: U.S. Federal	$1,238	$ 815	$1,422
Foreign	473	732	489
State	124	87	104
	1,835	1,634	2,015
Deferred: U.S. Federal	223	313	22
Foreign	21	(69)	(66)
State	21	1	2
	265	245	(42)
	$2,100	$1,879	$1,973
Tax rate reconciliation			
U.S. Federal statutory tax rate	35.0%	35.0%	35.0%
State income tax, net of U.S. Federal tax benefit	1.2	0.8	0.9
Lower taxes on foreign results	(7.9)	(8.0)	(6.6)
Tax settlements	–	–	(1.7)
Other, net	(2.3)	(1.1)	(1.8)
Annual tax rate	26.0%	26.7%	25.8%
Deferred tax liabilities			
Investments in noncontrolled affiliates	$1,120	$1,193	
Property, plant and equipment	1,056	881	
Intangible assets other than nondeductible goodwill	417	295	
Other	68	73	
Gross deferred tax liabilities	2,661	2,442	
Deferred tax assets			
Net carryforwards	624	682	
Stock-based compensation	410	410	
Retiree medical benefits	508	495	
Other employee-related benefits	442	428	
Pension benefits	179	345	
Deductible state tax and interest benefits	256	230	
Other	560	677	
Gross deferred tax assets	2,979	3,267	
Valuation allowances	(586)	(657)	
Deferred tax assets, net	2,393	2,610	
Net deferred tax liabilities/(assets)	$ 268	$ (168)	
Deferred taxes Included within:			
Assets:			
Prepaid expenses and other current assets	$ 391	$ 372	$ 325
Other assets	–	$ 22	–
Liabilities:			
Deferred income taxes	$ 659	$ 226	$ 646
Analysis of valuation allowances			
Balance, beginning of year	$ 657	$ 695	$ 624
(Benefit)/provision	(78)	(5)	39
Other additions/(deductions)	7	(33)	32
Balance, end of year	$ 586	$ 657	$ 695

For additional unaudited information on our income tax policies, including our reserves for income taxes, see "Our Critical Accounting Policies" in Management's Discussion and Analysis of Financial Condition and Results of Operations.

In 2007, we recognized $129 million of non-cash tax benefits related to the favorable resolution of certain foreign tax matters.

RESERVES

A number of years may elapse before a particular matter, for which we have established a reserve, is audited and finally resolved. The number of years with open tax audits varies depending on the tax jurisdiction. Our major taxing jurisdictions and the related open tax audits are as follows:

- U.S.—continue to dispute one matter related to tax years 1998 through 2002. Our U.S. tax returns for the years 2003 through 2005 are currently under audit. In 2008, the IRS initiated its audit of our U.S. tax returns for the years 2006 through 2007;
- Mexico—audits have been substantially completed for all taxable years through 2005;
- United Kingdom—audits have been completed for all taxable years prior to 2007; and
- Canada—audits have been completed for all taxable years through 2006. The Canadian tax return for 2007 is currently under audit.

While it is often difficult to predict the final outcome or the timing of resolution of any particular tax matter, we believe that our reserves reflect the probable outcome of known tax contingencies. We adjust these reserves, as well as the related interest, in light of changing facts and circumstances. Settlement of any particular issue would usually require the use of cash. Favorable resolution would be recognized as a reduction to our annual tax rate in the year of resolution. For further unaudited information on the impact of the resolution of open tax issues, see "Other Consolidated Results."

As of December 26, 2009, the total gross amount of reserves for income taxes, reported in other liabilities, was $1.7 billion. Any prospective adjustments to these reserves will be recorded as an increase or decrease to our provision for income taxes and would impact our effective tax rate. In addition, we accrue interest related to reserves for income taxes in our provision for income taxes and any associated penalties are recorded in selling, general and administrative expenses. The gross amount of interest accrued, reported in other liabilities, was $461 million as of December 26, 2009, of which $30 million was recognized in 2009. The gross amount of interest accrued was $427 million as of December 27, 2008, of which $95 million was recognized in 2008.

Notes to Consolidated Financial Statements

A rollforward of our reserves for all federal, state and foreign tax jurisdictions, is as follows:

	2009	2008
Balance, beginning of year	**$1,711**	$1,461
Additions for tax positions related to the current year	**238**	272
Additions for tax positions from prior years	**79**	76
Reductions for tax positions from prior years	**(236)**	(14)
Settlement payments	**(64)**	(30)
Statute of limitations expiration	**(4)**	(20)
Translation and other	**7**	(34)
Balance, end of year	**$1,731**	$1,711

CARRYFORWARDS AND ALLOWANCES

Operating loss carryforwards totaling $6.4 billion at year-end 2009 are being carried forward in a number of foreign and state jurisdictions where we are permitted to use tax operating losses from prior periods to reduce future taxable income. These operating losses will expire as follows: $0.2 billion in 2010, $5.5 billion between 2011 and 2029 and $0.7 billion may be carried forward indefinitely. We establish valuation allowances for our deferred tax assets if, based on the available evidence, it is more likely than not that some portion or all of the deferred tax assets will not be realized.

UNDISTRIBUTED INTERNATIONAL EARNINGS

As of December 26, 2009, we had approximately $21.9 billion of undistributed international earnings. We intend to continue to reinvest earnings outside the U.S. for the foreseeable future and, therefore, have not recognized any U.S. tax expense on these earnings.

Note 6 Stock-Based Compensation

Our stock-based compensation program is a broad-based program designed to attract and retain employees while also aligning employees' interests with the interests of our shareholders. A majority of our employees participate in our stock-based compensation program. This program includes both our broad-based SharePower program which was established in 1989 to grant an annual award of stock options to eligible employees, based upon job level or classification and tenure (internationally), as well as our executive long-term awards program. Stock options and restricted stock units (RSU) are granted to employees under the shareholder-approved 2007 Long-Term Incentive Plan (LTIP), our only active stock-based plan. Stock-based compensation expense was $227 million in 2009, $238 million in 2008 and $260 million in 2007. Related income tax benefits recognized in earnings were $67 million in 2009, $71 million in 2008 and

$77 million in 2007. Stock-based compensation cost capitalized in connection with our ongoing business transformation initiative was $2 million in 2009, $4 million in 2008 and $3 million in 2007. At year-end 2009, 42 million shares were available for future stock-based compensation grants.

METHOD OF ACCOUNTING AND OUR ASSUMPTIONS

We account for our employee stock options, which include grants under our executive program and our broad-based SharePower program, under the fair value method of accounting using a Black-Scholes valuation model to measure stock option expense at the date of grant. All stock option grants have an exercise price equal to the fair market value of our common stock on the date of grant and generally have a 10-year term. We do not backdate, reprice or grant stock-based compensation awards retroactively. Repricing of awards would require shareholder approval under the LTIP.

The fair value of stock option grants is amortized to expense over the vesting period, generally three years. Executives who are awarded long-term incentives based on their performance are offered the choice of stock options or RSUs. Executives who elect RSUs receive one RSU for every four stock options that would have otherwise been granted. Senior officers do not have a choice and are granted 50% stock options and 50% performance-based RSUs. Vesting of RSU awards for senior officers is contingent upon the achievement of pre-established performance targets approved by the Compensation Committee of the Board of Directors. RSU expense is based on the fair value of PepsiCo stock on the date of grant and is amortized over the vesting period, generally three years. Each RSU is settled in a share of our stock after the vesting period.

Our weighted-average Black-Scholes fair value assumptions are as follows:

	2009	2008	2007
Expected life	**6 yrs.**	6 yrs.	6 yrs.
Risk free interest rate	**2.8%**	3.0%	4.8%
Expected volatility	**17%**	16%	15%
Expected dividend yield	**3.0%**	1.9%	1.9%

The expected life is the period over which our employee groups are expected to hold their options. It is based on our historical experience with similar grants. The risk free interest rate is based on the expected U.S. Treasury rate over the expected life. Volatility reflects movements in our stock price over the most recent historical period equivalent to the expected life. Dividend yield is estimated over the expected life based on our stated dividend policy and forecasts of net income, share repurchases and stock price.

A summary of our stock-based compensation activity for the year ended December 26, 2009 is presented below:

Our Stock Option Activity

	Options[a]	Average Price[b]	Average Life (years)[c]	Aggregate Intrinsic Value[d]
Outstanding at December 27, 2008	103,672	$50.42		
Granted	15,466	53.09		
Exercised	(10,546)	39.48		
Forfeited/expired	(2,581)	59.49		
Outstanding at December 26, 2009	106,011	$51.68	4.91	$1,110,793
Exercisable at December 26, 2009	68,272	$46.86	3.21	$ 965,661

(a) *Options are in thousands and include options previously granted under Quaker plans. No additional options or shares may be granted under the Quaker plans.*
(b) *Weighted-average exercise price.*
(c) *Weighted-average contractual life remaining.*
(d) *In thousands.*

Our RSU Activity

	RSUs[a]	Average Intrinsic Value[b]	Average Life (years)[c]	Aggregate Intrinsic Value[d]
Outstanding at December 27, 2008	6,151	$63.18		
Granted	2,653	53.22		
Converted	(2,232)	57.48		
Forfeited/expired	(480)	62.57		
Outstanding at December 26, 2009	6,092	$60.98	1.33	$371,364

(a) *RSUs are in thousands.*
(b) *Weighted-average intrinsic value at grant date.*
(c) *Weighted-average contractual life remaining.*
(d) *In thousands.*

OTHER STOCK-BASED COMPENSATION DATA

	2009	2008	2007
Stock Options			
Weighted-average fair value of options granted	$ 7.02	$ 11.24	$ 13.56
Total intrinsic value of options exercised[a]	$194,545	$410,152	$826,913
RSUs			
Total number of RSUs granted[a]	2,653	2,135	2,342
Weighted-average intrinsic value of RSUs granted	$ 53.22	$ 68.73	$ 65.21
Total intrinsic value of RSUs converted[a]	$124,193	$180,563	$125,514

(a) *In thousands.*

As of December 26, 2009, there was $227 million of total unrecognized compensation cost related to nonvested share-based compensation grants. This unrecognized compensation is expected to be recognized over a weighted average period of 1.7 years.

Note 7 Pension, Retiree Medical and Savings Plans

Our pension plans cover full-time employees in the U.S. and certain international employees. Benefits are determined based on either years of service or a combination of years of service and earnings. U.S. and Canada retirees are also eligible for medical and life insurance benefits (retiree medical) if they meet age and service requirements. Generally, our share of retiree medical costs is capped at specified dollar amounts, which vary based upon years of service, with retirees contributing the remainder of the costs.

Gains and losses resulting from actual experience differing from our assumptions, including the difference between the actual return on plan assets and the expected return on plan assets, and from changes in our assumptions are also determined at each measurement date. If this net accumulated gain or loss exceeds 10% of the greater of the market-related value of plan assets or plan liabilities, a portion of the net gain or loss is included in expense for the following year. The cost or benefit of plan changes that increase or decrease benefits for prior employee service (prior service cost/(credit)) is included in earnings on a straight-line basis over the average remaining service period of active plan participants, which is approximately 10 years for pension expense and approximately 12 years for retiree medical expense.

Our adoption of the standard on accounting for defined benefit pension and other postretirement plans required that, no later than 2008, our assumptions used to measure our annual pension and retiree medical expense be determined as of the balance sheet date, and all plan assets and liabilities be reported as of that date. Accordingly, as of the beginning of our 2008 fiscal year, we changed the measurement date for our annual pension and retiree medical expense and all plan assets and liabilities from September 30 to our year-end balance sheet date. As a result of this change in measurement date, we recorded an after-tax $39 million decrease to 2008 opening shareholders' equity, as follows:

	Pension	Retiree Medical	Total
Retained earnings	$(63)	$(20)	$(83)
Accumulated other comprehensive loss	12	32	44
Total	$(51)	$ 12	$(39)

Notes to Consolidated Financial Statements

Selected financial information for our pension and retiree medical plans is as follows:

	Pension				Retiree Medical	
	2009	2008	2009	2008	2009	2008
	U.S.		International			
Change in projected benefit liability						
Liability at beginning of year	$ 6,217	$ 6,048	$1,270	$1,595	$ 1,370	$ 1,354
Measurement date change	–	(199)	–	113	–	(37)
Service cost	238	244	54	61	44	45
Interest cost	373	371	82	88	82	82
Plan amendments	–	(20)	–	2	–	(47)
Participant contributions	–	–	10	17	–	–
Experience loss/(gain)	70	28	221	(165)	(63)	58
Benefit payments	(296)	(277)	(50)	(51)	(80)	(70)
Settlement/curtailment loss	–	(9)	(8)	(15)	–	(2)
Special termination benefits	–	31	–	2	–	3
Foreign currency adjustment	–	–	130	(376)	6	(10)
Other	4	–	–	(1)	–	(6)
Liability at end of year	$ 6,606	$ 6,217	$1,709	$1,270	$ 1,359	$ 1,370
Change in fair value of plan assets						
Fair value at beginning of year	$ 3,974	$ 5,782	$1,165	$1,595	$ –	$ –
Measurement date change	–	(136)	–	97	–	–
Actual return on plan assets	697	(1,434)	159	(241)	2	–
Employer contributions/funding	1,041	48	167	101	91	70
Participant contributions	–	–	10	17	–	–
Benefit payments	(296)	(277)	(50)	(51)	(80)	(70)
Settlement/curtailment loss	–	(9)	(8)	(11)	–	–
Foreign currency adjustment	–	–	118	(341)	–	–
Other	4	–	–	(1)	–	–
Fair value at end of year	$ 5,420	$ 3,974	$1,561	$1,165	$ 13	$ –
Funded status	$(1,186)	$(2,243)	$ (148)	$ (105)	$(1,346)	$(1,370)
Amounts recognized						
Other assets	$ –	$ –	$ 50	$ 28	$ –	$ –
Other current liabilities	(36)	(60)	(1)	(1)	(105)	(102)
Other liabilities	(1,150)	(2,183)	(197)	(132)	(1,241)	(1,268)
Net amount recognized	$(1,186)	$(2,243)	$ (148)	$ (105)	$(1,346)	$(1,370)
Amounts included in accumulated other comprehensive loss (pre-tax)						
Net loss	$ 2,563	$ 2,826	$ 625	$ 421	$ 190	$ 266
Prior service cost/(credit)	101	112	20	20	(102)	(119)
Total	$ 2,664	$ 2,938	$ 645	$ 441	$ 88	$ 147
Components of the (decrease)/increase in net loss						
Measurement date change	$ –	$ (130)	$ –	$ 105	$ –	$ (53)
Change in discount rate	47	247	97	(219)	11	36
Employee-related assumption changes	–	(194)	70	52	(38)	6
Liability-related experience different from assumptions	23	(25)	51	(4)	(36)	10
Actual asset return different from expected return	(235)	1,850	(54)	354	(2)	–
Amortization of losses	(111)	(58)	(9)	(19)	(11)	(8)
Other, including foreign currency adjustments and 2003 Medicare Act	13	–	49	(135)	–	(1)
Total	$ (263)	$ 1,690	$ 204	$ 134	$ (76)	$ (10)
Liability at end of year for service to date	$ 5,784	$ 5,413	$1,414	$1,013		

Components of benefit expense are as follows:

Components of benefit expense	Pension						Retiree Medical		
	2009	2008	2007	2009	2008	2007	2009	2008	2007
	U.S.			International					
Service cost	$ 238	$ 244	$ 244	$ 54	$ 61	$ 59	$ 44	$ 45	$ 48
Interest cost	373	371	338	82	88	81	82	82	77
Expected return on plan assets	(462)	(416)	(399)	(105)	(112)	(97)	–	–	–
Amortization of prior service cost/(credit)	12	19	5	2	3	3	(17)	(13)	(13)
Amortization of net loss	110	55	136	9	19	30	11	7	18
	271	273	324	42	59	76	120	121	130
Settlement/curtailment (gain)/loss	(13)	3	–	3	3	–	–	–	–
Special termination benefits	–	31	5	–	2	–	–	3	–
Total	$ 258	$ 307	$ 329	$ 45	$ 64	$ 76	$120	$124	$130

The estimated amounts to be amortized from accumulated other comprehensive loss into benefit expense in 2010 for our pension and retiree medical plans are as follows:

	Pension		Retiree Medical
	U.S.	International	
Net loss	$108	$24	$ 5
Prior service cost/(credit)	12	2	(17)
Total	$120	$26	$(12)

The following table provides the weighted-average assumptions used to determine projected benefit liability and benefit expense for our pension and retiree medical plans:

Weighted-average assumptions	Pension						Retiree Medical		
	2009	2008	2007	2009	2008	2007	2009	2008	2007
	U.S.			International					
Liability discount rate	6.1%	6.2%	6.2%	5.9%	6.3%	5.8%	6.1%	6.2%	6.1%
Expense discount rate	6.2%	6.5%	5.8%	6.3%	5.6%	5.2%	6.2%	6.5%	5.8%
Expected return on plan assets	7.8%	7.8%	7.8%	7.1%	7.2%	7.3%			
Rate of salary increases	4.4%	4.6%	4.7%	4.2%	3.9%	3.9%			

The following table provides selected information about plans with liability for service to date and total benefit liability in excess of plan assets:

	Pension				Retiree Medical	
	2009	2008	2009	2008	2009	2008
	U.S.		International			
Selected information for plans with liability for service to date in excess of plan assets						
Liability for service to date	$(2,695)	$(5,411)	$ (342)	$ (49)		
Fair value of plan assets	$ 2,220	$ 3,971	$ 309	$ 30		
Selected information for plans with benefit liability in excess of plan assets						
Benefit liability	$(6,603)	$(6,217)	$(1,566)	$(1,049)	$(1,359)	$(1,370)
Fair value of plan assets	$ 5,417	$ 3,974	$ 1,368	$ 916	$ 13	$ –

Of the total projected pension benefit liability at year-end 2009, $564 million relates to plans that we do not fund because the funding of such plans does not receive favorable tax treatment.

Notes to Consolidated Financial Statements

FUTURE BENEFIT PAYMENTS AND FUNDING

Our estimated future benefit payments are as follows:

	2010	2011	2012	2013	2014	2015-19
Pension	$340	$360	$395	$415	$450	$2,825
Retiree medical[a]	$110	$120	$125	$125	$130	$ 695

(a) *Expected future benefit payments for our retiree medical plans do not reflect any estimated subsidies expected to be received under the 2003 Medicare Act. Subsidies are expected to be approximately $10 million for each of the years from 2010 through 2014 and approximately $70 million in total for 2015 through 2019.*

These future benefits to beneficiaries include payments from both funded and unfunded pension plans.

In 2010, we will make pension contributions of approximately $700 million, with up to approximately $600 million expected to be discretionary. Our net cash payments for retiree medical are estimated to be approximately $100 million in 2010.

PENSION ASSETS

Our pension plan investment strategy includes the use of actively-managed securities and is reviewed annually based upon plan liabilities, an evaluation of market conditions, tolerance for risk and cash requirements for benefit payments. Our investment objective is to ensure that funds are available to meet the plans' benefit obligations when they become due. Our overall investment strategy is to prudently invest plan assets in high-quality and diversified equity and debt securities to achieve our long-term return expectations. Our investment policy also permits the use of derivative instruments which are primarily used to reduce risk. Our expected long-term rate of return on U.S. plan assets is 7.8%, reflecting estimated long-term rates of return of 8.9% from our equity allocation and 6.3% from our fixed income allocation. Our target investment allocation is 40% for U.S. equity allocations, 20% for international equity allocations and 40% for fixed income

allocations. Actual investment allocations may vary from our target investment allocations due to prevailing market conditions. We regularly review our actual investment allocations and periodically rebalance our investments to our target allocations.

The expected return on pension plan assets is based on our pension plan investment strategy, our expectations for long-term rates of return and our historical experience. We also review current levels of interest rates and inflation to assess the reasonableness of the long-term rates. To calculate the expected return on pension plan assets, we use a market-related valuation method that recognizes investment gains or losses (the difference between the expected and actual return based on the market-related value of assets) for securities included in our equity strategies over a five-year period. This has the effect of reducing year-to-year volatility. For all other asset categories, the actual fair value is used for the market-related value of assets.

We adopted the new accounting guidance on employer's disclosures about postretirement benefit plan assets which requires that we categorize pension assets into three levels based upon the assumptions (inputs) used to price the assets. Level 1 provides the most reliable measure of fair value, whereas Level 3 generally requires significant management judgment. The three levels are defined as follows:

- Level 1: Unadjusted quoted prices in active markets for identical assets.
- Level 2: Observable inputs other than those included in Level 1. For example, quoted prices for similar assets in active markets or quoted prices for identical assets in inactive markets.
- Level 3: Unobservable inputs reflecting assumptions about the inputs used in pricing the asset.

Plan assets measured at fair value are categorized as follows:

		2009			2008
	Total	Level 1	Level 2	Level 3	Total
U.S. plan assets					
Equity securities:					
PepsiCo common stock[a]	$ **332**	$ 332	$ –	$ –	$ 302
U.S. common stock[a]	**229**	229	–	–	103
U.S. commingled funds[b]	**1,387**	–	1,387	–	513
International common stock[a]	**700**	700	–	–	463
International commingled fund[c]	**114**	–	114	–	47
Preferred stock[d]	**4**	–	4	–	6
Fixed income securities:					
Government securities[f]	**741**	–	741	–	724
Corporate bonds[d]	**1,214**	–	1,198	16	592
Mortgage-backed securities[d]	**201**	–	195	6	250
Fixed income commingled fund[e]	**–**	–	–	–	647
Other:					
Derivative instruments	**–**	–	–	–	(9)
Contracts with insurance companies[f]	**9**	–	–	9	15
Dividends and interest receivable	**32**	–	–	32	19
Cash and cash equivalents	**457**	457	–	–	302
Total U.S. plan assets	**$5,420**	$1,718	$3,639	$63	$3,974
International plan assets					
Equity securities:					
U.S. commingled funds[b]	$ **180**	$ –	$ 180	$ –	$ 128
International commingled funds[c]	**661**	–	661	–	429
Fixed income securities:					
Government securities[d]	**139**	–	139	–	123
Corporate bonds[d]	**128**	–	128	–	103
Fixed income commingled funds[e]	**363**	–	363	–	310
Other:					
Contracts with insurance companies[f]	**29**	–	–	29	26
Currency commingled funds[g]	**44**	–	44	–	17
Cash and cash equivalents	**17**	17	–	–	29
Total international plan assets	**$1,561**	$ 17	$1,515	$29	$1,165

(a) *Based on quoted market prices in active markets.*
(b) *Based on the fair value of the investments owned by these funds that track various U.S. large-and mid-cap company indices. Includes one fund that represents 25% of total U.S. plan assets.*
(c) *Based on the fair value of the investments owned by these funds that track various non-U.S. equity indices.*
(d) *Based on quoted bid prices for comparable securities in the marketplace and broker/dealer quotes that are not observable.*
(e) *Based on the fair value of the investments owned by these funds that track various government and corporate bond indices.*
(f) *Based on the fair value of the contracts as determined by the insurance companies using inputs that are not observable.*
(g) *Based on the fair value of the investments owned by these funds. Includes managed hedge funds that invest primarily in derivatives to reduce currency exposure.*

RETIREE MEDICAL COST TREND RATES

An average increase of 7.5% in the cost of covered retiree medical benefits is assumed for 2010. This average increase is then projected to decline gradually to 5% in 2014 and thereafter. These assumed health care cost trend rates have an impact on the retiree medical plan expense and liability. However, the cap on our share of

retiree medical costs limits the impact. A 1-percentage-point change in the assumed health care trend rate would have the following effects:

	1% Increase	1% Decrease
2009 service and interest cost components	$ 4	$ (3)
2009 benefit liability	$30	$(26)

SAVINGS PLAN

Our U.S. employees are eligible to participate in 401(k) savings plans, which are voluntary defined contribution plans. The plans are designed to help employees accumulate additional savings for retirement. We make matching contributions on a portion of eligible pay based on years of service. In 2009 and 2008, our matching contributions were $72 million and $70 million, respectively.

For additional unaudited information on our pension and retiree medical plans and related accounting policies and assumptions, see "Our Critical Accounting Policies" in Management's Discussion and Analysis.

Note 8 Noncontrolled Bottling Affiliates

Our most significant noncontrolled bottling affiliates are PBG and PAS. Sales to PBG represented approximately 6% of our total net revenue in 2009 and 7% of our total net revenue in both 2008 and 2007.

See Note 15 for information regarding our pending mergers with PBG and PAS.

THE PEPSI BOTTLING GROUP

In addition to approximately 32% and 33% of PBG's outstanding common stock that we owned at year-end 2009 and 2008, respectively, we owned 100% of PBG's class B common stock and approximately 7% of the equity of Bottling Group, LLC, PBG's principal operating subsidiary.

PBG's summarized financial information is as follows:

	2009	2008	2007
Current assets	$ **3,412**	$ 3,141	
Noncurrent assets	**10,158**	9,841	
Total assets	**$13,570**	$12,982	
Current liabilities	$ **1,965**	$ 3,083	
Noncurrent liabilities	**7,896**	7,408	
Total liabilities	$ **9,861**	$10,491	
Our investment	$ **1,775**	$ 1,457	
Net revenue	**$13,219**	$13,796	$13,591
Gross profit	$ **5,840**	$ 6,210	$ 6,221
Operating income	$ **1,048**	$ 649	$ 1,071
Net income attributable to PBG	$ **612**	$ 162	$ 532

Notes to Consolidated Financial Statements

Our investment in PBG, which includes the related goodwill, was $463 million and $536 million higher than our ownership interest in their net assets less noncontrolling interests at year-end 2009 and 2008, respectively. Based upon the quoted closing price of PBG shares at year-end 2009, the calculated market value of our shares in PBG exceeded our investment balance, excluding our investment in Bottling Group, LLC, by approximately $1.4 billion.

Additionally, in 2007, we formed a joint venture with PBG, comprising our concentrate and PBG's bottling businesses in Russia. PBG holds a 60% majority interest in the joint venture and consolidates the entity. We account for our interest of 40% under the equity method of accounting.

During 2008, together with PBG, we jointly acquired Russia's leading branded juice company, Lebedyansky. Lebedyansky is owned 25% and 75% by PBG and us, respectively. See Note 14 for further information on this acquisition.

PEPSIAMERICAS

At year-end 2009 and 2008, we owned approximately 43%, respectively, of the outstanding common stock of PAS.

PAS summarized financial information is as follows:

	2009	2008	2007
Current assets	$ 952	$ 906	
Noncurrent assets	4,141	4,148	
Total assets	$5,093	$5,054	
Current liabilities	$ 669	$1,048	
Noncurrent liabilities	2,493	2,175	
Total liabilities	$3,162	$3,223	
Our investment	$1,071	$ 972	
Net sales	$4,421	$4,937	$4,480
Gross profit	$1,767	$1,982	$1,823
Operating income	$ 381	$ 473	$ 436
Net income attributable to PAS	$ 181	$ 226	$ 212

Our investment in PAS, which includes the related goodwill, was $322 million and $318 million higher than our ownership interest in their net assets less noncontrolling interests at year-end 2009 and 2008, respectively. Based upon the quoted closing price of PAS shares at year-end 2009, the calculated market value of our shares in PAS exceeded our investment balance by approximately $515 million.

Additionally, in 2007, we completed the joint purchase of Sandora, LLC, a juice company in the Ukraine, with PAS. PAS holds a 60% majority interest in the joint venture and consolidates the entity. We account for our interest of 40% under the equity method of accounting.

RELATED PARTY TRANSACTIONS

Our significant related party transactions are with our noncontrolled bottling affiliates. The transactions primarily consist of (1) selling concentrate to these affiliates, which they use in the production of CSDs and non-carbonated beverages, (2) selling certain finished goods to these affiliates, (3) receiving royalties for the use of our trademarks for certain products and (4) paying these affiliates to act as our manufacturing and distribution agent for product associated with our national account fountain customers. Sales of concentrate and finished goods are reported net of bottler funding. For further unaudited information on these bottlers, see "Our Customers" in Management's Discussion and Analysis of Financial Condition and Results of Operations. These transactions with our bottling affiliates are reflected in our consolidated financial statements as follows:

	2009	2008	2007
Net revenue	$3,922	$4,049	$4,020
Cost of sales	$ 634	$ 660	$ 625
Selling, general and administrative expenses	$ 24	$ 30	$ 33
Accounts and notes receivable	$ 254	$ 248	
Accounts payable and other liabilities	$ 285	$ 198	

Such amounts are settled on terms consistent with other trade receivables and payables. See Note 9 regarding our guarantee of certain PBG debt.

We also coordinate, on an aggregate basis, the contract negotiations of sweeteners and other raw material requirements for certain of our bottlers. Once we have negotiated the contracts, the bottlers order and take delivery directly from the supplier and pay the suppliers directly. Consequently, these transactions are not reflected in our consolidated financial statements. As the contracting party, we could be liable to these suppliers in the event of any nonpayment by our bottlers, but we consider this exposure to be remote.

In addition, our joint ventures with Unilever (under the Lipton brand name) and Starbucks sell finished goods (ready-to-drink teas, coffees and water products) to our noncontrolled bottling affiliates. Consistent with accounting for equity method investments, our joint venture revenue is not included in our consolidated net revenue and therefore is not included in the above table.

Note 9 Debt Obligations and Commitments

	2009	2008
Short-term debt obligations		
Current maturities of long-term debt	$ 102	$ 273
Commercial paper (0.7%)	–	846
Other borrowings (6.7% and 10.0%)	362	509
Amounts reclassified to long-term debt	–	(1,259)
	$ 464	$ 369
Long-term debt obligations		
Short term borrowings, reclassified	$	$ 1,259
Notes due 2012-2026 (4.5% and 5.8%)	7,160	6,382
Zero coupon notes, $225 million due 2010-2012 (13.3%)	192	242
Other, due 2010-2019 (8.4% and 5.3%)	150	248
	7,502	8,131
Less: current maturities of long-term debt obligations	(102)	(273)
	$7,400	$ 7,858

The interest rates in the above table reflect weighted-average rates at year-end.

In the first quarter of 2009, we issued $1.0 billion of senior unsecured notes, bearing interest at 3.75% per year and maturing in 2014. We used the proceeds from the issuance of these notes for general corporate purposes.

In the third quarter of 2009, we entered into a new 364-day unsecured revolving credit agreement which enables us to borrow up to $1.975 billion, subject to customary terms and conditions, and expires in June 2010. We may request renewal of this facility for an additional 364-day period or convert any amounts outstanding into a term loan for a period of up to one year, which would mature no later than June 2011. This agreement replaced a $1.8 billion 364-day unsecured revolving credit agreement we entered into during the fourth quarter of 2008. Funds borrowed under this agreement may be used to repay outstanding commercial paper issued by us or our subsidiaries and for other general corporate purposes, including working capital, capital investments and acquisitions. This agreement is in addition to our existing $2.0 billion unsecured revolving credit agreement which expires in 2012. Our lines of credit remain unused as of December 26, 2009.

In addition, as of December 26, 2009, $396 million of our debt related to borrowings from various lines of credit that are maintained for our international divisions. These lines of credit are subject to normal banking terms and conditions and are fully committed to the extent of our borrowings.

Subsequent to year-end 2009, we issued $4.25 billion of fixed and floating rate notes. The issuance was comprised of $1.25 billion of floating rate notes maturing in 2011 (the "2011 Floating Rates Notes"), $1.0 billion of 3.10% senior unsecured notes maturing in 2015, $1.0 billion of 4.50% senior unsecured notes maturing in 2020 and $1.0 billion of 5.50% senior unsecured notes maturing in 2040. The 2011 Floating Rate Notes bear interest at a rate equal to the three-month London Inter-Bank Offered Rate ("LIBOR") plus 3 basis points.

We intend to use the net proceeds from this offering to finance a portion of the purchase price for the mergers with PBG and PAS and to pay related fees and expenses in connection with the mergers with PBG and PAS. Pending such use we invested the net proceeds in short-term, high-quality securities. If one or both of the mergers with PBG and PAS is not completed, we intend to use the remaining net proceeds from this offering for general corporate purposes, which may include the financing of future acquisitions, capital expenditures, additions to working capital, repurchase, repayment or refinancing of debt or stock repurchases.

Concurrently with the debt issuance after year-end, we terminated the commitments from lenders to provide us with up to $4.0 billion in bridge financing to fund the mergers with PBG and PAS.

Also subsequent to year-end 2009, we entered into amendments to PBG's revolving credit facility (the Amended PBG Credit Facility) and PAS's revolving credit facility (the Amended PAS Credit Facility). Under the Amended PBG Credit Facility, subject to the satisfaction of certain conditions to effectiveness, at the closing of the merger with PBG, Metro will be able to borrow up to $1,080 million from time to time. Borrowings under the Amended PBG Credit Facility, which expires in October 2012, are guaranteed by us. Under the Amended PAS Credit Facility, subject to the satisfaction of certain conditions to effectiveness, at the closing of the merger with PAS, Metro will be able to borrow up to $540 million from time to time. Borrowings under the Amended PAS Credit Facility, which expires in June 2011, are guaranteed by us.

Notes to Consolidated Financial Statements

LONG-TERM CONTRACTUAL COMMITMENTS[a]

	Total	2010	2011–2012	2013–2014	2015 and beyond
			Payments Due by Period		
Long-term debt obligations[b]	$ 7,400	$ –	$1,332	$2,063	$4,005
Interest on debt obligations[c]	2,386	347	666	500	873
Operating leases	1,076	282	356	203	235
Purchasing commitments	2,066	801	960	260	45
Marketing commitments	793	260	314	78	141
	$13,721	$1,690	$3,628	$3,104	$5,299

(a) *Reflects non-cancelable commitments as of December 26, 2009 based on year-end foreign exchange rates and excludes any reserves for uncertain tax positions as we are unable to reasonably predict the ultimate amount or timing of settlement.*

(b) *Excludes current maturities of long-term debt obligations of $102 million. Includes $151 million of principal and accrued interest related to our zero coupon notes.*

(c) *Interest payments on floating-rate debt are estimated using interest rates effective as of December 26, 2009.*

Most long-term contractual commitments, except for our long-term debt obligations, are not recorded on our balance sheet. Non-cancelable operating leases primarily represent building leases. Non-cancelable purchasing commitments are primarily for oranges and orange juice, packaging materials and cooking oil. Non-cancelable marketing commitments are primarily for sports marketing. Bottler funding is not reflected in our long-term contractual commitments as it is negotiated on an annual basis. See Note 7 regarding our pension and retiree medical obligations and discussion below regarding our commitments to noncontrolled bottling affiliates.

OFF-BALANCE-SHEET ARRANGEMENTS

It is not our business practice to enter into off-balance-sheet arrangements, other than in the normal course of business. However, at the time of the separation of our bottling operations from us various guarantees were necessary to facilitate the transactions. We have guaranteed an aggregate of $2.3 billion of Bottling Group, LLC's long-term debt ($1.0 billion of which matures in 2012 and $1.3 billion of which matures in 2014). In the first quarter of 2009, we extended our guarantee of $1.3 billion of Bottling Group, LLC's long-term debt in connection with the refinancing of a corresponding portion of the underlying debt. The terms of our Bottling Group, LLC debt guarantee are intended to preserve the structure of PBG's separation from us and our payment obligation would be triggered if Bottling Group, LLC failed to perform under these debt obligations or the structure significantly changed. Neither the merger with PBG nor the merger with PAS will trigger our payment obligation under our guarantee of a portion of Bottling Group, LLC's debt. As of December 26, 2009, we believe it is remote that these guarantees would require any cash payment. See Note 8 regarding contracts related to certain of our bottlers.

See "Our Liquidity and Capital Resources" in Management's Discussion and Analysis of Financial Condition and Results of Operations for further unaudited information on our borrowings.

Note 10 Financial Instruments

In March 2008, the FASB issued new disclosure guidance on derivative instruments and hedging activities, which amends and expands the disclosure requirements of previously issued guidance on accounting for derivative instruments and hedging activities, to provide an enhanced understanding of the use of derivative instruments, how they are accounted for and their effect on financial position, financial performance and cash flows. We adopted the disclosure provisions of the new guidance in the first quarter of 2009.

We are exposed to market risks arising from adverse changes in:

- commodity prices, affecting the cost of our raw materials and energy,
- foreign exchange risks, and
- interest rates.

In the normal course of business, we manage these risks through a variety of strategies, including the use of derivatives. Certain derivatives are designated as either cash flow or fair value hedges and qualify for hedge accounting treatment, while others do not qualify and are marked to market through earnings. Cash flows from derivatives used to manage commodity, foreign exchange or interest risks are classified as operating activities. See "Our Business Risks" in Management's Discussion and Analysis of Financial Condition and Results of Operations for further unaudited information on our business risks.

For cash flow hedges, changes in fair value are deferred in accumulated other comprehensive loss within common shareholders' equity until the underlying hedged item is recognized in net income. For fair value hedges, changes in fair value are recognized immediately in earnings, consistent with the underlying hedged item. Hedging transactions are limited to an underlying exposure. As a result, any change in the value of our derivative instruments would be substantially offset by an opposite change in the value of the underlying hedged items. Hedging ineffectiveness and a net earnings impact occur when the change in the value of the hedge does not offset the change in the value of the underlying hedged item. Ineffectiveness of our hedges is not material. If the derivative instrument is terminated, we continue to defer the related gain or loss and then include it as a component of the cost of the underlying hedged item. Upon determination that the underlying hedged item will not be part of an actual transaction, we recognize the related gain or loss in net income immediately.

We also use derivatives that do not qualify for hedge accounting treatment. We account for such derivatives at market value with the resulting gains and losses reflected in our income statement. We do not use derivative instruments for trading or speculative purposes. We perform assessments of our counterparty credit risk regularly, including a review of credit ratings, credit default swap rates and potential nonperformance of the counterparty. Based on our most recent assessment of our counterparty credit risk, we consider this risk to be low. In addition, we enter into derivative contracts with a variety of financial institutions that we believe are creditworthy in order to reduce our concentration of credit risk and generally settle with these financial institutions on a net basis.

COMMODITY PRICES

We are subject to commodity price risk because our ability to recover increased costs through higher pricing may be limited in the competitive environment in which we operate. This risk is managed through the use of fixed-price purchase orders, pricing agreements, geographic diversity and derivatives. We use derivatives, with terms of no more than three years, to economically hedge price fluctuations related to a portion of our anticipated commodity purchases, primarily for natural gas and diesel fuel. For those derivatives that qualify for hedge accounting, any ineffectiveness is recorded immediately. We classify both the earnings and cash flow impact from these derivatives consistent with the underlying hedged item. During the next 12 months, we expect to reclassify net losses of $124 million related to these hedges from accumulated other comprehensive loss into net income. Derivatives used to hedge commodity price risk that do not qualify for hedge accounting are marked to market each period and reflected in our income statement.

Our open commodity derivative contracts that qualify for hedge accounting had a face value of $151 million as of December 26, 2009 and $303 million as of December 27, 2008. These contracts resulted in net unrealized losses of $29 million as of December 26, 2009 and $117 million as of December 27, 2008.

Our open commodity derivative contracts that do not qualify for hedge accounting had a face value of $231 million as of December 26, 2009 and $626 million as of December 27, 2008. These contracts resulted in net losses of $57 million in 2009 and $343 million in 2008.

FOREIGN EXCHANGE

Financial statements of foreign subsidiaries are translated into U.S. dollars using period-end exchange rates for assets and liabilities and weighted-average exchange rates for revenues and expenses. Adjustments resulting from translating net assets are reported as a separate component of accumulated other comprehensive loss within common shareholders' equity as currency translation adjustment.

Our operations outside of the U.S. generate 48% of our net revenue, with Mexico, Canada and the United Kingdom comprising 16% of our net revenue. As a result, we are exposed to foreign currency risks. On occasion, we may enter into derivatives, primarily forward contracts with terms of no more than two years, to manage our exposure to foreign currency transaction risk. Exchange rate gains or losses related to foreign currency transactions are recognized as transaction gains or losses in our income statement as incurred.

Our foreign currency derivatives had a total face value of $1.2 billion as of December 26, 2009 and $1.4 billion as of December 27, 2008. The contracts that qualify for hedge accounting resulted in net unrealized losses of $20 million as of December 26, 2009 and net unrealized gains of $111 million as of December 27, 2008. During the next 12 months, we expect to reclassify net losses of $20 million related to these hedges from accumulated other comprehensive loss into net income. The contracts that do not qualify for hedge accounting resulted in a net gain of $1 million in 2009 and net losses of $28 million in 2008. All losses and gains were offset by changes in the underlying hedged items, resulting in no net material impact on earnings.

INTEREST RATES

We centrally manage our debt and investment portfolios considering investment opportunities and risks, tax consequences and overall financing strategies. We use various interest rate derivative instruments including, but not limited to, interest rate swaps, cross currency interest rate swaps, Treasury locks and swap locks to

Notes to Consolidated Financial Statements

manage our overall interest expense and foreign exchange risk. These instruments effectively change the interest rate and currency of specific debt issuances. Our interest rate and cross currency swaps are generally entered into concurrently with the issuance of the debt that they modify. The notional amount, interest payment and maturity date of the interest rate and cross currency swaps match the principal, interest payment and maturity date of the related debt. Our Treasury locks and swap locks are entered into to protect against unfavorable interest rate changes relating to forecasted debt transactions.

The notional amounts of the interest rate derivative instruments outstanding as of December 26, 2009 and December 27, 2008 were $5.75 billion and $2.75 billion, respectively. For those interest rate derivative instruments that qualify for cash flow hedge accounting, any ineffectiveness is recorded immediately. We classify both the earnings and cash flow impact from these interest rate derivative instruments consistent with the underlying hedged item. During the next 12 months, we expect to reclassify net losses of $6 million related to these hedges from accumulated other comprehensive loss into net income.

Concurrently with the debt issuance after year-end, we terminated $1.5 billion of interest rate derivative instruments, and the realized loss will be amortized into interest expense over the duration of the debt term.

As of December 26, 2009, approximately 57% of total debt, after the impact of the related interest rate derivative instruments, was exposed to variable rates compared to 58% as of December 27, 2008. In addition to variable rate long-term debt, all debt with maturities of less than one year is categorized as variable for purposes of this measure.

FAIR VALUE MEASUREMENTS

In September 2006, the FASB issued new accounting guidance on fair value measurements, which defines fair value, establishes a framework for measuring fair value, and expands disclosures about fair value measurements. We adopted the new guidance as of the beginning of our 2008 fiscal year as it relates to recurring financial assets and liabilities. As of the beginning of our 2009 fiscal year, we adopted the new guidance as it relates to nonrecurring fair value measurement requirements for nonfinancial assets and

liabilities. These include goodwill, other nonamortizable intangible assets and unallocated purchase price for recent acquisitions which are included within other assets. Our adoption did not have a material impact on our financial statements. See Note 7 for the fair value framework.

The fair values of our financial assets and liabilities as of December 26, 2009 are categorized as follows:

	2009			
	Total	Level 1	Level 2	Level 3
Assets(a)				
Available-for-sale securities(b)	$ 71	$ 71	$ –	$–
Short-term investments—index funds(c)	**$120**	$120	$ –	$–
Derivatives designated as hedging instruments:				
Forward exchange contracts(d)	$ 11	$ –	$ 11	$–
Interest rate derivatives(e)	177	–	177	–
Prepaid forward contracts(f)	46	–	46	–
Commodity contracts—other(g)	8	–	8	–
	$242	$ –	$242	$–
Derivatives not designated as hedging instruments:				
Forward exchange contracts(d)	$ 4	$ –	$ 4	$–
Commodity contracts—other(g)	7	–	7	–
	$ 11	$ –	$ 11	$–
Total asset derivatives at fair value	$253	$ –	$253	$–
Total assets at fair value	**$444**	$191	$253	$–
Liabilities(a)				
Deferred compensation(h)	**$461**	$121	$340	$–
Derivatives designated as hedging instruments:				
Forward exchange contracts(d)	$ 31	$ –	$ 31	$–
Interest rate derivatives(e)	43	–	43	–
Commodity contracts—other(g)	5	–	5	–
Commodity contracts—futures(i)	32	32	–	–
	$111	$ 32	$ 79	$–
Derivatives not designated as hedging instruments:				
Forward exchange contracts(d)	$ 2	$ –	$ 2	$–
Commodity contracts—other(g)	60	–	60	–
Commodity contracts—futures(i)	3	3	–	–
	$ 65	$ 3	$ 62	$–
Total liability derivatives at fair value	$176	$ 35	$141	$–
Total liabilities at fair value	**$637**	$156	$481	$–

(a) Financial assets are classified on our balance sheet within other assets, with the exception of short-term investments. Financial liabilities are classified on our balance sheet within other current liabilities and other liabilities.
(b) Based on the price of common stock.
(c) Based on price changes in index funds used to manage a portion of market risk arising from our deferred compensation liability.
(d) Based on observable market transactions of spot and forward rates.
(e) Based on LIBOR and recently reported transactions in the marketplace.
(f) Based primarily on the price of our common stock.
(g) Based on recently reported transactions in the marketplace, primarily swap arrangements.
(h) Based on the fair value of investments corresponding to employees' investment elections.
(i) Based on average prices on futures exchanges.

The effective portion of the pre-tax (gains)/losses on our derivative instruments are categorized in the tables below.

	2009		
	(Gains)/Losses Recognized in Income Statement	Losses/(Gains) Recognized in Accumulated Other Comprehensive Loss	(Gains)/Losses Reclassified from Accumulated Other Comprehensive Loss into Income Statement
Fair Value/Non-designated Hedges			
Forward exchange contracts[a]	$ (29)		
Interest rate derivatives[b]	206		
Prepaid forward contracts[a]	(5)		
Commodity contracts[a]	(274)		
Total	$(102)		
Cash Flow Hedges			
Forward exchange contracts[c]		$ 75	$(64)
Commodity contracts[c]		(1)	90
Interest rate derivatives[b]		32	–
Total		$106	$ 26

(a) *Included in corporate unallocated expenses.*
(b) *Included in interest expense in our income statement.*
(c) *Included in cost of sales in our income statement.*

The fair values of our financial assets and liabilities as of December 27, 2008 are categorized as follows:

	2008			
	Total	Level 1	Level 2	Level 3
Assets[a]				
Available-for-sale securities[b]	$ 41	$ 41	$ –	$–
Short-term investments—index funds[c]	98	98	–	–
Forward exchange contracts[d]	139	–	139	–
Interest rate derivatives[e]	372	–	372	–
Prepaid forward contracts[f]	41	–	41	–
Total assets at fair value	$691	$139	$552	$–
Liabilities[a]				
Forward exchange contracts[d]	$ 56	$ –	$ 56	$–
Commodity contracts—other[g]	345	–	345	–
Commodity contracts—futures[i]	115	115	–	–
Deferred compensation[h]	447	99	348	–
Total liabilities at fair value	$963	$214	$749	$–

(a) *Financial assets are classified on our balance sheet within other assets, with the exception of short-term investments. Financial liabilities are classified on our balance sheet within other current liabilities and other liabilities.*
(b) *Based on the price of common stock.*
(c) *Based on price changes in index funds used to manage a portion of market risk arising from our deferred compensation liability.*
(d) *Based on observable market transactions of spot and forward rates.*
(e) *Based on LIBOR and recently reported transactions in the marketplace.*
(f) *Based primarily on the price of our common stock.*
(g) *Based on recently reported transactions in the marketplace, primarily swap arrangements.*
(h) *Based on the fair value of investments corresponding to employees' investment elections.*
(i) *Based on average prices on futures exchanges.*

The carrying amounts of our cash and cash equivalents and short-term investments approximate fair value due to the short-term maturity. Short-term investments consist principally of short-term time deposits and index funds of $120 million as of December 26, 2009 and $98 million as of December 27, 2008 used to manage a portion of market risk arising from our deferred compensation liability. The fair value of our debt obligations as of December 26, 2009 and December 27, 2008 was $8.6 billion and $8.8 billion, respectively, based upon prices of similar instruments in the marketplace.

The preceding table excludes guarantees, including our guarantee aggregating $2.3 billion of Bottling Group, LLC's long-term debt. The guarantee had a fair value of $20 million as of December 26, 2009 and $117 million as of December 27, 2008 based on our estimate of the cost to us of transferring the liability to an independent financial institution. See Note 9 for additional information on our guarantees.

Note 11 Net Income Attributable to PepsiCo per Common Share

Basic net income attributable to PepsiCo per common share is net income available for PepsiCo common shareholders divided by the weighted average of common shares outstanding during the period. Diluted net income attributable to PepsiCo per common share is calculated using the weighted average of common shares outstanding adjusted to include the effect that would occur if in-the-money employee stock options were exercised and RSUs and preferred shares were converted into common shares. Options to purchase 39.0 million shares in 2009, 9.8 million shares in 2008 and 2.7 million shares in 2007 were not included in the calculation of diluted earnings per common share because these options were out-of-the-money. Out-of-the-money options had average exercise prices of $61.52 in 2009, $67.59 in 2008 and $65.18 in 2007.

Notes to Consolidated Financial Statements

The computations of basic and diluted net income attributable to PepsiCo per common share are as follows:

	2009		2008		2007	
	Income	Shares[a]	Income	Shares[a]	Income	Shares[a]
Net income attributable to PepsiCo	$5,946		$5,142		$5,658	
Preferred shares:						
Dividends	(1)		(2)		(2)	
Redemption premium	(5)		(6)		(10)	
Net income available for PepsiCo common shareholders	$5,940	1,558	$5,134	1,573	$5,646	1,621
Basic net income attributable to PepsiCo per common share	$ 3.81		$ 3.26		$ 3.48	
Net income available for PepsiCo common shareholders	$5,940	1,558	$5,134	1,573	$5,646	1,621
Dilutive securities:						
Stock options and RSUs	–	17	–	27	-	35
ESOP convertible preferred stock	6	2	8	2	12	2
Diluted	$5,946	1,577	$5,142	1,602	$5,658	1,658
Diluted net income attributable to PepsiCo per common share	$ 3.77		$ 3.21		$ 3.41	

(a) *Weighted-average common shares outstanding.*

Note 12 Preferred Stock

As of December 26, 2009 and December 27, 2008, there were 3 million shares of convertible preferred stock authorized. The preferred stock was issued only for an ESOP established by Quaker and these shares are redeemable for common stock by the ESOP participants. The preferred stock accrues dividends at an annual rate of $5.46 per share. At year-end 2009 and 2008, there were 803,953 preferred shares issued and 243,553 and 266,253 shares outstanding, respectively. The outstanding preferred shares had a fair value of $73 million as of December 26, 2009 and $72 million as of December 27, 2008. Each share is convertible at the option of the holder into 4.9625 shares of common stock. The preferred shares may be called by us upon written notice at $78 per share plus accrued and unpaid dividends. Quaker made the final award to its ESOP plan in June 2001.

	2009		2008		2007	
	Shares	Amount	Shares	Amount	Shares	Amount
Preferred stock	0.8	$ 41	0.8	$ 41	0.8	$ 41
Repurchased preferred stock						
Balance, beginning of year	0.5	$138	0.5	$132	0.5	$120
Redemptions	0.1	7	–	6	–	12
Balance, end of year	0.6	$145	0.5	$138	0.5	$132

Note 13 Accumulated Other Comprehensive Loss Attributable to PepsiCo

Comprehensive income is a measure of income which includes both net income and other comprehensive income or loss. Other comprehensive income or loss results from items deferred from recognition into our income statement. Accumulated other comprehensive loss is separately presented on our balance sheet as part of common shareholders' equity. Other comprehensive income/(loss) attributable to PepsiCo was $900 million in 2009, $(3,793) million in 2008 and $1,294 million in 2007. The accumulated balances for each component of other comprehensive loss attributable to PepsiCo were as follows:

	2009	2008	2007
Currency translation adjustment	$(1,471)	$(2,271)	$ 213
Cash flow hedges, net of tax(a)	(42)	(14)	(35)
Unamortized pension and retiree medical, net of tax(b)	(2,328)	(2,435)	(1,183)
Unrealized gain on securities, net of tax	47	28	49
Other	–	(2)	4
Accumulated other comprehensive loss attributable to PepsiCo	$(3,794)	$(4,694)	$ (952)

(a) Includes $23 million after-tax gain in 2009, $17 million after-tax loss in 2008 and $3 million after-tax gain in 2007 for our share of our equity investees' accumulated derivative activity.
(b) Net of taxes of $1,211 million in 2009, $1,288 million in 2008 and $645 million in 2007. Includes $51 million decrease to the opening balance of accumulated other comprehensive loss attributable to PepsiCo in 2008 due to the change in measurement date. See Note 7.

Note 14 Supplemental Financial Information

	2009	2008	2007
Accounts receivable			
Trade receivables	$4,026	$3,784	
Other receivables	688	969	
	4,714	4,753	
Allowance, beginning of year	70	69	$64
Net amounts charged to expense	40	21	5
Deductions (a)	(21)	(16)	(7)
Other (b)	1	(4)	7
Allowance, end of year	90	70	$69
Net receivables	$4,624	$4,683	
Inventories (c)			
Raw materials	$1,274	$1,228	
Work-in-process	165	169	
Finished goods	1,179	1,125	
	$2,618	$2,522	

(a) Includes accounts written off.
(b) Includes currency translation effects and other adjustments.
(c) Inventories are valued at the lower of cost or market. Cost is determined using the average, first-in, first-out (FIFO) or last-in, first-out (LIFO) methods. Approximately 10% in 2009 and 11% in 2008 of the inventory cost was computed using the LIFO method. The differences between LIFO and FIFO methods of valuing these inventories were not material.

	2009	2008
Other assets		
Noncurrent notes and accounts receivable	$ 118	$ 115
Deferred marketplace spending	182	219
Unallocated purchase price for recent acquisitions	143	1,594
Pension plans	64	28
Other	458	702
	$ 965	$2,658
Accounts payable and other current liabilities		
Accounts payable	$2,881	$2,846
Accrued marketplace spending	1,656	1,574
Accrued compensation and benefits	1,291	1,269
Dividends payable	706	660
Other current liabilities	1,593	1,924
	$8,127	$8,273

	2009	2008	2007
Other supplemental information			
Rent expense	$ 412	$ 357	$ 303
Interest paid	$ 456	$ 359	$ 251
Income taxes paid, net of refunds	$1,498	$ 1,477	$ 1,731
Acquisitions(a)			
Fair value of assets acquired	$ 851	$ 2,907	$ 1,611
Cash paid	(466)	(1,925)	(1,320)
Liabilities and noncontrolling interests assumed	$ 385	$ 982	$ 291

(a) During 2008, together with PBG, we jointly acquired Lebedyansky, for a total purchase price of $1.8 billion. Lebedyansky is owned 25% and 75% by PBG and us, respectively.

Notes to Consolidated Financial Statements

Note 15 Acquisition of Common Stock of PBG and PAS

On August 3, 2009, we entered into the PBG Merger Agreement and the PAS Merger Agreement.

The PBG Merger Agreement provides that, upon the terms and subject to the conditions set forth in the PBG Merger Agreement, PBG will be merged with and into Metro (the PBG Merger), with Metro continuing as the surviving corporation and our wholly owned subsidiary. At the effective time of the PBG Merger, each share of PBG common stock outstanding immediately prior to the effective time not held by us or any of our subsidiaries will be converted into the right to receive either 0.6432 of a share of PepsiCo common stock or, at the election of the holder, $36.50 in cash, without interest, and in each case subject to proration procedures which provide that we will pay cash for a number of shares equal to 50% of the PBG common stock outstanding immediately prior to the effective time of the PBG Merger not held by us or any of our subsidiaries and issue shares of PepsiCo common stock for the remaining 50% of such shares. Each share of PBG common stock held by PBG as treasury stock, held by us or held by Metro, and each share of PBG Class B common stock held by us or Metro, in each case immediately prior to the effective time of the PBG Merger, will be canceled, and no payment will be made with respect thereto. Each share of PBG common stock and PBG Class B common stock owned by any subsidiary of ours other than Metro immediately prior to the effective time of the PBG Merger will automatically be converted into the right to receive 0.6432 of a share of PepsiCo common stock.

The PAS Merger Agreement provides that, upon the terms and subject to the conditions set forth in the PAS Merger Agreement, PAS will be merged with and into Metro (the PAS Merger, and together with the PBG Merger, the Mergers), with Metro continuing as the surviving corporation and our wholly owned subsidiary. At the effective time of the PAS Merger, each share of PAS common stock outstanding immediately prior to the effective time not held by us or any of our subsidiaries will be converted into the right to receive either 0.5022 of a share of PepsiCo common stock or, at the election of the holder, $28.50 in cash, without interest, and in each case subject to proration procedures which provide that we will pay cash for a number of shares equal to 50% of the PAS common stock outstanding immediately prior to the effective time of the PAS Merger not held by us or any of our subsidiaries and issue shares of PepsiCo common stock for the remaining 50% of such shares. Each share of PAS common stock held by PAS as treasury stock, held by us or held by Metro, in each case, immediately prior to the effective time of the PAS Merger, will be canceled, and no payment will be made with respect thereto. Each share of PAS common stock owned by any subsidiary of ours other than Metro immediately prior to the effective time of the PAS Merger will automatically be converted into the right to receive 0.5022 of a share of PepsiCo common stock.

On February 17, 2010, the stockholders of PBG and PAS approved the PBG and PAS Mergers, respectively. Consummation of each of the Mergers is subject to various conditions, including the absence of legal prohibitions and the receipt of regulatory approvals. On February 17, 2010, we announced that we had refiled under the HSR Act with respect to the Mergers and signed a Consent Decree proposed by the Staff of the FTC providing for the maintenance of the confidentiality of certain information we will obtain from DPSG in connection with the manufacture and distribution of certain DPSG products after the Mergers are completed. The Consent Decree is subject to review and approval by the Commissioners of the FTC. We hope to consummate the Mergers by the end of February, 2010.

We currently plan that at the closing of the Mergers we will form a new operating unit. This new operating unit will comprise all current PBG and PAS operations in the United States, Canada and Mexico, and will account for about three-quarters of the volume of PepsiCo's North American bottling system, with independent franchisees accounting for most of the rest. This new operating unit will be included within the PAB business unit. Current PBG and PAS operations in Europe, including Russia, will be managed by the Europe division when the Mergers are completed.

Management's Responsibility for Financial Reporting

To Our Shareholders:

At PepsiCo, our actions—the actions of all our associates—are governed by our Worldwide Code of Conduct. This Code is clearly aligned with our stated values—a commitment to sustained growth, through empowered people, operating with responsibility and building trust. Both the Code and our core values enable us to operate with integrity—both within the letter and the spirit of the law. Our Code of Conduct is reinforced consistently at all levels and in all countries. We have maintained strong governance policies and practices for many years.

The management of PepsiCo is responsible for the objectivity and integrity of our consolidated financial statements. The Audit Committee of the Board of Directors has engaged independent registered public accounting firm, KPMG LLP, to audit our consolidated financial statements, and they have expressed an unqualified opinion.

We are committed to providing timely, accurate and understandable information to investors. Our commitment encompasses the following:

Maintaining strong controls over financial reporting. Our system of internal control is based on the control criteria framework of the Committee of Sponsoring Organizations of the Treadway Commission published in their report titled *Internal Control—Integrated Framework*. The system is designed to provide reasonable assurance that transactions are executed as authorized and accurately recorded; that assets are safeguarded; and that accounting records are sufficiently reliable to permit the preparation of financial statements that conform in all material respects with accounting principles generally accepted in the U.S. We maintain disclosure controls and procedures designed to ensure that information required to be disclosed in reports under the Securities Exchange Act of 1934 is recorded, processed, summarized and reported within the specified time periods. We monitor these internal controls through self-assessments and an ongoing program of internal audits. Our internal controls are reinforced through our Worldwide Code of Conduct, which sets forth our commitment to conduct business with integrity, and within both the letter and the spirit of the law.

Exerting rigorous oversight of the business. We continuously review our business results and strategies. This encompasses financial discipline in our strategic and daily business decisions. Our Executive Committee is actively involved—from understanding strategies and alternatives to reviewing key initiatives and financial performance. The intent is to ensure we remain objective in our assessments, constructively challenge our approach to potential business opportunities and issues, and monitor results and controls.

Engaging strong and effective Corporate Governance from our Board of Directors. We have an active, capable and diligent Board that meets the required standards for independence, and we welcome the Board's oversight as a representative of our shareholders. Our Audit Committee is comprised of independent directors with the financial literacy, knowledge and experience to provide appropriate oversight. We review our critical accounting policies, financial reporting and internal control matters with them and encourage their direct communication with KPMG LLP, with our General Auditor, and with our General Counsel. We also have a Compliance Department to coordinate our compliance policies and practices.

Providing investors with financial results that are complete, transparent and understandable. The consolidated financial statements and financial information included in this report are the responsibility of management. This includes preparing the financial statements in accordance with accounting principles generally accepted in the U.S., which require estimates based on management's best judgment.

PepsiCo has a strong history of doing what's right. We realize that great companies are built on trust, strong ethical standards and principles. Our financial results are delivered from that culture of accountability, and we take responsibility for the quality and accuracy of our financial reporting.

Peter A. Bridgman
Senior Vice President and Controller

Richard Goodman
Chief Financial Officer

Indra K. Nooyi
Chairman of the Board of Directors and Chief Executive Officer

Management's Report on Internal Control Over Financial Reporting

To Our Shareholders:

Our management is responsible for establishing and maintaining adequate internal control over financial reporting, as such term is defined in Rule 13a-15(f) of the Exchange Act. Under the supervision and with the participation of our management, including our Chief Executive Officer and Chief Financial Officer, we conducted an evaluation of the effectiveness of our internal control over financial reporting based upon the framework in *Internal Control— Integrated Framework* issued by the Committee of Sponsoring Organizations of the Treadway Commission. Based on that evaluation, our management concluded that our internal control over financial reporting is effective as of December 26, 2009.

KPMG LLP, an independent registered public accounting firm, has audited the consolidated financial statements included in this Annual Report on Form 10-K and, as part of their audit, has issued their report, included herein, on the effectiveness of our internal control over financial reporting.

During our fourth fiscal quarter of 2009, we continued migrating certain of our financial processing systems to SAP software. This software implementation is part of our ongoing global business transformation initiative, and we plan to continue implementing such software throughout other parts of our businesses over the course of the next few years. In connection with the SAP implementation and resulting business process changes, we continue to enhance the design and documentation of our internal control processes to ensure suitable controls over our financial reporting.

Except as described above, there were no changes in our internal control over financial reporting during our fourth fiscal quarter of 2009 that have materially affected, or are reasonably likely to materially affect, our internal control over financial reporting.

Peter A. Bridgman
Senior Vice President and Controller

Richard Goodman
Chief Financial Officer

Indra K. Nooyi
Chairman of the Board of Directors and Chief Executive Officer

Report of Independent Registered Public Accounting Firm

The Board of Directors and Shareholders
PepsiCo, Inc.:

We have audited the accompanying Consolidated Balance Sheets of PepsiCo, Inc. and subsidiaries ("PepsiCo, Inc." or "the Company") as of December 26, 2009 and December 27, 2008, and the related Consolidated Statements of Income, Cash Flows and Equity for each of the fiscal years in the three-year period ended December 26, 2009. We also have audited PepsiCo, Inc.'s internal control over financial reporting as of December 26, 2009, based on criteria established in *Internal Control—Integrated Framework* issued by the Committee of Sponsoring Organizations of the Treadway Commission (COSO). PepsiCo, Inc.'s management is responsible for these consolidated financial statements, for maintaining effective internal control over financial reporting, and for its assessment of the effectiveness of internal control over financial reporting, included in the accompanying Management's Report on Internal Control over Financial Reporting. Our responsibility is to express an opinion on these consolidated financial statements and an opinion on the Company's internal control over financial reporting based on our audits.

We conducted our audits in accordance with the standards of the Public Company Accounting Oversight Board (United States). Those standards require that we plan and perform the audits to obtain reasonable assurance about whether the financial statements are free of material misstatement and whether effective internal control over financial reporting was maintained in all material respects. Our audits of the consolidated financial statements included examining, on a test basis, evidence supporting the amounts and disclosures in the financial statements, assessing the accounting principles used and significant estimates made by management, and evaluating the overall financial statement presentation. Our audit of internal control over financial reporting included obtaining an understanding of internal control over financial reporting, assessing the risk that a material weakness exists, and testing and evaluating the design and operating effectiveness of internal control based on the assessed risk. Our audits also included performing such other procedures as we considered necessary in the circumstances. We believe that our audits provide a reasonable basis for our opinions.

A company's internal control over financial reporting is a process designed to provide reasonable assurance regarding the reliability of financial reporting and the preparation of financial statements for external purposes in accordance with generally accepted accounting principles. A company's internal control over financial reporting includes those policies and procedures that (1) pertain to the maintenance of records that, in reasonable detail, accurately and fairly reflect the transactions and dispositions of the assets of the company; (2) provide reasonable assurance that transactions are recorded as necessary to permit preparation of financial statements in accordance with generally accepted accounting principles, and that receipts and expenditures of the company are being made only in accordance with authorizations of management and directors of the company; and (3) provide reasonable assurance regarding prevention or timely detection of unauthorized acquisition, use, or disposition of the company's assets that could have a material effect on the financial statements.

Because of its inherent limitations, internal control over financial reporting may not prevent or detect misstatements. Also, projections of any evaluation of effectiveness to future periods are subject to the risk that controls may become inadequate because of changes in conditions, or that the degree of compliance with the policies or procedures may deteriorate.

In our opinion, the consolidated financial statements referred to above present fairly, in all material respects, the financial position of PepsiCo, Inc. as of December 26, 2009 and December 27, 2008, and the results of its operations and its cash flows for each of the fiscal years in the three-year period ended December 26, 2009, in conformity with U.S. generally accepted accounting principles. Also in our opinion, PepsiCo, Inc. maintained, in all material respects, effective internal control over financial reporting as of December 26, 2009, based on criteria established in *Internal Control—Integrated Framework* issued by COSO.

As discussed in Note 2 to the consolidated financial statements, the Company changed its method of accounting for business combinations and noncontrolling interests in 2009.

KPMG LLP

New York, New York
February 22, 2010

Selected Financial Data

(in millions except per share amounts, unaudited)

Quarterly	First Quarter	Second Quarter	Third Quarter	Fourth Quarter
Net revenue				
2009	$8,263	$10,592	$11,080	$13,297
2008	$8,333	$10,945	$11,244	$12,729
Gross profit				
2009	$4,519	$ 5,711	$ 5,899	$ 7,004
2008	$4,499	$ 5,867	$ 5,976	$ 6,558
Restructuring and impairment charges (a)				
2009	$ 25	$ 11	–	–
2008	–	–	–	$ 543
Mark-to-market net impact (b)				
2009	$ (62)	$ (100)	$ (29)	$ (83)
2008	$ 4	$ (61)	$ 176	$ 227
PepsiCo portion of PBG restructuring and impairment charge (c)				
2008	–	–	–	$ 138
PBG/PAS merger costs (d)				
2009	–	–	$ 9	$ 52
Net income attributable to PepsiCo				
2009	$1,135	$ 1,660	$ 1,717	$ 1,434
2008	$1,148	$ 1,699	$ 1,576	$ 719
Net income attributable to PepsiCo per common share—basic				
2009	$ 0.73	$ 1.06	$ 1.10	$ 0.92
2008	$ 0.72	$ 1.07	$ 1.01	$ 0.46
Net income attributable to PepsiCo per common share—diluted				
2009	$ 0.72	$ 1.06	$ 1.09	$ 0.90
2008	$ 0.70	$ 1.05	$ 0.99	$ 0.46
Cash dividends declared per common share				
2009	$0.425	$ 0.45	$ 0.45	$ 0.45
2008	$0.375	$ 0.425	$ 0.425	$ 0.425
2009 stock price per share (e)				
High	$56.93	$ 56.95	$ 59.64	$ 64.48
Low	$43.78	$ 47.50	$ 52.11	$ 57.33
Close	$50.02	$ 53.65	$ 57.54	$ 60.96
2008 stock price per share (e)				
High	$79.79	$ 72.35	$ 70.83	$ 75.25
Low	$66.30	$ 64.69	$ 63.28	$ 49.74
Close	$71.19	$ 67.54	$ 68.92	$ 54.56

(a) *The restructuring and impairment charge in 2009 was $36 million ($29 million after-tax or $0.02 per share). The restructuring and impairment charge in 2008 was $543 million ($408 million after-tax or $0.25 per share). See Note 3.*

(b) *In 2009, we recognized $274 million ($173 million after-tax or $0.11 per share) of mark-to-market net gains on commodity hedges in corporate unallocated expenses. In 2008, we recognized $346 million ($223 million after-tax or $0.14 per share) of mark-to-market net losses on commodity hedges in corporate unallocated expenses.*

(c) *In 2008, we recognized a non-cash charge of $138 million ($114 million after-tax or $0.07 per share) included in bottling equity income as part of recording our share of PBG's financial results.*

(d) *In 2009, we recognized $50 million of costs associated with the proposed mergers with PBG and PAS, as well as an additional $11 million of costs in bottling equity income representing our share of the respective merger costs of PBG and PAS. In total, these costs had an after-tax impact of $44 million or $0.03 per share.*

(e) *Represents the composite high and low sales price and quarterly closing prices for one share of PepsiCo common stock.*

Five-Year Summary	2009	2008	2007
Net revenue	**$43,232**	$43,251	$39,474
Net income attributable to PepsiCo	**$ 5,946**	$ 5,142	$ 5,658
Net income attributable to PepsiCo per common share – basic	**$ 3.81**	$ 3.26	$ 3.48
Net income attributable to PepsiCo per common share – diluted	**$ 3.77**	$ 3.21	$ 3.41
Cash dividends declared per common share	**$ 1.775**	$ 1.65	$ 1.425
Total assets	**$39,848**	$35,994	$34,628
Long-term debt	**$ 7,400**	$ 7,858	$ 4,203
Return on invested capital(a)	**27.2%**	25.5%	28.9%

Five-Year Summary *(continued)*	2006	2005
Net revenue	$35,137	$32,562
Net income attributable to PepsiCo	$ 5,642	$ 4,078
Net income attributable to PepsiCo per common share – basic	$ 3.42	$ 2.43
Net income attributable to PepsiCo per common share – diluted	$ 3.34	$ 2.39
Cash dividends declared per common share	$ 1.16	$ 1.01
Total assets	$29,930	$31,727
Long-term debt	$ 2,550	$ 2,313
Return on invested capital(a)	30.4%	22.7%

(a) *Return on invested capital is defined as adjusted net income attributable to PepsiCo divided by the sum of average common shareholders' equity and average total debt. Adjusted net income attributable to PepsiCo is defined as net income attributable to PepsiCo plus net interest expense after-tax. Net interest expense after-tax was $211 million in 2009, $184 million in 2008, $63 million in 2007, $72 million in 2006 and $62 million in 2005.*

- Includes restructuring and impairment charges of:

	2009	2008	2007	2006	2005
Pre-tax	**$ 36**	$ 543	$ 102	$ 67	$ 83
After-tax	**$ 29**	$ 408	$ 70	$ 43	$ 55
Per share	**$0.02**	$0.25	$0.04	$0.03	$0.03

- Includes mark-to-market net (income)/expense of:

	2009	2008	2007	2006
Pre-tax	**$ (274)**	$ 346	$ (19)	$ 18
After-tax	**$ (173)**	$ 223	$ (12)	$ 12
Per share	**$(0.11)**	$0.14	$(0.01)	$0.01

- In 2009, we recognized $50 million of costs associated with the proposed mergers with PBG and PAS, as well as an additional $11 million of costs in bottling equity income representing our share of the respective merger costs of PBG and PAS. In total, these costs had an after-tax impact of $44 million or $0.03 per share.
- In 2008, we recognized $138 million ($114 million after-tax or $0.07 per share) of our share of PBG's restructuring and impairment charges.
- In 2007, we recognized $129 million ($0.08 per share) of non-cash tax benefits related to the favorable resolution of certain foreign tax matters. In 2006, we recognized non-cash tax benefits of $602 million ($0.36 per share) primarily in connection with the IRS's examination of our consolidated income tax returns for the years 1998 through 2002. In 2005, we recorded income tax expense of $460 million ($0.27 per share) related to our repatriation of earnings in connection with the American Job Creation Act of 2004.
- On December 30, 2006, we adopted guidance from the FASB on accounting for pension and other postretirement benefits which reduced total assets by $2,016 million, total common shareholders' equity by $1,643 million and total liabilities by $373 million.
- The 2005 fiscal year consisted of 53 weeks compared to 52 weeks in our normal fiscal year. The 53rd week increased 2005 net revenue by an estimated $418 million and net income attributable to PepsiCo by an estimated $57 million ($0.03 per share).

Specimen Financial Statements:

The Coca-Cola Company

THE COCA-COLA COMPANY AND SUBSIDIARIES

CONSOLIDATED STATEMENTS OF INCOME

Year Ended December 31,	2009	2008	2007
(In millions except per share data)			
NET OPERATING REVENUES	$ 30,990	$ 31,944	$ 28,857
Cost of goods sold	11,088	11,374	10,406
GROSS PROFIT	19,902	20,570	18,451
Selling, general and administrative expenses	11,358	11,774	10,945
Other operating charges	313	350	254
OPERATING INCOME	8,231	8,446	7,252
Interest income	249	333	236
Interest expense	355	438	456
Equity income (loss) — net	781	(874)	668
Other income (loss) — net	40	39	219
INCOME BEFORE INCOME TAXES	8,946	7,506	7,919
Income taxes	2,040	1,632	1,892
CONSOLIDATED NET INCOME	6,906	5,874	6,027
Less: Net income attributable to noncontrolling interests	82	67	46
NET INCOME ATTRIBUTABLE TO SHAREOWNERS OF THE COCA-COLA COMPANY	$ 6,824	$ 5,807	$ 5,981
BASIC NET INCOME PER SHARE[1]	$ 2.95	$ 2.51	$ 2.59
DILUTED NET INCOME PER SHARE[1]	$ 2.93	$ 2.49	$ 2.57
AVERAGE SHARES OUTSTANDING	2,314	2,315	2,313
Effect of dilutive securities	15	21	18
AVERAGE SHARES OUTSTANDING ASSUMING DILUTION	2,329	2,336	2,331

[1] Basic net income per share and diluted net income per share are calculated based on net income attributable to shareowners of The Coca-Cola Company.

Refer to Notes to Consolidated Financial Statements.

THE COCA-COLA COMPANY AND SUBSIDIARIES
CONSOLIDATED BALANCE SHEETS

December 31,	2009	2008
(In millions except par value)		
ASSETS		
CURRENT ASSETS		
Cash and cash equivalents	$ 7,021	$ 4,701
Short-term investments	2,130	—
TOTAL CASH, CASH EQUIVALENTS AND SHORT-TERM INVESTMENTS	9,151	4,701
Marketable securities	62	278
Trade accounts receivable, less allowances of $55 and $51, respectively	3,758	3,090
Inventories	2,354	2,187
Prepaid expenses and other assets	2,226	1,920
TOTAL CURRENT ASSETS	17,551	12,176
EQUITY METHOD INVESTMENTS	6,217	5,316
OTHER INVESTMENTS, PRINCIPALLY BOTTLING COMPANIES	538	463
OTHER ASSETS	1,976	1,733
PROPERTY, PLANT AND EQUIPMENT — net	9,561	8,326
TRADEMARKS WITH INDEFINITE LIVES	6,183	6,059
GOODWILL	4,224	4,029
OTHER INTANGIBLE ASSETS	2,421	2,417
TOTAL ASSETS	$ 48,671	$ 40,519
LIABILITIES AND EQUITY		
CURRENT LIABILITIES		
Accounts payable and accrued expenses	$ 6,657	$ 6,205
Loans and notes payable	6,749	6,066
Current maturities of long-term debt	51	465
Accrued income taxes	264	252
TOTAL CURRENT LIABILITIES	13,721	12,988
LONG-TERM DEBT	5,059	2,781
OTHER LIABILITIES	2,965	3,011
DEFERRED INCOME TAXES	1,580	877
THE COCA-COLA COMPANY SHAREOWNERS' EQUITY		
Common stock, $0.25 par value; Authorized — 5,600 shares;		
Issued — 3,520 and 3,519 shares, respectively	880	880
Capital surplus	8,537	7,966
Reinvested earnings	41,537	38,513
Accumulated other comprehensive income (loss)	(757)	(2,674)
Treasury stock, at cost — 1,217 and 1,207 shares, respectively	(25,398)	(24,213)
EQUITY ATTRIBUTABLE TO SHAREOWNERS OF THE COCA-COLA COMPANY	24,799	20,472
EQUITY ATTRIBUTABLE TO NONCONTROLLING INTERESTS	547	390
TOTAL EQUITY	25,346	20,862
TOTAL LIABILITIES AND EQUITY	$ 48,671	$ 40,519

Refer to Notes to Consolidated Financial Statements.

THE COCA-COLA COMPANY AND SUBSIDIARIES
CONSOLIDATED STATEMENTS OF CASH FLOWS

Year Ended December 31,	2009	2008	2007
(In millions)			
OPERATING ACTIVITIES			
Consolidated net income	$ **6,906**	$ 5,874	$ 6,027
Depreciation and amortization	**1,236**	1,228	1,163
Stock-based compensation expense	**241**	266	313
Deferred income taxes	**353**	(360)	109
Equity income or loss, net of dividends	**(359)**	1,128	(452)
Foreign currency adjustments	**61**	(42)	9
Gains on sales of assets, including bottling interests	**(43)**	(130)	(244)
Other operating charges	**134**	209	166
Other items	**221**	153	99
Net change in operating assets and liabilities	**(564)**	(755)	(40)
Net cash provided by operating activities	**8,186**	7,571	7,150
INVESTING ACTIVITIES			
Acquisitions and investments, principally beverage and bottling companies and trademarks	**(300)**	(759)	(5,653)
Purchases of other investments	**(2,152)**	(240)	(99)
Proceeds from disposals of bottling companies and other investments	**240**	479	448
Purchases of property, plant and equipment	**(1,993)**	(1,968)	(1,648)
Proceeds from disposals of property, plant and equipment	**104**	129	239
Other investing activities	**(48)**	(4)	(6)
Net cash provided by (used in) investing activities	**(4,149)**	(2,363)	(6,719)
FINANCING ACTIVITIES			
Issuances of debt	**14,689**	4,337	9,979
Payments of debt	**(12,326)**	(4,308)	(5,638)
Issuances of stock	**662**	586	1,619
Purchases of stock for treasury	**(1,518)**	(1,079)	(1,838)
Dividends	**(3,800)**	(3,521)	(3,149)
Net cash provided by (used in) financing activities	**(2,293)**	(3,985)	973
EFFECT OF EXCHANGE RATE CHANGES ON CASH AND CASH EQUIVALENTS	**576**	(615)	249
CASH AND CASH EQUIVALENTS			
Net increase (decrease) during the year	**2,320**	608	1,653
Balance at beginning of year	**4,701**	4,093	2,440
Balance at end of year	$ **7,021**	$ 4,701	$ 4,093

Refer to Notes to Consolidated Financial Statements.

THE COCA-COLA COMPANY AND SUBSIDIARIES
CONSOLIDATED STATEMENTS OF SHAREOWNERS' EQUITY

Year Ended December 31,	2009	2008	2007
(In millions except per share data)			
EQUITY ATTRIBUTABLE TO SHAREOWNERS OF THE COCA-COLA COMPANY			
NUMBER OF COMMON SHARES OUTSTANDING			
Balance at beginning of year	2,312	2,318	2,318
Stock issued to employees exercising stock options	—	—	8
Purchases of treasury stock	(26)	(18)	(35)
Treasury stock issued to employees exercising stock options	17	12	23
Treasury stock issued to former shareholders of glacéau	—	—	4
Balance at end of year	2,303	2,312	2,318
COMMON STOCK			
Balance at beginning of year	$ 880	$ 880	$ 878
Stock issued to employees related to stock compensation plans	—	—	2
Balance at end of year	880	880	880
CAPITAL SURPLUS			
Balance at beginning of year	7,966	7,378	5,983
Stock issued to employees related to stock compensation plans	339	324	1,001
Tax (charge) benefit from employees' stock option and restricted stock plans	(6)	(1)	(28)
Stock-based compensation	238	265	309
Stock purchased by former shareholders of glacéau	—	—	113
Balance at end of year	8,537	7,966	7,378
REINVESTED EARNINGS			
Balance at beginning of year	38,513	36,235	33,468
Cumulative effect of the adoption of new accounting guidance for pension and other postretirement plans	—	(8)	—
Cumulative effect of the adoption of new accounting guidance for uncertain tax positions	—	—	(65)
Net income attributable to shareowners of The Coca-Cola Company	6,824	5,807	5,981
Dividends (per share — $1.64, $1.52 and $1.36 in 2009, 2008 and 2007, respectively)	(3,800)	(3,521)	(3,149)
Balance at end of year	41,537	38,513	36,235
ACCUMULATED OTHER COMPREHENSIVE INCOME (LOSS)			
Balance at beginning of year	(2,674)	626	(1,291)
Net foreign currency translation adjustment	1,824	(2,285)	1,575
Net gain (loss) on derivatives	34	1	(64)
Net change in unrealized gain on available-for-sale securities	(52)	(44)	14
Net change in pension liability	111	(972)	392
Net other comprehensive income (loss)	1,917	(3,300)	1,917
Balance at end of year	(757)	(2,674)	626
TREASURY STOCK			
Balance at beginning of year	(24,213)	(23,375)	(22,118)
Stock issued to employees related to stock compensation plans	333	243	428
Stock purchased by former shareholders of glacéau	—	—	66
Purchases of treasury stock	(1,518)	(1,081)	(1,751)
Balance at end of year	(25,398)	(24,213)	(23,375)
TOTAL EQUITY ATTRIBUTABLE TO SHAREOWNERS OF THE COCA-COLA COMPANY	$ 24,799	$ 20,472	$ 21,744
EQUITY ATTRIBUTABLE TO NONCONTROLLING INTERESTS			
Balance at beginning of year	$ 390	$ 342	$ 333
Net income attributable to noncontrolling interests	82	67	46
Net foreign currency translation adjustment	49	(25)	1
Dividends paid to noncontrolling interests	(14)	(20)	(23)
Contributions by noncontrolling interests	40	31	41
Disposal of subsidiaries	—	(5)	(56)
TOTAL EQUITY ATTRIBUTABLE TO NONCONTROLLING INTERESTS	$ 547	$ 390	$ 342
COMPREHENSIVE INCOME			
Consolidated net income	$ 6,906	$ 5,874	$ 6,027
Consolidated net other comprehensive income (loss)	1,966	(3,325)	1,918
CONSOLIDATED COMPREHENSIVE INCOME	$ 8,872	$ 2,549	$ 7,945

Refer to Notes to Consolidated Financial Statements.

APPENDIX C

Specimen Financial Statements:

Zetar plc

CONSOLIDATED INCOME STATEMENT
FOR THE YEAR ENDED 30 APRIL 2009

	Note	2009 Adjusted results £'000	2009 Adjusting items £'000	2009 Total £'000	2008 Adjusted results £'000	2008 Adjusting items £'000	2008 Total £'000
Continuing operations							
Revenue	3	**118,602**	—	**118,602**	109,216	—	109,216
Cost of sales		**(93,857)**	—	**(93,857)**	(83,938)	—	(83,938)
Gross profit		**24,745**	—	**24,745**	25,278	—	25,278
Distribution costs		**(4,777)**	—	**(4,777)**	(5,013)	—	(5,013)
Administrative expenses							
– Other administrative expenses		**(13,917)**	—	**(13,917)**	(11,541)	—	(11,541)
– One-off items	4	—	**(1,508)**	**(1,508)**	—	—	—
– Amortisation of intangible assets	14	—	**(456)**	**(456)**	—	(675)	(675)
– Share-based payments	9	—	**116**	**116**	—	(377)	(377)
Operating profit		**6,051**	**(1,848)**	**4,203**	8,724	(1,052)	7,672
Interest income	8	**47**	—	**47**	116	—	116
Finance costs	8	**(1,556)**	**(680)**	**(2,236)**	(1,733)	(144)	(1,877)
Profit from continuing operations before taxation		**4,542**	**(2,528)**	**2,014**	7,107	(1,196)	5,911
Tax on profit from continuing activities	10	**(1,241)**	—	**(1,241)**	(2,034)	179	(1,855)
Net result from continuing operations		**3,301**	**(2,528)**	**773**	5,073	(1,017)	4,056
Net result from discontinued operations	11	—	**(5,836)**	**(5,836)**	—	(811)	(811)
Net result for the period		**3,301**	**(8,364)**	**(5,063)**	5,073	(1,828)	3,245
Basic (losses)/earnings per share (p)	12			**(42.9)**			29.5
Diluted (losses)/earnings per share (p)	12			**(42.6)**			25.9
Adjusted basic earnings per share (p)	12	**28.0**			46.2		
Adjusted diluted earnings per share (p)	12	**27.8**			40.5		

CONSOLIDATED BALANCE SHEET
AT 30 APRIL 2009

	Note	2009 £'000	2008 £'000
Non-current assets			
Goodwill	13	30,821	32,363
Other intangible assets	14	623	1,002
Property, plant and equipment	15	15,283	18,545
Deferred tax asset	21	198	167
		46,925	52,077
Current assets			
Inventories	16	14,319	13,364
Trade and other receivables	17	19,190	15,253
Derivative financial asset	30	—	72
Cash at bank	26	5,405	3,175
		38,914	31,864
Total assets		85,839	83,941
Current liabilities			
Trade and other payables	18	(23,763)	(20,337)
Performance related contingent consideration		(220)	(876)
Current tax liabilities		(252)	(687)
Obligations under finance leases	19	(214)	(470)
Derivative financial instruments	30	(607)	—
Borrowings and overdrafts	20	(15,712)	(9,289)
		(40,768)	(31,659)
Net current (liabilities)/assets		(1,854)	205
Non-current liabilities			
Performance related contingent consideration		(300)	(2,555)
Deferred tax liabilities	21	(1,575)	(1,448)
Obligations under finance leases	19	(167)	(369)
Borrowings and overdrafts	20	(4,676)	(7,609)
		(6,718)	(11,981)
Total liabilities		(47,486)	(43,640)
Net assets		38,353	40,301
Equity			
Share capital	22	1,324	1,151
Share premium account	23	28,252	26,449
Merger reserve		3,411	3,411
Equity reserve	24	2,719	1,431
Retained earnings	24	2,647	7,859
Total equity attributable to equity holders of the parent		38,353	40,301

CONSOLIDATED STATEMENT OF CHANGES IN EQUITY
FOR THE YEAR ENDED 30 APRIL 2009

			Attributable to equity holders of the parent			
	Share capital £'000	Share premium account £'000	Merger reserve £'000	Equity reserve £'000	Retained earnings £'000	Total £'000
Balance at 1 May 2007	1,073	22,673	3,229	621	4,914	32,510
Profit for the year	—	—	—	—	3,245	3,245
Exchange gain on translation of foreign operation	—	—	—	557	—	557
Issue of new ordinary shares	78	3,776	182	—	—	4,036
Purchase of own shares	—	—	—	—	(300)	(300)
Share-based payment charge	—	—	—	377	—	377
Deferred tax on share-based payments	—	—	—	(124)	—	(124)
Balance at 30 April 2008	1,151	26,449	3,411	1,431	7,859	40,301
Loss for the year	—	—	—	—	(5,063)	(5,063)
Exchange gain on translation of foreign operations	—	—	—	1,404	—	1,404
Issue of new ordinary shares	173	1,803	—	—	—	1,976
Purchase of own shares	—	—	—	—	(149)	(149)
Prior year share-based payment reversal	—	—	—	(116)	—	(116)
Balance at 30 April 2009	**1,324**	**28,252**	**3,411**	**2,719**	**2,647**	**38,353**

CONSOLIDATED CASH FLOW STATEMENT
FOR THE YEAR ENDED 30 APRIL 2009

	Note	2009 £'000	2008 £'000
Cash flow from operating activities			
Profit on ordinary activities before taxation		2,014	5,911
Finance costs		2,236	1,877
Interest income		(47)	(116)
Share-based payments		(116)	377
Depreciation (including trademark amortisation)	15	2,346	1,989
Loss on sale of plant and equipment		22	6
Amortisation of intangible assets		457	675
One-off items		1,388	—
Net movement in working capital		(2,469)	(1,011)
Increase in inventories		(1,299)	(2,646)
(Increase)/decrease in receivables		(4,504)	4,075
Decrease/(increase) in payables		3,334	(2,440)
Cash flow from continuing operations		5,831	9,708
Cash flow from discontinued operations		(1,002)	(1,260)
Total cash flow from operations		4,829	8,448
Net interest paid	8	(1,510)	(1,646)
Tax paid		(782)	(1,682)
Cash generated from activities in continuing operations		3,539	6,380
Cash flow generated from operating activities in discontinued operations		(1,002)	(1,260)
Total cash flow from operating activities		2,537	5,120
Cash flow from investing activities			
Purchase of property, plant and equipment		(3,847)	(3,722)
Proceeds from sale of plant and equipment		42	26
Disposal of subsidiary	11	(220)	—
Total cash impact of acquisitions		(879)	(3,733)
Acquisitions of businesses (including contingent consideration)		(879)	(2,814)
Net borrowings assumed on acquisition		—	(919)
Net cash outflow from continuing investing activities		(4,904)	(7,429)
Net cash outflow from discontinued investing activities		—	(5,244)
Net cash flow from investing activities		(4,904)	(12,673)
Cash flow from financing activities			
Net proceeds from issue of ordinary share capital		1,976	3,851
Purchase of own shares		(149)	(300)
Proceeds from new borrowings		—	5,000
Repayment of borrowings		(3,536)	(4,819)
Finance lease repayments		(457)	(472)
Minority interest dividends paid		—	—
Net cash flow from financing activities		(2,166)	3,260
Net decrease in cash and cash equivalents		(4,533)	(4,293)
Cash and cash equivalents at beginning of the year		(3,331)	917
Effect of foreign exchange rate movements		(263)	45
Cash and cash equivalents at end of the year		(8,127)	(3,331)
Cash and cash equivalents comprise:			
Cash at bank	26	5,405	3,175
Bank overdraft	26	(13,532)	(6,506)
		(8,127)	(3,331)

APPENDIX D

Time Value of Money

Study Objectives

After studying this appendix, you should be able to:

[1] Distinguish between simple and compound interest.

[2] Identify the variables fundamental to solving present value problems.

[3] Solve for present value of a single amount.

[4] Solve for present value of an annuity.

[5] Compute the present value of notes and bonds.

Would you rather receive $1,000 today or a year from now? You should prefer to receive the $1,000 today because you can invest the $1,000 and earn interest on it. As a result, you will have more than $1,000 a year from now. What this example illustrates is the concept of the **time value of money**. Everyone prefers to receive money today rather than in the future because of the interest factor.

Nature of Interest

Interest is payment for the use of another person's money. It is the difference between the amount borrowed or invested (called the principal) and the amount repaid or collected. The amount of interest to be paid or collected is usually stated as a rate over a specific period of time. The rate of interest is generally stated as an **annual rate**.

The amount of interest involved in any financing transaction is based on three elements:

1. **Principal (p):** The original amount borrowed or invested.
2. **Interest Rate (i):** An annual percentage of the principal.
3. **Time (n):** The number of years that the principal is borrowed or invested.

Simple Interest

Simple interest is computed on the principal amount only. It is the return on the principal for one period. Simple interest is usually expressed as shown in Illustration D-1 on the next page.

Study Objective [1]
Distinguish between simple and compound interest.

Illustration D-1
Interest computation

Interest	=	Principal	×	Rate	×	Time
		p		*i*		*n*

For example, if you borrowed $5,000 for 2 years at a simple interest rate of 12% annually, you would pay $1,200 in total interest computed as follows:

$$\text{Interest} = p \times i \times n$$
$$= \$5,000 \times .12 \times 2$$
$$= \$1,200$$

Compound Interest

Compound interest is computed on principal **and** on any interest earned that has not been paid or withdrawn. It is the return on the principal for two or more time periods. Compounding computes interest not only on the principal but also on the interest earned to date on that principal, assuming the interest is left on deposit.

To illustrate the difference between simple and compound interest, assume that you deposit $1,000 in Bank Two, where it will earn *simple interest* of 9% per year, and you deposit another $1,000 in Citizens Bank, where it will earn compound interest of 9% per year *compounded annually*. Also assume that in both cases you will not withdraw any interest until three years from the date of deposit. Illustration D-2 shows the computation of interest you will receive and the accumulated year-end balances.

Illustration D-2
Simple versus compound interest

Bank Two				Citizens Bank		
Simple Interest Calculation	Simple Interest	Accumulated Year-End Balance		Compound Interest Calculation	Compound Interest	Accumulated Year-End Balance
Year 1 $1,000.00 × 9%	$ 90.00	$1,090.00		Year 1 $1,000.00 × 9%	$ 90.00	$1,090.00
Year 2 $1,000.00 × 9%	90.00	$1,180.00		Year 2 $1,090.00 × 9%	98.10	$1,188.10
Year 3 $1,000.00 × 9%	90.00	$1,270.00		Year 3 $1,188.10 × 9%	106.93	$1,295.03
	$ 270.00				$ 295.03	

$25.03 Difference

Note in Illustration D-2 that simple interest uses the initial principal of $1,000 to compute the interest in all three years. Compound interest uses the accumulated balance (principal plus interest to date) at each year-end to compute interest in the succeeding year—which explains why your compound interest account is larger.

Obviously, if you had a choice between investing your money at simple interest or at compound interest, you would choose compound interest, all other things—especially risk—being equal. In the example, compounding provides $25.03 of additional interest income. For practical purposes, compounding assumes that unpaid interest earned becomes a part of the principal, and the accumulated balance at the end of each year becomes the new principal on which interest is earned during the next year.

Illustration D-2 indicates that you should invest your money at the bank that compounds interest annually. Most business situations use compound interest. Simple interest is generally applicable only to short-term situations of one year or less.

Present Value Variables

The **present value** is the value now of a given amount to be paid or received in the future, assuming compound interest. The present value is based on three variables: (1) the dollar amount to be received (future amount), (2) the length of time until the amount is received (number of periods), and (3) the interest rate (the discount rate). The process of determining the present value is referred to as **discounting the future amount**.

In this textbook, we use present value computations in measuring several items. For example, Chapter 15 computed the present value of the principal and interest payments to determine the market price of a bond. In addition, determining the amount to be reported for notes payable and lease liabilities involves present value computations.

Study Objective [2]
Identify the variables fundamental to solving present value problems.

Present Value of a Single Amount

To illustrate present value, assume that you want to invest a sum of money that will yield $1,000 at the end of one year. What amount would you need to invest today to have $1,000 one year from now? Illustration D-3 shows the formula for calculating present value.

Study Objective [3]
Solve for present value of a single amount.

$$\text{Present Value} = \text{Future Value} \div (1 + i)^n$$

Illustration D-3
Formula for present value

Thus, if you want a 10% rate of return, you would compute the present value of $1,000 for one year as follows:

$$
\begin{aligned}
PV &= FV \div (1 + i)^n \\
&= \$1{,}000 \div (1 + .10)^1 \\
&= \$1{,}000 \div 1.10 \\
&= \$909.09
\end{aligned}
$$

We know the future amount ($1,000), the discount rate (10%), and the number of periods (1). These variables are depicted in the time diagram in Illustration D-4.

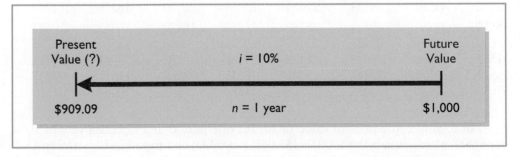

Illustration D-4
Finding present value if discounted for one period

Present Value (?)	$i = 10\%$	Future Value
$909.09	$n = 1$ year	$1,000

If you receive the single amount of $1,000 **in two years**, discounted at 10% [$PV = \$1{,}000 \div (1 + .10)^2$], the present value of your $1,000 is $826.45 [($1,000 ÷ 1.21), depicted as shown in Illustration D-5 on the next page.

Illustration D-5
Finding present value if
discounted for two periods

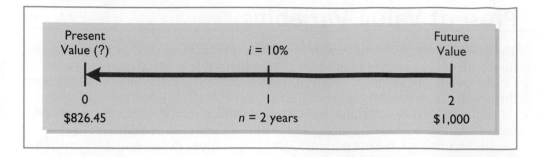

You also could find the present value of your amount through tables that show the present value of 1 for n periods. In Table 1, below, n (represented in the table's rows) is the number of discounting periods involved. The percentages (represented in the table's columns) are the periodic interest rates or discount rates. The 5-digit decimal numbers in the intersections of the rows and columns are called the **present value of 1 factors**.

When using Table 1 to determine present value, you multiply the future value by the present value factor specified at the intersection of the number of periods and the discount rate.

Table 1								
Present Value of 1								
(n) Periods	**4%**	**5%**	**6%**	**8%**	**9%**	**10%**	**11%**	**12%**	**15%**
1	.96154	.95238	.94340	.92593	.91743	.90909	.90090	.89286	.86957
2	.92456	.90703	.89000	.85734	.84168	.82645	.81162	.79719	.75614
3	.88900	.86384	.83962	.79383	.77218	.75132	.73119	.71178	.65752
4	.85480	.82270	.79209	.73503	.70843	.68301	.65873	.63552	.57175
5	.82193	.78353	.74726	.68058	.64993	.62092	.59345	.56743	.49718
6	.79031	.74622	.70496	.63017	.59627	.56447	.53464	.50663	.43233
7	.75992	.71068	.66506	.58349	.54703	.51316	.48166	.45235	.37594
8	.73069	.67684	.62741	.54027	.50187	.46651	.43393	.40388	.32690
9	.70259	.64461	.59190	.50025	.46043	.42410	.39092	.36061	.28426
10	.67556	.61391	.55839	.46319	.42241	.38554	.35218	.32197	.24719
11	.64958	.58468	.52679	.42888	.38753	.35049	.31728	.28748	.21494
12	.62460	.55684	.49697	.39711	.35554	.31863	.28584	.25668	.18691
13	.60057	.53032	.46884	.36770	.32618	.28966	.25751	.22917	.16253
14	.57748	.50507	.44230	.34046	.29925	.26333	.23199	.20462	.14133
15	.55526	.48102	.41727	.31524	.27454	.23939	.20900	.18270	.12289
16	.53391	.45811	.39365	.29189	.25187	.21763	.18829	.16312	.10687
17	.51337	.43630	.37136	.27027	.23107	.19785	.16963	.14564	.09293
18	.49363	.41552	.35034	.25025	.21199	.17986	.15282	.13004	.08081
19	.47464	.39573	.33051	.23171	.19449	.16351	.13768	.11611	.07027
20	.45639	.37689	.31180	.21455	.17843	.14864	.12403	.10367	.06110

For example, the present value factor for one period at a discount rate of 10% is .90909, which equals the $909.09 ($1,000 × .90909) computed in Illustration D-4. For two periods at a discount rate of 10%, the present value factor is .82645, which equals the $826.45 ($1,000 × .82645) computed previously.

Note that a higher discount rate produces a smaller present value. For example, using a 15% discount rate, the present value of $1,000 due one year from now is $869.57, versus $909.09 at 10%. Also note that the further removed from the present the future value is, the smaller the present value. For example, using the same discount rate of 10%, the present value of $1,000 due in **five years** is $620.92, versus the present value of $1,000 due in **one year**, which is $909.09.

The following two demonstration problems (Illustrations D-6 and D-7) illustrate how to use Table 1.

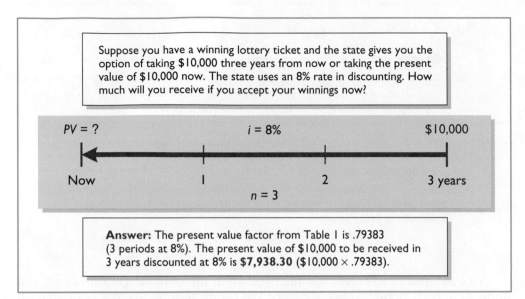

Illustration D-6
Demonstration problem—
Using Table 1 for *PV* of 1

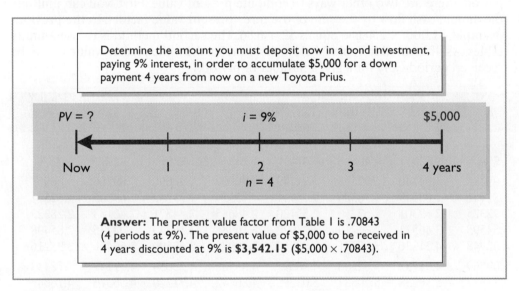

Illustration D-7
Demonstration problem—
Using Table 1 for *PV* of 1

Present Value of an Annuity

The preceding discussion involved the discounting of only a single future amount. Businesses and individuals frequently engage in transactions in which a *series* of equal dollar amounts are to be received or paid at evenly spaced time intervals (periodically). Examples of a series of periodic receipts or payments are loan agreements, installment sales, mortgage notes, lease (rental) contracts, and pension obligations. As discussed in Chapter 15, these periodic receipts or payments are **annuities**.

The **present value of an annuity** is the value now of a series of future receipts or payments, discounted assuming compound interest. In computing the present value of an annuity, you need to know: (1) the discount rate, (2) the number of discount periods, and (3) the amount of the periodic receipts or payments.

Study Objective [4]
Solve for present value of an annuity.

To illustrate how to compute the present value of an annuity, assume that you will receive $1,000 cash annually for three years at a time when the discount rate is 10%. Illustration D-8 depicts this situation, and Illustration D-9 shows the computation of its present value.

Illustration D-8
Time diagram for a three-year annuity

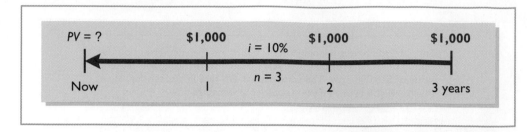

Illustration D-9
Present value of a series of future amounts computation

Future Amount	×	Present Value of 1 Factor at 10%	=	Present Value
$1,000 (one year away)		.90909		$ 909.09
1,000 (two years away)		.82645		826.45
1,000 (three years away)		.75132		751.32
		2.48686		**$2,486.86**

This method of calculation is required when the periodic cash flows are not uniform in each period. However, when the future receipts are the same in each period, there are two other ways to compute present value. First, you can multiply the annual cash flow by the sum of the three present value factors. In the previous example, $1,000 × 2.48686 equals $2,486.86. The second method is to use annuity tables. As illustrated in Table 2 below, these tables show the present value of 1 to be received periodically for a given number of periods.

Table 2 Present Value of an Annuity of 1									

(n) Periods	4%	5%	6%	8%	9%	10%	11%	12%	15%
1	.96154	.95238	.94340	.92593	.91743	.90909	.90090	.89286	.86957
2	1.88609	1.85941	1.83339	1.78326	1.75911	1.73554	1.71252	1.69005	1.62571
3	2.77509	2.72325	2.67301	2.57710	2.53130	2.48685	2.44371	2.40183	2.28323
4	3.62990	3.54595	3.46511	3.31213	3.23972	3.16986	3.10245	3.03735	2.85498
5	4.45182	4.32948	4.21236	3.99271	3.88965	3.79079	3.69590	3.60478	3.35216
6	5.24214	5.07569	4.91732	4.62288	4.48592	4.35526	4.23054	4.11141	3.78448
7	6.00205	5.78637	5.58238	5.20637	5.03295	4.86842	4.71220	4.56376	4.16042
8	6.73274	6.46321	6.20979	5.74664	5.53482	5.33493	5.14612	4.96764	4.48732
9	7.43533	7.10782	6.80169	6.24689	5.99525	5.75902	5.53705	5.32825	4.77158
10	8.11090	7.72173	7.36009	6.71008	6.41766	6.14457	5.88923	5.65022	5.01877
11	8.76048	8.30641	7.88687	7.13896	6.80519	6.49506	6.20652	5.93770	5.23371
12	9.38507	8.86325	8.38384	7.53608	7.16073	6.81369	6.49236	6.19437	5.42062
13	9.98565	9.39357	8.85268	7.90378	7.48690	7.10336	6.74987	6.42355	5.58315
14	10.56312	9.89864	9.29498	8.24424	7.78615	7.36669	6.98187	6.62817	5.72448
15	11.11839	10.37966	9.71225	8.55948	8.06069	7.60608	7.19087	6.81086	5.84737
16	11.65230	10.83777	10.10590	8.85137	8.31256	7.82371	7.37916	6.97399	5.95424
17	12.16567	11.27407	10.47726	9.12164	8.54363	8.02155	7.54879	7.11963	6.04716
18	12.65930	11.68959	10.82760	9.37189	8.75563	8.20141	7.70162	7.24967	6.12797
19	13.13394	12.08532	11.15812	9.60360	8.95012	8.36492	7.83929	7.36578	6.19823
20	13.59033	12.46221	11.46992	9.81815	9.12855	8.51356	7.96333	7.46944	6.25933

Table 2 shows that the present value of an annuity of 1 factor for three periods at 10% is 2.48685.[1] (This present value factor is the total of the three individual present value factors, as shown in Illustration D-9.) Applying this amount to the annual cash flow of $1,000 produces a present value of $2,486.85.

The following demonstration problem (Illustration D-10) illustrates how to use Table 2.

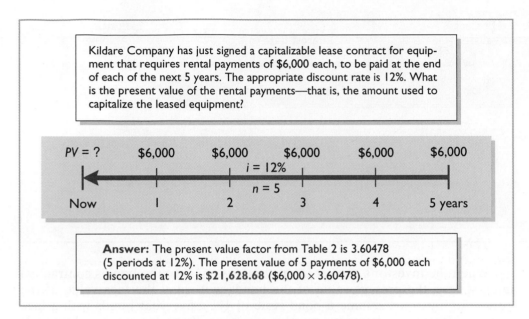

Kildare Company has just signed a capitalizable lease contract for equipment that requires rental payments of $6,000 each, to be paid at the end of each of the next 5 years. The appropriate discount rate is 12%. What is the present value of the rental payments—that is, the amount used to capitalize the leased equipment?

Answer: The present value factor from Table 2 is 3.60478 (5 periods at 12%). The present value of 5 payments of $6,000 each discounted at 12% is **$21,628.68** ($6,000 × 3.60478).

Illustration D-10
Demonstration problem—Using Table 2 for *PV* of an annuity of 1

Time Periods and Discounting

In the preceding calculations, the discounting was done on an *annual* basis using an *annual* interest rate. Discounting may also be done over shorter periods of time such as monthly, quarterly, or semiannually.

When the time frame is less than one year, you need to convert the annual interest rate to the applicable time frame. Assume, for example, that the investor in Illustration D-8 received $500 **semiannually** for three years instead of $1,000 annually. In this case, the number of periods becomes six (3 × 2), the discount rate is 5% (10% ÷ 2), the present value factor from Table 2 is 5.07569, and the present value of the future cash flows is $2,537.85 (5.07569 × $500). This amount is slightly higher than the $2,486.86 computed in Illustration D-9 because interest is paid twice during the same year; therefore interest is earned on the first half year's interest.

Computing the Present Value of a Long-Term Note or Bond

The present value (or market price) of a long-term note or bond is a function of three variables: (1) the payment amounts, (2) the length of time until the amounts are paid, and (3) the discount rate. Our illustration uses a five-year bond issue.

Study Objective [5]
Compute the present value of notes and bonds.

---

[1]The difference of .00001 between 2.48686 and 2.48685 is due to rounding.

The first variable—dollars to be paid—is made up of two elements: (1) a series of interest payments (an annuity), and (2) the principal amount (a single sum). To compute the present value of the bond, we must discount both the interest payments and the principal amount—two different computations. The time diagrams for a bond due in five years are shown in Illustration D-11.

Illustration D-11

Present value of a bond time diagram

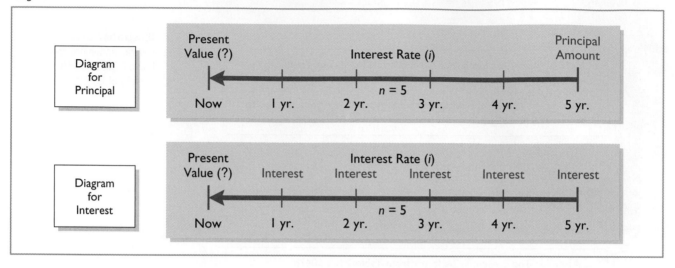

When the investor's market interest rate is equal to the bond's contractual interest rate, the present value of the bonds will *equal* the face value of the bonds. To illustrate, assume a bond issue of 10%, five-year bonds with a face value of $100,000 with interest payable **semiannually** on January 1 and July 1. If the discount rate is the same as the contractual rate, the bonds will sell at face value. In this case, the investor will receive the following: (1) $100,000 at maturity, and (2) a series of ten $5,000 interest payments [($100,000 × 10%) ÷ 2] over the term of the bonds. The length of time is expressed in terms of interest periods—in this case—10, and the discount rate per interest period, 5%. The following time diagram (Illustration D-12) depicts the variables involved in this discounting situation.

Illustration D-12

Time diagram for present value of a 10%, five-year bond paying interest semiannually

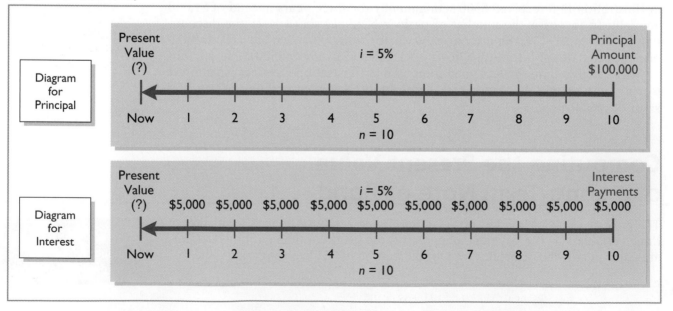

Illustration D-13 shows the computation of the present value of these bonds.

<table>
<tr><td colspan="2" align="center">**10% Contractual Rate—10% Discount Rate**</td></tr>
<tr><td>**Present value of principal to be received at maturity**
$100,000 × *PV* of 1 due in 10 periods at 5%
$100,000 × .61391 (Table 1)</td><td align="right">$ 61,391</td></tr>
<tr><td>**Present value of interest to be received periodically**
over the term of the bonds
$5,000 × *PV* of 1 due periodically for 10 periods at 5%
$5,000 × 7.72173 (Table 2)</td><td align="right">38,609*</td></tr>
<tr><td>**Present value of bonds**</td><td align="right">**$100,000**</td></tr>
</table>

*Rounded

Illustration D-13
Present value of principal and interest—face value

Now assume that the investor's required rate of return is 12%, not 10%. The future amounts are again $100,000 and $5,000, respectively, but now a discount rate of 6% (12% ÷ 2) must be used. The present value of the bonds is $92,639, as computed in Illustration D-14.

<table>
<tr><td colspan="2" align="center">**10% Contractual Rate—12% Discount Rate**</td></tr>
<tr><td>**Present value of principal to be received at maturity**
$100,000 × .55839 (Table 1)</td><td align="right">$55,839</td></tr>
<tr><td>**Present value of interest to be received periodically**
over the term of the bonds
$5,000 × 7.36009 (Table 2)</td><td align="right">36,800</td></tr>
<tr><td>**Present value of bonds**</td><td align="right">**$92,639**</td></tr>
</table>

Illustration D-14
Present value of principal and interest—discount

Conversely, if the discount rate is 8% and the contractual rate is 10%, the present value of the bonds is $108,111, computed as shown in Illustration D-15.

<table>
<tr><td colspan="2" align="center">**10% Contractual Rate—8% Discount Rate**</td></tr>
<tr><td>**Present value of principal to be received at maturity**
$100,000 × .67556 (Table 1)</td><td align="right">$ 67,556</td></tr>
<tr><td>**Present value of interest to be received periodically**
over the term of the bonds
$5,000 × 8.11090 (Table 2)</td><td align="right">40,555</td></tr>
<tr><td>**Present value of bonds**</td><td align="right">**$108,111**</td></tr>
</table>

Illustration D-15
Present value of principal and interest—premium

The above discussion relies on present value tables in solving present value problems. Many people use spreadsheets such as Excel or financial calculators (some even on websites) to compute present values, without the use of tables. Many calculators, especially "financial calculators," have present value (*PV*) functions that allow you to calculate present values by merely inputting the proper amount, discount rate, and periods, and pressing the PV key. Appendix E illustrates how to use a financial calculator in various business situations.

Summary of Study Objectives

[1] Distinguish between simple and compound interest. Simple interest is computed on the principal only, while compound interest is computed on the principal and any interest earned that has not been withdrawn.

[2] Identify the variables fundamental to solving present value problems. The following three variables are fundamental to solving present value problems: (1) the future amount, (2) the number of periods, and (3) the interest rate (the discount rate).

[3] Solve for present value of a single amount. Prepare a time diagram of the problem. Identify the future amount, the number of discounting periods, and the discount (interest) rate. Using the present value of a single amount table, multiply the future amount by the present value factor specified at the intersection of the number of periods and the discount rate.

[4] Solve for present value of an annuity. Prepare a time diagram of the problem. Identify the future annuity payments, the number of discounting periods, and the discount (interest) rate. Using the present value of an annuity of 1 table, multiply the amount of the annuity payments by the present value factor specified at the intersection of the number of periods and the interest rate.

[5] Compute the present value of notes and bonds. To determine the present value of the principal amount: Multiply the principal amount (a single future amount) by the present value factor (from the present value of 1 table) intersecting at the number of periods (number of interest payments) and the discount rate.

To determine the present value of the series of interest payments: Multiply the amount of the interest payment by the present value factor (from the present value of an annuity of 1 table) intersecting at the number of periods (number of interest payments) and the discount rate. Add the present value of the principal amount to the present value of the interest payments to arrive at the present value of the note or bond.

Glossary

Annuity   A series of equal dollar amounts to be paid or received at evenly spaced time intervals (periodically). (p. D5).

Compound interest   The interest computed on the principal and any interest earned that has not been paid or withdrawn. (p. D2).

Discounting the future amount(s)   The process of determining present value. (p. D3).

Interest   Payment for the use of another's money. (p. D1).

Present value   The value now of a given amount to be paid or received in the future assuming compound interest. (p. D3).

Present value of an annuity   The value now of a series of future receipts or payments, discounted assuming compound interest. (p. D5).

Principal   The amount borrowed or invested. (p. D1).

Simple interest   The interest computed on the principal only. (p. D1).

Brief Exercises

Use tables to solve exercises.

Use present value tables.

BED-1   For each of the following cases, indicate (a) to what interest rate columns, and (b) to what number of periods you would refer in looking up the discount rate.

1. In Table 1 (present value of 1):

	Annual Rate	**Number of Years Involved**	**Compounding Per Year**
(a)	12%	6	Annually
(b)	10%	15	Annually
(c)	8%	12	Semiannually

2. In Table 2 (present value of an annuity of 1):

	Annual Rate	**Number of Years Involved**	**Number of Payments Involved**	**Frequency of Payments**
(a)	8%	20	20	Annually
(b)	10%	5	5	Annually
(c)	12%	4	8	Semiannually

Determine present values.

BED-2   (a) What is the present value of $30,000 due 8 periods from now, discounted at 8%? (b) What is the present value of $30,000 to be received at the end of each of 6 periods, discounted at 9%?

BED-3 Ramirez Company is considering an investment that will return a lump sum of $600,000 5 years from now. What amount should Ramirez Company pay for this investment in order to earn a 10% return?

Compute the present value of a single-sum investment.

BED-4 LaRussa Company earns 9% on an investment that will return $700,000 8 years from now. What is the amount LaRussa should invest now in order to earn this rate of return?

Compute the present value of a single-sum investment.

BED-5 Polley Company sold a 5-year, zero-interest-bearing $36,000 note receivable to Valley Inc. Valley wishes to earn 10% over the remaining 4 years of the note. How much cash will Polley receive upon sale of the note?

Compute the present value of a single-sum zero-interest-bearing note.

BED-6 Marichal Company issues a 3-year, zero-interest-bearing $60,000 note. The interest rate used to discount the zero-interest-bearing note is 8%. What are the cash proceeds that Marichal Company should receive?

Compute the present value of a single-sum zero-interest-bearing note.

BED-7 Colaw Company is considering investing in an annuity contract that will return $40,000 annually at the end of each year for 15 years. What amount should Colaw Company pay for this investment if it earns a 6% return?

Compute the present value of an annuity investment.

BED-8 Sauder Enterprises earns 11% on an investment that pays back $100,000 at the end of each of the next 4 years. What is the amount Sauder Enterprises invested to earn the 11% rate of return?

Compute the present value of an annuity investment.

BED-9 Chicago Railroad Co. is about to issue $200,000 of 10-year bonds paying a 10% interest rate, with interest payable semiannually. The discount rate for such securities is 8%. How much can Chicago expect to receive for the sale of these bonds?

Compute the present value of bonds.

BED-10 Assume the same information as in BED-9 except that the discount rate is 10% instead of 8%. In this case, how much can Chicago expect to receive from the sale of these bonds?

Compute the present value of bonds.

BED-11 Berghaus Company receives a $75,000, 6-year note bearing interest of 8% (paid annually) from a customer at a time when the discount rate is 9%. What is the present value of the note received by Berghaus Company?

Compute the present value of a note.

BED-12 Troutman Enterprises issued 8%, 8-year, $1,000,000 par value bonds that pay interest semiannually on October 1 and April 1. The bonds are dated April 1, 2012, and are issued on that date. The discount rate of interest for such bonds on April 1, 2012, is 10%. What cash proceeds did Troutman receive from issuance of the bonds?

Compute the present value of bonds.

BED-13 Ricky Cleland owns a garage and is contemplating purchasing a tire retreading machine for $16,280. After estimating costs and revenues, Ricky projects a net cash flow from the retreading machine of $2,800 annually for 8 years. Ricky hopes to earn a return of 11% on such investments. What is the present value of the retreading operation? Should Ricky Cleland purchase the retreading machine?

Compute the value of a machine for purposes of making a purchase decision.

BED-14 Martinez Company issues a 10%, 6-year mortgage note on January 1, 2012, to obtain financing for new equipment. Land is used as collateral for the note. The terms provide for semi-annual installment payments of $78,978. What were the cash proceeds received from the issuance of the note?

Compute the present value of a note.

BED-15 Durler Company is considering purchasing equipment. The equipment will produce the following cash flows: Year 1, $30,000; Year 2, $40,000; Year 3, $60,000. Durler requires a minimum rate of return of 12%. What is the maximum price Durler should pay for this equipment?

Compute the maximum price to pay for a machine.

BED-16 If Carla Garcia invests $2,745 now, she will receive $10,000 at the end of 15 years. What annual rate of interest will Carla earn on her investment? (*Hint:* Use Table 1.)

Compute the interest rate on a single sum.

BED-17 Sara Altom has been offered the opportunity of investing $51,316 now. The investment will earn 10% per year and at the end of that time will return Sara $100,000. How many years must Sara wait to receive $100,000? (*Hint:* Use Table 1.)

Compute the number of periods of a single sum.

BED-18 Stacy Dains purchased an investment for $11,469.92. From this investment, she will receive $1,000 annually for the next 20 years, starting one year from now. What rate of interest will Stacy's investment be earning for her? (*Hint:* Use Table 2.)

Compute the interest rate on an annuity.

BED-19 Diana Rossi invests $8,559.48 now for a series of $1,000 annual returns, beginning one year from now. Diana will earn a return of 8% on the initial investment. How many annual payments of $1,000 will Diana receive? (*Hint:* Use Table 2.)

Compute the number of periods of an annuity.

BED-20 Minitori Company needs $10,000 on January 1, 2015. It is starting a fund on January 1, 2012.

Compute the amount to be invested.

Instructions

Compute the amount that must be invested in the fund on January 1, 2012, to produce a $10,000 balance on January 1, 2015, if:

(a) The fund earns 8% per year compounded annually.
(b) The fund earns 8% per year compounded semiannually.
(c) The fund earns 12% per year compounded annually.
(d) The fund earns 12% per year compounded semiannually.

Compute the amount to be invested.

BED-21   Venuchi Company needs $10,000 on January 1, 2017. It is starting a fund to produce that amount.

Instructions

Compute the amount that must be invested in the fund to produce a $10,000 balance on January 1, 2017, if:

(a) The initial investment is made January 1, 2012, and the fund earns 6% per year.
(b) The initial investment is made January 1, 2014, and the fund earns 6% per year.
(c) The initial investment is made January 1, 2012, and the fund earns 10% per year.
(d) The initial investment is made January 1, 2014, and the fund earns 10% per year.

Select the better payment option.

BED-22   Letterman Corporation is buying new equipment. It can pay $39,500 today (option 1), or $10,000 today and 5 yearly payments of $8,000 each, starting in one year (option 2).

Instructions

Which option should Letterman select? (Assume a discount rate of 10%.)

Compute the cost of an investment, amount received, and rate of return.

BED-23   Carmen Corporation is considering several investments.

Instructions

(a) One investment returns $10,000 per year for 5 years and provides a return of 10%. What is the cost of this investment?
(b) Another investment costs $50,000 and returns a certain amount per year for 10 years, providing an 8% return. What amount is received each year?
(c) A third investment costs $70,000 and returns $11,971 each year for 15 years. What is the rate of return on this investment?

Select the best payment option.

BED-24   You are the beneficiary of a trust fund. The fund gives you the option of receiving $5,000 per year for 10 years, $9,000 per year for 5 years, or $30,000 today.

Instructions

If the desired rate of return is 8%, which option should you select?

Compute the semiannual car payment.

BED-25   You are purchasing a car for $24,000, and you obtain financing as follows: $2,400 down payment, 12% interest, semiannual payments over 5 years.

Instructions

Compute the payment you will make every 6 months

Compute the present value of bonds.

BED-26   Contreras Corporation is considering purchasing bonds of Jose Company as an investment. The bonds have a face value of $40,000 with a 10% interest rate. The bonds mature in 4 years and pay interest semiannually.

Instructions

(a) What is the most Contreras should pay for the bonds if it desires a 12% return?
(b) What is the most Contreras should pay for the bonds if it desires an 8% return?

Compute the present value of bonds.

BED-27   Garcia Corporation is considering purchasing bonds of Fred Company as an investment. The bonds have a face value of $90,000 with a 9% interest rate. The bonds mature in 6 years and pay interest semiannually.

Instructions

(a) What is the most Garcia should pay for the bonds if it desires a 10% return?
(b) What is the most Garcia should pay for the bonds if it desires an 8% return?

APPENDIX E

Using Financial Calculators

Study Objective

After studying this appendix, you should be able to:

[1] Use a financial calculator to solve time value of money problems.

Business professionals, once they have mastered the underlying concepts in Appendix D, often use a financial (business) calculator to solve time value of money problems. In many cases, they must use calculators if interest rates or time periods do not correspond with the information provided in the compound interest tables.

To use financial calculators, you enter the time value of money variables into the calculator. Illustration E-1 shows the five most common keys used to solve time value of money problems.[1]

Study Objective [1]
Use a financial calculator to solve time value of money problems.

Illustration E-1
Financial calculator keys

where

N	=	number of periods
I	=	interest rate per period (some calculators use I/YR or i)
PV	=	present value (occurs at the beginning of the first period)
PMT	=	payment (all payments are equal, and none are skipped)
FV	=	future value (occurs at the end of the last period)

In solving time value of money problems in this appendix, you will generally be given three of four variables and will have to solve for the remaining variable. The fifth key (the key not used) is given a value of zero to ensure that this variable is not used in the computation.

Present Value of a Single Sum

To illustrate how to solve a present value problem using a financial calculator, assume that you want to know the present value of $84,253 to be received in five years, discounted at 11% compounded annually. Illustration E-2 (page E2) pictures this problem.

---

[1]On many calculators, these keys are actual buttons on the face of the calculator; on others, they appear on the display after the user accesses a present value menu.

Illustration E-2
Calculator solution for present
value of a single sum

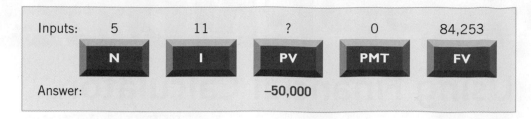

The diagram shows you the information (inputs) to enter into the calculator: N = 5, I = 11, PMT = 0, and FV = 84,253. You then press PV for the answer: −$50,000. As indicated, the PMT key was given a value of zero because a series of payments did not occur in this problem.

Plus and Minus

The use of plus and minus signs in time value of money problems with a financial calculator can be confusing. Most financial calculators are programmed so that the positive and negative cash flows in any problem offset each other. In the present value problem above, we identified the $84,253 future value initial investment as a positive (inflow); the answer −$50,000 was shown as a negative amount, reflecting a cash outflow. If the 84,253 were entered as a negative, then the final answer would have been reported as a positive 50,000.

Hopefully, the sign convention will not cause confusion. If you understand what is required in a problem, you should be able to interpret a positive or negative amount in determining the solution to a problem.

Compounding Periods

In the problem above, we assumed that compounding occurs once a year. Some financial calculators have a default setting, which assumes that compounding occurs 12 times a year. You must determine what default period has been programmed into your calculator and change it as necessary to arrive at the proper compounding period.

Rounding

Most financial calculators store and calculate using 12 decimal places. As a result, because compound interest tables generally have factors only up to 5 decimal places, a slight difference in the final answer can result. In most time value of money problems, the final answer will not include more than two decimal points.

Present Value of an Annuity

To illustrate how to solve a present value of an annuity problem using a financial calculator, assume that you are asked to determine the present value of rental receipts of $6,000 each to be received at the end of each of the next five years, when discounted at 12%, as pictured in Illustration E-3.

Illustration E-3
Calculator solution for present
value of an annuity

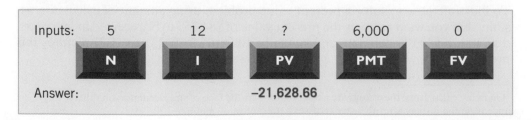

In this case, you enter N = 5, I = 12, PMT = 6,000, FV = 0, and then press PV to arrive at the answer of $21,628.66.

Useful Applications of the Financial Calculator

With a financial calculator, you can solve for any interest rate or for any number of periods in a time value of money problem. Here are some examples of these applications.

Auto Loan

Assume you are financing the purchase of a used car with a three-year loan. The loan has a 9.5% nominal annual interest rate, compounded monthly. The price of the car is $6,000, and you want to determine the monthly payments, assuming that the payments start one month after the purchase. This problem is pictured in Illustration E-4.

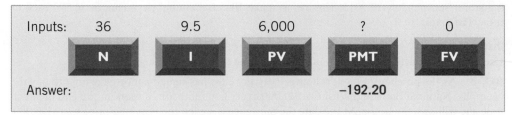

Illustration E-4
Calculator solution for auto loan payments

To solve this problem, you enter N = 36 (12 × 3), I = 9.5, PV = 6,000, FV = 0, and then press PMT. You will find that the monthly payments will be $192.20. Note that the payment key is usually programmed for 12 payments per year. Thus, you must change the default (compounding period) if the payments are other than monthly.

Mortgage Loan Amount

Let's say you are evaluating financing options for a loan on a house. You decide that the maximum mortgage payment you can afford is $700 per month. The annual interest rate is 8.4%. If you get a mortgage that requires you to make monthly payments over a 15-year period, what is the maximum purchase price you can afford? Illustration E-5 depicts this problem.

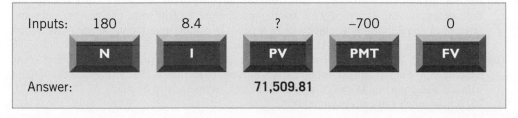

Illustration E-5
Calculator solution for mortgage amount

You enter N = 180 (12 × 15 years), I = 8.4, PMT = −700, FV = 0, and press PV. You find a present value of $71,509.81—the maximum house price you can afford, given that you want to keep your mortgage payments at $700. Note that by changing any of the variables, you can quickly conduct "what-if" analyses for different situations.

Summary of Learning Objective

[1] Use a financial calculator to solve time value of money problems. Financial calculators can be used to solve the same and additional problems as those solved with time value of money tables. One enters into the financial calculator the amounts for all but one of the unknown elements of a time value of money problem (periods, interest rate, payments, future or present value). Particularly useful situations involve interest rates and compounding periods not presented in the tables.

Brief Exercises

Determine interest rate.

BEE-1   Reba McEntire wishes to invest $19,000 on July 1, 2012, and have it accumulate to $49,000 by July 1, 2022.

Instructions
Use a financial calculator to determine at what exact annual rate of interest Reba must invest the $19,000.

Determine interest rate.

BEE-2   On July 17, 2012, Tim McGraw borrowed $42,000 from his grandfather to open a clothing store. Starting July 17, 2013, Tim has to make 10 equal annual payments of $6,500 each to repay the loan.

Instructions
Use a financial calculator to determine what interest rate Tim is paying.

Determine interest rate.

BEE-3   As the purchaser of a new house, Patty Loveless has signed a mortgage note to pay the Memphis National Bank and Trust Co. $14,000 every 6 months for 20 years, at the end of which time she will own the house. At the date the mortgage is signed the purchase price was $198,000, and Loveless made a down payment of $20,000. The first payment will be made 6 months after the date the mortgage is signed.

Instructions
Using a financial calculator, compute the exact rate of interest earned on the mortgage by the bank.

Various time value of money situations.

BEE-4   Using a financial calculator, solve for the unknowns in each of the following situations.

(a) On June 1, 2012, Shelley Long purchases lakefront property from her neighbor, Joey Brenner, and agrees to pay the purchase price in seven payments of $16,000 each, the first payment to be payable June 1, 2013. (Assume that interest compounded at an annual rate of 7.35% is implicit in the payments.) What is the purchase price of the property?

(b) On January 1, 2012, Cooke Corporation purchased 200 of the $1,000 face value, 8% coupon, 10-year bonds of Howe Inc. The bonds mature on January 1, 2022, and pay interest annually beginning January 1, 2013. Cooke purchased the bonds to yield 10.65%. How much did Cooke pay for the bonds?

Various time value of money situations.

BEE-5   Using a financial calculator, provide a solution to each of the following situations.

(a) Bill Schroeder owes a debt of $35,000 from the purchase of his new sport utility vehicle. The debt bears annual interest of 9.1% compounded monthly. Bill wishes to pay the debt and interest in equal monthly payments over 8 years, beginning one month hence. What equal monthly payments will pay off the debt and interest?

(b) On January 1, 2012, Sammy Sosa offers to buy Mark Grace's used snowmobile for $8,000, payable in five equal annual installments, which are to include 8.25% interest on the unpaid balance and a portion of the principal. If the first payment is to be made on December 31, 2012, how much will each payment be?

APPENDIX F

Standards of Ethical Conduct for Management Accountants

Management accountants have an obligation to the organizations they serve, their profession, the public, and themselves to maintain the highest standards of ethical conduct. In recognition of this obligation, the Institute of Management Accountants (IMA) has published and promoted the following standards of ethical conduct for management accountants.[1]

IMA Statement of Ethical Professional Practice

Members of IMA shall behave ethically. A commitment to ethical professional practice includes: overarching principles that express our values, and standards that guide our conduct.

Principles

IMA's overarching ethical principles include: Honesty, Fairness, Objectivity, and Responsibility. Members shall act in accordance with these principles and shall encourage others within their organizations to adhere to them.

Standards

A member's failure to comply with the following standards may result in disciplinary action.

I. COMPETENCE

Each member has a responsibility to:

1. Maintain an appropriate level of professional expertise by continually developing knowledge and skills.
2. Perform professional duties in accordance with relevant laws, regulations, and technical standards.
3. Provide decision support information and recommendations that are accurate, clear, concise, and timely.
4. Recognize and communicate professional limitations or other constraints that would preclude responsible judgment or successful performance of an activity.

---

[1]Reprinted by permission of the Institute of Management Accountants, *www.imanet.org/pdf/981.pdf*.

II. CONFIDENTIALITY

Each member has a responsibility to:

1. Keep information confidential except when disclosure is authorized or legally required.
2. Inform all relevant parties regarding appropriate use of confidential information. Monitor subordinates' activities to ensure compliance.
3. Refrain from using confidential information for unethical or illegal advantage.

III. INTEGRITY

Each member has a responsibility to:

1. Mitigate actual conflicts of interest. Regularly communicate with business associates to avoid apparent conflicts of interest. Advise all parties of any potential conflicts.
2. Refrain from engaging in any conduct that would prejudice carrying out duties ethically.
3. Abstain from engaging in or supporting any activity that might discredit the profession.

IV. CREDIBILITY

Each member has a responsibility to:

1. Communicate information fairly and objectively.
2. Disclose all relevant information that could reasonably be expected to influence an intended user's understanding of the reports, analyses, or recommendations.
3. Disclose delays or deficiencies in information, timeliness, processing, or internal controls in conformance with organization policy and/or applicable law.

Resolution of Ethical Conflict

In applying the Standards of Ethical Professional Practice, you may encounter problems identifying unethical behavior or resolving an ethical conflict. When faced with ethical issues, you should follow your organization's established policies on the resolution of such conflict. If these policies do not resolve the ethical conflict, you should consider the following courses of action:

1. Discuss the issue with your immediate supervisor except when it appears that the supervisor is involved. In that case, present the issue to the next level. If you cannot achieve a satisfactory resolution, submit the issue to the next management level. If your immediate superior is the chief executive officer or equivalent, the acceptable reviewing authority may be a group such as the audit committee, executive committee, board of directors, board of trustees, or owners. Contact with levels above the immediate superior should be initiated only with your superior's knowledge, assuming he or she is not involved. Communication of such problems to authorities or individuals not employed or engaged by the organization is not considered appropriate, unless you believe there is a clear violation of the law.
2. Clarify relevant ethical issues by initiating a confidential discussion with an IMA Ethics Counselor or other impartial advisor to obtain a better understanding of possible courses of action.
3. Consult your own attorney as to legal obligations and rights concerning the ethical conflict.

PHOTO CREDITS

Chapter 1 Page 3 Monica Wells/SuperStock Page 6 iStockphoto Page 8 Gemunu Amarasinghe/AP Photo Page 10 Toru Hanai/AP/Wide World Photos Page 12 Josef Volavka/iStockphoto

Chapter 2 Page 51 m63/ZUMA Press/Newscom/ NewsCom Page 55 Jonathan Daniel/Getty Images, Inc. Page 61 Sciencefaction/SuperStock Page 73 Enviromatic/ iStockphoto

Chapter 3 Page 99 James Lauritz/Digital Vision/Getty Images, Inc. Page 102 Dan Chippendale/iStockphoto Page 110 Apcuk/iStockphoto Page 114 Günay Mutlu/iStockphoto

Chapter 4 Page 153 Comstock/Getty Images, Inc. Page 165 Alex Slobodkin/iStockphoto Page 170 Christian Lagereek/ iStockphoto Page 172 Lowell Sannes/iStockphoto Page 173 Denis Vorob'yev/iStockphoto Page 174 Nikki Ward/ iStockphoto Page 175 Jorge Salcedo/iStockphoto Page 176 (top) Vladislav Gurfinkel/iStockphoto (bottom) iStockphoto

Chapter 5 Page 209 Stone/Getty Images, Inc. Page 213 Ben Blankenburg/iStockphoto Page 220 Maciej Noskowski/ iStockphoto Page 226 Heizfrosch/iStockphoto

Chapter 6 Page 261 Steve Dunning/Getty Images, Inc. Page 263 Alexey Dudoladov/iStockphoto Page 264 Yin Yang/iStockphoto Page 275 AP/Wide World Photos Page 279 Jaap Hart/iStockphoto

Chapter 7 Page 315 Terra Images/Age Fotostock America, Inc. Page 318 Sean Locke/iStockphoto Page 321 Niels Laan/ iStockphoto

Chapter 8 Page 361 Valerie Loiseleux/iStockphoto Page 371 (top) Tom Nulens/iStockphoto (bottom) Catherine Yeulet/iStockphoto Page 387 AFP Photo/Timothy A. Clary/ NewsCom

Chapter 9 Page 415 cogal/iStockphoto Page 427 Michael Braun/iStockphoto Page 430 iStockphoto Page 432 Andy Dean/iStockphoto

Chapter 10 Page 457 David Trood/Getty Images, Inc Page 461 iStockphoto Page 478 iStockphoto Page 480 Linda Steward/iStockphoto

Chapter 11 Page 509 Cary Westfall/iStockphoto Page 516 Steve Diblee/iStockphoto Page 527 Katie Nesling/iStockphoto

Chapter 12 Page 553 Charles Taylor/iStockphoto Page 556 Malcolm Romain/iStockphoto Page 559 PhotoDisc/Getty Images, Inc.

COMPANY INDEX